Descent into Barbarism:

A HISTORY OF THE TWENTIETH CENTURY 1934–1951

SIR MARTIN GILBERT is one of Britain's most distinguished historians. He was born in London in 1936, educated at Highgate School and spent two years in the army as a National Serviceman. He studied history at Magdalen College,  uate work at St Antony's College, to Randolph Churchill. After Ra bert succeeded him as the official b and wrote six of the eight volum of Churchill documents. His othe. 94), *Second World War* (1989), *The Holocaust* (1986), *In Search of Churchill* (1994) and *The Day the War Ended* (1995). He is married with three children and lives in London; his wife Susie has been his principal historical helper for more than two decades. Since 1962, he has been a Fellow of Merton College, Oxford (an Honorary Fellow since 1994).

More from the reviews:

'A mammoth, uncompromising enterprise . . . Grand strategy is given a lesser place than the actual experience of those who fought, or civilian victims. Accounts of battles and of air-raids are interspersed with the Holocaust – but it is not the six million Jews as an abstract figure but the sufferings of individual communities and of individual men, women and children that count. He is equally direct when it comes to Japanese atrocities in China and subsequently to their treatment of their Western captives when the Americans, British and Australians were drawn into the war. Partition in India is represented not as a question of a line on the map but as the occasion of intercommunal strife of a horrifying kind, with Gandhi as the period's final major victim of the assassin's gun . . . I find Gilbert's stance appealing and share his list of heroes – Churchill, Roosevelt, Marshall Truman – as well as villains, I would like to think that many, particularly among the young to whom Montgomery is as remote as Boadicea will read the book, despite its often gruesome subject matter. Gilbert's ability to switch from one scene to another helps create the desired sense of immediacy.'

MAX BELOFF, *TLS*

BOOKS BY MARTIN GILBERT

THE CHURCHILL BIOGRAPHY

Volume III: 1914–1916
Document Volume III: (in two parts)
Volume IV: 1917–1922
Document Volume IV: (in two parts)
Volume V: 1922–1939
Document Volume V: 'The Exchequer Years' 1922–1929
Document Volume V: 'The Wilderness Years' 1929–1935
Document Volume V: 'The Coming of War' 1936–1939

Volume VI: 'Finest Hour' 1939–1941
Document Volume VI: 'At the Admiralty' September 1939–May 1940
Document Volume VI: 'Never Surrender' May–December 1940
Volume VII: 'Road to Victory' 1941–1945
Volume VIII: 'Never Despair' 1945–1965

Churchill: A Photographic Portrait
Churchill: A Life

OTHER BOOKS

The Appeasers (with Richard Gott)
The European Powers 1900–1945
The Roots of Appeasement
Children's Illustrated Bible Atlas
Atlas of British Charities
Atlas of American History
Atlas of the Arab-Israeli Conflict
Atlas of British History
Atlas of the First World War
Atlas of the Holocaust
The Holocaust: Maps and Photographs
Atlas of Jewish History
Atlas of Recent History (in preparation)
Atlas of Russian History
The Jews of Arab Lands: Their History in Maps
In Search of Churchill
Descent into Barbarism: The History of the Twentieth Century 1934–1951

The Jews of Russia: Their History in Maps
Jerusalem Illustrated History Atlas
Sir Horace Rumbold: Portrait of a Diplomat
Jerusalem: Rebirth of a City
Jerusalem in the Twentieth Century
Exile and Return: The Struggle for Jewish Statehood
Auschwitz and the Allies
The Jews of Hope: The Plight of Soviet Jewry Today
Shcharansky: Hero of Our Time
The Holocaust: The Jewish Tragedy
The Boys, Triumph over Adversity
First World War
Second World War
The Day the War Ended
Empires in Conflict: The History of the Twentieth Century 1900–1933
Challenge to Civilization: The History of the Twentieth Century 1952–1999

EDITIONS OF DOCUMENTS

Britain and Germany Between the Wars
Plough My Own Furrow: The Life of Lord Allen of Hurtwood
Servant of India: Diaries of the Viceroy's Private Secretary 1905–1910

DESCENT INTO BARBARISM

A HISTORY OF THE TWENTIETH CENTURY
1934–1951

MARTIN GILBERT

HarperCollins*Publishers*

HarperCollins*Publishers*
77–85 Fulham Palace Road,
Hammersmith, London W6 8JB

First published in Great Britain by
HarperCollins*Publishers* 1998

This paperback edition 1999
1 3 5 7 9 8 6 4 2

ISBN 000 637662 2

Set in Garamond 3 by
Rowland Phototypesetting Ltd,
Bury St Edmunds, Suffolk

Printed in Great Britain by
Caledonian International Book Manufacturing Ltd, Glasgow

I dedicate this history to my mother, Miriam Gilbert, who was born in 1911, and who has lived through all but one decade of the century which is the subject of these volumes.

This second volume I dedicate to my children, Natalie, David and Joshua, in the hope that the century that lies ahead will be kind to them, and to all mankind.

CONTENTS

PART THREE

LIST OF ILLUSTRATIONS

Jacket photograph: The 'mushroom cloud' over Hiroshima

LIST OF MAPS

INTRODUCTION

Mankind's long search for a rule of law among nations.

PRESIDENT HARRY S TRUMAN

THIS VOLUME – the second of three – covers the nineteen years in the middle of the twentieth century, opening in 1933 and including the Second World War. Aspects of this and several other wars, among them the Sino-Japanese war that began in 1937 and the Korean War that began in 1950, dominate many of its pages, as they dominated the lives of those who lived through the period. It was on 24 September 1927 – six and a half years before this volume opens – that the League of Nations declared 'aggressive war' to be a crime. Germany and Japan were among the signatories of that declaration. A year later, under the Briand-Kellogg Pact, to which Germany and Japan were likewise signatories, the governments of sixty-one countries renounced aggressive war as an instrument of national policy. These two solemn agreements, negotiated at length and with the approval and applause of the war-weary nations, set the seal, within a decade of the end of the First World War, on the peaceful resolution of all disputes among nations.

The breakdown of the short-lived era of peace after only two decades is a dominant facet of the story of the twentieth century. Another is the consolidation and spread of totalitarianism, bringing with it persecution and war. If totalitarianism stalks the pages of this volume, it does so as an echo of the insistence with which it dominated the lives of so many hundreds of millions of people, and destroyed so many millions of lives. In the Soviet Union and Italy, Stalin and Mussolini were already at the repressive helm of their respective States. Hitler had been in power in Germany for only three months when this volume opens, but he had already announced his purposes to the world.

Democracy was not always its own most impressive advocate, but in the face of considerable pressures, internal and external, it strove to maintain its place in the world. The struggle between liberal, humanitarian values, supported by the rule of law and democratic institutions, and the counter-values of dictatorship, one-Party rule, the regime of secret police and informants, torture chambers and executions without trial, is a struggle which has pervaded the twentieth century. That struggle reached several climactic points in the years under review from 1933 to 1951. The rule of law and the misuse of law serve as opposing elements in the behaviour of nations and rulers. Racism, tyranny, ideologies like Nazism, Fascism or Communism, in leading to an abridgment of human rights, also restrict the potential of individual expression and creativity.

The years covered by this volume are dominated by the struggle between the rule of law and lawlessness; between the rights of the individual and the destruction of those rights. In 1937 President Roosevelt asked, of the people of the world: 'Surely the 90 percent who want to live in peace under law and in accordance with moral standards that have received almost universal acceptance through the centuries, can and must find some way to make their will prevail.' Roosevelt added: 'It seems to be unfortunately true that the epidemic of world lawlessness is spreading.'

Seven years later, in 1944 – in the midst of the Second World War – Churchill stressed both the rule of law and the rights of the individual when he asked the Italian people a series of questions about the form of government they would set up in the aftermath of the defeat of Fascism. One of his questions concerned the nature of the law courts that would be set up: 'Will these courts administer open and well-established laws which are associated in the human mind with the broad principles of decency and justice?' he asked. Another of Churchill's questions concerned the relationship between the State and the individual: 'Will the rights of the individual, subject to his duties to the State, be maintained and asserted and exalted?'

In the aftermath of the Second World War, President Truman was as emphatic as Churchill that human rights had to serve as a protector of the social system under which individuals lived and flourished. In contrasting the democratic and communist systems Truman stressed, in 1949: 'Democracy maintains that the government is established for the benefit of the individual and is charged with protecting the rights of the individual and his freedom in the exercise of those abilities.' Truman added that, by contrast, the 'actions resulting from the Communist philosophy are a threat to the efforts of free nations to bring about world recovery and lasting peace'.

The search for that peace, and for the means to halt the forward march of tyranny, was an integral part of national policy among the democracies, among neutrals, and among all states that were vulnerable to the power and avarice of stronger neighbours. Twice during the period covered by this volume – in the late 1930s and again in the early 1950s – considerable thought and effort was put into the search for means of avoiding war, and, when those means failed, into confronting aggression. In 1951, with the Korean War being fought in Asia, and the threat of the Soviet Union looming over the West, it was Truman who tried to draw on the lessons of the past in order to protect the future. 'The Kaiser and Hitler,' Truman said, 'when they started their great wars of aggression, believed that the United States would not come in. They counted on being able to divide the free nations and pick them off one at a time. There could be no excuse for making that mistake today.'

Despite the almost unbroken demands of war-making and national defence, the century continued to be one of great scientific and medical advance, of technical improvements in the way of life of hundreds of millions of people. But there were also the often desperate sufferings of the poor, the dispossessed, the outcasts – often within their own societies – and the refugees. In these pages, the refugees are omnipresent. Sometimes they are the victims of deliberate persecution, at other times they are caught inexorably in the crosscurrents – and often literally in the crossfire – of war, civil war and revolution.

Every historian brings to the study of a particular period perspectives formed from personal experience and reflection. In my own case I have for many years been conscious of the fact that several million people born, as I was, in the years immediately preceding the Second World War, were murdered in it and never grew to adulthood. Their talents, their creativity, their capacity for happiness and family life and friendship, was never allowed to develop. For those who were born in my particular year – 1936 – and were murdered, or killed in air raids, before they reached the age of ten, I feel a special affinity to their stories, and wish to make some reference to them in my pages: Europeans and Asians, Christians and Jews, Poles and Germans – the list could continue for a very long time without being exhausted.

Many episodes in this volume have been the subject of commemoration and reflection. Picasso's *Guernica* for instance, is an example of an artist's immediate response which continues to influence subsequent generations. Hundreds of the events in this volume, often of short duration in time, have been the subject of books: some have been the subject of many books. The 'Rape of Nanking' in 1937 is one example among many. The sinking of the American cruiser *Juneau* in a few minutes in 1944 is another. For virtually every episode described in these pages, usually in a short paragraph, a complete volume could be written. Novels have also reflected moments in time, moods and themes: among those from which I have taken extracts are those of Martha Gellhorn, Arthur Koestler, George Orwell, Alan Paton, Jean-Paul Sartre, Alexander Solzhenitsyn and John Steinbeck. Poems, films, music and paintings also have their place in chronicling the struggles and achievements of the century.

The scale of the loss of human life in wars, civil wars and natural disasters did not diminish after the first third of the century, indeed it escalated. The daily death tolls included those of the Sino-Japanese War, the Italian-Abyssinian War, the Spanish Civil War, the Second World War, and then the daily death tolls of the post-war conflicts, including the civil war in China, the Korean War, and the French wars in Vietnam and Algeria. More secret, but no less terrible, were the killings perpetrated by totalitarian regimes: the fate of millions of defenceless Russians, Chinese and Jews killed in cold blood is an almost unimaginable horror of these years.

Writing in 1973, in his *Bright Book of Life*, Alfred Kazin pointed to the period immediately after the Second World War as the one in which even the most optimistic intellectuals abandoned the hope that war − even the 'just war' of 1939−1945 − had really put an end to international evil and wrongdoing, or that there would be an end to war itself. There were, Kazin wrote, 'so many uncovered horrors, so many new wars on the horizon, such a continued general ominousness, that "*the* war" soon became War anywhere, any time − War that has never ended, War as the continued experience of twentieth century man.'

In quoting this passage in his book *The Great War and Modern Memory*, Paul Fussell notes that whereas in 1916 the image of never-ending war 'has about it, to be sure, a trace of the consciously whimsical and the witty hyperbolic', there was 'nothing but the literal' in this headline from the *New York Times* for 1 September 1972, which read: 'US AIDES IN VIETNAM SEE AN UNENDING WAR'. Fussell comments: 'Thus the drift of modern history domesticates the fantastic and normalizes the unspeakable.'

*   *   *

Nature also made a contribution to the suffering of the human species, through epidemics and earthquakes. As I write these words, the World Health Organization has just announced the deaths last year of three million people from tuberculosis, which can today be cured and even avoided. On the roads, each year saw slaughter that would be shocking, and even unacceptable, if it occurred in war. In the nineteen years covered by this volume, more than a quarter of a million United States citizens were killed in road accidents. These statistics relate to individual human beings, each of whom had a name, sorrowing family and friends, a career cut short, a life unfulfilled.

No chapters devoted to any year of the history of the twentieth century, if they are to be true to events, can be free from descriptions of violence. But the aims and instincts of so many of those living in the twentieth century, even when they have been propelled by the fiercest of national and ideological forces, have been to improve and enhance the pattern and quality of daily life. Those twentieth century men and women who prided themselves on their civilization did so because it had evolved and emerged from darker eras. In the words of E.H. Gombrich and E. Kris, written in 1940: 'Civilization has taught us to renounce cruelty and aggression, which once ran riot in atrocious reality and magical practices.' By tragic irony, as these words were published 'atrocious reality' had returned over much of the civilized globe to plague mankind.

There have always been victors in history, in the generally accepted sense of the word: those victorious nations which defeated their adversaries in battle and did well, territorially and even financially, out of their military success. But even for those countries that were victorious, the demons of fear, suffering and loss, and the memory of harsh times and bitter lessons, have never been far from the surface. The struggles that emerged after both the First and Second World Wars were the struggles to prevent future war, to create a mechanism and a state of mind conducive to the peaceful settlement of disputes. But the struggles, whether of nationalism in its extreme forms, or between the Communist and non-Communist world, or between the colonial rulers and those whom they ruled, repeatedly lurched towards violence, and the threat of violence. Ethnic hatreds also pulsated through the decades; in 1935 the historian H.A.L. Fisher commented, almost in despair: 'An insane racialism threatens to rupture the seamless garment of civilization.'

The most forceful threat of destruction – and certainly also the most powerful deterrent to destruction – emerging from the Second World War, and created during the war as a means of victory, was atomic power. This was a threat that led to intense anguish within democratic societies, where the anti-nuclear debate brought moral and medical arguments to bear upon the strategic arguments. It was the development of the Hydrogen Bomb that led seven Nobel Prize winners, among them Albert Einstein, to call in the 1950s for the renunciation of nuclear weapons by all governments possessing nuclear weapons, and for those governments 'to find peaceful means for the settlement of all matters of disputes between them'. The Nobel laureates stressed that 'a war with H-bombs might possibly put an end to the human race'.

The threats to the human race – or to vast areas of human habitation – have been recognized by those nations prepared to take a moral stance in the interest of the rule of law and the rights of the individual. For the first half of the century, Britain, even while an Imperial and Colonial power, took a lead in the defence of democracy. But the weakness of Britain in the 1930s, both militarily and in terms of commitment, threw a question mark over how far she would be willing or able to continue to shoulder that burden. As Churchill warned two years before the outbreak of the Second World War: 'If mortal catastrophe should overtake the British Nation and the British Empire, historians a thousand years hence will still be baffled by the mystery of our affairs. They will never understand how it was that a victorious nation, with everything in hand, suffered themselves to be brought low, and to cast away all that they had gained by measureless sacrifice and absolute victory – gone with the wind!' The forces of evil had filled the vacuum created by the withdrawal of those who could have been at the forefront of the defence of democracy. 'Now the victors are the vanquished,' Churchill commented, 'and those who threw down their arms in the field and sued for an armistice are striding on to world mastery.'

Britain took up her role in 1939, as she had done in 1914, and with an even stronger sense of moral purpose, though much weaker militarily. But it was the United States which, during the Second World War and after it, took over the mantle of British democratic concerns, and by the end of this volume had become in effect the world's policeman. The first war in which the United States took the leading part from the outset was the Korean War, which began in 1950, as the twentieth century entered its second half. Many other burdens were also shouldered by the United States in the half century following the Second World War, at a time when Britain lacked the military and financial – though never entirely the moral – strength to shoulder those burdens. The achievements of the United Nations agencies in many areas of welfare and support for the Third World would never have been possible in their past and current scale but for the direct involvement of the United States. The maintenance of the Cold War barriers against Communism likewise depended above all on United States participation in the Western defence systems. Other nations, most notably India, strove to take on the mantle of beneficent leadership, or to share it, while lacking the international strength. Canada likewise sought to make its contribution to upholding international morality. The emergence of European unity – at first confined to Western Europe – held a similar international aspiration.

The period covered in this volume is not only recent history; it is a history of which many elements continue to emerge almost every day. As a result of the research of historians, of interviews with eye-witnesses, of newly published memoirs, and the continual public and journalistic focus on the recent past, there is no end to the information, and even the perspectives, that come to light. During the writing of the first and second of these volumes no day passed without a newspaper or magazine article being published that contained material bearing directly on the episodes or personalities that are an integral part of the story of our century. Neither the fascination nor the importance of the Twentieth Century will allow its earlier years to be treated as dead or dry. The issues with which we live from day to day as the century ends have their past, and their echoes, in the events of each earlier decade.

Merton College
Oxford
15 July 1998

ACKNOWLEDGEMENTS

In the course of writing this volume I incurred many debts of gratitude. My main thanks are to the archivists, librarians, authors and fellow-historians whose holdings and whose writings have been my principal source over many years. I have listed in the bibliography all those works from which I have made direct quotation. Without the work of many hundreds of other writers – contemporaries, eye-witnesses, participants, bystanders, journalists and historians – no work such as this could be attempted. In particular, the researches of historians over many years form an indispensable bedrock of information.

Almost every book cited in the bibliography, especially in the biography and general works sections, was itself the result of many years of reading and research by its author. To take one example at random, Lawrence D. Walker's study of Hitler Youth and Catholic Youth in the first four years of the Hitler regime in Germany contains 115 items in its own bibliography. To take another example, for his book on the fate of primarily Americans held captive by the Japanese during the Second World War, Gavan Daws interviewed, or had access to the personal testimonies, of 178 former prisoners of war.

Interest in recent history is such that no day passes without several articles in the national newspapers in many lands, including Britain and the United States, on some past episode. I have drawn on a number of these articles, and have listed them in a special section of the bibliography. Newspaper obituaries also provide, on an almost daily basis, records of historical events and details of the lives of those who participated in them.

As well as the published works of others, I have been helped in this volume, as in its predecessor, by those who sent me material which I was able to use with regard to specific episodes. For such material I am grateful to Geoff Carver (the aftermath of the bombing of Dresden), Sam Chernawsky (the 'Rape of Nanking'), Harry Crooks (the incident at Imber Down), Ian Edwards, Department of the Environment, Transport and the Regions (British road deaths), Fred Gaffen, Canadian War Museum (Canada's participation in the Korean War), Lyn Cianflocco,

United States Department of Transportation (American road deaths), Ron Hoffman Sr (the battles for Peleliu and Anguar), Jan Hoser (the executions in Warsaw in February 1944), the late Wim van Leer ('Operation Tooth'), Vilém Precan (the fate of Archbishop Beran, Vilém Novy and Václav Nosek), Wallace Reid (Empire Training Scheme), Stan Rose (influenza and other epidemics) and Arno Surminski (the Soviet army's entry into East Prussia).

Many people have sent me information and material that I have used in this volume, and for this I would like to thank Dr Stanislaw Biernacki (Director of the Main Commission on Nazi Crimes, Warsaw), Leslie Blau, Dr Melvyn H. Brooks, Geraldine Cohen, Antony Copley, Robert Craig, Ellis Douek, John and Carol Garrard, David Gilbert, Richard Goldsmith (Chairman, The Richard Strauss Society), Richard Gott, Jane Gottlieb (Juilliard School Library), Zena Harman, Ben Helfgott, Renée Silberman Holt, Sir Michael Jay, Rick Kardonne, Brother James M. Kelly, Serge Klarsfeld, Tonk van Lexmond, David Littman, Sean McCoy, Len Mader, Cyril Mazansky, Valerie Nevin, George Newkey-Burden (*Daily Telegraph*), Esther Poznansky, Dr Jo Reilly, Jeremy Rex-Parkes (Archivist, Christie's), Sir Robert Rhodes James, Sam Mozes, Eric S. Root (The Claremont Institute), Professor Oleg Rzheshevsky (Centre for War History Studies, Russian Academy of Sciences), Colin D. Sells, Colin Shindler, Jeffrey Siegel, Barbara E. Spicer, M. Richard Strauss, Jan Thompson, Hugh Toye, Mike Tregenza, Sir Leslie Turnberg, Lord Williams of Elvel, and Guy Chalermsuk Yugala.

I am most grateful to those librarians and archivists who answered my queries and sent me material from their holdings. For help in this regard I would like to thank Lady de Bellaigue, The Royal Archives; Betty Austin, Archivist, Fulbright papers, University of Arkansas at Fayettville; the librarians and staff of the British Newspaper Library, Colindale; Lorraine Collett, Supporters' Information Team, Oxfam; Eamon Dyas, Group Records Manager, News International; Felice Betty Litchfield (Public Relations Officer) and Group Captain Bruce Wynn (Acting Secretary), Kwai Railway Memorial, Three Pagodas Group; Vernon W. Newton, Director, Franklin D. Roosevelt Library, Hyde Park, New York; Jorgen Diekmann Rasmussen, City Archivist, Esbjerg; Amanda Robertson, London Library; and Sarah West, Information Assistant, United Nations High Commissioner for Refugees, London. I was also helped in my search for material by Gary Allen, New Zealand Defence Staff, London; Putriga Ampaipan, Second Secretary, Royal Thai Embassy, London; Ewan Hyde, New Zealand Defence Force Library; His Excellency François Nordmann, Ambassador of Switzerland in London; and His Excellency J. H. R. D. van Roijen, Royal Netherlands Ambassador, London.

Personal recollections which I used in this volume were sent to me by Tom Fleming, Dr Harry Jacobi, Henry Miller, Professor Robert O'Neill, Baroness Park of Monmouth, Gerhard Schoenberner, Henry Schwab and Shippen Swift.

Friendship with some of those who reported this period or wrote about it at the time guided me many years ago to look closely at the contemporary newspaper record: in this regard I was much influenced by G.E.R. Gedye and Alexander Werth. In conversation with me in 1962, Professor Michael Polanyi stressed the need for freedom to find a popular base, as nationalism and socialism had done so readily. Jeremy Carver helped me with several conundrums with regard to international law, and Larry Arnn with a difficult point of United States constitutional history. Hugh Lunghi cast a 'Russian eye' over the Soviet sections. My former school teacher and friend, the historian Alan Palmer, scrutinized the typescript of this volume as he did its predecessor, and made many helpful suggestions. Morris J. Massel provided important newspaper and other historical material from the United States and was both patient and productive with my queries. Kay Thomson did the same in Britain, and also helped enormously with the search for information. I am grateful to the staff of the Hulton Getty Picture Collection, and in particular to Luigi Di Dio, for allowing me to roam their stacks in search of the photographic material which illustrates this book, and from which I also derived important historical information. Permission to reproduce the photographs was given by Churchill College, Cambridge (No. 5), the City of Esbjerg Archive (No. 19), the Imperial War Museum (Nos. 20 and 22), Hodder and Stoughton (No. 21), Yad Vashem, Jerusalem (No. 26), and the Hulton Getty Picture Collection for the rest.

Arabella Pike made many useful suggestions of form and content. Charlotte Sacher helped during a crucial week. As with the previous volume, Tim Aspden transformed my very rough map drafts into maps of the utmost clarity. Beccy Goodhart of William Morrow gave me encouragement from afar. My son Joshua helped me in the search for wall plaques and memorials in Paris. My son David helped me prepare the index. As with every one of my books over the past twenty-seven years, my wife Susie has been my main source of encouragement and inspiration.

PART ONE

CHAPTER ONE

1933

If fair-dealing be taken away,
what are kingdoms
but brigandage on a large scale.

SAINT AUGUSTINE

DURING 1933 much of the world was preoccupied with the consolidation of Nazi rule in Germany. There was intense curiosity, and even anxiety, about what the new German government really intended. The imposition of domestic tyranny went hand in hand with Germany's repeated public protestations of international peaceful intentions. Yet even as the tyranny within Germany was being directed at those who were considered enemies of the regime, a wave of skilfully organized enthusiasm led to widely reported demands for the carrying out of Nazi ideals. During the first days of May, Nazi students demonstrated against what they called 'non-German culture', demanding an end to what they characterized as alien, and especially socialist and Jewish, influences. Those influences had hitherto been an integral part of German life and culture. On 1 May 1933, the traditional May Day of the working classes, the National Socialist Workers Unions organized a Day of National Work, complete with demonstrations and banners, reminiscent of the great working-class spectacles of earlier years, but with a total hostility to the socialist work ethic and aspirations of the past. The traditional theme of international solidarity was replaced by the call for national renewal. In proclaiming a 'holy day of national labour', Hitler's Minister of Propaganda, Dr Josef Goebbels – the leading propagandist of Nazism – declared: 'Germans of all estates, lineages, and professions, join hands! In serried ranks we march into the new age.'

On the day after May Day, the buildings of the Socialist Trade Unions were occupied by the Nazis, and all German trade union leaders arrested.

This operation was organized by Robert Ley, a chemist by profession, and one of Hitler's earliest supporters, who established a German Labour Front, to be the sole representative of the German working man. In explaining the sudden destruction of the existing trade unions, Ley declared: 'Workers, your institutions are sacred and unassailable to us National Socialists. I myself am a poor son of peasants and have known poverty. I swear to you that we shall not only preserve everything you have, we shall extend the rights of the worker in order that he might enter the new National Socialist State as an equal and respected member of the nation.'

Not only the traditional ideals of organized labour but the century-old evolution of German culture was under attack, and not in Germany alone. In Vienna, on May 9, Nazi university students defied the Austrian authorities to raise the Swastika banner, and, as students left the lecture halls, to set upon them with truncheons and sticks studded with nails, crying out, in the words of the *Daily Telegraph* correspondent, G.E.R Gedye: 'Hail, Hitler. Perish the Jews.'* Gedye added: 'The students, including girls, were driven into the lecture room and tried to barricade the door against the Nazi attacks. Many jumped from first floor windows into the street, sustaining nasty injuries.'

On the following day, May 10, in Berlin, the Public Prosecutor ordered the immediate confiscation of all the property and funds of the Socialist Party and its allies. All Socialist newspapers were confiscated and the assets of all Socialist organizations seized. It was a final blow to such freedom of Socialist expression that remained: since Hitler had come to power three months earlier the number of Socialist newspapers had declined from well over a hundred to less than twenty.

That midnight, in the square facing the Berlin Opera House, and the university, a bonfire of books was lit, photographs of which were to appear within twenty-four hours on the front pages of hundreds of newspapers around the world. But many of the reports of the event poured scorn on it. Under the headline

'SYMBOLIC' HOLOCAUST'
DAMPED BY RAIN AND APATHY

the *Daily Telegraph* Berlin correspondent, Eustace B. Wareing, wrote:

---

* The first cry soon became universally known in its German form: *Heil, Hitler*. The second was *Juda verrecke*. (*Verrecken* is slang for To kick the bucket).

The symbolical burning at the stake of Jewish, 'Marxist' and pacifist books which took place here this evening must have been a disappointment to its organizers. The ceremony was damped not only by a heavy and prolonged shower of rain, but also by apathy on the part of the public.

As the Opera House Square in which the holocaust was accomplished was reserved for the students and their friends, the only part of the ceremony visible to the wider public was the torchlight procession by which the condemned volumes were escorted to the bonfire.

But, though the route followed was not more than two or three miles long, there were, even before the rain began, stretches of as much as one hundred yards on which not a single spectator was stationed.

It was quite obvious that the mass of the population is not interested in 'the fight against the un-German spirit'.

The procession itself was rather a poor spectacle. It was mainly composed of a few thousand young Nazis, some in the orthodox Storm Detachment uniform, some in the white shirts of the Nazi sporting students, and some, who were lucky in having overcoats, in ordinary civilian dress.

There was a small group of Steel Helmet youths, a smattering of girls, and a few dozen schoolboys as a tail to the procession. A Nazi band took the lead, and the students sang their patriotic songs as they marched.

'The condemned books were carried in two or three tradesmen's delivery vans,' the correspondent wrote. 'There can hardly have been more than one volume for each member of the escort. The total number collected was under 20,000, and a few hundredweight were sold to a dealer for pulping.'

The word 'holocaust' was being used in its literal sense, as a destruction by fire – the current use of the word only became widespread almost half a century later. The books that were thrown on the flames at midnight on May 10 had been judged according to the Nazi ideology to be harmful to the German spirit. They included books on philosophy and psychology, books of Communist, Socialist, democratic or humanistic outlook; books by Jews; books like Erich Maria Remarque's *All Quiet on the Western Front*, which failed to glorify war; or like Ivan Uksusov's two books *The Sisters* and *The Twentieth Century*, that glorified the wrong war. Uksusov, a Soviet writer living in Leningrad, had praised the heroism of the war effort of Bolshevik workers during the Russian Civil War.

Reflecting five years later on the burning of the books that night, any mocking of which had quickly evaporated, the novelist E.M. Forster noted that 'some of the books were by Jews, others Communist, others liberal, others "unscientific", and all of them were "un-German",' and he added:

It was for the government to decide what was un-German. There was an elaborate ritual. Nine heralds came forward in turn, and consigned an author with incantations to the flames.

For example, the fourth herald said: 'Concerning the corrosion of the soul by the exaggeration of the dangers of war! Upholding the nobility of the human spirit, I consign to the flames the writings of Sigmund Freud'.

The seventh herald said: 'Concerning the literary betrayal of the World War Soldier! Upholding the education of our people in the spirit of reality, I consign to the flames the writings of Erich Maria Remarque,' author of the novel *All Quiet on the Western Front*.

'There were holocausts in the provinces too,' Forster added, 'and students were instructed to erect "pillars of infamy" outside their universities; the pillar should be "a thick tree-trunk, somewhat above the height of a man", to which were to be nailed "utterances of those who, by their participation in activities defamatory of character, have forfeited their membership of the German nation".'

The expulsion of Jews from their positions in the German universities was as swift and complete as the burning of books. When Fritz Haber, the Nobel Prize-winning chemist, was deprived of his professorship, *The Times* reflected on the 'irony' that Germany's ability to carry on fighting during the four years of the First World War 'was in all probability due to him more than to any other man'. The leading German authority on civil law, Martin Wolff, was physically driven out of his lecture room by students wearing Swastika armbands. No Jewish painter or sculptor was allowed to exhibit at the annual Academy Exhibition; this prohibition included Jewish artists who had seen active war service at the front. On May 14 Goebbels' newspaper, *Der Angriff* (The Attack), published the following advice: 'When addressed by a Jew, act as though you did not hear properly and stare into the distance. If this should not prove effective let your gaze travel coldly up and down his outlandish body. If he still does not catch on, remark: "Sir, there must be some mistake. You have not yet emigrated".'

The excesses of Nazism inside Germany were shocking to the many members of the international community, but there seemed to be no immediate cause

for, or means of, external intervention. The debates that filled the deliberations of the League of Nations at Geneva, and had been the subject of
annual diplomatic exchanges and agreements since the end of war in 1918,
centred around how to avert a second 'Great War' between the former
victorious powers and those whom they had defeated, and punished.

Disarmament was to be the means whereby nations would avoid any
repetition of the bloodletting of 1914 to 1918, in which an estimated fifteen
million soldiers had fallen on the battlefields of Europe, Africa and Asia.
The very concept of war as a means of resolving disputes between nations
had been challenged in 1928 by the Kellogg-Briand Pact, outlawing war.
Secretary of State Frank Kellogg's leading part in that pact – to which
sixty-two nations adhered, and for which Kellogg had been awarded the
Nobel Peace Prize – associated the United States in the quest for permanent
peace at the highest level. Disarmament, the principal method envisaged at
Geneva for avoiding war, was to be effected by negotiations through the
good auspices of the League of Nations.

On May 16 President Roosevelt made a public appeal to all governments
to work towards a successful conclusion of the World Disarmament Conference at Geneva. It was a powerful call for an end to warmaking armaments.
During the course of his remarks, Roosevelt said:

If we ask what are the reasons for armaments it becomes clear that they
are two-fold – first a desire, disclosed or hidden on the part of Governments
to enlarge their territories at the expense of sister nations. I believe that
only a small minority of Governments and peoples harbour such a purpose.
Second – the fear of the nations that they will be invaded. I believe the
overwhelming majority of the peoples feel obliged to retain excessive
armaments because they fear some act of aggression against them, not
because they themselves seek to be the aggressors.

There is justification for this fear. Modern weapons of offence are vastly
stronger than modern weapons of defence. Frontier forts, trenches, wire
entanglements, coast defences – in a word, fixed fortifications – are no
longer impregnable to the attack of war planes, heavy mobile artillery,
land battleships called tanks, and poison gas. If all nations agree wholly
to eliminate from their possession and use weapons which make possible
successful attack, defences automatically will become impregnable and the
frontiers and independence of every nation will be secure.

The ultimate object of the Disarmament Conference must be the complete elimination of all offensive weapons. The immediate objective is a substantial reduction of some of these weapons and the elimination of many others.

On the day after Roosevelt's appeal, Hitler – who had become German Chancellor only eleven weeks after Roosevelt was elected President of the United States – made a conciliatory speech, in which he appeared to accept one of the proposals of the conference. This was the suggestion, hitherto unacceptable to Germany, that the existing regular German Army should be transformed into a short-service army. Germany did not wish to take any other path, Hitler declared, 'than that recognized as justified by the peace treaties themselves'.

The application of violence 'would have no favourable effect' on the existing political or economic situation; Hitler insisted, however, that neither the two million members of the SA – the *Sturmabteilung* (Storm Detachment), known as the Brownshirts – nor the quarter of a million members of the Stahlhelm, the strongly conservative association of German ex-servicemen, were military organizations. Hitler also excluded the thousand members of the SS – the *Schutzstaffeln*, Protection Squad – originally established as his personal bodyguard, commanded by Heinrich Himmler, from any head-count of German military strength. In March an SS military unit, the Leibstanddarte Adolf Hitler, had been set up under Sepp Dietrich. The sole purpose of these various forces, Hitler insisted, was 'to protect Germany against Communism'. Whatever arms they possessed could not therefore be counted in Germany's total, nor could their numbers be relevant to the proposed upper limit of 200,000 men each for the armies of Germany, France, Italy and Poland. Hitler was supported in his disingenuous, even brazen assertion by the governments of Italy, Austria and Hungary.

While welcoming the involvement of the United States into European relations 'as a guarantor of peace', Hitler nevertheless continued his speech with words of warning. 'The German Government and the German people,' he said, 'will under no circumstances allow themselves to be forced to sign what would mean a perpetuation of the degradation of Germany.' An attempt had been made 'in newspaper articles and regrettable speeches' to threaten Germany with sanctions, 'but such a monstrous step would only be our punishment for having pressed for the carrying out of the Treaties by our demand for disarmament. Such a measure could only lead to the definite moral and effective invalidation of the Treaties.'

Hitler went on to say that even if the treaties were to be 'invalidated' in this way, Germany 'would never abandon her peaceful claims'. But the political and economic consequences, 'the chaos which such an attempt would bring upon Europe, would be the responsibility of those who used such means against a people which is doing the world no harm'. He then raised the possibility of Germany withdrawing from the League, telling his German listeners: 'It would be difficult for us as a constantly defamed nation to continue to belong to the League of Nations.'

The United States continued to take a lead in trying to maintain a momentum of negotiations, and to work out an acceptable formula for disarmament. As a sign of America's commitment to the disarmament ideal, on May 22 the leader of the United States delegation at Geneva, Norman Davis, expressed his country's readiness to reduce its armed forces to the level provided by the post-war peace treaties, even though the United States Congress had voted, in 1920, against involvement with the treaties. As the negotiations continued, however, it became clear that France, suspicious of German intentions, was not willing to risk too small a discrepancy between her armaments, which were to be reduced, and those of Germany, which were to be increased to a level closer to that of France.

In July the British Foreign Secretary, Arthur Henderson, who was committed, with his government, to the success of the negotiations, made a 'disarmament pilgrimage' to various capitals, but failed to bridge the gap between them. When he was in Berlin he suggested to Hitler that a compromise might be found through a direct meeting between Hitler and the French Prime Minister, Edouard Daladier, but Hitler was not enthusiastic. Henderson also put to Hitler a French proposal intended to break the deadlock, for a 'probationary period' of a number of years during which a method of supervision would be tested, before the actual disarmament began. Hitler rejected any such supervision outright.

The continued search by the League of Nations for effective disarmament was supported publicly by those for whom pacifism was an ideology as tenaciously held as the nationalisms which regarded disarmament as 'sapping the moral fibre'. It was in indignation that a distinguished British author, Major Yeats Brown, commented that 'the whole pacifist case rests on the denial of nationality'. On July 25 a British pacifist, Beverley Nichols, wrote to the *Daily Telegraph*:

As for 'sapping the moral fibre', I should like to know exactly how the 'moral fibre' is improved by ascending into an aeroplane and dropping bombs of Lewisite on to hospitals, which will be the chief occupation of the dupes of the next war, in every country.

Whose moral fibre is likely to be improved by this little sport? The aviators or the invalids?

But of course it goes deeper than that, as those who do me the honour of reading my little book will realize. Major Yeats Brown hits the nail on the head when he writes that 'the whole pacifist case rests on a denial of nationality'. It does.

We pacifists must be honest enough to admit it. We have to lower flags that we love, to deny causes and movements that are glamorous and profitable, to be prepared to wear on our sleeves the badge, 'Traitor to His Country'. It isn't pleasant. It isn't easy. But we must do it. Somebody must begin, lest all should end.

Despite the popular appeal of the pacifist argument, the rulers of the nations around Germany had to contemplate the possibility that the accentuated and intensified German nationalism might pose a threat not only to their borders, but to their independence and way of life. Marshal Josef Pilsudski, Poland's Minister of War and virtual dictator, had by far the most dramatic proposal, which he put to the French Government: that Poland should occupy the Free City of Danzig, East Prussia and Silesia until Hitler had resigned and a new Chancellor given guarantees to maintain the Versailles settlement. The French turned Pilsudski down.

Disturbed by the implications of Hitler's call for the revision of the Treaty of Versailles, three nations of central Europe – Czechoslovakia, Yugoslavia and Roumania – under the leadership of the Czech Foreign Minister, Eduard Benes, strengthened their existing Little Entente, creating a Permanent Council, a Secretariat and an Economic Council – a virtual diplomatic federation. Winston Churchill, a Member of Parliament who had held high office before, during and after the First World War, but who had been without a place in government since 1929, set out the German danger as he saw it when he spoke to his parliamentary constituents near London on August 12. 'Nobody can watch the events which are taking place in Germany without increasing anxiety about what their outcome will be,' he said. 'At present Germany is only partly armed and most of her fury is turned upon herself. But already her smaller neighbours, Austria, Switzerland, Belgium, and Denmark, feel a deep disquietude. There is grave reason to believe that

Germany is arming herself, or seeking to arm herself, contrary to the solemn treaties exacted from her in her hour of defeat.'

Alarmed by the realization that German rearmament was already under way, Churchill, who had been First Lord of the Admiralty at the outbreak of the First World War, expressed his hope that the National Government, 'and especially the Cabinet Ministers in charge of the Navy and Army and Air Force, will realize how grave is their responsibility. They are responsible, like the Ministers before the War, for our essential safety'. Churchill added: 'I trust they will make sure that the forces of the Crown are kept in a proper state of efficiency, with the supplies and munitions factories which they require, and that they will be strong enough to enable us to count for something when we work for peace, and strong enough if war should come in Europe to maintain our effective neutrality, unless we should decide of our own free will to the contrary.'

'. . . if war should come to Europe'. Churchill knew that Hitler's appeal, and that of the Nazi Party, was not restricted to the existing post-1919 borders of Germany. Hundreds of thousands of Germans lived beyond those borders. Those living in Danzig, Memel and the Saar, and in the Polish Corridor, had been part of Imperial Germany before the defeat of 1918. Others had been part of the Austro-Hungarian Empire, or were members of German minorities in Denmark, South Tyrol (which had been transferred to Italy from Austria-Hungary in 1919) and elsewhere in central and eastern Europe. To many of these Germans the prospect of a revived, strong, trium- phant Germany made a strong appeal. In almost every case, the pro-Nazi movements began as small minorities, but they received constant funding and guidance from Germany to carry on their work. The overseas Nazi Parties – most vociferously those in Austria, the Sudetenland, the Saar and Danzig – struggled to win the support of all the German-speaking peoples within their regions. Many of these Germans were democrats, liberals, humanitarians, socialists or Jews; others were attracted by the shrill mixture of Pan-German, racist and nationalist appeals.

On October 1, Konrad Henlein, a former German subject of the Austro-Hungarian Empire (he was born in Bohemia in 1898), who had recently become the head of the German Gymnastics Association of Czechoslovakia, founded a pro-Nazi movement inside Czechoslovakia. Although he had been born in Bohemia, the German-speaking peoples he decided to lead, and if possible to bring into the Nazi orbit, were the Germans of the Sudetenland. These Germans had never been part of Germany, but of Austria-Hungary.

To help start Henlein's Sudeten German Party, the German Foreign Office, which monitored all pro-Nazi activity outside Germany, financed Henlein's newspaper and paid his Party debts. Within a year he was able to call his first mass meeting, to which 20,000 Sudeten Germans came.

Germany continued to assert her territorial demands throughout the autumn. One of these was for the return of the Saar to Germany: Hitler's Minister of Propaganda, Dr Joseph Goebbels, regularly demanded the return of this territory, which had been detached under the Treaty of Versailles, and for which a plebiscite was to be held in two years' time. Germany also demanded to be allowed to acquire at least 'samples' of the armaments which, under Versailles, she had been forbidden in their entirety. At the same time Hitler continued to reject the proposals for arms supervision for which France was pressing. On October 14, as a British proposal to find a rearmament formula acceptable to both Germany and France was being submitted, Germany suddenly and unexpectedly announced that, as she had been denied 'equality of rights' with regard to armaments, she was withdrawing from both the World Disarmament Conference and the League of Nations.

This act of defiance astounded those nations of the world for whom disarmament was an essential precondition to world peace. Hitler articulated his position in a radio broadcast. 'If the world decides that all weapons are to be abolished down to the last machine-gun,' he said, 'we are ready to join at once in such a convention. If the world decides that certain weapons are to be destroyed, we are ready to dispense with them immediately. But if the world grants to each nation certain weapons, we are not prepared to let ourselves be excluded from this concession as a nation with inferior rights.'

Anxious not to have Germany's withdrawal from the World Disarmament Conference seen as in any way threatening France, Hitler then spoke of the French soldier as 'our ancient and glorious opponent'. He continued, in pacific, mellifluous mode:

We and the whole German nation would rejoice at the thought that we might spare our children and children's children what we as honourable men had to watch and suffer in the long years of bitterness. The history of the last one hundred and fifty years should in its changing course have taught the two nations that essential and enduring changes are no more to be gained by the sacrifice of blood.

As a National-Socialist I, with all my followers, refuse by reason of our national principles to acquire by conquest the members of other nations, who will never love us, at the cost of the blood and lives of those who are dear to us.

It would be a great day for all humanity if these two nations of Europe would banish, once and for all, force from their common life. The German people is ready to do so. While claiming boldly those rights which the Treaties themselves have given us, I will say as boldly that there are otherwise for Germany no grounds for territorial conflict.

Hitler then spoke specifically of the Saar, which he, like Dr Goebbels, repeatedly demanded as an integral part of Germany, as it had been before 1918. 'When the Saar territory has been restored to Germany,' Hitler said, 'only a madman would consider the possibility of war between the two States, for which, from our point of view, there is no rational or moral ground. For no one could demand that millions of men in the flower of youth should be annihilated for the sake of a readjustment, indefinite in scope, of our present frontier.'

Hitler's protestations of peace came amid the flurry of the collapse of the disarmament talks. How could Germany's worried neighbours interpret his words? The very meaning of words was beginning to change, to take on a bizarre difference from reality. Language itself was being used as a weapon to deceive and to lull. Could there be any more noble ideals than to 'spare our children' and to 'banish' force?

The British Government was actively pursuing a policy of disarmament, whereby the well-armed nations, led by France, would reduce their arms substantially, to a level that Germany would find less threatening. Churchill, convinced that British pressure to secure French disarmament could only encourage Hitler to embark upon aggression across his borders, proposed in the House of Commons on November 7 that the League of Nations should seek 'some redress of the grievances of the German nation, and that this may be effected before this peril of disarmament reaches a point which may endanger the peace of the world.' He had already stated publicly, two months before Hitler came to power, that 'the removal of the just grievances of the vanquished ought to precede the disarmament of the victors'. Otherwise, he had warned then, the vanquished would be able to resort to war to obtain what they believed was theirs. Unless Germany's grievances were redressed while the former Allies remained strong, Europe would 'drift on, inch by inch and stage by stage, until once again vast combinations, equally matched, confront each other face to face'.

Within Germany, where the left-wing Parties had been suppressed during the first three months of Nazi rule, pressure on the centre and right-wing Parties was continuous throughout the summer and autumn. The Stahlhelm, the conservative association of German ex-servicemen whose members Hitler had insisted could not be counted as part of Germany's armed strength, turned its considerable political weight and military strength and allegiance from Hugenberg to Hitler. Abandoned by his most important organization, Hugenberg resigned.

Von Papen's Centre Party was under particularly strong pressure to give up its rights within Hitler's coalition; unable to resist that pressure, which was felt in the streets as much as in the Reichstag, the Centre Party dissolved itself. The coalition that Hitler had formed at the beginning of the year was at an end. On July 14, the day on which the people of France celebrated the overthrow of monarchy and the establishment of a parliamentary system, a German government decree made illegal the existence of any political party other than the Nazi Party. Four months later, at the General Election held on November 12, only the Nazi Party was allowed to campaign. The only candidates allowed were Nazi Party candidates. Not surprisingly Hitler obtained 95 per cent of the votes cast. Within a year of coming to power his power was absolute. His main financial support came from German industry and the banks. There were still four million unemployed, but in the three months since Hitler had come to power 1,300,000 former unemployed had been given work on public work projects.

Hitler's main instrument of control was one which Stalin had been using for several years inside the Soviet Union: the arrest and incarceration of all opponents, without trial or right of appeal. On the one hand, Stalin despatched his opponents to the remote regions of Russia – the labour camp zones that had been set up a decade earlier in North Russia and spread eastward vast distances to the Urals and Siberia. On the other, Hitler, having much less land at his disposal, created concentration camps within a few miles of Germany's main cities. These included Sachsenhausen near Berlin and Dachau near Munich.

In the first six months of Nazi rule more than 26,000 Germans had been taken into the 'protective custody' of concentration camps or Gestapo prisons. Most of those arrested had been members of the Social Democratic and

Communist Parties. Some were Christian priests who had spoken out in their pulpits against the racism of the regime. Among those taken to the concentration camps were lawyers who, during the years of the Weimar Republic, had defended trade union organizations and individual workers, often against Nazi violence. Jewish shopkeepers and businessmen were arrested at random, often denounced for an imaginary crime by some jealous local non-Jewish rival. At the beginning of August, in Regensburg, whose Jewish community numbered just over four hundred, more than a quarter of the community was taken into 'protective custody'. At Hamm, a leading trade unionist, Julius Rosemann – a Jew – was shot dead on August 22. That same week the Central Association for German Deaf expelled all its Jewish members. One of those expelled from the Berlin branch was an elderly woman who had been a member for fifty-seven years, since 1876. That same month, all Jewish deaf lost the monthly financial relief to which all German deaf were entitled as a result of the payment of their subscriptions over many years.

In October a new disciplinary and punishment code was introduced at Dachau concentration camp. The aim was to create a 'Model Concentration Camp' where compliance with orders would be absolute. The code was explicit: 'Agitators are to be hanged by virtue of the Law of the Revolution.' By the end of 1933 at least 100,000 Germans were being held in concentration camps, Dachau among them, subjected to forced labour, to constant indignities, brutality, and the danger of sudden violent death. It was widely known throughout Germany, and far beyond its borders, that several hundred Germans had been murdered in that first year of Nazism triumphant.

The ability of German Catholicism, and of the supporters of the Centre Party which had been so powerful in Germany for so many years, to act as a force for moderation was undermined in the early months of the Nazi regime when Hitler negotiated a Concordat with the Pope. Under its terms the Catholic Church agreed not to carry out any political activities. In return Hitler's government promised not to interfere with Catholic life inside Germany. The Concordat was signed on July 20. Five days later the German government published a decree which had actually been passed by Hitler's Cabinet eleven days earlier – on the day the Cabinet had approved the Concordat – under which compulsory sterilization was ordered for all individuals who were blind, deaf, deformed or suffering from mental disorders. When the Centre Party newspaper *Germania* published an article in support of the new decree, the Vatican condemned the article, and urged German

Catholics to adhere to an earlier Papal Encyclical which declared that 'public magistrates have no direct power over the bodies of their subjects . . . they can never directly harm or tamper with the integrity of the body, either for the reasons of eugenics or for any other reason.'

In a series of laws and regulations the position of the Catholic Church worsened, despite the Concordat. On July 29 Baldur von Schirach, who five weeks earlier had been appointed Youth Leader of the German Reich, announced that all members of Nazi youth organizations, including the Hitler Youth, were forbidden to hold membership in Church youth groups. As membership in the Hitler Youth was already necessary for many jobs, and for all civil service positions, this order fell particularly harshly on members of the Christian youth organizations, of which the Catholic Youth were the most numerous.

Hitler was confident that, through the instrument of the Nazi youth organizations, the racism he wished to promulgate would win wide acceptance. 'Only in our own day does the significance of the laws of race and racial heredity dawn upon mankind,' he declared in a speech at Nuremberg on September 2. Those laws would serve 'as the basis for the coming development'. Hitler was also confident that, as a result of Nazi efforts among the youth, Christian parents would soon lose control of the minds and beliefs of their children, telling an audience in the East Prussian town of Elbing on November 6: 'When an opponent declares, "I will not come over to your side, and you will not get me on your side," I calmly say, "Your child belongs to me already. A people lives forever. What are you? You will pass on. Your descendants, however, now stand in the new camp. In a short time they will know nothing else but this new community."' Von Schirach echoed his Leader's voice three weeks later, when he said in a public speech that the Nazi Party intended to educate German youth 'in the cult of race and nation' and would dissociate Catholic Youth from the Catholic organizations.

Hitler reiterated his confidence in the ultimate triumph of 'race and nation' when he spoke in Munich on November 10 at the tenth anniversary commemoration of the failed Beer Hall putsch. But the racism of the Nazi Party was anathema to many German churchmen. In a series of sermons, the Catholic Archbishop of Munich, Cardinal Michael von Faulhaber, spoke courageously against the racial policies of the Nazi regime. 'The individual must not be deprived of his own dignity,' he said, 'or be treated as a slave without rights of his own.' Other Catholic priests also protested against the new tyranny. For doing so, many were arrested and sent to concentration camps. The Protestant Evangelical clergy, having established a Pastors' Emergency League, publicly opposed the introduction of Nazi ideology into the Evangelical ranks. The inspiration for this act of defiance was a pastor of the church, Martin Niemöller, who, as a U-boat commander during the First World War, had been awarded Germany's highest decoration for bravery, the Pour le Mérite. Niemöller's appeal to his fellow pastors to join the League was made on September 21. Within four months 7,000 of Germany's 18,000 Protestant pastors had joined him.

Two days after Niemöller's appeal on behalf of the Emergency League he went to Wittenberg, where four centuries earlier Martin Luther had posted up his ninety-five theses (and where Luther was also buried). In Wittenberg, Niemöller posted up on tree trunks throughout the city a statement denouncing the adoption by the Church – at Hitler's urging – of an ordinance whereby only those of 'Aryan descent' could be ordained priests, and under which all clergy who were married to 'non-Aryans' were dismissed.

Following Germany's withdrawal from the League of Nations Disarmament Conference on October 14, the German Government further defied its former adversaries by refusing to make any further Reparations payments, or to pay more than 30 per cent of the interest due on moneys borrowed from foreign governments. For those Germans whom Hitler sought to imbue with heightened German national sentiment, this was stirring defiance. Other opportunities for self-pride came with a law whereby German peasant farmers were given ownership of their farms in perpetuity, and a guaranteed price for their farm produce.

Outside Germany, the first revelations of the cruel nature of Nazi policy were a feature of book publishing in 1933. Among the most powerful descriptions of the regime in Germany were a volume edited by the British publisher Victor Gollancz entitled *The Brown Book of the Hitler Terror*, and the American journalist Edgar Mowrer's *Germany Puts the Clock Back*, in which Mowrer wrote, not without a final hesitation which he indicated with three enigmatic dots: 'It is astonishing the way the people of Goethe repudiated everything he had stood for. Liberalism? A disruptive ideology of a bygone age! Europe? A geographical expression! The League of Nations? A cackle of geese! World peace? A dream of girls and pacifists and Jews! The only reality was the Nordic Race and its noble German incarnation. And yet . . .'

The consolidation of Nazi power during 1933 was matched by an upsurge in emigration. Many of those whom the Nazi rulers declared to be the enemies of the new Germany made their way abroad. By the end of 1933 more than 60,000 German citizens had found refuge in neighbouring lands. At least half of these were Jews. The Jewish death toll in 1933 was small compared with what it became within a decade – forty-five Jews were killed that year. This was frightening in itself. Everywhere towns and villages had put up placards, 'Jews not wanted', and in some villages the names of Jewish war dead had been erased from the war memorials. By the end of the year, 30,000 German Jews had left Germany, and been admitted into Britain, the United States and the countries of Western Europe. A further 5,000 had gained entry into Palestine.

On October 26 – twelve days after Germany's withdrawal from the League of Nations – the League established a 'High Commission for Refugees (Jewish and Other) Coming from Germany'. The man chosen as High Commissioner was a citizen of the United States, James G. McDonald. His instructions were to 'negotiate and direct' the international collaboration necessary to solve the 'economic, financial and social problem' of the refugees. Jewish and Christian philanthropic organizations worked closely with him. The German government put no serious obstacles in the way of emigration. The British Mandate authorities in Palestine continued to allow in up to 20 per cent of those leaving Germany. The rest found havens in the United States, Britain and the countries of Western Europe, as well as on other continents. Many of those refugees were the teachers, writers, intellectuals, scientists and professional people – thousands of doctors among them – who had constituted an essential element in German cultural, economic and intellectual life.

Among the first Jews to establish himself in exile was Albert Einstein. Not only was he a Jew, but in 1914 he had emerged in Berlin as one of the leading opponents of the war, an unforgivable sin in the new climate of national regeneration. On October 3, in London, he gave the 'science and civilization lecture' to a vast audience at the Royal Albert Hall. Another refugee in those early days was Ernst Chain, a twenty-seven-year-old Berlin-born biochemist. Chain had already done pioneering research in the Institute of Pathology at the Charité Hospital in Berlin before being forced, as a Jew, to leave his post. Finding refuge in Britain, he was to play a major part in enabling penicillin to be used as a cure for a wide range of infectious diseases; and to do so in time to save the lives of tens of thousands of Allied soldiers in the war against Germany. For his work on penicillin he received the Nobel Prize in 1945.

Aged thirty-one, Nikolaus Pevsner was a lecturer in art history and architecture at the University of Göttingen when Hitler came to power. As a
Jew – he had been born in Leipzig – he knew that he would not be able to
teach at a German university and made his way to Britain. During the course
of twenty-three years he published and edited a 46-volume architectural
history of the counties of England as well as editing the *Pelican History of
Art*. Not only those who were already making their careers, but tens of
thousands of youngsters who would have made their contribution to the life
and culture of Germany, were leaving for new lives as refugees. Claus Moser
was ten years old when Hitler came to power, living in his birthplace, Berlin.
He was to become the director of the British Government's Statistical Service,
head of an Oxford college, Chancellor of a British University, and Chairman
of the Royal Opera House. Had there been no anti-Jewish racial policy,
Claus Moser – like so many of the refugees from Hitler – might have been
among the leaders of modern German society.

Another exile in the early days of the Nazi regime was Helmuth von
Gerlach, President of the German League for the Rights of Man, and one
of the founders of the German Democratic Party. Von Gerlach had served
in the Prussian Republican Government in 1918, and, while an editor of a
weekly newspaper, had pursued since then an outspoken pacifist stand. He
also advocated the reconciliation of Germany and France. His chosen place
of exile was Paris, where he died two years later.

Not only individuals but institutions went into exile. A ship which arrived
in the Thames that year from Hamburg brought, as part of its cargo, a book
collection packed in six hundred boxes, as well as reading desks, iron shelving
and bookbinding machines, and six people familiar with the collection. This
was the library of the Warburg Institute in Hamburg, one of the finest art
history libraries in the world, totalling 60,000 books, the creation of Aby
Warburg – an art historian of distinction, and a member of the Jewish
banking family – who had died four years earlier. A home was found for
the library in a new, not yet fully occupied, office building overlooking the
Thames; among those who worked there, initially as a research assistant,
later as Director, was Ernst Gombrich, an art historian from Vienna, who
was to make his career as an art historian in Britain.

Another library that was sent to Britain for safety had been formed in
Berlin by Dr Alfred Wiener. He had been determined to assemble as comprehensive a collection as possible about the history and current fate of German

Jewry. It too found a home in London; six decades later the Wiener Library was still in use as an important source for a people and an era that was to be systematically destroyed within twelve years.

Another institution that Hitler's racial policies denied to Germany was the photographic archive collected by Otto Bettmann. When he left for the United States in 1933 he took with him on board ship two steamer trunks full of photographs which he had collected over several years. At the German customs control all his money was taken from him as a 'leaving-the-Reich tax' but his photographs, rummaged through by the German officials, were dismissed as worthless. In New York they were to become the basis of a 16-million-photograph rental library. Bettmann died in his new homeland in 1998, at the age of ninety-four.

Beyond the immediate borders of Germany, Hitler's propaganda machine, directed by Dr Goebbels, was untiringly and skilfully active in stimulating pan-German feeling. As a result of elections in the Free City of Danzig, the Nazis gained control of the city's administration. It was the first success of the Nazi party beyond the Versailles Treaty borders of Germany. On June 11, an Austrian Nazi, Franz Hofer, tried to assassinate Dr. Steidle, the leader of the right-wing but anti-Nazi Austrian Heimwehr Party. In Vienna, two citizens were killed in a Nazi bomb outrage. A week later, three Heimwehr militiamen were murdered by Austrian Nazis at Krems. Rescued by his followers from Innsbruck prison, Franz Hofer was smuggled across the border into Italy. Mussolini's officials refused an Austrian request to extradite him, and he travelled to Germany where he was welcomed as a hero.

On July 1 the German government carried out the first of a series of propaganda flights over Austria, when light aircraft dropped leaflets denouncing the Austrian Chancellor, Dr Engelbert Dollfuss. Austrian diplomatic protests were ignored. These propaganda air raids were intensified during the Salzburg music festival in August, when many German singers and musicians were prevailed upon by the local Nazis to cancel their contracts in the hope of preventing the festival from continuing. In September, determined to preserve the territorial integrity of Austria, and to prevent the Austrian Nazis from trying to overthrow the government, Dollfuss assumed dictatorial powers. He also set out to crush all popular manifestations of working-class and Communist political activity. The Austrian Social Democrat Party was also under continual pressure; its newspaper was repeatedly censored, and its defence organization was dissolved. As part of his new consolidation of power, Dollfuss appointed the Heimwehr Fascist leader, Major Emil Fey, as Vice-Chancellor.

On October 3 an Austrian Nazi storm trooper, Rudolf Dertil, attempted to assassinate Dollfuss as he left the parliament building in Vienna. Dollfuss was not badly wounded and returned to work within a few days. Dertil was sentenced to five years in prison. The court could not know that Austrian independence had less than five years to run.

The activities of Austria's Nazis were centred on their call for union with Germany – the *Anschluss* that was specifically forbidden in the post-war treaties. It was also robustly challenged by the Austrian government, which was determined to uphold the territorial integrity and sovereignty of Austria. The local Nazis sought to make their presence felt by continual protest. Anti-Dollfuss riots were organized in the universities. On the evening of November 5, when Dollfuss was about to speak in Klagenfurt, the Nazis cut off the electricity and plunged the city into darkness. Hitler's overwhelming victory in the General Election that he called in Germany a week later – the opposition Parties had all been banned from putting up candidates – was celebrated by the Austrian Nazis in a series of forbidden acts: pro-Nazi demonstrations, the ringing of church bells, and the raising of Swastika flags.

It was not only in Austria that German-speaking people were attracted to Nazism or stimulated by the flow of pan-German Nazi propaganda from Berlin. For several centuries people of German origin had lived in many lands in Central and Eastern Europe. Known as *Volksdeutsche* (Ethnic Germans), they were German speakers, with dialects that could sound outlandish to German ears. In the main they felt a sentimental affinity for the 'homeland', and were vulnerable to any appeal that stressed the weakness of their minority status or sought to stimulate their Germanness. There were Volksdeutsche in Roumania, Hungary, Yugoslavia, Poland and the Soviet Union. Other than those living behind the almost impenetrable Soviet border, they offered a fertile field for Dr Goebbels and the Nazi ideology.

Alarmed by the rise of Nazism in Germany, the Soviet government, which had hitherto denounced the Treaty of Versailles as the creation of 'capitalist highwaymen', suddenly discovered virtue in the Treaty, and in Germany's existing borders. This new-found concern with the status quo in Europe led to negotiations between the Soviet Union and several of its neighbours who were similarly alarmed at what Nazi foreign policy might entail. Soviet non-aggression pacts were signed with Poland, Czechoslovakia and Roumania, and negotiations were begun between Russia and France whereby France would help to organize the Soviet air force along modern lines, a task hitherto entrusted to Germany.

In the twelve months following Hitler's rise to power the Soviet Union made strenuous efforts to widen the range of countries with which it had diplomatic relations. Spain and Uruguay were two of these, but most important for Russia was the agreement of the United States to recognize Stalin's regime. Hitherto, the United States had refused to enter into diplomatic relations with a country which showed 'an active spirit of enmity to our Institutions'. On October 10 President Roosevelt – who had been President for less than a year – invited the Soviet Union to enter into negotiations, and on November 17 the United States officially recognized the existence and legitimacy of the Soviet Union. In a letter that day to the Soviet Foreign Minister, Maksim Litvinov, Roosevelt expressed the hope that the two nations would cooperate 'for their mutual benefit and for the peace of the world'.

Inside the Soviet Union the process of eliminating all opposition to Stalin's rule was continuous. As 1933 came to an end, more than a thousand Red Army officers and soldiers were arrested. In preparation for the first Party Congress in more than three years, it was announced from Moscow that it was necessary before the Congress met to 'purge' the party of 'undesirable' and 'incompetent' members. Within a few months almost a million Party members were deprived of their membership – and of the power and privilege that went with it.

Hunger had continued to follow in the wake of Communist determination to control and centralize all agricultural production. In October a British newspaper published an account of the situation in the Ukraine, the former granary of Russia: 'One cannot be in the countryside today without a sense of tragedy. When one sees empty huts, windows gutted, floors torn up – the former homes of fugitives and victims of starvation.' Every statistic available in the West gave credence to the severity of Russian life. There had been five and a half million horses in the Ukraine in 1929; in 1933 there were fewer than three million. The number of pigs and sheep had decreased even more dramatically: of more than six million sheep only one and a half million remained. Some farmers had no cows left: on October 14 Stalin himself promised that every effort would be made to provide cows to those farmers who had none. But the two regions from which these cows were principally to be drawn – the Lower Volga and White Russia – failed utterly to deliver the numbers required. Although the quota for White Russia was set at 40,000, fewer than 2,000 reached the Ukraine.

As Russian industry concentrated on military, naval and air force manufacture, the needs of the populace suffered. The economy was not strong enough to provide for both defence and domestic needs. Shortages of consumer goods of the most basic sort were reported throughout the Soviet Union, including forks and spoons, clothes, linen and soap.

The tendency to dictatorial action, especially in regard to minorities, was widespread in many regions of Europe. In Latvia the language rights of Germans, Russians and Jews – the three main national minorities – were under attack where they were at their most vulnerable, in the secondary schools. In Poland there were riots by the Ukrainian minority against discrimination. In Yugoslavia the Croats, seeking greater autonomy within the structure of the State, were unable to move the Serbs from their position of predominance: Belgrade did not want to devolve any effective power on Zagreb. The Muslim minority in Yugoslavia was also aggrieved, as were the Albanians of the Kosovo region. Most Albanian villagers in this remote area of Yugoslavia lacked land deeds. Four years later a Belgrade government document stated, of the maximum size of the land-holding permitted (0.4 hectares): 'This is below the minimum for subsistence. But that is and has been our aim: to make their life impossible, and in that way to force them to emigrate.' In addition to these land tenure pressures, the Albanian language was actively suppressed, and tens of thousands of Serb 'colonists' sent into the region.

In Hungary, the dominance of the majority manifested itself in anti-Jewish demonstrations on university campuses, where Hungarian students demanded that their Jewish co-students – who were likewise full citizens of Hungary – be restricted to the benches at the back of the classroom. Jewish students who defended themselves against physical attack were given the same punishments by the university authorities as those who attacked them. Propaganda emanating from Germany was a main factor in intensifying Hungarian anti-Jewish activity, both in Budapest and in several provincial towns.

In Roumania the government made serious efforts throughout the year to curtail the activities of the Fascist Iron Guard. But on December 30 a student member of the Iron Guard assassinated the Prime Minister, Ion Duca. As a result, martial law was declared in many towns. The Iron Guard continued, however, to serve as a focus for violent and fascist activities.

In Switzerland, its long border with southern Germany offering tempting access to Nazi propaganda, all Party uniforms had been forbidden by a Parliamentary vote on May 12. Among the groups to whom this ban applied was the Swiss National Socialist Front, which was hostile to Jews. The liberal traditions with which Switzerland had been closely associated since the revolutionary year 1848 were to be upheld. By the end of 1933 several thousand German Jews and other opponents of Nazism had been admitted to Switzerland as refugees.

In its role as international mediator, the League of Nations had not been idle in 1933. Its most effective intervention was to resolve the dispute between Norway and Denmark, which had followed the Norwegian occupation of East Greenland in 1931 and of South-East Greenland in 1932. The Permanent Court of International Justice at the Hague, to which the League submitted the dispute, ruled during 1933 that the occupations were 'contrary to law' and invalid. The only judge to dissent was the Norwegian one. In a gesture of reconciliation between the two peoples, King Haakon VII of Norway immediately sent a telegram to King Christian X of Denmark, congratulating him on the verdict. Norwegian democrats had further cause for congratulation in 1933 when, at the General Election on October 16, the Fascist Party led by Captain Vidkun Quisling failed to win a single seat.

In Afghanistan, the flag of Islamic revolt was raised in 1933 in the southern district of Khost. A leader, known as the 'Crazy Fakir', led not only the local Afghan tribes, but also several tribal groups living across the border in British India, in an attempt to seize power in Kabul on behalf of the exiled and defeated King Amanullah. The rebel forces were defeated by troops loyal to Amanullah's successor, Nadir Shah, and the Crazy Fakir fled into exile. But on November 8, during a school prize giving in the palace courtyard in Kabul, Nadir Shah was assassinated. His assassin was a servant loyal to a former rebel who had been executed exactly a year earlier. His motive was revenge. The assassin was himself executed before the end of the year. The new king, Zahir Shah, was the son of Nadir Shah. His three uncles – who were respectively Prime Minister, Minister for Foreign Affairs, and Minister of War – declared their allegiance to their nephew, and, one western observer noted, 'Kabul soon resumed its wonted aspect'.

Another region of Islamic ferment was Iraq, where several thousand Assyrian Christians were massacred. The British had brought the Assyrians into the Mandate of Iraq from southern Turkey for their own protection at the end of the First World War. Men, women and children were shot down in cold blood by Iraqi troops, who were aided by the Kurds, among whom the Assyrians – their age-old enemies – had been forced to settle. To prevent the growth of an Assyrian national movement, the Assyrian Patriarch, Mar Shimun, was deported to Cyprus and deprived of his Iraqi citizenship. The ruler of Iraq, King Faisal, who was in Europe being treated for heart disease, returned to Baghdad in August intent on curbing the anti-Christian violence, but ill-heath forced him to return almost at once to Switzerland, where he died on September 8. His body was brought in a British warship to Haifa, where the Muslim Arabs of Palestine – another British Mandate, with a common border with Iraq – hailed the dead king as the father of Arab unity and called for his burial in the special Muslim Pantheon that was being created in Jerusalem on the Haram al-Sharif. When the King's body was flown on by the British to Iraq there were Muslim riots in Palestine.

Both the Arabs and the Jews of Palestine were in ferment in 1933. The target of their anger was in both cases predominantly the British Mandate administration. Arab demonstrations against Jewish land purchase were broken up by the British in several towns, but not until twenty-four Arabs and one British policeman had been killed. The British authorities took two measures to assuage the Arab grievance: one was the prohibition of the removal of agricultural tenants from their lands unless suitable alternative land could be found for them, and the other was the purchase of land near the Arab town of Beisan on which to settle Arabs whose fields near the coast had been bought by Jews.

Confronted by an upsurge of Jewish immigration from Germany, and also from Poland, the British authorities took measures to increase vigilance at the points of entry to Palestine, and to turn away those who did not have legal entry papers. Throughout Palestine Jews protested; during a riot in Tel Aviv several Jews and several policemen were injured. A struggle also began that year between the Jews and the British, centred upon what became known as 'illegal immigration', as plans were made by Zionist emissaries to Germany and eastern Europe to organize clandestine entry into Palestine.

In the Far East, Japanese troops continued to advance into China, overrunning Jehol and reaching the Great Wall. Even as they consolidated their control over Manchukuo the Chinese were fighting bitterly among themselves. The Communists, advancing towards Amoy, pushed back the Nationalist forces

of Chiang Kai-shek almost to the coast, and succeeded in occupying Fukien.
They were then driven out by the Nineteenth Route Army, hitherto loyal
to Chiang Kai-shek, which proceeded to declare itself independent of the
Nationalists and, at Foochow, proclaimed a People's Revolutionary Government. In response, the Nationalists set up a blockade of the Fukien coast.

As the fighting continued, so did the ravages of nature, by which China
had frequently been cursed since the start of the century. During floods in
the Yellow River valley in the autumn of 1933, more than 2,000 villages
were destroyed.

Imperial rule was everywhere under attack. Since the beginning of the century
the subject peoples in Asia and Africa had aspired to throw off the rule of
the European Powers. That rule had varied enormously in its qualities: at
its best it brought economic advancement, civil and educational progress,
and opportunities to participate in commercial, professional and even political
life. At its worst it had led to the exploitation of the natural wealth and
physical labour of those being ruled from afar.

In British India, the home of 255 million Hindus and 94 million Muslims,
the Indian National Congress was demanding 'home rule' as a prelude to
independence. Under the leadership of Mahatma Gandhi, innumerable acts
of peaceful but effective civil disobedience caused havoc to the smooth working of the administrative machine. The British had brought in Indians to
the Viceroy's Legislative Council, but the Indian National Congress, in
their search for greater autonomy, also demanded an Indian presence on the
Executive Council where power resided. When this was refused, they declared
a boycott of the central legislature and took no further part in its work.

Elsewhere in the imperial domains the protests were more violent. In the
Netherlands East Indies, thirty-four Indonesian naval mutineers were killed
when the training ship they had commandeered was bombed from the air.
In Morocco, sixty French troops were killed during the final phase of the
'pacification' of the tribes of the Atlas district. The tribes of the Anti-Atlas
region in the south remained uncurbed.

Fighting continued throughout the year in South America, between Paraguay
and Bolivia, for possession of the Gran Chaco plain, at the foot of the Andes,
where rumours of oil deposits had led to frontier clashes in 1927 and full-scale
war in 1932. Two international oil companies were competing for the oil
rights: the Standard Oil Company of New Jersey, which had obtained oil

concessions in Bolivia, and Royal Dutch Shell, which was encouraging Paraguay to drill. In December 1933 the Paraguayan forces drove back the Bolivians and took 8,000 prisoner.

An armistice was concluded but the rival territorial claims remained unresolved. Bolivia felt aggrieved that – having been deprived of access to the Pacific coast by Chile in the 1880s, she could not press westward across the Chaco to the river Paraguay and the Atlantic. Not long after the armistice was signed, oil was discovered on the Bolivian side of the Chaco divide. The cost of the war had been high: Paraguay lost 50,000 men; the Bolivians – most of whose conscripts were Indians brought down from their homes in the high Andes – lost even more.

Three years after the war ended, a 'military-socialist' regime in Bolivia, headed by the President, German Busch, nationalized the oilfields: his was the first government to take such action against one of the oil companies that controlled the industry and its sources of supply.

In Cuba, the dictatorial regime of General Machado, who had become President at the end of 1930, was overthrown in 1933, and on August 12 Machado went by aeroplane into exile. Many of his secret policemen were tracked down and killed. When the army sought to seize power, the United States ordered warships to Havana to protect its citizens. A new government was formed, headed by a Havana University professor, the Dean of the Medical Faculty, Dr Ramon Grau San Martin. Those opposed to him, including the supporters of the army coup, took up arms in the National Hotel in Havana, but were bombarded by forces loyal to Grau San Martin and driven out.

The fighting that continued spasmodically in Cuba until the end of the year was overshadowed in its death-dealing by a cyclone which hit Cuba on November 9. One town, Santa Cruz del Sur, was almost totally destroyed, and eighty people were killed. In the new year a new government was formed by a former army sergeant, Fulgencio Batista, and what the historian of Cuba, Hugh Thomas, has called 'the Age of Democracy' began. It was to last almost twenty years, and to be gradually eroded by the growing corruption of the regime, and challenged by, among others, the Cuban Communist Party, which dreamed of entering Havana much as the Bolsheviks had entered Petrograd in 1917.

In the United States, President Roosevelt persevered with his New Deal designed to ensure the recovery of the American economy, and a continual reduction of unemployment from its peak of eleven million when he came into office. On May 7, in a nationwide radio address, he described his plan to give work to 'one-quarter of a million of the unemployed, especially the young men who have dependents, to go into the forestry and flood prevention work.' This, Roosevelt explained, 'is a big task because it means feeding, clothing and caring for nearly twice as many men as we have in the regular army itself'. In creating the civilian conservation corps 'we are killing two birds with one stone. We are clearly enhancing the value of our natural resources and second, we are relieving an appreciable amount of actual distress. This great group of men have entered upon their work on a purely voluntary basis, no military training is involved and we are conserving not only our natural resources but our human resources.'

During his radio address Roosevelt recalled a remark by his kinsman and predecessor as President, Theodore Roosevelt, who 'once said to me: "If I can be right seventy-five per cent of the time I shall come up to the fullest measure of my hopes".' Franklin Roosevelt was confident that since his inauguration in March he had made 'a wise and sensible beginning'. In June he submitted to Congress the National Industrial Recovery Bill, a milestone in his measures to increase employment. The use of child labour was to be abolished. Adult hours of work were to be reduced without a reduction in wages. Minimum rates of pay were to be maintained and exceeded. One of those who was most outspoken against the Bill in Congress was Senator Huey Long, the virtual dictator of Louisiana, who tried to talk the Bill out by filibustering. He spoke for fifteen and a half hours, but failed in his attempt.*

The National Recovery Act was passed by Congress on June 16. It gave Roosevelt extraordinary powers, unprecedented in the United States in peacetime. It was, Roosevelt said, 'the most important legislation ever enacted by the American Congress'. Its fourteen provisions were terse and to the point:

> To establish control over all industry with the view to fixing minimum wages and maximum hours of work, regulating production and otherwise to promote, encourage and require fair competition.

---

* Huey Long, known as 'The Kingfish', who had become Governor of Louisiana at the age of thirty-five, and Senator four years later, tyrannized those in Louisiana who opposed him. He was shot dead in the State House in Baton Rouge in 1935.

To set up a system of government licenses for business if necessary to require conformance to the above.

To initiate and direct, through a Federal director of public works, a $3,300,000,000 public works program as a further government contribution to re-employment.

To direct, through a Federal director of relief, expenditure of $500,000,000, supplied by the Reconstruction Finance Corporation, for relief of destitution.

To invoke the Presidential powers of the World War to regulate transactions in credit, currency, gold and silver, even to embargo gold or foreign exchange; to fix restrictions on the banking business of the Federal Reserve System irrespective of the Federal Reserve Board.

To eliminate the old system for compensation and allowances for veterans and set up an entirely new pension system, with himself at the head.

To reduce by executive order the salaries of government employees by an amount not to exceed 15 per cent upon the finding of commensurate reduction in cost of living.

To transfer, eliminate, consolidate or rearrange bureaus in the executive branch of the government in the interest of public economy.

To repeal by executive proclamation certain new taxes voted in the Industrial Recovery Act upon showing of restoration of business or in event of repeal of the Eighteenth Amendment.

To publish heretofore secret income tax returns to the extent he may deem in the public interest, and under such rules and regulations as he may prescribe.

To inflate the currency either by requiring open market operations in Federal securities, devaluing the gold dollar by not more than 50 per cent, issuing United States notes up to $3,000,000,000 or accepting up to $200,000,000 in silver in payment of the Allied war debts.

To employ more than 250,000 unemployed young men to reforestation operations as still further government contribution to re-employment.

To appoint a coordinator of railroads to effect economies among the carriers and increase service to the public.

To appoint a Tennessee Valley Authority to develop natural resources of Tennessee River basin, including completion of Muscle Shoals project.

Within two hours of the passage of the Act, Roosevelt set its provisions in train. Eight days later he invited the nation's employers to sign the Presi-

dent's Code. 'Send me a telegram if you will sign', he said. Those employers
who did so would be entitled to display a government badge with the
American eagle in blue, and the slogan, 'We do our part'. For several days
the telegraph companies and postal authorities were swamped with replies.
Among those who eventually agreed to participate was Henry Ford, thus
helping to lead the American motor car industry in 'setting its house in
order'. Slowly unemployment fell, though the drop of two million by the
end of the year was much less than Roosevelt had hoped.

Another of Roosevelt's economic devices to increase employment was the
increase of expenditure on defence. That summer the Navy Department was
allocated $238 million to build thirty-two new warships. Money was also
put up for 'public works' to the value of $500 million to be carried out
in various States and a further $400 million for road building and road
improvement. Over the coming two years, Roosevelt explained in a radio
address, he was prepared to accept a national debt of $31,000 million ($31
billion) in order to get Americans back to work.

The end of the year saw the end of Prohibition, when Utah became
the thirty-sixth State to ratify the twenty-first amendment, repealing the
eighteenth amendment which had established Prohibition, and with it all
the dangers and excesses of illegal liquor production and distribution. For
more than thirteen years the United States had suffered, and individual
citizens made their fortunes – or lost their lives in the associated violence
– from the ban on alcoholic beverages. In announcing Utah's decisive vote,
Roosevelt urged upon the citizens of the United States 'greater respect for
law and order by confining such purchases of alcoholic beverages as they
may make solely to those dealers or agencies which have been duly licensed
by State or Federal licenses'.

Under the direct authority of the National Recovery Act, other legislation
passed by Congress that year included an Act which guaranteed all bank
deposits under $5,000, a powerful protection to small savers and business
people. Most ambitious of all, a new government authority was set up, the
Tennessee Valley Authority (TVA) with the power and the money to build
a series of dams and hydro-electric plants across a wide geographic area
hitherto hard hit by the Depression. 'It will add to the comfort and happiness
of hundreds of thousands of people,' Roosevelt explained, 'and the incidental
benefits will reach the entire nation.'

The 'entire nation' was also a troubled one. On November 26 a crowd of
a hundred men broke into the county jail at San Jose, California, and

demanded two men, Thomas Thurmond and John Holmes, who had confessed to a recent kidnap and murder. As reported in *The Times*:

> Policemen and deputy sheriffs fought valiantly with tear gas bombs and clubs to defend their prisoners, but the infuriated crowd was not to be stayed. After having beaten the sheriff, Mr William Emig, into insensibility, the assailants brought into play as battering rams two lengths of heavy iron pipe. With these they broke down the outer and inner doors of the gaol. They beat a deputy sheriff, seized his keys, and unlocked the cells on the third floor, where Thurmond, Holmes and other prisoners were confined.
>
> Yelling and shouting, they dragged the two kidnappers across a wide street to the park. Thurmond, who had fainted was strung up without delay. Holmes, who had been stripped of all his clothes and badly beaten, fought desperately and threw the noose off his neck twice before he was overpowered.
>
> The lynchers made no attempt to conceal their identity, and after their victims had been hanged even encouraged photographers to make flashlight pictures of the scene.

When the Governor of California, James Rolph, was told what had happened, he commented with approval: 'This is the best lesson California has ever given the country. We show the country that the State is not going to tolerate kidnapping.'

The science of flight continued to make rapid strides; on July 15 an American aviator, Wiley Post, flew direct from New York to Berlin, the first aviator to do so. This was but a prelude to his complete aerial circumnavigation of the globe in seven days, eighteen hours and 49 minutes. In October a commercial flight from Britain to Australia was completed in the record time of six days, seventeen hours and 56 minutes. Above Moscow, a Soviet balloon with three people on board reached the record height of 19,000 metres (more than eleven miles).

In the world of ever-advancing consumer interests and demands, the first commercially produced synthetic detergent was marketed in 1933, in Britain, and in the United States the Ritz cracker was introduced.

CHAPTER TWO

1934

... the centre of our time was perhaps the violent,
incommunicable death of an innocent victim

STEPHEN SPENDER

FACED WITH THE SUCCESS and – to some people in every land – attractive-
ness, of German Nazism and Italian Fascism, the future of democratic institutions was under threat in many European countries. In France the
maintenance of democracy had been a matter of continual struggle. On
February 6 the government of Edouard Daladier had given permission for a
demonstration to be held in Paris, in the Place de la Concorde, by the
right-wing Union Nationale des Combattants (the UNC), which was
denouncing the failures of democracy.

Police were on hand to prevent any attempt by the demonstrators to
march across the river to the Chamber of Deputies. The American journalist
William Shirer was an eye witness to the events of the evening. In his diary
he wrote of how, reaching the Place at about seven, he saw steel-helmeted
Mobile Guards, on horseback, trying to clear the demonstrators away:

> Over by the obelisk in the centre, a bus was on fire. I worked my way
> over through the Mobile Guards, who were slashing away with their sabres,
> to the Tuileries side. Up on the terrace was a mob of several thousand
> and, mingling with them, I soon found they were not fascists, but Commu-
> nists. When the police tried to drive them back they unleashed a barrage
> of stones and bricks.
>
> Over on the bridge leading from the *Place* to the Chamber across the
> Seine, I found a solid mass of Mobile Guards nervously fingering their
> rifles, backed up by ordinary police and a fire-brigade. A couple of small

groups attempted to advance to the bridge from the quay leading up from the Louvre, but two fire-hoses put them to flight.

About eight o'clock a couple of thousand UNC war veterans paraded into the *Place*, having marched down the Champs-Elysées from the Round-Point. They came in good order behind a mass of tricoloured flags. They were stopped at the bridge and their leaders began talking with police officials. I went over to the Crillon and up to the third-floor balcony overlooking the square. It was jammed with people. The first shots we didn't hear. The first we knew of the shooting was when a woman about twenty feet away suddenly slumped to the floor with a bullet-hole in her forehead . . .

Now we could hear the shooting, coming from the bridge and the far side of the Seine. Automatic rifles they seemed to be using. The mob's reaction was to storm into the square. Soon it was dotted with fires. To the left, smoke started pouring out of the Ministry of Marine. Hoses were brought into play, but the mob got close enough to cut them. I went down to the lobby to 'phone the office. Several wounded were laid out and were being given first aid.

The shooting continued until about midnight, when the Mobile Guards began to get the upper hand. Several times the Place de la Concorde changed hands, but towards midnight the police were in control. Once – about ten o'clock it must have been – the mob, which by this time was incensed, but obviously lacked leadership, tried to storm the bridge, some coming up along the quays, whose trees offered them considerable protection, and others charging madly across the *Place*.

'If they get across the bridge,' I thought, 'they'll kill every deputy in the Chamber.' But a deadly fire – it sounded this time like machine-guns – stopped them and in a few minutes they were scattering in all directions.

Sixteen demonstrators were killed that night, and several hundred wounded. On the following day Daladier resigned. His successor was Gaston Doumerge, a former President of the Republic. 'They've dragged him from his village of Tournefeuille,' wrote Shirer, 'where he had retired with his mistress, whom he married shortly after stepping down from the presidency.' General Philippe Pétain, the man who had insisted that Verdun would not fall during the First World War, became Minister of War.

On February 12 there was a general strike throughout France in protest against the shootings in the Place de la Concorde. It lasted one day and led to no further civil strife. That same day, in Vienna, there was violence on a far heavier scale than in Paris as the Chancellor, Engelbert Dollfuss, leader of the Christian Socialist Party, tried to crush his principal rivals for power, the Social Democrats. Artillery and tanks were turned on the socialist strongholds in the city, the great residential apartment blocks – including the Karl Marx Hof and the Goethe Hof – built for the working classes in the aftermath of the First World War. The British newspaper correspondent Eric Gedye was a witness to the end of the fighting at the Karl Marx Hof. 'The building was as shell-shattered and bullet-scarred as anything I had seen in Arras or Albert in 1916,' he later wrote. 'In the courtyard in one window was hanging the body of a Socialist city councillor, who had lost his reason towards the end of that night of horror and committed suicide. The wife of another councillor was in the hands of the police as a prisoner – raving mad. She died soon after. But most of the defenders had gone down into the sewers from the interior of the building and escaped.'

A year earlier, William Shirer had interviewed Dollfuss, in company with his fellow-American journalist, John Gunther, and their British colleague Eric Gedye. 'I found him a timid little fellow,' Shirer noted in his diary as news of the fighting in Vienna reached Paris, 'still a little dazed that he, the illegitimate son of a peasant, should have gone so far. But give the little men a lot of power and they can be dangerous. I weep for my Social Democrat friends, the most decent men and women in Europe. How many of them are being slaughtered tonight, I wonder. And there goes democracy in Austria, one more State gone.'

Eric Gedye later recalled the grim aftermath of the Dollfuss victory. 'Hardly had the workers laid down their arms before an orgy of persecution and revenge began,' he wrote:

The first man hanged was Karl Münichreiter, a married shoemaker of forty-three, with three children. Badly wounded in two places, he was brought into court on a stretcher, tried and sentenced in an hour, and three hours later strung up in the courtyard. But let one of the Heimwehr papers itself describe this scene, typical of many others:

'It is 3.41. The executioner stands in his black suit with black top hat and black gloves. There stand the judges, the priest and a police-surgeon. The sentence is read over again. The corners of the man's mouth twitch. As the hangman draws the noose tight around his throat, Münichreiter shouts some Marxist phrases' (they were 'Long live Social Democracy — Freedom!').

'The hangman's assistants, who until now have been holding up the man, pull away the steps from beneath the feet of the dangling body. *After an interval of seven and a half minutes* the police-surgeon announces that he is dead.'

Ten others were hanged that day. The second victim was Georg Weissel, 'a brilliant and self-educated civil engineer', who had commanded the fire brigade at Floridsdorf, and been an officer in the workers' defence organization, the *Schutzbund*:

He was arrested for having given the order to fire on the forces attacking one of the Floridsdorf workers' tenement blocks. His bearing before the court was remarkable. When he declined to incriminate others, the judge told him: 'After your manly admissions concerning yourself, I shall not press you to involve others. Did you act in accordance with your inner convictions?'

'Yes. And we surrendered because we were outnumbered, otherwise we should never have done so.'

At midnight the same night, Weissel marched with upright step to the gallows and shouted as the noose was placed around his neck: 'Long live Revolutionary Socialism'. The judge, having watched the hanging of the young man of thirty-five whom he had sentenced to death, got into his car and drove to the humbling dwelling of the widow and, placing his hands on her shoulders, said in a broken voice: 'It is I who judged your husband, and I have come to tell you that he died like a man and a hero.' So did nine more.

The British government, indignant at the hangings, protested through its ambassador in Vienna, Walford Selby. Dollfuss gave Selby an assurance that no more hangings would take place in Vienna. 'He kept his promise,' wrote Eric Gedye, 'for when they caught Koloman Wallisch in the Alps a week later, they hanged him in Styria.'

Beyond Germany's borders a debate was raging about how best to deal with the awakened German nationalism. The French Government sought safety in armaments, and in drawing closer to the Soviet Union. The Polish

Government felt that it could come to some satisfactory agreement directly with Germany, and negotiated a non-aggression treaty. The British Government wanted to secure peace by a universal reduction of arms. Churchill, who was emerging as the most outspoken and persistent critic of the existing defence policy, disagreed. Unless Britain was in 'a proper state of security', he told the House of Commons on February 7, a diplomatic crisis would arise – 'within a measurable time, in the lifetime of those who are here' – when threats would be made, and pressure applied, and within a few hours 'the crash of bombs exploding in London and cataracts of masonry and fire and smoke will apprise us of any inadequacy which has been permitted in our aerial defences'.

Churchill advised the Government to prepare the nation so that if war came it would be able to face it. The very act of preparation could, he argued, deter a would-be enemy. 'We ought to begin the reorganization of our civil factories so they can be turned over rapidly to war purposes.' Every factory in Europe was being prepared so that it could be turned over quickly to war production, in order to produce the material 'for the deplorable and melancholy business of slaughter'; and he asked: 'What have we done? There is not an hour to lose.' Britain was an air power: 'I cannot conceive how, in the present state of Europe and our position in Europe, we can delay in establishing the principle of having an air force at least as strong as that of any Power that can get at us.'

For the British Government, Stanley Baldwin, a former and future Prime Minister – holding the Cabinet position of Lord President of the Council – replied that the Government's aim was 'an ordered arms limitation'. To this end less money would be spent by Britain on the Royal Air Force in 1934 than in previous years. Baldwin also spoke words of assurance: 'I do not think we are at all bound to have a war.'

Churchill believed that war could only be averted if Britain were seen to be both strong and determined to uphold the rule of law internationally. Because of the overwhelming parliamentary majority of the National Government, headed since 1931 by Ramsay MacDonald, with Stanley Baldwin as its senior Conservative, Churchill acted as an almost solo opposition voice on the Conservative benches. Month after month he pressed for a larger and more efficient air force, and for greater preparation of shadow factories for aircraft production, as well as tank and arms manufacture. Again and again during the next three years he was to challenge the government for its failure to rearm adequately in the air, or to match the known increases in German air strength, or to create the structure whereby at short notice factories could be converted to full-scale nation-wide war production. As he told the House of Commons on March 8, when the first tentative air increases were announced, and which he was convinced were inadequate: 'I dread the day when the means of threatening the heart of the British Empire should pass into the hands of the present rulers of Germany.'

Inside Germany the presentation of Nazi actions in the most favourable light possible involved two separate and contradictory approaches: the continual efforts by Goebbels to glorify and justify events, and the equally emphatic denial and denunciation of criticism. On Hitler's personal orders one of the most perceptive and outspoken American journalists in Berlin, Dorothy Thompson, was expelled from Germany and refused permission to go back. Returning to the United States, she published a newspaper column three times a week and made regular radio broadcasts denouncing the Nazi regime. Anti-Jewish excesses continued throughout the year. The Gauleiter (District Leader) of Franconia, Julius Streicher – who, like Hitler, had been awarded the Iron Cross, First Class, for his service in the trenches – filled a whole newspaper, *Der Stürmer* (The Stormer), with crude attacks on the Jews, portraying them as an evil force that had to be eliminated from German life.

The violence of language used by the German leaders was distressing and offensive to those who had earlier championed Germany's right for a fair deal in the councils of Europe. In his book *These Times*, the British journalist J.A. Spender wrote of 'something nasty and brutish in the German Revolution, which was worse than primitive savagery', and he commented about the frequent speeches by Hitler, Goering and Goebbels calling for German national unity and sacrifice: 'We should think an English Prime Minister or Foreign Minister mad if he spoke to us in these terms, and still more so, if at the same time he was appealing to his next door neighbour to disarm on the ground of his pacific disposition and intentions.'

Details of that 'savagery' appeared almost daily in the Western newspapers. On April 3 the *Manchester Guardian* reported that on Palm Sunday a member of Julius Streicher's personal bodyguard, Kurt Baer, had marched at the head of a squad of Stormtroops into Gunzenhausen, his parents' village and also the home of nineteen Jewish families – shopkeepers, craftsmen and innkeepers. Baer ordered the Jews to be dragged from their homes and from the cellars in which they had sought refuge. He himself dragged one Jewish woman through the streets by her hair. Throughout the night the Jews were beaten and whipped in the streets. On the following morning two Jews were found dead, one, a seventy-five-year-old man, had been stabbed to death; the other, a thirty-year-old man, had been hanged.

The murder of Jews was part of a sustained attempt to isolate, marginalize, hurt and humiliate them. On May 1 *Der Stürmer* produced a special fourteen-page issue in which the Jews were accused, as they had often been during the Middle Ages, of murdering Christian children in order to use their blood in the Passover bread and other 'Judaic rituals'. This was an outrageous libel on a whole people: no such rituals had ever existed. But this particular ritual murder accusation, tens of thousands of copies of which were displayed on public notice boards throughout Germany, reproduced the libel – a medieval engraving depicting four rabbis sucking the blood of a Christian child through a straw. The publication also included a photograph of a dead child, with the inflammatory caption: 'Slaughtered on 17 March 1929 near Manau shortly before the Jewish Passover.'

Throughout Germany, Jews left incensed, hostile villages – in many of which their ancestors had lived for generations – and settled in the towns, or left Germany altogether. By the end of 1934 some 50,000 Jews had emigrated, mostly to Britain, Western Europe, the United States and Palestine. But those 450,000 who remained did not necessarily feel the need to prepare to leave. In their study *The Jewish Refugee*, published in New York in 1944, and based on interviews with several thousand refugees, Arieh Tartakower and Kurt Grossman wrote of the first two years of Nazi rule: 'During this first period, the refugee movement had rather a tentative character. To many it seemed that the anti-Jewish excesses would pass, to be followed by a new Jewish policy, embodying moderate restrictions and disabilities.' Many Jews hoped 'that there would be only a limited exodus, and that the bulk of the Jewish population would remain in Germany'.

That spring a British writer, Stephen Spender, was on holiday in Yugoslavia, at the small resort town of Mlini, five miles from Dubrovnik. He later wrote of how, as he climbed up from his hotel to the coastal road he was almost run over by a large six-wheeled car, followed by four others:

The man in the first car, who turned his head and stared at me so that I met his eyes, was Goering.

Somewhere I felt that there was a place which was at the very centre of this world, some terrible place like the core of a raging fire. Perhaps it was in a cell where some helpless old man was being beaten to death, perhaps it was a café over some frontier where exiled leaders were plotting to return. If I could ever approach it, I felt it would be the centre where the greatest evil of our time was understood and endured. But at this thought I was appalled, for it made me realize that the centre of our time was perhaps the violent, incommunicable death of an innocent victim.

On May 25 the London *Daily Express* reported on an episode that had taken place in February, when Stormtroops entered the village of Arnswalde, in Pomerania, and at a given signal hurled stones at Jewish houses, shops and meeting halls. Breaking into the synagogue, and into the house of the rabbi, they destroyed the furnishings and tore up the holy books. During the night Jewish homes were attacked, and Jews, if caught, were beaten up in the street. On the following morning most of the Jews left the village. That same morning German children on their way to school helped themselves to toothpaste, soap and sponges lying in the wreckage of a Jewish chemist's shop, 'while', in the words of the report, 'parents and teachers looked on'.

In the German province of Franconia, which had also become a centre of anti-Jewish feeling, villages throughout the province competed during the summer of 1934 to be 'free of Jews'. On May 26 the *Frankische Tageszeitung* described the moment at which, a few days earlier, at precisely five in the afternoon, 'the swastika flag was hoisted on the property of the last Jew to leave Hersbruck. The Hersbruck district is now definitely purged of Jews. With pride and satisfaction the population takes cognizance of this fact.' The newspaper was certain that other districts would soon follow this lead, 'and that the day is not now far off when the whole of Franconia will be rid of Jews, just as one day that day must dawn when throughout the whole of Germany there will no longer be one single Jew.'

Between May 29 and 31 a synod of Evangelical churchmen was held at Barmen. Pastor Martin Niemöller was a prominent influence, and the anti-Christian excesses of the regime were denounced. The churchmen present – who formed themselves into a new Confessing Church to counter the official church subservience – pledged not to succumb to the prevailing anti-Christian ideology.

One of Niemöller's areas of conflict with the Nazi regime concerned the persecution of Jews who had already converted to Christianity. As he told the synod of the Prussian Protestant Church a year later, such Jews had to be helped, according to the precept laid down by St Paul in his Epistle to the Galatians, 'For ye are all children of God by faith in Christ Jesus. For as many of you as have been baptized into Christ have put on Christ. There is neither Jew nor Greek, there is neither bond nor free, there is neither male nor female: for ye are all one in Christ Jesus.' On this basis, Niemöller insisted, the Church must speak out and must intercede – even fight – for converted Jews.

As for the mass of German Jews, however, those who had not converted to Christianity, in Niemöller's view they bore God's curse for having 'rejected forgiveness'. It was a curse that carried with it, he said, 'as a fearsome burden the unforgiven blood-guilt of their fathers'. In addition, he later reflected, 'certain restrictions against the Jews seemed to me tolerable considering the great aims the Nazis were driving at.'

Those 'great aims' and the racial policy were being pursued simultaneously. On June 17 a special court at Nuremberg sentenced the non-Jewish wife of a Jew to four months in prison as a 'race-defiling female'. Three days later the German Vice-Chancellor, Franz von Papen – a leading Catholic statesman – spoke out against Nazi excesses. The occasion was an address to the University Association in Marburg. Papen's speech, which had been drafted by his assistant Edgar Jung, attacked the 'Brown Terror' tactics of the SA, criticized the 'rigid press manipulation' practised by Goebbels' Propaganda Department, suggested that single-Party rule was a 'transitional stage', and hinted at the restoration of the monarchy.

The historian Joachim Fest has commented about Papen's speech that it was 'not so much the outcry of a sense of justice outraged by the aims and methods of the National Socialist conquest and power, as the outcry of an infuriated accomplice finally brought to realize that he had no chance of putting his own plans into effect, and that if he had been given any role at all it was purely as a decorative element in the State which, after a fourteen-year interregnum, he considered as once more belonging to himself and his class, and which he had intended to govern'.

In response to Papen's attack, Goebbels used his own ministerial power to forbid either the radio or the newspapers to disseminate the speech. Papen threatened to resign as Vice-Chancellor but was dissuaded from doing so by Hitler. On June 21, Goebbels warned an audience in Berlin that once the masses were to challenge the 'dignified gentlemen' and 'ridiculous fools' who criticized Nazism, 'you will see them beat a cowardly retreat'.

Hitler had his own plans to consolidate power, including taking total control of the private army of his Nazi Party, the SA. Since the beginning of 1931 the SA had been commanded by Captain Ernst Roehm, a thrice-wounded veteran of trench warfare (half his nose had been shot away) who had been at Hitler's side during the failed Beer-Hall putsch in Munich in 1923. Swearing loyalty to Hitler as the 'Supreme Leader' of the SA, Roehm organized his men on rigid military lines, from himself as Chief of Staff down to the Battalions, Storm Troops, Troops and Bands. Known from their uniforms as Brownshirts, they were a much-feared instrument of Nazi control. By the start of 1934 they numbered more than two million.

Roehm wanted the SA to become the sole military arm of the regime, absorbing the regular armed forces within its structure. Hitler understood the need for the support of the regular army if the German State was to be transformed as he wished; the determination of Roehm to see the SA replace the army was therefore unacceptable to him. In preparation for a drastic outcome he ordered the SA to go on leave for the whole of the month of August, during which time its members were not to wear their uniforms. But he had decided to act before the August decree could create a backlash, and in the early hours of June 30 flew from Bad Godesberg to Munich, where an SA march had taken place the previous evening. He then drove, with an SS escort, to the resort town of Bad Wiessee, where Roehm and the other SA leaders were staying. Confronting Roehm directly, and accusing him of plotting rebellion, Hitler placed Roehm under arrest. A gun was later put in Roehm's cell and he was ordered to take the 'honourable' way out. He refused to do so, whereupon he was shot.

The murder of Roehm was decisive in giving Hitler full control of the SA. In Berlin, more than a hundred and fifty SA leaders were arrested, confined in a coal cellar and then taken out in batches to face an SS firing squad. The slaughter of the SA leadership was also the signal which enabled Hitler to settle scores with other opponents who had nothing to with Roehm. In particular he wished to eliminate the Socialist tendencies within the Nazi Party, that had been a strong element since its formation. The assassinations which began in the early hours of June 30, during what quickly became known as the Night of the Long Knives, were widespread. Among those who were shot was Gregor Strasser, one of the founders of the Nazi Party, a believer in 'undiluted socialist principles' who had earlier hoped to use Nazism to advance those principles. Since December 1932 he had lived in retirement, with no Party positions and no influence. This did not save him. Nor did retirement save a former German Chancellor, General Kurt von Schleicher. Six assassins shot him down. He had been in retirement since

Hitler came to power a year and a half earlier. His wife Elisabeth also died, hit by a single bullet in the hail of fire.

The long arm of vengeance spared neither those who had retired nor those who were elderly. Seventy-three-year-old Gustav von Kahr, who a decade earlier had led the troops against Hitler's Beer-Hall putsch, was dragged from his home and hacked to death with pickaxes. Several leading Catholics were also killed, among them Fritz Beck, the director of the Munich Students' Welfare Fund: when his naked body was found in the woods near the town of Passing, his face was a formless mass: he was identified by a Papal medal that he wore around his neck.

A well-known music critic, Willy Schmidt, was killed by mistake. He was confused with an intended victim named Wilhelm Schmidt. When the mistake was discovered, Hitler's deputy, Rudolf Hess, called on the music critic's widow to apologize. Another of those shot was Edgar Jung, who had drafted von Papen's anti-Nazi speech of thirteen days earlier. Dr Fritz Gerlich, a leading Catholic writer who had edited an anti-Nazi newspaper in Munich before 1933 was also shot.

'The French are pleased,' the American journalist William Shirer noted in his diary when the first news of the killings reached Paris. 'They think it is the beginning of the end for the Nazis.' But the Night of Long Knives ensured the primacy in the Nazi movement of Hitler, Goering, Himmler and Goebbels, who for the next decade were to direct the fate of the German nation, and of all those who came under its sway. Another of those who had participated in the organization of the killings of June 30 was Reinhard Heydrich, the head of the State Security Service (SD), whose loyalty to terror never wavered.

Hitler defended the killings of the Night of the Long Knives in a speech to the Reichstag in Berlin on July 13. Of his enemies, he said: 'Though worthless in themselves they are, nevertheless, dangerous, because they are veritable bacillus-carriers of unrest and uncertainty, of rumours, assertions, lies and suspicion, of slanders and fears.' The killing of these men, he asserted, 'belonged to a higher justice'. Of the moment that he had decided to take action, Hitler reflected: 'In this hour I was responsible for the fate of the German people, and therefore I became the Supreme Justiciar of the German people.' Hitler ended with a warning: 'Everyone must know that in all future time, if he raises his hand to strike at the State, then certain death will be his lot.'

To ensure that the ferocious executions and assassinations were 'lawful',

Hitler instructed Wilhelm Frick, the Reich Minister of the Interior, to draft a law that would make the killings legal. The law as drafted declared Hitler's actions during the Night of the Long Knives to have been both 'legal and statesmanlike'. It was passed by the Reichstag without dissent. A further law was passed, on August 1, combining the offices of 'Führer and Reich Chancellor' with that of President. This was done as eighty-six-year-old President Hindenburg lay dying. On the following morning, Hindenburg died. Goebbels then announced the new amalgamated office in a radio broadcast. Before the day was over the Minister of War, General Blomberg, issued an order whereby all German soldiers had to swear an oath of personal loyalty to 'the Führer of the German Reich and People, Adolf Hitler'. The Field Marshal was dead; the former corporal was supreme; the loyalty of the army to the Nazi leader was secured. One of Hitler's biographers, Konrad Heiden, wrote a decade after the executions:

By his gruesome deed of June 30, 1934, Hitler, in the eyes of the German people, definitely assumed the dimensions of an historical, superhuman being, whose rights and reasons could no longer be questioned. 'There won't be another revolution in Germany for the next thousand years', he proclaimed.

The belief in the necessity of evil, which slumbers in the lowest depths of the human soul, had been awakened by Hitler as by no other man in the history of Europe; the fact that he could do what he had done seemed like a confirmation of Hess's fanatical words: that through Hitler higher powers were fulfilling man's destiny.

Hitler now began to do frightful things easily, and the more frightful they were, the more easily he did them. He discovered the secret law of history which has made all bloody figures like himself bigger than life-size when the times were favourable: the law by which the most horrible deeds become less heavy to bear, the more monstrous and numerous they are, because in the end each horror wipes out its predecessor in the minds of the people.

Within a month of the Night of the Long Knives in Germany, Austrian Nazis, with the full support and encouragement of Berlin, initiated a campaign of terror throughout Austria. Power stations were blown up, administrative buildings and railway stations attacked, and supporters of Chancellor Dollfuss beaten in the streets. Anti-Dollfuss and pro-Nazi propaganda was broadcast daily into Austria from neighbouring Bavaria, calling for the absorption of Austria into Germany: the *Anschluss* that was specifically forbidden by the Allies in the postwar treaties.

On June 25, in great secrecy, a meeting was held in Zurich by four men who had as their aim nothing less than the assassination of Dollfuss and the victory of Austrian Nazism. One of the four, Fridolin Glass, was an Austrian Nazi with the rank of Captain in the SS. The other three were German citizens, chief among them Theo Habicht, Hitler's emissary to Austria, who at Hitler's urging had formed, in Bavaria, an Austrian Legion of 15,000 men. At the Zurich meeting, Glass explained that the assassination of Dollfuss would take place simultaneously with the capture of the entire Austrian Cabinet, after which an Austrian Nazi government would be put in its place.

Dollfuss, unaware of the plot being planned against him, announced, in an effort to curb Nazi terror, that all acts of violence against the State would be severely punished. Ironically, it was a twenty-year-old Socialist, Josef Gerl, who, denied a pardon by Dollfuss, was the first to be hanged after the new rule was announced. His execution took place on July 25. He had tried to blow up a signal pole on a little-used railway, and had wounded the policeman who came to arrest him.

Then, on July 25, in connivance with the German Government, the Austrian Nazis took dramatic action to advance their cause. That day an estimated 154 members of a German-trained Austrian Nazi formation, dressed deceptively in Austrian army uniforms, broke into the Federal Chancellery in Vienna. Dollfuss was shot in the throat. The man who shot him, Otto Planetta, had been a member of Dollfuss's regiment in the First World War, a sixteen-year-old volunteer, decorated for bravery on the Italian Front.

As Dollfuss lay bleeding, his attackers refused him any medical help. Quite untruthfully, they told him that the whole army, the police force and the country had risen against him. 'In this heartbreaking belief,' wrote Eric Gedye – who was present at the trial of the chief assassin – 'after lingering two hours and three-quarters without medical aid, he died at about 3.45 in the hands of his utterly callous Nazi captors – less than twenty-four hours after he had sent to the gallows the young Socialist, Gerl, for doing what thousands of Nazis had for months been doing almos‛ with impunity – trying to damage railway property with explosives.'

Dollfuss's last words before he died of his wounds were: 'Children, be good to one another. I always wanted to do only the best.'

*   *   *

The murder of Dollfuss was intended as the first stage of the seizure of power by the Nazis in Vienna, and of the annexation of Austria by Germany. But the plans laid by Hitler's 'Plenipotentiary for Austria', Theo Habicht, and the other conspirators, came to nothing. Austrian government forces led by the Minister of Justice, Dr Kurt von Schuschnigg, won control of the Chancellery, and the attempted coup was crushed. During the assassination of Dollfuss, and in its wake, 145 Austrian Nazis were either killed in action or executed for their part in the attempted coup.

Even as fighting was continuing in Vienna, Mussolini, fearing Hitler's annexation of Austria – a country which he regarded as his sphere of influence, and as a territorial buffer against Germany – mobilized four Italian Divisions on the Brenner Pass. Hitler had no choice but to abandon his current plans of a coup.

Summing up the contribution of Dollfuss to the concept of Austria as an independent State, Gordon Brook-Shepherd, one of his biographers, wrote, a quarter of a century after the assassination:

Abroad, Dollfuss's death fixed him in history as the person he will always remain, despite his own errors and the calumnies of his enemies: the incorporation of an Austrian way of living and thinking and therefore of an Austrian right to independent existence.

This ideal he snatched back from that Empire which his opponents despised and gave to the Republic which those same opponents had built. He thus put into the body of the young state the soul of the ancient nation.

'By his death,' wrote *The Times* in its obituary, 'Dr Dollfuss has proved that a German culture really exists that is worth saving.'

In Poland, the dictatorship of Marshal Pilsudski took an unexpectedly liberal turn that year. Following the assassination of Bronislaw Pieracki, who as Minister of the Interior had persued harsh measures towards Poland's minorities – particularly towards the Ukrainians – Pilsudski appointed as his successor Marjan Koscialowski. Known to want better relations with the minorities, Koscialowski proceeded to legislate for an improvement in their situation.

In the Soviet Union, the power of the State to impose its will was reaching areas hitherto untouched by the practice of Communism. On May 21 it was announced in Moscow that a thirteen-year-old schoolboy, Pronya Kolibin, had been given a cash prize for reporting to the authorities that his mother was stealing grain (in part to feed him) from a collective farm near Moscow. Theft of grain was a crime punishable by death. A poem by the young man, denouncing his mother, was published in *Pravda*. Two of its lines were:

> You are a wrecker, mother.
> I can live with you no more.

A young American diplomat in Moscow, George F. Kennan, recalled in his memoirs:

> ... no one, of course could have been fully prepared for the reality. If in earlier stages of the development of Soviet power there had been vestiges of belief that society would be genuinely benefited by all the cruelty and suffering, here, in the Russia of the purges, was cynicism, shamelessness, contempt for humanity – all triumphantly enthroned. Here was a great nation helpless in the toils of an unbelievably cunning, in many ways great, but monstrously ruthless and cynical man.
>
> So insistently were the evidences of Russia's degradation borne in upon me during the years of my residence in Moscow – so prolonged and incessant were the hammer-blow impressions, each more outrageous and heartrending than the other – that the effect was never to leave me.

The effects of enforced collectivization continued to be felt throughout Russia. After foodstuffs had been taken away from the peasants at extremely low prices, considerable pressure was applied to persuade them to sell part of what remained 'voluntarily'. Since the start of collectivization some years earlier, almost half of all Russian cattle had been lost, either slaughtered for meat or dying through shortage of fodder. Stalin promised that 1934 would see an improvement, but while a small increase in livestock was recorded, the number of cows did not increase, and the number of horses continued to decrease. From the Communist Party faithful, however, came nationally publicized and choreographed paeans of praise. At the Party Congress that opened in Moscow on January 26, Stalin was described as 'our genius leader' by the forty-year-old Second Secretary of the Moscow Party organization – Nikita Khrushchev – who in the same city, twenty-two years later, at another Party Congress, would denounce Stalin's crimes.

On March 31, in the introduction to his book *These Times*, J.A. Spender wrote of 'the hardships, the shortages, the dragooning and the martyrdom inflicted on millions of Soviet citizens by the Communist regime.' Communist economic theory, he reflected, 'is reckless of life or happiness, and in a semi-Oriental people takes on some of the characteristics of a Mohammedan holy war. *Das Kapital* is now as drenched in blood as the Athanasian creed.'*

In China, the Communist armed forces in the province of Kiangsi, from which in earlier years they had made several strong attacks on Nationalist towns, were unable to continue their military struggle against the Nationalists. Chiang Kai-shek's elite units were too strong for them. Following a series of defeats, Mao Tse-tung ordered a withdrawal. It began on October 16, when the Communist fighting forces embarked upon what was to be a journey of almost six thousand miles, across a harsh terrain, to the northern province of Shensi. This twelve-month ordeal, known as the Long March, established the leadership of Mao Tse-tung — who had earlier worked in tandem with the Nationalists — and who, when the march was successfully ended, became Party Chairman, committed to extending to the maximum the area under direct Communist control. Those who were prominent on the Long March became the future leaders of Communist China, among them the Commander-in-Chief of the marchers, Chu Teh, and Lin Piao, who commanded one of the two army corps.

As they prepared to leave Kiangsi the Communists were attacked by the Nationalists, and during five days' continuous fighting 4,000 Communist soldiers were killed. But repeated efforts by the Nationalists to trap the retreating forces as they began their marching, first westward more than eight hundred miles to Mougong, and then north-east a further seven hundred miles to Yenan, were unsuccessful. Under the organizational skills of Chou En-lai, 28,000 troops set off, divided into two army corps. They were poorly armed, with only 9,000 rifles, and a hundred cartridges per rifle. Their 300 machine guns, a pitifully small number, had ammunition for only ten minutes of high-speed firing each. Behind these troops were two columns,

* Latin Creed, expounding chiefly the doctrines of the Trinity and the Incarnation, regarded as authoritative by both the Roman Catholic and Anglican churches, and by some Protestant churches. Its central concept, the Trinity, was challenged in the 4th century by the followers of the priest Arius. The struggle between Arianism and the believers in the Athanasian creed was a bloody one.

each of about 14,000 men. A further 66,000 men defended the flanks and carried the rice and salt rations.

Hardly any women accompanied the march. One of those who did was Mao Tse-tung's second wife, who was pregnant. Another was Chu Teh's fourth wife: of his three previous wives one had died after childbirth, one had been killed by warlords, and one had been executed by the Nationalists, as had Mao Tse-tung's first wife.

An even greater setback to the Nationalists than the escape of their Communist adversary was their failure, in the longer term, to redress the balance of rural poverty. During 1934 it was announced by the Bank of China that in the previous year, on average, a farmer's income accounted for 80 per cent of his subsistence expenditure – a statistic that related to forty million families.

On the borders of China, both success and failure met Chinese imperial ambitions. The province of Kashgar, which had been captured by local Muslim tribesmen, was reoccupied by military forces loyal to the Nationalist government in Nanking. But an attempt by a Nationalist Chinese mission, headed by an army general, to persuade the Tibetans to put the new Dalai Lama under the tutelage of a Chinese Resident was rejected by the Tibetans, and the mission returned to China.

In the areas of China occupied by Japan, the Japanese rulers brooked no interference. Nor were they willing to see outside Powers become the protectors or defenders of China, however much the Chinese government might seek outside help. On April 17 the Ministry of Foreign Affairs in Tokyo announced that Japan would oppose any foreign projects for building aerodromes in China at the request of the Nanking government, or for supplying China with warplanes or military advisers. Five days later the Japanese ambassador in Washington issued a 'hands off' warning to the United States and all other interested Powers, insisting that no important transactions should be concluded with the Nanking government by other States without prior consultation with Japan. In May, the Japanese Minister for Foreign Affairs told a meeting of provincial governors in Tokyo that 'the gratuitous assistance of outsiders, animated by selfish motives' would not help China to realize her aspirations, nor could Japan remain indifferent 'to any act of conspiracy against the peace and order of eastern Asia'.

In Manchuria, under Japanese occupation, the Chinese Regent – and former boy emperor – P'u Yi, was proclaimed Emperor of Manchukuo. This proclamation was intended to show the world, and China, that P'u Yi was no longer primarily the claimant to the throne of China, but the ruler of a separate, independent entity. Reuter's correspondent described the scene:

> The officials having taken up positions north of the altar, the Emperor mounted the marble steps, and the ceremonies began. A thin column of smoke symbolized the passage of prayers to Heaven as the new Monarch made an offering of a jade amulet and a roll of silk.
>
> Then followed offerings of three goblets of sacrificial wine and a scroll bearing a message which P'u Yi read out. The great jade Seal of State was then handed to him, and he reverently raised it to Heaven.
>
> As the seal was handed back to the attendant the fire on the altar was rekindled while the Emperor silently invoked the blessing of Heaven and the spirits of his ancestors.
>
> While the Emperor was thus engaged in prayer, the priests killed a snow-white bull, which was offered in sacrifice.

Aeroplanes dropped Royal proclamations on a crowd of 15,000 Chinese who had assembled to witness the event, informing them that a reign of 'tranquillity and virtue' had begun.

The League of Nations refused to recognize the new 'empire', but the unanimity of the League in thus showing its disapproval of the Japanese conquest of Manchuria was broken when the Republic of San Salvador recognized Manchukuo. There was vexation at the League that one of its number, however small and remote, should have broken ranks.

Yet another of the hitherto Chinese-controlled regions of Asia, Inner Mongolia, came under Japanese rule that year, when Japanese troops occupied the province of Chahar, forcing the Chinese Governor to withdraw from the province. At the same time, Japanese control of Korea – in place since 1910 – was consolidated by the widespread arrest of Communists throughout the peninsula. By the end of 1933 twenty-two Korean Communist leaders had been brought to trial and sentenced to death.

On May 24 the Japanese fired an important warning shot across the bows of the United States and Britain, declaring that the limitations on naval construction laid down in the Washington and London Treaties were 'obsolete', and stating that because of her increased responsibilities in Manchuria, Japan must be strong enough at sea 'to safeguard her position in the Pacific Ocean'. The British government suggested that the Japanese demands be resolved through negotiations. The Japanese agreed and naval conversations opened in London on October 23. Japan was represented by Admiral Isoruku Yamamoto, who proposed that the existing restrictions be abolished, and that the three Powers be allowed to build their respective navies on a basis of equality. Naval armaments could be limited, he said, to such weaponry as was needed for defensive purposes only.

The London negotiations continued for almost two months. On December 19 they broke down, whereupon Japan formally abrogated the Washington Treaty. Henceforth, Japan would build her navy to whatever strength and scale she wished.

Two natural disasters struck Japan in 1934. In March, in a fire that swept through the town of Hakodate, almost two thousand people were killed. In September a tidal wave and typhoon struck Osaka, killing more than three thousand people.

Whatever the shocks that natural disasters brought to Japan, or the human shocks that Japanese political decisions portended to British naval power, the nature of the British Commonwealth and Empire was also changing. In New Zealand the racial pride of the Maoris was given a boost when, during celebrations to mark the ninety-sixth anniversary of the treaty between the British and the Maoris, a leading Maori politician, Sir Apirana Ngata (the New Zealand Minister for Native Affairs, who had been knighted in 1927) threw off his top hat and black coat and, stripping himself to the waist, put on Maori dress and led five hundred warriors in a war dance. Ngata had played a leading part in the resettlement of the Maori people on the land from which they had earlier, and most brutally, been driven.

In India, the decision by the British government to pass legislation through the British parliament that would promote Indian constitutional reform led to Indian politicians and civil servants being brought into even higher positions of authority than hitherto. As a result, Gandhi called off the civil disobedience movement. For a decade and a half he had used non-violent civil disobedience as his chosen weapon to push the British into concessions. On April 7, at Patna, he advised all members of the Indian National Congress to suspend civil disobedience with regard to home rule, and to restrict it to specific grievances. Gandhi's initiative led to the abandonment of the Congress boycott of all participation within the provincial legislatures. For its part, the Government of India withdrew its ban on various aspects of Congress activities.

Seeking, not the national demands of the Congress Party, but social revolution, was the Communist Party of India, which at the end of July called a strike of textile mill workers in Bombay. Another Communist Party initiative was taken among the agricultural workers of the Punjab, who were encouraged to demand higher prices for their labours. In answer to these acts of civil disobedience, the Government of India declared the Communist Party illegal, and forced the strikers back to work.

In the Indian province of Bengal there was relief among British government officials that the terrorist actions which had been a fearful feature of previous years were on the decline. A tremor of alarm was felt on May 8 when two Bengalis fired at the Governor, Sir John Anderson, at almost point blank range, when he was at the races near Darjeeling. Despite their proximity they failed to kill him. He was not even wounded. Anderson had already initiated a programme of reform, centred on a Rural Development Commission, to improve the chronic economic hardships of rural Bengal.

The principal short term challenge to the British and Indians alike in India was the challenge of nature. On the afternoon of January 15 an earthquake had struck northern India with a hitherto unrecorded ferocity; the human and economic effects were felt for the rest of the year. In Bihar and Nepal at least ten thousand people were killed. The first photographs of the disaster were flown to Britain by air for distribution to the newspapers, bringing scenes of the 'Great Indian Earthquake' – including harrowing scenes from the town of Monghyr – to the breakfast tables of the ruling nation.

In August there was severe flooding in the Ganges Valley, when many villages were totally submerged. But the general economy of India was improving, with the export of Indian-manufactured merchandise at a higher level than for more than twenty years. At the end of the year it was decided to establish a Reserve Bank of India, to manage the Indian currency and exchange free of political control. The governor of the new bank was to be a senior British civil servant, Sir Osborne Smith. One of his two deputies was an Indian, Sir Sikander Hayat Khan. South of Madras, a major advance in flood control and irrigation was made on August 21, with the opening of the Cauvery-Mettur irrigation dam.

In Delhi, the Indian Legislature, whose Indian members had given up their boycott, passed a Factory Act which reduced the maximum hours of work per week from sixty to fifty-four. Legislation was also passed giving greater protection to dock workers who were injured in loading and unloading ships. Convinced that the progress of constitutional reform would not be impeded, Gandhi retired from the leadership of Congress to devote himself to the improvement of the lot of the Harijans – known officially as the Depressed Classes, unofficially as the 'untouchables'. Under the leadership of Gandhi's successor Jawaharlal Nehru, the Congress, while working again alongside the British members in both the national and provincial Legislatures, reaffirmed its goal of complete independence.

Indianization was being pursued in the Indian Army; during 1934 an act was passed enabling Indian graduates of the Dehra Dun military academy to become officers. The Royal Indian Marine, which had come into existence more than three hundred years earlier, was given the full status and title of a Navy. The extension of radio broadcasting by means of a new transmitting station in New Delhi was intended as the first step in an all-India broadcasting system which would enable each of the provinces to have programmes in their own language and with full regard to local culture. These were significant advances not only in giving Indians greater authority and say in their own affairs, but in British attitudes. The traditional imperial concept of 'divide and rule', with its underlying sense of superiority over the 'native peoples', was giving way to a sense of partnership and of individual equality of rights.

The French Empire faced more direct challenges than the British in 1934, as the military revolt of Moroccan tribesmen flared up again at the beginning of the year in the south-west of the country. The soldiers sent by France against the tribesmen were almost entirely Moroccan and other Colonial troops, with the addition of French Foreign Legionnaires. Two military columns, 17,000 men in all, were sent into the interior, under two French generals, Catroux and Giraud, both of whom were to come to even greater prominence within a decade. After the main force of tribesmen had surrendered, the cavalry and mechanized formations searched for the others in the remotest regions. 'By March 16,' wrote one observer, 'the pacification of the entire Anti-Atlas region was completed with the submission of the last dissident tribesman.'

As a result of this French-led military success a further 200,000 tribesmen found themselves part of the French Empire. The French consolidation of their rule in Morocco was enhanced by the development of communications. On April 10 the opening of a small section of railway, from Fez to Taza, meant that it was possible to travel by rail without interruption from Tunis to Marrakech, a distance of 1,700 miles.

*   *   *

The assassination of the Archduke Franz Ferdinand of Austria-Hungary by a Serb nationalist in June 1914 had been the catalyst that precipitated the European war. Twenty years later, on 9 October 1934, another assassination caused a sudden tremor of fear: that of King Alexander of Yugoslavia, who was killed, together with the French Foreign Minister, Louis Barthou, at Marseille. The King was at the start of a goodwill visit to France. His assassin was a Macedonian who had been trained in terrorist activity by Croat extremists inside Hungary. The moments before and after the assassination were caught on film by a newsreel cameraman, and shown on cinema screens throughout the world. One of those who watched that film was the British novelist, Rebecca West. She described the scene in her book *Black Lamb and Grey Falcon*:

Now King Alexander is driving down the familiar streets, curiously unguarded, in a curiously antique car. It can be seen from his attempt to make his stiff hand supple, from a careless flash of his careful black eyes, it can be seen that he is taking the cheers of the crowd with a childish seriousness. It is touching, like a girl putting full faith in the compliments that are paid to her at a ball.

Then his preoccupation veils his brows and desiccates his lips. He is thinking of Yugoslavia again, with the nostalgia of an author who has been interrupted in writing his new book. He might be thinking, '*Heureux qui, comme Ulysse, a fait un beau voyage . . .*'

But then the camera leaves him. It recedes. The sound-track records a change, a swelling astonishment, in the voice of the crowd. We see a man jumping on the footboard of the car, a soldier swinging a sword, a revolver in the hand of another, a straw hat lying on the ground, a crowd that jumps up and down, up and down, smashing something flat with its arms, kicking something flat with its feet, till there is seen on the pavement a pulp covered with garments.

A lad in a sweater dodges before his captors, his defiant face unmarked by fear, although his body expresses the very last extreme of fear by a creeping, writhing motion. A view of the whole street shows people dashed about as by a tangible wind of death.

Rebecca West's account continued, as she described what she saw in the newsreel film:

The camera returns to the car and we see the King. He is lying almost flat on his back on the seat. . . . He does not know that anything has happened, he is still half rooted in the pleasure of his own nostalgia. He might be asking, 'Et en quelle saison Revoiray-je le clos de ma pauvre maison, Qui m'est une province, et beaucoup d'avantage?'

It is certain that he is dying, because he is the centre of a manifestation which would not happen unless the living had been shocked out of their reserve by the presence of death. Innumerable hands are caressing him. Hands are coming from everywhere, over the back of the car, over the sides, through the windows, to caress the dying King, and they are supremely kind. They are far kinder than faces can be, for faces are Marthas, burdened with many cares because of their close connection with the mind, but these hands express the mindless sympathy of living flesh for flesh that is about to die, the pure physical basis for pity. They are men's hands, but they move tenderly as the hands of women fondling their babies, they stroke his cheek as if they were washing it with kindness.

Suddenly his nostalgia goes from him. His pedantry relaxes. He is at peace, he need not guard against death any more.

Immediately following King Alexander's assassination, the Yugoslav government, as an act of retaliation, ordered the mass expulsion of Hungarians living on the Yugoslav side of their common border. Alexander's cousin, Prince Paul, who was appointed Regent, then appealed for justice to the League of Nations, pointing out that Yugoslavia had protested four months earlier to Hungary about specific Croat terrorists being trained on Hungarian soil, and even mentioning individuals who were later implicated in the Marseille crime.

The Yugoslav note to the League of Nations was a stern one. Fearing that Hungary would give an equally stern reply, and that tension might escalate as it had done steadily and inexorably in 1914, both Britain and France put themselves forward as mediators and prevailed upon Hungary to give a conciliatory reply. Yugoslavia accepted this, and ended the mass expulsions of Hungarians across the border.

King Alexander's funeral in Belgrade saw a galaxy of foreign dignitaries, among them the French Minister of War, General Pétain, and General Goering, Hitler's Air Minister. From his preparatory school in England came the new King, Peter II, who was only eleven years old. Hopes that in the aftermath of the assassination the Serb-dominated government might offer some gesture of conciliation to the Croats were not fulfilled. Press censorship and restrictions on freedom of assembly remained in force under the Regency as they had done under the King. Regent Paul did, however, order the Croat leader, Dr Vladko Macek, to be released from prison, and genuinely thought that his Prime Minister, Dr Milan Stojadinovich was the one Serb politician prepared to sit down and talk to Croats at the same table. Paul had experimented with three Prime Ministers in nine months before appointing Stojadinovich, hoping that he would reach agreement with the Croats. His failure to do so was one of the reasons for his dismissal four years later.

In Turkey the process of drastic modernization undertaken by Mustafa Kemal continued with the same intensity as hitherto. In July it became compulsory for all Turks to take family names. Kemal himself took the name Atatürk (Chief Turk). In November all titles and designations of social hierarchy – among them Aga, Bey, Effendi and Pasha – were abolished. Only 'Bay' and 'Bayan' (Mr and Mrs) were allowed before one's name. All civilian decorations and medals, so beloved of the pre-republican regime, were also abolished: only war medals could henceforth be worn. Education and social welfare were devised on the most progressive of western and secular models. Not the imam and the mosque, but the schoolteacher and the schoolroom, were held up as the model of the way forward. Higher education became a status symbol of the new Turkey: German Jewish refugees from Hitler were welcomed in to teach in the professions. Kemal personally took the campaign against illiteracy to dozens of villages.

As Republican Turkey moved towards western modernity, Republican Spain moved towards civil war. Throughout 1934 the forces of socialism and separatism sought to test their respective strengths against the centrist, Catholic-dominated government. In February, common cause was made in Madrid among Socialists, Syndicalists and Communists, and a series of strikes began in the capital. Anarchist bomb attacks in Saragossa led to widespread arrests, which were countered by a crippling general strike. In an attempt to protect itself from violent revolution the government instituted widespread searches for arms. In June more than 80,000 rounds of ammunition were discovered in Madrid, in the custody of trade union officials. In the home of one Socialist deputy, twelve parcels of pistols were seized. In July the Socialist leader, Indalecio Prieto, declared: 'Every town and village is replete with arms. Let all who will have to fight us take warning!'

In both Catalonia and the Basque country, separatist movements were demanding greater political authority. The Prime Minister of Spain from 1931 to 1933, Manuel Azana, had set up Municipal Committees which the separatists declared were an infringement of their existing autonomies. With the support of the Socialists, both Basque and Catalan separatists held mass demonstrations, which a new Prime Minister, Ricardo Samper, ordered to be broken up. In retaliation, on September 10, Catalan separatists set fire to the Law Courts in Barcelona. A day later, two Socialist deputies were arrested as they helped bring more than 100,000 rounds of rifle ammunition ashore at San Esteban, in the Asturias.

Samper's government fell, and he was succeeded by Alejandro Lerroux. The Socialists denounced the government as a mere faction and declared a general strike. There were armed attacks on police stations and army barracks. In Barcelona, Catalan independence was proclaimed. Lerroux declared martial law and appealed to the army to suppress the revolutionaries. In Madrid the Socialist forces were dispersed. In Barcelona the Catalan separatists surrendered or fled. But in the Asturias the miners were not quickly cowed. As many as 20,000 miners were under arms and equipped with the dynamite that was an integral part of their work. Isolated Civil Guard and Police posts in the coal-mining region were overrun and in several cases their defenders put to death. In the first week of October the revolutionaries gained two major successes, seizing Oviedo, the capital of the region, and Gijon, its principal port.

On October 6 a Communist government was proclaimed throughout the Asturias. Within three days much of the Asturias was in the hands of the miners, with almost every town and village controlled by revolutionary committees. The revolutionary committee of Grado declared: 'Comrades, we are creating a new society. It is not surprising that the world which we are forging costs blood, grief and tears; everything on earth is fecund, soldiers of the Ideal! Put up your rifles! Women, eat little, only what is necessary! Long live the social revolution!' The two arms factories in Oviedo were taken over by a committee of their own workers, who instituted a shift system for 24-hour working. Other factories and mines were deserted, however, as military recruitment offices called up all male workers between the ages of eighteen and forty for the 'Red Army'.

The Madrid government took immediate military action, much of it directed from Madrid by General Franco, who was in Spain on leave from his command in the Balearic Islands. Franco, a strong anti-Communist, was convinced that the workers' uprising in the Asturias had been 'deliberately prepared by agents from Moscow'. This conviction, although erroneous, gave Franco the moral confidence to use Spanish troops against Spanish citizens 'as if' – writes Franco's biographer Paul Preston – 'they were a foreign enemy'.

Gijon was retaken after a naval bombardment which Franco directed from Madrid over the telephone. The cruiser *Libertad* – Liberty – led the assault from the sea. But on land, troops seeking to reach Oviedo were unable to penetrate through the mountain passes, and it was left to troops of the Spanish Legion, and Moorish Regulars rushed at Franco's orders by sea from Morocco to Gijon, to advance from Gijon to Oviedo, causing considerable destruction of property and loss of life on their way. One of the commanders of the troops from Africa had expressed doubts that his men would fire on civilians. He was replaced by a general who had exhibited particular ferocity during the Moroccan campaign. The commander of the air base in Leon – Franco's cousin and childhood friend Major Bahamonde – who had ordered his pilots not to fire on the strikers in Oviedo, was replaced at Franco's insistence. Franco then gave orders for the bombing and shelling of working class districts in the town.

The advancing troops entered Oviedo on October 13, a week after the Communist regime had been established there. Two hundred soldiers and Civil Guard were killed in the assault. Vengeance was swift. Workers believed to have been leaders of the insurrection were arrested and shot. In all more than a thousand civilians were killed. All local trade unions, fifty in all, were dissolved, and Catalan autonomy suspended. When it was announced in Madrid that fifty-eight churches had been blown up by the Communists during their short rule, there was indignation among the Catholic defenders of law, order and Spanish unity.

In the aftermath of the defeat of the Catalans, the Madrid Government commuted the death sentences on those military officers who had supported the rebellion. Franco was indignant, telling the Italian Chargé d'Affaires in Madrid: 'The victory is ours, and not to apply exemplary punishments to the rebels, not to castigate energetically those who have caused so many casualties among the troops, would signify trampling on the just rights of the military class and encourage an early extremist response.' When, however, two of Franco's colleagues, General Fanjul and General Goded, suggested carrying out a military coup in order to prevent the death sentences being commuted, Franco advised against it, recognizing that the army did not have sufficient support to seize power.

The admission of the Soviet Union to the League of Nations took place in September. Moscow had for some months encouraged the idea that a united front might be formed in Europe between Communists and Socialists, insisting that their aims were not dissimilar, and that they could work amicably and productively together. There were rumours, likewise officially encouraged, of an imminent amnesty for the many thousands of Russian Socialists who had been deported to slave labour camps in Siberia, or to the penal colonies on the Solovki Islands in the White Sea. One western observer even noted a 'marked tendency' among Communist youth 'to adopt European ideas of personal cleanliness, of better dress, of smartness in appearance, and jazz-dancing, nose-powdering, lipstick, clean collars, shaving, and what was generally called by them "humanism",' and that these changes were discussed at Party meetings and voted for. 'In short, Russia showed definite signs of a cultural and intellectual awakening.' There was even 'much less fear' of the secret police – the NKVD – who were said to be relaxing their grip.*

The Soviet Union was indeed admitted to the League of Nations. But any internal relaxations were of short duration. On December 1 one of Stalin's closest colleagues, Sergei Kirov, a member of the Politburo with responsibility for heavy industry and the timber industry, was assassinated in Leningrad. Stalin, who was in Moscow, travelled immediately by special train to Leningrad, together with the head of the NKVD; on arrival in the city he struck the waiting head of the local NKVD in the face.

The Soviet authorities announced that the murder of Kirov was the work of the disgraced former revolutionary leaders, Trotsky, Kamenev and Zinoviev. The assassin, Leonid Nikolaev, was said to have been part of a secret 'Trotskyite-Zinovieite terrorist organization'. No such organization existed. Nikolaev was shot. Those closest to Kirov were also despatched. Borisov, a member of the secret police and the head of Kirov's bodyguard, was killed when the car taking him in for questioning crashed: none of the other passengers was hurt. The head of the local NKVD – whom Stalin had struck in the face at the railway station – and his deputy were both transferred for work in the Soviet Far East, and three years later, in 1937, were shot.

* The secret police under Soviet Communism had a succession of names, all of them acronyms of their function, or of a bland version of it: the first, from December 1917, was the Cheka (All-Russian Extraordinary Commission for Combating Counter Revolution and Sabotage). This was followed in 1922 by the GPU (State Political Administration), renamed OGPU (the United GPU) in 1923, later the NKVD (People's Commissariat for Internal Affairs); MVD (Ministry of Internal Affairs), MGB (Ministry of State Security) and finally the KGB (Committee of State Security).

The question of who ordered Kirov's assassination has not been resolved. Stalin's recent, post-Soviet biographer, General Dmitri Volkogonov – whose own father, an agrarian specialist, was also executed in 1937 – writes: 'Knowing what we know about Stalin, it is certain he had a hand in it. The removal of two or three layers of indirect witnesses bears his hallmark.'

On the day of Kirov's murder, while Stalin was in Moscow, a decree was issued amending the Soviet Criminal Code. It was done on Stalin's own initiative, without any discussion at the Politburo. Stalin was so determined to publish this decree without delay that he did not even submit it for the necessary formal signature by M.I. Kalinin, the nominal head of the Soviet Government. The decree read:

i. The investigating authorities are instructed to expedite cases of those accused of planning or carrying out terrorist acts.

ii. Judicial bodies are instructed not to delay carrying out death sentences involved in crimes of this category on the assumption of possible clemency, as the Presidium of the Central Executive Committee considers clemency in such cases to be unacceptable.

iii. Agencies of the Commissariat of Internal Affairs are instructed to carry out the death sentence on criminals in the above category as soon as possible after sentence has been pronounced.

Within hours of this draconian decree being published – denying those accused by the State either the right to defence counsel, or the right of appeal – cases already under investigation were speeded up. Arrests were carried out and trials prepared. At public meetings held across the Soviet Union demands were made for action against 'terrorists'. The personnel of the secret police was substantially increased. The public were warned of the possibility of sabotage everywhere, and of the need for vigilance. Enemies of the people were said to be lurking in every factory and collective farm, in every educational and technical institute. Newspapers stressed 'the need to strengthen awareness'. The preparation of public show trials intensified. From every region came accounts of enemies unmasked, admissions of guilt, accusations against those who denied their guilt, continual interrogations, and sentences of death.

Of the 1,225 Communist delegates at the Seventeenth Party Congress in February 1934, 1,108 were arrested within a year. Most of them died under interrogation in NKVD prisons, or in the slave labour camps of Siberia. Of the 139 members and candidate members of the Central Committee elected at the Seventeenth Congress, ninety-eight were arrested and shot. Meanwhile, Kirov was elevated into a hero: his name was attached to myriad institutions and towns, including the Leningrad ballet, and main roads everywhere.

The evils of the Nazi and Soviet regimes are closely parallel in the human suffering that they caused. Historians at the end of the Twentieth Century have calculated that Stalin's victims numbered even more than those of Hitler. In part this was made possible because Stalin's tyranny lasted almost twice as long as that of Hitler: twenty-five years as against twelve. But in the atmosphere of the 1930s, many of those who were anti-Fascist and anti-Nazi often saw in Soviet Communism a beacon of hope, or could at least delude themselves that while tyranny was in the very nature of the Fascist and Nazi ideology, Communist tyranny was an aberration and could be seen as a passing phase.

When Einstein, then living in the United States as a refugee from Hitler, was asked to speak out against the 'medieval bloodbath improvised by Stalin', he declined to do so. In a letter dated December 10, while stating that 'I, too, regret immensely that the Russian political leaders let themselves be carried away to deal such a blow to the elementary demands of justice by resorting to political murder', he went on to write that 'the Russians have proved that their only aim is really the improvement of the lot of the Russian people, and that they can in this regard already show achievements. Why then direct the attention of public opinion in other countries solely to the blunders of this regime? Is such a choice not misleading?'

The question of why there had to be a choice was not easily resolved. Churchill was to ask, three years later, whether there might not be somewhere between the points of view of Communism and Nazism in which 'there ought to be room for you and me, and a few others, to cultivate opinions of our own'. But for many people, listening to the protestations and demands of the European leaders, the concept of the middle way, of a liberal, demo-cratic, humanitarian half-way house, was not as attractive as the ideology either of the Right or of the Left. Polarization was the tendency of the age. The great achievement of democracy in Britain and the United States was to ensure, despite deep divisions of political opinion, that the ideological extremes that had come to dominate European thinking did not cross either the English Channel or the Atlantic Ocean. The confidence of the United States in its constitution and way of life was shown on June 19, when the National Archives were opened in Washington. Above the portals were inscribed in stone the proud assertion: 'This building holds in trust the records of our national life and symbolizes our faith in the performance of our national institutions.'

The workings of democracy in the United States were typified by two events that year, both of which had their origins in the mid-West. The first of these two events took place – unnoticed at the time – at four o'clock in the morning of March 14 in a room in the Pickwick Hotel, Kansas City. It was then that an American who had served as an artillery officer on the Western Front, whose post-war clothing store venture had gone bankrupt, and who had been elected a county judge, made the decision to run for the United States Senate. His honesty as a judge had led to his being asked to run. That night he wrote in his diary: 'I am to make the most momentous announcement of my life. I have come to the place where all men strive to be at my age, and I thought two weeks ago that retirement on a virtual pension in some minor county office was all that was in store for me.' The diarist was a future President, Harry S Truman. He won the Senate seat and became a staunch supporter of Roosevelt's New Deal.

The second event that year which was a pointer to peaceful, democratic change in the United States was the first performance of William Levi Dawson's *Negro Folk Symphony*. The magazine *News-Week* wrote that Dawson had written 'a musical history of his race in three movements – "The bond of Africa", "Hope in the Night", and "O! Lem-me Shine",' and added: 'The cafe-au-lait musician started his career as a bootblack.' When Dawson had graduated from music school he was not allowed to sit on the platform with the other – White – graduates, but had to watch from the gallery while the Kansas City Orchestra played one of his early compositions.

In explaining what he intended in his symphony, Dawson wrote: 'I have never doubted the possibilities of our music, for I feel that buried in the South is a music that somebody, some day, will discover. They will make another great music out of the folksongs of the South. I feel from the bottom of my heart that it will rank one day with the music of Brahms and the Russian composers.'

The American Communist Party had a recruit that year who was to be among those later disillusioned, a contributor in 1950 to *The God That Failed*. For Richard Wright, however, the prospects in 1934 of advancing his talents in the United States seemed dogged by the colour of his skin. As a Communist, this former mail clerk and digger of ditches became editor of the Harlem edition of the Communist Party newspaper, the *Daily Worker*. Ten years later he was to write an account of his childhood, *Black Boy*, which made a strong impact on those Americans who wished to see prejudice brought to an end, not by Communist revolution but by legislation and a change in the public mind.

Richard Wright's four grandparents had been slaves. Paul Robeson, a Black American singer who visited Europe that year, was the youngest son of a slave. While in Germany, on his way to the Soviet Union, he was the object of racial taunts from Nazi stormtroops. Reaching Moscow he was feted as a cultural hero. He had made his first film, *Body and Soul*, a decade earlier and had played the title role in Shakespeare's *Othello* in London in 1930: at that time no Black actor had been invited to play the role with a White cast on Broadway. It was to be three decades before the inequalities of colour were to be overcome through Congressional legislation and a slowly changing public mood. Robeson's talents, like Wright's and Dawson's, would eventually be accepted as part of mainstream American culture.

CHAPTER THREE

1935

> That long, dismal catalogue of the fruitlessness of
> experience and the confirmed unteachability of
> mankind.
>
> WINSTON S. CHURCHILL

Following the murder of Sergei Kirov in Leningrad at the end of
1934, the year 1935 was dominated in the Soviet Union by a drive of the
secret police, under Stalin's personal direction, to eliminate every trace of
political opposition or potential opposition. Zinoviev and Kamenev, both of
whom had stood at the very centre of the revolutionary effort since 1917,
were sentenced to death. Only a direct appeal to Stalin from Lenin's widow
led to their death sentences being commuted to prison terms instead. This
proved a short-term respite: they were both shot within a few years.

Other death sentences had no chance of appeal. In regular reports to Stalin,
the NKVD chiefs informed him of the death sentences that had been carried
out. A typical example was a trial of three people – a man and two women
– who were alleged to have queried the circumstances of the death of Kirov.
They were accused on March 9, executed on March 10, and the report of
their fate sent to Stalin on March 11.

During 1935 Stalin authorized the publication in the Soviet Union of an
interview he had given to H.G. Wells a year earlier. The two men had been
discussing coercion. 'Isn't your propaganda old-fashioned?', Wells asked him,
'inasmuch as it is the propaganda of coercive methods?' To this Stalin replied
defending the coercive method. Communists, he told Wells, 'do not at all
idealize the use of coercion. But they do not wish to be caught unawares,
they cannot count on the old world leaving the scene of its own accord, they
can see that the old order is defending itself with force, and therefore the
Communists say to the workers, "Be prepared to answer force with force."'

Stalin went on to ask Wells: 'What's the good of a military leader who lulls his army's alertness, an army leader who does not understand that the enemy will not surrender and that he must be finished off?' In quoting this passage, Stalin's biographer General Volkogonov has commented: 'How he loved that phrase, "to finish off". In countless speeches he called for the opposition, or the remnants of the exploiting classes, or the kulaks, the degenerates, the double dealers, spies and terrorists to be finished off. And finish them off he did, as well as his potential rivals.'

On April 5 the Soviet writer Ivan Uksusov was arrested. Five years earlier, at the age of thirty, he had been unreservedly praised by the Soviet authorities during the Kharkov International Writers' Conference. Later his books had been burned in Berlin by the Nazis. After his arrest Uksusov was kept in prison for sixty-two days and severely tortured. His interrogators wanted to know 'which country or countries' he was spying for. Sentenced to three years 'administrative exile' in Siberia, he was sent eastward in a prison train made up of five goods wagons, with as many as two hundred other Leningrad prisoners. 'There were thirty-seven men packed into his car,' write John and Carol Garrard – the historians of the Soviet Writers' Union, of which Uksusov had been an honoured member – 'but no one said a word because, as Uksusov later realized, each was innocent and thought all the others were guilty.'

On the lap of the journey between Sverdlovsk and Omsk, 'Uksusov saw other freight trains full of prisoners from all over the country. At Tobolsk, he observed a column of about 100–150 old men and women and younger women, some carrying babies, and children. These were relatives of men like himself who had been arrested by the NKVD; they had been forced to walk along a 320-kilometre road from Tyumen to Tobolsk (there was no railroad). As the column halted near a stream a woman stepped toward it and began drinking thirstily. One of the vicious guard dogs, an Alsatian (*ovcharka*), pounced on her and ripped off her left breast. The dying woman was picked up and dumped at the end of the column.'

On April 7 – two days after the arrest of Uksusov – a decree was made public whereby all penalties, including the death penalty, were extended to Soviet citizens as young as twelve. Stalin's biographer Robert Conquest, reflecting on the 'bad propaganda' which this decree made for the Soviet Union abroad, noted that as it could easily have been passed and kept unpublished, 'the purpose was clearly to put heavy pressure on the oppositionists with children, like Kamenev and Zinoviev'. The public announcement was 'a sign that the State's intention was serious.' Conquest added –

writing in 1991: 'The decree would be put into force in a number of cases. The light it throws on Stalin's ruthlessness is obvious. It also serves to illustrate the distinction between his words and the reality: in August 1936 he publicly rebuffed any idea that in Soviet circumstances children should answer for their parents' sins. A few weeks later dozens of relatives of Zinoviev and others were arrested, and many were shot. This is only one of many occasions in which Stalin's pronouncements were very different from his practice.'

From the nature of the denunciations, arrests and executions in the Soviet Union during the early months of 1935 it was made to appear that thousands, even tens of thousands of foreign spies, saboteurs, criminals and enemies of the people had infiltrated into the Soviet Communist Party in the previous fifteen years, reaching positions of authority at the centre, and throughout the country. The prisons and labour camps received them all.

The Russian Orthodox Church was likewise singled out for a new assault. In every city, ancient churches were demolished, to make way for roads and parks. The vast empty lot on which the great cathedral in Moscow had stood before its demolition was designated a municipal swimming pool. Soviet Communism also set itself up as the pinnacle of modernity and efficiency. The Moscow underground railway system was completed, some of its spacious stations being marble palaces of working class achievement and municipal pride. Individual industrial output was increased by groups of workers providing the back-up to a colleague who, as if working on his own, would then break all individual work norms. The original example of this super-productivity was a coal miner, Alexei Stakhanov. The term Stakhanovite became one of the highest praise. Goals were set to encourage spectacular achievements in factories and work places. On November 7, the eighteenth anniversary of the Bolshevik revolution, Russian railwaymen 'celebrated' the day by loading a total of 86,742 trucks. The statistics of such achievements became the focal point of daily newspaper and radio coverage and exhortation. Seeking to excel in cinema, the authorities planned a Russian Hollywood in the Crimea, just as Mussolini was to set up the Cinecitta studios at Rome two years later, and also to paraphrase a slogan of Lenin: 'For us the cinema is the strongest weapon'.

Soviet films justified – and glorified – the denunciations which were pervading the whole society. Sergei Eisenstein's film *Bezhin Lug* (Bezhin Meadow), based on the story of Pavel Morozov, justifies a son's betrayal of his father. The young Morozov, even more than Pronya Kolibin, was being held up to youngsters throughout the Soviet Union as an ideal: he had told the authorities where his father and grandfather were hiding grain. In Alexander Dovzhenko's film *Aerograd* (Air Town) a man shoots his best friend because he was revealed to be a traitor. In Ivan Pyriev's film *Partiinyi Bilet* (Party Card) a wife shoots her husband, exposed as the 'hidden enemy' of the State: the film historian Peter Kenez has called this 'perhaps the single most distasteful film of the decade'.

The power of propaganda to impress visitors to the Soviet Union was enormous. In their book *Soviet Communism: A New Civilization?* – the question mark was only added to the title after the first printing – the veteran British social reformers Sidney and Beatrice Webb, wrote of Stalin, 'whom foreigners are apt to think of as a dictator, being merely principal secretary of the organization, a post from which he could at any moment be dismissed by the highest committee'. The names of those on this 'highest committee' were, it seems, unknown: a cynic (from the Webbs' perspective) would doubtless say that they would all be executed by Stalin before they could dismiss him.

The League of Nations was confident that it could be an effective instrument of fairness and world order. On January 13 it supervised the plebiscite in the Saar, under which the inhabitants of this coal-rich region were to decide whether to be part of France or of Germany. To ensure the maximum possible control, should there be difficulties, the League Council remained in session during the plebiscite. When the voters of the Saar, who were German-speaking and part of the German Empire before 1918, decided by an overwhelming majority – ninety per cent of the votes cast – that they wished for union with Germany, the League Council agreed unanimously to transfer the whole territory to Germany, and to do so within six weeks.

With the imminent imposition of Nazi rule and ideology, many liberal and left-wing Saarlanders fled to France, among them Max Braun, the Saar Socialist leader. The German Front – made up of the German National and Saar People's Parties, and for a year before the plebiscite incorporating the Nazi Party – had skilfully campaigned for the massive vote in favour of union with Germany. In an attempt to allay fears of how the Saar would be Nazified by the change – as indeed it was – the leader of the German Front, the industrialist Hermann Röchling, told a visiting Englishwoman, Elizabeth Wiskemann: 'My dear young lady, you must try to understand that National Socialism is built upon a basis of love.'

*   *   *

Only three days after the Saar plebiscite, the League suffered a setback when Paraguay refused an offer of mediation in its war against Bolivia in the Gran Chaco. As a result of Paraguay's action the League lifted the arms embargo with regard to Bolivia. Fierce fighting ensued for the next three months, with the Paraguayan advance across almost the whole territory being repulsed, and the Paraguayan forces being driven out of the Chaco. The next phase of negotiations was undertaken, not by the League, but by five Western Hemisphere nations – the United States, Argentina, Brazil, Chile and Uruguay. After a month of negotiation in Buenos Aires, an armistice was agreed and peace negotiations begun.

One agreement that was effected by the League in the early months of 1935 came in the aftermath of the Yugoslav-Hungarian dispute following the assassination of King Alexander of Yugoslavia the previous year. With the agreement of both countries, the League established a Committee of Experts, charged with preparing an international convention for the repression of terrorist outrages. The League also ruled that several legislative decrees issued by the Nazi-controlled Senate of the Free City of Danzig were 'not consistent with the Constitution' of the Free State. The decrees were withdrawn.

The League was also able to maintain its opposition to the introduction of Nazi racist laws to Upper Silesia, a region that had been under League supervision prior to the plebiscite that returned it to Germany. A Mixed Commission of the League, headed by a Swiss citizen, Felix Calonder, had ensured since 1933 that the Jews of Upper Silesia could practice law and medicine, as well as receive official funds for education. Calonder, a former President of the Swiss Confederation, and Swiss Minister of Foreign Affairs (1918–19) had been posted in the Upper Silesian city of Katowice since 1922, in the service of the League of Nations. The protection which he supervised continued until the expiry of the League's responsibility for Upper Silesia two years later.

Another contribution by the League, financial help, enabled the future of the Assyrian Christians of Iraq to be resolved. After they had been the victims of Iraqi Muslim violence in 1933, they had sought some other area in which they could settle. At first Brazil was suggested, then British Guiana, but a transatlantic solution was given up in return for an Asian one, and the Assyrians were settled, at the suggestion and with the encouragement of France, in the French mandated territory of Syria. The only French condition was that France should not have to bear any of the cost of the transfer.

The greatest challenge to the League in 1935 came beyond Europe. A clash between Abyssinian soldiers and Italian colonial troops had been submitted by Abyssinia to the League at the end of 1934. On 5 December 1934, Abyssinian troops on the border of Italian Somaliland had attacked an Italian frontier garrison, which withdrew. On the following day Italian military reinforcements, supported by aeroplanes and tanks, had driven the Abyssinians back and inflicted heavy casualties. In the first week of January 1935 the Abyssinian government asked Italy to proceed to arbitration, as provided for under the Italo-Abyssinian treaty of 1928.

In mid-January, as a result of secret negotiations at the League headquarters in Geneva, the Abyssinians agreed to withdraw their complaint and to enter into direct negotiations with Italy. The Italian government demanded reparations for the losses inflicted on its soldiers during the clash. Abyssinia demanded a full enquiry into the incident before it would agree to any such payments. On January 29, while talks were still going on at Geneva, another border clash took place and five Italian soldiers were killed.

The Italian government took immediate action, mobilizing two divisions and calling for Blackshirt volunteers. On February 22 the first of these troops embarked for Africa. The Abyssinian government thereupon asked the League of Nations to apply Article 15 of the League Covenant to Italy, to prevent the further despatch of Italian troops. Meanwhile, there were a number of Abyssinian raids across the border into Italian Somaliland, and in the Ogaden. The Italians mobilized a further army division and two further Blackshirt divisions. Then, in the second week of March, all Italian men born in 1911, 1912 and 1913 were mobilized. On March 17, Abyssinia complained about this to the League, but nothing was done, Italy insisting that there was no cause for League intervention.

As the military build-up continued, it took considerable efforts by the League, and in particular by Anthony Eden, the British Minister for League Affairs, to persuade the Italians to accept League-appointed arbitrators. Italy agreed to this on May 25. A date was set three months hence – August 25 – by which the arbitrators would give their decision. Both sides agreed to abide by it. But even as the arbitrators were meeting in neutral Holland, Abyssinia protested to the League that 'the situation has gone from bad to worse' and that 'an aggression upon the independence and integrity of Ethiopia seems imminent'. Any such aggression, the Abyssinians declared, must call into being the collective action in defence of victims of unprovoked aggression, as laid down in the Covenant of the League.

Mussolini had no intention of being deprived of what he considered Italy's rightful colonial conquest, and on July 7 he announced: 'There can be no turning back. Government and nation are now engaged in a conflict which we have decided to carry on to the bitter end.' In Geneva, the Italian delegate to the League, Baron Aloisi, reflected his leader's contempt for his African adversary by demanding that Abyssinia should be excluded from the negotiations. On August 1 a British Member of Parliament, Colonel Josiah Wedgwood – who had fought at Gallipoli in 1915, and also as an armoured car officer with the Russian army in South Russia in 1917 – warned the House of Commons: 'If one dictator cannot be stopped from attacking Abyssinia, nothing can stop another dictator from attacking Lithuania, and Memel, and Austria.' If the League of Nations failed to prevent war, Wedgwood added, 'security will leave, not only the small nations, but France, and Czechoslovakia, and Italy as well'. A month later, on September 5, the National Convention of British Trade Unions voted by 2,962,000 to 770,000 in favour of military sanctions in support of Abyssinia, should she be attacked.

The Sixteenth Assembly of the League of Nations opened in Geneva on September 11. The British Foreign Minister, Sir Samuel Hoare, spoke forcefully of the need 'for the collective maintenance of the Covenant in its entirety, and particularly for steady and collective resistance to all acts of unprovoked aggression'. Other nations, including France and the Soviet Union, joined in the call for decisive action in defence of Abyssinia. Canada, Australia, New Zealand and South Africa, as well as the Irish Free State, gave their support to the strong British stance.

The United States took no part in these deliberations, but it too was edging away from the absolute neutrality to which it had adhered since the end of the First World War and the withdrawal of American troops from their intervention against Bolshevik Russia in 1919. In a statement to the newspapers on September 12 the Secretary of State, Cordell Hull, intimated that even for the United States there might be a limit. 'Armed conflict in any part of the world,' the statement read, 'cannot but have undesirable and adverse effects in every part of the world. All nations have the right to ask that any and all issues, between whatsoever nations, be resolved by pacific means. Every nation has the right to ask that no nations subject it and other nations to the hazards and uncertainties that must inevitably accrue to all from resort to arms by any two.'

The League Council set up a Committee of Five to prepare a report. The report, which was submitted on September 26, made every possible concession to Italy: a mission of foreign specialists would examine the need to reform the Abyssinian government departments, Italy's 'special interest' in the economy of Abyssinia was recognized, and Britain and France would help secure territorial adjustments in Italy's favour on the border between Abyssinia and the Italian colonial territories to the east and south. At the same time, the arbitrators set up to report on the border clashes absolved both Abyssinia and Italy from blame.

For Italy, none of this was enough. Mussolini rejected the compromise proposals of the Committee of Five, and the League Council ordered a report to be drawn up, as a matter of urgency, with regard to the future of Abyssinian sovereignty. On October 3, before the report could be completed, Italian troops advanced into Abyssinia on three separate fronts.

The League Council, meeting in emergency session on October 7, declared Italy to be the aggressor. Only Austria, Hungary and Albania refused to join this condemnation. The League Council then activated Article 16 of the League Covenant, under which sanctions could be imposed by member States, with a view to stopping aggression. A Committee of Eighteen was appointed to propose specific measures. By the end of the month four sets of sanctions were suggested: an arms embargo, financial measures including the refusal of loans and credits, the refusal to take imports from Italy, and an embargo on the export to Italy of materials needed to make war, including oil.

These sanctions were imposed on Italy from November 18. On December 5, Samuel Hoare told the British House of Commons: 'I am glad to tell the House that the League machinery is working well, and that Member-States for the most part are playing their part.' Hoare said nothing to the House of Commons about the French government's non-cooperation. The French Prime Minister, Pierre Laval, who was also Foreign Minister, was particularly concerned about the need to maintain good relations with Italy. This had been a cornerstone of his foreign policy and a counterweight to Germany. In secret conversations with Hoare in Paris, Laval persuaded his British opposite number to support a 'peace plan' very much in Italy's interest.

The Hoare-Laval pact was meant to be a secret basis for a joint Anglo-French approach to Italy. But after it was leaked to the newspapers it could no longer be denied, and was officially published in Paris on December 13. Those who had supported the League of Nations' strong stand against Italian aggression were shocked by the cynicism of the Pact. Abyssinia was to be partitioned, and part of her territory transferred to Italy. Italy was also to have a large zone within Abyssinia for economic expansion and settlement. Abyssinia was to have a corridor to the sea, but without the right to build a railway on it. There was an outcry of indignation from the League States, and in Britain. Samuel Hoare resigned. He was replaced as Foreign Secretary by Anthony Eden, who was known to be strongly in favour of sanctions. Mussolini, who rejected with contempt the plan which was meant to help him, also warned that any embargo on oil for Italy would be regarded as an 'act of hostility', and that he would reply to it with 'acts of war'.

Throughout the year, Mussolini had been attempting to strengthen Italian war-making potential. In January compulsory pre- and post-military instruction was introduced, starting in schools at the age of eight and continuing to the age of thirty-two; 17,000 army officers were delegated to supervise this training. In April a school of aerial warfare was established in Rome. In June a decree was promulgated, introducing compulsory military training for factory workers on Saturday afternoons. In September a new national loan was launched. With the opening of hostilities in October a 'gold crusade' was inaugurated, under which Italian women were urged to give up not only their gold jewellery, but their wedding rings, 'for the Nation'.

On the battlefield, the Italian troops faced fierce opposition from the Abyssinians. On the Tigre front, those advancing from Adowa were driven back in mid-December. On the Somaliland front two of the three Italian mobile columns were forced back. In the air, however, the Italians held virtual mastery. Among the bomber pilots in action was Mussolini's son Vittorio. In his memoirs he described the glee he felt while watching the devastating effect on the tribesmen below of the anti-personnel mines that he dropped; two years later he co-scripted a film which paid homage to the 'bravery' of the Italian pilots in what was very much a one-sided conflict.

In France the year 1935 witnessed an intensification of the political and social divisions. Municipal elections in May showed a marked swing to the Left. In the suburbs of Paris the Communist Party made impressive gains. On July 14, during the public holiday, competing demonstrations took place in the centre of Paris between the right-wing Croix de Feu and the left-wing Popular Front. The Popular Front, which denounced the Fascist tendencies of the Croix de Feu, presented the unusual, and for its members inspiring, spectacle of the three main left-wing Parties – the Socialists, led by Léon

Blum, the Radical-Socialists and the Communists – united under the same banner of the 'protection of the Republic'.

Among the Popular Front demands were a forty-hour working week, large-scale public works to be financed by a tax on the wealthy, the nationalization of heavy industry, and the dissolution of the 'Fascist Leagues'. At Limoges there were violent clashes between the Popular Front and the Croix de Feu. On December 6, during a dramatic debate in the Chamber of Deputies, a member of the Croix de Feu proposed the 'disarmament of all Leagues'. The Popular Front accepted this, and agreed to dissolve all organizations within its own orbit that were of a para-military nature. That same night, with Laval's energetic intervention, three Bills were presented with the aim of dissolving the associations. All three were passed. The danger of escalating street violence had been averted.

In Northern Ireland there was violence during 1935 between Catholic and Protestant extremists. Following the Orange Day celebrations in July – commemorating the Protestant victories of 1690, two hundred and forty five years earlier – there were clashes between Protestants and Catholics and two people were shot dead. Within a week, another seven people had been killed. Legislation, the Summary Jurisdiction Bill, was introduced to speed up the sentencing of troublemakers. Local Catholics protested that it abolished one of the safeguards of popular rights. In the British General Election, eleven Protestant Members of Parliament were elected for Northern Ireland, and two Catholics. The Catholics, members of the Nationalist Abstentionist Party, were pledged not to take their seats at Westminster, as an act of protest and defiance. They therefore stayed away.

In the Irish Free State there were those who wanted to take reprisals against the Protestants in their midst, for the killing of Catholics in Belfast. The Free State leader, Eamon de Valera, opposed such reprisals and took effective measures to prevent them. There were also calls in the Free State for the establishment of a Republic, and protests when the Free State celebrated the Silver Jubilee of the accession of King George V. Members of the Irish Republican Army (the IRA) sought to gain popularity by endorsing a transport strike which had already brought Dublin to a halt. The government at once arrested the leaders. When De Valera supported Britain at the League of Nations, republicans reminded him of their slogan: 'England's Difficulty is Ireland's Opportunity', but he continued to give Britain his support.

South Africa was another country where the influence of Britain had survived through membership of the British Commonwealth, after the establishment of independent institutions. Here too there were demands for a complete breakaway and the establishment of a republic. When the leader of the would-be republicans, Dr Malan, told Parliament in Cape Town that the ultimate destiny of South Africa was 'undoubtedly to be a republic' he was answered by a fellow-nationalist and former ministerial colleague Colonel Creswell: 'Do you realize that there are 800,000 English-speaking people in the Union to whom the British connection and the Commonwealth ideal are as real an affection and sentimental attachment as any of your sentiments?' The issue was put to the vote, and Dr Malan defeated by 83 votes to 19. The South African Prime Minister, General Hertzog, then sailed to Britain to participate in the Silver Jubilee celebrations.

Britain had no intention of giving the Africans of the three native protectorates – Bechuanaland, Swaziland and Basutoland – control over their internal affairs. Indeed, it was their eventual transfer to South African rule that was envisaged, albeit as a distant eventuality, in the South Africa Act of 1909. The British government was reluctant to move towards transfer. 'We have the right to be proud that the native peoples are reluctant to leave our tutelage,' the British High Commissioner, Sir William Clark, declared on July 10, 'unless, as in the case of India, they can claim that the time has come when they should be entrusted with the control of their own destinies.'

On August 2, British Royal Assent was finally given by King George V for the coming into force of the Government of India Act. For several years there had been a vigorous debate in Britain as to what measure of self-government could be accorded, and in India as to what would be sufficient. The central feature of the Act was the establishment of provincial autonomy. Many Indian nationalists, hitherto opposed to any scheme that excluded them from political control of the central government, accepted that their most effective course was to secure their election to the provincial legislatures, and to press from within those legislatures for the widest possible measures of Indianization and further constitutional reform. Gandhi focused his political efforts on an all-India campaign for the improvement of the conditions of village life, and on his campaign for the abolition of 'untouchability'. On June 25 a Hindu who opposed equality for the untouchables – known to Gandhi and his followers as the Harijans, or Children of God – had thrown a bomb into a car, mistakenly believing that Gandhi was in it.

In the Punjab there were violent religious clashes between Hindus and Muslims, and between Sikhs and Muslims. During riots in both Karachi and Lahore, forty people were killed. To reduce the possibility of further killings, the government forbade the carrying by Sikhs of the dagger that is one of the five symbols of their faith. Insulted by this, many Sikhs embarked upon a campaign of civil disobedience.

An upsurge of protest against British rule came in north-western India, on the frontier of Waziristan. A local Muslim leader, the Haji of Turangzai, raised the Islamic banner of revolt, raided the Peshawar district, and urged other local Muslim tribes to challenge British rule. A substantial force of Indian troops was sent against him: 15,000 men commanded by General Auchinleck. One of Auchinleck's advance columns was ambushed and two British officers and twenty-seven Indian soldiers were killed. The leader of the ambushed column, Captain Godfrey Meynell, was wounded five times. As he lay dying he called out to his men, 'Be brave'. He was posthumously awarded the Victoria Cross. When the main Indian Army columns arrived the rebellion was crushed and the tribes of the region made their submission.

It was not inter-communal violence, however, or the Muslim uprising in Waziristan, but the ravages of nature, that led to by far the greatest loss of life in India in 1935. On the last day of May an earthquake struck northern India – for the second year in succession – and more than 30,000 Indians were killed, 20,000 of them in the city of Quetta.

Within the British Foreign Office there was mounting concern at the information reaching it about Germany's growing air strength. When the British Government made efforts to minimize the danger, this information was passed on to Churchill by several members of the Foreign Office who knew that he would use it to good advantage. Churchill did so, warning the House of Commons that the British rate of aircraft production was such that Germany would catch up within three years, and that after that the German superiority would grow, unless dramatic British increases were agreed to.

While increasing the number of aircraft being produced, the British Government was not prepared to do so sufficiently to catch up and overtake Germany. The plans agreed upon by a special Cabinet Committee on Defence Requirements on April 30 were, as the Prime Minister, Ramsay MacDonald, explained to his colleagues, that in two years time – that is, by April 1937 – 'Germany would have 1,512 aircraft, and we should have 740'. Sir John Simon, the Foreign Secretary, pointed out to the meeting that Germany already had '250 more than us, and 382 more next year, and the longer the expansion went on, the farther ahead would Germany get'.

Churchill's forecast of continuing and growing German air superiority, though strenuously denied and belittled in public by government spokesmen, was correct. Despite a subsequent revised British air expansion scheme, on the outbreak of war in September 1939 the German minimum first-line air strength was 4,300 mobilizable aircraft, while the maximum British first-line mobilizable strength was under 2,000. This was an even greater German lead than at the time of the Munich Conference in September 1938, when the maximum first-line British air strength was 1,606 (not all of them mobilizable), and the minimum first-line German strength was 3,200.*

Churchill's concerns were based on the reality of the situation inside Germany, both its growing rearmament and Hitler's political aims. In the privacy of his entourage Hitler spoke openly of what he intended to do. On March 22, from what he described as a 'reliable source', the British Ambassador to Germany, Sir Eric Phipps, had informed the Foreign Office in London that Hitler 'talks not only about Russia but also about Czechoslovakia whose existence he considers a regrettable smudge on the map of Europe. The German minorities numbering 3,000,000 must be restored to the Reich when Austria joins Germany.' Phipps added: 'The problem of disposing of the Czechs is exercising him.'

Churchill made a strenuous effort on May 2 to alert the House of Commons and the British public to Hitler's intentions, and also to Britain's weakness in the air. He was distressed that the European powers, which in his view were threatened by Germany, did not work together and build up an adequate deterrent force. That could have been done as soon as Hitler came to power, he believed, and it could have been centred upon 'collective security'. But, Churchill declared:

> When the situation was manageable it was neglected, and now that it is thoroughly out of hand we apply too late the remedies which then might have effected a cure.
>
> There is nothing new in the story. It is as old as the sibylline books.

---

* The British figures were provided for Churchill after the war by the RAF Historian, Denis Richards (on 21 September 1947); the German figures by the Commanding General of the US Army Air Forces, Carl Spaatz (on 17 July 1947). The German figures were taken from the files of the Luftwaffe Quartermaster by Royal Air Force Intelligence agencies, and given to the to the United States Army Air Force: reference number ADI(K)352/1945.

It falls into that long, dismal catalogue of the fruitlessness of experience and the confirmed unteachability of mankind. Want of foresight, unwillingness to act when action would be simple and effective, lack of clear thinking, confusion of counsel until the emergency comes, until self-preservation strikes its jarring gong – these are the features which constitute the endless repetition of history.

Churchill had his own vivid memories of the coming of war in 1914, and of the narrow margin by which the German army had been halted on the Marne forty days after it had crossed into Belgium and France. His mother had been in Paris at the time of the Prussian siege in 1870. Churchill himself, in 1883, at the age of nine, on the way to an Austro-Hungarian spa with his father, had been driven through the Place de la Concorde. 'Being an observant child,' he later recalled, 'I noticed that one of the monuments was covered with wreaths and crepe and I at once asked him why. He replied, "These are the monuments of the provinces of France. Two of them, Alsace and Lorraine, have been taken from France by the Germans in the last war. The French are very unhappy about it and hope some day to get them back." I remember quite distinctly thinking to myself, "I hope they will get them back".' Once more, Germany was in the ascendant.

Inside Germany, thousands of German Jews continued to lose their jobs as a result of the continuing legislative measures to 'purify' German professional life. All teachers and professors in Germany were part of the civil service structure. On the day of Churchill's speech, Victor Klemperer, Professor of Romance Languages at the University of Dresden, wrote in his diary: 'On Tuesday morning, without any previous notification, two sheets of paper delivered by post. "On the basis of para. 6 of the Law for the Restoration of the Professional Civil Service I have recommended your dismissal. Notice of dismissal enclosed".' Klemperer added: 'At first I felt alternatively numb and slightly romantic: now there is only wretchedness and bitterness.'

In accordance with his mastery of the diplomacy of deception, Hitler continued in public to make considerable efforts to express peace-loving sentiments, and to reassure those who might fear that Germany intended to use its growing armaments for war. On May 3, the day after Churchill's warnings in the House of Commons, Hitler sent an open letter to the owner of the *Daily Mail*, Lord Rothermere – two of whose three sons had been killed in action on the Western Front – and whose newspapers in Britain were advocating good relations with Germany. In his letter, Hitler wrote:

Nine-tenths of the blood poured out on battlefields during the last three hundred years in Europe has been wasted. In those three hundred years Germany has lost from twenty to twenty-five million lives in wars which were intrinsically without benefit to the nation, if benefit is estimated in terms of practical advantage rather than dubious prestige.

All hope for the future is dead, so far as the human eye can see, unless it comes from England and Germany.

I am no new advocate of an Anglo-German understanding. In Germany I have made between four and five thousand speeches to small, large, and mammoth audiences, yet there is no single speech of mine, nor any line that I have written, in which I have expressed anything contrary to this conception, or against an Anglo-German understanding.

So far as I am concerned, the world may reproach me with what it will; one reproach, however, it can never make – that I have vacillated in my views or been unfaithful in my work. Had an unknown man with such defects set himself to win a nation in fifteen years, he could never have succeeded. This perhaps is the basis of what may, to many, seem the exaggerated faith inspired by my personality.

I believe that my consistent mental attitude, my invariable principles, and my unshakable resolution will in the end succeed in enabling me to play a great and historical part towards the re-establishment of sound and permanent relations between the two great Germanic nations.

'Such an agreement between England and Germany,' Hitler wrote to Lord Rothermere, 'would represent the weighty influence for peace and common sense of 120,000,000 of the most valuable people in the world. The historically unique colonial aptitude and naval power of Britain would be combined with that of one of the first military nations of the world.'

If this understanding between Britain and Germany could be 'still further enlarged by the adhesion of the American nation,' Hitler told one of Rothermere's leading journalists, G. Ward Price, 'it would be absolutely impossible to see who in the world could disturb a combination for peace which would never, of set purpose or intent, neglect the interests of the white peoples.' Hitler then quoted what he called a 'fine' German proverb: 'The gods love and bless those who seem to strive for the impossible,' and he told the British journalist: 'That is a divinity in which I believe.'

The treatment of those who were judged to be enemies of the Nazi State and movement lay outside the reach of this 'divinity'. On May 7, only three days after Hitler's mellifluous letter to Lord Rothermere, the *Manchester Guardian* published an account that had reached it of the treatment of political prisoners in an unnamed town in northern Germany:

Those taken to the remand prison are habitually struck across the face so that the blood flows from ears and mouth. The rooms and corridors are often bespattered with blood. A girl prisoner (most of the prisoners are young) was pushed and knocked from one end of a room to the other so that she kept on dashing against the walls. Her whole body was bruised and her head was so severely bumped that she lost consciousness. She was taken back to her cell and was left lying there for a whole day.

Another girl prisoner, eighteen years of age, was kicked in the abdomen and lost consciousness. She was carried to her cell. There she came to and was left in extreme pain for a day and a night.

The next day the prison doctor came to see her. She told him how she had been treated. He said 'It couldn't have been as bad as that' and gave her an injection. Because she had told the doctor, she was again ill-treated, besides being sentenced to a week's detention in a special cell and to nine weeks' solitary confinement.

The 'special cell' is in a filthy condition. The stench is almost unbearable. The window can be opened about an inch wide. There are only wooden planks to sleep on. There is a hot meal every third day – the other days is only bread and water . . .

Particularly unbearable to prisoners who are nervous or uninjured is the perpetual whimpering and groaning of those who have been beaten.

Some of the prisoners are only sixteen or seventeen years old. One prisoner, aged twenty, has been in chains for two weeks. The bridge of his nose was broken and his hands have been cut about with a knife. Another has been beaten about the face with a bunch of keys. Another has a broken ear-drum. Several women have been chained up at night.

For racial rather than political reasons, the Jews, more than any other group of Germans, faced continued discrimination. Sometimes a voice was raised in support of them, always a risk to whoever dared speak out. On June 17

the composer Richard Strauss wrote to the Jewish novelist and poet Stefan
Zweig – who had written the libretto for Strauss's opera *Die schweigsame
Frau* (The Silent Woman) – expressing his anger that Zweig's name was not
to be allowed on the programme, as the Nazis insisted, and refusing to let
the opera be performed without it. Strauss added that for him there were
only two types of people, those who had talent and those who did not,
regardless of who they were or from where they came. Strauss's letter was
intercepted by the Gestapo, passed to Hitler, and led to the banning of the
opera throughout Germany. That same year all jazz of Black or Jewish origin
was banned over the national radio.

Violence against Jews was commonplace throughout Germany. On July
15 in Berlin, several Jews were attacked and beaten up as they walked in
the street. Twelve days later an SA magazine, in an article entitled 'Finish
up with the Jews', urged what were called 'German' girls – hitherto Jewish
girls in Germany had also been 'German' girls – 'not to go with Jews any
longer'. This article marked the start of a newspaper campaign demanding
legislation to forbid sexual relations between Jews and non-Jews. An SA
newspaper in Mannheim, the *Hakenkreuzbanner* (The Swastika Flag) devoted
a series of articles to this theme throughout August. At the same time, as
more and more firms, offices and institutions dismissed their Jewish
employees, the search to dismiss Jews, even Jews who had converted to
Christianity – as tens of thousands of Jews had done in the previous decades
– was continuous.

By September 1935 at least a quarter of all German Jews – some
100,000 in all – had been deprived of their livelihood. More than 10,000
Jewish health officials and social workers had been driven from their posts,
4,000 lawyers were without the right to practice, 2,000 doctors had been
expelled from hospitals and clinics, 2,000 actors, singers and musicians had
been refused permission to continue their work in theatres, cafés and clubs,
and 1,200 editors and journalists had been dismissed, as had 800 university
professors and 800 schoolteachers.

Then, on September 15, Hitler personally signed two decrees, known
as the Nuremberg Laws, which redefined German citizenship and set out
regulations 'for the protection of German blood and German honour'. Under
the first of the two laws, German citizenship could only belong to 'a national
of Germany or kindred blood'. Under the second law, all Jews were defined
as being 'not of German blood'. Marriages between Jews and German
'nationals' were forbidden. All marriages conducted 'in defiance of this law'

were invalid. Sexual relations outside marriage were forbidden between Jews and Germans. Jews were forbidden to fly the German flag.

Under the headline 'The Shame of Nuremberg', the *New York Herald Tribune* described the two laws as 'a signal victory for the violent anti-Jewish wing of the Nazi Party, led by Julius Streicher', and as the realization 'of nearly the whole anti-Semitic portion of the Nazi programme'. In London *The Times* declared: 'Nothing like the complete disinheritance and segregation of Jewish citizens, now announced, has been heard since medieval times.'

The Nuremberg Laws made it clear that the Jews were to be allowed no further part in German life: no equality under the law, no further citizenship, no chance of slipping back into the mainstream of German life in which for so many generations they had been an integral part. Following the Nuremberg Laws, every further move against the Jews could be made with the backing of legal segregation. Such moves began at once. Only a week after the Nuremberg Laws were promulgated, Jews were forbidden access to any holiday resort in Bavaria.

On October 6 two Englishmen, Eric Mills, the Commissioner for Migration and Statistics in Palestine, and Frank Foley, the British Passport Control Officer in Berlin, met members of the German Economics Ministry in Berlin to discuss the financial aspects of emigration of German Jews to Palestine. What they heard gave them an insight into the German government's mood and intentions. 'German policy', they wrote in their report to the Foreign Office in London, 'is clearly to eliminate the Jew from German life, and the Nazis do not mind how this is accomplished. Mortality and emigration provide the means.'

In a private letter that day, Mills wrote: 'While before I went to Germany I knew that the Jewish situation was bad, I had not realized as I now do that the fate of German Jews is a tragedy, for which cold intelligent planning by those in authority takes rank with that of those who are out of sympathy with the Bolshevik regime, in Russia; or with the elimination of Armenians from the Turkish Empire. The Jew is to be eliminated and the state has no regard for the manner of his elimination.'

In Paris, the German writer and dramatist Kurt Tucholsky, a Jew who had devoted his life to anti-militarism, committed suicide on December 21. He was forty-five years old. Since 1924 he had been an exile, first in France and then in Sweden, warning, even when Germany was disarmed, that German militarism was a phoenix that would rise again. That year tens of thousands of German Jews emigrated, many of them to Palestine. To facilitate their emigration had been the task of the League of Nations High Commissioner for Refugees, James G. McDonald. But on December 27 McDonald resigned. He had come to the conclusion that the cause of that emigration – Nazi racial policy – ought to be challenged directly by the League. Amelioration of the plight of the refugees was not, in McDonald's view, any longer adequate. It was the racial policies that ought to be opposed.

In his letter of resignation, McDonald gave a clear picture of the scale and intractability of the problem, and of the way in which it could only worsen as a result of the Nuremberg Laws. As a direct result of these laws, he wrote, 'not only the Jews, who now number about 435,000, but also tens of thousands of Christian "non-Aryans" who are classified as Jews, lost their citizenship, were disfranchised, and made ineligible to hold public office. Indirectly, through this new law, a constitutional basis was laid for unrestricted discriminations against all those whom the Party may wish to penalize.' McDonald added: 'The denationalization by the German Government of thousands of German citizens has added to the hardships both of those remaining in Germany and of the refugees, and is an increasing burden on States which have admitted the refugees while in possession of German nationality.'

McDonald's protest continued with a survey of the situation of the Jews inside Germany. 'Relentlessly the Jews and "non-Aryans" are excluded from all public offices, from the exercise of the liberal professions, and from any part in the cultural and intellectual life of Germany,' he wrote. 'Ostracized from social relations with "Aryans", they are subjected to every kind of humiliation. Neither sex nor age exempts them from discrimination. Even the Jewish and "non-Aryan" children do not escape cruel forms of segregation and persecution.'

In Nazi Party publications, McDonald went on to explain, '"Aryan" children are stirred to hate the Jews and the Christian "non-Aryans", to spy upon them and to attack them, and to incite their own parents to extirpate the Jews altogether.' There was no area of German life in which this distinction and discrimination was not being imposed:

It is being made increasingly difficult for Jews and 'non-Aryans' in Germany to sustain life. Condemned to segregation within the four corners of the legal and social Ghetto which has now closed upon them, they are increasingly prevented from earning their living. Indeed, more than half of the Jews remaining in Germany have already been deprived of their livelihood. In many parts of the country there is a systematic attempt at starvation of the Jewish population.

In no field of economic activity is there any security whatsoever. For some time it has been impossible for Jewish business men and shopkeepers to carry on their trades in small towns. The campaign against any dealings with Jews is now systematically prosecuted in the larger towns. Despite the restrictions upon migration from the provinces into the few largest cities where Jewish economic activity is not yet completely excluded, the Jews are fleeing to those cities because there only can they hope to escape, at least for a time, from the more brutal forms of persecution.

McDonald went on to warn that this forced influx of Jews from the hundreds of villages and small towns in which they had lived for generations had 'exhausted already the resources of the Jewish philanthropic and educational institutions in Germany. The victims of the terrorism are being driven to the point where, in utter anguish and despair, they may burst the frontiers in fresh waves of refugees.'

McDonald was in no doubt that there ought to be active international intervention. The developments since Hitler came to power, he wrote, and in particular those following the Nuremberg Laws, called for 'fresh collective action' with regard to the problem created by persecution in Germany. The moral authority of the League of Nations and of Member States of the League 'must be directed towards a determined appeal to the German Government in the name of humanity and of the principles of the public law of Europe. They must ask for a modification of policies which constitute a source of unrest and perplexity in the world, a challenge to the conscience of mankind, and a menace to the legitimate interests of the States affected by the immigration of German refugees'.

It was not only through the racist laws promulgated at Nuremberg that Nazism defined its purpose and its plan. At the Nuremberg rally that September 54,000 representatives of the Hitler Youth marched past Hitler in the stadium. Afterwards Hitler told the youngsters that what was required of them was quite unlike what had been required of previous generations. The dull, philistine youth of yesterday had been replaced by the upright athlete, 'swift as a greyhound, tough as leather, hard as Krupp steel'. The Nazi movement would replace 'yesterday's degenerates' and would educate the new youth 'in strict discipline and perfect self-respect'.

The previous year's Nuremberg rally had seemed to Hitler the ideal vehicle for nationwide propaganda, using documentary film with artistic presentation. He entrusted this task to a former actress and fiction film maker, Leni Riefenstahl, who worked to turn the 1934 rally into an epic paean of praise for the 'Leader'. Her film *Triumph of the Will* (*Triumph des Willes*) was finished in 1935, and gave German audiences an almost mystical view of Hitler's charismatic appeal: the film opens with Hitler in an aeroplane flying to Nuremberg, and descending through the clouds to the city and the rally, where the Nazi Party officials proclaim repeatedly: 'Hitler is Germany, the Party is Germany, thus Germany is Hitler and the Party is Germany.' The film historian Charles Musser writes: 'The exchange of looks and salutes creates a bond of obedience between these different levels, one in which the identity of self is only found through identifying with the nation and the Party. In the process, Hitler and the various troops are eroticized by Riefenstahl's adoring vision.'

Before coming to power, Hitler had made much of the 'humiliation' of the Treaty of Versailles, particularly with regard to those prohibitions designed to prevent the re-emergence of the German Army. On March 16, he struck a body blow at these prohibitions when he announced the introduction of compulsory military service. The new youth were part of his future military programme. Henceforth, German rearmament, which since 1918 had been carried out in conditions of the utmost secrecy, often disguised as civilian sports activities such as amateur flying clubs, would be in the open. Hitler was convinced that the Versailles Powers would take no action, and he was right.

Hitler took the opportunity of the introduction of national military service to repeat his peaceful intentions with regard to those who might take alarm at his action, telling the German people and the world:

What the German Government, as the guardian of the honour and interests of the German nation, desires is to make sure that Germany possesses sufficient instruments of power not only to maintain the integrity of the German Reich but also to command international respect and value as co-guarantor of general peace.

For in this hour the German Government renews before the German people, before the entire world, its assurance of its determination never to proceed beyond the safeguarding of German honour and freedom of the Reich, and especially does it not intend in rearming Germany to create any instrument for warlike attack, but, to the contrary, exclusively for defence and thereby for the maintenance of peace.

Through rearmament, Hitler declared, 'the German Reich's Government expresses the confident hope that the German people, having again reverted to their own honour, may be privileged in independent equality to make its contribution for the pacification of the world in free and open co-operation with other nations and their Governments'.

On November 1 all German males aged twenty-one – those born during 1914 – who were physically fit, were called up for military service. Twelve months service was to be compulsory; volunteers could serve for longer. Jews were excluded from national service (in 1914–18 more than 12,000 Jews had been killed on active service with the German forces). Under the new plans, the German Army would consist of thirty-six Divisions – a total of 550,000 men. Without the agreement of the League of Nations, the four main classes of weapons forbidden by the Treaty of Versailles were to be re-introduced: tanks, heavy artillery, aeroplanes and submarines.

The new army was far from ready to make war, but its training was robust and the expansion of its equipment continuous. Within a year aircraft production reached a scale that outstripped that of Britain and France. Hitler became the Supreme Commander of the German Defence Forces, in addition to President, Chancellor and Reich Leader. At the same time, the Stahlhelm ex-servicemen's organization and the German Student Corps were both disbanded. A new ex-servicemen's union recognized by Hitler, and the National-Socialist Student organizations, alone remained with their uniforms and their marches and their rallies. That November the Swastika flag was recognized as Germany's only official flag.

Persecution of the German Catholic Church proceeded without abatement. There were mass arrests of monks and nuns accused of conspiring to smuggle money out of the country (they were in close contact with branches of their orders outside Germany) and sentenced to long terms of hard labour. Heavy fines effectively secured the confiscation by the authorities of a large part of the church's property. In the German Protestant community, the Union of Opposition-Pastors refused to allow the Nazi theories of race to replace the Christianity of the Bible.

In July, a Minister for Church Affairs was appointed, who was given supreme authority over the Evangelical Church. Church Committees were established under the Ministry's auspices, which sought to impose the Nazi doctrines in churches and church schools. The leading Opposition-Pastors were arrested and sent to concentration camps.

Refugees from Nazism had begun to make their experiences known. One of the first to do so was a journalist, Stefan Lorant. A Hungarian-born Jew who had been a pioneer of illustrated magazines in Germany, he was incarcerated in prison in Munich for six and a half months between March and September 1933. Two years later, having been given refuge in Britain, he published *I Was Hitler's Prisoner*, in which he wrote of an especially degrading aspect of Nazi racial and political pressure, one which served as a magnet for destructive action:

In New Germany, whenever anyone wants to get rid of a competitor in trade, or give an enemy something to think about, or revenge himself on a lover, he simply denounces the person in an anonymous letter to the Political Police. The rest follows as a matter of course. The person is arrested. No one inquires whether he is innocent or guilty.

Envy, hate, tale-bearing, falsehood, every kind of human baseness, triumph. The prison is full of innocent men. In political custody. They are not allowed to defend themselves, for they are never granted a hearing. They are not permitted to see a lawyer. Most of them have never troubled themselves about politics. They are the victims of denunciation.

Others as well as Jews had become refugees on a large and increasing scale. In June 1935 the British historian H.A.L. Fisher was reaching the end of his history of Europe from earliest times to the modern age. 'Refugees from tyranny flock into the free countries,' he wrote in his final section: 'Greeks in flight from Asia Minor, Jews in flight from Nazi Germany, Russians who crowd into Prague and Constantinople, Paris and London, rather than endure the rigour of Soviet rule.' Of the tyranny of Stalin − who had effectively sealed the borders of the Soviet Union against any further emigration − Fisher wrote: 'At the cost of its civil liberties, a vast population is enabled to enjoy a prison ration of the goods of life.' As to Germany under Hitler: 'Nordic paganism assails Christianity. An insane racialism threatens to rupture the seamless garment of civilization.'

In China, the struggle between the Communists and the Nationalists continued throughout the year. The Communists were in retreat, the Long

March moving steadily further westward away from the areas that Mao Tse-tung had earlier controlled, but on several occasions they were able to take the initiative and attack. In March they came within ten miles of the Kweichow provincial capital of Kweiyang, and were only beaten off after a two-day pitched battle.

The Long March was beset with problems. During the crossing of the Great Snow mountains, Mao Tse-tung was suffering so badly from malaria that he had to be carried on a litter. Chu Teh repeatedly fainted from the thin air. At times the marchers – as many as eighty thousand had set off the previous year – were having to cross terrain at 16,000 feet. The Nationalists bombed them from the air. When they reached Mougong in June their numbers were half what they had been when they had set off eight months earlier. But it was only in September that the Long March was forced northwards, into southern Kansu, thus giving the Central Government control over four provinces in which it had hitherto been largely powerless: Kiangsi, Kweichow, Hunan and Szechwan.

When the Long March reached Wuqizhen, a hundred miles east of Yenan, on October 20, less than ten thousand – one in eight – of the troops who had left Shansi were still marching. But they had at last reached an area they could hold, particularly as the warlord Marshal Chang Hsueh-liang, based in Sian, was mainly interested in fighting the Japanese. Mao Tse-tung established his new headquarters in Yenan. That December he declared defiantly that, despite its heavy losses, the Long March 'has proclaimed to the world that the Red Army is an army of heroes, while the imperialists and their running dogs, Chiang Kai-shek and his like, are impotent.' But it was to be another fourteen years before the impotent ones could be driven out of China.

Some anarchy still prevailed in areas nominally under Nationalist control. On the Yangtse River, pirates seized a Chinese Navigation Company steamer, the *Tungchow*, which was taking seventy-three British and American children from Shanghai back to school in Chefoo. British warships were sent up river in pursuit. But it took several days before the pirates agreed to let the children go. Six months later the commander of the Chinese Government's anti-piracy troops and his Chief of Staff were found guilty of helping rather than suppressing the pirates. Both men were executed.

Once again it was the ravages of nature that brought death and destruction to China on a far larger scale than human conflict. During heavy rains in May the Yellow River burst its banks and hundreds of square miles of countryside were flooded. More than 50,000 peasants were drowned. In July the River Yangtse likewise overflowed, with a death toll as high.

In the United States, President Roosevelt pursued his New Deal despite continued Republican hostility to what was denounced as Federal 'interference'. In his address to Congress at the beginning of the year he stressed the need to use the nation's resources for life and not for profit. There were still at least ten million unemployed. More than sixteen million people were receiving Federal, State or Municipal relief. But there were setbacks to the New Deal when some of Roosevelt's programmes were rejected by the Federal Courts.

The most serious of these setbacks concerned the enforcement of codes of fair competitive practices on industry, and the enforcement of agreements with regard to hours and wages. On May 27 the Supreme Court held that these aspects of New Deal legislation (specifically in the National Industrial Recovery Act) were unconstitutional.

Roosevelt persevered. In June, by Executive Order – whereby the President had the power to execute a law passed by Congress under his constitutional rights as Chief Executive – he created the National Youth Administration (NYA). Its aim was to provide jobs for hundreds of thousands of youngsters who had been forced out of work, and even out of school, by the depression. The man chosen to be the director of the NYA in Texas was Lyndon Baines Johnson, at twenty-seven the youngest director in the United States. It was as a result of his two years in this position that Johnson was able to stand for, and to win election to, Congress.

In August, after more than seven months of struggle in Congress, Roosevelt obtained the passage of a Social Security Bill. This established, for the first time in United States history, something for which both Germany and Britain had legislated before the First World War: the provision of several essentials of State support for those who did not have more than a minimum of independent means (or had no independent means at all). These were unemployment insurance, health insurance, non-contributory old age pensions, maternal and child welfare, vocational rehabilitation, and pensions for the blind. The Act provided that the Federal government would match, more or less equally, State funds allocated to these measures. Signing on August 14 in the full glare of the newsreel cameras, Roosevelt used twenty pens in signing his name: a means of providing souvenirs for the faithful which has persisted to this day. 'This social security system,' he said at the signing of the Act, 'will give at least some measure of protection to 30 million of our citizens who will reap direct benefits.'

Other citizens – citizens by conquest – were beneficiaries of Roosevelt's legislation that year. It was almost forty years since the United States had acquired the Philippines from Spain. On November 14, following legislation enacted by Congress the year before, the New Commonwealth of the Philippines was inaugurated. For ten years the Philippines would have a large measure of self-government, after which they would become 'automatically free'. The Filipinos, in a vote which included women's suffrage, supported the new constitution by 20 to 1. The first act of the new President of the Philippines, Manuel Quezon, who was inaugurated on November 14, was to ask Roosevelt to lend the Chief of Staff of the United States Army, General Douglas McArthur, to reorganize the Philippine defence forces. Roosevelt agreed. Six years later, McArthur was to defend the Philippines against Japanese attack, to capitulate, and in due course to return as victor.

In Canada, the influence of President Roosevelt was seen when the Prime Minister, Richard Bennett, announced a 'New Deal' for Canada, which would provide for unemployment and social insurance, maximum hours and minimum wages in industry, federal support for farm credits, and a federally supported agricultural marketing board.

Roosevelt proceeded with yet further stages of his own New Deal. A Resettlement Administration was set up to help farm owners and tenants move to better land: one of its decisions was to hire a film maker, Pare Lorentz, to make films showing what the New Deal was achieving. The first film, *The Plough that Broke the Plains*, was opposed by Hollywood as undesirable government competition, but when the film did well in independent cinemas – its final dust storms sequence was a cinematographic masterpiece – Paramount agreed to distribute its successor, *The River*. Following this second success, Roosevelt set up the United States Film Service, as a well-funded vehicle to portray the efforts of government departments, as well as the serious problems confronting those who were struggling to overcome economic hardship.

A Works Progress Administration (WPA) was established to provide public work programmes. A Rural Electrification Administration (REA) gave federal loans to companies who would construct electricity supply networks in rural areas. The Social Security Act, which came into law on August 14, provided pensions for those over sixty-five, federal financial help for the blind and the disabled, and – starting in seven years time – unemployment assistance paid from individual contributions rather than from taxation. A Federal Arts Project was set up, which was to employ tens of thousands of artists for public works of art: they were paid by the federal exchequer. Among those whose works were thus commissioned were Jackson Pollock and Ben Shahn.

Amid the challenges of conflicting ideologies and national ambitions, the lives of millions of individuals continued to be centred upon everyday and pleasurable pursuits. Many inventors and composers had leisure activities in mind, as when a new game was launched, 'Monopoly', invented by Charles B. Darrow of Philadelphia, or when George Gershwin's opera *Porgy and Bess* was given its first performance. Among the films launched were *Anna Karenina*, starring Greta Garbo, *The Bride of Frankenstein* with Boris Karloff, and *A Night at the Opera* with the Marx Brothers. In Britain, the first streamlined steam locomotive was introduced on the main railway line from London to Newcastle. It set the world train speed record twice, travelling at 108 miles per hour in March and reaching 112 miles per hour in September.*

In 1935 the League of Nations did not only concern itself with disputes among sovereign States. During the Sixteenth Assembly, the Australian delegate, Stanley Bruce, opened a discussion on 'nutrition'. He and his government felt that it was necessary to increase the world consumption of fresh food products, in order to improve global health. But somehow the shadow of an impeding clash of nations and armies was always in evidence. In Britain, the first practical radio equipment was constructed for detecting aircraft in flight: radar. Ten years later radar was to provide vital warning of incoming enemy aircraft intent on mass destruction.

* This record was beaten by the Germans in February 1936, with 124 miles per hour, and then by the London North-Eastern Railway's newly constructed Mallard engine in July 1938, with 125 miles per hour. In 1998 the London to Paris Eurostar regularly reached 186 miles per hour on the French side.

CHAPTER FOUR

1936

> The fact of progress is written plain and large on the
> page of history; but progress is not a law of nature.
> The ground gained by one generation may be lost by
> the next. The thoughts of men may flow into the
> channels which lead to disaster and barbarism.
>
> H.A.L. FISHER

HERBERT FISHER, whose *History of Europe*, first published in January
1936, is quoted above, had been an advocate of liberal values in the post-war
British government and a British delegate to the League of Nations in its
first years. 'I begin this book,' he noted, 'with Neolithic man and conclude
with Stalin and Mustapha Kemal, Mussolini and Hitler. Between these rough
and rugged frontiers there are to be found some prospects flattering to human
pride which it is a pleasure to recall to memory . . .' That same month the
American journalist John Gunther wrote: 'This is the age of great dictatorial
leaders. Millions depend for life or death on the will of Hitler, Mussolini,
Stalin.'

Gunther commented that culture itself, the civilization on which Europe
had been built, was being overshadowed. 'What books in the realm of art,'
he asked, 'have had the sales or influence of Hitler's *Mein Kampf?*' As to
science and technology, he added, 'Who is a greater engineer than Stalin?'

Both Hitler and Stalin had a deepening interest that year in the future
governance of Spain, distant though it was from their respective frontiers.
In the elections which were held in Spain on February 16 victory went to
the Popular Front coalition of the Parties of the Left. They obtained 265
seats, as against 165 for the Right, including Basque Nationalists, and 66
for the Centre Parties. By far the largest Left-wing grouping was the Left
Republicans with 136 seats. The Socialists won 87 and the Communists

only 15. The Right Parties, headed by Gil Robles, tried at once to prevent the formation of a government of the Left. Robles went to see the Prime Minister, Manuel Portela, and urged him to declare martial law. The success of the popular front, Robles warned, meant violence and anarchy.

Robles also sent a messenger to General Franco, Chief of the Spanish General Staff, who during the election campaign had been in Britain representing Spain at the funeral of King George V. Robles hoped that Franco would lead the army in preventing the formation of a new government. For his part, Franco tried to institute a decree of martial law throughout Spain, although this had not been formally agreed by the President or the Prime Minister. Another senior army officer, General Goded, tried to bring out the troops from their barracks in Madrid, but they were unwilling to find themselves in confrontation with the Civil Guard. On February 18 the Civil Guard made its position clear: 'The Civil Guard will oppose any coup attempt,' and proceeded to surround those army barracks in the capital from which it was thought a military coup might be launched.

On the afternoon of February 19, Franco made one last attempt to persuade the Prime Minister to declare martial law, but Portela declined to do so. That same afternoon Portela handed over the premiership to Manuel Azana. Three days later, Franco was relieved of his position as Chief of Staff and sent to the Canary Islands as Military Governor, a virtual exile. General Goded was sent to govern the Balearic islands.

On February 20 the new Prime Minister announced his commitment to wide changes. Land reform was to favour the small holders. Taxation and rents were to be reduced. Some State control of industry would be secured. Large scale public works would be introduced to combat unemployment. Regional autonomy would be restored to Catalonia.

Azana then appealed to the working classes for unity in the work of reform and reconstruction. Above all, he said, there should be no disturbances. But prison riots forced him to bring forward a proposed amnesty without first submitting it for parliamentary approval. Other rioters attacked those whom they blamed for their distress during the previous three years: right-wing political clubs were looted and some land on the large estates in Extremadura was occupied by farm labourers who did not wish to wait for the slow process of legislation to transfer the land. They wanted to be in possession of the soil in time to plant their grain. The only way to achieve this was to seize the land without delay. The government accepted the seizures by special decree.

Churches were also burnt, and property belonging to the rich was destroyed. In reaction to the activities of the Left, which were denounced as a Red Terror, Fascist vigilante groups, the Falange Espagnola, took up arms and went on a rampage of their own. On April 3, after expressing his understanding of the needs of the 'hungered multitudes' fresh from prison or repression, Azana appealed for an end to all extra-parliamentary activity by whatever extreme group. This, he said, was the last chance for Spain to make progress by parliamentary methods. He was supported in this appeal two days later by Francisco Largo Caballero, the Marxist leader.

The political crisis came to a head on April 10, when, on a Socialist motion, the President of Spain, Niceto Alcalá-Zamora, was dismissed. For a month there was political as well as social chaos. Fascists and Socialists fought in the streets. On April 17 a government decree made all Fascist groupings illegal. On April 20 an emergency Bill was passed forbidding anti-Republican activity in the Army.

On May 10 the Prime Minister, Azana, accepted the Presidency. Three days later a senior Marxist, Santiago Quiroga, became Prime Minister. In his first appeal to the nation, Quiroga spoke of 'the excesses which I know are committed by local authorities and which must cease forthwith.' Those excesses continued, however, and from the Right the call grew for the army to take over, restore social discipline and 'save Spain'.

For several weeks, however, it looked as if Quiroga's appeal would be effective. Similar calls for moderation came from Moscow, with regard to the role the Spanish Communists should play. But on July 12 a police officer, Lieutenant Castillo, who was known to have Socialist sympathies, was murdered by a Rightist. On the following day the police went to the home of a leading Rightist, Calvo Sotelo, intending to arrest him. In the struggle, Sotelo was shot dead. As public anger mounted on both sides of the political divide, Parliament was suspended for a week to prevent violence in the chamber.

The army decided that the time had come to act. The first shots were fired on July 18, when the Spanish Moroccan Army, led by the exiled General Franco, seized the city of Melilla after a fierce fight, and then took control of all Spanish Morocco. Spanish government submarines in the Free Zone of Tangier were bombed by the insurgents. Army officers led by General Mola then sought to take over power in Spain itself, and Moroccan troops crossed over from Africa as part of the insurgent plan. The Left had a particular hatred for the Army of Morocco because of the ferocity with which, under Franco's overall direction, it had suppressed the revolt in the Asturias the previous year – an episode which, but for the murder of Sotelo and the subsequent suspension of its debates, Parliament would have been investigating during the very week of the uprising.

'The whole country' declared the Communist journalist Dolores Ibárruri in a broadcast from Madrid on July 18, 'is shaking with indignation, faced with these heartless men who, with fire and terror, want to plunge popular and democratic Spain into an inferno of terror. But they shall not pass!' That phrase, 'they shall not pass!' – *no pasarán* – became the rallying cry and motto of the Republic. Dolores Ibárruri, known as La Pasionaria – passion flower – became the eloquent mouthpiece of the Republic. She had acquired the name in Passion Week 1918 when, as a woman of twenty-three, she had needed a pseudonym for an article supporting the claims of the Basque coal miners. In 1934 she had made her name championing the miners of the Asturias against the assault upon them by the army, and by Franco. In a peroration in her broadcast at the start of the Spanish Civil War she referred to those miners. 'The whole of Spain is on a war footing,' she said. 'In Madrid the people are on the streets, warning the government with their decisiveness and spirit of combat so that the crushing of the reactionaries and fascists who have rebelled will be achieved. Women, heroic women of the people, remember the heroism of the Asturian women! Fight alongside the men to defend the bread and security of your threatened children.'

There were military uprisings in a number of cities in Spain itself on July 18, as the army seized control of Seville, Cadiz, Saragossa and Pamplona. Franco, at Tetuan, placed himself at the head of the insurgent government. On the morning of July 19 the Prime Minister, Santiago Quiroga resigned. His successor, Martinez Barrio, refused the Socialist demands to arm the workers and tried to open negotiations with General Mola, but Mola refused to negotiate, and Barrio's government fell. Under pressure from the Socialist, Syndicalist and Communist trade unions, and with the authority of President Azana, trade unions throughout Spain were authorized to call general strikes wherever the army sought to impose martial law. In Madrid and Barcelona, there was severe fighting between the army and forces loyal to the government. In both cities the government gained the upper hand, and the rebels withdrew.

In Madrid, General Fanjul – who had contemplated an army coup two years earlier – was captured, tried and shot. When General Goded – another of those who had contemplated an army coup in 1934 – reached Barcelona from the Balearic Islands, to which he had been effectively exiled, the army uprising in Catalonia was already defeated. Taken prisoner, the general was forced to broadcast an appeal to his followers to surrender. A further blow to the rebellion came when one of its main organizers, General Sanjurjo, was killed in an aeroplane crash shortly after taking off from Lisbon, on his way to Spain.

Supporting the Madrid Government were those who had welcomed the Republic of 1931: Liberals, Catholics, Socialists, Communists, Anarcho-Syndicalists, members of the Civil Guard, the navy, and as many as 12 per cent of army officers (some of whom had fought alongside government troops in the first battles in Madrid and Barcelona). Also loyal to the Republic were the Basque nationalists, who, while often strongly Conservative, had an even stronger stake in a republic that had promised them regional autonomy. Basque support meant that the government had access to the industrial resources, including iron and steel, of the Bilbao region, and of Catalonia.

The Junta could call upon the support of Monarchists, landowners and the Catholic Church hierarchy, small-holders in certain Catholic provinces, the peasants in the traditionalist region of Navarre, as well as the bulk of the army officers, and the middle and business classes, for whom Republican government seemed to offer only anarchy and chaos. The fact that the army had failed to seize power in Madrid did not deter the insurgents. On July 27, Franco told Jay Allen, an American journalist who interviewed him in Tetuan: 'There can be no compromise, no truce. I shall go on preparing my advance to Madrid. I shall advance. I shall take the capital. I shall save Spain from Marxism at whatever cost.' Rebutting the suggestion that there was a stalemate, Franco told Allen: 'I have had setbacks, the defection of the Fleet was a blow, but I shall continue to advance. Shortly, very shortly, my troops will have pacified the country, and all of this will soon seem like a nightmare.' When Allen commented about the pacification, 'That means you will have to shoot half Spain', Franco told him: 'I repeat, at whatever cost.'

Franco appealed to the Western world to take his side, telling Allen: 'Europe must see that Spain cannot be allowed to become a second Communist Power in Europe, using her strategic position to disseminate "Red" propaganda in Morocco, Algeria, Tunis and even America. The Powers must see this. France must see this.'

In cities where the Madrid Government had retained control, committees of Anti-Fascist Militia were set up, to carry out all police and transport duties, and to hunt down 'Fascists'. A report in *The Times* on August 1, headed 'RED RULE IN BARCELONA', gave an account of an episode which was part of what it described as a 'war of extermination' widely regarded as 'a necessary stage in the consolidation of the anti-Fascist revolution'. It had taken place four days earlier:

> On the morning of July 27 the local Revolutionary Committee at Vallvidrerea, a suburb of Barcelona on the Tibidabo ridge, tried unsuccessfully to stop a large motor-car containing three armed men and six women, which was speeding through.
>
> When the car returned later without the women, a search was made for them, and the bodies of four, who had been shot dead, were found among undergrowth and trees. Another was too seriously wounded to be moved. The sixth was still conscious and was taken to the local Red Cross hospital.
>
> The women were nuns of the Dominican Convent in Barcelona and had been taken from there on the pretext that they were to be put in a safe place. The dead lay on the ground all night and were taken to Barcelona the next day.

More than 30,000 such executions were committed: each side contributed almost equally to this horrendous total.

The government in Madrid, headed from September 4 by the working class leader Francisco Largo Caballero, ruled through a Cabinet that included five Socialists, two Communists, and three Republicans, as well as representatives of the Catalan and Basque Nationalists. Within a few weeks of the government being established the Anarcho-Syndicalists were also represented in it. The insurgent government, the Junta de Defensa Nacional, functioned from Burgos – the city to which General Sanjurjo had been going when his plane had crashed.

Franco and the Nationalist Junta appealed to Germany and Italy for war supplies. A constant flow of weaponry also reached the Nationalists from across the land border with Portugal. For its part, the Madrid Government turned the factories of Bilbao and Barcelona to war production. Outside Spain, the struggle was portrayed as one of Fascists against Democrats and Communists. Supporters of democracy and Communism in many lands hurried to participate in the struggle. 'We are plunging into a tunnel of anguish,' André Gide wrote in his journal on September 6, 'the end of which cannot yet be seen.'

The Basques were the first to gain politically and nationally from the Spanish divide. On October 1 the government in Madrid adopted a Basque Home Rule Statute. A week later, on October 8, the first Autonomous Basque Government was called into being. The ceremony was held under the historic tree at Guernica where their ancient assembly had once met – an assembly praised by Rousseau in the eighteenth century as a model of popular democracy.

At first the Junta's armed forces made rapid advances, as Franco had predicted. The outskirts of Madrid were reached on November 6. It was said that Franco hoped, as a dramatic gesture of defiance, to enter the capital on November 7, the anniversary of the Bolshevik revolution in Russia. But Madrid held out, its defences augmented by volunteers of the International Brigade, who came from many lands, including France, the United States, Britain and the Soviet Union. In his breakdown of the different nationalities fighting in the Brigade, the historian Hugh Thomas puts the French as the largest – about 10,000, of whom a thousand were killed in action. Of the 5,000 German and Austrian volunteers, 2,000 were killed. There were also 5,000 Poles, among them General Swierczewski, Poland's Minister of Defence from 1945 until his assassination in 1947 by Ukrainian anti-Communists. There were 3,350 Italians fighting on the Republican side, contrasting with at least 40,000 Italians serving with the Nationalists, among them – as a bomber pilot – Mussolini's son Vittorio.

As many as three thousand Russians came from the Soviet Union to fight for the Republic, among them a thousand pilots. They included ten future Soviet Marshals, one of whom, Marshal Rokossovki, later became Polish Defence Minister. Of the 2,800 volunteers from the United States, many of them serving in the Abraham Lincoln battalion – 900 were killed. A third of the American volunteers were Jews, mostly the children of turn-of-the-century immigrants from Russia. Of the 2,000 British volunteers, 500 were killed. Among the other volunteers in the Brigade were 1,500 Yugoslavs – twenty-four of whom later became Generals in the post-war Yugoslav Communist Army. There were 1,500 Czech volunteers and a thousand Hungarians, including Pal Maleter, who played a leading part in the anti-Communist uprising in Hungary in 1956. A thousand Scandinavians volunteered – including 500 Swedes – and several hundred Swiss, seventy-six of whom fell in action. A thousand Canadians volunteered, as did ninety Mexicans – crossing the Atlantic Ocean to serve with the Brigade. One of the Albanian volunteers, Mehmet Shehu, became President of the Albanian Communist Government after 1945. One of his volunteer colleagues in Spain, Enver Hoxha, ruled post-war Albania with an iron fist for several decades. Other volunteers came from Ireland, China, Korea, Japan and Peru, as well as Jews from Palestine.

The American journalist Louis Fischer, who enlisted in the International Brigade at the start of the battle for Madrid, recalled in his memoirs the atmosphere of the first days of the siege:

> In ten days, Madrid had changed its aspect. Frivolity gone! Barricades instead! Streets had been torn up and the granite blocks used to build walls across streets and in front of big buildings. Avenues were dug up to obstruct tanks.
>
> Most Madrileños refused to leave the city. The government actually arrested several noted artists and professors and took them to the coast where they were released. It did not want them to be hurt or killed.
>
> The art treasures of the Prado and other museums were moved out. This was no simple task. Some of the big Velasquez and Goyas could not be rolled without cracking the varnish and colour. If they were transported in their frames in ordinary trucks they might be bombed or machine-gunned from the air. The Loyalist government therefore used specially armoured trucks for this purpose.

Louis Fischer recalled how the first 1,900 men of the International Brigade who joined the defence of Madrid in early November were greeted by the citizens with the cry 'Viva Rusa.' But, he commented, 'most of them were French'. The same was true of the 1,550 who arrived a week later and reached the front on November 14. 'These fighters had left peaceful jobs and peaceful countries to die or lose their eyes and arms in the struggle against Fascism. But nobody used big words in the Brigade. It was a big, dirty, costly job. Flags were furled. The flags waved in the heart.'

In the Soviet Union a 'Spanish levy' was imposed on all trade union members, and later on the peasant farmers in the collective farms, for the supply of food and war materials to the Madrid government. One of those who gave succour to the troops of the International Brigade was the Black

American singer Paul Robeson. 'I saw the connection between the problems of all oppressed peoples and the necessity of the artist to participate fully,' he explained a decade later when his left-wing sympathies were under attack.

The British writer Stephen Spender, who was living in Vienna when the Spanish Civil War began, found that the Austrian socialists living there in fear of arrest and persecution no longer felt alone and abandoned. For them, as for anti-Fascists throughout Europe, the cause of republican Spain became a rallying point of activity and hope. Later he reflected on how the war in Spain 'offered the twentieth century an 1848: that is to say, time and place where a cause representing a greater degree of freedom and justice than a reactionary opposing one, gained victories.' It became possible, Spender added, 'to see the Fascist/anti-Fascist struggle as a real conflict of ideas, and not just as the seizure of power by dictators from weak opponents. From being a pathetic catastrophe, Spain lifted the fate of the anti-Fascists to heights of tragedy. Since the area of struggle in Spain was confined, and the methods of warfare comparatively restrained, the voices of human individuals were not overwhelmed, as in 1939, by vast military machines and by propaganda. The Spanish war remained to some extent a debate, both within and outside Spain, in which the three great political ideas of our time – Fascism, Communism, and Liberal-Socialism – were discussed and heard.'

In Portugal, the government of General Salazar, which had been in power since the summer of 1932, feared that the Spanish republican cause might have echoes among those in Lisbon for whom the Salazar dictatorship represented a repression of individual liberty. Press censorship was severe, but some sense of the excitement of the republican experiment in Spain could not be stopped. On September 8 the crews of two Portuguese warships stationed in the River Tagus set sail for the open sea, with the intention of joining the naval forces of the Spanish Republic. Salazar's government had, however, received prior intelligence of this move, and the forts on both sides of the estuary were ordered to open fire. For half an hour ships and shore batteries exchanged fire, until both ships were so badly damaged that they were forced ashore. The rebels were brought to trial and condemned to long periods of forced labour in a Portuguese colonial penal settlement.

On October 24 the Portuguese government broke diplomatic relations with the government in Madrid: the first foreign government to turn its back on the elected rulers of Spain.

*   *   *

In Germany, parallel with the imposition of Nazism, the process of modernization which Hitler had promised continued. Motor roads were built (the precursors of today's motorways) which enabled Germans to drive between the major cities without traffic lights or crossroads to impede their progress. On February 26, Hitler personally opened the first factory – many more were planned – to make the 'People's Car' (the *Volkswagen*), to enable Germans of modest means to be able to afford to drive.

The pace and pattern of Hitler's actions were swift, unpredictable, and above all effective. On March 6 the Soviet Embassy in Berlin was holding a reception at which the high point was a film 'Russian army manoeuvres in the Ukraine'. High ranking German officers had accepted invitations, including several from the General Staff. All foreign military attachés were present, as was the Spanish General Sanjurjo, who was in Berlin buying arms. At 5.15 the German generals sent a message to their Soviet hosts to say that they were delayed because of important discussions with Hitler – the film should start without them. Three quarters of an hour later the Belgian Military Attaché, General Schmidt, hurried back to his embassy and reported to Brussels that German troops were at that very moment entering the Rhineland.

At his meeting with the German General Staff, Hitler had listened to warnings that the French would react strongly against the remilitarization, which was forbidden under the Versailles Treaty. He had answered their fears with the words: 'France won't move an inch.'

The Rhineland had been a sovereign and integral part of Imperial, Weimar and Nazi Germany. It had been demilitarized after the First World War, as part of the Versailles Treaty. France in particular feared the presence of German troops on German soil so close to the French border. When Hitler sent German troops into the Rhineland it was not only a violation of the Versailles Treaty, but also of the Locarno Pact, which had been signed freely by Germany eleven years earlier with Britain, France, Belgium and Italy. At a conference in London on March 13 the German delegate, Joachim von Ribbentrop, declared that the German people desired henceforth to cooperate in building up a real European solidarity. On behalf of the British Government, Anthony Eden welcomed this declaration, and offered British help in the work of reconstruction.

That same day, Churchill commented in the *Evening Standard* that with the remilitarization of the Rhineland, Europe was presented simultaneously with 'Hope and Peril'. Were the League of Nations able to seize the opportunity to re-establish 'a reign of law' in Europe then it might still be possible to stop 'the horrible, dull, remorseless drift to war in 1937 or 1938' and bring to an end the 'preparatory piling up' of armaments in every European country. France had appealed to the League of Nations. It was essential for the League to give her justice and 'satisfaction'. If the League proved powerless to act, if no means 'of patient, lawful redress' could be found to put at rest the fears not only of France but also of Belgium, 'the whole doctrine of international law and cooperation, upon which the hopes of the future are based, would lapse ignominiously'. There was only one way to preserve peace: 'the assembly of overwhelming force, moral and physical, in support of international law'.

The British Cabinet rejected Churchill's argument. 'Our own attitude', the secret notes of its meeting on March 17 recorded, 'had been governed by the desire to utilize Herr Hitler's offers in order to obtain a permanent settlement'.

To show that his action in remilitarizing the Rhineland had total national support inside Germany, Hitler dissolved the Reichstag and called new elections. Once more the Nazi Party was the only Party on the list of candidates. Propaganda against the candidates, or in favour of any other Party, was forbidden. The election was held on March 29. When it was announced in Berlin that 99 per cent of the votes had been cast for the Nazi Party, there was derision outside Germany.

The remilitarization of the Rhineland had not involved the firing of a single shot, or the confrontation of troops or armies. Although there was indignation in France and Britain that Germany had taken such unilateral action, there was no widespread call for sanctions or military measures against Germany. In an editorial headed 'A Chance to Rebuild', *The Times* suggested that the shock of Hitler's unilateral action could be turned to good effect if Britain and Germany were to seek means of drawing more closely together. The editor of *The Times*, Geoffrey Dawson, made continuous efforts not to offend the Germans. A year later he wrote to a friend: 'I should like to get going with the Germans. I simply cannot understand why they should apparently be so much annoyed with *The Times* at this moment. I spend my nights in taking out anything which I think will hurt their susceptibilities and in dropping in little things which are intended to soothe them.'

Following the remilitarization of the Rhineland, Hitler adopted a forceful foreign policy that overshadowed international unease over the Rhineland. On the very day of his Rhineland bombshell he offered Non-aggression Pacts, each of them to last twenty-five years, between Germany and France, Germany and Belgium, and Germany and Britain. Having abolished one demilitarized zone, he proposed the establishment of another, on both sides of the Franco-German and Belgian-German frontiers.

Amid the roller-coaster aspects of remilitarization and offers of non-aggression, pacifists in Britain retained their determination to seek European peace through unilateral disarmament. That summer, in an interview with a young writer – Alan Campbell Johnson – the pacifist writer Beverley Nichols stressed the ideological aspects of the pacifist creed. 'I am coming now to believe that to follow Christ all the way is the only way,' he stressed. 'There is much to be said for the conduct of the Quakers. One must be prepared in the last resort to submit to Force. It is no use resisting Force with Force.'

Beverley Nichols went on to ask his questioner: 'Why not Great Britain disarm completely? One nation must make the first gesture to the world. Great Britain should make it. There is, of course, no harm in keeping a few boys in red tunics to march up and down in front of the Palace.' Campbell Johnson noted that there was 'a hardness in his voice and bitter implication in his smile as he looked up to see how I reacted to this phrase'. Beverley Nichols continued: 'Let us lose our Empire if it must be so, let the Germans come and rule over us if they will, Force only breeds Force. If you are going to describe this talk of ours at all, I would ask you to stress this above everything, that the world today is perishing of security and expediency.'

There was a growing gulf in Britain between those who wanted to come to terms with Hitler and those who wanted to deter any future aggression by armaments and the alliance of all threatened States. Much of the argument centred on whether Hitler did in fact pose a threat beyond Germany's borders. Those who felt that he did not saw no reason for rapid or accelerated rearmament, and even feared that any such rearmament would give a hostile signal to Germany. Fear of Communism led many Britons to look to Hitler as the main bastion between the Red Army and the White Cliffs of Dover. Others, hostile to France, regarded a strong Germany as Britain's natural ally.

Within British Government circles were those who saw an Anglo-German economic arrangement, even an economic 'condominium', as providing not only Britain and Europe, but Africa and Asia, with a powerful focus for development and prosperity. If there was to be war, Baldwin confided to a group of senior Conservatives that year, he would 'rather see' it between Hitler and Stalin (or as he phrased it, 'between the Bolshies and the Nazis').

The appeasement of Germany as a constructive way forward for European harmony and security meant giving Germany some redress for her grievances, as long as those grievances could be characterized as legitimate. In this regard, revision of the Versailles Treaty had been a clarion call in many circles for the previous fifteen years. Hitler's call for the unity of all German-speaking peoples within one national border seemed a reasonable one: according to such a perspective, the countries that had been created after 1918 and contained German minorities would have to accept frontier rectification.

Even those at the centre of the British Government who were made aware of the extent of German military preparations were reluctant to respond fully. After a secret British government report recommended 'a far more effective standard' of defence preparedness, a Cabinet Committee presided over by Baldwin concluded that to organize for war in peacetime 'is unthinkable in a democratic country like ours', and that any interference with normal trade in order to accelerate armaments would not only 'adversely affect the prosperity of the country' but also 'attract Parliamentary criticism'. Churchill, who opposed this line of thought, believed that if the truth about German preparations were put before Parliament by the leaders of the government, the response would be immediate. On April 23 he pointed out in the House of Commons what was being done in Germany. 'A veto prevails in Germany on all expansion of private plant for purely economic purposes,' he said. 'The capital expenditure of Germany other than for residential buildings may, therefore, be regarded as almost exclusively devoted to warlike preparations, in which, of course, I include the preparation of those great military roads where four columns of troops can march abreast, which may play a greater part in a future war than the fortifications that are being built.'

Those in Britain, like the journalist Francis Hirst, who doubted Hitler's warlike intentions, denounced Churchill's 'panic statistics'. But the details Churchill set out in each of his speeches warning of the extent of German preparations and military expenditure – and the rapid increase in expenditure on armaments – were based on material he himself was receiving from individuals in the British Foreign Office and Air Ministry who continued to be distressed that in framing its policy the government was ignoring their own warnings and information.

The main thrust of Churchill's arguments, in his public speeches and articles throughout the year, was that Hitler could be deterred from making war if the European democracies, and in particular Britain, were adequately armed to resist him; and that all rearmament should be coordinated through the League of Nations and the working together of all the threatened States. On May 21 he asked the British government to set up a Ministry of Supply to coordinate the arms purchases of all three Services, and to plan for army, navy and air force expansion on a war basis. This did not mean that he was 'in favour of war', he told the House of Commons, indeed, that was a 'foul charge', and he went on to ask: 'Is there a man in the House who would not sacrifice his right hand here and now for the assurance that there would be no war in Europe for twenty years?'

As a first step to prevent war, Churchill proposed on May 25, to the newly created Anti-Nazi Council – for which six days earlier he had been the first speaker – 'a strictly limited regional pact among the Western States, Holland, Belgium, France and Britain for mutual aid in the event of unprovoked attack, and for keeping in being a force great enough to deter Germany from making such an attack'.

In the aftermath of his Rhineland challenge Hitler not only accelerated his war preparations at home, but began a new foreign policy initiative, seeking Italian support as a counterweight to the closer cooperation of France and the Soviet Union, which had signed an alliance a year earlier. The Franco-Soviet Pact gave Hitler a theme for speech after speech: the threat of Bolshevism and encirclement. It was easy to conjure up the nightmare shades of 1914 when France and Russia had been Imperial Germany's military adversaries in a two-front war. Such a spectre made the call for German rearmament all the more logical, urgent and acceptable.

The German rapprochement with Italy had a price. On July 11, at the expense of his previous support for the disruptive tactics of the Nazi movement in Austria, which was demanding the annexation of the Italian South Tyrol, Hitler reached an understanding with Austria. The Austrian Nazis lost their patron, and the embargo on German travellers to Austria was lifted. Henceforth, the main target of German propaganda outside its borders was the neighbouring State of Czechoslovakia. Hitler began to demand greater rights, powers and even autonomy for the German-speaking peoples of the Sudetenland.

Although these German speakers had never been a part of Germany –

before 1918 the Sudetenland was within the Austro-Hungarian Empire – Hitler saw a means of weakening Czechoslovakia by putting himself forward as the champion of the Sudeten Germans. Nazi Party activity inside the region increased. The Sudeten Germans, many of whom regarded every aspect of Nazism as vile, found that local leaders were also affected by the pressure and appeal of Hitler's Reich. The Sudeten German Party led by Konrad Henlein had begun to demand autonomy for the Sudetenland. The Czech President, Eduard Benes, rejected this call, fearing that it was but a prelude to separation from Czechoslovakia and annexation to Germany. Henlein's Party, which continued its call for autonomy, could not be discounted. In the Czech parliament his 45 deputies (elected in 1935) represented 60 per cent of the German-speaking citizens of the State. He was also well-funded, receiving a monthly subsidy from the German Foreign Office.

The Czech Government was denounced for inequalities which did not exist. It also found that any act towards the Sudeten Germans which was in any way discriminatory was blown up into a major accusation of tyranny. At the same time Czechoslovakia – which had signed its own Pact with the Soviet Union – was denounced from Berlin as an 'outpost of Bolshevism'. In September, Dr Goebbels – whose philosophy of propaganda was that if one told a lie often enough it would be believed – declared that the Soviet Union had military aircraft and airfields in Czechoslovakia. This was untrue, and was officially denied. But a few days later the accusation was repeated during that year's Nuremberg rally. The Czech government protested, but the accusation continued to be used inside Germany as proof of the imminence of the Bolshevik threat.

Poland was also watching with alarm the way in which Germany exacerbated the dispute over the Polish Corridor, the strip of land given to Poland by the victorious Allies after the war, but containing many Germans. The exacerbation took the form of an official German refusal to pay transit fees for trains that crossed the corridor in order to reach East Prussia – German territory which, as a result of the creation of the Corridor, was cut off territorially from the rest of the Reich. Poland also took action against members of the German-financed National Socialist Workers Movement in Katowice (formerly Kattowitz), who were demanding the transfer of Upper Silesia from Poland to Germany. This region had earlier been transferred from Germany to Poland as a result of a post-war plebiscite. The Poles were determined not to allow agitation in favour of yet another change.

The Latvians were also taking action against an organization known simply as the Movement, likewise inspired by Germany, that was propagating Nazi ideology in the Latvian capital, Riga. In the Free City of Danzig, the League of Nations High Commissioner complained to the League about the 'unconstitutional activities' of the Nazi Party of Danzig, whose leader, Albert Forster, a German citizen, declared openly that members were subordinate to the Nazi Party of Germany. But the protest was in vain. The League took no action; and in October, using terror tactics learned in Germany, the Danzig Nazi Party forced its two main rivals, the Socialists and German Nationalists, to dissolve.

Roumania was more well-disposed towards Germany, having her own concerns about the day when the Soviet Union might be strong enough to reclaim the province of Bessarabia, which Roumania had acquired after the collapse of the Tsarist Empire. There was also sympathy with the general aims of German Nazis. Early in 1936 a new political Party had been formed, made up of several well-established existing Parties, whose aim was the elimination of Jews and Hungarians from Roumanian public life. Starting on June 21, nationalist students organized a series of anti-Jewish demonstrations in Bucharest. In a further demonstration in the capital on November 8, there were calls – led by Professor Cuza of the Christian League – for closer relations between Germany and Roumania.

Communist activity was treated harshly. That year one of the leaders of the Roumanian Communist Party, Anna Pauker, was sentenced to ten years in prison. Many more such sentences were imposed on other Roumanian Communist leaders that same year. In Poland also, the Communist Party was at the centre of political conflict. On March 26 it organized the occupation of the coal mines at Chropaczowa, and a hunger strike. The police moved in and broke up the strike: they also arrested the Communist leaders, among them Wladyslaw Gomulka, who was sentenced to eight years in prison. For the first year and a half he was kept in solitary confinement. He was later to spend five years as a prisoner of Stalin, before emerging as the undisputed leader of Communist Poland in 1956 – twenty years after his first imprisonment.

In France, the General Elections that were concluded on May 3 brought to power a coalition of Parties of the Left, the Popular Front. Its largest single component was the Socialists, with 146 seats, followed by the Radicals with 116 and the Communists with 72. This was the first time in French history that the Socialists were the largest single parliamentary Party. Léon Blum, the Socialist leader, became Prime Minister. But the Communist party, alongside which he had campaigned, declined to join his government, and, before the end of May – and before Blum had actually taken up office – called for a strike of metal workers in the capital.

In factories working for the national defence, and in the large motor car factories, 100,000 men went on strike, occupying the factory floors. Within a week a further 200,000 workers were out on strike. Although the occupation of the factories was illegal, Blum took no action to end it, unwilling to risk the electoral unity of the Popular Front.

Arbitration began at Blum's official residence, the Matignon Palace. It ended with the Matignon Agreement, whereby the employers agreed to recognize collective labour contracts negotiated by the unions, and to wage increases of between seven and fifteen per cent. For their part, the workers agreed to end the occupation of the factories and to start work. At the same time, Blum introduced to Parliament a series of wide ranging measures of social reform. There would be a forty hour week, collective labour agreements, levies on the salaries of civil servants, and holidays with pay.*

Inside Germany, Hitler continued to strengthen the basis of Nazism throughout the year. All German youngsters had to join the Hitler Youth Movement, which had hitherto been voluntary. As a result of this, the Church Youth Movement lost almost all its former influence. Within the Hitler Youth, as also within the SS, the Christian religion – which had been at the centre of German life for almost a thousand years – was being replaced by a pagan cult exemplified by the slogan 'Blood and Soil'. Racism was a central feature, with emphasis put on the 'purity' of German 'Aryan' blood. No such blood is known to anthropology or to medical science.

German Jews continued to try to lead such lives as could be called normal, given their segregation and isolation. On May 27 a Jewish boy by the name of Heinz reached his thirteenth birthday and celebrated his Barmitzvah – the traditional Jewish coming of age – in the town of Fürth. Two years later, together with his parents, he left Germany as a refugee. After a distinguished academic career in the United States, culminating as Professor of Government at Harvard, he was made Secretary of State in 1973. His name then: Henry. As a result of Nazi racial policies, the achievements of Henry Kissinger were to the benefit of a country other than that of his birth.

* When, eight years later, Blum was being held in a German concentration camp (as a 'privileged' prisoner), his trousers were returned from the camp laundry with a note in one of the pockets, written by French forced labourers working in the laundry: 'Thank you for paid holidays.'

One eye-witness to the atmosphere in Germany in 1936 was a young American, Tom Fleming, who was making his first journey to Europe, before entering Harvard. Sixty-two years later he set down his recollections. 'When I got off the train at Cologne, my entry-point in Germany, I was immediately aware of groups of two's and three's of Brown-shirted SS men,' he wrote. The uniforms and Swastika insignia which were soon to become fearful were not yet recognized as such, and this, Fleming reflected, gave advantage to Hitler. 'Those brown shirted oafs,' he wrote, 'looked slightly silly to an American, who thought they looked like overgrown boy scouts. In the United States, Hitler was the subject of parodies in vaudeville skits, radio jokes, and movie spoofs. A fellow in my class in high school liked to take out his pocket comb put it on his upper lip to simulate Hitler's toothbrush moustache, and pop a Heil Hitler salute. His Nazi movement seemed rather ludicrous to my young contemporaries. Of course it was yet another plus for Hitler.'

The visitor could not be perpetually amused, however, as Fleming recalled:

That there was more to Hitler's Germany than comedy soon became evident. My cousin, Richard Stebbins, saw a piano in the hotel lounge, and sat down to play a piece of Mendelssohn he liked. While I was admiring his musicianship, an officious German rushed over to the musician, and rapped loudly on the piano with his knuckles. 'Stop that!' he shouted. 'That is decadent Jewish music!'

I had never before seen or heard such verbal viciousness first hand. Richard made eye contact with this member of the master race, and said 'Prove it!' The weight of his tiny brain pressed down on this Teuton's eyebrows and he was momentarily non-plussed. Richard got up and we left, the fun of playing eliminated.

My trip on the Rhine to Koblentz was highlighted by boats of Germans on 'Strength Through Joy' excursions. The groups sang lustily like some light opera performance, out of a Jeanette McDonald/Nelson Eddy movie. The castles on the high points along the river's east bank were in the middle of rolling vineyards. The whole thing was romantic as billed, until I saw openings in the bluffs. Were they gun emplacements?

Heidelberg was the place where I got the clearest views of the 'show' Hitler was putting on. There were any number of uniformed soldiers strolling through the city with family members. Hitler Youth, giving continuity to Nazism's future, paraded through the streets in disciplined ranks. Truck loads of conscript workers, singing loudly, showed up regularly. I had never seen workers in the US singing as they went to their work assignments. It seemed staged.

The most unsettling action came when German troops on a route march, came past my hotel the second evening I was there. They wore field kit, and steel helmets were on their backpacks. Motorcycles with side cars zipped up and down the ranks to keep order and discipline along the route of march. It went on for hours and I was really concerned that I was in the middle of something I didn't understand. When I asked the hotel manager, he looked off into space and said it was something he couldn't be concerned about.

Fleming returned to the United States, and to Harvard. 'It was distressing,' he wrote, 'to hear instructors at Harvard state that Hitler was trying to do what Americans were doing with the New Deal, only in German ways. Lebensraum was understandable, etc., etc. Hitler's bluff was of historic dimensions.'

On June 17, in further consolidating the power base of Nazism, Hitler placed all German police forces under the direct control of Heinrich Himmler, who was already chief of the SS. This brought the forces of law and order of both the Nazi Party and the German State under one roof: a roof beneath which terror was already well-established through the concentration camp system. That summer, in an ostentatious gesture designed to separate Nazism and religion yet further, Himmler publicly left the Catholic Church. His example was quickly followed by Hitler's personal bodyguard, and within a year by eight other senior SS leaders, by 214 of the SS guards at Dachau, and by all 250 SS-men at Sachsenhausen concentration camp, just north of Berlin.

Hitler wanted to show the German Nazi achievements to the world. His opportunity came in August, when Berlin was host to the Olympic Games. Never before had the Games been staged with such elaborate ceremonial. The Swastika flag seemed to be the ornament of a new civic grandeur. That a 'non-Aryan', the Black American runner Jesse Owens, won four gold medals was galling to the self-proclaimed 'master race', and to Hitler personally. But many of those who came from abroad to the Games were struck by all that was most modern and efficient in Nazi Germany. The former British Prime Minister, David Lloyd George, was even taken as an honoured visitor to Dachau concentration camp, where he expressed himself impressed by the hard work being done there by the prisoners of the Reich – whom he was shown at work, stripped to their waists in the hot sun, spades in hand, digging drainage ditches.

As he had done two years earlier with the Nuremberg Rally, so again with the Berlin Olympics Hitler decided to have a film made that would stress the Aryan and Germanic aspects of the Games. Once more his choice of producer was Leni Riefenstahl. It took her more than a year to complete the film, but when *Olympia* was finally shown, it too gave an incredibly vigorous and inspirational view of Nazi youth and its physical and national aspirations. But as in her earlier film *Triumph of the Will*, it is Hitler himself who is the central, and dominant figure, and symbol. The film historian Eric Rentschler writes: 'The prologue begins in Greece at the Temple of Zeus and ends in Berlin with an image of Hitler's profile. The leader stands as an unrivalled master of ceremonies, the Supreme Being who grants shape to a nation and its people.'

In September the annual Nazi Party Congress was held at Nuremberg. The theme was the launching of a crusade against the 'world danger of Bolshevism'. Germany would, according to the Nazi vision, become the world centre for Fascists and conservatives everywhere to fight 'Bolshevism, Socialism and the Jews'. The first diplomatic fruit of this crusade was an agreement signed before the end of the year (on November 24) between Germany and Japan, in which both signatories undertook to make 'common cause' against Communism. The first practical manifestation of the crusade was the German help sent to the Junta in Spain. This help included not only German aircraft and munitions, but German pilots, engineers and technical advisers. By the end of the year several complete battalions of German troops – amounting to at least 10,000 infantrymen – had arrived in Spain to fight for Franco. On November 18 both Germany and Italy recognized the Junta at Burgos, and General Franco, as the legitimate government of Spain.

As a result of its victories in Abyssinia in the first three months of 1936, Italy was also able to give considerable help to the Junta in Spain. In April the Abyssinian forces, rather than fall back towards the capital, Addis Ababa, decided to risk all in a direct military confrontation with the advancing Italians. The Emperor, Haile Selassie, took charge of the battle, seeking to push the Italian forces back. But within four days he and his troops were forced to retreat.

There was anger at the League of Nations when the first details of the Italian success reached Geneva. It appeared that this had been due in large measure to the use by the Italians of poison gas. Anthony Eden, who was in Geneva, demanded an inquiry, but before anything could be done, the Emperor abandoned his capital. No inquiry, however vigorously conducted, could save him or Abyssinia from defeat. The Emperor made his way to the port of Djibouti, on the Red Sea, and then by ship to Palestine, an exile appealing in vain to the world for the restoration of his kingdom. Italian troops entered Addis Ababa. In a mass rally in Rome, Mussolini announced the end of hostilities and the annexation of Abyssinia to Italy. The King of Italy was proclaimed Emperor of Abyssinia. An Italian Viceroy was appointed, Marshal Rodolfo Graziani.

Mussolini's top secret instructions that summer to Graziani ensured that the last pockets of resistance would be ruthlessly attacked. On June 5 he telegraphed: 'All rebels taken prisoner are to be shot', and three days later: 'Use gas to clean up the rebels.' A telegram on July 8 reiterated the policy of ruthlessness and sought to justify it. 'I once again authorize Your Excellency to initiate and systematically carry out a policy of terror and extermination against the rebels and their civilian accomplices,' Mussolini wrote. 'Unless the law of an eye for an eye is enforced the wound will not heal.'

With the conquest of Abyssinia, Italy controlled a large swathe of East Africa: Abyssinia, Eritrea and Somaliland. When the deposed Emperor, Haile Selassie, rose to address the League of Nations Assembly, the Italian journalists present made loud and disruptive interjections. They were arrested, and then expelled from Geneva. But the reality of power had passed to Italy, and economic sanctions, which had been but fitfully imposed on her during the hostilities, were lifted.

'Pacification', the word used to describe the military efforts of Britain, Germany, France and Spain before the First World War to extend their imperial control into the various hinterlands, was undertaken by Italy in Abyssinia throughout the summer and autumn. Even the main railway line between Addis Ababa and Djibouti was subject to spasmodic 'rebel' attacks. At the same time, Mussolini wanted to be seen as a model and enlightened ruler. On July 4 his Council of Ministers established special colonial administrative units for the whole region – known as Italian East Africa – with an autonomous road department, a corps of civil engineers, a sanitary corps, and a postal and telegraphic corps as examples of the determination to improve the conditions of the conquered peoples. Another corps created that same day, the political police, indicated that Fascist rule might not be entirely benign.

Mussolini also intended to promote widespread Italian immigration to Abyssinia. Italian factory corporations – ironworks, brickworks and cement works among them – were encouraged to transfer their productive enterprises to the new territory. Italian farmers were encouraged to emigrate to Abyssinia, with the promise that at a later stage the land which they cultivated there would become their own property. Mussolini had hoped that the Italian soldiers who had fought in Abyssinia would remain there, constituting the first substantial wave of colonization, but when pressure grew in the ranks for a return to Italy, that hope was abandoned. New troops and workmen, as many as 100,000, were then sent out, and encouraged to settle. At the same time, echoing Hitler's Nuremberg Laws of the previous year, strict rules were introduced – in this case to prevent a mingling of White Italian and Black Ethiopian blood.

German rearmament, and German preparations to wage war – activities which the Treaty of Versailles was meant to have ended for all time – were both becoming more and more evident. On October 3 the German Government launched a battle-cruiser, the *Scharnhorst*. At 35,000 tons, it was 10,000 tons above the Versailles Treaty limit. Sixteen days later Goering was appointed by Hitler to carry out a Four-Year Plan, the aim of which was to make Germany entirely independent of the supply of raw materials from abroad. In theory, this would give Germany enhanced warmaking powers from the early months of 1941. As Goering was widely known as 'the hero of 30 June 1934' – the Night of the Long Knives – his appointment also signified a determination to brook no opposition or disruptive tactics.

That November, Germany unilaterally denounced the section of the Versailles Treaty which established international control over five waterways that flowed through Germany: the Rhine, the Danube, the Elbe, the Oder and the Niemen. The French government hoped to obtain a collective protest against this by the signatories of the Versailles Treaty, but no such protest was forthcoming. For France, the need for increased military vigilance dominated the political agenda. The Maginot Line was strengthened, and in September, army manoeuvres were held: defence against a German invasion was their secret objective. Churchill was invited both to witness the manoeuvres and to inspect the Maginot Line. He did so and was impressed, writing to his wife Clementine on September 13: 'The officers of the French army are impressive by their gravity & competence. One feels the strength of the nation resides in its army.'

Hitler tried to persuade his German critics that there was no alternative to Nazism. On November 4 he spent three hours in conclave with the Catholic Archbishop of Munich, Cardinal Michael von Faulhaber, who had continued to express in public his dislike of Nazi methods. 'The Catholic Church should not deceive itself', Hitler told the Cardinal. 'If National Socialism does not succeed in defeating Bolshevism, then both Church and Christianity are finished in Europe.' Once more, as in *Mein Kampf* ten years earlier, Hitler portrayed himself as doing 'the Lord's work'.

On November 24 there was a sign of the contempt with which the western democracies held Nazism when the Nobel Peace Prize was awarded to one of Hitler's most outspoken opponents, the leading German pacifist Carl von Ossietzky, who had been held in the concentration camp at Esterwegen since 1933. Thomas Mann, from his exile in Switzerland, wrote to a friend when he learned the news: 'At last a stirring announcement, a sign of courage, of opposition in the world after all the soft-stepping and all the timid retreating.'

Under Goebbels's orchestration, the award to Ossietzky was described in the German newspapers as 'an insult to the new Germany'. Ossietzky himself died in hospital in Berlin two years later, broken by his concentration camp treatment, at the age of sixty-one.

During November the city councillors of Leipzig took the opportunity of the absence abroad of the Mayor, Dr Carl Goerdeler, to remove the statue of the composer Mendelssohn from its pedestal facing the town hall. Goerdeler had refused to 'penalize' Mendelssohn for being of Jewish ancestry. On his return from abroad he realized that he could no longer be effective in trying to maintain his anti-racial stance. He therefore resigned as mayor, and began an outspoken, and also clandestine career in opposition to Nazism that was to lead eleven years later to his execution.

In a further centralizing measure by the German government, on December 2 all tax-gathering powers, especially the all-important regional Land Tax, were taken away from the German States and placed under the Central Government in Berlin. In the sphere of propaganda, Dr Goebbels excelled himself. Food shortages were justified under the slogan: 'The German people must temporarily do without butter in order to produce the guns necessary for their defence!' Food shortages in Germany created discontent, however. In an attempt to alleviate this the German government abandoned its boast – and hope – that Germany was to be self-sufficient in foodstuffs, and began to import large quantities of butter, eggs, lard, pigs and cattle from neighbouring Denmark.

On December 8 a second battle-cruiser, the *Gneisenau*, was launched. Slowly but with definite intent, Germany was becoming a Great Power again. But in 1936 Germany's military preparations seemed puny when contrasted with those of the Soviet Union. The Soviet Union felt itself threatened on two fronts: the western front with Germany and the eastern front with Japan. Germany's introduction of conscription and Japan's consolidation of her position in Manchuria – along Russia's Far Eastern border – gave the impetus to a massive militarization. Russia's peacetime strength was set at 1,300,000 men (a hundred Divisions), 6,000 aeroplanes and 3,000 tanks. The military budget was doubled, and the age of conscription lowered from twenty-one to nineteen. In December a new Commissariat was established, that of Industry and Military Defence.

Inside the Soviet Union, forced labour, hitherto confined to the labour camps of North Russia and Siberia, was extended throughout the country as an unprecedented road-building plan was launched. A government decree of March 3 established for the inhabitants of all villages and farms six compulsory days' labour a year. All men between the ages of 18 and 45 and all women between the ages of 18 and 40 had to participate. Two ambitious canal systems, the White Sea-Baltic Canal in the north, and the Caspian-Black Sea Canal on the south, employed tens of thousands of slave labourers from the prison camps. Many thousands were to die while working on these canals, in conditions of extreme hardship, privation, and the lack of adequate food or shelter.

Trials and purges, that had marked and marred the previous year, continued, as ripple after ripple, fanning out in the aftermath of Kirov's murder two years earlier, turning into a tidal wave of destruction. Stalin was determined to eliminate all those who might rival or challenge his leadership or criticize his policies. From his exile in Norway, Leon Trotsky was issuing a chorus of complaints against the tyranny and failures of the Soviet regime. Stalin used this as an excuse to arrest all those who had been associated with Trotsky in the past at the highest level of government – men who had devoted their working lives to the establishment and maintenance of Soviet Communism since its early years. Suddenly these leaders were accused of seeking to destroy the Soviet Union from within, and of being the 'lackeys' of foreign powers. Seventeen leading Communists were put on public trial.

Among the accused was Mikhail Tomsky, who in the ten years following the revolution had been President of the Central Council of Soviet Trade Unions. In 1936 he was head of the State Publishing House. He committed suicide as the police came to arrest him.

On August 22, the last day of the trial, the prosecutor, Andrei Vyshinsky, demanded that all sixteen of those who stood in the dock should be shot. 'This society of political murderers, these beasts, must pay with their heads for their monstrous crime against the Fatherland,' he said. 'And this must be the fate of all other traitors who are ready to knife the Soviet Government in the back. Dreadful and monstrous are the aims and crimes which the accused directed against our Socialist Fatherland. Dreadful and monstrous is the guilt of these criminals and murderers who raised their hand against the leaders of our party.'

What *Pravda* described as 'stormy applause' greeted Vyshinsky's final demand, 'Shoot all the sixteen mad dogs'. He then shouted at the prisoners: 'Mad Fascist police dogs! Despicable rotten dregs of humanity! Scum of the underworld!' The accused were said to have been working with the Gestapo. They were all executed, or died soon afterwards in prison and labour camps.

Communists from the West frequently visited the Soviet Union and, having been well-feted and entertained, returned home to publish positive impressions of what they had seen. In 1936, however, the propaganda value of sympathetic visitors was dealt a blow when, on his return from a visit to the Soviet Union, André Gide published a pamphlet, *Retour de l'URSS*, in which, writing as a former Communist sympathizer, he poured ridicule on the claims made by Soviet apologists that the deportations, exploitations and lack of democratic freedoms were provisional – but essential – measures if the gains of the 1917 revolution were to be maintained. Gide's denunciation was especially powerful because, eight years earlier, he had established his radical credentials in two outspoken denunciations of French colonial exploitation in the French Equatorial Africa.*

The German attempt the previous year to undermine the Austrian government having failed, the Austrian Chancellor, Kurt von Schuschnigg, adopted dictatorial powers. Democratic and Socialist activity was sternly suppressed.

* *Voyage au Congo* in 1927 and *Retour du Chad* in 1928.

The new diplomatic orientation was towards Italy and Hungary, with both of whom Schuschnigg signed a Three Power Pact in March.

In the greatest secrecy Germany had been putting pressure on Austria for closer links with Germany. Hitler's intermediary in the final negotiations was von Papen, who two years earlier had spoken out against Nazism, but who now did the Chancellor's bidding. Hitler was also supported within Austria by a former officer of the Austro-Hungarian General Staff, Colonel Edmund Glaise-Horstenau, who, like Hitler, had been born at Braunau on the River Inn. Glaise-Horstenau was a militant Catholic turned Austrian Nazi.

On July 11 an agreement was signed, announced that day over the radio, whereby, while both Austria and Germany pledged not to 'seek to influence' the internal policies of the other, Austria promised that her policy would always be based on the recognition that she was 'a German State'. An amnesty was granted to Austrian Nazis who were then in prison, and Schuschnigg agreed to take two pro-Nazi Austrians into his Cabinet. One of them, Dr Guido Schmidt, was made Foreign Minister. The other, Colonel Glaise-Horstenau, was made Minister of the Interior, with control of the police.

Britain and France, and democrats everywhere, looked with alarm as the Swastika emblem was again allowed to be flown in Austria, as banned Nazi newspapers made their reappearance, and as the Nazi anthem, the Horst Wessel Song, was again heard in the streets (though according to the agreement only those who were German subjects were allowed to sing it).

Encouraged to do so by both Hitler and Mussolini, on October 1, Austria re-introduced conscription, as Germany had done the previous year, and called up 8,000 men. This was a violation of the Treaty of St Germain, just as Germany's conscription had been a violation of the Versailles Treaty. As with the German violation, the victorious powers of 1918 took no action. A month later Austria formally recognized the Italian conquest of Abyssinia, and pressed for Hungary's right to rearm to be allowed by the Versailles Powers.

Almost all of Europe was being disturbed by the collapse of the Versailles settlement – after less than twenty years – and by the strident claims of German Nazism. Without threatening war, without firing a shot, without crossing a border, Hitler's Germany had become to those who lived beyond its borders an object of fear and anger. No occasion was lost by Germany to assert its new-found confidence and its nationalistic demands. On December 9 a trial began in Switzerland which focused Nazi energies southward. The accused man was a Yugoslav Jewish medical student, David Frankfurter, the son of a rabbi. He had studied medicine in Germany from 1929, fleeing in 1933 and continuing his studies in Switzerland. He was charged with shooting dead Wilhlem Gustloff, Hitler's emissary in Switzerland. Frankfurter told the court that he had murdered Gustloff in order to 'avenge' fellow-Jews persecuted by the Nazis and to draw public attention to the fate of German Jews.

The German newspapers fulminated as much against Switzerland as against Frankfurter, trying to implicate the Swiss authorities in the murder. A 'Jewish-Marxist' organization, based in Switzerland and never apprehended by the Swiss, had used Frankfurter as a tool. The Swiss had allowed this to happen. None of this was true, but it was trumpeted from Germany, and made a bad impression on the Swiss. The German newspapers also demanded the death penalty for Frankfurter, but the criminal code of the Canton in which he was tried did not allow the death penalty. The maximum penalty for the crime was twenty-five years in prison. There was anger in Germany when Frankfurter was sentenced only to eighteen years.*

In Britain, the Fascist movement under the leadership of Sir Oswald Mosley took to the streets wearing black shirts in imitation of Mussolini, and promoting anti-Jewish sentiment in imitation of Hitler. Provocative marches were organized through the predominantly Jewish areas of London's East End. The Jews defended themselves, and on October 11, a week after a Fascist march through the East End, took part in what they described as a 'victory march' of their own. *The Times* reported on the following day:

Heavily escorted by mounted and foot police, a long procession marched from Tower Hill to Victoria Park, where meetings were held round three main platforms in the presence of big crowds. The demonstrators assembled and marched in orderly fashion, and the only disturbances on the route occurred in the neighbourhood of Victoria Park, where there were a few scuffles between the police and groups of Fascists who sought to interrupt the procession or expressed their hostility too freely.

Nine arrests were made in connection with the demonstration, the

* David Frankfurter was pardoned in 1945 and expelled from Switzerland. He went to Palestine, fought in the Israel War of Independence, studied sciences and joined the Israel Ministry of Defence. When the ban on entering Switzerland was lifted in 1969 he returned for a visit. He died in Israel, in 1982.

charges including wilful damage, assault, and obstructing the police.

At one point, it was reported, a party of about fifty young men, shouting 'Up with Fascism,' charged into the ranks of the procession and pulled down a Communist banner. A free fight began for possession of the banner, and the crowds began to surge forward. A short baton charge by a strong body of foot police put an end to the fight.

Further along the route groups of Fascist youth shouted the name of Mosley and raised their arms in the Fascist salute. The Jewish and Communist marchers responded by the clenched fist salute and chants of 'Ban the Blackshirt Army.' Finally the marchers drew near to their destination:

At the head of the procession were a number of ex-Service men, many wearing medals and carrying banners inscribed: 'National Ex-Service Men's League Against Fascism.'

Marching behind a uniformed band which set off from Tower Hill playing 'The Red Flag' the ex-Service men also displayed half a dozen Union Jacks. Others in the procession carried scores of Communist red flags, and there were other banners on which were anti-Fascist slogans and caricatures of Sir Oswald Mosley . . .

A party of fifty or more young Fascists made some attempt to interrupt the meeting a few minutes after it had begun. They advanced shouting towards the platforms, but when they were still about a hundred yards away the police charged them, and they turned and ran to another part of the park. Here they tried to reassemble, but the police again dispersed them without drawing their batons. Two of the Fascists were left lying on the grass after the scuffle, and had to receive first aid.

Within three months the British Government passed a Public Order Act, banning uniforms in street processions, and giving the police the power to forbid such processions altogether. The Fascist Movement, without a single seat in parliament, was increasingly held up to mockery and obloquy. There was no constituency in which a Fascist candidate could secure the votes of anything approaching a majority of the local electorate.

Beyond Europe, but still within the control of a European power, the violence that broke out within British Mandate Palestine in 1936 was the worst since Britain had pledged herself almost twenty years earlier to the creation in

Palestine of a Jewish National Home. The violence first took the form of Arab attacks on Jews and Jewish property. It developed into a series of bloody clashes between the Arabs and the British. In some instances Arabs killed Arabs: the Mayor of Hebron was shot dead outside his house because he had opposed the acts of violence by his fellow-Arabs.

More than 30,000 British troops were deployed throughout Palestine. They could not maintain control even of the main roads. One of their adversaries was a Syrian soldier, Fawzi Kawakji, who led a band of armed men calling themselves the Army of Southern Syria. Escaping from Palestine when the fighting died down, he was welcomed in Baghdad as a hero. Twelve years later he was to return to Palestine, and die in another war, the Israeli War of Independence.

The death toll when the disturbances ended in 1936 was 187 Muslim Arabs, 80 Jews and 28 British soldiers and police. Some of the Arabs were killed by machine gun fire from British aeroplanes. A Royal Commission, sent to examine the cause of the disturbances, and to recommend what should be done to avoid them in future, produced the radical proposal of partition: the creation in Palestine of two separate States, one Jewish and one Arab, with Britain retaining control of Jerusalem. The Jews of Palestine were tempted by Statehood, even if it was in less than a third of the country, and excluded the city they regarded as holy. The Arabs rejected the idea of partition altogether: they wanted sovereignty throughout Palestine. No solution was reached, beyond a curtailment of Jewish immigration which the British hoped would mollify Arab hostility. Britain rejected outright the principal Arab demands: an end to all Jewish immigration and the prohibition of the sale of land to Jews.

Britain would remain the ruler, and maintain law and order as best she could. Some Jewish immigration could continue. Those Jews who sought to enter Palestine without permits, the 'illegals', would be arrested and deported. Jews could continue to buy land and, as they had done every year, build new settlements.

Palestine lay on the western edge of Asia. On the eastern edge the vast mass of China continued to witness the twin struggles of Communist against Nationalist Chinese, and Communist and Nationalist Chinese against the Japanese. The five northern provinces of China seemed to the Japanese — already masters of Manchuria — to be a natural area of imminent control, and Japanese military reinforcements were sent to the area. The Chinese protested. In anti-Japanese demonstrations in August, two Japanese were killed. Further killings followed. Chiang Kai-shek apologized, but when the Japanese asked him to accept Japanese military help against the Chinese Communists, he refused.

For ten years the Nationalist centre of power had been divided between Nanking, where Chiang Kai-shek ruled supreme, and Canton and the south, where various senior generals controlled the Nationalist regions. In June, Nationalist generals based in Kwangtung and Kwangsi provinces, combined their forces to form an Anti-Japanese Salvation Army which, marching northwards, ostensibly to challenge the Japanese, was seen by Chiang Kai-shek as aimed against himself. He immediately sent his own troops to block their advance. Negotiations began, but broke down; it looked as if civil war would break out between the Nationalists and Communist Chinese. But Chiang Kai-shek's leading opponent in Canton, Hu Han-min, died in Canton, and the anti-Chiang Kai-shek grouping began to fall apart. The first to defect to Chiang Kai-shek were the Cantonese air pilots, followed by some of the Kwangtung Army commanders. A Pacification Commission was established, and the Canton Nationalists agreed to accept Chiang Kai-shek's overall control. He entered Canton itself on August 11, for first time in ten years.

In the north, the Communists were more successful, crossing the Yellow River into Shansi, defeating the government forces there, and besieging the towns of Pingyang and Hungtung. Frightened that the Japanese would use this Communist success to move down from the north and intervene militarily, Chiang Kai-shek sent 100,000 troops to Shansi and regained control of the province for the Nationalists.

There was an internal political drama in China that year when, on December 8, Chiang Kai-shek flew from Nanking to Sian, the capital of Shensi Province, to inspect the Nationalist troops. They were commanded by a local warlord, Marshal Chang, and Chiang Kai-shek intended to urge Chang to take action against Communist columns that were even then escaping the Nationalist net and making for the safety of Yenan. Immediately on reaching Sian, however, Chiang Kai-shek was arrested, as were those with him: these included the Pacification Commissioner, the Minister of the Interior and the Vice-Minister for War. Chang then announced that the aim of his coup was to form a common front with the Chinese Communists against the Japanese.

Marshal Chang had been reluctant to fight the Communist armies, despite repeated urgings to do so by the Nationalists. He preferred to fight the

Japanese, who had earlier defeated him both in Manchuria and south of the Great Wall. He allowed Chiang Kai-shek to establish a small headquarters in the hills outside Sian. From there, far from his own armies and supporters, the Generalissimo urged Marshal Chang to join forces against the Communists.

At dawn on December 12, units of Marshal Chang's army attacked Chiang Kai-shek's headquarters. Most of Chiang Kai-shek's bodyguards were killed, but the Generalissimo escaped over a wall, fleeing in his night clothes to a cave on the mountainside. He was soon captured. The Nanking Government, fearing that their leader was lost, appointed a new Generalissimo of the Nationalist forces. In Sian, Marshal Chang continued negotiations with his prisoner. Intent on forming a united front against the Japanese, Chang invited Chou En-lai to Sian and flew him to Sian to put pressure on Chiang. Chou En-lai did so willingly: he had received a telegram from Stalin telling him that the whole episode might have been 'engineered' by the Japanese to drive a wedge between the various Chinese factions and stimulate a civil war that could only benefit Japan.

After his discussion with Chou En-lai, Chiang Kai-shek offered to 'review the situation' and to continue negotiations with both Marshal Chang and the Communists in Nanking. He made this offer while still in his prison cell, completely cut off from any source of rescue. His confidential adviser, an Australian, W.H. Donald – who had earlier held the same position with Marshal Chang – undertook the task of mediation.

On December 25 Chiang Kai-shek was released. Marshal Chang then went to Nanking to accept Chiang Kai-shek as his leader, and, in a letter to Chiang Kai-shek, described himself as 'naturally rustic, surly and unpolished'. He regretted his 'impudent and surly act' and offered to submit to any punishment. He was sentenced to ten years' in prison, but immediately pardoned.

The agreement reached at Sian was very much to the advantage of the Communists. There were to be no attacks on Communist columns, but, instead, joint Communist-Nationalist attacks on the Japanese. For their part the Communists also agreed to curb their attacks on the Nationalists. The popular Communist poet Ting Ling, who had earlier seen some of her closest colleagues shot by the Nationalists, called for Communist cooperation with the Nanking Government against Japan.

The dangers to China from Japan were put in high profile during 1936, as the militarists in Tokyo demanded greater expenditure on the army and an even more forward policy in China. On February 26 a group of junior officers, supported by more than a thousand troops of the Tokyo garrison, broke into the houses of several leading statesmen and industrialists. The Prime Minister was fortunate to escape. But the Lord Keeper of the Privy Seal, Admiral Saito, was murdered, as were the Minister of Finance and the Inspector-General of Military Training.

The government took rapid action, throwing a cordon of loyal troops around the area held by the mutineers and placing Tokyo under martial law. After two days of negotiation, the soldiers surrendered. Several of their leaders committed suicide. Thirteen were condemned to death. But the cause of militarism was not lost, and in the government that was formed after the mutiny two leading militarists were given senior posts: General Terauchi as Minister of War and General Isogai as Director-General of the Military Affairs Bureau of the War Office. But the attempted continuation of an aggressive forward policy in Manchuria, aimed at the conquest of Outer Mongolia, was challenged by the Soviet Union, and there was fighting at several places along the Soviet-Manchurian border between Japanese and Soviet troops.

In the international sphere Japan was becoming more sharply aligned with Germany, and with potential territorial expansion. In November a Japanese-German Convention was signed in Berlin to 'combat the subversive activities' of the Moscow-based Communist International, the Comintern. Also that year Japan withdrew from the London Naval Disarmament Conference after its proposal for a 'common upper limit' of naval strength was rejected. The Japanese navy could henceforth build without restrictions. In Tokyo, the Navy Minister declared that Japan had at last been 'released from the naval ratio bondage'. A new area of Japanese naval interests was defined, including the Japanese Mandated islands – that had belonged to Germany before 1918 – extending as far south as the equator and as far east as the 180th meridian. The publishing in Britain that February of Lieutenant-Commander Tota Ishimaru's book *Japan Must Fight Britain* caused ripples of alarm: the author, an officer of the Imperial Japanese Navy, set out a scenario in which Japan declared war on England and, by skilful use of her naval power, was victorious.

'Manchuria alone is not enough,' Ishimaru warned. 'With it Japan cannot go on.' As for China, she was 'anti-foreign, inclined to turn Red, and in a state of disorder'.

*　　　*　　　*

On August 26, Egypt's sovereignty and independence were recognized by treaty with Britain. It was fifty-four years since the British bombardment of Alexandria, which heralded the start of British control. Even as negotiations for independence began in the early months of 1936, anti-British rioting had provided a violent background. But Britain's one strategic demand, to retain control of the Suez Canal, was accepted. British troops would be responsible for the defence of the Canal until such time as the Egyptian government 'was able to undertake the defence itself'. No specific time when this might happen was mentioned. In the event, Britain was to have twenty more years astride the Canal.

King Fuad having died during the year, the new King, under whom Egypt faced independence, was his sixteen-year-old son Farouk, who was still at school in England. The young king soon returned home and began to assert his authority. Within a year of coming to the throne he demanded the dissolution of the Blueshirts, a private army loyal to the Muslim religious organization, the Wafd. When the Prime Minister opposed him on this issue, Farouk had him replaced, and the Blueshirts were made illegal.

In the United States, social distress found eloquent voices to make it known. In her novel *The Trouble I've Seen*, Martha Gellhorn depicted the poverty which led to child prostitution. A young girl, Ruby, after her grim encounters with the men who use her body, wants to live with her mother, but the courts will not allow it:

> 'I can't take you, Ruby.'
> Ruby's body went hard in her mother's arms.
> 'They won't let me take you home. They say I'm not fit to keep you. They say I should have known what you were doing, and if I didn't then I'm not a good mother,'
> Her voice stopped, as if there was no more breath inside; came to a stop from emptiness, as if there was nothing to say anymore, ever.
> Ruby wept . . .

Martha Gellhorn was herself deeply involved in the New Deal, working as an investigator for the Works Progress Administration, which would have an average enrolment of two million jobs during its seven-year history. This was its second year. The projects chosen, which were intended to make a genuine contribution without competing with private business, included street and highway building, public housing and slum clearance, restoring forests, extending electrical power to rural communities, and the construction of public buildings and even airports.

Roosevelt continued to find his New Deal legislation being undermined by the Supreme Court. During 1936 the Agricultural Adjustment Act was declared unconstitutional. The basis of the act was a tax imposed on the manufacturers and processors of farm produce, the proceeds of which would be given to the farmers as payment for withholding certain land from culti- vation or reducing their livestock, so as not to create unmarketable surpluses. It was a skilful piece of economic engineering, designed to meet the need of the hour, but the Supreme Court ruled that the Federal government had no right to impose it on individual States.

Faced by the hostile decision of the Court, Roosevelt was not without a stratagem of his own. New legislation was introduced, and passed through Congress, the Soil Conservation Act, which effectively preserved the Govern- ment's control of farm surpluses, as envisaged under the Act that had been declared unconstitutional. The central logic of the new Act was that over- farming was leading to the creation of enormous dust storms which dispersed thousands of tons of top soil. In some areas the pasture for cattle had been completely destroyed, creating 'dust bowls' where nothing would grow.

Under the Soil Conservation Act as many as 30 million acres were to be transferred from intensive cultivation of soil-exhausting crops into grassland and vegetable cultivation. Special stress was put on crops that would preserve the fertility of the soil. Farmers received a Federal grant for every acre of land which they were prepared to transform. To avoid a further conflict with the Supreme Court over the rights of the federal government to act nationally in this way, the Act specifically laid down that after two years its operation and financing would be taken over by individual States. 'Rural rehabilitation: in itself a magnificent idea,' Martha Gellhorn wrote in *The Trouble I've Seen*. 'A chance for men to be again self-supporting; their own masters; captains of their destinies, souls, pocket-books.'

The intensity with which Roosevelt's policy of Federal intervention was resented by those who believed in the powers and legitimacy of laissez faire was enormous. In June, the Supreme Court struck down another of the central planks of Roosevelt's legislation, the New York State Minimum Wage Law for women and children. As a result of the imposition of a minimum wage, the Supreme Court ruled, the property rights of the employers were being violated. As a result of this ruling, minimum wage laws in seventeen States were made unconstitutional, and had to be revoked.

Roosevelt continued on his course, devising economic measures that would boost the economy, such as the opening of the Hoover Dam on the Colorado River to provide hydro-electricity, and shrugging off the complaints of men like the newspaper proprietor William Randolph Hearst that his policies smacked of 'communism'. At the Republican Convention, held in Cleveland on June 10 the Party platform warned that as a result of Roosevelt's interventionist policies the character of American men and women as free citizens, and their individual opportunities, 'for the first time are threatened by the Government itself.' To such criticisms Roosevelt answered ascerbically that he at least was 'trying to do something', and at the Democratic Convention on June 27, held in Philadelphia, the party platform declared with pugnacious pride: 'We have taken the business man out of the red. We have saved his bank, and given it a sounder foundation; we have extended credit; we have lowered interest rates; we have undertaken to free him from the ravages of cut-throat competition. We will keep him on the road to freedom and prosperity.'

Electioneering had begun. Roosevelt toured the country addressing large audiences. He was also an effective radio speaker. But the main newspapers, led by those controlled by Hearst from coast to coast, attacked him without respite. Democrats feared that this barrage of contempt might be effective. But when the nation went to the polls on November 3 it cast an astounding sixty per cent in favour of the President. In 1932 he had won twenty-two million votes. In 1936 he polled twenty-seven million, against his Republican rival's sixteen million. Under the electoral college system, Roosevelt carried every State but two.

The United States could not be unaffected by the growing military power of Nazi Germany. Despite the vast ocean that lay between Europe and the Americas, it was only twenty years since American troops had been sent to Europe and had fought to defeat that same Germany. On September 7 the Secretary of State, Cordell Hull, issued a serious public warning that 'a general war now would set loose forces that would be beyond control – forces which might easily bring about a virtual destruction of modern political thought, with all its achievements, and possibly a veritable shattering of our civilization.'

Many of Roosevelt's supporters in Congress demanded a policy of strictest neutrality with regard to Europe. There were persistent demands that, in the event of war breaking out in Europe, the United States should impose a complete embargo on arms sales to either side in the conflict. Not only munitions, but all material capable of sustaining a war economy, was to be included in this embargo. A minority of Roosevelt's supporters wanted the United States to have the right to help one side against another: the intervention of Germany and Italy in support of the Junta in Spain seemed to create a one-sided foreign involvement that the United States ought to be in a position to rectify, if it decided to do so. The German verbal attacks on Czechoslovakia throughout the year also created sympathy for the Czechs. But the proposed legislation would prevent American help being sent to Czechoslovakia if she were to be attacked by Germany. Those sympathetic to Czechoslovakia wanted Roosevelt to be given some latitude in deciding to help a nation that was under attack. At least, they said, the country for whom the United States had sympathy ought to be permitted to buy the supplies it needed, short of actual munitions, in the United States, and pay for, and transport them to Europe at its own risk. This was known as the 'cash and carry' policy.

As the debate on neutrality versus cash and carry raged, Roosevelt kept his views to himself. But he was known to favour some form of American involvement wherever 100 per cent neutrality 'threatened the destruction of democratic States'. The existing Neutrality Law was, however, strengthened by Congress on the last day of 1936, when the 'one hundred percenters' — as they were known — obtained a clause which prevented the shipment of war material to either side in the Spanish Civil War.

The First World War was remembered that summer, when both the German and French governments agreed to establish a preserved area around Vimy Ridge, on French soil, as a permanent war memorial to the war dead of all the combatants. When the Canadian monument at Vimy was unveiled, four thousand Canadian veterans gathered at the ceremony of dedication. Three days later they were addressed in Westminster Hall, London, by the British Prime Minister, Stanley Baldwin. 'I am confident of this,' he told them. 'If the dead could come back today there would be no war. They would never let the younger generation taste what they did. You all tasted that bitter cup of war. They drank it to the dregs.'

Baldwin went on to warn that 'if Europe and the world can find no other way of settling disputes than the way of war, even now when we are still finding and burying the bodies of those who fell twenty years ago — if they can find no other way, the world deserves to perish.'

The world could not live on past sorrows any more than on future promises. An exciting prospect was on offer for those who wanted to enjoy the most recent achievements of culture and communications. In March, Imperial Airways began a weekly commercial service from Croydon airport, just south of London, to Hong Kong, via Penang in Malaya. The flights took ten days. On June 25 the first twice-daily non-stop commercial air service was opened between New York and Chicago. The flight brochure noted that at the 'christening ceremonies' of the new service it was 'acclaimed by socialites, prominent business men, public officials and Naval officers'. The journey eastbound took three hours and fifty-five minutes.*

On November 23 a new illustrated magazine, *Life*, was launched in the United States. It was to introduce millions of Americans to the visual world of politics, art, fashion, sports and travel. The first issue included what was described as 'the first air photograph ever published of the future gold fortress of the United States' – Fort Knox, where the Treasury Department was about to concentrate its gold reserves, valued at $10,000 million. Among more than twenty articles was one about the 12,000 Chinese living in San Francisco, and another about relief works in north-eastern Montana, which was given the enticing headline: 'Franklin Roosevelt has a wild west'. A photograph showed the sheriff of one Montana town, Wheeler, 'toting' his gun.

In Britain, television transmissions began on a daily basis in November (they were to be suspended three years later on the outbreak of the Second World War). In the world of music, the 'swing' era of jazz had begun, with band leader and broadcaster Benny Goodman the widely-proclaimed King of Swing. In the world of art, while the Nazi, Fascist and Communist regimes of Europe imposed strict rules on what could be exhibited, and censored those works of art judged to be unsuitable or degenerate, in the United States no such prohibitions applied. Among the exhibitions at the Museum of Modern Art in New York during 1936, one was of 'Cubism and Abstract Art' and another of 'Fantastic Art, Dada and Surrealism'.

Initiatives in art, as in music, sculpture, architecture, town planning and travel, exciting though they were, had nevertheless to compete in the public consciousness with a growing fear, which had been expressed by Siegfried Sassoon four years earlier when he warned that 'poor panic-stricken hordes'

---

* A typical commercial journey time from Chicago to New York in 1998, allowing for manoeuvering above and around the airports, was two hours.

would hear the 'hum' of aircraft and that 'fear' and 'flight' would become synonymous. When a Welsh correspondent protested to David Lloyd George, against the establishment of an aerial bombing school near Lloyd George's own former Welsh home at Criccieth – the former wartime Prime Minister wrote:

> I live in Surrey, in a neighbourhood where military aeroplanes are humming night and day over my house, but I should not join in a petition from the inhabitants of the neighbourhood to remove this nocturnal torment to some other part of the country where it would disturb the rest of others.
>
> If there is to be bombing there must be a bombing school somewhere. Where would you put it? My remedy would be to abolish it altogether by international agreement.
>
> The nations very nearly came to terms once; why not make another real effort? Bombing experiments before war are bad, but the real horror is the use to which it is contemplated they should be put if war unfortunately breaks out amongst the nations.

Air rearmament, not international agreement to phase out or to abolish bombing, was at the top of every national agenda. When Albert Einstein was invited to contribute a message to a time capsule on paper that was guaranteed to last a thousand years, his message began: 'Dear Posterity! If you have not become more just, more peaceful, and generally more rational than we are (or were), – why then, The Devil take you.'

CHAPTER FIVE

1937

> What is it really worth, this wonderful machine
> civilization, if it has no inherent force to prevent a
> destruction like this?
>
> J. GUNNAR ANDERSSON

THE TWENTIETH CENTURY was never free from the plight and burden of refugees, and their personal suffering. In 1937 there were an estimated 700,000 refugees worldwide. It was the League of Nations that set itself the task of ameliorating their plight. But not all governments were willing to cooperate: particularly those who were the cause of a continuous flight of refugees. The Soviet government was particularly emphatic that the League had no right to intervene with regard to refugees from Russia, towards whom the Soviet authorities expressed nothing but contempt, and for whose well-being it felt no responsibility whatsoever.

Colonial rule remained an object of challenge, despite the superior military forces, and the administrative experience, of the rulers. In French Morocco the nationalist movement continued to challenge French rule. On September 2, during a nationalist demonstration at Meknes, ten people were killed. Rioting spread to Marrakech, Casablanca and Fez. It was only when French troops managed to trap a number of the ringleaders of the revolt in the narrow lanes of the old city of Fez that the disorders subsided.

On the Waziristan frontier of India, Muslim insurgents continued to attack British outposts. In May, Britain's main adversary, the Fakir of Ipi, was driven from his stronghold near the Afghan border, but local tribal disturbances continued. A British military contingent of more than sixty thousand men was assembled to pacify the region, and a programme of emergency roadbuilding was begun, to provide more rapid access to the disaffected areas. More than two hundred British troops were killed and several hundred wounded before the British judged it possible to withdraw, leaving a civil administration to assert such British authority as it could over the region.

In another British colony, Barbados, there was discontent as the worldwide economic slump led to the collapse of sugar prices and widespread unemployment and hardship. The price of sugar had fallen precipitately, from twenty-six shillings a hundredweight to five shillings in five years. On March 27 a young labour organizer, Clement Payne, arrived on the island from Trinidad. A historian of Barbados, Hilary Beckles, writes of how Payne 'did not confine his fiery speeches to the labour question' but also spoke of race relations and Black cultural oppression. Arrested by the British, Payne was brought to trial in the capital, Bridgetown, and found guilty on July 22 of making a false claim that he had been born in Barbados. The conviction was reversed by the Court of Appeal on July 26. On the following day, as Payne's supporters prepared to take him from jail, the British deported him to Trinidad.

As soon as the news that Payne had been spirited away reached the crowd outside the jail, there were riots which continued all night. Barbadan workers clashed with police, and cars and property were destroyed. On the following day groups of workers, armed with sticks, stones and bottles, attacked the city's commercial centre. The police took drastic action, opening fire on the rioters, and killing fourteen of them. Payne's successor as leader of the discontented Barbadans was Israel Lowell. He told his followers: 'We cannot steal from the white man, because if we take anything it would only be some of what they have stolen from our fore-parents for the past two hundred and fifty years.'

The rebellion in Payne's name was the last rebellion on the island, which twenty-nine years later became an independent republic.

Italy, a colonial power in both North and East Africa, found that its rule in Abyssinia, so recently conquered, was under continual challenge. In mid-February an attempt was made in Addis Ababa on the life of the Italian Viceroy, Marshal Graziani. As a reprisal, several thousand Abyssinians were massacred. Later that month, when the Abyssinian guerrilla leader, Ras Desta Damtou, was caught, he was immediately shot.

Among the international protests against Italian rule was a conference organized by two newspapers, *The Times* and *Ethiopia News*, at Central Hall, Westminster, on September 9, entitled 'Abyssinia and Justice'. The speakers included Sylvia Pankhurst, daughter of the pre-First World War suffragette leader Emmeline Pankhurst – a co-fighter with her mother for women's rights, who had made the cause of African independence her main task in life.* She was photographed at the conference talking to a Kenyan then living in London, Jomo Kenyatta, of the Kikuyu tribe, whose book *Facing Mount Kenya*, published the following year, helped establish him as a national leader of his people.

Inside Abyssinia, small guerrilla groups continued to attack the occupying forces. An Italian military communiqué of October 13 told of fifty-eight Italians being killed during a reconnaissance operation.

One small, disputed territory whose fate was thrust into the international consciousness in 1937 was the former Ottoman Sandjak of Alexandretta. Both Turkey and Syria claimed control over this area, Hatay, which included the most north-easterly port in the Mediterranean, Alexandretta (in Turkish, Iskenderun). In an attempt to prevent the territory being given to either side, and thus offending the other, France, as the former Mandatory Power, established the Sandjak as an independent republic. This was distressing to Turkey, but was upheld by the League of Nations. Kemal Atatürk had no intention of accepting this verdict as the final one, and his methods of protest could be unconventional. While dining at a restaurant in Ankara he saw the French Ambassador, Monsieur Ponsot, at a nearby table. He at once, in the words of his biographer Lord Kinross, 'called upon the ladies at his table to raise their hands and shout, "We want Hatay!" One of his adopted daughters chanced to have a toy revolver in her bag and he made her fire it off. The explosion took M. Ponsot aback and Atatürk playfully sent for the police and had her arrested for the illegal use of firearms.' He then informed his Prime Minister, Ismet Inönü, 'that the women of Turkey must have Hatay' and instructed him to make representations on their behalf to the French Government.

Turkey planned to take unilateral action. When, a year later, Atatürk sent his troops into Hatay and annexed it, there was no force that Syria or the League of Nations felt able to apply to dislodge them.

In the United States, where President Roosevelt's efforts to introduce New Deal legislation were meeting with increasing opposition from the Supreme Court, several Acts had already been declared to be unconstitutional. The

* In 1956, at the age of seventy-four, Sylvia Pankhurst went to live in Ethiopia, where she died four years later.

bias of the Court was clearly opposed to the various Federal schemes and Federal interventions which lay at the basis of the legislation. American conservatism had always rejected the interventionist approach by government. It was a persistent theme in preventing what was seen by many American constitutionalists as too great a power being vested in the central government, over both individual States of the Union, and over the individual citizen.

On February 6, Roosevelt decided to strike at the root of this problem. In a message to Congress that day – a message described by the newspapers as 'sensational' – he demanded a reorganization of the whole Federal judiciary. The gravamen of Roosevelt's charge was this: 'It matters not that Congress has enacted the law, that the executive has signed it, and that the administrative machinery is waiting to function. The judiciary, by postponing the effective dates of Acts of Congress, is assuming an additional function and is coming more and more to constitute a scattered, loosely organized and slowly operating Third House of the National legislature.' This immense power, Roosevelt added, was being wielded by old men who, 'assuming that the scene is the same as it was in the past, cease to explore or to inquire into the present or the future'.

Roosevelt proposed that he be given power to appoint extra judges whenever a Federal judge (each of whom who had life tenure) who had reached seventy and had served for ten years failed to resign or retire. Under the plan that he proposed, the nine judges of the Supreme Court could be expanded to fifteen. Clearly he would only appoint those who were supportive of his ideas and plans. Angrily, the Republicans claimed that Roosevelt was aiming to 'pack' the Supreme Court with his nominees. The scheme was denounced in the Hearst newspapers as 'fascism' and a step towards what they described as the president's goal of 'dictatorship'. The American Bar Association, a bastion of conservatism, passed a series of resolutions condemning the scheme. The Chief Justice of the Supreme Court, Charles Evans Hughes, issued a public statement in which he warned the United States against 'the most unwise fervour of crusaders which may carry a dominant majority over into oppression, destroying the basic values of democratic government.'

Roosevelt stood his ground. Then, with no new judges having been appointed, the Supreme Court itself reversed its decision. On March 29, while Roosevelt's Bill for judicial change was still being debated, the Supreme Court voted by five justices to four to declare the Minimum Wage for Women Act of the State of Washington to be a legal and constitutionally valid piece of legislation. This was less than a year after the same Supreme Court had thrown out a similar minimum wage act for the State of New York. Nor was this the only New Deal legislation that suddenly found favour in the eyes of the hitherto hostile justices: a Moratorium Act for keeping down farm mortgages was likewise judged to be in keeping with the constitution, even though it took away the same 'property rights' of the mortgage companies (by forcing them to keep down mortgages) as the collective bargaining sections of the previous year's Railway Labor Act had done, which the Supreme Court had reversed.

Roosevelt's Bill to change the judiciary was not making good progress in Congress. But the judiciary itself seemed to have found new inspiration in the legality of the New Deal concept of Federal intervention to protect the weak and the poor, so much so that on May 24 it approved the Social Security Act, one of Roosevelt's most revolutionary measures.

Roosevelt's proposal of February 5 to change the basis of the senior judiciary was defeated in Congress on July 22. The aim of its passage, however, had been achieved. The Supreme Court was no longer setting itself up as a political opponent.

On February 27 the French government took measures designed to protect France against a German attack: the creation of a Ministry of Defence, a further extension of the Maginot Line of forts, and the nationalization of the Schneider-Creusot arms factory. In Czechoslovakia, Thomas Masaryk's successor as President, Eduard Benes, was taking steps to strengthen the frontier with Germany that ran along the northern, western and southern boundaries of the State.

Benes had also to take into account the growing influence of Nazi Germany on the Bohemian Germans living mostly in the Sudeten mountain border regions. These Czechoslovak citizens had been citizens of Austria-Hungary before 1918: they had never been part of the German Reich. Although they were known as Bohemian Germans, the Nazis across the border called them *Sudetendeutsch* – Sudeten Germans – and under this name those of them who wanted union with Germany campaigned with growing verbal violence against the Czechoslovak State and its democracy.

The British writer, Elizabeth Wiskemann, who visited the predominantly German-speaking town of Cheb – known in German as Eger – shortly after Masaryk's death, recalled in her memoirs: 'For many years Eger had been a pan-German centre: nevertheless I had not expected to see Germans spit at photographs of Masaryk which Czechs had displayed. Coming from the grief of Prague, I was startled by this, but it showed me how unafraid the Sudeten Germans were. Of all the minorities in inter-war Europe, they were indubitably the best off.'

The only fighting in Europe during 1937 was in Spain. Throughout the year the Spanish civil war raged and the armies clashed in increasing intensity. During January small territorial gains were made by both sides, but no one side could gain the ascendancy. On January 13 Hitler sent General Faupel to Spain to report what should be done so that Germany could 'derive the utmost advantage' from the civil war. Faupel recommended the despatch of 80,000 more men from Italy and Germany. His advice was taken.

Madrid, though it faced no immediate danger of being overrun in the first month of the year, suffered from repeated bombing and artillery attack, so much so that the seat of government was moved to Valencia. In February there was a fierce battle on the Jarama River, south-east of Madrid. A British Communist member of the International Brigade, Jimmy Younger, wrote to a friend:

> The Battle of Jarama, on 12 February 1937, was one of the toughest of the whole Civil War. The Moors and the International Brigade clashed head-on in the hills. It was slaughter. At the end of the first day my Battalion, the Saklatvala, 400 strong to start with, was reduced to less than one hundred. I could hear the wounded moaning and calling to us as they lay between the lines.
>
> At the end of a week I knew the meaning of war. I can still see the blood and the dead faces; worse still, the expression in the eyes of the dying. I felt no anti-Fascist anger, but only overwhelming pity.

The Saklatvala Battalion was named after the first British Communist Member of Parliament, Shapurji Saklatvala, a Bombay-born Parsi who before the First World War had helped to establish India's largest iron and steel works. He had died on the eve of the Spanish Civil War.

Also fighting on the Jarama were 373 officers and men of the Abraham Lincoln Battalion. These American volunteers were sent into the attack for the first time on February 23. Their attack was supported by two Soviet tanks, which took the bulk of the defenders' fire, until one tank was hit and the other turned away. The combat was ill-fated. Not one of the eight machine guns – the Americans' most effective weapon – was in working order. The men were forced to retreat. Twenty of their number lay dead on the battlefield. Even back in their trenches hazards lurked: one volunteer, Bob Norwood, was shot in the head and killed by sniper fire as he drank from a coffee urn.

A second attack by the Americans four days later was equally unsuccessful, the artillery barrage that was intended to support them beginning three hours late and falling wide of its objectives. Twenty Republican planes had been promised to assist the attack: only three appeared. Of the 263 men who went into battle that day, only 150 returned. One of the dead was a young actor from Boston, John Lenthier, who, wounded as he ran forward, died with his full pack still strapped to his back, pressing him down. The *New York Times* correspondent, Herbert Matthews, told his readers that the American volunteers 'knew nothing of soldiering and had precious little time to learn it'. They were, he wrote, 'still raw as soldiers, but they were ripe in spirit'. Robert Merriman – later Chief of Staff of the brigade – had been badly wounded in the second attack. He recalled being taken to a front-line medical station: 'It was a butcher's shop. People died on stretchers in the yard . . . Went to the operating room. Pulling bullets out of a man who had become an animal. Several doctors operating on stomach exploring for bullets while others died.' Merriman was a graduate in economics at the University of California at Berkeley.

Supported by a naval bombardment, and with the participation of Navarese Traditionalists (*requetés*), Moroccan troops and Spanish Legionaries, the Junta captured Malaga. An Italian military column took part in the triumphal entry into the city, and throughout Italy the 'Italian victory' was proclaimed. As the fighting near Malaga continued, 150,000 refugees, fearful of the impositions of army rule, fled towards Almeria.

The loss of Malaga caused the government to reconsider the organizational structure of national defence. Hitherto, volunteers had made up the bulk of the government forces. After Malaga, conscription was introduced. Hitherto, four separate groups of forces – defending the Madrid, Cordoba, Teruel and Aragon fronts – had operated as best they could according to their respective local needs. After Malaga, a single military command was established. These changes were made as a result of pressure from the Communist Party leaders in the government. They were encouraged in maintaining an active resistance

by the Soviet Ambassador in Madrid, Marcel Rosenberg. But Stalin had no
intention of taking too visible a part in the conflict, or in risking a direct
confrontation with Germany and Italy. On February 19, Rosenberg was
recalled. He later disappeared without trace, a victim of the purges. His
'crime', apparently, was to have tried to arrange an exchange of prisoners –
Nationalists held by Republicans for Republicans held by Nationalists. For
such sane humanity there could be no forgiveness.

Although Soviet war material continued to reach the Republican forces,
the number of Soviet citizens who were allowed to participate in the fighting
was no more than 3,000, most of them technicians and pilots. The number of
Italian soldiers sent to Spain, 40,000, included complete military formations
commanded by Italian officers. The number of German participants on the
side of the Insurgents was at least 10,000. These included large numbers of
German airmen based in Spanish Morocco. For them, the Spanish Civil War
was to be an ideal training ground for future combat in a more deadly war.
One result of the German presence in Spanish Morocco was an upsurge in
feeling against the Jews of the region, who had been there since before the
expulsion of the Jews from Spain in 1492.

Towards the end of February, the Insurgents announced that they were
in control of thirty-three out of Spain's fifty provincial capitals. This was
true, but the three main capital cities, Madrid, Barcelona and Bilbao, as well
as the most heavily populated and prosperous areas, remained loyal to the
Republican government. An Insurgent attempt to seize the mercury mines
at Almaden, in the south, was beaten back. Eye-witnesses both marvelled
at the enthusiasms of rival patriotisms, and were shocked by the callousness
of war. The French aviator, Antoine de Saint-Exupéry, visiting the battle
fronts near Madrid and Barcelona, recalled two years later:

Fields have been turned into charnel-houses and the dead are burned in
lime or petroleum. Respect for the dignity of man has been trampled
under foot. Since on both sides the political parties spy upon the stirrings
of man's conscience as upon the workings of a disease, why should the
urn of his flesh be respected? This body that clothes the spirit, that moves
with grace and boldness, that knows love, that is apt for self-sacrifice –
no one now so much as thinks of giving it decent burial.

I thought of our respect for the dead. I thought of the white sanatorium
where the light of a man's life goes quietly out in the presence of those
who love him and who garner as if it were an inestimable treasure his last

words, his ultimate smile. How right they are! Seeing that this same whole
is never again to take shape in the world. Never again will be heard exactly
that note of laughter, that intonation of voice, that quality of repartee.
Each individual is a miracle. No wonder we go on speaking of the dead
for twenty years.

'Here, in Spain,' Saint-Exupéry added, 'a man is simply stood up against a
wall and he gives up his entrails to the stones of the courtyard. You have
been captured. You are shot. Reason: your ideas were not our ideas.'

In the first week of March an attempt by the Junta to cut the road and
rail links between Madrid and Valencia was defeated. There was considerable
rejoicing in Republican ranks – and among supporters of the Republic in
Britain and France – when the Italian troops taking part in the assault
abandoned their positions on the battlefield and fled. On March 13 the
government forces captured the town of Brihuega, gaining large quantities
of war material, including several hundred sub-machine guns.

Giving up his efforts to separate Madrid from Valencia, Franco decided
to focus his main military efforts on completing the conquest of the Basque
provinces. He also, emulating the decision of the Republicans a month
earlier, put his forces under a single command, merging the Traditionalist
militias (the Carlists) with the Phalangists. On both sides of the divide,
greater centralization and an intensification of control signified the growing
intensity of the conflict.

In late March and throughout April, as Franco's forces advanced slowly
and with mounting difficulty through the Basque country, aircraft of the
German Condor Legion bombed the towns through which they believed the
Basque troops were passing. In the bombing of Durango on March 31 the
number of dead was 258, most of them civilians.

On April 26 the German target was the historic Basque capital of Guernica, whose peacetime population of 7,000 was swelled to 10,000 by refugees.
A thousand Basque soldiers were stationed north of the town. No troops
were retreating through it. April 26 was the weekly market day, a Monday.
The first attack was made by German Heinkels dropping bombs near the
station and machine-gunning the area around it. A British journalist, George
Steer, who reached Guernica that night, pieced together from survivors of
the raid an account of the moment when the next wave of bombers, the
heavier Junkers 52s, came over the town 'so clumsy that they seemed to
clang rather than to fly':

... they dispersed their load a ton at a time. They turned woodenly over Gernika,* the bombs fell mechanically in line as they turned. Then came the crack of the explosions; smoke stood up over Gernika like wool on a Negro's head. Everywhere it sprouted, as more heavy bombers came.

Besides many fifty- and hundred-pound bombs, they dropped great torpedoes weighing a thousand. Gernika is a compact little town, and most of these hit buildings, tearing them to pieces vertically from top to bottom and below the bottom. They penetrated refuges. The spirit of the people had been good, but now they panicked.

An escort of Heinkel 51s, the same perhaps that had molested us that afternoon, were waiting for this moment. Till now they had been machine-gunning the roads round Gernika, scattering, killing or wounding sheep and shepherds. As the terrified population streamed out of the town they dived low to drill them with their guns. Women were killed here whose bodies I afterwards saw. It was the same technique as that used at Durango on March 31, nearly a month back.

The little fighting planes came down in a line, like flashing dancing waves on shingle. They burst in spray on the countryside as they merrily dived. Twenty machine-guns working together in line, and the roar of breakers behind them from ten engines. Always they flew nose towards Gernika. For the pilots it must have been like surfing. The terrified people lay face down in ditches, pressed their backs against tree trunks, coiled themselves in holes, shut their eyes and ran across sweet green open Meadow. Many were foolish, and fled back before the aerial tide into the village. It was then that the heavy bombing of Gernika began.

'It was then,' Steer added, 'that Gernika was smudged out of that rich landscape, the province of Vizcaya, with a heavy fist.'

The bombing of Guernica continued for three hours. According to the Basque government 1,645 people were killed, many of them shot down as they fled, by the machine guns of the Heinkels. Among the dead was Antonia Izar de la Fuente, one of La Pasionaria's school teachers more than a quarter of a century earlier. No full count of the dead could be made, as the National-ists entered Guernica three days later, before all the bomb damage and debris

---

* In a note in his article, Steer explained: 'This is the Basque spelling of Guernica'. He preferred to use the Basque rather than the Spanish form.

had been cleared. Despite the bombing, both the crucial bridge on the road through the town and the local small arms factory were intact.

Outside Spain the impact of the bombing of Guernica was immediate. George Steer's account, sent from Bilbao early the following morning, was published in both *The Times* and the *New York Times*, causing great indignation. One British Foreign Office official later noted that Guernica 'told us what to expect from the Germans'. Pablo Picasso's large black and white mural *Guernica* was to fix the bombing of the town in the public mind as one of the terrible and deliberate evils of the century. Among its anguished forms can be seen a wounded horse – made of newsprint – a screaming woman, a burning house and a dead baby. 'Painting is not done to decorate apartments,' Picasso later explained. 'It is an instrument for war, for attack and defence against the enemy.' His first sketch for *Guernica* was made on May 1 when he read, in Paris, the press accounts of the attack. After Guernica he never returned to Spain – his birthplace.

On May 3, in London, the *New Statesman and Nation* published a poem by Sagittarius (Olga Katzin):

> Who shall avenge Guernica? None will avenge her,
> it is not the blood of our children that cries from the ground.
> Death has no summons to call from the sky the revenger,
> the murdered make no sound.
> Over our shifts and surrenders, connivance unending,
> hover the smoke and the reek of that smouldering pyre.
> We will remember Guernica when black birds descending
> *Our* cities set on fire.

Behind the lines, the Spanish Republic was faced with a severe crisis in Barcelona, where the Communists, who held sway over the allegiance of the workers in the city, were confronted by Anarcho-Syndicalist, dissident Communists and Trotskyists contemptuous of what they saw as the 'petite bourgeoisie'. Verbal violence was intense, threatening to break out into physical violence. But from Madrid, the conduct of the war continued with vigour.

On May 29, government air forces, flying to the Balearic Islands, bombed a German battleship, the *Deutschland*, which was unloading military supplies for Franco. Thirty-one German sailors were killed. In revenge, German war-ships carried out a ferocious naval bombardment of Almeria.

The Soviet involvement in the Spanish Civil War took a cruel twist in May, when fighting broke out within the Republican ranks between the Communists, one of whose leaders, Rodriguez Sala, seized the Barcelona telephone exchange, and the Anarcho-Syndicalist trades unionists and their allies the Catalonian Marxists – the POUM (*Partido Obrero de Unificacíon Marxista*). Guided from Moscow, the Communists sought to eliminate these other Left-wing elements from control or power. The Anarcho-Syndicalists and POUM resisted. In the ensuing four-day battle as many as a thousand were killed. The Republican Prime Minister, Largo Caballero, refused to allow the formal suppression of POUM. Under pressure from Stalin he was replaced by Dr Juan Negrin. Several Comintern representatives in Spain played their part in this change of government, including the future Italian Communist Party leader, Palmiro Togliatti, and the future Hungarian Communist leader Erno Gerö.

As soon as Negrin became Prime Minister, orders went out for the arrest of the POUM leaders. Dolores Ibárruri (La Pasionaria) was active in upholding this order, sending troops to arrest the POUM leadership in Catalonia. The climax came on June 16, when Andrés Nin, the Political Secretary of POUM – and former Secretary of the Red Trade Union International in Moscow – who had served as Minister of Justice in the Catalan autonomous government, was arrested, interrogated and then tortured: his face beaten literally to a pulp. Whether he died under interrogation, or was shot, is not known.

With the death of General Mola in a plane crash near Burgos on June 3, General Franco emerged as the undisputed leader of the Junta. Two weeks later, his troops entered Bilbao. Immediate steps were taken to humiliate Basque nationalism, including the cancellation of taxation privileges which the Basques had long enjoyed. For almost three months Basque guerrillas fought on in the mountains. On August 25 Franco's forces entered Santander. Two months later they had eliminated almost all Basque resistance. In the centre of Spain, however, government forces made considerable gains, winning back more than 350 square miles of territory from the insurgents.

The Republican government did its utmost to function as an elected body. In October the parliament met in Valencia. It was widely expected that the Nationalists would make a renewed offensive against Madrid, and even capture it. Instead, it was the Republicans who took the military initiative, seizing back the town of Teruel and the strategic area around it. A Nationalist counter-offensive failed to recapture the town. British soldiers of the International Brigade were among those who participated in Teruel's defence. After a visit by the leader of the British Labour Party, Clement Attlee – who had fought at Gallipoli in 1915 – they named one of their companies the 'Major Attlee Company'. In thanking them, Attlee wrote: 'I shall try to tell the comrades at home of what I have seen. Workers of the World unite!'

On October 17 the Nationalists entered Gijon, in the Asturias, gaining control of Spain's coal industry. As Franco already controlled the iron ore of the Basque region, he could immediately accelerate his military production. In their preliminary assault on Gijon, the Nationalists had carried out an intensive aerial bombardment, in which a combination of incendiary bombs and petrol created an early form of napalm. The photographs of Gijon after its capture, with scenes of buildings destroyed by aerial bombardment and citizens distracted by the destruction, shocked the outside world almost as much as the photographs of Guernica had done six months earlier.

As the year came to an end the Republicans remained in control of Madrid, and much of the centre, east and south of Spain: those regions that were linked geographically with the Mediterranean. Franco and the Nationalists were in control of the western and northern regions, linked with the Atlantic Ocean. Recognizing Franco's ascendancy in the north, Britain sent a diplomatic mission to the Nationalist authorities in Santander to represent British interests in the Basque country.

It was as a result of the representations of the British Government that the Hungarian-born journalist Arthur Koestler was released from a Nationalist prison in Malaga, where he had been held for four months. The owner of the British newspaper for which he was reporting, the *News Chronicle*, had intervened on his behalf, and had successfully enlisted Winston Churchill's support. Koestler later recalled, of his prison days: 'My companion of patio exercises, Garcia Atadell, was garrotted shortly after my liberation. Pity for the little Andalusian and Catalan peasants whom I heard crying and calling for their *madres* when they were led out at night to face the firing squad.'

As well as contributing to Franco's struggle throughout 1937, the German and Italian governments were also creating a wider set of alignments designed to increase their power in Europe. They were helped in this by their respective increase in armaments production, and in their joint efforts to win the support of the Muslim world, and thus embarrass both Britain and France, who had many Muslim subjects in their respective empires, and many problems with regard to them.

On September 25 the Italo-German rapprochement was celebrated in lavish style when Mussolini visited Hitler in Munich. Together they travelled to German army manoeuvres in Mecklenburg and visited German armaments factories at Essen. Then, on September 28, in the grounds of Olympic City in Berlin, before a crowd estimated at no less than three million, Hitler and Mussolini received an address affirming the 'fraternity' of the two regimes.

It was fifteen years since Mussolini had come to power, less than five since Hitler had become Chancellor: but it was clear that Germany held the balance of power. On November 6, Italy joined the Anti-Communist Pact which had already been signed by Germany and Japan. But neither Hitler nor Mussolini were able to persuade Austria or Hungary to join the Rome-Berlin Axis. At a meeting with Mussolini in Venice, the Austrian Chancellor, Dr Schuschnigg's suggestion, that the Habsburg monarchy should be restored, in order to prevent the incorporation of Austria into Germany, was dismissed by Mussolini with contempt.

Mussolini wanted to be the master of the Mediterranean. But it was Britain, with her naval, military and air bases at Gibraltar, Malta, Cyprus and Palestine, and her military presence on the Suez Canal (through which Italian ships had to pass on their way to Italian East Africa), that was the leading Mediterranean power. A series of anti-British actions that year showed Italy's hostility: the expulsion of British traders and missionaries from Addis Ababa, the prohibition of most English newspapers inside Italy, and the anti-British propaganda beamed to Muslim countries from the Italian radio transmitter at Bari.

Most tempting of all to Mussolini was to exploit the continuing anti-British campaign among the Arabs of Palestine. During a visit to the Italian territory of Libya, he proclaimed himself the 'Protector of Islam'. He also signed a Treaty with Yemen, the Muslim Arab country bordering on Britain's Aden Protectorate. Hitler was likewise active seeking to stir up Pan-Islamic feeling among the Arabs, and to turn them even more actively against both the Jews and the British. Letters exchanged between the German Ministries of War and Propaganda at the end of the year stressed that if unrest or disorder could be created in Palestine, Britain would have to send troop reinforcements which would then be unavailable to her in the event of war with Germany in Europe.

A month after Mussolini's visit to Germany, Hitler welcomed another foreign visitor, the Duke of Windsor, England's former king, who had abdicated the previous December in order to marry a twice-divorced American, Wallis Simpson. The newly-wed couple travelled to Hitler's mountain villa at Berchtesgaden, where Hitler treated them with the deference due to the member of a royal house, and a man who had expressed interest, even sympathy, with aspects of Nazism. The Duke was taken around Germany by Robert Ley, head of the German Labour Front, to study working conditions in factories and farms. 'A curious thing for the Duke to do,' William Shirer noted in his diary, 'to come to Germany, where the labour unions have been smashed, just before he goes to America.'

In the Soviet Union, the purges of 'enemies of the State' intensified during 1937. Any manifestation of political opposition – real or imaginary – was treated as a criminal offence of the gravest order. Arrests were made daily: accusations of 'Trotskyite', 'Fascist', 'Lackey of Germany', even 'Lackey of Japan' were made against people whose whole life had been spent in the service of Soviet Communism. Among the institutions from which more and more members were arrested and taken away to execution, prison or labour camp were the main sources of Communist activity and zeal: the Young Communist Movement, the Trade Unions, the Academy of Sciences, and the Union of Soviet Writers.

It was shortly after his release from a Spanish prison that Arthur Koestler, who had joined the Communist Party in Germany six years earlier, learned of the fate of some of those closest to him. That knowledge turned him for ever against his former mentors in Moscow:

I learned that in the Russian mass-purges, my brother-in-law and two of my closest friends had been arrested. My brother-in-law, Dr Ernst Ascher, was a doctor who worked at a State hospital in the Volga German republic. Though a member of the German CP, he was politically naïve and indifferent.

The accusation against him, as I later learned, was that he was a saboteur who had injected syphilis into his patients, and he had demoralized the people by pretending that venereal diseases were incurable, and thirdly, as a matter of course, that he was the agent of a foreign power.

He has never been heard of since his arrest twelve years ago.

On January 23 the trial began in Moscow of men who had been at the centre of the establishment and the perpetuation of Soviet Communism. All of them were accused of being 'Trotskyite terrorists, wreckers, murderers and spies': among them was G.L. Pyatakov, a former Vice-Commissar for Heavy Industry, who had played a major part in the industrialization of the Soviet Union – one of Lenin's chief objectives – and Karl Radek, who had stood at Lenin's side from the early days of the revolution. The trial ended on January 30. On February 1, thirteen of the accused were shot, among them Pyatakov. Radek was sentenced to ten years in prison. He too was later shot.

The purveyors of terror themselves became the next victims of the regime of terror. On April 3, G.G. Yagoda, who had operated the Cheka secret police system with all the ruthlessness that Stalin required of him, was arrested and accused of having committed crimes while in office. While he was held in prison awaiting trail, mass executions were carried out of those accused of sabotaging factories and military installations. These executions were publicized in the Soviet newspapers. One such mass execution, in October, was of fifty-four 'criminals' at Ulan Ude, the capital of the Buryat-Mongol Republic.

Often the arrest and trial of 'criminals' was only made public after they had been sentenced. This was the case in June, when a military court, meeting between June 1 and 4, sentenced to death one of Stalin's leading military commanders, Marshal Tukhachevsky, and seven other generals, all of whom had been charged with treason and spying 'on behalf of an unfriendly State'. The trial began at nine in the morning on June 10 and sentence was passed shortly after lunch. The sentences were made public on June 11. The executions took place on the following day. According to the decree of 1 December 1934, the accused were denied defence counsel or the right of appeal.

Not everyone was prepared to act as a cat's-paw for the regime. One of those who had been asked to sit in judgement on the accused generals was their fellow-soldier, General Gamarnik. Another of the military tribunal, General Blucher, had been to see Gamarnik, to tell him to join the tribunal – inevitably its verdict would be a guilty one. 'But how can I?', Gamarnik replied. 'I know they're not enemies.' Blucher replied that if he did not agree to participate he could be arrested. Fifty years later, Gamarnik's daughter – who was aged twelve at the time – recalled the sequel: 'Blucher came again briefly on the 31st. Then some other people came and put a seal on my father's safe. They told him that he had been removed from his post and that his assistants, Osepian and Bulin, had been arrested. He was ordered to stay in the house. As soon as the NKVD people left we heard a shot in his study. When mother and I rushed in it was all over.'

General Gamarnik's wife was arrested and sentenced to eight years in prison as 'the wife of an enemy of the people' and simultaneously to another ten years in labour camp for 'aiding an enemy of the people'. Her daughter never saw her again. 'Apparently she died in camp in 1943. I was sent to a children's home. When I reached sixteen in 1941 I was given six years as "a socially dangerous element".'

Another of those accused, the veteran Bolshevik, General Dybenko, who had been a Communist Party member since 1912, and who at the time of the revolution was the Chairman of the Central Committee of the Baltic Fleet, organizing revolutionary activity among the sailors, protested direct to Stalin about the accusations being made against him. His letter survives in Stalin's archive and is reproduced by General Volkogonov in his biography of Stalin. In his letter, the old Bolshevik listed the accusations against him and answered each one, making a mockery of them. His letter began:

Dear Comrade Stalin,

It seems the Politburo and government have decided I am an enemy of our Motherland and our Party. Politically isolated, I am a living corpse. But why, for what? How could I know that those Americans who came to Central Asia with official representatives of the NKVD and OGPU were special intelligence agents? On the way to Samarkand I was not alone with them for a second. Anyway, I don't even speak American.

At the end of his letter General Dybenko asked Stalin: 'I beg you to look again at all these facts and to remove the badge of shame from me.' After reading the letter, Stalin noted on it two words: 'For Voroshilov.' The letter was then shown to Kliment Voroshilov, Politburo member and one of the most enthusiastic architects of the purges. Dybenko was arrested, tried and later shot.

The removal of those who had helped to establish, maintain and defend Soviet Communism was continuous and frenetic. Among those who were expelled from the Communist Party in the summer of 1937 were Aleksei

Rykov, who had succeeded Lenin as Prime Minister of the Soviet Union –
and who had served, most recently, as Commissar of Posts and Telegraphs
– and Nikolai Bukharin, the former editor of the government newspaper
Izvestia. Even close friends of Stalin could not count on his goodwill. One
such was a fellow-Georgian Bolshevik, Avel Yenukidze. From 1920 until
March 1935 he had been Secretary of the Central Executive Committee of
the Communist Party. In June 1935 he had been expelled from the Party
for 'political and moral corruption'. On 19 December 1937 he was shot for
'high treason'.

A fierce attack on religion was likewise accompanied by denunciations,
arrests, imprisonment and executions. The enemy in this case was declared
to be 'counter-revolutionary religious organizations'. Christian and Muslim
religious leaders were charged with subversive activities, espionage and even
'terrorism', usually in the service of Germany or Japan. A counter-religious
organization, the League of the Militant Godless, which had boasted five
million supporters in 1933, revealed in 1937 that its numbers had fallen to
less than two million. The campaign against the churches was intensified.

On July 31 a Soviet Politburo directive instructed the commandants of
all labour camps to submit lists of prisoners who 'continued to conduct
anti-State agitation' inside the camps. This 'arrest quota' was diligently
filled. Tens of thousands of names were submitted by zealous camp commandants who did not dare to be thought slacking in their duties. The directive
laid down that twenty-eight per cent of those whose names were put forward
should be shot, and the rest given eight to ten years additional labour camp
sentences. The number to be shot was listed precisely: 72,950. They were
taken in closed lorries marked 'Meat' or 'Vegetables' to places where pits
had been dug to receive their corpses.

The arrests and executions during 1937 affected every branch of Soviet
life, from the highest echelons of politics and administration to the essential
services on which the daily running of national life depended. Fifty years
later a former Commissar of Communications, I.V. Kovalev, told Stalin's
biographer, General Volkogonov: 'In 1937 I was appointed head of the
western railway. I arrived in Minsk and went to the administration office.
It was empty. There was no one to hand over the job to me. My predecessor,
Rusakov, had been arrested and shot. I called for his deputies. There weren't
any. They'd been arrested. I looked for anyone, but there was only a strange
and terrible silence. It was as if a tornado had passed through. I was amazed
that the trains were still running . . .'

Kovalev went to the home of an acquaintance who worked in the railway administration. 'Why aren't you at work?' he asked, even before greeting him. The acquaintance replied: 'I'm waiting. They said they'd come for me today. See, I've got some clean shirts packed.' Kovalev telephoned Moscow and spoke to a member of Stalin's secretariat. 'I told him of the situation. Somehow the rampage was rapidly brought to a halt. Anyway, there was no one left to put in gaol.'

One area where the disaffection with the Soviet regime was both real and still openly expressed was the non-Russian Republics. Here, as the arrests began, the charge of 'nationalism' was added to that of 'Trotskyism'. Of the eleven Soviet Republics, ten had their Heads of Government removed from office during 1937. The Declaration on Nationalities of 1917, issued when Stalin was Chairman for Nationality Affairs, had enshrined in Soviet theory the right of the many and diverse national groups within the former Tsarist Empire to their own national self-expression. Stalin's own writings had earlier extolled the virtues of a vigorous national identity. According to the original Bolshevik orthodoxy, the annexation of non-Russian territory by the Tsars had been a historical evil, part of the universal evil of nineteenth century imperialism. To resist the control of St Petersburg was a progressive act, one in keeping with the revolutionary ethic. One of those who had contributed most to this theory, and to the Declaration on Nationalities, was a Russian historian, Professor Pokrovsky. By 1937, five years after Pokrovsky's death, his theory, and the regional nationalism that flourished with it, were considered, in the words of the Central Asian expert Sir Olaf Caroe, 'too productive of national pride', and on August 27 a decree was issued, denouncing Pokrovsky as 'the slave of a defective anti-Marxist convention'.

The decree of August 27, which was issued in conjunction with the search for a single, standard historical text book for the whole Soviet Union, stated that although the Tsarist regime had indeed been repressive against the many nationalities that made up the empire, it had been less evil and less oppressive than the alternative available at the time – annexation to the Turkish Empire then bordering on the Caucasus, or to the British Empire in India, with its northern frontier so close to Central Asia. Nor would independence have been the right historical path for these nationalities: the decree made it clear that it was only by becoming part of the Tsarist Empire that the scattered peoples had been able to take part in the revolutionary process which culminated in the 1917 triumph of the Bolsheviks. It appeared that the national movements had therefore gained from Soviet Communism, and from Soviet rule. Pokrovsky's enthusiasm for national liberation was misplaced. The new truth stated that liberation existed within the Soviet borders, and only within the Soviet borders. This new truth was taught to the diverse peoples and nationalities of the Caucasus and Central Asia.

The intense hardships resulting from Soviet rule were not confined to the Russian heartland; in Central Asia the nationalities whose best interests lay within the Soviet system were as much the victims of forced collectivization as any other Soviet citizens. In Kazakhstan many collective farms were without even the herd of cattle that had earlier characterized the Kazakh way of life, and livelihood. During six years of intensive collectivization ending in 1934, 73 per cent of the cattle, 83 per cent of the horses and 87 per cent of the sheep had disappeared. They had not been restored in the four years since then.

Expulsions and arrests also took place throughout the two western Republics of White Russia and the Ukraine. Here too the enemies were declared to be 'Trotskyite wreckers'. Here too the men who had played the leading part in establishing the Soviet system were its principal victims. In June, the President of White Russia, A.G. Cherviakov, killed himself when the arrests began of 'Jewish nationalist elements' in the White Russian government. In August, the Chairman of the Council of People's Commissars in the Ukraine, Lyubchenko, killed himself so as to avoid arrest as an 'enemy of the USSR and a betrayer of Ukrainian interests'. His successor Bondarenko – appointed by Stalin – was arrested three months later, and charged with maintaining treasonable contact with Ukrainian separatists in an 'anti-Soviet' centre in Berlin. In November, the acting President of White Russia – another Stalin appointment – and the Vice-President, were both removed from office. Similar purges of the leaders of the peripheral Republics took place in the Caucasus, the most dramatic being the trial of thirteen senior members of the Abkhazian Government on a charge of 'counter-revolutionary conspiracy'.

Another group of servants of the Soviet regime who were caught up in the purges were the diplomats. In the autumn of 1937 all the Soviet diplomatic representatives to the border States were summoned back to Moscow, never to reappear again in any diplomatic list. Several Soviet ambassadors, on being ordered home, killed themselves rather than obey the summons to return. One of those who had been a stalwart of Soviet foreign policy for many years, the former Vice-Commissar for Foreign Affairs, Leo M. Karakhan, an Armenian, was executed on December 19 for 'high treason'.

Since the failure of Communist revolutions outside Russia after 1918, several hundred European Communist activists had found refuge in Moscow. There they were made welcome in an impressive hotel facing the Kremlin, and from time to time spoke lyrically of the achievements of their Soviet hosts, and of Stalin. In 1937 they too became the victims of the purges, accused of 'spying and wrecking'. One of those victims was Bela Kun, who had led the Hungarian Communist government in 1919.

Among the many descriptions that were published of the Stalin terror, and the world of the labour camps, after the disintegration of the Soviet Union in 1991, one of particular poignancy is that of General Dmitri Volkogonov. A professional soldier, in Soviet times he had risen to the position of Deputy Chief of the Main Political Section of the Soviet Army and Navy, a loyal and centrally-placed Communist functionary. In 1988, three years before the collapse of the Soviet Union, he published a highly critical biography of Stalin, in which – almost hidden at the end of the book – he recalled his own memories of the pre-war years, when he was a boy of nine:

I grew up in the village of Agul, Irbei district, in the south of Krasnoyarsk region. In the distance one could see the majestic snows of the Sayan mountains and their spurs jutting out towards the Yenisei, the Kana and the Agala. This was the genuine, drowsy taiga, the land of the Kerzhaks, indigenous Siberians who had migrated from the western territories of Russia a century or two earlier.

In 1937 or 1938 some soldiers turned up in our little village, followed by columns of prisoners. They started cordoning off zones, and in some six months camps were established in Agul and a number of neighbouring settlements. Barbed wire appeared and high fences behind which one could just make out the huts, the armed sentries on watch-towers and the guard dogs.

The locals soon began seeing long columns of exhausted people constantly arriving on foot from the railhead sixty miles away. It seemed the camps must be infinitely expandable. Later they understood what was happening. Long ditches started appearing beyond the outskirts of the settlements, and the corpses of dead prisoners would be taken on carts or sleighs, covered with tarpaulins, and buried there at night. Many died from the sheer hardship. Many were shot out in the taiga.

General Volkogonov's recollections of his childhood continued:

Boris Frantsevich Kreshchuk, who was living then in Agul and whose father, a blacksmith, and elder brother had been shot, told me of the time he and some other boys were out looking for pine nuts when they suddenly heard the crack of gunfire nearby, 'just like the sound of a large canvas being ripped apart'. They ran to the place and from behind some bushes watched as the firing squad threw some twenty executed prisoners into a ditch. 'I remember one of them was clinging to the grass, obviously he wasn't dead. We ran away.'

My mother was the head of a primary school (for children aged seven to fourteen). The authorities allowed two prisoners to come and help put her library in order, repair bindings and so on. Life was very hard for us, especially after they arrested and executed my father and exiled us to Agul. As we were already living in the Maritime region, there was nowhere further east to send us, so they sent us west, to Agul. There were no teachers in the place, so the authorities allowed my mother to teach. She had graduated from university after the revolution.

When there was no one else around, my mother used to have long conversations with one of the prisoners, whose name I cannot recall. Once, he took a bit of rag from inside his shirt and quickly unwrapped a photograph and showed it to my mother. We were in the long, low room that served as the library, and I was standing on tiptoe and looking over my mother's shoulder. The small photograph was mounted on board and there was some foreign writing below. The prisoner spoke in a low whisper: 'We were in emigration then. In Switzerland. That's Lenin, that's me next to him with my wife, and those two were German Communists.'

I couldn't help wondering how someone so shabby and emaciated could have known Lenin personally. He was brought under escort to the school on two further occasions and then he vanished. Either he died or he was shot in the forest, like the others. Those childhood impressions have never left me.

Stalin and Hitler were both imposing their dictatorships to a degree hitherto unprecedented even in the Twentieth Century. On April 1 the Enabling Law of 1933, by which Hitler had ruled by decree throughout the previous four years, expired. It was this Enabling Law (two of Hitler's predecessors had resorted to the same device) that he regarded as the legal basis for his dictatorship. To cover his actions in the continuing mask of legality, Hitler had the law extended by a further four years – until 1941. The mask of legality was ever-present in the actions of the Nazi dictatorship.

On July 15 the Geneva Convention in respect of Upper Silesia expired. The international protection accorded the Jews of that province through the League of Nations disappeared overnight. From that day, German Jews whose families had lived in the area for generations were suddenly and without exception subjected to the full rigours of all German racial legislation: expelled from their jobs, losing the right of citizenship, and subjected to the Nuremberg Laws, which prevented marriages between Jews and non-Jews.

These laws were rigidly applied. By the beginning of 1937 about three hundred Jews were being held in Dachau, accused of 'race defilement'. An American lawyer, David Glick, from Pittsburgh, negotiated with the Gestapo for the release of 120 of them. He was successful; the only Gestapo condition was that the released men must leave Germany at once, which they did. This was made possible by the efforts of the British Consul-General in Munich, John Carvell, who issued Palestine Certificates, as he was entitled to do, thus enabling the men to emigrate to Palestine. But while small rescue efforts were permitted – the money raised going directly to the German exchequer – anti-Jewish legislation and anti-Jewish propaganda did not abate.

Hitler was also determined to impose Nazi values on art and artists throughout the Reich, and to drive out those who did not uphold and glorify the Nazi perspective. To this end, an Exhibition of Degenerate Art (*Entartete Kunst*) was opened in Munich on July 19. In an appeal to the Austrian President, Kurt von Schuschnigg, the artist Oscar Kokoshka, an Austrian citizen and a Jew, noted that his paintings were among those being displayed as 'degenerate'. Hitler's representative at the exhibition had denounced the artists whose paintings were on show as 'these ruffians, the lackeys and pacemakers of international Jewry'. They had, he said, 'committed crime after crime against German art'. Hitler himself, in his speech at the exhibition, declared that the pilloried artists, 'in so far as they are not swindlers, who should therefore be brought to trial as such, suffer from defective vision', and called upon the Ministry of the Interior to establish 'whether this defective vision is congenital or acquired. If congenital, steps must be taken to ensure that it becomes impossible for them to pass on, and thus propagate, the defect.'

'In other words', Kokoshka told Schuschnigg, 'the German Chancellor threatened to have these artists sterilized.' Many of the artists whose work was being pilloried subsequently went into exile, including Kokoshka, who made his home in London. As refugees they made their artistic contribution to many other lands. One of them, Hans Feibusch, whose work was much-mocked at the Munich exhibition, had left Germany as soon as Hitler came to power. He became a British citizen, and was still exhibiting his paintings in Britain in 1997, at the age of ninety-nine.

In the early months of the year, Catholic priests, monks and nuns were brought to trial in Germany on a series of spurious charges which were given massive publicity by Goebbels and his propaganda machinery. The favourite charges, being the most salacious, were of sexual depravity. Others were of 'complicity with Communism'.

Catholic parents whose children went to religious schools were encouraged to remove them. Special 'plebiscites' were held among parents to hasten this decision. On May 27, Pope Pius XI, who six years earlier had criticized as 'pagan' the worship of the State by the Italian Fascists, issued an encyclical on the condition of the Catholic church in Germany. It was entitled *Mit brennender Sorge*: 'With Deep Anxiety'. In it he sought to remind Hitler that man, as a human being, possessed rights that had to be preserved against every attempt by the State to deny, suppress or hinder them. The encyclical deplored the persecution of Catholics in Germany as 'illegal and inhuman'. That same week Pope Pius also issued a condemnation of atheistic Communism.

Undeterred by Papal protest, Hitler lost no opportunity of weakening all opposition. The churches were a main target, with their centuries-old influence on German life and thought. On June 25 a special decree deprived the Protestant Church of control of its finances. That summer more than a hundred Protestant clergymen were arrested, among them, on July 1, Pastor Niemöller, the former U-boat commander, who had spoken out against the anti-Christian facets of Nazism. He was to remain in prison and concentration camp for almost eight years – until the final week of the war.

Neither Niemöller nor his Evangelical Confessing Church had been willing to speak out on behalf of the Jews, only on behalf of those Jews who had converted to Christianity. 'Its major concern was churchly jurisdiction and administration,' the historian Theodore S. Hamerow has commented on Confessing Church – so courageous in defence of its own Christianity, and in its reaction to Nazi racist ideology: 'Only on the issue of religious governance did it disagree sharply with National Socialism. Otherwise it was prepared to tolerate or even support the Hitler dictatorship. It sought not to overthrow or even reform the established system but to find a secure and recognized place within it. Ultimately, its inability to rise above confessional expediency reflected the lack of an ideal expressing the transcendent moral responsibility of religious faith.'

In October 1937 the British journalist G. Ward Price tried to set the record straight with regard to what he saw as unjust criticism of Hitler's foreign policy and intentions. In his book *I Know These Dictators* he wrote of Hitler's sincerity in his protestations that he desired peace. Despite appearances such as the remilitarization of the Rhineland, 'not a solitary shot has been fired and not a single incident has occurred on any frontier of Germany'. Hitler remained determined to achieve 'closer and more cordial' Anglo-German relations.

In his book, Ward Price drew a veil over Hitler's anti-Jewish measures. On September 7 a German government decree imposed a 25 per cent tax on all Jewish wealth. On November 8 an exhibition opened at Nuremberg entitled *Der ewige Jude* – 'The Eternal Jew'. It portrayed Jews as the 'taskmasters for international Bolshevism' whose aim was to enslave Germany within the Soviet system. The exhibition was the creation of Goebbels. It was replete with grotesque allegations of universal Jewish corruption and immorality. With a bravery born of desperation a group of Austrian anti-Nazis, led by a devout Christian, Irene Harand, entered the exhibition hall and stuck labels showing Jewish 'benefactors of humanity' on the walls and display cases.

Anti-Jewish measures were not confined to Germany. In the Free City of Danzig, nominally under League of Nations supervision, but in effect under the control of local Nazis, Jewish shops were often attacked and looted during 1937, and the assets of many Jewish firms seized by the authorities. In Poland that year there was a spate of anti-Jewish actions. That September, in the town of Bielsk, every Jewish shop was looted. In the Polish universities, Jewish students – men and women – were physically attacked. At the university of Lvov, the Rector, a devout Catholic, who tried to prevent anti-Jewish violence, was himself attacked. The Polish government – whose royal predecessors had welcomed the Jews to Poland three centuries earlier – began negotiations that December with the French government, with a view to facilitating Jewish emigration to the French colonial territory of Madagascar, in the Indian Ocean.

*   *   *

It was to the Far East that the main focus of international attention turned during the second half of 1937. In mid-February, the Kuomintang Central Executive Committee had rejected all proposals to join with the Communist Chinese forces against possible Japanese aggression. This decision was helped by Nationalist fears that if they did ally with the Communists, the Japanese would regard this as a hostile and provocative act. Everything should be done, the Nationalists argued, to avoid giving Japan an excuse for further armed intervention in China.

On July 7, Japanese troops who had been carrying out night manoeuvres at Lukouchiao, a town only twenty miles from Peking, clashed with a battalion of Chinese troops that was guarding the border at that point. In the clash, heavy casualties were inflicted by both sides. Declaring that this was a local problem, of no relevance to the Nationalist Chinese Government in Nanking, the Japanese sent reinforcements to the Peking area. In reply to this, Chiang Kai-shek, his authority as Generalissimo restored after the setbacks of the previous year, ordered Chinese troops northward, into Hopei, and issued a proclamation insisting on China's sovereign rights over the northern provinces.

The Japanese, declaring that they had no further quarrel with China with regard to the Lukouchiao incident, demanded that the Chinese troops withdraw from Hopei. The Chinese refused. On July 26 the Japanese issued an ultimatum demanding withdrawal. When this demand was also rejected, the Japanese army began full-scale war. Although, man for man, the Chinese could match the forces that the Japanese had stationed in North China, they could not match the equipment. As Japanese aircraft, tanks and troops pressed relentlessly forward, the Chinese forces withdrew, evacuating Peking without a struggle, and withdrawing southward in a series of defensive actions.

On August 30 the Chinese government brought the Sino-Japanese dispute to the League of Nations at Geneva. What Japan had done, the Chinese alleged with justification, was 'a case of aggression pure and simple'; a continuation of the aggression against China that had started six years earlier with the Japanese invasion of Manchuria. The Japanese aggression, China insisted, was a violation of the League Covenant and the Kellogg-Briand Pact, both of which Japan had signed. It was an attempt 'to destroy all the work of reconstruction which the Chinese nation had so steadily and assiduously undertaken during the past ten years'.

The Chinese case was presented verbally to the League Assembly on

September 15. China's spokesman was her ambassador to the League, Dr Wellington Koo. His speech, which was in English, and the interpretation into French, were applauded loudly by the representatives of fifty nations, an unprecedented gesture of support. But when it came to action, the only decisions reached were to reduce China's financial contribution to the League, and to pay £30,000 towards the fight against epidemic diseases inside China. There was great unease among several European Powers, including Britain and France, but also Poland and Czechoslovakia, that if too many commitments were made to give assistance to China, or to take a military initiative, this would give Germany – in particular – a chance to wreak mischievous damage behind the cloak of Far Eastern diversions.

On October 10 the Chinese forces, having fallen back from Peking, were defeated in a fixed battle along a forty-mile stretch of the River Puto. As many as 30,000 Chinese soldiers were killed. Those who survived, 200,000 in all, fled southward in disarray. There were a few more efforts to hold up the Japanese advance, but all were defeated. By the end of October the Japanese had driven the Chinese Nationalist Army out of Hopei, Chahar and the northern part of Shansi province.

It was not only in the north of China that the Japanese army attacked. Shanghai was also a target. For several weeks the Chinese forces defended the city. In an attempt to protect as many Chinese as possible from the Japanese, a French priest, Father Jacquinot de Bessage, prevailed upon the Japanese to allow the European community in Shanghai to set up a neutral zone into which almost half a million Chinese whose homes had been destroyed were able to find refuge. The British Ambassador to China, Sir Hughe Knatchbull-Hugesson, who was making his way from Nanking to Shanghai by car with several members of his staff, including his military attaché, was fired upon by Japanese warplanes from the air and badly wounded.

The fate of Shanghai, like that of every Chinese city attacked and over-run by the Japanese, was terrible. One eye witness was a Swedish mining engineer, J. Gunnar Andersson, who had served as a mining adviser to the Chinese Government after the First World War, and had returned to China in 1936, to take up residence in the International Settlement in the city – which was defended by British, American, French and Italian troops. In his account, Andersson described the intensification of the fighting on August 14 and the horrors of aerial warfare:

Two Japanese seaplanes attacked the Hungjao aerodrome, while the Chinese bombers tried to hit the Japanese flagship *Idzumo*, which was moored quite near the Japanese Consulate General.

An event which overshadowed all other happenings on that 'Bloody Saturday', at any rate in the interest of foreigners, was the double catastrophe within the non-Japanese section of the International Settlement. Between four and five in the afternoon two Chinese planes each dropped a bomb, one on the traffic circus at the junction of the Avenue Edward VII – Yu Ya Ching Road and the Boulevard de Montigny, the other at the corner of Nanking Road and the Bund.

The effect of the first-named explosion was terrible; it has even been suggested that it was a world's record in the destruction of a civil population in aerial warfare.

The traffic circus was filled with refugees trying to get away from the district occupied by the Japanese. The bomb made a huge crater in the street paving. The destruction was so appalling, wreckage of falling houses, paving-stones and exploding motor-cars were so intermixed with fragments of human bodies that it was never possible to calculate the exact number of casualties. One thousand and forty-seven persons killed and three hundred and three wounded are thus minimum figures.

Two of the city's big hotels suffered severely from the Nanking Road bomb: the Cathay Hotel and the Palace Hotel, which face each other at the end of that road. Here the number of victims was over two hundred, including more than one hundred and forty-five killed. Almost all the victims of these two explosions were Chinese, but among the few foreigners were some well-known persons.

The Chinese army command published an explanation of what had happened, to the effect that the pilots had been wounded by Japanese anti-aircraft shells and that the bomb-racks were damaged, so that their releasing was quite involuntary. This interpretation did not satisfy the opinion of the foreign colony. The unparalleled catastrophes in the midst of a neutral population and one favourably disposed to the Chinese naturally created a feeling of panic, which expressed itself in arrangements for the speedy evacuation of British women and children to Hong Kong and of American women and children to Manila.

Fighting inside Shanghai continued for ten more days. In a bombing attack on August 23, a further 173 Chinese were killed in the city's largest department store. It was not known whether Chinese or Japanese bombers were responsible: both were dropping their bombs on areas believed to be held by the other's forces. On the night of August 26/27 matters came to a climax, as Andersson recalled:

For once the Japanese bombers joined in the work that night: air-bombs, guns, trench-mortars, machine-guns and rifles, every means of destruction this powerfully mechanized enemy had at his disposal was let loose in a rain of explosives, fire and steel over this quarter of the city that had been tortured for months and was now doomed to destruction.

On the morning of the 27th the firing ceased; the Chinese divisions which, deeply dug in, had held up the Japanese for more than two months, had slipped out during the night under cover of darkness, and in the opinion of European and American officers on the spot the retreat was accomplished with exemplary regularity and was so dogged and complete that the Japanese found simply nothing in the way of military supplies.

In order to cover the retirement the late defenders set fire to the town. From dawn on the 27th throughout the whole day we saw from our lofty lookout fire after fire flare up and spread, till we had before us a continuous front of fire the length of which was estimated by different observers at from four to six miles.

I cannot even guess at the depth of this conflagration, and it is quite likely that here and there in the sea of fire there were islands which escaped destruction; but it appears probable that four square miles would be a very cautious estimate of the urban area that was wiped out by the fire.

As this was one of the most thickly populated quarters of Shanghai, it has been conjectured that something like a million people lost their homes, even if large numbers had fled at an earlier stage from this inferno of street fighting.

When at last night descended upon this day, which surely no dweller in Shanghai will forget, then and not till then did we see the full extent of this abominable destruction. The glowing wall of fire stretched all the way from north-north-east to west-south-west, reckoned from our point of vision; part of it quite near, part of the north-west disappearing behind Soochow Creek. Fortunately enough the wind carried the immense volume of smoke to the northward during the whole of that critical day; otherwise the foreign city would have been in immediate danger, and we should certainly have been smoked out of our swallow's nest.

There is no doubt that night of the burning of Chapei will be reckoned as one of the great conflagrations in the history of the world.

'On me personally the sight of the unparalleled zone of fire made a strangely nauseating impression,' Andersson wrote. 'My thoughts were split up into tens of thousands of little pictures of all the poor, thickly clustered homes where only a few months ago an industrious and peace-loving population went about its daily work. Where are they now, all these small tradesmen and workers who have lost all? How many old people, pregnant women and little children were left to be roasted to death among the glowing ruins?'

Andersson ended his account with a cry of anguish. 'What is it really worth, this wonderful machine civilization, if it has no inherent force to prevent a destruction like this?' he asked. 'Will it never be possible to create an international power, not talk and resolutions which are not worth the paper they are written on, but a power higher than war, a power that treats the aggressor as society deals with a man-eating tiger or a dangerous criminal?'

The United States Ambassador in Tokyo, Joseph Grew, described the bombing of Shanghai in his diary as 'one of the most horrible episodes in modern times'. Following the capture of the city, the Japanese army continued to advance inland, determined to reach the Nationalist capital, Nanking. As they advanced they subjected towns and villages to a ferocity of violence extreme even by the harsh precedents of conflict on Chinese soil.

On October 5 President Roosevelt spoke in Chicago of how 'the peace, the freedom and the security of ninety percent of the population of the world is being jeopardized by the remaining ten percent who are threatening a breakdown of all international order and law,' and he went on to ask:

Surely the ninety percent who want to live in peace under law and in accordance with moral standards that have received almost universal acceptance through the centuries, can and must find some way to make their will prevail . . .

It seems to be unfortunately true that the epidemic of world lawlessness is spreading.

When an epidemic of physical disease starts to spread, the community approves and joins in a quarantine of the patients in order to protect the health of the community against the spread of disease.

The reaction in the United States to Roosevelt's remarks was not favourable to American intervention. Of what he called the 'quick and violent' response of American opinion, Cordell Hull wrote in his memoirs: 'As I saw it, this had the effect of setting back for at least six months our constant educational campaign intended to create and strengthen public opinion toward international cooperation.' Hull added:

> Those of us who had been carrying on this campaign, through speeches, statements, and actions wherever possible, had been working as actively as we could; but we were always careful not to go too far lest a serious attack by the isolationist element throw us farther back than we were before.
>
> If we proceeded gradually and did not excite undue opposition, our words and actions, although not so dynamic or far-reaching as we might wish, had more effect on the world at large than if we made startling statements or took precipitate action and then, because of the bitter reaction we aroused, presented the world with the spectacle of a nation divided against itself.

Hull noted that following Roosevelt's speech, 'six of the major pacifist organizations issued a declaration that the President "points the American people down the road that led to the World War". The American Federation of Labor resolved: "American labor does not wish to be involved in European or Asiatic wars." Two Representatives, Fish and Tinkham, threatened to have the President impeached. A *Philadelphia Inquirer* telegraphic poll of Congress showed more than two to one against common action with the League toward the Far East. A campaign was launched to secure 25,000,000 signatures to a "Keep America Out of War" petition.'

Hull commented: 'All this reaction, of course, received wide publicity and was dulcet to the ears of Hitler, Mussolini, and the Japanese war lords. It undoubtedly emboldened the aggressor countries, and caused the democracies of Europe to wonder if we could ever be with them in more than words.' In the opinion of Winston Churchill, who had been passed over the previous year for a place in the government – his supporters had wanted him to be given the newly created post of Minister for Coordination of Defence – the aggressor countries were being equally emboldened by Britain's failure to rearm at a more effective rate. 'Mere declarations of readiness to spend money over a five-year period,' Churchill told the House of Commons on March 4 – after a British Government decision to spend £1,500 million on defence between 1937 and 1942 – 'do not affect the realities through which we will have to live in 1937, 1938, and 1939.'

Churchill then spoke of several specific areas of military and defence planning in which he believed insufficient progress was being made, in particular the provision of anti-aircraft guns with trained crews, and the re-equipment of the Territorial Army. 'I must say I am astounded,' he said, 'at the wave of optimism, of confidence, and even of complacency, which has swept over Parliament and over public opinion. There is a veritable tide of feeling that all is well, that everything is being done in the right way, in the right measure and in the right time,' and he went on to ask:

> When a whole Continent is arming feverishly, when mighty nations are laying aside every form of ease and comfort, when scores of millions of men and weapons are being prepared for war, when whole populations are being led forward or driven forward under conditions of exceptional overstrain, when the finances of the proudest dictators are in the most desperate condition, can you be sure that all your programmes so tardily adopted will, in fact, be executed in time?

Hitler and Mussolini, Churchill went on to point out, were 'welding entire nations into war-making machines', and they were doing so 'at the cost of the sternest repression of all the amenities and indulgences of human existence'. Such fanatical efforts could not be combated 'merely by going along in the present comfortable manner without any decisive impingement upon private trade or profit-making or demanding any temporary sacrifices of comfort and changes in our way of living'. Financial sacrifices were not enough: 'the whole nation must pull together'.

Churchill ended his speech by appealing for a genuine British commitment both to the military potential of the League of Nations, and to the moral forces which it embodied. Of those moral forces he declared: 'Do not let us mock at them for they are surely on our side. Do not mock at them, for this may well be a time when the highest idealism is not divorced from strategic prudence. Do not mock at them, for these may be years, strange as it may seem, when Right may walk hand in hand with Might.'

On May 26 Neville Chamberlain succeeded Stanley Baldwin as British Prime Minister, and head of the predominantly Conservative National Government. He offered no place to Churchill in his new administration, thereby leaving

in the political wilderness the man who had most forcefully urged rearmament and collective security within the Covenant of the League of Nations.
Speaking to the Anti-Nazi Council on June 14, in London, Churchill told
those who shared his concerns: 'I feel our country's safety is fatally imperilled
both by its lack of arms and by the Government's attitude towards the Nazi
gangsters.' German intentions were being made clear in every report from
Germany. On October 18 Anthony Rumbold, a young British diplomat
whose job was to study these reports – and who had been in Berlin in 1933
when his father was Ambassador there – minuted, about the German Army:
'Great strides are being made in mechanization, even at the expense of great
casualties.' The German Army, Rumbold added, was 'being prepared to
deliver a knock-out blow in any direction that may be required'.

In November, in the search for an understanding with Germany, Chamberlain sent Lord Halifax – soon to become Foreign Secretary – to Germany.
Reporting to the Cabinet about his talk with Hitler in Berlin, Halifax
confided, on November 24, that 'he had encountered friendliness and a desire
for good relations'. The Germans, he said, 'had no policy of immediate
adventure'. All would be well with Czechoslovakia if she treated 'the Germans
living within her borders well'. In conclusion, Halifax told his colleagues,
he would expect 'a beaver-like persistence' on the part of the Germans 'in
pressing their aims in Central Europe, but not in a form to give others cause
– or probably occasion – to interfere'. Halifax also pointed out that Hitler
'had suggested an advance towards disarmament', and had also 'strongly
criticized widespread talk of an imminent catastrophe and did not consider
that the world was in a dangerous state'.

Commenting on Halifax's visit, Neville Chamberlain told the Cabinet
that as a result of what Hitler had said, 'the most hopeful prospect' for
disarmament 'was in a qualitative rather than a quantitative direction; that
is to say, some limitation of the size and power of weapons such as guns,
tanks or aeroplanes'.

Chamberlain believed that Hitler would respond to a British approach
along these lines, and rejected Churchill's argument that Britain ought to
work with the League of Nations. Chamberlain told his Cabinet that with
regard to the League he 'took the same view as Herr Hitler. At present it
was largely a sham, owing more particularly to the idea that it could impose
its views by force'.

The parliamentary debate which was held to discuss Halifax's visit to
Germany raised fundamental differences in the approach towards Germany

between the British Government and its critics. Churchill focused on the persecution of the Jews in Germany. 'It is a horrible thing', he said, 'that a race of people should be attempted to be blotted out of the society in which they have been born', and he went on to express his unease about Halifax's visit to Berlin. 'We must remember,' he said, 'how very sharp the European situation is at the present time,' and he continued:

> If it were thought that we were making terms for ourselves at the expense either of small nations or of large conceptions which are dear, not only to many nations, but to millions of people in every nation, a knell of despair would resound through many parts of Europe.

> It was for this reason that Lord Halifax's journey caused widespread commotion, as everyone saw, in all sorts of countries to whom we have no commitments other than the commitments involved in the Covenant of the League.

Churchill also told the House of Commons that it would be wrong to ignore 'the moral forces involved' in public opinion. 'For five years I have been asking the House and the Government to make armaments – guns, aeroplanes, munitions – but I am quite sure that British armaments alone will never protect us in the times through which we may have to pass.'

In China those who represented the 'moral forces' which Churchill believed to be so important were under continuous physical attack. On November 19 the Japanese troops, advancing in their war of conquest, reached Souchow, one of China's oldest cities, known because of its canals and bridges as 'the Venice of China'. For four days Souchow was looted and burned. Thousands of Chinese women were raped, or taken away by force to Japanese army brothels. Thousands more were murdered. Three weeks later, on December 10, the advancing Japanese reached the outskirts of the Nationalist capital, Nanking. The Chinese government moved further up the Yangtse, to Hankow. Nanking was surrounded and besieged.

Wherever the Japanese advance continued, it was characterized by a fierce campaign of air and sea bombardment. Although Peking was spared destruction – there had been no attempt by the Chinese to defend it – the nearby city of Tientsin was heavily bombed and the university there destroyed. Deep in the interior, Hankow, the new Nationalist capital, was also bombed. Far to the south, Canton was likewise attacked repeatedly from the air. Many towns and villages that were not directly in the line of the Japanese advance were also bombed. The world's newspapers reported day-by-day the horrors of aerial bombardment.

On December 12 Japanese aircraft bombed and sank an American gunboat, the *Panay*, in the Yangtse River. Four men on board were killed. In their note of apology the Japanese government blamed over-zealous junior officers. The United States was not mollified, and in a formal note to the Japanese government asked that Emperor Hirohito himself be informed 'of the indiscriminate bombing' of American and other non-Chinese vessels on the Yangtse: among the non-Chinese dead in a similar incident was a British sailor killed on board HMS *Ladybird*. The Japanese were offended by the American request, but eventually agreed to pay an indemnity and to punish those responsible for the attacks.

Even as the American government and people fulminated against the sinking of their gunboat, the advance of the Japanese forces along the Yangtse reached a climax with the entry of Japanese forces into Nanking, the former Nationalist capital, on December 13. This was the entry of a conquering army into a foreign capital, an event with which the world was to become familiar in the course of the next five years; but in 1937 it was something hardly seen since the First World War. With an intensity that shocked even those familiar with the savagery of war, the Japanese soldiers who entered Nanking attacked the Chinese civilian population in an orgy of destruction. The 'Rape of Nanking' was to take its place among the massacres not only of the century, but of modern times.

When the Japanese entered Nanking the total Chinese population was estimated at between 600,000 and 700,000, of whom 150,000 were soldiers. In the ensuing slaughter more than 200,000 civilians and 90,000 soldiers were killed. The first to be killed were the soldiers who had surrendered. The orders for their execution were specific: 'All prisoners of war are to be executed. Method of execution: divide the prisoners into groups of a dozen. Shoot to kill separately.' Japanese company commanders were instructed to meet 'to exchange opinions on how to dispose of POWs.' One official army suggestion was to carry out the executions 'in groups of fifty'. To lull the Chinese soldiers into surrendering, the Japanese offered them 'fair treatment'. Once they had submitted to having their hands bound, writes the historian Iris Chang, 'the rest was easy'.

Japanese officers used their swords to chop off the heads of their prisoners. Soldiers bayoneted prisoners to death, often tying them up in batches first. A Japanese officer, Tominaga Shogo, later explained the bayoneting of live men. 'When I was a company commander, this was used as a finishing touch to training for the men and a trial of courage for the officer,' he said. 'After that, a man could do anything easily. The army created men capable of combat. The thing of supreme importance was to make them fight. It didn't matter whether they were bright or sincere. Men useless in action were worthless. Good soldiers were those who were able to kill, however uncouth they were.'

A Japanese war correspondent wrote of the brutal behaviour of the Japanese troops in China: 'It is their reward for taking a town; the officers promise three days to do what they like when a town is captured.' In Nanking those three days were extended to almost two months. With the soldiers taken captive – and killed – the civilians had no one to protect them. Old people, women, children, and wounded soldiers were shot down in the streets. Shopkeepers, having been ordered to open their shops, were then killed, and the shops looted. In the weeks that followed at least 20,000 rapes were committed by the Japanese soldiers in Nanking – one Chinese estimate puts the figure at 80,000. A Japanese soldier, Takokoro Kozo, later recalled: 'Women suffered most. No matter how young or old, they all could not escape the fate of being trapped. We sent out coal trucks to the city streets and villages to seize a lot of women. And then each of them was allocated to fifteen to twenty soldiers for sexual intercourse and abuse.' Takokoro added: 'After raping we would also kill them. Those women would start to flee once we let them go. Then we would "bang!" shoot them in the back to finish them up.'

As news of the mass rapes in Nanking reached the outside world there was an outcry. In response, the Japanese army instituted a system of military brothels into which women from the nationalities and races under Japanese rule – starting with Korea and those parts of China already conquered – were forced to service the sexual demands of the soldiers. These women were designated 'comfort women' by their captors and abusers. The first of the buildings set aside as 'facilities of sexual comfort' was opened near Nanking within a few months of the city's capture.

On December 17 General Matsui, the commander of the Japanese troops who had entered Nanking four days earlier, issued a victorious proclamation. 'Now the flag of the Rising Sun is floating high over Nanking, and the Imperial Way is shining in the southern ports of the Yangtse,' he declared. The general added: 'The dawn of the renaissance of the East is on the verge of appearing.'

The atrocities committed by the Japanese in Nanking were witnessed by the twenty-two foreigners — mostly Europeans and Americans — who were members of the small foreign community there. As well as witnessing, these twenty-two sought to do what they could to offer protection to the Chinese in whose midst they lived. A Presbyterian minister from the United States, W. Plumer Mills, who had heard of the efforts of Father de Bessage in Shanghai, suggested that a similar protected zone be set up in Nanking. He received support from the Americans, English, Danes and Russians in the city, as well as from several German residents, who were members of the Nazi Party.

Among those foreign residents who intervened to save the lives of the Chinese in the Nanking Safety Zone was the man who was elected its head, John Rabe. A German, and the leader of the Nazi Party in Nanking, Rabe had lived in China for more than thirty years, mostly as the representative of Siemens, selling telephones and electrical equipment. As a quarter of a million Chinese entered the Safety Zone, a telegram which Rabe sent to Hitler asking for his intervention in support of the zone may have been the cause for Japanese reluctance to enter it. But that reluctance was shortlived. Several thousand Chinese soldiers, having laid down their arms, were given sanctuary in the zone. The Japanese came and took them out: in the first search 1,300 were found, taken away, and executed.

The Japanese took thousands more men from the zone, and killed them. These men had not been soldiers, but were rickshaw pullers and manual labourers. The Japanese soldiers who searched the zone said that the calluses on these men's hands were proof that they were soldiers. An eye witness of one such search was the YMCA representative in the city, George Fitch, who wrote in his diary: 'The men were lined up and roped together in groups of about 100 by soldiers with bayonets fixed; those who had hats had them roughly torn off and thrown to the ground — and then by the lights of our headlights we watched them marched away to their doom.'

John Rabe protested to the Japanese about the raping of women inside the zone. He also intervened to stop individual rapes. George Fitch noted in his diary that when Rabe confronted Japanese soldiers he 'thrusts his Nazi armband in their face and points to his Nazi decoration, the highest in the country, and asks them if they know what it means. It always works!' Another Nazi Party member in Nanking, Eduard Sperling, used his Swastika armband to order four Japanese soldiers to desist from raping and looting.

Two other foreigners who made a particularly strong impact on the petrified Chinese in Nanking were both Americans: a surgeon, Robert Wilson – whose uncle had founded the University of Nanking – and Minnie Vautrin, the head of the education department of the Ginling Women's Arts and Science College in the city. Both made extraordinary efforts to protect the Chinese within the zone, especially from the soldier-rapists. In his diary for December 18, Wilson wrote: 'Today marks the 6th day of modern Dante's Inferno, written in huge letters of blood and rape. Murder by the wholesale and rape by the thousands of cases. There seems to be no stop to the ferocity, lust and atavism of the brutes.'

One survivor of the massacre at Nanking, Xia Shuqin – who set down her recollections sixty years later – was eight years old when the Japanese entered the city. Her grandparents and her parents were shot before her eyes. Her older sisters were also killed, and she herself was bayoneted three times and left for dead. Tens of thousands of children were bayoneted and killed. Tens of thousands of soldiers, and young men of military age – or younger – were machine-gunned, bayoneted or decapitated. The Japanese company commander, Tominaga Shogo, later explained how, after decapitating a Chinese prisoner with his sword 'I felt something change inside me. I don't know how to describe it, but I gained strength somewhere in my gut.'

'How our modern civilization drifts back towards medievalism,' the United States Ambassador to Germany, William Dodd, wrote in his diary on December 14, shortly before returning to the United States after more than four years in Berlin. His last three official visitors at the Embassy all told the same tale, from their different national perspectives:

Today the Czechoslovak Minister called, tremendously concerned about the fate of his country because democratic countries do nothing and thus give Mussolini, Hitler and Japan increasing sway over the world. He said Russia, though an ally of his country and France, is helpless.

Yesterday the Russian Chargé d'Affaires came to see me and insisted that democratic countries, England, France and the United States, wish his country to save China without their assistance. Russia, said he, will not do that, but she would co-operate with those countries if they would help China.

After the Czechoslovak Minister left this morning, the Chinese Ambassador came to talk again about his country's dangerous condition. He repeated information I had received from Washington over the radio: that the Japanese had destroyed American and English vessels in Chinese rivers, even killing Americans, and that our President had demanded complete restoration and apologies from the Emperor of Japan. He wanted to know whether the United States would really do anything.

I could not give any assurance though I agreed with him that the democracies must save China or themselves soon come into grave danger.

Dodd added: 'We parted sadly, he saying his country might have to be subjugated and I acknowledging that modern civilization seemed to be on the verge of disaster.'

CHAPTER SIX

1938

... a quarrel in a faraway country between people of
whom we know nothing.

NEVILLE CHAMBERLAIN

THE FIRST DAY of 1938 saw the Japanese forces in China continue their
advance, capturing a number of coastal towns. The possibility of total mastery
of Japan over much of the land mass of China, with all its resources, was
within Tokyo's grasp. In February, the troops who had so savagely imposed
Japanese rule on Nanking also advanced further inland. Everywhere the
Nationalist forces under Chiang Kai-shek resisted; and were able at one or
two points to counterattack, but the Japanese superiority in aircraft and
tanks was decisive. The Chinese were also unfortunate that a number of
military advisers lent to it earlier by Germany were recalled: Germany was
not going to contribute in any way to the discomfiture of Japan.

A British journalist, Harold Timperley, sought to alert the world to what
was happening in China. His book, *Japanese Terror in China*, would not have
been written, he explained in his preface, written on March 23, 'had it not
been for the fact that telegrams reporting the outrages committed against
Chinese civilians by the Japanese troops which occupied Nanking in
December of last year were suppressed by the censors installed by the Japanese
in the foreign cable offices at Shanghai'. Among the 'suppressed or mutilated'
messages, Timperley explained, were several telegrams which he himself
'attempted to send to the *Manchester Guardian*'. His book was the first account
published in the West which conveyed the full scale and horror of the
suffering of the Chinese during the Nanking massacre. It also gave copious
details of the continuing atrocities as other cities fell to the Japanese army,
including Hankow, Wuhu and Souchow.

From Britain, a word of encouragement for the Chinese came from Winston Churchill who, although not holding government office for almost a decade, had a wide regular readership. In an article in the *Daily Telegraph* on May 26 he wrote, about Chiang Kai-shek: 'He may well become a world hero, as a patriot and a leader who, amid a thousand difficulties and wants, does not despair of saving China from a base and merciless exploitation. It may thus be that from the opposite side of the earth will come that exemplary discomfiture of a brutal aggression which will cheer the democracies of the Western world and teach them to stand up for themselves while time remains.'

After five months uninterrupted fighting the Japanese reached the city of Kiukiang, only 138 miles by river from the seat of the Chinese government at Hankow. The Japanese troops then paused, as a result of the hot August weather, but in September renewed their drive towards the capital. The Chinese planned to make a fierce defence, and in the event of being about to be overwhelmed, to raze Hankow to the ground. But following heavy Japanese bombing attacks there was a sudden collapse of Chinese morale, and the city was abandoned to the Japanese on October 26. Five days earlier, Japanese forces had entered Canton, their warplanes having carried out a series of heavy bombing raids on the city. Japanese troops, landing at Bias Bay, marched 125 miles in nine days to enter the city in force.

A European eye-witness to the Japanese capture of Hankow was Albert Dorrance, the manager of the Standard Oil Company offices in the city. He watched from the deck of one of the four United States gun boats in the Yangste River as Japanese troops forced Chinese soldiers in groups of three and four to walk a gangplank and then threw them into the river. As their heads appeared above the water the Japanese soldiers opened fire on them.

Following the capture of both Canton and Hankow, the Japanese were able to control the whole length of the Canton-Hankow railway, one of the main commercial arteries of China, and the route along which the Chinese forces had received most of their arms and ammunition from overseas. The only route open after October was a mountain road from India, through Burma to Yunnan, known as the Burma Road. From Yunnan the road was open to the Yangstse, where the river was under Nationalist control to Chungking, Chaing Kai-shek's third capital in less than a year.

A United States Army engineer, Major John E. Ausland, supervised the technical aspects of the Burma Road's construction. In the first disastrous month of full-scale work, 1,300 of the 2,000 labourers on one section of the road died of malaria. It was only the arrival of a Field Sanitary Engineer, 'Doc' Wright, sent by the Rockefeller Foundation from New York, that led to the elimination of malaria among the workers: Wright had been in charge of controlling malaria during the construction of the Panama Canal in 1904.

A *Life* magazine correspondent, George Rodger, who travelled the road in its early days, recalled how the Chinese workers 'learned to report sickness among those who still lived, but those who died were beyond consideration and they threw them into the jungle, where they lay rotting until Doc Wright could trace them by their stench and have them buried'.

On December 29 the United States Ambassador to China, Nelson T. Johnson, made the first motor car journey over the newly opened Burma Road. Even after the exertions of the engineers and their teams of labourers the road was not suitable for heavy artillery. But once motor cars and lorries were able to negotiate it, at any one time the road was being travelled by up to 5,000 trucks and 8,000 pack mules. Maintaining the winding, often precipitous 620-mile road, and the railway track that was being built along it from Lashio to Yunnan, involved the continuous work of a quarter of a million Chinese labourers.

In the fighting against the Japanese, a million Chinese soldiers were killed or wounded during 1938. Tens of thousands of Chinese civilians were killed in Japanese air raids. The Chinese themselves, in desperate attempts to halt the Japanese advance, burned everything they could as they left, thereby also depriving millions of Chinese peasants of their means of existence. Floods on the Yellow River added to the terrible human suffering, with as many as sixty million Chinese being brought to the verge of starvation – and several million dying of hunger.

Chinese resistance continued behind the lines of the Japanese advance. A Chinese Political Council, headed by Chiang Kai-shek, contained representatives of all the groups actively fighting, including the Communist leader, Mao Tse-tung. In eastern and central Hopei province, which was nominally under Japanese control, the remnants of the 8th Route (Communist) Army controlled an area estimated at 90,000 square miles.

The European Powers were divided in their attitude to the war in the Far East. Germany and Italy were sympathetic to the Japanese; Britain and France to China. When Japan closed the Yangstse River from Hankow to the sea to all foreign traffic, the United States as well as Britain and France protested.

It was the stance of Hitler's Germany in Europe, however, that seemed the most dangerous factor for disruption. At the start of 1938 a Committee of Seven was set up in Vienna by a group of Austrian citizens, whose declared purpose was the reconciliation of the Austrian government with the Austrian Nazis. When, however, on January 26, the Austrian police raided the committee's headquarters, they discovered documents, initialled by Rudolf Hess, Hitler's Deputy Führer, calling for the Austrian Nazis to stage a revolt against the government in the spring. The plan explained in the documents was that, once the 'spontaneous' revolt began, the German Army would cross the border into Austria 'to prevent German blood being spilled by Germans'.

Hitler was not deterred by the exposure of his Austrian plan. The master of improvization, he was likewise the master of steady consolidation. He also knew that there was no automatic alignment of threatened States willing to make common cause against him. Indeed, on January 27 Neville Chamberlain explained to the Cabinet's Foreign Policy Committee in London his ideas for 'an entirely new chapter in the history of African colonial development' whereby Germany would be 'brought into the arrangement by becoming one of the African Colonial powers'. Chamberlain explained that his plan was to offer Hitler several African territories for Germany to administer, telling his colleagues that he rejected the 'pessimistic' view of Professor Stephen Roberts, in his recent book *The House that Hitler Built,* that there was a German threat to Britain, and a malign element in Nazism that could only lead to war.

Events as they unfolded seemed to confirm what Roberts had written. On February 4 Hitler declared himself Commander-in-Chief of the German Army. Soldiers already swore a personal oath of loyalty to him. That same day he replaced the diplomat Konstantin von Neurath as Foreign Minister with a Nazi activist, Joachim von Ribbentrop, who for several years had held the rank of Colonel in the SS. As German Ambassador to Britain, Ribbentrop had been offended by the failure of British society to embrace him; and had been mocked for having given the Nazi salute to King George VI at a court reception. His rancour against Britain, which was intense, did not bode well for diplomatic moderation. Nor did Hitler appoint him to his post in order to be a force for moderation.

The future and fate of Austria was being discussed throughout Europe from day to day. 'The independence of Austria should be maintained,' wrote the French journalist Geneviève Tabouis, in a widely syndicated column in her newspaper *L'Oeuvre* – it was banned in Germany – 'for with it is bound up the independence of Czechoslovakia, and it constitutes the basis for the equilibrium in Central Europe.'

A nineteen-year-old Austrian Jew, George Weidenfeld, a student at the Diplomatic Academy in Vienna – later to be a distinguished British publisher and man of letters – recalled after half a century how, 'while Austria began to burn, its youth danced':

> The winter before the Anschluss was especially gregarious and festive. The season started in the middle of December, resumed after Christmas and culminated in the great Viennese Carnival just before Lent, the *Wiener Fasching*, consisting of a veritable avalanche of balls – the Opera Ball, the Architects' Ball, the Lawyers' Ball, the ball in the Konzerthaus, the Academicians' Ball, masked balls and costume balls in period attire, balls for all ages and all classes, public balls for charity and private balls so select that exclusion could mean social ostracism for the hapless member of the set in question.
>
> The ball of the Konsularakademie was a special event because members of the diplomatic corps, the leading figures in the Government and Viennese society were invariably present and lent it international distinction.

Two things happened, Weidenfeld later wrote, which made February 12 'a night to remember':

> While we waltzed and tangoed, rumba'd and self-consciously partook in rather stilted rural *Laendlers*, polkas and gavottes, a chilling rumour suddenly spread that Chancellor Schuschnigg had been summoned to Hitler's alpine eyrie and could not therefore be present. Instead, at a late hour, a senior minister, Guido Zernatto, appeared in the somewhat operatesque uniform of the Austrian Storm Squadrons, one of the innumerable variants of fascist gala dress. He made an appearance to reassure us. However, foreign diplomats were whispering to one another. The old guard of the Ballhausplatz, the Austrian foreign ministry, who had only minutes earlier admired the graceful spectacle of the young couples on the dance floor, now clustered in corners with long faces and frightened miens.
>
> Yet I danced with imperturbable abandon because I had fallen in love for the first time in my life, and for the last time in Austria.

It was on February 12 that Hitler had invited the Austrian Chancellor, Kurt von Schuschnigg to Berchtesgaden. Schuschnigg was told by his deputy Foreign Minister, Dr Guido Schmidt – a pro-Nazi – that the meeting was to be 'a friendly visit to clear up misunderstanding'. Schuschnigg agreed to go provided his journey was kept secret. Hardly had Schuschnigg reached Berchtesgaden, however, than the Nazis announced the visit to the world.

Far from finding himself on a 'friendly visit', Schuschnigg found himself facing demands by Hitler that all Nazis serving sentences in Austrian prisons should be amnestied, that the Nazi Party should have full freedom of movement inside Austria, and that the Ministry of the Interior should be handed over to a leading Austrian Nazi, Artur Seyss-Inquart. Hitler was not making these demands as a basis for negotiation, or for prolonged discussion. Indeed, he addressed Schuschnigg as if he were a despised adversary rather than a Head of State, screaming at him that he was a 'murderer' and a 'dwarf'.

He, Hitler – 'the greatest German that ever lived', as he described himself to a bewildered Schuschnigg – wanted compliance. And he wanted it at once, telling the Austrian Chancellor: 'I demand obedience, and I shall enforce it, if necessary with my armies.' Hitler then called General Walther von Reichenau – Commander of the Munich Defence District – into the room, and told Schuschnigg that Reichenau 'will be the Commander of my Armies of Occupation in Austria'.

After laying an ultimatum to Austria on the table in front of Schuschnigg, Hitler told Reichenau: 'Before Herr Schuschnigg studies my ultimatum I want you to take him into the next room and show him the whole of your strategic plan for the occupation and garrisoning of Austria.' Reichenau did so. This was the German plan for the invasion of Austria which the Austrian police had discovered at the end of January.

By the end of the afternoon Schuschnigg had rejected eight of Hitler's eleven points. Under the 'Berchtesgaden Agreement', Schuschnigg would remain Chancellor, but the Nazi influence in his government would be increased to the point at which true independence would be a figment. Schuschnigg returned to Vienna in the early hours of February 13. Three days later – for Hitler had given him three days to comply – he carried out Hitler's demands, appointing Artur Seyss-Inquart as Minister of the Interior and Guido Schmidt as Foreign Minister, and releasing all those Nazis who had earlier been imprisoned. Among the Austrian Nazis who emerged into prominence overnight was Odilo Globocnik: four years later, as an SS Major-General, he was to establish four death camps in German-occupied Poland for the mass murder of more than two million Jews.

Hitler addressed the German people on February 20, speaking for three hours to a packed audience at the Kroll Opera House in Berlin. While boasting of his Austrian triumph he also focused attention on another region adjoining Germany, telling the Reichstag that it was 'imperative' that the three and a half million German-speaking peoples in Czechoslovakia and in the Sudetenland should be given the 'right of self-determination'. The 'unnecessary torture' of the German-speaking minority in Czechoslovakia must cease.

Speaking of ten million Germans living outside the Reich, and linking them to the sixty-six million Germans under his rule, Hitler declared: 'It is intolerable for a self-conscious world-Power to know that at its side are co-racials who are subjected to continuous suffering because of their sympathy and unity with the whole German race and its ideology.' Those inside Austria who did not accept that ideology were 'race traitors'.

Among those who were in the Opera House when Hitler spoke was Francis Yeats-Brown – the film of whose novel *Tales of a Bengal Lancer* was Hitler's favourite film. Yeats-Brown later wrote:

The whole speech was read, and read very quickly, with no pauses, except during the applause. Even during a solid hour of statistics, he kept every one galvanized by the cadence of his sentences.

During the rhetorical passages his voice mounted to the pitch of delirium: he was a man transformed and possessed: we were in the presence of a miracle: fire might have fallen from Heaven or the chandelier of the Opera House might have come crashing down; the tension was almost unbearable until the passionate voice was drowned by the cries of those who listened.

The delirium was real – Hitler was in a frenzy at these moments, but he was able to create this atmosphere – this curious sense of collective hysteria – without losing his own self-control: whatever his emotion, a steady hand turned the pages of his speech. He possesses that rarest of mental combinations, intense passion harnessed to a cool brain.

The British journalist Eric Gedye, who had listened to Hitler's speech over the radio in his room in Vienna, later recalled how, when the speech was over: 'Up to the windows of my flat rose for the first time that insane, threatening, rhythmic howling which was to echo in day after day . . . "Sieg Heil! *Sieg Heil!* SIEG HEIL! *Heil Hitler!* HEIL HITLER!"'

Taking a taxi to the German Legation, Gedye heard that chant again:

The dam of four years had been pierced by the Hitler speech, and the Brown flood was beginning to trickle into the streets of Vienna. It was only a trickle of stormtroopers and SS guards in plain clothes that I saw that night, shouting and singing the Horst Wessel song, but it was enough to send nervous citizens scurrying home in all directions from the cafés where they had been listening to Hitler's speech.

On the Karlsplatz was a young man directing the illegal formations in stentorian tones: 'Stormtroopers on the right – SS Guards on the left', wearing a surprisingly shabby raincoat over an incongruously smart suit.

Next day I received by a roundabout route a message from a member of the French Legation staff who had been watching the demonstration from a window of the Legation. He had recognized quite unmistakably this young man as one of the attachés of the German Legation – in charge of the Austrian revolutionary Nazis!

It was assumed among those in Berlin who had listened to Hitler's speech that the annexation of Austria was imminent. Starting on February 15, in strictest secrecy, the Austrian Nazis had made preparations to take over every Jewish-owned shop and factory, with 'managing commissars' – many of them employees – appointed to take charge when the annexation came. But Schuschnigg felt that there must be some way to uphold the independence of Austria, even if, at Hitler's insistence, the Nazi influence within his government was to be so strong. On February 27 he ordered troops, airplanes and armoured cars to Graz, where they stopped a planned march on the city of 60,000 Austrian-Nazi Storm Troopers. He also asked Seyss-Inquart to go to Graz on March 1 to point out that the Berchtesgaden Agreement did not mean an end to Austrian sovereignty.

At the very moment that Seyss-Inquart made the journey to Graz, a court in Berlin was about to pass judgment on Pastor Martin Niemöller for his outspoken criticism of Nazism. To the surprise of many observers, the court, which reached its verdict on March 2, gave him a short sentence – eight months – which was exactly the time he had already spent in prison since 1 July 1937 awaiting trial. This meant that he would be released. Then, without further charges being laid against him, and with no prospect of another trial, he was re-arrested that same evening and taken to Sachsenhausen concentration camp.

As Niemöller began his seven-year ordeal, Seyss-Inquart was in Graz, where, instead of defending Austrian independence, he took the salute at a torchlight procession of 15,000 Austrian Nazi Storm Troopers who were pledged to see that independence come to an end.

The German and Nazi pressure on Austria mounted. Four days after his provocative performance in Graz, Seyss-Inquart repeated it in Linz. Schuschnigg realized that he must appeal direct to the people of Austria to prevent the slide to annexation, which might possibly come through a sudden German military attack, or an attempt by the Austrian Nazis to seize power from within. He therefore opened negotiations with the Austrian workers, apologized to them for their sufferings under the Dollfuss regime, allowed them to meet freely in Vienna, and offered to restore the Trade Union rights which Dollfuss had taken away from them.

Even as his discussions with the workers continued, Schuschnigg decided to take a dramatic initiative. On March 9, in Innsbruck, he announced that in four days' time – on March 13 – there would be a nationwide plebiscite to decide whether or not the people wanted an independent Austria. It would be for the Austrian people to decide for or against a 'free Austria'. On hearing of the plebiscite, Hitler gave top secret orders for the German army to prepare 'Operation Otto', the longstanding military plan for the occupation of Austria.

Hitler could not risk a vote that would support continuing independence. On the morning of Friday March 11 he ordered the German border with Austria to be closed at Salzburg, and then sent an ultimatum to Schuschnigg, demanding the cancellation of the plebiscite. The ultimatum was delivered by Seyss-Inquart. Schuschnigg rejected the cancellation of the plebiscite, but offered to change its wording to include the possibility of his own resignation. Hitler rejected this. 'The situation has become untenable,' he told Franz von Papen, the German Ambassador in Vienna, who had flown from Vienna to Berlin that morning. Hitler went on to explain: 'Schuschnigg has betrayed the Greater German ideal. He cannot be allowed to succeed and he will not succeed.'

Those to whom Austria might have looked for support were unable or unwilling to give it. France was in the midst of a political crisis and for three days had been without a Prime Minister. From London, Lord Halifax telegraphed in confidence to Vienna that the British Government could not 'take the responsibility' of advising Schuschnigg to take any action 'which might expose his country to dangers against which his Majesty's Government are unable to guarantee protection.' For its part, the Italian Government issued a public announcement that it would do nothing to intervene.

Hitler had no need to fear outside intervention. At 4 p.m. that afternoon a second German ultimatum was delivered to Schuschnigg. It demanded not only that the plebiscite be cancelled, but that Schuschnigg resign. A time limit for the reply was fixed at 7.30 p.m. From Berlin, Field Marshal Goering told Seyss-Inquart over the telephone two hours before the ultimatum was due to expire that unless Schuschnigg resigned and appointed Seyss-Inquart as Chancellor, 'then this very night the troops massed against and moving towards the whole length of the border will march on, and Austria's existence will be at an end.'

Having made certain that Mussolini would not intervene to protect Austria, Hitler had sent 200,000 German troops to the border, with instructions to enter Austria in force if ordered to do so. Then, as the ultimatum was about to expire, Schuschnigg broadcast to Austria, and to the world, accepting the ultimatum, but seeking to put the record straight:

> I declare before the world that the reports put into circulation concerning disorders by the workers, the shedding of streams of blood and the allegation that the situation had got out of the control of the Government, are lies from A to Z.
>
> President Miklas asks me to tell the people of Austria that we have yielded to force, since we are not prepared even in this terrible situation to shed blood. We decided to order the troops to offer no serious – to offer no resistance.
>
> So I take leave of the Austrian people, with the German word of farewell, uttered from the depth of my heart – 'God protect Austria'.

One of those listening to Schuschnigg's broadcast was the eighteen-year-old George Weidenfeld – soon to leave Austria for Britain as a refugee – who recalled:

> His closing word was the salute 'Austria', and then, turning to the small band of followers in the studio with, it seemed, his back to the microphone, he was heard repeating it: 'Austria. Gentlemen, good luck.' Then the

Austrian anthem was played for the last time, slowly and languidly, as laid down by Haydn.

Silence fell, but after a seemingly endless minute or two another recorded version, with quickening tempo and a triumphalist tone, the same music but with a different text – 'Deutschland, Deutschland, Über Alles' – began. And, to complete the ritual, the sounds of the Horst Wessel song, the Nazi Party anthem, that blend of political triumphalism and folkloric romanticism signalling the beginning of a new era, rang out: 'The Thousand Year Reich'.

That night, Hitler's forces crossed into Austria. There was no resistance, and no fighting. In many places the Germans were welcomed with Swastika flags and flowers.

As evidence that the harshest measures were to be expected once Austria came into the German orbit, Heinrich Himmler travelled by air to Vienna on Saturday March 12. That day, Seyss-Inquart, who at Hitler's insistence had succeeded Schuschnigg as Chancellor, issued a decree making Austria part of the German Reich. The prohibition on Anschluss – one of the main prohibitions of the Treaty of Versailles – had been swept aside.

The British writer Francis Yeats-Brown was in the Austrian ski resort of Kitzbühel when the proclamation of the annexation of Austria was read over the wireless by Dr Goebbels. He recalled:

We were just an average Kitzbühel crowd: people from the village, hotel guests, ski instructors, and some of us, I know, were by no means ardent Nazis when Doctor Goebbels began to speak in his resonant voice. But a miracle occurred when he said: 'This morning the soldiers of the armed forces of Germany are marching across the Austrian frontiers, while in the blue sky above our German aeroplanes are soaring!'

The audience was German. There was magic in the name. Never have I felt so unmistakably the influence of unseen forces as in that little room, the scene of many careless hours, now suddenly being filled with history. Under the sway of a common emotion the audience rose to its feet and sang 'Deutschland über alles.' . . .

No one was coerced. The joy of the people was real; they felt that everyone must be delighted at the swift movement of troops, at this dramatic, decisive ending of uncertainty. No longer was Austria a lone child; now she was part of the most powerful nation in Europe. Austria was German and answered the call of the blood.

Such was the enthusiastic view of those both inside Austria and outside it for whom Pan-Germanism was a creed and an inspiration. As soon as he learned of the rousing reception of his troops at every point along the road from Linz to Vienna, Hitler hastened to follow them. It was almost thirty years since he had left Austria-Hungary for Germany, serving in the German Army, challenging the German political system, and rising to become German Chancellor. On reaching Linz he told the ecstatic crowd of Austrian Nazis who turned out to greet him: 'When I first set out from this town I felt in the depth of my soul that it was my vocation and my mission given me by destiny that I should bring my home country back to the great German Reich. I have believed in this mission and I have fulfilled it.'

Travelling by car from Linz to Vienna, Hitler was greeted by the leader of the Catholic Church in Austria, Cardinal Innitzer. Without ordering a shot to be fired, without having to test the effectiveness of his army, and without fighting a battle, Hitler had secured his first territorial gain. Austria became a German province.

Yeats-Brown had hurried to Vienna from Kitzbühel to witness the scene of Hitler's arrival. 'I made my way to the balcony of the Bristol Hotel,' he wrote. 'From here I saw the greatest crowd that has ever been assembled in Vienna . . . All Vienna was not rejoicing – the Jews, for instance – but the scene below me left no doubt about what the majority were thinking. Hitler came almost unexpectedly as dark was falling. I had thought that there would be some elaborate pageantry; instead, there he stood alone in a big grey car. Vienna has seen the ebb and flow of many conquests, but never a conqueror who once shovelled snow in her streets.'

Throughout March 13, the day on which the plebiscite was to have been held, a swift and terrible vengeance was already being taken by the German and Austrian Nazis against all those who had led the struggle to maintain Austrian independence. Two-thirds of the officers in the Austrian army were interned; many of them favoured the return of the Archduke Otto von Habsburg to the throne. Thousands of Austrians – democrats, patriots, trade unionists – were arrested and sent to concentration camps in Germany.

Within a few days, under Himmler's vigilant eye, and with his black-shirted SS – often called at that time the Nazi Black Guards – the masters of the streets, every aspect of German Nazism was introduced into Austria, most visibly the anti-Jewish laws and practices which had evolved over the previous five years in Germany. In Austria those laws and practices were imposed overnight. Jewish shops and homes were looted. Large red placards were placed on all Jewish enterprises – and even on Jewish-owned cafés – and any non-Jew who was caught by stormtroopers entering was made to wear a placard around his or her neck stating: 'I, Aryan swine, have bought in a Jewish shop.'

Several thousand Jews were attacked and beaten up in the streets. At the Jewish Community Centre in Vienna, uniformed stormtroopers decided to amuse themselves. 'I was given a bucket of boiling water,' one community leader, Moritz Fleischmann, later recalled, 'and I was told to clean the steps. I lay down on my stomach and began to clean the pavement. It turned out that the bucket was half full of acid and burned my hands.' Also ordered out of the building and made to brush the pavement was the Chief Rabbi, Dr Taglicht, a man of seventy. 'In order that he should feel the full force of the degradation and humility of it,' Fleischmann recalled, 'he was thrown out wearing his gown, and with his prayer shawl on.'

The Jews of Vienna, who made up a sixth of the city's inhabitants, were immediately deprived of the right to own property, were refused the right to be employed or to employ others, were forbidden to participate in any of their professions, and were refused entry to any public bath or public park. Suicides were a frequent occurrence among Jews who did not know how to face a future made suddenly so bleak and dangerous. Among those who killed themselves were several well-known writers and lawyers. A British dental student who was studying in Vienna wrote in a private letter five days after the Anschluss: 'A family of six Jews have just shot themselves, a few houses down the street. They are well out of it.'

Eric Gedye, who was in Vienna when the German soldiers and stormtroopers marched in, recalled seeing the occupiers 'gloating over the daily suicide lists'. After the suicide of a young Jewish doctor and his mother in the block of flats in which he lived, Gedye, wrote: 'From my window I could watch for many days how they would arrest Jewish passers-by – generally doctors, lawyers or merchants, for they preferred their victims to belong to the better-educated classes – and force them to scrub, polish and beat carpets in the flat where the tragedy had taken place, while insisting that the doctor's non-Jewish maid should sit at ease in a chair and look on.'

Of Austria's 200,000 Jews, 30,000 were arrested and sent to German concentration camps. They could only secure their release if a friend provided them with the necessary documents for emigration. As many as ten thousand of those being held in the camps are believed to have killed themselves, as terrible torture, and the threat of torture, intensified. Tens of thousands of Austrian Jews managed to make their way as refugees to whatever countries would receive them. Many found refuge in Czechoslovakia, Holland, Belgium and France, unable to know that within two years and two months their safe havens would be overrun by that same Germany that had overrun Austria.

Having been expelled from Vienna, the British journalist Eric Gedye went to the Ambassador Hotel in Prague, where he found 'several faces with the bewildered, apologetic look of emigrés, uncertain of themselves and their welcome, homeless, futureless – most of them to be penniless when the loose cash they had in their pockets when they fled is gone.' And yet, Gedye added, 'these homeless men and women are the millionaires of the emigration – they can at least for a few days find the price of a cup of coffee in this hall where the new arrivals seem automatically to come first for news of who is saved, who is lost. The others have saved – quite literally – their naked lives.'

Among those who fled from Vienna was Sigmund Freud, who, at the age of eighty-two, made his way to Britain. There he was made a Fellow of the Royal Society in recognition of his services to psychoanalysis. German radio propaganda mocked at the 'degeneracy' of Britain in giving such an honour to such a 'degenerate'. Clifford Allen, a former pacifist, who had long sought to give Nazi Germany the benefit of the doubt in international affairs, told the House of Lords: 'Germany has said that British democracy is degenerate. Well, I for one was never more proud of British democracy than when Professor Freud, that great scientist, aged and infirm, became an exile from his country and was welcomed within our shores.'

Like a growing number of Englishmen, Clifford Allen had come to recognize that the racism of the German government was an integral part of its national philosophy, which must affect its wider relations. 'I have known myself, as a guest of the German Government,' he said, 'what it is to be taken through the lovely countryside in Germany, and then to feel the profound discomfort which comes from seeing those placards of hatred against the Jews which encounter you as you pass through the country.' Allen went on to speak of the racial aspect of the Nazi Germany whose actions and aspirations he had sought so hard to understand:

Some of us have known in Germany, even when we have been the guests of the German Government, what it is to have in our hands the hand of a little German child, a child which in school has been compelled to sit upon benches separate from its school-fellows, an object of contempt, for no other reason than that it is the child of its Jewish parents.

I cannot conceive anything more cruel than to try to stir up hatred between child and parent. That is not a persecution of opinion, that is not an attempt to put down sedition, that is persecution of blood, from which there is no escape; and, for a child to be brought up under that form of persecution, I think must stir the heart of anyone who has passed through that experience in Germany.

As well as the Jews, thousands of Austrians who were active Catholics, Democrats, Socialists or Communists were arrested and sent to concentration camps. There were also Austrian zealots for the new ideology. On April 6 a leading professor of anatomy, Eduard Pernkopf, at his inaugural lecture as Dean of the Medical Faculty at Vienna University, called on his colleagues to take charge of the 'national body' both in what he called 'the positive sense, in the sense of promoting the industrious', and 'in the negative sense, extermination of the inferior and the weak'.

Returning to Vienna on April 9, Hitler spoke at the disused North-West Station to a gathering of 20,000 members of the Austrian Nazi Party. 'I stand here,' he said, 'because I flatter myself that I can do more than Herr Schuschnigg. I have shown through my life that I can do more than these dwarfs, who ruled this country into ruin. Whether in a hundred years' time anyone will remember the names of my predecessors here, I do not know, but my name will stand as the name of the great son of this country.' Hitler even made great play of the fact that while he had been born in Austria, Schuschnigg had been born in Italy. This was not strictly true: Schuschnigg had been born at Riva, at the northern end of Lake Garda: it was indeed part of Italy in 1938, but it had been inside Austria-Hungary at the time of Schuschnigg's birth.

During the gathering of April 9, as a climax of the ceremonial events, messages of allegiance were brought to Hitler from all thirty-one German provinces. One of those provinces was the 'Ostmark', the new name for the region around Vienna: the very word Austria was about to disappear from the Nazi lexicon. The country whose independence had been guaranteed by the victorious powers in 1919 had not only become a German province, but was given a name last used almost a thousand years earlier, when the Ostmark had been the eastern region of Charlemagne's empire. The provinces of Upper

Austria and Lower Austria were renamed in riverine terminology *Oberdonau* and *Unterdonau*: Upper Danube and Lower Danube.

On April 10, in a cynical echo of Schuschnigg's call for a plebiscite in Austria, Hitler held a plebiscite throughout Greater Germany: the name that was given to Germany and Austria combined. The German people were asked to say that they approved the union with Austria. Robert Ley, head of the German Labour Front, told an audience in Stettin that voters would indicate, by their support for the union, their faith in Hitler as 'the blessed messenger of God'. When the vote was counted, it was said to have been 100 per cent in favour. Hitler's Minister of Justice, Hans Frank – who had taken part as a Nazi stormtrooper in the failed Beer Hall putsch in Munich in 1923 – called the result 'a prayer of thanks of the entire German people'.

God and prayer were an integral part of the Nazi message to people who were seeped in almost a thousand years of Christianity. 'In the Germany of the Twentieth Century,' declared the State-controlled Christian newspaper when the result was known, 'Adolf Hitler's fist is God's fist, and the battalions of the Third Reich who have marched into Austria have become God's military might.'

Inside Austria, hoping that the new Nazi authorities would look with favour on their Church activities, the bishops of the Roman Catholic Church had invited the Catholic population to vote for the Anschluss. But this act of submission did not help the church in the months ahead. The introduction of the Nuremberg Laws in Austria meant that Hitler's definition of a Jew (a person with one Jewish grandparent) would have precedence over the Roman Catholic belief that a convert to Roman Catholicism (even if Jewish by birth, let alone with a single Jewish grandparent) was a full and protected member of the Church.

A series of anti-Roman Catholic measures swiftly followed the Anschluss. In May, the Roman Catholic bishops were forbidden to attend the Eucharistic Congress in Budapest. In August the Catholic Volksbund was dissolved. In October, when a large number of Catholic youth tried to demonstrate in favour of religious principles outside St Stephen's Cathedral in Vienna, they were attacked by Nazi youth who stormed the nearby episcopal palace, destroying and burning its furniture, attacking the priests seeking shelter in it, and throwing one of them out of the window – he later died of his injuries. A week after the demonstration the Austrian Catholic Church was publicly denounced for its 'treacherous attitude', as being 'pro-Jew and pro-

Czech'. As a punishment and a warning, five Catholic priests were sent to Dachau concentration camp.

In the aftermath of the Anschluss, resentment inside the Austrian Nazi Party that most of the top administrative jobs were going to German Nazis led to a revolt within the Austrian Nazi rank and file. The leader of the revolt was Captain Leopold, who in February had been one of the recipients of the Rudolf Hess plan for the overthrow of the Schuschnigg regime. He was opposed by the specially appointed Reichskommisar for Austria, Josef Buerkel, who obtained Hitler's permission for a repeat in miniature of the Night of the Long Knives of 1934. Several hundred disaffected Nazi Party members were arrested and sent to Dachau; 135 of them were shot, Captain Leopold among them.

The ruthless imposition of Nazi terror throughout Austria, and the ever-present threat of incarceration in Dachau, continued to lead to suicides for many months after the arrival of Hitler in Vienna. On the night of March 19 sixty people had killed themselves. In the weeks that followed that number rose to more than a hundred a day. A leading Viennese Jewish furniture manufacturer, Max Bergmann, committed suicide with his wife, his son and daughter, and his son-in-law. The author and journalist Dr Kurt Sonnenfeld, a member of the staff of the *Neue Freie Presse*, took poison together with his wife and father. His paper's editor, Dr Stefan von Mueller, also killed himself. The former Attorney General in Schuschnigg's Government, Dr von Winterstein, shot himself in May to avoid arrest. Schuschnigg's secretary, Dr von Froehlichsthal, took his own life by throwing himself in front of a train when he learned that the Gestapo were looking for him. Industrialists, professors, doctors, lawyers, civil servants, writers, journalists – people whose names were well-known and whose patriotism and liberal outlook was an integral part of inter-war Austria – killed themselves rather than submit to incarceration and torture.

German confidence in the long-term future of Greater Germany was seen in the plans being developed in Berlin for a new University City which would be ready in 1945. That summer a British visitor, Charles Domvile-Fife, was shown the architectural drawings of a three-mile-long central avenue for Berlin – 'tree, shrub and flower-embellished' – that would link two new railway stations, the North and South stations, designed to replace the existing five main stations, which would be pulled down. In front of the North Station a 'huge lake' was planned, flanked by new, monumental headquarters of the President of the Police and the political centre of the Nazi Party.

Domvile-Fife was sympathetic to the plans of the new Germany, and also to the German search for new territories to control. 'They are a military race, and are proud of this fact,' he wrote on his return to Britain. 'I venture to express the opinion that if denied this outlet for their inherited character- istics, ninety out of every hundred German men would feel that the true spirit of their country was being crushed.'

As a result of the German annexation of Austria, Czechoslovakia was sur- rounded on three sides by Germany. Those areas closest to the German border were the ones in which most of the three and a quarter million German- speaking population of Czechoslovakia lived – almost a quarter of the Czecho- slovak population.* The Sudeten mountains were the natural defensive barrier for Bohemia and Moravia. The predominantly German-speaking towns of the Sudetenland contained most of Czechoslovakia's arms factories.

From the first moments of Hitler's increased pressure on Austria in Febru- ary, the Czechs had realized that their turn would be next. In a reply to Hitler's speech of February 20, raising the question of the Sudeten Germans, the Czechoslovak Prime Minister, Milan Hodza – himself a Slovak – told the Chamber of Deputies in Prague on March 4 that, if attacked, Czechoslo- vakia would defend itself 'to the very last'. Any claim by Germany to protect the Sudeten German minority would, he said, be regarded as 'interference' in the internal affairs of Czechoslovakia. But the Sudeten German leader, Konrad Henlein, was confident that, as a result of Hitler's pressure, the Sudeten Germans would be able to gain autonomy, telling his followers on March 13: 'Victory is certain'.

During the debate in the British House of Commons on March 14, to discuss the German annexation of Austria, Churchill warned the government that if resistance to Hitler were to be delayed for too long, a point might well be reached 'where continued resistance and true collective security would become impossible'. His speech continued:

The gravity of the event of the 11th of March cannot be exaggerated.

Europe is confronted with a programme of aggression, nicely calculated and timed, unfolding stage by stage, and there is only one choice open,

---

* The 1930 Czechoslovak census gave a total population of 14,479,565, of which the German minority was 3,231,688.

not only to us, but to other countries who are unfortunately concerned – either to submit, like Austria, or else to take effective measures while time remains to ward off the danger and, if it cannot be warded off, to cope with it.

Churchill went on to ask what would become of Britain by 1940, when the German Army 'will certainly be much larger than the French Army', and when all the small nations of Europe would have abandoned the League of Nations 'to pay homage to the ever-waxing power of the Nazi system, and to make the best terms they can for themselves'. He then spoke of the country which was likely to be threatened next, Czechoslovakia, which, he pointed out, manufactured the munitions on which two other countries, Roumania and Yugoslavia, depended for their defence. Yet Czechoslovakia had been isolated politically and economically as a result of Hitler's annexation of Austria, and, surrounded as a result on three sides by German-controlled borders, found both her communications and her trade suddenly in jeopardy.

'To English ears,' Churchill said, 'the name of Czechoslovakia sounds outlandish. No doubt they are only a small democratic State, no doubt they have an army only two or three times as large as ours, no doubt they have a munitions supply only three times as great as that of Italy, but still they are a virile people; they have their treaty rights, they have a line of fortresses, and they have a strongly manifested will to live freely.'

Churchill feared that Chamberlain's promise to accelerate British rearmament would not, in itself, be enough to preserve peace. The small nations of Europe had to be brought in to a system of collective defence. They had to feel that they could rely upon Britain's word. Churchill then addressed the Conservative Party benches in the parliament:

I know that some of my hon Friends on this side of the House will laugh when I offer them this advice. I say, 'Laugh, but listen.' I affirm that the government should express in the strongest terms our adherence to the Covenant of the League of Nations and our resolve to procure by international action the reign of law in Europe.

Churchill then reiterated the point he had been making since Hitler came to power: 'There must be a moral basis for British rearmament and British foreign policy.'

There had also to be, in Churchill's view, a 'common cause in self-defence' with France. 'But why stop there?' he asked. 'Why be edged and pushed farther down the slope in a disorderly expostulating crowd of embarrassed States? Why not make a stand while there is still a good company of united, very powerful countries that share our dangers and aspirations?'

Churchill's view that Czechoslovakia needed to be defended was supported by the French Government – which offered to go to Czechoslovakia's aid if she were attacked – was not shared by the senior members of Chamberlain's Cabinet. On March 18 Sir Thomas Inskip, the Minister for Coordination of Defence – the post many felt should have gone to Churchill – told the Cabinet's Foreign Policy Committee that he believed Czechoslovakia to be 'an unstable unit in Central Europe', and that he could see 'no reason why we should take any steps to maintain such a unit in being'. According to the Chancellor of the Exchequer, Sir John Simon – a former Foreign Secretary – 'Czechoslovakia was a modern and very artificial creation with no real roots in the past.'

Unlike Churchill – who welcomed the French Government's strong declaration in support of Czechoslovakia – both Chamberlain and Halifax were worried by the thought of a French commitment to Czechoslovak independence. Chamberlain, as the minutes of the meeting of March 18 noted, 'wondered whether it would not be possible to make some arrangement which would prove more acceptable to Germany'. Halifax stressed the weakness of France as an ally for Czechoslovakia. He also told his colleagues: 'Mr Winston Churchill had a plan under which the French Army was to act on the defensive behind the Maginot Line and there detain large German forces while Czechoslovakia engaged Germany's remaining forces. This seemed to have no relation to the realities of the situation.'

Halifax went on to warn that 'the more closely we associated ourselves with France and Russia the more we produced on German minds the impression that we were plotting to encircle Germany'. Halifax added, in the words of the official record of the meeting, that 'He (Lord Halifax) distinguished in his own mind between Germany's racial efforts, which no one could question, and a lust for conquest on a Napoleonic scale which he himself did not credit.'

On March 22 Chamberlain and his Cabinet agreed that pressure should be put on Czechoslovakia by Britain to make concessions to its Sudeten minority. 'It is a disagreeable business,' Halifax wrote to a friend, 'which has to be done as pleasantly as possible.' Not knowing what had been decided in the secrecy of the Cabinet room, Churchill called for exactly the opposite policy. Unless German pressure were countered by joint Anglo-French firmness and an arrangement for mutual defence, he told the House of Commons two days later, 'Czechoslovakia will be forced to make continuous surrenders, far beyond the bounds of what any impartial tribunal would consider right or just, until finally her sovereignty, her independence, her integrity, have been destroyed.' Churchill ended his speech with a cry of anguish:

If mortal catastrophe should overtake the British Nation and the British Empire, historians a thousand years hence will still be baffled by the mystery of our affairs. They will never understand how it was that a victorious nation, with everything in hand, suffered themselves to be brought low, and to cast away all that they had gained by measureless sacrifice and absolute victory – gone with the wind!

Now the victors are the vanquished, and those who threw down their arms in the field and sued for an armistice are striding on to world mastery.

Inside Czechoslovakia, the Sudeten Nazi campaign gathered daily momentum, as Henlein warned the Sudeten Germans that anyone who continued to cooperate with the Czech authorities would be treated as a traitor when the 'day of reckoning' came. On March 22, the two Sudeten German Parties – the Clericals and the Agrarians (known as the German Activist Parties) – which objected to this provocative attitude and had been terrorized by Henlein's supporters, were forced by Henlein to resign their positions in the Czech Cabinet. Two days later he persuaded them to join his Party, making it the largest single Party in the Czech parliament. Only the German Social Democrat Party, which was implacably opposed to Henlein's separatist policies, refused to join him, though they too were forced by his pressure to leave the Czech Cabinet.

Another force for disruption, and for the potential disintegration of Czechoslovakia, was the Slovak Autonomist Party. Although it did not have the support of more than a third of the Slovak people in the Republic, who themselves formed fifteen per cent of the Czech population, it used Henlein's tactics to press within Parliament for greater autonomy. Two other, far smaller, minorities – the Hungarians, slightly over five per cent of the Czech population, and the Poles, just over half of one per cent – joined the cacophony of calls for autonomy, with strong undercurrents of separatism. The Poles, living mostly in Teschen, were contiguous to Poland. The Hungarians, in the south and east, lived in a region contiguous to Hungary. The one minority that was not attracted by the idea of joining its ethnic neighbours was the Ruthenians; their fellow Ruthenians were part of the Soviet Union, under the strict eye of repression.

On April 10, during Hitler's Austrian plebiscite, there were demonstrations among the Sudeten Germans. Six days later, in a gesture of conciliation, President Benes declared an amnesty under which Sudeten Germans who had been imprisoned, many of them for high treason, were released. The German-language newspapers controlled by Henlein denounced the gesture as 'quite worthless'. Then, on April 24, speaking in Karlovy Vary (Karlsbad), Henlein announced eight demands which, he said, were the minimum that his party would accept.

The Karlsbad Programme rejected 'minority rights' for the Sudeten Germans, and demanded instead that Czechoslovakia give up its 'Czechoslovak character' and become a State of 'nationalities'. What Henlein called the Sudeten Folk Group must, he said, be recognized as a 'legal personality'. Reparations must be paid for 'all the injustices suffered' by the Sudeten Germans since 1918. There must be complete autonomy for the Sudetenland, and special legal guarantees for the Germans living elsewhere in Czechoslovakia. Only Sudeten Germans should be employed as State officials in the German-speaking areas. The eighth point was that all Germans must live 'according to the tenets of Nazism'.

The Karlsbad Programme also contained a radical demand with regard to the foreign policy of Czechoslovakia. The existing alliances with France and Russia, which had been the cornerstone of Benes' diplomacy aimed at preserving Czech independence, must, Henlien insisted, be abandoned, and the State make itself 'subordinate' to the foreign policy of Germany.

The Czech government rejected the Karlsbad Programme on the day after it was issued, while at the same time pledging itself to continue with plans to satisfy all minority claims. When Henlein reiterated his demands on May 1, he stated that they were 'the very minimum' and could not be the subject of compromise or diminution. Then, on May 7, a blow was struck at the determination of the Czech government not to concede to Henlein, when Britain and France, both of whom looked with alarm at the prospect of a Czech-German conflict, suggested that there might after all be some basis of negotiation on the Karlsbad Programme. The Czech government rejected this pressure, but realized that pressure would continue to be applied.

Henlein, with the encouragement of Berlin, travelled to Britain on May

13, where he told all those whom he met that the Karlsbad Programme was in fact capable of modification. This confirmed the British government in its view that the best way to calm the crisis was to persuade the Czechs to make concessions. Critics of the official British approach were convinced that firm support for Czechoslovakia on the part of Britain and France would not only save the territorial integrity of the Czech State, but could have serious repercussions inside Germany. 'If the Powers present a united defence against the plan of aggression,' wrote a British journalist, Sheila Grant Duff, who was then in Prague, there would be an 'explosion' inside Germany itself, 'and the German people will have their chance to rid themselves of their present rulers'.

In mid-May, rumours began to circulate in Prague that a German invasion of Czechoslovakia was imminent. On May 20 there was Intelligence information that several German divisions were concentrating behind the Czech frontier with Saxony. The Sudeten German Party began to demonstrate and create disturbances. The Czech government took immediate action, mobilizing all specialist troops of the reserve, and sending 400,000 troops to garrison and patrol the frontier districts. The demonstrations ceased. Henlein, travelling from Berlin to Prague, warned Hodza on May 23 that there must be immediate demobilization. Hodza refused. The Slovaks also sought to exploit the German threat by a demand for autonomy: 70,000 Slovaks demonstrated in Bratislava for autonomy on June 5. But Hodza travelled to Bratislava on the following day and defended the unity of Czechoslovakia before a sympathetic crowd of 100,000 Slovaks.

German pressure on Czechoslovakia mounted almost daily – the technique of constantly increasing pressure that was being perfected through practise. In Berlin the German Foreign Ministry – at Ribbentrop's insistence – warned the senior Czech diplomatic representative in the German capital that unless Czechoslovakia changed its policy towards the Sudeten Germans, Germany would be forced to 'march to the rescue' of the German minority. In vain did the Czech diplomat point out that the German minority was not persecuted, that it constituted the largest single political grouping in the Czech Parliament, and that it was making demands that would effectively mean the disintegration of Czechoslovakia.

When municipal elections were held throughout Czechoslovakia on June 12, the Henleinists won 90.9 per cent of the votes cast in the Sudetenland, although in some industrial areas the German-speaking vote against Henlein was as high as 30 per cent. Henlein was convinced that he had the full support of Hitler in continually raising his demands. Six days after the municipal elections, in a private conversation, Hitler told the Head of the German Armed Forces, General Keitel: 'I will decide to take action against Czechoslovakia only if I am firmly convinced, as in the case of the demilitarized zone and the entry into Austria, that France will not march, and that therefore England will not intervene.'

In case France should be tempted to stand by Czechoslovakia, Hitler ordered emergency measures to be taken to build a line of fortresses along his western frontier. To obtain the workers needed for such a task, a decree was issued on June 23 making labour service on essential government projects compulsory. Under the decree, factory owners on the Rhine had to transfer ten per cent of their workforce to fortification construction. On the day of the German labour service decree, Churchill warned Germany, in an article in the *Daily Telegraph*, that if Czechoslovakia were attacked she would not be left to struggle alone. France, Russia and eventually Britain would be drawn in to help her. The Sudeten Germans, he wrote, must also realize that their future would be far more secure inside a tolerant Czechoslovakia than 'swallowed whole by Berlin and reduced to shapeless pulp by those close-grinding mandibles of the Gestapo'.

In conformity with the British Cabinet's decision to pressure the Czechs to make concessions, on July 2 the British Government urged the Czechs to produce a Nationalities Statute – that had been under discussion for some time – aimed at giving greater powers to the regions. Benes did not want to go forward precipitately along such a radical course, and resented the warning element that was present in the tone of the British request. That same day the Henleinists demanded the withdrawal of the State police in the Sudetenland, and their replacement by Czech National Socialist storm-troopers, as well as the establishment of a legislative parliament (the Volkstag).

On July 23, following Anglo-German talks in London, the British government announced that it was intervening directly to find a solution to the Sudeten crisis. Neville Chamberlain had decided on an initiative which he hoped would satisfy the German government, and thus avert a Czech-German war into which Britain might be drawn. He therefore sent out a senior politician, Lord Runciman, as British 'adviser' – his title was later changed to that of 'conciliator and mediator' – to examine the situation in the Sudetenland and to make recommendations. Henlein welcomed the Runciman Mission, stating that its very presence constituted for the first time the recognition of him and his movement 'as a negotiating partner on an equal footing with the Czechoslovak government'.

Runciman reached Prague on August 3. His first meeting was with two Henleinist leaders, Kundt and Sebekowsky, both of whom were members of the Czech parliament. He then made brief calls on Benes and Hodza, and on the Czech Foreign Minister, Dr Krofta, before holding further long talks with the Sudeten German leaders. Many Czechs protested: these first steps of the Runciman mission, they said, were as if in 1916, at the height of the Easter Rebellion, the French government had sent an elderly retired states-man to Dublin, first to negotiate with the Irish rebels and the British government on an equal footing, and to start by giving most of their time to the rebels.

Among those who attended the first press conference given by Runciman on the day he reached Prague was William Shirer, who wrote in his diary on August 4:

Lord Runciman arrived today to gum up the works and sell the Czechs short if he can. He and his Lady and staff, with piles of baggage, proceeded to the town's swankiest hotel, the Alcron, where they have almost a whole floor. Later Runciman, a taciturn thin-lipped little man with a bald head so round it looks like a misshapen egg, received us – about three hundred Czech and foreign reporters – in the reception hall.

I thought he went out of his way to thank the Sudeten leaders, who, along with Czech Cabinet members, turned out to meet him at the station, for *their* presence.

Runciman's whole mission smells. He says he has come here to mediate between the Czech government and the Sudeten Party of Konrad Henlein. But Henlein is not a free agent. He cannot negotiate. He is completely under the orders of Hitler. The dispute is between Prague and Berlin. The Czechs know that Chamberlain personally wants Czechoslovakia to give in to Hitler's wishes. These wishes we know: incorporation of all Germans within the Greater Reich.

The discussions that began between Runciman, the Henleinists and the Czechs were overshadowed from the start by the question of Hitler's inten-tions. On August 7 the British Military Attaché in Berlin, Colonel Mason-Macfarlane, reported secretly to the Foreign Office that Hitler had already decided to attack Czechoslovakia in September, whatever agreement Benes might reach with the Sudeten Germans. Six days later a Conservative Member of Parliament, Charles Taylor, who had just returned from Germany, informed the Foreign Office that massive German troop movements were taking place between Nuremberg and the Czech frontier. That same day Churchill wrote to David Lloyd George, Britain's Prime Minster during the last two years of the First World War: 'Everything is overshadowed by the impending trial of will-power which is developing in Europe. I think we shall have to choose in the next few weeks between war and shame, and I have very little doubt what the decision will be.'

Pressure on the Czech Government to make concessions to Germany came from many countries that wished not to offend Germany, or to seem in any way to be impeding German territorial ambitions. When King Carol of Roumania visited Turkey he expressed to Atatürk the feelings of more than one national leader. Their discussion revealed a pugnacious attitude on Atatürk's behalf:

King Carol: The President of Czechoslovakia, Dr Benes, is complicating the situation by his obstinacy, and the result is that there might be war in Europe.

Atatürk (to his Foreign Minister): Ask His Majesty this. What sort of attitude does he expect from a President of a republic who is the person mainly responsible for the independence of his country?

As the German troop movements grew, with more than one and a half million men under arms, Hitler announced that he was holding the German army's annual peace-time manoeuvres. His announcement was widely accepted by the British and French public, for, as a British diplomat, Orme Sargent, noted on August 15, the French newspapers had probably received the same government 'hint' as the British newspapers 'to write down the German mobilization as much as possible so as not to create a sudden panic'. Churchill, however, in an article in the *Daily Telegraph* on August 18, warned that it 'would be only common prudence for other countries besides Germany to have these same kind of manoeuvres at the same time and to place their precautionary forces in such a position that, should the optimists be wrong, they would not be completely ruined'.

Commenting on the work of the Runciman mission in Prague, Churchill expressed the hope that a 'practical working compromise' could be secured whereby, within the existing boundaries of Czechoslovakia, the Sudeten Germans would be given 'a free and equal chance with other races'. He warned, however, that any attempt to bring about the 'trampling down' of Czechoslovakia 'would change the whole current of human ideas, and would eventually draw upon the aggressor a wrath which would in the end involve all the greatest nations of the world'.

The presence of the Runciman mission gave great encouragement to the Sudeten Germans, so much so that on August 17 the Henleinist leaders rejected the draft Nationalities Statute that Benes had produced, legislation that would have given the Sudeten Germans a substantial measure of autonomy (though not the right to police the region exclusively with National Socialist stormtroopers, as they had demanded).

The Czechs were even more alarmed when, on August 19, a day after Runciman had met Henlein for the first time, it was a communiqué issued by the Runciman Mission that made public the news that Hodza had appointed a number of Henleinists to important administrative posts. Runciman then put forward, through his Chief of Staff, Frank Ashton-Gwatkin, a proposal for 'cantonal self-government', which would give the Sudeten Germans even greater autonomy than under the Nationality Statute. In a mood of exhilaration at what they saw as their eventual victory, the Henleinists rejected this, while issuing inflammatory calls for 'self-defence to put an end to the provocations of Marxist and irresponsible Czech elements'. But the provocations were elsewhere: at the end of August the Czech government seized several consignments of arms and ammunition being smuggled into the Sudetenland from Germany.

As the Czech crisis intensified, the stream of refugees from Germany and Austria grew ever larger. It was difficult to obtain visas, and strenuous efforts had to be made by would-be refugees to find friends, relatives, and people willing to give them employment – in Britain even the most highly trained professional had to agree to take menial work. Among those who left Germany on August 20 were Henry Kissinger and his family. They went first to London, where they stayed with relatives, and then, after two weeks, to the United States. 'When I came here in 1938,' he told an American audience thirty-nine years later, 'I was asked to write an essay at George Washington High School about what it means to be an American. I wrote that . . . I thought that this was a country where one could walk across the street with one's head erect.'

*   *   *

The German government was convinced that it could annex the Sudetenland without serious international repercussions. Formal approaches were made by Berlin to Moscow, Bucharest and Belgrade, asking for neutrality in the event of a Czech-German conflict. Moscow replied that it would regard an attack on Prague as a casus belli, but there was no evidence of any Soviet military preparations on a meaningful scale. In Berlin, Goering boasted to the French ambassador that he had 'definite assurances' from Britain that in the event of an armed conflict between Germany and Czechoslovakia, 'Britain would not lift a finger'.

The British government discussed, in the secrecy of the Cabinet room at 10 Downing Street, what course to take. On August 30, Lord Halifax reported a suggestion by Churchill of 'the possibility of a joint note to Berlin from a number of Powers'. Halifax himself deprecated any such joint policy, warning his Cabinet colleagues that 'if we were to invite countries to sign a joint note, they would probably ask embarrassing questions as to our attitude in the event of Germany invading Czechoslovakia'. Chamberlain was likewise hesitant, warning his colleagues that the policy 'of an immediate declaration or threat might well result in disunity, in this country, and in the Empire'. He did not think that war was a prospect which the Defence Ministers 'would view with great confidence'. Sir Thomas Inskip, the Minister for Coordination of Defence, then explained why Britain was not in a position to stand up to Hitler. 'On the question whether we were ready to go to war,' he said, 'in a sense this country would never be ready owing to its vulnerable position. With a country as formidable as Germany so close to us we would be bound to go through a period of suffering and serious injury and loss. It was obvious, however, that at the present time we had not reached our maximum preparedness and should not do so for another year or more.' Inskip added, as a decisive argument for not contemplating military action in support of the Czechs: 'We had based our rearmament programme on what was necessary for our own defence. We had concentrated on Navy and the Air. We could not put an army into the field for many months after the outbreak of war.' Thus, in the privacy of the Cabinet room, a senior member of the government admitted the logic of Churchill's five-year campaign for increased armaments in order to be able to deter German aggresssion, and his warning that neglect of armaments had fatally weakened Britain's ability to stand up to Hitler on behalf of the Czechs.

During the British Cabinet meeting on August 30 three Ministers urged a firm policy. Alfred Duff Cooper, the First Lord of the Admiralty (with responsibility for the Royal Navy), wanted to send the Fleet to Scapa Flow as a sign of British naval preparedness. The Secretary for the Dominions, Oliver Stanley, argued that the time to make a stand had come, and that in two years time Germany would be even stronger relative to Britain than she was then. The Chancellor of the Duchy of Lancaster, Lord Winterton, stated that Chamberlain's attitude underestimated the capability of the Czechs themselves to resist an attack. The Cabinet concluded, however, that no threats should be uttered, and no multi-power cooperation attempted.

Despite the Henleinist rejection of the British proposal for 'cantonal self-government', the British Government decided to persevere with this solution. At Runciman's urging, Henlein agreed to see Hitler and to put the British proposal to him. But after Hitler had seen Henlein at Berchtesgaden on September 1, the Henleinist newspapers denounced the proposal as totally inadequate. On September 2, Benes put the British plan to the Henleinist deputies Kundt and Sebekowsky. Once more, it was rejected.

On September 6, which the Nazis had designated Nazi Party Day, Hitler presented himself at the annual mass rally in Nuremberg as the champion of the Sudeten Germans against an imaginary Czech enemy. On the following day *The Times* commented that 'it might be worth while for the Czechoslovak Government to consider whether they should exclude altogether the project, which has found favour in some quarters, of making Czechoslovakia a more homogeneous state by the cession of that fringe of alien populations who are contiguous to the nation to which they are united by race'.

In this single paragraph *The Times* gave its support to the most extreme of the German and Henleinist demands, the complete cession of the Sudetenland. If met, this demand would condemn Czechoslovakia to disintegration, and place a majority of the Sudeten Germans, as well as those Jews and Czechs who lived in the Sudetenland, under the grim rigours of Nazi rule. That same day, the British Foreign Office publicly disassociated itself from the leading article which was already causing consternation in Prague. But the damage had been done. Throughout Europe it was believed that *The Times*, in advocating a German annexation of the Sudetenland, spoke for the British Government, and that as a result Britain would clearly not fight to protect the frontiers of Czechoslovakia against German attack

Despite the Foreign Office firmness against *The Times* leader, Neville Chamberlain decided to hold back a warning which he had contemplated sending to Hitler, and to seek instead direct negotiations with him; negotiations from which the Czechs were to be excluded.

Desperate to avoid war with Germany, on September 8 Benes made a further offer to the Henleinists of a massive loan to benefit local Sudeten industry, local police autonomy, and absolute language equality, as well as the full cantonal self-government proposed by Britain. Not only was this rejected, and the negotiations broken off by the Henleinists, but there were riots throughout the Sudetenland, and demonstrations in favour of annexation by Germany.

The prospect of a German invasion of Czechoslovakia, and of that being followed by a wider war, led to an upsurge of emigration of German citizens from Germany. One couple who left in the second week of September were Gerhard Leibholz, a Jew by birth, and his wife Sabine. Their two daughters, Marianne and Christiane, went into exile with them. Sabine Leibholz was the twin sister of pastor Dietrich Bonhoeffer, who had encouraged her and her husband to leave and helped organize their escape. Their daughter Marianne later recalled the moment of their departure:

> The morning of September 9th was gloriously sunny in Göttingen. As usual our Nanny woke my seven-year-old sister Christiane and me at half past six and began to help us dress for school. Suddenly my mother came into the night nursery in a great hurry and said, 'You're not going to school today, we're going to Wiesbaden.' And to our Nanny, 'We'll be back on Monday. The children are to wear two lots of underclothes each.'
>
> I knew at once that something very serious was happening to us. My parents never went to Wiesbaden, this was obviously said to mislead our Nanny, and never before had we had to wear two lots of underclothes. I said to myself: We're leaving; as we can't take more out of the country than goes into the car and we have hardly any money abroad, wearing two lots of underclothes is an inconspicuous way of getting some extra clothes out of the country.
>
> I tore downstairs and ran round the whole of our huge garden, saying goodbye to it. I wanted to say goodbye to all the rooms in the house but feared the adults would guess I knew what was up and confined my goodbyes to one floor. I collected two finger-length dolls, their passports and certificates of birth and baptism which I had previously made, crayons, my diary; these would go into my pocket. I realized that any big toys would take up valuable car space.

My best friend Sybille came rushing up the stairs; we always walked to
school together. 'You aren't ready! We'll be late for school! 'I'm not coming,
we're going to Wiesbaden for three days.' She stared at me, astonished and
disappointed. 'Oh, well, goodbye then, I must dash.' I looked after her hard,
thinking I must remember forever what she looked like.

Pastor Bonhoeffer accompanied the would-be emigrants by car almost to the
border with Switzerland. The Leibholz family crossed the border at night.
'My mother had put on a long, very brown suede jacket, whose brownness
was meant to pacify the German officials,' Marianne Leibholz later wrote.
'They let our car through and the Swiss let us in.'

The war crisis intensified. On September 10, in a speech at Nuremberg,
Goering – who had brought the German Air Force to a high point of combat
readiness – fulminated against the Czech people, telling an ecstatic German
audience: 'This miserable pygmy race without culture – no one knows where
it came from – is oppressing a cultured people, and behind it is Moscow
and the eternal mask of the Jew devil.'

Czechoslovakia looked to Britain and France to give assurances to warn
Hitler that, if German troops crossed the Czech border, Britain and France
would act, if necessary by going to war. Unlike Britain, France had an alliance
with Czechoslovakia which would involve declaring war on an aggressor. But
on September 10 Lord Halifax told the French Ambassador in London that
'although Great Britain might feel obliged to support France in a conflict,
if only because our interests were involved in any threat to French security,
it did not mean that we should be willing automatically to find ourselves
at war with Germany because France might be involved in discharge of
obligations which Great Britain did not share and which a large section of
opinion in this country had always disliked.'

Britain was making it clear that it had no intention of going to war in
order to prevent Hitler acquiring the Sudetenland. On September 11 Churchill wrote to a friend, reiterating the sentiments that had tormented him
throughout the crisis: 'Owing to the neglect of our defences and the mishand-
ling of the German problem in the last five years, we seem to be very near
the bleak choice between War and Shame. My feeling is that we shall choose
Shame, and then have War thrown in a little later, on even more adverse
terms than at present.'

*   *   *

Speaking at Nuremberg on September 12, in a speech broadcast throughout Europe, Hitler declared that the 'oppression' of the Sudeten Germans by the Czechs must end. 'I am speaking of Czechoslovakia. It is a monstrous formation.' Benes was 'a liar' in offering to seek a fair solution (it was scarcely seven months since Hitler had called Schuschnigg a liar). The Sudeten Germans must be given 'self-determination'. The whole power of the German Reich would be behind them in this.

Taking as an analogy the British Mandate in Palestine, Hitler declared: 'I am in no way willing that here in the heart of Germany through the dexterity of other statesmen a second Palestine should be permitted to arise. The poor Arabs are defenceless and perhaps deserted. The Germans in Czechoslovakia are neither defenceless nor are they deserted, and folk should take notice of that fact.'

Then, referring to his annexation of Austria earlier that year, Hitler spoke of how the 'Germans of Austria know best how bitter a thing it is to be separated from the Motherland. They will be the first to recognize the significance of what I have been saying today.'

As Hitler spoke, men and women all over Europe listened, hoping to gather from his arguments and his tone what they might expect in the days and weeks ahead. Listening to the wireless had become a way of life for millions of people, a desperate attempt, almost always in vain, to find some crumbs of comfort. In France, André Gide was among Hitler's listeners. 'The call to arms permits a facile eloquence,' he wrote in his journal, 'and it is easier to lead men to combat and to stir up passions than to temper them and to urge them to the patient labours of peace.' Listening in Prague, William Shirer wrote in his diary:

> The Great Man has spoken. And there's no war, at least not for the moment. That is Czechoslovakia's first reaction to Hitler's speech at Nuremberg tonight. Hitler hurled insults and threats at Prague. But he did not demand that the Sudetens be handed over to him outright. He did not even demand a plebiscite. He insisted, however, on 'self-determination' for the Sudetens.
>
> I listened to the broadcast of the speech in the apartment of Bill and Mary Morrell overlooking Wilson Station. The smoke-filled room was full of correspondents . . .
>
> I have never heard the Adolf quite so full of hate, his audience quite so on the borders of bedlam. What poison in his voice when at the

beginning of his long recital of alleged wrongs to the Sudeteners he paused: *'Ich spreche von der Czechoslovakei!'* His words, his tone, dripping with venom.

Everyone in Czechoslovakia seems to have listened to the speech, the streets being deserted tonight from eight to ten. An extraordinary meeting of the Inner Cabinet Council was convoked immediately afterwards, but Benes did not attend.

Hitler's Nuremberg speech was taken by the Henleinist as a call for revolt. 'Some six thousand Henlein enthusiasts, wearing Swastika arm-bands, paraded the streets of Karlsbad, afterwards,' noted Shirer. They were shouting: 'Down with the Czechs and Jews! We want a plebiscite!'

In many of the towns of the Sudetenland bombs were set off, public buildings attacked, and Czech and Jewish homes wrecked. In a single day of rioting, twelve people were killed. On the following day, September 13, as the riots continued, a further eleven people were killed. The Czechs declared martial law. Henlein told members of the Runciman Mission who called on him at his headquarters in Asch that his Karlsbad Programme demanding autonomy was superseded by Hitler's speech calling for self-determination.

The British government was not ready for war, and convinced itself that war would not be justified to prevent the Sudeten Germans from being given the self-government that Hitler had demanded for them. No democracy could refuse to accept a plebiscite, Chamberlain told his Cabinet on September 14. On the following day, travelling by air for the first time in his life, Chamberlain flew to see Hitler at Berchtesgaden — where six months earlier Schuschnigg had been summoned to such ill-effect. Hitler assured Chamberlain that, while he would accept the results of a plebiscite in the Sudetenland that called for annexation with Germany, he 'did not wish to include Czechs in the Reich'. For his part, Chamberlain told Hitler that he was not opposed to the separation of the Sudetenland from Czechoslovakia, if that were the result of a plebiscite.

Chamberlain returned to London, where, on September 18, he received the French Prime Minister, Edouard Daladier, and his Foreign Minister, Georges Bonnet. It was a stormy meeting. Alarmed by Chamberlain's effective acceptance in his talk with Hitler of the transfer of the Sudetenland to Germany, Daladier warned Chamberlain that it was not the Sudetenland alone that Hitler wanted, but that 'Germany was aiming at something far greater'. Daladier wanted Britain to join with France in setting up an international guarantee for Czechoslovakia against aggression. Chamberlain rebutted this idea. Britain had 'no army which could march to Czechoslovakia,' he said, 'and it was a long way to send an air force'. As for the Sudetenland, Chamberlain told Daladier that mediation between Czechs and Sudeten Germans was no longer possible: there would have to be a plebiscite.

The French emissaries were surprised at how emphatic Chamberlain was: no international guarantees for Czechoslovakia, and a plebiscite – these seemed to be the approaches most favourable to Hitler's designs. But France did not feel that it could act alone, and before returning to Paris, Daladier agreed that France would join with Britain in pressing upon the Czech Government the need to transfer all areas with a German-speaking majority to Germany. Chamberlain and Daladier were agreed that once that transfer was made, there should be a joint Anglo-French guarantee for the remainder of Czechoslovakia: that is, for Bohemia, Moravia, Slovakia and Ruthenia.

The plebiscite, and the inevitable transfer that would follow it, had become the cornerstone of Anglo-French policy. On September 19 a British Foreign Office official noted that 'every pressure is being applied to Benes to accept and accept quickly'. That day, in the British Cabinet, the Secretary of State for War, Leslie Hore-Belisha, warned that Czechoslovakia might not be able to survive as an independent State without the Sudeten German areas. Chamberlain answered him by pointing out that, during the Berchtesgaden meeting, Hitler had assured him that Germany had no designs on Czechoslovakia itself, and that he, Chamberlain, was convinced that Hitler 'would not deliberately deceive a man he respected'.

On September 20 Britain and France prepared a plan which they believed would satisfy Hitler: a plebiscite, followed by the cession to Germany of those German-speaking areas of Czechoslovakia that voted for it. This plan was telegraphed to the British and French Ministers in Prague – Basil Newton and Victor de Lacroix – who, on the instructions of their respective governments, went to see Benes at two o'clock on the morning of September 21. Despite the lateness of the hour he received them and listened to their governments' joint and emphatic advice: Czechoslovakia should accept the British and French proposals for the cession of the Sudetenland. Were Benes to refuse to do so, the Ministers told him, it would produce a situation 'for which France and Britain could take no responsibility'.

On September 22 Chamberlain flew for a second time to see Hitler, who was then at Bad Godesberg, on the Rhine. His mission was to tell Hitler about the Anglo-French plan, and to secure Hitler's approval. While accepting in principle – for the plan was essentially his own – Hitler made heavy weather about the timetable, which (logically) put the plebiscite first, followed by the transfer of territory to Germany. The Anglo-French plan, Hitler said, was 'unacceptable on the grounds that its operation would be too slow'. German troops must be allowed to occupy the German-speaking areas at once, without a plebiscite.

Chamberlain stayed at Bad Godesberg overnight. Then, on the following morning, he agreed with Hitler's demand that there need be no plebiscite in areas with more than 50 per cent German speakers. He also assured Hitler that he would urge the Czech government to accept this plan. On his return to London he did just that, while at the same time pressing the Czech Government to agree to Hitler's further demand that all fortifications and war materials in the Sudeten areas should be handed over to Germany intact. Unaware of the pressure being put on Czechoslovakia by Britain – but fearing that the British Government might not be willing to take a firm line – demonstrators marched through London on September 25 with banners declaring: 'Stand By Czechoslovakia', 'Stand by the Czechs', and 'Stop Hitler'.

On September 27, while awaiting the Czech Government's response to its essentially pro-German initiative, the British Government took a further initiative, aimed at accelerating the timetable of the transfer of Czech territory to Germany. The British plan was that the Czechs should withdraw from the frontier towns of Eger and Asch on October 1 – in four days time – and from all the other areas with more than fifty percent German speakers on October 10. Any further withdrawals, as determined by plebiscite, must be completed by October 31. At that point, Britain and France and Germany would begin negotiations to guarantee the new frontiers of Czechoslovakia.

Chamberlain believed that the British plan, which conceded Hitler's basic demands – and went far beyond Henlein's Karlsbad Programme of mere autonomy – would be sufficient to prevent a German invasion of Czechoslovakia. Yet in case war came, defence preparations were being made throughout Britain. 'How horrible, fantastic, incredible it is that we should be digging trenches and trying on gas-masks here,' Chamberlain broadcast over the radio on September 27, 'because of a quarrel in a faraway country between people of whom we know nothing', and he added: 'It seems still more impossible that a quarrel which has already been settled in principle should be the subject of war.'

Chamberlain's listeners could not know just how much that 'quarrel' had already been settled. On the afternoon of September 28 Hitler invited

Chamberlain to fly to Munich, with the French Prime Minister Edouard Daladier, and Mussolini, for a conference to settle the Sudeten question along the lines already agreed by Britain, France and Germany. The Czechs were not invited to participate in the discussion. As Chamberlain prepared to fly to Munich – his third flight to Germany in fourteen days – Lord Halifax telegraphed to Basil Newton in Prague: 'It is essential that Czechoslovak government should at once indicate their acceptance in principle of our plan and timetable. Please endeavour to obtain this without delay.'

This telegram was sent from London to Prague at 8 p.m. on September 28. As soon as it reached him, Basil Newton went to see Benes. At 10.40 that same evening Benes accepted in principle the Anglo-French and German plan.

On the morning of September 29, Chamberlain flew to Munich. There – during twelve hours of talks – he, Daladier, Mussolini and Hitler worked out the details of the transfer of the Sudetenland from Czechoslovakia to Germany. The Czech representatives were given no place in the conference hall. Chamberlain asked that they should be present, but Hitler refused. Kept in a room near the conference hall, it was only when the decision had been finalized after midnight that the Czechs were told what had been decided and asked to accept it. When they asked if they could make some comments on the agreement, they were told that there was no point, as everything had been settled. In his turn, Benes, who had remained in Prague, was also asked to accept, but given no opportunity to make any changes whatsoever. He accepted at noon on September 30, shortly before Chamberlain flew back from Munich to London.

Echoing Jaroslav Hasek's satire in *The Good Soldier Schweik* on the eve of the First World War, Jean-Paul Sartre wrote in *The Reprieve*:

The small soldier came up to Gros-Louis waving a newspaper.
  'It's peace!'
Gros-Louis set down his bucket. 'What did you say, mate?'
  'I said it's peace'
Gros-Louis eyed him dubiously.
  'Peace? – but there hasn't been a war.'
  'They've signed a peace, old thing. You've only got to read the paper.'
He handed it to Gros-Louis, who pushed it away.
  'I can't read.'

1. Munich, November 1933: Hitler is hailed by
stormtroopers at the celebrations of the first
anniversary of Nazi power.

2. *(left)* Stalin at his desk

3. Roosevelt at the microphone,1937

4. Addis Ababa, October 1935: Abyssinian cavalrymen on their way to the front after the Italian invasion.

5. Churchill, accompanied by French generals, en route to witness French manoeuvres, September 1936.

6. Mao-Tse-tung talking to peasants in the early months of the Sino-Japanese War in 1937.

7. The 'Burma Road', along which British and American supplies were transported from Burma to the Chinese Nationalists in western and central China.

8. Japanese troops entering a Chinese village south of Hsuchow in June 1938.

9. In the aftermath of battle, a Chinese soldier looks at a comrade killed during a Japanese attack.

10. China: Chungking after a Japanese air raid, May 1939.

11. Madrid: Republican militiamen in a trench dug round the Model Prison which was cleared of prisoners and transformed into a fortress to keep out the rebels.

12. Spain: Gijon is in ruins after its surrender to Franco's forces. White sheets of surrender hang from the balconies of unbombed houses, 27 October 1937.

13. London, September 1938: communists call on the Government to 'Stand By the Czechs'.

14 *(left)* The return from Munich, October 1938: Neville Chamberlain at the window of 10 Downing Street.

15. *(right)* Churchill in his bricklaying clothes, t Chartwell, his home in Kent. This ohotograph was published in *Picture Post* on 5 February 1939 as part of a call to bring him ack into government.

16. Berlin: Axis leaders salute the crowd after the signing of an Italo-German military alliance – the Pact of Steel – on 22 May 1939. (Left to right) the German Foreign Minister, von Ribbentrop, the Italian Foreign Minister, Count Ciano, Hitler and Field Marshal Goering on the balcony of the recently completed Reich Chancellery.

17. June 1939: two German-Jewish child refugees returning to Europe, having been refused entry to the United States.

'Is that so?' said the lad sympathetically. 'Well, look at the picture.'

Gros-Louis reluctantly took the paper, went up to the stable window and looked at the picture. He recognized Daladier, Hitler, and Mussolini, all smiles: they seemed to be good friends.

'Well I never!' he said.

He frowned at the lad, then said with a sudden chuckle: 'So they've made it up, have they? And I didn't even know why they'd fallen out!'

During his discussion with Chamberlain at Munich, Hitler had insisted that while he wanted 'justice' he was entirely in favour of a peaceful solution to the crisis. If the Czechs were foolish enough to resist the Munich agreement by force, he told Chamberlain, he would 'try to spare the civilian population and to confine himself to military objectives.' Hitler added that he 'hated the idea of little babies being killed by gas bombs'.

On his return from Munich to Britain – echoing Disraeli after the Congress of Berlin in 1878 – Chamberlain spoke of bringing back 'peace in our time'. Bertolt Brecht, who had been forced to flee from Germany to Denmark in 1933, had heard Hitler protest his desire for peace many times. His comment on such protestations was full of foreboding:

> When the leaders speak of peace
> The common folk know
> That war is coming.
> When the leaders curse war
> The mobilization order is already written out.

> It is night
> The married couples
> Go to their beds. The young women
> Will bear orphans.

> Those at the top say: peace and war
> Are of different substance.
> But their peace and their war
> Are like wind and storm.

War grows out of their peace
Like a son out of a mother
He bears
Her terrible features.
Their war kills
Whatever their peace
Has left over.

———————

On the wall was chalked:
They want war.
The man who wrote it
Has already fallen.

In London, Chamberlain was met by large and enthusiastic gatherings, first at Downing Street and then outside Buckingham Palace. 'Vast crowds in the street, hysterical cheers and enthusiasm,' Oliver Harvey noted in his diary. 'But many feel it to be a great humiliation.' When Frank Ashton-Gwatkin, who had been one of the main negotiators of the final agreement, was awarded the CB (Companion of the Order of the Bath) for his efforts, a fellow Foreign Office official commented dourly that the initials stood for 'Czechoslovakia Betrayed'.

Chamberlain was confident that, as a result of the Munich agreement, the danger of an Anglo-German war had receded. As the minutes of the Cabinet meeting on October 3 recorded (in the third person, as usual): 'He thought that we were now in a more hopeful position, and that the contacts which had been established with the Dictator Powers opened up the possibility that we might be able to reach some agreement with them which would stop the armaments race.'

The Munich agreement was, and has remained, one of the most controversial agreements of the Twentieth Century. Many years later, politicians in many lands would declare a particular diplomatic surrender of which they did not approve to be a 'Munich betrayal'. The very word 'Munich' came to represent craven surrender to threats and blandishments. This was also a widespread view at the time. Despite many speeches in the British House of Commons in support of Chamberlain, there were also many which opposed what he had done. The Leader of the Labour Party, Clement Attlee, warned: 'This has not been a victory for reason and humanity. It has been a victory for brute force.' The Leader of the Liberal Party, Sir Archibald Sinclair, was as emphatic, telling the House: 'A policy which imposes injustice on a small and weak nation, and tyranny on free men and women, can never be the foundation of lasting peace.'

Speaking on October 5, Churchill warned that the Munich Agreement would not lead, as Chamberlain had told parliament, to a reduction of European tension. 'It must now be accepted,' he said, 'that all the countries of Central and Eastern Europe will make the best terms they can with the triumphant Nazi power.' In a speech which stressed the moral aspect of the Czech crisis, and Britain's failure to take a stand for what was right and just, Churchill declared:

> The Prime Minister desires to see cordial relations between this country and Germany. There is no difficulty at all in having cordial relations with the German people. Our hearts go out to them. But they have no power.
>
> You must have diplomatic and correct relations, but there can never be friendship between the British democracy and the Nazi Power, that Power which spurns Christian ethics, which cheers its onward course by a barbarous paganism, which vaunts the spirit of aggression and conquest, which derives strength and perverted pleasure from persecution, and uses, as we have seen, with pitiless brutality the threat of murderous force.
>
> That Power cannot ever be the trusted friend of the British democracy.

Under the Munich Agreement, the Sudeten German districts of Czechoslovakia were ceded to Germany. The transfer would take place without a plebiscite, except in those areas where the linguistic majority was uncertain. The timetable was a swift one. German troops began their occupation on October 1, and completed it ten days later. Hitler had gained yet another territory for Germany. As with the annexation of Austria, no shot was fired, no armies fought, and there was no resistance. The two annexations increased Germany's size from 186,000 to 225,000 square miles, and its population from 68 million to 79 million. Considerable gains were also made in raw materials (particularly coal) and in industrial power.

Of the 3,850,000 people ceded to Germany by the Munich Agreement, almost 850,000 were Czechs. More than a third of the land area of Czechoslovakia was transferred to Germany. Benes resigned as President and went to England as an exile. In a further weakening of the authority of Prague, two 'Autonomist' administrations were set up, one in Slovakia and the other in

Ruthenia. On November 2 there was a further diminution of the territory
of the rump Czechoslovakia, when Germany and Italy, under the Vienna
Award, allocated territory in southern Slovakia and western Ruthenia to
Hungary. Among the towns transferred to Hungary was the Ruthenian
capital, Uzhgorod. One further territorial humiliation was yet to come: on
November 21 the Czech government agreed to cede to Germany a corridor
through its heartland, linking Breslau with Vienna, and to give jurisdiction
over this road to Germany.

The aftermath of Munich was as divisive among the democracies as it was
traumatic for the Czechs. Those who resigned from the British and French
governments on the grounds that Munich had been a betrayal of Czechoslovakia faced the obloquy of those who felt that what had been at stake was
no less than the preservation of peace in Europe. Both Paul Reynaud and
Georges Mandel resigned from the French Cabinet, as did Duff Cooper from
the British Cabinet. On October 2, Eric Gedye wrote to Duff Cooper from
Prague, where he was the correspondent of the *Daily Telegraph*:

> Please allow a complete stranger to write and thank you for your action
> in dissociating yourself from the Chamberlainite treachery. Your action
> makes it just a little easier to bear the shame – one which is felt by
> everyone of my colleagues here on all newspapers from Right to Left – of
> having to bear the name of Englishman in Prague today among a gallant
> little people which has displayed every fine quality in which England has
> shown herself miserably lacking.
>
> If you can use this letter in any way to stir up some sense of shame and
> of their senseless applause of what in the end is the betrayal also of
> themselves among my fellow countrymen – of course without involving
> the actual name of my newspaper – I shall be more than happy.

The poet Louis Macneice expressed his indignation in verse:

> But once again
>   The crisis is put off and things look better
> And we feel negotiation is not in vain –
>   Save my skin and damn my conscience.
> And negotiation wins,
>   If you can call it winning,
> And here we are–just as before–safe in our skins;

> Glory to God for Munich.
> And stocks go up and wrecks
>   Are salved and politicians' reputations
> Go up like Jack-on-the-Beanstalk; only the Czechs
> Go down and without fighting.

A leading Social Democrat, Wenzel Jaksch, flew to London to ask for visas for his fellow Sudeten German Social Democrats. Almost no visas were granted. To escape the imposition of Nazi rule, many Social Democrats fled across the Sudetenland border into rump Czechoslovakia. They were sent back to Germany, where many were immediately arrested and sent to concentration camps. The agreement that led to them being sent back was signed two weeks after Munich. The British and French governments acceded to it. The German civil servant who drafted the agreement, Dr Hans Globke, had drafted the official commentary for the Nuremberg Laws three years earlier (in 1962 he was appointed a Secretary of State in the German Federal Republic).

Even as Hitler's administrators, soldiers and followers began to absorb the benefits which the annexations of Austria and the Sudetenland had brought them, Hitler decided on another dramatic move against the Jews. All Polish-born Jews who lived in Germany – many of them immigrants from the 1920s – were to be expelled from Germany. Beginning on October 28, first 12,000 and then a further 8,000 were ordered out of their homes, taken by train and truck to two crossing points on the German border with Poland, Neu Bentschen/Zbaszyn and Konitz/Chojnice, and driven over the border. They could take with them only what they could carry: a suitcase or a bundle. All their other possessions – including their homes and livelihoods – had to be left behind. There were plenty of Germans, often neighbours or business associates, who had no hesitation in acquiring what had been abandoned.

When one of the Polish-born Jews who had been expelled, Sendel Grynszpan, wrote to his seventeen-year-old son, Herschel, who was in Paris, describing the suddenness and humiliations of the expulsion, the indignant son went to the German Embassy in Paris and shot and seriously injured the Third Secretary there, Ernst vom Rath. 'My dear parents,' Hershel Grynszpan wrote on a postcard that was found on him when he was arrested. 'I could not do otherwise. May God forgive me. My heart bleeds at the news of 12,000 Jews' suffering. I must protest in such a way that the world will hear me. I must do it. Forgive me. Herschel.'

Before vom Rath finally succumbed to his injuries, Hitler approved a massive physical attack on the homes and synagogues of the Jews of Germany, Austria and the Sudetenland – the Greater Germany that he had created. Starting in the early hours of November 10, this Twentieth Century pogrom was as violent and wide-ranging as any perpetrated in Tsarist Russia half a century earlier. Members of the Gestapo, of the Nazi Automobile Corps, and of Robert Ley's German Labour Front were summoned to local Nazi Party headquarters everywhere. From these headquarters they fanned out through the towns, setting fire to Jewish shops and synagogues. In Vienna, which had been under Nazi control for less than eight months, twenty-two large synagogues and eighty small houses of prayer were blown up or set on fire. A further ninety synagogues were set on fire throughout Germany: seventy-six of them were destroyed.

Ruth Gross, then a young child in Berlin, walked with her father along Oranienburger Strasse on the morning of 10 November 1938. She later recalled passing near the great nineteenth-century synagogue, the pride of the Jewish community (Bismarck had been present at its opening): 'Glass shards, Bibles, and prayer books lay in heaps on the sidewalk. I wanted to pick up one of the holy books since it is a sin to throw them in the dirt, but my father pulled me back with a frightened start. I couldn't understand this – I was seven years old then. He knew the danger that surrounded us; I only slowly came to realize it.'

The *Kristallnacht* (the Night of the Broken Glass), as it became known, revealed several unexpected acts of courage. In Munich, the Catholic Archbishop, Cardinal Michael von Faulhaber, showed his sympathy for the Jews by providing a truck for the city's Chief Rabbi to rescue religious objects from the main synagogue before it was pulled down.* In Berlin, as the Gestapo prepared to set the Oranienburger Strasse synagogue on fire, the head of the local police precinct, Police Lieutenant Wilhelm Krützfeld, insisted that they stop, citing the fact (for it was a fact) that the synagogue was a protected municipal building. It had been so for many years because of its historic importance in the architecture of the city. The Gestapo went away, and there was no fire. Krützfeld was severely reprimanded. Ten months after the Kristallnacht, in September 1939, the Jewish New Year services were held in the synagogue.

*   *   *

---

* A plaque at the site today records the location and fate of the synagogue, but makes no mention of the Cardinal's act.

The Kristallnacht marked a turning point in how the Nazi Party was perceived abroad. 'Jews aren't a lovable people, I don't care about them myself,' Neville Chamberlain confided to one of his sisters, 'but that is not enough to explain the pogrom.' The leading article in *The Times* on November 11 declared: 'No foreign propagandist bent upon blackening Germany before the world could outdo the tale of burning and beatings, of blackguardly assaults upon defenceless and innocent people, which disgraced that country yesterday.'

In the course of a fifteen hour orgy of destruction, as many as 7,500 Jewish-owned shops had been looted. Many Jewish homes were ransacked, and the furniture that was not looted was piled in the streets and set on fire. A hundred Jews were murdered that night. Twenty thousand were arrested during the following few days and sent to Sachsenhausen, Buchenwald and Dachau concentration camps. In order totally to impoverish the Jews who were still living in Germany, on November 13 General Goering issued a decree ordering the Jews to make good at their expense the cost of the damage done to them. All money received by German Jews as a result of insurance claims for the damage done was to be handed over to the German government. In addition, a massive one billion mark fine was imposed on the whole German Jewish community.

In the Soviet Union, behind a cloak of secrecy quite unlike the daily Western newspaper publicity for the events in Germany, the death toll from the purges continued to rise. Of the eight military judges who had tried Marshal Tukachevsky and the other senior army officers in 1937, at least four were disgraced by the end of 1938, including the Chief of Staff of the Soviet Air Force and Vice-Commissar for Defence (General Alksnis), the Supreme Commander of the Leningrad District (General Dybenko) and the commander of the Caucasian Military District (General Kashirin).

As the Stalinist terror mounted in intensity, consuming in its wake so many army officers, the Soviet Union had to confront a military threat in the Far East. At the point where the frontiers of Japanese-held Manchukuo and Korea met the Soviet Union, an area of high ground, the Changkufeng Hills, lay, according to Russo-Chinese Treaty of 1886, inside Russia. For many years they had remained virtually unoccupied, save for a small Soviet guard post, but on July 26, a force of Japanese soldiers, supported by tanks and artillery, overran the guard post and occupied the hills.

Stalin ordered his troops to retake the hills, reinforcements were sent, and fighting began. Japan offered to withdraw its troops if Russia would leave the hills unoccupied and submit the dispute for arbitration. The Soviet Foreign Minister, Maksim Litvinov, refused to consider this. Fighting spread throughout the area around the hills. When the Japanese were forced to retreat, they called for an armistice. This the Soviets accepted.

The Japanese had hoped that Russia would be so weakened by the military purges that she would have no heart to defend such a remote area. A Soviet secret police defector had spoken in Tokyo of seven hundred Red Army officers in the Far East being arrested during the purges. This number was correct. Limited though the conflict was, it was also a signal from Moscow that the Soviet Union would not, despite its internal turmoil, surrender territory without a fight.

Yet the purges continued. Neither successful oldtimers nor keen newcomers were immune. The successful Soviet general in the recapture of the Changkufeng Hills, Marshal Blucher, was recalled to Moscow soon after the victory, dismissed from his command, and given a minor post in the Ministry of Defence. Even the newest member of that bastion of Soviet conformity, the Writers' Union – whose members were pathetically and wisely eager to praise every aspect of Soviet life – was caught up in the net. Fifty-one years later the magazine *Ogonyek* gave, for the first time, the facts of this one writer's fate:

> On February 23, 1938, D.I. Gachev was admitted into the Union, then arrested the following day and accused of Trotskyite counter-revolutionary activities. He served eight years in the camps of Kolyma, but a few months before he was scheduled for release his sentence was rolled over for another ten years.
>
> He died at the beginning of 1946, but how exactly is not known.

The climax of the public trials came with the 'Trial of the Twenty-One'. Among the accused were two founding members of Soviet Communism, Aleksei Rykov and Nikolai Bukharin, both of whom had been expelled from the Communist Party in 1937. 'As I write', Bukharin protested to Marshal Voroshilov on learning that charges were being prepared against him, 'I am experiencing a sense of half-reality: is it a dream, a mirage, a madhouse, a hallucination? No, it is reality.'

Also brought to trial was the former head of the secret police, G.G. Yagoda, who had master-minded so many of the previous trials, and several other leading Communists, among them Christian Rakovsky, who had established Soviet rule in the Ukraine after the revolution, and was later the first Soviet ambassador to Britain. In the course of his confession, which like all those made at the trial flew beyond the borders of the fantastic, Rakovsky said that he had spied for Britain at the request of Lady Muriel Paget. In saying this in court, Rakovsky must have realized that his 'admission' would cause the trial to be held up for mockery outside the Soviet Union, for Lady Paget was well-known as a leading charitable worker and philanthropist who had organized the Anglo-Russian hospital in Petrograd during the First World War, and had later established free kitchens in Latvia, Estonia, Lithuania and Czechoslovakia. The British Prime Minister, Neville Chamberlain, formally denied that she had ever been involved in espionage.

Unlike the hundreds of trials which lasted a few hours, and were held in secret, the Trial of the Twenty-One lasted ten days, in the presence of journalists from all over the world. Each of the accused, having been subjected to a range of physical and mental tortures over many months, confessed to a series of bizarre crimes: espionage against the Soviet Union, being an agent of foreign powers, seeking to wreck Soviet industry. Each was cross-examined with humiliating cruelty. Each admitted, over and over again, to being an enemy of the State. All were sentenced to death, with the exception of Rakovksy, on behalf of whom the British Labour Party leadership, headed by Clement Attlee, appealed direct to Stalin. Great play was made in Britain of Stalin's generosity when Rakovsky, aged seventy, was not sentenced to death but to twenty years penal servitude. He was shot a few years later.

During the Trial of the Twenty-One there were many extraordinary moments. In the preliminary, secret investigation, at which the confessions were extracted, a former member of the Central Committee secretariat, N.N. Krestinsky, had admitted that he had 'entered into treacherous contact' with German Intelligence in 1921, and that he had been paid 250,000 Marks a year by the German Army to carry out 'Trotskyist work' inside the Soviet Union. When, during his public cross-examination at the trial, he was asked if he was guilty, he retracted his confession and began, point by point, to deny the charges against him.

The court, in turmoil, was adjourned. Stalin was told, and demanded that no such retraction take place again. Krestinsky was taken away for the night and subjected to further interrogation of a sort that can only be guessed at. The next morning, when the trial resumed, the following exchange took place between him and the principal prosecutor, Andrei Vyshinsky:

Krestinsky: 'I completely confirm the testimony I gave at the preliminary inquiry.'

Vyshinsky: 'In that case, what is the meaning of your statement yesterday, which can only be seen as a Trotskyite provocation to the trial?'

Krestinsky: 'Yesterday, under the influence of a momentary sharp sense of false shame, caused by being in the dock and the depressing effect of hearing the charges read out, and aggravated by my ill health, I was not in a condition to tell the truth, not in a condition to say that I was guilty.'

Vyshinsky: 'Is this an automatic response?'

Kretinsky: 'I request that the court minute my statement that I completely and entirely acknowledge that I am guilty of all the serious charges levelled against me personally, and I hold myself completely responsible for the treason and treachery committed by me.'

Even as the Trial of the Twenty-One was still in progress, and being reported daily in the world's newspapers, it was announced in Moscow that a further trial of eleven more 'enemies of the people' was being prepared. It would consist of former Communist Party activists, including members of the Central Committee. The head of the NKVD, Nikolai Yezhov, who had operated the terror system since replacing Yagoda, was himself among the victims. He was replaced in his turn by Lavrenti Beria, who proceeded to arrest and imprison – or in many cases condemn to death by shooting – those who had been most closely associated with the earlier terror. In the archives of the secret police is a brief note sent by one of the military prosecutors, V.V. Ulrich, to Beria, informing him of the previous two years' sequence of arrests and their result. The note read:

During the period 1 October 1936 to 30 September 1938, the military collegium of the Supreme Court of the USSR and the circuit college of sixty towns sentenced

33,514 to be shot
5,643 to prison
_____
39,157 total

The Soviet destruction was internal. The borders of the Soviet Union were sealed, very few Soviet citizens could travel abroad. All visitors to the Soviet Union were the subject of close supervision and scrutiny during their visits. On the western border of the Soviet Union, only a few miles away in distance, but seemingly a thousand miles away in freedom, the Baltic States were celebrating the twentieth anniversary of their independence. In Estonia, a celebratory Week of Song was attended by three British bishops. In Latvia, a Neutrality Law was passed by which belligerents were refused permission to use any part of Latvia or Latvian waters for military operations. But the tensions inside the Baltic States were not conducive to a quiet life. In Estonia, the Head of State, Konstantin Paets, ruled by emergency decree. In Latvia there was a state of semi-dictatorship. In Lithuania there were frontier clashes with Poland – which since 1920 had ruled over the Lithuanian capital Vilnius – and disaffection with the German-speaking population of Memel, which looked to neighbouring Nazi Germany for inspiration.

Local elections in Memel on December 11 showed that a German crisis was imminent. All the German candidates there stood as National Socialists, demanding autonomy, as the Sudeten German National Socialist Party had done a few months earlier. As a result of the election the Germans won twenty-five seats (59,000 votes) and the Lithuanians four seats (9,300 votes). On the night that the results were announced a torchlight procession marched through Memel chanting 'We want to return to the Reich'.

As a result of the Munich Agreement, several frontiers had been redrawn. Not only did Germany acquire the Sudetenland from Czechoslovakia, but other countries also found it expedient to make territorial gains. After Munich, the Polish government demanded the Teschen district of Czechoslovakia, with its Polish minority. Teschen was occupied by Poland on October 4. Poland also occupied the important Czech railway junction of Bohumin, to prevent the Germans from doing so. The land transferred to Poland contained 132,000 Czechs, 77,000 Poles and 20,000 Germans.

The turmoil created in Europe by Hitler's successes, and the grim news of the continuing purges in Russia, could not overshadow the turmoil elsewhere. In Spain, the Madrid government continued to defend the capital, and the considerable regions under its control, despite the constant acquisition by Franco and the Nationalist Army of arms and war supplies from Germany and Italy. A blow for the Republic was the loss of the town of Teruel, which had been held throughout the winter but was then surrounded by the Nationalists and captured. As many as fourteen thousand Nationalist soldiers perished on the battlefield; the Republican dead may have amounted to more than twenty thousand.

It was air power which the Germans and Italians urged Franco to exploit to the full, despite the widespread international outrage at the bombing of Guernica the previous year. On January 11 the first sustained air raids of 1938 took place, on Barcelona, Tarragona, and several coastal towns where there were no military objectives. Similar air raids were repeated eight days later. Then, on January 28, nine Italian bombers, striking again at Barcelona, killed 150 of its citizens in the course of a single swoop on the city which lasted only a minute and a half.

Neither an appeal from Britain and France for an end to the bombing of civilians, nor a similar appeal from the Pope, had any effect. Starting on March 16 there was a new series of bombing raids on Barcelona in which 815 people were killed. The British journalist F.A. Voigt wrote in indignation of how the city was being bombed 'in a manner that no city in the world could long endure'. Leaflets dropped over Barcelona after the first raid stated: 'We shall bomb you every three hours unless you surrender.'

Barcelona refused to surrender, but on April 8 Nationalist forces in the north, capturing Balaguer, Tremp and Camarasa, cut off the city's hydro-electric supply lines in the Pyrenees, a severe blow to what was still functioning of the city's industry. Then, in a renewed military offensive towards the Mediterranean, on April 15 – Good Friday – the insurgent forces reached the sea at the small fishing town of Vinaroz, thereby driving a wedge between the Barcelona province and the rest of Spain, and cutting the area still under the control of Madrid into two. In their delight the first of Franco's soldiers who reached the sea waded out into it. By April 19 they had fanned out to capture forty miles of the coastline. That day Franco announced: 'The war is over, these are the last days of conquest.'

Franco's triumphant enthusiasm was premature. In what was intended as a swift, twelve day assault on the coastal towns of Castellon and Sagunto, it took the insurgents fifty days to reach Castellon, but they were stopped short of Sagunto. In July the Republicans, in a sustained counter-attack, crossed the River Ebro, holding their positions there against repeated assault, and halting the Nationalist advance on Valencia. Visiting Spain on the eve of the Battle of the Ebro was Jawaharlal Nehru. Two years earlier he had described the gates of Madrid as 'the symbols of human liberty', and had organized fund-raising in India for the purchase of food grains and an ambulance unit for the Republic. In Barcelona he had his first experience of air raids. Travelling to the front he spent an afternoon with the British and American battalions of the International Brigade. He was so inspired by them that he wrote in the Indian *National Herald* of how 'something in me wanted to stay on this inhospitable looking hill-side which sheltered so much human courage, so much of what was worth while in life'.

In October, after Franco had ordered the heaviest artillery and aerial bombardment of the two-year struggle – and of the struggle in the months ahead – the Republicans were driven back across the Ebro. The historian Raymond Carr has written of Franco at this time: 'He had become the Haig of the Civil War; his repeated attacks on a narrow front had bled his enemy to death and destroyed material which could not be replaced.' That month, Franco's younger brother Ramón was killed while on a bombing mission against the Republican-held docks at Valencia. 'It is nothing to give a life joyfully for the *Patria*,' Franco telegraphed to the Nationalist Air Force, 'and I am proud that the blood of my brother, the aviator Franco, should be united to that of many aviators who have fallen.'

The nature of Franco's orders in the field could shock even a seasoned observer of the military scene. A British Field Marshal, Sir Philip Chetwode, who negotiated successfully with Franco for the exchange of a hundred British prisoners-of-war held by the Nationalists for a hundred Italian prisoners-of-war held by the Republicans, was unable to mitigate the plight of the Republican prisoners-of-war whom he saw. 'I can scarcely describe the horror that I have conceived since my interview with Franco three days ago,' he wrote to Lord Halifax in London on November 14. 'He is worse than the Reds and I could not stop him executing his unfortunate prisoners.'

On December 23 the Nationalists launched a massive offensive against Catalonia. From the first hours the defenders were overwhelmed by Franco's artillery barrage. The scale and superiority of German military supplies was proving decisive. Shocked by the speed of Franco's advance, the French government, whose political instincts were on the side of the Republic, opened the Pyrenees frontier to allow military equipment across, to help sustain the Catalan defences. The Italians, whose troops were fighting alongside Franco's, took immediate diplomatic action, warning that in the event of this open border continuing, Italy would 'make war on France' on Spanish soil. France closed the border.

Confident of victory in a struggle that had continued for two and a half years, on December 31 Franco gave a published interview in which he referred to the Republicans as 'criminals' for whom there could be neither amnesty nor reconciliation. Those who had committed minor 'crimes' could expect prison and labour camp. Others could expect only exile or death. Franco's cold fulminations boded ill for hundreds of thousands of Spaniards, and for Spain.

British rule in Palestine continued to be threatened by the Arab revolt, as most predominantly Arab towns, including Jaffa and Hebron, passed completely out of the control of the authorities. To defend the Jewish settlements, a British army officer, Orde Wingate, created a Special Night Squad which was first in action on June 3. It consisted of seven armed Jews led by Wingate himself. The aim of each Squad was not to defend the perimeter of a settlement, but to go out beyond it and attack Arab saboteurs who had hitherto used the darkness to destroy water pipes with impunity.

In the cities, Arab and Jewish terrorists competed in an escalating spiral of violence. After nine Jews had been killed in a series of individual murders throughout Palestine, a Jewish terrorist bomb killed twenty-five Arabs in Haifa. On July 21 four Jewish workers were killed at the Dead Sea potash works – located near what was believed to be the site of the biblical city of Sodom. Four days later a Jewish terrorist planted a bomb in the melon market in Haifa, killing thirty-nine Arabs. A leading Jewish newspaper in Palestine, *Davar*, denounced the Jewish terror as both 'shameful and calamitous'. The head of the Jewish Agency for Palestine, David Ben-Gurion, called the Jewish terrorists 'miserable cowards'. But a cycle of violence had begun which the most strenuous indignation and active counter-measures (which both the Jews and the British undertook) could not entirely curb.

At a conference in London, held at St James's Palace, the British government found itself under heavy pressure from the governments of Egypt, Iraq and Saudi Arabia to curtail Jewish immigration into Palestine. But the governments of Poland and the United States pressed Britain to allow an increase in the number of Jews entering the mandated territory: Poland because it wanted to facilitate the departure of as many Jews as possible, and the United States because it did not want to have to increase its own immigration quotas.

Within six months, the British deferred to the pressure from the Arab States, and imposed far stricter barriers to emigration, as well as an upper limit of 75,000 more Jews and a further 25,000 more in emergency cases.

At the point when this total of a maximum of 100,000 Jews had entered, or after a period of five years, majority rule would be established: that is, power would be transferred to the Arab majority.

Under this British plan – embodied the following year in a Palestine White Paper which the Parliament at Westminster approved – there could never be a Jewish majority in Palestine, for the Jewish population, which stood at 445,457 in 1939, could rise under the new legislation only to 545,475. But the Arab population already stood at 1,501,698. Under the White Paper restrictions, demography – political demography – would prevent the emergence of a Jewish State in Palestine. Alfred Duff Cooper, who had resigned from the government in protest at the Munich Agreement, spoke in the House of Commons against the restrictions on future Jewish immigration. 'It is the strong arm of the British Empire that has opened the door to them when all other doors are shut,' he said. 'Shall we now replace that hope – that we have revived – by despair, and shall we slam the door in the face of the long-wandering Jew?'

Ironically, while the debate on Palestine was at its height, the death was announced, at the age of eighty-six, of Karl Kautsky, the historian of socialism and friend of Karl Marx, who, in one of his last books, *Are the Jews a race?* had prophesied the defeat of Zionism and expressed his confidence that the Jews would turn their backs on 'the futile aspiration of an antiquated nationalism' to take what he considered to be 'the only path to salvation that is open to them: an energetic participation in the class struggle of the proletariat'. As a Jew, Kautsky had emigrated in 1933 from Germany, seeking refuge in Austria. From Austria he had emigrated to Prague. From Prague he had emigrated to Holland, where he died. Had he lived another year and a half, he might have found himself a refugee once more. During his own search for a safe haven in Europe, tens of thousands of Jews had found refuge in Palestine. But a growing number were being denied it, as pressure on the British Government from the Arab States near Palestine – chiefly Saudi Arabia and Egypt – led to more and more restrictions on the categories of Jews allowed entry.

Far removed from the European, Middle Eastern and Chinese conflicts, and yet concerned about how they might spread, the United States remained cursed by its high level of unemployment: eleven million when the year began. But Roosevelt's measures to create employment were slowly having their effect, with just over a million of the unemployed finding work by the end of the year. This improvement could not mask the fact that an estimated twenty-three million people were receiving some form of public relief. Uncertainty with regard to the economy was reflected that year by the fact that almost a third of the railway companies in the United States were in the hands of the receivers or the courts. But the underlying strength, both of the economy and of the democratic base of the American people, was also evident, as the country avoided the path that led to violent civil unrest and dictatorship.

In an attempt to stimulate the economy, Roosevelt announced a massive Federal programme of 'spending and lending'. Under the Emergency Relief Appropriations Act $3.75 billion was allocated by Congress to public works and industrial expansion. Two industries, textiles and steel, took immediate advantage of this 'pump-priming' (as Roosevelt called it), and saw a rise in production. The boot and shoe industry followed, as did the building industry. By the end of the year the construction of residential homes was breaking all recent records. Even the much-troubled railway companies were able to take advantage of the Federal injection of cash, with the result that they were able to abandon a 15 per cent wage cut already announced, that could only have added to hardship.

The New Deal legislation continued, highlighted by the Fair Labor Standards Act which provided a minimum wage and maximum hours of work for all industries whose products were sold across State borders. During the Bill's passage through Congress, the Southern States opposed it on the grounds that their struggling industries could not afford to pay out minimum wages, but the balance of power in Congress made sure that the Act came into force on October 24. Some Southern factories, unable to pay the increased wages needed to reach the minimum (of 25 cents an hour, rising to 40 cents an hour after seven years) were forced to close down, including pecan-shelling enterprises, tobacco and lumber mills, and garment factories.

It was in foreign policy, however, that the greatest changes took place in the United States in 1938. Hitherto, bolstered by the Neutrality Act of 1935, the American people could contemplate the problems of the rest of the world from afar, without any serious sense of potential danger to themselves. But on January 9, as the Japanese advance through China accelerated, and as German bombers continued to attack Republican-held towns in Spain, a proposal in Congress to insist on a national referendum before war could be declared was defeated by 209 votes to 108.

Five months later, after Hitler had annexed Austria, Secretary of State

Cordell Hull, speaking in Nashville, Tennessee, on June 3, warned that isolation during a period of totalitarian advance was a 'bitter illusion'. His words were a dramatic departure from earlier cautious references to the relevance of European and Asian conflicts. 'It is my firm conviction that national isolation is not a means of security, but rather a fruitful source of insecurity,' he said. 'For, while we may seek to withdraw from participation in world affairs, we cannot thereby withdraw from the world itself. Attempts to achieve national isolation would not merely deprive us of any influence in the councils of nations, but would impair our ability to control our own affairs.'

Hull ended his speech with a bold assertion. 'There was never a time in our national history,' he said, 'when the influence of the United States in support of international law was more urgently needed than at present – to serve both our own best interests and those of the entire human race.' Thomas Mann, an exile from German Nazism, lectured in the United States that spring. He spoke with a sense of urgency about America's place in the disintegrating European scene. 'I am convinced,' he said, 'that if Europe continues for a while to pursue the same course as in the last two decades, many good Europeans will meet again on American soil. I believe, in fact, that for the duration of the present European dark age, the centre of Western culture will shift to America. America has received much from Europe, and that debt will be amply repaid if, by saving our traditional values from the present gloom, she can preserve them for a brighter future that will once again find Europe and America united in the great tasks of humanity.'

In September, during the Munich crisis, Roosevelt had appealed direct to Hitler not to break off negotiations with the Czechs. In November, after the pogrom against the Jews, he had taken the unusual course of handing to the newspaper correspondents, at a Press Conference in the White House, a written statement that 'The news of the past few days from Germany has deeply shocked public opinion in the United States'. Roosevelt added: 'I myself could scarcely believe that such things could occur in a twentieth-century civilization.'

Roosevelt told the journalists: 'With a view to gaining a first-hand picture of the situation I have asked the Secretary of State to order our Ambassador in Berlin to return at once for report and consultation.' Three days later, Hitler retaliated by ordering home the German Ambassador, with instructions 'to report on public sentiment in the United States and the singular attitude towards domestic affairs in Germany manifested in various declarations by President Roosevelt and other important United States personalities'.

With so many German, Austrian, and Czech refugees seeking entry to the United States, Roosevelt ruled that the 12,000 to 15,000 German refugees who were already in the country under visitors' permits would not be forced, despite the condition of their permits, to return to Germany. He did not feel that it was politically possible, however, to ask Congress for revision of the immigration quotas to allow a larger number of refugees to enter. Isolationism may have suffered a blow as a result of the actions of Hitler, Franco and Hirohito, but prejudice and conservatism were far from dead. When the State Department helped to finance an international committee – the Evian Committee – which, meeting by the shores of Lake Geneva, sought a solution to the international problem created by Hitler's anti-Jewish measures, it emerged that very few countries indeed were willing to open their gates, and many, frightened by what were characterized in the national newspapers in many lands as 'a flood of refugees', actually closed their gates more tightly than hitherto.

The Evian Conference revealed hesitations and qualifications that marked a low point in the moral stature of the participants. The United States would still allow its existing quota of 27,370 refugees a year to be maintained, but make no extra entry permits available for the accelerating number of applicants. Most countries opposed almost any immigration. The Australian delegate was emphatic that as Australia did not yet have a 'racial problem' it had no intention of importing one.

Only three countries, the Netherlands, Denmark and the Dominican Republic, agreed to allow refugees in without restrictions. Britain would still allow up to 20,000 Jews a year to enter Palestine over the coming five years, but no more. The Jewish response was to begin to smuggle refugees into Palestine illegally, by sea. The British took immediate steps to intercept these ships, and to deport those caught, not back to Europe, but to the Indian Ocean island of Mauritius. There, though conditions were harsh, the internment camps were at least far away from the European turmoil. Those 'illegals' who were allowed to land in Palestine were deducted from the annual quota.

There was a warmer welcome in Britain itself for those who fled Nazi persecution. On December 2 a boat docked at Harwich with 5,000 Jewish children on board, part of a British Government scheme to bring over children whose parents wished them to find an immediate safe haven in the aftermath of Kristallnacht. They were taken to a camp at Dovercourt, to begin their new lives. Their parents had remained behind: few of the children were to see them again.

The people of the United States became alarmed during 1938 at reports in the newspapers of German Nazi influence in South America, and of the presence of uniformed German Nazi and Italian Fascist groups, and of German espionage, inside the United States itself. A trial in New York City, at which several German spies were convicted, fuelled the unease. That year, the House Un-American Activities Committee was established, to probe into the links between American citizens and potentially hostile foreign governments. During the final discussion on May 26 at which it was agreed to set up the committee, the *New York Times* reported that 'both communism and Nazism were vigorously assailed'.

Target number one during the final debate was the German-American Bund, an organization with 480,000 members who flew the Swastika flag at their meetings and marches. At one of their meetings a speaker had advocated the assassination of Roosevelt. The second target was the American Communist Party, the influence of which inside the Post Office and the New York Fire Department was commented on adversely. 'No one was safe on the WPA in New York unless he joined the Communist Party,' one speaker alleged. The WPA – the Works Progress Administration – had been established by Roosevelt three years earlier to provide public work programmes.

The most unusual event of the year for the United States came on October 30, when the radio broadcast an hour and a quarter long dramatic account of the invasion of New Jersey by alien, gigantic creatures, believed to have landed from Mars. Hundreds of thousands of listeners throughout New Jersey and New York State were petrified by the urgent bulletins coming over the radio each minute, describing how the National Guard had been called out to fight against terrifying, ruthless figures who were marching through so many towns. Several hundred people left their homes with wet handkerchiefs and towels over their faces to flee from what they believed to be a gas raid. A high point of the terror came when the radio announcer told of a meteor landing near Princeton, New Jersey and killing 1,500 people. It was then 'discovered' that the meteor was a metal cylinder containing creatures from Mars armed with 'death rays' and intent on making war.

The listeners who took fright were unaware that what they were listening to was a dramatization by a young producer, Orson Welles, of *War of the Worlds*, a novel by H.G. Wells. The *New York Times* commented on the following day: 'Despite the fantastic nature of the reported "occurrences", the programme, coming after the recent war scare in Europe and a period in which the radio frequently had interrupted regularly scheduled programmes to report developments in the Czechoslovak situation, caused fright and panic throughout the area of the broadcast.'

In the real world, aerial record-breaking continued to exercise pioneers and to excite all who read about it. A British luxury 'Empire' flying boat service made its first regular commercial flight from Southampton on June 26, with only eighteen passengers. It reached Darwin on July 3 and landed at Sydney on July 6. Eight days later the American aviator and inventor Howard Hughes, with four companions, set off in a monoplane to fly around the world. They completed the journey in 3 days 19 hours and 17 minutes, beating the previous world record, set up by Wiley Post in 1933, by almost four days. In October an Italian aviator, Lieutenant-Colonel Mario Pezzi, set a new height record by reaching 56,017 feet. The longest non-stop flight yet recorded was made in November, when three British bombers flew from Egypt to Australia in forty-eight hours: a distance of 7,162 miles, at an average speed of 149 miles an hour. Transatlantic shipping continued to set records: that year the ocean liner *Queen Elizabeth* was launched: it was ten feet longer than the *Queen Mary*, and weighed 85,000 tons.

A new patent ballpoint pen was introduced in 1938, the invention of two Hungarians, J. Ladisla and Georg Biro. It was the latter who gave the pen its name.

Among those who died in 1938 was the Nobel Prize winner Carl von Ossietzky, the German pacifist who had never recovered from his ill-treatment in Nazi concentration camps. Otto Bauer, who had been the Austrian Foreign Minister when the Republic was proclaimed in 1918, also died in 1938. He had fled from Austria to Czechoslovakia when Dollfuss came to power in 1934, and had moved from Czechoslovakia to France in the spring of 1938, when the Czech government – struggling against a host of enemies – curtailed the full liberty of expression to political refugees.

In the United States the oldest surviving general of the Civil War died that summer, one month short of his 101st birthday. Aaron Simon Dagget had received his generalship on 12 March 1865 for 'gallant and meritorious service'. He had retired from the army in the first year of the century. When, also in the United States, Walt Disney launched his film *Snow White and the Seven Dwarfs*, there were protests from many who watched it that the dwarves were too ugly to be shown to children.

In India the struggle for independence entered a radical new phase in the autumn, when Mohammad Ali Jinnah, the Muslim leader who had hitherto supported Indian independence – provided there were safeguards for India's sixty million Muslims – turned from the concept of safeguards to that of separation. His new demand was for a 'separate nationhood' that would allow the followers of the Prophet to acquire their own 'national homelands' in those large areas of north-eastern and north-western India where Muslims were in a majority. As a result of Jinnah's change of policy, the call for an independent united India was replaced, for Muslims, by one of a Muslim State, or States.

The poet Muhammed Iqbal had written of a Muslim entity called Pakistan – the name was made up of the initials for the Punjab, the North-West Frontier region, Kashmir and Bengal. Thenceforth, through a decade of disputes, aspirations and struggle, the word Pakistan became the watchword of millions of Muslims throughout the subcontinent. Communal violence was never far from the surface, and easily provoked. On April 17 three Hindus and a Muslim were playing cards in a public garden in Bombay. They had been drinking, and began to quarrel. An official report described the sequel:

> Rumour of a Hindu-Moslem disturbance spread in the city, resulting in panic which was taken advantage of by hooligans, and stray assaults, stabbing and stone-throwing commenced . . .
>
> Orders were issued prohibiting the carrying of lethal weapons and pre-scribing the routes for Hindu and Moslem funeral processions. Troops were also asked to stand by . . .
>
> A clash that threatened to assume serious proportions was soon brought under control. Sporadic assaults, however, continued for a few days and altogether there were fourteen deaths and injuries to ninety-eight persons.

The police arrested 2,488 people. The riot was over. But the tinder box remained dry.

The year 1938, which saw the twentieth anniversary of the ending of the First World War, was a year in which all the elements of a peaceful, cooperating, evolving international polity were breaking down. Civil wars in Spain and China, brutal war between Japan and China, the destruction of Austrian independence, the dismemberment of Czechoslovakia – these were the pointers to a renewed catastrophe. Purge trials in the Soviet Union, the intensification of totalitarian rule in Germany – marked by violence against Jews and the persecution of Catholics – these betokened a further disintegration of the rule of law, and a further erosion of the rights of the individual.

CHAPTER SEVEN

1939

JANUARY TO AUGUST

> ... each of the two peoples will fight confident of its
> own victory. But surely Destruction and Barbarism
> will be the real victors.
>
> EDOUARD DALADIER

IN A NEW YEAR SPEECH welcoming 1939, Adolf Hitler stated that the year would be devoted to 'forging the complete National-Socialist unity of the German people' and to building up its armed forces. In the previous year he had acquired both Austria and the Sudetenland with a minimum show of force. But for the steps he planned for the new year he was prepared to contemplate military activity of a sort not embarked upon by Germany for more than twenty years.

In pursuit of his goal of a larger army, on January 21 Hitler replaced the President of the Reichsbank, Dr Hjalmar Schacht, by the German Minister of Economics, Walther Funk. In an attempt to prevent inflation and preserve Germany's gold reserves, Schacht had insisted on a policy of reduction of armaments and economy in public works. Neither of these were what Hitler wanted if there was to be war. Funk (whom Schacht denounced in private as 'a harmless homosexual and alcoholic') was a compliant replacement who understood what was needed of him, and was willing to dip deeply into the national resources in order to provide the guns and tanks and planes – and submarines – that Hitler required. No budget figures for this arms expenditure were ever made public: Funk's first budget statement (on April 2) stated blandly: 'The Reich Minister of Finance is authorized, in agreement with the competent Reich Ministers, to allot to the respective Reich administrations the necessary working funds and to determine their mode of employment.'

On January 22, a day after Funk's appointment, Hitler issued a decree in which all men over seventeen were required to undertake some form of 'defence education'. All soldiers who had completed their military service must take part in continuation courses. Labour conscription was also extended, with every worker in Germany having to take up any work which the State might require. A militarized, disciplined nation was being brought into being. It was also a nation that contained critics of the regime whose voices Hitler and the Nazi Party were determined to silence. Among those arrested early in the new year were a number of leading pastors of the Confessional Church who had spoken out in public against the anti-Jewish excesses unleashed the previous November.

The ideals of Christianity continued to be a threat and a thorn in the side of the Nazi movement. In Baden, the Ministry of Education ordered the censoring of the Gospel of St John: the phrase 'salvation is of the Jews' had to be deleted from all Bible readers. In Austria, Reich Controllers confiscated all property belonging to the Catholic Church. Convents were taken over by Party members to serve as their headquarters. Many monks and nuns, made homeless as a result, joined the growing emigration of those for whom Nazism had no place. The confiscation of so much property touched on an aspect of Nazism that was to expand in the years ahead: its greed. Homes, shops, institutional buildings, factories, savings – the list was long of valuable assets which Nazi Party members accrued easily as 'enemies' of the regime were driven out of the country, or taken off to prison and concentration camp.

Outside observers waited on Hitler's words to try to work out what he intended. On January 30 – the sixth anniversary of his coming to power – he gave the Reichstag in Berlin an extraordinary prophesy, that to observers outside the ideological insanities of the German Reich seemed beyond the bounds of credibility. 'If the international Jewish financiers within and outside Europe,' Hitler warned, 'succeed once more in hurtling the peoples into a world war, the result will be, not the Bolshevization of the world and with it a victory of Jewry, but the annihilation of the Jewish race in Europe.'

Hitler also told the Reichstag that day that in order to acquire the food-stuffs needed to feed its population, Germany would need *Lebensraum* – living space. He gave no indication of where, or in which direction, he contemplated finding that space, or in what form it would be found. A clue to his intentions came early in late February and early March, when, in a number of speeches, Hitler made a series of demands on the Czechoslovak government in Prague.

One of Hitler's demands – which he claimed as part of Germany's 'right' in the Sudetenland – was the delivery to Germany of one-third of the gold reserves in the Czechoslovak National Bank. He also demanded that the Czech government, which had lost its principal frontier defences to him the previous October with the loss of one third of its territory, reduce the size of its army, give him overall control of its foreign policy, and provide him with whatever raw materials he required. Another demand that Hitler made on the government in Prague was that it introduce his own Nuremberg Laws of 1935 with regard to the Jews of Czechoslovakia, to turn them into second-class citizens, forbidden to marry non-Jews and forbidden to participate in national life. Prague rejected all these demands, but the fact that they had been made gave a clear danger signal – to those who had ears to hear – for the continuing independence of the much-weakened State.

The very nature of Czechoslovak independence was put at risk by Hitler's demands, for Germany declined, unless these demands were met in full, to sign the agreement reached at Munich for the triple guarantee by Britain, France and Germany of the new, already truncated Czechoslovak frontiers. In Britain, Churchill was calling for a 'strong foreign policy' in which the opinions of 'the working people' would be taken into account. Although he was in his tenth year without political office, the call for his return to government was growing. On February 25 the magazine *Picture Post* published photographs of him working – and bricklaying – at Chartwell, his home in Kent. In Berlin, Field Marshal Goering asked the British Ambassador, Sir Nevile Henderson, what 'guarantee' Germany had that Chamberlain might not be succeeded by a Churchill or an Eden government. This question, Goering told the Ambassador, was Germany's 'main preoccupation'. Chamberlain was not alarmed. 'I myself,' he wrote to his sister on February 19, 'am going about with a lighter heart than I have had for many a long day. All the information I get seems to point in the direction of peace & I repeat once more that I believe we have at last got on top of the dictators.' While agreeing to an increase in defence expenditure, Chamberlain declined to set up a Ministry of Supply to coordinate and accelerate munitions production.

In the second week of March, two areas of German-Czech dispute arose, both stimulated from Berlin. In areas of mixed German-Czech populations, especially in the town of Moravska-Ostrava, there were clashes between German-speakers and Czechs. On March 9, William Shirer wrote in his diary (he was then in Rome for the funeral of Pius XI): 'A storm brewing in what is left of poor Czechoslovakia. Dr Hacha the weak little President – successor to the great Masaryk and the able Benes – has proclaimed martial law in Slovakia and dismissed Father Tiso and the Slovak Cabinet. But Tiso, I know, is Berlin's man.' Four days later, Tiso, although no longer Slovak Prime Minister, was received in Berlin with official acclaim. In his speech of welcome he demanded an independent Slovak State.

A sense of crisis pervaded Europe. On March 13, the day on which Father Tiso spoke in Berlin, special gas masks – designed for children under the age of two – were demonstrated at Holborn Town Hall in London. March 13 was also the day on which Hitler summoned the President of Czechoslovakia, Dr Hacha, to Berlin. Hacha was the third foreign statesman to make the journey to the German capital in order to receive a virtual ultimatum. Schuschnigg had been first, after which, following a prolonged crisis, Austria had been annexed by Germany. Henlein had been the second, after which, again following a prolonged and nerve-wracking crisis, the Sudetenland had been annexed.

On the morning of March 14, while Hacha was preparing to leave for Berlin, the Slovak Diet, meeting in Bratislava, called for the separation of Slovakia from Czechoslovakia – of which it had been an integral part since the founding of the State twenty years earlier. The Diet then adopted a Declaration of Independence. That same day, Father Tiso, who had just returned to Bratislava from Berlin, sent a telegram to Hitler asking him to act as the protector of the new Slovak State.

On March 14 Dr Hacha and the Czechoslovak Foreign Minster, Dr Chvalkovsky, made the journey to Berlin. They were received in the German capital with full military and diplomatic honours: national flags, national anthems, and all the impressive protocol of a State visit. Then, in an interview with Hitler that lasted until four in the morning, they were presented – as Schuschnigg had been a year earlier without the ceremonial welcome – with Germany's demands. The Czech Republic, already deprived of the Sudetenland, must be divided into three separate States: Bohemia and Moravia (as a single entity), Slovakia and Ruthenia. The Czech heartland, Bohemia and Moravia, must become a 'Reich Protectorate' within the orbit of Greater Germany. If these changes were not accepted, Hitler told the Czech President, he would reduce Prague to 'a heap of ruins' by aerial bombardment.

Dr Hacha was familiar with the fate of Guernica, the work primarily of German pilots, and of the effects of the bombing of Barcelona in 1938. He also knew what terrible damage could be inflicted on cities from the air: the bombing of Nanking and Canton by the Japanese air force in the previous year was clear evidence of that. Telephoning from Berlin to Prague, for several hours Hacha discussed with members of his government what he should do. But even as the German ultimatum was being discussed on the telephone line between Berlin and Prague, German troops marched into Moravska-Ostrava. They did so, Hitler declared, to protect the German-speaking population there from possible attack by the local Czechs.

On March 15 the Czech government capitulated. An official communiqué that day stated: 'The Führer, at their request, and in the presence of the Reich Foreign Minister, Joachim von Ribbentrop, had received the Czecho-slovak State President and the Czechoslovak Minister for Foreign Affairs, who had trustfully laid the fate of Czechoslovak people and country into the hands of the Führer of the German Reich.' The German newspapers were triumphant. Their message that day was succinct: 'From now on Germany is again an Imperial Power, seeing that a foreign nationality has placed itself under German protection.'

The deceptive use of words, at least in public, by Hitler and the Nazi Party, was once again to constitute a major distortion of reality. The words 'German protection' enabled many to be lulled into feeling that everything could not really be that bad. Six months earlier, during the Munich crisis, when Hitler handed Chamberlain a document with his latest demands, Chamberlain told the Führer indignantly, 'But this is an ultimatum'. Hitler took the document back from him, studied it for a moment, and then said: 'Ultimatum? Not at all. Look, it is headed "Memorandum".' In the same way, the use of the word 'Protectorate' masked the total imposition of German rule and of Nazi ideology.

The deliberate misuse of language deceived the outsider: those who were sent to concentration camps had no illusions on learning that the places of their terrible incarceration were called 'Camps of Protective Custody'.

On March 15 German troops marched into Bohemia and Moravia. As with the earlier annexations of Austria and the Sudetenland no shots were fired. On instructions from the Czech Government in Prague, no resistance was offered. The Czech armed forces laid down their arms. The new region of

Germany was 18,000 square miles in extent, with a population of nearly seven million people. Of considerable importance for Germany's military strength, it contained enough military supplies, some of the most modern type, to arm and equip a million and a half soldiers.

Travelling to the Czechoslovak Government's former seat of government on Castle Hill, in Prague, Hitler proclaimed Bohemia and Moravia a Protectorate of the Reich. All German-speaking inhabitants were to become German nationals. All others were to be 'protected peoples' – in effect, subject peoples. The gold reserves in the Czechoslovak National Bank were taken charge of by Reichsbank officials from Berlin.

William Shirer, who was then in Paris, wrote in his diary: 'Complete apathy in Paris tonight about Hitler's latest coup. France will not move a finger. Indeed, Bonnet told the Chamber's Foreign Affairs Committee today that the Munich guarantees had "not yet become effective" and therefore France had no obligation to do anything.' This was also the British government's view. As Chamberlain explained to the House of Commons that same day, March 15: 'The condition of affairs which was always regarded by us as being only of a transitory nature has now ceased to exist, and His Majesty's Government cannot accordingly hold themselves any longer bound by this obligation.'

The national existence and human realities of post-Munich Czechoslovakia had become reduced to a 'condition of affairs'. Within a few days of the establishment of the Protectorate that condition followed the pattern of the imposition of Nazi rule anywhere. Many hundreds of Czechs were imprisoned. Thousands more were rounded up and taken into Germany as forced labourers. The universities were closed. Jewish disenfranchisements were introduced according to the full severity of the Nuremberg Laws. Businesses owned by Jews were taken over by Germans. All manifestations of Czech culture were suppressed.

With Germany's agreement, Slovakia retained the independence which it had declared during the break-up of Czechoslovakia: indeed, it was the Slovak declaration of independence that had effectively sealed the geographic fate of the country which Masaryk and Benes had established two decades earlier. Slovakia was allowed to create an army, fortify her borders, and promulgate her own laws. She also provided the military bases for the tens of thousands of German troops which, as the summer months proceeded, began to mass along the southern Polish border.

Ruthenia also took the opportunity of the disintegration of Czechoslovakia to declare its independence. There had been a Ruthenian national movement at the end of the First World War, but during the creation of Czechoslovakia, Ruthenia became the new country's eastern province. Its population was mixed: Ruthenians (Sub-Carpathian Ukrainians), Hungarians, Jews and Germans. The Prime Minister of the new State was a Ruthene, Father Volosin. But he did not even have time to form a government before Hungarian troops, who were already in occupation of the main cities adjacent to Hungary, marched in. There were still Czech troops stationed in the province, but the Hungarians demanded that these withdraw, and they left at once. The Ruthenes had no army of their own with which to offer resistance. Father Volosin fled across the border into Roumania. Hungary declared the annexation of Ruthenia.

Among those in Prague when Czechoslovakia was dismembered was Marina Tsvetayeva, born in Moscow, one of many thousands of Russians who had found exile from Soviet Communism in democratic Czechoslovakia, and felt a deep bond with the country that had taken them in. She wrote in her *Poems to Czechoslovakia*:

> They took quickly, they took hugely,
>   took the mountains and their entrails.
> They took our coal, and took our steel
>   from us, lead they took also and crystal.
>
> They took the sugar, and they took the clover
>   they took the North and took the West.
> They took the hive, and took the haystack
>   they took the South from us, and took the East.
>
> Vary they took and Tatras they took,
>   They took the near at hand and far away.
> But worse than taking paradise on earth from us
>   they won the battle for our native land.
>
> Bullets they took from us, they took our rifles
>   minerals they took, and comrades too:
> But while our mouths have spittle in them
>   The whole country is still armed.

On March 20, five days after the German Protectorate was proclaimed over Bohemia and Moravia, the Roumanian government – which many observers felt might be the next to succumb to Hitler's pressure – agreed to set aside for Germany's exclusive use one half of Roumania's considerable petrol production. Soon afterwards, in a secret visit to Berlin, King Carol of Roumania told Hitler that Roumania was 'predisposed against Russia but cannot say so openly because we are neighbours.' However, the King added, 'Roumania will never allow the passage of Russian troops, although it is often asserted that she is supposed to have promised Russia to allow her troops in. This is not the case.'

On March 21, the day after Roumania's oil pledge to Germany, the Lithuanian Foreign Minister was invited to Berlin for the following day as a matter of urgency, and there, in the course of a few hours, signed an agreement whereby the territory of Memel was ceded to the German Reich. Hardly had Hitler acquired Memel than Mussolini was making plans for another Italian conquest, this time in Europe, and on April 7, Good Friday, the first of 30,000 Italian troops disembarked at several Albanian ports and advanced towards the capital, Tirana. Albania was already much dependent on Italy, including its banking system.

The ruler of Albania, King Zog, had made plans to resist an Italian attack. But as Italian troops moved towards his capital he fled, seeking refuge in Greece with his queen – a Hungarian aristocrat, Geraldine Apponyi – who had just given birth to their son. For the loss of only twelve Italian soldiers in action, Albania was conquered. On April 13 King Victor Emanuel III of Italy – who was already Emperor of Abyssinia – accepted the throne of Albania as well, and declared the 'personal union' of his two kingdoms. In London and Paris, the Italian action caused anger and alarm. On the day that Victor Emanuel accepted the Albanian throne, the British and French Governments hurriedly gave guarantees to Greece and Roumania.

While Hitler and Mussolini strode forward in Europe, the Spanish civil war entered its final fighting phase. In the first three weeks of January, three thousand square kilometres fell to the Nationalist forces under Franco. On January 15 the capture of the town of Tarragona opened the way for a nationalist assault on Barcelona, the Catalonian capital. On the following day, Franco issued an order to accelerate the pace of the advance, with 'no quarter' to be given. On January 25 the government in Madrid, headed by Dr Juan Negrin, decided that it could no longer defend Barcelona, and left

Catalonia to its fate. On the following day Franco's forces entered Barcelona. In the bloodletting that followed, several thousand Republicans were killed.

On February 6 the President of the Republic, Don Manuel Azana, fled to France and exile, refused all calls that he return to Spain, and urged the Republicans to surrender. Dr Negrin followed him into exile on February 9. By the following day Franco's forces were in control of the whole of Catalonia. The demoralization of the Republican forces was nearly complete. It was heightened further when several Italian divisions played a prominent part in the triumphal Nationalist victory parade in Barcelona, while Italian and German warplanes flew above the ceremony.

In and around Madrid the Communist forces within the government ranks wanted to fight on. Thirty per cent of the land area of Spain was still under government control. But the departure of the President and the Prime Minister was a serious blow. When Diego Martinez Barrio, who was himself in exile, was appointed successor to the President at the end of February, he refused to return to Spain. From Burgos, Franco continued to act as the imminent ruler of all Spain. On February 13 he showed his contempt for his Republican opponents not only by issuing a Law of Responsibilities in which all supporters of the Madrid government were declared 'guilty' of supporting the 'illegitimate' Republic, but made the law retrospective to 1934. Under the law, membership of left-wing political parties was made a crime, as was 'serious passivity'.

In the first week of March those Republicans who wanted to fight on suffered a massive blow when the Commander of the Republican Central Army, Colonel Segismundo Casado, set up a Council of Defence in Madrid. Its task was to end the war and make the best possible terms with the Nationalists.

Colonel Casado's aim was to make peace before the Republican forces were wiped out. He was supported in this by the seventy-year-old Socialist leader and philosopher, Julian Besteiro, who had refused to leave Madrid throughout the conflict. Both Casado and Besteiro believed that if they could throw off the Communist influence in the Republican ranks, they would be able to negotiate a reasonable compromise with Franco. They might even be able to get some credit from Franco by their attempt 'to save Spain from Communism'. One of those who cast their lot with Casado was General Rafael Calzada, the twenty-four-year-old scion of an aristocratic Galician family, who had led a battalion in the defence of Madrid at the start of the war. He shared Casado's belief that it might be possible to negotiate a peace with the Nationalists in order to fight the common enemy, Communism.*

On Casado's orders the arrest of Communists in Madrid began on March 6. The Communists, denouncing Casado's rebellion as treason to the Republic, fought back. Those on whom the defence of the Republic had for so long depended were again at each others throats, with a ferocity intensified by the imminence of defeat. On March 7 the pro-Communist commander of one of the Army Corps under Casado, Major Luis Barceló, ordered his troops to surround Madrid. Casado and his supporters were trapped inside the capital. On March 10, after four days of intense fighting, another Army Corps commander, Cipriano Mera, an anarchist, won the military initiative. Barceló and several other Communist officers were arrested and shot. Casado and Calzada escaped and sailed for England in a British warship.

On the coast, at Cartagena, another Communist officer, Major Francisco Galán, took control of the naval base for the Republic. He was then attacked by Republicans who, like Casado in Madrid, hoped to negotiate a settlement with Franco. The Nationalists in the port appealed to Franco for help. He responded by sending two divisions to Cartagena by sea. The troopships were unescorted. When Republican shore batteries opened fire on them, one troop transport was sunk and more than one thousand Nationalist troops were drowned. It was the first wartime naval disaster of the year, but it was not to be the last.

Those European States which had looked with sympathy on the Republican efforts hastened to come to terms with Franco. Both Britain and France sent their envoys to see him in Burgos, and to offer their recognition to the Junta. The French emissary was eighty-three-year-old Marshal Pétain, one of whose uncles had fought in Spain with Napoleon's army, against the British. In France's hour of need in March 1918, Pétain's had been the voice of courage and resistance. He was to remain the French representative with Franco – first in Burgos and then in Madrid – until called back to France in its second hour of need in May 1940.

On March 23, Colonel Casado, having secured the upper hand once more in Madrid, sent emissaries by air to Franco at Burgos. Their mission was to get Franco to accept their surrender, on the basis of no reprisals, and a twenty-five day period of grace for the departure from Spain for anyone

---

* In exile in London, Rafael Calzada became a distinguished restaurateur. In December 1997, when he was being rushed to hospital (aged 83) in the last moments of his life, and was asked by the paramedics if he was allergic to anything, he replied: 'Penicillin and Communism.'

wishing to leave the country. One of Franco's conditions was the immediate surrender of the Republican Air Force. When for technical reasons this condition was not met in time, Franco refused to set a second deadline and broke off all negotiations. He then announced that he would accept only unconditional surrender. At the same time, in a radio broadcast from Burgos, he promised 'a generous pardon for all who have not committed crimes'. Merely serving with the Republican forces, or being a member of an anti-Nationalist political Party, would not, Franco explained, be considered a crime.

Colonel Casado was deeply disappointed that his conditions for surrender were not to be met. He decided to take unilateral action, and, on March 25, announced 'the self-demobilization of the Republican Army'. For two days Franco's forces advanced through abandoned trenches and deserted fortified positions. Then, on March 27, they entered Madrid. The remaining Republican-held cities, among them Cartagena, fell in rapid succession. On March 28, as if to make clear that any further Republican resistance would have been futile, fresh Italian troops landed at Cadiz, to replace their colleagues who had been fighting alongside Franco in the very forefront of the action. By March 31 all Spain was under Nationalist control.

Thirty-two months of civil war was over. Going quite against the word and the spirit of his Burgos broadcast about 'a generous pardon', Franco imprisoned – among others – those who had opposed the 'National Movement' by what the Law of Responsibilities had described in February as 'grave passivity'. In Catalonia and the Basque country, regional liberties were suppressed with rigour. One rule laid down that the Catalan language was not to be used for commerce. The restoration of the land to its 'rightful owners' – one of the main pieces of legislation of the Negrin government – was halted and then reversed. As a sign of how ruthless the new ruler would be, the moderate Socialist leader Professor Julian Besteiro, then aged seventy, was sentenced to thirty years in prison.

The Church was an ally that Franco sedulously wooed. One of his earliest laws was to require every Spanish citizen to be a Catholic. On May 8, Spain withdrew from the League of Nations, thus aligning itself with Germany and Italy as a pariah State among the would-be enforcers of non-aggression. Eleven days later, on May 19, Franco held a victory parade in Madrid. Two hundred thousand troops paraded in front of him, among them a battalion of black-shirted Italian soldiers, their daggers raised in a Roman salute. Also in the parade were many of the Portuguese volunteers who had fought for the Nationalists. Headed by their German Chief of Staff, General Wolfram von Richthofen, were the men of Hitler's Condor Legion.

During his triumphal speech, Franco declared that Spain would remain alert against 'the Jewish spirit which permitted the alliance of capital with Marxism'. As a gesture of solidarity with his fellow Dictators he joined the Anti-Comintern Pact, pledged to resist all the blandishments of Communism at home and abroad. But Franco did not want his shattered country to be drawn into a European war, and both Hitler and Mussolini were disappointed that he would not make any strong statements in support of them, or contemplate any action at their side. When Mussolini's son-in-law and Foreign Minister, Count Galeazzo Ciano – who on May 22 had stood with Hitler on the balcony of the new Chancellery in Berlin for the signing of an Italian-German military alliance, the 'Pact of Steel' – visited Madrid for five days in July to secure a similar alliance between Italy and Spain, he was unable to do so, and returned to Rome greatly disappointed. Hitler was also annoyed when one of Franco's closest colleagues, General Aranda, during a visit to Berlin at the head of a large Spanish Military Mission, declined to make any greater commitment to the German-Italian Axis than to offer Spain's 'benevolent neutrality'.

In August, Franco – having raised himself to the rank of Generalissimo – announced the nature of the new Spanish government and regime. It would be a National Syndicalist State, with himself as *El Caudillo* (the Spanish equivalent of *Führer*): the National Chief of the Single Party. At the same time, he was Head of State, with full autocratic powers, responsible 'only to God and to history'. He was also Commander-in-Chief of the Armed Forces, with more than a million men under his command, even after demobilization. Criticism of Franco's regime would be rigorously opposed. Strict Press censorship became an integral feature of the new Spain.

In a gesture of friendship to his neighbour on the Iberian Peninsula, Franco awarded the Prime Minister of Portugal – his fellow-dictator Dr Salazar – the Grand Cross of Isabella. More than six thousand Portuguese officers and men had fallen on the battlefield alongside Franco's forces – a larger number of war dead than of any other foreign participant in the Nationalist ranks.

The Spanish exiles waited, most of them in France, for the day when they could return home. It was to be a long and demoralizing wait. Louis Fischer, who had fought alongside them, wrote a year after the Republic had been destroyed: 'There is a measure of bitterness engendered among Spanish

Republicans by the fight against Fascism. The Loyalists exile now entered upon the sad role of émigrés. The law of all emigrations is: Man eats Man, Friend Assails Friend. Parties split into fractions, the fractions into factions, the factions into groups, the groups into grouplets.' Fischer added: 'Everybody blamed everybody else for the defeat. Everybody made wild accusations. Everyone thinks the Spain of the future is his. Meanwhile many must fret about their permit to stay in the country of asylum and worry about the next meal. A nation died when Franco won. But nations have been reborn.'

Returning to the Soviet Union, those who had led the Russian effort on behalf of the Republic both militarily and diplomatically were almost all arrested, imprisoned and shot. Stalin wanted no-one to live who had participated in the Spanish struggle. Among those who vanished without trace on his return to Russia was the Soviet Consul in Barcelona, fifty-five-year-old Vladimir Antonov-Ovseenko – who had been at the centre of the destruction of the POUM Marxists in Catalonia in May 1937. Antonov-Ovseenko had been active in the 1905 Revolution, was one of the organizers of the seizure of the Winter Palace in 1917, and had been Lenin's first Commissar for Military Affairs. The two men who respectively headed the Soviet Military Mission in Spain – General J.P. Berzin and Brigade Commander Skoblevsky – were also among those 'completely liquidated' (as Nikita Khrushchev later phrased it). Skoblevsky, who was known in Spain as General Gorev, had taken a leading part in winning the Battle of Madrid for the Republic, and on his return to the Soviet Union had been hailed as the 'Hero of Madrid'. This did not save him: like hundreds of thousands of other Soviet citizens that year he was denounced as a traitor, a wrecker, a spy or a Trotskyite, and shot. His arrest took place, according to one account, only two days after he received the Order of Lenin for his services in Spain.

In the laconic words of the historian Robert Conquest, 'Spain was a bad posting for all Soviet personnel'. Among those who fought in Spain and were later shot by Stalin were the future Generals Pavlov and Kulik, as well as General Shtern, a future Army Commander in the Far East, and General Smushkevich – an air ace in Spain who became Head of the Soviet Air Force. All four were shot in 1941, for alleged 'treacherous activity' in the Russo-German War.

In the Far East, the Japanese advances deep into Chinese-held territory had continued from the first days of the new year. Parallel with their military thrusts the Japanese had pressed forward with their policy of heavy aerial bombardment of the Chinese cities, including Chungking, in which the Nationalist Government had established its capital. By the beginning of May, half a million Chinese troops stood between the Japanese forces and Chungking itself.

The Japanese, unable to break through the line, sent their bombers against Chungking. During the air raid of May 4 more than 1,500 Chinese were killed in the city, and in the raid on May 23 at least 5,000, many of them refugees from the fighting elsewhere. 'For seven years,' wrote the Nobel Peace Prize winner Sir Norman Angell, 'Japan has been proclaiming to the world that her military operations against China (which are not war at all, be it remembered, only an "incident"), the laying waste of great cities, the slaughter of helpless civilian populations, the bombing and machine gunning of British ambassadors, all these Japan, probably with complete sincerity, is persuaded are but incidents of her defence.'

Despite the Japanese bombardment, Chungking remained under Nationalist control, but in the south, the Japanese continued to capture port after port – including Swatow, Fuchow and Wenchow – thus further depriving the Nationalists of the possibility of sea-borne supplies. In yet another military success, the Japanese captured the southern city of Nanning, thereby cutting off the Nationalists from one of their main land-borne supply routes, the road and rail link with French Indo-China. This left Chiang Kai-shek almost entirely dependent for his supplies on the longest and most precipitous route of all, the Burma Road linking him across high mountains and deep valleys with British Burma and India.

One barrier to an even swifter Japanese success, and to the consolidation of the Japanese military conquests, was the growth throughout 1939 of Chinese guerrilla activity that had begun the year before. In Hopei province in the north the Japanese completely failed to suppress the activities of the Communist-led guerrilla forces, which, in a direct military assault upon the Japanese positions, inflicted heavy loss of life. More than a million Chinese were participating in some form of guerrilla activity. There were also, however, repeated clashes between the Kuomintang and Communist forces – an ongoing civil war.

The scale of the casualties in the Sino-Japanese War was massive. According to Japanese figures, issued with a chilling precision, 94,358 Chinese had been killed in guerrilla battles during 1939, and 1,218,462 Chinese had been killed in the fighting since 1937. But the Japanese aim, to destroy the Chinese armies in the field, had been denied them.

The death toll of Chinese civilians from Japanese air raids during the first nine months of the year was estimated by the Chinese at 20,000. There were those who thought that Chiang Kai-shek and the Kuomintang forces under his command would not be able to hold out against the combined pressures of Japanese attack and Chinese Communist power. The Swedish mining engineer, J. Gunnar Andersson, who had served as a mining adviser to the Chinese Government after the First World War, and had returned to China in 1936, wrote in July 1939, in the preface to his book *China Fights the World*:

In the course of the war Chiang has explained on occasion that it is hard for him to follow *the middle course*.

One extreme, repeatedly offered to him, is to accept the Japanese terms and hand over China to totalitarian rule and to co-operate in forming a Tokyo-Nanking axis, making the war chariot of the dictatorial States a four-wheeled vehicle.

The other extreme is to throw in the lot of the Chinese with Bolshevik rule, a terrible temptation in this hour when all the resources of China are strained to uphold the national cause.

But in spite of all allurements from Tokyo and from Moscow, the Kuomintang government of China still stands firm in upholding the middle course, its democratic rule, and in doing so it fights for a principle that ought to be supreme in all democracies of the world, the right of every people to live its own national life.

Andersson noted that when the Chinese Nationalist struggle against both Japan and the Chinese Communists was presented to the democratic countries of the world, they responded 'with moral support, a sympathetic voice, and material help'.

The Japanese government decided in 1939 to take a step which would end its naval inferiority in the Pacific. A six-year naval expansion programme was begun, through which it was envisaged that the Imperial Japanese Navy would, by 1945, be as large as that of the strongest naval power. In fact, at the end of those six years, Japan would find herself reduced to physical ruin and military impotence, something inconceivable in the confident atmosphere of 1939, when friendship with Germany and Italy seemed to place Japan on the winning side in any future conflicts.

In Manchuria, there were further clashes that year between Japanese and Soviet forces. On July 5 the Japanese Government published photographs of captured Russian soldiers under Japanese guard. When a truce was signed in September both sides agreed to remain on the respective side of their common border. Reflecting on the life of the Chinese living under Japanese rule, Jung Chang has written:

> The teachers said that Manchukuo was a paradise on earth. But even at her age my mother could see that if the place could be called a paradise it was only for the Japanese. Japanese children attended separate schools, which were well equipped and well heated, with shining floors and clean windows. The schools for the local children were in dilapidated temples and crumbling houses donated by private patrons. There was no heating. In winter the whole class often had to run around the block in the middle of a lesson or engage in collective foot stamping to ward off the cold.
>
> Not only were the teachers mainly Japanese, they also used Japanese methods, hitting the children as a matter of course. The slightest mistake or failure to observe the prescribed rules and etiquette, such as a girl having her hair half an inch below her earlobes, was punished with blows. Both girls and boys were slapped on the face, hard, and boys were frequently struck on the head with a wooden club. Another punishment was to be made to kneel for hours in the snow.
>
> When local children passed a Japanese in the street, they had to bow and make way, even if the Japanese was younger than themselves. Japanese children would often stop local children and slap them for no reason at all. The pupils had to bow elaborately to their teachers every time they met them. My mother joked to her friends that a Japanese teacher passing by was like a whirlwind sweeping through a field of grass – you just saw the grass bending as the wind blew by.

'Many adults bowed to the Japanese, too,' Jung Chang wrote, ' for fear of offending them.'

In French Indo-China, the Communist Party – founded nine years earlier and led by Ho Chi Minh – was concerned not to encourage the Japanese to set themselves up as the allies of national independence. Ho Chi Minh sensed danger in the Japanese attempt to champion the rights of those in South East Asia who were under French, Dutch or British colonial rule. In July, in his report to the Communist International, he warned: 'For the time being, the Party cannot put forth too high a demand (national independence, parliament, etc.). To do so is to enter the Japanese fascists' scheme.' He suggested the creation of a broad-based Democratic National Front. The Communist Party, he advised, 'must assume a wise, flexible attitude with the bourgeoisie, strive to draw it into the Front, win over the elements that can be won over, and neutralize those which can be neutralized'.

In the United States, Roosevelt continued to show that strong leadership did not have to become dictatorship: indeed, neither Congress nor the Supreme Court would have allowed excessive use of Presidential power. Hitler, Mussolini and Stalin each saw himself as the model of successful use of the mechanism of the State to get things done. But, among the Great Powers, it was in the United States that the most harmonious combination of power and the national good could be seen in action. This was all the more impressive in that even many Democrats in Congress were opposed to the continuing 'recovery and relief' programme, based as it was on high government spending and increased taxation. Every measure that did go forward did so only as a result of prolonged debate and modification, rather than being steamrolled through a complacent or bullied legislature.

The most imaginative of Roosevelt's schemes that year, and one which would involve an expenditure of $400 million, was the construction of 'super-highways'. These revolutionary-style roads would provide fast inter-State links for private cars, buses and commercial vehicles.*

The continuing problems besetting rural life in the United States were highlighted that year with the publication of John Steinbeck's novel *The Grapes of Wrath*. The scenes portrayed, like those by Martha Gellhorn three years earlier, made an indelible impression on those Americans who were desperate to see their country prosper, and its citizens flourish. A migrant from Oklahoma is in search of work in California: '. . . he saw the golden oranges hanging on the trees, the little golden oranges on the dark green trees; and guards with shotguns patrolling the lines so a man might not pick an orange for a thin child, oranges to be dumped if the price was low.'

In Steinbeck's novel, the spokesman of the cotton owners explains that there is no more work:

* In the summer of 1962 I was driven by a Republican politician through pleasing countryside in New Jersey, until we came to a deep cutting, in which lay a broad and busy inter-State highway. Pointing to it with a contemptuous gesture, my host exclaimed: 'I blame this on Roosevelt.'

The squatting men raised their eyes to understand. Can't we just hang on? Maybe the next year will be a good year. And with all the wars — God knows what price cotton will bring? Don't they make explosives out of cotton? And uniforms? Get enough wars and cotton'll hit the ceiling. Next year, maybe. They looked up questioningly.

We can't depend on it. The bank — the monster has to have profits all the time. It can't wait . . .

With the worsening situation in Europe and Asia, the United States found itself drawn in more and more to debates on foreign policy. Although the general concept of isolationism, of keeping clear of foreign entanglements prevailed, it was foreign policy that had begun to overshadow the domestic scene. In his speech to Congress at the beginning of the year, Roosevelt intimated that the concept of perpetual neutrality, much as it might seem to be enshrined in the Neutrality Acts, could not survive the conflicts that were arising across the Atlantic and the Pacific oceans. 'We have learned,' he said 'that the God-fearing democracies of the world, which observe the sanctity of treaties and good faith in their dealings with other nations, cannot safely be indifferent to international lawlessness anywhere. They cannot forever let pass, without effective protest, acts of aggression against sister nations — acts which automatically undermine all of us.'

The very concept of neutrality was one which Roosevelt wished to question. 'We have learned,' he said, 'that when we deliberately try to legislate neutrality, our neutrality laws may operate unevenly and unfairly — may actually give aid to the aggressor and deny it to the victim. The instinct of self-preservation should warn us that we ought not to let that happen any more.' That month, as a result of a $25 million loan, American aeroplanes, pilots and machine guns were beginning to reach the Chinese forces in their struggle against Japan. Later that year the American Trade Treaty with Japan, which dated from 1911, was abrogated, ending America's primacy as the provider of raw materials for Japan's munitions of war. Also in January, Roosevelt made it known — as a result of a casual remark — that he had given permission for a Military Mission from the French government to purchase United States warplanes.

The German occupation of Bohemia and Moravia led to a definite change in the public voice of the administration in Washington. The German action, according to a State Department spokesman, had resulted 'in the temporary extinguishment of the liberties of a free and independent people'. On March

20, five days after Hitler's forces entered Prague, Roosevelt informed the German ambassador in Washington that the United States 'declined' to recognize the German occupation. He then issued a direct challenge to Hitler. Roosevelt's main point was put in the form of a question to Hitler, listing thirty-one countries whose independence the United States seemed to wish to protect.

Roosevelt's question read: 'Are you willing to give assurance that your armed forces will not attack or invade the territories or possessions of the following nations: Finland, Estonia, Latvia, Lithuania, Sweden, Norway, Denmark, The Netherlands, Belgium, Great Britain and Ireland, France, Portugal, Spain, Switzerland, Liechtenstein, Luxembourg, Poland, Hungary, Roumania, Yugoslavia, Russia, Bulgaria, Greece, Turkey, Iraq, the Arabias, Syria, Palestine, Egypt, and Iran?' This was not the sort of question usually put by any Head of State to another, and certainly not to Hitler. Yet Hitler answered it thirteen days later, in a speech that lasted more than two hours. During his speech he offered to make a Non-Aggression pact with any of the countries mentioned in Roosevelt's list that wanted to do so. Hitler added contemptuously that Roosevelt had apparently not noticed 'that Palestine is at present occupied not by German troops but by the English'.

Few outside observers imagined that some German move, against a nearby country, was not in prospect. On April 1, in Berlin, William Shirer wrote in his diary: 'Off to Warsaw tomorrow to see when the German attack is expected.' On the following day Shirer attended what he called a 'pitiful' Polish air show, 'my Polish friends apologizing for the cumbersome slow bombers and the double-decker fighters – all obsolete. They showed a half-dozen modern fighters that looked fast enough, but that was all. How can Poland fight Germany with such an air force?'

Throughout 1939 the nature of the Nazi regime in Germany was the subject of innumerable books and pamphlets. Among those which made a particular impact in both the United States and Britain was the 319-page memoir of Martha Dodd, the daughter of Roosevelt's first ambassador to Hitler. Her book was published in April. In the chapter entitled 'Torture' she wrote:

I can never forget what I know about German concentration camps, for I have been in contact, both in Germany and outside, with people who have suffered untold agony and tortures for periods of months and years in these hellholes.

When I read in the papers almost daily of new executions, new arrests, new attacks, new imprisonments, new secret police examinations, I can only feel renewed horror, fresh pain and pity, and an overpowering sense of indignation.

Though it is well known what men and women suffer in concentration camps, many people seem to think those who tell the stories are hate-mongers or sensation seekers. I know these stories to be true and I have spent days with people who have endured their service in purgatory and watched others of their kind do so. Some of them escaped, others were released after the spirit and body had been broken, many watched their comrades killed or tortured to death.

The people I have talked to have been socialists, artists, or writers who were completely innocent of any charges made against them.

Martha Dodd stressed that in the lives of prisoners in the concentration camps, experiences 'either too horrible or nauseating to relate are everyday occurrences'.

Even exiles were unable to contemplate the intensification of Nazism and the onward march of Fascism without traumatic responses. On May 22 the German dramatist, poet and revolutionary Ernst Toller – one of the leaders of the Bavarian Communist revolution in 1918 – took his own life in New York. He had served five years in prison in Germany for his part in the Bavarian uprising. Fleeing Germany in 1934, he came to the conclusion that all force, in whatever cause, had to be rejected. His last two plays, *No More Peace!* and *Pastor Hall*, had been cries of pain against Nazi totalitarianism and the Nazi obsession with war. In New York, he had devoted considerable time to trying to help Spanish Republican exiles. The catalyst to his suicide was the fall of Madrid.

Anti-Jewish measures did not completely depend upon the German Nazi Party for their promulgation. In April the Hungarian Government introduced a law under which the many Jews who had fought in the First World War in the ranks of the Austro-Hungarian army, and Jewish war widows and orphans, were to be deprived of the benefits granted to their fellow-Hungarian veterans, widows and orphans. Jews were to be forbidden to participate any further in government service, in newspaper offices, film studios or the theatre. Jewish working men and women were no longer to be allowed to be members of working associations.

In an attempt to discredit these proposed anti-Jewish measures, and to prevent the law from being put on the statute book, Hungarian liberals declared that the Prime Minister, Dr Bela Imredy, was himself of Jewish ancestry. In order to disprove this, and thus to proceed with the discriminatory legislation, Imredy caused a detailed search to be made into his family records. Then, in a public speech, he announced in triumph that, as far back as his mother's grandfather, there was no Jewish blood. But the researches which Imredy had instituted were pressed further, until it emerged that his mother's grandmother had been a Jewess. She had been baptized at the age of seven, in 1814. Under Jewish religious law, Jewishness descends through the female line, despite baptism.

Dr Imredy felt compelled to resign as Prime Minister. He was succeeded by Count Paul Teleki, who was shown to have no Jewish antecedents, and the anti-Jewish law was enacted. When, within a few weeks of the passage of this legislation, elections were held, the Liberal and opposition Parties were reduced to an impotent minority: 57 as against 183 for the government. Count Teleki pursued what he called a 'constructive, social, Christian, and national, policy'. This put him at odds with the largest of the opposition Parties, the Arrow Cross – the Hungarian Nazis – who held 33 seats. But it did not disturb his essentially pro-German alignment.

At the request of Germany, Italy and Japan, Hungary also agreed to join the Anti-Comintern Pact.

Neville Chamberlain had been outraged when Hitler went back on his assurance of less than six months earlier that he wanted 'no Czechs' under his rule. Any attempt by Germany 'to dominate Europe', Chamberlain warned after the German occupation of Prague, 'would rouse the successful resistance of this and other countries who prize their freedom'. The German government replied with an invitation to Britain – published in the SS newspaper – to 'join hands with Germany in dictating the peace of the entire world'.

The British Government began negotiations with other countries that it felt might be in danger of German hostility, and within a few weeks Britain signed agreements with Poland and Turkey. The German Government immediately protested that these agreements constituted 'encirclement'. German commentators pointed out that Germany had signed a Non-Aggression Pact with Poland five years earlier, and that this pact still had five years to run. Poland ought therefore to be in no danger at all. But in a speech on April 28, Hitler – who so often announced his intentions in public speeches before ecstatic German audiences – denounced the Non-Aggression Pact and accused Poland of seeking to join Britain in the encirclement of Germany.

A new direction of urgent German interest had been signalled: Hitler assured the Poles in his speech that all Germany wanted was the return of Danzig and the Polish Corridor – both with their predominantly German populations. But he could tolerate no longer, as the Leader of the German people, that East Prussia should be cut off territorially from Germany. The very creation of Poland in 1919, like that of Czechoslovakia the same year, had involved great injustices to the German people. Twenty years earlier, when these borders had been established, Germany was a defeated, weak nation. She was weak no longer.

On June 6 the German volunteers of the Condor Legion returned from Spain – 15,000 men in all – and paraded through the streets of Berlin. Hitler took the salute, and in his speech of welcome told them that their success in Spain was 'a lesson to our enemies'.

A German newspaper campaign began, in which Poland was portrayed as the enemy and the obstacle to German unity. Just as, at Munich, Hitler had assured Neville Chamberlain that he wanted 'no Czechs' in the German Reich, so he insisted throughout the summer of 1939 that he had no desire to rule over a single Pole. His sole aim was the restoration of German sovereignty over German people. If Poland continued to resist these just demands, the German newspapers warned, she would be 'wiped off the map with a mailed fist'.

Despite his anger at having been deceived with regard to Prague, Chamberlain was not entirely hostile to the German demands on Poland. On July 15, in the privacy of a letter to his sister, he wrote that while he doubted if any solution short of war was 'practicable' as far as Danzig was concerned, 'if Dictators have a modicum of patience I can imagine that a way could be found of meeting German claims while safeguarding Poland's independence and economic security'. But Hitler did not intend to call on Britain to help him secure his claims. Ribbentrop pointed out to him, which was true, that the Anglo-Polish agreement was not a binding alliance. Ribbentrop was confident that Britain would not go to war on behalf of Poland.

An appeal to Hitler came from an unexpected quarter that month, when Gandhi wrote to him from India on July 22: 'You are today the one person who can prevent a war which may reduce humanity to a savage state. Listen to the appeal of one who has deliberately shunned the method of war not without inconsiderable success.' Hitler made no reply.

One of those who knew the working of Hitler's mind, Hermann Rauschning, a former member of the Nazi Party whom he had earlier installed in
Danzig to secure the nazification of the Free City, warned that summer, in
his book *Germany's Revolution of Destruction*: 'The German riddle is not only
growing more sinister, it is threatening men's lives'. Nazism stood for 'the
destruction of all traditional, spiritual values'. Before turning his back on
Nazism and Germany, Rauschning had received orders for 'arresting incon-
venient Catholic priests, disenfranchising the Jewish population, and suppressing all rival Parties'. He had appealed direct to Hitler to have these
orders rescinded. Hitler had refused to do so.

Such aspects of life that could be called normal during such abnormal times
continued to rouse interest and to give pleasure. Millions of Americans
followed the news as, on May 2, the baseball player Lou Gehrig retired after
making his 2,130th consecutive appearance for the New York Yankees.
Lovers of travel everywhere were thrilled when, on June 26, a streamlined
locomotive, travelling on the Hamburg-Berlin line, reached a new world
record speed of 133.6 miles an hour.

There was another leap forward in the cause of communications – of the
letter-writing which linked families and friends across oceans and continents
– on August 6, when the first British transatlantic airmail service was
inaugurated, and a flying boat, the *Caribou*, flew from Newfoundland to
Foynes with 40,000 letters on board. Seventeen days later, in the ever-active
competition to break motor car land speed records, an Englishman, John
Cobb, drove his Railton Red Lion motor car at 368.85 miles an hour over
the Bonneville Salt Flats in Utah. Four days later a Swedish long distance
swimmer, Sally Bauer, swam the English channel from France to Britain in
15 hours and 23 minutes: the challenge and thrill of record-breaking crossed
all national barriers.

In addition to the challenge of the unknown – the search for the fastest,
the longest, the highest, the boldest – war was also a beneficiary of the
competitive spirit. In Britain, a Spitfire fighter flew on January 16 from
Paris to London in forty-one minutes, at an average speed of 300 miles an
hour. Nine days later an aeroplane factory was opened at Southampton which
had taken only sixty-four days to build. In Germany, a German fighter plane,
flying near Augsburg on April 26, reached a new world speed record of
469.11 miles an hour: but even this remarkable feat was not the last German
record that year in the skies; the air speed record for 1939 went to the first

Messerschmitt military jet plane, the Me 109, which in a test flight reached 481 miles an hour.

In the intensification of military preparations, accidents brought home to the public in every land the human cost of war-making activity. On June 1 the British submarine *Thetis* sank during a test dive in Liverpool Bay, and was unable to rise to the surface. A faulty torpedo tube was the cause of the accident. Ninety-one people in all – fifty crew members and forty-one naval and civilian observers – were drowned. Only the captain and three others managed to escape the submarine and survived.

One young submariner, Richard Gatehouse, had arrived at the shipyard to join the trials just as the *Thetis* was ready to sail. He was told to his disappointment that there were already enough officers on board and was invited instead to spend the rest of the day playing golf. He had thus to watch and wait, with the whole British people, for four days, as the repeated attempts to raise the *Thetis* failed.*

The uncertainties facing those in search of an escape from German racial policy was highlighted in June, when 927 German-Jewish refugees sailed from Hamburg on board the ocean liner *St Louis*, bound for the New World. The United States immigration quota numbers which 734 of the refugees possessed were not valid for another three years. Despite steaming within sight of the Florida coast, the refugees failed to persuade the United States Government to let them in. Twenty-two were allowed to land in Cuba, whereupon, on June 2, the Cuban Government ordered the ship to leave Cuban territorial waters. On the following day the State Department in Washington rejected a Jewish proposal that those refugees with valid United States immigration quota numbers should be allowed to land in the United States.

The *St Louis* sailed along the coast of Florida. On June 6 Roosevelt received a telegram asking him to reconsider the appeal to let the quota-holding refugees in to the United States. He made no reply. That day, after the Colombian, Paraguayan, Argentinian and Chilean Governments declined to open their doors to the refugees, the *St Louis* set course back to Europe. On June 17 her passengers disembarked in Antwerp. More than six hundred

* During his subsequent naval career, Richard Gatehouse was awarded the Distinguished Service Cross three times: for sinking an Italian submarine off the North African coast in 1941, for sinking a German troop transport off Crete in 1944, and for his contribution to operations off the Korean peninsula in 1952.

were allowed into Holland, Belgium and France – where within twelve months they were to come under German rule. It is thought that only 240 of them survived the war. A further 288 were given refuge in Britain.

Also finding refuge in Britain were 235 Jewish children from Vienna who reached the port of Harwich from the Hook of Holland on July 14, and were taken by train to London. These children were part of the continuing, and that summer almost daily, rescue effort undertaken by charitable organizations and individuals, as a result of which ten thousand German, Austrian and Czech Jewish youngsters were saved. Known as the *Kindertransporte*, they made a full contribution in the decades ahead to British life and culture. Among them, Alf Dubs became a Member of Parliament, Karel Reisz a film-maker, and Hella Pick a journalist and author. Although the new arrivals were mostly helped by Jewish organizations – principally the Central British Fund – the Quakers and the Christian Council for Refugees looked after about 20 per cent. Those who rescued them included many selfless individuals, Jewish and non-Jewish: of the latter, a notable example was Nicholas Winton, a young stockbroker, who visited Prague to accelerate the children's departure.

On July 18 another refugee arrived in Britain: Eduard Benes, President of Czechoslovakia until its disintegration and conquest four months earlier. Around him in Britain he gathered a government in exile – the first of what would be several such governments – awaiting the day when his country would be free and he could return.

At the beginning of August the holiday season in Europe was in full swing. The British historian A.J.P. Taylor was in the South of France, confident that nothing would interrupt his summer break. The August issue of *Cook's Continental Timetable* offered a wide range of rail journeys for the European travellers on both business and pleasure. Night sleepers for the International Wagon Lits Company could be booked in Cracow and Bordeaux, in Paris and Oslo, in Brussels and Warsaw; even in Berlin at offices in the Unter den Linden and the Kurfürstendamm. Travellers to Germany were warned that the one item that could not be brought into the country was 'preserved meats'. The guide book listed sixty golf courses available to travellers in Germany – two were near Vienna and one in the former Czech spa town of Marienbad (formerly Marianske Lazne).

The Orient Express left London at two o'clock each afternoon: travelling to Dover, with a cross-Channel ferry to Calais, then on by train through

France, Germany – including Vienna – Hungary, Roumania and Bulgaria, it reached Istanbul after three days and three nights. From London, at eleven each morning, the Golden Arrow Luxe took passengers to Paris in under seven hours, where they could connect with trains running as far east as Moscow and as far south as Rome.

Air services were reaching a new peak of efficiency and comprehensiveness. A daily flight leaving Rotterdam at 10.45 in the morning and touching down in Vienna, ended its flight in Budapest just before four o'clock that afternoon. The one hint that everything in Europe was far from normal was a note in the guide book about this particular flight, stating: 'Not at present calling at Prague'. The daily flight from London to Berlin, with onward flight to Warsaw, was, however, unchanged.

On August 4 the Polish Government issued an ultimatum to the Danzig Senate. The aim of the ultimatum was to end a long-standing refusal by the Danzig authorities to recognize Polish customs inspectors. The Poles also demanded an end to the open frontier between Danzig and East Prussia, an act that was in defiance of the Danzig's Free City status, and a flaunting of the city's desire to be part of Germany.

The Polish Government gave the Danzig Senate twenty-four hours to comply. The President of the Danzig Senate, Arthur Greiser, a committed Nazi, gave way. The Polish, British and French newspapers trumpeted the German 'climb down'. Hitler ordered German troops to concentrate along the Polish border. A senior British diplomat, Orme Sargent, commented, as German and Polish troops faced each other across the frontier defences: 'If it had not been one thing it would have been another. Hitler wanted his pretext and he would have found it even if he had been dealing with the Archangel Gabriel.'

The German newspapers began a campaign of denunciation of Poland. Any future Polish ultimatum on Danzig, they declared in unison, would be met by an 'appropriate reply'. On August 10 William Shirer, from his vantage point in Berlin, wrote in his diary:

How completely isolated a world the German people live in. A glance at the newspapers yesterday and today reminds you of it.

Whereas all the rest of the world considers that the peace is about to be broken by Germany, that it is Germany that is threatening to attack Poland over Danzig, here in Germany, in the world the local newspapers create, the very reverse is being maintained. (Not that it surprises me, but when you are away for a while, you forget.)

What the Nazi papers are proclaiming is this: that it is Poland which is disturbing the peace of Europe; Poland which is threatening Germany with armed invasion, and so forth. This is the Germany of last September when the steam was turned on Czechoslovakia.

'POLAND? LOOK OUT!' warns the *BZ*, headline, adding: 'ANSWER TO POLAND, THE RUNNER-AMOK (AMOKLAUFER) AGAINST PEACE AND RIGHT IN EUROPE!'

Or the headline in *Der Führer*, daily paper of Karlsruhe, which I bought on the train: 'WARSAW THREATENS BOMBARDMENT OF DANZIG— UNBELIEVABLE AGITATION OF THE POLISH ARCH-MADNESS (POL- NISCHEN GROSSENWAHNS)!'

For perverse perversion of the truth, this is good. You ask: But the German people can't possibly believe these lies? Then you talk to them. So many do.

On August 11 Hitler summoned Professor Carl Burkhart, the League of Nations High Commissioner to Danzig, to the Chancellery in Berlin, and told him: 'If the slightest incident happens I shall crush the Poles without warning in such a way that no trace of Poland can be found afterwards.'

William Shirer was in Danzig during the Hitler-Burkhart meeting. After spending two days there he noted in his diary on August 12: 'I have more and more the feeling that Danzig is not the issue and I'm wasting my time here. The issue is the independence of Poland or German domination of it.' Also on August 12 Stalin's ambassador in Berlin telegraphed to Moscow: 'The conflict with Poland is escalating at a growing rate. Decisive events may occur at the shortest notice.'

Poland, like Czechoslovakia a year earlier, was vulnerable to a German attack on three separate fronts: from East Prussia in the north, from the direction of Berlin in the west, and from the recently occupied Sudetenland in the south. Britain, hoping to secure Poland's eastern frontier, and to deter Germany from aggression, began negotiations with the Soviet Union. Previous hesitations about coming to an agreement with the hated Commu- nists were being set aside in the interest of a common front against Nazi aggression. But Stalin had no particular desire to fight for the maintenance of Polish independence. The eastern third of Poland had been acquired from Russia by conquest in 1921 – under the Treaty of Riga – and contained, outside the cities, a majority of White Russians and Ukrainians, both of whom had their own Soviet republics within the Soviet Union.

In strictest secrecy, Stalin began negotiation with Hitler's Germany. Even while the British negotiators were in Moscow, Russian negotiators in Berlin were in the closest conclave with their German opposite numbers. The British negotiators did not have the enthusiastic backing of their Prime Minister. In a letter to one of his sisters he confided: 'I am so sceptical of the value of Russian help that I should not feel that our position was greatly worsened if we had to do without them.' Hitler had no such hesitations. For him, the chance of neutralizing Russia made the prospect of an attack on Poland extremely tempting. In return for Russia taking no action against him, he would cede to the Soviet Union the eastern provinces of Poland, and partition the country between the two dictators. The partition of Poland between Germany and Russia would echo the partitions of the eighteenth century, in which Austria (which Hitler now ruled) had also been a part.

On August 19, at a secret meeting of his Politbureau, Stalin made clear that a momentous decision faced the Soviet Union, and that an arrangement with Nazi Germany was a definite possibility. On the following day it was announced that Germany had concluded a Commercial Agreement with the Soviet Union, advantageous to Soviet trade. In Moscow, the head of the British negotiating team had asked for a meeting with the Soviet negotiators in two days' time, on August 23. But the meeting that was held that day at the Kremlin on the day of the British request was with a German delegation.

The offers that had been made to Stalin from Berlin were a far greater attraction to him than those from London. In essence, London wanted him to align himself in a grouping that, in defence of Poland, might find itself at war with Germany within a matter of weeks. Berlin offered a means both to keep out of war, and to extend Soviet territory. For Stalin, one of the most attractive features of the German offer was that it gave him control of the three Baltic States – Estonia, Latvia and Lithuania – which until then, with their considerable German minorities and Baltic coastline, had been much championed by Hitler as part of the German patrimony.

Stalin was about to commit the Soviet Union to an agreement with the ideology to which he had been most implacably opposed, and which had most fiercely and crudely abused him and his system. But he knew that to join a western alliance would be to take incredible risks. One of his trusted assistants, B.A. Dvinsky, had showed him earlier that summer the most recent Intelligence reports about the size and state of the German army. As many as 3,700,000 million German soldiers were under arms, almost half of them in mechanized formations. Germany possessed 3,195 tanks and more than 4,000 warplanes. Against such numbers the Red Army and Red Air Force, if for any reason Russia found itself without active allies in the West, would be in danger of defeat.

In a telegram which he sent to Stalin on August 20, Hitler pressed for a decision. 'The tension between Germany and Poland,' he warned, 'has become insupportable. Poland's behaviour towards a great Power is such that a crisis may occur any day.' Hitler went on to ask Stalin to receive Ribbentrop in Moscow in two days' time, on August 22, 'or at the latest on Wednesday 23 August'. Stalin replied that he would receive Ribbentrop on August 23. Meanwhile, an obstacle had occurred in the Soviet talks with Britain and France with regard to the defence of Poland. The Polish government had refused one of the Soviet conditions for an Anglo-Franco-Soviet agreement: the right of passage of Soviet troops across Polish soil, to be able to reach the eastern border of Germany in the event of war.

As negotiations on this point continued between London, Paris and Warsaw, Stalin made his decision to come to terms with Germany. 'Assistance to Poland,' Stalin's biographer General Volkogonov has written, 'was hampered not only by Warsaw's attitude, but also by the Soviet Union's unpreparedness.'

On August 22, Hitler made it clear to his confidants how he intended to proceed against Poland, and how he considered that the world would react. 'I shall give a propaganda reason for starting this war, no matter whether it is plausible or not,' he said. 'The victor will not be asked afterwards whether he told the truth or not. When starting or waging war it is not right that matters, but victory.'

On August 23, Ribbentrop flew from Berlin to Moscow. The Nazi-Soviet pact was signed that same day. It was guided, according to its preamble 'by the desire to strengthen the cause of peace' between Germany and the Soviet Union. Each Power agreed to refrain from any act of force, or aggressive act, or attack 'against each other or in conjunction with any other Powers'. Each agreed to settle any dispute between them 'by friendly exchanges of views, or if necessary by arbitration commissions.' The pact was to last for ten years: the same time scale, observers noted, as the defunct German-Polish Non-Aggression pact.

As a result of the Nazi-Soviet Pact – which was also known, from its two signatories, as the Molotov-Ribbentrop Pact – the fate of Poland was sealed. Although the facts of the agreement were made public, the map which accompanied it remained secret, as did the clauses explaining it. Poland was to be divided between Germany and the Soviet Union. In the event of a German invasion of Poland, the Soviet Union was to occupy the eastern side of the line drawn on the map.

On August 24, not knowing about the map but aware of the suddenly increased danger to Poland from the Nazi-Soviet Pact, President Roosevelt appealed to both Hitler and the Polish President, Ignacy Mosticki, to settle their differences at the conference table. The Pope and the King of the Belgians did likewise. But Hitler had no reason to fear any military reaction if he were to march against Poland. Stalin was his ally. Britain and France would not, in his considered opinion – reinforced by Ribbentrop's confident assertions – take any action on Poland's behalf. But on August 25 the British government, under considerable public and parliamentary pressure not to let Hitler achieve yet another bloodless conquest, signed a formal treaty of alliance with Poland. The new alliance committed Britain to coming to Poland's aid in the event of Poland being attacked by Germany. France had a similar alliance already in place. Suddenly Hitler was confronted by the same possibility that had confronted the Kaiser in 1914: a two-front war, this time against Poland in the east and Britain and France in the west.

Britain was facing an internal scare that month which had been a recurring factor since the beginning of the year. On August 25, as tension mounted on the German-Polish border, a bomb detonated by the Irish Republican Army killed five passers-by in Coventry. This Irish nationalist campaign on mainland Britain had earlier led to bombs in London, Manchester, the Midlands and Northumberland. The IRA campaign created unease in Britain at what would happen internally in the event of a European war. The terror campaign was in fact to continue until February 1940, when there was a hiatus of thirty-two years.

Inside Germany, the anti-Polish campaign was mounting in intensity. In the Polish Corridor, according to one German newspaper headline on August 26, there were 'MANY GERMAN FARMHOUSES IN FLAMES'. This was completely untrue. The newspapers were also insisting that Germany required not only Danzig and the Polish Corridor, but also the Poznan (formerly Posen) province and that part of Silesia which had been transferred to Poland by plebiscite in 1922.

Hitler made one last effort, on August 26, to persuade Mussolini to commit himself to the coming battle. Mussolini did not reject the call outright. Instead, he promised to enter the war at the side of Germany as soon as he had been sent 17,000 train loads of materials to complete his rearmament. Denis Mack Smith, one of Mussolini's biographers, comments: 'The amount had been calculated in just a few minutes and some of the requirements had been doubled or trebled to make them quite impossible to meet.' All Hitler could do was to beg Mussolini to keep his impending neutrality secret. This Mussolini promised. At the same time Mussolini informed the British Government, in strict secrecy, that he would 'in no circumstances' initiate war against France or Britain.

On August 27, Edouard Daladier sent a message to Hitler asking him to hold back from war. Poland was a 'sovereign nation', Daladier pointed out, and France would stand by its alliance and its obligations to her. Daladier ended with an appeal that went beyond the formalities of diplomacy: 'If', he wrote, 'French and German blood is now to be spilled, as it was twenty-five years ago, then each of the two peoples will fight confident of its own victory. But surely Destruction and Barbarism will be the real victors.'

Among those seeking to escape the barbarism that had already been unleashed was a leading Berlin neurosurgeon, Ludwig Guttmann. His expertise – which since 1933 he had not been allowed to exercise in non-Jewish hospitals – was the rehabilitation of people suffering from paraplegia and paralysis. An invitation to come to Britain enabled him to leave that August. At Stoke Mandeville hospital he was to treat over the coming six years many thousands of those with severe spinal injuries incurred in battle and in bombardment, reducing the death rate from such injuries from 80 per cent to 10 per cent, and enabling many of the survivors to lead much fuller lives than they might otherwise have done. In 1945 a British Government Minister remarked: 'Thank you, Hitler, for sending us men like these.'

On August 29, Britain sent Germany a formal note, warning her not to seek to conquer Danzig by force. That same day, in the style of the previous Sudeten, Austrian and Czech crises, Hitler demanded that a Polish negotiator, equipped with full powers to come to a final agreement about the transfer of Danzig and Pomerania to Germany, arrive in Berlin 'by midnight' of

August 30. The British felt that a solution might be reached if the Germans would list their demands in detail, and the Poles agree to discuss them. At midnight on August 30 the British Ambassador in Berlin, Sir Nevile Henderson, told Ribbentrop that his government 'could be counted upon to do their best in Warsaw to temporize negotiations'.

The Polish Ambassador in Berlin, Jozef Lipski, was afraid that Britain would put similar pressure on Poland as had been put nine months earlier on Czechoslovakia, to cede territory in return for German guarantees of making no further claims. The transfer of the Polish Corridor, Lipksi told the British Embassy in Berlin at midday on August 31, 'was a breach of Polish sovereignty and was quite out of the question'. It would be 'fatal' for a Polish plenipotentiary to go to Berlin. 'We must for heaven's sake stand firm and show a united front, and Poland if deserted by her allies was prepared to fight and die alone.'

The British Ambassador continued to believe that British pressure on Poland could avoid war. Just after midday on August 31 he telegraphed to Lord Halifax from Berlin, commenting that the German terms 'sound moderate to me and are certainly only so in view of German desire for good relations with Britain'. Henderson added: 'This is no Munich, since we are behind Poland who will never get such good terms again guaranteed as they will be internationally.' The Polish Government should 'be insistently told' to give Lipski 'immediate instructions' to open negotiations.

The Polish Government was unwilling to be forced into negotiations without having seen the German terms in advance. It therefore declined either to ask its ambassador to open negotiations, or to send a negotiator-plenipotentiary to Berlin. Petrified of being drawn in to a European war, that afternoon Mussolini put himself forward as a mediator. He would sponsor a conference, to be held on September 5, to revise the eastern frontiers of the Versailles Treaty by negotiation. Poland would transfer land at the conference table – as Czechoslovakia had done – and war would be avoided. The British drew back from a second Munich. There could be no value, Chamberlain told Halifax, in a conference held 'under the threat of mobilized armies'.

Hitler was also unwilling to follow the Munich path of negotiation. When Bernardo Attolico, the Italian ambassador in Berlin, saw him on the evening of August 31, to urge his acceptance of Mussolini's conference, Hitler refused. Was 'everything now at an end', the ambassador asked. 'Yes' Hitler replied. Not knowing that Hitler had made up his mind to invade Poland, the

British government made one last attempt on August 31 to persuade the Poles to send a minister-plenipotentiary to Berlin, as the Germans had demanded. When the British Ambassador in Warsaw, Howard Kennard, warned that the demand for the plenipotentiary's presence constituted an ultimatum, Lord Halifax replied that Ribbentrop had 'vigorously repudiated' this suggestion. 'If negotiations are initiated,' Halifax telegraphed to Kennard later that night, 'His Majesty's Government will at all times be ready, if desired, to lend any assistance in their power to achieve a just settlement.'

'Berlin is quite normal in appearance tonight,' William Shirer wrote in his diary on August 31. 'There has been no evacuation of women and children, not even the sandbagging of windows. We'll have to wait through still another night, it appears, before we know. And so to bed, almost at dawn.' While Shirer slept, the German government informed the world that Polish troops had broken into a German radio station in the city of Gleiwitz, in Upper Silesia, and, after killing a number of Germans in the radio station, had broadcast an appeal to the Polish people calling the population to war.

No such Polish provocation had taken place. The Polish troops were in fact Germans dressed up as Poles. The dead German – for there was indeed one – was a common criminal taken from a concentration camp and killed by his fellow-Germans in order to give credence to the tale of a Polish attack. The attack was a crude fabrication, but in the early hours of September 1, citing this bogus incident as the reason, Hitler ordered the German army to cross into Poland, and German aircraft to set off on their first bombing missions of the Second World War. That morning Hitler broadcast to the German people:

Since 5.45 a.m. we have been returning the fire, and from now on bombs will be met with bombs. Whoever fights with poison gas will be fought with poison gas. Whoever departs from the rules of humane warfare can only expect that we shall do the same. I will continue this struggle, no matter against whom, until the safety of the Reich and its rights are secured.

For six years now I have been working on the building up of the German defences. Over 90 milliards have in that time been spent on the building up of these defence forces. They are now the best equipped and are above all comparison with what they were in 1914. My trust in them is unshakable. When I called up these forces and when I now ask sacrifices of the German people and if necessary every sacrifice, then I have a right to do so, for I also am to-day absolutely ready, just as we were formerly, to make every personal sacrifice.

I am asking of no German man more than I myself was ready throughout four years at any time to do. There will be no hardships for Germans to which I myself will not submit.

'My whole life henceforth belongs more than ever to my people,' Hitler declared. 'I am from now on just the first soldier of the German Reich. I have once more put on that coat that was the most sacred and dear to me. I will not take it off again until victory is secured, or I will not survive the outcome.'

For two days, throughout September 1 and 2, Britain and France hesitated to declare war in honour of their respective alliances to Poland. The British government sought a formula whereby Hitler would agree to halt his forces at the point they had reached after twenty-four hours, and then open negotiations with Poland with a view to some territorial adjustments in favour of Germany. But when these behind-the-scenes activities became known, they were rejected by the British Cabinet and Parliament.

From the first hours of the advance of the German army across the Polish frontier, and the falling of German bombs on Warsaw, the conflict that began that September 1, whatever the initial hesitations in London and Paris, was clearly going to be far more than a local one, restricted to the disputed German-Polish borderlands. But whether it was going to be a war that would match the so-called Great War of 1914–18 in geographic scale or human suffering, and perhaps even exceed the Great War in its devastation, no one could know.

Only one thing seemed certain, that the Jewish people had been singled out to be the target of the strongest power – the designated enemy of the nation that had initiated the most recent aggression, against Poland, the home of more than three million Jews. An American journalist, Lothrop Stoddard, travelling in Germany shortly before the outbreak of war, published on his return to the United States a stark account of what he had personally seen and heard. 'In Nazi Germany,' he wrote, 'the resolve to eliminate the Jews is further exacerbated by theories of race. The upshot, in Nazi circles, is a most uncompromising attitude. If this is not oftener expressed, the issue is already decided in principle and the elimination of the Jews will be completed within a relatively short space of time.' Stoddard added that the subject of the fate of the Jews did not 'ordinarily' arise. 'But it crops up at unexpected moments. For instance, I have been stunned at a luncheon or dinner with Nazis, when the Jewish question had not even been mentioned, to have somebody raise his glass and casually toast: *Sterben Juden!* – "May the Jews Die!"'

PART TWO

CHAPTER EIGHT

1939
SEPTEMBER TO DECEMBER

A war . . . to establish and revive the stature of man.

WINSTON S. CHURCHILL

THE SECOND WORLD WAR has dominated the Twentieth Century: the fighting that took place on the battlefields, by land, sea and air between 1939 and 1945, and the killings that were perpetrated behind the front lines, saw the greatest loss of military and civilian life in so short a time in recorded history. Yet the date 1939–1945 is in many ways arbitrary. War in China had been a daily and brutal feature of life in eastern Asia since 1937. The civil war in Spain, ending in 1939 a few months before the 'world' war began, had been a three-year ordeal for those living on the Iberian peninsula. A Euro-Asian war, in many ways a civil war, was being fought behind a cloak of secrecy inside the Soviet Union: the war of Stalin and his instruments of terror against several million Soviet citizens.

When yet another war began on 1 September 1939 it was between two States only, Germany and Poland. It was this German-Polish war, spreading slowly, and only becoming truly global more than two years later, that is known as the Second World War. The Soviet Union, which was not invaded by Germany until the summer of 1941, has designated its period of hostilities as the Great Patriotic War. Yet the Soviet invasion of Finland at the end of 1939 can be seen as an integral part of the Second World War.

One thing seemed certain, however – as certain inside Germany as beyond it – that without Hitler there would not have been war. Writing in the spring of 1941, William Shirer reflected:

The primary cause of the Continent's upheaval was one country, Germany, and one man, Adolf Hitler. Most of my years abroad were spent in that country in proximity to that man. It was from this vantage-point that I saw the European democracies falter and crack and, their confidence and judgment and will paralyzed, retreat from one bastion to another until they could no longer, with the exception of Britain, make a stand.

From within that totalitarian citadel I could observe too how Hitler, acting with a cynicism, brutality, decisiveness, and clarity of mind and purpose which the Continent had not seen since Napoleon went from victory to victory, unifying Germany, rearming it, smashing and annexing its neighbours until he had made the Third Reich the militant master of the Continent, and most of its unhappy people his slaves.

On that first morning of September the peoples of Germany, Austria, Bohemia and Moravia were the 'slaves'. Among them, though far fewer in Bohemia and Moravia than elsewhere, were also many willing followers, full of high hopes of conquest and mastery. Millions of others were to be the instruments, and in due course the victims of that conquest. Yet millions more were to be silenced and suborned. And, within hours of the advance of the German armies into Poland, new victims, and new cruelties, were to mark the pages of that 'terrible Twentieth Century' of which Churchill had spoken in 1922, and of which he had warned then that the 'destructive tendencies have not yet run their course'.

With the outbreak of war, after ten years in the political wilderness, Churchill was brought back into the British Government as First Lord of the Admiralty. 'This is not a question of fighting for Danzig or fighting for Poland,' he told the House of Commons on the morning that Britain declared war on Germany:

We are fighting to save the whole world from the pestilence of Nazi tyranny and in defence of all that is most sacred to man.

This is no war of domination or imperial aggrandizement or material gain; no war to shut any country out of its sunlight and means of progress.

It is a war, viewed in its inherent quality, to establish, on impregnable rocks, the rights of the individual, and it is a war to establish and revive the stature of man.

The German advance into Poland was swift, and on three fronts: from Greater Germany in the west, from East Prussia in the north, and from Slovakia in the south. Germany's use of air power proved to be decisive. In the very first hours of the attack, German planes destroyed many Polish aircraft while they were still on the ground. Bombers struck not only at Polish military lines of communications, munition dumps and supply depots, but at civilian centres, causing panic and confusion. On the afternoon of September 1, forty-one German bombers took part in the first German bombing raid on Warsaw. Two of them were shot down and their crew taken prisoners-of-war. As many as a hundred civilians were killed in this raid. On the following day, more than a hundred Polish refugees were killed when their train, which was evacuating them from the border area, was bombed while standing at a railway station. Parallel with the continuous assault in the air, German tanks and armoured vehicles – the panzers of Hitler's modern army – advanced in force against battered and often bewildered defenders.

From the first days of the German advance into Poland, a new dimension entered into the hitherto predominantly military aspect of wars between States. This was the deliberate singling out of civilians for ill-treatment and execution. On the day that the German army began marching into Poland, a meeting was held at Sachsenhausen concentration camp, just north of Berlin, at which Theodor Eicke, the commander of the SS Death's Head regiments, explained to his assembled officers – before they too set off for Poland – that the SS would have to 'incarcerate or annihilate' every enemy of Nazism. This task, he explained, would test even the 'absolute and inflexible severity' for which the Death's Head regiments had become famous within the German concentration camp system. 'It is the duty of every SS man,' Eicke told them, 'to identify himself body and soul with the cause. Every order must be sacred to him and he must carry out even the most difficult and the hardest of them without hesitation.'

These orders were for the killing of Polish civilians, day after day, in every Polish city, town and village. Prominent local Poles – priests, teachers, municipal officials – were executed in order to deprive the citizens of those who would be their natural leaders in adversity. Random arrests were made of Polish civilians to be shot as a reprisal for an attack – often not a fatal attack – on a German soldier. For the death of a single German soldier, ten, twenty, thirty, even more people could be taken out of their homes and summarily killed.

Polish Jews were also killed at random from the first days of the war. On

September 3, in the border town of Wieruszow, twenty Jews were rounded up, among them sixty-four year old Israel Lewi. They were then taken to the market place, lined up and shot. When Liebe Lewi, Israel Lewi's daughter, tried to intercede on behalf of her father, she was ordered to open her mouth wide for her 'impudence', and then shot through the mouth. She fell dead on the spot.

Sunday September 3 was the third day of the German attack on Poland. That morning neither Britain nor France had yet declared war on Germany. Both had, however, issued an ultimatum to Germany to stop hostilities or face war. Above Poland the German Air Force had begun its third day of operations. A young schoolboy, Ben Helfgott, whose father had taken him a day earlier from their home town of Piotrkow to the nearby smaller town of Sulejow, for safety, later recalled:

People were walking around in the warm sunlight as though life was as serene as the sun made it seem. I started playing with the local boys. Within minutes I had new friends. A lovely, lovely day – until as the sun began to go down we heard the sound of planes overhead. They swooped down and started dropping incendiary bombs. Seconds later, this pretty little village was a mass of flames. At ten years of age, I had never seen anything like it before. I have also seen nothing like it since – not even Dante's inferno could have been visualized in this form.

No one knew where to go, but they were all running in different directions, some with their clothes on fire. Blindly running. Cats, dogs, horses, cows, all of them aflame, too, all running. Madly, pointlessly, agonizingly. Instantly, whole families were consumed by flames. That we managed to escape unhurt was a real miracle. As we ran into the nearby woods, I could see people falling all around us – picked off by machine-guns from the aircraft ahead. There was the terrible sound of screaming. Sometimes just screams. Sometimes names – 'Moishe!' 'Gittel!' Names that might never be heard again, but which at that moment were being called in other towns and villages all over Poland.

Then there were those looking for their children, for parents, for grandparents, for brothers, for sisters. About three thousand people were burnt and killed within a very short time, whole families wiped out and many decimated. By a miracle our family of five was saved. Our horse was killed, our carriage destroyed. So my father led us on foot away from the village.

At midday on September 3 the British ultimatum expired and Neville Chamberlain broadcast over the wireless that Britain was at war with Germany. France issued her declaration of war a few hours later. In New Delhi, Gandhi wept as he spoke with the Viceroy of the possible destruction of the Houses of Parliament and Westminster Abbey. He could not speak for his colleagues, he said, but he viewed the war 'with an English heart' and would personally favour 'full and unquestioning' support for the British war effort.

That evening, in the Atlantic Ocean two hundred and fifty miles north-west of Ireland, the passenger liner *Athenia*, on its way from Liverpool to Montreal, was torpedoed without warning by a German U-boat. Of the 1,418 passengers and crew on board, 112 were killed, most of them American students who were returning home, and refugees from Europe seeking a new life in Canada and the United States. In the First World War it had been the persistent sinking of American ships, starting with the ocean liner *Lusitania*, that had eventually drawn the United States into the war. But the sinking of the *Athenia* in 1939 – like the sinking of the *Lusitania* in 1914 – while it caused anger and outrage, did not lead to war.

A few hours after the sinking of the *Athenia*, Roosevelt broadcast from the White House. 'Passionately though we may desire detachment,' he said, 'we are forced to realize that every word that comes through the air, every ship that sails the sea, every battle that is fought does affect the American future. Let no man or woman thoughtlessly or falsely talk of America sending its armies to European fields. At this moment there is being prepared a proclamation of American neutrality.' Roosevelt ended his broadcast:

This nation will remain a neutral nation, but I cannot ask that every American remain neutral in thought as well. Even a neutral has a right to take account of facts. Even a neutral cannot be asked to close his mind or close his conscience.

I have said not once but many times that I have seen war and that I hate war. I say that again and again.

I hope the United States will keep out of this war. I believe that it will, and I give you assurance and reassurance that every effort of your Government will be directed toward that end.

As long as it remains within my power to prevent, there will be no blackout of peace in the United States.

That night ten British bombers flew from their bases in southern England across the North Sea to Hamburg, Bremen and nine other cities in the Ruhr. They carried with them more than five million leaflets, denouncing Germany's action in invading Poland. There were no losses on the raid. The next morning twenty-nine British bombers were sent on a mission to bomb German warships in harbour at Wilhelmshaven and Brunsbüttel, at the mouth of the Kiel Canal.

During the raid on Brunsbüttel, owing to a navigational error, four bombs were dropped on the Danish town of Esbjerg – more than a hundred miles to the north – and one Danish citizen was killed, Edel Hansen, whose block of flats was hit. She was the first civilian victim of British aerial warfare.

In the British bombing raid on Wilhelmshaven that night three bombs hit the pocket battleship *Admiral Scheer* but failed to explode. No bombs hit the cruiser *Emden*, but several German sailors were injured when one of the British bombers was hit by anti-aircraft fire and crashed on the ship. The anti-aircraft guns of another of the German warships, the *Admiral Hipper*, shot down a bomber, killing the pilot, Flight Lieutenant F.W. Barton and his crew of two, Flying Officer J.F. Ross and Corporal J.L. Ricketts: they were the first British military casualties of the Second World War.

On September 5 four British and one French merchant ship were sunk by German U-Boats; these U-boat sinkings were to see a daily loss of life and cargo, reflecting the German determination to make war on the two powers that had declared war on her. That day the British War Cabinet discussed the bombing of military targets in German cities. This was opposed by the Chancellor of the Exchequer, Sir Kingsley Wood, on the grounds – as a War Cabinet colleague reported – 'that it would be entirely wrong for us to bomb even German munitions works as in doing so we were bound to kill women and children and thereby provoke reprisals from the Germans'. To do anything that would lead to the bombing of Britain by Germany, said the Chancellor of the Exchequer, 'be a fatal error'.

German bombers attacked Warsaw each day without respite. Also converging on the city were the badly wounded soldiers whom it was hoped could find some succour in the city's hospitals. Among the nurses in the capital was Jadwiga Sosnkowska, a Polish Red Cross Reserve Nurse who had worked in the same hospital in 1920, as a volunteer during the Russo-Polish war. She later described the days of 'just waiting' until, on September 6, transports of wounded men began suddenly to arrive at the hospital gates. 'They were carried in horse-drawn peasant carts,' she wrote, 'and their wounds, unattended for several days, were a terrible sight. My first patient was a young boy from Lancut, whose leg was torn off by a bomb above the knee; the gaping wound was tied up with a dirty piece of cord. His tortured, bloodless face showed only his young, feverishly burning eyes, and as I stooped over him he whispered: "Sister, shall I ever be able to march again?"'

On September 6, Hitler, who was following the battle from a war room in his special train, went by car to the village of Tuchola in the Polish Corridor, where he watched the final phase of the destruction of a Polish army corps that had been surrounded there. While he was watching the battle, a message was brought to him that German forces had entered Cracow, Poland's historic capital, and a city with more than a quarter of a million inhabitants. German rule in Cracow was to be severe from its first hours. On September 7 the head of the SS, Reinhard Heydrich, told the commanders of the *Einsatzgruppen* (Special Task Forces): 'The Polish ruling class is to be put out of harm's way as far as possible.'

Executions by Eicke's SS units took place every day. Many volumes could be filled with the story of the fate of the Poles. Travellers in Poland today are struck by how many roadside markers and wall plaques record the execution on that spot of one, or several, or many Polish citizens. On September 8, in the village of Ksiazki, thirty-three Polish civilians were executed. Their memorial plaque is but one of tens of thousands which, sixty years after the event, remind the passer-by of the dark night that had befallen Poland. Even before the struggle on the battlefield had been resolved, this war against civilians had taken on a ferocity of its own, and was fought, unlike the battle between soldiers, by armed men against the unarmed, and by able-bodied men against people of all ages: men, women, children, the aged and the infirm. When Hitler's Army Chief of Staff, General Halder, discussed Hitler's intentions with a number of senior officers, one of them – Colonel Eduard Wagner – wrote in his diary: 'It is the Führer's and Goering's intention to destroy and exterminate the Polish nation.' Colonel Wagner added, ominously: 'More than that cannot even be hinted at in writing.'

Although Britain and France were both at war with Germany, they saw little scope for a meaningful military initiative that might help the Poles. On September 7, French troops did cross the German frontier at three points in the Saar, but there was little fighting, and the Germans were content to let France hold a few square miles of German territory.

With the daily U-boat sinkings of merchant ships, the British and French were themselves under attack. On September 7 the convoy system was introduced for ships crossing the Atlantic, but there were not sufficient destroyer escorts to maintain the convoys more than four hundred miles into the Atlantic.

The member of the War Cabinet responsible for the Royal Navy was Winston Churchill. 'Each day I reported to the Cabinet the Admiralty tale,' he later recalled, 'which usually consisted of a list of British merchant ships sunk by the U-boats.' On September 11 Churchill had to report to the War Cabinet the sinking of a British submarine 'which had been torpedoed by another of our own submarines in mistake for an enemy'.

In his recollection of the early days of the war Churchill also wrote of how the morning briefings by the Chief of the Imperial General Staff, General Ironside, who demonstrated the position on the map, 'very soon left no doubt in our minds that the resistance of Poland would speedily be crushed'. But the call by many members of the British public that Britain should intervene militarily was rejected. On September 12, at the first meeting of the newly constituted Anglo-French Supreme War Council, at Abbeville, on the River Somme, Neville Chamberlain told his French opposite number, Edouard Daladier that – in the words of the official record of the meeting – he 'thought the decision not to undertake large-scale operations as yet in France had been wise'. In Chamberlain's view there 'was no hurry as time was on our side. Moreover, the Allies required time to build up their full resources, and in the meantime it might well be that the morale of Germany would crumble'.

The Commander-in-Chief of the French Land Forces, General Gamelin, told Chamberlain that the military operations then being carried out by the French army in western France were designed 'to help Poland by distracting the Germans', but that they were confined to an offensive in the no-man's land between the two armies, and that he had 'no intention of throwing his army against the German main defences'. Gamelin told Chamberlain he had already 'issued specific orders forbidding anything of the kind'.

The Poles fought with great bravery against an enemy that was far superior in artillery power, and in armour. In the battle for the Polish industrial city of Lodz, an SS fighting unit (as opposed to the SS Special Task Forces) noted the courage of its Polish adversaries. 'The Poles launched yet another counter attack. They stormed over the bodies of their fallen comrades. They did not come forward with their heads down like men in heavy rain – and most attacking infantry come on like that – but they advanced with their heads held high like swimmers breasting the waves. They did not falter.'

Machine-gun and artillery fire destroyed that wave upon wave of attackers. Lodz, like every western Polish city, was occupied by the invader. In the defence of Warsaw, the Poles took up their positions along the River Bzura, but were outnumbered, outgunned and outflanked. Nineteen Polish divisions were surrounded, and 170,000 Polish soldiers taken prisoner.

Behind the lines, the killings of civilians continued. On September 10, Admiral Canaris – head of the Secret Intelligence Service of the German armed forces, travelled to the war zone. Wherever he went he was told by his Intelligence officers of the 'orgy of massacre' that was being carried out against Polish civilians. On September 12 he went to Hitler's headquarters train, which was then at Ilnau, in Upper Silesia, intent on protesting. Before seeing Hitler he explained the cause of his protest to General Keitel, the Chief of the Armed Forces High Command, telling Keitel: 'I have information that mass executions are being planned in Poland, and that members of the Polish nobility and the Roman Catholic bishops and priests have been singled out for extermination.'

Keitel advised Canaris: 'If I were you I would not get mixed up in this business. This "thing" has been decided by the Führer himself.' Every army command in Poland would, Keitel explained, have a civilian chief alongside its military commander. This civilian would be in charge of the 'racial extermination' programme. Canaris listened to Keitel's explanation and then went to see Hitler. They spoke about the course of the war, but Canaris said nothing about the killings.

On September 14, Warsaw was heavily bombed. On the following day a new German system of attack against the capital was introduced: artillery bombardment. A colonel in the Warsaw Defence Command described the new technique in his diary: 'Every minute two shells struck the city, each directed at a different quarter. We are constantly faced with the possibility of having one dwelling after another destroyed. It matters little to soldiers, but after twenty-four hours of this the nerves of the civilians are beginning to get frayed.' At the same time, a German attack on the Warsaw suburb of Wola was driven off, and Polish morale boosted by the capture of several German tanks, field-guns and machine guns.

In southern Poland the Polish forces were retreating eastward, towards the River San. The 11th Infantry Division, which had escaped a German attempt to encircle it north of Jaslo, was among the mass of troops intent on crossing the River San and regrouping in the region of Lvov. As it moved eastward, a rapid German thrust eastward cut off the Division from its hospitals and main ammunition store.

During the retreat towards the river, the Division discovered a group of German soldiers who were preparing to disguise themselves as Polish soldiers and to cause diversionary havoc behind the lines by misdirecting the Polish troops. 'They were destroyed to the last man,' recalled a Colonel on the Divisional Staff, and he added, in defence of the Germans not being held as prisoners-of-war: 'Where could one find staff officers, military police or unit police in this war, which was so different from any other war?'

The Division retreated to the River San at Przemysl, and began the eastward crossing. The colonel later wrote:

The river crossing – but how unnecessary the words seemed on those beautiful September days of 1939! The rivers were all dried up; the San was a trickling rivulet which artillery and caterpillars could ford wherever they wished. The battalion fulfilled its task splendidly, shattering several of the Germans' caterpillars, and the Division marched on.

The German aeroplanes raided us at frequent intervals. There was no shelter anywhere: nothing, on every side, but the accursed plain. The soldiers rushed off the road, trying to take cover in the furrows, but the horses were in a worse plight. After one of the raids we counted thirty-five dead horses, and a few days later the divisional artillery lost eighty-seven horses in a single raid. Such a march was not like the march of an army; it was more like the flight of some Biblical people, driven onward by the wrath of Heaven, and dissolving in the wilderness.

As the Division approached Mosciska, some eighteen miles from Przemysl, the Commander stood at the side of the road and watched the men as they wearily trudged by.

There was no question here of a march past; but as the soldiers turned their heads in the 'Eyes right!' the Colonel asked them simply:

'Can you stick it, lads?'

And he could still see the gleam in their eyes, the spark of that fire with which Szczot's company had shattered the armoured column near Blazow, with which the 48th Regiment had set out to cut off Bircza, before it shed its blood in defence of the Krzywiecki Hills, and with which the 49th Infantry Regiment had made its nocturnal bayonet charge near Lentownia.

'We'll stick it!'

All along the River San, Polish troops were struggling to cross before the German forces arrived. Travelling in his train to Jaroslaw, another of the towns on the San, Hitler watched while German soldiers followed across the river in pursuit.

Such Polish forces as had managed to cross the river were prepared to regroup in Eastern Poland and to use the city of Lvov as a base from which to counter-attack. But on September 17, just as these plans were being worked out, and the morale of the Polish army rising, a bombshell arrived: in a statement issued from Moscow, Molotov declared that as the Polish government had 'ceased to exist' – he made no mention of the fact the capital, Warsaw, was still in Polish hands – Soviet troops had been ordered to occupy Eastern Poland, in accordance with a secret clause in the Nazi-Soviet pact. This pact had been signed only twenty-five days earlier. The secret clause gave the Soviet Union the right to move its forces forward as far as the River San. The city of Lvov was among the many towns in Polish Eastern Galicia that would come under Soviet rule. It was a Soviet general who, in Lvov, ordered the Polish soldiers to lay down their arms.

On September 19, Hitler took the march past in Danzig, which his troops had overrun in the first few days of the war. During his speech he referred to 'Almighty God, who has now given our arms his blessing'.

On the following day, in a hotel in the nearby resort town of Zoppot, Hitler signed, in strictest secrecy, a decree legitimizing the murder of any German judged to be 'incurably ill'. This included the mentally ill. Seven special institutions were established, and a euthanasia programme put in force at once. Its headquarters was in Berlin, at a villa at No. 4 Tiergartenstrasse, an address which gave its name to the operation itself: T4. More than 100,000 Germans, many of them babies and young children, were killed during the coming two years, mostly by gas.

Within three weeks of the meeting at Zoppot, census forms were prepared, to be sent out from Hitler's Chancellery to all hospitals and doctors, asking them 'for statistical purposes' to list all patients who were senile, criminally insane, or of non-German blood. These forms would then be studied by assessors – appointed by T4 – who would decide which patients were to be subjected to euthanasia. The head of Hitler's Chancellery wanted the procedure codified as part of German law. Hitler refused to do so.

One of the first institutions set up specifically for the purpose of killing people who were mentally ill was located on former Polish soil, at Piasnica, in what had been the Polish Corridor. The new institution was only twenty miles from Zoppot, where the evil decree had been signed. As well as Poles and Jews from the Danzig region, 1,200 Germans were sent to Piasnica from psychiatric institutions inside Germany, and killed.

A pattern for the systematic murder of civilians was being established, even before Poland had been defeated. While Hitler was still at Zoppot, a meeting was held in Berlin at which Reinhard Heydrich spoke to as many commanders of SS units in Poland as could be taken away from their work. Those who could not be present were sent a top secret account of the meeting, which concerned the Jews. Heydrich spoke of the 'ultimate aim' of German policy with regard to the Jews, which must be kept 'strictly secret' and would take 'a prolonged period of time'. Meanwhile, the Jews under German rule in Poland must be restricted to a number of cities, and all other Jewish communities – of which there were several thousand – deported to those cities. Within the cities in which Jews would be allowed to live, they would be confined to a particular area of the city. All Jews living outside that area would be taken from their homes and moved to the new area. Jewish Councils would be created, through which the Jews could govern their internal affairs, and transmit the German orders. Jewish Councils which sought to sabotage those orders 'would be threatened with the severest measures'. A medieval term was decided upon for what was being created: ghetto. The last ghetto, that of Venice, had been abolished by Napoleon.

Warsaw had still not fallen to the Germans, although the death toll from the daily aerial bombardment was rising steadily. Wherever the German army had established itself, the SS Special Task Force killings continued. On September 22 the SS Brandenburg Division entered Wloclawek and for four days looted Jewish shops, blew up the city's synagogues, and rounded up and shot several dozen of the leading Jewish citizens. Half of the Division was then ordered to nearby Bydgoszcz to conduct a further 'action' against Polish intellectuals and local leaders. Within two days, 800 Poles had been shot.

With the German and Soviet armies having met along the River Bug to the east of Warsaw, the Polish capital was completely isolated. Hunger was turning to starvation. Electricity and water supplies were both destroyed. Aerial bombardment continued to be joined by artillery fire. The 140,000 Polish soldiers inside the city could do nothing except suffer with the rest of the inhabitants and await the main German assault. It came on the evening of September 26, and was so ferocious that the Polish garrison commander asked for a truce. The Germans refused; they would only accept complete surrender. Within twenty-four hours the German demand was met: Warsaw surrendered unconditionally. The 140,000 Polish soldiers in the capital were taken away as prisoners-of-war. More than a quarter of them were already wounded. They were to spend the rest of the war in captivity, during which time many of them died of their injuries, of privation, or at the slave labour tasks to which they were set.

With the fall of Warsaw, Poland's twenty-year-old independence was over. Isolated groups of Polish troops fought on, but one by one their enclaves were overrun. The killing of civilians continued: Poles and Polish Jews being equally subjected to Nazi terror. In one Church diocese, 214 of the 690 priests were shot. In Czestochowa, 180 Jews were shot in a single day. A new German concentration camp was set up, the first on Polish soil, at Stutthof near Danzig. Among those sent there before the end of the year, and executed, was every Polish inmate of the mental hospital at Stralsund, on the German Baltic coast.

As the last Polish forces were still in action on the battlefield, Poland was being partitioned. Soviet forces moved rapidly up to the demarcation line, covering 250 to 350 kilometres in a single week. In those places where German troops had already pushed further eastward, the Germans withdrew. Hundreds of thousands of Polish soldiers surrendered to the Russians. They were despatched to prisoner-of-war camps deep inside the Soviet Union. Hundreds of thousand more Poles, and Polish Jews, also fled eastward, seeking what they hoped would be the greater security of Stalin's protective hand.

If the Twentieth Century has claims to be the century of the refugee, the events of September 1939 added powerfully to that claim. As the German army drove into Poland, tens of thousands of refugees reached the zone of Soviet occupation and continued eastward into the Soviet Union. There, many of them were subsequently despatched to Stalin's labour camps. Others fled to Lithuania, hoping that Lithuanian independence would provide a safe haven. Others fled southward into Roumania – including most members of the Polish government, who made their way to Paris, where they established a Polish government in exile.

Even in Roumania, a place of refuge that month, there were ominous signs of political and ideological turmoil. On September 21 the Prime Minister, Armand Calinescu, was assassinated while being driven through one of the main streets of Bucharest. His assassins were members of the fascist Iron Guard, which, during the six and a half months of his premiership, he had rigorously sought to suppress. After his death as before it, the Iron Guard continued to be trained by German army officers who had entered Roumania ostensibly as teachers in the German schools.

On September 26, as the extent of the Nazi-Soviet collaboration in the destruction of Poland became clear, the French government outlawed the Communist Party in both France and the French colonies. This had its impact as far away as French Indo-China, where the French police arrested more than a thousand Party members. Those on the Communist Party Central Committee who could do so fled to China, including the young revolutionary Vo Nguyen Giap, who was later to command the Vietnamese Communist forces against both the French and – three decades later – the Americans. While those who had escaped were given military training by the Chinese Communists, Giap's wife, Minh Thai, who had been arrested, was tortured and died in captivity. Their three-year-old daughter also died in prison. His wife's sister, Minh Khai, a member like himself of the Central Committee, was guillotined.

A month after he had flown to Moscow to sign the Nazi-Soviet Pact for Germany, Ribbentrop returned to the Soviet capital. During two days of intense negotiations, agreement was reached for the partitioning of Poland, as envisaged in the secret protocol a month earlier. Germany would rule all Poland that lay to the west of the River Bug and the River San, and the area between the Vistula and East Prussia: this was the home of more than two-thirds of the Polish people – 22 million in all – and most of Poland's industry and raw materials. The Soviet Union would rule everything to the east, including the cities of Bialystok, Vilna and Lvov. The Eastern Galician region of Poland, once a province of the Austro-Hungarian Empire, was part of the area annexed by the Soviet Union; it was incorporated into the Soviet Ukraine. It contained the oilfields of Drohobycz. Stalin agreed that in return for these coming under Soviet control, he would supply

Germany with 300,000 tons of oil a year. This agreement was scrupulously observed.

Although the new treaty, signed at five o'clock on the morning of September 29, destroyed Polish sovereignty, its name made no reference to Poland. It was called the Soviet German Boundary and Friendship Treaty. Neither the boundary nor the friendship were to survive the next two years.

In the immediate aftermath of the partition of Poland, Stalin moved to secure control of the three Baltic States, each of which had been under Russian rule in Tsarist times, and each of which (like Poland) had achieved its independence at the end of the First World War. On September 29, as Ribbentrop was flying back to Berlin, the Soviet Union signed a Treaty of Mutual Assistance with Estonia, giving Soviet forces the right to occupy all four of Estonia's naval bases. Six days later a similar treaty was signed with Latvia, and eleven days after that with Lithuania. Under the Lithuanian-German Treaty, the Vilna region, which had been assigned to Poland by the League of Nations in 1923, became part of Lithuania, and Lithuania's capital.

Hitler accepted that the homes and livelihoods of the Baltic Germans — a minority whose rights he had championed — would pass under Soviet Communist rule. He went so far as to negotiate a treaty whereby these Baltic Germans could be brought to Germany. Their families had, for the most part, left Germany several centuries earlier. Quite why it was in order for the Baltic Germans to be uprooted and taken to Germany, when the Sudeten Germans had to remain in the Sudetenland and become the beneficiaries of a German annexation, Hitler did not explain. But his plans for military action in western and northern Europe depended upon a peaceful eastern front. By the sacrifice of the Baltic Germans, and of any German interests in the Baltic States, he had secured this. He also made sure, by a Führer Directive on September 30, that his new Polish frontier with the Soviet Union 'will be constantly strengthened and built up as a line of military security towards the East'.

In the month-long battle for Poland, 60,000 Polish soldiers had been killed — 6,000 of them Jews. In the aerial and artillery bombardment of cities, principally Warsaw, 25,000 Polish civilians had been killed, 3,000 of them Jews. On the battlefield, 14,000 German soldiers had laid down their lives: a total death toll of 99,000 in thirty days. Several thousand more Poles and

Polish Jews had been killed by the SS killing squads: on October 4, in Berlin, Hitler signed a secret amnesty whereby those SS men who had been arrested by the German Army authorities on charges of brutality to the civilian population were all released.

Hitler hastened to visit Warsaw, the third capital city – Vienna was the first and Prague the second – that had become part of his empire. On October 5 he flew to Warsaw and took the salute at a march past of German troops. At the airport before flying back to Germany, he told the foreign journalists who had been invited to witness his triumph: 'Take a good look round Warsaw. This is how I can deal with any European city.'

The German war machine hardly paused after the conquest of Poland. At sea, the sinking of British merchant ships brought home to the British people that the 'German war' was a real one. In the third week of September the British aircraft carrier *Courageous*, employed on convoy duty, had been torpedoed in the Western Approaches, and more than 500 of its crew were drowned. But despite the sinkings – which were intended to show the British that they were not invincible at sea – Hitler tried to suggest that peace might be possible. 'Why should this war in the West be fought?' he asked in a public speech in Berlin on October 6, the day after his triumphant return from Warsaw. 'For the restoration of Poland? The Poland of Versailles will never rise again.' Hitler suggested that there was no reason for war except Poland, and that all issues still dividing Britain and France from Germany could be settled at the conference table.

On the day before Hitler's question, a Swedish businessman, Birger Dahlerus – a friend of Goering – had visited Lord Halifax in London, and asked him if some form of accommodation with Germany might not be possible. On October 8, while Dahlerus was on his way back to Berlin, via Sweden, with Halifax's answer, Hitler proceeded to annex the Polish frontier regions to Germany, enlarging both East Prussia and Silesia, and incorporating the western provinces of Poland into the Third Reich. What was left of Poland, including Warsaw, he set up as a 'General Government', to be ruled by Dr Hans Frank, the legal adviser to the Nazi Party. Frank's instructions – which were not made public, and which he carried out scrupulously to the end – were that 'Poland shall be treated like a colony' and that 'the Poles will become the slaves of the Greater German Empire'.

On October 8, the day after the annexations were announced, Dahlerus saw Hitler in Berlin. He presented Hitler with the British terms: the restoration of Polish statehood, the 'immediate destruction' of all weapons of aggression, and a plebiscite inside Germany on Hitler's foreign policy. Hitler asked Dahlerus to see him again on the following day. He then gave the Swede his reply, and asked him to convey it back to the British: Germany had the right to fortify her new eastern frontier against Russia, and she wanted the return of the German colonies of which Germany had been deprived at Versailles, or 'suitable substitute territories' given to Germany in their place.

Hitler saw Dahlerus twice that day, October 9. Between the two meetings he issued a Führer directive to his Chief of Staff, General Keitel, and to the Army, Navy and Air Force commanders, setting out the details of a new military campaign, Operation Yellow: a German offensive through Holland, Belgium, Luxembourg and Northern France, 'to serve as the base for the successful prosecution of the air and sea war against England'. On the following morning, at a meeting in the Chancellery with his senior commanders, Hitler told them that the aim of Operation Yellow was 'the destruction of the power and ability of the Western Powers ever again to oppose the State consolidation and further developments of the German people in Europe'.

The war against Western Europe, Hitler explained, would succeed because there would be no eastern-front war to be fought at the same time. The pact with Stalin had ensured that. But, he warned, there was no treaty or pact that could ensure 'with certainty' the lasting neutrality of the Soviet Union. A 'prompt demonstration of German strength' was needed in the West.

On the day after Hitler gave his army commanders the reasons for an attack in the West before the Soviet Union abandoned its neutrality – or before, though he did not say so, Germany attacked the Soviet Union – Albert Einstein, one of the most prominent refugees from Nazi Germany, sent an emissary to President Roosevelt with a letter. In it, Einstein set out to explain to Roosevelt a new scientific development: atomic energy. By turning atomic energy to the needs of war, he wrote, a man would be able 'to blow up his neighbour' on a hitherto unimagined scale. Roosevelt understood that this was no theoretical fantasy. 'This requires action', was his comment. Ten days later an advisory committee on uranium held its first meeting in Washington.

Even as action was being taken to advance an aerial bomb of unprecedented power, the writer H.G. Wells, who before 1914 had predicted the violent clash of civilized nations, was setting out in his book *The Common Sense of War and Peace* his thoughts on the future abolition of aerial warfare. His answer was world disarmament, something that he had strongly favoured between the wars:

> One world-wide federation there must certainly be after this war, and that is a federation to put a stop to air war for ever. Plainly that at least must stop, or civilized life must stop, and the one and only way to stop it is to set up a world commission with full powers to control the air everywhere, powers of search, powers of instant suppression.
>
> No single country can be left out of that. If necessary, countries must be compelled to come in. And no simple treaties or conventions will meet the case. There will be no more treaties because there is no more good faith. Germany has killed that for ever. The air commission must be a commission with full powers, a world air police. All over the world reasonable people and common people will be in favour of that.

H.G. Wells also hoped that 'contagious, creative liberalism' would play its part in the post-world war in helping to stop future wars. There would be a Standing Armistice. The United States and the Soviet Union – 'Have you thought of such a combination?' he asked – might insist upon it. But what Wells called the 'backbone' of his hopes for permanent peace after the war was 'the possibility of a world-wide coalescence of all the scattered forces of creation and protest in the human heart, into one consciously revolutionary movement based on the declared rights of men'. By the time that Wells' book was published in the first week of 1940 the collective rights of man, like the individual lives of men, had been subjected to several further and considerable setbacks.

The war at sea took a turn for the worse for Britain on October 14, when the battleship *Royal Oak* was torpedoed, and 833 sailors drowned, while the warship was at anchor in Scapa Flow. Two days later the Germans mounted their first air attack on British territory, when German aircraft attacked warships at Rosyth, in the Firth of Forth. Two British cruisers and a destroyer were damaged. On the following morning, October 17, Scapa Flow was bombed.

On October 18 Hitler issued another Führer directive (his seventh since the start of the war) authorizing German submarines to attack all passenger ships that were travelling in convoy, or were proceeding without lights. He was confident that he could bend Europe to his will. On October 20 the first of the Baltic Germans who had hoped to find him their protector reached Danzig from Estonia. They would never learn that, on the following day, in a speech to senior Nazi Party officials, Hitler set out his long-term aim: once Britain and France had been brought to their knees he would turn his attention to the East 'and show who was the master there'. The Russian soldiers, he said, were badly trained and poorly equipped. Once he had dealt with the East 'he would set about restoring Germany to how she used to be'. Meanwhile, with no delay, starting on October 22, many thousands of Poles were expelled from Poznan, the largest city in what had been western Poland. It was intended by the masters in Berlin that within a decade vast regions hitherto with Polish majorities would become 'pure and Germanic provinces'. Albert Forster, who had imposed Nazi rule on Danzig in the three years before the outbreak of war – he was only thirty-seven when war broke out – was made the ruler of the annexed areas. 'I have been appointed by the Führer as a trustee of the German cause in this country with the express order to Germanize it afresh,' he declared in his first public speech, given in the annexed city of Bydgoszcz. 'It will therefore be my task to do everything possible to remove every manifestation of Polonism within the next few years, no matter what the kind.' A brutal start was being made in this direction with the driving from their homes and expulsion into central Poland of 120,000 Poles from the newly created Posen District, 35,000 from Danzig-West Prussia and 15,000 from East Upper Silesia.

Thousands of Jews were also being expelled by the Germans – out of Poland and across the River Bug and the River San into the newly-acquired territories of the Soviet Union, and from hitherto Polish towns and villages in the regions annexed by Germany. Jews from the German Baltic coast were also driven out: they were sent by train to a region set aside for them near Lublin, in the eastern part of the General Government. Here, under the watchful eye of Hans Frank, they were subjected to harsh conditions and near starvation. As SS and Police Leader of the Lublin District, Frank appointed Odilo Globocnik, the zealous Austrian Nazi who had been one of the activists during the annexation of Austria a year and a half earlier. He was well-known as an extreme anti-Semite.

One of Globocnik's first acts in Lublin was to take the books from the library of the recently completed Talmudic Academy – a source of pride for religious Jews around the world – and burn them. The destruction took twenty-four hours. 'The Lublin Jews assembled round and wept bitterly, almost silencing us with their cries,' a German eye-witness recalled. 'We summoned the military band, and with joyful shouts the soldiers drowned out the sounds of the Jewish cries.'

Frank's rule of the General Government, and Globocnik's zealous organization, was to bring death and privation to millions of Poles and Polish Jews alike. One of Frank's first acts was to set up forced labour camps for Jews throughout the General Government. This was announced on October 25 in his first official gazette – through which all laws were to be promulgated. All Jewish males between the ages of fourteen and sixty would be 'obliged to work' at special labour projects. By the end of the year, seventy-five labour camps had been set up. Two days later, another General Government ordinance was directed at Poles. All Poles must leave the pavement free for Germans to walk on. 'The street belongs to the conqueror, not to the conquered.' All Polish men must raise their hats to German soldiers. 'Whoever annoys or speaks to German women or girls will receive exemplary punishment. Polish females who speak to or annoy German nationals will be sent to brothels.'

In Germany plans were being made to breed a 'master race'. On October 28 Himmler issued a 'Procreation Order' to the members of the SS, which described as the 'sublime task of German women and girls of good blood, acting not frivolously but from a profound moral seriousness, to become mothers to children of soldiers setting off for battle'. Special human stud farms were set up where young girls, selected for their allegedly perfect 'Nordic' traits, could 'procreate' with SS men. Their children would be taken care of in special maternity homes, and receive special benefits.

On November 4, following a six-week-long series of discussions in Congress, Roosevelt was able to sign into law a new Neutrality Act, whereby the United States could sell arms to belligerents. Those taking advantage of the Act would have to pay in cash, and transport the arms in their own ships – no American credit or naval protection would be available to them – but this 'cash and carry' policy brought immediate succour to both France and Britain. It also ended an arms embargo which, as a result of the earlier Neutrality Act, had been in force since the outbreak of war two months earlier.

It would clearly take a long time – perhaps a year – before American supplies to Britain and France could add meaningfully to the balance of power. Most of the war material which the two purchasing missions ordered after November 4 had first to be manufactured and then to be shipped across the Atlantic. Hitler had hoped to launch his attack on Western Europe on November 12. That date was known to the British and French through two German officers, both working in Admiral Canaris's Army Counter Intelligence department, who had separately passed it on to the British.

The weather was a serious factor against the planned date. Winter was approaching, and the German Air Force had calculated that it would need five consecutive days of good weather in order to destroy the French Air Force. The weather forecast on November 7 indicated that no such seven day respite was in prospect. Hitler set the date aside. But the search for a new date began at once.

On November 8, Hitler went to Munich for the annual celebration of the 1923 Beer Hall putsch. Under Nazi rule, Hitler told those gathered at the scene of the abortive coup, Germany had achieved more in six years than Britain had achieved in many centuries. Because he had to get back to Berlin – by overnight train – to discuss with his generals a new date for the Western offensive, Hitler left the beer hall more than half an hour earlier than scheduled. Eight minutes after he left a bomb exploded inside the pillar next to where he had been speaking. Seven people were killed and more than sixty injured. Hitler was given the news on the train. He commented: 'Now I am completely content. The fact that I left the beer hall earlier than usual is corroboration of Providence's intention to let me reach my goal.'

The would-be assassin was a carpenter and furniture maker, Johann Georg Elser. He had recently been released from Dachau, where he had been held as a Communist sympathizer. Before 1933 he had been a member of the Red Front Fighters' Association. After planting the bomb he had taken the train to Konstanz, intent on crossing into Switzerland, but he had been caught trying to cross the border. He was incarcerated in Sachsenhausen concentration camp, designated as 'Hitler's special prisoner'.

Reaching Berlin the following morning, Hitler continued his planning of the invasion of Western Europe, holding almost daily discussions. On November 20, after talking to one of his favourite generals, Erwin Rommel – the commander of his personal bodyguard battalion – Hitler issued a directive to all military commanders with regard to the invasion of Belgium and Holland. 'Where no resistance is offered,' Hitler wrote, 'the invasion will assume the character of peaceful occupation.'

Hitler's use of language encapsulated the double face of Nazi propaganda. An ultimatum was a memorandum, aggression was defence, attacks were counter-measures, invasion was peaceful occupation: yet behind every linguistic deception was an iron fist. This was nowhere more evident than at sea. Even during the inhospitable storms and wicked weather of winter, the German U-boats waged a pitiless war on merchant ships. A further element of danger was added to the work of the merchant seamen bringing food and raw materials across the oceans by a new German weapon: the magnetic mine. This was dropped into the water by aeroplane, and exploded on contact with a ship's metal hull, to which it was magnetically attracted.

On November 18 the Dutch ocean liner *Simon Bolivar* hit a magnetic mine and sank, with the loss of 120 lives. On November 19, of five merchants ships sunk that day, two were British, one French, one Swedish and one Italian. The magnetic mine, like the U-boats, was indiscriminate. It also blew up British minesweepers and minelayers, as well as merchant ships. When one of these devices was found intact, washed up on the mudflats of the Thames Estuary, work began at once on an antidote. It was dangerous, secret and urgent work, and it was successful: the effective de-magnetizing of the ships by means of metal coils wrapped around their hulls.

By chance, on the day that the British found the unexploded mine – November 23 – and began the work of discovering how to neutralize it, Hitler was giving his generals a survey of his military thought with regard to the coming offensive. He was confident that Belgium, Holland and France would swiftly succumb, as Poland had done, to a direct military attack. As to Britain, he did not envisage the need for actual invasion. Britain, he said, 'could be forced to her knees by the U-boats and the mines'.

On the day after this confident assertion by Hitler, the battle cruiser *Scharnhorst* – the first warship to be built after Hitler had broken the Versailles Treaty prohibition on German warship construction – sank the armed British merchant cruiser *Rawalpindi* after a fourteen-minute bombardment: 270 British naval officers and ratings were drowned.

In establishing the General Government of Poland, Hitler did not rule out the possibility of finding a Polish leader willing to act as the head of a puppet regime. Several distinguished Poles were approached and asked if they would serve. One of Europe's leading jurists, Professor Stanislas Estreicher, Professor of Western Jurisprudence at Cracow University, was offered the post of President in a Polish government that would be loyal to (and subservient to) Germany. He refused. Several other distinguished professors were offered the post. They too refused. Then, in an attempt to destroy all intellectual opposition, 167 Polish professors and lecturers at Cracow's Jagellonian University were arrested and sent to Sachsenhausen concentration camp. There, seventeen died of the torture to which they were subjected. Professor Estreicher was among those who died.

November 11 was Polish independence day. That day, German soldiers took 350 Poles from a labour camp near Gdynia, where they were working, to a prison yard in the nearby town of Weherowo. First they were ordered to dig a number of deep pits. Then they were divided into groups, and one group forced to watch as the other was taken to the edge of the pit and shot. As each group was brought to the edge of the pit they cried out, 'Long live Poland!' Then they were shot. That week fifty Polish officers, prisoners-of-war, were led through the town of Ciechocinek with their hands held above their heads. Later that day all of them were shot. Such incidents became commonplace.

The German policy of reprisals ensured that for every German killed, the number of Poles executed would be on a much higher scale. At the village of Wawer, just outside Warsaw, two German soldiers were killed that winter by two Polish criminals seeking to evade arrest. Two hours later 170 men and boys were rounded up in Wawer and the nearby village of Anin and taken to a railway tunnel where they were forced to stand for several hours with their hands above their heads. They were then taken out in groups of ten and shot. The last ten were reprieved: they were then ordered to dig a mass grave for those who had been killed. Among the dead were two Poles – a father and his sixteen-year-old son – who held United States citizenship. Their American passports had been of no avail.

The killing of Poles, and of Polish Jews, did not abate for a single day. When Himmler saw Hitler in Berlin on November 19 he told him – as Himmler's notes of the meeting record – of the 'shooting of 380 Jews at Ostrow'. Three days later, fifty-three Jews, all of whom lived in the same apartment block in Warsaw, near which a policeman had been killed, were arrested. They would be shot, said the Gestapo, unless a ransom was paid. The Warsaw Jewish Council collected the ransom and took it to Gestapo headquarters. The Council was then told that the hostages had already been shot. The money was not returned. Among those who had been executed was Samuel Zamkowy, one of Warsaw's leading gynaecologists. He was forty-five.

On the newly established German-Soviet demarcation line, thousands of Polish Jews were taken from their homes and driven eastward into the Soviet

Union. Sometimes the Soviet officials on the eastern side of the line allowed them to enter, sometimes they did not. Hundreds were killed trying to cross the River Bug, shot by frontier troops on both banks. Thousands more were killed by sadistic SS guards as they were being driven towards the river. In the town of Chelm, just inside the new German area, the patients at the local mental hospital – both Poles and Polish Jews – were lined up in the hospital grounds and shot by SS troops. Those few inmates who managed to run off were chased through the grounds, hunted down, and killed.

That November, in Warsaw, a German Army staff officer, Major Helmuth Stieff, was appalled by what he saw, writing to his wife: 'The wildest fantasy of horror propaganda is as nothing to the reality, the organized gangs who murder, rob and plunder with what is said to be the tolerance of the highest authorities.' Stieff added: 'It shames me to be a German!'

This was not the only voice of protest. On November 23 the German military commander in the newly created Warthegau, General Petzel, wrote a report, which was sent on to Hitler's Chancellery, in which he said that the SS and Gestapo were carrying out 'public shootings' in all major localities in German-occupied Poland. The general commented: 'Selection is entirely arbitrary and the conduct of the executions is in many cases disgusting.'

Such protests did not deter the ideologists of racism. On November 25 two senior officials in the Racial Policy Office in Berlin, Gerhard Hecht and Eberhard Wetzel, sent all the Nazi leaders, including Himmler, a policy document with regard to their intentions for the future of the Polish people. 'Medical care from our side must be limited to the prevention of the spreading of epidemics to Reich territory,' they wrote. As to the Polish Jews under German rule, numbering two and a half million: 'We are indifferent to the hygienic fate of the Jews.' As to the future generations of all Poles – Christians and Jews alike – 'their propagation must be curtailed in every possible way'.

Ten days after this policy document, which envisaged the deliberate physical reduction of two branches of the human family, Goebbels went to see Hitler in Berlin, together with Hans Frank, to report on the journey Goebbels had just made through the German-occupied regions of Poland. In his diary Goebbels noted: 'I tell him about my trip. He listens to everything very carefully and shares my opinion on the Jewish and Polish question. We must liquidate the Jewish danger. But it will return in a few generations. There is no panacea for it. The Polish aristocracy must be destroyed. It has no links with the people, whom it regards as existing purely for its own convenience.'

Goebbels also noted in his diary that Hans Frank 'has an enormous amount to do', and was 'framing a series of new plans'. The General Government, that was to become the destination of hundreds of thousands of Jews deported from Germany, Austria and Czechoslovakia, was also to become their killing ground. Nor was it only the Jews who were to perish on a scale hitherto unimaginable. Anyone whom the Nazi power regarded as its enemy, whether on political, national or racial grounds, faced persecution and death. Two days after his meeting with Goebbels and Frank, Hitler issued a top secret decree which authorized the seizure without warrant or explanation of any person 'endangering German security'. It was known as the 'Night and Fog' (*Nacht und Nebel*) decree: those arrested under it were not to be executed at once, but were to 'vanish without trace into the night and fog'. Their destination was a concentration camp. In the precise and detailed registers of the camps, the initials *NN* against the name of a prisoner signified that he had been taken out of his barrack and shot.

The confidence of total victory and total control of the conquered populations is evident in the diaries of all those who set the policy for Nazi domination. Two weeks after his meeting with Hitler and Goebbels in Berlin, Hans Frank confided to his diary: 'We cannot shoot 2,500,000 Jews, neither can we poison them. We shall have to take steps, however, designed to extirpate them in some way – and this will be done.'

On November 28 the Soviet Union renounced the Non-Aggression Treaty which it had signed with Finland seven years earlier. Two days later, Stalin's forces launched an air, land and sea attack on Finland. Marshal Shaposhnikov, the Chief of the Soviet General Staff, warned Stalin that it would be wrong to underestimate the Finnish capacity for resistance. But Stalin, knowing that 460,000 Soviet troops were facing only 130,000 Finnish soldiers, and that a thousand Soviet aircraft were facing 150 Finnish warplanes – was confident that victory would be swift. In this he was mistaken.

Just as Hitler had ordered the bombing of Warsaw in the hope of creating panic and demoralization in the 'enemy' capital, so Stalin ordered the bombing of Helsinki. More than sixty Finns were killed during the first aerial attack on the first afternoon of the war. A British journalist who was in Finland when the war broke out, Geoffrey Cox, later wrote: 'On every front that I was to visit later, man after man spoke angrily of this afternoon of

November 30. I saw newspapers and photographs of the burning streets of
Helsinki in peasants' homes and workers' flats all over the country. Not a
little of the steel strength of Finnish morale in this war was due to the raid
on Helsinki.'

Before the evidence of the battlefield was clear, Stalin announced the
establishment in Moscow of the government of the Finnish Democratic
Republic. It was thought to be only a matter of weeks before it would be
installed in Helsinki, headed by the Finnish Communist – then in Moscow
– Otto Kuusinen. Within a few days it became clear, however, that the
Finns were not going to be defeated quickly. One device used by the Finnish
troops was a bottle filled with petrol, with a rag stuffed into the neck of
the bottle: the rag was then ignited with a match and thrown against the
tracks or into the turret of a Soviet tank. This simple but devastatingly
successful incendiary grenade was soon given the name 'Molotov cocktail'.

In many lands, sympathy for Finland was strong. On December 7, only
a week after the Soviet offensive had begun, Neville Chamberlain announced
that Britain would be selling thirty fighter aircraft to Finland. From France,
Daladier ordered the despatch of 145 warplanes, five thousand machine guns,
and large quantities of hand grenades, rifles and ammunition. British, French
and Italian volunteers presented themselves at the Finnish embassies in
London, Paris and Rome, and were sent to Finland with their governments'
approval. On December 14, after a four day emergency debate at Geneva,
the Soviet Union was expelled from the League of Nations.

What the Finns call the Winter War continued into 1940, with the main
Finnish line of defence, the Mannerheim Line, resisting all Soviet efforts to
break through it. While Hitler was imposing his iron rule inside western
Poland, and regrouping, rearming and re-equipping his land, sea and air
forces within the yet larger confines of the Greater Reich, Stalin was struggling to avoid humiliation at the hands of his northern neighbour. On
December 22 Stalin received a telegram of congratulation from Hitler: it
was Stalin's sixtieth birthday. That day the Soviet forces in Finland were
confronted by the start of a tenacious Finnish counterattack, in temperatures
of 35 degrees centigrade below zero.

The Soviet soldiers were unprepared for such ferocity, either of the attacking force or the weather. For four days the Finns hammered home their
advantage, driving two Soviet divisions back to the Soviet frontier, and then
across it. The Soviet commander, General Vinogradov, was later executed
by Stalin for his failure. When the battle came to an end on the fourth day,

more than 25,000 Soviet troops lay dead under the snow, killed in action or frozen to death.

The war between Britain and Germany continued in two very different spheres. In the air, British bombers made regular sorties across the North Sea, dropping tens of millions of leaflets over Germany denouncing the Nazi regime. There was also a sustained attempt on December 18 by twenty-two British bombers to attack German warships off Wilhelmshaven. But a German radar station on the nearby island of Wangerooge was able to detect the incoming force when it was still seventy miles away, and the fighters sent up to intercept it shot down twelve of the twenty-two attackers.

At sea, as in the air, the struggle was one of life and death. In early December, in the South Atlantic, the German pocket battleship *Graf Spee* sank three British merchant ships in five days. She was then tracked down by two British and a New Zealand cruiser and sought safety in Uruguayan territorial waters. Four days later her captain ordered the ship to be scuttled. He then shot himself in a hotel bedroom in Montevideo. The loss of the *Graf Spee* was a blow to Germany and gave a boost to British morale. But the sinking of British merchant ships continued.

Hitler spent the week before Christmas 1939 visiting German positions on the Western Front. At the point where the German border was opposite the French village of Spicheren he was able to cross over on to French soil: in September the German troops had driven back a French skirmish at this point. It was the first time Hitler had been on French soil since his military service in the First World War.

On December 30, Hitler issued a New Year message for the German people. In it his obsession with the Jews was expressed without prevarication. 'The Jewish-capitalist world,' he wrote, 'will not survive the Twentieth Century.'

Beyond Europe, there were harbingers of death other than war. On December 27 an earthquake struck Turkey, wiping out dozens of villages in eastern and north-eastern Anatolia, and killing more than 15,000 people. The town of Erzincan was completely laid waste. Further tremors during the following days, and the extreme cold, led to thousands more deaths. On December 31 severe tremors hit the Aegean Coast of Turkey, followed by floods, in which there were many more deaths. The British and French governments were among those that made financial provision for the survivors.

Disease was another killer which had continued to work its destructive course throughout the second half of the 1930s. In Java, in four years ending in 1934, 70,000 people died from plague. In Madagascar plague killed 12,000 people in the four years ending in 1937. In Brazil a malaria epidemic killed 26,000 in the three years beginning in 1938. In China, cholera killed at least 55,000 people in 1939 alone. In Chad, part of French Equatorial Africa, there were 6,500 deaths from meningitis between 1937 and 1939; outbreaks of the disease, with further high mortality, continued annually in Chad for the next forty years. Enormous efforts were being made by the Rockefeller Foundation of New York to combat the cause of the disease; in several regions the mosquitoes responsible for it were eliminated by means of an insecticide spray.

Fighting disease in order to save life continued uninterrupted, particularly in Africa, even as men fought in Europe to destroy life. For every sick person cured by medical science, tens, hundreds, even thousands, died through the steady, ceaseless and ruthless application of the art of war.

CHAPTER NINE

1940

JANUARY TO MAY

> One seems to hear the echoing tramp of twenty-five
> years ago.
>
> FREYA STARK

THE YEAR 1940 opened at the height of what had become known in Britain and France as the Phoney War (in French, *Le Drole de Guerre*). Both countries were at war with Germany, and had been for four months. But although German U-boat sinkings of their merchant ships and warships, and their own counter-attacks, were a regular feature of the war at sea, no land battles had been fought, and no attempt had been made by either side along the Franco-German frontier to launch a military offensive. Such was the sense of a lack of danger that on January 8 the last of 316,192 British child evacuees were allowed back to London by the British government, which had evacuated them on the outbreak of war, fearing a German air bombardment on the capital.

Other conflicts were far from 'phoney'. In Finland, the Finnish army continued to resist the enormous pressure of repeated Soviet efforts to break through the Finnish defences. Inside Poland, there was no respite in the daily persecution of Poles, and of Polish Jews: indeed, knowledge of the murder of civilians was creating a growing anti-German feeling among the British and French which worked against any attempt by Hitler to seek a compromise peace in the West. At the beginning of January a train made up of cattle trucks reached Warsaw. It had been thirteen days on its journey – a journey that could easily have been accomplished in three or four hours. Locked inside the trucks were two thousand Polish prisoners-of-war, who had been captured during the fighting three months earlier, and were being returned home. When the trucks were unlocked it was found that more than two hundred of the prisoners had frozen to death. Others had been driven insane by their ordeal.

News of this atrocity reached the West through Polish underground sources which reported to the Polish government in exile in Paris. Other atrocities were kept secret by the Germans, and only come to light after the war. On January 9 the Chief of the SS and Police of the province of Greater Danzig-West Prussia, Dr Hildebrandt, informed Himmler by letter that two of the units of SS stormtroopers under his command had carried out 'the elimination of about 4,000 incurable patients from Polish mental hospitals', as well as the 'elimination' of a further 2,000 German mental patients at mental hospitals in Pomerania.

During January, Gestapo agents in Warsaw captured Andrej Kott, the leader of a clandestine Polish youth organization. Kott's family had converted from Judaism to Catholicism several decades earlier, and he was a practising Catholic. To warn others not to participate in clandestine activities, on January 18 the Gestapo rounded up 255 Warsaw Jews – among them doctors, teachers, chemists, musicians, businessmen, engineers and industrialists – and took them to a wood outside Warsaw, where they were shot. It was estimated by Polish underground sources that 15,000 Poles had been executed in the previous four-and-a-half months.

On January 22, Pope Pius XII broadcast from the Vatican: 'The horror and inexcusable excesses committed on a helpless and a homeless people have been established by the unimpeachable testimony of eye-witnesses.' That same day the Chief of Staff of the German First Army, Major-General Friedrich Mieth, told the officers on his staff: 'The SS has carried out mass executions without proper trials.' These executions, he warned, had 'besmirched' the honour of the German army. When Hitler was informed of Mieth's speech, the general was dismissed.

The German conquest of Poland provided the German war effort with a mass of forced labourers who were quickly exploited. Under an order issued by Hans Frank from Cracow – the headquarters of the General Government – on January 25, more than a million Polish workers were to be deported to Germany to work in factories and fields. Czech civilians were already being taken to Germany as forced labourers. Thousands of these deportees died in the harsh conditions. Others returned home after the war broken in body and embittered.

*   *   *

One of Germany's sources of essential war materials was Sweden. The Swedish government had no compunction in supplying this material, without which the German war-making powers would have been curtailed. With the Baltic Sea frozen during the winter, this material – most of it iron ore – was sent by rail from the Swedish ore-fields at Gällivare to the northern Norwegian port of Narvik, and then by ship through Norwegian territorial waters to Germany.

In the first week of January the British Government warned the Norwegians of its intention to lay mines inside Norwegian territorial waters, in order to force the German ore-ships out into the North Sea, where they could be attacked. But the mines were not laid, and the ore-ships continued on their way. Neville Chamberlain's Government, though pressed by Churchill to act swiftly, hesitated. Chamberlain's own instinct was to send British troops across Norway and through Sweden, not primarily to secure the ore fields, but to reach Finland and help the Finns in their war against Russia.

In mid-January Soviet bombers began a massive attack on army depots, road and rail junctions, and dockyards throughout southern Finland. On January 14, thirty-five towns and villages were bombed. But it was becoming clear that the defeat of Finland would not take place, and two weeks later Stalin authorized secret negotiations to begin in Sweden, agreeing that the Soviet Union would abandon its support for a Communist Government in Finland, and would be willing to accept modifications to the Russo-Finnish border that would give extra defence to Leningrad, but not impinge on Finnish sovereignty except along a strip of border territory.

Even as the secret negotiations were under way, Stalin ordered a new offensive to be launched against the Finnish defences along the Mannerheim Line. Soviet tanks and infantry, with air support, made a determined effort to break through, but the line did not break. Two days later, on January 20, at the Anglo-French Supreme War Council, the British and French Prime Ministers, Chamberlain and Daladier, agreed to send an expeditionary force of at least three divisions to Finland, to take their place in the line against the Soviet forces. Chamberlain told his colleagues, in explanation of the Allied decision: 'Finland must not be allowed to disappear off the map.' In order to reach Finland, the force would land at three Norwegian ports – Stavanger, Bergen and Trondheim – and march eastward across Sweden to the Finnish border. A date was set for this initiative: March 20.

The Supreme War Council also agreed that, in order to deprive Germany of Swedish iron-ore, an Anglo-French force should land at the northern

Norwegian port of Narvik, cross into Sweden, and take control of the Swedish iron-ore fields at Gällivare. This same force could then continue eastwards to Finland, to assist the Finns, thus, in Chamberlain's words, 'killing two birds with one stone'.

Whether the war in Finland would still be being fought in March was unclear. On February 10 the Soviet forces, persevering with their renewed offensive, broke through the Mannerheim Line. The Finns beat a hasty but well-ordered retreat to a second defence line that had been prepared during the winter. But only three days after the first line had been breached the second line was attacked. This was the moment when Finnish military effort reached a climax. Henceforth, despite innumerable acts of bravery, and an ever-tenacious Finnish defence, the Soviet forces were able to exploit their superiority in numbers, and slowly but inexorably push back the Finnish defenders.

Terrible errors compounded the savagery of war. During a Soviet artillery barrage on Finnish front-line trenches on the night of February 28, the Soviet artillery shells, fired from the heaviest sixteen- and eighteen-inch guns, fell more than half a mile short, killing 400 Soviet soldiers. The dead men were the members of a fresh battalion that had just reached the front and were resting, eating their bread. 'All through the day,' a Finnish officer later wrote, 'we heard voices from no-man's land. They were voices of men in pain.' These were the few survivors of the Soviet barrage. When the Finns saw them crawling about, they themselves opened fire with artillery and mortars. Finally only a single voice was heard, screaming 'Stalin, Stalin, Stalin!' The Finnish officer described the sequel: 'We decided that if the Russians were coming to rescue the man we would let them do it. But nobody came. Since we did not want to send any of our men, a quick machine-gun burst was fired at the man and the screaming stopped.'

On March 4 the Soviets launched an offensive against the Finnish city of Viipuri. Making use of the frozen waters of the Gulf of Finland, Soviet artillery took up its positions offshore, bombarding Viipuri from the frozen sea. The artillery bombardment continued throughout the night, assisted by repeated bombing attacks by the Soviet Air Force. The next morning the Soviet government announced that it was 'once more' willing to sit down at the negotiating table with the Finns.

On March 7 the Finnish Prime Minister, Risto Ryti, flew to Moscow. While he was still in the Soviet capital, it was announced from Helsinki that the second Finnish line of defence had been broken. On March 13 a

Treaty was ready to be signed. Finland retained its independence, and most of its territory. The Soviet Union annexed Finnish territory which extended its Baltic border more than fifty miles further from Leningrad. The Soviet Union also acquired a swathe of Finnish territory in the north, and secured a thirty-year lease on the Finnish naval base at Hango, at the entrance to the Gulf of Finland.

Another war was over: it had lasted for three and a half months. The bloodletting had been high – 58,000 Russian and 27,000 Finnish dead. The territorial and strategic gains for the Soviet Union had been adequate to its purpose, to push the Soviet-Finnish border further away from Leningrad, Lake Ladoga and the White Sea. Finland's resistance was widely admired. Hitler, reading into the war the proof of weakness in the Soviet army, looked forward with even greater confidence to the second phase of the plan that he had outlined to his generals a few months earlier: first Holland-Belgium-France-Britain and then – East. At a meeting with Mussolini on March 18 at the Brenner Pass, Hitler reiterated his confidence that once France was defeated Britain would come to terms without Germany having to invade.

Early in 1940 the British won a major success in the sphere of Intelligence that was, in due course, to transform many aspects of war-making, both in terms of strategy and tactics, first helping to avert defeat and then proving a decisive element in victory. During January, British cryptographers began to read, with some frequency, messages sent by the most secret system of German communication, the Enigma machine.

This Signals Intelligence breakthrough was not a British effort alone. For many months French cryptographers had been equally active in what was essentially a joint Anglo-French effort, working against the clock. Both the British and the French were indebted in their turn to pioneering work done across more than a decade by Polish mathematicians. The Enigma machine was a German invention. It had originally been intended for commercial use, but the moment its wartime potential was recognized it was taken over by German Intelligence and put under a blanket of the most formidable secrecy. By chance, a Polish engineer had been among those in Germany who originally worked on the design of the machine, and it was also a Pole, Marian Rejewski, helped by material obtained by a French secret agent – Asché – who made the crucial breakthrough in Poland before the war. On 16 August 1939, two weeks before the outbreak of war, Polish Intelligence handed its British counterparts the latest model of a rebuilt Enigma machine.

The breakthrough of January 1940 was one of method; it had no immediate benefit for the Allied cause. The cypher which had been broken, after prodigious effort, was the German Army Enigma key used more than two and a half months earlier on a single day, October 28. It was to take nearly nine months before the Enigma keys used by the German Air Force were to be broken regularly. At times they were broken almost simultaneously with the despatch of the message from Berlin to the field commanders. Within a year of first being broken, 'Enigma', Germany's most secret means of communication, was to become a powerful weapon in the British – and subsequently in the Allied – armoury.

It was a slow process whereby Enigma – which to the very last day of the war the Germans were convinced was still intact – was broken. Progress came initially as a result of good fortune. On February 12 the British minesweeper *Gleaner* sank a German U-boat, the *U-33*. From the U-boat, which had settled at thirty fathoms, the British recovered three Enigma machine rotors. Unfortunately for Britain, and luckily for Hitler, the naval Enigma keys themselves could not be broken. But the rotors gave the British government's cryptanalysts at Bletchley Park, north-west of London, an important insight into German operating procedures.

Hitler also had a Signals Intelligence success early in 1940, for it was from his Intelligence services' reading of British top secret naval signals at that time that he learned of the threat to Germany in Scandinavia: the Anglo-French plan to land a military force in Stavanger, Bergen and Trondheim, as decided upon by Britain and France on February 5. At German Army Headquarters at Zossen, near Berlin, a special unit under Hitler's personal supervision, headed by a naval officer, Captain Theodor Krancke, worked to organize a counter-move. The plan which the unit evolved was to land German troops at seven points: not only at Stavanger, Bergen, Trondheim and Narvik, to forestall the British, but also at Arendal, Kristiansand and Oslo – the Norwegian capital. This latter landing would enable Germany to replace the Norwegian Royal government with a government of its own choosing.

On February 21 Hitler appointed General Nikolaus von Falkenhorst to command the Norway invasion. Von Falkenhorst soon widened the plan to include the invasion of Denmark, in order to secure the lines of communication between Germany and Norway.

A new war was in the offing; British and German naval, air and army personnel were in training for the same objective. British troops who had been preparing to go to France were told that they had a new destination involving different climatic conditions, including ice and snow.

The Gestapo and SS-led tyranny inside German-occupied Poland continued to grow more ferocious with every month. Hans Frank was able to call on both the SS and German Police units to control the civilian population, round up Poles for forced labour, and impose the harshest penalties on any Pole who criticized the regime, or who showed the slightest manifestation of national feeling. On February 2 the German Commander-in-Chief of the Frontier Sector South, General Ulex, sent a letter of protest to his senior officer, General Blaskowitz, the Commander-in-Chief of the German Army of Occupation in Poland. In his letter, Ulex wrote: 'The recent increase in the use of violence by the police shows an almost incredible lack of human and moral qualities; the word "brutish" is almost justified.' General Ulex continued: 'The only solution I can see to this revolting situation which sullies the honour of the entire German people, is that all police formations together with all their senior commanders, should be dismissed in a body and their units disbanded.'

General Blaskowitz was not unsympathetic to this complaint – the rivalry between the SS and the German Army had existed from the earliest days of Hitler's regime. Shortly after receiving Ulex's letter he drew up a list of SS crimes, citing in detail thirty-three incidents of the murder and rape of Poles and Jews, and the looting of Polish and Jewish property. As to the German Army officers and men under his command, Blaskowitz noted on February 6 that their attitude to the SS and German police 'alternates between abhorrence and hatred. Every soldier feels disgusted and repelled by these crimes committed in Poland by nationals of the Reich and representatives of our State.'

Angered by these accusations, on February 13 Hans Frank travelled to Berlin to ask Hitler for Blaskowitz's dismissal. Two days later Blaskowitz reiterated his charges in a letter to the Commander-in-Chief of the German Armed Forces, General von Brauchitsch. His protest was to no avail, however, and incidents such as those of which he had complained continued on a daily basis, against individuals, and against those forced to serve in labour gangs. This included Poles and Jews. 'The humiliations and tortures inflicted upon the Jewish workmen', the *Manchester Guardian* reported on February 18, 'who are compelled by their Nazi overseers to dance and sing and undress during their work, and are even forced to belabour each other with blows, show no signs of abating.'

Not only Polish Jews, but all Poles were subjected to the harshest cruelty. On February 21, Richard Gluecks, head of the German Concentration Camp Inspectorate, informed Himmler that he had found a suitable site for a new 'quarantine' camp, in which Poles could be held, punished and put to work for any 'acts of rebellion or disobedience'. The site was a former Austro-Hungarian cavalry barracks, a series of imposing brick buildings on the outskirts of the Polish town of Oswiecim, a town which, having been annexed to the German Reich after Poland's defeat, was known once more by its earlier German name, Auschwitz.

It was not initially intended to use Auschwitz as a place of incarceration for Jews. Its sole initial purpose was as a punishment camp for Poles. Work began to convert the barracks to a camp, and to find from the existing German concentration camps suitable personnel to administer and supervise a regime which was intended from the outset to be of the utmost severity. Two months after the site had been found, a thirty-nine-year-old SS man, Rudolf Hoess – who in the First World War had won the Iron Cross First Class on the Turkish Front – was sent there from Dachau, where he had been on the camp staff. With him on this new assignment were five other SS men. Calculating the future size of the camp, and the nature of the punishments and hard labour that were to be to be imposed on the Polish prisoners, they sent for thirty German convicted criminals from Sachsenhausen concentration camp to serve as barrack chiefs (Kapos) in the new camp.

Imprisonment in Auschwitz was not the only punishment imposed upon the Poles. On March 8 a Polish workman in Cracow was walking in the street humming the tune of the Polish national anthem 'Poland has Not Yet Perished'. He was overheard by a member of the Gestapo, and shot dead in the street.

The Anglo-French plan to occupy Narvik and deny Swedish iron ore to Germany was about to go ahead. Trondheim, Bergen and Stavanger would also be occupied in order to forestall a German counter-attack. The British War Cabinet gave its final approval to the plan on March 12. The Norwegians were not to be informed until the invading force was already offshore. A million and a half tons of iron ore was even then in warehouses and at the quayside in Narvik, awaiting shipment to Germany.

The Allied Scandinavian plan was briefly abandoned as a result of the Soviet-Finnish peace agreement, as that aspect of it involving the despatch of the expeditionary force to Finland was no longer needed; but when, on March 20, Daladier was replaced by Paul Reynaud as Prime Minister of France, the plan was revived. The new plan was, however, a much truncated version of the old one. There would be no troop landings, only the laying of mines in Norwegian territorial waters. Two minelaying operations would be launched simultaneously, one in southern and the other in northern Norwegian waters. A new date, April 5, was set for the minelaying, which it was hoped would force the ore-bearing ships out to sea. Hitler, his Intelligence services alerted to the original Anglo-French plan for a military landing, decided to anticipate it. On April 2 he gave the order that the German invasion of Norway was to begin in five days' time.

Without having intended to make any moves other than those against Belgium, Holland and France, Hitler switched his army's and navy's planning and organizational skills to Norway, and did so with remarkable speed. On April 3 three German supply ships, camouflaged as colliers, moved through the Kattegat and Skagerrak and then northward along the Norwegian coast towards Narvik. Artillery and ammunition were hidden under their tarpaulin. That same day, two thousand German troops were put aboard ten destroyers, ready to be sent to Narvik as soon as the signal was given. Other warships were alerted to be sent with troops to ports further south, and to Oslo itself.

On April 5, as British ships set off across the North Sea to begin their minelaying operations along the Norwegian coast, Chamberlain declared with triumph: 'Hitler has missed the bus.' Throughout April 6 the British ships steamed towards Norwegian waters. That night, while they were still forty-eight hours away from their destination, aircraft of British Bomber Command reported seeing 'intense shipping activity and brilliantly lit wharves' at Eckernförde, near Kiel. This was another last-minute operation on which Hitler had decided, in conjunction with the invasion of Norway – the invasion of Denmark. The two operations would be carried out simultaneously.

On April 7, as the British minelaying armada was on its final day's journey to the Norwegian coast, the ten German destroyers destined for Narvik left their Baltic harbours and steamed northward, carrying below decks the first troops intended to land on Norwegian soil. When details of this German move reached the Admiralty in London during April 8 they were not believed, the Admiralty Intelligence Division concluding: 'All these reports are of doubtful value and may well be only a further move in the war of nerves.' When, a few hours later, incontrovertible news of several other seaborne troop movements reached London, the southern minelaying force was ordered to turn back. It did so just in time. It would have been no match for the destroyers which were even then in its path.

As dawn broke on April 9, German warships were in position off Trondheim, Bergen and Stavanger – the three ports that Britain and France would have occupied on March 20 under the original Supreme War Council plan. Other German warships were entering Oslo Fjord. Another war had begun – the war between Germany and Norway, and with it, also the war between Germany and Denmark – successors to the German-Polish and Russo-Finnish wars. With Austria, Czechoslovakia and Poland having fallen to Germany, two more sovereign States were about to face the full force of German power.

At Narvik, ten German destroyers landed the troops that had been held in readiness for the past week for the Norwegian campaign. Instead of resisting the invaders, the local Norwegian commander ordered his own men to lay down their arms. He was a supporter of Norway's leading fascist sympathizer, Vidkun Quisling, a former Foreign Minister whose ambition was to lead Norway into the German orbit.

Elsewhere along the Norwegian coast – at Bergen, Kristiansand and Trondheim – the German forces faced stiff opposition that morning. But at each port their superior fire power, artillery, and air support, enabled them to land and push up the fjords and valleys. German forces also landed that morning in Copenhagen. The King of Denmark, Christian X, knew that his army could not resist the Germans and ordered the Commander-in-Chief of the Danish forces, General Pryor, to declare an immediate ceasefire. Pryor, however, wanted to continue the fight, and refused to pass on the order. It was left to the King's adjutant to bypass the general, and all fighting ceased. Denmark was Hitler's second military conquest, six months after Poland.

With the fall of Oslo to the Germans on the afternoon of April 9, Vidkun Quisling was installed as head of government and appealed to all Norwegians to lay down their arms and to welcome the invader. The mass of the Norwegian people refused to do so. Fleeing Oslo, the legitimate government moved inland to Hamar, seventy miles to the north.

At Narvik, five British destroyers under the command of Captain Warburton-Lee managed to penetrate the port's defences in the early hours of

April 10 and sank six invasion transports and two of the ten German destroyers. In the ensuing German chase, two British destroyers were also sunk, and Warburton-Lee was mortally wounded. He was posthumously awarded the Victoria Cross, the first of the war.

In London, it was decided on April 12 to send a military force to land in Narvik, not only to drive out the Germans and form a focal point for continuing Norwegian resistance, but to serve as a base to carry out the original Supreme War Council plan of advancing across the border into Sweden and occupying the iron-ore fields at Gällivare. On the day after this decision, another British naval attack into Narvik harbour resulted in the remaining eight German destroyers being sunk. That same day, British troops landed at two other Norwegian ports, Andalsnes and Namsos, to the north and south of Trondheim. Hitler, fearing a reverse in central and northern Norway, ordered his troops to evacuate Narvik.

Fighting was taking place along the whole Norwegian coastline. Inland in the south, troops led by the Norwegian Chief of Defence, General Otto Ruge, fought a series of rearguard actions. More than 13,000 British troops were ashore north of Narvik, and north and south of Trondheim. French troops, troops of the French Foreign Legion, and Polish naval units – which had escaped capture by the Germans six months earlier, were also in action. But the Germans had two advantages that were to prove decisive: air superiority which enabled them to mount repeated dive bombing attacks on the Allied forces and shipping, and the ability – secured by skilful cryptography – to read more than thirty per cent of the British naval signals in the North Sea and Norwegian area, enabling them to attack ships carrying troops and munitions that might otherwise have evaded them.

Hitler was confident of victory, and of enlisting his newly conquered people to his cause. On his fifty-first birthday, April 20, he ordered the establishment of a new SS regiment, Norland, in which Norwegians and Danes would serve alongside Germans. Four days later, unwilling to risk any weakening of Berlin's dominance over its imminent conquest, he appointed Josef Terboven, a senior German Nazi Party official from Essen, to take effective control of Norway as Reich Commissioner. After only fifteen days of power over his fellow Norwegians, Vidkun Quisling had been pushed aside.

The Germans were winning the battle for Norway. On April 29, as the British began their withdrawal from Andalsnes, General Ruge warned that without 'further Allied intervention' Norway would have to sue for peace.

Each episode of the struggle was a reminder of how pitiless war could be. On May 4 a Polish destroyer, the *Grom*, was hit by German bombs near Narvik and fifty-two Polish sailors killed. As the wounded men waited in the water to be rescued by a British battleship that was steaming towards them, German machine gunners opened fire from the shore, killing many of the wounded men as they tried to keep afloat.

Hitler did not want to wait for the Norwegian surrender before embarking on the next phase. On April 30 he gave instructions for the final preparations to be made for the attack on Belgium, Luxembourg, Holland and France. On May 9, having given orders for the attack to begin on the following day, he left Berlin on his special train. To maintain secrecy and deception it was said that he was on his way to Oslo, to review his troops in the conquered Norwegian capital. In fact, he went westward, reaching the small town of Euskirchen, less than thirty miles from the Belgian border, shortly before dawn on May 10.

The size of the German force attacking on May 10 was in itself an indicator of a rapid victory: 136 German divisions were advancing against half that number of British, French, Belgian and Dutch troops. Holland and Belgium, as neutrals, were not prepared to wage war, or even to defend their frontiers for more than a few hours. Nor could any of the countries whose independence was threatened that day match – even when combined – the German air forces ranged against them. Even as the British and French forces moved forward through Belgium – the Belgian government having forbidden them to do so earlier – 2,500 German aircraft launched a ferocious blitz on the Allied and neutral airfields, destroying many aircraft on the ground. At the same time, 16,000 German airborne troops were parachuted over Holland.

This was the start of the *Blitzkrieg*, or Lightning War, which had been devised to create havoc and panic as the advancing forces pushed rapidly forward before their opponents could establish a system of trench lines – it was the trenches from the North Sea to the Swiss border that had created the war of attrition and stalemate from September 1914 to August 1918. The key to Blitzkrieg was armour: light armoured vehicles, supported by air strikes on both the gathering and the retreating armies that were seeking to defend their native lands. The strategist who had devised the operational plan for this Lightning War was the senior quartermaster on the German Army General Staff, General Erich von Manstein. As a reward for his efforts he was created Field Marshal.

In Britain, Neville Chamberlain realized that this new crisis made a National Government necessary: hitherto he had governed without the services of the opposition Labour Party. The Labour Party, which was at that very moment holding its annual conference, was willing to join the administration and participate in the making of war policy, but refused to serve under Chamberlain, who was regarded as an implacable enemy of the Labour Party and the man who had, in the immediate pre-war years, pursued the policy of appeasement beyond the bounds of wisdom.

After several hours of crisis, Winston Churchill – who was acceptable to Labour because of his consistent opposition to appeasement before the war – became Prime Minister. That day a squadron of bombers flew over the German town of Freiburg-in-Breisgau, twelve miles from the Franco-German border. In the raid that followed, fifty-seven people were killed, among them thirteen children in a school playground. The citizens of Freiburg believed that the French or British had carried out the raid. It was in fact carried out by a squadron of German bombers, flying over the town as a result of a navigational error, and mistaking it for a target in France.

With the Germans having occupied Denmark, there was a danger that they would also occupy the Danish Dependency of Iceland and threaten Britain's transatlantic lifeline. On his first day as Prime Minister, Churchill authorized British forces to occupy Iceland, both to deny it to the Germans and to establish British naval and air bases there. That night, May 10/11, thirty-six British bombers struck at the town of München Gladbach, seventeen miles inside Germany across the Dutch frontier. Four people were killed in the town centre. One of them was an Englishwoman.

Even as the new war front opened in western Europe, the war in northern Norway continued. On the morning of May 11 it was learned in London that the Allied base which had been secured at Harstad, north of Narvik, was being severely bombed by German aircraft. It was also learned that German troops, taking advantage of the Nazi-Soviet Pact, were being moved by rail from Leningrad to Murmansk, as part of a possible attack into northern Norway around the North Cape. Plans were made to land an Allied force at Narvik itself, to hold northern Norway against any such move.

On the Western Front the German commanders vied with each other during May 11 on how far they could advance. 'Everything wonderful so far', General Rommel, commanding the 7th Panzer Division, wrote to his wife that day, and he added: 'Am way ahead of my neighbours.' In Holland, after a march of a hundred miles from the German border, the German Eighteenth Army linked up on May 12 with the paratroops who had been dropped two days earlier. That evening, the British War Cabinet were told that seventy-six British aircraft had been lost in the previous two days of fighting.

On May 13 Queen Wilhelmina of Holland sought refuge in Britain. That afternoon Churchill told the members of his new Government: 'I have nothing to offer but blood, toil, tears and sweat.' He repeated those words a few hours later in the House of Commons, telling the Members of Parliament 'You ask, what is our policy? I will say. It is to wage war, by sea, land and air, with all our might and with all the strength that God can give us; to wage war against a monstrous tyranny, never surpassed in the dark lamentable catalogue of human crime. That is our policy.' As to Britain's aim, Churchill was equally emphatic: 'It is victory, victory at all costs, victory in spite of all terror, victory however long and hard the road may be; for without victory there is no survival.'

The danger confronting Britain was not only the fall of Belgium, Holland and France, and German troops in occupation of the North Sea and Channel coastlines, but the invasion of Britain itself. That evening the British Air Staff estimated that sixty fighter squadrons were needed for the 'adequate defence' of Britain, but that only thirty-nine squadrons – of ten to twelve aircraft each – were available. But the number of serviceable fighter aircraft ready for immediate combat was less than fifty.

Confronted on the morning of May 14 by a stronger Dutch defence than he had envisaged, Hitler ordered: 'This resistance must be broken quickly.' German aircraft were then diverted from the battle for the Belgian frontier 'to facilitate the rapid conquest of Fortress Holland'. Their target was the bridges over the Rhine at Rotterdam. Many bombs, missing their target, fell on the city centre, more than a square mile of which was totally destroyed. More than eight hundred Dutch civilians were killed.

Rumour, and Allied propaganda, quickly multiplied the figure of eight to nine hundred civilian dead in Rotterdam – the highest estimated figure is 980 – to 25,000, even 30,000. The reality was harsh enough. The widely-circulated rumour gave added terror to those in France and Belgium who were as yet unbombed.

At midday on May 14, news reached the Allied commanders that across the Franco-German border, near Sedan, the Germans had greatly enlarged their bridgehead. With substantial British and French forces pinned down by the battle in Belgium, the Germans would be able to use this bridgehead as a base for operations to sweep behind the Allied armies, pushing in a broad semi-circle to the three principal Channel ports, Dunkirk, Calais and Boulogne. This was Hitler's plan. 'The progress of the offensive to date', he noted in his Directive No. 11, issued that day, 'shows that the enemy has failed to appreciate in time the basic idea of our operations.'

In Norway, the sustained German air bombardment made it impossible for Britain to hold Harstad, and a general evacuation began. There was no way that Norwegian sovereignty could be restored. 'The small countries are simply smashed up one by one, like matchwood,' Churchill telegraphed to Roosevelt. On the following day, May 15, British troops landed at the Dutch port of Ijmuiden in an attempt to bolster Dutch resistance. As they landed, six buses reached Ijmuiden from Amsterdam. On them were two hundred Jews, mostly children, being brought to the port by a Dutch woman, Geertruida Wijsmuller. Many of her charges were German-Jewish children who had reached Holland as refugees before the war. Now they were on the move again. 'At ten to eight in the evening we sailed away,' one of the boys, Harry Jacobi, later wrote. 'At nine p.m. news came through, picked up by the ship's radio. The Dutch had capitulated. My last impressions of Holland were gigantic clouds of black smoke from the burning Shell oil refinery, which the Dutch had ignited so as not to let them fall into the hands of the enemy.' After four days at sea, the children found safety in Britain. 'The Germans had broadcast that our ship had been bombed and sunk, causing grief to all our relatives. The BBC promptly broadcast a denial.'

With the Dutch capitulation Hitler was the ruler of yet another European State. In Holland, Harry Jacobi's grandparents, for whom there had been no place on the crowded coaches, were to be among the many thousands of Dutch Jewish victims deported to their deaths in the years ahead.

On the night of May 15, for the first time since the German Army had struck in the West five days earlier, British bombers attacked German industrial targets in the Ruhr. In all, ninety-nine bombers set off, to sixteen different targets. Twenty-four of the bombers found oil targets, some of which were seen by the crews burning fiercely as they turned for home. Blown off course by an unexpected wind during the return flight, one bomber crashed into high ground in France, killing the pilot and his four crewmen. All the other bombers returned safely.

Britain's ability to continue at war, and to resist the invasion that was thought to be imminent, depended on a rapid increase in bomber and fighter aircraft. Roosevelt wanted to help, but was unable to breach American neutrality by shipping aircraft to Britain uncrated and ready to fly. He therefore devised, on the night of May 15, a way round the Neutrality Act. This was to fly the aircraft to the American side of the Canadian border, 'push' them across the border, then fly them on to Newfoundland, where they could be put on board ship. By this device, they would not technically have 'flown' out of the United States.

This plan was secret. On the following day, May 16, Roosevelt sent a message to Congress in which he stated: 'I should like to see this nation geared up to the ability to turn out at least 50,000 planes a year.' The mention of this figure 'electrified Congress and the nation', one of Roosevelt's advisers, Edward R. Stettinius Jr later wrote. The number of military planes produced in 1939 had been 2,100. Stettinius added: 'Fifty thousand planes a year seemed at first like an utterly impossible goal, but it caught the imagination of the Americans, who have always believed they could accomplish the impossible.' It also made clear just how seriously Roosevelt regarded the defence situation, and the vulnerability of the United States.

'The battle is fighting fiercely and the history of our world beats itself out in Flanders,' the British explorer Freya Stark wrote in her diary on May 16, in Aden – more than two thousand miles from the battlefield. 'One seems to hear the echoing tramp of twenty-five years ago. Yesterday, in the wireless report from the RAF correspondent, one heard the thud of bombs.'

Throughout May 16 the German advance continued deep into French territory east of Sedan. That day the commander of the French land forces, General Gamelin, ordered French forces to leave Belgium. Churchill, while on his way to Paris to seek a joint Anglo-French strategy, gave orders for the emptying of all oil-storage tanks in the immediate line of the German advance. This included the successful draining off 150,000 tons of fuel into the River Scheldt near Antwerp. Reaching Paris that afternoon, Churchill urged an Allied military stand on the line from Antwerp to Namur. 'We have lost Namur' was Reynaud's comment.

Fears of an imminent German breakthrough led to panic in the French capital. Bundles of official documents thrown from the windows of the French Foreign Ministry were set alight on the Ministry lawn. But it was not towards Paris that the German mechanized forces were advancing. Instead they turned north-west and by noon on May 17 had reached the River Oise, driving towards the Channel Coast. Attacking them, but unable to halt them, were the tanks of the French 4th Armoured Division, commanded by a pioneer of armoured warfare, Colonel Charles de Gaulle. In recognition of his bravery that day he was promoted to the rank of brigadier-general.

On every sector of the front the German forces were succeeding beyond their hopes. On May 17 they entered Brussels, the fifth capital to be occupied by the German military machine in nine months. Among the British troops falling back from Brussels towards the Channel Coast was the 3rd Division, commanded by General Bernard Montgomery. Only at Hitler's headquarters did there seem to be a moment of doubt. 'A very disagreeable day!' General Halder noted in his diary. 'The Führer is excessively nervous. He mistrusts his own success; he's afraid to take risks; he'd really like us to stop now.'

For the Belgian refugees fleeing in front of the advancing German army, there was no respite. One of those who witnessed the terrible scenes of flight, José Antonio de Aguirre, was himself a recent refugee from the Spanish Civil War. On May 17 he and his children, and a fellow-Spanish refugee, Cesaro Asporosa, were fleeing in the direction of La Panne, on the Channel Coast. Five years later, from his subsequent place of refuge in Britain, he recalled that day:

Before we had come to the outskirts of La Panne, there was a terrific bombardment. Just ahead of us streets were torn open wide – and before our children's eyes other children were blown into bits and crushed beneath a building which crumbled sadly, in a dejected fashion, like a house made of cards . . .

It was terrible; the sound and the smell; the awful noise of the suddenly wounded. We were at first frozen to the ground where we stood, and then the planes began circling and swooping down, with their machine-guns singing out their merciless pursuit of anything that lived – however small . . .

We had seen all of it before. It was such an old story to us now, we were not so afraid as some others. But our women were terrified. Some of the children became quite ill, vomiting in the street from what they had seen. We had to make them get under a tree and we had to encircle them so they would not try to escape. The noise and the sight of a bombardment make the power of reason leave quickly. Since it was impossible to take refuge from the bombs, at least to keep under the trees was to keep from being a target for the machine-gunning pursuit planes.

The firing grew more intense. A German pilot, whose plane had been downed by anti-aircraft guns, descended suddenly in a parachute. Everyone with a gun shot at him. He was killed there in the square a thousand times — riddled over and over again. Asporosa, watching with me, said, 'It's too bad, you know, that now they are wasting so many bullets.'

I could only think of how frugally and cautiously our men and our citizens had been trained to use those precious bullets.

That night 130 British bombers made a second heavy raid on German cities, striking mostly at oil refineries and railway yards. In Hamburg, where several factories were hit, bombs also fell by mistake on one of the city's main streets, the Reeperbahn, and thirty-four people were killed.

Hitler's nervousness of May 17 was misplaced. On the following day General Rommel reached Cambrai and General Guderian — the master of armoured warfare — occupied St Quentin. The way to the Channel Coast was open. When one of France's senior commanders, General Giraud, entered Le Cateau that day with the remnants of the French Ninth Army, he was captured by the Germans. Unknown to his Intelligence services, German troops had reached the town a few hours earlier.

Also on May 18, Belgium's principal port, Antwerp, fell to the Germans. 'I do not need to tell you about the gravity of what has happened,' Churchill telegraphed that day to Roosevelt. 'We are determined to persevere to the very end, whatever the result of the great battle raging in France may be. We must expect in any case to be attacked here on the Dutch model before very long and we hope to give a good account of ourselves.' The 'Dutch model' was the use of parachute troops to seize the vital points.

That night Churchill broadcast to the British people. It was his first broadcast since becoming Prime Minister eight days earlier. 'This is one of the most awe-striking periods in the long history of France and Britain,' he said. 'It is also beyond doubt the most sublime.' The British and French peoples, side by side, 'have advanced to rescue not only Europe but mankind from the foulest and most soul destroying tyranny which has ever darkened and stained the pages of history'. Behind the armies and fleets of Britain and France there gathered 'a group of shattered States and bludgeoned races: the Czechs, the Poles, the Norwegians, the Danes, the Dutch, the Belgians

– upon all of whom the long night of barbarism will descend, unbroken even by a star of hope, unless we conquer, as conquer we must, as conquer we shall'.

How Britain and France could conquer was, at that moment, unclear. It was they, not Germany, that seemed about to succumb. That morning, as the German thrust threatened to drive a wedge between the British and French forces north and south of the River Somme, Churchill ordered the British Admiralty to assemble 'a large number of vessels' in readiness to cross over 'to ports and inlets on the French coast'. It had become clear, he told the Admiralty, that plans must be made at once, in case it became necessary 'to withdraw the British Expeditionary Force from France'. Hitler, his moment of hesitation behind him, was elated by the rapid advance of his armies against the two most powerful forces in Western Europe, telling one of his generals that night: 'The British can have their peace as soon as they return our colonies to us.'

Events followed with a rapidity that made the adversaries gasp. On May 21, German troops reached the Channel Coast at Le Crotoy, at the mouth of the River Somme, cutting off the British Expeditionary Force from all avenues of escape southward. In Britain there was a growing sense of resolve, a collective feeling of fellowship and determination. On May 23 the poet Siegfried Sassoon, whose First World War poems had stressed the barbarity and callousness of war, wrote a poem which reflected the new mood. He called it 'Silent Service':

> Now, multifold, let Britain's patent power
> Be proven within us for the world to see.
> None are exempt from service in this hour;
> And vanquished in ourselves we dare not be.
> Now, for a sunlit future, we can show
> The clenched resolved endurance that defies
> Daemons in dark, – and toward that future go
> With earth's defended freedom in our eyes.
> In every separate soul let courage shine –
> A kneeling angel holding faith's front-line.

On the terrestrial front line there were nothing but setbacks and withdrawals for the Anglo-French forces. 'My estimate is that the war will be won in a fortnight,' Rommel wrote to his wife on May 24.

That day Hitler issued his Directive No. 13. 'The next objective of our operations is to annihilate the French, British and Belgian forces which are surrounded,' it began. The evacuation of those Allied forces began that day, first from Boulogne – which was quickly occupied by the Germans – and then from Dunkirk. British warships, merchant ships and even pleasure craft steaming across the North Sea from London and the seaside towns, converged on Dunkirk and helped take off the men.

Above the Dunkirk beachhead a ferocious air battle took place, as the Germans tried to prevent the evacuation. In nine days, 176 German aircraft and 106 British aircraft were shot down over the beaches. Among the Allied pilots who fought to keep the German aircraft at bay were British, Canadians and Poles. The British air losses over France were beginning to exceed the productive capacity of the aircraft factories. Between May 19 and June 1, a total of 151 Hurricanes had been produced in Britain, and 119 lost in action. In that same period, thirty-nine Spitfires had been produced and seventy-five shot down.

In an attempt to accelerate aircraft production, Churchill had appointed one of his closest friends, the Canadian-born newspaper proprietor Lord Beaverbrook – who had been Minister of Information during the First World War – as Minister of Aircraft Production. In reporting to Churchill after his first month in office that, as a result of the efforts of his ministry there were 1,040 operational aircraft ready for service, Beaverbrook wrote: 'I would remind you that there were 45 aircraft ready for service when your Administration began.' This reflected the consequences of the British Government's pre-war defence policies, of which Churchill had been the main critic. Yet when Churchill's son Randolph remarked to his father that the leaders of the former Government ought to be punished, Churchill replied: 'We don't want to punish anybody now, except the enemy.'

As the evacuation continued from Dunkirk, British bombers struck at German railway lines and marshalling yards leading from Germany to the battlefield. Night after night the bomber pilots and crews sought out road and rail bridges, and German troop concentrations, including those converging on Dunkirk. Oil targets in Germany were also a priority. Such was the German ingenuity, however, that when three bombs hit a group of oil tanks at Harburg, near Hamburg, causing 3,000 tons of oil to leak through the holes, all but 32 tons were later reclaimed and pumped back into the tanks.

*   *   *

On May 26, as the evacuation from Dunkirk gathered momentum, ninety-seven British troops who had been captured at the village of Paradis while defending the perimeter were lined up by their German captors – a unit of the SS Death's Head Division – and shot. Those who had only been wounded were then killed by pistol shot and bayonet. Two survived unnoticed among the bodies. Later their wounds were tended by a French farmer's wife, but they were then captured again and sent to a prisoner-of-war camp in Germany. After the war, when their story was told, the perpetrator of the massacre, SS Captain Fritz Knochlein, was tried by a British military tribunal in Hamburg, condemned to death and hanged.

Two days after the massacre at Paradis, a second massacre took place at Wormhout, when SS soldiers shot dead eighty British soldiers who had already surrendered to them. SS Captain Mohnke, who ordered the executions later became an SS Major-General, and the Citadel Commandant of Hitler's bunker in Berlin. Fifty years after the war he was a retired bank manager living near Hamburg, the scene of SS Captain Knochlein's trial.

The Dunkirk evacuation continued. On one of the small ships that had come across the North Sea from Britain – the former pleasure steamer *Mona's Isle* – forty of those being evacuated were killed as she reached the open sea and was struck by a German bomb. Still the British, French and Belgian troops were fighting a strong rearguard action, enabling more and more soldiers to reach Dunkirk and be taken back to Britain. But on May 27 the King of the Belgians asked the Germans for an armistice. When the Germans demanded unconditional surrender, he accepted. At four on the morning of May 28 the ceasefire came into effect. Belgium – neutral until eighteen days earlier – was no longer a belligerent.

As the first 30,000 British soldiers were taken off the beaches of Dunkirk to safety, the last act in the Norwegian war was taking place. On May 28 a combined British, French, Polish and Norwegian force landed at Narvik. In the battle for the port, 150 of the Allied attackers were killed, but the port was theirs. What they did not know was that, because of the desperate Allied situation in France, a decision had already been made – three days before they landed – to withdraw them. The successful landing did not alter that decision. They were to leave Norway within ten days, as was the other Allied force still ashore, at Bodö.

The landing at Narvik on May 28 was the first Allied attack on territory that had been conquered by Germany. In view of this fact, the French commander had allowed a Norwegian battalion to be the first to land and to challenge the German occupation forces. 'They went in at 5 p.m.,' the historian Kingston Derry has written, 'the tiny vanguard of all the armies of European liberation.'

Despite this Norwegian initiative by the Allies, the defeat of France did not seem a particularly onerous task for the Germans whose advance remained unaffected. 'Perhaps France will give up her now hopeless struggle', Rommel wrote to his wife on May 29 – the day on which 47,310 men were taken off from Dunkirk, including many French soldiers. 'If she does not, we'll smash her to the last corner.'

In Washington, at noon on May 30 – it was already late afternoon in embattled Europe – seven members of the United States Defence Advisory Commission met at the White House. So important were their deliberations that day that the meeting was presided over by President Roosevelt. The issues to be discussed included labour and employment, farm production, transportation, prices, and industrial materials. When Roosevelt spoke it was to focus the Commissioners' attention on the war in Europe, and the response of the United States. He told them, the minutes of the meeting recorded, 'of the crucial necessity for speeding up the arms programme. America's material resources must be mobilized to provide our own defences and to furnish the weaponry so desperately needed by the forces which stood between us and Nazi aggression.'

With these words, Roosevelt made a commitment – unknown to Congress or to the hard-pressed French and British troops in France – that was within a year to ensure the survival of what was left of the democratic alliance.

Unknown to the embattled Western Allies, or to the Polish Government in exile in France, the fate of 15,000 Polish officers who had surrendered to the Soviet Union the previous September and October was in the balance even as the battle in France reached its climax. These Polish captives had been taken to three prison camps inside the Soviet Union: Kozelsk near Smolensk, Starobelsk near Kharkov, and Ostashkov near Kalinin. As well as regular Polish army officers there were many reservists, medical doctors – many of them Jews – customs officers, police, military police and prison officers: they had all been captured when the Soviet forces moved up to the Nazi-Soviet partition line following the German defeat of Poland. Some had surrendered to the Soviets rather than fall into German hands.

Throughout April and the first days of May, these 15,000 prisoners were taken from their respective camps under NKVD guard. It was rumoured that they were being sent back to Poland. Every day the details of their actual fate was telephoned from the three camps to the NKVD headquarters in Moscow. They were being taken to execution sites. Those at Kozelsk were taken to the forest of Katyn, where their hands were tied behind their backs with wire. They were then shot in the back of the head.

Not one of the 4,400 Poles taken to Katyn survived. Nor were there any survivors of the other two massacres. The mass graves at Katyn were discovered by the Germans when they overran the area in 1943. The other two mass graves were uncovered by the Soviet authorities in the summer of 1990 – a year and a half before the disintegration of the Soviet Union. Becoming known in 1943, the Katyn massacre soured Polish-Soviet relations for half a century. One of the first decisions of the post-Communist Polish government in Warsaw was to inscribe the names 'Katyn', 'Starobelsk' and 'Ostashkov' on the Polish Unknown Soldier's war memorial in the centre of the capital.

CHAPTER TEN

1940
JUNE TO DECEMBER

... the great arsenal of democracy.

FRANKLIN D. ROOSEVELT

By MIDNIGHT on 2 June 1940 the Dunkirk evacuation was completed: 338,226 men had been evacuated in the space of seven days. British, Dutch and French ships, including 665 British civilian craft, had assisted in the evacuation. Hundreds of soldiers has been killed by German bombs during the evacuation. The worst single disaster was the death of more than three hundred men when the *Waverley*, a paddle steamer that had previously been converted into a minesweeper, was subjected to half an hour of unremitting air attack. From Narvik, 25,000 British, French and Polish troops, some of whom had only just landed, were still to be evacuated.

'Wars are not won by evacuations': Churchill's comment reminded the British people that a sense of deliverance was not a victory. More than 34,000 British soldiers had been captured in the Dunkirk perimeter. Considerable quantities of arms and ammunition, heavy guns and armoured vehicles, had to be left behind, including 475 tanks, 38,000 motor vehicles, 400 anti-tank guns, 1,000 heavy guns, 8,000 Bren guns, 90,000 rifles and 7,000 tons of ammunition (in Britain there were less than 600,000 rifles and 12,000 Bren guns). Most of the equipment captured by the Germans was usable by them as they turned their attentions southward, thrusting towards to Paris. 'Now that Britain will presumably be willing to make peace,' Hitler told one of his generals, 'I will begin the final settlement of scores with Bolshevism.'

On June 3, at the start of a campaign to force France to capitulate, German bombers struck at Paris: 254 people were killed. That day, in passionate, heartfelt words, the philosopher Michael Polanyi – who had left Germany at the start of the Nazi era – wrote, in the preface to his book *The Contempt of Freedom*, of how crucial it was for the cause of freedom 'to rely on popular tradition and patriotism'. Hitherto freedom's cause lacked 'the dynamic, the vital, the promise of a great future of social redress'. The constructive, vital ideology of freedom needed active defenders as much as the negative ideologies of revolutionary socialism or destructive dictatorship. 'Only now that the peril of freedom has become deadly,' Polanyi wrote, 'has its value been recognized.'

How deadly that peril had become was seen the day after Polanyi's warning, when, on June 4, sensing a quick victory, Hitler moved his headquarters to Brûly-de-Pesche, a Belgian village only a few miles from the French border. As his troops began their advance towards Paris, the sheer weight of numbers was on their side: 143 German divisions facing 65 French divisions. The first breakthrough came on June 6. In Berlin, Dr Goebbels was triumphant, but he was also looking at another element of the Nazi plan as the fall of France seemed imminent. 'After the war,' he wrote, 'we shall deal quickly with the Jews.'

On June 6 King Haakon of Norway broadcast to his people from Tromsö, in the far north of Norway, to say that all military operations were at an end. He then embarked in a British warship for England, and exile. The Norwegian Chief of Defence, General Ruge, had been captured by the Germans. During the Allied evacuation from Narvik, which was completed on June 8, two British warships, the destroyer *Acasta* and the aircraft carrier *Glorious*, were sunk by German bombers and 1,515 officers and men were drowned. There was only a single survivor on *Acasta*, forty-five on *Glorious*.

More than 24,000 troops were evacuated safely from Narvik and a dozen other evacuation points along the Norwegian coast: British, French, Foreign Legion, Polish and Norwegian troops among them. On Norwegian soil, remnants of the Norwegian Army prepared to fight on against the German occupiers from the forests and mountains.

The German-Norwegian war was ended. The German-French and German-British wars continued. After Dunkirk, there were still more than 150,000 British troops in northern and western France, west of the German thrust that had encircled their comrades. But as the Germans began to push westward, these troops were also evacuated. Paris was also threatened. On June 10, after the publication of that morning's newspapers, the French journalists left for the south, together with the military censor and his staff.

That day, realizing that France's days of fighting were nearly over, Mussolini announced that Italy was at war with France, and moved his troops forward into the French provinces along the Italian border. 'First they were too cowardly to take part. Now they are in a hurry so that they can share the spoils,' was Hitler's comment. Roosevelt was also stung to a caustic comment by the news. 'On this tenth day of June 1940,' he said, 'the hand that held the dagger has stuck it into the back of its neighbour.'

Roosevelt also pledged that day 'the material resources of this nation' to those who were 'the opponents of force'. For France the speed of the battle was such that there was no way it could take advantage of this pledge: a week later all France's munitions contracts being fulfilled in the United States were transferred to Britain.

Italy had not only declared war on France, but also on Britain. Italian bombers struck immediately at a range of British bases within flying distance of Italy, Libya and Italian East Africa. Within a few days, Malta and Aden were both bombed. The British retaliated by using bases in southern France to bomb Genoa and Turin. On the desert border between Libya and Egypt, Britain – having evacuated its troops from France and Norway – faced a new war zone.

The fate of France hung in the balance. In the week of fighting after the Dunkirk evacuation, thirty-five French divisions had been lost in their entirety. Others had been reduced to half their strength. No such losses had affected the Germans. When Churchill flew to Paris on June 11 and suggested that a stand be made inside the capital, which could be fought street by street, and which could 'absorb immense armies', the French Deputy Prime Minister, Marshal Pétain, said angrily that to make Paris 'a city of ruins' would not affect the issue.

While Churchill was still in Paris, General de Gaulle, who had been brought in to the French government as Minister of War, suggested making a stand in Brittany, where British troops could be landed to fight alongside the French. But the Reynaud government was divided; there were those who questioned the wisdom of fighting on, and wanted to get the best terms possible from the Germans while Paris was still intact.

Every setback on the battlefield was a cause for further French demoralization. On June 12 more than 38,000 French troops, and 8,000 British troops who were about to be evacuated from St. Valery-en-Caux on the Channel Coast, were subjected to such a fierce German artillery barrage, including fire directed on to the beaches themselves, that they surrendered. The senior

British general was General Fortune: he was to spend the rest of the war in captivity. The German victor was Rommel, who wrote in triumph: 'No less than twelve generals were brought in as prisoners.' That evening, contrary to what Churchill had advised, General Weygand, who had commanded the French troops in northern France – and in 1920 had advised the Poles in the defence of Warsaw – ordered the French Military Governor of Paris to declare the capital an open city. After negotiations with the Germans, the French agreed that there would be no barricades and no sniper fire – not only in Paris but, as the Germans insisted, in the towns around it, including Versailles.

When Churchill returned to France on June 13 the French government had left Paris and was at Tours. Reynaud, who had hoped to find some basis for continuing the fighting, told Churchill that France had given 'her best, her youth, her lifeblood; she can do no more'. She was entitled to make a separate peace with Germany. Churchill persuaded Reynaud to appeal to Roosevelt, and not to seek an armistice until Roosevelt had replied. Reynaud agreed, asking the President by telegram 'to declare war if you can, but in any event to send us every form of help short of an expeditionary force'.

Later that day, before Roosevelt could reply, the French government left Tours for Bordeaux. Several Ministers, led by the Minister of the Colonies, Georges Mandel, wanted to go to French North Africa and carry on the fight from there. General Weygand urged his colleagues to seek an armistice. Reynaud urged them to wait for Roosevelt's reply to his appeal. That reply came a few hours later. The American government, Roosevelt said, was doing 'everything in its power to make available to the Allied Governments the material they so urgently require, and our efforts to do still more are being redoubled'. Reynaud felt that this offer, and how it was phrased, might counter the growing feeling in favour of capitulation, provided it were published. But while Roosevelt was willing to have it made public, his Secretary of State, Cordell Hull, was not. Hull feared that publication of the offer might constitute a step on America's road to war.

Churchill still urged Reynaud to fight on, telegraphing to him on June 13 that if France did continue to resist, an American declaration of war against Germany 'must inevitably follow', and with it would be created a 'sovereign opportunity of bringing about the world-wide oceanic and economic coalition which must be fatal to Nazi domination'.

The French political leaders no longer had the will to fight, and the United States had no intention of declaring war on Germany (she was in fact never to do so; it was Germany that eventually declared war on the United States, a year and a half later). Churchill's advocacy was in vain. On the morning of June 14, German troops entered Paris. They were unopposed. That same morning twenty-two Gestapo functionaries entered the city to establish their headquarters. Among the telegrams of congratulation reaching Hitler that day was one from his new-found Soviet ally, Vyacheslav Molotov.

In the Polish city of Cracow, also under German rule, the station announcer interrupted the information about incoming and departing trains to tell those waiting on the platforms that Paris was in German hands. One train whose passengers heard the announcement as they were on their way through Cracow station had just arrived from the town of Tarnow. On board – prisoners being deported under armed guard – were 728 Poles, including twenty Jews, who were being sent to prepare the barracks at the new concentration camp at Auschwitz – not much more than an hour further west by train. Some of them had earlier been caught trying to cross the border into Slovakia and been arrested. Others were chosen in order to deprive the local Polish and Jewish communities of their leaders – among them priests and schoolteachers, including the director of the local Hebrew school. On reaching Auschwitz later that day they were sent out to work digging ditches and moving earth. None of the Jews and only 137 of the Poles were to survive the war.

Within nine months, more than three thousand Poles had been murdered at Auschwitz, or had died there during the winter of exposure and cold. The name of the camp quickly became a byword throughout Poland for cruelty and death. One of those who ensured that Poland's intellectuals were arrested, incarcerated and killed there, and elsewhere, was Dr Josef Bühler, who had received his Doctorate in law at a German university in 1932 and joined the Nazi Party a year later. In May and June, as Under-Secretary of the Governor-General of the General Government – with its headquarters in Cracow, only thirty miles from Auschwitz – Dr Bühler was in charge of a special 'pacification operation' in which 3,500 Polish intellectuals – writers, journalists, university professors, philosophers – were murdered.

At the beginning of the third week of June, Churchill still hoped to persuade the French Ministers to remain at war, but he realized that the only remaining factor that might influence them was the United States. On June 15 he appealed to Roosevelt to make a declaration of war on Germany. 'When I speak of the United States entering the war,' Churchill explained to the

President, 'I am of course not thinking in terms of an expeditionary force, which I know is out of the question. What I have in mind is the tremendous moral effect that such an American decision could produce, not merely on France, but also in the democratic countries in the world, and, in the opposite sense, on the German and Italian peoples.'

Britain's own ability to continue the war in France was collapsing. Of the 261 British fighters sent to France in the ten days up to June 15, seventy-five had been shot down or destroyed on the ground. A further 120 were unserviceable, or lacked the fuel needed to fly back to Britain. In those ten days seeking to challenge German air power in France, the Royal Air Force had lost a quarter of its fighter strength. That day, German forces entered Verdun, the fortress town whose defence in 1916 had become a symbol of unflinching resistance, whatever the human cost, and where Pétain had won his fame.

On June 16 the Germans entered Dijon, almost half way between Paris and the Mediterranean. Southwest of Paris they had reached the River Loire and were pushing rapidly towards Tours. French forces in retreat were caught up in the mass of refugees fleeing south and west; several refugee columns were machine-gunned by the Germans from the air. That day, at Bordeaux, Reynaud asked Britain to release France from their agreement not to make a separate peace. Britain had no choice but to agree.

Reynaud resigned. That evening Marshal Pétain succeeded him as Prime Minister, and immediately asked the Germans for an armistice. The Belgians had been offered only unconditional surrender. The Dutch, Norwegians and Danes had come under the full military rule of Germany. But Hitler did not wish to impose such a draconian plan on France. He was concerned that if his terms were too harsh, Pétain might be overthrown and a new French government move to North Africa and continue the war from there. This would give Britain the whole French colonial empire as a base against Germany.

Hitler therefore proposed terms that he knew Pétain could accept: defeat, but not humiliation. Germany would have control of the Channel Coast and the northern industrial regions, but not of the whole of France, or of its overseas empire. He would agree both to an armistice and to the survival of a government lead by Pétain in the central and southern part of the country: 'Unoccupied France' (known to the French as the *Zone Libre*), with the remote spa town of Vichy as its capital, and with an Empire in Africa, Asia, the Pacific and the Americas, an area almost as large as that of the British Empire, and under Vichy rule.

As the negotiations for an armistice began, the remaining British and Canadian soldiers, as well as many Polish military units, were evacuated from western France, where, if General de Gaulle had been allowed to carry out his plan, they would have formed part of a French redoubt, fighting on with their backs to the Atlantic. In eight days, 163,225 troops were taken away from the French Atlantic ports and brought safely to Britain. But when, on June 17, a German bomber attacked one of the evacuation ships, the passenger liner *Lancastria*, just as she was leaving St Nazaire, the *Lancastria* sank in a few moments, and nearly three thousand of those on board were drowned. Even as France was seeking peace, her territorial waters were witness to one of the worst maritime disasters of the war.

That day, as news was made public that France had asked for an armistice, Churchill broadcast to the British people. 'Whatever has happened in France makes no difference to our actions and purpose,' he said. 'We shall defend our Island home, and with the British Empire we shall fight on until the curse of Hitler is lifted from the brows of mankind. We are sure that in the end all will come right.'

On June 18, General de Gaulle reached Britain, where he took up the banner of defiance, calling on all Frenchmen who wanted to fight on to join him. 'Today we are crushed by the mechanized forces hurled against us,' he said, 'but we can still look to a future in which even greater mechanized forces will bring us victory.' Four years later, almost to the day, de Gaulle was to be among those taking part in the greatest mechanized amphibious landing in the history of warfare. Slowly at first, but with growing momentum, he was joined by Frenchmen already in Britain and outside Europe, and by those who came, often amid great danger, to join him from France.

One of the first well-known Frenchmen to join de Gaulle in London was Maurice Schumann, the author of an anti-Nazi book published in 1938, who was also to be among the first Frenchmen to set foot on the soil of Normandy alongside de Gaulle four years later. That summer, however, only one serving French army general joined de Gaulle: General Georges Catroux, the Governor-General of French Indo-China, who was dismissed from his post by Pétain, and subsequently condemned to death in absentia by Vichy for joining the Free French.

On the day on which de Gaulle made what seemed to most people at the time a quixotic appeal and far-fetched forecast of victory, Hitler invited Mussolini to Munich. Mussolini's son-in-law, the Italian Foreign Minister

Count Galeazzo Ciano, was present at their meeting. He was surprised to find Hitler talking of making peace with Britain. That evening Ciano wrote in his diary: 'Hitler is now the gambler who has made his big scoop, and would like to get up from the table risking nothing more.'

A few days earlier an incident had taken place in Paris which was reported in *The Times* on June 18. It was an indication of the depth to which national antagonisms could plunge. A group of French prisoners-of-war, under German guard, were being marched through Paris. They marched quietly until they saw the United States Ambassador's car, decorated with a large Stars and Stripes. The sight was too much for them. These men had fought 'the battle of civilization' against impossible odds until they had dropped from exhaustion. Seeing the flag they burst into shouts of rage and shook their fists at the once admired, but suddenly hated symbol of detached neutrality.

Yet the United States and its democratic way of life seemed all the more precious in the eyes of many of those watching the collapse of Western Europe. One of them, the German-born Socialist writer Tosco Fyvel, wrote an article that week in Britain which asked 'which way is the battle turning?':

The British Empire and America under new leadership hold the key to immense reforms and changes in society, which can release hundreds of millions of people in Asia, in Africa, in South America and let them bring their fresh contribution to a new world civilization.

Alas, Spengler was right, the critics who questioned his *Decline of the West* were wrong. Europe is physically and nervously shattered. The old nations are tired. Yet they still have so much to give; above all, it is their task to call the new world in. Can they do it?

May not the very insanity of the Nazi challenge be the means of creating the faith in a new world community of equal nations of whatever colour, race or creed? We have the modern technique. But have we what is much more difficult to preserve — the faith?

Which way? The issue is balanced on the knife-edge.

During June 18, the armistice negotiations, which had begun a day earlier, reached their foregone conclusion. In triumph, Hitler went to the clearing in the Forest of Compiègne, near the village of Rethondes, where, on 11 November 1918, the German plenipotentiaries sent from Berlin had signed the armistice ending the First World War, and a sense of humiliation had spread through Germany.

Among the foreign journalists who had been brought to witness the scene of Germany's vengeance was William Shirer, who wrote in his diary:

The time is now three-eighteen p.m. Hitler's personal flag is run up on a small standard in the centre of the opening.

Also in the centre is a great granite block which stands some three feet above the ground. Hitler, followed by the others, walks slowly over to it, steps up, and reads the inscription engraved in great high letters on that block. It says:

HERE ON THE ELEVENTH OF NOVEMBER 1918 SUCCUMBED
THE CRIMINAL PRIDE OF THE GERMAN EMPIRE,
VANQUISHED BY THE FREE PEOPLES WHICH IT
TRIED TO ENSLAVE.

Hitler reads it and Göring reads it. They all read it, standing there in the June sun and the silence.

I look for the expression on Hitler's face. I am but fifty yards from him and see him through my glasses as though he were directly in front of me. I have seen that face many times at the great moments of his life. But today! It is afire with scorn, anger, hate, revenge, triumph.

He steps off the monument and contrives to make even this gesture a masterpiece of contempt. He glances back at it, contemptuous, angry – angry, you almost feel, because he cannot wipe out the awful, provoking letters with one sweep of his high Prussian boot. He glances slowly around the clearing, and now, as his eyes meet ours, you grasp the depth of his hatred. But there is triumph there too – revengeful, triumphant hate.

Suddenly, as though his face were not giving quite complete expression to his feelings, he throws his whole body into harmony with his mood. He swiftly snaps his hands on his hips, arches his shoulders, plants his feet wide apart. It is a magnificent gesture of defiance, of burning contempt for this place now and all that it has stood for in the twenty-two years since it witnessed the humbling of the German Empire.

Finally Hitler leads his party over to another granite stone, a smaller one fifty yards to one side. Here it was that the railroad car in which the German plenipotentiaries stayed during the 1918 armistice was placed – from November 8 to 11. Hitler merely glances at the inscription, which reads: 'The German Plenipotentiaries'.

The stone itself, I notice, is set between a pair of rusty old railroad tracks, the ones on which the German car stood twenty-two years ago.

The same railway car in which the Germans had signed the armistice in 1918 had been brought out of its nearby museum building and prepared for this second signing. When the French delegates arrived for the signing ceremony, Hitler was already sitting at the very seat which, in 1918, Marshal Foch had used. But he did not remain there long. After two or three minutes, while General Keitel was reading the preamble to the armistice terms, he remained in his seat. But as Keitel began to set out the detailed terms, Hitler left the railway car, walked past a German guard of honour, and was driven away.

Three hours later the French delegates signed. 'Down the road, through the woods,' Shirer wrote in his diary, 'I could see the refugees, slowly, tiredly, filing by – on weary feet, on bicycles, on carts, a few on trucks, an endless line. They were exhausted and dazed, those walking were footsore, and they did not know yet that an armistice had been signed and that the fighting would be over very soon now.'

The ending of the fighting brought an end to yet another heavy toll of youthful death: more than 100,000 corpses lay on the battlefields of northern Europe, after a twenty-two year respite in killing. Among the dead were 92,000 Frenchmen, 7,500 Belgians and 2,900 Dutchmen. The British had lost 3,500 soldiers killed in action in Belgium and France. The German dead numbered more than 5,000. On the day that the armistice came into effect, General Rommel wrote to his wife: 'How wonderful it's all been.'

The fall of France, accomplished so swiftly by German armoured and motor-ized units, and by German air mastery, sent shock waves through all the remaining democracies. That a great nation should be laid so low in so short a time was almost unbelievable. It had happened in 1870, but that was seventy years earlier: there were few people alive who could remember that moment of trauma for France. In 1914–18 the balance had been far more evenly, and bloodily matched. In London, John F. Kennedy, the son of the American Ambassador, wrote that summer in the introduction to his book *Why England Slept*:

It was a great shock to America to wake up one morning in May and find that her supposedly invulnerable position between two large oceans was invulnerable no longer. America's armoured position showed a startling similarity to England's after Munich. Like England, we had less than one hundred modern planes. Like England, we had few anti-aircraft guns. Like England, our mechanized equipment was almost nil. And yet, like England, we had voted what we considered to be large appropriations and we had felt perfectly secure.

And, unlike Britain's leader, Stanley Baldwin, America's Roosevelt had been far ahead of public opinion in this country in his opposition to the dictatorship. Since his 'Quarantine the aggressor' speech in 1937, he has introduced larger defence estimates than Congress was prepared to accept. In fact, his 1940 Naval appropriation was cut by over 500 million dollars not four months ago. I point this out as I wish to show that we should not dismiss England's position as being merely a question of lack of leadership. Our leadership has been outspoken, yet our positions still show a remarkable similarity.

The young Kennedy warned his readers: 'A defeat of the Allies may simply be one more step towards the ultimate achievement – Germany over the world.' The position of the United States was clear in Kennedy's mind. If 'the decision' that summer went in favour of the British, he wrote, 'we must be prepared to take our part in setting up a world order that will prevent the rise of a militaristic dictatorship.' Even as Kennedy wrote these words, however, it was just as likely that the decision, and the war, would go against Britain.

On June 20 Roosevelt indicated the determination of the United States to confront the European crisis with a cross-Party Cabinet when he appointed two Republicans to senior positions: Henry L. Stimson as Secretary of War and Franklin Knox as Secretary of the Navy. On the following day, the Polish Government, which had found its first home exile in Paris, reached London, where it served as a rallying point for Poles who had managed to leave Poland, and wanted to serve the Allied cause.

Mussolini did not want to be outdone by Hitler: on June 22 Italian troops advanced along the French Riviera and occupied Menton. Britain was Hitler's only adversary still at war. That night was the first night since the opening of the German offensive in the West that no British bombers set off across the North Sea. They had carried out forty-four continuous nights of operations. But on the following day they began again, when twenty-six bombers struck at targets in the Ruhr – and three were lost.

On June 23, in the immediate aftermath of the Franco-German armistice, Hitler made his only visit to Paris, flying from his headquarters at Brûly-de-Peche to Le Bourget, and being driven around the city early in the morning to see the main monuments. After visiting Napoleon's tomb he told one of those with him: 'That was the greatest and finest moment of my life.' While in Paris, Hitler ordered two monuments which he drove past to be destroyed: the statue of General Mangin, one of the victors of 1918, and the monument to Edith Cavell, the British nurse who had been shot by the Germans in Brussels in 1915.

Three days after visiting Paris, Hitler travelled from Brûly-de-Peche to the First World War battlefields of the Western Front, where he visited his own former front-line trenches with two of his wartime comrades-in-arms. But on the drive back he was disturbed by an incident which he recalled sixteen months later, when he told one of his generals: 'I still have before me the mental picture of that woman in Lille who saw me from her window and exclaimed: "The Devil!"'

'The Devil' was master of Poland, Denmark, Norway, Belgium, Luxembourg, Holland and France. Whether Britain could fight off an invasion or survive being so isolated was not certain. 'I shall myself not enter into any peace negotiations with Hitler,' Churchill confided in the Canadian Prime Minister, William Mackenzie King, on June 24, 'but obviously I cannot bind a future government, which, if we were deserted by the United States and beaten down here, might very easily be a kind of Quisling affair ready to accept German overlordship and protection.'

Fears of a 'Quisling affair', and of possible Fifth Column activity, led on June 25 – as a result of pressure from the British Chiefs of Staff – to the internment of 50,000 German and Austrian 'enemy aliens' in Britain, and also more than 10,000 Italians. Those below the age of seventeen and over sixty were exempt. Many of the Germans and Austrians who were taken into custody were Jewish refugees from Nazi persecution who had been admitted into Britain during the previous year and a half. Most of the Italians had been living in Britain for many years, spoke English as their first language, and thought of themselves as British.

Five thousand of those arrested were interned in an unfinished housing estate at Huyton in Lancashire. Fourteen thousand were taken to internment camps on the Isle of Man, most of them established in hotels on the sea front at Douglas. The whole camp area was surrounded by barbed wire. Men

326 · DESCENT INTO BARBARISM

and women were kept separate. Of the 4,000 women interned that summer, 300 were pregnant. Among the internees – men and women – Jewish and anti-Nazi Germans were in the majority; the pro-Nazi Germans, though fewer in numbers, were more vocal and assertive. There were times in the men's camps when the hatred between Nazis and anti-Nazis led to fighting.

Some of the internees were to have distinguished careers in post war Britain, among them the Nuremberg-born industrialist Ronald Grierson, the art historian Nikolaus Pevsner, who had been a lecturer in the history of art at Göttingen when Hitler came to power, and the Czech-born historian Geoffrey Elton. Most were released from internment within a few months and allowed to undertake war work. Among the non-Jewish internees were the Italian-born Charles Forte, who established an international catering empire, and the German-born R.W. ('Tiny') Rowland, who became the head of the Lonrho business consortium.*

Britain's overriding fear following the fall of France was of a German invasion. The whole southern coast was vulnerable to a rapid attack. Barbed wire and pill-box defences were erected as swiftly as possible, but were far from adequate to hold up a determined adversary for long. On June 30 German troops landed on British soil for the first time: on the Channel Islands. They were unopposed. The Union Jack was lowered and the Swastika flag raised in its place.

Nazi terror had not been suspended for the duration of the battle for France. On June 21, while the armistice negotiations were taking place at Compiègne, a German pacifist and conscientious objector, Hermann Stöhr, who had been held in prison since the previous August and brutally tortured, was executed at Ploetzensee prison in Berlin.† In German-occupied Poland, Polish politicians, intellectuals and potential leaders were being executed every day at the Palmiry forest outside Warsaw. On June 26 the Polish Socialist leader Mieczyslaw Niedzialkowski was among those taken to the forest and shot.

---

* As the war spread, so did the number of nationalities interned on the Isle of Man. At the beginning of 1942 there were 340 Finnish and 90 Japanese civilian internees. The Japanese were from the small Japanese business community in London, including several senior officials of the Yokohama Bank.
† On 4 January 1998, the 100th anniversary of Stöhr's birth, a memorial to him was opened in Berlin, the first of its kind in Germany. A month earlier, the guilty verdict on him had been formally reversed by a Berlin court.

There was also terror of a different kind taking place in Germany. On June 30 the Ministry of the Interior announced that in psychiatric institutes throughout Germany, for the mentally ill, the schizophrenic, those totally incapable of work or those who had been hospitalized for a long time, 'under the direction of specialists, all therapeutic possibilities will be administered according to the latest knowledge'.

This deceptive language masked a harsh reality. In most cases those to be 'administered' were taken in groups of eighteen to twenty to false 'shower rooms' where they sat on benches while gas was inserted along the water pipes. Hitler's personal physician, Dr Brandt, had expressed himself satisfied with this method, as had the head of the euthanasia department of Hitler's Chancellery, Dr Brack. Mentally ill Jews were among the first to be submitted to this procedure. Even before the soothing official announcement from the Ministry of the Interior, two hundred Jewish men, women and children had been brought in six buses from a mental institution in Berlin to a special centre at Brandenburg, where they were all gassed.

Neither the power of the Nazi ideology nor the threat of the Gestapo could deter those few people who were both indignant at the euthanasia programme and brave enough to speak out against it. That summer a German Protestant pastor, Paul-Gerhard Braune, who was the administrator of a medical institution in Berlin, wrote Hitler a letter protesting against the euthanasia programme, which, he said, constituted a 'large-scale plan to exterminate thousands of human beings'. The killings 'gravely undermine the moral foundations of the whole nation' and were 'simply unworthy' of institutions dedicated to healing. Braune added that the euthanasia killings had, in his knowledge, already been extended to people who were 'lucid and responsible', and that they endangered 'the ethics of the people as a whole'. He went on to ask: 'Whom if not the helpless should the law protect?'

Pastor Braune was informed by the head of Hitler's Chancellery, Hans Lammers, that the euthanasia programme could not be stopped. A month later Braune was arrested. The arrest warrant, signed by Heydrich, charged him with having 'sabotaged measures of the régime in an irresponsible manner'. After being held for ten weeks in the Gestapo prison in Berlin, Braune was released on condition that he took no further action against the policies of the German government or the Nazi Party.

With the establishment of the Vichy government in France, Hitler was in a stronger position with regard to Britain. Pétain's rule extended throughout

French North Africa. Further east along the North African coast, Mussolini was master of Libya, effectively ensuring that, despite Britain's control of its naval bases at Gibraltar and Malta, the Mediterranean constituted a German-Italian lake.

That spring the Norwegian Vidkun Quisling had given his name to treachery and servility. By the autumn, the name of Pétain laid claim to an even more sinister betrayal. Anyone naming even the 'longest' list of those who represented the culture and civilization of France could be answered, wrote Rebecca West, 'with the single word, "Pétain"'. The closing months of 1940, she reflected, 'saw the Continent sink into a state of degradation not paralleled in any other age. In Scandinavia, in the Low Countries, and in Czechoslovakia men who had yesterday enjoyed freedom and dignity were dumb beasts of burden, to be hit in the mouth by German soldiers if they showed any recollection of their former state; and the continuing martyrdom of Poland was a warning against the sin of saying nay to evil'.

Both the Phoney War and several fighting wars were over: the only European countries still at war in the late summer of 1940 were Britain and Germany, and Britain and Italy. Behind the British war effort lay two other Allies: the British Dominions, of which Canada had already sent troops to France (they had been among those evacuated in the last days), and the United States, which, while still neutral, was steadily providing Britain with a growing mass of war supplies. Every day, and sometimes several times a day, a British merchant ship left an American East Coast port bound for Britain, carrying arms, ammunition or aircraft on board. Not only did Roosevelt insist that help should be sent, but General George C. Marshall, Chief of Staff of the United States Army, was emphatic that Britain's war effort had to be sustained.

The losses of the war at sea never abated. When the passenger liner *Arandora Star*, carrying civilian internees who were being deported from Britain to Canada, was torpedoed on July 2 off the coast of Ireland, 714 of the deportees were drowned. A Canadian destroyer rescued the remaining 868. Most of the deportees were German and Italian 'enemy aliens'. Some were Jewish refugees from Germany who had been classed as aliens. Also on board were more than a hundred German merchant seamen who had earlier been captured by the British from German ships. Among those who were drowned was a German spy, known as No. 3528 in the German Intelligence service listing. When he and his brother – a fellow-spy – had been caught by the British, his brother agreed to work for the British as a double-agent. No. 3528 refused to turn against his country, and hence found himself on board ship as a deportee.

On July 2 – the day of the sinking of the *Arandora Star* – and unknown to the British, Hitler ordered his army, navy and air forces to make preparations for an invasion 'provided that air superiority can be obtained and certain other necessary conditions fulfilled'. It was not only German air superiority, but German naval strength, that alarmed the British. Following the fall of France, the French fleet represented a powerful potential addition to the German invasion fleet. Under the armistice terms, the French were forbidden to allow their fleet to be transferred to neutral ports or to French colonial territory outside the range of German control.

The British needed to be certain that the French fleet would not be part of a German invasion armada. Churchill knew that Germany's chances of a successful invasion would be much improved if the French ships were at the disposal of the German navy. He was determined to deny the ships to the Germans. On July 3 a British plan was put into operation to seize or neutralize all French ships wherever they might be, and to prevent them being taken over by Germany.

Those French ships in British ports, and at the Egyptian port of Alexandria, were taken over without difficulty, with the exception of one French submarine in a British port on which, because of a misunderstanding, one French and one British sailor were killed. The French warships at Casablanca and Dakar decided to remain loyal to Vichy. The two battleships there were put out of action for several months by a British torpedo boat and air attack by torpedo-carrying aircraft.

The largest single concentration of French warships was at Mers-el-Kebir, near Oran. Their commander was offered four options: to sail his ships to British harbours and fight thereafter alongside the Royal Navy, to sail them to British ports and hand them over to British crews, to demilitarize them in such a way that the Germans could not use their armaments, or to scuttle them. When each of these four options was rejected, the British offered a fifth, to sail them to the French West Indies where they would either be disarmed or handed over to the United States until the end of the war. When this option was refused, the British naval force outside Mers-el-Kebir opened fire. Most of the French ships were still at anchor. Three were destroyed. Seven managed to get up steam and sail across the Mediterranean to the safety of Toulon, where they remained under the protection of Germany.

During the British bombardment more than 1,250 French sailors were killed. The former ally had become the enemy, acting in desperation in order to lessen the chances of a successful invasion. If the Royal Navy had not acted, Churchill told the House of Commons on July 4, 'mortal injury' might have been done to Britain. The British action, he reflected nine years later – while writing his memoirs – 'at any rate showed where we stood unmistakably and convinced the world that Germany had to face an indefinitely long war'.

Many French people felt betrayed: 'Oran' and 'Mers-el-Kebir' could be heard as terms of anti-British abuse in France many years later.* But Pétain's use of Oran to stir up anti-British feeling was far from universally successful inside France, any more than were his attempts to placate Germany. Five days after the sinkings, Albert Camus wrote to his wife, in criticism of Pétain:

> Cowardice and senility, that's all we are being offered. Pro-German policies, a constitution like those of totalitarian regimes, horrible fear of a revolution that will not happen, all this as an excuse for sweet-talking enemies who will crush us anyway, and to preserve privileges which are not threatened.
>
> Terrible days are in store: famine and general unemployment along with the hate they bring, which won't be prevented by an old geezer's speeches. Military dictatorship and the censor will not keep me from saying as much as I please. We must also be aware of anti-British propaganda, which hides the worst motivations.

In the immediate aftermath of Oran, the Vichy government broke off relations with Britain. But for Roosevelt – who had been Secretary of the Navy in the First World War – the action was decisive. He at last recognized the extent to which Britain was prepared to take desperate measures to avoid being overrun. With Roosevelt's personal approval, and indeed insistence, United States aid to Britain continued to cross the Atlantic, and did so in ever-increasing measure, despite the constant threat of U-boat attack.

Roosevelt had also to keep a watchful eye on the Pacific. Both Britain and the United States had cause for alarm in the Far East. With France and

---

* In 1972, while I was doing research in France, a French landowner – who had lent his chateau to Churchill in 1917 – asked (through his son) to be excused from meeting me, on the grounds that he had not spoken to any Englishman since Oran.

Holland both under German control, the future of the French and Dutch colonial possessions was much in doubt. The Dutch possessions – principally the Netherlands East Indies, were being ruled by the Dutch government in exile in London; the French possessions – principally French Indo-China, by the Vichy government. But Japan, as Germany's ally, felt that these European colonial possessions were 'enemy' territories which ought – given their non-European population – to be within the Japanese sphere.

Immediately following the establishment of the Vichy regime in France, the Japanese occupied certain strategic ports in French Indo-China, extending Japanese influence southward. In answer to this, on July 5, the United States Congress passed the Export Control Act, forbidding the export to Japan of aircraft parts, minerals and chemicals that might be used for war purposes. Similar prohibitions were later imposed for aviation fuel, lubricants, and iron and steel scrap. On July 19 Roosevelt signed the Two-Ocean Navy Expansion Act, authorizing a substantial increase in United States naval strength in both the Atlantic and the Pacific. With 358 warships already in service, and 130 under construction, the Act provided for a further 200 warships, including a hundred destroyers.

The Japanese, neutral in the European war but linked through the Axis with Germany and Italy, put pressure on Britain to close the Burma Road supply link to China. The British government wanted to resist this, and to continue to help the Chinese in their struggle to maintain control of the regions still under their rule. But the British Ambassador in Japan warned that failure to do as Japan wanted would lead to the real possibility of a Japanese attack on British possessions in the Far East, especially Hong Kong, which was vulnerable to a Japanese assault from both mainland China and the sea. Britain therefore agreed to close the road; as a country at war, facing possible invasion, she had no choice.

A new government, coming to power in Tokyo on July 22, did not make the British dilemma any easier. The Prime Minister, Prince Konoye, in explaining the policies that his government would pursue, warned that it did not rule out the use of force to attain its goal. That goal, Konoye explained nine days later, was the setting up of 'a New Order in Greater East Asia'.

The question of a German invasion of Britain was imminent. On July 6 the first German daylight bombing raid over England, on the army barracks at Aldershot, caused the death of three Canadian soldiers. Four days later, seventy German bombers struck at dockyard installations in South Wales. The incoming raiders were detected before they crossed the British coast – and even while they were still flying over their French and Belgian air-fields – by a series of twenty-one operational radar stations, the first of which had been set up three years earlier. Despite several pre-war German photo-reconnaissance flights, the most recent by a Zeppelin in August 1939, the German Air Force was unaware of the nature of the 350-feet high steel transmitting towers and 250-feet high wooden receiving masts that marked the continuous coastal radar cover from the Isle of Wight to the Orkneys.

The ability of the Royal Air Force to plot the incoming raiders was in contrast to its means of challenging them. As the attacks began, Britain possessed only 600 serviceable fighters. In order to involve the public, and to heighten the very real sense of urgency, Lord Beaverbrook issued an appeal over the radio and in the newspapers to every household in Britain for the aluminium needed in the construction of the fighters. Issued on July 10, it stated: 'We will turn your pots and pans into Spitfires and Hurricanes, Blenheims and Wellingtons. Everyone who has pots and pans, kettles, vacuum cleaners, hat pegs, coat hangers, shoe trees, bathroom fittings and household ornaments, cigarette boxes, or any other articles made wholly or in part of aluminium, should hand them over at once.'

In London, General de Gaulle was building up the Free French movement, calling on all Frenchmen and women to support him, and asking all those who could to join him. On July 14, Bastille Day, he laid a wreath at the Cenotaph in London and promised to continue the struggle until France was liberated. That day Churchill broadcast to the British and French people: 'A year ago, in Paris,' he said, 'I watched the stately parade down the Champs Elysées of the French Army and the French Empire. Who can foresee what the course of other years can bring?' There were, he added, 'vast numbers' not only in Britain but in every land 'who will render faithful service in this war, but whose names will never be known, whose deeds will never be recorded. This is a War of the Unknown Warrior, but let all strive, without failing in faith or in duty, and the dark curse of Hitler will be lifted from our age.'

On July 16 Hitler issued his secret Directive No. 16, setting out the 'preparations for a landing against England'. The plan was codenamed Operation Sea Lion. The assault was to start on August 5 with an aerial attack on all British fighter aerodromes, in order to make it impossible for the Royal Air Force – in Hitler's words – 'to deliver any significant attack against the German crossing'. On August 1, in Berlin – four days, though he did not know it, before the German attack on the British airfields was to start – William Shirer noted in his diary: 'Everyone impatient to know when the invasion of Britain will begin. I have taken two new bets offered by Nazis in the Wilhemstrasse. First, that the Swastika will be flying over Trafalgar Square by August 15. Second, by September 7.'

Hitler hoped that he could first destroy the Royal Air Force and then, with Britain defenceless, swiftly secure a British surrender, either through intensive bombing of British cities, or by bombing followed by invasion. But in the long term his main objective remained the defeat of the Soviet Union. On July 21, the day on which Stalin formally annexed the three Baltic States – Estonia, Latvia and Lithuania – Hitler told his military commanders of his intention to invade Russia. On the following day he ordered a special staff under General Erich Marcks to be set up, to develop an outline plan of attack and to submit it to him in three weeks' time.

Hitler's commanders, having only received the Sea Lion directive five days earlier, were puzzled as to how the invasion of Russia fitted in with the invasion of Britain. Hitler told them, with what several of those present regarded as a distinct lack of enthusiasm, that the plans for the invasion of Britain were still on, but that without air superiority there could be no cross-Channel landings. He added that unless the first wave of landings could be completed by mid-September, the worsening weather would make it impossible for the German Air Force to provide adequate air cover for the invading force. 'If preparations cannot be completed with certainty by the beginning of September it is necessary to consider other plans', he said.

The invasion of the Soviet Union, however, was a certainty, and plans for it made rapid progress. The date 'May 1941' soon appeared in the inner circles of Hitler's senior military advisers as the one most favoured. The head of the planning section of the German General Staff, Colonel Warlimont, was informed on July 29 that Hitler wanted the attack on Russia 'as soon as possible'. That day, the Chief of the German Naval Staff, Admiral Schniewind, warned Hitler, with regard to the invasion of Britain, that the Navy would not be ready 'to accept responsibility for any such operation during the current year'. When the Naval Commander-in-Chief, Admiral Raeder, went to see Hitler on July 21, it was to warn him that the navy's earliest preferred date for invading Britain was May 1941 – the very month, though Raeder did not know it, which Hitler had already chosen for his invasion of Russia.

On July 31 Hitler issued his Directive No. 17 'for the conduct of air and sea warfare against England'. Repeating what he had told Admiral Raeder, he stressed that a successful German air offensive was the prerequisite of a seaborne landing. The next Directive, issued on August 1, called for an 'intensification of the air war' on or after August 5: 'The Day of the Eagle'. British Intelligence learned of the code-name but did not know what it stood for.

According to Hitler's instruction, the air attacks were to be directed 'primarily against flying units, their ground installations and their supply organizations, but also against the aircraft industry, including that manufacturing anti-aircraft equipment'. But there was a warning, and potential setback that day, when a German pilot reported to Goering that the British Spitfires which he had encountered in his recent forays over England were fully as good as the German fighter planes. Goering replied tersely: 'If that is so, I will have to send my Air Inspector-General before the firing squad.' The Air Inspector-General, the First World War flying ace Ernst Udet, who was present, smiled politely.

Another insult was hurled over the radio on August 2 by an Irishman (and British passport holder), William Joyce, who, based in Germany, had made himself a fountain of German radio propaganda. Known derisively to his British listeners, on account of his nasal accent, as Lord Haw-Haw, Joyce spoke mockingly over Radio Bremen: 'The glorious Royal Air Force was too busy dropping bombs on fields and graveyards in Germany to have any time available for the Battle of France.'

The British were in no mood to be abused, or even to be wooed. When, on the day of Joyce's broadcast, King Gustav of Sweden secretly offered his services to both Hitler and King George VI with a view to setting up contacts for a negotiated peace, George VI noted in his diary: 'Until Germany is prepared to live peaceably with her neighbours in Europe, she will always be a menace. We have got to get rid of her aggressive spirit, her engines of war, and the people who have been taught to use them.'

British preparations against invasion, supervised with vigilance by Churchill, were continuous. On August 3 a large contingent of Canadian troops arrived in Britain. Among them were several United States citizens who had volunteered for service. On the following day a draft of Australian troops arrived, followed two days later by a contingent of pilots and aircrew from Southern Rhodesia. None of this boded well for Hitler's invasion plans, if indeed he still believed Goering's Air Force could really create the necessary conditions for a landing that would be unopposed from the air.

The German air offensive against British air targets that had been meant to begin on August 5 was postponed for four days because of bad weather. But on August 5 Hitler was presented with the plan which, less than three weeks earlier, he had asked a special staff under General Marcks to draw up – for the invasion of Russia.

The postponed German air offensive against Britain was launched on August 9. That day – the first day of what became known as the Battle of Britain – three hundred German aircraft flew over South-East England and the Channel coast. Their targets were the radar stations at Portland Bill and Weymouth which enabled the British to 'see' the raiders in time to intercept them. In the battle that followed with the British fighters that were – as a result of these very radar stations – sent to intercept them, eighteen German aircraft were shot down. On August 11 and again on August 12 there were further attacks on radar targets. Then, on August 13, with Britain's radar defences still essentially intact, the German Air Force launched 'The Day of the Eagle'. On that day, wave after wave of German aircraft flew in search of the air stations and aircraft factories which they had been ordered to destroy, and to destroy quickly, in order that the invasion forces could follow.

The Day of the Eagle launched Germany's fourth major military campaign in less than a year. But unlike the three previous series of attacks – on Poland, on Norway and Denmark, and on France and the Low Countries – this one had to begin as an air attack without any ground-based advances. From the outset the German pilots – to whom the warning given to Goering had not been passed – were surprised by the skill of the British pilots who opposed them. Of the 1,485 German aircraft which crossed the English Channel that day, forty-five were shot down, for the loss of only thirteen British fighters. Almost all the German aircrew were killed, or captured where they had parachuted or crash-landed. Only seven British pilots were killed, the rest crash-landing or parachuting to safety on British soil.

On the second day, August 14, poor weather limited the number of the attacking aircraft to five hundred. Even so, seventy of them, an even larger number than on the previous day, were brought down, for the loss of twenty-seven British fighters. Once again, the British planes were shot down mostly over British soil, giving those pilots who baled out, or who survived the crash landings – as most of them did – a chance to fly again, and in most cases to fly again the next day, or even the same day.

Encouraging news reached Britain on August 14 from across the Atlantic, when Roosevelt agreed to give Britain fifty American destroyers, in exchange for the use by the United States of British naval bases in the Caribbean and western Atlantic. August 14 was also the day on which General Halder recorded in his diary that the German Army was looking for a site in East Prussia which could serve as Hitler's headquarters during the invasion of the Soviet Union.

August 15 was the third consecutive day of the German air offensive against British airfields and installations. This was the day on which the German Air Force was determined to put its strength and tactics to the crucial test. If the attack that day could succeed, then it might still be possible to mount an invasion before the autumn storms. In all, 520 German bombers and 1,270 fighters crossed the English Channel between 11.30 in the morning and 6.30 in the evening.

Seventy-five German aircraft were shot down on August 15, for a British loss of thirty-four. It was a German rate of loss which could not be long sustained. In three days of air combat the Germans had lost 190 machines. But the Germans had not been without successes of their own: in the first three days of the German attacks, a hundred British aircraft had been destroyed on the ground, one-sixth of the available machines.

Despite the severe setback on August 15, Goering gave orders for a fourth consecutive day of full-scale aerial attack. On August 16, however, an equally heavy raid was similarly mauled, even though it succeeded in destroying forty-seven British aircraft on the ground at Brize Norton and thirteen at airfields elsewhere in southern England. Churchill went to the Operations Room of No. 11 Group Fighter Command, at Uxbridge, to watch the battle as it was being plotted minute by minute on maps set out on tables in the centre of the room. The head of Churchill's Defence Staff, General Ismay, later recalled: 'There had been heavy fighting throughout the afternoon; and at one moment every single squadron in the group was engaged; there was nothing in reserve, and the map table showed new waves of attackers crossing the coast. I felt sick with fear.'

The German attackers were challenged in the air and again badly mauled. At the very moment when no extra British planes were available to go up against them, no further wave of attackers crossed the coast. It had been the closest imaginable margin of safety – and survival. That night, 150 British bombers made a raid deep into Germany, bombing oil targets at Jena,

Leuna and Augsburg, as well as industrial installations in the Ruhr and at Frankfurt-on-Main. During the raid, seven British aircraft were lost.

In the skies of southern England the Battle of Britain was becoming a battle of wills as well as of aircraft and their pilots. Hitler and the German High Command were prepared to risk extraordinary losses in the hope of being able to destroy Britain's capacity to fight on in the air. Churchill and the British Chiefs of Staff were equally prepared to send even the last available fighter into the sky to shoot down the attackers, while at the same time continuing the bomber offensive against Germany without respite. But on August 17 the Germans were forced to reduce the level of their attack. Some of their fighters, the Stukas, had proved too vulnerable and were withdrawn. That night, 105 British bombers flew over the Channel and the North Sea in the same direction that the German daytime raiders had returned, striking at five separate airfield targets in northern Germany.

During August 17 a secret tally was made of all those British servicemen and civilians who had been killed since the first day of the war. By far the largest category were the sailors, 8,266 in all. In Norway and France, 4,400 British soldiers had fallen in action. In Britain, 729 civilians had been killed in German air attacks. The number of British pilots and air crew killed, or missing and believed killed, was 3,851.

Acts of courage were widely reported, and at Churchill's urging were rapidly given official recognition. The first Military Medal to be won in Britain by a member of the Women's Auxiliary Air Force (the WAAF) was awarded to Sergeant Elizabeth Mortimer. When German aircraft bombed Biggin Hill airfield on August 18, and before the 'All Clear' siren sounded, she picked up a bundle of red flags and ran all over the airfield marking the site of each unexploded bomb, thus enabling Hurricane and Spitfire pilots returning from combat to land safely. Her citation stated that she had 'displayed exceptional courage and coolness which had a great moral effect on all those with whom she came in contact'.

Elizabeth Mortimer never married: the fighter pilot to whom she was engaged was killed in action.

On August 19 there was no German air attack on Britain. 'They are making a big mistake', Churchill told one of his Secretariat that night, 'in giving us a respite.' Speaking in the House of Commons on the following day he told of how the gratitude 'of every home in our island, in our Empire, and indeed throughout the world, except in the abodes of the guilty, goes out to the British airmen who, undaunted by odds, unwearied in their constant challenge and mortal danger, are turning the tide of the war by their prowess and by their devotion'.

Churchill went on to say, of those airmen: 'Never in the field of human conflict was so much owed by so many to so few.' In five days of intense air attack, Hitler had failed to fulfil the one condition that he had set for the invasion of Britain – the breaking of Britain's air power. At the same time, the British bomber offensive against Germany, although not on a very large scale, was continuous. Hardly a night passed without a British bombing raid against German military and industrial targets. During his speech on August 20 Churchill warned that British bombers would continue to strike at German military industries and communications, as well as at the German air bases and storage depots used to launch air attacks on Britain, and would strike 'upon an ever-increasing scale until the end of the year, and may in another year attain dimensions hitherto undreamed of'. The bombing of Germany, Churchill declared, if not the shortest, was 'most certain of all the roads to victory'.

Churchill did not know that Hitler was already deep in his preparations for an attack on Russia. He knew however that such an attack was likely, and wanted Hitler to know that Britain would not stand idly by. 'Even if Nazi legions stood triumphant on the Black Sea,' he said in his speech on August 20, 'or indeed the Caspian, even if Hitler were at the gates of India, it would profit him nothing if at the same time the entire economic and scientific apparatus of German war power lay shattered and pulverized at home.'

Yet another German air raid on a massive scale was launched against Britain on August 23. The main targets were aircraft factories and oil storage tanks. One flight of bombers, twelve in all, flying off course, dropped its bombs on London. Nine civilians were killed. Two nights later British bombers struck at Germany. Their target was a group of armaments factories north of Berlin. Some of the hundred aircraft, confused by the low cloud ceiling, flew off course, dropping their bombs on the centre of Berlin. Although no Germans were killed, and only two people slightly injured, a pattern of the bombing of city centres had been established – by accident. William Shirer was an eye-witness on the ground of the Berlin raid. 'The concentration of anti-aircraft fire was the greatest I've ever witnessed,' he wrote in his diary. 'It provided a magnificent, a terrible sight. Not a plane was shot down; not one was even picked up by the searchlights, which flashed back and forth frantically throughout the night.'

Some of the British bombs had fallen by mistake on the large farms owned by the city of Berlin in the countryside south of the city. This led Berliners to joke: 'Now they are trying to starve us out.' Three nights later another British raid on Berlin killed ten civilians, including four men and two women who, Shirer noted in his diary, 'unwisely, were watching the fireworks from a doorway'.

On August 30 the German Air Force made yet another attempt to destroy British air power, and to enable the sea-borne invasion to begin. Eight hundred German aircraft took part. Their main targets were the aerodromes from which the British fighters had caused such high losses to the attackers on previous raids since The Day of the Eagle three weeks earlier. The British fighter pilots rose to intercept the attackers in a combat that was often watched from the ground in mesmerized awe. One of the airmen, Richard Hillary, wrote: 'The fighter pilot's emotions are those of the duellist – cool, precise, impersonal. He is privileged to kill well. For if one must either kill or be killed, as now one must, it should, I feel, be done with dignity.' The squadron in which Hillary served first went into action on August 27. A week later he was shot down, suffering terrible burns.

Over Biggin Hill, one of the main airfields attacked on August 30, seventeen German aircraft were shot down for the loss of only a single British plane. The British pilot, parachuting to safety, returned later that day to the battle. That night German bombers dropped incendiary bombs on London. A new phase of the air battle had begun: the London Blitz. The main targets of the German bombers were no longer the airfields and aircraft factories, but the capital city itself: its docks, railway yards and railway stations, and factories.

As the night bomber raids over London increased in frequency, Hitler and Goering hoped that British morale could be broken, even if the Royal Air Force could not be reduced to powerlessness. On September 4, Hitler reduced an audience in Berlin to spasms of laughter when, talking about the much-mooted invasion of Britain, he said: 'In England they're filled with curiosity and keep asking, "Why doesn't he come?" Be calm. Be calm. He's coming! He's coming!'

The first full-scale bomber offensive against British cities was launched on September 7. Goering went in his special train to the Pas-de-Calais to take personal charge of the attack. Three hundred German bombers, escorted by six hundred fighters, flew in two waves over the London docks. Many bombs fell on residential areas around the docks and 448 civilians were killed. A second raid on the following day against London's electricity power stations and railway lines met tenacious British fighter opposition: 88 of the 200 incoming attackers were shot down. The British fighter losses were twenty-one. A second night raid the following night brought more deaths, more German losses, and the first signs of widespread unease among the population under bombardment.

In the first week of the London Blitz 1,286 people were killed. Polish, Czech and Canadian pilots joined the British defenders in inflicting losses on each incoming raid. But the raids continued. So also did the British air raids on Berlin. During an attack on the German capital on the night of September 9 one bomb fell in Dr Goebbels' garden.

It was not only London that was subjected to German air bombardment. In September the docks in Liverpool, Cardiff and Swansea were also attacked. The German bombing of British cities had become Hitler's main warmaking effort. The civilian population was subjected to an intensity of aerial bombardment, over a longer period of time, unsurpassed even during the German and Italian bombing of Republican-held Spanish cities two years earlier, or the Japanese bombing of Chinese cities the previous year. A year later, while the bombing of Britain, though lessening, still continued, Rebecca West wrote, of the civilians under bombardment in the autumn of 1940:

> . . . though their knees knocked together, though their eyes were glassy with horror, they joked from sunset, when the sirens unfurled their long flag of sound, till dawn, when the light showed them the annihilation of dear and familiar things.
>
> But they were not merely stoical. They worked, they fought like soldiers, but without the least intoxication that comes of joy in killing, for they could only defend themselves, they could not in anyway attack their assailants. In this sobriety, men and women went out and dug among the ruins for the injured while bombs were still falling, and they turned on fire, which it is our nature to flee, and fought it at close range, night after night, week after week, month after month.

On September 15 German bombers again attacked London, causing massive damage. The docks at Southampton were also a target during the day. That night Bristol, Cardiff, Liverpool and Manchester were attacked. In all, 230 German bombers and 700 fighters took part in the battle. Fifty-six were shot down, a rate of loss that could not long be sustained. The Royal Air

Force also suffered losses, but less than half those of the Germans. Twenty-three British planes were shot down.

On September 16 President Roosevelt signed the Selective Training and Service Act, which established peace-time military service for the first time in American history. Almost all the Democratic Senators and Congressmen supported it, as did half the Republicans: the final draft was passed by the Senate by 47 votes to 25 and by the House of Representatives by 232 to 124, majorities large enough to send a clear message to the American people that the situation was serious. Under the Act, sixteen million American men between the ages of twenty-one and thirty-five were liable to be taken away from their work and careers for a year's military training and military service.

On the day the Selective Training and Service Act became law in the United States, the German Air Force used a new method of aerial warfare over Britain – the magnetic mine – intended to intensify the terrors of the Blitz, and to create panic. Hitherto these mines had been dropped into the sea by aircraft, where their magnetic properties attracted them to the hulls of ships, with devastating effect. But an antidote had been found for them in the early months of 1940 – a metal coil around the ship that de-magnetized the hull and rendered the mines useless.

By the summer of 1940 a new use was found for the magnetic mines: they were dropped from aircraft by parachute on to cities. Known as land mines, they drifted to the ground and could not be directed on any particular target, but they caused considerable damage, especially in residential districts. News of their existence was kept secret by the British Government for almost four years. Those who knew the nature of the weapon feared that the use of such an indiscriminate method of destruction and the killing of civilians – the mines were clearly not being directed against docks or railways or factories – might, if it became known, create the very panic the Germans intended.

Britain tried to fight back elsewhere, encouraging de Gaulle, that September, to attack the port of Dakar and wrest it from Vichy control, in an attempt to win French West Africa to the Allied cause. The attempt failed. Unexpectedly, the Vichy authorities at Dakar put up a fight, and de Gaulle's forces were forced to withdraw. In North Africa, Italian soldiers crossed from Libya into Egypt, creating Britain's first 'front line' since the fall of France and introducing the words 'Western Desert' into the vocabulary of the war.

On September 13 a pre-war ocean liner, the 11,000-ton *City of Benares*, had set sail in a convoy from Liverpool. On board were two hundred passengers, leaving the perils of the Blitz for the United States. The passengers included English, Canadian, Hungarian, French, Indian and Polish citizens, as well as several anti-Nazi Germans, and ninety-three British children between the ages of five and fifteen. The children, who were accompanied by an escort of nurses, teachers and a clergyman, were part of a British government scheme to evacuate children to the United States and Canada.

Four days after leaving Liverpool, the *City of Benares* was judged to be out of the danger zone and was able to leave the convoy – which had hitherto seriously restricted her speed – and to proceed westward. Soon afterwards, she was struck by a torpedo, and began to sink. One of the Polish passengers, F.B. Czarnomski, a diplomat who had fled twice from the onrush of war – from Poland in September 1939 and from Paris in May 1940 – later described the sight of the ship as he looked back from his lifeboat:

I saw that the upper deck was brilliantly lit by reflector lamps and noticed that she was settling down heavily by the stern. Suddenly the lights went out, the bows rose high out of the water, and then the huge hull vanished under the surface. All that we could do now was to find one of the other ships as quickly as possible; but we could see nothing.

After a while we were approached by several of our shipmates who were clinging to a raft. We took them into our boat, and from them we learned that two of the lifeboats had capsized on being lowered.

For five days this lifeboat was at sea. On the fifth day a ship was spotted on the horizon, but its crew did not see the lifeboat and steamed away. On the seventh day, one of the crewmen fell into the sea and drowned. That evening, the oldest of the children, a fifteen year old boy, was 'seized with a fit of madness' and had to be tied down. On the eighth day, after their small supply of water had run out, a flying boat spotted them, and summoned a warship to rescue them.

A second lifeboat had been found after twenty-four hours. Several of those in it had died of exhaustion. In all, seventy-seven of the children and seventy-two of the adults on board the *City of Benares* when it was hit had died, either when the ship went down or at sea. Fifteen children and eighteen adults were saved. On learning of the disaster Churchill told his Cabinet colleagues that he was 'anxious that the scheme for evacuating children overseas should now be discontinued.' This was accepted without dissent. No more sea evacuations took place.*

In Roumania, the coming to power on September 6 of General Ion Antonescu, the Minister of War, initiated all the ferocity of a Fascist regime. Roumania, despite admiration for Hitler's achievements, had been the loser in a series of territorial changes. Following the Nazi-Soviet Pact, she had lost Bessarabia and the northern Bukovina to the Soviet Union. She had also lost southern Dobruja to Bulgaria, and been forced, under the second Vienna Award, to give up two-fifths of Transylvania to Hungary. Following these considerable – and in many ways humiliating – losses, and Antonescu's rise to power, King Carol abdicated and went into exile. He was succeeded as ruler by Crown Prince Michael. Four months later Antonescu proclaimed himself 'Conducator' (Leader) following in the style of Führer and Duce. The new regime used as its weapon of control and terror the Iron Guard organization which had hitherto been largely kept under strict control.

Within hours of Antonescu coming to power, leading democratic politicians were arrested and murdered, and hundreds of Jews were killed in the streets of Bucharest by members of the Iron Guard. Between September 13 and October 5, all Jewish employees were removed from public office and private enterprises. Jewish professors and students were barred from attending courses at Roumanian universities. The Director General of the Bucharest Gas and Electricity Company, Martin Bercovici, himself a Jew, who was in charge of the electrification of the whole country, was among those dismissed from his post. Watching with alarm the sudden ending of educational opportunities for Jewish pupils, he managed to obtain permission from the authorities to open a Jewish polytechnic.

Despite continual pressures and harassment, Bercovici's school, which opened on December 11, survived the war. Within two years it had fifty professors and five hundred students. With complete disregard for his own safety, as the war spread Bercovici would gather young Jews from the streets. Many of them had fled from Moldavia, where deportation, labour camp and death awaited those who remained.

In German-occupied lands, tyranny and terror continued to go hand in hand. In Belgium a punishment camp was opened by the SS in Fort Breen-

---

* The author (then not quite four) having travelled from Liverpool on the *Duchess of Bedford* a few weeks before the *City of Benares* set sail, was already in Canada.

donk, on the outskirts of Antwerp. The number of Germans and Poles in concentration camps that autumn exceeded 100,000. On September 23, unknown except to a small circle within the SS, Himmler signed a decree ordering that 'all teeth, gold fillings and bridgework should be taken out of the mouths of camp inmates'. This was the crudely-named Operation Tooth. On arrival at a camp, new prisoners were examined for dental gold and a note taken of the location of the teeth – and of the estimated monetary yield. A small tattoo was then made on the upper left arm of the prisoners, for easy identification in due course in the camp morgue. The gold collected was delivered to the Reichsbank and credited to the SS.

In October, in the German-occupied countries of Europe, Alfred Rosenberg established a special task force to seize and transport valuable cultural objects to Germany. More than five thousand paintings, including works by Rembrandt, Rubens, Goya, Gainsborough and Fragonard, were removed from museums and private homes, as were thousands of porcelain objects, bronzes, old coins, icons and seventeenth- and eighteenth-century furniture. At Frankfurt, Rosenberg set up the Institute for the Investigation of the Jewish Question, declaring in his opening speech: 'Germany will regard the Jewish Question as solved only after the last Jew has left the Greater German living space.' Meanwhile, so-called 'ownerless Jewish property' could be taken at will, from hundreds of Jewish homes and shops in France, Belgium and Holland.

On October 3 the 150,000 Jews of Warsaw, some of whom lived in every district of the capital, were ordered to move to the predominantly Jewish district of the city, which was to be walled in, forcing more than 400,000 Jews to live in the already crowded space where 250,000 had lived before. Those Jews who had to move to this specially created 'ghetto' could take with them only what they could carry, or load on handcarts. The rest of their possessions, the heavy furniture, home furnishings, stoves, ovens, shop furnishings, stock, had all to be abandoned. More than 100,000 Poles, living in the area now designated a 'ghetto', had likewise to move, and to abandon all their possessions except those which they could carry with them.

'Black melancholy reigned in our courtyard,' the historian Emanuel Ringelblum, who lived in the Jewish quarter of Warsaw, wrote in his diary when details of the move to the ghetto were made public. On the following day Jews from the suburb of Praga, across the river from Warsaw, were expelled from their homes and ordered into the new ghetto. 'Today was a terrifying day,' Ringelblum wrote, 'the sight of Jews moving their old rags and bedding made a horrible impression. Though forbidden to remove their furniture, some Jews did it.'

Tosha Bialer, a Jewish woman who eventually managed, as an American citizen, to leave the ghetto, wrote (in *Collier's* magazine two years later), of the establishment of the ghetto: 'The narrow, crooked streets of the most dilapidated section of Warsaw were crowded with pushcarts, their owners going from house to house asking the inevitable question: Have you room? The sidewalks were covered with their belongings. Children wandered, lost and crying, parents ran hither and yon seeking them, their cries drowned in the tremendous hubbub of half a million uprooted people.'

At first, humiliation was the theme of German behaviour within the ghetto. At one street corner, Ringelblum saw German soldiers tearing up paper into small pieces, scattering the pieces in the mud, ordering Jews to pick the pieces up, and then 'beating them as they stoop over'. On another street a German soldier 'stopped to beat a Jewish pedestrian' and then ordered him 'to lie down and kiss the pavement'. A 'wave of evil', Ringelblum commented, 'rolled whole over the whole city'.

'The war is won!' Hitler told Mussolini when they met at the Brenner Pass on October 4. 'The rest is only a question of time.' The British people, Hitler explained, were under 'an inhuman strain'. 'Only the hope of American and Russian aid, he commented, 'kept them in the war.'

The British hope of American aid was real: on October 12, speaking in Dayton, Ohio, Roosevelt made a public pledge. 'Our decision is made,' he said. 'We will continue to pile up our defence and our armaments. We will continue to help those who resist aggression, and who now hold the aggressors far from our shores.' Roosevelt added that the courage of the British people under air bombardment would be 'perpetual proof that democracy, when put to the test, can show the stuff of which it is made'.

Hitler was confident that the British would fail the test – to which he was putting them with relentless severity – telling another Italian visitor two days after Roosevelt's speech: 'Let's wait and see what London looks like two or three months from now. If I cannot invade them, at least I can destroy the whole of their industry.' On the following night, October 15, German bombers caused nine hundred fires in London, and the deaths of four hundred Londoners. By the end of October, 6,334 British civilians had been killed in that one month, of whom 643 were children under sixteen. The poet Roy Fuller began his poem *October 1940*:

No longer can guns be cancelled by love,
Or by rich paintings in the galleries;
The music in the icy air cannot live,
The autumn has blown away the rose.

Can we be sorry that those explosions
Which occurring in Spain and China reached us as
The outer ring of yearning emotions,
Are here as rubble and fear,
as metal and glass . . .

Despite the daily battering of British cities, and the daily loss of civilian life in them, not everything went as Hitler intended. When he met General Franco at Hendaye on October 23, on the border with Spain, he was angered by Franco's refusal to enter into an alliance with Germany, or to allow German troops to pass through Spain should they decide to attack the British in Gibraltar. Had not German airmen, soldiers and munitions been an important factor in Franco's victory scarcely a year earlier? But Franco was immovable, so much so that Hitler later told Mussolini: 'I would rather have three or four teeth extracted than go through that again.'

On his way back to Germany, Hitler stopped at Montoire, just inside the German-occupied zone of France, to try to persuade Marshal Pétain to join in the war against Britain in the future 'in the most effective way possible'. Pétain proved as obdurate — or as cautious — as Franco. He even refused Hitler's request to use Vichy troops to drive General de Gaulle from his Free French base of operations that, following the failed attack on Dakar, had been set up in French Equatorial Africa. Those whom Hitler had imagined to be his friends did not want to be his allies, or to take on the enmity of Britain — even when the British cities were being bombed so heavily night after night. Hitler's failure to launch his invasion had given many of his potential supporters reason to pause.

There was no pause inside Germany in the anti-Jewish measures that had begun more than seven years earlier, and were accelerating as a result of Germany's new territorial conquests and control. Starting on October 22, a total of 6,500 German Jews from the western provinces of Baden, the Saar and the Palatinate were taken from their homes, allowed to bring with them only what they could carry, and sent by train across France. Their destination was a number of internment camps in the French Pyrenees, under control of Vichy French police and guards. All the property of those deported – their homes, furniture, businesses, shops and possessions – was seized by the local German authorities. These Jews came from some of the oldest Jewish communities in Germany. Two thousand of them were from Mannheim, where the first synagogue was built in 1664. Thirty-four were from Alt Breisach, where the first Jews had settled in 1301.

There were four camps in the Pyrenees to which the deportees were sent: Gurs, Noé, Récébédou and Rivesaltes. Gurs was the largest. Some of those interned there had been living in the Palatinate but were born outside Germany: several in Warsaw. One deportee, Lieba Lust, had been born in 1875 in the then Austro-Hungarian frontier town of Auschwitz: she died at Gurs, six weeks after deportation, three weeks before her sixty-fifth birthday.

'From this camp Gurs,' a German Protestant pastor, Heinrich Grüber, later recalled, 'we had – in Berlin – very bad news, even worse news than reached us from Poland. They did not have any medicaments or any sanitary arrangements whatsoever.' Grüber had tried to go to Gurs, to do what he could to ameliorate the situation, but instead he was arrested, and sent as a prisoner first to Sachsenhausen and then to Dachau.

Tens of thousands of Indian troops were serving under the British flag, and millions of Indians were being asked to help the war effort, but on October 13 the Indian National Congress, in its desire for independence from Britain, adopted a plan for nation-wide civil disobedience. Individual congressmen, personally selected by Gandhi, launched the campaign by shouting the slogan: 'It is wrong to help the British war effort with men or money: the only worthy effort is to resist all war with non-violent resistance.'

The British reacted by arresting the Congress leaders: Nehru was sentenced to four years in prison. As the protests against supporting the war effort spread throughout the country, 14,000 Indians were arrested and jailed.

On October 28 another war zone opened, when Mussolini ordered Italian troops based in Albania – which Italy had occupied a year and a half earlier – to invade Greece. Greece was the fifteenth European country to have been annexed, invaded or attacked in just over two years.*

---

* The other fourteen were (by Germany) Austria, Czechoslovakia, Poland, Denmark, Norway, Holland, Belgium, Luxembourg and France; (by the Soviet Union) Finland, Estonia, Lithuania and Latvia; (by Italy) Albania.

Mussolini had not told Hitler in advance of his plan to invade Greece. Instead, he greeted Hitler on his arrival in Florence that day with the triumphant words: 'Fuhrer, we are on the march!' Hitler was appalled, recognizing at once the serious strategic mistake of attacking a country that could well resist successfully, and even be helped from outside if her independence were really at risk. Only Roosevelt gave Hitler some comfort when, two days after the Italian invasion of Greece, he told an audience in Boston, as part of his campaign to be re-elected the following month: 'I have said this before, but I shall say it again and again and again: Your boys are not going to be sent into any wars.'

Roosevelt said nothing in his speech about the secret Anglo-American Agreement signed six days earlier – on October 24 – whereby his administration agreed 'to equip fully and maintain' ten additional British Divisions, their weapons to be manufactured in the United States, and everything to be ready to send them into combat in time for 'the campaign of 1942'. The agreement also contained a pledge by the United States that it would 'ensure priority' for the material needed to maintain these divisions in the field. Roosevelt told the head of the British Purchasing Mission in Washington, Arthur Purvis, that henceforth his 'rule of thumb' would be to make munitions available to Britain on a fifty-fifty basis with the United States.

Half of all munitions produced in the United States would go to Britain, irrespective of America's own defence needs. Roosevelt would also requisition for Britain, as a result of the continuing high U-boat sinkings of British merchant ships, seventy American 'war boats' that had been kept in store since the end of the First World War, and for which he, as Secretary for the Navy, had been responsible. In addition, the United States would build for Britain three hundred new merchant ships. As Britain's financial resources, and in particular her gold reserves, were rapidly dwindling, Roosevelt proposed that the United States would pay for the construction of these vessels, which she would then 'rent' to Britain. A similar system – which later became known as Lend-Lease – might also be applied for arms purchases.

In a single commitment, Roosevelt had extended to Britain the means of survival. Within two weeks, on November 5, he was re-elected to an unprecedented third term as President, a matter of considerable relief to the British government. His rival was a wealthy Republican businessman, Wendell Willkie, who, while offering in foreign policy 'all aid to the Democracies short of war', attacked what he called the 'socialism' of Roosevelt's domestic policies. The vote was 25,694,747 to 21,427,832. Under the American electoral system Roosevelt carried thirty-nine of the forty-eight States.

On the day of Roosevelt's re-election a British convoy of thirty-eight merchant ships was making its way across the Atlantic. It was attacked by the German pocket battleship *Admiral Scheer*. Nine of the merchant ships were sunk before the escorting armed merchant cruiser, *Jervis Bay*, was able to engage the *Admiral Scheer* while the convoy made its escape. During the last phase of the battle *Jervis Bay* was hit and set on fire. After two hours she blew up and sank. Only sixty-five of her crew of 254 survived.

That November, Britain continued the bomber offensive over Germany. On November 8, the anniversary of the Beer Hall putsch in Munich in 1923, Hitler had to bring his celebratory speech forward an hour to avoid it being disrupted by a British bombing raid which would have forced all the celebrants to retire to the air raid shelters.

A British pilot who took part in that night's raid on Munich broadcast his impressions on the BBC the following evening. His target had been a railway marshalling yard 'It was so light that we could see houses and streets quite clearly,' he said. 'It was a bomb-aimer's dream of a perfect night. Altogether we stayed for twenty minutes checking on our target. All the way down I could see those big, black locomotive sheds coming up in front us. And the front gunner was shooting out searchlights . . .'

There was also a British bombing raid over Berlin that night, in which 169 aircraft took part. Eleven Berliners were killed, but twenty-one of the attacking aircraft were lost, most of them shot down by German anti-aircraft fire. This rate of loss – 12.4 per cent – was judged too high, and it was to be more than a year before the next large-scale raid on the German capital. Also bombed that night were Cologne, Mannheim and Essen, by a further 150 bombers. Another sixteen aircraft were lost, many of them crashing into the North Sea because of bad weather conditions. On the following night, during a raid by 103 aircraft on Hamburg when thirteen civilians were killed – and only one bomber was lost – great disappointment was caused to the citizens because the Post Office store containing express parcels was set on fire. It was film change-over day, and the entire stock of new films for the Hamburg area was destroyed.

Within a week of the Italian invasion of Greece, the Greeks halted the Italian advance scarcely fifty miles inside their border. They then launched a counter-offensive that within five months would drive the Italians back across the border and deep into Albania, almost to the capital, Tirana. From the outset of the Greek conflict, Britain – which had signed a guarantee of support for Greece in April 1939 – tried to give what small help it could, sending several hundred troops, a squadron of fifteen aircraft, some anti-aircraft guns and a coastal defence battery from its forces stationed in Egypt – forces which were themselves facing an Italian army which was entrenched sixty miles inside the Egyptian border.

The re-election of Roosevelt, despite his commitment not to send any American 'boys' to fight overseas, was a tremendous relief for the British and the Greeks – the two European nations that were then under attack – and also to the many captive nations, all of whom recognized that their survival and victory – in the case of Britain and Greece – and their liberation – in the case of the captive peoples – must depend upon an eventual direct military confrontation between the United States and Germany. The equipment which Roosevelt had already arranged to be sent to Britain, and the British determination that much more such equipment should be secured, provided the one realistic answer to those who could not see how Hitler could ever be defeated. This was even the perspective in Germany, where William Shirer wrote in his diary on November 6, when news of Roosevelt's re-election reached Berlin: 'It is a resounding slap for Hitler and Ribbentrop and the whole Nazi regime' and he went on to explain:

> I'm told that since the abandonment for this fall of the invasion of Britain, Hitler has more and more envisaged Roosevelt as the strongest enemy in his path to world power, or even to victory in Europe. And there is no doubt that he and his henchmen put great hope in the defeat of the President . . .
>
> But now the Nazis face Roosevelt for another four years – face the man whom Hitler has told a number of people is more responsible for keeping up Britain's resistance to him than any other factor in the war except Winston Churchill. No wonder there were long faces in the Wilhelmstrasse to-night when it became certain that Roosevelt had won.

Roosevelt did not wait more than forty-eight hours after his re-election before making his next commitment to Britain. On November 7 he spoke at the White House with Arthur Purvis about what equipment Britain would need in order to put into the field – as Churchill hoped – a fifty-five

Division army, the minimum needed to contemplate landing an invasion and liberation force in Northern Europe.

Over southern Italy, twenty-four British torpedo-bombers carried out a daring raid on November 11, when, from their aircraft carriers, they attacked the Italian fleet at anchor in Taranto harbour, sinking one battleship and badly damaging two, and also damaging two Italian cruisers. The surprise of the attack, its comprehensive results, and the effective use of torpedo-bombers, was noted in Japan by the Commander-in-Chief of the Japanese Combined fleet, Admiral Yamamoto, who saw how he could use exactly that technique to eliminate American naval predominance in the Pacific. Within a year and a month, under Yamamoto's guidance, the Japanese were to effect a similar, and far more destructive such coup at Pearl Harbor.

The United States Secretary of the Navy, Frank Knox, also saw the dangers that an emulation of the Battle of Taranto would pose for the United States, noting for his naval advisers: 'The success of the British aerial attack against ships at anchor suggest that precautionary measures be taken to protect Pearl Harbor against surprise attack in the event that war should break out between the United States and Japan. The greatest danger will come from aerial torpedoing.' There could not have been greater clarity and greater foresight. But the alarm bells sounded by Knox failed to lead to any preventative action taking place.

On November 13, Hitler took an important step forward in his plans for the invasion of Russia. He told Goering – whose bombers were still causing nightly havoc over Britain – that the long-term needs of the war against Britain required Germany to have control of the Soviet oilfields in the Caucasus. The war against Russia could be won in a few months, Hitler declared, and he expected Goering to prepare his air forces for a massive eastern offensive beginning on May 1.

Hitler's army commanders were also given their instructions: one third of all Germany's divisions were to be motorized, giving a total of seventy armoured and motorized divisions, far in excess of what the Soviet Union possessed. Ironically, on the day that Hitler was setting the date for the invasion of Russia, Molotov was in Berlin for talks with Ribbentrop. Molotov noted that the Germans whom he met 'were assuming that the war against England has already been won'. What made this confidence seem somewhat misplaced was that Molotov's celebratory dinner for Ribbentrop that night, which was held in the Soviet Embassy, had to be broken off early. Because of an air raid alarm in anticipation of a British bombing raid, their discussion had to continue in Ribbentrop's air raid shelter at his own home. In fact, no British bomber flew over Berlin that night.

Hitler had been so angered by the British bombing raid on Munich on the night of his anniversary celebrations of the Beer Hall putsch that he ordered a series of counter-raids to be mounted as soon as possible. On November 14 five hundred German bombers set off across the North Sea. Their target was the factory zone around Coventry, but in the course of the raid – during which seven vital war factories were hit and production stopped for many months – the city centre was also bombarded, and 568 men, women and children killed. A new verb entered the German language, *Koventrieren* – 'to Coventrate', or raze to the ground. Of the 75,000 buildings in the city centre, 60,000 were destroyed or badly damaged. So many fires had been started that the fire services, which had been sent to Coventry from the whole surrounding area, were unable to bring them under control. The fires linked up, causing what later came to be called a firestorm. The Coventry raid, reflected Air Marshal Harris – then at the Air Ministry in London – taught the British air raid planners the 'principle' of starting 'so many fires at the same time'.

Coventry was as much the precursor of the air raids on Hamburg in 1943 and Dresden in 1944 – which killed between them more than 100,000 people – as Taranto was the precursor of Pearl Harbor. In each case the link was not accidental, but the careful learning of a tactical lesson, as well as the use of greater technical skills and a much more powerful armoury.

The bombing of Coventry was not the only retaliation for the bombing of Munich – in which less than a dozen German civilians had been killed. That same week, 484 civilians were killed in London and 228 in Birmingham. The British at once retaliated in their turn. In a bombing raid on Hamburg, where cloud cover and severe icing made accurate bombing impossible, 233 German civilians were killed. Slowly, and terrifyingly, the civilian deaths from bombing were mounting. That November, the British civilian death toll for the month was 4,588. Many more were injured. Tens of thousands of people were made homeless. Apart from death and injury, sleepless nights, worry, and the daily visible aftermath of destruction were the cruel realities of a war that no longer respected the historic parameters of soldier against soldier, sailor against sailor and, since the first decade of the century, airman against airman.

Four months later, a former admirer of Hitler's Germany, Francis Yeats

Brown, who had been walking on a British beach with a friend, wrote in his diary:

> We saw an object on the beach, hunched on the shore, lying on its face with arms in sand, as if it was trying to crawl up. It was the body of a German airman, washed up by the last tide. His uniform was more or less intact, and his parachute on his back unopened. They took him to Martle-sham, where they found his identity disc and a photograph of himself; quite a good-looking young man. They thought he belonged to the machine which crashed in the creek last November. It certainly did not look a four-months-old body.
>
> There it lay in the soft spring sun, with bare white skull looking somehow old and wise, but someone is grieving for him in Germany.

One of Hitler's fears in the winter of 1940 was that – with the Greeks beginning to drive the Italians back across the Albanian border – Britain would be able to use air bases on Greek soil to bomb the Roumanian oilfields. Hitler needed this oil for his invasion of Russia. But in November he began to realize that he might have to postpone the attack on Russia in order to attack Greece first. Mussolini had created an Allied belligerent that would have to be defeated, in order to secure German air power in the Balkans. On December 13 Hitler therefore issued a secret directive for the reinforcement of the German troops already in Roumania. They were not, in the first instance, to take part in the attack on Russia, but to occupy northern Greece and deny it to the British bombers. An important part of the Directive was the seizure of the air bases which Britain had established on the Greek islands. After this task was completed, Hitler explained, 'the forces engaged will be withdrawn for new employment'.

That 'new employment', the impending German invasion of Russia, was taking up more and more of Hitler's time and thought. On December 5 he had held a four-hour conference with his senior military commanders, to discuss his ideas of how to capture the main 'Bolshevik breeding grounds', which he argued were Leningrad and Stalingrad rather than Moscow. Hitler told his commanders: 'Hegemony in Europe will be decided in the battle against Russia.' Nor did he envisage the defeat of Russia as a long or difficult task. The Red Army was, he said, 'leaderless'. The Russian soldier was 'mindless'. Russia had nothing but 'badly armoured ' units to face the superior German armour.

Hitler ordered his military planners to prepare a detailed plan for the total defeat of Russia. It was given the code name Operation Fritz. Work began on it on December 6. Hitler quickly changed the name to Operation Barbarossa. The Holy Roman Emperor Frederick Barbarossa – Red Beard – who had drowned in 1190, would (according to legend) return to life when he heard his fellow-countrymen's call to lead them back to glory. The place where he had remained hidden since his death, the legend had long related, was Berchtesgaden: the very mountain on which Hitler's Bavarian retreat was built.

The new Barbarossa was working at fever pitch. On December 18, in Hitler's detailed eleven-page Directive No. 18, he instructed his senior military commanders to make their preparations 'to crush Soviet Russia in a quick campaign'. The preparations must be started at once, and be completed by 15 May 1941. The 'final objective' was to 'erect a barrier against Asiatic Russia' along the geographic line 'Volga-Archangel'.

The Molotov-Ribbentrop line had enabled Hitler to conquer Poland with Stalin's quiescence (and participation). The Volga-Archangel line would destroy Stalin's Russia, and push what was left of Soviet organization, industry and culture to the Ural mountains, 750 miles east of Moscow, making Russia an entirely Asiatic nation.

Inside Germany, the euthanasia programme had become the object of growing public unease. Not only had a number of written protests reached Hitler's Chancellery, but others were circulating clandestinely. On December 19 the two architects of the programme within the Chancellery, Dr Brack and Dr Brandt, were castigated by Himmler for the way in which knowledge of the euthanasia activities had leaked out. 'If Operation T4 had been entrusted to the SS, things would have happened differently,' he told them. 'When the Führer entrusts us with a job, we know how to deal with it correctly, without causing useless uproar among the people.'

The euthanasia programme had to be abandoned; those carrying it out had already killed 50,000 Germans deemed 'useless defectives'. This had included several thousand children and many babies.

Himmler and his SS were not, however, without work to do. Plans were being made by the army, navy and air force for the defeat of Russia in the field. The SS was also making plans, and training SS personnel, for the revival and expansion of the Special Task Forces – which came to be known as the Special Killing Squads – that had murdered tens of thousands of Jews in Poland in September and October 1939. Their new sphere of operations would be in Russia, and their principal target the Jewish population. Not tens of thousands, as hitherto in Poland, but as many as two million, were to be their victims in the East.

Meanwhile, December saw no respite in the Nazi terror in Poland, where almost every day both Jews and Poles were murdered in cold blood and often at random. On December 6 a Warsaw Jew, Chaim Kaplan, wrote in his diary of occasions 'when courageous Jews were shot in full view of their entire family, and the murderers not held responsible, because the excuse was that the "filthy Jew" cursed the Führer and it was the duty to avenge his honour.' Four days later Emanuel Ringelblum noted in his diary that a German soldier 'sprung out of a passing automobile and hit a boy on the head with an iron bar. The boy died'.

Poles were also daily victims of the Nazi terror. That month several hundred telegrams reached individual Polish families, reporting in the briefest telegraphic language the death of a husband, a father or a son who had earlier been taken off by the Gestapo to a concentration camp. Most of these telegrams referred to deaths in one particular camp, Auschwitz, the name of which was beginning to impose itself on the Polish consciousness as a place where Poles were being subjected to especially hard labour and barbaric treatment.

That winter there was hardly any halt in the respective bomber offensives carried out by Britain and Germany. Their bomber forces often went in opposite directions on parallel paths. Some of the raids were heavy ones, such as the British raid on Düsseldorf on December 7 and the German raid on Sheffield four days later. In response to the British public's continuing indignation at the German raid on Coventry, the War Cabinet authorized 'the maximum possible destruction in a selected town' in Germany. The town selected for this reprisal raid was Mannheim, which was bombed on December 16. But there was disappointment, to those who wanted massive revenge, that only twenty-three German civilians were killed.

In the land war, Italy was being driven back, first in Greece, and then, following a British military offensive, in Egypt, where 75,000 Italian soldiers were pushed out of Egypt by 36,000 British and Indian troops. As in Greece, Hitler was suddenly forced to contemplate German military action to prevent the rout of his Italian ally and the victory of the British in North Africa.

On December 17 the British force crossed onto Italian soil in the eastern Libyan province of Cyrenaica.

Those in the British Government who were privy to Germany's own most secret signals communications – via the Enigma machine – knew that a German invasion of Britain had been postponed. But it could not be certain that invasion might not re-emerge as a German priority in due course. On December 23 Hitler visited Boulogne to inspect the invasion preparations. His special train had to be shunted into a tunnel as British bombers attacked a nearby German military installation.

A potentially serious threat for Hitler at the end of 1940 – his year of triumphs – came six days later, on December 29, when Roosevelt broadcast to the American people. 'The people of Europe who are defending themselves do not ask us to do their fighting,' he said. 'They ask us for the implements of war, the planes, the tanks, the guns, the freighters, which will enable them to fight for their liberty and for our security.' The United States, 'must be the great arsenal of democracy'.

Roosevelt's words 'arsenal of democracy' gave courage in Britain, in particular to those who wondered how they could survive the continuing aerial bombardment. That very night, in London, a German air raid destroyed or severely damaged many famous buildings and churches, and engulfed St Paul's Cathedral in flames. It also brought the civilian death toll in Britain that month to 3,793. In sending photographs of the scenes of destruction to the newspapers, one photographic agency captioned them: 'The mark of the Hun.'

Among those whose place of work was destroyed that December 29 was a British-born telephonist from south London, Violette Szabo. The telephone exchange where she worked was within a few hundred yards of St Paul's. That night's experience spurred her to do something more active for the war effort, in which her husband was a serving army officer. A year later, on reaching twenty, she joined the Auxiliary Territorial Service. Within another three years she was to be parachuted into France to help the Resistance; and to be executed by the Gestapo.

Far from the European war, on August 21, in Mexico – on Stalin's orders – Leon Trotsky had been murdered, his head cut open with an axe. The former Bolshevik revolutionary had for more than a decade been denouncing Stalin in letters, speeches and books. Moving from country to country, he had been an implacable opponent of the way in which Soviet Communism had developed. His assassination caused few tears among those who remembered his own harsh rule. But it showed how long the arm of vengeance could be.

Nor did vengeance stop there; as soon as news of Trotsky's death reached Moscow, Beria issued an order for the 'liquidation of active Trotskyites in the camps'. Yet again the labour camp regions were combed and victims extracted. General Volkogonov has commented: 'Pechora, Vorkuta, Kolyma and Solovki became the silent witnesses of a bloody vengeance carried out "in pursuit" of the murdered leader of the Fourth International.'

Throughout the year in which Hitler was trying to transform the fate of Europe, the Japanese continued to try to defeat the Chinese forces they had pushed so far into the interior since the start of their attack almost three years earlier. The Chinese fought back with tenacity and skill; in a counter-attack in western Hupei province in mid-May more than 20,000 Japanese soldiers were killed. When on June 12 the Japanese captured the city of Ichang, on the Yangste, it was at a cost of 9,000 Japanese dead.

Japanese air superiority continued to bring death and destruction to those cities under Chinese control, and in particular to the temporary Chinese capital, Chungking, where at least 500 people were killed during an air raid on May 29 – at the height of the Dunkirk evacuation on the other side of the globe. For the first half of the year the Japanese had been helped in their military operations by friction between the Chinese Nationalists and the Chinese Communists, who were unable to resolve their respective territorial jurisdictions. But in mid-August agreement was reached. Communist troops would control the military operations in Shensi, Shansi, northern Shantung and Hopei. Communist troops operating in other provinces – as they were in Anhui – would be moved to the provinces within their sphere. The Communists were also assigned a political district in part of Shensi.

Within the areas of China under their control the Japanese established Wang Ching-wei, a former associate of Chiang Kai-shek, as head of a newly created Central Government of China. The new government was immediately denounced by Chungking as a 'puppet organization created by Japanese militarists'. Assurances were quickly given by both the United States and Britain that their loyalty was to Chiang Kai-shek. When Wang Ching-wei signed a treaty of 'basic relations' between his government and Japan on November 30, giving Japan effective control of China's mineral resources, and declaring its aim to be 'for defence against Communist activities', it was mocked by Chungking. On the day of its signature Roosevelt announced a considerable increase in American financial aid to Chiang Kai-shek's China.

As a result of the German defeat of France, the Vietnamese Communist leaders who had earlier fled to China, and had been learning military and political techniques at Chinese Communist headquarters at Yenan, in northern China, returned to Vietnam. There, just beyond the Chinese border, they established a training camp and began to seek converts to Communism from among the tribes living along the border. Under the auspices of Vo Nguyen Giap – one of those who had returned from China – a 'self-defence' unit was set up, initially of only a few dozen men, poorly armed, but intent on challenging French rule and on spreading Communism. Giap also set up a training course for a local tribal group, the Nung. As the strength and determination of the Vietnamese Communists grew they ambushed French military patrols, assassinated Vietnamese officials whom they denounced as 'reactionary', and continued to make Communist propaganda among the local peasantry. A new battleground was in the making.

The year 1940 was the first year of the century since 1918 that had been fully dominated by war. The arts reflected the world's renewed preoccupation with armed conflict. Charlie Chaplin's film *The Great Dictator*, with its mocking depiction of Hitler, gave amusement and even courage to those for whom Hitler's bombs brought only daily death and misery. But the *New York Times* warned, while the film was being made: 'If the public will accept as a comedy character a figure who is popularly regarded as responsible for the greatest slaughter in history, then Chaplin has little about which to worry. But if the public's revulsion is carried into the theatre, the reaction against Chaplin and the industry will be intense.'

In France, at the very moment when the humiliation and uncertainties of Vichy rule were being imposed, a group of schoolboys exploring a cave at Lascaux discovered Paleolithic paintings that were greatly to enhance knowledge of some of humanity's first ancestors. Below ground were depictions of the simple weapons of the hunt, and above ground, the reality of the far deadlier weapons developed by the modern age.

Even as the war continued, the interests of the consumer flourished in regions that lay beyond the conflict: in the United States the world's first record chart was published, setting the path for what was to become one of the greatest pleasure-giving and money-making devices of the century. Also in the United States, nylon stockings were marketed for the first time; an

American southerner, Colonel Sanders, created the recipe for Kentucky Fried Chicken; Bugs Bunny made his film debut; Walt Disney produced *Pinocchio*; and colour television was demonstrated. For sportsmen the world over, however, there was disappointment: the 12th Olympic Games, which was to have been held in Tokyo that year, were cancelled because of the war.

The number of refugees for whom a safe haven was found in 1940 were numbered in the tens of thousands. Among those reaching the United States – despite the imposition of quotas that kept many refugees out – was the photographer Philippe Halsman, a Jew born in Riga who had fled from Paris, his home and place of work since 1930. Once in the United States he joined *Life* magazine, for which he was to produce a record number of covers – 101.

Based in Marseille, an American citizen, Varian Fry, worked tirelessly after the German defeat of France to build up a network of rescue throughout the Vichy area. He took this initiative as the representative of a private American relief organization – the Emergency Rescue Committee. Under Article Five of the Franco-German Armistice, the Germans had imposed a 'surrender on demand clause'. Fry made strenuous efforts to circumvent it, enabling more than 1,500 people, many of them politicians, scientists, artists, writers and musicians, to leave France for the United States. In Kaunas, the inter-war capital of Lithuania, at least 1,600 transit visas across the Soviet Union were given to Jewish refugees from Poland by the Japanese consul, Sempo Sugihara. 'I cannot allow these people to die, people who had come to me for help with death staring them in the eyes,' Sugihara explained. 'Whatever punishment may be imposed upon me, I know I should follow my conscience.' Amid the growing tempest of evil, tiny sheltered corners of courage survived.

CHAPTER ELEVEN

1941
JANUARY TO JUNE

... without mercy or pity.

SS GENERAL EICKE

EVERY WEEK OF THE WAR was sated with fighting and suffering. On January 5 the British drove the Italian army out of the Cyrenaican fortress of Bardia. The Greeks, having repelled the Italian invaders, were fighting the Italian army on Albanian soil. On the British cruiser *Southampton*, on convoy duty from Gibraltar to Malta, eighty sailors were killed during a German bombing attack. In London, 111 civilians who had taken refuge in one of the underground railway stations being used during the air raids as places of safety were killed when a bomb brought down the tunnel on top of them.

In the Warsaw ghetto, deaths from starvation were reaching 2,000 a month. An American citizen, Mary Berg – who was shortly to be repatriated from Warsaw to the United States, recorded in her diary seeing 'a Nazi gendarme "exercise" a Jewish policeman . . . The young man finally lost his breath but the Nazi still forced him to rise and fall until he collapsed in a pool of blood'.

In Paris, the German Social Democrat, Rudolph Hilferding – who had twice been Finance Minister in the Weimar government, and who had sought refuge in France after 1933 – died in prison as a result of torture by the Gestapo. In the Polish town of Grudziadz, a Catholic woman, Pelagia Bernatowicz, who had been caught listening to a Polish radio broadcast from London, was sentenced to death and shot. In Amsterdam, SS troops and German police opened fire on Dutch workers who were protesting against the round-up of 400 Jews for deportation. Eleven of the Dutch strikers were killed. The Jews were then deported to Buchenwald and Mauthausen, and to their deaths. Three weeks later the Germans sentenced eighteen members of the growing Dutch resistance to death by shooting. On their way to the execution site they sang, alternating Psalms with the Dutch national anthem. In German-annexed western Poland, two Polish artisans, Edward Lembicz, a saddler, and Jan Mikolajczyk, a carter, who were overheard singing the Polish national anthem, were shot.

These are but a few examples from the daily reports of murder that were reaching the West from German-occupied Europe. In the face of this terror and horror, on January 6 President Roosevelt issued a clarion call for decency, describing the 'four essential human freedoms' on which he believed the post-war world must be based. These were freedom of speech and expression, freedom to worship God, freedom from want, and freedom from fear. Freedom from fear, he said, 'translated into world terms, means a world-wide reduction of armaments to such a point and in such a thorough fashion that no nation will be in a position to commit an act of aggression against any neighbour, anywhere in the world'.

Ironically, it was not the reduction of armaments, as envisaged by Roosevelt, but their continued increase and development, that was to be the main basis for the avoidance of global war by Roosevelt's successors, from Truman to Reagan.

Roosevelt's immediate efforts in the first months of 1941 were to persuade Congress to allow the Allies – principally Britain, but also Greece, and the French, Polish, Norwegian, Dutch and Belgian governments in exile, to acquire arms from the United States under a leasing agreement that would not involve any cash payments while the war was being fought. To assure himself that Britain had the willpower to continue at war, and that American supplies would not be sent over the Atlantic only to become part of an even wider German conquest, Roosevelt sent his close friend Harry Hopkins as his personal emissary to Britain, with instructions to report back on British moral and prospects. Hopkins' report gave Roosevelt the assurance he sought. 'The people here are amazing, from Churchill down,' Hopkins informed the President, 'and if courage alone can win, the results are inevitable. But they need our help desperately, and I am sure you will permit nothing to stand in the way.'

As the Lend-Lease Bill made its way through Congress, offering the hard-pressed Allies the prospect of being able to continue at war, and perhaps one day even to turn the tide, Hitler faced his first difficulty. He would have to come to Mussolini's aid both in Greece and in North Africa if he were to prevent the British from exploiting these Italian setbacks to Germany's disadvantage.

Hitler's Directive No. 22, dated January 11, set out clearly that 'Tripolitania must be held and the danger of a collapse on the Albanian front must be eliminated.' German troops would therefore be sent both to Greece and to North Africa, and German aircraft, operating from Italian air bases in Sicily, would undertake substantial and continuous operations against the British in Malta and the central Mediterranean. Within weeks, the bombardment and effective siege of Malta was begun. But despite great privation, the morale of the Maltese did not break. The attempt to prevent British seaborne supplies reaching Malta, though often almost devastating in its severity, never succeeded in totally cutting the island off from help and the means of survival.

Hoping to enlist Bulgaria's support against Greece in the Balkans, Hitler invited King Boris to join the Axis, but the King refused to do so. First Franco, then Pétain and finally King Boris had declined to align themselves against Britain. But Hitler's woes continued to be mostly those that his Italian ally inflicted on him as a result of military setbacks. On January 19, the day on which Mussolini arrived at Berchtesgaden as Hitler's guest, British forces broke into Italian East Africa and, entering Abyssinia as liberators, converged on Addis Ababa. Pressed to do so by Mussolini, Hitler agreed to accelerate the arrival of German troops in North Africa: he would send the 15th Armoured Division, commanded by Rommel.

On January 22, before Rommel could arrive, British and Australian troops broke into Tripoli, taking 25,000 Italian soldiers prisoner. Within two weeks the Italians had been defeated again, at the Battle of Beda Fomm, and 20,000 more Italian soldiers were taken prisoner. Entering Benghazi, Australian soldiers captured eighty Italian tanks and seven Italian generals. The total number of Italians taken prisoner-of-war had mounted to 130,000. They had also lost more than 400 tanks. Rommel's arrival would be none too soon. Hitler saw him personally to inspire him.

As well as the struggle of Allied and Axis armies, a battle of wills continued to develop between Hitler and Churchill, and between Hitler and Roosevelt. On February 6 Hitler issued his Directive No. 23, in which he ordered an increase in the U-boat sinkings of British merchant ships. The cutting of Britain's supply lifeline across the Atlantic could, he wrote, 'bring about the collapse of British resistance in the near future'. But on the following day, by 260 votes to 165, the House of Representatives passed the Lend-Lease Bill, which was steadily making its way into law. Churchill at once broadcast to the British people: 'It now seems to be certain that the Government and people of the United States intend to supply us with all that is necessary for victory.' In the First World War, Churchill reminded his listeners, the United States had sent two million fighting men to assist in the defeat of Germany. The need in the Second World War was for arms and ammunition. He was confident that these would be forthcoming, and in ten words expressed to the Americans the heart of so much of what he and Britain needed from them: 'Give us the tools and we will finish the job.'

Churchill, visiting the scenes of destruction in the aftermath of bombing raids, understood the tenacity of the British people in adversity. He said of them, referring to that tenacity as if it were salt water: 'The British people are like the waters of the ocean. You may put a bucket in the sea, and pull it up, and always find it salt.' Examples of individual heroism strengthened the public mood of unified endeavour. A special award, the George Cross, gave civilian bravery the same status as that of military heroism 'over and above the call of duty' as recognized by the Victoria Cross. An early recipient of the George Cross was Dr Hannah Billig, a London physician known as 'The Angel of Cable Street'. During a bombing raid early in 1941 a bomb blast threw her down some stairs in a dockside shelter and she broke her ankle. She strapped the ankle up, left the shelter, and gave assistance to the wounded in the street, binding tourniquets and, where necessary, operating. Despite her pain, and the continuation of the bombing – one bomb fell twenty yards from her – she carried on with this work for four hours.

The Germans understood that in the lands under their occupation, and among the neutrals, collaboration and compromise were also emotions which could be exploited. Switzerland made it possible, and profitable, to act as a conduit for German gold deposits and payments. Swedish ball-bearings were a crucial component of Germany's warmaking capacity. On February 21 a Stockholm furrier wrote to a German firm with which it wished to do business: 'Our firm is pure Aryan and there is, thank God, not a single drop of Jewish blood in it.'

Between 1937 and 1943 Swedish ore provided the raw material for four out of every ten German guns that were in action on the war fronts.

*   *   *

As Germany's plans to invade the Soviet Union gained momentum, and with the attack still set for May, Hitler decided that the time had come to prepare to occupy northern Greece. His aim was to prevent the Greek airfields from falling under British control, and being used as bases to bomb the essential oil fields and fuel oil refineries in Roumania. When the British learned of Hitler's plans through their daily eavesdropping on the German's most secret messages, it was decided to send 100,000 British troops to Greece, to defend their ally and to keep Hitler out of the Balkans.

The British decision to send troops to Greece – a decision for which Churchill obtained the approval of every Cabinet Minister and all his senior military advisers – ensured that Hitler would not be able to force Greece to a rapid capitulation. It also made it inevitable that he would have to postpone his invasion of the Soviet Union until Greece was subjugated. The likelihood was high, however, that an invasion of Russia that began later than May would be caught up in the terrible harshness of the Russian winter.

Hitler dismissed the doubts of his generals as to the difficulties that would face them in Russia if the invasion had to be delayed in order to defeat Greece first. He was still thinking about the civil administration that he would set up in Russia. 'The Jewish-Bolshevik intelligentsia must be eliminated,' he told General Jodl on March 3, and in a special decree issued later that week, known as the Commissar Order, Hitler stated bluntly: 'The war against Russia cannot be fought in knightly fashion. The struggle is one of ideologies and racial differences, and will have to be waged with unprecedented, unmerciful and unrelenting harshness.'

Those whom Hitler called 'the commissars' held views, he said, 'directly opposed to those of National Socialism. Hence these commissars must be eliminated. Any German soldier who breaks an international law will be pardoned. Russia did not take part in the Hague Convention, and therefore has no rights under it'. Even as this order circulated among Hitler's senior military commanders, SS units were undergoing a rigorous training in the methods of mass murder at a camp near the village of Pretzsch, on the Elbe. During their training, ten SS men were accidentally killed.

Despite the overriding importance to Hitler of the war against the Soviet Union, it was on the imminent war in the Balkans that he had to focus his attention and his skills in March. His first success was to persuade King Boris of Bulgaria to agree to allow German troops to use Bulgarian soil for one prong of their attack on Greece. To facilitate the passage of German troops through Bulgaria, German military engineers who were already stationed in Roumania built three bridges across the Danube from the Roumanian to the Bulgarian shore. Churchill and his advisers knew all about these bridges through Enigma. British troops began to arrive in Greece from March 5. The efforts of the Italian Air Force, from its bases in the Dodecanese Islands, to halt the passage of these troops was unsuccessful, despite the sinking of twenty-four of the troopships.

Like King Boris of Bulgaria, the Regent Paul of Yugoslavia was under strong German pressure to allow German troops through Yugoslavia on their way to attack Greece. For many weeks, he resisted. But on March 25, hoping to avert a German invasion of Yugoslavia itself, he gave way, and, together with the Yugoslav Prime Minister, Dragisa Cvetkovic, travelled to Vienna, where he signed Yugoslavia's adherence to the Tripartite Pact of Germany, Italy and Japan. The Japanese Ambassador in Berlin, Count Oshima, who was also a General in the Imperial Japanese Army, travelled specially to Vienna to take part in the ceremony.

Inside Yugoslavia there were immediate and widespread public protests against the alignment with Germany. The British Embassy in Belgrade was active in encouraging Yugoslav opposition. In the early hours of March 27 there was a coup d'état in Belgrade and the Cvetkovic government was overthrown. The new Prime Minister, the Air Force Commander, General Dusan Simovic, pledged his government to oppose the passage of German troops through Yugoslavia. Hitler, having made certain less than forty-eight hours earlier that his troops could attack Greece from the north as well as from the east, was suddenly and unexpectedly cheated of his unimpeded advance from the north. Summoning his military commanders, he opened up yet another war front. Their task, he said, was 'to smash Yugoslavia militarily, and as a State,' and he added: 'Politically it is especially important that the blow against Yugoslavia be carried out with merciless harshness and that the military destruction be done in Blitzkrieg style.'

Plans were made at once to carry out Hitler's orders. But on the day of Yugoslavia's defiance, which would inevitably further postpone the invasion of Russia, it was yet again the military performance of his Italian ally that gave Hitler cause for alarm. In Eritrea, Italian forces were driven out of Keren. Off the coast of Greece, in a ferocious naval engagement with Britain which took place off Cape Matapan, five out of the eight Italian cruisers in the battle were sunk, and 2,400 Italian sailors drowned. Britain lost two naval aircraft. As a result of the Battle of Matapan, the Italian navy could take no significant part in the struggle for the future of Greece and Yugoslavia that was about to begin.

On March 27, Hitler decided Yugoslavia and Greece would be invaded simultaneously. In his Directive No. 25 he ordered that the city of Belgrade 'will be destroyed from the air by continual night and day attack'. He also postponed the date of the invasion of the Soviet Union until June 22, telling a gathering of two hundred of his commanders and their staffs, at a meeting in Berlin on March 30, that once Yugoslavia and Greece had been defeated, Germany would have 'the chance to smash Russia while our own back is free. That chance will not return so soon. I would be betraying the future of the German people if I did not seize it now!'

Not only the German army, but also the SS were called on to participate in the Yugoslav and Greek campaigns. As the German army advanced, the SS Special Task Forces would have unrestricted power behind the lines. On April 3, at a briefing with Himmler in Berlin, they were told that their specific task was 'to take executive measures affecting the civilian population'. Once again the use of deceptive language in the printed (though strictly secret) version of the discussion was deliberate: 'executive measures' were, first and foremost, executions. But most of the Special Task Forces were not to go to Greece and Yugoslavia. They had an even vaster area in which they would have to operate within the coming three months, and training for that task continued – the planning of mass murder on a scale not hitherto seen in the Twentieth Century.

On the day of Himmler's briefing to the SS about their role in Greece and Yugoslavia, the Hungarian Regent, Admiral Horthy, agreed to join with Germany in its Balkan offensive. In protest against this decision, the Hungarian Prime Minister, Count Paul Teleki, committed suicide. Hitler proceeded to offer Hungary and Bulgaria, his two new allies, some of the territory that he was about to invade with their help. Hungary would acquire the Yugoslav province of the Backa. Bulgaria would acquire the Yugoslav province of Macedonia and the Greek province of Thrace.

Italy would also move against Yugoslavia, and acquire territory along the Dalmatian coast, but Mussolini insisted rather cautiously, and successfully, that his troops would not have to advance against Yugoslavia until the German attack 'begins to be effective'.

On the morning of April 6, German bombers attacked Belgrade. Another war front had been opened. In a single day, 17,000 Yugoslav civilians were killed: the capital was packed with villagers and people from other towns celebrating Palm Sunday. Simultaneously with the attack on Belgrade other German warplanes attacked the Yugoslav airfields, destroying almost the whole of their unsuspecting adversary's air fighting power while it was still on the ground. That same day, German troops based in Bulgaria advanced on the Greek port of Salonika, and bombed the main Greek supply port of Piraeus. Six British cargo ships carrying military supplies were sunk before a seventh ship, the *Clan Fraser*, which was carrying explosives, was hit by German bombs and blew up. The explosion was so fierce that it devastated the port and sank ten more British supply ships.

As Mussolini waited for some clear sign of victory before entering the battle for Yugoslavia and Greece, his troops were finally defeated in Eritrea, and at the Battle of Massawa surrendered their imperial possession to Britain. They had not given up without a struggle: of the 13,000 defenders of Massawa, 3,000 were killed in action. In North Africa, Rommel had succeeded in reversing the Italian defeats and was marching eastward through Cyrenaica, driving the British in front of him. But it was the battle for Yugoslavia and Greece that was the most savage and the most decisive.

On April 8 the German army occupied Salonika. A British army patrol that crossed over the northern border of Greece into Yugoslavia found only Yugoslav troops in retreat, who reported that all Yugoslav resistance was at an end. That day in the House of Commons, Churchill warned that however far Hitler might go, 'or whatever new millions, or scores of millions he may lap in misery, he may be sure that, armed with the sword of retributive justice, we shall be on his track'.

The night of April 8/9 saw a deliberate British act of retribution: the despatch of eighty aircraft to bomb Berlin in response to the bombing of Belgrade. Several buildings in the centre of Berlin were hit and Hitler was forced to spend part of the night in his air raid shelter. No Berliners were killed – although 125 Germans had been killed the night before in a raid on Kiel. In a German counter-retaliation on London on April 16, more than 2,300 Londoners were killed. Among the dead were forty Canadian servicemen who were on leave in the capital.

On April 10 the German army entered Zagreb, and then handed the city to the Croat nationalist, Ante Pavelic, who immediately declared a separate Croat State. The Italians entered the Slovene capital of Ljubljana and the Hungarians advanced on Novi Sad. Yugoslavia was being torn apart.

In the Atlantic, the German attempt to cut Britain off from her United States supply line was being sharply challenged. But the United States, while still neutral – and still represented in Berlin by diplomats and journalists – was becoming more involved on the British side. On April 10, in the first military action authorized by Roosevelt since the outbreak of war more than eighteen months earlier, the American destroyer *Niblack* dropped depth charges against a German U-boat that had earlier sunk a Dutch merchant ship. On the following day United States forces occupied the Danish colony of Greenland, while Roosevelt, in order to give greater protection to transatlantic convoys, announced that the patrol and security zone of the United States was extended as far eastward as the 25th Meridian.

The need for greater action against the U-boats was urgent. In the three days before the extension of the United States patrol zone, 31,000 tons of Allied shipping was sunk.

On April 13 German forces occupied Belgrade. Including Vienna, this was the ninth European capital to be occupied by Germany in a little over three years. The new conquest involved new terrors. According to one account, the first civilian to be shot in cold blood in Belgrade was a Jewish tailor who, as the German troops passed him in the street, had spat at them and shouted out: 'You will all perish.' When the Hungarians entered Novi Sad they seized 500 Serbs and Jews whom they then shot and bayoneted to death.

In northern Greece a stand was being made along the defensive line established along the Aliakhmon River. For a few days the German forces, pushing down from Yugoslavia, were checked, but by April 16 the line was breached in so many places that the Greek Commander-in-Chief, General Papagos, contemplated surrender, and urged all British and Allied forces to leave Greece at once in order to save her from 'devastation'. They declined to do so. As the Aliakhmon Line crumbled, New Zealand troops were among those making a final, desperate stand along it.

On April 17 the Aliakhmon Line was completely overrun. The Greek Prime Minister, Alexander Koryzis, fearing defeatism and even treachery in Greek government circles, killed himself. That day, in Belgrade, the Yugoslav government signed a formal act of unconditional surrender. Hitler, working in his train at Mönichkirchen, near the Austrian-Yugoslav border, spent part of the day discussing with his architect Albert Speer the proposed new government centre in Berlin, which he was determined would outshine Paris.

On April 20, in Paris, a German soldier was shot and fatally wounded; as a reprisal twenty-two French civilians were shot. That day, Hitler celebrated his fifty-second birthday. Three days later, the Greek army surrendered.

Several Greek officers took their own lives rather than hand over their swords and side arms to the Germans. To avoid capture, the Allied troops – British, Australians, New Zealanders and Poles – began their evacuation on the following day from the ports of Attica. In order to stop the Germans reaching the ports before the evacuation was completed, British, Australian and New Zealand troops held the narrow, four-and-a-half-mile-long pass at Thermopylae – where in classical times a small Greek force under Leonidas had held off the Persian invaders for three days, until they were outflanked. The modern soldiers also held the pass against heavy odds, while the evacuation of their colleagues continued, until they themselves were forced back on the evacuation ports.

In all, more than 50,000 Allied soldiers were evacuated from Greece. Most of them were transferred by ship to the island of Crete. On April 24, as the Greek evacuation was in its final stages, Hitler ordered German Air Force units to begin their move from the Channel Coast facing Britain to the Polish border facing the Soviet Union. But he had not yet finished with the unfortunate defenders of Greece. On April 25, as the last evacuations to Crete were taking place – of the men who had held the pass at Thermopylae – Hitler issued his 28th Directive of the war: the invasion of Crete.

German troops entered Athens on April 27. They had lost fewer soldiers in the campaign than any of the contending armies. The Greeks had lost the most: 15,700 Greek soldiers had been killed on the battlefield. In the other armies fighting on Greek soil, 13,755 Italians, 3,712 British and 2,232 Germans had been killed. The Allied troops on their way from Greece to Crete were subjected to continuous aerial bombardment while at sea. During April 27 the seven hundred survivors of a troopship that had been bombed and sunk were dive-bombed again as they took refuge in the two destroyers that had picked them up. Both destroyers were sunk, and all but fifty of the seven hundred survivors were drowned.

Continuing his advance through Cyrenaica, at the end of April, Rommel crossed the Libyan border into Egypt, as the Italians had done before him. But he was determined not to be pushed out again as they had been. His aim was to reach Cairo and the Suez Canal. When a British cruiser and several merchant ships were sunk in the Atlantic, Goebbels could not contain his delight at so many successes, writing in his diary: 'Bad days for London. Let us have more of them! We shall soon bring John Bull to his knees.'

Hitler had been cheered since March by a distant ally who was taking action against Britain. In Iraq, General Rashid Ali had seized power in Baghdad, threatening the desert approaches to Palestine, and the supply of oil from Iraq to the Haifa refineries. German military experts were flown to Baghdad to give guidance to Rashid Ali. The most senior of them, Major Axel von Blomberg, who was sent out as Liaison Officer with the rebels, reached Baghdad airport at the very moment when a 'dogfight' was underway between British and Iraqi planes. He was hit by a stray British bullet and killed. The Mufti of Jerusalem, Haj Amin al-Husseini, was also in Baghdad stimulating anti-British feeling. It was four years since he had fled from Jerusalem to escape arrest for fomenting anti-British riots.

On April 28 Rashid Ali surrounded the British air base at Habbaniya, trapping 2,300 fighting men and 9,000 civilians. It took two weeks before the garrison could be relieved. Succour came when the Transjordanian Frontier Force, led by Major John Glubb (later Glubb Pasha) crossed three hundred miles of desert. On the way, however, one of his Bedouin squadrons mutinied, declaring that it had 'no quarrel with the Iraqis' and that the British 'made others fight for them'.

Over the cities of Britain, renewed German bombing raids caused the deaths of more than six thousand civilians that month. In the Atlantic nearly 400,000 tons of Allied merchant shipping had been sunk, precious cargoes of arms and food bound from the United States to Britain. Seventy-three Canadian soldiers had also been killed when their troop transport, on its way from Canada to Britain, was torpedoed; they were the only Canadian soldiers to be lost at sea on their way across the Atlantic.

As Hitler's plans to capture Crete and then invade the Soviet Union moved into high gear, his obsession with the Jews also intensified. On May 4 he declared to a vast audience in Berlin: 'In the Jewish-capitalist age the national Socialist State stands out as a solid monument to common sense. It will survive for a thousand years.'*

In the ghettos of Warsaw and Lodz the combined death toll from starvation had reached more than 15,000. 'The children are no longer afraid of death,' Emanuel Ringelblum wrote in his diary on May 11. 'In one courtyard, the children played a game tickling a corpse.' In the Lodz ghetto, a mentally-ill

---

* The Thousand Year Reich had, in fact, only four years and four days more to run.

woman, Cwajga Blum, who was often seen wandering at the edge of the ghetto, was ordered by a German sentry to dance in front of the barbed wire. 'After she had performed a little dance,' the ghetto chronicle recorded, 'the sentry shot her dead at nearly point-blank range'. Cwajga Blum was forty-one years old.

In China, the Japanese were still masters of half the country, continually seeking further military advantage. But neither in Britain nor the United States did the Chinese struggle get much attention. In May, at the request of her newspaper, Martha Gellhorn reached the Chinese capital, Chungking. The Sino-Japanese war had been going on 'so long and was so far away', she wrote, 'that it ranked more as an historic fact than a war. Compared to the survival of Britain, the Far East was stale and stifling.'

Martha Gellhorn was received by Chiang Kai-shek and his wife. 'The Generalissimo and Madame Chiang, to whom power was all, feared the Chinese Communists not the Japanese,' she wrote. 'They were not fools. The Japanese would disappear some day; historically the Japanese were like an attack of boils. The true threat to the Chiangs' power lay in the people of China and therefore in the Communists who lived among and led the people.'

The Nationalists could not give up their hopes of defeating the Communists militarily, despite a series of truces. Shortly before Martha Gellhorn's arrival, Nationalist troops ambushed the southern wing of the Communist Fourth Route Army – one of its two major military forces. In six days of battle, 3,000 Communist troops were killed and many others shot by the Nationalists after they had been captured.

May 10 was the first anniversary of Hitler's successful invasion of Belgium, Holland and France. That day in 1941 he launched a massive air raid over Britain; 1,436 civilians were killed and the debating chamber of the House of Commons was destroyed. That same day, like a bolt from the blue, Hitler's deputy, Rudolf Hess, made a dramatic solo flight to Britain. He had taken an incredible risk flying solo across the North Sea, and had narrowly missed being shot down as an unidentified intruder into British air space.

For several years Hess had been without any real influence in the Nazi hierarchy. It was assumed by Stalin, however, that Hess was on an official mission to persuade the British to join in the German attack on the Soviet Union, an attack which both Stalin and Churchill knew to be imminent. In fact Hess had no mission at all. To his British interrogators he produced a garbled set of ideas about how Hitler was in the right, and how the British people ought to realize this.

Hess was imprisoned, and his conversations monitored, but he volunteered nothing approaching a political initiative or proposal. Those who continued to question him came to the conclusion that he was deranged.

On May 20 Hitler launched the German invasion of Crete. With overwhelming air superiority the German forces attempted an entirely airborne landing, in which 493 transport planes took part. It was the largest parachute and glider landing that had ever been undertaken. At first it seemed that the Germans might be defeated by the land forces arrayed against them. But German air power proved decisive, and German dive bombing deadly. On May 22, dive bombers sank two British cruisers and four destroyers. On the cruiser *Gloucester* 725 sailors were killed: several of them were machine-gunned from the air while clinging to pieces of wreckage.

In one of the land battles on Crete the Germans were counter-attacked in no fewer than twenty-five bayonet charges. But by May 27 it was clear that the Germans had won mastery of the island, and the order was given for the Allied forces to evacuate. Several Allied units were without ammunition. Every unit was at the mercy of German aerial attacks. A total of 17,000 men were evacuated in five nights. But the evacuation ships were themselves subjected to fierce dive-bombing. The British and Commonwealth war dead in the land battle was 1,742 – New Zealanders taking a major part in the fighting. But a further 2,265 men were killed while they were on the high seas, their hopes of reaching a safe haven in Egypt destroyed by German air power, and by German air policy.*

An attempt to disrupt the German airfields established on Crete was made by a small British-organized undercover force that was landed by submarine. It was commanded by a Frenchman, Georges Bergé, who three months earlier had undertaken a clandestine mission in German-occupied France. Bergé and his group succeeded in blowing up more than twenty German aircraft at an airfield outside Heraklion. On the way back to rendezvous with the

---

* It is in the nature of a general history covering nineteen years that few episodes can be described in the detail they merit. Histories exist of almost every campaign of the Second World War: for the Battle of Crete there are several, including Antony Beevor's *Crete: The Battle and the Resistance*, first published in 1991. Among important earlier histories are those by D. Davin – part of the New Zealand official war history – (1953), Ian Stewart (1955) and Alan Clark (1962).

submarine, however, he and his men ran into superior German forces and, after a fierce firefight, were forced to surrender. Bergé spent the rest of the war as a German prisoner.*

The Germans resorted to what was becoming their standard response when such acts of sabotage and resistance took place: reprisals. On June 14, the day after the attack on the airfield, they executed fifty Cretan hostages. These included a former Governor-General of the island, Tito Georgiadis, as well as a seventy-year-old Greek Orthodox priest and several Jews who were already being held in prison. Cretan anger at the reprisals turned in part against the British, for having ordered the sabotage. But as the historian Antony Beevor notes, 'Cretan groups never ceased to demand arms to attack the Germans'. Morale, he adds, 'as one might expect under the occupation, could be very mercurial'.

On May 24, while the battle for Crete was at its height, in the distant North Atlantic, off the coast of Greenland, the German battleship *Bismarck* opened fire with its 15-inch guns on the British battlecruiser *Hood*. For twenty-one years the 44,000-ton *Hood* had been the biggest warship in the world. The 'battle' lasted eight minutes, the shells from the *Bismarck* piercing the *Hood's* deck and blowing up her munitions magazine. The British warship sank immediately. All but three of her 1,418 officers and men were killed.

Three days later, on May 27, the *Bismarck* was herself tracked down and attacked by a ring of British warships. As she burned, her captain gave orders to scuttle the ship: 2,107 of her crew of 2,222 were drowned. A member of Hitler's Chancellery noted: 'Mood very dejected. Führer melancholy beyond words.'

The pride of Hitler's navy was at the bottom of the sea. Hitler also learned that day, from one of President Roosevelt's 'Fireside Chats' broadcast over the radio to the American people, that the ports of the United States 'are helping now to ensure the delivery of needed supplies to Britain'. The United States would also take the 'necessary measures' to ensure the delivery of these supplies, Roosevelt added. 'This can be done. It must be done. It will be done.' Then, in yet another clarion call to the struggling Allies – defeated in Greece and being driven rapidly and violently from Crete – Roosevelt declared: 'The only thing we have to fear is fear itself.'

---

* After the war Bergé returned to France, where he pioneered the use of helicopters in the military attack role.

At the end of May the focus of battle in the Libyan desert turned briefly but intensely to the remote outpost of Bir Hakeim. When Rommel was approaching the border with Egypt, he had left Bir Hakeim besieged behind his line of advance. On May 27 an Italian force, commanded by Colonel Prestissimo, attacked those who were besieged in Bir Hakeim – French Foreign Legion and Free French soldiers, among them Bretons, Tahitians, Algerians, Moroccans, Lebanese, Cambodians, Mauritians, and men from Madagascar and Chad. The Italians were driven off and Prestissimo captured. The Germans then sent a column of tanks to capture the fort. It too was driven off, by the inspired leadership of a young French captain, Pierre Mesmer – who many years later was to be Prime Minister of France.

As another German attack was being prepared, the defenders of Bir Hakeim broke out, making their way across the desert to the British lines. In the breakout, seventy-two French soldiers were killed, but 2,500 reached safety. The defence of Bir Hakeim inspired those Frenchmen who, in exile, or under Vichy, or under German occupation, dreamed of the day when France would be free.

Two months after Bir Hakeim an international civil servant, Harold Butler, an Englishman who had been for eighteen years the director of the International Labour Office in Geneva, wrote: 'The Vichy period is a purgatory through which France is condemned to pass, but once the nation is freed from its fetters its old faith in liberty will flare up with a purer fire. The tribulations through which it is now living, the bitter taste of tyranny and brutality, the suppression of the values which France prized most, are experiences which will fortify the old devotion to freedom for generations to come.'

In an attempt to prevent the Vichy regime in Syria supporting the anti-British revolt in Iraq, an expeditionary force commanded by General Catroux, made up of Free French forces, Australian, British, and Indian troops, as well French Legionaries, Arab Legionaries and Palestinian Jews, entered Syria and Lebanon. For five weeks the Vichy forces resisted the Allied armies, but in due course both Beirut and Damascus were in Allied hands. The flag of the Free French flew throughout yet another French overseas territory.*

* * *

* It was during the advance into Syria that Moshe Dayan, a twenty-six year old Palestinian Jewish volunteer (later Israel's Minister of Defence and Foreign Minister) lost an eye.

The final German preparations for the invasion of the Soviet Union were under way. Since January, 17,000 trains — on average more than a hundred every day — had moved troops from Greater Germany and the German-occupied regions to the Polish-Soviet border.

On June 1 the SS Special Task Force leaders, 120 in all, were briefed by Heydrich on their task. The 'eastern Jews' were the 'intellectual reservoir of Bolshevism', he told them, and were 'in the Führer's view' to be 'liquidated'. Two days later the SS Death's Head Division left its base at Bordeaux and travelled for four days and nights to its new base at Marienwerder in East Prussia. On arrival, its commander, General Eicke, stressed that the war that was about to begin was an ideological war, 'a life-and-death struggle between National Socialism and Jewish Bolshevism'. The Division must be 'fanatical and merciless', he said. Each soldier must act 'without mercy or pity'.

In the last two weeks of May, Stalin received two particular warnings of the build-up of German forces. On Churchill's instructions, on May 21 Stalin was sent a summary of the most recent German Enigma messages. This made it clear that the German preparations for war against the Soviet Union 'will be completed by the end of the month'. The British report added that special Commissariats had been established in Berlin for the future governance of the Ukraine, the Caucasus and the three Baltic States — Estonia, Latvia and Lithuania.

The second intelligence report that Stalin was sent before the end of May also came from London, and was likewise sent on Churchill's authorization. It was from a top secret diplomatic message intercepted by British Intelligence, which had been sent from the Japanese Consul in Vienna to the Japanese Foreign Ministry in Tokyo. It stated that the Germans intended to make war against the Soviet Union 'by the second part of June' in order to complete the conquest in six to eight weeks, in time for the autumn harvest. In sending these warnings to Stalin, Churchill was risking disclosure of by far the most important source of British Intelligence. But he recognized the crucial importance to Britain's survival that the Soviet Union should not be caught by surprise and defeated, thereby enabling Hitler to turn all his vast, and vastly augmented, resources against Britain.

Hitler sought out two more partners to assist his plan for Russia. On June 8, the Government of Finland having agreed to join in the assault and to allow the German army to use its territory as a base, German troops entered Finland. Three days later Hitler told the Roumanian leader General Antonescu that while he was not asking for Roumanian participation, he 'merely expected of Roumania that in her own interest she do everything to facilitate a successful conclusion to this conflict'. Antonescu did not need persuading. The defeat of Russia would enable Roumania to regain Bessarabia, which she had been forced to cede to the Soviet Union following a Soviet ultimatum a year earlier, in June 1940. The Hungarians, Italians and Bulgarians also offered to send troops to fight against the Soviets; and Franco was eventually persuaded to do the same.

On June 9 the Chief of Staff of the German Army, General Halder, visited the German Fourth Army to discuss special measures for 'surprise attack': artillery, smoke-screens, rapid movement and the evacuation of Polish civilians from the operational zone. June 10 was the 751st anniversary of the drowning of Emperor Frederick Barbarossa in 1190; the day on which, according to legend, the dead Frederick began to await his countrymen's call to lead them back to glory. That day the Germans put into effect a ten-day programme of minelaying in the Baltic. It was designed to prevent the Soviet Baltic Fleet from escaping through the Kattegat into the North Sea. On the following day, June 11, in Directive No 32, Hitler laid down his plans for the German Army, Navy and Air Force 'after the destruction of the Soviet armed forces'.

Hitler's plans were wide-ranging. Operation Isabella would secure the Atlantic coastline of Spain and Portugal. The British would be driven from Gibraltar with Spanish help or without it. In the Middle East, strong pressure would be exerted on both Turkey and Persia to participate 'in the struggle against England'. The British would be driven from Palestine and the Suez Canal by two 'converging attacks', one of them launched from Libya through Egypt, the other from Bulgaria through Turkey.

In this Directive, Hitler stressed that it was 'important that Tobruk should be eliminated'. He ordered the attack on the besieged Libyan fortress to take place in November. If the 'collapse of the Soviet Union' had created the 'necessary conditions', he added, then preparations should be made for the despatch of a German expeditionary force from Transcaucasia against the oilfields of northern Iraq. He would also enlist Arab support in this. The position of the British in the Middle East would be 'rendered more precarious, in the event of major German operations,' Hitler pointed out, 'if more British forces are tied down at the right moment by civil commotion or revolt'.

Quite apart from these Middle Eastern and Mediterranean operations, there was, Hitler wrote, another objective to be borne in mind: 'The "Siege of England" must be resumed with the utmost intensity by the Navy and Air Force after the conclusion of the campaign in the East.'

The eventual defeat of Britain was Hitler's ultimate aim. The defeat of Russia was the penultimate step on that path. He did not expect it to take more than a few months. By the end of 1941, with Russia captive and Russia's military and raw material resources – including the Caucasian oilfields at Maikop, Grozny and Baku – at his disposal, he would be making his plans to invade Britain.

Churchill had no intention of waiting to see what would happen in Russia. On the very night of Hitler's Directive No. 32, British bombers struck at industrial targets in the Ruhr, the Rhineland and the German North Sea ports. In the attack on the railway yards at Cologne much damage was caused, and fourteen people killed. Behind the lines in France, British agents were at work co-ordinating acts of resistance. Churchill himself gave a clarion call to the occupied countries on June 12, telling them in a broadcast picked up on many thousands of secret radio sets listened to, and in great danger, throughout German-occupied Europe: 'We shall aid and stir the people of every conquered country to resistance and revolt. We shall break up or derange every effort which Hitler makes to systematize and consolidate his subjugation. He will find no peace, no rest, no halting place, no parley.' Churchill's advice to those entrusted with clandestine operations behind German lines was: 'Set Europe ablaze'.

Hitler's plans for the invasion of Russia had reached their final stages. On June 19 the SS established a special fund for the care of widows and orphans of SS men killed in action. Throughout June 20 and June 21 the German forces in the eastern borderlands of Greater Germany were brought up to the border itself. On the night of June 21, Hitler, who was entertaining Albert Speer and Admiral Raeder in Berlin, put on a gramophone record and played his guests a few bars from *Les Préludes* by Liszt. 'You'll hear that often in the near future,' he told them, 'because it is going to be our victory fanfare for the Russian campaign.'

CHAPTER TWELVE

1941
JUNE TO DECEMBER

To see sovereign rights and self-government restored
to those who have been forcibly deprived of them.

THE ATLANTIC CHARTER

THE GERMAN INVASION of the Soviet Union began at fifteen minutes after four o'clock on the morning of 22 June 1941. The most gargantuan of all the conflicts of the Second World War had begun. Millions of soldiers and millions of civilians – also millions of soldiers who had been taken prisoner-of-war – were to be its victims, as were more than a million Russian Jews.

The conflict and conflagration in Russia were to last for more than three years. During the first day of the war, as an indication of what was to come, whole Russian villages were burned down after the German army had passed through them. Many of their civilian inhabitants were massacred – Russian peasants and Russian Jews – on the spot. The Red Army was in no position to hold the border. By midnight on the first day, German aircraft had destroyed a quarter of the Soviet air force – more than a thousand planes – either on the ground or in combat.

'We have only to kick in the door and the whole rotten structure will come crashing down,' Hitler told General Jodl at his new headquarters, named the Wolf's Lair, at Rastenburg in East Prussia. Dr Goebbels sounded an unexpected note of caution, however, when he wrote in the privacy of his diary on June 23: 'The public mood is one of slight depression. The nation wants peace, though not at the price of defeat, but every new theatre of operations brings worries and concerns.'

The new theatre of operations was unlike any other: 3,200,000 German soldiers were advancing eastward, along a 930-mile front, faced by 2,000,000 Russians, with a further 2,200,000 Russians in reserve protecting Moscow, Leningrad and the factories of the Donetz basin and the Urals. Not only tanks and armoured vehicles, planes and artillery, machine guns and rifles, but the instruments of terror, were part of the German armoury. Stalin's crimes of the previous decade – the deportations to labour camps, the executions of several million citizens for non-existent opposition, the deaths at slave labour – these were overshadowed by new horrors.

On the fourth day of the German invasion, the commander of the 47th Panzer Corps, General Lemelsen, protested to his subordinates about what he characterized as the 'senseless shootings of both prisoners-of-war and civilians' and ordered the shootings to stop. His order was ignored. Five days later he protested that 'still more shootings' had taken place 'conducted in an irresponsible, senseless and criminal manner. This is murder! The German Army is waging war against Bolshevism, not against the Russian peoples'.

General Lemelsen was wrong. The war was being waged against all the Russian peoples: Russians, Ukrainians, Armenians, Georgians, Mongols, and above all Jews. It was being waged against millions of soldiers fighting to defend their native soil, and against millions of civilians who had laboured so hard and suffered so much under the Soviet regime. In protesting against the executions of Russian prisoners-of-war and civilians, and in saying that the Soviet soldier who fought well was entitled to 'decent treatment', even General Lemelsen made an exception to his sense of fair play. No such 'decent treatment', he explained, need apply to 'commissars and partisans' who were captured. They were to be interrogated, identified and then led outside and shot on the order of an officer. Christian Streit, a German scholar who has studied the fate of the Soviet prisoners-of-war in German hands, writes: 'It was quite obvious that even for Lemelsen, who adhered to the traditional military code of honour, the long-cherished military principle of giving quarter to an enemy who surrendered did not apply to Communists.'

On June 26 the German army had penetrated 185 miles inside the Soviet border along the Baltic and White Russian areas of the front. That day Finland declared war on the Soviet Union. Like Italy during the war against Greece and Yugoslavia, Finland had waited until she judged that victory would fall to Germany. A day later Hungary declared war on the Soviet Union. Roumania, while expressing total support for Germany's action in invading Russia, still hesitated to join Germany on the battlefield.

Several defence lines were created by the Soviet High Command. From Leningrad more than thirty thousand people, most of them women, were taken towards Luga to build anti-tank ditches, dugouts and tank traps. As they worked, low flying German fighters, and higher altitude bombers, bombed and strafed them day after day. 'How many thousands were killed?' asked the American war correspondent – and historian – Harrison Salisbury. 'No one knows. There was no accurate account of those engaged on the job and no way of identifying who returned and who did not.'

The fate of hundreds of Russian towns that were overrun, of the soldiers defending them, and of the Jews living in them, was gruesome. On June 27 the White Russian capital, Minsk, was surrounded. There were 300,000 Soviet soldiers encircled in the trap. Tens of thousands were killed in the fighting. The rest were taken prisoner, but denied the most elementary rights accorded to prisoners-of-war. Many were taken to a former collective farm on the outskirts of Minsk, at the village of Maly Trostenets, where they were put into the fields without any form of cover and surrounded by barbed wire and guards. Refused any medical attention, refused food and even water, in the course of a few weeks they were deliberately starved to death. Other Russian prisoners-of-war, who were marched to the rear, or taken off to camps far away from where they were captured, were beaten and shot down as they marched. When winter came they were given no shelter and froze to death in their hundreds of thousands.

From the first days of the German invasion of the Soviet Union the SS Special Task Forces moved steadily and ruthlessly behind the armies, taking Jews out of their homes to the nearest wood or ravine, and shooting them down. Tens of thousands of Jews were murdered in the first few weeks; hundreds of thousands in the months ahead. This was the beginning of the Holocaust – the mass murder of Jews with a view to destroying not only their lives as individuals but obliterating their life as a people: the deliberate and system-atic destruction of their homes and culture, their way of life and language, their future from generation to generation. As the executions spread from town to town and village to village, babies and small children were thrown alive into the pits on the edge of which their parents had been shot.

Amid the slaughter there were acts of bravery on the part of the victims, who for the most part were killed even as they sought to resist. When the Germans entered the town of Lutsk on June 25 the soldiers found Dr Benjamin From, a Jewish surgeon, in the hospital operating room. He was performing an operation on a Christian woman. They ordered him to stop the operation at once. Jews could not operate on Christians, it was against the racial policy of the Third Reich. Dr From refused. He was immediately dragged out of the hospital, taken to his home, and killed with his whole family.

In the early hours of June 27 the Germans entered Bialystok, a city which they had occupied briefly in September 1939, before handing it over to the Soviet Union under the terms of the Nazi-Soviet Pact. Since September 1939 ten thousand Jewish refugees from German-occupied Poland had found refuge in the city, raising its Jewish population to more than fifty thousand. At eight on the morning of the German entry into the city – 'Red Friday' in the annals of the Jewish community of Bialystok – a large German motorized unit gathered at one end of the Jewish Quarter and began drinking 'To death!'. A few minutes later they besieged the Szulhojf quarter around the Great Synagogue. The slaughter started at once. The Germans, in small units, armed with automatic pistols and hand grenades, started chasing Jews through the narrow, winding streets around the Great Synagogue.

'Dante-esque scenes', the Bialystok Jewish historian Szymon Datner later wrote, 'took place on these streets. Jews were taken out of the houses, put against the walls, and shot. From everywhere, the unfortunate people were driven in the direction of the Great Synagogue, which was burning with a great fire, and from which horrible cries came out.' At least eight hundred Jews had been locked into the synagogue, before it had been set on fire.

The Germans then forced further victims to push one another into the burning synagogue. Those who resisted were shot, and the dead bodies thrown inside the burning building. 'Soon the whole quarter around the synagogue was burning,' Datner wrote. 'The soldiers were throwing hand grenades inside the houses, which being mostly wooden, burned easily. A sea of flames which embraced the whole Szulhojf overflowed into the neighbouring streets.'

Until late in the afternoon Jews were driven into the burning synagogue, or shot on the streets and in their houses. The noise of exploding grenades, Datner has written, 'mingled with the shots from the pistols, and with the drunken cries of the Germans, and the horrible cries of the murdered victims'. Among those who died in the burning synagogue were a celebrated chess player, Zabludowski, and a popular comedian, Alter Sztajnberg.

At one moment, when the Germans were not watching, a Pole – his name is not known, he was the porter of the synagogue – opened a small window at the back of the synagogue, and several dozen Jews managed to escape.

By the end of that day of burning and shooting, two thousand Jews had been murdered.

For the conquerors, the murder of Jews and the murder of captured Soviet soldiers went in tandem. On June 27 the Germans entered the town of Nieswiez. A Jewish youngster, Shalom Cholawski – who survived the war as a partisan in the forests – later described the fate of a group of captured Red Army men that day:

> Groups of Russian prisoners-of-war were brought into the synagogue court-yard. They lay hungry and exhausted. The Germans moved among them, kicking them with their heavy shoes.
>
> One of the soldiers began beating a prisoner. He raised the man to his feet and cursed him with every punch. The prisoner, a short fellow with dull Mongolian features, did not know why the German had singled him out or what he was raving about. He stood there, not resisting the blows. Suddenly, he lifted his hand and, with a terrific sweep, slapped his attacker powerfully and squarely on the cheek. Blood trickled slowly down the German's face.
>
> For a moment they stared at each other. One man seething with anger, the other calm. Several Germans brusquely shoved the man to a place behind the fence. A volley of shots echoed in the air. I witnessed the scene from my window.

As the Soviet army retreated it left behind groups of men who were instructed to remain armed and ready to start partisan actions against the German occupiers whenever the orders came to do so. One of those who organized this system in the early days was a senior Communist Party official in the Ukraine, Nikita Khrushchev, who was later ruler of the Soviet Union. On June 27 he gave instructions for groups of between ten and twenty men each to prepare to remain behind in Kamenets Podolsk. Similar small groups were set up in the first week of the war in at least twenty other locations. Some were taken up to the front line and infiltrated into areas already under German control.

On June 29 Stalin ordered the destruction of everything that could be destroyed, in order to deny it to the Germans. This 'scorched earth' policy was to be carried out in every locality that was about to be abandoned. What could not be evacuated must be destroyed, 'leaving the enemy with not a single locomotive, not a truck, not a loaf of bread, not a litre of fuel'. At the same time, the newly-formed partisan groups were instructed to blow up bridges, railway tracks, telephone and telegraph wires and installations behind the lines.

That day Hitler approved the formation of national SS Legions, to be recruited in the occupied countries for the 'battle against Bolshevism'. Those who were designated 'Germanics' – Norwegians, Dutch, Swedes, Danes and Flemings – would serve with the elite Waffen SS units. Others – Croats, Spaniards and Frenchmen – would serve with the German Army. Recruitment was to be voluntary. The first such formation to be created was the Danish Legion, for which 480 men volunteered. The Danish Government, in a remarkable act of defiance, branded as traitors all those who joined, and deprived them of their personal rights as Danish citizens.*

On the day of the Stalin and Hitler decrees of June 29, the German army entered Lvov, the main city of Eastern Galicia. Each group of its mixed population of Poles, Ukrainians and Jews was singled out for privation, persecution and execution. On entering Lvov the Germans found 3,000 Ukrainians who were still confined in the prison cells and secret police cellars as enemies of the Soviet Union. Overnight, to their own disbelief and distress, the enemies of the previous rulers became enemies of the new rulers. Most of them were killed within a few hours of the Germans' arrival. As for the Jews, it was not only the members of the Special Task Forces who killed them; when the German army entered the city of Kaunas (Kovno) they discovered that more than two thousand Jews had been massacred by local Lithuanians in the few day gap between the departure of the Soviet authorities and the arrival of the Germans.

The Latvian capital, Riga, fell to the Germans on July 1. That day the Japanese rejected a request by Ribbentrop that Japan enter the war and attack the Soviet Union in the Far East. On the following day the Roumanians agreed to enter the war, and advanced into the Ukraine. The industrial heartland of the Donetz was suddenly threatened. On July 2 an extraordinary decision was made in Moscow. Factories that were on the line of the German advance – all the factories, in fact, in the vast industrial regions of southern Russia – would be evacuated: the light and heavy plant, the raw material stockpiles, and the factory workers and their families. The first factory to

---

* No Swedish SS Legion was ever created. By the end of July, 1,164 Norwegians, 1,100 Dutchmen and 600 Flemings (from Belgium) had volunteered to serve in their respective national SS Legions.

be moved was the armoured-plate mill in Mariupol, on the Sea of Azov. It was to be taken to the Urals, to the city of Magnitogorsk, and re-erected there. On the following day, July 3, twenty-six other armaments factories were given the order to move. Even factories in Moscow and Leningrad were sent eastward to the Urals.

Stalin had not spoken to the Russian people when the German armies attacked. He did so for the first time on July 3, the fourteenth consecutive day of the German assault. His words were stern ones: 'A grave threat hangs over our country,' he said. 'Military tribunals will pass summary judgments on any who fail in our defence, whether through panic or treachery, regardless of position or rank.' This was no idle threat. Even the highest ranking officers whom Stalin felt were deficient in courage were shot: among them Generals Pavlov, Kulik and Shtern, each of whom had served in the Spanish Civil War.

Stalin's threat of shooting seemed to the Germans proof that his armies and his people would indeed panic, and betray their leader. 'It is no exaggeration to say that the campaign against Russia has been won in fourteen days', was General Halder's reflection on July 3. He was wrong. All that was certain that day was the violence and cruelty of the struggle, its deranged brutality, and the mounting numbers of civilian victims as the German army and the SS Special Task Forces moved ever eastward.

Hitler shared General Halder's sense of victory. On July 5 he spoke to his staff of how he would make 'the beauties of the Crimea' accessible to all Germans by means of a specially-built motor road linking it with Germany. 'For us Germans, that will be our Riviera'.

The scourge of Nazi racism was not confined to Germany. On July 8 the Roumanian dictator, General Ion Antonescu, confronted by spontaneous acts of killing of Jews by the Iron Guard, especially in the city of Jassy, told his Cabinet:

> I beg you to have no mercy. At the risk of being misunderstood by some traditionalists, who might be among you, I am supporting the idea of the compulsory eviction of Jews from Bessarabia and Bukovina. They shall be pushed outside the borders. The same shall be done to the Ukrainian element, which has nothing to do there . . .
>
> I do not know when, in how many centuries, the Roumanian nation will benefit from the same liberty of action for its ethnic purification.

Nowadays we are owners of our territory. Let us make use of it. It does not matter if we are treated as barbarians . . .

We never had a more proper moment . . .

If necessary, fire with machine-guns . . .

I give you the full liberty. I assume all the responsibilities and I am declaring again: the law does not exist.

While thirty Roumanian divisions fought alongside the Germans on the Eastern front, Roumanian soldiers and police were expelling Jews from the conquered areas, stealing their possessions, looting their homes, and killing those who resisted eviction. Roumanian troops, advancing deeper into Russia, wreaked terrible destruction – on life as well as on property – on the Jews whom they found in every town. When Antonescu was told that in the occupied areas of southern Russia two hundred Jews were being shot for every Roumanian soldier killed, and a hundred Jews shot for every Roumanian soldier wounded, he remarked approvingly: 'Go on with this, because I am taking it on me, before the country and history.' And he added, derisively: 'Let American Jews call me to account.'

Realizing that if the Soviet Union were defeated, as she might be before the late autumn, Hitler would then turn against Britain, the British Government, at Churchill's urging, and with his daily scrutiny, prepared to send whatever military help it could. Churchill asked Stalin what he wanted, and his needs were met. Those needs were formidable, so much so that Britain transferred direct to Russia military equipment of the highest quality which had just arrived from the United States, intended as part of Britain's war arsenal. Roosevelt not only accepted this, but extended the area of the Atlantic over which American naval patrols would operate to within four hundred miles of the coast of Scotland. To ensure that there would be a permanent American presence in the new area of operation, a United States Marine Brigade was landed in Iceland.

Another British plan to help Russia – a plan which Churchill strongly endorsed – was to intensify the bombing of German cities, with the aim of disrupting even further than before German munitions production and communications, and of forcing Hitler to bring back German warplanes from the Russian front to defend the German cities. Churchill announced the new policy when he broadcast to the British people on July 14: 'In the last few weeks alone we have thrown upon Germany about half the tonnage of bombs thrown by the Germans upon our cities during the whole course of the war. But this is only a beginning. Starting that same day, a series of even heavier bombing raids was launched from Britain. Several industrial areas of Hanover were bombed on July 14, followed by two more raids in the next nine days, during which factories in Hamburg, Frankfurt and Mannheim were also bombed.

Hitler was not impressed by the threat from Britain. On the day of Churchill's speech he issued a supplementary directive in which he looked at what German policy would be 'after the overthrow of Russia'. But the Russians themselves were finding extraordinary reserves of strength and tenacity as their native land was being overrun and ravaged. The very word native land (*rodina*) which the Communists had banished from the vocabulary as being a bourgeois affectation, was reinstated on Stalin's orders. Individual German units were being pushed back. Attacks by the most mechanized and highly trained German divisions were being repulsed. Although the German front continued to move forward, it was meeting defence lines that did not break as easily as had been expected.

On July 14, the day of Hitler's confident directive – and of the intensification of British bombing raids over Germany – a Soviet army officer, Captain Flerov, experimented with a new type of anti-tank rocket launcher. It was a simple but effective device, that fired 320 rockets in a twenty-five second burst. Known as the Katyusha, it was quickly to take its place in the Soviet arsenal, and in the Soviet Army's unyielding determination not to abandon the motherland.

As the daily massacre of Jews continued, one such massacre was recorded in his diary by SS Sergeant Felix Landau. One of the Austrian Nazis who had carried out the murder of the Austrian Chancellor, Engelbert Dollfuss, in 1934, Landau a member of an SS Special Task Force in the Eastern Galician town of Drohobycz. On July 14 his unit rounded up more than a hundred Jews:

We drive a few kilometres along the main road till we reach a wood. We go into the wood and look for a spot suitable for mass executions.

We order the prisoners to dig their graves. Only two of them are crying, the others show courage. What can they all be thinking? I believe each still has the hope of not being shot. I don't feel the slightest stir of pity. That's how it is, and has got to be.

My heart beats very faintly when I recall being in the same position once. In the Federal Chancellery on 25.7.1934, I was also in peril of my life. At that time I was younger and thought it was all over. Yet I had the firm conviction that my death won't be in vain. It happened differently, however. I stayed alive, and now I stand here and shoot others.

Slowly the grave gets bigger and deeper. Two are crying without let-up. I let them dig more so they can't think. The work really calms them. Money, watches and valuables are collected. The two women go first to be shot; placed at the edge of the grave they face the soldiers. They get shot.

When it's the men's turn, the soldiers aim at the shoulder. All our six men are allowed to shoot. Three prisoners have been shot in the heart.

The shooting goes on. Two heads have been shot off. Nearly all fall into the grave unconscious only to suffer a long while. Our revolvers don't help either. The last group have to throw the corpses into the grave; they have to stand ready for their own execution. They all tumble into the grave.

While horrendous scenes like this were being enacted behind the lines throughout the Eastern Front, in Holland one of the leading Dutch statesmen, Hendrikus Colijn, was arrested by the Gestapo. A former Prime Minister, Foreign Minister and Minister of War, he had become chief editor of the Calvinist newspaper *De Standaard* in 1939. After the German conquest of Holland he had momentarily shown himself to be impressed by Germany's inevitable victory and had published a pamphlet describing democracy as a 'deadly disease'.

Within a short time, however, Dr Colijn had begun to support the Dutch Resistance, emerging as an uncompromising opponent of Nazism. Within a year of his arrest he was sent to Germany and interned; he died while still in internment two years later, at the age of seventy-five.

On July 16 the last defence line before Moscow was broken and the German encirclement of Smolensk was begun. Hitler was jubilant. 'We must now face the task of cutting up our cake according to our needs in order to be able, first to dominate it, second to administer it, third to exploit it.' He welcomed the Russian partisan activity behind the lines because, he told General Keitel and the others who had come to his East Prussia headquarters, 'it enables us to exterminate everyone who opposes us'. On the following day Hitler entrusted Himmler with full autonomy for 'police security in the newly occupied territories'. The SS would rule supreme.

The struggle between Hitler and his Western adversaries had many turning points. On July 20 a British naval vessel, a minelayer, set off across the North Sea on its way to the Arctic Ocean and the Soviet port of Murmansk, bringing military supplies. This was the first step in what was to become a veritable armada of supply ships, many of which were sunk by German U-boat attack, and by German planes using bases in German-occupied northern Norway. With the Baltic Sea under German control, and the Russian shore of the Black Sea falling rapidly to the German and Roumanian armies, the British merchant ships, escorted by warships, could only reach Russia by using the perilous Arctic Sea route.

Three days after that first minelayer set sail, a large British naval force of two aircraft carriers, two cruisers and six destroyers set off at Stalin's urgent request to attack German ships taking war supplies between the Norwegian port of Kirkenes and the Finnish-controlled port of Petsamo, for military operations against the Germans in the Murmansk region. These, and later other British warships, fought far above the Arctic Circle to prevent German war materials being used against Russia in the far north.

Hitler was becoming impatient. He wanted Leningrad 'finished off speedily,' as he demanded on July 20 during a visit to his forces in Russia. On July 21, German bombers struck at Moscow for the first time. It was the day before the British handed over the secrets of jet propulsion to an American aviation mission, leading to the manufacture of jet engines in the United States. Three years later, Germany's jet aircraft factories were to be vulnerable to repeated Allied attack. The factories in the United States had no such impediment.

German troops had been advancing eastward through Russia for a month. In neutral Sweden, the Chief of the General Staff, General Olof Thornell, informed his superiors: 'A German victory and defeat for the Soviet Union has invaluable advantages for Sweden.' When, however, the Japanese Government was again pressed by Hitler to help the German war against Russia by attacking the Soviet Far East, it again declined to do so. Japan had other priorities and imperial aspirations. In French Indo-China, the Communist movement led by Ho Chi Minh had organized an armed uprising against Vichy rule on June 6. The French had crushed it and arrested its leaders. Sixteen days later, on July 24, Japanese forces issued a demand that they be allowed to occupy Indo-China.

The Vichy authorities in Indo-China agreed to let in 40,000 Japanese troops. The Japanese sent in 125,000. The United States bases in the Philippines, as well as Britain's base at Singapore, were within eight hundred miles of the new forward Japanese positions. In retaliation for the Japanese occupation of French Indo-China and the threat it seemed to pose to America's Far Eastern interests, Roosevelt ordered the seizure of all Japanese assets in the United States. The British seized all Japanese assets in Britain and the British Empire. The Dutch government in exile in London, whose Dutch East Indies territories were equally threatened, seized all Japanese assets in the Dutch East Indies. Japan was suddenly deprived of ninety per cent of her oil imports. Her own oil resources could last only another three years at the most. In an added measure of disapproval of the occupation of French Indo-China, the United States closed the Panama Canal to Japanese merchant ships.

On the Eastern Front, as Hitler's forces advanced, a Soviet military order announced the execution of nine senior Soviet generals. In case the call of patriotism was not enough, Stalin had decided to use the technique of pre-war terror to create military discipline through fear. At that very moment, his first-born son Yakov was captured on the Eastern Front. He was thirty-four years old. On July 24 the Germans circulated a photograph of their prize captive. They also used his capture to seek a propaganda victory, dropping leaflets over the German lines with the exhortation:

To Red Army soldiers. Follow the example of Stalin's son! He has surrendered and is a prisoner. He is alive and feels fine. Why do you want to die when already the son of your leader gave himself up and is our prisoner? Peace to your tormented Motherland! Stick your bayonets in the earth!

When the Germans tried to exchange Stalin's son for German civilian internees being held in the Soviet Union, Stalin's only comment was that he had no son called Yakov. He did however arrest Yakov's wife Yulia Mel'ster, of whose marriage – she was Jewish – he had disapproved. She was kept in prison for two years. Yakov was shot by a guard in a German prisoner-of-war camp when, in suicidal mood, he ran to the camp wire.

'They have been bombing Moscow for the third night running,' Boris Pasternak wrote to his wife and mother on July 24. 'How often during the course of last night, with high-explosive bombs coming down and bursting on every second and third house, and incendiaries setting entire street blocks almost instantaneously alight – as if at the wave of a magic wand – did I mentally say good-bye to you both.'

On July 29 a final defence line for Moscow was created, less than 150 miles west of the capital. That day, in addition to the British help that was already arriving in North Russia in a steady stream – at the very ports where in 1919 the British anti-Bolshevik forces had landed – the United States, which had also sent troops to fight the Bolsheviks in the immediate aftermath of the revolution, despatched two hundred American fighter planes by ship to Archangel. A leading American expert in the operation of these planes had already reached Moscow.

In the Bessarabian city of Kishinev, a German SS Special Task Force killed 10,000 Jews in fourteen days of continuous executions. They had set a gruesome record: the first 'five figure' execution of the war. The Jews of Kishinev were taken to pits and machine-gunned. The executions ended on July 13. Sometimes the killers were so exhausted by the effort of shooting that they pushed children and old people into the pits alive. 'The Führer is to be kept informed continually from here about the work of the Special Task Forces in the East,' the Gestapo chief Heinrich Müller wrote to the Task Force commanders from Berlin on August 1.

Hitler was not content to learn of the killing of those Jews who lived east of the Polish-Russian border of 1940 – the Jews whom his Special Forces could murder behind the turmoil of war. He wanted the hundreds of thousands of Jews in Western and Central Europe, the Jews walking the streets of Paris, Amsterdam, Brussels and Berlin, as well as the two million Jews confined in the Polish ghettos, to be destroyed as well. On July 31, as the Kishinev killings came to an end, Field Marshal Goering wrote to Reinhard Heydrich, Head of the Reich Security Service, setting out a more comprehensive 'solution' of the future of the many millions of Jews under direct German rule, and elsewhere in Europe.

In his letter, Goering instructed Heydrich 'on the Führer's instructions, to make all necessary preparations as regards organization and actual concrete preparations for a general solution of the Jewish problem within the German sphere of influence in Europe'. Not written of in the letter, but clear from the events on the ground, it was not mass killing on the spot, but deportation to a remote location and death by gas in a special van or chamber, that was emerging as the preferred method. Such gas vans had been used in Belgrade, against Serbian Jews.

It was to take six months before the 'general solution' – to be known within six months as the 'Final Solution' (*Endlösung*) – could be put in operation. But tests in killing by gas were carried out that autumn at Auschwitz using a commercial pesticide, Zyklon-B. In its commercial form the pesticide had an added noxious smell so that those who were killing insects with it would be alerted to it and stand clear. For the purpose of killing human beings, the smell was removed, so that the gas could not be detected. Its human victims would not therefore be alerted to anything untoward. The modified gas was first used at Auschwitz, experimentally, late that autumn, against Soviet soldiers being held as prisoners-of-war. The experiment was hailed as a success by those who devised it.

On August 12, at their first wartime meeting, held on board ship in Placentia Bay, off Newfoundland, Churchill and Roosevelt agreed to give immediate aid to the Soviet Union 'on a gigantic scale'. That day, forty British fighters, with their pilots, reached Murmansk. Nearby were two British submarines, about to go into action against German troop transports and coastal shipping off the coast of northern Norway and Finland. Each shipment, whether of planes or war material, and each transit of warships or submarines, ran enormous risks. The losses in British shipping on the Murmansk-Archangel route was extremely high. The merchant seamen who maintained the lifeline to northern Russia were among the unsung heroes of the Second World War: there were many such, unsung, unnamed and – except by their loved ones – mostly unremembered.

Stalin's behaviour towards those who were bringing help to Russia caused considerable anger. He refused to allow visas to Royal Air Force personnel who were to have flown their fighter-bomber aircraft from bases in Northern Russia against the German planes and submarines attacking the convoys. He also refused to allow visas for special medical detachments that had been sent out from Britain to establish naval hospitals in the Soviet ports to treat the casualties from the convoys. Eventually he allowed one hospital to be established, in Polarnoye, but not the larger one that was to badly needed in Archangel.

While off Newfoundland, Churchill and Roosevelt issued the Atlantic Charter, setting out a joint Anglo-American commitment – to which every Allied power was invited to subscribe – that there would be 'no aggrandizement, territorial or other', as a result of the war. To those already under occupation, the Atlantic Charter stressed the Allied wish 'to see sovereign rights and self-government restored to those who have been forcibly deprived of them'.

That these rights were not to be restricted to Whites was stressed by the Britain's Deputy Prime Minister, Clement Attlee, when he told a group of Black West African students in London on August 15: 'Our enemies, the Nazis, set up a monstrous and ridiculous racial doctrine. They declare themselves to be a master-race to which the rest of us are inferior, and if they assert that claim in respect to Europeans you may be quite assured they are going to apply it to everyone else – Asiatics, Africans, and everyone.'

From Burma, the British Governor sent a message to London that the Burmese would certainly use the Atlantic Charter to press for full self-government after the war. Within the inner circles of the British Colonial Office and administration, there were limits, however, to what the Charter implied, a senior official writing direct to Churchill's office: 'Gibraltar, Aden, Mauritius, Seychelles, Fiji, the Western Pacific islands, the Falklands, British Honduras, Bermuda, the Gambia, Hong Kong. All these Colonies, and probably others (Cyprus, Malta, the dependencies in Borneo, and even Malaya) are too small or too important strategically ever to become independent self-governing units.'

Fifty-six years later, with the transfer of Hong Kong to China, only three territories in the above list – Gibraltar, the Falklands and Bermuda – remained within the orbit of British rule. But as the war continued, it became clear that the fighting would not end with an upsurge of decolonialization. Speaking in New York six months after the Atlantic Charter was promulgated, the American writer Pearl Buck warned that Britain and the United States 'walking together side by side in majesty' – words used by Churchill – might only mean to 'coloured' peoples 'a formidable white imperialism, more dangerous to them than anything even a victorious Japan could threaten'. But towards India, by far the largest of the British imperial possessions, Britain was within a year of offering self-government and the prospect of post-war independence. Inside British India, laws were being promulgated to lessen the worst aspects of the Indian caste system and the wider economic imperative. Under a series of Shops and Establishments Acts passed since the outbreak of the war, and affecting Bombay, Karachi and Ahmedabad among the larger manufacturing centres, the employment of children under the age of twelve was forbidden, and a week's annual holiday with pay provided for all workers – only three years after it had been introduced in France.

In the second week of August, from his headquarters in East Prussia, Hitler gave orders for Leningrad, the Crimea and the Donetz industrial region to be captured first, and then Moscow. Each of these objectives seemed within the realm of possibility before winter set in. He also received a visit from Goering which touched on matters of mass murder. First, Goering pointed out that the euthanasia programme, which had started up again, was being criticized openly and widely. In the city of Münster, the bishop, Count Clemens von Galen, had denounced it from his pulpit. Hitler, unwilling to face widespread criticism at home on a matter that concerned 'Aryan' Germans, when he needed all the loyalty and unity he could get for the Russian campaign, ordered the programme to be halted.

Goering also spoke to Hitler of the need to 'get rid' of the 72,000 Jews living in Berlin: those who had not managed to emigrate before the outbreak of war. It was wrong, Goering insisted, that German soldiers, returning to Germany after Russia was defeated, should find Jews still in residence. Hitler agreed that 'as soon as the first transport possibilities arise, the Berlin Jews will be deported from Berlin to the East. There they will be taken in hand under a somewhat harsher climate'. Starting on October 18, ten thousand Berlin Jews were deported eastward. Only nine trains were needed to uproot so many people. Some were sent to the Lodz ghetto, where they stayed for two to three months, sharing the fate of the starving ghetto inhabitants before being deported again and murdered. But most of the Berlin deportees were sent direct from Berlin to Riga, Minsk and Kovno, where they were murdered within a few hours of arrival. Gas vans which had been used that summer in Belgrade against Serbian Jews, had been transferred to the Baltic for use against the Jews of Berlin; and also to kill several thousand Jews deported at the same time from Vienna and other German cities.

On the night of August 20, German forces on the northern sector of the front reached to within twenty-five miles of Leningrad. On August 22 the Germans advancing towards Moscow entered Vitebsk, whose church spires and wooden houses had been made famous by the painter Marc Chagall. After the Bolshevik revolution of 1917, Chagall had briefly been the town's Commissar for the Arts. Like virtually every town in the path of the advancing army, Vitebsk had been set ablaze by the German artillery bombardment.

On August 26, German troops on the southern sector entered the industrial city of Dnepropetrovsk, in the Ukraine. Although the coveted region was theirs, much of its industry and movable raw materials had already been evacuated to the Urals. On the following day, having ordered a scorched earth policy inside the Baltic port of Tallinn (Reval), the Russians began the evacuation of 23,000 soldiers from the city by sea. More than five thousand Russians were drowned when German dive bombers struck at the troop transports.

Moscow itself was under continuous German air attack, with fifteen or twenty bombers flying over it almost every day and dropping their bombs. On August 27 it was announced in Moscow that 750 people had been killed and 2,000 seriously injured during the previous month – in the course of twenty-four air raids.

Behind the lines, tens of thousands of Jews were being killed every week. At one town in Lithuania – Kedainiai – the Special Task Force noted with precision on August 28 that it had killed '710 Jewish men, 767 Jewish women, 599 Jewish children'. The mind can hardly grasp either the scale of the killings or the desire of the perpetrators to keep such precise statistics. That day, Hitler flew with Mussolini from Rastenberg to Uman, where the two leaders saw another town still burning as a result of the German advance, and inspected captured Russian tanks and artillery.

On September 1 the German forces attacking Leningrad cut the city off from all rail connection with Moscow. To assist the Germans, the Finns destroyed part of the Murmansk-Leningrad railway, cutting the city off from any supplies from the north. When the Russian forces made a small counter-attack, Hitler let it be known to the commander of Army Group North that he had no objection to Leningrad – with its million or more civilian inhabitants, including tens of thousands of refugees – being bombed from the air or pounded without respite by artillery fire.

In the first sustained bombing raid on Leningrad, in the second week of September, two hundred citizens were killed. But as the German commander prepared to break into the city, Hitler called off the attack, unwilling to face the ravages of street-by-street fighting that might destroy utterly the city he hoped to conquer and display. Instead, he instituted a state of siege, and moved away the best of the tank and air forces that were poised to attack. He had decided that the main thrust that September must be to Moscow.

In Moscow, Stalin found time among the demands of the battle to settle old scores. Such opposition to his rule as had existed in the past had long been crushed, and those accused of opposing him, if not shot, had all been sentenced to long terms in labour camps. On September 5 Stalin signed a list on which were the names of 170 people. Most of them were already prisoners. All of them were sentenced to be shot. One of those executed as a result of this signature was Christian Rakovsky, the former Soviet Ambassador to Britain who had been spared the death sentence three years earlier as a result of the intervention of the British Labour Party leadership. At the time of his execution Rakovsky was seventy-three.

Also executed as a result of Stalin's order of September 5 was Maria Spiridonova. In 1906, at the age of twenty, her assassination of one of the senior policemen involved in suppressing the peasant revolt in the Tambov province had made her a revolutionary hero, and earned her a long spell of punitive Tsarist exile in Siberia. After the October revolution she had become the leader of a new Party, the Left Socialist Revolutionaries (Internationalists), and in 1918 was the joint Bolshevik-Left Socialist Revolutionary candidate for the chairmanship of the Constituent Assembly. In July 1918, after the Assembly had been precipitately closed down by Lenin, she had led an anti-Bolshevik uprising. For this, she had again been imprisoned. At the time of her execution she had spent a total of more than twenty-two years in prison and Siberian exile.

Hitler had failed to defeat the Soviet Union in a few weeks, as he had hoped. A new adversary loomed over the battlefield that month: the onset of winter. 'We are heading for a winter campaign,' one German general wrote in his diary on September 9. 'The real trial of this war has begun.' Three days later the first snow flurries fell on the battlefield, though none of the snow settled. Hitler remained confident of victory before the full force of winter set in. To Otto Abetz, his ambassador in Paris, who visited Rastenburg on September 16, he set out his vision of the future. Leningrad would be razed to the ground; it was the 'poisonous nest' from which for so long 'Asiatic venom had spewed forth'. The 'Asiatics' and the Bolsheviks must be hounded out of Europe, bringing an end to 'two hundred and fifty years of Asiatic pestilence'. The Ural Mountains would become the new frontier. Russia west of the Urals would be Germany's 'India'. The iron-ore fields at Krivoi Rog alone would provide Germany with a million tons of ore a month.

Hitler assured Otto Abetz that as soon as the Vichy government agreed to take part in the defeat of Britain, France would have its share of the economically self-sufficient German New Order. Inside that New Order a young German Army officer, Lieutenant Erwin Bingel, was at Uman, in the Ukraine, on September 16. Four years later he recalled the scene as SS troops and Ukrainian militiamen murdered several hundred Jews, who were taken outside the town, lined up in rows, forced to undress, and mowed down with machine-gun fire. In Lieutenant Bingel's words: 'Even women carrying children a fortnight to three weeks old, sucking at their breasts were not spared this horrible ordeal. Nor were mothers spared the sight of their children being gripped by their little legs and put to death with one stroke of the pistol butt or club, thereafter to be thrown on the heap of human bodies in the ditch.' Two of Lieutenant Bingel's men suffered a 'complete nervous breakdown' as a result of what they saw. Two others were sentenced to a year each in a military prison for having taken 'snapshots' of the action.

On the day of this massacre at Uman – a scene that was being repeated somewhere in German-occupied Russia every day – Field Marshal Keitel, the chief of the High Command of the German Armed Forces, issued an order to all German troops that they must act with special severity against partisans, both in Russia and in Serbia. In Serbia, after five months of German occupation, partisan actions against German troops were becoming more and more frequent. Keitel's order stated that for every German soldier killed by partisans, fifty to a hundred 'Communists' were to be executed as a reprisal. Keitel explained the severity of this order on the grounds that 'a human life in these countries often counts for nothing and a deterrent effect can be achieved only through unusual harshness.'

Hitler focused his mind on the aftermath of victory. On September 17 he told his visitors at Rastenburg that with the defeat of the Soviet Union, the Crimea would provide Germany with its citrus fruits, cotton and rubber. The Ukraine would be Germany's to exploit. 'We'll supply grain to all in Europe who need it.' The conquered Russian people would be denied any access to education. They would become the tillers of the soil for Germany. German settlers and rulers would control the whole region. 'The least of our stable lads must be superior to any native.'

The German road to conquest was costly, however, and far from smooth. On September 15, after a fierce Soviet counter-attack, Red Army troops led by General Timoshenko recaptured the town of Yelnya and two villages south-east of Smolensk – Ushakovo and Ustinovka – 'perhaps the first villages, the first towns recaptured from the monstrous German war machine on the continent of Europe,' wrote the British newspaper correspondent

Alexander Werth, who was taken from Moscow to see them. 'And all that was left,' he added, 'was rubble and ashes.'

Sixteen miles of Russian territory was recaptured in Timoshenko's counter-offensive, and fifty villages and hamlets. Rumours swept Moscow that Smolensk itself had been recaptured, but these rumours were false. In the third week of September, however, it was announced from Berlin that 86,000 German soldiers had been killed since the invasion of the Soviet Union almost three months earlier – an average of more than a thousand soldiers a day.

For Hitler, waiting on German soil at Rastenburg, victory appeared to be coming closer, despite the cost. The Timoshenko counter-offensive was pushed back, and on September 19, repeating their eastern triumph of 1918, German troops entered Kiev, the capital of the Ukraine. Half a million Soviet soldiers were taken prisoner. Almost all of them were to die in the months ahead as a result of deliberate starvation and cruelty. Such cruelty was a daily occurrence. When three SS sentries were killed in a Russian village near Krasnaya Gora in mid-September, all the villagers – several hundred old men, women and children – were lined up and machine-gunned.

On September 22 the German commanding general in Serbia, Franz Böhme, issued an order to his troops which referred to events that had taken place before most of them were born. Their mission lay, he said, in the country 'in which German blood flowed in 1914 through the treachery of Serbs, women and children. You are the avengers of these dead. An intimidating example must be created for the whole of Serbia, which must hit the whole population most severely.'

That intimidation began on the following day, and within ten days 1,126 Serbs accused of Communist sympathies had been killed and many villages burned to the ground. Women and children were spared at the last moment so that the harvest could be brought in – to help feed the German army. Later General Böhme carried out reprisal actions for Serb partisan attacks on his troops, executing – in accordance with Keitel's order of September 16 – a hundred hostages for every one German killed. At Sabac camp the hostages were Jews who had been seized in Belgrade, most of whom had found refuge there in 1939 after fleeing from Austria. The historian Christopher Browning writes of how at Sabac 'these executions were particularly absurd and grotesque, in that predominantly Austrian troops gunned down central European Jewish refugees mostly from Vienna in retaliation for Serbian partisan attacks on the German army'.

Ten days after the German occupation of Kiev the largest massacre of the war thus far began, when, during the course of three days, more than thirty thousand Jews were ordered out of the city and taken to a ravine at nearby Babi Yar. A twelve-year-old Russian boy, Anatoli Kuznetsov, then living in Kiev, recalled the sound of distant shooting and his grandfather's horrified comment: 'Do you know what? They're not deporting 'em. They're *shooting* 'em.' In all, 33,771 Jews were killed in those three days, shot down into the ravine, many of them buried alive under the mound of bodies that fell down on top of them. A massacre on a similar scale took place later that week in the Black Sea cities of Nikolayev and Kherson. The Special Task Force Report – Operational Situation Report No. 101 – gave, with its usual precision, the number of victims there as 35,782.

As Roosevelt and Churchill had promised, Allied aid to the Soviet Union was intensified. In the last week of September the whole of that week's British tank production was sent to Russia. Also that week, all the fighter planes (1,800), tanks (2,250), anti-tank guns (500) and Tommy guns (23,000) that were on their way from the United States to Britain were also diverted to Russia, special convoys being despatched direct from Iceland to Archangel, starting on September 28. Enormous quantities of war supplies, including medicines, were earmarked for Russia. Britain and the United States between them agreed to send 600,000 pairs of army boots and shoes a month, and more than a million doses of the newly discovered antibiotics. Within a month, Roosevelt had approved $1 billion of Lend-Lease aid to Russia, with no interest to be charged. Nor would the first repayments have to be made by Russia until five years after the end of the war.

For its part, the Soviet Union had moved, in anticipation of the German advance, more than a thousand heavy industrial plants from western and southern Russia to the Urals, Siberia and Central Asia. But Allied aid and Soviet ingenuity might both prove in vain if Hitler could achieve his goal of victory before the winter. On October 2 he launched the would-be victorious onslaught, Operation Typhoon – the capture of Moscow. 'Today begins the last, great, decisive battle of the war,' he announced in a communiqué broadcast from Rastenburg. Returning to Berlin for a single afternoon, Hitler told an enormous crowd in the Sportpalast on October 4: 'The enemy has already been routed and will never regain his strength.'

As the German armies moved eastward towards Moscow, and in the south reached the Sea of Azov, the killing of civilians – Russians, Ukrainians and Jews – intensified. On October 10, Hitler told his visitors at Rastenburg:

'The law of existence prescribes uninterrupted killing, so that the better may live.' That day Field Marshal Walther von Reichenau, commander of the German Sixth Army, issued a directive which stated: 'The most essential aim of the campaign against the Jewish-Bolshevist system is the complete crushing of its means of power, and the extermination of Asiatic influences in the European region.' Reichenau went on to explain that this aim 'poses tasks for the troops that go beyond the one-sided routine of conventional soldiering'. The German soldier 'must have full understanding for the necessity of a severe but just atonement on Jewish sub-humanity'.

On October 14 the temperature on the Moscow front fell to below zero for the first time that year. On the battlefield melting snow and heavy rain began to cause the Germans severe difficulties, creating a thick, glutinous mud that slowed down and could even halt the German tanks. The Soviet T-34 tank, by contrast, had a wider tread deliberately designed to overcome the mud. But still the advance continued, and on October 15 Stalin ordered the evacuation of all government offices from Moscow to the city of Kuibyshev, on the Volga.

The evacuation of all the factories in and around Moscow was also begun that day. Hitler was certain that, even with the mud, he would enter Moscow within the month. But within a few days the obstacles created by the mud were compounded by thick snow. 'Everything is bogged down in a bottomless quagmire,' the Deputy Chief of Staff of the German Air Force, General von Waldau, noted in his diary on October 16. 'The temperature drops to eleven degrees, a foot of snow falls, and then it rains on top of the snow.'

In front of Moscow, anti-tank ditches — one of them four miles long — were being dug by labour detachments of women brought from the capital. Within a week half a million Muscovites had been mobilized for this work. Millions of men were also being called up. On October 18 twenty-four-year-old Alexander Solzhenitsyn, who had been born a year after the Bolshevik revolution, was among those who joined the army. Serving as an artillery officer, he was twice decorated for bravery.

On October 19 Stalin declared that Moscow was under siege and issued an Order of the Day: 'Moscow will be defended to the last.' The nearest German troops were only sixty-five miles away. Six days later, the first deep snow fell on the Moscow front. It offered the prospect of growing difficulties for the attackers and a protective shield for the defenders.

*   *   *

The enormous demands of the battlefield did not prevent the Germans from carrying out vicious reprisals behind the lines. In the Yugoslav town of Zasavica several hundred Jews and Gypsies were murdered on October 12. In its Operational Situation Report No. 120 of October 21, the Special Task Force operating in Serbia reported that as a reprisal for an attack on a train near Topola, when twenty-two German soldiers lost their lives, 2,200 Serbs and Jews had been shot, and a further 1,738 of the local population, as well as 'nineteen Communist women', executed at Kraljevo. The report added that further south, in Greece, two villages near the Strumen estuary which were 'proved' to have given support for Greek partisans had been burned down, and that 'all the male inhabitants were shot'.

On October 21, in France, the Germans shot fifty hostages at Nantes, as a reprisal for the assassination the previous day of the German military commander of the region, Lieutenant-Colonel Hötz.* On October 26 two men and a woman were executed in Minsk. They had been active in the Russian partisan movement since the German occupation four months earlier. The men were Kiril Trus and Vlodia Shcherbatsevich, both Belorussians. The woman was a seventeen-year-old Jewish girl, Masha Bruskina. The public had been ordered to watch the proceedings, following a German Army directive that 'the population must be more frightened of our reprisals than of the partisans'.

Three nooses were prepared. Masha Bruskina was the first to be hanged. An eye-witness later recalled: 'When they put her on the stool, the girl turned her face towards the fence. The executioners wanted her to stand with her face to the crowd, but she turned away and that was that. No matter how much they pushed her and tried to turn her, she remained standing with her back to the crowd. Only then did they kick away the stool from under her.'

On the following day, October 27, in the inter-war Lithuanian capital, Kovno, a German Roman Catholic woman, Margarete Sommer, protested to the Cardinal about the murder that day of 9,000 Jews in the city. A thousand of them had recently been deported from Germany. In her protest she noted that before the Jews were machine gunned they had been forced to undress in a temperature of eighteen degrees below freezing.

On November 2, while snow lay thick on the ground at Rastenburg,

---

* The murdered hostages are remembered today in the name of one of the main streets of Nantes, the Rue des Cinquantes Otages.

Hitler again spoke to those in his entourage of looking forward to the time – not long distant, he believed – after the Soviet Union was defeated. He would give the Russian regions German names: the Crimea might be called Gothenland. Aryan names as well as Aryan values would spread and be vaunted from the Baltic to the Black Sea.

In Berlin that week there was a human tragedy arising from the Aryan fixation. Since the outbreak of war in 1939 one of Germany's most popular young actors, Joachim Gottschalk, had been ostracized because his wife was Jewish. The authorities had urged him to divorce her, but he refused. As pressure mounted on him, she was accused of 'race defilement', and given one day to pack her bags and leave Germany without him, together with their eight-year-old son. She would not do so; on November 6 she and her husband, after killing their child, killed themselves.

Returning briefly once more to Germany, on November 8 Hitler told the annual Beer Hall commemoration in Munich: 'We are deciding the fate of Europe for the next thousand years.' That day the cold was so intense on the Moscow front that the mud itself was frozen: this gave the German tanks an advantage, as, with the mud frozen solid, they could move forward again with ease. But the low temperatures – on November 12 they fell to twelve degrees below centigrade on the Moscow front – also brought frostbite which was a nightmare to the German soldier. No provision had been made to fight at such low temperatures, as it had been assumed by the planners in Berlin that the war would be over, and won, well before the onset of winter. By contrast, the Russian army, whose training had always included winter fighting, possessed specially trained ski troops, who first went into action on November 16.

Far behind the new battle lines, the tyranny of occupation continued. On the morning of November 17 the Jews of the Warsaw ghetto were shocked to learn of the death sentence carried out on eight people who had left the ghetto 'without permission'. Six of those executed were women. All had been caught after crossing into 'Aryan' Warsaw in search of food. 'One of the victims,' Chaim Kaplan noted in his diary, 'a young girl not quite eighteen, asked the Jewish policeman who was present at the execution to tell her family that she had been sent to a concentration camp and would not be seeing them for some time. Another young girl cried out to God imploring Him to accept her as the expiatory sacrifice for her people and to let her be the final victim.'

'All past experience', Emanuel Ringelblum noted, 'pales in the face of the fact that eight people were shot to death for crossing the threshold of the ghetto.' The execution 'has set all Warsaw trembling'. A few SS officers had attended, 'calmly smoking cigarettes and behaving cynically all through the execution'. One of the six executed women was a beggar, another was a woman with three children.

The deaths from the severe winter weather were mounting inside the Warsaw ghetto. 'In the streets', Mary Berg noted in her diary on November 22, 'frozen human corpses are an increasingly frequent sight'. Sometimes, she wrote, a mother 'cuddles a child frozen to death, and tries to warm the inanimate little body. Sometimes a child huddles against his mother, thinking that she is asleep and trying to awaken her, while, in fact, she is dead'.

Horrific news became known during November, when Heniek Grabowski, a Jew from Vilna, managed to reach Warsaw and reported that many thousands of Jews had been taken out of the Vilna ghetto throughout the autumn to the nearby pre-war holiday resort of Ponar, where they had been executed in the sand pits there. The German statistics, meticulously recorded after each round up and execution, reveal that of more than 3,900 Jews taken to Ponar and murdered there during October, 885 were children. By November 30, the commander of the SS killing squads in Lithuania, SS Lieutenant-Colonel Karl Jaeger, recorded that 21,381 Jews had been murdered at Ponar in the previous five months. The Jews of Vilna, the 'Jerusalem of Lithuania' – one of the most vibrant Jewish communities of the previous century, and earlier – were being systematically and barbarically destroyed.

During the third week of November the temperature on the Moscow front continued to fall. German sentries who fell asleep at their post were found in the morning frozen to death.

On November 18 the first Siberian division, together with a Siberian armoured brigade, joined the Russian defenders of the capital, halting a German attack at Venev, south of Moscow. These Siberian troops had been transferred from the Soviet Far East in the sure knowledge that Japan was not going to enter the war against Russia, despite repeated German urgings. Japanese troops, ships and planes were indeed preparing for action, but a Soviet spy in Tokyo, Richard Sorge, had sent convincing evidence to Moscow that their destination was not the Soviet Union.

*   *   *

In Manchuria, Japanese rule proceeded upon its tyrannical course, largely unnoticed by the distant world of Europe's contending armies. Jung Chang has recounted an episode from that period, while Japan was still neutral in Asia:

> One day in late 1941 Dr Xia was in his surgery when a man he had never seen came into the room. He was dressed in rags, and his emaciated body was bent almost double. The man explained that he was a railway coolie, and that he had been having agonizing stomach pains. His work involved carrying heavy loads from dawn to dusk, 365 days a year. He did not know how he could go on, but if he lost his job he would not be able to support his wife and newborn baby.
>
> Dr Xia told him his stomach could not digest the coarse food he had to eat.

Two years earlier, on 1 June 1939, the Japanese Government had announced that henceforth, in all Japanese-occupied areas of China, rice was reserved for the Japanese and the small number of Chinese collaborators. Thereafter, most of the local population had to subsist on a diet of acorn meal and sorghum, which were difficult to digest. 'Dr Xia gave the man some medicine free of charge, and asked my grandmother to give him a small bag of rice which she had bought illegally on the black market.'

Not long afterwards Dr Xia heard that the man had died in a forced labour camp. 'After leaving the surgery he had eaten the rice, gone back to work, and then vomited at the railway yard. A Japanese guard had spotted rice in his vomit and he had been arrested as an "economic criminal" and hauled off to camp. In his weakened state, he survived only a few days. When his wife heard what had happened to him, she drowned herself with her baby.'

In an attempt to draw off German aircraft, including troop transports, from the Eastern Front, Churchill ordered a new military offensive, Operation Crusader, in Cyrenaica. It was launched on November 18 by British and British Commonwealth troops, including soldiers from South Africa. The attack forced Rommel to withdraw westward, and also to call for reinforcements from the Eastern Front. These were sent to him by means of troop transport aircraft that had to be taken away from their Eastern Front duties. The diversion gave crucial help to the Soviet struggle. But the British and

Commonwealth forces suffered heavy losses in and around Sidi Rezegh, when both German and Italian troops put up a fierce resistance.

On the southern sector of the German thrust into Russia, the Eleventh Army under General Erich von Manstein had overrun the Crimea, besieged Sebastopol and advanced along the northern shore of the Sea of Azov, towards the River Don. On November 20, von Manstein issued an Order of the Day to his soldiers, reiterating other commanders' orders that each soldier was 'not merely a fighter according to the rules of the acts of war, but also the bearer of a ruthless ideology'. Each soldier should therefore 'understand the necessity for a severe but just revenge on sub-human Jewry'. That month, the Special Task Force allocated to the Crimea wiped out every Jewish community there, including farming communities that had been set up in the 1920s as the Bolshevik answer to Zionism: Jews tilling the soil. One by one these farms were located and the farmers and their families murdered.

The sub-zero winter temperatures in the East proved the salvation of Leningrad. As the German siege lines tightened, 400 Leningraders a day had been dying of starvation – in the Warsaw ghetto that winter, the Jewish deaths from hunger exceeded 4,000 a day. But in mid-November the waters of Lake Ladoga froze so hard that convoys of Russian trucks — sixty a day for eight consecutive days – were able to make their way to Leningrad across the ice, bringing food supplies and fuel oil for heating.

Among those who were in Leningrad during the siege was the composer Dmitry Shostakovich. Five years earlier, at the opening night of his opera *Lady Macbeth of the Mtsensk District*, Stalin had been present and had found the opera not 'optimistic' enough. The opera had immediately been withdrawn from further performance, and Shostakovich's work was consigned to limbo. During the siege of Leningrad, Shostakovich composed his *Seventh Symphony*. It caught a mood of defiance and was instantly successful. Stalin, desperate for patriotic uplift, approved it.

On the Moscow front the struggle was reaching a climax. South of the capital the Siberian defenders of Venev were pushed back on November 25 almost to the River Oka. North of the capital the main road to Kalinin was cut, as was the Moskva-Volga canal, raising the prospect of Moscow being surrounded. But Hitler was beginning to grasp that something terrible was going wrong in his calculations. In the depth of winter his troops were fighting in conditions they had never before experienced, against soldiers for whom the severity of a Russian winter was an annual phenomenon. On November 25 he confided his new-found fears to his adjutant, Major Engel:

'We started one month too late.' In his diary, Engel commented: 'Time is his greatest nightmare now.'

On November 27 the Soviet defenders of Leningrad managed at certain points to push the Germans back two or three miles. Several hundred German soldiers were taken prisoner. North of Moscow twelve newly created Soviet ski battalions were forming up ready to engage in battle. To the south-east of Moscow a complete Soviet Army – more than ten thousand men – was being brought forward by rail to Ryazan. Soviet partisan activity was also increasing. When, in the village of Petrishchevo, just behind the Moscow front, the Germans prepared to hang an eighteen-year-old girl, Zoia Kosmodemianskaya, for setting fire to houses in the region, her last words were: 'You can't hang all 190 million of us.'

It was not only the Soviet resistance on the battlefield and behind the lines that boded ill for Hitler. The Reich Minister for Armaments and Munitions, Dr Fritz Todt, who as head of Operation Todt had also mobilized millions of labourers from all the conquered territories, East and West, warned Hitler on November 29: 'Given the arms and industrial supremacy of the Anglo-Saxon powers, we can no longer militarily win this war.'

In southern Russia the German armies were being forced to retreat. In an attempt to hold the southern line, reinforcements had to be sent from the Moscow front. For the first time since the outbreak of war in 1939, Germany's resources were at their utmost stretch. A desperate German attempt on December 1 to break through the defences of Moscow was unsuccessful. When ordered to renew their efforts, many of the German soldiers screamed out in agony that they could not go on.

Despite a ferocious blizzard on December 2, the German commanders ordered the offensive to be continued through the snow storm. Some German troops did manage to enter the village of Khimki, twelve miles north of the centre of Moscow, but were pushed back. A German tank attack to the west of the city was likewise unable to break through the Moscow defences. The freezing weather was breaking the German morale. So too was the high scale of casualties: in the last two weeks of November and the first four days of December, 85,000 German troops had been killed in action on the Moscow Front. This was the same number as had been killed on the whole Eastern Front between mid-June and mid-November. The rate of deaths in action had risen from an average of just over 400 day to an average of almost 5,000. When fresh Russian divisions that had gathered east of Moscow were thrown into the front line immediately south of the city on December 5, a further 30,000 German soldiers were killed.

Hitler knew that he must capture Moscow, or face a prolonged and possibly interminable war. A further German attack was ordered against Moscow's defences on December 4. The temperature had fallen to almost its coldest ever recorded in the Moscow area: thirty-five degrees centigrade below zero. In that temperature the German tanks could not be started, nor could the German artillery pieces fire. They were utterly frozen. Even after lighting a fire underneath a tank, it took four hours before an engine could be made to start. Thousands of men also died, not from the battle but from frostbite. They were frozen to death in the fields and trenches.

The turning point came on December 5. That day there was a blizzard so fierce that the German soldiers could hardly stand up, let alone fire their guns. In places the snow was three feet deep. That same day the Russians began a determined counter-attack along a 500-mile front. From Kalinin, north of Moscow, to Yelets, south of the capital, eighty-eight Russian divisions, fresh to battle, advanced against sixty-seven German divisions, almost all of them totally weary and in many cases demoralized. Hitler ordered his troops to hold on 'at all costs'. But by nightfall the German front line had been driven back, everywhere at least two miles, and – where it mattered most, north of Moscow where the threat had been the closest – eleven miles.

Hitler would not enter Moscow that year in triumph, as Napoleon had done in 1812. Nor, as Hitler had often told his listeners at Rastenburg, would he be able to burn the Soviet capital to the ground.

In Washington on November 26, as the battle for Moscow intensified, Cordell Hull had summoned the Japanese ambassador, Nomura, and the Japanese Government's special envoy, Kurusu, to the State Department. There, he insisted, as part of the United States terms to end the oil embargo, that all Japanese armed forces withdraw from China and French Indo-China.

Both Roosevelt and Hull already contemplated the possibility of a surprise Japanese attack somewhere in the Far East. An attack on the Philippines would, they told the commanding Admiral there on the following day, be 'most embarrassing'. The British felt that Malaya was most probably the Japanese target. The Dutch government in exile in London feared that the Dutch East Indies were soon to be attacked. The commander of the United States base at Oahu – which included Pearl Harbor – was discussing sending his warships to Midway and Wake Islands – the latter a thousand miles closer to Japan – in case those islands might be the ones in danger. 'Hostile action possible at any moment,' the War Department in Washington warned General McArthur in the Philippines on November 27.

On the morning of December 6 – the day on which Hitler was forced to accept that Moscow was not about to fall – a secret committee met in Washington, charged with ascertaining, within the next three six months, whether the United States would be able to produce an atom bomb. That day, also in Washington, a member of the United States Navy's Cryptographic Department, Dorothy Edgers, translated an intercepted secret Japanese diplomatic message that had been sent four days earlier from Tokyo to the Japanese Consul-General in Hawaii. The message asked the Consul-General to send regular reports on all shipping movements, berthing positions and torpedo-netting at Pearl Harbor. Alarmed by what she read, Dorothy Edgers translated three more messages that had been decrypted. All contained similar questions. That afternoon she took her translations to the head of the Translation Department. He read them, made a few minor criticisms of her translations, and told her: 'We'll get back to this on Monday.' The Monday in question was December 8. By then it did not need an Intelligence analyst to be shown the messages.

On Sunday December 7, a total of 366 Japanese bombers and fighters, brought by aircraft carriers 3,500 miles across the Pacific, attacked the United States warships at anchor in Pearl Harbor. Four American battleships were blown up, or sank where they lay at anchor. Four more were damaged. Eleven other warships were sunk or disabled. The airfields at Pearl Harbor were also attacked, and 188 American aircraft destroyed on the ground.

In all, in the course of that sudden, unexpected, whirlwind attack, 2,403 Americans were killed. Sixty-eight of them were civilians, and 2,008 of them were sailors, of whom 1,777 were on the battleship *Arizona*. The Army lost 218 men and the Marines 109. With Roosevelt's concurrence, the full extent of the destruction was withheld from the American newspapers.*

There had also been Japanese air attacks during December 7 on United States airfields in the Philippines, where 86 of the 160 American aircraft on Luzon had been destroyed; and on the main British airfield in Hong Kong, where all but one of the aircraft lined up on the tarmac were likewise

---

* Roosevelt did send Churchill the detailed story and full death toll. Churchill wrote in the margin of Roosevelt's message: 'What a holocaust!'.

destroyed. In a Japanese bombing raid on Singapore, sixty-one civilians were killed. The airfields of three other United States island possessions – Guam, Midway and Wake – were also bombed. Batan, the northernmost island in the Philippines, was occupied by Japanese amphibious forces.

At 00.25 local time on December 8 – seventy minutes before the attack on Pearl Harbor across the International Date Line – a Japanese fleet carrying 24,000 combat troops from Indo-China had reached the shores of Malaya at Kota Bharu, where, despite heavy seas, a landing was effected within two hours. The British Empire had been attacked by Japan. When the British Governor was woken by a telephone call from the Army Commander, informing him of the landing, he is said to have replied: 'Well, I suppose you'll shove the little men off!' On the China coast, Japanese troops seized the small American garrisons at Shanghai and Tientsin. The Second World War had entered a new, destructive and all-encompassing phase. Hitler, whose troops had just suffered their first setback in front of Moscow, was elated when the news of Japan's attacks reached him. 'Now it is impossible for us to lose the war,' he told a German diplomat. 'We now have an ally who has never been vanquished in three thousand years.'

On the day after the Japanese onslaught on Pearl Harbor, Roosevelt told Congress: 'Yesterday, December 7, 1941 – a day which will live in infamy – the United States of America was suddenly and deliberately attacked by naval and air forces of the Empire of Japan. No matter how long it may take us to overcome this premeditated invasion, the American people in their righteous might will win through to absolute victory.'

As Japan went on the offensive, Hitler ordered his troops in Russia to take up defensive positions. Russia would be his military preoccupation until he could launch another offensive, perhaps in six months' time. He could no longer plan to invade Britain in 1942. On his return to Berlin on December 9 he was told that Roosevelt would do all he could to avoid war with Germany, and thus not have to wage war on – and across – two oceans. Hitler ought to have been encouraged at this news. The United States and Germany were not at war, and with America forced to focus all her energies on the war with Japan, Hitler might not have to face even America's existing naval activity in the Atlantic in support of Britain.

Hitler felt no sense of relief at the thought of continuing American neutrality. Instead, he was about to make what was arguably his single greatest mistake of the war. On December 9 he told the German naval commanders that they could begin operations against American ships even within the Pan-American Security Zone in the western Atlantic. Still he did not declare war on the United States. But he had moved, like the Kaiser before him, into dangerous waters. Germany's action against American ships in 1916 had brought the United States into the war as Germany's newest, freshest, and ultimately most effective enemy.

In Berlin the American diplomats waited, uncertain as to what would happen. One of them, George F. Kennan, recalled in his memoirs how for four days after Pearl Harbor 'we lived in excruciating uncertainty as the Germans deliberated whether or not to support their Japanese associates by declaring war on the United States. Realizing that we would look like fools if the declaration of war did not come, but also realizing that we would appear as worse than fools if it did come and we had failed to take this step, we burned our codes and our classified correspondence during the night from Tuesday to Wednesday.'

On Thursday December 11, Joachim von Ribbentrop, the German Foreign Minister, summoned Leland Morris, the American Chargé d'Affaires in Berlin, to the German Foreign Ministry. It was a fateful encounter. Ribbentrop read out to Morris the German declaration of war on the United States. He then shouted at the American diplomat: 'Your President has wanted this war; now he has it.'

Hitler had declared war on the United States. By this single act he made the United States a belligerent in the struggle for the mastery of Europe that was then entering its third year. Within two and a half years of Hitler's challenge, a vast American army was to land against Hitler in Northern Europe and to pursue his forces into the heart of Germany.

In declaring war on the United States, Hitler – so close to victory over Russia and yet having had that victory temporarily denied him – did not wish to be seen to stand aside in what he was convinced would be Japan's victorious confrontation with the United States. He remained confident that within twelve months he would be the victor in the East against Russia. Britain would be isolated and alone. Japan would be master of the Pacific and of South East Asia. The Hitler-Hirohito Axis would divide the world and share the spoils.

Britain was reeling from the Japanese onslaught. On December 10, off the coast of Malaya – two days after the Japanese troop landing at Kota Bharu – eighty-four Japanese torpedo-carrying aircraft sank the British battleship *Prince of Wales* and her sister ship *Repulse*; 840 officers and men were killed. By this victory at sea, Japan completed her naval mastery of the Pacific and South East Asian waters which had been all but secured by the attack on Pearl Harbor three days earlier. The Japanese conquests were rapid, yet they were never allowed to go unchallenged. On December 11, during the invasion of Wake Island, two Japanese troop-carrying destroyers were sunk by American aircraft and 5,350 sailors and soldiers on board were drowned: it was one of the worst maritime disasters of the war.

The war at sea had continued to have its daily toll of loss in all the theatres of war. In the Ionian Sea, off the Italian-occupied Greek island of Cephalonia, a British submarine, HMS Perseus, was on a routine patrol on December 12 when it hit an Italian-laid mine and plunged to the sea bed, 170 feet below the surface. Of her crew of sixty, only one survived. John Capes is the only person known to have escaped from a shipwreck at such a depth. Hitherto it had been believed that the Davis Submerged Escape Apparatus which he used was only effective at depths less than a hundred feet.

Capes later recalled how he had tried to drag three wounded men with him out of the submarine, having fitted the same rubber escape sets to them before he swam to the surface. They did not survive. Capes' own experiences were dire:

> As I rose the pain became frantic, my lungs and my body were fit to burst. Agony made me dizzy. I was coming up too quickly and unrolled the small apron in front of me designed to act like a reverse parachute. Bursting to the surface I wallowed in a slight swell with whitecaps here and there.
>
> There was nothing in sight. At some distance, maybe ten miles, I saw a broken line of cliffs. I started to swim immediately. Hour after hour I kept going. I never lost faith. The will to live kept me going. Finally I clutched solid rock. I dragged myself over and on to a sandy beach. I lapsed into oblivion.

Capes had reached the shore of Cephalonia. Greek villagers hid him from the occupying forces – first Italian and then German – for more than a year, after which the Greek resistance was able to smuggle him to neutral Turkey. After the submarine sank his mother was informed that Capes was 'missing, presumed dead'. Two years after she began to mourn his loss she received a brief message, forwarded by the Red Cross: 'All well, Johnny.'

The deaths of 57 Britons off Cephalonia, the deaths of 5,350 Japanese off Wake Island – the death of any one man, woman or child anywhere in the war zones and behind the lines – constitute the daily burden and loss of war. On December 11, the day on which so many Japanese soldiers and sailors died in the Pacific Ocean, a British pilot, John Gillespie Magee, also lost his life. He had been born in Shanghai, the son of Episcopalian missionaries to China. His father was American and his mother British. During the Battle of Britain he had enlisted in the Royal Canadian Air Force. A Spitfire pilot, he was first in action, north of Dunkirk, on November 8 when, as he wrote to his parents, 'I had a crack at Jerry, but didn't see any results so I'm not claiming it.' On December 11 he was killed in a mid-air collision with another British plane, whose pilot was also killed.

Pilot Officer Magee was nineteen years old when he was killed. Four months earlier he had written some verses which were to become among the most read and quoted of the Second World War, and after it. Following the *Challenger* Space Shuttle disaster in 1986 – forty-five years after Magee's death – part of his poem, *High Flight*, was quoted by President Reagan. It read, in full:

> Oh! I have slipped the surly bonds of Earth
> And danced the skies on laughter-silvered wings;
> Sunward I've climbed, and joined the tumbling mirth
> Of sun-split clouds, – and done a hundred things
> You have not dreamed of – wheeled and soared and swung
> High in the sunlit silence. Hov'ring there,
> I've chased the shouting wind along, and flung
> My eager craft through footless halls of air.
>
> Up, up the long, delirious, burning blue
> I've topped the wind-swept heights with easy grace
> Where never lark or even eagle flew -
> And, while with silent lifting mind I've trod
> The high, untrespassed sanctity of space,
> Put out my hand, and touched the face of God.

On December 12 a force of 500 Japanese troops broke through the British defences at Jitra, in northern Malaya, driving 8,000 British and Indian troops in retreat before them. The British commander, General Percival, learned with disbelief that the British line had collapsed. The Japanese officer in charge of the attack, Colonel Masanobu Tsuji, was amazed by what the defenders left behind them. 'Our officers and men,' he later wrote, 'who since embarkation had been living on dry bread and salt, found tobacco, cakes and tinned food, piled-up chock-full in a storehouse. We had to be grateful to General Percival not only for provisions for the men but also for the cars and gasoline abandoned in abundance.'

With a rapidity that stunned the victims, the American island of Guam was overrun, then Hong Kong, then the Dutch East Indies, then Malaya, and finally the Philippines. Everywhere the defenders were overwhelmed by greater Japanese manpower and air mastery. 'The Japanese are occupying all the islands, one after another,' Hitler told Himmler on December 18. 'They will get hold of Australia too. The white race will disappear from those regions.'

In Europe, Hitler and Himmler were doing their utmost to ensure that the Jewish race would disappear. Starting on the day after Pearl Harbor a new method was adopted. This method replaced the mass slaughters on the outskirts of several hundred towns and villages: slaughters that were even then leading to the murder of as many as a million Jews throughout German-occupied Russia. The new method was the systematic deportation of Jews – from their ghettos throughout Poland, and in due course from towns throughout Western Europe – to remote camps where they were murdered by gas. The first such camp was established in a forest near Chelmno, in German-occupied western Poland. The first deportees to be sent there were from the small villages in the neighbourhood, and from the ghetto that had been set up in the nearby industrial city of Lodz.

Local Polish Jews, as well as German and Austrian Jews who had earlier been deported to Lodz, and several thousand Gypsies who had been sent to the Lodz ghetto, were all taken by train and truck the short distance to Chelmno, where they were murdered by gas in specially designed vans. The camp commandant boasted that he could kill a thousand people a day by this method, and he did so day after day until several hundred villages and towns had completely lost their Jewish inhabitants, and as many as 300,000 Jews had been murdered. Only two Jews survived from that time; both had been forced to take the dead bodies from the gas van and bury them in pits; both had escaped; both recorded the horrors they saw.*

---

* One of the two escapees, Yakov Grojanowsky, wrote down his experiences in diary form immediately after his escape. I published his diary in full in *The Holocaust, The Jewish Tragedy* as chapter 16, 'Eye-witness to mass murder', pages 252–79.

Had Chelmno been the only death camp set up for the mass murder of Jews, it would have become one of the names synonymous with evil in the Twentieth Century. But as more death camps came into being in the months ahead, the scale of its destructive work, the torments enacted there, and even its name, slid into virtual oblivion. Several other camps – among them Auschwitz and Treblinka – were to exceed Chelmno's destructive power. Their names would be more widely remembered.

In the Far East, different torments and tortures were being enacted. With each Japanese conquest, British, American, Australian and other Allied soldiers were captured. The names of the prison and labour camps into which they were put – Changi Jail in Singapore was one – also became synonymous with terror, slow starvation, brutality and violent death. Just as the Soviet soldier could expect none of the laws of war to be applied to him after he fell into German captivity, so the prisoners-of-war of the Japanese quickly learned that their captors did not consider them as worthy of any form of decent treatment, let alone the protection laid down in the various pre-war Geneva Conventions.

The first Western soldiers to experience Japanese methods were the British and Canadian soldiers captured in Hong Kong. After capture, first twenty – on December 18 – and then fifty-three – on Christmas day – were roped together and then bayoneted to death. Even the staff of an Army Medical Corps station at which the wounded were being treated were taken away and shot or bayoneted to death.

In the immediate aftermath of the Japanese attack on Pearl Harbor, and the rapid advance of Japanese forces throughout South-East Asia and the Pacific, tens of thousands of Japanese Americans were interned in the United States. The British deprived the Emperor Hirohito of the Order of the Garter, the symbol of his earlier recognition by Britain as a senior and respected sovereign.

In China, as the Japanese advance was renewed, there were further atrocities whenever Chinese soldiers surrendered. On the Japanese march from Hankow to Changsha two hundred Chinese soldiers who had been taken prisoner were lined up and machine-gunned. Not one survived. When the Japanese reached Changsha, several thousand Chinese soldiers surrendered. They too were shot, and hundreds of Chinese women were forced into prostitution in military brothels.

*　　*　　*

The year 1941 had been a year of human suffering on an unparalleled scale. As the year came to an end more than four thousand Jews were dying every month inside the Warsaw ghetto, their deportation to the death camp at Treblinka having to wait for the camp's completion. On December 19, in the Russian town of Vitebsk, a Special Task Force reported having killed 4,090 Jews 'of both sexes', as well as sixteen mentally ill Russian and Jewish children whose hospital had been declared by the chief German military physician in the area to be 'an epidemic centre of the first degree, sufficient reason for their shooting'.

In the Baltic States it was the Gypsies who were singled out for death, having been described by the German civil governor, Hinrich Lohse, as 'a double danger' because they were carriers of disease, 'especially typhus', and they were 'unreliable elements who cannot be put to useful work'. Their fate was set out by Lohse on December 24: 'I therefore determine that they should be treated in the same way as Jews.' Thus began the mass murder of many thousands of Baltic Gypsies. Polish Gypsies were already being rounded up and sent with Jews to the gas vans of Chelmno.

At one prisoner-of-war camp in German-occupied Poland, 100,000 Soviet soldiers died during the winter after being herded together in a vast open field, surrounded by barbed wire and guards, and given no food. They dug holes in which to try to get shelter from the wind and snow, and ate grass and roots to try to keep alive. But it was not long before all the grass and roots were used up. Any Polish villager who was caught trying to throw them food was shot.

The battle front also had horrors other than war itself. In a single day in December on the Eastern Front 14,000 German soldiers submitted to the amputation of their frozen, gangrenous limbs. Not all of them survived more than a few hours. 'The immobile wounded inexorably died as stiffened blocks of ice,' the historian Alan Clark has written of the fighting on the Kerch Peninsula that winter, when the temperature fell to minus twenty degrees centigrade. 'Some men took their own lives with a hand grenade held against the stomach . . .' In Leningrad, still besieged by the Germans despite one precarious supply line over the ice, three to four thousand people were dying every day of starvation; 3,700 on Christmas Day alone.

Behind the lines in what had been Czechoslovakia, Greece and Yugoslavia, continual reprisals were being carried out by the German occupation authorities against the local populations. In Yugoslavia the reprisals for partisan attacks had turned into an all-out war against unarmed and defenceless Serbs,

Jews and Gypsies. The German army's own statistics gave the figure of 11,164 for the numbers killed in reprisal shootings during the three months from October to December, but it is known that not all German Army units reported the numbers of their victims. The correct figure was probably closer to 15,000.

So severe were the reprisals in and around Prague that on December 28 two Czech agents were parachuted into Bohemia from Britain to coordinate activities with the local anti-German resistance. Within a few months they received their assignment: to assassinate Reinhard Heydrich, whom Hitler had just sent as Reich Protector to Bohemia. His rule as 'protector' was one of severe repression for all forms of Czech national sentiment.

In the winter in which Hitler failed to defeat the Soviet Union, and declared war on the United States, the Allies decided to declare their war aims. The declaration was drafted in Washington by Roosevelt and Churchill together. Twenty-six countries, many of them represented by governments in exile in London, and calling themselves the 'United Nations', signed it. Issued on 1 January 1942, the declaration stated that the aim of the struggle, and of their own unity, was 'to ensure life, liberty, independence and religious freedom, and to preserve the rights of man and justice'.

The Soviet Union was a signatory to this declaration. But the extent to which the Soviet Union failed to observe the 'rights of man and justice' was widely known, not least by those former Communist Party members in Europe and beyond who had become disillusioned by the tyrannies of Moscow. One of those who made his disillusionment known was the Hungarian-born Arthur Koestler, whose novel *Darkness at Noon* was first published in May 1941. In it was a graphic portrayal of the process of the interrogation – and confession to absurd and imaginary crimes – of a loyal Party member. At one point the interrogator tells the accused:

Whole sets of our best functionaries in Europe had to be physically liquidated. We did not recoil from crushing our own organizations abroad when the interests of the Bastion required it. We did not recoil from co-operation with the police of reactionary countries in order to suppress revolutionary movements which came at the wrong moment. We did not recoil from betraying our friends and compromising with our enemies, in order to preserve the Bastion.

That was the task which history had given us, the representative of the first victorious revolution. The short-sighted, the aesthetes, the moralists did not understand. But the leader of the Revolution understood that all depended on one thing: to be the better stayer.

In the world conflict that was proceeding that year, and was so intensified in the months after Koestler's book was published, the Soviet Union had been deceived by Hitler, had seen its much-vaunted Nazi-Soviet Pact torn to shreds, had taken heavy military blows, and had been pushed to the very edge of defeat. But the primacy of the Communist Party and its leader, Stalin, remained as secure as that of the Nazi Party and Hitler: and the Soviet capital, Moscow, although evacuated by the Soviet government, remained unconquered. The 'Bastion', though massively assaulted, was intact.

CHAPTER THIRTEEN

1942

> This is not an occasion on which we are expressing
> sorrow and sympathy to sufferers from some terrible
> catastrophe due unavoidably to flood or earthquake, or
> some other convulsion of nature. These dreadful events
> are an outcome of quite deliberate, planned, conscious
> cruelty of human beings.
>
> HERBERT SAMUEL

O N 10 JANUARY 1942, in the strictest secrecy, between twenty and thirty German medical doctors, nurses and office personnel left Germany by train for the Eastern Front. They were all members of T4 – the euthanasia operation established more than two years earlier at No. 4 Tiergartenstrasse in Berlin. Since then they had been responsible for the deaths of at least 100,000 German children, those judged too chronically mentally ill to merit life, who had been murdered, mostly by gas, in institutions throughout Germany.

The team that had carried out this barbaric policy was setting off to a new area of action, setting up their first operational base near Minsk. Two tasks awaited them. One was to apply their techniques of euthanasia to German soldiers who had been horrifically wounded and were judged by the team to have no chance of leading normal lives again. The other was to devise similar techniques for the mass murder of Jews who had hitherto been confined to ghettos throughout Poland and western Russia, and had been marked out – as a people – for death. Within a few months, one of the doctors of this eastern task force, Dr Irmfried Eberl, became the commandant of the death camp at Treblinka, in which more than three quarters of a million Jews from Warsaw and central Poland were murdered. Another, Dr Horst Schumann, went to Auschwitz, where he carried out medical experiments on Soviet prisoners-of-war, Poles and Jews.

At the very moment when German Jewish refugee doctors who had reached Britain before the war were active in the medical fight to save the lives of badly injured soldiers and civilians, German Nazi doctors who had been through the same medical training in the same German medical school system were destroying life.

In the fighting on the Eastern Front the German army was being pushed back from the outskirts of Moscow. Accepting that the Soviet capital was for the time being beyond his grasp, Hitler devised a new strategy, whereby his armies would hold a defensive line west of Moscow, and would attack the Caucasus, in order to seize the Russian oilfields and reach the Caspian Sea. Hitler also hoped that many of the national groups that had been absorbed into Soviet rule in the Caucasus – most of them by conquest first during Tsarist times and then for a second time after the 1917 revolution – would rally to the German cause. Stalin, anticipating this strategy, deported these national groups en bloc to Siberia and Central Asia. The deportations were conducted with considerable brutality.*

Although Hitler had no foreboding of defeat, small signs everywhere were pointers to what might lie ahead. In Yugoslavia two resistance movements had emerged. One was led by a Serb, Drazha Mihailovic, a former army colonel who had been promoted to General by the Royal Yugoslav government in exile in London. The other was led by a Croat, Josip Broz, a Yugoslav communist who had trained in Moscow, and who fought under the name Tito.

On January 13, as more and more news of German reprisal actions and mass murder reached the Allies, the representatives of nine occupied countries met in London and signed a declaration that all those guilty of 'war crimes' would be punished after the war. Among their principal war aims, the signatories wrote, was 'the punishment, through the channels of organized justice, of those guilty of, or responsible for, these crimes, whether they have ordered them, perpetrated them, or participated in them'. The boldness of the declaration did not, however, stop the reprisals or the killings.

With Japanese troops rapidly completing the conquest of the Philippines, and the German navy striking at American vessels wherever it could, the United States was forced to adapt to the needs of a two-ocean war. Early

* The deported Caucasian nationalities were the Karachais, the Meskhetians, the Chechen-Ingush and the Kalmyks.

the previous December, with military supplies for Britain the main concern, an all-America manufacturing target of 12,750 new operational aircraft had been established. On January 2 this was increased to 45,000. The December figure for tanks, 15,450, was likewise increased to 45,000. The manpower needs were doubled and then redoubled.

The first United States Congressman to enlist in the armed forces after Pearl Harbor was Lyndon Baynes Johnson, from Texas, who entered the navy. He served for twelve months, until Roosevelt issued an order that all Senators and Congressmen were to return to their duties on Capitol Hill. During his service Johnson was sent on a mission of inspection to the Australian battle area. On his way there his plane was almost shot down, and he was awarded a Silver Star. He was to wear the battle ribbon on his lapel for the rest of his life, first as Senator and then as President.

It was the fate of Allied soldiers captured by the Japanese that marked out the early months of 1942 in the Pacific and the Far East as months of evil. On January 21, in Malaya, a group of badly wounded Australians who had been left behind under some trees during the retreat were taken by their captors to a nearby hut and bayoneted or shot. On New Guinea, after 6,000 Japanese troops landed and attacked the Australian garrison of 1,000 men, most of those who surrendered were then killed. On Amboina Island, in the Dutch East Indies, Lieutenant Nakagawa of the Imperial Japanese Army later described the fate of thirty Australian soldiers whom his men had captured. First, 'they were taken out one by one to the spot where they were to die, and made to kneel down with a bandage over their eyes.' Then Nakagawa's own soldiers 'stepped out of the ranks, one by one as his turn came, to behead a prisoner-of-war with a sword, or stab him through the breast with a bayonet.'

Within a month, Nakagawa had ordered the mass execution of another 120 Australian prisoners-of-war. They were made to kneel down with their eyes bandaged, and then either decapitated or shot. 'The whole affair took from 6 p.m. to 9.30 p.m.', he recalled. 'Most of the corpses were buried in one hole, but because the hole turned out not to be big enough to accommodate all the bodies, an adjacent dug-out was also used as a grave.' Scenes such as these were repeated in many hundred different localities all over the Japanese areas of conquest.

In German-occupied Poland, more than 4,500 Jews had been murdered at Chelmno between early December and mid-January. On January 19 an escapee from the camp, Yakov Grojanowsky, reached the village of Grabow – only twelve miles from Chelmno – and told the story of the gas-van killings to the rabbi of the village. Their conversation was the last entry in Grojanowsky's diary of his thirteen days at Chelmno:

'Who are you? he asked. 'Rabbi I am a Jew from the nether world!' He looked at me as if I was mad. I told him: 'Rabbi, don't think I am crazed and have lost my reason. I am a Jew from the nether world. They are killing the whole nation Israel. I myself have buried a whole town of Jews, my parents, brothers and the entire family. I have remained lonely as a piece of stone.

I cried during this conversation. The rabbi asked, 'Where are they being killed?' I said, 'Rabbi, in Chelmno. They are gassed in the forest and buried in mass graves.' His domestic (the rabbi was a widower) brought me a bowl for my swollen eyes. I washed my hands. The injury on my right hand began to hurt. When my story made the rounds many Jews came, to whom I told all the details. They all wept.

Hitler's ambition with regard to the Jews went far beyond Poland. On January 20 – the day after Grojanowsky was recounting the story of Chelmno – a meeting of senior German officials was convened in a lakeside villa at Wannsee, outside Berlin. The purpose of the gathering was to prepare a plan for the continued and systematic destruction of European Jewry. At a private talk before the formal meeting began, Dr Josef Bühler, the chief representative of the General Government, urged the meeting's convenor, Reinhard Heydrich, that 'the final solution of this question should begin in the General Government, where transportation problems play only a minor role, and questions pertaining to deployment of labour would not impede the course of this operation'.

At the start of the meeting Heydrich asked one of the most conscientious of Germany's wartime bureaucrats, SS Lieutenant-Colonel Adolf Eichmann, who had previously been in charge of Jewish emigration from Germany and Austria, to present the statistics for the number of Jews in every country of Europe, with a view to bringing them to camps in areas under German control, and murdering them there. The Jews on Eichmann's list included those from countries allied to Germany, and even from neutral Sweden, Ireland, Portugal and Switzerland. The statistics noted that Estonia was already 'Free of Jews', and that in Lithuania only 34,000 of the 135,000 Jews who were living there six months earlier were still alive.

Following the Wannsee meeting, plans were drawn up to bring as many Jews as possible from throughout Europe into German-occupied Poland. The deportees were told that they were going 'to the East' to help with the harvest, or to 'resettlement' in labour camps and farms 'in the East' (the deportation trains were often called 'resettlement trains'). They were in fact deported to death camps that were being set up on the Chelmno model, but using specifically designed gas chambers instead of vans crudely adapted to become murder vehicles. Including Chelmno there were five such death camps. The most destructive during 1942, in terms of the statistics of mass murder, was Treblinka, where more than three quarters of a million Jews were killed, brought there from the Warsaw ghetto and more than a hundred towns and villages in a wide circle around Warsaw – as well as Jews from as far away as Greece. The next most destructive camp was Belzec, where more than 360,000 Jews from Eastern and Western Galicia were deported from the ghettos in which they had been confined and starved for more than a year, and killed. Many thousands of Jews from Greater Germany were also brought to Belzec and murdered. Also murdered at Belzec were 1,500 Poles who had been deported to the camp 'for helping Jews', many Gypsies, and several thousand Soviet prisoners-of-war.

An hour's drive from Belzec was Sobibor, where more than 250,000 Jews from the surrounding region were likewise murdered, together with several thousand Jews brought from Holland. The fifth death camp was Maly Trostenets, on the outskirts of Minsk, the only camp not on former Polish soil. In the autumn and winter of 1941 it had been used for the mass murder of Soviet prisoners-of war. More than 300,000 Jews, many of them German, Austrian and Czech, were murdered on arrival at the camp in 1942; the first deportees reached it on May 10. There are no known survivors of the deportees who reached Maly Trostenets.

To keep secret the true nature of the destination of the deportees, language was again used by the Nazis as an important aspect of deception. In mid-April, Himmler's personal secretary informed the Inspector of Statistics of the Reich that the phrase 'special treatment for the Jews' should no longer be used in official reports. The phrase to be used in its place was 'transportation of the Jews towards the Russian East'. The careful use of language was maintained at every level, with the stress on the technological aspects of the work. Six months after the first use of a gas van a Chelmno, and the use of similar vans at Riga, a senior civil servant in Berlin set out details, in an internal memorandum, of the required 'technical modifications of special vehicles put into service'.

Since December 1941, the civil servant explained, 'using three vehicles, 97,000 persons have been "processed" without any defects occurring in these vehicles. The explosion which is known to have occurred in Chelmno should be considered as an isolated case, a technical failure. Special instructions have been sent to the depots involved, in order to prevent such accidents in future'. The civil servant mentioned one further 'problem': the 'merchandise' in the van at Chelmno had displayed during the operation a regrettable if natural 'rush towards the light' which was hampering the efficiency of the procedure. This fault would be 'rectified'.

The German military campaigns were proceeding in different and contradictory ways. On January 22, two days after the secret gathering at Wannsee was determining the fate of the Jews of Europe, Goebbels wrote in his diary: 'The anxiety of the German people about the Eastern Front is increasing. Deaths owing to freezing are an especially important factor in this connection. The number of cases of freezing revealed by transports from the Eastern Front back home is so enormous that it is causing great indignation here and there.'

The number of civilians murdered behind the lines in the East had been far more 'enormous', but was reported only in the strictest secrecy. When sending to Berlin his summary of the mass murder of Jews in Lithuania during the previous seven months, the head of the Gestapo there, SS Colonel Karl Jaeger, itemized the shootings day by day, and then added them up for his superiors to see at a glance: the figure he gave was 138,272 Jews murdered, of whom 34,464 were children. His careful analysis of those murdered also listed those who were not part of his mission: forty-four Poles, twenty-eight Russian prisoners-of-war, five Gypsies and one Armenian.

Returning to Berlin from his headquarters at Rastenburg, on January 30 Hitler celebrated the ninth anniversary of his coming to power. That day he told a vast crowd in the Sportpalast in Berlin: 'The war will not end as the Jews imagine it will, namely with the uprooting of the Aryans, but the result of this war will be the complete annihilation of the Jews.' On the following day the Special Task Force operating behind the lines in the Crimea, having completed its work, sent Berlin a summary of the most recent executions it had carried out, during the previous six days. They totalled 3,601. The report went on to explain: '3,286 of these were Jews, 152 Communists and NKVD agents, 84 partisans, and 79 looters, saboteurs, and asocial elements.' The report then added a succinct and precise note of its killing efforts since entering the Crimea in the wake of Field Marshal von Manstein's victorious army three months earlier: 'In all, to date, 85,201.'

The Germans made every effort inside Russia to win over non-Russian nationalities to their cause. In this they were sometimes successful, making use of every device. On January 30 Goebbels wrote in his diary:

It is interesting to observe what importance the clever exploitation of religion can assume. The Tatars at first had a none-too-gratifying attitude toward the German Wehrmacht. But they changed about completely when permitted to sing their religious chants from the tops of minarets. Their change of attitude went so far that Tatar auxiliary companies which fought actively against the Bolsheviks could be formed.

Our efforts were supported by our propaganda companies who distributed a picture showing the Grand Mufti of Jerusalem visiting the Führer. That was extremely successful.

The exiled Mufti of Jerusalem, Haj Amin al-Husseini, had twice visited Hitler seeking help against the British in Palestine. Travelling to Bosnia, he helped to raise a Muslim SS formation that fought alongside the German army. Later, when he learned that there was a possibility of several thousand Bulgarian Jewish children being allowed out of Bulgaria and into Palestine, he intervened successfully in Berlin to prevent this.

In Norway, the Protestant Church was seeking means of opposing the Nazi puppet government headed by Vidkun Quisling. On February 1 the Provost of Trondheim Cathedral was suspended, and then dismissed from his post. In protest, all the Norwegian bishops resigned from their official positions, continuing only to attend to the spiritual needs of their congregations. The Germans responded by announcing the formation of a Norwegian version of the Hitler Youth. This led to the resignation of a thousand schoolmasters. Inspired by Bishop Berggrav, all parish priests then abandoned their livings. Occupation had not weakened the courage of the church in Norway.

In North Africa, Rommel had begun a new advance through Cyrenaica, aiming once more for the Egyptian frontier, and moving rapidly towards it.

'We have got Cyrenaica back. It went like greased lightning', he wrote to his wife on February 4. The Jews of Palestine feared that Rommel's next forward move would take him across the Suez Canal and into Palestine. The British authorities in Palestine, recognizing that such a fear was not far-fetched, authorized the Jews to arm themselves in preparation for the battle.

The German military success in the Western Desert was overshadowed by the almost daily victories of Germany's ally, Japan, in the Far East. The Japanese prize in Malaya was the city and fortress of Singapore, against which a formidable assault had been mounted. On February 15, with only twenty-four hours' water left for the garrison, with little petrol for transport, and under incessant Japanese shelling and bombing, Singapore surrendered. The British Empire's largest city east of India had fallen. The soldiers who surrendered at Singapore included 32,000 Indians, 16,000 British and 14,000 Australians. In the months and years ahead, more than half of them were to die as prisoners-of-war in circumstances of the harshest deprivation and cruel treatment.

The European and other civilians who lived and worked in Malaya also faced terrible times. 'I knew one planter,' writes Cecil Lee, who had worked in Malaya from 1934, 'a jovial fellow named Bill Harvey who was in a party of four (three planters and one Australian) who stayed behind the Japanese lines after the capitulation and did valuable work. They were finally caught and imprisoned in Pudu jail, Kuala Lumpur. The Japanese decreed that anyone trying to escape would be executed. Despite this, these four men made the attempt and were caught, brought back to Pudu jail, and then after being ordered to dig their own graves were beheaded at Cheras cemetery. The horror of that final scene haunts me to this day.'

On February 16 twenty-five British soldiers who had surrendered to the Japanese in Malaya were taken to the shore, bayoneted and shot. Sixty-five Australian nursing sisters who were with them were ordered to march into the sea. Japanese machine gunners then opened fire on them. Only one nurse survived. Two days later, on Singapore Island, 5,000 Chinese civilians – most of them prominent members of the island's thriving Chinese community – were rounded up and taken into captivity. After two weeks all of them had been killed: first their hands were tied behind their backs and then their heads cut off with a sword. An Australian soldier, Colin Brien, who miracu-lously survived an attempted decapitation, was subsequently pointed out by the Japanese in his prisoner-of-war camps as a 'novelty'. He survived the war, and was to give testimony at the Tokyo War Crimes Trials in 1946 about the mass executions of which he was meant to have been a part.

The Japanese military advances continued. On February 19 the Japanese carried out an air raid on the Australian city of Darwin. All seventeen ships in Darwin harbour, including an American destroyer, were sunk, and, in the air battle, twenty-two Australian and American planes were shot down, for the loss of only five Japanese planes. The death toll on the ground was 240. Within two weeks there was another Japanese air attack against Western Australia. The objective was the port of Broome, to which soldiers and refugees taken off Java were being brought by flying boat. Twenty-three aircraft – Australian, American, Dutch and British – were destroyed during the raid, and seventy people killed, most of them refugees. In a series of naval battles off Java, several hundred Allied sailors were drowned, including 352 on the Australian cruiser *Perth*. Of the survivors who were picked out of the sea by Japanese ships, more than a hundred died while prisoners-of-war.

That February, Roosevelt issued an Executive Order with regard to Japanese immigrants living on the West Coast of the United States, and their children. They were instructed to leave the West Coast area, for fear that they might form a pro-Japanese fifth-column in the event of a Japanese landing, or otherwise act against the national interests of the United States, whose citizens they were. They were asked to go voluntarily, but when most of them – about 120,000 – refused, they were rounded up by American troops and removed by force to isolated detention camps. Most were held in these camps until the end of 1944.*

On February 21, as Japanese forces on Luzon pressed southward down the Bataan Peninsula, as the battle for Java turned against the Allied forces, and as Japanese troops crossed the border of Thailand into British Burma, Roosevelt told the American people: 'We Americans have been compelled to yield ground, but we will regain it. We and other United Nations are committed to the destruction of the militarism of Japan and Germany. We are daily increasing our strength. Soon we, not our enemies, will have the offensive; and we, not they, will win the final battles; and we, not they, will make the final peace.'

On the Eastern Front, Russian partisans, often many hundreds of miles

---

* In 1988, as a result of pressure from Japanese Americans, including Senator Daniel Inouye of Hawaii, the American Government issued a formal apology for the internment and agreed to pay $40 million, half to compensate those who had been interned and half to fund educational programmes to teach the American public about the internment.

behind the front line, had begun to control large areas of forest and swamp, destroying German army stores and disrupting rail and road communications. Armaments, and even armed soldiers, were parachuted to them by the Soviet army. But Hitler, despite confirmation at the beginning of March that more than 200,000 soldiers had already been killed in Russia – and more than 100,000 permanently incapacitated by frostbite – was preparing for an offensive in the spring. The siege of Leningrad continued: 100,000 of the million people in the city died of starvation, frostbite or shelling during February. The human cost of the war between Germany and the Soviet Union had already exceeded, in nine months, that of all the other European conflicts since September 1939 combined.

High though the military losses were on the Eastern Front, they were far exceeded by the murder of civilians. Between March 2 and March 4, in five separate localities, 12,000 Jews were killed, some by Special Task Force members and others in the gas vans at Chelmno. Three days later Goebbels wrote in his diary: 'The situation is ripe for a final settlement of the Jewish question. Later generations will no longer have either the will-power or the instinctive alertness. That is why we are doing good work in processing radically and consistently. The task we are assuming today will be an advantage and a boon to our descendants.'

Goebbels knew that the mass executions in the East, effective though they were in killing hundreds of thousands – perhaps already as many as a million – were about to be superceded by a new method to be applied to all the Jews in Western and Central Europe and in the Balkans. On March 13 the death camp set up at Belzec, in a remote forest in eastern Poland, began operation. The first Jews to be murdered there were 6,000 from the southern Polish town of Mielec. They were told that they were needed for agricultural work. All of them were murdered on arrival at Belzec. Also sent to Belzec and murdered there, were thirty-three German Jewish orphans who were deported on March 22 with their teacher, Dr Isaak Halleman, from the German town of Fürth, in which Henry Kissinger had lived before the war. The orphans had been held before their deportation in the synagogue where Kissinger used to pray.*

Responsibility for the preparation and operation of the new system –

---

* Thirteen of Henry Kissinger's close relatives were murdered in the gas chambers or died in concentration camps, among them three of his aunts – Ida, Sara and Fanny – and their husbands, and also his great uncle Simon, and his great uncle's two sons Ferdinand and Julius (all three were teachers).

which involved, in Poland, the deportation of more than three million Jews from their confinement in ghettos to death camps and slave labour camps – was given to Odilo Globocnik, one of the Austrian Nazis who had facilitated the German annexation of Austria four years earlier. Globocnik was carrying out this work in Poland, Goebbels noted on March 27, 'with considerable circumspection and in a way that does not attract too much attention'. Goebbels added:

> Though the judgement now being visited upon the Jews is barbaric, they fully deserve it. The prophecy which the Führer made about them for having brought on a new world war is beginning to come true in a most terrible manner.
>
> One must not be sentimental in these matters. If we did not fight the Jews, they would destroy us. It's a life-and-death struggle between the Aryan race and the Jewish bacillus.
>
> No other government and no other regime would have the strength for such a global solution as this. Here, once again, the Führer is the undismayed champion of a radical solution, which is made necessary by existing conditions and is therefore inexorable. Fortunately a whole series of possibilities presents itself to us in wartime which would be denied to us in peace. We shall have to profit by this.

On March 21 the impressively named Reich Plenipotentiary-General for Labour Mobilization, Fritz Sauckel, was instructed by Hitler to obtain, by whatever methods needed, a labour force that could bring German war industry to its highest possible productive capacity. Labourers could be brought from all the occupied lands. If necessary they could be seized on the streets and deported to Germany.

The new demands of the war economy also affected the Jewish deportees. Under a Labour Decree promulgated on March 31, Jews who had been deported were henceforth to be divided into two types: 'fit' to work and 'unfit'. A new camp was being set up in which this categorization would apply; a camp where, while many of the deportees would be murdered on arrival, others would be taken to forced labour. The place chosen for this murder-labour combination was adjacent to the penal camp for Poles that had been operating with particular cruelty at Auschwitz since the summer of 1940.

In order to provide the means of murdering the deportees who were expected to be sent to Auschwitz from all over Europe, a special section of

Auschwitz – itself the scene for almost two years of hundreds of executions and terrible tortures – was built during the early months of 1942. It was located in the nearby hamlet of Birkenau, across the main railway line from Auschwitz camp. More than a million Jews were to be brought to Birkenau by train from all over Europe, mostly in sealed cattle trucks in conditions of the utmost squalor, during which many died.

The first deportation of Jews to Auschwitz took place on March 26, when 999 Jewish women from Slovakia were sent there, with the assistance of the Slovak authorities in rounding them up and putting them on board the trains. On the following day 1,112 Jewish men and women from France, having been rounded up by the French police, were put on board what was called a 'special train' (*Sonderzug*) and sent eastward. Of those 1,112 deportees only twenty-one survived the war. 'The procedure is pretty barbaric', Goebbels noted in his diary on March 27, 'and is not to be described here more definitely. Not much will remain of the Jews. About 60 per cent of them will have to be liquidated; only about 40 per cent can be used for forced labour.'

During the coming two and half years more than half of the deportees who reached the Birkenau section of Auschwitz were murdered within a few hours of their arrival in four specially constructed gas chambers, with crematoria attached. Those who were not murdered were put to forced labour in the camp itself and in the industrial region around it. The conditions in which they were made to work led to the deaths of many hundreds of thousands of them. A dozen major German industrial enterprises benefited from the use of Jewish slave labour at Auschwitz. When British bombing of the Ruhr intensified, complete factories were moved to the Auschwitz region – which until the summer of 1944 lay beyond the Allied bombing range – to make use of the slave labour force there.

Also at Auschwitz, as in the other death camps, the suitcases and bundles which the deportees had been allowed to bring with them were taken away on arrival. Their clothing was taken from them a few moments before they were to be murdered. The women were shaved before being killed, and their hair carefully set aside: it had a value to the Third Reich. After the Jews had been killed and their bodies dragged out of the gas chambers, any gold teeth were extracted. The Jews were cremated naked, every item of value having been systematically taken from them: this included the shoes they arrived in and the glasses they were wearing. Babies' prams and push chairs were likewise set diligently aside.

The material that was taken from the arrivals on the threshold of their destruction, after they had been murdered, and sometimes even while they were being murdered – was taken the short distance from the gas chambers to a group of large wooden huts known as 'Canada'. The name was chosen because it represented the concept of a wealthy place, of a prosperous land. One of the Jewish prisoners at Auschwitz who worked in this Canada, Rudolf Vrba – a Slovak Jew – later described the scene:

It was incredible sight, an enormous rectangular yard with a watchtower at each corner and surrounded by barbed wire. There were several huge storerooms and a block of what seemed like offices with a square, open balcony at one corner. Yet what first struck me was a mountain of trunks, cases, rucksacks, kitbags and parcels stacked in the middle of the yard.

Nearby was another mountain, of blankets this time, fifty thousand of them, maybe one hundred thousand. I was so staggered by the sight of these twin peaks of personal possessions that I never thought at that moment where their owners might be. In fact I did not have much time to think, for every step brought some new shock.

Over on the left I saw hundreds of prams. Shiny prams, fit for a firstborn. Battered prams of character that had been handed down and down and down and had suffered gladly on the way. Opulent, ostentatious, status-symbol prams and modest, economy prams of those who knew no status and had no money. I looked at them in awe, but still I did not wonder where the babies were.

Another mountain, this time of pots and pans from a thousand kitchens in a dozen countries. Pathetic remnants of a million meals, anonymous now, for their owners would never eat again.

Then I saw women. Real women, not the terrible, sexless skeletons whose bodies stank and whose hearts were dead.

These were young, well-dressed girls, with firm, ripe figures and faces made beautiful by health alone. They were bustling everywhere, running to and fro with bundles of clothes and parcels, watched by even healthier, even more elegant women kapos.

It was all a crazy jigsaw that made no sense to me and seemed sometimes to verge on lunacy. Beside one of the storerooms I saw a row of girls sitting astride a bench with zinc buckets on either side of them. One row of buckets was filled with tubes of toothpaste which the girls were squeezing out on to the bench and then throwing into the other, empty buckets.

To me it seemed thoroughly anti-German, an appalling waste of labour and material; for I had yet to learn that perhaps one tube in ten thousand contained a diamond, a nest egg that some pathetic trusting family had felt might buy privilege or even freedom.

Heinrich Grüber, the German Protestant pastor who had been sent to Dachau for having spoken out against the murder of Jews, later recalled the arrival in Dachau of railway carriages full of clothes which had reached the camp from Auschwitz. 'We were shaken to the depths of our soul', he recalled, 'when the first transports of children's shoes arrived – we men who were inured to suffering and to shock had to fight back tears.' Later they saw yet more thousands of children's shoes: 'this was the most terrible thing for us, the most bitter thing, perhaps the worst thing that befell us.'

In the Far East, Japanese forces had entered Burma and were approaching the capital, Rangoon. On March 7 a British General, Harold Alexander, who had been the last officer to leave the beaches of Dunkirk in 1940, ordered Rangoon's evacuation. That day the Dutch High Command on Java surrendered to overwhelming Japanese military and air attack, and 100,000 Dutch, British, Australian and American troops were taken prisoner. More than 80,000 Dutch civilians were also interned; of them, 10,000 were to die in captivity.

Tens of thousands of refugees fled northward from Rangoon. Many of them were Indian families whose community had been living and working in Rangoon for several generations. George Rodger, the American journalist reporting for *Time* magazine, watched them hurrying northward, towards the Indian border:

There must have been 50,000 to 60,000 of them. Dock labourers, coolies, and bearers plodded side by side with clerks and government servants, their women folk and children trailing beside them. In endless streams they came – women tired out and hobbling along by the aid of sticks; men carrying babies slung in panniers from their shoulders, others carrying small children on their backs.

Some of the women carried bundles of dry wood on their heads for, with such a large party, it was not easy to find fuel for their fires wherever they stopped for the night, and it was not safe to forage in the jungle where Burmans might be lurking.

These people were already about 150 miles from Rangoon and still had another thirty miles to go. Most of them were already lame. The older people were obviously exhausted and they had not yet learned of the disappointment that awaited them in Prome. Some of the men pulled heavy carts in which their women and children perched on top of their household goods, but the majority had been unable to bring more than a small bundle of personal things with them.

I was struck by the incongruity of the articles that some of them had chosen to salvage from their homes when nothing but the most indispensable things could be carried. One man had a cross-cut saw over his shoulder, another lugged along a large tom-tom, several had umbrellas, and one carried a bicycle with the back wheel missing.

They were all Indians; part of the 200,000 who formerly provided ninety per cent of Rangoon's labour strength – that was fifty-one per cent of the total population.

George Rodger explained that this was 'the second mass evacuation' since Burma had been given her new constitution, independent of India, in 1937. 'First they fled one year after independence had been given the country, when the Premier, Ba Maw had refused to stop the anti-Indian riots fostered by the Thakins – the leftist hooligans from Tharrawaddy. Today they fled from the Japanese terror, and Burman uprisings put them in danger of their lives.' They fled by day, Rodger added, 'under the burning pitiless sun and, when they camped at night, they were preyed on by Burman bandits'.

A few days later George Rodger and the journalists who were with him were themselves forced to hurry northward, as the Japanese, advancing from Rangoon, captured Prome. Fifty miles north of Prome the journalists caught up with the fleeing Indian refugees. 'Cholera and typhoid had broken out among them,' Rodger wrote, 'and we saw them dead and dying by the roadside. So great was their fear of the menace behind them that none dared delay to tend the sick. They cried out as we approached and we gave them water, though it might have been kinder to have put a bullet through their brains.'

In a prisoner-of-war camp at Bandung, on Java, a British medical officer, Colonel Edward Dunlop, recorded in his clandestine diary how three Dutch prisoners-of-war who had been caught while trying to escape were 'tied to poles and bayoneted to death like pigs before their comrades'. Each man, before being bayoneted, was asked if he had a final request. One man asked to have the bandage on his eyes removed. His request was granted. He then called out 'God Save the Queen!' The other two did likewise.

On March 11 General MacArthur left Luzon, and made his way by motor torpedo boat through 560 miles of Japanese-controlled waters to Mindanao, from where he flew on to Australia. To the newspaper reporters who met him at Darwin he declared: 'I came through, and I shall return.' On March 19 General Dwight D. Eisenhower, the head of the War Plans Division in Washington, wrote in his diary: 'MacArthur is out of Philippine Islands. Now supreme commander of "Southwest Pacific Area". The newspapers acclaim the move – the public has built itself a hero out of its own imagination.'

As British Intelligence obtained through Enigma the details of a new German offensive against Russia, Churchill offered Stalin a British bomber offensive against German industrial targets. The first such raid took place on the night of March 3/4, against a French factory that was known to be producing as many as 18,000 lorries a year for the German army. The factory, which before the war had been owned by Renault, was at Boulogne-Billancourt, in the west of Paris. A total of 223 aircraft bombed the target, at which there were no anti-aircraft defences. It was the largest Royal Air Force bombing raid over a single target since the bombing of Kiel almost a year earlier. A record tonnage of bombs was dropped – more than 412 tons.

Forty per cent of the factory was destroyed, and production halted for four weeks. The German production loss before the factory became operational again was estimated at 2,300 lorries. But the civilian cost of the raid was high. When the air raid sirens had sounded, many workers ignored it; similar sirens had gone off too frequently before as British bombers flew overhead on their way to Germany and back. The factory was not thought to have been at any risk. In one block of flats which was hit, seventy-two French civilians were killed. The total French death toll was 367, more than twice the number of people killed in the heaviest British bombing raid on Germany to date. Almost 10,000 French men and women lost their homes.

French bitterness threatened to revive the intensity of anti-British feeling of the summer of 1940, after the death of more than a thousand French sailors at Mers el-Kebir. But a prominent citizen of Billancourt, Georges Gorse, who was then with the Free French forces in London – and who after the war was elected Mayor of Billancourt – wrote shortly after the raid, in defence of what had happened: 'If we want the liberation of France, we have to clench our teeth and accept that the English bomb occupied Paris just as the Germans bombed London, that some French people perish under Allied bombs, just as much the victims of Germany as the casualties of the 1940 campaign and the men shot at Nantes or Paris.' Gorse added: 'The workers of Boulogne-Billancourt truly saw in the raids of March a promise of liberation. And those who have died have also brought "their own contribution to the coming dawn".'

The next British bombing raid was on Essen on the night of March 8/9. Industrial haze over the city prevented accurate bombing and the Krupp factory that was the target was not hit. During the raid, in which 211 aircraft took part, ten German civilians were killed. Essen was bombed again on the following night, when twenty-four other Ruhr towns were also attacked. Ten more people were killed in Essen and seventy-four in the other towns. A third consecutive raid on Essen likewise failed to do serious damage. But a raid on Kiel on the night of March 12/13 caused damage in two U-boat factories, and a raid on Cologne the following night seriously damaged an important rubber works, leading to a month's loss in production. Sixty-two civilians were killed in this raid on Cologne, including forty-six in a block of flats that collapsed when it was hit by 4,000-pound bombs. Two children who had been in the block were rescued alive after sixty-five hours of digging by rescue workers.

Speaking in Berlin on March 15, Hitler promised the German people that Russia would be 'annihilatingly defeated' in the coming summer. This promise caused the British to intensify their bombing of German industry. The Germans made skilful efforts to minimize the damage. During a British raid on Essen on the night of March 25/26 much of the attacking force of 254 aircraft was drawn off by decoy fires started by the Germans at a special site that had been prepared near the town of Rheinberg, eighteen miles to the west of Essen, on the other side of the River Rhine.

In Riom, in Vichy France, the pre-war Prime Minister Léon Blum was brought to trial on March 11. His trial lasted two days. All his judges were Frenchmen, as were the President and Vice-President of the Supreme Court. Convicted of 'neglecting the national defences' before the war, Blum was sentenced to life imprisonment. Other pre-war patriots and political leaders were also convicted and sentenced, among them the former Minister of War and Prime Minister Edouard Daladier, and the former Commander-in-Chief of the French Armies, General Gamelin. The trials were intended by Vichy to pour scorn and contempt on those who had led France before the collapse in 1940. It succeeded in doing so only among those who did not regard Vichy as a subservient tool of the Germans.

'By a cruel irony,' Blum told his accusers, 'it is our loyalty which has become treason. Yet this loyalty is not spent, it still endures. And France will reap the benefit of it in the future, in which we place our hope, and for which this very trial, this trial directed against the Republic, shall help to prepare.' Handed over by Vichy France to the Germans, Blum was held in a concentration camp for the rest of the war. Writing in 1943 in the introduction to the transcript of Blum's trial, Clement Attlee, the British Deputy Prime Minister and Labour Party leader wrote:

> The men of Vichy failed to break Léon Blum's spirit. After months of imprisonment he never wavered in his faith in the victory of civilization over barbarism or in his hope in the final victory of Socialism.
>
> The last message I received from him just before he was taken to Germany breathed the same unconquerable spirit. There was no word of his personal sufferings or danger. His whole thoughts were devoted to plans for the future of the world when victory should have been won and civilization saved. His enemies may enslave his body, they cannot subdue his soul.

On the Eastern Front the German army was preparing for its coming offensive. A series of attacks on Soviet partisan units behind the lines was launched on March 19. Dozens of Russian villages were set on fire and their inhabitants killed. The murder near Bobruisk of at least 3,500 villagers over a period of a few days only served to strengthen the determination of the partisans to continue their operations, and to intensify them. A German army report warned, at the end of March, that the strength of the partisan units near Vitebsk had been 'bolstered by individual units of regular troops': Soviet soldiers who had been ordered to remain behind the lines, and who were trained in the use of heavy weapons, artillery and anti-tank guns.

As resistance gathered momentum throughout Europe, the local populations under German rule everywhere were under constant threat of reprisals. In Yugoslavia a German army directive ordered the destruction of houses, and even of whole villages, wherever partisan activity had taken place. 'Removal of the population to concentration camps can also be useful,' the directive pointed out. In Poland, after a German patrol was attacked on March 20 in the town of Zgierz, a hundred Poles working in a nearby labour camp were taken to the market place in Zgierz and hanged. All six thousand inhabitants of the town, and hundreds more Poles from the surrounding villages, were brought to the market place and forced to watch the executions.

On March 22 the Italians suffered a setback at sea, when, in the Gulf of Sirte, a strong Italian force consisting of the battleship *Littoria*, three cruisers and eight destroyers – confident of success – attacked a British convoy bound for Malta. The convoy's escort of five cruisers and seventeen destroyers, commanded by Rear-Admiral Philip Vian, was heavily outgunned by the Italians, but Vian's naval tactics were such – including the skilful use of smoke – that the convoy got away unscathed. Later, however, Italian aircraft sank two of the British merchantmen at sea and two more in harbour at Malta, so that only 20 per cent of the convoy's cargo was landed.

On the Atlantic coast of France a British raid on the German battleship and U-boat base at St Nazaire on March 28 led to the destruction of the lock gates, and a short but welcome reduction in the capacity of the German submarine forces for action against Allied shipping. The British destroyer that rammed the lock gates loaded with tons of explosives, HMS *Campbell-town*, was one of the hundred First World War American destroyers given by Roosevelt to Britain a year and a half earlier in exchange for United States control of the British Caribbean bases. At the time of the transfer she had been the USS *Buchanan*.

Another of the bartered United States destroyers, the USS *Meade*, was to achieve the wartime endurance record of 250,000 miles at sea without a single breakdown.

The German summer offensive in Russia, planned to begin in the first week of May, was designed to achieve what the previous year's offensive had so narrowly failed to achieve: the total defeat of the Soviet Union. Hitler expressed his complete confidence that this second offensive could succeed, telling the Reichstag, whose members were still in shock from the failure of the 1941 winter offensive: 'When Napoleon retreated from Moscow in 1812 and his army was finally wiped out, the worst cold was 25 degrees below zero. But the severest frost we experienced was 52 degrees! We have mastered the fate that broke another man 130 years ago.'

In an attempt to draw back as many Russian soldiers as possible to the Far East, and to tie them down there, on March 28 Ribbentrop urged

the Japanese ambassador in Berlin to persuade his government to attack the
Soviet Union simultaneously with Germany's own 'crushing blow'. But, as
in the previous year, the Japanese declined. They had the whole of South
East Asia to conquer, to rule and to defend. In Burma, the Chinese 5th
Army commanded by General T'u participated in the British defence of the
Irrawaddy Front, as the main Japanese attack moved northward from Ran-
goon and Prome. British and American aircraft were continually in action,
but after a heavy Japanese air raid on the main Anglo-American air base at
Magwe on March 22, they were forced to move their base of operations to
Loiwing, near the Chinese border, and to Akyab, on the coast.

The fighting on the Irrawaddy Front was witnessed by the Allied journalists who retreated with the troops. George Rodger, the American journalist
reporting for *Time* magazine, described the scene at Yedashe, where the
Chinese hoped to make a stand:

... wounded Chinese soldiers kept breaking out of the jungle into the
roadway and limping off towards Yedashe. Some of them were terribly
shot up and supported themselves with sticks cut from the jungle. I am
sure no white man could have lived with such wounds.

One young soldier, who looked about eighteen, sank down by the side
of the road opposite us. His left arm was broken in two places, and he
had a bullet through his throat as well as a gaping hole in his stomach.
Not a murmur came from his parched lips as we lifted him into the shade
of a bush and gave him water.

Nobody seemed to pay any attention to the wounded. There were no
stretcher parties or ambulances to take them back to the dressing station.
They had to drag themselves along the road and they passed us without
a word; without a whimper or a plea for help; just wandering wrecks of
humanity battered and torn by a war that few of them knew why they
were fighting. Only their stoic endurance drove them on, for with such
loss of blood the strength of their bodies had already gone.

Forsaking all thought of getting more pictures that day, we drove the
jeep out of its concealment, loaded the worst cases into the back and drove
them to the village. Then for the rest of the day we ferried back and forth
between the front line and the dressing station, taking our pitiful passengers with all possible speed to the meagre comfort of iodine and bandages.

At the end of the day deep blood sloshed in the back of the jeep and
the stench was nauseating. We went to bed that night sick at heart.

On March 27 the increased intensity of the Japanese air attacks forced the British to move their air base from Akyab into India. The Allied troops in Burma could no longer receive close air support. A sustained Japanese air attack on the Burmese village and railway junction of Thazi threatened to open up the road to Mandalay. George Rodger, and his fellow journalist Burchett of the London *Daily Express* drove into Thazi immediately after the main Japanese attack. Rodger wrote:

I shall never forget the next hour that passed – the heartrending cries of the wounded; the screams of those who were caught in the flames, and the animal-like look of gratitude in the eyes of those we were able to rescue.

Two Indians, one with his feet blown off and another with his legs broken, were dragging themselves over the smouldering rubble of a fallen house by their hands when we found them. The loose brick gave no purchase to their clawing fingers, and they came on like seals, their legs dragging behind them, and flames threatening to engulf them from behind. We dashed in and dragged them to safety, leaving them in the road till we had rescued others in more imminent danger.

All those who could get out of the houses unaided were already gathered in the roadway or trying to make their own way out of the town, but there were still a few with leg and back injuries who were unable to help themselves. We dragged out a small child and a Burman girl whose leg was completely severed just below the knee, and loaded them into the jeep.

Then we picked up the two Indians. The girl's dangling leg, held only by tissues was obviously distressing her. It would be impossible for any surgeon to save it so I cut it off with my knife and sat beside her in the jeep, holding up the dismembered stump with my thumb on the main artery to stop the bleeding, while Burchett drove the gruesome load to the dressing station.

Several times we made trips into the village bringing the wounded out as fast as we could. There was no time to be gentle or soft-hearted, and if someone died on the rough journey we just unloaded his body and picked up another who had a better chance of survival.

As part of the British scheme to help the Soviet Union, the port city of Lübeck, on the Baltic, was bombed on the night of March 28/29. Eighty per cent of the medieval city was destroyed, including the Marienkirche, known as the 'mother church of Northern Germany'. A factory making U-boat components was also destroyed. 'This Sunday has been thoroughly spoiled by an exceptionally heavy raid by the Royal Air Force on Lübeck,' Goebbels complained in his diary.

The Royal Air Force also had a technical reason for carrying out the raid as it did. 'The main object of the attack was to learn to what extent a first wave of aircraft could guide a second wave to the aiming point by starting a conflagration,' the head of Bomber Command, Sir Arthur Harris, later recalled, and he went on to explain: 'I ordered an half-an-hour interval between the two waves in order to allow the fires to get a good hold. Lübeck was not a vital target, but it seemed to me better to destroy an industrial town of moderate importance than to toil to destroy a large industrial city.' Harris also recalled another reason: 'I wanted my crews to be well "blooded" as they say in fox-hunting, to have a taste of success for a change.'

That night 312 citizens were killed in Lübeck. It was the highest German civilian death toll thus far in a British bombing raid, although less than the number of French civilians who had been killed at Boulogne-Billancourt at the beginning of the month. Hitler retaliated for the raid on Lübeck, sending German bombers against British cities with medieval town centres. The raids were known as Baedeker raids, after the German guide books – among the best guides to British cities – which had been published in Leipzig for many decades by Karl Baedeker. In the raids on Bath, Norwich and York, starting on April 23, many ancient buildings were destroyed and 938 civilians killed. In the raid on York the medieval Guildhall was destroyed.

During the same night as the German raid on Bath, the British carried out a raid on the Baltic port of Rostock. The target was not only the Heinkel aircraft factory there, but also the medieval city centre. Like so many bombing raids however, the objectives were not attained: the aircraft factory was not hit and most of the bombs intended for the city centre fell between two and six miles away. In a second raid on Rostock two days later, the first hit was scored on the factory, and considerable damage done in the town. That night Goebbels wrote in his diary that the English 'have now chosen the expression "to lübeck" in place of the expression "to coventrize" invented by us. We are going to do everything possible to prevent this expression from being used in international terminology.'

A third raid on Rostock on the night of April 26/27 was so successful that the official history of Bomber Command described it as 'the masterpiece'

of the April raids: 1,765 buildings were destroyed and sixty per cent of the
central part of the city was reduced to rubble. During the raid more than
two hundred civilians were killed – there would have been many more had
they not fled after the first two raids. 'Community life there is practically
at an end,' wrote Goebbels in his diary. 'The situation in the city is in some
sections catastrophic.'

It was during the April raids on Germany that the phrase 'Terror raid'
(*Terrorangriff*) was first used in Germany. When details of the third Rostock
raid reached Berlin, Hitler told Goebbels that – as Goebbels recorded in his
diary – 'our task now must be to reply to terror with terror, and to respond
to the attempted destruction of German centres of culture by razing English
cultural shrines to the ground'.

Even as the Germans had been making their final plans for the Baedeker
raids, the British were practising low-level tactical air attacks on tanks, motor
vehicles and dummy soldiers. One such practice, with live ammunition, was
held at Imber Down on April 13, in preparation for a further exercise at
which Churchill was to be present. The practice exercise consisted of Hurricane fighters swooping down on the targets, which were laid out in three
parallel lines: a line of lorries, a line of dummy soldiers – made of wood –
and a line of tanks. The spectators formed a fourth parallel line 400 yards
long and 88 yards from the nearest target.

Five Spitfires made the first attack, with success. Then, as a Hurricane
approached, it became clear to those on the ground that something was
wrong: it opened fire, not on the targets, but on the spectators. Twenty-seven
people were killed. The pilot, a young Canadian sergeant, was absolved from
blame. He was later killed in action. Three days after the disaster, Churchill
was present at the final exercise. In a nearby hospital, doctors and nurses
were still struggling to save the lives of those who had been badly wounded.

The Japanese forces in the Far East were reaching their extreme limit of
conquest. On March 31 they reached British-ruled Christmas Island, Christmas Island, south of Java. The garrison of a hundred British troops surrendered. It was the most southerly Japanese conquest of the war. Four days
later, Japanese aircraft launched from five aircraft carriers that had crossed
the Indian Ocean, attacked the harbour at Colombo, the main city of Ceylon.
Four British warships were sunk, including the cruisers *Dorsetshire* and *Corn-
wall*, and more than five hundred sailors drowned.

Japanese aircraft flying from the same carrier-borne force also attacked the northern Ceylonese port of Trincomalee, sinking two more British warships, one of them the aircraft carrier *Hermes*, and killing three hundred sailors. It was a veritable Pearl Harbor; indeed, the Japanese aircraft carriers involved had all taken part in the Pearl Harbor attack. During this same raid, twenty-three Allied merchant ships were sunk in the Bay of Bengal.

On April 6 the Japanese air force carried out a bombing raid on two towns in southern India, Cocanada and Vizagapatam. A week later, during a Japanese air attack on the city of Mandalay in Burma, 2,000 Burmese were killed and much of the city set on fire. South of the city, British, American and Chinese troops were being pushed back relentlessly, fighting a series of brave but ultimately ineffective rearguard actions against the steady Japanese advance. But the main effort of the Japanese war machine at the beginning of April was to complete the conquest of Luzon, where American and Filipino troops had continued to fight on the Bataan peninsula and, after the evacuation of Bataan, on the island fortress of Corregidor.

On April 9 the Japanese overran Bataan, taking 76,000 prisoners, of whom 12,000 were American servicemen. The captives were then marched northward for sixty-five miles. The brutality practised against them on the march was such that at least 5,000 Filipinos and more than 600 Americans died. Many of the dead had been too weak to walk, or had stumbled and fallen along the line of march. They were clubbed or bayoneted to death as they lay on the ground. The march became known as the March of Death.

The prisoner-of-war camps to which the Filipinos and Americans were taken were run with sadism and without the slightest concern for the health or survival of those in them. In their first few weeks behind barbed wire, a further 16,000 Filipinos and at least a thousand Americans had died of starvation, disease and the brutality of the Japanese guards.

In Australia there were fears that the Japanese might bomb Sydney or Melbourne. In a radio broadcast to Britain on April 28, John Curtin, the Australian Prime Minister, uttered a dire warning:

> Like Britain after Dunkirk, we find that we have not enough arms, not enough aeroplanes. You did not have enough aeroplanes nor enough arms, but you did have the will to resist. It was the spirit of the people that freed Britain, and it will be the spirit of the Australian people that will not only save Australia but send us marching forward to victory.
>
> Dangerous days lie ahead of us, but under this threat the Empire is more united than ever before. The people of Australia have no illusions

about this struggle. They know that this is not a fight for Australia, nor for the Empire, nor for any other section of the world, but a fight for the world itself.

Reflecting on the Australian fear of invasion, Robert O'Neill, then a youngster of five, recalled: 'It did not last long, but long enough for most families to have built their own air raid shelters in the garden.'

That April there were several episodes that led to an upsurge in Allied morale. While it was clear that the war would go on for a long time, and that no prospect yet existed of a clear or rapid road to the defeat of Germany and Japan, such successes as there were from day to day served to point a way forward to eventual victory. In April, the first trams ran again in besieged Leningrad – where in each of the winter months at least 100,000 citizens had died. In a British low-level air raid on Augsburg – although seven of the twelve attacking bombers were shot down – the fact that a raid had been made so deep into Germany, and by planes flying at only five hundred feet, gave the British public a sense of pride. In Bordeaux harbour, two British commandos, entering the port in a canoe, blew up a German tanker.

The escape of General Giraud, who had been captured by the Germans in 1940, from a maximum security prisoner-of-war castle prison at Königstein in Saxony, gave pleasure to all anti-Nazi French men and women, wherever they lived. In the First World War Giraud had also escaped from a prisoner-of-war camp in Germany. Goebbels reported that Hitler was in a 'black rage' at Giraud's escape, and that 'anyone who extends aid and protection to him is to be punished by death'. But the General avoided capture, making his way first by German passenger trains, and finally in a British submarine, to North Africa, where he became a focal point of French patriotism.

The Americans also had a morale-boosting success that April, a risky enterprise that succeeded. Sixteen American bombers, commanded by the test pilot and international air racer Lieutenant-Colonel James H. Doolittle, were instructed to carry out a bombing raid over the Japanese mainland. The aircraft were taken across the Pacific by sea on the aircraft carrier *Hornet*, the newest carrier in the United States Navy, and launched on April 18. They then flew five hundred miles across the Pacific to bomb naval and oil installations in Tokyo, Kobe, Yokohama and Nagoya. 'It is the first time in history,' Roosevelt pointed out, 'that Japan has suffered such indignities.'

As the American bombers did not have a long-enough range to fly back to their carrier, they flew on to air bases in Nationalist-held China. Two of the bombers crash landed in one of the Japanese-occupied provinces of China. Of the eight crew members who were captured, three were executed. In the hope of preventing further raids, the Japanese occupied the Chinese coastal province of Chekiang, to which some of the bombers had flown.

The Japanese forward march in the Far East was not yet over. On April 29, Japanese troops in Burma seized the terminus of the Burma Road, at Lashio, ending the possibility of any further overland supplies being sent to Nationalist China. As the Japanese grip on Burma increased, 100,000 Chinese troops were withdrawn over the mountain passes into India. On April 30 the British had to give up the Burmese port of Akyab, less than a hundred miles from the border of British India.

The Japanese capacity to cause momentary havoc was greater than their ability to conquer the whole Pacific region. On the last day of May two Japanese 'midget' submarines, each with a two-man crew, entered the harbour of Diego Suarez, in Madagascar – which the British had just captured from Vichy France. The submarines then torpedoed and sank the merchant ship *British Loyalty*, and severely damaged the British battleship *Ramilles*. In the ensuing action all the submariners were killed. Theirs had been in effect a suicide mission; there was no way in which they could have obtained the fuel needed to return to a Japanese-held port.

Six thousand miles further west of Madagascar, two other Japanese submarines, each likewise with a two-man crew, penetrated the harbour defences of Sydney and fired their torpedoes at the American cruiser *Chicago*. They missed the cruiser but hit the Australian depot ship *Kuttabul*: twenty sailors were drowned when the depot ship sank. One of the submarines was sunk and its crew killed; the other was captured, every member of its four-man crew killing themselves to avoid the perceived humiliation of capture. The four bodies were cremated in Sydney with full military honours and the ashes returned to Japan. Such courtesies were inconceivable on the victorious Japanese battlefields and in the prisoner-of-war camps where Allied soldiers, sailors and airmen were being murdered and tortured.

A daring Japanese raid took place that summer, when a single Japanese submarine reached the estuary of the Columbia River on the Pacific coast of the United States, surfaced, and opened fire on a military depot at Fort Stephens, Oregon. It was the first time since the British attacks in 1812 that a foreign power had opened fire on an American military installation in the continental United States. Little damage was done and no further such attack took place. There was, however, one Japanese air attack on the continental United States, also on Oregon, when a single small plane, launched from the deck of a submarine, dropped its incendiary bombs on a forest near Brookings. The result was a small fire, but no casualties.

A form of combat new to the Twentieth Century took place on May 2, when American warships intercepted a Japanese invasion fleet that was on its way to both Tulagi in the Solomon Islands and Port Moresby in New Guinea. A four-day battle ensued that was fought entirely by the aircraft from the aircraft carriers of the respective fleets. No shots were fired by ships against ships. The entire battle was fought in the air: plane against plane and plane against ship. The American aircraft carrier *Lexington* was so badly damaged by aerial bombs and aerial torpedoes that she had to be scuttled. During the onslaught against her, 216 of her crew were killed. The Japanese light aircraft carrier *Shoho* was also sunk.

In the battle between plane and plane, seventy Japanese and sixty-six American planes were shot down. The Japanese losses made it impossible for the invasion fleet to continue. The battle of the Coral Sea had been America's first naval victory against Japan. During a radio broadcast four months later, Roosevelt told the story of a United States Navy lieutenant, John James Powers, who, before going into action, had told his fellow pilots: 'Remember, the folks back home are counting on us. I am going to get a hit if I have to lay it on their flight deck.' Powers then flew down from 8,000 feet to less than 200 feet above the deck of a Japanese carrier before releasing his bomb. His plane was destroyed in the explosion of his own bomb. After telling this story, Roosevelt continued: 'I have received a recommendation from the Secretary of the Navy that Lieutenant James Powers of New York City, missing in action, be awarded the Medal of Honour. I hereby and now make this award.'

In Japanese-occupied Manchuria, the wider war had begun to impinge on daily life. Jung Chang has recounted her mother's experiences as a schoolgirl:

> As part of their education, my mother and her classmates had to watch newsreels of Japan's progress in the war. Far from being ashamed of their brutality, the Japanese vaunted it as a way to inculcate fear. The films showed Japanese soldiers cutting people in half and prisoners tied to stakes being torn to pieces by dogs. There were lingering close-ups of the victims' terror-stricken eyes as their attackers came at them.
>
> The Japanese watched the eleven- and twelve-year-old schoolgirls to

make sure they did not shut their eyes or try to stick a handkerchief in their mouths to stifle their screams. My mother had nightmares for years to come.

During 1942, with their army stretched out across China, Southeast Asia, and the Pacific Ocean, the Japanese found themselves running short of labour. My mother's whole class was conscripted to work in a textile factory, as were the Japanese children. The local girls had to walk about four miles each way; the Japanese children went by truck. The local girls got a thin gruel made from moldy maize with dead worms floating in it; the Japanese girls had packed lunches with meat, vegetables, and fruit.

The Japanese girls had easy jobs, like cleaning windows. But the local girls had to operate complex spinning machines, which were highly demanding and dangerous even for adults. Their main job was to reconnect broken threads while the machines were running at speed. If they did not spot the broken thread, or reconnect it fast enough, they would be savagely beaten by the Japanese supervisor.

The girls were terrified. The combination of nervousness, cold, hunger, and fatigue led to many accidents. Over half of my mother's fellow pupils suffered injuries. One day my mother saw a shuttle spin out of a machine and knock out the eye of the girl next to her. All the way to the hospital the Japanese supervisor scolded the girl for not being careful enough.

Just as in Poland the Germans had failed to find a distinguished Polish citizen willing to act as their puppet ruler, so in the Philippines the Japanese were equally frustrated. Like the Germans in Poland, they wreaked their vengeance on those who refused to be their Quislings. The Chief Justice of the Philippines, José Abad Santos, refused to serve in a pro-Japanese government. He was executed on May 7. In German-occupied Russia that day, the SS hanged Isai Kazinets, a leading partisan who had been caught and tortured, but had betrayed none of his colleagues. As a Jew, he had also been in contact with the Jewish underground in the city of Minsk. Their secrets died with him.

There was an Allied execution that month, of José Key, a citizen of Gibraltar, who was shot as a spy on May 18 at Wandsworth Prison, London. He had given the Germans information about the movement of Allied ships and aircraft entering and leaving the Mediterranean.

German air power faced two setbacks that month. Repeated bombings of

Malta failed to break the will of the Maltese, who continued to deny the island to the Germans, and to whom two aircraft carriers, the Royal Navy's *Eagle* and the United States Navy's *Wasp*, brought vital air reinforcements – sixty-two fighters. They were conveyed near enough to the island for them to reach it by air, and then to join in the air battle within thirty-five minutes of landing (the time needed to refuel).*

A second setback for the Germans was their failure for more than a month to overcome the continuing resistance of the Crimean port city and fortress of Sebastopol, thereby holding up the imminent German offensive against southern Russia. Both Malta and Sebastopol were rewarded, much as fighting men might be. Malta received the highest British civilian award for bravery, the George Cross, and Sebastopol was declared a Hero City. But the heroism of Allied cities and islands did not shake the long-term confidence of the rulers of Germany. On May 19 Goebbels wrote in his diary of one of his visions of the future. It concerned the cinema. 'We must take a similar course in our film policy as pursued by the Americans on the North American and South American continents,' he wrote. 'We must become the dominant film power in Europe. Films produced by other States should only be allowed to have local and limited character.'

Visible to the Nazi leaders and administrators, as well as for all citizens, anti-Nazi posters had begun to appear in the streets of Berlin that May. In addition to the posters, fires had been started at several of the displays in an anti-Soviet exhibition. Twenty-seven people were arrested for these acts of defiance. Led by Herbert Baum, a German Communist, they were all Jews, living in Berlin. Between October 1941 and January 1942 the city's Jewish population had been reduced from 72,000 to 60,000 as a result of the deportations to Riga, Minsk, Kovno and the Lodz ghetto. The remaining Jews had every expectation of being unmolested. Even the Yellow Star had not yet been imposed.

Among the Baum group were two sisters, Alice and Hella Hirsch, aged nineteen and twenty-two respectively, and Baum's sister, Marianne. Baum himself is thought to have been tortured to death. All but two of the others were beheaded or sent to concentration camps, where they died. Two survived in Auschwitz, where they were eventually liberated by the Soviets.

---

* The *Wasp* was later transferred to the Pacific, where it was sunk in the New Hebrides on 15 September 1942 by Japanese submarines.

As a reprisal for the arson at the exhibition, the Gestapo rounded up five hundred Berlin Jews, of whom half were shot immediately and the others sent to Sachsenhausen concentration camp north of the capital, where they too were eventually killed. On June 6 the first of 15,000 Berlin Jews – many of them the elderly and the infirm – were taken by train southward to the eighteenth century garrison town of Terezin, in Bohemia. Known by its German name of Theresienstadt, the town become a ghetto: the place of incarceration of 140,000 German, Austrian and Czechoslovak Jews, more than 33,000 of whom died there, mostly of starvation. Almost all the others, 88,191 in all, were deported from Theresienstadt to the East during the course of the next two years, and murdered.

To prepare for the second German offensive against the Soviet Union, an attack was launched on May 17 to close the Soviet pocket at Izyum, in the eastern Ukraine. On the second day of the attack the pocket was closed, with the capture of 214,000 Soviet soldiers and 1,200 tanks. On May 24, as part of the plan to protect the supply lines to the front, once the main offensive had begun, the Germans launched a massive anti-partisan operation north of Bryansk: 45,000 German soldiers took part, against an estimated 20,000 Soviet partisans. Thousands of partisans were caught and killed.

Determined to see the partisans engage the Germans as widely as possible behind the lines, on May 30 Stalin set up a 'General Staff of the Partisan Movement' to coordinate all sabotage activities, and to maximize the effectiveness of partisan attacks.

Further German attacks on the partisans continued during the summer. In the Polotsk-Borisov-Lepel area, partisans had declared a 'Republic of Palik' It took 16,000 German troops to overrun them. Another anti-partisan sweep had to be carried out between Roslavl and Bryansk, where 5,000 German troops searched for an estimated 2,500 partisans. Although, in the course of a four-week sweep, more than a thousand partisans were killed for the loss of only fifty-eight German troops, the partisans made use of the forests with which they were so familiar to move their base of operations elsewhere.

Western newspapers were provided with a stirring picture of life on the Eastern Front, from an optimistic Allied perspective. On May 23 the British evening papers published a photograph of Sergeant Korneiko. He was the armourer of a Soviet Naval-Air unit, and was shown loading a bomb onto a Russian bomber. The bomb bore the chalked inscription, in Russian: 'A present for Hitler.'

During May the Danish SS Legion, then numbering a thousand men, was in action on the Eastern Front for the first time, serving as a replacement unit with the elite SS Death's Head Division. The Danish volunteers were commanded by SS Major Christian von Schalburg, a former officer in the Danish Army. As a result of his new role, von Schalburg was ostracized by almost all his fellow officers in Denmark.

The Germans did not accept all offers of help: when the Indian nationalist leader Subhas Chandra Bose met Hitler at the Reich Chancellery in Berlin on May 29, and offered his services as the leader of Indian soldiers disaffected with Britain, he was rebuffed, Hitler telling him that what Indians needed on their path to modernity and independence was another fifty years of British rule. Hitler's one constructive suggestion was that Bose seek the support of the Japanese. To this end a German submarine was put at his disposal, and took him to the Indian Ocean, where he transferred to a Japanese submarine. In Japan, Bose found sympathy and support for his ideas, and was allowed to set up an Indian National Army to fight against the British in Burma.

The diversion of German forces from the Russian Front as a result of the Allied military effort in North Africa had come to an end during the winter with the end of the British offensive. In the early summer Stalin demanded an Allied 'Second Front' in Northern Europe. The implacable British bombing of German cities was not enough for him. Nor were Britain's frequent naval engagements in the Mediterranean.

A British naval attack on a German-Italian convoy of four supply ships on May 10 boded well for the British attackers. But on the following day, in a German air attack, three British destroyers were sunk and 112 British sailors killed. Stalin reiterated his call for a cross-Channel landing, and demanded it that year. Churchill travelled by air to Moscow, via Egypt and Iran, to explain to him face to face that the Western Allies did not have the resources for such a massive undertaking that year. In fact, two years were to pass before the landings were possible, and even then they faced a high risk.

Even before his journey to Moscow, Churchill took a personal interest in the means whereby such a massive cross-Channel landing could eventually be launched. In May he was shown a proposal for an artificial harbour which could be towed across the Channel a hundred miles to the invasion point. Reading about the piers that were to be constructed for such a harbour,

Churchill wrote to his advisers on May 30: 'They *must* float up and down on the tide', and he added: 'The anchor problem must be mastered. The ships must have a side flap cut in them and a drawbridge long enough to overreach the moorings of the piers. Let me have the solution worked out. Don't argue the matter. The difficulties will argue for themselves.'

As part of the immediate British attempt to take pressure off the Eastern Front, the heaviest bombing raid yet carried out over Germany was launched on the night of May 30/31, against Cologne. It was known as 'the thousand bomber raid'. In all, 1,047 aircraft were despatched from Britain. Hitherto, between 250 and 350 bombers had been considered an extremely large force, the largest that could be put against a single city target in the time needed before anti-aircraft activity intensified. Even the heaviest German air raid launched against Britain had seldom exceeded five hundred planes.

Cologne was selected as a target that night because the weather over most of Germany was cloudy. The factories of Cologne were the objective. Within the space of ninety minutes, 1,455 tons of bombs were dropped by 900 of the bombing force (some of the aircraft on the raid were fighters that bombed German airfields along the route; others were bombers that carried out small diversionary attacks). The damage done was enormous. Thirty-six factories were unable to continue production, and 600 acres of built up area was destroyed or severely damaged. This was almost the equivalent of the total (780 acres) of all the destruction caused in all previous British bombing raids over Germany, including those on Lübeck and Rostock.

As many as 2,500 separate fires were started in Cologne that night; 3,330 buildings were destroyed and more than two thousand seriously damaged. Among the buildings totally destroyed were nine hospitals, seventeen churches, sixteen schools, six department stores and two cinemas. More than 45,000 people were made homeless. The number of dead was between 469 and 486 – the highest yet caused by a British bombing raid. British civilian deaths in the Blitz had been much higher. The German civil defence authorities had gained a full extra year to construct deep and effective air raid shelters.

The Royal Air Force also broke another record that night: the highest rate of its own loss of any raid hitherto. Forty-one aircraft were lost. Sixteen were known to have been shot down by anti-aircraft fire from the ground, four were shot down by German night fighters, and two collided.

Within the harsh confines of the Warsaw ghetto, where more than four thousand Jews were dying each month of starvation, the news of the Cologne raid had a noticeable effect on morale. The Polish Jewish historian, Emanuel Ringelblum – who was later to be betrayed while in hiding and shot – wrote in his diary of the jubilation throughout Warsaw at the news of the raid. He added:

> The Jewish jubilation was quite different from the general one. Day in, day out in hundreds of cities throughout Poland and Russia, thousands upon thousands of Jews are being systematically murdered according to a preconceived plan, and no one seems to take our part. The bombing of Cologne, the destruction of thousands of buildings, the thousands of civilian victims, have slaked our thirst for revenge somewhat.
>
> Cologne was an advance payment on the vengeance that must and shall be taken on Hitler's Germany for the millions of Jews they have killed. So the Jewish population of tortured Europe considered Cologne its personal act of vengeance.
>
> After the Cologne affair, I walked around in a good mood, feeling that, even if I should perish at their hands, my death is prepaid!

On the day after the Cologne raid a new forced labour camp that had been under preparation for some months was ready to be opened at Monowitz, on the outskirts of Auschwitz, one mile from Auschwitz town and two miles from the existing concentration camps there. It was planned to make use of the Polish and Jewish prisoners already in those camps, of new prisoners who would be brought there, of forced labourers from western Europe including Belgium, and of British prisoners-of-war, for whom a special camp was built alongside the Polish and Jewish ones.

The factory that would use this mass of forced labour – more than 10,000 men at any given moment – was the Buna synthetic rubber and synthetic oil factory, owned and operated by I.G. Farben. The repeated British bombing of factories in the Ruhr, and the unceasing German army and air force demand for rubber and fuel oil, made the development of this, and several other synthetic factories elsewhere in Greater Germany, an essential part of the German war effort.

The importance of setting up the synthetic oil factory – which was not expected to be able to produce oil in large quantities for at least a year – was underlined on June 12 when American bombers, using Egypt as their base, flew more than nine hundred miles to bomb the Roumanians oilfields at Ploesti. It was Roumanian oil on which Germany was principally dependent.

There was, however, another source of oil, by far the most substantial on the continent of Europe, that lay within the German grasp. This was the oil in the Caucasus, in the Soviet republic of Azerbaijan. Two cities, Grozny and Baku, were the main prizes awaiting the German army and the German warmaking machine as the summer offensive was launched.

As the German army prepared its new eastern onslaught, it secured a dramatic victory in the Western Desert, when Rommel overran Tobruk, taking 30,000 Allied prisoners. When news of the battle reached Hitler, he awarded Rommel a Field Marshal's baton. When Churchill, who was then in the United States, told Roosevelt of the disaster at Tobruk, the President responded with a quiet question: 'What can we do to help?' The urgent need, Churchill replied, was bomber aircraft. Roosevelt immediately ordered the diversion to Egypt of an American bomber squadron that was about to be sent to China, and ordered forty fighter bombers that were then in Basra on their way to Russia to be sent to Egypt instead.

The fall of Tobruk was followed ten days later by the fall of Sebastopol. The German army was moving forward both to the Suez Canal and the Caucasian oil fields. It was to reach neither. But in the fighting for both it was to bring the Allies to the brink of disaster.

Following the Allied loss of Tobruk, the Germans employed prisoners-of-war to unload supply ships in the harbour. Many of these prisoners were Black South Africans, members of the Native Corps of the South African armed forces. The Germans kept them in an open barbed-wire compound at night, and marched them to the docks each morning. One of their number, Lance-Corporal Job Masego, surreptitiously collected unexploded cartridges in the sand, and diligently made a small bomb with them. He then used it to blow up a ship loaded with drums of fuel oil.

Masego was awarded the Military Medal for his exploit. Later he escaped from captivity and rejoined the South African forces. After the war he returned to the mining community of Benoni from which he came, and all trace of him was lost. Forty-six years after his exploit, however, and following the collapse of apartheid in South Africa, the South African navy named one of its most modern coastal strike vessels in his honour.

In Prague, the two Czech patriots who had been parachuted into Bohemia some months earlier joined forces with their fellow-Czech partisans to assassinate Reinhard Heydrich. He was ambushed on May 27 as he was being driven to Prague from his villa ten miles north of the city. After his death, reprisals were begun, the details of which, reaching the West through a series of shocked messages from the Czech Resistance, so perturbed were the Allies that there was intensive discussion about placing a ban on all future assassinations of Nazi leaders.

The German reprisals began even while Heydrich lay dying. The first to be killed were what Goebbels called 'a whole crowd of Jews' who were then in Sachsenhausen concentration camp north of Berlin. 'The more of this filthy race we eliminate, the better things will be for the security of the Reich,' he wrote in his diary. Two days later a thousand Viennese Jews were taken by train to Minsk. There, all trace of them was lost: they were almost certainly taken from the station by truck the few miles further east to Maly Trostenets, the camp in which the first deaths of Jews in gas vans had taken place a few weeks earlier. Not one of the thousand was ever seen again.

Further killings took place in the week after Heydrich's death that were given the name of reprisals, though they conformed to the pattern of mass murder that had been established for many months. In Warsaw, 110 Jews were rounded up on June 3 and taken to a prison on the edge of the ghetto, where they were shot. Those killed included several women, two of whom were pregnant. Three days later, Adolf Eichmann ordered the deportation of 450 German Jews from the Koblenz area, including the inmates of a mental institution. In order to maintain secrecy, Eichmann insisted that the words 'deportation to the East' should not be used. Instead, those who had been deported were described as 'people who emigrated elsewhere'. None of the deportees was ever seen again. They were probably sent to Belzec and murdered there.

On June 10, at Heydrich's State Funeral in Berlin, Himmler told the SS mourners that it was their 'holy obligation' to avenge Heydrich's death 'and to destroy with even greater determination the enemies of our nation, mercilessly and pitilessly'. Renewed reprisals began the following day with the execution of 199 men from the Czech village of Lidice, near Prague. The eighty-eight children of the village, and their mothers – sixty women in all – were sent to various concentration camps. The mothers were separated from their children and sent to Ravensbrück north of Berlin, and to Mauthausen, where they were killed. The children were sent to Chelmno, where they were gassed.

In another Czech village, Lezaky, seventeen men and sixteen women were shot, and fourteen children sent to concentration camps. Only two of the children of Lezaky survived. As a further reprisal, on the day of Heydrich's funeral the SS began 'Operation Heydrich': the systematic deportation of Jews from hitherto undeported communities to the death camps in the East. The operation lasted for many months. On that first day a thousand Jews were sent to 'the East' from Prague. Only one person out of the thousand deportees survived the war: a man who managed to jump out of the train early in its journey and evaded the shooting of the guards.

On June 12 and 13 two more trains left for the East as part of Operation Heydrich. They took Jews from the ghetto that had been set up at the small garrison town of Theresienstadt on the Sudeten border – into which tens of thousands of Czech Jews had been confined since the end of the previous year – and despatched them likewise to 'the East'. Each train carried a thousand deportees. From these two trains there was likewise only a single survivor, a man who also managed to jump from the train early in the journey. In the course of three days, three thousand people disappeared in 'the East'. Their destination was almost certainly the death camp at Maly Trostenets, six hundred miles from Prague. Not one of them survived.

That summer Admiral Wilhelm Canaris, the chief of the Abwehr – the military intelligence service of the High Command of the German Army – and his deputy, Hans von Dohnanyi, managed to save the lives of fourteen German Jews by sending them to Switzerland, on the pretext that they were being employed as counter-intelligence operatives. To save these fourteen it had taken a year of careful planning and subterfuge, culminating in persuading the Gestapo Chief, Heinrich Müller, that the departure of these Jews was in the German national interest.

Also that summer, in the ranks of the German army, a young officer, twenty-five year-old Michael Kitzelmann, who had won an Iron Cross second class for bravery as a company commander, spoke out against the atrocities being committed on the Eastern Front, and against the Nazi leadership. 'If these criminals should win,' he told his fellow officers, 'I would have no wish to live any longer.' His remarks were reported to his superiors, and Kitzelmann was arrested. He was tried by court martial, and shot by a firing squad at Orel on June 11.

Within three weeks of Kitzelmann's execution, Himmler addressed the officers of the SS Das Reich Division to explain why they, the SS troops, and not the German Army, were the ones who must wage the race war. 'The German soldier has in the past frequently operated under long-outmoded conceptions that once went unquestioned; these he carried with him to the

battlefield in 1939,' Himmler told them. He added that, from the very
moment that 'the enemy was taken captive, this erroneous notion of what
war is all about showed itself unmistakably. Thus, for instance, it was thought
that one had to say that even a Jew was a human being and that, as such,
he could not be harmed. Or, in the case of a Jewess – even if she had been
caught harbouring partisans at the time – one couldn't touch her; she was,
after all, a lady. The same held for this Eastern campaign too, when the
whole German nation took to the field, their heads filled with such absolute
rubbish and over-refined, civilized decadence'.

Himmler then confided: 'We SS men were less encumbered, one might
even say practically unencumbered, by such rubbish. After a decade of racial
education we, the entire cadre of the SS, entered this war as unshakeable
champions of our Germanic people.'

In the summer of 1942, both Germany and Japan were confident of further
victories. But neither was able to achieve its aims without losses so high
that they cast serious doubt over the possibility of ultimate success. In the
first week of June, alerted by the daily reading of Japan's top secret radio
signals, American warships intercepted a Japanese invasion fleet on its way
to Midway Island, the two square mile indispensable stepping stone for the
planned Japanese invasion of the Hawaiian Islands, and the last outpost
between Japan and Hawaii that was still under American control.

Four Japanese aircraft carriers and eighty-six warships were en route to
Midway from Japan, together with 5,000 soldiers on board twelve troop
transports. It was the largest Japanese task force ever assembled. Four sustained American aircraft attacks against the invasion fleet failed to hit their
targets, and sixty-five American aircraft were shot down. The fifth American
attack, on the morning of June 5, sank three of the four Japanese aircraft
carriers. The fourth carrier was destroyed that afternoon. Three of the carriers
sunk had been among the five that had taken part in the attack on Pearl
Harbor six months earlier.

A Japanese cruiser, the *Mikuma*, was also sunk. In all, the Japanese lost
332 aircraft and 3,500 men. American losses were one carrier – the *Yorktown*
– fatally damaged, 150 aircraft destroyed and 307 men killed. The Battle
of Midway was not only a defeat for Japan; like the Battle of the Coral Sea
a month earlier it was also a defeat in the arm of warfare that Japan had
chosen for conquest: air power.

*   *   *

Those conquered peoples who had looked to Japan as the liberator from British, French and Dutch colonial rule were quickly and cruelly disappointed. The Filipinos had already met the implacable enmity which led to the deaths of thousands of their prisoners-of-war. The Indonesians, Malaysians, Burmese and Indo-Chinese were to be confronted with similar cruelty and exploitation. Even Korea, which had been under Japanese control for more than twenty-five years, was expected to provide forced labourers for Japanese enterprises, and to send Korean women and girls – the crudely-named 'comfort women' – to specially established Japanese military brothels, where the captives were used, and abused, by the Japanese armed forces.

In the Japanese treatment of Europeans, racial and punitive motives were intermingled. In a civilian internment camp in Borneo the Japanese commanding officer told his British civilian prisoners – some of whom had been in the colonial service for many years: 'You are a fourth-class nation now. Therefore your treatment will be fourth class, and you will live and eat as coolies. In the past you have had proudery and arrogance! You will get over it now!'

On June 23 a group of three hundred British prisoners-of-war was taken to a base in Thailand and ordered to build both their own camp and a camp for their Japanese guards. Three months later, 3,000 Australian prisoners-of-war were sent to a camp in Burma. Between the two camps lay hundreds of miles of jungle and ravines. The Japanese wanted to have a railway between the two, along which they could move troops and military supplies from Thailand to Burma. Prisoners-of-war of all nationalities were to be the builders. Fifteen thousand were to perish on the railway. One of the first accounts of a prisoner-of-war camp in Thailand to reach the outside world came in a broadcast made from Singapore to Britain by Padre J.N. Duckworth on 12 September 1945, more than three years after the work and the torment had begun. He described how the labour force had been collected.

The Japanese told us we were going to a health resort! *We* were delighted. They told us to take pianos and gramophone records – *they* would supply the gramophones. We were overjoyed, and we took them. Dwindling rations and a heavy toll of sickness were beginning to play on our fraying nerves and emaciated bodies.

It all seemed like a bolt from the tedium of life behind barbed wire in Changi, Singapore. They said 'Send the sick – it will do them good'.

And we believed them, so we took them all.

Padre Duckworth went with 1,680 men to a camp in northern Thailand. Less than 250 of those men survived the war. His account of conditions in the camp gives a picture of their torments:

Our accommodation consisted of bamboo huts without roofs. The monsoon had begun and the rain beat down. Work (slave work, piling earth and stones in little skips onto an embankment) began immediately. It began at five o'clock in the morning, and finished at nine o'clock at night (or even later than that). Exhausted, starved and benumbed in spirit we toiled, because if we did not, we and our sick would starve. As it was, the sick had half-rations because the Japanese said 'No work, no food'.

Then came cholera. This turns a full-grown man into an emaciated skeleton — overnight twenty, thirty, forty and even fifty deaths were the order of the day. The medical kit we had brought could not come with us. We were told it *would* come on. It never did. We improvised bamboo holders for saline transfusions, and used boiled river water and common salt to put in to the veins of the victims.

Cholera raged. The Japanese still laughed and asked 'How many dead men?' We still had to work, and work harder. Presently there came dysentery and beriberi — that dread disease bred of malnutrition and starvation. Tropical ulcers, diphtheria, mumps and smallpox all added to the misery and squalor of the camp on the hillside where water flowed unceasingly through the huts at the bottom.

A rising feeling of resentment against the Japanese, the weather and general living conditions, coupled with the knowledge that the officers could do little or nothing about it, made life in the camp full of dreams that each day would bring something worse.

The lowest daily death rate, Duckworth explained, came down to seventeen in September 1943, 'when the weather improved and things began to get a little better'. His account continued:

Yet we had to work — there was no way out of it. Escape through the jungle, as many gallant parties attempted, would only end in starvation and disease; if the party survived and were eventually captured, the torture which followed was worse than death itself.

We were dragged out by the hair to go to work, beaten with bamboo poles and mocked at. We toiled, half-naked in the cold unfriendly rain of

Upper Thailand. We had no time to wash, and if we did it meant cholera. By day we never saw our bed spaces (on long platforms in those bleak one-hundred-metre huts).

'Our comrades died,' Duckworth said, 'and we could not honour them even at the graveside because we were still working.'

This account, broadcast in 1945, was available fifty-three years later on the internet, put there by the Kwai Railway Memorial, Three Pagodas Group. For them, the suffering of the prisoners-of-war on the River Kwai railway, and in all Japanese prisoner-of-war camps, is one of the neglected aspects of the Second World War. As a result of this memorial initiative, Duckworth's words continue to reverberate. 'No medical officer or orderlies,' he said, 'ever had to contend with such fantastic, sickening, soul-destroying conditions of human ailment. No body of men could have done better. We sank low in spirit, in sickness and in human conduct, but over that dark valley there rose the sun of hope which warmed shrunken frames and wearied souls.'

In the European theatre of war, the German drive towards the Caucasus opened on June 26 with its objective the road and rail junction at Rostov-on-Don. This gateway to the whole Caucasian region had been occupied by Germany but then recaptured by the Russians the previous year. Such hopes as had earlier been entertained in Berlin of a two-pronged attack, with Rommel pushing through into the Caucasus from Egypt, Palestine, Syria, Iraq and Iran, were dashed, however, that week when the German advance into Egypt was halted at El Alamein. There, a combined force of British, Indian, South African and New Zealand troops barred Rommel's way on Egyptian soil. With daily reinforcements of American supplies that had been flown from West Africa or brought around the Cape of Good Hope, the line was held and strengthened. Mussolini, who had flown to Libya in order to enter Cairo in triumph, returned to Italy.

The Allies felt considerable relief at Rommel's failure to push through to Cairo. But every day also brought grave news in human terms for the Allied cause. When an American submarine sank a Japanese merchant ship off Luzon on July 1, among those drowned were 849 Australian prisoners-of-war who had been captured in New Guinea six months earlier and were being taken to Japan. Three days later, one of the British convoys – PQ 17 – that was taking British and American supplies to Russia, was attacked by German aircraft based in northern Norway and forced to scatter. German U-boats and torpedo-bombers then attacked the ships one by one. Twenty-one were sunk, and 153 merchant seamen drowned. Of the convoy's cargo, which included 594 tanks and 297 aircraft, 430 tanks and 210 aircraft were lost. Only eleven of the ships reached Archangel.

Hitler had cause to be elated when news of the fate of Convoy PQ 17 reached him. It was he who had intervened personally to prevent the despatch of four of his most powerful battleships from their Norwegian fiord bases to the scene of the battle, not wanting to risk them. He had further cause for elation in the days ahead, as the German thrust towards the Caucasus made rapid progress, approaching Rostov-on-Don.

Sensing victory, and wanting to be closer to his troops, on July 16 Hitler left his Wolf's Lair headquarters at Rastenburg – which remained available to him whenever he needed it – and moved to headquarters which had been prepared for him in the Russian town of Vinnitsa, closer to the front. This new headquarters was given the name 'Werewolf'. On Hitler's first day there, Himmler arrived. The two men discussed the future of the Caucasus, which seemed so nearly in the German grasp. Himmler noted in his diary: 'The Führer's view is that we should not physically incorporate this territory into the German sphere of power, but only militarily secure oil sources and borders.'

From Vinnitsa, Himmler flew to Cracow, from where he was driven to Auschwitz. There he watched as two thousand Dutch Jews, who had just arrived from Holland, were taken off the train: 1,551 were tattooed on the forearm and sent to the barracks at Birkenau as slave labourers. The remaining 449, mostly the elderly, the sick, and the children, were taken to the gas chambers and murdered. Himmler watched the whole process. On the following day he was shown the Polish punishment camp at Auschwitz, where he asked to see some beatings 'to determine their effects'. He also ordered the 'total cleansing' of Jews from the General Government.

The camp that had been prepared at Treblinka, near Warsaw, was ready to begin operation. The commandant, Dr Eberl, was the thirty-two-year-old German doctor who had earlier been involved in the euthanasia programme, when he had personally ordered the murder, over a period of a year and a half, of 18,000 German patients in the clinics under his control. On July 22 the SS in Warsaw, commanded by SS Major Hermann Höfle, and helped by Ukrainian and Latvian SS volunteers, rounded up 6,250 Warsaw Jews and deported them to Treblinka, and their deaths. The Chairman of the

Warsaw Jewish Council, Dr Adam Czerniakow, was asked to provide lists of names. He killed himself rather than comply with the order. His grave in the Warsaw Jewish cemetery – the largest Jewish cemetery in Europe – is today a place of frequent pilgrimage.

The elderly and distinguished educator, Dr Janusz Korczak, who had looked after several hundred orphans in the ghetto, insisted on being deported with them, as did his assistants. They and their charges were all murdered on reaching Treblinka, where the only memorial stone – erected in the final decade of the century – that records the name of a person rather than of a town is the memorial stone for Korczak. On the wall of Korczak's pre-war orphanage, outside the ghetto limits, is a memorial plaque to Stefania Wilczynska, one of the helpers who insisted on being deported with him and the children. She had worked at the orphanage for thirty years.

On July 23 the number of Jews seized by the SS and their helpers, and deported to Treblinka, was 7,300. In the ten succeeding days it never fell below five thousand a day. In the first round-ups, those Jewish prostitutes who had survived the ravages of hunger were seized and deported. Starting on July 29, families were offered a free issue of three kilogrammes of bread and up to one kilogramme of jam for any family that would go voluntarily. The temptation for thousands of starving families was too much, and they presented themselves at the deportation place. To ensure that the ruse was not cut short through lack of supplies, the Germans allocated 180,000 kilogrammes of bread and 36,000 kilogrammes of jam for the purpose. In all, 20,000 people took up the offer of a few days' meagre food.

Emanuel Ringelblum understood why they did so. They were, he wrote, 'driven by hunger, anguish, a sense of hopelessness of their situation'; they were people who 'had not the strength to struggle any longer', or who 'simply had no place to live'. Another eyewitness, Vladka Meed, recalled how, for many people, 'the possibility of assuaging their hunger just once, and the Germans' repeated promises of employment, were enough.' One deportee told Vladka Meed: 'After resettlement we might perhaps survive in another town.' So many hundreds of Jews were shot down in cold blood as they were asked for their papers – prior to deportation – that there were those who preferred to go unbidden rather than face the risks of these random shootings. No one knew what the destination would be. The Jews from more than a hundred other towns and villages in the region were also deported to Treblinka and killed, including 22,000 from the city of Piotrkow.

The scenes of terror during the course of the daily deportations from

Warsaw were witnessed by several hundred people who survived the war. Vladka Meed later recalled an incident which – like so many in that time of horror – has the power to disturb after more than half a century:

> Several horse-drawn vans went by, loaded with Jews, sitting and standing, hugging sacks that contained whatever pitiful belongings they had managed to gather at the last moment. Some stared straight ahead vacantly, others mourned and wailed, wringing their hands and entreating the Jewish police who rode with them. Women tore their hair or clung to their children, who sat bewildered among the scattered bundles, gazing at the adults in silent fear. Running behind the last van, a lone woman, arms outstretched, screamed:
> 'My child! Give back my child!'
> In reply, a small voice called from the van.
> 'Mama! Mama!'
> The people in the street watched as though hypnotized. Panting now with exhaustion, the mother continued to run after the van. One of the guards whispered something to the driver, who urged his horses into a gallop. The cries of the pursuing mother became more desperate as the horses pulled away. The procession turned into Karmelicka Street. The cries of the deportees faded and became inaudible, only the cry of the agonized mother still pierced the air. 'My child! Give back my child!'

In seven weeks, more than a quarter of a million of Warsaw's Jews were seized in the ghetto, deported to Treblinka, and killed on arrival at the camp. It was the largest, swiftest murder of a single community, Jewish or non-Jewish, in Europe or in Asia, in the Second World War. The camp commandant, Dr Eberl, was dismissed from his post after only a month. His failure to arrange for the rapid enough disposal of the bodies of those who had been killed had created panic among the Jews in the incoming trains.

As the second German campaign in Russia gained momentum, the German armies drove back the Russians to the south and to the east. On July 23, the day of the capture of Rostov-on-Don, Hitler set out the aims of the campaign. These were: control of the Black Sea coast as far as the Turkish border; occupation of the oilfields of Maikop, Grozny and Baku; control of the western shore of the Caspian Sea; and the capture of the city of Stalingrad,

on the River Volga. That done, the capture of Leningrad was next on Hitler's
list of priorities.

Hitler's generals were concerned at the over-ambitious nature of this plan,
which was issued to them as Directive No.45. The first danger, which came
rapidly to pass, was that Stalingrad would be reinforced and that the battle
for Stalingrad would therefore take men away from the Caucasus front. There
was also alarm at the failure to capture any large number of Soviet soldiers
during the battle for Rostov-on-Don, the defenders of which were able to
get away, and to regroup.

Stalin was exerting firm, even draconian, control of the Soviet fighting
troops and their commanders. On the day after German troops crossed the
River Don south of Rostov he issued an Order of the Day that did not
prevaricate: 'Panic-makers and cowards must be liquidated on the spot. Not
one step backward without orders from higher headquarters! Commanders,
commissars, and political workers who abandon a position without an order
from higher headquarters are traitors to the Fatherland, and must be handled
accordingly.'

By the despatch of orders from capital cities – orders written in calm
offices, amid a panoply of secretarial and deferential assistance – the lives of
thousands of people could be put in immediate jeopardy. On August 6 one
such order was issued from Berlin, by Field Marshal Goering. It was sent
to the Reich Commissioners and Military Commanders of all the territories
under German military occupation, from Cape Matapan in Greece to the
North Cape in Norway; from Brest on the Atlantic to Riga on the Baltic.
'In all the occupied territories,' Goering wrote, 'I see the people living there
stuffed full of food, while our own people are going hungry. For God's sake,
you haven't been sent there to work for the well-being of the peoples
entrusted to you, but to get hold of as much as you can so that the German
people can live. I expect you to devote your energies to that. The continual
concern for the aliens must come to an end once and for all.'

Goering concluded emphatically: 'I could not care less when you say that
people under your administration are dying of hunger. Let them perish so
long as no German starves.'

Germany and Japan were both in celebratory mood at the end of July. In
New Guinea the Japanese seized Kokoda from the Australians and were
confident that they could take the capital, Port Moresby. Five days later the
Germans reached the North Caucasus capital, Stavropol. But the fortunes of

war did not always follow smoothly the victories that caused elation. On August 7 the Americans launched their first land-based offensive in the Pacific. Less than a year after the start of Japanese territorial expansion throughout the Pacific region, Japanese control was being challenged.

The turn of the tide in the Pacific began with the landing of 16,000 American troops on Guadalcanal in the Solomon Islands. Although, in the initial landing, four Allied heavy cruisers were sunk and more than a thousand men killed, the landings succeeded. The Japanese fighting method, however, was formidable in the extreme: essentially and literally to fight to the death. In one month of fighting on the island, much of it hand-to-hand fighting, 1,600 Americans and 9,000 Japanese were killed. When capture was imminent, most Japanese soldiers committed suicide rather than face the personal humiliation of captivity. 'These people refuse to surrender,' Major-General Alexander A. Vandegrift wrote to the Marine commandant in Washington after witnessing the landings on four other, smaller islands. 'The wounded will wait till men come up to examine them, and blow themselves and the other fellow to death with a hand grenade.'

On August 9 the German army reached the oilfields of Maikop. The oil wells had been blown up by the Soviet defenders as they withdrew. The same destruction was carried out at Krasnodar. But the German advance to the much larger oil wells of Grozny and Baku continued.

Hitler was much heartened on August 19 when an Allied raid on the French channel port of Dieppe – in which 4,963 Canadian and 1,075 British troops took part – was driven off. More than a hundred British planes were shot down during the raid, for a cost of forty-eight German planes. During the raid a British Flight Sergeant, Jack Nissenthall, led a small task force to a German radar station on the cliffs above Dieppe and extracted crucial information for future British jamming and deception.

The cost of the Dieppe raid was high: 907 Canadians and more than a hundred British soldiers were killed; 345 of the German defenders were also killed, and four German soldiers were taken back to Britain as prisoners. Two thousand of the attacking force were taken prisoner. During the withdrawal, their vehicles and equipment had to be left behind. 'This is the first time that the British have the courtesy to cross the sea to offer the enemy a complete sample of their weapons,' Hitler scoffed. But he also recognized that the raid had a wider purpose than a mere pin-prick. 'We must realize that we are not alone in learning the lesson of Dieppe,' he informed his commanders. 'The British have also learned. We must reckon with a totally different mode of attack at a quite different place.'

Dieppe had proved a costly but important prelude to the cross-Channel landings for which Stalin was continually pressing. It showed him, and the Anglo-American planners, what a long way there was to go before a permanent Allied foothold could be secured in northern Europe, or the chance opened up to drive the Germans back to the borders of the Reich.

In India the British offered, in March, to establish self-governing institutions at the end of the war. A mission from London, headed by a leading left-wing Socialist, Sir Stafford Cripps, a member of Churchill's government, proposed that 'immediately on the cessation of hostilities' an Indian elected body would be asked to frame a constitution, and to establish an Indian Union that would be entitled to make treaties with other sovereign States, to secure the removal of British troops, and even to disown its allegiance to the Crown. Penderel Moon, a British administrator who was sympathetic to Indian national claims, wrote with approval:

> This looked like business. India's independence was no longer relegated to the Greek kalends; the time and manner of achieving it were precisely specified. Moreover, it was to be real independence. For it was made clear that the new Indian Union would be fully entitled, if it so wished, to disown allegiance to the Crown.
>
> As for British obligations and interests in India, these were to be settled by a treaty negotiated between the British Government and the constitution-making body. Congress demands as regards the future could hardly have been more fully met.
>
> Provision was also made for the satisfaction of the Muslim League. Any Provinces which did not wish to accept the new Constitution were to be entitled to remain out of the Indian Union and to frame separate constitutions for themselves, giving them the same full status as the Indian Union. Thus partition was accepted in principle, should the Muslims really desire it.
>
> As regards the immediate present, 'leaders of the principal sections of the Indian people' were invited to participate forthwith in the counsels of the country, of the Commonwealth, and of the United Nations. Clearly the intention was that Indian members of the Executive Council should be nominated not by the Viceroy, but by the various political parties; and

that in their share in the common deliberations of the United Nations they should be on an entirely equal footing with the representatives of other countries.

'Here at last,' Moon wrote, 'was real statesmanship; but statesmanship so long postponed that it seemed hardly distinguishable from panic. Such deathbed repentance excited suspicion. Concessions so long refused were now suddenly offered when India's position was desperate. They were not offered freely; they were not (it was unfairly suggested) genuinely meant.'

Not only were the Cripps proposals rejected; the British were confronted during August by an upsurge in Indian nationalist activity. On August 7 Gandhi told a meeting of Indian National Congress leaders: 'We shall get our freedom by fighting. It cannot fall from the skies.' On the following day Congress passed a resolution demanding that the British leave India at once. This 'Quit India' resolution electrified the nationalist fervour of tens of millions of Indians, although the Muslim League refused to have any part in it.

On August 9 the British responded to the Quit India call by arresting all fourteen members of the Congress Working Committee – the Party's governing body. The imprisoned Committee members – among them Jawaharlal Nehru – encouraged a Civil Disobedience Movement throughout India and the jails were quickly filled as the non-violent protesters were arrested. The most distinguished prisoner was Gandhi; it was his fourth time as a prisoner of the Raj.

Aware of the strength of British military presence, the Working Committee urged all Congress Party members to avoid violence. These appeals were ignored. Mobs on the rampage killed as many as a hundred people associated directly or indirectly with British rule – soldiers, administrators and passers-by. 'One particularly brutal and distressing case,' Nehru later wrote, 'was the murder of two Canadian airmen by a mob somewhere in Bihar. But generally speaking the absence of racial feeling was very remarkable.' Police posts and railway signalboxes were burned down. Telephone and telegraph wires were cut. Railway lines were dislocated and war industries were cut off from their coal supplies. In the resulting police and army actions, including the machine-gunning of rioters from the air, more than a thousand Indians were killed.

In his account of the revolt and its aftermath, Nehru wrote:

The external evidences of rebellion having been crushed, its very roots had to be pulled out, and so the whole apparatus of government was turned in this direction in order to enforce complete submission to British domination. Laws could be produced overnight by the Viceroy's decree or ordinance, but even the formalities of these laws were reduced to a minimum.

The decisions of the Federal Court and the High Courts, which were creations and emblems of British authority, were flouted and ignored by the executive, or a new ordinance was issued to override those decisions. Special tribunals (which were subsequently held by the courts to be illegal) were established, functioning without the trammels of the ordinary rules of procedure and evidence and these sentenced thousands to long terms of imprisonment and many even to death.

The police (and especially the Special Armed Constabulary) and the secret service were all powerful and became the chief organs of the state, and could indulge in any illegalities or brutalities without criticism or hindrance. Corruption grew to giant proportions. Vast numbers of students in schools and colleges were punished in various ways and thousands of young men were flogged. Public activity of all kinds was prohibited unless it was in favour of the government.

'But the greatest sufferers,' Nehru recalled, 'were the simple-hearted, poverty-stricken villagers of the rural areas. Suffering, for many generations, had been the badge of their tribe; they had ventured to look up and hope to dream of better times; they had even roused themselves to action; whether they had been foolish or mistaken or not, they had proved their loyalty to the cause of Indian freedom. Their effort had failed, and the burden had fallen on their bent shoulders and broken bodies. Cases were reported of whole villages being sentenced to sentences ranging from flogging to death.'

Nehru went on to quote a statement made on behalf of the Government of Bengal that 'Government forces burnt 193 Congress camps and houses in the sub-divisions of Tamluk and Contai before and after the cyclone of 1942', and he commented bitterly: 'The cyclone had worked havoc in that area and created a wilderness, but that made no difference to the official policy.'

Gandhi, confident that India would eventually win its freedom, wrote on the first anniversary of the Atlantic Charter direct to Roosevelt:

I venture to think that the Allied declaration that the Allies are fighting to make the world safe for the freedom of the individual and for democracy sounds hollow, so long as India and for that matter Africa are exploited by Great Britain, and America has the Negro problem in her own home. But in order to avoid all complications, in my proposal I have confined myself only to India. If India becomes free the rest must follow, if it does not happen simultaneously.

In order to make my proposal fool-proof I have suggested that if the Allies think it necessary they may keep their troops, at their own expense, in India, not for keeping internal order but for preventing Japanese aggression and defending China.

So far as India is concerned she must become free even as America and Great Britain are.

Gandhi's proposal was that any Allied troops that needed to be on the subcontinent as part of the war against Japan would be put under a 'free treaty' with the independent Indian Government. Roosevelt made no reply.

The Quit India movement continued active for another year, led by Congress socialists under Jayprakash Narayan and supporters of the nationalist leader Subhas Chandra Bose, who was already in Japan raising an anti-British military force from among Indian prisoners-of-war, many of whom had been captured at Singapore.

On August 21 the Swastika flag was raised by German soldiers on the peak of Mount Elbrus, the highest mountain in the Caucasus. Two days later, German soldiers reached the River Volga just north of Stalingrad. Inside Egypt, however, Rommel was about to be confronted by the one enemy against which he had no control: the British ability to follow his most secret communications.

From their headquarters in Cairo – Rommel's objective – British cryptographers were learning through Enigma and the similarly top-secret Italian codes, of the sailing dates, routes and cargoes of every ship being sent to the German and Italian forces; including every despatch of munitions and fuel oil. As a result of Britain sinking the crucial ships one by one, Rommel was deprived of the fuel oil needed by his tanks.

On August 31 Rommel attacked. Once more the defending force was drawn from the wide arc of the British Empire. Among the defenders were troops from Britain, New Zealand, Australia, South Africa and India.

Rommel was forced back. Cairo and the Suez Canal would never be his. Behind him lay the vast expanses of the Western Desert which he had crossed in triumph, but which he was soon to have to traverse in gloom. A new British commander, General Montgomery, availing himself of the fruits of Enigma, devised a battle plan that was intended within two months to regain the Allied initiative in the Western Desert. When Churchill's wife, querying Montgomery's appointment, told her husband that the general was said to be a disagreeable character, Churchill replied that he was confident he would also be 'disagreeable to the enemy'.

Hitler, unaware of the triumph of British Intelligence at Rommel's expense, had set his sights on the capture of Stalingrad. As always before a battle, he made his intentions clear to those closest to him. On August 31 General Halder noted in his diary: 'The Führer has ordered that, upon penetration into the city, the entire male population must be eliminated, since Stalingrad with its one million uniformly Communist inhabitants is extremely dangerous.' Halder added that the female population would be 'shipped off'. Where they would be 'shipped off' to was not recorded.

Stalin recognized that if the Germans could be held at Stalingrad, and forced to send more and more troops to hold their positions there, the Caucasus offensive would be seriously weakened. 'Attack the enemy without delay. No delay can be tolerated. Delay at this moment is equivalent to a crime,' he telegraphed to the Chief of the Soviet General Staff, Marshal Zhukov on September 3. Two days later the Soviet forces counter-attacked at Stalingrad, but were driven back. One of the most ferocious and prolonged military confrontations of the Second World War had begun.

Once more, in an attempt to take German pressure off the Russian front, the Royal Air Force – as Churchill had promised Stalin in Moscow when he flew to see the Soviet leader three weeks earlier – launched another sustained bombing offensive against German cities and war industries. The first of the new targets was Düsseldorf, on which, for the first time in aerial warfare, bombs weighing two tons were dropped. They were known as 'block busters' because a single bomb could destroy a whole apartment block. Almost five hundred aircraft took part in the raid. More than fifty industrial enterprises were badly damaged and 20,000 people made homeless; seventy people were killed. Three days later, in British raids on and around Essen, eight factories were destroyed, one by a bomber loaded with incendiary bombs that crashed on the factory. That day, seventy-four Germans were killed.

On the Russian Front, German troops were fighting their way into the very centre of Stalingrad. But they met opposition in every street and building and cellar. Thousands of civilians and wounded Russian soldiers were evacuated across the Volga to the eastern shore. German units which had reached the western bank of the river opened fire with their artillery against the evacuee ships. When the river steamer *Borodino* was hit, several hundred wounded soldiers were killed. More than a thousand civilians died when the river steamer *Iosif Stalin* was sunk.

Soviet reinforcements, reaching Stalingrad from across the river on September 18, drove back ten German attacks on the city's giant grain elevator in a single day.

In Berlin, those who were planning for the future of a totally German-dominated Europe continued to see Russia as an area for German settlement, and to seek means of reducing the local populations. On the day that the German troops in Stalingrad were being denied control of the grain elevator and access to that part of the Volga that lay beyond it, the German Minister of Justice, Otto Thierach, who was also a General in the SS, concluded an agreement with Himmler that in order to make the newly conquered eastern territories 'fit' for German settlers, 'Jews, Poles, Gypsies, Russians and Ukrainians convicted of offences should not be sentenced by ordinary courts but should be executed.' The Thierach-Himmler agreement gave formal German governmental sanction, and legality, to a killing process that had been in operation for more than a year.

Inside Stalingrad, despite their penetration to the very heart of the city, German troops were unable to break the resistance of its defenders. In the Caucasus the German advance had been halted on the outskirts of Grozny, whose oilfields were never to fall into German hands. Hitler was so furious at both setbacks that he dismissed General Halder, who had been Chief of the Army General Staff since the outbreak of war three years earlier.

On September 23 two thousand fresh Siberian troops were ferried across the Volga to Stalingrad to reinforce the exhausted defenders. A few hours later the Russian counter-attack began, driving the Germans from the cellars and devastated buildings for which they had fought at heavy cost. Two days later the Germans counter-attacked, using tanks to push their way back to the river bank. On September 27 the Swastika flag was raised over the headquarters of the Stalingrad Communist Party. Hitler, again elated, flew back from Vinnitsa to Berlin to await the moment – which he expected within twenty-four hours – when he could announce the fall of Stalingrad.

That moment never came. Even as Hitler was on his way back to Germany, yet more fresh Soviet troops were being ferried across the Volga to push the Germans out of the city.

While awaiting news that Stalingrad was his, Hitler spoke to a mass meeting in Berlin to launch the Nazi Party's Winter Aid Programme. Triumphantly he told his cheering audience: 'I said that if Jewry started this war in order to overcome the Aryan people, then it would not be the Aryans but the Jews who would be exterminated. The Jews laughed at my prophesies. I doubt if they are laughing now.'

Even as Hitler spoke, his prophesies of 1939 were being carried forward with the utmost savagery. At Auschwitz that week, four thousand Jews were gassed. They had been brought to the camp from Slovakia, France, Holland and Belgium. That same week, six thousand German, Austrian and Czech Jews were deported to Maly Trostenets from the ghetto at Theresienstadt. There were no survivors. On September 28, on one of the trains that was leaving Paris every few days, a hundred Jewish children under the age of sixteen were deported to Auschwitz and killed. Among them were two five-year-olds, Zizi Adoner and Soida Wiorek. The youngest child on the train, Lucien Oster, was five months old.

Since the earliest days of the war, Jews had found refuge in Switzerland. The Hungarian-born conductor Georg Solti was among the 28,512 registered Jewish refugees, many of whom were kept in harsh internment camp conditions; others, like Solti, were able to work in their professions, though he later recalled a Swiss police officer arriving while he was practising at home for a piano competition and warning him – intimating that he could be expelled from the country – 'You must stop playing. You are disturbing Swiss citizens'.

Those Jews who had found refuge in Switzerland were safe. But as a result of a police regulation of August 13 other Jews, crossing into Switzerland from France to escape deportation, were being turned back by the Swiss police. As a result of this regulation, at least 9,751 Jews were turned back, a Swiss police guideline of September 25 explaining: 'Under current practice refugees on the grounds of race alone are not political refugees.' Once taken back to the French border, and forced over it, these same refugees were then, entirely on the grounds of race, sent by the German authorities – with French Vichy police assistance – to Auschwitz and to their deaths.

One witness of the fate of these Jews was a Swiss woman, Madame Francken, who lived on the French side of the border at the village of Novel, near the border town of Saint-Gingolph, facing mountain peaks that rose above 6,000 feet. Recalling two Czech Jews, a brother and a sister, who had managed to cross from Novel to Swiss soil, over the River Morge, Madame Franken wrote:

We never found out what became of those two! The notorious Sergeant Arretaz of Saint-Gingolph turned people back like a sadist, whereas his confrère, a customs officer, ran and hid so as not to see the agonizing cortège of those sent back to the border, straight into the hands of the French militia.

Two of these poor wretched creatures slit their wrists on the bridge on the same day, while a woman (whom we had seen being hunted down in L'Haut de Morge) threw herself from the fourth storey of the hotel in Saint-Gingolph where she was staying.

Another Jewish couple who crossed into Switzerland at Novel, but had been turned back, were Elli and Jan Friedländer, Czechoslovak Jews who had managed, while refugees in France, to find their son Saul a safe haven with Catholic nuns. Saul survived the war, brought up as a Catholic; he later received the copy of two letters and a telegram written by his parents to those who were looking after him. The first letter was dated September 30:

We reached Switzerland after a very tiring journey and were turned back. We were misinformed. We are now awaiting our transfer to the camp at Rivesaltes, where our fate will be decided in the way that is already quite familiar to you.

There are no words to describe our unhappiness and our despair. Moreover, we don't have our baggage. Can you imagine our physical and mental state?

Perhaps if you could intervene at Vichy we would be spared the worst. It is not the camp that we are afraid of. You know that. If there is the slightest possibility of helping us, do not hesitate, we beg you. Act quickly. There must be a solution at Vichy that would be less catastrophic for us. Don't forget the little one!

On October 3 the Friedländers telegraphed from the internment camp at Rivesaltes: 'Without intervention Minister Interior, our imminent departure inevitable.' Two days later they were taken by train from Rivesaltes to

Drancy. They believed they were on their way to Germany. From the train they threw out their second letter, the first few lines written in ink, the rest in pencil. It was addressed to the Director of the Catholic Boarding School to whom they had entrusted their son for baptism and for survival:

> Madame, I am writing you this in the train that is taking us to Germany. At the last moment, I sent, you, through a representative of the Quakers, 6,000 francs, a charm bracelet, and, through a lady, a folder with stamps in it. Keep all of this for the little one, and accept, for the last time, our infinite thanks and our warmest wishes for you and your whole family. Don't abandon the little one! May God repay you and bless you and your whole family. Elli and Jan Friedländer.

Publishing this letter thirty-four years later, their son asked bitterly, 'What God was meant?'

Jan and Elli Friedländer were taken to Drancy. From there, with a thousand other Jews, they were deported to Auschwitz. Of those thousand, only four men, and no women, survived. The Friedländers were among those who perished. Among those deported with them, and gassed on arrival at Auschwitz, were more than two hundred children, among them the three-year-old Solange Zajdenwerger and her four-year-old brother David.

On September 30, in the Caucasus, the local German commander reissued to his men Field Marshal von Manstein's Order of the Day of the previous winter, stressing that the German soldier was 'not merely a fighter according to the rules of the acts of war, but also the bearer of a ruthless ideology' who must understand 'the necessity for a severe but just revenge on sub-human Jewry'. Executions followed immediately; but on October 1 the German advance through the North Caucasus was halted.

Inside Stalingrad, having reached the landing stages on the Volga, the Germans were nevertheless unable to dislodge the defenders from the city's factories – especially from the Tractor and Barricade factories whose ruins had been massively fortified. Nor could they prevent what had become the nightly crossing of re-inforcements from the eastern bank of the river. By October 5 more than 160,000 Russian soldiers had joined the city's defenders.

Increasing quantities of military aid were reaching Russia from both Britain and the United States. Some of it came via the North Cape to Archangel, but a growing amount was arriving through Persia, being taken by truck and rail from the Persian Gulf to the Caspian Sea, and from there across the Caspian and up the Volga, straight to the outskirts of Stalingrad. Among the American supplies sent through Persia in the six months from May to October were more than 80,000 Thompson machine guns.

On October 14 the Germans inside Stalingrad made a renewed attempt to drive the Russian soldiers from their cellars and strongpoints. Three hundred German tanks took part in the assault against the Russian positions, particularly the Tractor and Barricade factories. But although the ruined buildings between the factories were overrun, had been retaken, and were then overrun again several times, the two factories themselves held out. Then, on October 20, the Tractor factory was captured, and German soldiers reached the river bank beyond it. Soviet soldiers were in possession of a thousand yards of shoreline. Hitler believed victory to be imminent. 'The Führer is convinced the Russians are collapsing,' Field Marshal Keitel reported on October 21. 'He says that twenty million will have to starve.'

Behind the German lines south of Stalingrad, Soviet partisans were being parachuted in to disrupt German communications between the Stalingrad and Caucasus fronts. The Germans enlisted the help of a local Cossack cavalry squadron to hunt the partisans down, but soon reported despondently that while the partisans would withdraw 'temporarily' it was only to make 'new sallies from their hideouts' later on.

Further behind the German lines the mass murder of Jews was unceasing. Starting on October 15 the 20,000 Jews who had been confined for more than a year in the ghetto set up by the Nazis in Brest Litovsk were taken by train to specially prepared pits at Bronnaya Gora, on the main Brest-Minsk railway line near Baranovichi. There they were forced to undress and were then executed: mown down by machine-gun fire. In all 50,000 Jews were shot at Bronnaya Gora, brought there from ghettos throughout the region. Among the dead for whom documentation survives were at least eighty-seven with the surname Kagan – a Russian version of Cohen. Among the oldest was Ester Kagan, aged seventy-six. Lina Kagan was fifteen.

On October 23, while Hitler waited with growing impatience to learn of the fall of Stalingrad, his forces at El Alamein, astride the road to Cairo, were attacked. On the first day of the British offensive, the German commander, General Stimme, died of a heart attack. Field Marshal Rommel, who was in Germany on leave, was flown back to the battlefield of which he had earlier been the master. But he could do nothing to mitigate the fury of the Allied attack, in which British, Australian, New Zealand and South African troops took part.

The new commander, General Montgomery, proved to be a formidable adversary. After five days Rommel had to pull his forces back: 2,300 of his men, both Germans and Italians, had been killed and 27,900 taken prisoner. This was not the only serious setback for the Axis cause that week. On the third day of the Battle of El Alamein, when a series of German and Italian counter-attacks were being beaten off, the Japanese launched a sustained attack in the Pacific on the American positions on Guadalcanal, but were likewise repulsed, and several thousand Japanese soldiers were killed.

A Japanese fleet bringing reinforcements to Guadalcanal was attacked off the Santa Cruz Islands. As at the Battle of the Coral Sea six months earlier, fighting was entirely between the aircraft of the opposing fleets. The American aircraft carrier *Hornet* was sunk, but it was the shooting down of a hundred Japanese aircraft by the Americans that made it impossible for Guadalcanal to be reinforced. The Americans had lost seventy-four planes, but they had emerged the victors.

In New Guinea, the Australians had not only defended Port Moresby but had gone over to the offensive, retaking Kokoda on November 3 and moving steadily eastward. When a group of Japanese defenders tried to hold up the Australian troops with a bayonet charge, the Australians held their ground, and 580 of the Japanese were killed.

Bad news was reaching the Axis leaders with startling rapidity, as they struggled to accept that they could no longer expect continual advances, successes, victories and conquests. Indeed it was setbacks, defeats and the loss of territory that had begun to stare them in the face. Even Rommel's retreat in North Africa was made more difficult by a shortage of supplies reaching him across the Mediterranean. One reason for this was the interruption for six weeks of the flow of supplies along the railway running down through Greece to the port of Piraeus. This route had been broken by a daring raid on the Gorgopotamus railway viaduct, a spectacular operation commanded by a British officer, Brigadier Eddie Myers, who had been parachuted into Greece from Egypt, and who succeeded in uniting the right-wing and left-wing Greek resistance groups for this one task. Myers was to stay on in Greece as liaison between the British and the Greeks fighting behind the lines to disrupt the German war effort.

There was more bad news for the Germans on November 5, when the British landed ten tons of military stores on the coast of French North Africa, hitherto loyal to Vichy and subservient to Germany. The stores were for the use of the Algerian Resistance, which had been alerted to the news of an imminent task.

On the night of November 6, Hitler was making the long journey by train from his headquarters at Vinnitsa to Munich, for the annual celebration of the Beer Hall putsch of 1923. A message was brought to him while the train was still in Russia, informing him that the German troops in the North Caucasus had been halted and pushed back on the outskirts of Ordzhonikidze, the town which barred their route to the oilfields of Baku. The next morning, November 7, his train was halted again, this time by a signalman at a small railway station in eastern Poland. A message was brought to the Führer's carriage. It had been sent by radio from the German Foreign Ministry in Berlin, as a matter of top priority, to inform Hitler that the BBC had just announced that an American invasion force was at that very moment landing in French North Africa – at Algiers, Oran and Casablanca.

The Allied landings in North Africa – Operation Torch – transformed the balance of power throughout the Mediterranean. More than 100,000 men were put ashore and within three days the Allies were in control of 1,300 miles of coastline along both the Atlantic and the Western Mediterranean. The Vichy regime in North Africa collapsed.

When Hitler made his Beer Hall speech that evening he spoke mostly about Stalingrad, expressing his confidence that the German troops holding on inside the city would not be driven out. Indeed, he said, there was hardly much more of the city to be captured. As Hitler phrased it: 'There are only a few more tiny pockets!' He also reiterated his characterization of the fate of the Jews under German rule. 'Of those who laughed then,' he said, referring once more to his annihilation prophesy of 1939, 'countless already laugh no longer today; and those who still laugh today will probably not laugh much longer either.'

A week earlier, although Hitler did not say so, the largest ever single regional deportation of the Jews had taken place: the rounding up of 110,000 Jews throughout the Bialystok region, and their deportation to nearby Treblinka, and also to more distant Auschwitz, where they were murdered. When, in the village of Marcinkance, all 360 Jews resisted deportation, they were shot down and killed in the village itself. Another camp was also activated that week: on November 9 four thousand Jews were taken from the Lublin ghetto to the nearby concentration camp at Majdanek. Within a year, as many as a hundred thousand Jews, including several thousand Jewish prisoners-of-war who had fought in the Polish army in 1939, were to be murdered at Majdanek.

By November 9, Rommel had been driven back two hundred miles, and was defending Sidi Barrani. On the following day Churchill told an audience in London – his speech was broadcast nationwide, and filmed: 'Now this is not the end. It is not even the beginning of the end, but it is perhaps the end of the beginning.'

To try to prevent the fall of Tunisia, and Germany's ejection from North Africa, Hitler ordered several hundred German transport aircraft to be flown there at once with military reinforcements. To carry out his order the aircraft engaged in ferrying troops to Stalingrad and the Caucasus had to be taken away from the Eastern Front. Of the five hundred fighter aircraft also moved to Tunisia, four hundred had to be brought from Russia.

Hitler was determined not to give up North Africa, despite the considerable setbacks there. But in order to hold North Africa, even to hold Tunisia, he had to face for the first time all the problems of a tenaciously fought two-front war. Other German aircraft which were moved to Tunisia included torpedo-bomber units that had been based in northern Norway, and were one of the main scourges of the Arctic convoys taking Allied aid to Russia. Hitler also took the precaution of occupying Vichy France. He could no longer trust Pétain to keep out the Allies. This new area of direct German military control created its own problems of increased military presence, attacks by the French Resistance, sabotage and reprisals.

The first blow to Hitler following his annexation of Vichy France was the decision of the commander of the French fleet, Admiral Jean de Laborde, to scuttle his ships, which were then in Toulon harbour, rather than let them fall into German hands. As SS troops began to take over the Toulon naval base, the order was given, and a veritable armada settled on the sea bed: two battleships, two battle-cruisers, four heavy cruisers, two light cruisers, an aircraft carrier, thirty destroyers and sixteen submarines. Not one of them could be used by Germany. Three French submarines, putting to sea, crossed the Mediterranean and joined the Allied naval forces in Algiers.

On November 11 Rommel was driven out of Sidi Barrani and had to withdraw into Libya. Two days later he was driven out of Tobruk, the loss of which that summer had been such a blow to Britain. Realizing that the German position in North Africa had become precarious, and that sooner or later the American troops pushing in from the west and the British from the east must prove fatal, Rommel asked Hitler for permission to withdraw his troops from North Africa altogether, otherwise they would be destroyed. Hitler refused. It was a 'political' necessity, he told Rommel, for Germany to have a bridgehead in North Africa.

Hitler's decision to insist upon holding North Africa was to involve him in a constant drain of manpower and munitions, transport planes and fuel oil, that were increasingly needed by his troops in Russia, particularly if they were to be in a position to launch an offensive in 1943 – Hitler's much vaunted third Russian campaign.

In the Pacific, in further attempts by the Japanese to reinforce their isolated and besieged garrison on Guadalcanal, heavy casualties were inflicted by both sides. There was a disaster at sea for the Americans in the Pacific on November 13, when the light anti-aircraft cruiser *Juneau*, badly damaged during the battle on the previous night, and unable to steam at speed, was hit by a torpedo from a Japanese submarine (the torpedo had been misfired: it was intended for the heavy cruiser *San Francisco*). There was a massive explosion below decks and the *Juneau* blew up, sinking beneath the waves in a matter of seconds: 560 men were killed outright.

Those who witnessed the explosion were convinced that there could be no survivors on the *Juneau*. Of the captain of the *Helena*, Gilbert Hoover – who was later disgraced for leaving the scene – the writer Dan Kurzman narrates: 'Like most other men who viewed the blast, Hoover was overwhelmed by the image of that awesome cloud emanating, it seemed, from the guts of the ocean, maybe from hell itself, raging, roaring, smouldering, seething, churning.' Aside from the atom bomb, Kurzman adds, 'this was perhaps the greatest single explosion of the war.'

Not wanting to risk the possibility of another torpedo attack if they were to search the area, no rescue effort was mounted by the onlookers. 'Let's get the hell out of here!' was the cry of Captain Hoover's sailors, and they praised him for leaving the dangerous waters so swiftly. In fact 140 of the *Juneau* crewmen had survived. They managed to cling to the wreckage, but after seven days adrift all but ten of them were dead. Most had been eaten by sharks. Others, without food or water, had gone mad and drowned. The ten survivors were rescued and told the story of that horrendous week. Among the dead were the five Sullivan brothers – Albert, Francis, George, Joseph and Madison – from Waterloo, Iowa. Against naval policy they had been serving together in the same ship.

The captain of the *Juneau*, Captain Swenson, who had doubted the combat readiness of his ship, was posthumously awarded the Navy Cross. Two years later a warship, the *Lyman K. Swenson*, was named after him; his son Robert, graduating from the Naval Academy in 1944, served on it.

The war in Russia took a decisive turn on November 19, when the Red Army launched a counter-offensive north of Stalingrad. The first Axis troops to be overwhelmed were the Roumanians; 65,000 were taken prisoner. Hungarian and Italian troops in the line were driven back. Then, a day later, the Red Army attacked south of Stalingrad, and the Russian plan was revealed: nothing less than the encirclement of all the German forces inside Stalingrad and around it – the German Sixth Army. Hitler broadcast that day to the men who had been fighting for so long, and in vain, to conquer Stalingrad: 'Hold on!'

As soon as it became clear that the Russian encirclement plan might succeed, the German commander, General Friedrich von Paulus, asked permission to withdraw before the trap was closed around him. Hitler did not even deign to reply. When he did so three days later, having assumed 'personal command' of the German Army, it was to insist that Paulus remain in the city. The German forces inside Stalingrad were completely surrounded. A sustained German attempt to break in to besieged forces was a failure. As the Russians renewed their attacks on the main body of the German forces west of Stalingrad, a whole military force of one of Hitler's military allies in the fighting in Russia, the Italian Eighth Army, was wiped out, and another military force fighting alongside the Germans, the Roumanian Third Army, was partly destroyed.

Inside Stalingrad, the German Sixth Army remained under siege. To the south of Stalingrad, the German forces in the Caucasus were being driven back. Soviet partisan activity intensified, making even retreat precarious. German reprisals took the form of the murder en masse of villagers who were suspected of having helped the partisans with food or shelter. But the partisans, acting under military discipline, and receiving their orders from Moscow, continued to attack German military convoys and to destroy telegraph lines, signalling equipment, bridges and railway tracks throughout the area under German control.

Field Marshal Keitel had always realized the effectiveness of partisan activity. 'If the fight against the partisans in the East, as well as in the Balkans, is not waged with the most brutal means,' he reiterated in an Order of the Day on December 16, 'we shall shortly reach the point where the available forces are insufficient to control the area. It is therefore not only justified, but it is the duty of the troops, to use all means without restriction, even against women and children, as long as it ensures success'. Any consideration shown to the partisans,' Keitel warned, 'is a crime against the German people'.

On December 17, a day after this anti-partisan order, the Allies issued a solemn declaration in London, Washington and Moscow, denouncing the mass murder of the Jews. The declaration associated not only Britain, the Soviet Union and the United States, but also de Gaulle's French National Committee, and the Governments-in-Exile of Belgium, Czechoslovakia, Greece, Luxembourg, Holland, Norway, Poland and Yugoslavia, in condemnation 'in the strongest possible terms' of what it called 'this bestial policy of cold-blooded extermination'.

'I regret to have to inform the House,' Anthony Eden told the House of Commons in introducing the Declaration, 'that reliable reports have recently reached His Majesty's Government regarding the barbarous and inhuman treatment to which Jews are being subjected in German-occupied Europe.' A Labour Member of Parliament, William Cluse, an orphan since the age of five, asked the Speaker if all members present could 'rise in their places and stand in silence in support of this protest against disgusting barbarism'.

In the House of Lords a Jewish peer, Lord Samuel, the former leader of the Liberal Party, commented: 'This is not an occasion on which we are expressing sorrow and sympathy to sufferers from some terrible catastrophe due unavoidably to flood or earthquake, or some other convulsion of nature. These dreadful events are an outcome of quite deliberate, planned, conscious cruelty of human beings.'

In Tunisia, on Guadalcanal and New Guinea, in the Caucasus – from which Hitler ordered a complete withdrawal on December 27 – and in South Russia, the Axis powers were in difficulties and in retreat. Yet they were still in control of vast territories and captive peoples, and were still carrying out atrocities against civilians and prisoners-of-war. In an act or terror against Bialowola, a tiny Polish village which had sheltered partisans, all sixty-nine of the villagers were driven into the schoolhouse and shot.

In the Polish town of Poniatowa, 18,000 Russian prisoners-of-war who were being held in an enormous enclosure behind barbed wire died that winter. Most of them starved to death. They had literally been refused all food. Nor were they allowed any shelter. When the temperature fell particularly low, the guards would amuse themselves by hosing the prisoners down with cold water. By morning, hundreds of them were found frozen to death.

When Himmler visited Hitler at Rastenburg on December 31, he brought with him the precise statistics compiled in Berlin for the number of 'Jews executed' in the four months August to November. The figure was 363,211. This murdering had been done, and much more remained to be done, in the name of the 'Aryan race' and of 'racial purity'. Yet even as the worst recorded killings in the name of race were being carried out, the very concept of purity of race and racial differences was being challenged. During 1942 a British writer, A.G. Russell, wrote at the conclusion of his book *Colour, Race and Empire*:

> That theory of unmixed races must be abandoned, for the world has progressed because of the diversity of the races and their sub-divisions. No doubt some qualities are more highly developed in one race than in another, but these qualities themselves are often the result of mixture, and the 'area of overlap' is tremendous.
>
> No race has a monopoly of one virtue – or of one vice. Competition has hitherto prevented races from working out a synthesis of their natural endowments, gifts and predispositions – it is an internecine warfare on a world-wide scale; the harmony and integration which we find in a work of art are sadly lacking from what might be the grandest of all creative efforts – the ordered, balanced Human Society, into whose brilliant radiance of white light would be blended the rainbow hues of its many parts.

The killings in the name of race could only end when the regime that was carrying out those killings was itself destroyed. But during 1942 Germany's warmaking powers were still growing, with the mass production of weapons of war at its highest since Hitler had come to power nine years earlier, despite the ever-intensifying Allied bombing raids on German cities. Industries that were destroyed in one place were repaired, or rebuilt elsewhere.

The military strength of all the belligerents was on the increase. During 1942 the Canadian Government provided training facilities for 138,000 British and Allied pilots and aircrew under the Empire Training Scheme, and then wrote off the $425 million cost of the scheme as part of its war effort. The Canadian Government also gave Britain an outright gift of $1 billion for the purchase of war materials.

In the United States that year there was a secret but dramatic development in the weaponry of war. On December 2, in an atomic pile located in a squash court beneath the University of Chicago's disused football stadium, an order for an experiment was given, in strictest secrecy, by an Italian émigré scientist, Enrico Fermi, who had fled from Italy because his wife was Jewish. So uncertain was Fermi as to whether he would be able to control the reaction once it was started that he and his staff established a 'suicide squad' to destroy the atomic pile if anything went wrong with the experiment.

Fermi gave the order at ten that morning. By mid-afternoon he had produced what he was looking for: the first self-sustaining nuclear chain reaction. The next step was to find and process the necessary uranium for the manufacture of an atom bomb.*

---

* Today a twelve-foot bronze sculpture stands on the site of the experiment. Entitled 'Nuclear Energy', it is the work of the British sculptor Henry Moore.

CHAPTER FOURTEEN

1943

The massed, angered forces of common humanity are
on the march.

FRANKLIN D. ROOSEVELT

IT WAS NOT ONLY those peoples and groups singled out by the Germans
for 'special treatment', but every captive nation under German rule, that
suffered the privations of war: not only the deliberately lower ration scales
forced on them by the Germans, but chronic food shortages as a result of
their total isolation from the sea-borne trade that had sustained them in
peacetime. The Allied blockade was relentless, preventing any merchant
ships from reaching German-controlled ports. In the case of Greece, as famine
conditions spread, and at least 300,000 Greeks died of famine, the Allies
were being pressed by the Greeks themselves, and by their own publics, to
open an avenue of supply on humanitarian grounds. Roosevelt responded,
and the British, reluctantly, followed. Food would be allowed into Greece
to prevent further starvation, even if its arrival would relieve the Germans
of their own humanitarian obligations.

In Britain an organization was established to collect the money needed
for Greece from public charity. The Oxford Committee for Famine Relief –
known later as Oxfam – raised £12,700 in a 'Greek Week' appeal. The food
was bought, and sent, and allowed through the Allied blockade.

In the Pacific, on the fringes of their newly won conquests, the Japanese
had begun to retreat, challenged without respite by American carrier-borne
aircraft attack and infantry assault. The cost to the Americans was always
high: on January 6 a senior pre-war bombing instructor, Brigadier General
Kenneth N. Walker, was lost in combat while leading a formation of bombers
over Rabaul. The citation of his posthumous Congressional Medal of Honour

made the point, upon which much of the American bombing effort was devised, that a 'well organized, well planned and well executed bomber attack, once launched, cannot be stopped'.

On orders from Tokyo the Japanese forces on Guadalcanal, to which repeated Japanese efforts at reinforcement had been beaten off, were overrun, although some troops refused to surrender and fought on to the last man. The most south-easterly shore of New Guinea was also evacuated. As the last Japanese stronghold there, Buna Mission, surrendered, many of the garrison swam out to sea to drown of their own volition rather than be taken prisoner. At Sanananda, on New Guinea, a combined American and Australian force took nine days to defeat the Japanese defenders, who refused to surrender: all three thousand were killed. During the month-long campaign at Sanananda, three thousand American and Australian soldiers, and seven thousand Japanese, were killed. In Burma the Japanese also suffered their first reverse when a British counter-attack succeeded in pushing their forces back along the coast from Chittagong almost to Donbaik.

On the day that the Japanese successfully repulsed the attack on Donbaik, the ground was broken on a ninety-two acre site at Oak Ridge, Tennessee. To protect the utter secrecy of the work, a thousand local families were moved away. The engineers and scientists – headed by the physicist Robert J. Oppenheimer – who came in their place were to operate the first ever manufacturing plant for uranium-235, a crucial step on the path to the atom bomb.

Many of the scientists who worked under Oppenheimer were German-Jewish refugees from Hitler. Oppenheimer himself was the son of German-Jewish immigrants who had come to the United States at the beginning of the century. He had gained his doctorate in Germany five years before Hitler came to power.

The Germans, like the Japanese, were facing a new situation of unremitting struggle and gradual but definite retreat at every extremity of their conquests. In North Africa, Rommel's hopes of conquest had been totally dashed. 'The times have grown very grave, in the East also,' he confided to his wife. 'There's going to be total mobilization for every single German without regard for place of residence, status, property or age.' On the Eastern Front to which Rommel referred, the severity of winter did not deter the Russian partisans from creating continual disruption behind the German lines, so much so that three separate military operations were launched against them in January.

West of Stalingrad, German troops who had come within thirty miles of their trapped colleagues were driven back 120 miles. On January 8 the Russians sent an ultimatum to the trapped men to surrender. Von Paulus, obedient to Hitler's command, refused to do so. As the Soviet offensive was renewed, 490 German transport and bomber-torpedo aircraft that tried to bring reinforcements and supplies to the trapped army were shot down.

On January 13, while the German forces inside Stalingrad continued to fight, the German siege of Leningrad was broken. Soviet troops, pushing through the German siege lines, reached a point south of Lake Ladoga, creating a narrow corridor along which men, munitions and food could reach the city. It was a decisive moment not only in the morale of Leningrad but in Soviet morale, and in the Allied sense of a turning tide.

On the following day, January 14, Roosevelt and Churchill met at Casablanca, in recently liberated French North Africa, to coordinate the next stage of their joint war policy. During the meeting they publicly reaffirmed that the 'unconditional surrender' of Germany and Japan was their unalterable policy. They also agreed, in strictest secrecy, that as a result of a clear warning by the Combined Chiefs of Staff with regard to the problems of supply and preparation, no cross-Channel liberation of German-occupied Europe could be launched until the early summer of 1944.

A principal theme of the discussions at Casablanca was the part to be played by air power in the defeat of Germany. Roosevelt and Churchill agreed that the bombing of Germany both by day and by night, and on a massive scale, should be intensified. By this means they hoped to achieve not only 'the progressive destruction and dislocation of the German military, industrial and economic system' but also – as their secret directive explained – 'the undermining of the morale of the German people to a point where their capacity for armed resistance is fatally weakened'. On January 16, five days before this directive was finalized, British bombers carried out their first heavy raid on Berlin for more than fourteen months. As the city was covered by haze, however, it proved impossible to make accurate strikes on industrial targets.

Almost two hundred people were killed during this Berlin raid, among them fifty-two French prisoners-of-war and one English prisoner-of-war. The 10,000 Berliners who were packed into the largest hall in Europe for the yearly circus were evacuated just in time. Hardly had the last person – and the last of the performing animals – left the hall than it was hit by incendiaries and completely burnt out.

Hitler was always agitated after an air raid on Berlin, and Goebbels even more so. A series of reprisal raids were ordered, and in a single week of renewed German aerial bombardment, mostly low-level daylight attacks, 328 British civilians were killed. Among the dead were six teachers and thirty-eight school children, killed when their school in South London – Sandhurst Road, Catford – took a direct hit before they had time to go to their shelter. The youngest of the dead was four-year-old Pauline Carpenter. One of the schoolboys who was injured, Eric Brady, recalled the bomb twenty years later:

I was in the dining room with about seventy-five other children when the bombers struck. Nearly two hundred other children were in the playground or other parts of the school – a lot of them waiting to go to see *A Midsummer Night's Dream*. In the dining room the teacher screamed at us to get under the tables. We wouldn't make it to the shelter.

As my older sister Kitty dashed towards me the plane returned, dropping his bomb and the school collapsed on top of us. I had only been able to get partly under the table. The whole of my left side was exposed. A lump of masonry hit me over the left eye, knocking me unconscious and pinning my left hand down. Another smashed my left ankle.

Over the next hours I came round, then lost consciousness several times. They reached the dining room at about 4.30 p.m., but got to Kitty and me much later. Kitty's injuries, especially to her head, were terrible. She died as she reached hospital.

When I arrived at Lewisham Hospital I was found to have a smashed ankle, a dislocated elbow, a paralyzed arm and spinal injuries.

The Sandhurst Road school was not the first school to be bombed with high casualties – thirty-one schoolchildren had been killed when a school in Petworth, West Sussex, was bombed four months earlier – but the public, surprised by the renewal of bombs over London after so many months, was convinced that this was a deliberate attack on a school. This was almost certainly not so, although other bombs dropped in the raid were carefully and accurately targeted, including one on the President's House at the Royal Naval College, Greenwich, one on the Deptford West Power Station and several on the Surrey Commercial Docks, which were set ablaze. But more than any other bomb dropped that year, whether deliberate or not, the one on the school stirred up a wave of anger and hatred towards the Germans, more so even than during the Blitz.

Anger was intensified when, in a broadcast the next day over German radio, one of the pilots who had been on the raid said – with typical pride after any such action – 'we dropped our bombs where they were to be dropped', and another pilot described the attack as 'quite a jolly enterprise'. Both pilots were later killed in action.

In spite of the military setbacks in Russia and the Western Desert, the deportation of Jews to their deaths remained a Nazi priority. In the end the mass murder of the Jews was the only element in Hitler's war policy that succeeded. In a top secret letter to the German Minister of Transport on January 21, Himmler wrote of 'the removal of Jews' from both Eastern and Western Europe: 'I need your help and support. If I am to wind things up quickly, I must have more trains for transports. I know very well how difficult the situation is for the railways and what demands are constantly made of you. Just the same, I must make this request of you: help me get more trains.'

Those trains were forthcoming. On the day of Himmler's letter, two thousand Jews were deported from the ghetto at Theresienstadt to Auschwitz, where 1,760 of them were gassed on their arrival. Another train left Holland that day. Among the deportees were several hundred patients from a Jewish mental hospital. Before the train left Holland, the Germans called for nurses to volunteer to accompany the patients. They were offered the choice of returning home after the journey or of working in a 'really modern mental home'. Twenty nurses volunteered. On reaching Auschwitz both they and their patients were taken straight to the gas chambers and killed.

To accelerate the 'final solution', on January 30 Hitler appointed Ernst Kaltenbrunner as head of the Reich Central Security Office (the *Reichssicherheitshauptamp*, or RSHA). His task was to take charge of the round-ups and deportations of Jews throughout Germany, the occupied areas, and those States that were willing to cooperate with Germany in the deportations. For the States which did cooperate – such as Slovakia and Croatia – as well as for those that were under direct German rule – such as Holland, France and Belgium – it was Adolf Eichmann, a longtime official at the RSHA, who was in charge of the day to day coordination.

Kaltenbrunner, Hitler's choice to speed up the mass murder of the Jews, was forty years old. He had been born in Ried im Innkreis, a small village in Austria near to Hitler's birthplace at Braunau. He held an Austrian law degree and had run a small law office in Linz before joining the Austrian Nazi Party in 1932. It was Kaltenbrunner who, in the summer of 1942, had been appointed after Heydrich's assassination to carry out the reprisals against Czechs and Jews. It was also Kaltenbrunner who encouraged local people to kill Allied parachutists. He relished his new task, and rapidly intensified the deportation of Jews from a dozen European countries.

An indication of the scale of these deportations can be seen from a report sent to Himmler a week after Kaltenbrunner's appointment – and reflecting the scale of mass murder before the 'acceleration'. The report concerned the clothing of Jewish victims collected from Auschwitz and from the camps in the Lublin region. The list included 22,000 pairs of children's shoes, 155,000 women's coats and 3,000 kilogrammes of women's hair. The clothing of the murdered Jews was to be sent to the Reich: it filled 825 railway wagons. This process was still in its early stages. Within a week of this report, at least four thousand more Jews had been murdered at Auschwitz. Among them were 123 Jewish children from France, many of them deported without their parents, and all of them under twelve years of age.

On January 27 the United States Eighth Air Force, based in Britain, carried out its first bombing raid over Germany. Sixty-four bombers took part. Their targets were warehouses and factories at the North Sea port of Wilhelms-haven. In the air battle that developed during the raid, twenty-two German aircraft were shot down, for the loss of only three of the American planes.

January 30, three days after this first American raid, marked the tenth anniversary of Hitler coming to power. Whatever dreams he might have had then of becoming the master of Europe within a decade, he can hardly have anticipated what did happen on that anniversary: a small but dramatic and unusual British daylight bombing raid on Berlin. Only six aircraft took part. But this was the first time Berlin had been bombed in daylight. British planners also had another surprise in store. The first part of the raid, with three of the aircraft, was timed to take place just as Goering was about to speak at a large rally in the capital. As a result of the raid, his speech had to be postponed for an hour. The second part of the raid, with the next three aircraft, took place as Goebbels was due to speak. But the German defences had been alerted and one of the aircraft was shot down. Both the pilot, Squadron Leader D.F. Darling and his navigator, Flying Officer W.

Wright, were killed. Their graves are today at the British war cemetery in Berlin, a few hundred yards from the former Olympic Stadium.

Compared to the conflict on the Eastern Front, the raid on Berlin was like a pinprick. On January 31, as the German troops in southern Russia were driven further back, losing Voronezh and their positions on the River Don, the German soldiers trapped in Stalingrad reached the end of their capacity to fight on, losing even the last airstrip on which – albeit with difficulty – supplies could be flown in to them. Their commander, General von Paulus, sent a radio message that day to Hitler asking for permission to surrender. Hitler replied: 'The Sixth Army will hold its positions to the last man and the last round.' To encourage Paulus to continue fighting, on January 31 Hitler appointed him a Field Marshal, the coveted rank at the top of the military hierarchy. That same day, Paulus surrendered.

The surrender of the German forces trapped inside the Stalingrad pocket was a humiliation for Hitler and a blow to the prestige of Germany. The army which had come to the end of its fighting abilities was the same army – the Sixth – which had conquered Belgium and Holland in 1940. The scale of loss was almost catastrophic for Germany: a quarter of a million men had been either killed or captured: 160,000 lay dead on the battlefield and 90,000 were taken into captivity. The wounded and those suffering from frostbite were alike led away on foot, eastward to Siberia. Tens of thousands died on the march. Tens of thousands more died in captivity. The remnant were not allowed back to Germany until almost a decade after the war. For the most part they were broken men.

After the Stalingrad surrender, the Germans were driven from Kursk on February 8. It was one of the main German north-south communication centres in Russia. Among those who took part in the battle were four thousand Jews, soldiers in the Lithuanian Division of the Red Army; during the course of the fighting more than a thousand of them were killed.

On February 12, in North Africa, Montgomery's Eighth Army drove Rommel back across the border into Tunisia from the south. American troops already stood on the western edge of Tunisia, having been briefly pushed back at the Kasserine Pass, but holding their ground behind it, and preparing to advance again. Just as Hitler had ordered Paulus to hold on in Stalingrad, so Rommel was ordered to hold on in Tunisia. As he was driven back towards Tunis, he was ordered to hold the Tunisian Tip, the promontory that was the nearest African land to Sicily and Italy.

If Tunisia were lost, the unthinkable might happen − the launching of an Allied invasion of Europe through Italy, the weakest member of the Axis. Hitler saw clearly that it would fall to him to defend Italy. Mussolini, who scarcely a decade earlier had been the scourge of the European Powers, was a broken reed, full of bombast but lacking the substance of military strength or will power.

Hitler needed to reassert German military prowess, and above all stop the rapid erosion of his position in Russia. If Rommel could hold Tunisia, the troops in the East would not have to come back to defend Italy. If they could advance in the East, regaining at least some of the Soviet territory that had been lost, a line of defence could be established to hold Stalin at bay while Hitler turned, as he still hoped to turn, against Britain.

For this third German offensive against the Soviet Union within two years the goal was no longer Moscow or Baku, but the eastern Ukrainian city of Kharkov. The attack began on February 21. British Signals Intelligence, reading the German Enigma, was able to alert the Russians to the precise German plan, and within twenty-four hours the Red Army was able to counterattack. Hitler, in urging his people to have confidence in victory, returned, as he always did when speaking to the German people − this time over the radio − to the theme and obsession of his early rise to power, the Jews. 'We shall smash and break the might of the Jewish world coalition,' he said, 'and mankind struggling for its freedom will win the final victory in this struggle.'

On the day after the new German offensive had begun, an agreement was reached between Bulgaria and Germany, with regard to the 11,000 Jews living in the two territories occupied by Bulgaria in 1941 − Yugoslav Macedonia and southern Serbia, and Greek Thrace. All thirty-two communities would be 'evacuated'. Beginning on March 3 they were rounded up by Bulgarian police under German supervision, put in cattle trucks, and taken, in twenty trains, a thousand miles across the Balkans and Central Europe to the death camp at Treblinka. There were almost no survivors.

The trains, manpower and organization required for the successful despatch of tens of thousands of Jews to their deaths was considerable; but it nowhere approached the transportation needs of the battlefield. While the racial policy of the Reich was succeeding day by day, its military initiatives were failing. When Soviet partisans surprised a large unit of Hungarian and German soldiers at Orlov on March 1 they killed a hundred soldiers before disappearing into the woods. On March 3 the Red Army captured Rzhev, one of the closest German positions to Moscow, and begun pushing the German forces westward, away from the capital. The siege of Leningrad had been completely broken. Russian partisan activity behind the lines, such as that at Orlov, had continued to grow. In Tunisia, a strong counterattack by Rommel was repulsed: the British had learned of what was impending by their reading of Rommel's own most secret radio messages.

On the night of March 3/4, as British bombers were flying against Hamburg, a German air raid on London led to a panic at the entrance to an air raid shelter in an area where no bombs were falling. The shelter was a deep one at Bethnal Green underground station. In the crush of people seeking to enter it after the alert was sounded, a woman carrying both a bundle and a baby tripped near the foot of a flight of nineteen steps. Her fall tripped an elderly man, who likewise fell. Others pushing behind then fell over him. As more and more people, unaware of the reason for the blockage, tried to get down the stairs into the shelter, and fell down in their turn, 173 people were killed.

In the British bombing of Hamburg that night, twenty-seven Germans were killed. The next night, March 5/6, the pledge that Roosevelt and Churchill had given at Casablanca at the beginning of the year, that the bombing offensive against Germany would be accelerated, was brought into full effect when British bombers struck at Essen. This was the first night of what became known as the Battle of the Ruhr. It was to last four months, and was by far the most intensive British bombing campaign to date. On that first night, 442 aircraft took part – the raid also contained a bomber whose participation constituted the 100,000th individual sortie by Bomber Command since the outbreak of war. Within the Krupp Works at Essen – the principal target – 160 acres of factories, railways and stores were hit, and 53 separate factory buildings destroyed or damaged. In addition, three thousand houses were destroyed and at least 457 workers and citizens were killed.

Goebbels complained in his diary: 'The city of Krupp has been hit. The number of dead too is considerable. If the English continue their raids on this scale, they will make things exceedingly difficult for us.' Goebbels was also indignant that day when, as the deportation began of Berlin Jews from an Old Age Home, there were what he described as 'regrettable scenes . . . when a large number of people gathered and some of them even sided with the Jews.'

On the night of March 8/9, diverting briefly from the battle for the Ruhr, 335 British bombers struck at Nuremberg, the home of the great rallies at which, a decade earlier, Hitler had inspired the German people with his calls for national honour and the revenge for the defeat of 1918 and the Treaty of Versailles. It was one of the longest range missions by so many aircraft. Six hundred buildings were destroyed, several important factories damaged, and more than 284 citizens killed.

On the return flight the crew of one plane, which had been damaged, believing that they were over France, baled out. They were in fact over the English Channel, and were drowned. A single member of the crew, Sergeant D.R. Spanton, one of the gunners, had not heard the order to bale out and was still on board. When he realized that he was alone (and the plane on automatic pilot) he parachuted out while over British soil, leaving the pilotless plane to crash land in the Thames estuary. The fortunate Sergeant flew on twelve more bombing missions, but was killed three months later during the thirteenth mission.

On the night after the Nuremberg raid, Munich was bombed. As a result of a strong wind, the main weight of bombs missed their targets. Among the buildings damaged were the cathedral, four churches, and eleven hospitals. More than two hundred people were killed. Goebbels was again perturbed, writing in his diary: 'Again one asks: How is this to go on? If the English are in a position night after night to attack some German city, one can easily imagine how Germany will look after three months unless we take effective counter-measures.'

It was not only the British who had incurred Goebbels's anger. As he wrote in his diary: 'The scheduled arrest of Jews on one day failed because of the shortsighted behaviour of industrialists who warned the Jews in time.' The part played towards the Jews by industrialists on whom the German war effort depended was sometimes remarkable. A year earlier, Oskar Schindler had helped to save more than a thousand Jews in Cracow by taking them into his factory. Other 'Schindlers', most of them unsung, were at work in Germany. One of them, Otto Weidt, who had a small brush factory in a courtyard in the centre of Berlin, took in several hundred blind Jews and, in his discussions with the deportation authorities, insisted that the work they did for him was essential for the German war economy. Today, at the entrance to his courtyard, a plaque records his courage and notes: 'Many men thank him for having survived.'

There were 27,260 Jews still living in Berlin. The fate of most of them had been sealed when mass round-ups began, starting on February 27. Unknown to those seized, and taken to railway sidings at Grunewald, just outside the city, their destination was Auschwitz. Within four months, Goebbels noted in his diary that only 6,800 Jews were left in the city. 'Berlin's liberation from the Jews,' he commented, was one of the regime's 'most important achievements'.

The war at sea continued remorselessly from day to day. At the beginning of March, when the Japanese tried to send reinforcements to New Guinea, their movement was betrayed by the interception of their own top secret radio signals – which they could not conceive were being read by the Americans, any more than the Germans could conceive that the British were reading their most secret operational orders and tactical secrets. As a result of this knowledge, on March 4 a force of 137 American bombers was despatched to intercept the invasion fleet. In the battle that followed, the Americans sank all eight of the Japanese troop transports: 3,500 Japanese soldiers were drowned. Of the 150 Japanese warplanes that took part in the battle, 102 were shot down. Ten years earlier to the day, Roosevelt had been inaugurated President. That day he received a telegram from Churchill: 'Accept my warmest congratulations on your brilliant victory in the Pacific, which fitly salutes the end of your first ten years.'

On March 13 the ocean liner *Empress of Canada,* on her way to South Africa with 1,400 Greek and Polish refugees and Italian prisoners-of-war on board, was torpedoed by an Italian submarine off the coast of West Africa. She sank in twelve minutes. Despite this, a large proportion of those on board were saved. But forty-eight sailors, eight soldiers and 340 passengers were drowned. That same day the British submarine *Thunderbolt* was lost off Sicily with all her crew. This particular submarine had been sunk before, raised and renamed. In her previous existence she had been the ill-fated *Thetis*, which had failed to resurface during a practise dive shortly before the war with the loss of ninety-nine of those on board. Twice in four years she had proved to be a graveyard.

On the day of the loss of the *Thunderbolt* an incident took place in German-occupied Russia that might have shaken the German war-making power to its depths, perhaps even brought the war to an end. It was known to those who were in on the secret as Operation Flash. For many months, and with particular intensity since the disaster at Stalingrad, several senior German army officers had discussed among themselves what had hitherto been inconceivable: how to get rid of Hitler. The enthusiasms of 1939 and 1940 were over. The prospect of rapid military campaigns, followed by swift victory and long years of peace and national rejuvenation, was no longer an inspiration, or even within the realm of possibility. Retreat was the reality on all fronts, and after retreat it was defeat that loomed. There was particular anger in senior German military circles that Hitler had refused to allow Paulus to retreat, and thus escape the humiliation and loss of capture.

The conspirators knew that Hitler, then visiting his troops at Zaporozhe, in southern Russia, was due to fly on March 13 to his headquarters at Rastenburg in East Prussia. He would fly first to his headquarters at Vinnitsa, then make a short stop at Smolensk, towards which the German troops nearest to Moscow were being forced back. It was while Hitler was at Smolensk that Major-General Henning von Tresckow and his staff officer, Lieutenant Fabian von Schlabrendorff, the leaders of the disaffected officers, devised a plan that would kill Hitler. A parcel bomb was given to one of the officers accompanying Hitler during the final leg of the flight, from Smolensk to Rastenburg. This officer was not in the plot. He had been told that the parcel contained a gift of two bottles of liqueur for one of the senior officers at Rastenburg.

The officer with the parcel was taken on the plane, and Hitler flew westward. Meanwhile, in Berlin, other conspirators, among them Colonel Hans Oster, the Chief of Staff of the German Armed Forces Counter-Intelligence service, and his deputy, Hans von Dohnanyi, waited for the code word 'Flash'. This would mean that Hitler was dead and that the conspirators should take control in the capital. The bomb was timed to go off as the plane was flying in the region of Minsk. But two hours after leaving Smolensk the plane reached Rastenburg without incident. The conspirators, recovering the parcel, discovered that the detonator had been defective. Operation Flash had failed.

Not only German Army officers and aristocrats, but students and liberals, had been spurred after Stalingrad to protest against the Nazi régime. In Düsseldorf, sixty-one people were arrested that March for distributing anti-Nazi leaflets. Other arrests were made in Dortmund, Görlitz, Chemnitz, Nuremberg, Saarbrücken and Weimar. On March 15 a German Security Police report complained that the German population was 'no longer meeting such manifestations as before, by, for instance, the prompt removal of the inflammatory writings or the handing over of leaflets, but instead read the contents and hands them on'.

There were several other manifestations of discontent inside Germany. For many months a twenty-four-year-old medical student at Munich University, Hans Scholl, had led a small group, including his twenty-one-year-old sister Sophie, that called itself the White Rose. They set as their aim 'to strive for the renewal of the mortally wounded German spirit', and made contact with students in other universities, pledged to oppose the 'dictatorship of evil'. In mid-February they had gone out at night and painted the words 'Freedom' and 'Down with Hitler' in large white letters on a wall in one of the main streets. Two days later they had scattered anti-Nazi leaflets in the main entrance to the university. One sentence in the leaflets read: 'Germany's name will remain disgraced for ever unless German youth rises up immediately, takes revenge, and atones – smashes its torturers, and builds a new, spiritual Europe.'

The White Rose had been much affected by the stories told to them by those of their members, including Hans Scholl, who had served with the German forces on the Eastern Front and been shocked at what they saw of the barbarous treatment of the Jews. Scholl had been so upset by what he saw in German-occupied Poland that he had gone up to cattle trucks in which Jews were being deported and shaken their hands, as a public – and dangerous – gesture of sympathy.

The members of the White Rose were quickly tracked down and arrested. Three of them were sentenced to death by decapitation. As Hans Scholl was being led to the scaffold inside the prison, he cried out in a voice heard by those in the cells: 'Long live liberty!' Sophie Scholl, who had been tortured by the Gestapo, appeared in court with a broken leg. She had to hobble to the scaffold in great pain.

On March 15, two days after the failure of the assassination attempt on Hitler, and while the last Jews of Thrace and Macedonia were still on their way to death, the German occupation authorities in the Greek port of Salonika rounded up all 56,000 Jews of that city, in which there had been a Jewish community at the time of St Paul (himself a Jew – Saul). A large Jewish community had lived in Salonika since the expulsion of the Jews from Spain in 1492. All were deported to Treblinka and Auschwitz. It took nineteen trains to uproot and destroy a whole community.

The Bulgarian parliament, angered by the German-organized deportations from Bulgarian-occupied territory, refused, in a vote on March 17, to allow the deportation of Bulgarian Jews. Hitler did not have the means to occupy

Bulgaria and organize the deportation using German troops and police. The Jews of Bulgaria therefore survived the war. Among those who had intervened on their behalf was the Bulgarian king, Boris, the head of the Orthodox Church in Bulgaria, the Archimandrite Cyril, and the Papal Nuncio in neighbouring Turkey – who had earlier served in Bulgaria – Angelo Roncalli, later Pope John XXIII.

The German military conspirators did not allowed their failure on March 13 to deter them. A new plan was devised, and devised quickly, as Russian troops on the Moscow front – where once the Soviet capital had seemed within hours of capture – continued to push back the German forces towards Smolensk. The conspirators decided to act on March 21, eight days after their failed attempt. Hitler was still in Berlin, and would be attending that day the annual memorial ceremony to the German dead of the First World War. After the ceremony, it was intended that he would be shown a collection of weapons captured from the Russians. The military conspirators decided to make use of this demonstration to assassinate him. One of their number, Major-General Baron von Gersdorff, was to be on duty at the exhibition. He proposed that he would carry out a suicide mission: putting a bomb into his greatcoat pocket, he would detonate it as Hitler passed him.

Major-General von Tresckow approved the plan and asked Lieutenant von Schlabrendorff to find a bomb with a specially devised short time fuse which would go off after ten minutes. Among those who were privy to this attempt on Hitler's life was Pastor Dietrich Bonhoeffer. He, his wife and children, and his closest friends, were together in Berlin when the attempt was being made. They were practising a cantata to be sung on the seventy-fifth birthday of Bonhoeffer's father in ten days' time. Among those present was Bonhoeffer's brother-in-law Hans von Dohnanyi, a leading member of the conspiracy. Bonhoeffer's biographer, Mary Bosanquet, has written:

> Dietrich, conducting, was pleasant and composed. Patiently he worked to bring the performance up to the high standard that was a *sine qua non* on special occasions. As the young voices rose up, disciplined and trim, the page of music trembled in Christine's hand, but Hans von Dohnanyi's fine tenor voice never faltered, though his car stood at the door with the engine warmed up, and any minute could bring a telephone call which would mean an immediate dash to the *Abwehr* headquarters.
>
> To the rest of the family he appeared as usual, and no one looking at

Dietrich's broad cheerful face would have guessed that he was listening for anything more dramatic than the balance of voices as they competently wove into a seamless whole the pattern of their several parts.

The hours went by; the singers worked diligently. No sound came from the next room where the telephone stood. And when at last the family folded up their music and dispersed, three of them knew that another attempt on Hitler's life had failed.

Unknown to Bonhoeffer, von Schlabrendorff had failed in his search for a suitable bomb, and the attempt had been called off. Ironically, Hitler had only stayed at the exhibition for eight minutes after the dedication ceremony ended, and had ignored the demonstration of captured equipment. As during the Munich Beer Hall assassination attempt in November 1939, he would have left the building just before the explosion.

The German military setbacks and defeats continued. On March 27, after struggling for seven days to hold the Mareth Line, Rommel was forced to pull back deeper into Tunisia. That night 396 British bombers raided Berlin. Although most of the bombs fell between seven and seventeen miles outside the target area, and the raid did not cause the damage that had been intended, many factories suffered some damage. Bombs hitting the Anhalter Station in the centre of the city killed eighty soldiers who were on their way back from the Russian front on leave. A flying school was also hit, and several service personnel killed. Some bombs fell, entirely by accident, on a secret German Air Force store depot at Tetlow, eleven miles outside Berlin (the bombs were five or six miles off their intended target). A large quantity of radio and radar equipment was destroyed. German Air Force Intelligence was much impressed that such a remote, hidden and secret location had been targeted and hit with such accuracy.

The British bombing raids against German cities continued without interruption. On April 10 one of the main targets was Frankfurt. More than five hundred bombers took part. Twenty-one of the attacking aircraft were shot down; the first was attacked by German fighters shortly after crossing the French coast. One of its crew, Group Captain John Whitley, managed with great difficulty to parachute out of his bomber and was given shelter by a French family. Typical of many hundreds of those who were shot down over France he was spirited across the Pyrenees down the 'Comet' escape line. In Whitley's case he was back in Britain, via Gibraltar, a mere forty-five days after he had been shot down. His squadron having assumed that he was either dead or a prisoner-of-war, no one recognized him when he entered the officers' mess in civilian clothes. 'Good God! Doesn't anyone know me here?' he called out. After a while someone said: 'Bloody hell! It's Group Captain Whitley.'

After the war Whitley returned to France to thank those who had sheltered him and helped him to escape. Several of them had survived the war; but two had been deported by the Germans and died in a concentration camp, four had been executed in France, one had been starved and tortured to death, and another had been crippled by machine-gun fire in both legs.

The British bombing offensive intensified. In an attack on Stuttgart on the night of April 14/15, one bomb scored a direct hit on an air raid shelter in which prisoners-of-war had been taken for safety: 257 French and 143 Russians were killed. The total death toll that night was 619, the highest number of deaths yet recorded in an air raid over Germany. Two nights later, 130 people were killed in Mannheim, and nearly seven thousand made homeless. In a raid on Stettin – a flight of more than six hundred miles from Britain – a hundred acres of mostly industrial property was destroyed, and a large chemical factory forced to halt production. That night 586 people were killed in Stettin. Almost imperceptibly, and yet by definite gradations, the death toll from bombing raids was growing.

It was not only over Germany that the Allied bombers sought their targets. On April 4 an American daylight air raid on port installations at Naples left 221 Italian dead. When American bombers struck the next day at the Renault assembly lines near Paris, 228 French civilians were killed. Also on April 5, an American daylight raid on Antwerp, the aim of which was to destroy an aircraft factory, failed, because of a navigational error, to find the factory. Most of the bombs fell on a built-up area of the city, killing 936 civilians. Among the dead were 209 schoolchildren who were at school – as the thirty-eight British schoolchildren had been in January in South London.

Goebbels was quick to seek advantage from the Antwerp deaths, noting in his diary a week after the raid: 'An imposing funeral has been arranged.' The fact that neither the British nor American radio had mentioned the civilian casualties 'supports our idea of making a first-class propaganda matter of the Antwerp incident'. Goebbels needed as much propaganda as he could obtain. That week, inside Germany, the scale of anti-war feeling was under- lined when the Gestapo arrested Dietrich Bonhoeffer, on suspicion of being involved in an anti-Hitler plot. He was charged with 'subverting the armed forces'. Imprisoned first of all in Berlin, he remained in prison and concentration camps until a month before the end of the war, when, on 9 April 1945, two years after his arrest, he was tried by summary court-martial at Flossenbürg concentration camp and executed.

Another of those arrested in April was Bonhoeffer's brother-in-law, Hans von Dohnanyi, the Deputy Chief of Staff of the German Armed Forces Counter-Intelligence service who had been involved in the attempt to kill Hitler at Smolensk. After two years in Sachsenhausen concentration camp, he too was murdered.

The bravery of those who resisted was undoubted. But the many thousands of acts of collective and individual resistance were without any hope of success. The Jews who drove off the deportation squads inside the Warsaw ghetto in January 1943, and then took up such arms as they could acquire when the full force of the German army was turned against them in April, had little chance of survival. But the instinct to resist was omnipresent. It was matched only by the determination of the German occupation authorities to destroy those whom they ruled.

Not only was the deportation of Jews to the death camps accelerated that spring; the deportation of forced labourers from Western Europe also intensified. Fearing an Allied attempt to land substantial armed forces in northern Europe, Hitler ordered these forced labourers to work on the construction of the 'Atlantic Wall': a fortified line of gun emplacements and strongpoints that stretched from the North Cape of Norway to the French coast of the Atlantic. In addition to the hundreds of thousands of people taken from their homes and sent to work on the Atlantic Wall, 1,293,000 forced labourers were sent to Germany to work in factories there. Another type of deportee was the person considered to be a potential source of opposition: for them, the concentration camps on German soil were a place of incarceration and torment. A quarter of a million Frenchmen were arrested and sent off to these camps: of them, only 35,000 survived the war. How often the traveller comes across a memorial in France with the three words: 'Mort en Deportation' inscribed on it.*

More than 65,000 Belgians, Dutch, Luxembourgers, Norwegians and

* Walking though a small mountain village in southern France in 1975, I came across one such memorial tablet which gave the place of death of a local deportee as Johanngeorgenstadt. A number of villagers who watched me read the plaque asked me to show them the town on the map. It is also in the mountains: on the German side of the German-Czech border south of Chemnitz. In 1943 it was one of the many sub-camps of Buchenwald, fifty miles to the north-west.

Danes were likewise deported, of whom as many as 10,000 were killed in the concentration camps or died of ill-treatment and deliberate neglect. Collaboration was also a daily feature of life under occupation. The historian Richard Cobb, a lover of France, who began that year regular broadcasts from Britain into France and Belgium, has written in his account of the wartime occupation:

> By the middle of 1943, eighty thousand Frenchwomen – one would so much like to know of what classes and social origins, whether urban or rural, whether Parisian or provincial – had claimed children's' benefits from the German military authorities and had requested German nationality for their offspring – and this was only from the Occupied Zone; and Amouroux considers this figure to be only the tip of the iceberg.
>
> More banally, for the girl concerned with only short-term benefits, a German boy-friend could offer immediate and solid advantages not just to the working-class girl, but to the *lycéenne* from the XVIme and the VIIIme: *le prestige de l'étranger*, the hint of perversity and adventure, the wonderfully persuasive white dress uniform of a young *Luftwaffe* pilot, dinner in sumptuous surroundings, the best linen, starched napkins *en dindon*, fresh flowers on the table, heavy silver tableware, the obsequious deference of the waiters (one's own contemptible compatriots), the attentiveness and elaborate politeness of the officer in the uniform of the Master Race.
>
> This would add a delectable spice to the pleasure, the first step towards collaborationism, whether at a personal or at a public level, being a desire to opt out of one's own nationality and to cross the frontiers of an alien and adopted one.

On August 6, in a belated gesture of defiance, Pierre Laval – then President of the Council, Minister of Foreign Affairs and Minister of Information of Vichy France – rejected a German request for a further half million French workers to be sent to Germany. Fritz Sauckel, the German Plenipotentiary-General for Labour Mobilization, who had been ordered by Hitler to secure the workers, summoned Laval to Paris and argued with him for six hours, but in vain. 'His refusal constitutes a pure and simple sabotage of the struggle for life which Germany has undertaken against Bolshevism,' Sauckel reported to Hitler. But the deportation of French Jews, rounded up in every corner of France, continued without respite. On September 2 the fifty-ninth deportation train left France for Auschwitz. Many of the deportees were Jewish patients from psychiatric hospitals in the Paris area. One woman, who was described as 'violently insane', was deliberately chloroformed before being carried to the railway station at Bobigny where the deportation train was being loaded.

Among those deported that day was a three-month old baby, Albert Elbaz, and his two brothers, Marcel aged five and Maurice aged four: they were deported without their parents, and murdered on reaching Auschwitz.

In the Pacific war, the cruelty of those who captured Allied servicemen knew no bounds. On March 29 an American flight-lieutenant was shot down over New Guinea by Japanese anti-aircraft fire. He was sentenced to be decapitated. A Japanese officer described the sequel: 'The unit commander has drawn his favourite sword. He taps the prisoner's neck lightly with the back of the blade, then raises it above his head with both arms, and brings it down with a sweep. All is over. The head is dead white like a doll's.'

Against increasing American, Australian and New Zealand air power and military steadfastness, the Japanese were unable to make further advances of any significance. An air attack on American merchant ships off Tulagi on April 7 succeeded in sinking one American and one New Zealand warship, but only three merchant ships were then sunk, and the bulk of the convoy proceeded on its way. A Japanese bombing raid on Port Moresby four days later did no serious damage: the Japanese would not be able to regain their earlier position of apparently imminent mastery in New Guinea. On the day after the Port Morseby attack, an intercepted top secret Japanese radio message enabled the Americans to shoot down the plane carrying the Commander-in-Chief of the Combined Japanese Fleet, Admiral Yamamoto, while he was on a visit of inspection to Japanese bases on Bougainville Island.

In the Japanese-occupied areas of China, there was no relaxation of Communist partisan activity. The main partisan bases were more than centres of military activity. The Chinese Communists also provided educational facilities for women and children, and organized the collectivization and cultivation of land behind Japanese lines. At the same time, Japanese demands for grain, an essential component of the food needed for the occupation army, were resisted. In some regions, no more than ten per cent of what the Japanese called for was handed over. An American woman, Agnes Smedley, wrote about this defiant activity in her book *Battle Hymn of China*, published in the United States in 1943. Edgar Snow did likewise a year later; his book was called *People on Our Side*. In it he wrote:

While it is true the Japanese have failed to destroy the partisan forces, or to stop their increase, they have carried out literally thousands of large- and small-scale punitive expeditions against them. They have looted and burned thousands of villages, raped the womenfolk and slaughtered count- less civilians, in a terror aimed to wipe out all thought of resistance. The guerrillas have always found ways to overcome the demoralizing effects of these tactics, but not without sacrifices as bitter as any endured in Russia.

It is true the Japanese are now unable to control any village much beyond the range of their garrisons along North China's railways and roads. But it is also true that their fortified points have greatly increased and can now be seized only at a very heavy cost.

Partisan leaders were sometimes disparaged because they did not more often attack large fortified enemy strongholds. Such criticisms were usually based on ignorance of their circumstances. Lack of munitions industry was a basic weakness which ingenuity and improvisation could not wholly overcome.

While the main forces of the Eighth Route and New Fourth armies, comprising perhaps twenty divisions, were relatively well equipped with machine guns and rifles, and some mortars, they were always short of artillery, ammunition, high explosives and transport. Consequently they had to select engagements which could be quickly terminated and promised the capture of more supplies than might be expended.

Judged on the basis of the millions they have mobilized, their combat efficiency may seem low; but contrasted with the inactivity of troops in China sitting in secure bases and receiving important Allied help, their performance is impressive.

Among those who sympathized with the Chinese Communist efforts was Roosevelt's emissary to Chiang Kai-shek, General Joseph Stillwell. While based in Chungking – one of the 'secure bases' characterized by Edgar Snow – he was outspokenly critical of what he regarded as Chiang Kai-shek's failure to mobilize the people against Japan, warning Roosevelt that the Nationalist leader was 'a vacillating, tricky, undependable old scoundrel'.

Stillwell was particularly critical of the unwillingness of the Chinese Nationalist troops to fight against the Japanese in northern Burma. Today a museum in Communist Chungking contains a sign which praises Stillwell. 'Sympathizing with the Chinese people,' it declares, 'he detested the corrupt and incompetent government of old China and criticized the Kuomintang for being passive in its resistance against Japan but active in fighting the Communists.'

In Tunisia, the Germans under Rommel, though driven back, were still able to counterattack. On the night of April 20/21 the Hermann Goering Parachute Division led a German attack on a British position known as Banana Hill. The British defenders were almost overwhelmed, losing radio contact with their battalion headquarters and outnumbered. As so often in battle, a man emerged who was able to inspire the defenders, raise their morale, and in this case even lead them in a counter-attack of their own. At Banana Hill that man was Peter Faulks, who three years earlier had been in the retreat from Dunkirk.

In the counter-attack which Faulks launched, twenty-one Germans were taken prisoner. For his tenacity in defence and attack he was awarded the Military Cross. Later, at Anzio, he was shot in the head (in the dressing station he heard his sergeant say, 'I've got the Major here. He's a gonner.'). Faulks survived; after the war he became a solicitor and later a judge. When he died two years before the end of the century, at the age of eighty, a friend wrote of him: 'Though he was a gentle, peace-loving man, the pressure of war made him a formidable soldier, scornful of anyone less committed to the cause.'

On the last day of April the Germans deported two thousand Polish Jews by rail from the town of Wlodawa to the nearby death camp at Sobibor. On reaching the camp the Jews, alarmed by the intimation of their imminent destruction, attacked the SS guards with pieces of wood torn from the carriages. All were shot down by machine-gun fire or blown up with grenades. It was a courageous and a hopeless act of resistance. During the previous year the machinery of tyranny, deception and mass murder had been perfected and the forces at the disposal of the conquerors were overwhelming. The murderers were too many, their forces too well armed, and their determination to destroy too deeply rooted, for them to be challenged effectively.

There also continued to be enormous profit in the massive destruction of human life. In the three months up to the end of April, the personal belongings of murdered Jews that had been delivered to Germany included 94,000 men's watches, 33,000 women's watches, 25,000 fountain pens, 14,000 propelling pencils and 14,000 pairs of scissors. In sending these details to Himmler, Hans Frank reported from General Government headquarters in

Cracow that the men's watches were being distributed to combat troops, to men of the submarine service, and to guards in concentration camps. The five thousand 'most expensive' watches, as well as watches with gold or platinum cases or partly fitted with precious stones, were either to go to the Reichsbank in Berlin 'for melting down', or were to be retained by the SS 'for special use'.

In the Atlantic the fortitude of the Allied merchant seamen and the growing effectiveness of their naval escorts was to be rewarded that May. Success came as a result of the British cryptographers' success in breaking the German U-boat Enigma key which had earlier been broken but had subsequently proved impossible to decrypt: as many as half of the Enigma keys used by the Germans were not decrypted at any point during the war. Fortunately for the Allies, the main ones were. The re-breaking of the German U-Boat key was a crucial turning point in the Allies' favour. Its effect was seen on May 4 when a German U-boat which was about to attack a transatlantic convoy was sunk by depth charges dropped by a Royal Canadian Air Force aircraft. On the following day a second U-boat was destroyed by a British corvette.

More than thirty U-boats had gathered for the attack on this convoy, Even prior knowledge could not help avert their onslaught. By the evening of May 6 eleven merchant ships had been sunk. An officer of the Royal Naval escort, who knew nothing of the Enigma exposure of U-boat movements, noted in his log book: 'The convoy seemed doomed to certain annihilation.' The facts revealed by Enigma were, however, to alter the whole nature of the confrontation. Four U-boats were sunk in quick succession, and as a further twenty-five prepared to attack the convoy, details of their movements derived from Enigma, combined with local radar, the combat skills of the Royal Navy escort, and individual courage, enabled the convoy to be well protected, and only one more merchant ship was sunk.

For the Supreme Commander of the German Navy, Grand Admiral Karl Doenitz – who had been appointed to his post five months earlier – the loss of four U-boats in a single attack was a disaster. It was compounded when two more U-boats collided and sank. Even worse was to come. On the next Allied transatlantic convoy it was the German naval Enigma that alerted Allied Intelligence to the whereabouts of the submarine packs, and not a single merchant ship was sunk. At the same time, five more U-boats were destroyed. In one of them Doenitz's son was killed.

Doenitz never knew that his most secret radio signals, the orders sent often hourly from U-boat bases to U-boat commanders, were being intercepted and read hourly by the British. But he knew that somehow the U-boat war was being lost, as surely as the land battle in North Africa. 'The enemy holds every trump card, covers all areas with long-range air patrols, and uses location methods of which we still have no warning,' he wrote in his diary that autumn, and he added what for him – as well as for his army and air force colleagues – was the terrible truth: 'The enemy knows all our secrets and we know none of his.'

The Battle of the Atlantic had become a disaster for Germany. So too had the battle for Tunis. On May 4, as a result of the precise details sent in an Enigma message to Rommel, and decrypted simultaneously in Britain, British destroyers were able to find and sink a large Italian merchant ship that was taking fuel and military supplies to the Axis forces. On the following day, also as a result of an Enigma decrypt, American bombers sank a second Italian merchant ship on its way to Tunis. These were the last two merchant ships of any size that attempted to bring supplies to Rommel's beleaguered army.

On May 6 the British First Army began the final assault on Tunis. To the south and north, French and American troops joined in the attack. That same day, Allied bombers attacked the main harbours in Sicily, as well as the Italian mainland port of Reggio di Calabria, the terminal of the ferry and supply system to Sicily. After desperate German and Italian resistance, Tunis was captured on May 7, as was the port of Bizerta. Those Axis troops who managed to escape capture withdrew into the Cape Bon peninsula: the 'Tunisian Tip'.

The port of Hammamet was still open for German and Italian warships and other vessels. But on May 8 three Italian supply ships crossing from Sicily to Hammamet with essential fuel for Rommel's tanks and aircraft were sunk before they could unload. That same day the German Air Force abandoned its remaining North African airfields and withdrew to Sicily. Despite these severe setbacks, bringing to an end the earlier German mastery of North Africa from Tunis to the Western Desert of Egypt, Goebbels noted in his diary on May 8, after talking to Hitler in Berlin: 'The Führer expresses his unshakeable conviction that the Reich will one day rule all of Europe. We will have to survive a great many conflicts, but they will doubtless lead to the most glorious triumphs. And from then on, the road to world domination is practically spread out before us. For whoever rules Europe will be able to seize the leadership of the world.'

Such was Hitler's confident belief on 8 May 1943. This was two years to the day before the remnant of his once-victorious armies were to surrender unconditionally, amid the ruins of the Reich and the rubble of Berlin itself. On May 9 the German forces in the Tunisian Tip surrendered unconditionally to the Allies.

The defeat of the Germans and Italians in North Africa enabled two Allied projects to be devised with the aim of turning the tide of war still further against Germany. One, made possible by the successful breaking of top secret German Enigma military codes being used on the Eastern Front, was to defeat the next German offensive in Russia – the planned attack on the Russian-held Kursk salient – by anticipating and forestalling it. The other was to use the victory in Tunisia as the launching pad for the invasion first of Sicily and then of the Italian mainland, while deceiving the Germans that Greece was the actual Allied objective after Tunis.

This deception was successful, and Hitler ordered reinforcements to Greece. But his repeated insistence that there should be no strategical withdrawals and no surrenders meant that every Allied forward movement was costly in both German – and Allied – lives and time.

A third Allied initiative following the defeat of the Germans in North Africa was the yet further intensified bombing of industrial targets in Germany. In anticipation of the Sicily and Kursk battles, the Ruhr remained the main focus of these attacks. In a raid on Duisburg on the night of May 12/13, four of the Thyssen steel factories were damaged and 273 people killed. In a raid on Bochum on the following night German decoy markers drew the bombers away from the targets, but many buildings were destroyed and more than three hundred people were killed.

Although the Ruhr raids were severe, greater severity was to come. On May 14 the British and American Chiefs of Staff, meeting as a unified body, agreed to Operation Pointblank: a combined Anglo-American bomber offensive, from bases in Britain, under which the Americans would bomb German industrial targets by day and the British by night. The purpose of this round-the-clock bombing was set out by the Joint Chiefs of Staff as 'the progressive destruction and dislocation of the German military and economic system, and the undermining of the morale of the German people to a point where their capacity for armed resistance is fatally weakened'.

This was to be done with an aim that was new to Allied thinking: 'to permit initiation of final combined operations on the continent'.

The objective of Operation Pointblank was nothing less than the prelude to an Allied landing in northern Europe. The specific daily targets were carefully chosen to reduce Germany's capacity either to combat an invasion force or to continue to fight the war from a position of strength. Among the key targets were U-boat construction yards and bases, aircraft factories, oil production and storage facilities, synthetic rubber and tyre factories, and army vehicle factories and stores. There was to be no delay in implementing the programme; but even before it could be put into effect, the British bombing missions of the Battle of the Ruhr continued unabated.

On the night of May 16/17 a spectacular raid on the Möhne and Eder dams – making use of a new invention, the 'bouncing bomb' – led to a massive loss of water needed for the industries of the Ruhr, and widespread flooding which disrupted road, rail and canal communications. The cost of the raid in human terms was high, on both sides. The attack had been made by nineteen planes. Eight failed to return. Of the fifty-six crew members in these planes, fifty-three were killed. The Germans who died that night were mostly drowned when the dams were breached. Among the dead were 493 forced labourers – mostly women who had been brought from the Ukraine to work on farms in Germany, and who were in a camp five miles downstream from the Möhne Dam. The total death toll of more than 1,260 people was the highest thus far in the war during any air raid on Germany.

To repair the damage done, 50,000 forced labourers had to be taken off their work constructing the Atlantic Wall and brought to the areas around the dams. Anti-aircraft guns were also transferred from the cities of the Ruhr and brought to defend other dam sites, though no other raids took place. On May 24, a week after the dams raid – of which the British film *The Dambusters* was later made – an 826-bomber raid was launched on Dortmund. This was the largest raid in the Battle of the Ruhr. Large areas of Dortmund were devastated, the Hoesch steelworks partly destroyed, and more than six hundred people killed.

With the danger of an Allied amphibious landing in either Greece or Italy – or possibly Sardinia – Hitler was forced to contemplate the defection of Italy from the Axis. He knew from Intelligence reports how unpopular the war was among the Italian people, who realized that their soil could become the next battleground. 'Europe must be defended at its margin,' he told his senior generals on May 15. 'We cannot allow a second front to emerge on the Reich's frontiers.' In case the Allied objective was in fact

Greece – as the British deception plan had indicated – Hitler sent Rommel to Greece with reinforcements. He also brought troops back from Russia, reducing his chances of destroying the Kursk salient, even if his plans had not been known to the Allies.

Other German troops were engaged, albeit briefly, in defeating the Jewish insurgents in Warsaw, and in blowing up every building in the ghetto. During the month-long fighting in Warsaw, which had begun on April 18, the Germans used machine guns, artillery and flamethrowers against pistols and hand-made Molotov Cocktails. In the course of the revolt, 14,000 Jews were killed, or were rounded up while the fighting was still going on and sent to their deaths in Treblinka. Almost all those who were still alive in the city when the revolt was finally crushed on May 16 – 42,000 in all – were sent to labour camps in the Lublin region, where, before the end of the year, they too were murdered, or sent to Auschwitz as slave labourers. Very few survived the succession of deportations and camps. The SS Brigadier who crushed the Warsaw ghetto revolt, SS Brigadier Jürgen Stroop, was awarded the Iron Cross, First Class, for his services.

On May 17 the British and Americans created a unified system of pooling the Signals Intelligence that they had been gathering almost from the outset of the war, and with growing clarity, from the German Enigma, the Japanese Purple and the Italian C38m systems. For this mass of assorted Intelligence, the volume of which was growing as much as its quality, the code name Ultra was introduced. The information derived from the Ultra decrypts included the top secret and 'unbreakable' teleprinter (*Geheimschreiber*) messages passing between German army headquarters at Zossen, south of Berlin, and both the Mediterranean and Eastern Fronts.

Like aircraft, warships, tanks, artillery, partisan activity and infantry, Ultra had become an essential weapon in the Allied armoury. No one outside the inner circle of strategic policymakers knew about it – in the field it was restricted to the Commanders-in-Chief and their small Signals Intelligence staff – but its impact on the course of the war, already often formidable, was rapidly becoming crucial. Among the Americans who went to Bletchley to analyze the Ultra material was Telford Taylor, one of Roosevelt's New Deal legal draftsmen. He was also able to act as a liaison between the two countries, and to satisfy both the military and Intelligence chiefs in Washington that the United States was receiving everything it required, and could use it to immediate and often decisive military effect.

Travelling to the United States as the unified Intelligence agreement was being signed, Churchill spoke to a joint session of Congress on May 19. He had some words of warning, telling the Senators and Representatives: 'It is in the dragging out of war at enormous expense, until the democracies are tired or bored or split, that the main hopes of Germany and Japan reside.' Unknown to Congress, that very day, at a meeting in the White House, Churchill and Roosevelt agreed that the cross-Channel landing should take place no later than 1 May 1944. It was a target that enabled the most ambitious Allied operational plan of the war to be put into high gear.

That week Hitler also made a plan. It was so secret that he did not even put it into one of his top secret Directives. It envisaged, not advancing Germany's war effort, or taking a military initiative against one of his enemies, but shoring up the failure of an ally and partner. The plan was for the German occupation of Italy, should Italy defect to the Allies.

That summer, Germany intensified its anti-partisan activities, both in Russia and in Yugoslavia. This effort drained off fighting men, and weaponry, needed in Russia, and also needed for the defence of Sicily, the invasion of which had become an Allied priority. In Yugoslavia, 67,000 German troops were engaged in operations against Tito's Communist partisans, to whose side a small British mission had been parachuted on May 22. There were also 43,000 Italian and 11,000 Croat soldiers waging the anti-partisan war. For their part, the partisans numbered 16,000, a far smaller force than their occupiers and adversaries, living, moving and fighting in rough terrain which they knew well, but in which the armies sent against them could be isolated and trapped.

Italy's contribution to the war in the Balkans was mocked by its German allies. The Western Allies were also scathing of Italian military prowess, and chances. When Mussolini was photographed visiting the Italian defences in Albania, looking out to sea, the photograph – sent by radio from Switzerland to Britain and the United States on May 26 – was given the belittling caption: 'Mussolini takes a long view of the Mediterranean war.'

For the Germans, warmaking at sea continued to go badly. In the first twenty-two days of May, twenty-one U-boats had been destroyed in the North Atlantic. The Allied naval and air forces had been guided to them by Enigma as surely as if they had received their instructions direct from German naval headquarters – which in a sense they had. On May 24 Admiral Doenitz had to call his U-boats back from the Atlantic convoy routes. Six more were sunk while they returned to their bases on the Atlantic coast of France.

One aspect of German war policy flourished. On May 24, the day on which Doenitz was forced to call off the U-boat attacks on the North Atlantic convoys, a thirty-two-year-old German doctor reached Auschwitz. His name was Josef Mengele. He had a doctorate in medicine, and was a second-lieutenant in the SS. As a student in Germany he had studied philosophy as well as medicine, and had developed a theory that human beings, like dogs, had pedigrees, and that it would be as possible to breed blond, blue-eyed Nordic giants as it was to breed pedigree Rotweilers or Spaniels.

While at Auschwitz, Dr Mengele was to be present at the arrival of at least seventy-four trains reaching the camp from all over Europe. The first of these trains came in on the day after he arrived, with 2,862 Dutch Jews. Mengele was assisted in the medical side of his work by a doctor already in the camp, Professor Karl Clauberg, a distinguished German gynaecologist, who was about to report to Himmler that he had worked out a method of sterilizing a thousand women in one day, using a single doctor and ten assistants. It had taken him almost a year of experimentation, at Himmler's request, to reach this rapid rate of effectiveness.

During Mengele's first week at Auschwitz more than eight thousand Jews arrived from Holland, two thousand from Zagreb, ten thousand from Salonika and 395 from Berlin. On their arrival, Mengele was one of those who, day after day, decided whether each person should be sent straight to the gas chambers, or to the barracks instead. At each selection he wore a white medical coat and white gloves. As well as the selections which he conducted or took part in at the side of the incoming trains, Mengele also carried out at least thirty-one selections inside the camp infirmary, pointing out who should be taken from the sick room to the gas chambers, or shot, or killed with a lethal injection. His medical block was the scene of horrendous medical experiments, many of them on crippled people, young women, and identical twins. The reason he gave for the experiments – all of which were on Jews, and most of which killed those being experimented on – was that he was searching for the best medical means of multiplying the pure Nordic race, on behalf of the German future.

Two days after Mengele reached Auschwitz he also determined the fate of more than a thousand Gypsies, who had their own barracks in Birkenau, and who were then suffering from a typhoid epidemic. All of them were dragged out of the barracks and taken to the gas chambers. Against their names in the official camp register were written the letters 'SB' *Sonderbehand-lung* (Special Treatment), a Nazi camp euphemism for murder.

The mass murder at Auschwitz was carried out under the strictest rules of secrecy and skilfully devised deception. The Allies knew that deportation trains were leaving the main European cities almost every day, but they only knew the destination as 'somewhere in Poland' or 'somewhere in the East'. The Allied bombers, whose range did not reach anywhere near Auschwitz, were relentless in their raids over Germany. After the Dortmund raid of May 24, Goebbels noted in his diary that heavy industry and munitions factories had been particularly badly damaged. He added: 'One can only repeat about air warfare: we are in a position of almost hopeless inferiority and must grin and bear it as we take the blows from the English and the Americans.'

The Germans who lived in the Ruhr and in the cities in western Germany most frequently attacked were, Goebbels confided in his diary, 'gradually beginning to lose courage. Hell like that is hard to bear for any length of time, especially since the inhabitants along the Rhine and the Ruhr see no prospect of improvement'. Churchill did not need to read these words to realize that the bombing offensive was having its effect. At a press conference in Washington on the day after the Dortmund raid he told the assembled journalists who asked him about the Allied air bombardments of Germany: 'This was the weapon with which they boasted – the Germans boasted – they would terrorize all the countries of the world. And it is an example of poetic justice that this should be the first weapon in which they should find themselves most out-matched and first out-matched in the ensuing struggle.'

A British air raid on the night of May 29/30 on Wuppertal, in the Ruhr, created a firestorm in the narrow streets of the old town. A thousand acres of built up area were destroyed, including five of the six largest factories, and as many as 3,400 people were killed. This was by far the highest death toll yet in a single British bombing raid on Germany: five times greater than any earlier one. British newspapers commented on how much higher the Wuppertal death toll was than that of the notorious German raid on Coventry in 1940, when 568 civilians had been killed, and so much outrage had been caused in Britain.

As a preliminary to the German offensive against the Russian forces in the Kursk salient, planned for early July, the Germans began a series of air attacks on the salient on June 2. But on the following day the German army had to launch yet another anti-partisan offensive behind the lines. More than five thousand Russians, including many women and children, were murdered because partisans had been reported receiving food or shelter in their villages. The hatred which this policy of mass murder caused among the Russians was intense, making all the harder any German attempt to control partisan movements and attacks.

The first Allied forward move of the summer took place on June 11 when British troops from their base in Tunis captured four Italian islands between Tunisia and Sicily: Pantelleria, Lampedusa, Linosa (which surrendered two days later, on June 13) and Lampione (which was uninhabited).

While awaiting the moment when the invasion of Sicily could begin, the British pressed ahead with the bombing of German cities. On the night of the seizure of the Italian islands a bombing raid on Düsseldorf destroyed 130 acres of factories, industrial buildings and homes, starting more than eight thousand fires and killing 1,292 people. The next night, in Bochum, 449 buildings were destroyed in the centre of the city and 312 people killed. Raids which a year earlier would have been considered severe ones became classed as moderate. During a raid on Cologne on the night of June 16/17, sixteen factories were damaged, and bombs fell on five churches, five hospitals, and two cinemas: the death toll was 147.

For Cologne it was a terrifying night, but for many of those in Berlin or London who read about it, it no longer had the power to shock or to alarm. On June 27, however, while Churchill was watching a Royal Air Force film taken above the Ruhr cities to give a picture of the raids, the Australian representative in the British War Cabinet, Richard Casey, who was sitting next to him, noted that Churchill suddenly 'sat bolt upright and said to me: "Are we beasts? Are we taking this too far?"'

Casey recalled in his memoirs: 'I said we hadn't started it, and that it was them or us.'

The Allied attempts to turn the tide of the war against the Axis were continuous and varied. On the night of June 16/17, when British bombers were flying against Cologne, two aircraft flew across the Channel to land British agents in France. Their task was to work with the French Resistance. One of those who was flown in that night was Noor Inayat Khan, a great-great-great-granddaughter of Tipu Sultan, the last Moghul Emperor of southern India. She was the first woman operator to be infiltrated into

German-occupied France. For three and a half months she maintained radio contact with London. Then she was betrayed to the Gestapo, and sent to prison in Germany, where she was later shot.

The German offensive against the Kursk salient was about to begin. In a message to his troops on July 4, Hitler told them: 'This day you are to take part in an offensive of such importance that the whole future of the war may depend on its outcome. More than anything else, your victory will show the whole world that resistance to the power of the German Army is hopeless.' But two hours and twenty minutes before the offensive began the next morning, the Russians opened a massive artillery bombardment on the positions where the German troops were forming up to attack, and on their artillery positions. The German element of surprise was lost, and much damage inflicted on the German forces before they started to advance.

The largest tank battle in history had begun, with a total of six thousand tanks on the battlefield. In the skies, four thousand aircraft were in combat. A sign of the growing military activity of the Free French under General de Gaulle was that French pilots, members of the Normandy Squadron, fought alongside the Russian pilots in the Kursk salient.

Hitler failed to push out the salient, or to take Kursk, or to advance as he had hoped to the River Don, and to Voronezh, which he had captured a year earlier. Despite the heavy daily losses, however, he insisted that the fight continue, just as he had insisted that the fight in the Tunisian Tip go on.

On July 10, the fifth day of the battle of Kursk, when it might still have been possible for the Germans to reverse the setbacks, the Allies launched their invasion of Sicily. Hitler was suddenly fighting a massive war on two fronts simultaneously. Neither war went his way. Sicily – the stepping stone to Italy – was captured by the Western Allies, and Kursk was held by the Russians. In German-occupied Lithuania, the torments of the Jews of the Kovno ghetto were for a brief moment assuaged by the news of these distant battles. Avraham Tory, the official ghetto diarist, noted:

Yesterday afternoon the mood in the ghetto was excellent. The British radio had just broadcast the news about the invasion of Sicily by the Allied armies. This news had been brought by workers returning from the city; in no time it spread throughout the ghetto.

Everyone was certain that the end is near; deep in our hearts we were very glad. Everyone regarded the invasion of Sicily as a most unusual event which might bring our own liberation closer.

Optimists spoke about the surrender of Italy in the near future; about clashes between units of the Italian and German armies, and about the fiasco of the new German offensive in Russia.

In a final attempt to close the southern part of the Kursk salient, on July 12, near the village of Prokhorovka, the Germans attacked with nine hundred tanks against a Russian force that was also of nine hundred tanks. Among the German tanks were a hundred Tiger tanks which were in many ways superior to the Russian T-34. The battle was among the fiercest of the Second World War. In the words of the Russian general responsible for preventing the Germans from breaking through: 'The earth was black and scorched with tanks like burning torches.'

By nightfall, the Russians had driven the Germans from the battlefield, leaving three hundred German tanks destroyed, including seventy Tigers. The Russians had lost more tanks than the Germans, but had halted the German advance. That day, just north of the salient, the Russians launched a counter-attack on the German-held city of Orel. The Russian advance was slow – the German soldiers had orders not to yield – but the initiative on the Eastern Front had turned, in that one day, in favour of Russia.

The German initiatives were increasingly those of soldiers against civilians. On July 12, as the Battle of Prokhorovka was proving that German armour was not invincible, in Poland, in the village of Michniow, all two hundred villagers were killed, including babies and expectant mothers, as revenge for partisan activity in the region; and on the following day, at the village of Sikory, forty-eight villagers – including fourteen children – were killed by a German military detachment for the failure of the village to deliver its quota of agricultural produce to the occupying authorities. The agony of Poland was infinite. The memorial plaques in today's Polish countryside, indicating these and so many thousands of other such executions, are mute testimony.

In German-occupied France, British agents were parachuted almost every week to make contact with partisans and resistance fighters. One of those who was sent on such a mission more than once, and finally failed to return, was Hugh Dormer. He was twenty-one years old, newly married, with his first child expected in a few months. During July, on the eve of what was to be his final mission into German-occupied France, he wrote in his diary:

If one is caught by the Germans, one is tortured incessantly and scientifically until by pain and hunger the will is broken and that priceless information concerning the safety of other men's lives is finally extracted. In my own head lies the fatal knowledge which could send many brave men and women in France to their deaths and it is at times a terrifying responsibility.

There is none of the glamour of the scaffold and the guillotine, no opportunity for the last words of Charles I standing bareheaded in the falling snow and crying that he died for the liberties of England. It is all done so secretly that the world will never know whether you faced your torturers with closed lips to the end, or whether you broke down and screamed for mercy at the first blow.

And the result either way will be the same, death – shoddy and ignominious – in a civilian suit of clothes, like a rat finally hunted to exhaustion by its persecutors. Few people in England realize the shabby truth behind those stirring lines in a newspaper: 'Twelve Patriots were executed at Lille for subversive activities to the German State'.

A man must not lose the sublime vision of his ideals in the inevitable sordidness and technicalities of their mechanism among men. Too often we see only the selfishness and pettiness of the individual architects of those ideals, and forget those more transient moments of sacrifice and heroism. Things appear romantic enough in prospect and retrospect, that at the time are only monotony, and sweat, and thirst, and sickening fear.

On July 14, even as the murder of civilians behind the lines continued without a pause somewhere or other in the German-occupied lands of Europe, the first war crimes trial of the Second World War was held in the Russian city of Krasnodar, in the Caucasus. The Soviet authorities accused eleven Germans of mass murder during the occupation of the city. The victims had been Jews, and also the patients at the Municipal Hospital. The method of murder had been in gas vans.

That same week at Auschwitz, on July 17, ten Polish political prisoners who had been accused of trying to escape from Auschwitz were executed against the camp's notorious 'Wall of Death'. Two days later another twelve Polish political prisoners at Auschwitz, who had been held in the punishment bunkers there for almost two months, were taken out, handcuffed, and taken to be hanged in the presence of all their fellow Polish prisoners. Danuta

Czech, a leading historian of Auschwitz, has written: 'The nooses are placed around the necks of the condemned prisoners, and Commandant Hoess steps forward from the group of SS men present and starts to read the sentences. He does not finish, however; as an expression of protest, the prisoner Janusz Skrzetuski pushes away the stool on which he is standing. SS officers and subordinates then run to the condemned men, yank the stools from under their feet, and in this manner finish the execution.'

Three days later, on July 20, of a thousand French Jews who arrived that day at Birkenau, 440 of them – almost entirely the old people, women and children among them – were sent to the gas chambers. Arrested in France, where they had earlier made their homes and livelihoods, they had been born in cities as far away as Beirut, Jerusalem, Constantinople and Algiers. Among those who were murdered that day were Michael and Laja Feder and their six children: Salomon aged fourteen, Henri aged eleven, Sophie aged nine, Leon aged six, Laja aged four and Rachel, who had not yet reached her first birthday.

On July 22, American forces entered Palermo, the largest town on the northern coast of Sicily. Two days later the Fascist Grand Council, meeting in Rome, with Mussolini presiding, took a stand against Mussolini which left him bewildered and helpless. After a ten hour meeting, the Council agreed by nineteen votes to seven to ask King Victor Emmanuel to assume 'effective command' of the Italian armed forces. The Council also called for the responsibilities of both Crown and Parliament, which Mussolini had undermined, to be restored. Count Ciano, Mussolini's son-in-law, was among those voting for Mussolini's dismissal.

Mussolini followed these decisions with almost no anger, and with no will to resist them. Yet they marked the end of his dictatorship. On July 25 he was told by the King that the Government of Italy had been placed in the hands of Marshal Badoglio. 'By midnight,' writes Mussolini's biographer Denis Mack Smith, 'the news had spread through Rome and the whole complex fabric of fascism, which people had taken to be so strong and durable, disintegrated within minutes.' Arrested by the new government, and frightened of public hostility that might turn to physical assault, Mussolini was taken secretly from Rome in an ambulance, to a penal colony on the island of Ponza, where he was held under house arrest.

Many Italians expected that King Victor Emmanuel and Marshal Badoglio would call for an end to the war. Instead they announced that Italy would continue to fight at Germany's side. This gave no comfort to the German leaders. On July 26 Rommel – who was awaiting a possible Allied landing in either Greece or Italy – wrote in his diary: 'In spite of the King's and Badoglio's proclamation we can expect Italy to get out of the war, or at the very least, the British to undertake further landings in northern Italy.'

After a week on the island of Ponza, Mussolini was moved to another island, La Maddalena. Security was tight, there being a danger that Hitler might try to rescue him. While he was on La Maddalena, Mussolini celebrated his sixtieth birthday. He was reading a life of Jesus, and found in it what he described as 'astonishing analogies' between the betrayal of Jesus and his own betrayal.

As German forces were being pushed out of western Sicily and driven back from the Kursk salient, the Allied bombing of Germany reached a climax. During July there had been several German air raids on Britain, and 167 British civilians were killed. But by far the heaviest weight of bombs was that thrown against German cities. Two operations were carried out simultaneously, the American daylight raids and the British night-time raids, ensuring that there was no respite in the bombing.

On the night of July 24/25 the first British raid of what was codenamed Operation Gomorrah took place against Hamburg, when 791 aircraft dropped more than two thousand tons of bombs in the space of fifty minutes. More than 1,500 German civilians were killed. A new device, known as 'window' – strips of aluminium foil – created a snowstorm effect on German radar screens, reducing the number of aircraft that were shot down from an average of seventy or eighty (in an 800-bomber raid) to ten or twelve.

On the following night, when Essen was again the target, the Krupp works suffered their most extensive damage of the war. Among the five hundred people who were killed that night were twenty-two children, forty-two Allied prisoners-of-war and 131 foreign workers. The next Operation Gomorrah raid was carried out on the night of July 28/29. The target was again Hamburg, which had been bombed four nights earlier. This second raid lasted forty-three minutes, seven minutes less than the previous one. As at Wuppertal a month earlier, a firestorm was created in the city centre, as hundreds of fires merged into one, drawing the air out of the deep air raid shelters and suffocating everyone inside them. In the fires above, the intensity of the flames was such that no fire-fighting equipment could counter it: indeed, most of the city's fire engines were still working to damp down the fires of the earlier raid, and could not get to the region of the fire-storm because fallen buildings and debris, the result of high explosive bombs early in the raid, blocked their path. One of the British pilots later recalled:

The burning of Hamburg that night was remarkable in that I saw not many fires but one.

Set in the darkness was a turbulent dome of bright red fire lighted and ignited like the glowing heart of a vast brazier. I saw no flames, no outlines of buildings, only brighter fires which flared like yellow torches against a background of bright red ash.

Above the city was a misty red haze. I looked down, fascinated but aghast, satisfied yet horrified. I had never seen a fire like that before and was never to see its like again.

For three hours the centre of Hamburg burned, until, in the words of the Bomber Command diaries, 'all burnable material was consumed'. Eight square miles of the city were reduced to blackened ruins and ashes. A third of all Hamburg's residential buildings were destroyed: thirty-five thousand apartments and houses being consumed in the inferno. But the most extra-ordinary and terrible statistic of those forty-three minutes was the number of civilians killed: it was in the region of 42,000. So many of those who died were burned to death in the raging fires that the precise number will never be known. Civilians, soldiers billeted in the city, foreign workers in the factories, Allied prisoners-of-war on labour tasks: no one was spared the raging fire.

More civilians were killed in this one raid on Hamburg than in all the German raids on London combined. When details of the extent of the casualties became known, there was a sense of despair in Germany. 'German hopes of victory are completely dwindling,' commented the Swiss newspaper *Neue Züricher Zeitung*. 'They have been replaced by a deep anxiety, as the people are convinced that the Party will not give in, even if more towns like Hamburg are erased.' Rommel, awaiting a British invasion of either Greece or Italy, was determined not to be influenced by the bombing of civilians, writing to his wife: 'The casualties in Hamburg must have been very high. This must simply make us harder.'

In the aftermath of the Hamburg raid, even though he was able to get factory production back to normal fairly quickly in the outer suburbs, Albert Speer – who was about to be appointed head of a single authority to control all German raw material and industrial production – warned Hitler that if three or four other cities were bombed as Hamburg had been it could lead to 'an end of the war'. But no city was to be bombed in this way, with a firestorm leading to tens of thousands of deaths, until the bombing of Dresden in February 1945. In the summer of 1943 most of the large German cities lay beyond the range of such a massive and intense bombardment.

As Hamburg burned, Roosevelt was giving one of his regular Fireside Chat broadcasts to the American people. His words were full of confidence: 'Over a year and a half ago I said this to the Congress: "The militarists in Berlin, and Rome and Tokyo started this war, but the massed, angered forces of common humanity will finish it. Today that prophesy is in the process of being fulfilled. The massed, angered forces of common humanity are on the march. They are going forward – on the Russian Front, in the vast Pacific area, and into Europe – converging upon their ultimate objectives: Berlin and Tokyo. I think the first crack in the Axis has come. The criminal, corrupt Fascist regime in Italy is going to pieces.'

Roosevelt made no reference to the current Anglo-American bombing offensive over Germany. News of the destruction of Hamburg, and the massive death toll there, reached him only after he had spoken. Two nights later Hamburg was bombed again. The death of 800 people that night – including 370 who were asphyxiated when a large department store was hit and collapsed, blocking the exit to their air raid shelter – does not often merit the attention of historians, any more than it impinged too much on contemporaries. The quality of concern, of shock and of recording had all been weakened by the ever-mounting scale of death and destruction.

Air power was being used with the full knowledge of those wielding it of the cost to themselves. When 177 American bombers flew on August 1 from their bases in North Africa to bomb the Roumanian oil fields at Ploesti, fifty-four bombers were lost and 532 aircrew killed. But twenty more such raids were mounted, until twelve months later all oil production at Ploesti was brought to a halt. In two American bomber raids in August, one on the German ball-bearing factory at Schweinfurt and the other on the Messerschmitt aircraft works at Regensburg, sixty of the five hundred attacking aircraft were shot down, and more than six hundred aircrew killed. In the factories that these bombers attacked, 967 workers were killed, including

164 forced labourers who had been brought from Belgium, France, Russia, Czechoslovakia and Hungary.

Within the Soviet Union, Stalin had continued to order the arrest and execution of those charged with opposing his regime and being the agents of hostile foreign powers. Among those arrested in August was his own brother-in-law, Alexander Svanidze, whom he had known since before the First World War. Svanidze was accused of having been 'planted' on Stalin by German Intelligence. On Stalin's direct orders, the People's Commissar for State Security, V.N. Merkulov, told Svanidze that if he confessed he would not be shot. Svanidze refused, and was executed. Stalin commented to the Politburo: 'Well, what a proud man Alyosha turned out to be! I didn't expect it.'

The German army was in retreat on two fronts. The evacuation of Sicily began on August 11 and continued for six days: 60,000 men were brought back to the Italian mainland. On the Eastern Front, Hitler gave the order that week for the construction of a defence line – the Panther Line – more than a hundred miles further west than the existing front line. Roosevelt was concerned that, as the German forces fell back, the Russians might reach Berlin before the British and Americans.

The American forces then on the western shore of Sicily – looking across the Straits of Messina to the 'toe' of Italy – were only 1,000 miles from Berlin. The Soviet troops then driving the Germans from the Russian city of Orel were 950 miles from the German capital. Roosevelt was concerned by this fact, telling Churchill on August 23 that he wanted the troops of the western Allies 'to be ready to get to Berlin as soon as did the Russians'. In that simply phrased request lay the soon-to-be-germinated seeds of the Cold War.

On August 22 the Germans withdrew from Kharkov, the main city of the eastern Ukraine. Three days later the Royal Air Force launched a new bombing campaign, the Battle of Berlin, sending more than seven hundred bombers against the German capital and killing 854 people. More than a hundred of the dead were foreign workers – eighty-nine of them women. The cost of the raid, like the first American raid on Ploesti at the beginning of the month, was high: 298 airmen were shot down and killed, and 117 others taken prisoner.

A second American raid was carried out against Ploesti eight days after the first: 225 aircrew were killed and a further 108 captured. During the second raid of the Battle of Berlin, the German death toll, sixty-seven, was almost a quarter lower than that of the British airmen. As a result of the raid, Goebbels for the first time ordered the evacuation of all children, and adults not engaged in war work: they were sent to towns and villages further east, beyond the range of the British bombers.

In Greece, partisan activity had been growing with every month. The largest of the resistance groups was the left-wing EAM (the National Liberation Front) and its military arm ELAS (the Greek People's Liberation Army). With their slogan 'People's Rule' and their emphasis on social justice, they mounted attacks on German patrols, storehouses and communications, derailed trains and seized stocks of raw materials needed for the German war effort. In the organizational structure of EAM, the Greek Communist Party was predominant. A leading woman activist in the Communist ranks was Chrysa Chadzivasileiou, a former schoolteacher who had spent many years in island exile during the pre-war regime. At grass roots level, support for EAM spread far beyond Party considerations and appeals. Smaller resistance groups, among them EDES (the National Republican Greek League), also attempted to disrupt the pattern of occupation.

Faced with this hostile national activity, and the rejection by the Greeks of any part in the German New Order – those Greeks attracted by that New Order were soon cold-shouldered by the Germans – the occupation authorities used the harshest and cruellest measures against the Greek *andartes* (guerrillas). But the andartes had resources of their own, and were given – and at times extorted – food and supplies from the local population. They also received outside support: by the spring of 1943, several British agents, led by Brigadier Myers, were working alongside them.

With Italy was no longer a part of the Axis, German occupation was extended to the whole of Greece. Resistance increased, and so did reprisals. A new German Army Group Commander, General Alexander Löhr – 'a short, dapper, taciturn man ... stoic, asthmatic', as the historian Mark Mazower describes him – belied his appearance by the savagery of his actions. The total destruction of the andartes was his aim. In the course of a year, more than a thousand villages were burned to the ground, a million homes looted or destroyed, and as many as ten thousand civilians killed. Not only the buildings in a village, but its inhabitants, became the targets of mass destruction. On August 16, in Komeno, above the Ionian Sea, 317 villagers were shot. Four months later, after the andartes had abducted and killed 78

German soldiers, twenty-five villages in the region where the abduction took place were burned to the ground, and 696 villagers killed, including the entire male population (511 men) in the village of Kalavryta, to which the abducted men were said – by informants – to have been taken.

A guerrilla war had begun. But the power of the German Army was such that it was an unequal war. In October 1943, during one of the periodic sweeps against the andartes, the Germans lost nineteen men in an attack which left 755 Greeks dead. In November twenty-one Germans were killed and 700 guerrillas. The burning down of villages continued.

Resistance activities were also growing in Denmark, and were likewise met with the severest of responses. On August 30 a Danish writer, Carl Henrik Clemmensen, who had been active in the Danish resistance, was shot dead. His three executioners were not Germans but Danes, members of a Danish SS formation made up of Danish volunteers. One of the three executioners was Soren Kam, twenty-three years old, and the head of a school in which Danish Nazis received special training. Kam had been trained for his task at an SS school in Germany, and held the SS rank of lieutenant.

Following Clemmensen's execution, Kam was taken to Berlin and put on trial for murder by the SS High Court. After hearing the evidence the court concluded that what had occurred had not been murder but an 'act of war'. Kam later served with the Waffen SS on the Eastern Front with an Austrian unit. After the war he did not return to Denmark but settled in Bavaria. In 1997 – fifty-four years after Clemmensen's execution – Kam attended a reunion of Austrian Waffen SS members in Carinthia wearing his SS uniform.

At the end of August a conference was held in Quebec at which Churchill, Roosevelt and their military advisers, and the Canadian leaders, worked out the Allied strategy for the year ahead. The date of the cross-Channel landings on the coast of France was confirmed for the early summer of 1944. The Italian campaign would be pursued as far north as the Pisa-Ancona Line. Both these decisions were kept secret. Equally secret, if not more so – for it was known only to a dozen of the hundreds of participants at the conference – the manufacture of the atom bomb would go ahead.

On August 31, while still in Quebec, Churchill spoke about the war in a radio broadcast to the Canadian people. The broadcast was transmitted to the United States and Britain, and, by the BBC, to German-occupied Europe.

'We did not undertake this task,' Churchill said, 'because we had carefully counted the cost, or measured the exact duration. We took it on because duty and honour called us to it, and we are content to drive it on until we have finished the job.' In June 1940, he reflected, the 'odds and omens seemed very favourable to Fascist ambition and greed' and he went on: 'It is not given to the cleverest and most calculating mortals to know with certainty what is their interest. Yet it is given to quite a lot of simple folk to know every day what is their duty.'

On September 3, four years to the day after Britain had declared war on Germany, a joint force of British and Canadian troops landed on mainland Italy. The Italian government immediately agreed to an armistice under which no Italian troops would go into action against the invaders. The Germans were alone in the battle for Italy. The first scourge of the postwar European democracies – the nation that had marched into Albania, Greece and Ethiopia – was out of the war. The Germans had to take rapid action to prevent the Allies taking advantage of Italy's defection, occupying as quickly as they could those areas and cities in Greece which had been under Italian occupation, including Athens. This was a further drain on the resources needed by Germany to hold even the new defensive line on the eastern Front.

On the night of the Allied invasion of mainland Italy, the third air aid of the Battle of Berlin took place. Several factories were hit, and, causing a setback for local morale, one of Berlin's largest breweries was put out of action. Almost six hundred people were killed in the raid, among them several German criminals who were earning remission of their sentences by volunteering to work on unexploded bombs, and 123 foreign workers, of whom ninety-two were women: 150 British airmen were also killed.

As workers throughout Western Europe were being sent to Germany to repair the damage of Allied bombing and work in the factories whose German workers had been sent to the war fronts, several thousand Jews were being deported each week from Western Europe to Auschwitz and to their deaths. Those being deported were unaware of their destination or their fate. On August 24, twenty-seven-year-old Etty Hillesum wrote in her diary, in Westerbork camp, in north-east Holland: 'We are left with just a few thousand. A hundred thousand Dutch members of our race are toiling away under an unknown sky or lie rotting in some unknown soil.'

When yet another train with more than a thousand Dutch Jews left Westerbork on September 7, Etty Hillesum was one of those on board. As the journey began she managed to write a postcard to her parents, telling them: 'We have left the camp singing'. Her destination was as unknown to her as it was to hundreds of thousands of Western European Jews. It was Auschwitz, were she died within three months. Also deported from Westerbork to Auschwitz were many of the 181 German Jews from the *St Louis* who in 1939 had been refused entry to the United States but had been admitted to Holland on their return to Europe: those reaching Holland had been among the first Jews to be sent to Westerbork after the German occupation.

In the Pacific on the first day of September, American troops landed on Baker Island, defeating the Japanese garrison there and starting the work of transforming the island into a base for further operations against Japan. Four days after the Baker Island landings, a joint American and Australian parachute landing at Nazdab, in New Guinea, opened the way for the advance on the Japanese garrison at Lae.

After two weeks the Japanese abandoned Lae, and withdrew further north. But they fought, as the Germans were preparing to do in Italy, for every village and every track. In the first year of fighting on New Guinea, 12,161 Australians had been killed. But still they had to fight and die to take each of the ports still held by Japan, and to fight for those ports beach by beach and quayside by quayside. In a defiant gesture, a small Japanese bomber force flew across the Indian Ocean to the west coast of Australia, to attack an Allied airstrip at Drysdale Mission. They failed to find the airstrip, but destroyed the Mission instead.

With the Japanese in firm control of Burma, the rice which used to be imported from Burma to India was no longer available. For the people of Bengal, rice was the staple food. There were also tens of thousands of Indian refugees from Burma and Malaya who had reached Calcutta at the time of the Japanese invasion. They too were dependent on rice for their diet. In the summer of 1943, as supplies of rice ran out, famine spread through Bengal. Its ravages were savage and swift. The poor, and villagers in the remoter regions, were its main victims, not only in Bengal, but in neighbouring Orissa and distant Malabar. Within a few months, as many as 1,500,000 Indians had died.

The Bengal famine was one of the worst famines of the century. With it came a series of epidemics, in particular cholera and malaria, which spread far beyond Bengal. 'Even today,' wrote Jawaharlal Nehru in September 1946, 'they are taking their toll of scores of thousands of lives.' Nehru, who was in prison from August 1942 to March 1945 as a result of his continued public demands for Indian independence, commented:

> The famine brought out both the good qualities and the failings of the Indian people. Large numbers of them, including the most vital elements, were in prison and unable to help in any way. Still the relief works organized unofficially drew men and women from every class who laboured hard under discouraging circumstances, displaying ability, the spirit of mutual help and co-operation and self-sacrifice.
>
> The failings were also evident in those who were too full of their petty rivalries and jealousies to co-operate together, those who remained passive and did nothing to help others, and those few who were so denationalized and dehumanized as to care little for what was happening.

The official British inquiry into the Bengal famine concluded that society, including the British administration, 'failed to protect its weaker members. Indeed there was a moral and social breakdown, as well as administrative breakdowns'. The inquiry stated that it had been within the power of the Government of Bengal 'by bold, resolute and well-conceived measures at the right time, to have largely prevented the tragedy of the famine as it actually took place'.

Quoting this verdict, Nehru reflected that 'the tragedy of Bengal and the famines of Orissa, Malabar, and other places, are the final judgement on British rule in India. The British will certainly leave India, and their Indian Empire will become a memory, but what will they leave when they have to go, what human degradation and accumulated sorrow?' Nehru went on to quote from Rabindranath Tagore, who 'saw this picture as he lay dying', and had asked: 'But what kind of India will they leave behind, what stark misery? When the stream of their centuries' administration runs dry at last, what a waste of mud and filth they will leave behind them!'

German forces entered Rome on September 8. Escaping to the southern port of Brindisi, King Victor Emmanuel and Marshal Badoglio set up an Italian anti-Fascist government. Throughout the regions where Italian officers and men had been fighting alongside the Germans as their Allies, they were ordered by the Germans to disarm, and where they refused to do so, were subjected to ferocious cruelties.

On the Greek island of Cephalonia, 1,646 Italian soldiers were killed by their former comrades-in-arms. In Albania, a British officer, Major David Smiley, who was with the local partisans behind German lines, noted in his diary on November 5 of the mass grave of sixty-five Italian officers 'brutally murdered by the Huns'. The villagers who had been made to bury them said: 'Their hands had been tied and they had been machine-gunned and bayoneted to death.'

In army camps throughout Russia and German-occupied Poland similar killings took place. In the woods at Borki, just outside the Polish city of Chelm, several hundred Italian soldiers were executed by the Germans. Today, a memorial deep in the wood pays silent testimony to their fate. Other Italian soldiers were taken by ship through the Aegean and the Adriatic as prisoners-of-war to Germany. The Allies, unaware of the nature of the human cargo, bombed the ships, and three thousand Italians were drowned. More than a hundred thousand other Italian soldiers were deported to labour camps in Germany.

Italian warships, leaving the ports of La Spezia and Genoa to join the Anglo-American fleets in North Africa – warships that until a few days earlier had been the target for Allied bombers – were bombed instead by the very German aircraft that had hitherto protected them. The battleship *Roma* was sunk and 1,552 of its crewmen drowned.

Faced with the need to take over so much Italian territory, on September 11 Hitler decided that even with his policy of standing firm on every line, he did not have the resources to hold Corsica. All 27,347 German troops on the island were evacuated. The Allies gained back the first French sovereign territory in the Mediterranean region, a fact of considerable psychological impact for the Free French forces eager to participate in the liberation of France.

In Italy, the Allies were advancing rapidly northward. The Germans had not been able to bring enough troops into Italy in time to halt the advance. The German troops on Capri surrendered on September 12: among the Anglo-American force that captured them was a United States naval lieutenant who was also one of Hollywood's best known actor film stars, Douglas Fairbanks Jr.*

*   *   *

* Just over a month later, far from the battlefield, history was made in the United States when another actor, Paul Robeson, opened on Broadway – on October 19 – in the title role of Shakespeare's *Othello*. He was the first Black actor to play the role with a White supporting cast, and did so to ecstatic reviews.

Details of German destruction behind the lines on the Eastern Front were widely publicized by the Russians, and widely circulated in the Allied newspapers. On September 14 an American officer serving in the Pacific made a private note of 'German atrocities', in which he referred to the complete destruction of Tolstoy's village – Yasnaya Polana – the desecration of churches, and the massacre of civilians. His conclusion was terse: 'Attempt to put Russia back in Dark Age.' That officer was Richard Nixon, later the thirty-seventh President of the United States.

The German army was being pressed back by Soviet forces whose Commander-in-Chief, Stalin, was prepared to accept high casualties. His armies were also inflicting high casualties: that September the German military death toll on the Eastern Front reached more than half a million men. On September 14 – the day of Nixon's note about German atrocities – Hitler agreed to a substantial military withdrawal. 'It is a curious thing,' Goebbels wrote in his diary six days later, 'that although every individual soldier returning from the Eastern Front considers himself personally superior to the Bolshevik soldier, we are still retreating and retreating.'

Hitler's racial policy – of which Goebbels was a firm supporter – continued unimpeded by the reverses of war. Indeed, those reverses were turned to good effect by those for whom the destruction of European Jewry was the priority. Having occupied northern Italy, the full powers of the SS were used to deport the Italian Jews who, throughout the previous year, Mussolini had refused to send to Germany. The first to be deported were twenty-four Jews from Merano. They were sent direct to Auschwitz by train. One of those who was murdered on arrival at the camp was a six-year-old boy.

Following the Italian surrender, Hitler also made plans to 'liberate' Mussolini. From the island of La Maddalena he had been moved again, for the third time, in the hope of keeping his whereabouts secret. Italian army officers loyal to King Victor Emmanuel were holding him captive in a ski resort hotel on the 9,000-foot Gran Sasso d'Italia, in the Abruzzi mountains. On September 12, in a daring raid by ninety German soldiers using gliders and a small plane, the German commando leader, SS Colonel Otto Skorzeny, landed on the mountain, outwitted the 250-strong Italian garrison – not one of whom fired a shot – and flew off with Mussolini to a small airstrip near Rome.

From Rome, Mussolini was flown, first to Vienna, then to Munich, and finally, exhausted and bewildered by both the rescue and the journey, to Hitler's headquarters at Rastenburg in East Prussia. Hitler then established the former Italian dictator as ruler of a small puppet administration in northern Italy: the Italian Social Republic, known as the Republic of Salo.

In southern Italy, Allied troops were advancing on Naples. On the Eastern Front the Germans fell back behind the River Dnieper, which they had crossed in triumph two years earlier. In Denmark, the SS were cheated of a prize they had long coveted – Denmark's 7,000 Jews. On the night of September 29, twenty-four hours before the intended deportation, Danish fishermen worked through the night to smuggle almost all the potential victims across the narrow water to the safety of neutral Sweden. Among those who were saved was Niels Bohr, the atomic scientist, who was to put his expertise at the disposal of the Americans.

In newly-occupied Athens, the Gestapo also hunted for Jews to deport to Auschwitz. As in Denmark, however, they were cheated of most of their prize that September by the Athenian people. A Greek underground newspaper called on the population to offer asylum to the Jews of Athens: 3,000 were given shelter. Princess Andrew of Greece, a great-granddaughter of Queen Victoria – and the mother of Prince Philip of Greece, later the husband of the British Queen Elizabeth II – was one of those who took in a Jewish family and hid them from the eyes of the Gestapo until the end of the war.

The killing at Auschwitz went on, not only of those who were deported to the camp and were taken straight to their deaths, but from among those who had earlier been taken to the barracks as slave labourers. On October 3, during a regular inspection of the barracks, 139 Jewish forced labourers were judged by an SS doctor to be too sick to work any further. They were taken away and gassed. Speaking in Poznan on the following day, Himmler told a gathering of SS group leaders, many of whose Special Task Force squads had, in the previous two years, been at the centre of the mass murder of as many as two million Jews in western Russia:

> Most of you know what it means to see a hundred corpses lying together, five hundred, or a thousand. To have stuck it out – and at the same time – apart from exceptions caused by human weakness – to have remained decent fellows, that is what has made us hard.
>
> This is the page of glory in our history which has never been written and shall never be written.
>
> We have fulfilled this most difficult duty for the love of our people. And our spirit, our soul, our character has not suffered injury from it.

In his speech at Poznan, Himmler did not limit his reflections and exhortations to the mass murder of Jews. He also spoke of other civilian victims of the SS. 'What happens to the Russians, what happens to the Czechs is a matter of utter indifference to me', he said. 'Such good blood of our own kind as there may be among the nations we shall acquire for ourselves, if necessary by taking away the children and bringing them up among us. Whether the other people live in comfort or perish of hunger interests me only in so far as we need them as slaves for our *Kultur*. Whether or not 10,000 Russian women collapse from exhaustion while digging a tank ditch interests me only in so far as the tank ditch is completed for Germany.'

Himmler also spoke about decency, telling the SS killing squad leaders: 'We shall never be rough or heartless where it is not necessary; that is clear. We Germans, who are the only people in the world who have a decent attitude to animals, will also adopt a decent attitude to these human animals, but it is a crime against our own blood to worry about them.'

On the day after Himmler's speech, 1,260 Jewish children, who had earlier been sent by train from the ghetto in Bialystok to the ghetto in Theresienstadt, were ordered to embark once more on a railway journey. Volunteer doctors and nurses were called for from among the German, Austrian and Czech Jews of Theresienstadt to accompany them. In order to encourage these volunteers, the Germans announced the destination of the children as Palestine, or possibly Switzerland. Fifty-three volunteers came forward. The train set off, not south to Palestine, or west to Switzerland, but eastward.

On October 6, Himmler once more addressed the senior SS men gathered at Poznan. Once again, he spoke of the mass murder of the Jews, telling his listeners: 'Then the question arose, what about the women and children?' I decided to find a perfectly clear-cut solution to this too. For I did not feel justified in exterminating the men – that is, to kill them, or have them killed – while allowing the avengers, in the form of their children, to grow up in the midst of our sons and grandsons.'

On the day of this second speech, the train with the 1,260 orphans from Bialystok and their guardians reached Auschwitz. Every one of them, orphans and guardians alike, was taken away and gassed. The future 'avengers' had been destroyed.

It was the vengeance of the Germans themselves that was felt with particular severity that autumn. After each act of sabotage by resistance or partisan forces in every land under occupation, mass executions were the response of the occupier. Thousands of Greek civilians were killed in German reprisal actions as the Greeks sought to resist the new conquerors, whose severity so exceeded that of their Italian predecessors. Behind the ever-contracting German lines in Russia, further anti-partisan sweeps led to the deaths of thousands more Russian villagers, and the burning down of whole villages. Polish acts of resistance – which Goebbels noted in his diary on September 17 had 'increased enormously' – were met by executions and reprisals.

In France, following the execution by French Resistance fighters on September 27 of the German official responsible for rounding up and arresting Frenchmen for forced labour, fifty Parisians were seized, held for a few days as hostages, and then shot. In Italy as a reprisal for the capture of two German soldiers by Italian partisans in the village of Boves, thirty Italian civilians were shot on October 7. That same day, on the other side of the globe, ninety-six Allied prisoners-of-war being held by the Japanese on Wake Island were made to sit down on the beach in one long line with their backs to the sea. They were then blindfolded and, with their hands tied behind their backs, shot dead.

In the North Borneo capital of Jesselton, local Chinese and the native Suluk people rose in revolt against Japanese rule and tyranny. There was fighting, and forty Japanese were killed. Reprisals were swift. On one occasion 189 suspects were rounded up and then executed. On another occasion several dozen Suluk women and children, their hands tied behind their backs, were attached by a rope to the pillars of a mosque. A machine-gun was then set up in front of them, and fired at them until they were all dead.

The Japanese had cause for celebration in October: the completion, on the 25th, of the Burma-Thailand railway. Of the 46,000 Allied prisoners-of-war who had been forced to work on its construction, 16,000 had died of starvation, disease, gross neglect and brutality. Also dying on the 'Railroad of Death' were more than 50,000 Burmese forced labourers. Their Japanese taskmasters had shown no respect for their race or fate. The Burmese were as much slaves of the Japanese as were the soldiers of those who had once been their colonial rulers.

In Poland, the defiance of those under German occupation was continually finding new means of showing itself. October saw the twenty-fifth anniversary of the expulsion of the Germans from Warsaw in 1918, the essential prelude to the establishment of an independent Poland. That month slogans were painted up on walls in Warsaw with the single word: 'Oktober'. The aim, a member of the resistance commented, was to remind the occupiers 'that history sometimes repeats itself'. On other walls, Warsaw citizens painted the words: *Polska Zwyciezy!*: 'Poland will win!' and *Deutschland caput*: 'Germany is finished'.

As an occupier and a tyrant, 'Germany' was far from finished. The coming of sunset on October 8 marked the start of the most holy day in the Jewish calendar, *Yom Kippur* – the Day of Atonement – a day of prayer and fasting. That day the SS doctors carried out a special 'Yom Kippur' selection in the barracks at Auschwitz and in the camp infirmary. Several thousand Jews were picked out and sent to their deaths. Three days later it was the Poles at Auschwitz who were selected for a mass execution. The fifty-four Polish prisoners who were taken out of their punishment bunkers that day, having been horribly tortured for more than two weeks, were military men, politicians and public figures of distinction in pre-war Poland. They were all taken to the execution wall and shot.

Those who were incarcerated in camps, facing death at any time, followed as best they could the news of the war, usually through the occasional lapse of their guards when talking amongst themselves. When, on October 13, the government of Italy, based at Brindisi, declared war on Germany, it was a red letter day in German-occupied Europe. Germany had lost its former Axis ally and partner. Italian soldiers would henceforth join in the battle to defeat Germany. The Allies also offered a long-term beacon of hope to the captive peoples of both Europe and Asia. On October 20 a United Nations War Crimes Commission was set up, committed to bring to trial all those responsible for war crimes. It was hoped that the mere fact that such a commission existed would deter the perpetrators of those crimes. But the executions, reprisals, deportations and gassings continued, sometimes even on an accelerated scale, as the Germans saw their areas of military control growing smaller, their enemies becoming bolder, and their racial policy uncompleted.

That racial policy was also being foiled by the sympathy of local populations, churches and whole regions. When the SS seized more than a thousand of Rome's Jews for deportation to Auschwitz, many more – an estimated four thousand – were given shelter in private homes, monasteries and convents; 477 of them were taken in by the Vatican. In Milan, 600 Jews were seized and deported by train to Auschwitz, but more than six thousand were given shelter in Christian homes and survived.

One of the worst civilian massacres of the war took place at the beginning of November. The Germans gave it the codename 'Harvest Festival'. Jews from the camps and ghettos of the Lublin region of Poland were brought to the concentration camp at Majdanek, a suburb of Lublin, and murdered. During a single day of killing, November 3, an estimated 18,400 Jews were shot down. The killings continued for another day, while a further 20,000 Jews were killed in two nearby camps, Trawniki and Poniatowa. Many of those killed were survivors of the Warsaw ghetto revolt.

The perpetrators of the Harvest Festival killings continued to be tracked down and brought to trial over many years. Fifty-five years after the killings, a German State Prosecutor ordered the arrest – in Stuttgart on 3 March 1998 – of Alfons Goetzfried, charged with personally shooting five hundred people in Majdanek during the two days November 3 and 4.

While Nazi tyranny, racism and reprisals brought death to every corner of German-occupied Europe, the armies of the Allies were slowly and steadily pushing back the borders of German rule. In a nine day period in mid-October, nine thousand German soldiers were killed on the Eastern Front. On November 2 Goebbels noted in his diary: 'We cannot sustain the drain much longer. We are in danger of slowly bleeding to death in the East.'

Four days later the Red Army entered Kiev, the capital of the Ukraine, one of the mother cities of Russia, and the centre of a major road and rail communications network. Two days later, in understandable elation, the Red Army created two new medals. One was the Order of Victory, to be awarded to senior commanders who had carried out military operations that had resulted 'in a radical change of the situation to the enemy's disadvantage'. The other, to be awarded to lower ranks and also air force lieutenants, was the Order of Glory, for individual deeds of personal valour. The recipients of both orders would have the right to a pension for life, and to free education for their children.

The Russians were advancing westward so fast that in early November they overran part of the 'Panther' defence line which Hitler had set up two months earlier. On November 9 the Russians reached Zhitomir, eighty miles beyond the Panther Line, and only seventy-five miles from the pre-war Polish-Soviet frontier. That week, 20,000 German soldiers were killed in action on the Eastern Front. In despair, Goebbels wrote in his diary: 'Where will it ever end! The Soviets have reserves of which we never dreamed even in our most pessimistic estimates.' Hitler was being driven out of Russia with almost the same speed which Napoleon had been 131 years earlier.

The Japanese were facing a similar bloodletting in the Pacific. Just as the

German soldiers were being ordered to fight – and to die – rather than pull back to safer lines, so the Japanese soldiers refused to give themselves up, preferring suicide, often mass suicide. When more than six thousand Americans landed on Makin Island on November 20, only three hundred Japanese soldiers were on the island. Instead of surrendering, they fought to the last man. On Tarawa Atoll five thousand Japanese met the same fate after a seventy-six-hour battle, during which a thousand Americans were killed, and only one Japanese officer and sixteen men were still alive. The rest had been killed in the fighting or had committed suicide to avoid capture.

With every island captured, the ability of the Americans to bomb closer and closer to Japan, and more and more effectively, was increased. When American bombers attacked an airfield on Formosa on November 25, all forty-two Japanese aircraft at the airfield were destroyed, some in the air, others on the ground. But at every stage of the growing United States successes, there were tragedies which the American soldiers, sailors and airmen who witnessed them were never to forget. Writing his memoirs forty-five years later, Richard Nixon recalled the return to its base on a Pacific island of a badly damaged B-29 bomber. 'It was dusk, almost dark, and we all cheered as the plane came in on its belly,' he wrote. 'Then we watched in horror as it crashed head-on into a bulldozer and exploded. The carnage was terrible. I can still see the wedding ring on the charred hand of one of the crewmen when I carried his body from the twisted wreckage.'

While the Americans intensified their bombing of Japanese airfields, the British renewed the heavy air raids on Berlin. On November 22 Hitler's Chancellery and much of his special train were damaged during a raid by 764 bombers. Damage was also caused to the Admiralty, the Air Ministry and the Ministry of Armaments and War Production. Severe damage was caused to the Berlin Zoo, to much of the Unter den Linden, to the deserted British Embassy in the Wilhelmstrasse, and to the Japanese and Italian Embassies in the Tiergartenstrasse, as well as to the *Kaiser-Wilhelm-Gedächtniskirche* – the Kaiser Wilhelm Memorial Church – which has been kept a ruin to this day as a memorial.

It was the largest British bombing raid on Berlin thus far. Three thousand homes and twenty-three industrial premises were completely destroyed. Five hundred Berliners were killed when a large shelter in Wilmersdorf received a direct hit. In another shelter next to the Neuköln gasworks more than a hundred people were killed when there was a massive explosion. Other suburbs also suffered extensive damage. 'My mother and my mother-in-law were bombed out completely in Moabit,' Goebbels wrote in his diary: 'Their homes have simply vanished. The house in which they lived was transformed into one vast shambles. But what is that at a time of universal misfortune which has now fallen on this city of four and a half millions!' In all, about 2,000 Berliners were killed that night. In the skies above the city and on the approaches to it 167 British aircrew were shot down and killed.

More raids on Berlin followed in quick succession. On the night of November 23/24 Berlin was covered in cloud, but the crews aimed their bombs through the cloud at the glow of the eleven major fires that were still burning from the previous night. Both the State Playhouse and the Reichstag building were set on fire. The area around the Potsdamer Platz was completely destroyed.* Goebbels's official residence was hit and its upper rooms destroyed, and Hitler's private apartments at the Chancellery were damaged. Goebbels wrote in his diary: 'Hell itself seems to have broken loose over us. Mines and explosive bombs keep hurtling down on the government quarter. One after another of the important buildings begins to burn.' On going to look at the damage, Goebbels found, among the buildings still burning, his own Propaganda Ministry.

More than 1,300 people were killed in Berlin that night. Again the loss to the British and Canadian aircrews was high: 196 were shot down and killed. Two nights later there was a third raid on Berlin in four days. Thirty-four war industry factories were destroyed, as were the main workshops of the Allkett tank factory, one of the most important in Germany. Part of a factory making radar sets was also destroyed. More than seven hundred people were killed in Berlin that night, including 157 foreign workers and twenty-six Allied prisoners-of-war. Almost a hundred deaths were caused when a bomber that had been shot down crashed on a building and destroyed the building's air raid shelter.

Many senior German Army officers were becoming appalled by the continual retreats and heavy losses. After consultation with the military conspirators who had already failed twice to kill Hitler, Baron Axel von dem Bussche, who was serving on the Eastern Front, undertook to be the 'model' for a new type of army greatcoat that Hitler wished to see. With a third winter of the war in the East about to bring severe privations to his men, Hitler

---

* It was this area around the Potsdamer Platz that became, from 1994, the centre of the massive rebuilding of central and east Berlin. In 1998 it was being called 'the largest building site in Europe'.

had reason to see if a warmer, sturdier coat could be designed. Von dem Bussche proposed putting a bomb in one of the pockets. He would then detonate it while Hitler was inspecting the coat, killing them both.

Unfortunately for the conspirators, the demonstration dates were repeatedly postponed, and then, by a bizarre mischance, all the prototypes of the coat were destroyed in one of the November British bombing raids on Berlin. Meanwhile, von dem Bussche had returned to the Eastern Front, where he was severely wounded.

While Berlin burned, the Russians reached Gomel, four hundred miles from Hitler's headquarters at Rastenburg. They were within striking distance of East Prussia. In ten days, more than six thousand German soldiers had been killed in action. 'That is bearable,' Goebbels wrote in his diary. 'On the other hand, sickness has increased, and, above all, the troops' morale has sunk, physically and spiritually, because of our continuous retreat.'

On November 29 Stalin, Churchill and Roosevelt – the Big Three – met at Teheran, the Persian capital. Speaking of the post-war frontiers of Europe, Stalin told Churchill and Roosevelt that 'the Russians did not want anything belonging to other people, although they might have a bite at Germany'. As to the Poles, Stalin assured the other two leaders, they 'could not be extirpated'. The Soviet Union would re-acquire the eastern third of Poland that had been taken by the Poles at the time of the Treaty of Riga in 1921 – and subsequently transferred to the Soviet Union under the Nazi-Soviet Pact of 1939. Poland would be given a large swathe of east German territory in compensation, including the industrial region of Upper Silesia. Stalin also promised that the Soviet Union would enter the war against Japan 'the moment' that Germany was defeated. For Churchill and Roosevelt, this was a crucial pledge.

During their talks at Teheran, Churchill explained to Stalin that the launching of the cross-Channel landings would depend upon a 'satisfactory reduction' of German fighter and military strength in north-west Europe during the coming six months. When Stalin asked if this meant that Churchill and the British Chiefs of Staff did not really believe in the operation, Churchill replied that if the conditions were met 'it will be our stern duty to hurl across the Channel against the Germans every sinew of our strength.' Meanwhile, Churchill assured Stalin, the British bombing of Germany, and in particular of Berlin, would continue.

In a raid on Berlin on December 2, when munitions factories were the target, 228 British airmen were shot down and killed; 150 Berliners also died. On the following night factories in Leipzig were the target, but many of the bombs fell wide. In his diary Goebbels recorded the damage: 'The centre of the city was especially hard hit. Almost all public buildings, theatres, the university, the Supreme Court, exhibitions halls etc., have either been completely destroyed or seriously damaged.'

Berlin was again the target on December 16, when railway stations and marshalling yards were the main focus of the attack. Air crew losses were again high, with 294 British and Canadians being shot down and killed. Among the dead on the ground were 438 Berliners and 279 foreign labourers, mostly Poles and Ukrainians. Another raid on Berlin took place on Christmas Eve, when 178 Berliners and 104 aircrew were killed. It was a relentless toll.

To the American people, whose soldier sons, fathers, fiancés and friends were fighting that winter in southern Italy and in the Pacific, Roosevelt gave a warning in a broadcast on Christmas Eve. 'The war is now reaching the stage when we shall all have to look forward to large casualty lists – dead, wounded and missing. War entails just that. There is no easy road to victory. And the end is not yet in sight.'

Before the year even came to an end, more Americans – and even more Japanese – died when American troops landed on the Japanese-held island of New Britain. Other Americans were battling against the Germans in Italy for control of Cassino, but the Germans could not be driven back. At sea, where the Germans had already lost the battleship *Tirpitz*, badly disabled in September by three British midget submarines while in a Norwegian fjord, further disaster struck on the Sunday night after Christmas when British warships confronted the battlecruiser *Scharnhorst*.

The launching of the *Scharnhorst* in 1936 had been a proud moment in Hitler's rearmament of Germany. The ship's location had been betrayed by her own top secret radio signals, listened to and decrypted in Britain. For several months the British Admiral, Sir Bruce Fraser, had practised for just such a night action in foul weather, involving the close coordination of numerous naval forces, as well as the protection of two convoys being used as bait. The *Scharnhorst*, illuminated by star shell, was sunk and two thousand German sailors drowned.

As 1943 came to an end, civilians all over Europe continued to be as much the casualties of war as soldiers. More than six thousand Italian civilians had been killed in the first three months during which Italy was the battleground between Germany and the Western Allies. Another group of victims were the Soviet soldiers captured by the Germans. The sites of their mass murder can be visited today in many dozens of remote locations in Poland.*

The fate of these Soviet prisoners of war – the total number murdered was in excess of three million – is one of the least written about aspects of the Second World War. The monuments to their fate are also among the least visited. In the last decade of the Twentieth Century many Jews make a journey of memorial and reflection to the death camp at Treblinka. Most go by bus or car from Warsaw. On this relatively short journey – a drive of two hours – with its own solemn purpose for them, they pass through several towns and villages from which many thousands of Jews were taken to their deaths at Treblinka. They also pass the Wyszkow Forest where Jewish partisans fought and fell, and the dense wood of the Puscsza Biala, where Polish partisans likewise struggled against the occupier. Then, at the small town of Ostrow Mazowiecka, where they turn off to Treblinka, they are within one mile of the site of a camp in which 13,000 Soviet prisoners-of-war were murdered. If they wish, they can also make a short detour of a few miles to Komorowo, one of the largest of the camps in which captured Soviet soldiers were confined during the war years. When the remains of those who had perished there were exhumed after the war from the mass graves, 41,592 bodies were counted.

Just over a hundred miles to the south of Komorowo is the Polish village of Karpiowka. There, on the last day of 1943, as a reprisal for the participation of some of the villagers in acts of sabotage, fifty-nine old men, women and young children were rounded up and taken to a granary on the edge of the village. The granary was then set on fire and all fifty-nine were burned alive. This site too is indicated today with a memorial marker.

The terrors of war had intensified; so too had the determination of the Allies to destroy the Axis. The concept of unconditional surrender, to which Churchill, Roosevelt and Stalin had formally committed themselves, was about to be given its operational thrust. In Britain and the United States, amid intense preparations and the accumulation of a vast armoury of tanks,

---

* Among the mass murder sites in Poland of Soviet prisoners-of-war are Bukowka (10,000 murdered), Blizyn (10,000), Swiety Krzyz (12,000), Barycz (7,000), Skrodow (7,000), Krzyzwolka (46,000), Zambrow (12,000), Guty (24,000), Ostrow Mazowiecka (13,000), Komorowo (41,592) and Tonkiele (10,000). Tonkiele was one of the first points of attack of the German army into Russia in June 1941.

artillery, vehicles and weaponry, 1,600,000 American soldiers, sailors and airmen were poised to participate in the invasion and liberation of northern Europe. A further 1,800,000 Americans were already in action against Japan, intent on continuing the island by island advance across the Pacific, until the Philippines had been wrested from Japanese control, and the Japanese Home Islands themselves overrun.

Millions of Soviet troops, British and Commonwealth troops, the armies-in-exile of all the conquered lands, the navies and air forces of a dozen nations, were likewise poised to renew the attacks which had already begun seriously to weaken the German and Japanese war power. But in Berlin and Tokyo, those who had the authority to demand that waging of war continued unabated had no intention of bowing to the inevitability of defeat, or even to accepting its inevitability. The war would be fought to the finish, in every town and village, in every region, on every sea, in every city, river by river, road by road and street by street.

Fuelling the German warmaking capacity were four neutral States: Portugal, Spain, Sweden and Turkey, each of which accepted gold bullion from Germany – some of it revealed many years later to have included dental gold taken from the teeth of those murdered by the Nazis – and to accept that gold in return for crucial armaments. Portugal and Spain provided almost all the wolfram needed for steel alloys used in armour-piercing shells. Sweden exported more than 90 per cent of the iron ore needed by Germany for weaponry and ball bearings. Turkey provided Germany with most of the chromate needed for hardening the steel used for shells, tanks, aircraft and U-boats. There were only five to six months' stockpile of chromate in Germany, Albert Speer told Hitler in November. 'Almost the entire gamut of artillery would have to cease from one to three months after this deadline,' he warned, 'since by then the reserves and distribution channels would be used up'.

But the neutrals continued to supply Germany with many of its essential warmaking needs: for which Germany paid in gold.

CHAPTER FIFTEEN

1944
JANUARY TO JUNE

The air power was the weapon which both the
marauding States selected as their main tool of
conquest. This was the sphere in which they were to
triumph. This was the method by which the nations
were to be subjugated to their rule. I shall not
moralize further than to say that there is a strange,
stern justice in the long swing of events.

WINSTON S. CHURCHILL

IN THE ENORMOUS SWATHE OF LAND that had been under Japanese
occupation for almost two years, native uprisings gained momentum. In the
Philippines an American mining engineer, Wendell Fertig, led a force of
several thousand Filipinos. In Burma, an Englishman, Hugh Seagrim, organized a guerrilla force of two thousand Karens. So savage were the Japanese
reprisals on Karen villagers that Seagrim gave himself up to spare them
further executions. Seagrim was executed. The Karen revolt continued.

In New Guinea, many thousands of Japanese soldiers and civilians were
retreating continuously, on a two-hundred-mile march through the jungle,
from Lae to Madang, in an attempt to escape the American and Australian
troops advancing towards them. During the march, ten thousand men and
women perished. One place of refuge that was denied them was the port of
Saidor. In an American seaborne landing there on January 2, fifty-five Americans were killed capturing the port, for the loss of more than a thousand
Japanese lives.

It was information filtering out of South-East Asia about Japanese atrocities against Allied civilians and prisoners-of-war that intensified the hatreds which had been growing steadily since the fall of Manila, Hong Kong and Singapore two years earlier. On January 30 the British Member of Parliament and satirist A.P. Herbert, recalling the worldwide sympathy for Japan after the Yokohama earthquake in 1923, published a poem entitled *This is Bushido* – the Japanese warrior code – which expressed the pent-up anger:

> This is Bushido. These are they
> Who show the West a nobler way.
> Do you remember, long ago,
> When earthquakes crumbled Tokyo?
> We passed the plate, we filled our caps
> With hard-won pennies for the Japs.
>
> This is Bushido. This is how
> Our children are rewarded now.
> When God again afflicts Japan
> Let her not look to mortal man;
> And God bless those who mean to make
> The whole of that vile island quake.

In the war of armies and front lines it was the Soviet-German struggle that became the first to swing violently against the Axis when, on January 2, the Soviet army, advancing along a two-hundred-mile front westward through the Ukraine, reached to within a few miles of the pre-war Polish border.

In Western Europe two days later a sustained Anglo-American air drop of munitions and supplies was inaugurated to help resistance groups in France, Belgium, Holland and Italy. In Italy itself, the few remaining supporters of Mussolini and his German-dominated Republic of Salo exercised terror to try to impose their will. Even Mussolini's son-in-law Galeazzo Ciano, the Italian signatory of the Pact of Steel with Germany – who had been handed over to a Fascist court in northern Italy and sentenced to death for treason – was shot. Four other former Fascist leaders were executed with him, including an Italian war hero, Marshal de Bono.

In Denmark, a series of executions were carried out by a special German squad whose task was to create docility through terror. Among the first people to be executed – on January 4 – was the clergyman and poet, Kaj

Munk. Far from deterring further resistance, Munk's death only served to stimulate it: his funeral procession became a demonstration of Danish defiance. The executions continued. In France a similar policy of swift, indiscriminate and bloody reprisals was in operation. Five days after the execution of Munk in Denmark, twenty-two Frenchmen who were being held as hostages in prison in Lyon were shot dead as a reprisal for the death of two German soldiers.

Among those in Lyon at that time was Victor Basch. He was eighty-four years old. A Jew born in Hungary, he had lived for many years in France, having been National President of the League for the Rights of Man since 1926. Basch had defined the League's goals as 'the defence of human rights and the promotion of self-determination, peace, democracy, and the rights of women and children'. During the era of the Popular Front he had been an advocate of the intervention of the democracies in the Spanish Civil War. On the night after the prison executions in Lyon the German Gestapo and French Milice, acting together, arrested him and his seventy-nine-year-old wife Hilona. They were shot a day later.

The Red Army crossed into Poland on January 6, and advanced six miles inside the inter-war border. Stalin not only celebrated the military achievement this represented, but understood that he could obtain political advantage from it. Five days earlier he had established a Communist-controlled Polish National Council, which was to be the 'supreme organ of democratic elements' in Poland. The London Poles, including many members of the pre-war Polish government, were to be by-passed. Communism would come to Poland behind the tank tracks of the Red Army. Even as the London Poles continued to encourage resistance inside Poland with their Armia Krajowa (the National Army), the Polish National Council promoted a rival anti-German movement, the Armia Ludowa (the People's Army). Both were supplied with arms and help by their respective patrons in London and Moscow. Both fought tenaciously against the Germans and suffered massively in German reprisals. Both had regions within Poland in which they were especially active and could count on local support. Both saw a struggle ahead for the mastery of post-war Poland, and fought each other.

In London, Churchill recognized that the Soviet involvement in Poland marked the beginning of a new era, one that Roosevelt had hinted at earlier, and subsequently known as the Cold War. Even as the 'hot' war was still

8. Moscow: the Soviet Foreign Minister, Molotov, and Stalin, watch as von Ribbentrop signs the Nazi-oviet Pact, August 1939.

20. A German fighter plane shot down over Britain.

19. Esbjerg, Denmark, September 1939: the aftermath of a British bomb dropped in error. One Danish woman was killed.

21. Norwegian sharpshooters in the snow, April 1940.

22. Dunkirk, May-June 1940: British soldiers awaiting evacuation defend themselves against German planes.

23. Coventry, November 1940: A firestorm caused by a German air raid the night before is still blazing.

24. Inside the Soviet Union, two German soldiers clear the way for their car stuck in the Russian mud.

25. Dead German soldiers in the snow.

26. Thrace, March 1943: five hundred Jews are deported in cattle trucks to a death camp in German-occupied Poland, several thousand miles to the north.

27. Sant'Agata, Sicily, August 1943: three Sicilians watch as a US medical soldier gives blood plasma to a wounded American, half a mile behind the front line.

28. Japanese kamikaze pilots ready for action.

29. *(below)* A kamikaze pilot tries to manoeuvre his plane onto the deck of an American warship.

30. *(above)* Industrial Tokyo after an Allied saturation raid in September 1945.

31. *(left)* Emperor Hirohito surveys the damage to his capital, October 1945.

32. The 'Big Three' at Potsdam, August 1945: (front row) Attlee, Truman and Stalin (back row) Admiral Leahy and the three Foreign Ministers, Britain's Bevin, America's Byrnes and Russia's Molotov. Following the Conservative defeat at the June General Election, Churchill and Eden were replaced by Attlee and Bevin in the middle of the conference.

33. Hiroshima after the bomb, August 1945.

being fought, this new spectre was visible to those who had control of the Allied destinies. At the beginning of February Churchill told his senior military advisers: 'Now that the Russians were advancing into Poland, it was in our interest that Poland should be strong and well-supported. Were she weak, and overrun by the advancing Soviet armies, the result might be great dangers in the future for the English-speaking peoples.'

A similar struggle between the forces of Communism and anti-Communism – between future national independence and Soviet hegemony – was taking place inside Yugoslavia, where two resistance groups, one headed by Mihailovic and the other by Tito, competed for support from the Allies and struggled to drive the Germans out of areas in which they then established their respective political control. On January 15 the Germans launched their sixth military offensive against Tito's partisans in just over three years, driving them from their headquarters at Jajce. But Tito, to whom the British, the Americans and the Russians were sending weapons, ammunition and advisers, moved the centre of his operations forty miles, to Drvar, and continued to fight over an ever-widening area.

In Greece, partisan activity had also increased considerably, as German rule was imposed with severity. On January 18 a German intelligence officer, Austrian-born (and later Austrian President) Kurt Waldheim, sent his superiors his estimate of the number of Greek partisans active in northern Greece. There were, he reported, as many as 25,000 of them, and he pointed out that they were being helped by some four thousand Italian soldiers. The German authorities reacted to this partisan activity with repeated anti-partisan sweeps, executions, and the murder of villagers suspected of supporting the partisans. On April 23 a member of the Greek Resistance, Anastasia Siouli, a schoolteacher in the village of Katranitsa, was captured during a German raid and executed the following day together with six men. On May 1 two hundred Greek hostages were shot in Athens.

With regard to Greek villagers, as with all civilian victims, merely to list the numbers of those executed in each location is to provide a testimony to the depravity of human behaviour in the Twentieth Century. On May 5, as a reprisal for partisan activity in Greek Macedonia, 215 villagers were shot in the village of Klisura, including fifty children under ten years old. On May 10 more than 270 villagers were murdered in their homes in the Attica village of Distomon by a Waffen-SS unit that entered the village in search of guerrillas. When a Red Cross team arrived in Distomon from Athens two days later it found bodies hanging from the trees that lined the road into the village. On May 17 a hundred hostages were shot in Khalkis, on the island of Euboia.*

The search for the few Jews who had managed to find hiding places during the round ups and deportations of 1942 and 1943 was also a feature of the early months of 1944. On January 18 a sweep was carried out in the Buczacz area of Eastern Galicia, in which the German SS troops used tanks and aircraft to search out those in hiding – some hidden with farmers, others in isolated barns and even ditches. They had been in hiding for nine months, since the deportation of almost 3,000 Jews from Buczacz to their deaths in Belzec at the end of 1942 and the murder of 4,000 during 1943 in the surrounding fields. For those in hiding, the winter of 1943–44 had been a time of incredible hardship and harshness. In all, three hundred were discovered, including many young children. All were killed. In the search for hidden Jews – even for this last remnant of the Jews of central and eastern Europe – no mercy was shown, nor any human decency.

On January 22 – as the Anglo-American bombing of German cities and factories continued, and a day after a factory in Berlin making radar components for the German Air Force was put out of action – an Anglo-French army was put ashore at Anzio, half way between the Allied front line in Italy and German-held Rome. Within twenty-four hours more than 36,000 Allied troops were ashore for the loss of only thirteen of the attacking force. But when the American commander, General Lucas, decided to dig in rather than advance – the same decision that had been made by the British commanders at Suvla Bay on the Gallipoli peninsula in 1915 – the Germans took full advantage of the lull, and counter-attacked in force. The bridgehead was pushed back, and the Germans were besieging the men who were meant to be a strike force linking up with the Allied line further south and then pushing on to Rome.

To try to prevent an Allied breakthrough from Anzio, and to hold the front line further south, Hitler decided to move troops to Italy from the Eastern Front. He had also to move troops from the Eastern Front to the Balkans, where Yugoslav partisan activity was threatening to liberate

---

* Among other reprisal actions that took place was one at Pogonion, where 325 villagers were killed, and one at Kastelli (on Crete), when two hundred were shot. In his book *Inside Hitler's Greece: The Experience of Occupation, 1941–44*, Mark Mazower gives many poignant examples of the German reprisal policy in Greece.

large areas and cut off the German forces in Greece and the Aegean. In all, thirty-five German divisions were moved: they had been badly needed in the East to prevent further Russian inroads into Poland.

The rise of resistance in German-occupied Europe had created a third war front. On January 27 Hitler urged his generals to combat resistance with severity, telling them: 'You can't smash terror by philosophizing, you have to smash it by even greater terror.' Among those who were already obeying this order was Franz Kutschera, the SS General commanding the German police forces in Warsaw. Since his arrival in the city five months earlier he had ordered the execution of 4,300 Poles. On October 26 fifty Poles had been hanged from a balcony overlooking Leszno Street, after which the Germans forced passers-by to look at the bodies. In an attempt to strike at senior German officials, on January 8 Polish resistance fighters attacked a convoy of five German cars, including one with the governor of Warsaw, General Fischer, on his way back into Warsaw from a hunting trip. Nine Germans were wounded but no one was killed.

Twenty-four hours after Hitler's call of January 27 for 'greater terror' General Kutschera ordered more than a hundred Polish patriots who had been arrested in Warsaw during the previous few days to be shot. Thirty-three of them were taken to Jerusalem Avenue in the centre of the city and executed in public. At the same time it was announced that thirty Polish civilians had been taken hostage and would be executed if there were any further attacks on Germans in the city. Four days later Kutschera was killed by Polish partisans. As a reprisal for his assassination, not thirty but 1,600 Poles were executed by the SS and German police. Many of them were seized on the streets of the Warsaw suburb where Kutschera had been shot. On February 11 a teenage Polish resistance fighter, Julian Kulski, wrote in his diary:

On my way to Leszno Church today, I saw a crowd of people standing in front of the Wall. They were gazing at something above the Wall, on the Ghetto side of it. As I got closer, I could see for myself – hung from the upper storey balconies of what had been an apartment house were the bodies of twenty-two of our Freedom Fighters.

I was horrified, and cold with anger, yet at the same time amazed that the Germans couldn't see that such actions only encouraged us to fight back even harder than before.

On February 15 there was another public execution in Warsaw at the corner of Senatorska and Miodowa Streets. In reaction, Poles risked harsh punishment by lighting candles at the scene and laying flowers. Such was the strength of popular emotion and silent protest that the Germans decided not to hold further public executions in the city.

The air battle being fought daily in the skies of Western Europe followed a pattern increasingly damaging to German morale. Several German bombing raids were launched against London, but Goering's much-vaunted and once much-feared German air force no longer had the necessary air mastery to do great damage. Flying in the opposite direction to the German raiders, British bombers continued – although almost always at heavy cost to the aircrews – to bomb Berlin every few nights.

In a British bombing raid on Berlin on the night of January 29/30 many public buildings were hit, including four theatres and six hospitals. So great was the destruction of property that an estimated 180,000 people were made homeless. The death toll was also high, although the destruction of so many aspects of administrative life in Berlin had made the earlier attempts at accurate recording impossible to repeat – rather as in the First World War the British War Office had to admit in 1917 that it lacked the 'clerk power' to register the growing number of deaths in the trenches on any regular basis. It was known that more than a thousand Berliners – perhaps as many as 1,400 – were killed that night, and more than a hundred British aircrew.

On the following night, when Goebbels's Propaganda Ministry in the centre of Berlin was again hit, another thousand Berliners were killed, as well as 193 British aircrew. American bombers struck almost every day at German industrial targets. Their aircrews also suffered heavy losses. But considerable damage to the German war effort was inflicted. On February 1 Dietrich Bonhoeffer, from his prison cell in Berlin, wrote to his parents:

> Something that repeatedly puzzles me as well as other people is how quickly we forget our impressions of a night's bombing. Even a few minutes after the all-clear, almost everything that we had just been thinking about seems to vanish into thin air. With Luther a flash of lightning was enough to change the course of his life for years to come. Where is this 'memory' today?
>
> Is not the loss of this 'moral memory' (a horrid expression) responsible for the ruin of all obligations, of love, marriage, friendship, and loyalty? Nothing

sticks fast, nothing holds firm; everything is here today and gone tomorrow. But the good things of life – truth, justice, and beauty – all great accomplishments, need time, constancy, and 'memory', or they degenerate.

The man who feels neither responsibility towards the past nor desire to shape the future is one who 'forgets', and I do not know how one can really get at such a person and bring him to his senses. Every word, even if it impresses him for the moment, goes in at one ear and out at the other. What is to be done about him? It is a great problem of Christian ministry. You put it very well recently when you said that people feel so quickly and so 'shamelessly at home'.

In the Pacific the steady American advance into the still substantial Japanese area of control was accelerated on February 1, when there were landings on three of the Marshall Islands. In all, for the loss of fewer than a thousand American soldiers, 15,000 Japanese were killed and the islands overrun.

The Russian forces that had entered Poland the previous month had begun to drive the Germans out of several important Polish towns, among them Rovno and Lutsk. Churchill, apprehensive of future Soviet political control in these regions, and seeking to support the government of Poland in exile in London, tried over many hours of negotiations to persuade the Polish exile leaders to accept a return of Russian sovereignty to the eastern third of Poland (where Poles were in a minority of the population) in return for Soviet recognition of an independent Poland with Warsaw as its capital, and with territory in the west secured from Germany.

Despite Churchill's strenuous efforts, the London Poles refused to agree to give up the sovereignty of the eastern regions, which they had acquired in 1921 under the Treaty of Riga, after defeating the Bolshevik forces in battle. In the aftermath of the First World War, especially when the Red Army was within a few miles of Warsaw, the British had favoured a far more westerly line – known, after the name of the British Foreign Secretary at that time, as the Curzon Line.

Considerable effort was being made in London by both Churchill and his Foreign Secretary Anthony Eden to persuade the Poles to accept that line again, and to allow Stalin the eastern region. The London Poles declined to accept any diminution of their interwar territory. It was an impasse that would be decided, not at the conference table – though it was to dominate several Big Three conferences in the year ahead – but on the battlefield. And on that battlefield, the Soviet forces were in the ascendant.

In the Indian Ocean the power of the Germans still to wreak havoc at sea was shown when a German U-boat sunk the British troopship *Khedive Ismail*. After two massive explosions the troopship sank beneath the waves in two minutes. Six hundred East African artillerymen were among those drowned, as were sixty-seven women – mostly in their twenties – including Queen Alexandra army nurses, Wrens and members of the Kenyan ATS.* The tragedy of the sinking was compounded by the need of the destroyer escort to try to locate and destroy the U-boat by ferocious – and ultimately successful – depth charging. This may well have caused further casualties among those survivors swimming in the sea. But it ensured that the other troop transports in the convoy were unmolested.

On the Italian front, despite repeated attacks by British, American, Polish and other Allied troops, the town and monastery of Cassino were held by the Germans, while at the same time the Anzio beachhead was confined by a German ring of armour. There would be no swift linking up of the two Allied forces. To drive the Germans from Cassino, it would be necessary to bomb their most effective strongpoint, the early medieval monastery on Monte Cassino. As well as the German soldiers defending the mountain top from within the monastery confines, the bishop and more than five hundred civilian refugees were sheltering there. On February 12, Allied aircraft showered leaflets on the monastery, addressed to 'Italian friends'. The message in the leaflets was spelt out clearly. The monastery was about to become a target. 'The time has come when we must train our guns on the monastery itself,' the leaflet explained. 'We give you warning so that you may save yourselves. We warn you urgently: Leave the monastery. Leave it at once. Respect this warning. It is for your benefit.'

Two days later the Allies struck, not with guns but with bombs. In four hours more than four hundred tons of bombs were dropped – a fifth of the tonnage usually dropped during a night raid on the city of Berlin – reducing the monastery to ruins, and killing the bishop and 250 of the Italian civilians who had declined to leave after the leaflet raid. But an Allied infantry attack later that day in which Maori troops from New Zealand as well as Gurkhas from Nepal and Indian soldiers took part, fighting bayonet to bayonet, failed to drive the German defenders out. The Germans even found the strength

---

* The Wrens were the women's service of the Royal Navy; the ATS the Women's Auxiliary Transport Service of the Army.

to counter-attack, driving two Maori companies back down the slopes and across the Rapido River from which the assault had begun.

On the night of the Allied setback at Cassino, the British suffered a setback in the continuing air raids over Berlin, when 265 airmen – out of more than five thousand airmen participating in the raid – were shot down and killed. The quantity of bombs dropped that night was a record, 2,642 tons, and several important factories were hit. The death toll on the ground was more than five hundred, of whom 260 were civilians who were recorded as having been 'buried alive', and eighty were foreign workers.

Three nights later there was a British bombing raid on Leipzig. Eighty of the attacking bombers were shot down by German anti-aircraft fire, and nearly four hundred aircrew were killed: the largest aircrew deaths in a single bombing raid over Germany. Four of the British aircraft were lost after they collided in the air. The next morning American bombers struck the burning city. In the two raids, 969 citizens were killed, and as many as fifty thousand were made homeless.

By far the greatest death toll that week in any war zone was the one inflicted on the German army. It was a last attempt, at Hitler's insistence, to hold on to the west bank of the River Dnieper, at Korsun, south of Kiev. But the position was overrun, and at least twenty thousand Germans killed.

In the Pacific, American Marines drove the Japanese from Eniwetok Atoll in the Marshall Islands. In all, 2,677 Japanese defenders were killed for the loss of 195 Americans, and the island air base was secured. In an attack on the Island of Truk, in the Carolines, known as the 'Gibraltar of the Pacific', the American victory was even more spectacular, and a strong boost to the morale of the American people. In the battle for Truk, American warplanes – flying from eleven aircraft carriers – sank sixty Japanese warships. They also destroyed 265 Japanese aircraft, most of them while still on the ground. This was at the cost of twenty-five American aircraft.

Despite these setbacks for Japan, the Japanese continued to conduct the war with zeal and ferocity. When Japanese torpedo bombers launched their torpedoes at two American warships off Iwo Jima, 242 of those on board were killed. On the following day a Japanese submarine sank a British merchant ship in the Indian Ocean. The submariners then machine gunned the survivors from the deck of the submarine as they swam in the water and clung to the wreckage. Four days later the survivors of another torpedoed British merchant ship were likewise machine gunned as they tried to cling to the rafts and wreckage. In another such incident between Colombo and Diego Suarez, all but eight of the fifty-two survivors of a torpedoed British merchant ship were machine gunned in their lifeboats.

A few German bombers still managed to get through to London: their raid on the night of February 20/21 was the heaviest raid on the British capital since May 1941. Four people were killed in Whitehall at the entrance to Downing Street. But even as the German bombers had been preparing to set off, the Allies launched another substantial Anglo-American air offensive against Germany. Known as 'Big Week', its targets were German aircraft factories, airfields, air storage parks and ball-bearing factories as far east as the Baltic and as far south as the Adriatic.

The Big Week raids were planned as an essential preliminary to any cross-Channel landings, planned for just over three months' time. German air power had first to be significantly reduced. In this regard, the raids were effective, but both the British and Americans suffered heavy losses in aircrew killed. On February 22, as the raids of Big Week were still taking place – with seven separate targets that day – Churchill told the House of Commons that since the start of the war 38,300 British pilots and aircrew had been killed, and more than ten thousand aircraft shot down. He also sought to answer critics of the moral aspect of British bombing policy. One of the most outspoken of these was Bishop Bell of Chichester, who in May 1942 had travelled to Sweden to make contact with Dietrich Bonhoeffer and to find out about the German opposition to Hitler. Reflecting on the bombing both of Germany and Japan, Churchill commented: 'The air power was the weapon which both the marauding States selected as their main tool of conquest. This was the sphere in which they were to triumph. This was the method by which the nations were to be subjugated to their rule. I shall not moralize further than to say that there is a strange, stern justice in the long swing of events.'

Big Week continued, but in spite of the formidable weight of bombs thrown on the aircraft factories, extraordinary efforts were made by the Germans to restore production, and to move production elsewhere. In the last half of 1943 the average German monthly production of single-engine fighters was 851. By the summer of 1944 it had risen, despite the destructive work of Big Week, to 1,581 – it had almost doubled.

It was not only aircraft factories that were destroyed or damaged during Big Week. In the British air raid on factories at Augsburg on the night of

February 25/26, in which more than seven hundred citizens were killed, almost the whole of the medieval centre of the city was destroyed. The weather was so cold – at minus 18 degrees Celsius – that the water in many of the fire-fighting hoses froze, as did the river from which much of the water had to be pumped.

Slave labourers worked without respite throughout the Reich. Some were still building the Atlantic Wall against what was recognized in Berlin as an increasingly imminent Allied landing. On February 22 a secret German survey noted with precision that in the Auschwitz region there were 73,669 Jewish slave labourers, of whom 24,637 were women. More than six thousand of these slaves – each with an Auschwitz number tattooed on their forearm – were working in I.G. Farben's synthetic rubber and oil factory at Monowitz, six miles from the gas chambers and crematoria of Birkenau, where many hundreds of Jewish deportees were still being killed every week.

On the day of the secret German survey, a train left the detention camp of Fossoli, in northern Italy. On board, under German guard, crammed into cattle trucks, were 650 people – called by the Germans 'pieces'. They were destined for Auschwitz. One of the few who survived was Primo Levi, a young chemist from Turin who had fought with the Italian partisans and been captured. As a Jew, he was sent to Auschwitz. Of the final stages of the three-day journey he wrote:

Through the slit, known and unknown names of Austrian cities, Salzburg, Vienna, then Czech, finally Polish names. On the evening of the fourth day the cold became intense: the train ran through interminable black pine forests, climbing perceptibly.

The snow was high. It must have been a branch line as the stations were small and almost deserted. During the halts, no one tried any more to communicate with the outside world: we felt ourselves by now 'on the other side'.

There was a long halt in open country. The train started up with extreme slowness, and the convoy stopped for the last time, in the dead of night, in the middle of a dark silent plain.

On both sides of the track rows of red and white lights appeared as far as the eye could see; but there was none of that confusion of sounds which betrays inhabited places even from a distance. By the wretched light of the last candle, with the rhythm of the wheels, with every human sound now silenced, we awaited what was to happen . . .

That train from Italy had arrived at the Auschwitz-Birkenau siding, to which as many as a million Jews were brought during the two and a half years when the gas chambers were in operation, and from which only a few thousand survived:

The climax came suddenly. The door opened with a crash, and the dark echoed with outlandish orders in that curt, barbaric barking of Germans in command which seems to give vent to a millennial anger.

A vast platform appeared before us, lit up with reflectors. A little beyond it, a row of lorries. Then everything was silent again. Someone translated: we had to climb down with our luggage and deposit it alongside the train.

In a moment the platform was swarming with shadows. But we were afraid to break that silence: everyone busied himself with his luggage, searched for someone else, called to somebody, but timidly, in a whisper.

A dozen SS men stood around, legs akimbo, with an indifferent air. At a certain moment they moved among us, and in a subdued tone of voice, with faces of stone, began to interrogate us rapidly, one by one, in bad Italian. They did not interrogate everybody, only a few: 'How old? Healthy or ill?' And on the basis of the reply they pointed in two different directions.

Everything was as silent as an aquarium, or as in certain dream sequences. We had expected something more apocalyptic: they seemed simple police agents. It was disconcerting and disarming.

Someone dared to ask for his luggage: they replied, 'luggage afterwards'. Someone else did not want to leave his wife: they said, 'together again afterwards'. Many mothers did not want to be separated from their children: they said 'good, good, stay with child'.

They behaved with the calm assurance of people doing their normal duty of every day. But Renzo stayed an instant too long to say good-bye to Francesca, his fiancée, and with a single blow they knocked him to the ground. It was their everyday duty.

'In less than ten minutes,' Primo Levi recalled, 'all the fit men had been collected together in a group.' His account continued:

What happened to the others, to the women, to the children, to the old men, we could establish neither then nor later: the night swallowed them up, purely and simply. Today, however, we know that in that rapid and summary choice each one of us had been judged capable or not of working usefully for the Reich; we know that of our convoy no more than ninety-six men and twenty-nine women entered the respective camps of Monowitz-Buna and Birkenau, and that of all the others, more than five hundred in number, not one was living two days later.

We also know that not even this tenuous principle of discrimination between fit and unfit was always followed, and that later the simpler method was often adopted of merely opening both the doors of the wagon without warning or instructions to the new arrivals. Those who by chance climbed down on one side of the convoy entered the camp; the others went to the gas chamber.

This is the reason why three-year-old Emilia died.

The 'Jewish problem' of Nazi terminology impinged personally on Hitler that February. For a number of years his meals had been cooked for him by Frau Marlene von Exner, a dietician from Vienna who had been recommended to him by the Roumanian dictator, Marshal Antonescu. While cooking for Hitler, Frau von Exner fell in love with an SS officer at Hitler's headquarters, and they were engaged to be married. As was obligatory whenever an SS man was about to marry, detailed enquiries were made as to his fiancée's ancestry. It was discovered that one of Frau von Exner's great-grandmothers had been Jewish. Hitler was distraught. 'You will understand that I must pay you off,' he told the woman whose cooking he had so appreciated, and who had been a valued member of his domestic staff. 'I cannot make one rule for myself and another for the rest.'

Nazi racial policy not only meant that Frau von Exner had to leave Hitler's employ, but that several of her relatives who were members of the Nazi Party had to resign from it – because they too had a Jewish great-grandmother. Nothing further happened to Frau von Exner or her relatives. On February 23, however, twenty-six Jews who were discovered in hiding in Warsaw were deported to Auschwitz. Two days later they were followed there by thirty-seven Jews who had been arrested in Frau von Exner's own city, Vienna.

On March 3 it was the turn of 732 Jews from Holland and then 1,501 Jews from France, to be deported, as part of the regular weekly deportations from Western Europe. Of those two deportations, nearly two thousand of the deportees were gassed on reaching the camp. On the following day, in Warsaw, the Germans took eighty Poles and four Jewish women who had been caught while in hiding and led them to the ruins of the ghetto. They were then shot, and their bodies thrown into a basement in the ruins of the ghetto, doused with petrol and set on fire. Not all of them had been killed in the hail of bullets. The historian of this episode, Wladyslaw Bartoszewski – who was later Foreign Minister in post-Communist Poland – has written: 'For four to six hours there could be heard the screams of the wounded as they burned alive.'

As the Western Allies came to within three months of the planned cross-Channel landings, intense efforts were being made for the preparation of what was to be the largest ever amphibious landing. As part of that effort, the bombing of German industry, of which the Big Week raids had been a prelude, ranged over the whole industrial capacity of the Reich, and as far east as the bombers could go, whether from airfields in Britain or in southern Italy. The industrial region around Auschwitz still lay outside the range of the Allied bomber forces. But in March more than 27,000 tons of bombs were dropped on four main industrial cities: Stuttgart, Frankfurt-on-Main, Essen, Nuremberg and Berlin. A new bomb, weighing 4,000 pounds, was used for the first time during these raids.

There was hardly a single night without a bombing raid against Germany. At Stuttgart, on the night of March 1/2, serious damage was done to the Bosch and Mercedes Benz factories. On the night of March 3/4 a Polish bomber squadron took part in a minelaying sortie against the river estuaries and port exits along the North Sea. On the night of March 5/6 seventeen bombers dropped arms and ammunition to resistance groups in France that were also preparing to disrupt German lines of communication in the run-up to the Allied cross-Channel landings.

The cross-Channel landings, finally set for June, were becoming the main focus of Allied planning, from Churchill and Roosevelt to the private soldiers of their respective forces, drawing in also the commanders and troops of a dozen other Allied and associated powers. An intensification of the assault preparations came on the night of March 6/7, with the start of a sustained air assault on railway marshalling yards, bridges and communication centres in northern France. The target for the British bombers that night was the railway centre at Trappes, to the west of Paris. After 263 bombers had dropped more than a thousand tons of bombs, the railway lines, engine sheds and railway wagons were so badly damaged that the centre was unable to operate for more than a month.

In a raid on the marshalling yards at Le Mans on the following night, however, some bombs fell outside the immediate target area and thirty-one French civilians were killed. In a second raid on the marshalling yards at Le Mans six nights later, fifteen railway engines and 800 wagons were destroyed, but forty-eight French civilians were killed. In two raids on railway yards at Amiens that month, thirty-six French civilians were killed. There was growing bitterness in France that this was part of the cost of the Allied preparations.

Berlin was bombed again on the night of March 24/25. 'We had another very lively time last night,' Dietrich Bonhoeffer wrote to his parents from prison the following day, and he added: 'The view from the roof here over the city was staggering.' More than eight hundred British bombers took part in the raid, of which seventy-two were shot down. So much damage was done in the city that it looked as if it could never become a flourishing metropolis again.

Strong winds which had not been forecast accurately that night carried much of the attacking force away from the target. Bombs fell on 126 small towns and villages outside Berlin, killing thirty civilians. In Berlin, forty-seven people were killed. The British aircrew deaths were far higher – 392 – the largest death toll in all nineteen major raids on Berlin. No further such raids on Berlin were mounted. Among the buildings hit in the German capital were nine important war industry factories, the Swedish Embassy, the offices of the National Milk and Fat Industry, and Himmler's bunker. The SS chief was not inside it.

Despite Britain's growing air superiority, the Germans were able to carry out six retaliatory raids over London, Hull, North-East England and South Wales, and in the month of March, 279 British civilians were killed. So many incendiary bombs fell on London on the night of March 14/15 that it was known as the 'scalded cat' raid. In a raid a week later, eighteen civilians were killed when a stick of bombs fell on Strood, in Kent – the county known locally as Hell's Corner. In London that night sixty-two people were killed.

In a British bomber raid on Nuremberg on the night of March 30/31 – the night before all British bomber operations would have to centre on the needs of the cross-Channel landings – fifty-nine of the attacking bombers were shot down before they reached the target, which was covered by thick cloud. The death that night of 545 British airmen was the highest of any single Allied air raid over Germany: more airmen died over Germany on that one night than had been killed in action during the whole of the Battle of Britain.

The bombs which were dropped on Nuremberg killed 110 German civilians and fifty-nine foreign slave labourers. Nineteen German airmen also died attacking the incoming bombers, which were first intercepted by German fighters before they had even crossed the Belgian-German border. Eighty two of the 786 British bombers were shot down before they reached their target. By an error of navigation, 120 of the attacking force bombed Schweinfurt, a town fifty miles north-west of Nuremberg, but the inaccuracy of the initial bombing markers there was such that few bombs fell on the town and only two people were killed.*

Using the Nuremberg raid as a cover, a single British bomber had flown to Belgium with the Belgian resistance leader Robert Deprez and several other people who were to participate in resistance activities inside Belgium. This bomber was among those shot down, and five of the ten people on board were killed, including Deprez. Three of the surviving airmen were captured and sent to prisoner-of-war camps. Two others, the pilot and co-pilot, were helped by Belgian families in the village of Zelzate, on the Belgian-Dutch border. Forty-seven Allied airmen were already in hiding in that one village, part of a finely coordinated evading system whereby, in almost every case, the airmen were able to travel southward through Belgium and France to the Pyrenees, then cross into Spain, and make their way back to Britain, to fly again.

These escape lines were a remarkable feature of the Allied war effort. They were dependent on the good-will and great courage of the Dutch, the Belgians and the French, and this was evident in large measure. Thousands of aircrew made their way back to Britain as a result of the evasion lines. Jews were also the beneficiaries of these lines, one of which, run by a Dutch Seventh Day Adventist, John Weidner, arranged for both Allied airmen and Jews to be moved from Holland to Switzerland. There they were safe for the rest of the war, although the airmen could not then get back to Britain. An estimated 150 people assisted Weidner in operating the route of his 280-mile long evading line. Forty of them were arrested by the Gestapo and killed, among them Weidner's sister Gabrielle.

* Many of the individual episodes of the Second World War recounted in these pages have been the subject of their own book, even of several books. The Nuremberg raid of 30/31 March 1944 is no exception. Martin Middlebrook's *The Nuremberg Raid*, was published by Allen Lane in London in 1973.

Allied escapees and evaders found different ways of helping the war effort. An American airman, Lieutenant Charles F. Kingsman, who was shot down over northern Italy, and hidden by an Italian family, gave lessons to Italian partisans in the area as to how to use and maintain the machine guns which they had diligently gathered from crashed Allied aircraft.

In the war in the Far East, more than nine thousand British and Indian officers and men were gathering as much as a hundred miles behind the lines in Burma, mostly sent in by glider. They were joined by several thousand more men who infiltrated across the India-Burma border on foot. These included Gurkhas and Kachin tribesmen. The leader of this substantial force, Major-General Orde Wingate, who made two glider-borne descents to guide the operation, told them when all was in place for offensive action: 'We have inflicted a complete surprise on the enemy. All our columns are inside the enemy's guts. The time has come to reap the fruit of the advantage we have gained.'

Wingate was not to see the victory that his tactics and inspiration made possible. He was killed in an air crash before the end of March. That month, eighty-four of the 104 passengers and crew from the British merchant ship *Behar*, which the Japanese had sunk in the Indian Ocean on its way from Calcutta to Australia, were taken by their Japanese rescuers – who had saved them from certain death in shark-infested waters – on board the Japanese heavy cruiser *Tone*, which had rescued them. Later, fifteen of those rescued were transferred to another ship. On the night of March 18/19 the sixty-nine who remained on the *Tone* were brought on deck one by one, as if for interrogation, blindfolded, and knocked unconscious by members of the warship's judo class. They then had their throats cut by members of the warship's fencing class, each one of whom was a graduate of the Japanese Naval Academy. When all sixty-nine had been killed, their bodies were thrown into the sea.

In Europe, the Soviet forces which entered the Roumanian city of Czernowitz on March 2 were within a hundred miles of the border of Hungary. The Germans realized that their Hungarian ally might have neither the military means nor the political will to resist a Soviet thrust. There was fear in Berlin that the Hungarian Regent, Admiral Horthy, might seek an agreement with Stalin, rather than risk the destruction of his country and his regime. Even if Hungary were forced to give up the province of Ruthenia – taken from

Czechoslovakia four years earlier – to the Soviet Union (many of its inhabitants were Ruthenes of Slav race and language) – Stalin might still allow an independent Hungary to survive.

Hitler understood this line of thought among his allies. He therefore prepared to occupy Hungary and take over its defences. The prospect of a German occupation of Hungary caused considerable pleasure in Department VI of the Reich Central Security Office. Admiral Horthy had twice refused, in personal confrontations with Hitler, to deport the Jews of Hungary to their deaths. As a result of his refusal, three quarters of a million Jews were alive in the heart of Europe. A German occupation of Hungary would enable Eichmann and his team to carry out the main unfulfilled aspect of the Wannsee Conference plan of January 1942, more than two years later, but still not too late for their purposes. As German troops prepared to enter Hungary, Eichmann established a small team of experts – experts in deception and deportation – to enter Hungary within hours of the German army.

On March 17 – the day on which Soviet forces reached Dubno, twenty-five miles inside the pre-war Polish frontier – Hitler summoned Admiral Horthy to Klessheim castle, just outside Salzburg, and within sight of the mountain of Berchtesgaden in which the Führer had brow-beaten Neville Chamberlain six years earlier. Confronting Horthy without prevarication, Hitler set out his terms. There must be a new government in Budapest headed by a Hungarian politician sympathetic to Germany. German troops must be allowed into Hungary. Germany must be given full control of all Hungary's raw materials, including the oil wells at Nagykanizsa. Hungary must also allow the Germans to deport all three quarters of a million Hungarian Jews. Horthy could remain Regent.

Horthy accepted Hitler's terms. Two days later, in the early hours of March 19, German troops entered Hungary. In a repetition of what had happened in Austria, the Sudetenland and Prague in 1938 and 1939, the German troops entered unopposed. Hitler, albeit late in the day, was master of yet another European sovereign State. Eichmann and his team did not delay. Within two weeks of the German army entering Hungary, the Jews were being forced to leave their homes in more than five hundred towns and villages and move into ghettos – often the most run-down part of their town, or a brickworks or factory. Within another six weeks they were being deported to Auschwitz.

The pattern and pace under which the Jews of Hungary were caught up in the extermination process so late in the war is evidence of Eichmann's determination to act while there was still time. The fate of the Jews of the village of Bonyhád was typical. On April 3, fifteen days after the German invasion of Hungary, the public drummer – through whom the village administration always passed on its instructions – announced that no Jews could leave their homes between six in the evening and seven in the morning, and that none could leave the village. All radios, cameras and telephones were to be handed over. Two days later it was announced that Jews were to wear a yellow star on their clothing. Non-Jews were forbidden to work in Jewish households. On April 11 the heads of the local Jewish religious community were ordered to draw up a list 'of all Jewish persons and their families, marking their respective addresses'.

The historian of the Jews of Bonyhád, Leslie Blau – who had earlier been taken away from the village to serve as a forced labourer – writes: 'I heard from a reliable witness that as the two Jewish leaders signed this document, they both broke down and cried. Now they knew for sure; this was the beginning of the end.' What that end might be was unknown to the Jews. On April 20 the fifteen local Jews who had permission to carry firearms had their licenses revoked and had to give up their guns. On May 5 all Jewish communal and religious organizations were dissolved. On May 11 all Jews were ordered to leave their homes and move into the specially created ghetto, in 'rooms' four metres by four metres with at least three people in each.

In a gesture of sympathy for the incarcerated Jews, a number of local Gypsies threw freshly baked bread over the ghetto fence. The leaders of the local Catholic, Evangelical and Reform Churches also tried to help. But the final stage, when it came, was the swiftest of all: on June 28 the inhabitants of the ghetto were ordered to prepare small packages for themselves, containing two sets of underwear and some food. They were then moved from the ghetto into the two synagogues. Here they spent the night on the floor. One of them managed to throw a note to a passer-by, addressed to a relative in Budapest: 'We are about to start our journey to an unknown destination. God bless you all and may He help us to be able to endure it.'

On July 1 the Jews were taken from the two synagogues to the railway station, where a train made up of cattle trucks was waiting. Between seventy and eighty people were forced into each wagon. On July 2 the train reached the town of Pecs, to which almost six thousand Jews had been brought from similar small towns and villages throughout the region. All of them were confined in a military barracks until, on July 6, they were deported to Auschwitz. There, amid the destruction of hundreds of Hungarian Jewish communities, 1,096 Jews from Bonyhád were killed. Fewer than a hundred survived.

During April and May, while awaiting the time when the Jews of Hungary could be put on trains and sent northward, Eichmann's emissaries organized the deportation from Greece to Auschwitz of more than four thousand Jews who were seized in towns and villages throughout Greece. It was the most distant deportation of the war. But for every Jew who was caught and deported, another managed to escape the round up and find shelter with local villagers. More than a thousand Jews joined the Greek partisans.

In Italy, Monte Cassino was still being held by the Germans, frustrating the Allied hope of reaching Rome and pushing northward to the River Po, and even into north-western Yugoslavia and southern Austria. In a massive bombing raid on the monastery on March 15, almost a thousand tons of bombs were dropped. Some bombs fell several miles from the target, killing 96 Allied soldiers and 140 Italian civilians.

Neither the subsequent artillery bombardment of 195,000 rounds – probably the largest number ever fired into a single building – nor a second assault by British, New Zealand Maori, Indian and Gurkha troops, were able to drive the Germans out. More than a thousand Indians and 863 New Zealanders were killed, including more than thirty Maoris, but the German defenders, fighting amid ruins, far from home, and with no chance of reinforcements, obeyed Hitler's order that every inch of soil must be held for as long as possible.

In the German-occupied areas of Italy, hundreds of Italian partisans were hunted down and shot. On March 23, after an Italian partisan threw a bomb at an SS unit in Rome, killing thirty-three SS men, the Germans rounded up 335 Italian men and boys and took them to the Ardeatine caves. There, all of them were shot. The massacre sent a shock wave of fear and anger throughout Italy. Of those executed in the caves, 253 were Catholics and 70 were Jews. Twelve were never identified. Fifty-four years later the two main perpetrators of the massacre, SS Captain Erich Priebke and his colleague Karl Hass, were sentenced to life imprisonment by a court in Rome. Both men were then in their eighties. During the trial Priebke admitted to killing two of the victims, and to ticking off the names of others from a list. His defence was that he was 'only carrying out orders'.

On the day of the Rome killings, which achieved immediate notoriety, an event unseen except by a handful of people, and unreported, took place in the village of Voiron, in the French Alps. Sixteen Jewish children, orphans who had been hidden in various safe houses for the previous two years, having been refused entry into Switzerland by the Swiss border police, were betrayed by a local villager and handed over to the Gestapo. All sixteen were taken first to Grenoble, then to Paris, and finally to Auschwitz, where they were murdered. Among them were two brothers born in Colmar, in Alsace, Simon Rovinsky, aged fourteen and Jacques aged seven.

Also in the French Alps, two days after the Voiron deportation, 8,000 German soldiers, supported by two air squadrons, set out to track down and destroy a French Resistance unit numbering about four hundred and fifty men and women, who were operating from the mountains above Annecy. In the resulting, unequal battle, more than four hundred of the French fighters were killed.

Hitler's intense irritation at military setbacks was becoming more noticed by his subordinates. When seventy-nine Allied airmen escaped through a tunnel from their prisoner-of-war camp at Sagan, south-east of Berlin, an outraged Hitler burst out at Himmler: 'You are not to let the escaped airmen out of your control!' Three of the escapees, a Dutch pilot and two Norwegians, reached the Baltic port of Stettin, boarded a boat to Sweden, and from there made their way back to Britain to fly their bombing missions again. All the others were captured, one of them as far west as Saarbrücken.

On March 25, the day after the Sagan escapes, Russian forces drove the Germans out of Proskurov, one of the most westerly towns of the Ukraine, less than fifty miles from the East Galician border of Greater Germany. The commander of Army Group South, Field Marshal Erich von Manstein – the conqueror of the Crimea who in 1940 had masterminded the dramatically successful Blitzkrieg against France – asked Hitler if he could retreat further westward. In fury, Hitler dismissed Manstein from his command. On the following day, on a fifty-six-mile front, Russian forces reached the River Pruth, the pre-war border between Russia and Hitler's ally Roumania. That day, in a radio broadcast, Churchill said of the Russian advances – more than nine hundred miles in the previous twelve months – that they 'constitute the greatest cause of Hitler's undoing'.

By the end of March, Russian troops were on the borders of both Eastern Galicia and Roumania. Having already had to enter Hungary in order to prevent a Hungarian defection, Hitler ordered his troops to enter Roumania. But the urgency of the need to protect the borders of Germany itself did not halt the mass murder of Jews. On March 27, the day on which Russian troops overran a 1941 mass murder site at Kamenets Podolsk, to the north, at Kovno, two hundred miles behind the rapidly approaching front line, there was a round-up of all surviving Jewish children under the age of fourteen: several thousand in all. The SS ordered the commander of the Jewish police in the ghetto, his two deputies and thirty-four other Jewish policemen to assist them in the round-up. The Jewish policemen refused. They were shot dead on the spot. Very few of the children were able to find a hiding place. The SS then took them in trucks to one of the former Tsarist forts outside the city, and murdered them there.

When the Japanese besieged the Indian town of Imphal in April, 13,000 of them were killed before they were forced to withdraw. Several thousand more Japanese were killed when, seventy miles north of Imphal, they besieged the town of Kohima for three months: many of them were killed when British bombers carried out more than two thousand sorties against them.

At the end of his 217-page account of the battle of Kohima, the historian John Colvin writes: 'Men had been fighting on these hills and ridges for sixty-four days in conditions of mud, rain, fire and blood as bad as the Somme and Passchendaele. But now the battle of Kohima had been won.' The British and Indian victory at Kohima ensured that the Japanese army, hitherto unbrokenly victorious in Burma, would not penetrate into Assam and reach the Brahmaputra and Ganges valleys of the Indian subcontinent.

When, in the third week of April, the Americans attacked Hollandia and Aitape, the last two Japanese-held towns on the northern coast of New Guinea, the 15,000 Japanese defenders, many of whom were administrative and not combat troops, fought against heavy odds for more than three months, refusing to surrender, and when the struggle for the towns was over, 12,811 Japanese lay dead. Less than six hundred Americans were killed.

Soviet forces were fighting inside the border of Greater Germany, as established within a few weeks of the German invasion of the Soviet Union in the summer of 1941. When one German army was trapped inside the Eastern Galician town of Skala at the end of March, 26,000 Germans were killed.

The scale of reprisals behind the lines was also high. On April 1 the Germans hanged sixteen Poles in the town of Suwalki: they had been accused of being members of the resistance. One of them was a boy of fourteen. In France, after a German troop train was derailed at Ascq, near Lille, on April 2, eighty-six villagers were taken from their homes and shot. No German soldiers had been killed in the derailment. One of those killed in the reprisal was the village priest, Henri Gilleron, who was shot outside his church. His curate, Maurice Cousin, was beaten to death in the street. Another of those executed was a French soldier, Lucian Albert, who had been a prisoner-of-war in Germany since 1940, but had been allowed to return home a month earlier on account of illness before the reprisal.

The pattern of reprisals and executions was unrelenting. On April 5, six British commandos were captured by a German naval patrol boat in the Aegean as they were on their way to the German-occupied Alimnia Island. They were taken to the mainland, interrogated, and then sent by the army authorities to the Gestapo for 'special treatment'. All six were executed. That same day, 559 Jews were deported from northern Italy to Auschwitz and murdered there, among them several small children, including a three-year-old boy, Roberto Zarfatti, who had been born in Rome. On the following day, April 6, German soldiers and French Milice went to the village of Izieu, where forty Jewish children were being looked after in a local school by a Jew, Miron Zlatin, and five teachers. Two of the children were deported with Zlatin by train to the Estonian city of Tallinn and shot. The other children, with their five teachers, were taken to Auschwitz, where all the children and four of the teachers were killed.

In the second week of April, between the towns of Lepel and Borisov, and Lepel and Polotsk, during an anti-partisan sweep in the rapidly dwindling areas of German-occupied Russia, more than seven thousand Russians were killed. Most of them were villagers who had taken no part in partisan activity. In the German city of Brandenburg a Catholic priest, Max Josef Metzger, who had served in the First World War as an army chaplain, was executed for having written privately to a fellow clergyman that a new government was needed. He was found guilty of 'assisting the enemy'.

Criticisms like those of Metzger were becoming widespread. A top secret German Security Service report on April 6 warned that many Germans 'are asking themselves whether the many sacrifices and hardships which the war demands, and will continue to demand, are worth it'. The German people were, according to the report, 'gradually beginning to long for peace'.

On April 10 the German shore batteries along the Normandy coast of France were attacked by American bombers. To deceive the Germans that somewhere other than Normandy was the intended target of a cross-Channel landing,

German anti-aircraft batteries between Rouen and Dunkirk were also bombed. To ensure that the deception worked – as indeed it did – two batteries outside the real landing area had to be bombed for every battery inside it.

These raids continued for more than a month. Other Allied air raids were mounted against railway marshalling yards throughout northern France, including Paris. During a raid on April 21 against the marshalling yards of St Denis and the Gare de la Chapelle, 640 Parisians were killed. Three days later, during an American daylight raid on the railway yards at Rouen, many bombs were dropped in error on the medieval centre of the town, and four hundred citizens were killed.

There were other casualties in the preparation for the Normandy landings that were kept secret. On the night of April 28 an invasion exercise was carried out on the south coast of England, at Slapton Sands near Dartmouth. As the Allied ships gathered in the Channel to launch the mock landing they were seen by seven German torpedo boats that were on a routine patrol from Cherbourg. During the torpedo-boat attack, two of the American Tank Landing Ships were sunk, and 638 American soldiers were killed. Many of them were specialist engineers whose skills could not easily be replaced. Among the American officers drowned were ten who knew the true location of the cross-Channel landings.

A massive search was undertaken to retrieve as many bodies as possible, to ensure that none of the ten men had been picked up by the Germans. More than a hundred bodies were never found, but those of the ten officers were recovered from the sea. The secrecy of where the Allies would land had been preserved. Richard Meredith, one of the Americans who took part in the exercise, and six weeks later was in the Normandy Landings themselves at Utah Beach, commented on his return to Slapton Sands fifty years later, for a commemorative church service: 'The casualties on the exercise were five times greater than the real thing.'

Inside France, as partisan activity increased in the two months leading up to the Allied landings, a German anti-partisan sweep in the Auvergne was followed by the public hanging of ninety-nine of those who were caught. Inside Germany, a journalist, Erich Knauf, a veteran of the First World War, who had called Goebbels 'this little rat', stated publicly that German victory would be 'the greatest misfortune', and alleged that Himmler only kept his job 'by ordering between eighty and a hundred executions a day', was sentenced to death. Such money as Knauf possessed was taken from him before his execution as both a 'fee' to the court for the carrying out of the death penalty and a charge 'for prison maintenance'.

The Allied reading of Germany's most secret Signals Intelligence messages was bearing enormous dividends for the forthcoming cross-Channel landing. The work of more than five thousand cryptographers and their helpers in reading and analyzing the Ultra material enabled a map to be drawn showing the bases and identity of almost every German military unit in France.

The Ultra material revealed to the Allies the imminent creation of a fortified area at the base of the Cotentin Peninsula. It indicated that the Germans were not expecting the attack to come 'for some time'. It made clear that the Germans did not suspect that beaches of Normandy were the intended landing places. And it showed how far the German High Command – at Zossen in Berlin – and Hitler – at Rastenburg and Berchtesgaden – were convinced that the landing would be elsewhere: possibly between Dieppe and Calais.

This mistaken German belief was the result of persistent Allied deception techniques, including the creation of a totally non-existent invasion force, the First United States Army Group (FUSAG) based in East Anglia, commanded by General Patton, complete with its own communications network, staff, and training activities consistent with the main invasion effort. Churchill was a strong advocate and supporter of this deception plan, which had been devised by Colonel John Bevan, a member of the inner circle of war policy, whose headquarters were immediately below Churchill's rooms in Whitehall.

One of those who managed to convince the Germans that the First United States Army Group was the nucleus and spearhead of the true invasion force was Juan Pujol Garcia, a Spaniard living in Britain whom the Germans believed was working for them, but who was operating entirely for the Allies. Hitler was so convinced of Garcia's good faith and brilliant detective work that he awarded him the Iron Cross. The British, in their turn, made him a Member of the Order of the British Empire.

The First United States Army Group and its supposed Pas-de-Calais objective was not the only deception plan mounted to protect the Normandy Landings. The East Anglian forces whose training exercises were regularly reported to Germany – by German spies who had been 'turned' and were working diligently for the Allies – also included an equally fictitious Twelfth British Army, which boasted among its component forces the 15th British Motorized Division, the 34th British Infantry Division, the 8th British Armoured Division, and the 7th Polish Infantry Division. These could be put ashore either at the Pas-de-Calais alongside the Americans or further west, in the area of Boulogne, or across the North Sea along the Dutch coast. The up-to-date equipment for these well-armed divisions, their deployment in East Anglia, their training exercises and continuous communications with their own units and with headquarters were all plentiful – and fictitious.

In all there were nine separate British deception plans, each involving the apparent training of considerable military forces, each with very different military objectives, all of them the brainchildren of a small staff of planners working in an annex to the underground Cabinet War Rooms in London. These warlike enterprises – each with its naval and air components – were Operation Fortitude North against central Norway, centred on Trondheim; Operation Graffham against central Sweden; Operation Royal Flush against the triply deceptive coastlines of southern Sweden, Spain or Turkey; Operation Zeppelin, a triple assault against the Roumanian Black Sea coast, Crete, and the western coastline of Greece and Albania; Operation Ironside against Bordeaux; Operation Vendetta against Marseille; Operation Ferdinand against Rome; and Operation Fortitude South against Calais and Boulogne.

A careful scrutiny at Bletchley of the Ultra decrypts revealed just how seriously the Germans were taking these non-existent threats. The first indication that the deception was working came in two Ultra messages, both sent on February 9, in which German troops in the Balkans were ordered from Split to Skoplje, and from Mostar to Sarajevo, in order, the message explained, to be available for rapid movement in the event of an Allied landing in Greece. It was clear that this move was being taken in order to counter part of Operation Zeppelin.

On February 13 Churchill told General Wilson, the Commander-in-Chief of the British forces in the Mediterranean, that reports had been received 'that the islands off the Dalmatian coast are being equipped with naval guns'. Although he did not say so, Ultra was his source. That same day the Allied planners finalized both sections of Operation Fortitude – against the Pas-de-Calais and the Norwegian coast. The planners of the deception explained to Churchill that the aim was not only to persuade the German

Army 'to make faulty strategic dispositions in north-west Europe' before the cross-Channel invasion, but also to induce it to make 'faulty tactical dispositions' both during and after the Normandy landings – which were intended to appear as a mere feint for one of the deception plan assaults.

In the air, the Germans were losing the power which had hitherto given them the ability to support and sustain the battles on land. In the first four months of 1944 more than three thousand fighter planes had been shot down and their pilots either killed or taken prisoner. An attempt to deceive the British into believing that new airfields were being opened, and thus to divert Allied bombing raids on useless targets, was a failure. The order to set up these spurious airfields was sent by Goering in a top secret Ultra message. This message was decrypted at Bletchley and Goering's deception exposed. The Allied bombing effort could continue to be against real airfields. This bombing was intensified as the date of the cross-Channel landings drew near.

Hitler's insistence that he would not allow a strategic retreat in Italy was also known to Allied Intelligence through Ultra. As a result, three weeks before the intended cross-Channel landing, Churchill and his Chiefs of Staff authorized a massive air offensive on the Italian front, knowing – correctly – that such an offensive would lead Hitler to send reinforcements into Italy just when they were needed in France.

The Allied military offensive in Italy began on May 11. It was commanded by General Sir Harold Alexander, who had earlier been the officer in charge both of the Dunkirk evacuation and the withdrawal from Burma. This was his opportunity to lead his men forward, to overrun the fortress which the German army had created at Cassino, and drive northward to Rome and beyond. The troops under Alexander's command represented a full panoply of the Allied forces: British, American, Indian, French, Polish, and Moroccan among them. He also had a force of Palestinian Jews, fighting under the symbol of the Star of David.

It took seven days before Cassino was overrun. Meanwhile, on May 12, a massive American air attack was also launched on the seven most productive German synthetic oil factories. Three of them were so badly damaged that they had temporarily to be shut down. In German-occupied France, with British support, an act of sabotage was carried out by the French Resistance on an armaments factory at Bagnères-de-Bigorre, in the Pyrenees. Production was brought to a halt for six months. The factory produced the carriers for self-propelled guns, a mobile artillery piece of considerable versatility.

On May 18 the monastery of Cassino was finally in Allied hands. The flag that was raised on the ruins was that of the Polish troops who had been prominent throughout the battle. In all, more than eight thousand Allied troops were killed in the last phase of the six-month struggle to break the German line at Cassino.

In the Pacific, the steady advance of American troops from island to island was following a bizarre pattern, as each Japanese garrison, loyal to the Emperor and the virtues inculcated into it by the Japanese military code of honour, refused to surrender even when confronted by overwhelmingly larger forces. When the Admiralty Islands were overrun – at the height of the Cassino battle in Italy – it was announced from Washington that 3,820 Japanese soldiers had been killed, but that only seventy-five had surrendered.

Most of those who surrendered had been far too badly injured to be able to kill themselves. In the battle for the island, 326 American soldiers had been killed. Two days later, on May 20, Wake Island was conquered for the loss of fifty-three American lives. All eight hundred of the Japanese defenders had been killed in battle, or had killed themselves to avoid capture.

As the Allied army in Italy advanced northward from Cassino, the troops who had been trapped in the Anzio bridgehead for four months broke out, and on May 25 the two forces were at last able to link up. The Normandy landings were only two weeks away. With Churchill's insistence on the most careful and cautious detail, enormous efforts had been made in both training the soldiers and in technical preparation. At his initial suggestion, an artificial harbour had been devised to enable ships to anchor off the Normandy coast and unload men and supplies, without the need to depend on the small and vulnerable quaysides of the Normandy villages. A pipe line had been prepared through which fuel oil could flow under the Channel from Britain to Normandy for the Allied tanks and armoured vehicles, unassailable by German aircraft. It was given the code name Pluto (Pipe Line Under the Ocean).

At Churchill's request, working closely with Colonel Bevan and the British deception planners – themselves disguised as the innocuous sounding London Controlling Section – Stalin agreed to postpone the Soviet army's summer offensive until after the Normandy landings, so that Hitler would not be able to transfer troops from the Eastern Front at the very moment when they were needed in the West.

This coordinated Allied plan boded well for the year ahead: there were hopes in London, Moscow and Washington that Germany could be defeated in the course of the coming year. For many of the captive peoples, however, this time scale was too late. On May 26, when the Allied forces were twenty-five miles from Rome, the senior German official in Hungary, SS Brigadier-General Edmund Veesenmayer, reported to the German Foreign Office in Berlin that in the previous ten days 138,870 Hungarian Jews had been deported to their 'destination'. That destination was Auschwitz, where more than half of them had been taken on arrival to the gas chambers and murdered there.

It was on the very day of Veesenmayer's report that Hitler, relaxing at Berchtesgaden, told the German generals whom he had summoned there: 'Hungary! The entire country subverted and rotten, Jews everywhere, Jews and still more Jews right up to the highest level, and the whole country covered by a continuous network of agents and spies waiting for the moment to strike, but fearing to do so in case a premature move drew us in. Here too I intervened, and this problem is going to be solved too.' Even as Hitler spoke that 'problem' was being 'solved': by mass murder. Determined to complete the task before news of it reached the Allies, the SS were making use of all four gas chambers at Birkenau – murdering 4,000 people every day.

On the night of May 26 a group of several hundred Hungarian Jews who were being led by their SS guards to the two most distant gas chambers in Birkenau – located at the edge of the birch wood which gave the place its name – sensed that something terrible was wrong and ran towards the wood. The searchlights that had been installed around the gas chamber were turned on by the SS, who opened fire with their machine guns on all those who were trying to flee, pursuing them, in the words of the post-war *Auschwitz Chronicle*, 'like hunters'. Not one of those who managed to reach the woods survived the hail of bullets. A similar act of defiance three days later was likewise crushed.

By the end of the May, after fourteen consecutive days of the arrival at Auschwitz of Jews from Hungary, fifty kilogrammes of gold had been extracted from the teeth of those who had been murdered. In one of the two trains that arrived from Hungary on the last day of the month, having been three and a half days on its journey with neither food nor water, beyond what the deportees had managed to take with them, fifty-five had died and two hundred had gone mad. On arrival at Auschwitz, a hundred were taken to the barracks and a thousand to the gas chambers.

*   *   *

As the final Allied preparations were being made for the Normandy landings, British Intelligence was able to decrypt a top-secret message from Rommel, which he had sent to Zossen six days earlier, in which he informed the German High Command that one of the SS Panzer divisions in France had no tanks and was not expecting any. It was also seriously short of officers, motor transport, and spare parts. Some of its officers – and this was an armoured division – were having to use bicycles and horses to move around the divisional area.

Rommel's message gave the British planners an insight into the grave shortages that would impede the German defenders. It also stimulated one final effort to disrupt German road and rail communications leading to the Normandy region. An air raid on railway lines and marshalling yards in and around Lyon, which was intended to impede the movement of German re-inforcements from southern France to the Normandy area, was successful in destroying many of the designated targets, but the cost of the raid was high: 717 French civilians were killed in it. They had spent four years almost to the day as the subjects first of Vichy and then of Germany. They could not know that within four months Lyon would be liberated and free.

By the last week of May, more than three thousand French civilians had been killed as a result of the Allied bombardments judged essential if the Normandy landings were to succeed. 'You are piling up an awful load of hatred,' was Churchill's comment to the Allied air force commander when he was told by the Air Staff that no lesser scale of bombing would be effective. On June 2 there was a second Allied air raid on the railway marshalling yards at Trappes, just west of Paris. This was the last of the raids that had begun almost three months earlier. German communications had indeed been severely damaged. Even the German land telephone line between German air force headquarters in Paris and its air bases around Rennes and Caen was totally cut for three consecutive days.

The original plan for the Normandy landings had placed D-Day on June 5. But weather and Intelligence altered the final date in a way that was entirely favourable to the Allies. In a top-secret message to Zossen, Field Marshal von Rundstedt told the High Command that the Allies would not launch the attack unless they could be certain of four days of clear weather. Rundstedt's message was known to the British as a result of Ultra. It was also known to the British, through the reading of less secret German radio signals, that the German weather forecast on June 3 predicted bad weather for the following three or four days. This meant that the German military planners would rule out June 4, June 5, June 6 and June 7 as days on which the Allies would launch their attack.

By carrying out the landings on June 6, the Allies would therefore catch the Germans unawares. The decision was therefore made to attack that day. Even a slightly improved German weather forecast on June 4 did not give the four clear days that were regarded in Germany as the minimum for an Allied decision to launch the attack.

On the evening of June 4, American troops reached the centre of Rome. On the following morning, June 5, confident in the knowledge that the poor weather forecast meant that there would be no Allied landing in Northern France for the next four days, Rommel left his headquarters at La Roche Guyon, a few miles north-west of Paris, to return to Germany. He intended to see Hitler and to impress upon him 'the extent of the manpower and material inferiority we would suffer in the event of a landing'. He also intended to ask for the immediate despatch of two more Panzer divisions and substantial air reinforcements.

At nine-thirty that evening, June 5, a message sent to Rommel's head-quarters by German Intelligence warned that a long series of radio messages had been sent out during the night instructing the French Resistance to cut railway lines throughout France. In Rommel's absence, the message was not decrypted. Of the 1,050 planned acts of rail sabotage, 950 were carried out.

Shortly before midnight, British Intelligence received important confirmation, through Ultra, of the desperate shortage of fuel oil among the German air force units in France. That confirmation took the form of an instruction from German High Command in Zossen, near Berlin, to the First Parachute Army, based at Nantes, to conserve its fuel oil a much as possible, reducing training flights to a minimum and even using rail rather than air for the transfer of supplies and 'duty journeys' by airmen.

That night almost a thousand British bombers struck at ten separate German gun batteries in the invasion area. Five thousand tons of bombs were dropped, the greatest tonnage in one night so far in the whole war. At the same time, in a final act of deception, thirty-six bombers dropped hundreds of dummy parachutists and explosive devices over areas to the east of the actual landing grounds, to simulate the landings there. A vast naval armada was on the move: 2,727 merchant ships and steamers, most of them towing landing craft (of which there were 2,500) and escorted by 700 warships.

At five minutes to midnight, as June 5 came to an end, the first wave of the invading-liberating force was put ashore: several hundred British infantrymen, commanded by Major John Howard, who went in by glider at the village of Bénouville. Howard's men captured the two bridges, code-named Pegasus and Horsa, that were needed to secure the eastern flank of the imminent bridgehead. Three hours later these glider-borne troops were reinforced by 150 parachute troops, after which a massive parachute operation was put into force, so that by dawn on the following morning 18,000 British and American parachutists were on the ground.

A deception operation, codenamed Titanic, was also launched that night, against the beaches south of Boulogne. It was carried out by ten members of the Special Air Services, a group formed more than two years earlier to operate behind enemy lines and carry out tactical deception. The Boulogne landing was part of the wider 'Fortitude' deception that had successfully persuaded the German High Command that Normandy was not the main target. So successful were the ten men in simulating a larger landing that a whole German regiment – more than a thousand men – was deployed throughout the morning of June 6 to oppose them.

As June 6 began, the Normandy landings, codenamed Operation Overlord, were under way. The war in Europe had taken a decisive step towards the defeat of Germany.

CHAPTER SIXTEEN

1944
JUNE TO DECEMBER

The hated Swastikas have been torn down and burned.

JULIAN KULSKI

WITH THE DESCENT of the British parachutists between midnight and dawn on 6 June 1944 the Normandy landings had begun, and several bridges along which German troops would have to pass to reach the landing beaches were in Allied hands. At 6.30 that morning the first ground troops landed. They were Americans, supported by amphibious tanks, landing under fire at the most westerly point of the beachhead, code named Utah beach.

Within the hour the first British troops landed at Gold and Sword beaches, followed by more Americans at Omaha beach and the Canadians at Juno beach. Some of the Canadians came ashore at the small coastal village of Bernières, whose 'house on the beach' towards which they advanced was being shown within a few days in every Allied cinema newsreel. The German defenders did what they could to challenge the landings, but were out-numbered and outgunned.

In the air the Allies had virtually total control. 'Allied air cover over the fleet and beachhead is very complete,' reported the Toronto *Globe and Mail* of the situation by ten o'clock, when the Canadian troops who had gone ashore at Juno beach were more than a thousand yards inland. 'Every few minutes Spitfires or Lightnings sweep past in the sunshine which has now come out.'

It was not until after ten o'clock – three and a half hours after the first troops had landed – that the news of the landings reached Rommel. The German commander on whose skill and judgement so much depended was still in Germany, hoping to gain Hitler's attention with regard to the urgent needs of his suddenly embattled army. He immediately flew back to France, Hitler having instructed him to drive the invaders back 'into the sea' by midnight. But when midnight came, 155,000 Allied troops were ashore. Their losses had been expected to run into the tens of thousands, and messages had been prepared to announce heavy losses; but less than a thousand men had been killed in each of the British and American armies, and 355 in the Canadian army.

Hitler was not convinced that this was the main thrust of the Allied attack. The deception schemes that had been mounted so carefully convinced him that the real landings would come either in the area of Dieppe, or near Calais, or perhaps even on the Belgian coast. He knew that the First United States Army Group had not moved from East Anglia: in fact, as it did not exist as a fighting force, it was only as a figment of Britain's conniving and of Hitler's imagination. Fearing, however, that the Normandy landings were a deception, that evening Hitler alerted all German units in the Channel and North Sea to be prepared to meet attacks elsewhere. The British, decrypting this instruction, realized that they still had time to put men ashore before the full force of the German defenders was brought to bear on the actual landing grounds.

On the night of June 6/7 a thousand British bombers struck at German lines of communication throughout the Normandy area. Considerable damage was done to railway lines near Lisieux and Coutances, but the two towns were also hit. In Coutances more than half of the town centre was destroyed and 312 French civilians killed. Hitler and his military advisers still could not convince themselves that Normandy was the main Allied target. Even the previous night's bombing of the railway lines leading to Normandy could be a skilful deception.

On June 7, as the Allied positions on the beachhead were steadily consolidated, the German Air Force High Command was still warning its units throughout Western Europe that further landings might take place at any moment either towards Belgium, or on the western side of the Cotentin peninsula (across the peninsula from Utah beach), or on the French Atlantic coast near Lorient, or even on the Norwegian coast.

During the morning of June 7, Primo Levi, then a slave labourer at the Monowitz synthetic oil factory near Auschwitz – tattoo number 174517 – was among many thousands of Jewish slave labourers who saw a group of

British prisoners-of-war marching from the camp next to theirs on the way to work in the same factory. Watching them – as he did every morning – Levi recalled that 'there was something different about them: they marched well aligned, chests thrust forward, smiling, martial, with a step so eager that the German sentinel who escorted them, a territorial no longer young, had difficulty keeping up with them. They saluted us with the V-sign of victory. The next day we found out that from a clandestine radio of theirs they had learned about the Allied landings in Normandy, and that was a great day for us too: freedom seemed within reach.'

During the fighting on the Normandy beachheads on June 7 there was a reminder of the savagery of earlier encounters in 1940 between Allied and German troops. Thirty-four Canadian soldiers had been captured near the villages of Buron and Authie. Although severely wounded, they were shot or bayoneted to death. During the next forty-eight hours a further forty-three Canadians were likewise killed after being taken prisoner. The commanding officer of the SS regiment which captured them was heard to ask his men, after the Canadians had been captured: 'What should we do with these prisoners? They only eat up our rations.'

On June 8 the British troops who had landed at Gold beach linked up with the Americans at Omaha beach. Their greatest hazards were the German Panzer troops – experienced and ruthless. When the radio communication of Panzer Group West was decrypted at Bletchley it enabled the decrypters and Intelligence analysts to identify exactly the Group's headquarters, at La Caine. The headquarters was then bombed so severely that seventeen staff officers were killed and the counter-attack which had been planned for the following day had to be put off for twenty-four hours.

During June 8, Stalin telegraphed to Churchill: '"Overlord" is a joy to us all.' He also informed Churchill that he would be launching his own offensive soon, as he and Churchill had agreed six months earlier that he would, so that at the very moment when Hitler ought to be transferring troops from the Eastern Front to the West, he would have to keep them in the East to meet the new Soviet offensive.

In the immediate aftermath of the June 6 landings, the French Resistance answered the call from London to take action against German lines of communication throughout France. Some of this action was coordinated by agents who had earlier been sent in from Britain, among them the British-born shop assistant from south London, Violette Szabo, who had been parachuted south-east of Limoges on the night of June 6/7. Her husband, a soldier with the Free French, had been killed in the Western Desert two years earlier.

Violette Szabo and the three agents parachuted with her – one was an American wireless operator, Jean-Claude Guiet – had the task of preventing the Second SS Panzer Division – the SS Das Reich Division – from moving to the Normandy beachheads from southern France. In the ordinary course of military movement this transfer would have taken three days, and constituted a severe challenge to the Allied troops, already in harsh combat. As a result of the Resistance sabotage in blowing up road and railway bridges, and the simultaneous Allied air force destruction of the bridges across the Loire between Orléans and the Bay of Biscay, it took the Panzer Division seventeen days to make the journey.

The fate of those who were caught carrying out acts of resistance was harsh. Violette Szabo was among those ambushed three days after she had parachuted in: for the next five days she was interrogated by the Gestapo in Limoges, and then taken to Paris. A Resistance plan to rescue her from the prison in Limoges was frustrated by her move to Paris. She did not survive the war.

Two hundred miles south-east of the Normandy beachhead, the civilian Resistance leaders in the town of Saint-Amand decided to seize control of their town. They did so without difficulty, occupying the Milice headquarters and executing two militiamen whom they had arrested outside the building. This act of defiance was premature. On June 8 other French Milice forces from outside attacked the town, burnt down part of it, and shot nineteen of the Resistance members. The remaining fifty members managed to escape to the countryside, taking with them thirteen militiamen as hostages. Later, as German troops closed in on them, they were forced to flee from their hiding places. Unable either to guard or feed their prisoner-hostages while on the run, and not wanting to give their position away by shooting them, they hanged them with parachute cords. As a reprisal, the regional Milice and Gestapo rounded up seventy Jews in Saint-Amand and threw them into deep wells where they perished.

On the night of June 8/9 a special 12,000-pound bomb was dropped 125 miles south of the Normandy battle area to destroy the exit to a railway tunnel near Saumur through which units of the SS Das Reich Division was about to move towards the battlefield. Behind the lines, members of the French Resistance continued to sabotage bridges and railway lines. One active Resistance unit was operating near the town of Tulle. On June 9, as a reprisal for its activities, and hoping to deter any further Resistance activity, the Das Reich Division seized two hundred men at random in Tulle and, forcing wives and children to watch, hanged them on the lamp posts and balconies outside their homes.

Acts of resistance throughout France continued, and on a growing scale. So too did the British bombing attacks on German airfields in the area south of the battle. The main British bombing target on the night of June 9/10 was the railway junction and railway marshalling yards at Etampes. During the raid, bombs falling short of the target severely damaged more than twenty per cent of the town, destroying between 400 and 500 houses and killing 133 civilians.

The Germans still felt that the Normandy landings were not the main ones. On June 8 a message had been received from the double-agent Juan Pujol Garcia that the Normandy landings were 'a diversionary manoeuvre designed to draw off enemy reserves in order to make a decisive attack in another place'. In sending its report to Hitler, German Intelligence noted that it 'confirms the view already held by us that a further attack is to be expected in another place'. At German Army Headquarters at Zossen, the Chief of the Army General Staff's Intelligence Division, Colonel Alexis von Roenne, informed the Chief of the Army Operations Staff, General Alfred Jodl, on June 9, that an attack 'must be expected at any moment in the Pas-de-Calais'.

Among the soldiers fighting alongside the Germans in Normandy were Russian Cossack troops who had defected from the Soviets, and Indian troops loyal to one of the fiercest opponents of British rule, the Bengali national leader Subhas Chandra Bose. Troops loyal to Bose were also fighting that week alongside the Japanese troops in Burma, hoping to secure the liberation of India on the bayonets of the Japanese – and on their own bayonets. Cossack troops in France were used by the Germans to help carry out reprisals against acts of local resistance. German SS units could also carry out reprisals unaided. When a German military formation in central France was attacked while on its way to Normandy, a small village, Oradour-sur-Glane was surrounded by SS troops, who then murdered 642 of the villagers, of whom 190 were schoolchildren.

Only two villagers managed to escape. Among the dead were several Polish and Hungarian-born Jews, and an eight-year-old Jewish boy who had been born in Strasbourg: they had been given shelter in the village more than a year earlier, and were by any foreseeable prospect as safe from molestation as the villagers whose fate they shared. The Germans did not know or care that on this occasion there were Jews among those whom they decided to murder as a reprisal. The aim was to frighten villagers elsewhere in France from giving support to the Resistance, and even to turn the local French people against the Resistance in order to protect themselves from future reprisals. This did not work; acts of resistance continued, and as the Allies pressed deeper and deeper into France, they spread more and more widely, so much so that within two months of the Normandy landings whole towns were being liberated by Resistance groups.

On the night of June 12/13 more than six hundred British bombers attacked German communications along routes leading to Normandy, including road and rail junctions at Amiens, Arras, Caen, Cambrai and Poitiers. Another three hundred bombers flew to Germany to bomb the synthetic oil plant at Gelsenkirchen, in the Ruhr. The raid was so effective that all oil production ceased, depriving the German air force of a thousand tons of aviation fuel a day for several weeks. Many bombs fell in a nearby working class district, killing 270 German civilians and also twenty-three foreign workers. Twenty-four workers in the oil plant were also killed, as were six schoolboys who had been conscripted to help with anti-aircraft duties.

The ability of the Americans and the British to bomb German industry was an integral part of the plan to advance from Normandy through France to the German border, and into Germany. Bombing policy was tied in closely with the strategic objectives and tactical needs of the invasion.

In the Pacific War, in the third week of June, following the landings on Biak Island off the north-western coast of New Guinea – from which, on any western-based strategic plan the Japanese defenders ought to have been ordered to withdraw by their superiors – it took the Americans three weeks before the Japanese were defeated on the battlefield. But instead of surrendering, they retreated into caves. When they again refused to surrender, flame throwers were used against them. By the end of the battle more than five thousand Japanese were dead, for the loss of 525 American lives.

The ratio of Japanese dead to the dead of their adversaries was everywhere unequal. During the three and a half months fighting at Imphal and Kohima, inside the Indian frontier, 2,700 British and Indian troops were killed in action, and 30,000 Japanese. A military system that encouraged fighting to the death and suicide rather than surrender was leading to the destruction of a whole military, and human, class: the ordinary fighting man.

The last remnants of European Jewry under German rule were also being destroyed. On June 14 the deportation took place of 1,795 Greek Jews from the island of Corfu. They were taken by ship to mainland Greece, and then by sealed train the whole length of the Balkans and much of central Europe, a journey of seven hundred miles, to Auschwitz. They were told that they were going to be 'resettled' in Poland. On their arrival, two hundred of them were sent to the barracks as slave labourers, and 1,600 to the gas chambers and to their deaths.

The deception methods still worked, so much so that when the surviving Jews of the Lodz ghetto were told in June that volunteers were needed to go to Germany 'for the clearing away of debris in cities that have been bombed' they volunteered to go. What could be more logical? Hundreds of thousands of non-Jewish labourers – Poles and Czechs among them – were being used to remove the rubble caused by Allied air attacks on Germany. The Germans added, as an extra touch of verisimilitude, that the first three thousand to volunteer would be sent to Munich.

The Jews were also told that whoever volunteered could, before leaving for Germany, collect their food rations without having to wait their turn. As the ghetto inhabitants were permanently on the edge of starvation, this was also a powerful, inducement to volunteer. Three thousand volunteers came forward. They were taken away by train, but instead of travelling the 420 miles to Munich, the train went to Chelmno, less than thirty miles away. There, the former death camp had just been reopened with a gas chamber instead of the gas van. All three thousand volunteers were dead within a few days.

From the moment that he returned from Germany to the Normandy battle-field, Rommel made a sustained attempt to prevent the Allies from breaking out of the bridgehead. He succeeded for far longer than the Allies had believed possible, confining the attackers to a much smaller and therefore more vulnerable perimeter than they had anticipated.

The fighting for Caen was particularly fierce. The city of Caen, a crucial German communications centre, and the chief Allied objective for the fourth day of the landings, was not to be taken for another two months. Among those who fought in the battle for Caen was one of de Gaulle's first supporters in London in 1940, Maurice Schumann, and a young British officer, Edward Heath, with whom Schumann was later to be closely linked – when Heath was Prime Minister of Britain, and Schumann Foreign Minister of France.

As the battle for Caen began, the Germans were preparing to launch a new weapon: a pilotless, jet-propelled plane, just over twenty-five foot long, with a wing span of seventeen and a half feet, which carried a ton of explosives that would detonate on impact. It was known as the VI – the 'V' standing for *Vergeltungswaffe* (Reprisal Weapon). On mainland Britain, against which it was first launched on June 14, it was known as the flying bomb, Doodlebug and Buzz Bomb. The only one to cause casualties that day killed six people in London: the youngest was an eight-month-old baby, Tom Woodcraft, killed with his mother.

The German plan had been to launch a massive bomber attack on London on the same day as the first flying bombs. But by chance, the bomber force allocated for this task was destroyed on the ground at the military airfield at Beauvais by Allied bombers on their regular daily attack on German airfields in Northern France.

Always wanting to be as near to his troops as possible, but also to be safe, on June 17 Hitler went to a Führer Bunker which had been specially constructed for him at Marival, near Soissons, north east of Paris. It had been built more than six months earlier as part of the work on the Atlantic Wall for Fortress Europe. It was Hitler's first visit to France since he had come briefly, as a conqueror, in the summer of 1940. This time he came to prevent his conquest from being lost, issuing an order from the bunker: 'The fortress Cherbourg is to be held at all costs.' But he refused to allow the German Fifteenth Army, which was then in reserve at the Pas-de-Calais, to be moved to Normandy, as he wanted it to remain near Calais to repel the invasion his spy had told him was still to come.

On the day that Hitler reached his new headquarters at Marival – a decade later it was to be the headquarters of NATO – two flying bombs which fell on London killed thirty-seven people. One of the bombs, falling on a hospital – there was no way in which the flying bomb could be directed onto a specific target – killed thirteen patients, most of them children, and five members of the hospital staff. By a quirk of poor design, one of the flying bombs sent against London that day went accidentally and wildly off course, falling near Hitler's headquarters.

On the following day, a Sunday, several more flying bombs hit London. One of them hit the Guards' Chapel in Birdcage Walk, within sight of Big Ben, during a church service: 121 members of the congregation were killed – fifty-eight civilians and sixty-three Service personnel, including many American soldiers. Among the dead was the Commanding Officer of the

Scots Guards, Lieutenant Colonel John Cobbold, a veteran of the First World War. One of the British worshippers, a subaltern in the Women's Auxiliary Transport Service, Elizabeth Sheppard-Jones, whose spine was fractured, paralyzing her from the waist down, later recalled:

'Here endeth the first lesson,' the Guards' colonel who had been reading it must have said. The congregation rose to its feet. In the distance hummed faintly the engine of a flying bomb. 'We praise Thee, O God: we acknowledge Thee to be the Lord,' we, the congregation, sang. The dull buzz became a roar, through which our voices could now only faintly be heard. 'All earth doth worship Thee: the Father everlasting.' The roar stopped abruptly as the engine cut out . . .

The Te Deum soared again into the silence. 'To Thee all Angels cry aloud, the Heavens, and all the Powers therein.' Then there was a noise so loud it was as if all the waters and the winds in the world had come together in mighty conflict and the Guards' Chapel collapsed upon us in a bellow of bricks and mortar . . .

One moment I was singing the Te Deum and the next I lay in dust and blackness, aware of one thing only – that I had to go on breathing.

Elizabeth Sheppard-Jones's account reflected the experiences of the millions of people who were injured by bombs all over Europe between 1939 and 1945:

I felt no pain, I was scarcely aware of the chunks of massed grey concrete that had piled on top of me, nor did I realize that this was why breathing was so difficult. My whole being was concentrated in the one tremendous effort of taking in long struggling breaths and then letting them struggle out again. It may have been an hour later, perhaps two or three or more, that I was suddenly aware that somewhere above me, above the black emptiness, there were people, living, helpful people whose voices reached me, dim and disembodied as in a dream. 'Please, please, I'm here,' I said, and I went on saying it until my voice was hoarse and my throat ached with the dust that poured down it . . . Somewhere not far away from me someone was screaming, screaming, screaming, like an animal caught in a trap . . .

My eyes rested in horror on a blood-stained body that, had my hands

been free, I could have reached out and touched . . . the body of a young
soldier whose eyes stared unseeingly at the sky . . .

I tried to convince myself that this was truly a nightmare, one from
which I was bound soon to wake up. I think I must have been given a
morphia injection for I still felt no pain, but I did begin to have an inkling
that I was badly injured. I turned my freed head towards a Guardsman
who was helping with the rescue work, and hysterically I cried out: 'How
do I look? Tell me how I look!' Madam,' he said, 'you look wonderful to
me!'

The German High Command was still waiting for another Anglo-American
invasion force. On June 17, the eleventh day after the Normandy landings,
possible 'subsidiary operations' were still being discussed at Zossen. The
Pas-de-Calais, south-west France, Norway, the Dutch-Belgian coast, and the
South of France were all thought of as possible and imminent Allied points
of attack, even as the main point of attack.

A landing in the South of France was indeed about to take place. It was
primarily an American assault on the French Riviera. The Americans who
trained for it did so on the same beach at Salerno which many of them had
attacked in real and bloody combat more than a year earlier. 'Abandoned,
rusted landing craft were still bobbing their sterns as the tide changed,'
wrote the war cartoonist Bill Mauldin, 'and you would find skeletons washed
up on the beaches. It was a very grim place and we all lost friends there.'

Despite the tenacity of the German soldiers on the battlefield, and the
daily death toll from flying bombs over London, the Allied successes were
continuous. On June 19, a British bombing raid at Watten, inland from
Calais, destroyed a large number of flying bombs as they were being prepared
for launching. Three days later an American bombing raid on a flying bomb
depot at Nucourt, north-west of Paris, was likewise successful.

By midnight on June 20, half a million Allied soldiers were ashore at
Normandy, but still they were being held in a narrow perimeter by Rommel's
troops. In the first two weeks' fighting, still within the bridgehead, 4,000
Allied soldiers had been killed in action.

Behind German lines in the East, at least half a million Soviet partisans
were harassing German road and rail communications, attacking German
troops on the move, and destroying sections of railway line that were needed
to move German troops from one section of the front to another, on the eve

of what was clearly to be a massive Soviet offensive. That offensive was launched on June 22, three years to the day since the German invasion of the Soviet Union. It confronted Hitler with the worst form of a two-front nightmare: half a million troops in the West – their numbers doubled within three weeks – and 1,700,000 troops in the East.

Both sets of Allied armies that were moving against Germany in the third week of June had superior fuel resources and superior air power. Both had as their objective the conquest of Germany itself. When Germany signed the armistice on 11 November 1918 not a single Allied soldier stood on German soil. The Allied intention was to avoid this perceived error and to press on to Berlin. Not only was this a military imperative, but, as far as Stalin was concerned, it had a political dimension – the imposition of Communist rule as far West as the Vistula, the Oder and the Elbe.

While the battle for Normandy continued in the West – with heavy casualties on both sides as the Germans fought to retain their hold on Caen, the Cotentin Peninsula and Falaise – the battle in the East proceeded with a swiftness that left Germany no time to establish meaningful defence lines. By the end of the first week, 38,000 German troops had been killed and 116,000 taken prisoner. Having lost 2,000 tanks, German Army Group North, which had expected to hold the line in White Russia, broke into two and retreated, one half towards the Baltic States, where it was to be surrounded and isolated, the other half into East Prussia.

In the West, American troops reached the suburbs of Cherbourg on June 25. The German commander of the fortress, General Karl Wilhelm von Schlieben, appealed to Rommel to be allowed to surrender. 'Among the troops defending the town', he explained, 'there are two thousand wounded who cannot be treated. Is the sacrifice of the others still necessary?' Rommel replied: 'In accordance with the Führer's orders, you are to hold out to the last round.' That day more than a hundred German fighters flew from their bases in France to support General Schlieben's defence. All were beaten back, whereupon Allied warships bombarded Schlieben's positions from the sea.

Field Marshal von Rundstedt remained unconvinced that Normandy was more than a diversion. In his weekly situation report on June 25 he referred to the non-existent First United States Army Group as being ready to embark for Europe. This force, in his view, was even larger than that which had been put ashore at Normandy, and might be used at any moment for landings between the mouths of the Somme and Seine, to encircle and capture Le

Havre. In order to be able to challenge this army as it tried to come ashore, von Rundstedt insisted on keeping in the Pas-de-Calais area many thousands of German soldiers who might otherwise have tipped the balance in Normandy, and for whom Rommel clamoured in vain.

On June 26 the German naval commander at Cherbourg, Admiral Hennecke, ordered the destruction of all port facilities. For this act, Hitler awarded him the Knight's Cross to add to his Iron Cross. That day, on the Eastern Front, following a heavy air bombardment by 700 Russian bombers, Soviet forces entered Vitebsk. In the streets of the city they found the bodies of 6,000 German soldiers who had been killed during the bombing raid. The German forces at Vitebsk, like those at Cherbourg, had been ordered by Hitler to fight to the last. But for the German soldiers – and for their Leader – the stage had been reached in the war when after every fight there came defeat.

In Germany, a twenty-five-year-old sergeant in the Army Medical Corps, Heinz Bello, who held the Iron Cross Second Class, the East Medal and the Badge for wounded soldiers, expressed his hostility to Nazism and militarism while he was on fire-watching duty in Berlin. He was denounced, found guilty of 'undermining morale' and sentenced to death. He was executed on a machine-gun range. That same week, Professor Walther Arndt, a physician and zoologist, was also executed. His crime was to have remarked after a particularly heavy Allied bombing raid: 'This is the end of the Third Reich, and the guilty can now be brought to punishment.'

The 'guilty' still had work to do. On the day of Professor Arndt's execution, 485 Italian Jews were sent from Fossoli and Verona to Auschwitz. Four days later 1,153 French Jews were deported from Paris. Earlier that month 496 Dutch Jews had been deported from Westerbork camp in Holland. From Hungary a total of 381,000 Jews had reached Auschwitz in six weeks. More than a quarter of a million of them had been gassed, the highest rate of mass murder recorded during the Second World War.

In order to alert the world to the killings at Auschwitz, four Jewish prisoners there – Rudolf Vrba, Alfred Wetzler, Arnost Rosin and Czeslaw Mordowicz – had managed to escape, Vrba and Wetzler in April and Rosin and Mordowicz in May. With extraordinary luck and courage they brought news of the gas chambers to the Slovak town of Zilina, from where it was smuggled first to Bratislava and then to Berne, in neutral Switzerland. From Berne the terrible details were sent, on June 24, to both Washington and London, with an appeal by the British diplomats who forwarded it – Clifford

Norton and Elizabeth Wiskemann – that the Allies should bomb the railway lines leading to Auschwitz.

The names of twenty railway stations on those lines was included in the bombing appeal. On June 27, when Churchill was shown the report, he responded, in a note to Anthony Eden: 'What can be done? What can be said?' Eden then told Churchill of the request for the bombing of the railway lines. Churchill replied: 'Get anything out of the Air Force you can, and invoke me if necessary.'

The bombing would have to be done in daylight, by American bombers based in southern Italy. Churchill was told that the American air force commander in Europe, General Ira C. Eaker, was sympathetic to the request. But in Washington, the Assistant Secretary of War, John J. McCloy, rejected four separate appeals to bomb the lines. His instruction on receiving each request was, his deputy noted, 'to "kill" this'.

The deportations continued throughout the last week of June. Although no plans had yet been made to bomb the lines, other plans were made which were to prove effective. On July 2, two days before Churchill's instruction that something should be done, there was a heavy American bombing raid on oil refineries and oil storage tanks in Budapest. As well as dropping bombs, the bombers dropped leaflets informing 'the authorities in Hungary' that the United States government was following the persecution of the Jews with 'extreme gravity', and warning that 'all those responsible' for carrying out the orders to persecute the Jews would be punished.

The air raid of July 2 frightened the Hungarian leadership. Not only did the leaflets indicate that it might well be the prelude to a reprisal, but the damage done during the raid itself was considerable. As well as hitting the oil refineries and oil storage tanks, hundreds of bombs had fallen on residential areas – in error, as it happens, but the Hungarian authorities could not know this – and several hundred Hungarian civilians had been killed. Admiral Horthy at once summoned SS General Veesenmayer and informed him that the deportations must stop.

Veesenmayer argued in vain that the deportations must continue, but Horthy did not want another Allied bombing raid on Budapest. Nor did the Germans have the resources, at that particularly testing time of the war, to bring more troops into Hungary. Indeed, the troops already there were urgently needed on both the Eastern and Western Fronts. The Germans therefore halted the deportations. No more Hungarian Jews were sent to Birkenau. That one bombing raid had saved as many as a hundred thousand

Jewish lives. Adolf Eichmann, his work cut short before it was completed, was awarded the Iron Cross Second Class. His request to be promoted above the rank of Lieutenant-Colonel was rejected.

With the halt of the deportations from Hungary, the 170,000 surviving Jews – most of them in Budapest – sought protective documents against the possibility of Hungarian fascist attack. These documents were given by several foreign diplomats in Budapest, including the Swede, Raoul Wallenberg, a great-great-grandson of Michael Benedics, one of the first Jews to settle in Sweden: Benedics had come from Lithuania, across the Baltic Sea, at the end of the eighteenth century, and was a convert to Lutheranism.

In the Far East the Japanese were driven across the Indian border and back into Burma. On the Eastern Front the Russians continued to advance rapidly. By the end of the second week of their offensive a further 100,000 German soldiers had been killed. Hitler, having returned from France to Berchtesgaden, was confronted by both Rommel and von Rundstedt, who, after begging for a massive reinforcement of aircraft and anti-aircraft guns, asked their Commander-in-Chief how he imagined the war 'could still be won'. Three days later von Rundstedt was relieved of his post. The new commander in the West was Field Marshal Günther Hans von Kluge, charged by Hitler with holding the Falaise pocket – in which Canadian troops were fighting with noted bravery.

Although the prospects of a German victory had all but vanished in both the West and the East, Germany's warmaking activities did not cease. In Italy, during a German anti-partisan sweep between Parma and Piacenza at the end of June, two hundred partisans were killed, and forty-three captured. After capture, those forty-three were tortured and then shot. Over Britain, a flying bomb which fell on London on June 30 killed forty-eight people in the Strand. Another flying bomb that day killed twenty-four babies under a year old at a children's home at Westerham in Kent, and eight members of staff. Five of the babies were only a month old. They had mostly been evacuated from London to Kent for safety. By the last day of June, almost two thousand British civilians had been killed by the new weapon.

The largest flying bomb death toll was yet to come, when on the morning of July 3 a large group of American servicemen gathered outside their army billets in Turk's Row, Chelsea, waiting to be taken in trucks to help dig out the victims of a flying bomb that had fallen south of the river about half an hour earlier. As the Americans were preparing to go to the aid of the wounded, a flying bomb hit the truck in which the first batch were about to drive off. Sixty-four Americans were killed, as well as ten British civilians who happened to be in the street at the time.

Three days later Churchill told the House of Commons that the drug penicillin, which had hitherto been restricted for the use of service personnel, would be made available to civilians.

On July 7, in France, while the battle was being fought in Normandy, the Vichy militia took the former French Colonial Minister, Georges Mandel, to a wood near Paris. He had been handed over to them by the Gestapo, which was holding several of Mandel's pre-war Cabinet colleagues, including Reynaud, Daladier and Blum, as 'prominent' prisoners in various concentrations camps in Germany. They survived; Mandel did not. He was shot that day in his own country by his fellow-countrymen.

Thirty years earlier Mandel had been close to the French war leader Georges Clemenceau. He was hated by Vichy for having been one of the leading politicians in June 1940 – when Minister of the Interior – arguing in favour of continuing the war with Germany. This, combined with the fact that he was a Jew, had made him a focus of vengeance.

The German army officers whose efforts to kill Hitler just over a year earlier had so badly miscarried tried again in July. Their first plan was to smuggle a bomb into Berchtesgaden on July 2, and to kill Hitler, Himmler and Goering in a single blast. By chance Hitler was alone that day, and the assassination attempt was called off. It was the day on which the Allies put the millionth soldier ashore at Normandy, and on which 40,000 German soldiers, encircled on the Eastern Front, were killed while trying to break out of the trap. On the following day the Russian Army entered Minsk, taking more than 150,000 German soldiers prisoner and capturing 2,000 tanks.

On the day of the Russian entry into Minsk, and with the massive scale of German losses known to the German High Command, one of the leading military plotters, Count Claus von Stauffenberg, went to Berchtesgaden. There, in Hitler's own headquarters, he went to see Major-General Helmuth Stieff, the head of the Organization Branch of the Army High Command, who gave him a small bomb with a silent fuse. The bomb was small enough to hide inside a brief case.

As the renewed preparations for Hitler's assassination were being made, and the conspirators were planning how to establish an alternative government, Hitler was ordering the German soldiers still holding Caen not to withdraw. He also warned, in a Führer Directive to his senior officers, that if the Normandy bridgehead were to increase in size, 'our forces would prove inadequate to contain it, and the enemy will break out into the interior of France, where we do not possess any comparable technical mobility with which to oppose him'. Were the Normandy bridgehead to become a spearhead, not only German control of France, but also of Belgium, Holland and even Germany itself might be at risk. On the Eastern Front, the Russians were already about to break in to East Prussia.

On July 11 Count von Stauffenberg took his brief-case bomb to Berchtesgaden, whither he had been ordered by Hitler to give an account of the military situation. From Berchtesgaden, Hitler was about to go to his East Prussian headquarters at Rastenburg. Stauffenberg had also been summoned to Rastenburg, on July 15, and decided to take the bomb with him, and use it there instead. There would be a greater opportunity, he judged, to put the brief case closer to Hitler at Rastenburg than he had been able to do at Berchtesgaden.

In the four days between the Berchtesgaden briefing and the briefing to be held at Rastenburg, the German army suffered further disasters. During the Russian advance to Lvov, forty thousand German soldiers were encircled in the fortress town of Brody, of whom thirty thousand were killed during the seven-day battle. On July 15, the day on which Stauffenberg was to present himself at Rastenburg – and the day on which he intended to place his bomb – Hitler received a letter from Rommel warning that as a result of lack of adequate reinforcements, and given the Allied air and artillery superiority, 'even the bravest army will be smashed piece by piece, losing men, arms and territory in the process'. Rommel's unease was compounded by the fact that the German High Command remained convinced that the First United States Army Group – that masterpiece of Allied deception – was still waiting to be sent across the English Channel to cut off the German forces in Normandy by landing further east.

At Rastenburg on July 15, Hitler unexpectedly shortened the length of the conference. Stauffenberg had therefore to give up his plan, and decided to use his bomb at the next Rastenburg briefing to which he had been summoned, five days later. Not knowing of this last-minute change of plan, one of the senior officers at the centre of the conspiracy, General Friedrich Olbricht, who was in Berlin, ordered the troops of the Reserve Army to march on the city and seize the main government buildings. When he and his men approached the Wilhelmstrasse he realized that something had gone wrong. He had the presence of mind to tell his immediate superior, General Fromm, that he was just carrying out a practise manoeuvre. He was given a reprimand and returned to his desk in the War Ministry.

General Olbricht, a man of deep religious conviction who regarded the Nazi regime as 'a disgrace to the Fatherland', had been Chief of the General Staff of the Army High Command in 1940, and since 1943 the deputy commander of the Reserve Army. He and his fellow-conspirators decided to use the extra time between July 15 and July 20 to win Rommel over to their cause. Rommel was known to be despondent about Hitler's refusal to accept that Normandy was lost. 'The troops are everywhere fighting heroically, but the unequal struggle is approaching its end,' Rommel wrote to Hitler on July 16, in explaining why he wanted the 28,000 German troops then stationed in the Channel Islands to be brought over to Normandy to reinforce his men. But Hitler refused. Just as he had insisted a year earlier in holding on to the Tunisian Tip, so he would not contemplate giving up the Channel Islands. Every extremity of the regions under his control was to be held, even at the expense – as Rommel saw it – of the main battle and most dangerous battlefields.

The conspirators felt on confident ground when they decided to approach Rommel for support. But on July 17, Rommel was driving from the Normandy battlefield to his headquarters, through the village of Livarot, when he was severely wounded by machine-gun fire from an Allied fighter bomber. He was taken to hospital, no longer able to serve either as a commander or a conspirator.

On the day of Rommel's accident, 57,000 German prisoners-of-war were paraded through the streets of Moscow. The procession was headed by nineteen German generals. On July 18 the Soviet forces in the East reached Augustow, a small lakeside town on the Polish side of the pre-war Polish-German border. Rastenburg was only eighty miles away.

In Normandy, Rommel was no longer able to direct the battle. But the lack of German reinforcements and air power was something even he could not have overcome, as the Allies opened their assault on Caen itself. Four hundred Allied artillery pieces opened fire, as did the fifteen-inch naval guns of the monitor *Roberts*, which had last fired its guns in action at the Battle of Jutland in 1916. Two British cruisers also joined the bombardment, in which several thousand German soldiers and three thousand French civilians were killed. Too late Hitler agreed to move to Normandy the German forces further east that were still awaiting the phantom First United States Army.

On July 20 the German ring around the Allied forces in Normandy was broken. It had held for more than six weeks. What remained – and it was to involve continuing heavy fighting and loss of life on both sides – was the application of Allied superior resources against the tenacity of the German defenders. Those defenders were being pushed steadily back towards Paris, eastern France, and the border of Germany. With the Allied forces on the move in the West, and with the Russians pressing in upon Germany from the East and about to cross into the Reich, Hitler, still at Rastenburg, held his July 20 briefing. Among those present, and ready to act the moment the Führer was dead, was General Erich Fellgiebel, Chief of Communications for the Armed Forces, whose task was to close down all the signal circuits linking Rastenburg with German units elsewhere, so that a counter-attack on the conspirators could not be mounted.

Hitler was in a wooden hut near his bunker studying a map on a large table when Stauffenberg activated the fuse of the bomb in his briefcase. Stauffenberg then pushed the briefcase under the table with his foot, and hurried out of the room. When he was about two hundred yards away the bomb went off. Watching the hut exploding into the air, he assumed that Hitler was dead and drove rapidly to the airfield at Rastenburg, then flew to Berlin. What he did not know was that one of those present around the table, General Brandt, in trying to get a better look at the map, had inadvertently pushed the briefcase with his foot to the far side of the wooden frame holding up the table.

It was the wooden frame that saved Hitler from being killed outright. Four officers closer to the bomb were killed. Not only was Hitler not dead, but he would not allow his wounds to prevent him from greeting a long-awaited visitor – Mussolini – and showing him the ruins of the hut and how closely he had escaped assassination. After the war, one of the German generals who was present when Hitler and Mussolini took tea that afternoon told his Allied interrogator:

All of a sudden the Führer leapt up in a fit of frenzy with foam on his lips, and yelled out that he would be revenged on all traitors, that Providence had just shown him once more that he had been chosen to make world history, and shouted about terrible punishments for women and children, all of them would have to be put inside concentration camps!

Mussolini found it most unpleasant. Meanwhile more tea was served by the footmen in white gloves.

To a group of German railway workers whom he passed while taking Mussolini to the railway station, Hitler said: 'I knew from the first that men of your sort were not involved. It's my deep conviction that my enemies are the "vons" who call themselves aristocrats.'

As soon as von Stauffenberg reached Berlin he went to see the Commander of the Reserve Army – and Chief of Armaments – General Friedrich Fromm, who had been undecided whether to join the conspiracy or not. By chance Fromm had just telephoned Rastenburg to speak to General Keitel, and had learned from him both of the assassination attempt, and that Hitler was alive. When Stauffenberg entered Fromm's room in the War Ministry, Fromm ordered his arrest. Stauffenberg was indignant: 'General Fromm,' he said coldly, and with the confidence of a man who is about to share the reins of power, 'I myself detonated the bomb. No one in that room could possibly be alive.' Fromm replied: 'Count Stauffenberg, the assassination attempt has failed. You should shoot yourself at once.' Stauffenberg declined to do so.

Despite their failure to kill Hitler, the conspirators decided to go ahead with their plan. General Fromm was arrested, and orders were then given by another officer who was in the plot, the Berlin Fortress commander General von Hase, to surround the government offices in and around the Wilhelmstrasse, including Gestapo headquarters and the Ministry of Propaganda office in which Goebbels was at that very moment working.

The man to whom this crucial order was given was Major Otto Ernst Remer, in command of the Guards Battalion Grossdeutschland, then stationed in Berlin. The thirty-two-year-old Remer, a former Hitler Youth leader, had already obeyed the instructions of the plotters to use his troops to guard essential public buildings, believing that the instructions were part of a training exercise. Intent on obeying the order to arrest Goebbels, he confronted him at the Propaganda Ministry and was about to take him into custody when Goebbels suggested that they telephone Rastenburg and speak direct to Hitler.

The connection was made and Remer heard Hitler's voice. Hitler then, over the telephone, promoted Remer to the rank of Colonel, and ordered him to move at once against the conspirators. Remer obeyed. That evening,

Goebbels broadcast over German radio to tell the German people that their Leader was alive and in full possession of his faculties.

Remer's action has been seen as a turning point in history. The historian David Childs writes: 'Had Remer taken a different line, it is possible the plot would have succeeded. Although Hitler had survived the plotters' assassination attempt, which killed some of his entourage in a bomb explosion, if the plotters had succeeded in taking control of Germany the war would have ended nearly a year before it did.'

An hour and a half after Goebbels had spoken over the radio, a message was sent out to all army units in the name of Field Marshal Erwin von Witzleben: 'The Führer is dead. I have been appointed Commander-in-Chief of the Armed Forces, and also – '. At that point the message broke off. Some of the conspirators were still not aware that Hitler was alive. At German army headquarters in Paris the conspirators there, headed by General Karl Heinrich von Stuelpnagel, the Military Governor of occupied France, and his aide-de-camp Caesar von Hofacker – a cousin of Stauffenberg – had received a telephone call from Stauffenberg in Berlin at about four o'clock in the afternoon telling them that the bomb had exploded and that Hitler was dead. General Stuelpnagel had immediately ordered the arrest of all senior Gestapo and Security Service officers in the French capital. His order was obeyed.

Stuelpnagel had then set off for the headquarters of Field Marshal von Kluge at La Roche Guyon, fully expecting to gain Kluge's support for the conspirators. By the time he arrived, Kluge had learned from Berlin that Hitler was alive, and had only been lightly hurt. Stuelpnagel returned to Paris. From Rastenburg, Hitler gave orders for the arrest all the conspirators.

Stuelpnagel was among those who were summoned at once to Berlin. He drove back as far as the battlefield of Sedan, where he had fought in the First World War, and tried to commit suicide by shooting himself in the head. He succeeded only in blinding himself. General Fromm, whom the conspirators had arrested, proceeded that very evening to act with all the severity that he hoped – wrongly as it turned out – would save him from Hitler's suspicion that he had contemplated joining the conspirators. At Fromm's orders, Stauffenberg was arrested that evening and put before a firing squad in the courtyard of the War Ministry building, in front of a large pile of sand used to put out incendiary fires. With the scene illuminated by the headlights of a few trucks, Stauffenberg was executed. Shot at his side was Fromm's deputy, General Olbricht.

General Fromm proved an eager enthusiast for Hitler's acts of vengeance. One of those whom he arrested that night was General Ludwig Beck, whom the conspirators had designated Head of State in place of Hitler. As Chief of the Army General Staff in 1938, Beck had resigned in protest against the plan to invade Czechoslovakia. Brought to the War Ministry building, Beck was given the opportunity to shoot himself. Twice he attempted to blow his own brains out, but twice he failed. Gravely wounded by his own unsuccessful attempts, he was then shot at his own request by an army sergeant.

That night Hitler broadcast to the German people. His words were confident, and full of warning that the war would go on:

German racial comrades!

I do not know how many times an assassination attempt against me has been planned and carried out. If I speak to you today, I do so for two reasons: first, so that you may hear my voice and know that I myself am uninjured and well. Secondly, so that you may also learn the details about a crime that has not its like in German history.

A very small clique of ambitious, wicked and stupidly criminal officers forged a plot to eliminate me and along with me virtually the entire staff of the German leadership of the armed forces. The bomb which was planted by Colonel Count von Stauffenberg burst two metres to the right of me. It very seriously injured a number of associates dear to me; one of them has died.

I myself am completely uninjured except for some very small scrapes, bruises or burns. I regard it as a confirmation of my assignment from Providence to continue to pursue my life's goal as I have done hitherto . . .

The group represented by these usurpers is ridiculously small. It has nothing to do with the German armed forces, and above all with the German army. It is a very small coterie of criminal elements which is now being mercilessly extirpated . . .

Hitler added: 'We will settle accounts the way we National Socialists are accustomed to settle them.'

In the months ahead, more than five thousand Germans were executed for their part in the conspiracy, or for their alleged sympathy with the conspirators. As had happened at the time of the Night of the Long Knives ten years earlier, many of those whom Hitler considered his enemies, against whom he had scores to settle, and even those who were already his prisoners, were also killed, under the shadow and terror of vengeance for Rastenburg. To the final days of the Third Reich a '20th of July Special Commission' worked to find and to expose those who were the enemies of the regime. Four hundred investigators, and all the apparatus of torture developed by the Gestapo over the previous eleven years, were brought to bear on these enemies, real and imagined, and on those against whom the long arm of tyranny reached without mercy.

Among the first to die, hanged by the neck not with rope but with wire, and not dropped from the scaffold but pulled slowly up to it, were Field Marshal von Witzleben, who had authorized the message saying that Hitler was dead, and General Erich Hoepner, who had been dismissed from his command in 1941 for having carried out a withdrawal on the Russian front in defiance of Hitler's orders, and who had agreed to become War Minister following Hitler's overthrow. Before his execution Hoepner was offered a pistol with which to commit suicide. He refused it, saying: 'I am not a swine, that I should have to condemn myself.'

Also executed was General Erich Fellgiebel, Chief of Communications for the Armed Forces, who had been at Rastenburg at the time of the assassination attempt, ready to close down the signal circuits that might have been used against the plotters; and Colonel Caesar von Hofacker, aide-de-camp to General von Steulpnagel in Paris. It was von Hofacker who, under extreme torture, revealed that Rommel had not been unsympathetic when approached by the conspirators shortly before his accident, but had asked the conspirators to pass back the message: 'Tell the people in Berlin they can count on me.' Stuelpnagel, who had blinded himself in his suicide attempt after having been summoned back to Berlin, was also hanged. Because of his blindness he was led to the scaffold by hand. Rommel was given the choice of suicide – and a military hero's funeral – or a public trial and execution as a traitor. He chose suicide.

Another of those hanged was Adam von Trott zu Solz, a German diplomat who had studied at Oxford University before the war. A strong anti-Nazi, he had held secret talks with British and American diplomats in Switzerland at the beginning of the war. On his mother's side he was descended from John Jay, the first Chief Justice of the United States. In a book published in the third year of the Nazi era he had written in support of 'the sense of decency of the individual citizen' and had warned that 'the divine destiny of man has been trampled down into the dust'. He too was hanged on a wire noose.

The Allies had not believed in the conspiracy or taken it seriously once it came to light, although men like Adam von Trott were well-known in Allied Intelligence and intellectual circles. 'There is no subversive organization', British Intelligence had concluded on February 18, five months before the final assassination attempt. In his book *Changing Enemies*, Noel Annan, who was a member of British Military Intelligence in 1944, reflected that the officials of the British Foreign Office 'had no wish to be confronted by a group of Prussian Junkers who, they considered, would be scarcely less nationalistic than the Nazis when putting forward conditions for peace.' Half a century later the historian Thomas Power reflected: 'But the failure of the resistance and the Allies to understand each other should not surprise us; they had different goals in mind. The resistance was trying to end the war, while the Allies were trying to win it, and they did.'

Some of the Germans who had committed themselves to the conspiracy recognized that their defiance had been made too late. One of those who was imprisoned after the July plot, Albrecht Haushofer, wrote a series of sonnets while in the Moabit prison in Berlin. One of them contained the lines:

> Yes I am guilty otherwise than you think,
> I should have recognized my duty sooner,
> more sharply named disaster as disaster –
> I withheld my judgement much too long . . .
>
> Today I know what I was guilty of.

In the Pacific, during July, the Americans were driving the Japanese from island to island. Suicide was considered by the Japanese to be the honourable – and sole – reaction to defeat. Following the American invasion of the Marianas Islands, the Japanese refusal to surrender confronted the American soldier with the prospect of unceasing combat. In the fighting for Saipan Island, on which 20,000 American troops landed, 3,426 Americans were killed before the Japanese were overrun. Twenty thousand Japanese were killed in battle. A further seven thousand committed suicide, many of them on a single day – July 7 – in deliberately suicidal rifle and bayonet charges against the American troops facing them.

This mass suicide was insisted upon by General Yoshitsugu Saito, who, having been wounded by shrapnel, ordered his soldiers to make a final mass attack with 'each soldier to take seven enemy lives in exchange for his own'. He then killed himself by cutting open his stomach with his sword and ordering his adjutant to shoot him in the head. Of the 20,000 Japanese civilians on Saipan, at least 8,000 were killed in the fighting and 4,000 killed themselves rather than be captured by the Americans – the ultimate humiliation. To avoid being captured, mothers jumped off the cliffs with their children in their arms, or walked into the sea to drown. 'The Americans had never seen anything like that,' wrote the historian Gavan Daws. 'As for what happened after that, the Saipan Japanese would never have seen anything like it either: From the time the Americans secured the island to the end of the war, Seabees were cruising around in boats decorated with Japanese skulls skewered on stakes like shish kebabs.'

A Japanese attempt to attack the American naval forces which were protecting the Saipan landings was mounted by a force of nine aircraft carriers and more than five hundred aircraft. The attack was beaten off with the destruction of 346 of the Japanese aircraft, for the cost of thirty American aircraft shot down. Three of the Japanese aircraft carriers were also sunk, and four thousand Japanese sailors drowned.

An American bombing raid on July 14 – the first sustained bombing raid against mainland Japan – gave particular encouragement to the American people as well as to the soldiers, sailors and airmen, and to the strategic planners in Washington. The systematic capture of Pacific islands from the Japanese had made such a bombing offensive possible, although this first raid, carried out by sixty bombers, was mounted from the Chinese city of Chengtu. The target was the iron and steel works at Yawata, on Honshu Island.

Although little damage was done, the news that the raid had taken place was a boost to American morale, bringing nearer the prospect that Japan, like Germany, would soon face the spectre of a direct invasion. From what the Anglo-American bomber force had done to the cities of Germany, it was clear that bombing, even without invasion, would wreak a terrible toll. In the battle for Guam, which the Japanese had captured at the end of 1941 for the loss of only a single Japanese soldier, 18,500 Japanese defenders were killed or committed suicide rather than suffer the perceived humiliation of surrender. More than two thousand Americans also fell in the twenty-day battle, which began on July 21.

Three days after the landings on Guam, other American troops landed on Tinian. More than six thousand Japanese soldiers were killed, and 290

Americans. On Tinian there were also five thousand Korean labourers working for the Japanese. 'So as not to have hostiles *at their back* when the
Americans invaded,' writes Gavan Daws, 'the Japanese killed them.'

On the Eastern Front, Soviet forces had crossed the River Bug, having
overrun the whole area of eastern Poland which Stalin intended to annex to
the Soviet Union. On July 22, as soon as his troops reached the first Polish
town west of the Bug – the town of Chelm, best known for its humorous
stories of Jewish fools – Stalin set up a Polish Committee of National
Liberation. This was the government that he wished to install in Poland
after the war. Almost all its members were Communists, most of them
trained in Moscow. Another step towards the Cold War had been taken, in
the immediate wake of a military success.

A few days later Soviet troops reached Majdanek, the concentration camp
on the outskirts of Lublin in which hundreds of thousands of Poles, Soviet
prisoners-of-war and Jews had been murdered. Photographs of the gas
chamber, the crematorium and the corpses, taken by Soviet photographers
and by Western war correspondents travelling with the Russian army, were
shown all around the world. Hitler was furious, cursing 'the slovenly and
cowardly rabble in the Security Services' who had not erased the traces in
time. Not only the traces, but some of the perpetrators, were exposed: four
months after the Soviet troops entered Majdanek, four SS men and two
German Kapos were tried, sentenced to death and hanged. The gallows were
set up outside what had been the camp crematorium. A vast crowd, estimated
at 150,000, came from Lublin to watch the executions.

In Warsaw, with the Soviet army only a few hundred miles away – in
normal circumstances it was an easy day's drive from Chelm to the capital
– there was concern throughout July that the Soviet Union would impose
a Communist government as soon as its troops reached the capital. On
July 25 the commander of the Home Army, Lieutenant-General Tadeusz
Bor-Komorowski, telegraphed three terse sentences to the Polish government
in London, to which his underground forces were loyal: 'Be prepared to
bomb the aerodromes around Warsaw at any moment. Be prepared to bomb
the aerodromes around Warsaw at our request. I shall announce the moment
of the beginning of the fight.'

A new, violent and unequal struggle was about to begin. It was to draw
the Germans, already hard-pressed only a few hundred miles to the east,
deeper and deeper into a cruel and sustained conflict. It was to produce

among the Poles extraordinary examples of the most remarkable courage. The Warsaw revolt, like the Warsaw ghetto uprising that had taken place in the spring of 1943, stands as one of the heroic benchmarks of the war. Those who decided to challenge the German might wanted to make sure that it could not be said that they had not tried to wrest victory from the occupier. While the Jews, fourteen months earlier, had no chance of outside help – the nearest army, that of the Russians, was then more than five hundred miles away – the Polish insurgents did have hope that those same Russians who were drawing ever closer to Warsaw, would intervene, cross the Vistula, and link forces with the Polish fighters. Those fighters wanted first, however, to establish an independent Polish administration. They were encouraged in the early days of their defiance by a broadcast over radio Moscow urging them to rise up.

For the insurgents inside Warsaw, help from the British and Americans was within the realm of practical aspirations, although it was far away. Volunteer crews, many of them piloted by Poles who had been fighting alongside the British forces since the fall of Poland almost five years earlier, flew from both Britain and from Foggia in southern Italy to drop arms and supplies over Warsaw. The length of the return flights – more than 1,500 miles – was such that almost half the planes failed to make it back. When Churchill asked Stalin to make Soviet airfields fifty miles east of Warsaw available to these planes to refuel, Stalin refused. He did not want to create any difficulties for his own Communist Polish nominees whom he wanted to see installed in power. When the Soviet Army entered Lublin, Stalin formally established the Polish Committee of National Liberation there, as the interim Polish government, and declared Lublin to be the temporary capital of Poland.

The Lublin Poles, with Stalin's support, sought totally to undermine the standing and authority of the London Poles, and those in Poland who took orders from them, and who wished them to return as the government of Poland as soon as the war was over. The Warsaw insurgents were caught in the middle of a political feud which the London Poles could not win. It was Stalin who could close his airfields to the Allied rescue missions. It was Stalin who would halt his armies on the eastern bank of the Vistula, within sight of the burning city. He did so, despite a message from the Soviet Army liaison officer with the insurgents, who called for help from the Soviet Army, but who called in vain.

On July 29 Soviet tanks had reached the town of Wolomin, twelve miles east of Warsaw. The capital was so close that the Soviet tank commanders could hear the sound of firing. At that moment the Soviet tanks were suddenly confronted by German reinforcements that had been hurried eastward across the Vistula. Outnumbered, the Soviet tanks took up a defensive position along a line that ran twelve miles east of the embattled city. As they did so, a combined force of partisans and civilians, members of the Home Army loyal to London, and the Communist People's Army, joined forces and seized two thirds of the city. But an attempt by the insurgents to take Okecie airport, to the south of the city, as a base into which the British and Americans could fly supplies, was defeated by the German forces guarding the airfield.

The Germans pulled back and waited until they could counter-attack in force. That moment was not long in coming. On August 1 Himmler gave the order: 'Destroy tens of thousands.' Four days later the Germans took the offensive. Entering one hospital in the area that had been controlled by the insurgents, German troops killed the chief doctor, then ordered all the patients to leave the building, and then shot them all.

For the Polish resistance fighters there was seldom a moment of respite. Julian Kulski noted in his diary on August 2:

Just after passing Bielany, 'Baron's' hand grenade exploded on his belt, making a terrible wound in his stomach. It was one of the homemade grenades which had often proved to be very unsafe. Fragments of the grenade also wounded 'Akropolites'. 'Baron' begged with us, and we could not leave him for the Germans to find.

Leaving 'Baron's' body behind us, we continued our march in downcast spirits.

A heavy weight of German armour and military manpower was deployed against the citizens of Warsaw, including SS troops under a much feared anti-partisan fighter, General von dem Bach Zelewski; a brigade – the Kaminski Brigade – made up of Russian Cossack prisoners-of-war who had thrown in their lot with the Germans; and a force commanded by General Dirlewanger, consisting of German criminals who had been offered their discharge from prison in Germany if they agreed to fight – the Dirlewanger Brigade.

When Churchill asked Stalin on August 4 to join in helping the insurgents, Stalin declined to do so. It was his first but not his last refusal. In replying to Churchill, he contrasted the military strength of the Poles with

596 · DESCENT INTO BARBARISM

that of the Germans in an off-hand and belittling way, telling Churchill: 'I think that the information that has been communicated to you by the Poles is greatly exaggerated and does not inspire confidence.'

That night, flying from their base at Foggia in southern Italy, thirteen British bombers, mostly manned by volunteer crews, reached central Poland, a distance of more than 750 miles, which was at the far limit of their range. Only two of them were able to get as far as Warsaw, where they dropped twenty-four containers of arms and ammunition. Twelve of the containers fell into the hands of the insurgents. The other twelve fell into German-controlled parts of the city. Five out of the thirteen bombers failed to return. Neither then nor later would Stalin let them make the fifty mile flight beyond Warsaw to a Russian air base.

On July 29, at the very moment when Soviet tanks had come within twelve miles of Warsaw, the United States bombing missions in the Far East flew for the first time over Japanese-occupied Manchuria. Jung Chang has recorded her mother's recollections of the first appearance of American B-29 bombers over Chinchow:

> The Japanese ordered every household to dig air-raid shelters, and there was a compulsory air-raid drill every day at school. One day a girl in my mother's class picked up a fire extinguisher and squirted it at a Japanese teacher whom she particularly loathed. Previously, this would have brought dire retribution, but now she was allowed to get away with it. The tide was turning.
>
> There had been a long-standing campaign to catch flies and rats. The pupils had to chop off the rats' tails, put them in envelopes, and hand them in to the police. The flies had to be put in glass bottles. The police counted every rat tail and every dead fly.
>
> One day in 1944 when my mother handed in a glass bottle full to the brim with flies, the Manchukuo policeman said to her: 'Not enough for a meal.' When he saw the surprised look on her face, he said: 'Don't you know? The Nips like dead flies. They fry them and eat them!' My mother could see from the cynical gleam in his eye that he no longer regarded the Japanese as awesome.
>
> My mother was excited and full of anticipation . . .

In German-occupied Eastern Europe, with Warsaw in revolt, the German armies were almost everywhere falling back. But the search for Jews to deport and kill never ceased. On August 4, as the agony of Warsaw was in its early yet already terrifying stages, an episode took place seven hundred miles to the west, in Amsterdam. It has been recorded by the Czech-born Victor Kugler. Before the outbreak of war, Kugler had been living and working in Holland. In the apartment building that he rented, and which he kept after the German invasion of Holland in 1940, eight Jews were hiding. He helped them with food and news, and kept their hiding place – in the attic of the building – secret from the Gestapo, who were deporting Jews from Amsterdam every week. After the war, Kugler recalled 'that fateful Friday' of August 4 when:

. . . while working in my office, I heard an unusual commotion. It sounded like several people were running up and down the first floor corridor. I opened my office door and saw four policemen. One was a uniformed Gestapo man . . . an Austrian named Karl Silberbauer . . .
'Who's the owner of this building?' he snapped.
I gave him the name and address of the owner since, indeed, we did not own the property on 263 Prinzengracht. We only rented it.
'No, no!' he said impatiently. 'I want to know who is responsible here?'
'I am,' I replied.
'Now,' Silberbauer ordered, 'show us the rooms in the building.'
I started with my office, and to appear cooperative, I opened, for his inspection, all the bookcases and cabinets. Next I led him to the back of the building and showed him the office of the 'Travies Company', where Mr Kleiman worked. I even showed him the washroom and our little kitchen.
Outwardly I showed great calm, but inwardly I was terrified. I wondered why these men were here. Had they found out that I had been taking pictures for the Dutch underground? Or were they searching for the secret hiding place? Had we been betrayed?

Silberbauer ordered Kugler up to the next floor. He followed him, and was himself followed by the three other policemen. Kugler went first to the stockroom in the first part of the building. Silberbauer's three helpers stayed behind, in the corridor:

'Now,' said Silberbauer, 'let's look for secret weapons.'
Next we went to the corridor in the back and my heart was in my

mouth. We had come to the crucial place. In this area was the bookcase which concealed the entrance to the Secret Annexe. Next to this bookcase, along the side of the wall, there was a similar bookcase and some boxes. I noticed that this bookcase and the boxes had been moved from their original place. Obviously it was the work of the three Dutch policemen. To my horror I now saw these same men tampering with the bookcase which hid the entrance to the Secret Annexe.

However, the bookcase did not yield an inch. Again and again they tried to move it but they failed. Finally, they found the hook which kept the bookcase in its place. The hook was unfastened and they moved the bookcase. The door leading up to the staircase and rooms above were now exposed.

My heart sank.

The moment I had dreaded for two years had now arrived.

I realized the object of this search. I knew we had been betrayed. The secret had been revealed and our plans had failed. The eight people in the Secret Annexe were now doomed. A terrible fate awaited them all.

One of the policemen took a gun (a flat Browning) out of his jacket, and ordered me up the stairs. The other three, with their guns drawn, followed me upstairs.

The first person I saw was Mrs Frank, sitting motionless in the living room. I whispered 'Gestapo' as I entered, but she did not move. Now the dreaded moment had arrived. She seemed stunned. The others came slowly from the other room, and down from the top floor.

Mrs Frank was Edith Frank, the mother of Anne Frank: two of the eight people who were taken immediately from their hiding place. Their first destination was Westerbork internment camp in Holland, then Auschwitz – where Edith Frank died – and finally – in the case of Anne and her sister Margot – Bergen-Belsen, where the two sisters died. Only Otto Frank, Anne's father survived.

In Warsaw, the Polish insurgents fought on virtually unaided. Among those who helped them were several thousand Jews who had been hiding in cellars and attics since the destruction of the ghetto a year and a half earlier. They joined the fight, and more than a thousand fell alongside their fellow Poles.

Also joining the Warsaw insurgents were 348 Jews whom the Germans had brought to Warsaw from Auschwitz in order to sift through the rubble of the ghetto and find anything in it that might be of value to the Germans. These prisoners had been kept in a special camp near the ruins of the ghetto which was liberated by the insurgents. They included Jews from Greece, Belgium, France, Roumania and Hungary. One of them was a German-born Jew, Hans Robert Martin Korn, who had fled from Germany before the war to the safety of Finland. In 1939 he had fought as a volunteer with the Finnish forces against the Russians during the Winter War. In 1942 he had been one of only a few Jews deported from Finland to Auschwitz (before the Finnish authorities refused to allow any further deportations). From Auschwitz he had been brought as a slave labourer to Warsaw. Joining the uprising, he did not survive it.

The Warsaw uprising was a fight that the Poles were prepared to fight to the finish, and to do so with incredible energy after almost five years of debilitating occupation. On August 4 Julian Kulski wrote in his diary:

> Much of Warsaw is ours again! In many areas, the red and white flag of Poland is flying over the scarred but proud city for the first time in almost five years, and the hated Swastikas have been torn down and burned.
>
> Since early this morning, the civilian population has been working with the army in building barricades and in digging anti-tank and communications trenches throughout Zoliborz. The barricades consist of everything imaginable: overturned streetcars, all types of furniture from nearby houses, garbage cans, even mounds of trash. Some of the barricades are so high that they reach up to the second floors of adjacent buildings.
>
> The civilians are really eager to help, and work on the fortifications is proceeding swiftly and exceedingly well. The life of the citizens has been quickly 'normalized' since the enemy withdrew to the perimeter of Zoliborz.

By August 5 more than 15,000 Poles had been killed, many of them women and children. That evening General von dem Bach Zelewski gave the order for the killing of women and children to stop. But men were to be killed whether they were insurgents or not. His orders about the men were obeyed; his orders about the women and children were not. The Cossack troops and the troops in the German criminal brigade drove a brutal path through the suburbs still under insurgent control, killing another thirty thousand civilians, including hundreds of patients in the hospitals and casualty stations in their path.

On August 6, as the slaughter of the insurgents in Warsaw continued, the Germans began the deportation of the remaining fifty thousand Jewish inmates of the ghetto of Lodz, just over seventy miles to the south west of Warsaw. They had been kept alive throughout 1942, 1943 and the first seven months of 1944 in order to work in factories in the ghetto that had been set up to support the German war machine. They were the last substantial group of Jews left alive on Polish, German or Russian soil. In June, twenty thousand Jews had been taken from Lodz to Chelmno and murdered there: the camp had been reopened for this purpose. The fifty thousand still in the ghetto in August were taken to Auschwitz. Half of them were killed immediately on arrival. Those who were not killed were used as slave labourers in and around Auschwitz, many of them in the synthetic oil factory at nearby Monowitz. Germany still hoped to retain its ability to make war.

At the start of the Warsaw uprising, eleven Soviet partisans were parachuted several hundred miles further south into German-occupied Slovakia. They had with them the weapons and radio-transmitters needed to create a base for a large Soviet air drop. Stalin wanted both to defeat the Germans and their allies, and to create regimes sympathetic to the Soviet Union wherever his forces could take control. They would come as liberators, and save millions from the continuing tyranny and terror of Nazism, but they would remain as the ultimate guarantors of political subservience, and would introduce a tyranny and terror of their own.

Within six months of the independent national challenge of the Warsaw uprising, Soviet power was to be the dominant force in Poland, Slovakia, Roumania, Bulgaria, Yugoslavia, Hungary and Czechoslovakia, and was to remain so, with the exception of Yugoslavia, for more than four decades. The Western Allies, for whom the defeat of Germany was the priority, gave what help they could to the Soviet partisans. Within five weeks of the establishment of the Soviet bases deep inside Slovakia, in one of the most dangerous flying missions of 1944, two American bombers, flying from Foggia in southern Italy, landed on a partisan controlled airstrip at Tri Duby, deep in Slovakia – while the forty-one fighter planes which had accompanied them remained circling in the air above as a defensive shield – and, in a mere forty-five minutes on the ground, unloaded four and a half tons of military supplies for the Slovak and Soviet partisans in the area.

This flight, and a second similar one mounted within the month, had a second purpose, to bring back to southern Italy a number of Allied airmen

– mostly Americans – who had been shot down over Central Europe and had managed to make their way to Slovak-partisan held areas. Throughout Europe, the partisans themselves were always at grave risk. German military sweeps against resistance groups in France and northern Italy continued to be mounted throughout the autumn, and to result in many hundreds of executions. In Poland and Slovakia, many hundreds more partisans were executed as soon as they were caught, often left hanging on lampposts as a would-be deterrent.

Terror could not halt the advance of the Allied armies. On August 3 General Jean Piron, a Belgian officer commanding the Belgian brigade 'Liberation' – which had been formed in Britain of Belgians in exile – landed with his men at the mouth of the Seine, liberating Honfleur. By August 10, with the first forward Allied troop movements south of Normandy, towards Orléans, the German attempt to hold back the forces in Normandy threatened to collapse.

Only in the Falaise pocket were German troops refusing to surrender, and holding up the Allied forward thrust. A vast Allied force of more than a million men was poised to advance. Two Allied armies were ready to move: the 12th Army commanded by General Omar N. Bradley, which had been set Paris as its initial goal, and the 21st Army Group commanded by General Bernard Montgomery, which was to take the more northerly route towards Belgium and Holland.

Hitler's orders to stand and fight continued to be obeyed. On August 6, during a week when those who had considered his leadership the path to defeat and ruin were still being systematically executed in Berlin, he ordered the soldiers holding out in the Falaise pocket not to retreat. His orders were obeyed, the troops continuing to resist all efforts of the British, Free French, Canadian and Polish troops to dislodge them.

On August 12, after ten days of continuous fighting, the Warsaw insurgents were still in action against the Germans. Not only were they being attacked by German forces inside the city, they were also being bombarded by German artillery. That day the insurgents appealed to London: 'The soldiers and the population look hopelessly at the skies, expecting help from the Allies. On the background of smoke they see only German aircraft. They are surprised, feel deeply depressed, and begin to revile.'

Churchill had failed to persuade Stalin to let British aircraft use the Soviet air bases to the east of Warsaw at which to refuel. Had Stalin agreed to do so, many missions could have been mounted. The volunteer crews were eager to try. But Stalin was adamant. Churchill, knowing that some of the Soviet operational airfields were only twelve or fifteen minutes flying time from Warsaw, sent Stalin a further appeal on August 12, telegraphing to the Soviet leader: 'They implore machine guns and ammunition. Can you not give them some further help, as the distance from Italy is so very great?'

Stalin continued to decline. For his part, Roosevelt was reluctant to press Stalin too hard, as he had just concluded a secret agreement with Stalin to enable American bombers on their way to Japan to use Soviet airfields in eastern Siberia. Roosevelt did not want to jeopardize this agreement, crucial for the bombing of Japan, for the sake of the ultimately hopeless cause of Warsaw. 'I do not consider it advantageous to the general war prospect for me to join with you in the proposed message to UJ,' was Roosevelt's reply to Churchill's reiterated appeals.

UJ – Uncle Joe – was Stalin. He had divided the Western Allies. Recognizing that Britain would have to act alone with regard to Warsaw, and accepting the risks involved, on August 12 Churchill authorized the Royal Air Force to despatch twenty bombers from their base at Foggia. Each bomber carried twelve large containers of arms and ammunition to be dropped by parachute. Twenty-eight bombers in all set out on this dangerous mission. Among those who volunteered for it were Polish, British and South African crews. Fourteen of the bombers reached the skies above Warsaw, where three were shot down by German anti-aircraft fire. The rest dropped their containers. Of the thirty-five tons of supplies that had been loaded on the bombers at Foggia, less than five tons reached the insurgents. But even five tons gave them assistance in fighting on, as they were determined to do.

The Soviet Union continued to oppose and belittle the efforts of the Poles battling inside Warsaw, and refused to support them. The British and American ambassadors to Moscow went to see the Soviet Deputy Foreign Minister, Andrei Vyshinsky, on August 15, to ask for the despatch of Soviet help to the insurgents. They were shocked, as the American Ambassador, Averell Harriman, reported back to Washington, that the Russians 'clung' to the view that the Warsaw uprising 'was an ill-advised and not a serious matter, and that the future course of the war would not at all be influenced by it'.

That night a further ten British bombers set off from southern Italy on the flight to Warsaw. Six failed to return. Among the aircrew killed that night were twenty South Africans.

*   *   *

On August 14 Canadian troops and armour made a sustained attempt to drive the Germans from the Falaise pocket, where they were holding up the whole Allied advance from Normandy. By midnight the Canadians were within four miles of the town of Falaise. A Canadian officer wrote: 'It was an evening silent as death – only the crackling noise of flaming tanks and buildings.' But the Germans in the town still held out against the next assault.

That day, August 14, the Allies launched another amphibious landing, in Southern France. In one day 94,000 men and 11,000 vehicles were landed between Toulon and Cannes. Within twenty-four hours the troops had advanced inland almost twenty miles. The Germans did not have the troops to spare from the continuing battle in Normandy to halt the advance in the south. On August 16 the Canadians fighting in Normandy entered Falaise. For twenty-four hours they were forced to fight inside the town street by street and house by house, but finally, on August 17, Falaise was in Allied hands. 'When the bulldozers were called in to clear passages for the incoming vehicles,' writes the historian John North, 'it was not always easy to determine just where the roadways had once run.'

On the day of the fall of Falaise, Hitler ordered the evacuation of southern France. As a result of reading the secret message to this effect, British Intelligence knew the exact line to which the Germans would withdraw – running from Sens through Dijon to the Swiss frontier. This line could therefore be reached without fighting. Within two weeks the South of France, Provence and the Rhone Valley were liberated, and units of the Allied force had pushed north of Lyon.

On the day Hitler ordered the evacuation of southern France, he dismissed Field Marshal Günther Hans von Kluge – whose troops had occupied the Polish corridor in the first days of the war – for having failed to hold the Allies in the Falaise pocket. Kluge travelled to one of the battlefields of 1870 where the Prussian Army had been victorious over France, and decided to kill himself there. In common with all the German people, he had been told by Hitler of secret weapons that would turn the tide of war. One of those weapons was the flying bomb. It had killed more than four thousand Britons and was killing a further fifty or sixty every week, but it had in no way altered the course of the battle in France.

Following the collapse of German resistance at Falaise and on the Cotentin Peninsula, the Allies were poised to liberate Paris. In a final letter to Hitler before ending his life with a cyanide pill, Kluge declared: 'If your new weapons, in which such burning faith is placed, do not bring success, then, my Führer, take the decision to end the war. The German people have suffered such unspeakable ills, that the time has come to put an end to these horrors.'

Field Marshal Kluge was replaced by Field Marshal Walther Model, who had sent Hitler an enthusiastic telegram after the Rastenburg bomb congratulating him on his escape, and vowing 'eternal allegiance'. But Model had neither the time nor the means to halt the Allied advance to Paris. On August 19 an uprising by Resistance fighters in Paris was initiated under the command of Colonel Henri Tanguy – known by his codename as Colonel Rol – a French Communist who had fought with the International Brigade in Spain eight years earlier. The French police in the capital at once declared their loyalty to the Resistance, seized the Préfecture of Police and raised the tricolor flag.

When a German armoured vehicle appeared and opened fire, the Parisian police returned the fire. There was fighting between Resistance groups and German soldiers in different parts of the city. By the end of August 19, six hundred German soldiers had been taken prisoner. This was the first of six days of sniping, barricades and death in Paris. It was also the beginning of a struggle of wills and arguments over the future of the city. Hitler wanted the German commandant, General Dietrich von Choltitz – who in May 1940 had supervised the destruction of Rotterdam – to fight street by street and deploy the utmost savagery if necessary. As far as Hitler was concerned Paris could be razed to the ground. But the Swedish Consul-General in Paris, Raoul Nordling, persuaded Choltitz to take a more conciliatory course, starting on the evening of August 19 with a temporary truce to allow both the Germans and the French Resistance to collect their wounded.

Throughout France, Resistance forces were challenging the occupier. A British officer, Major Roy Farran, who led sixty men and twenty jeeps in a daring raid which penetrated several hundred miles behind German lines in the third week of August – from Orléans to Belfort – later wrote: 'I was most impressed by the bellicose air of the French partisan'. The imminent sense of liberation also impressed Farran. During a skirmish with a German military patrol east of Orléans he saw, as he later wrote, 'a pretty girl with long black hair and wearing a bright red frock put her head out of a top window to give me the "V" sign. Her smile ridiculed the bullets'.

Hitler had intended the V-bomb to be the terror of his enemies, but it was the V-sign, the symbol not of vengeance but of victory, that was proving the greater inspiration. Vengeance, however, was a daily feature of the occupation forces everywhere even as they were in retreat. One of the last acts of the Gestapo in Lyon was to take a hundred Frenchmen and women who were being held in prison on suspicion of being connected to the Resistance, drive them to a disused fort outside the city, and shoot them down.

In Paris, General von Choltitz was preparing to use tanks against the barricades put up by the Resistance. Again Consul-General Nordling intervened, and persuaded him not to do so, arguing that as an officer, a European and a Christian, the General had a duty to disobey orders that would lead to the destruction of the city, and to further loss of life in France, where the battle was lost. Choltitz deferred to the reasoning of his Swedish interlocutor.

On the battlefield, the Germans were everywhere in retreat. When, in the third week of August, Russian troops crossed into Roumania, 300,000 German soldiers surrendered. During the final resistance in the Falaise pocket 10,000 German soldiers had been killed and 50,000 taken prisoner. The Supreme Commander of the Allied Forces, General Eisenhower, later recalled how, when walking over the Falaise battlefield a few days after it was overrun, it was 'literally possible to walk for hundreds of yards at a time, stepping on nothing but dead and decaying flesh.'

With an Allied victory in Europe certain, if not by Christmas, then almost certainly by the following spring or summer, the Foreign Ministers of the Allied powers met at Dumbarton Oaks, just outside Washington, on August 21. Determined to avoid what was seen as the weakness of the League of Nations after the First World War, they established a post-war system of collective security designed – as indeed the League Covenant had been designed twenty-six years earlier – to make future war impossible.

The organization set up at Dumbarton Oaks was called the United Nations Organization: the UNO – later abbreviated to UN. Its main instrument of authority was to be a Security Council consisting of five of the founding member States: Britain, the Soviet Union, the United States, France and China. On their shoulders would lie the responsibility to take military action against any aggressor. Built into their structure, however, was a veto. If any one member of the Security Council refused to accept the decision of the majority, that decision would have to be set aside.

At the very moment when the United Nations and the Security Council were being set up, Germany and Japan were still fighting to retain as much territory as possible. But the fighting in Roumania was turning rapidly against the German forces and their Roumanian allies. On August 22 the Russians overran the city of Jassy. On the following day the Roumanian dictator, Marshal Antonescu – who in the summer of 1941 had sent thirty Roumanian divisions to fight alongside the Germans in Russia – was summoned to the Royal Palace in Bucharest by twenty-three-year-old King Michael and ordered to call for an armistice. Antonescu refused to do so and was promptly arrested.

Under the influence of King Michael, who hoped to preserve both his dynasty and the independence of his country, Roumania then abandoned the Axis and signed an armistice with the Russians, the second of Hitler's allies to defect: Italy had been the first, almost a year earlier. Michael then declared war on Germany and declared Roumania an ally of Britain, the United States and Russia. His gesture could not save Roumania from being overrun by Soviet troops and incorporated into the Soviet sphere of influence. Hitler did not have the resources to occupy Roumania, as he had occupied Hungary five months earlier. The power to control events, or even to influence them, was slipping away from the leader of the Third Reich.

Hitler ordered his troops in Roumania to fight on without the support of their former Roumanian colleagues-in-arms. In the course of a further week of battle, several thousand German soldiers were killed. There was also bad news for Hitler that week from northern Italy, where Italian partisans were preventing the Germans from maintaining control over large areas. In a pitched battle, partisan forces overran an Italian Fascist mountain stronghold in the village of Bacena. The Germans were unable, or unwilling, to make the effort to wrest it back.

On the Italian battlefield, the Allied line had moved northward from Rome to the River Arno. In the Balkans, Greek and Yugoslav partisans were creating increasing difficulties for all German troop movements. The defection of Roumania from the Axis cut Germany off from the oil of Ploesti, and opened up a line of advance for the Soviet forces from the Danube to the Adriatic. British aid to the Yugoslav partisans was increased. Hitler, having made his first major concession to the need for withdrawal when he pulled back from the South of France, agreed to his generals' further request for a fall back in the Balkans. Athens, Salonika and Skoplje were to be abandoned, and a defence line established between the Albanian port of Scutari on the Adriatic coast and the Iron Gates on the Danube.

Only the flying bombs over Britain seemed evidence of the German capacity for continued military initiatives, but their impact on the movement of armies was nil. Very carefully, so as not to give Hitler and his flying bomb units any idea of their success, details of the casualties and damage were strongly censored, and the death toll from each flying bomb kept secret. There could therefore be neither advantage nor satisfaction for Berlin when on August 23 a flying bomb hit a factory in London and killed 211 factory workers. The Germans knew nothing either of the damage or of the death toll. Photographs of the incident were only released to the British press after they had been carefully cropped and doctored to disguise both the location and the impact.

That same day an American B-24 bomber, attempting to land in a violent storm at the Warton air base in Lancashire, overshot the runway and crashed in the centre of the tiny village of Freckleton. Thirty-eight children and nine adults were killed in the local school: it was the worst such incident in Britain of the entire war. The three American airmen in the bomber, and four RAF personnel were also killed, as were seven Americans and three adults – one of them an evacuee from London – in the village café, the Sad Snack Bar, which had been specially opened for the local American community far from home.

The main Allied bombing offensive in August was against German synthetic oil plants. One of those hit, in an American daylight raid on August 20, was at Monowitz, within a few miles of the gas chambers at Auschwitz. During the raid thirty-eight of the British prisoners-of-war being forced to work at Monowitz were killed. In an Allied daylight raid on an armaments factory at Gustloff – named after the Nazi leader in Switzerland who had been assassinated by a Jew before the war – bombs falling wide of their target hit the nearby Buchenwald concentration camp. Four hundred prisoners – most of them Jews – and eighty SS men, were killed. Also killed were several 'privileged' prisoners who were being held as possible hostages, among them the tyre manufacturer Marcel Michelin – a French citizen – and Princess Mafalda, the daughter of the King of Italy.

In an act of retaliation for the death of the eighty SS men at Buchenwald, the camp commandant, SS Major Pfister, ordered sixteen British and French officers, members of the British Special Operations Executive, who had been captured while on clandestine missions inside France, to be hanged. Another of those executed in Buchenwald that day as a reprisal was Ernst Thaelmann, the German Communist leader who had challenged Hitler for the Presidency in 1932. First sent to a concentration camp on 28 February 1933, at the time of his execution Thaelmann had been a prisoner for more than eleven years.

The anger of the local population at the daily Allied bombing of German cities was seen on August 24 when eight American crew members, who had been shot down on their return from a bombing mission over Hamburg, were set upon by German civilians while being marched through the town of Rüsselheim. The town had just been attacked by British bombers, with the deaths of 179 local people. The locals who attacked the Americans were being evacuated from the damaged part of the town. They attacked the captive airmen with clubs, rocks, bricks and stone. Six of the Americans were beaten to death.

On that day, August 24, a Free French armoured force entered Paris from the south. The British and Americans had deliberately arranged for the liberators of Paris to be French soldiers. On the evening of August 25, as sniper fire continued in different parts of the city General von Choltitz surrendered. Colonel Rol, who had launched the uprising six days earlier, was the Frenchman who signed the instrument of surrender. Half an hour later General de Gaulle entered the city. For four years he had been the standard bearer of French independence. Paris welcomed him with enthusiasm, but during the fighting that was still talking place in several parts of the city, prolonged by small groups of German soldiers and German snipers, more than five hundred members of the French Resistance were killed, as well as 127 civilian Parisians – bystanders.

Even as sniper fire continued, de Gaulle addressed a large crowd of Parisians from the Prefecture of Police. 'France is a great nation,' he said, 'and she has rights which she will know how to make heard. She has the right to insist that she be never again invaded by the enemy who has so often invaded her.' Recalling the Allied failure, as he believed it to have been, to cross onto German soil in 1918, de Gaulle declared: 'It is not enough that with the aid of our dear and splendid allies we should drive the enemy from our soil. After what has happened to France we will not rest or be satisfied until we enter, as is only right, upon the enemy's own territory as conquerors. We are going to fight on the last day, to the day of total and complete victory.'

In the days after the liberation of Paris several thousand Frenchmen and women who had collaborated with the German authorities during the occupation were killed in acts of savage vengeance. The elation of victory could not spare those who had served the cause of the conqueror.

In Poland, as the last resistance of the Warsaw insurgents was being beaten down, Stalin ordered his forces, as they advanced into Poland, to arrest the leaders of the underground Polish Home Army. In answer to this, on August 28 the British and Americans announced that they regarded the Home Army in Poland as a 'responsible belligerent force'.

In the liberated areas of central and southern Italy, the British were supervising the establishment of a new Italian administration. Churchill, who had just spent two weeks travelling through the areas, issued a message to the Italian people on August 28 in which he sought to answer the question, 'What is freedom?' Churchill suggested that there were a number of 'quite simple, practical tests' by which freedom could be known in the modern world, in peace conditions. He explained those tests in the form of seven questions:

Is there the right to free expression of opinion and of opposition and of criticism of the Government of the day?

Have the people the right to turn out a Government of which they disapprove, and are constitutional means provided by which they can make their will apparent?

Are their courts of justice free from violence by the Executive and from threats of mob violence, and free of all association with particular political parties?

Will these courts administer open and well-established laws which are associated in the human mind with the broad principles of decency and justice?

Will there be fair play for poor as well as for rich, for private persons as well as Government officials?

Will the rights of the individual, subject to his duties to the State, be maintained and asserted and exalted?

Is the ordinary peasant or workman who is earning a living by daily toil and striving to bring up a family free from the fear that some grim police organization under the control of a single party, like the Gestapo, started by the Nazi and Fascist parties, will tap him on the shoulder and pack him off without fair or open trial to bondage or ill-treatment?'

These 'simple, practical tests', Churchill stressed, 'are some of the title-deeds on which the new Italy could be founded.'

By the end of August no corner of the ever-diminishing territory under the control of the Third Reich was beyond the range of Allied bombers, although some areas were still at the far extremity of the bombers' range. On the nights of August 26/27 and 29/30, British bomber forces flew 950 miles across the North Sea and the Baltic to drop their bombs on factories in the hitherto intact medieval city of Königsberg. As a result of the two attacks, 134,000 of the citizens of Königsberg were made homeless and a fifth of the city's industries destroyed. Of the 363 bombers that took part in the two raids, nineteen were lost, a much lower ratio than would have been the case a year earlier.

Other targets on those two nights – 'diversionary sweeps' to distract the German fighter defences – included Berlin, Kiel and Hamburg. The Königsberg raids were especially galling to Hitler, who was then at Rastenberg, only fifty-five miles away.

At the beginning of September, following Hitler's order to evacuate the Balkans, more than 300,000 German troops made their way northward. To impede their progress, and to capture as many as possible, Tito's Yugoslav partisans launched a series of offensives, closely coordinated with an Anglo-American bomber offensive against the roads and railways along which the Germans must travel.

The Germans were everywhere in retreat, often in precipitate retreat. On September 2, British forces crossed into Belgium. A day later Brussels was liberated. Among the liberators was the Belgian Liberation Brigade commanded by General Piron. As Brussels celebrated its freedom, Field Marshal von Rundstedt, who had led the victorious German armies in the West in May 1940, but had been temporarily dismissed from his command after the Normandy landings, was appointed by Hitler to command the retreat. Watching a specially-formed Hitler Youth Division pulling back through Belgium, Rundstedt commented: 'It is a pity that this faithful youth is sacrificed in a hopeless situation.'

In an attempt to force the besieged German garrison at Le Havre to surrender – it was more than a hundred miles behind the Allied lines on September 5 – a massive British bombing raid was carried out that day. During the raid a firestorm broke out, reminiscent of those that had earlier been created in German cities, caused by a combination of the intensity of the bombardment and the dry weather. As a result, 2,500 French civilians were killed.

On September 6 the Soviet forces advancing through Roumania reached the Danube, and crossed into Yugoslavia. On the following day, still hoping to make some impact on the course of the war, Hitler ordered the firing of his second secret weapon, the V2 (Revenge Weapon-2). This time it was not a pilotless plane but a rocket that carried the explosive charge.

That day ought to have been a landmark in the history of science, for the death-dealing rocket was a precursor of the rocket – designed by the same scientists – that eventually took Man to the moon. The V2 had a more mundane and warlike purpose, to cause havoc and destruction in the cities of Britain. But the British Government lessened the impact of the new weapon by keeping its existence, and its depredations, secret for a whole month – until they were revealed in the *New York Times*.

The 'revenge weapon' was destined to fail in its purpose, but revenge itself was unceasing. On September 9, in the concentration camp at Mauthausen, thirty-nine Dutchmen, seven Englishmen and an American who had been captured while helping the resistance forces behind German lines, were forced to carry out near-impossible tasks carrying blocks of quarry stones up the camp's notorious 186 steps, after which, exhausted and repeatedly beaten with clubs by the zealous guards, they were all shot. In Italy, by the end of the month, during a German anti-partisan sweep commanded by an SS Major, four hundred partisans were killed.

The Japanese had begun to evacuate the Philippine Islands. Among those being taken by ship to Japan were many thousands of Allied prisoners-of-war. They were put in the holds of the ships, allowed almost no food or water, and reduced to near starvation and madness. On September 7 an American submarine sank a large Japanese freighter, the *Shin'yo Maru*, hugging the coastline of Mindanao on its way towards Japan. The submarine commander did not know that there were 675 American prisoners-of-war on board, deep in the bowels of the ship. Only eighty-five survived the sinking. They were fortunate to be able to swim ashore, where they were sheltered by Filipino guerrillas.

Dozens of Japanese transport ships were sunk by the Americans during September. Many of them had prisoners-of-war in their holds, battened down, starving, tormented by thirst and fear. On September 12 two such ships on their way from Singapore to Japan were torpedoed off Hainan Island. There were more than 2,200 British and Australian prisoners-of-war on board. A few hundred were rescued by Japanese submarines. The rest were left in the shark-infested waters. More than 1,500 perished.

Six days later, on September 18, came one of the worst maritime disasters of the Second World War. When a British submarine sank the Japanese freighter *Jun'yo Maru* off Sumatra, 5,620 of those on board were drowned: of the dead, 1,377 were Dutch and Indo-Dutch civilian internees being taken to Japan, sixty-four were British and Australian internees, a few were American merchant seamen, and the rest were Asian slave labourers. There were 723 survivors.

On September 15 a ten-week battle began for the small islands of Peleliu and Angaur, two of the Palau Islands in the western Caroline Islands. Although American war correspondents who followed in the wake of the first landings took photographs of the dead American soldiers on the beaches, these were not allowed to be published in the United States; they were only seen by the public after the war.

Peleliu island is only two miles by six miles in extent. The Japanese defended it yard by yard, losing more than ten thousand men. Just over a thousand Americans were killed. One of the American radio operators in the battle, Staff Sergeant Ron Hoffmann, noted that – in view of the expenditure by the American soldiers of more than fifteen million rounds of ammunition – on average the Americans fired 1,589 bullets for every Japanese soldier killed.

The nearby Angaur island, only two miles by three in extent, was attacked at the same time as Peleliu. Both were considered essential as forward bases for the next phase of the island advance towards Japan. On Angaur 370 American soldiers were killed. More Medals of Honour were awarded for the Angaur/Peleliu battle than for any other engagement in the Second World War.*

Another American success in the Pacific during September was the first massive air raid on Japanese docks and shipping lanes in the Philippines.

---

* The Marines who fought at Peleliu and Angaur feel unhappy that their battle has not become an integral part of the knowledge of the Pacific War. On 16 August 1994 Ron Hoffmann wrote to President Clinton to ask why the islands had been omitted from the group of newly issued commemorative postage stamps of 1944 that included stamps for Tinian and Guam, where fewer American soldiers had been killed.

The raid was mounted in preparation for an amphibious landing and the eventual reconquest of the islands. The American carrier-based aircraft on the raid flew 145 miles from their carriers. In the course of their mission they destroyed or damaged more than four hundred Japanese aircraft and sank more than a hundred Japanese warships. Only fifteen American aircraft were lost.

The seas which the Japanese navy had dominated for almost three years were no longer safe for them. When, in the last week of September, an American submarine torpedoed a Japanese transport ship off Okinawa – it was on its way from Singapore to Japan – more than two thousand of its 2,350 passengers were drowned. Among the dead was a young, would-be leader of the Indian National Army, Bishan Singh, who was on his way with a group of like-minded Indians to fight as a volunteer with the Imperial Japanese forces against the forces of the British Empire.

On September 10 the first Allied soldier in Western Europe crossed from Belgium into Germany, reaching the German village of Roetgen. Two days later, Noor Inayat Khan – one of several British agents captured in France a year earlier – was executed at Dachau. According to one account, as she was forced to kneel before being shot she spoke the single word '*Liberté*'. She was posthumously awarded the Croix de Guerre with Gold Star, and the George Cross.*

On September 13, Allied Intelligence learned, through its reading of a radio signal sent from Berlin to Tokyo, that shortage of fuel oil would henceforth prevent the German Air Force from 'attaining the anticipated objective of regaining control in the air'. But in the daily British operations against Germany there were continual casualties. On the night of September 12/13 four of two hundred British bombers on their way to attack Stuttgart were shot down. One of them was reported 'missing without trace'. Its pilot, Pilot Officer John Oxborrow, and his crew of seven, were never seen again. Oxborrow was twenty-three years old. It was his twenty-seventh bombing mission in less than three months.

The war diary of Oxborrow's squadron reported: 'From all reports it appears that this was a successful attack. Fires could be seen a hundred miles

---

* Another British woman agent, Diana Rowden, who had been executed at Natzweiler on July 6, was awarded the Croix de Guerre. Vera Leigh, who was also executed that day at Natzweiler, received a posthumous King's Commendation.

away from the target.' During the raid, the northern and western parts of the city centre were destroyed by a firestorm and 1,171 people killed. It was Stuttgart's highest fatal casualty figure of the war.

At the end of the second week of September, Stalin finally allowed his pilots to fly air supplies to the Warsaw insurgents. But his help came a month too late to be of any real assistance. On September 14 his forces reached the bank of the Vistula opposite Warsaw. More help was parachuted in, but the insurgents were in their final days of being able to hold out against the German forces still destroying their strongholds one by one and laying the city to waste. An attempt by General Berling, a Polish General fighting with the Russians, to reach the beleaguered insurgents, was beaten off by the Germans after Berling had managed to cross the Vistula south of the city on the night of September 16, and advance several miles into the southern suburbs of the city.

Repeated German infantry and tank assaults forced Berling and his men back to the river. Two days later, Stalin at last allowed the Americans to fly over Warsaw with supplies and then land at Soviet air bases, but it could no longer save the insurgents, and within two weeks Stalin had rescinded his permission. The Allied losses had been high. Of the 306 aircraft which had set off from southern Italy or from East Anglia, forty-one were shot down, and at least two hundred airmen killed. One American airman, captured by the Germans outside Warsaw, was beaten to death by his captors.

The imperative to escape had led the Germans to set up a special prisoner-of-war camp at Colditz castle, in which those Allied officers who had escaped from other camps were confined in a virtually escape-proof fortress. Even from there several successful attempts were made. Some escapees from Colditz reached the safety of neutral Switzerland or the Baltic, others were caught within a few miles – even within a few hundred yards – of freedom. But for most prisoners the camp could not be breached. P.R. Reid, who was imprisoned in Colditz and later wrote its history, recalled a desperate escape attempt by a fellow British officer, Mike Sinclair, an Ulsterman who had been taken prisoner at Calais in 1940. Sinclair had already tried to escape several times from Colditz and had failed, though he had on different occasions reached Cologne, the Swiss frontier and the Dutch frontier:

On September 20th 1944 Mike went down to the recreation ground and walked the well-trodden path around the periphery inside the wire with Grismond Scourfield.

In half an hour the guards had settled down. They suspected nothing. This hour of recreation would be the same as the hundreds that had gone before it.

At the most vulnerable point in the wire, Mike stopped suddenly, turned and shook hands with Scourfield. 'Good-bye, Grismond,' he said quietly. 'It's going to be now or never.'

He was ashen-pale. Even the gigantic courage of his spirit could not conceal from his own brain the awful risk he was about to take. The subconscious reactions of the nerves and cells of his frail body rebelled and would not be controlled. His hand trembled as he grasped surreptitiously the hand of his friend. His whole body seemed to quiver. His eyes alone were steady and bright with the fire of a terrible resolve.

In the next instant he was at the wire, climbing desperately, climbing quickly, spread-eagled in mid-air. To those nearby, his progress seemed painfully slow, yet it was fast for a man mounting those treacherous barbed strands.

He had reached the top and was balanced astride the swaying wires when the Germans first saw him. They began shouting: 'Halt! Halt!' and again, 'Halt oder ich schiesse!' came echoing down the line of sentries.

He took no notice. Freeing himself from the top strands he jumped down to the ground and stumbled at the nine-foot drop. He picked himself up as the first shot rang out. There were shouts again of 'Halt!' and then a fourth time 'Halt! Halt!'

He was running. The hill was against him. He was not travelling fast. He dodged once, then twice, as two more shots rang out and he ran straight for the outer wall. But the Germans had his range by now and a volley of shots spattered around him. He dodged again. He could still have turned and raised his hands.

He was nearing the wall but he was tiring. Another volley echoed among the trees of the park and he fell to his knees and a gasp of horror rose from the men watching behind the wire. Then, slowly, he crumpled forward amongst the autumn leaves.

He lay still as the sentries rushed forward, swooping on their prey. He did not move when they reached him. A sentry, bending down turned him over while another quickly opened his shirt and felt with his hand over the heart. He was dead.

The Red Fox had escaped. He had crossed the last frontier and would never be brought back to Colditz again a recaptured, spent, defeated prisoner. He had made a 'home-run'. He was free.

On September 17, in northern Europe, British and American parachute troops, together with Polish troops, and British and American infantrymen and tanks, took part in Operation Market Garden. It was an attack launched with high expectations, designed to outflank the German defensive line known as the West Wall by establishing a bridgehead across the lower Rhine at the Dutch town of Arnhem. If successful it would bring the Allied armies almost to the Ruhr, and might, in the view of General Montgomery who planned it, bring the war to an early end.

The operation had two aspects: Market, the seizure by airborne troops of bridges across eight water barriers, and Garden, the advance of troops and tanks across the bridges. The total distance for the advance was fifty-nine miles. The airborne landings were successful, but two much battered German Panzer divisions were in the area, refitting. By ill-chance for the Allies, these two divisions had just completed a military exercise on how to repel an airborne landing. More than six thousand of the 35,000 airborne force were taken prisoner, and 1,400 were killed. Nearly half of the prisoners had been wounded in the battle.*

This Allied effort, so costly and so disappointing, took place as the mass murder machinery which had been in place at Auschwitz for more than two years (and for longer elsewhere) continued to take its grim toll. On September 20 a deportation began of 4,000 Jews from the Theresienstadt ghetto. Before being deported they were made to appear in a German propaganda film entitled 'The Führer donates a town to the Jews'. The film was designed to be shown throughout Germany and in neutral countries such as Switzerland and Sweden as an example of German goodwill towards the Jews, and as proof that rumours of the mass murder of Jews were false.

In the film the inmates of the ghetto were shown reading in a library, sunbathing by a swimming pool, watching a football match between two ghetto teams, eating bread, cheese and tomatoes in a canteen, and at a dance.

---

* A book by Cornelius Ryan, *A Bridge Too Far* (1974), and a film of the same name, made the drama of the Battle of Arnhem widely known.

Scenes were then shown of German soldiers at the front, while a commentator remarked: 'While the Jews in Theresienstadt enjoy their coffee and cakes and dance, our soldiers bear the brunt of this terrible war, suffering death and deprivation in defence of the homeland.'

It was not 'death and privation', but only death, which was to be the imminent fate of almost all those who had been made to play a part in the film. Deported to Auschwitz, they were either gassed on arrival or died there within a few months. The Auschwitz camp register which recorded their deaths, also recorded the deaths of two hundred Gypsies who had earlier been sent from Auschwitz to Buchenwald, but were then returned to Auschwitz. The victims, deceived as to where they were going, weak from hunger and the long journeys, denied even the semblance of medical attention or proper nourishment, surrounded by armed guards, driven at the point of the gun, by the lashes of whips and the snarling of SS trained dogs, were able, in the few instances that have been recorded, to raise the voice and spirit of revolt.

Sometimes a group that were being forced to undress next to the gas chamber would fight back, until their guards had shot them all down. Sometimes an individual would seize the dagger or gun of an SS man and turn it on him, before being killed by the other guards. In October there was an uprising by the Jewish slave labourers inside Auschwitz who were being forced to take out the corpses from the gas chambers to the crematoria. They succeeded in blowing up three of the gas chambers. The explosives which they used had been smuggled into the camp by five Jewish women slave labourers working in an ammunition factory just beyond the camp perimeter.

The revolt inside Auschwitz was crushed by armed force and all those who had taken part in it were killed. The five women who had made it possible were also executed: hanged in front of the whole camp. Despite severe torture they refused to betray their accomplices. From the cell in which she was being held before her execution, one of the women, Roza Robota, managed to smuggle out a message: 'You have nothing to fear – I shall not talk.'

Hitler was almost at the end of his ability to conduct the war. A senior German army officer, General Nikolaus von Vormann, who visited him at Rastenburg on September 26, noted in his diary: 'It was a tired, broken man who greeted me, then shuffled over to a chair, his shoulders drooping, and asked me to sit down. He spoke so softly and hesitantly, it was hard to understand him. His hands trembled so much he had to grip them between his knees.'

That day, Hitler signed a decree setting up a People's Army for the defence of German soil. Every able-bodied man between the age of sixteen and sixty was to be called up. On the following day, on receiving a report from Himmler that the Warsaw uprising had finally been crushed, and that 200,000 Poles — mostly civilians — had been killed, he awarded the much-coveted Knight's Cross to both General von dem Bach Zelewski and General Dirlewanger.

The Warsaw insurgents were taken by train, sixty men to a cattle truck, to concentration and slave labour camps. As they left, the final, flimsy, defiant *Information Bulletin* of the Home Army was passed from hand to hand throughout the city. 'The battle is over', it declared, 'but the defeat is the defeat of one city, of one stage in our fight for freedom. It is not the defeat of our nation, of our plans and historical ideals.' The bulletin continued:

From the spilled blood, the common hardship and difficulties, from the suffering of bodies and of souls, there will rise a new Poland — free, strong, and great.

With this faith we will live in forced, homeless wanderings or in prison camps, just as we live with it in our work and battles. This faith is the most real, the highest testament written with the blood of the many thousands of victims and heroes of the Uprising.

Poland 'free, strong and great' was a hope that was to sustain the captives, and their fellow-countrymen, for another half century.

As winter approached, and the Allies continued to press forward on to the soil of Germany, unceasing efforts were still being made to find and punish enemies of the people and of the regime. In October seventeen Post Office employees in Vienna were caught taking chocolate and soap from badly wrapped army parcels that were being sent through their sorting office. All seventeen were marched to a central square and executed in public.

There was fighting every day on every war front: not only the offensives, the attempts to break through the opposing lines, the efforts to change or to accelerate the course of the war, but the daily confrontations of millions of armed men, and the daily death and injury of those confrontations. For many years to come, until the end of the century, many families remembered first and foremost not the historical dates through which the war is usually recounted, but the date of their own personal loss. On September 29 a nineteen-year-old American soldier, Private First Class Jochanan Tartakower, was killed in action in France. In dedicating a book to him two months later, his father wrote that his son was one 'whose sacrifice is typical of the many thousands of Jewish refugees who have given the last full measure of devotion to their people and to the countries that gave them refuge.'

On October 4 the first British parachutists landed in Greece, at Patras, on the Gulf of Corinth. Their instructions were to secure an all-Party provisional government for Greece which would organize national, democratic elections, at the very moment when the Greek Communists were hoping to seize control of the country.

The German armies were being driven back on every front, but were fighting for every mile. In Yugoslavia, Soviet troops were advancing along the Danube. In the Baltic States they were driving the remnants of the German army to the sea and to captivity. In northern Europe, Canadian and Free French troops were among those pushing the Germans eastward. In Italy, the Allied troops of a dozen nations – with British, American and Polish troops predominant – had crossed the River Arno and were facing the Germans north of liberated Pisa. In eastern France, American troops were battling towards the German border and the Rhine.

What did such verbs – 'landing', 'advancing', 'driving', 'pushing', 'facing', 'battling towards' – really mean? On October 4 General Eisenhower distributed – to the senior officers of all the Allied combat units under his command in Europe – a report by the Office of the United States Surgeon General which indicated the answer to some of these questions, in regard to the strains and burdens of combat, not only physical but psychological. 'The key to an understanding of the psychiatric problem', the report explained, 'is the simple fact that the danger of being killed or maimed imposes a strain so great that it causes men to break down. One look at the shrunken, apathetic faces of psychiatric patients as they come down stumbling into the medical station, sobbing, trembling, referring shudderingly to "them shells" and to buddies mutilated or dead, is enough to convince most observers of this fact.'

The Surgeon General's report stressed that there was 'no such thing as "getting used to combat". Each man "up there" knows that at any moment he may be killed, a fact kept constantly before his mind by the sight of dead and mutilated buddies around him. Each moment of combat imposes a strain so great that men will break down in direct relation to the intensity and duration of their exposure. Thus psychiatric casualties are as inevitable as gunshot and shrapnel wounds in warfare'.

Every army made calculations with regard to the staying power of its soldiers when in combat. In Italy the American forces estimated that an infantryman could 'last' for about two hundred regimental combat days. The British commanders endeavoured to pull their men out of the line after every twelve days of combat, for a four day rest period, and estimated that their men could remain unaffected for up to four hundred days of combat. In giving these figures in his report, the United States Surgeon General noted: 'A wound or injury is regarded, not as a misfortune, but a blessing. As one litter bearer put it, "Something funny about the men you bring back wounded, they're always happy . . . they're sure glad to be getting out of here". Under these circumstances it is easy for a man to become sincerely convinced that he is sick or unable to go on. This in turn leads to the premature development of genuine psychiatric disability and to needless loss of manpower. It also leads to self-inflicted wounds and to misbehaviour before the enemy.'

Two days after this report was circulated, a new enemy presented itself to the Allied forces in the West: German jet aircraft. The first one to enter combat, however, above the Dutch-German border, was spotted by a Royal Canadian Air Force squadron and shot down. An older secret weapon – by one month – the V2 rocket, was being fired against the recently liberated city of Antwerp in mid-October, a particularly unpleasant act of vengeance on men and women who had been captives of the Germans for more than four years.

Within a week, ninety of Antwerp's citizens had been killed. Another seventy-one were killed before the end of October, and 295 in November, of whom thirty-two were children in an orphanage that had been converted into an emergency hospital. Thirty-two of the victims were nuns killed when a rocket bomb hit their convent.

On October 14, American troops besieged the German city of Aachen, once the capital of the Holy Roman Empire of Charlemagne. Forty-eight hours later, Soviet and Yugoslav partisan troops entered Belgrade. On the day of Belgrade's liberation, Hitler took action to prevent Admiral Horthy opening negotiations for the surrender of Hungary and – as with Roumania after its surrender almost two months earlier – its entry into the war on the side of the Allies. For the second time in seven months, German troops were ordered to enter Hungary in force. On October 15, as they prepared to do so, Horthy broadcast an announcement that Hungary was seeking an armistice with the Allies. Almost two weeks earlier, in strictest secrecy, a Hungarian armistice delegation had arrived in Moscow. Other Hungarians had gone to British military headquarters in Italy to raise the question of an end to hostilities. Hitler had no intention of debate or negotiation on this point. Instead, he ordered the immediate abduction of Horthy to Germany. His order was carried out by two experts in German kidnapping tactics. One of them was General Skorzeny, who had kidnapped Mussolini in 1943; the other was General von dem Bach Zelewski, who had crushed the Warsaw uprising less than a month earlier.

On the day after Horthy's kidnapping, a pro-German government came to power in Budapest, pledged to continue the fight at Germany's side. Soviet troops were already within a hundred miles of Budapest. On October 16 the first Soviet troops crossed on to German soil, entering Schirwindt, just inside the border of East Prussia. Hitler had finally to face a two-front war on German soil, as well as a thrust from the south that threatened to reach the southern borders of the Reich.

The warmaking powers of Japan were about to take a bizarre turn, as Japanese pilots volunteered to crash their planes on the decks of American warships. These suicide pilots were known as *kami-kaze* – from the Japanese characters for 'God-wind' or divine wind. They swore undying loyalty to the Emperor and died as their ultimate proof of that loyalty. They were inspired in their suicidal endeavours by Admiral Takijiro Onishi, who, as a young officer before the First World War, had studied naval warfare in Britain, and who, during the First World War, achieved fame in Japan as a successful air ace. In December 1941 Onishi had led the air assault on the Philippines.

Confident that with kamikaze suicide attacks the offensive power of the United States Pacific Fleet could be destroyed, and the invasion of the Japanese Home Islands averted, Admiral Onishi assembled a suicide squad which was ready for action in October. On October 20 he addressed the first twenty-six pilot volunteers:

My sons, who can raise our country from the desperate situation in which she finds herself?

Japan is in grave danger. The salvation of our country is now beyond the power of the Ministers of State, the General Staff, and lowly commanders like myself. It can come only from spirited young men such as you. Thus on behalf of your hundred million countrymen, I ask you this sacrifice, and pray for your success.

You are already gods, without earthly desires. But one thing you want to know is that your crash-dive is not in vain.

Regrettably, we will not be able to tell you the results. But I shall watch your efforts to the end and report your deeds to the Throne. You may all rest assured on this point. I ask you to do your best.

The first of the kamikaze suicide attacks took place on October 24, on the first day of the three-day Battle of Leyte Gulf, off the Philippines. The first suicide pilot hit the aircraft carrier *Santee*, killing sixteen men. But the *Santee* was not disabled, and was able to stay in formation. Several of the kamikaze planes were shot down before they reached their targets. Any hope Admiral Onishi might have had when October 25 dawned of a one-day knock out blow was misplaced. But the new 'weapon' created much havoc and considerable damage. On the cruiser *Nashville* 131 men were killed. The number American dead was to rise steadily month by month.

Despite the unexpected appearance of the kamikaze pilots, the Battle of Leyte Gulf was a failure for the Japanese, whose own warships were no match for the American carrier-born aircraft that assailed them. Twenty-six Japanese warships were sunk during the battle, including the super-battleship *Musashi*, launched two years earlier, with its hitherto unprecedented eighteen-inch naval guns, shared only by its sister ship *Yamato*. During a sustained American assault the *Musashi* was hit by twenty torpedoes and seventeen bombs, and blown to pieces.

On the day of the first kamikaze attack, October 24, a Japanese freighter, the *Arisan Maru*, steaming in convoy 225 miles off Hong Kong, was torpedoed by an Allied submarine. As it began to sink the Japanese shut the rear hatches and abandoned ship. There were 1,810 Allied prisoners-of-war in the hold. Many had been killed when the torpedo exploded. Some of the survivors managed to make a pyramid of the corpses and reach the hatch, which they forced open. As they swam in the sea hoping for rescue from the Japanese convoy escort destroyers, the destroyer crews, using long poles, pushed them under the water.

Only eight of the 1,810 prisoners-of-war survived. 'So the POWs, who suffered so much on land,' writes Gavan Daws, 'suffered again at sea. They died in the holds, of starvation, suffocation, dehydration, and disease. They were killed by bombs and torpedoes aimed at them by their allies, their countrymen. The Japanese killed them in the water, or they drowned, or they died on the rafts. Or, most terrible of all, they killed each other.' On one ship, the *Oryokku Maru*, more than a thousand American officers could not stop fellow-Americans from killing each other by the second night of their unbearable journey locked in the hold.

'Was it simply that the *Oryokku Maru* had the absolute worst level of unbearable heat,' Daws has asked, 'the worst lack of water, the worst lack of oxygen, prisoners in the worst shape when they were loaded aboard, and the worst stress from being attacked? In other words, was everything simply over the human physical edge? Who can say?'

The sea transfers were a horrific story: of 50,000 Allied prisoners-of-war who were transported on board ship – or rather, locked in the deep cargo holds and bilges of ships – by the Japanese, during 1944 and the early months of 1945, 10,800 died at sea.

Fearing that the advancing Soviet forces would come across the mass murder machinery at Auschwitz, in the last week of October Himmler ordered the whole vast camp to be dismantled: the murder machinery and the perimeter wire. Hundreds of thousands of prisoners who were in the barracks and the surrounding slave labour camps were sent away, at first on foot, then by truck and train. Their destination was other slave labour camps further west.

Yet trains were still being sent into Auschwitz. When a train carrying more than five hundred Slovak Jews reached Auschwitz on November 5, from the slave labour camp at Sered, the Auschwitz administration office contacted Mauthausen concentration camp in Austria, three hundred miles away, by telephone. 'We have a transport here; could you handle it in your gas chambers?' asked the Auschwitz administrator who made the call. His opposite number at Mauthausen replied: 'That would be a waste of coal burned in the locomotive. You should be able to handle the load yourself.' Because the gas chambers at Auschwitz that had not been blown up in the October uprising were being dismantled, the Jewish men from the camp at

Sered were sent to various factories in the area. The women and children were sent to the barracks. Those children were among the very few children who survived deportation to Auschwitz.

As Soviet troops came within fifty miles of Budapest, the German army was crushing the Slovak revolt less than two hundred miles to the north. Of two thousand Slovak partisans who were killed in action, 269 were Jews.

German troops were still fighting to hold every town and every fortified position. At the beginning of November they were defending the Dutch island of Walcheren, which guarded the mouth of the River Scheldt and the entrance to the port of Antwerp, which the British badly needed to supply their troops trying to press forward into Germany. In the battle above the island, the Germans shot down fifty-one British aircraft, and thirty-one pilots were killed. But after a total of ten thousand air sorties had been mounted against the German defenders by rocket-firing aircraft, Canadian troops were able to land on the island and secure Antwerp's sea lanes. Germany's fuel oil reserves were insufficient to mount an adequate counter-attack in the air or on land.

Only the V2 attacks on Britain continued, the rockets needing relatively little fuel, not needing pilots, and not having to be directed with any precision. When a V2 hit a Woolworth department store in South London in the last week of November, 160 lunchtime shoppers were killed.

President Roosevelt was elected to an unprecedented fourth term as President of the United States on November 7. For almost three years his Presidency had been dominated by the two-ocean war. He had committed American resources to win the war in Europe first, and that commitment was finally moving towards fulfillment. He could also look forward to an early British transfer of resources to the Far East, and an intensification of Britain's war effort there.

Two days after Roosevelt's re-election American troops near Aachen found themselves under heavy German artillery fire. Among them was Private Henry Kissinger, on German soil for the first time since he had left as a refugee six years earlier.

On November 12, British bombers finally managed to sink the *Tirpitz* in its Norwegian fiord. At least a thousand German sailors were drowned. The sinking of Germany's last warship in Western waters released several powerful

British warships for service against the Japanese in the Pacific. Roosevelt had promised Churchill that the defeat of Hitler would have priority over the defeat of Japan. The sinking of the *Tirpitz* enabled Britain to transfer an element of her warmaking powers hitherto needed in Europe to the Pacific side of the global war.

In the Far East, the Japanese were still managing to launch the occasional advance into China. On November 17 they pushed the Nationalist forces back towards Kweiyang, the railhead for the Nationalists' vital Burma Road supply line. But that same day, in the Yellow Sea, an American submarine sank one of the last Japanese escort carriers still afloat. Nor was the Japanese scientific war going well. In Tokyo a gathering of Japanese atomic scientists, called to discuss progress towards the making of a Japanese atom bomb, was told that 'since February of this year there has not been a great deal of progress'. It emerged from the meeting that Japan would not be able to develop an atom bomb in time to influence the outcome of the war. Unknown to the Japanese scientists at this meeting, the United States was making rapid progress towards that very goal.

Kamikaze attacks on American ships were frequent and much feared. On November 24 a kamikaze pilot crashed his plane on the deck of the aircraft carrier *Intrepid*. It was the third time the *Intrepid* had been hit by a suicide pilot. She was an inevitable target, her guns and planes having sunk eighty Japanese ships and destroyed 650 Japanese planes in fifteen months. *Intrepid* survived the war: today she is docked in the Hudson River, serving as New York's own naval museum.*

The fate of American prisoners-of-war in Japanese hands remained horrific. On the Philippine island of Palawan, 150 prisoners-of-war were warned by their captors that an American air raid was in progress and were ordered into the deep air raid shelters. There was no raid on its way and the order was a trick. As soon as the men were inside the shelters they were doused with petrol which was then set alight. As the Americans, many of them on fire, fled from the burning shelters, they were shot, bayoneted and clubbed to death. Some badly burned men were buried alive as they cried out in agony. Only five of the 150 survived – to give evidence after the war to this atrocity.

The native populations of the areas occupied by Japan fared no better than

---

* Five weeks before his assassination in 1995, the Israeli Prime Minister, Yitzhak Rabin, was the guest of honour at a dinner on board *Intrepid*.

the American prisoners-of-war. Brutality towards Filipinos was common. On December 19 a Japanese private noted in his diary: 'Taking advantage of darkness we went out to kill natives. It was hard for me to kill because they seemed good people. The frightful cries of the women and children were horrible. I myself killed several persons.'

Inside China, the Japanese army continued to advance, still extending the work of conquest which it had begun seven years earlier, and entering the city of Nanning before the end of November. In Burma, however, the British and Indian troops who had faced the Japanese on the border with Burma for almost three years, broke through into Burma itself on November 19, and linking up with the forces that had been dropped behind Japanese lines, advanced swiftly to the Chindwin River and across it.

In Western Europe, French forces reached the Rhine on November 19, at the village of Rosenau, near the border with France and Switzerland, across the river from Germany. A day later German forces were driven out of Sarrebourg, which they had acquired during the Saar plebiscite of 1935. An area predominantly German had passed into Allied control.

In East Prussia, the Russians continued to advance through one of the areas of medieval German settlement, the scene also of Hindenburg's victory over the Russians at the Battle of Tannenberg in August 1914. On November 20 Hitler judged it prudent to leave Rastenburg and return to Berlin. He was never to see Rastenburg or East Prussia again. In the areas which his armies had to give up, war crimes trials had begun. On the day that Hitler left Rastenburg, a Belgian collaborator was tried for inhumane behaviour at Breendonk camp by the new Belgian authorities, and sentenced to death.

American and French troops entered Strasbourg on November 23. The capital of Alsace returned to France for the second time: it had been annexed by Germany in 1870, and again in 1940.

Despite the imminence of defeat, the tyranny of Nazism knew no pause. On November 25, having demolished the last gas chamber, the Germans at Auschwitz murdered all two hundred Jews who had been forced to take the bodies of murdered Jews to the crematoria. One of those two hundred, a French Jew, Chaim Herman, who knew that his wife and daughter were alive in France, in hiding, managed to scribble a note to them three weeks before his own execution: 'I am going away calmly, knowing that you are alive, and our enemy is broken.'

The 'enemy' was indeed breaking, but not yet broken. On November 30, three executions took place in Plötzensee prison in Berlin, when a woman, her husband and her mother were beheaded at two minute intervals. The woman was thirty-one-year-old Lilo Gloeden, an opponent of the Nazi dictatorship. After the July Plot she had given shelter for six weeks to General Fritz Lindemann, one of the plotters with a substantial reward on his head. Earlier, she had helped the former mayor of Leipzig, Dr Carl Goerdeler, to find refuge. Her execution, and that of her husband and mother, were given wide publicity but the Gestapo in an attempt to deter any further shielding of 'traitors to the Third Reich'.

The British bombing raids on the Third Reich continued throughout December. In the first and only major raid of the war on Heilbronn, on the night of December 4/5, a firestorm was started, eighty-two per cent of the town's built up area was destroyed by fire, and 7,147 German civilians killed. The city had been chosen as a target because it lay on a main north-south railway line. That night severe damage was also caused at Karlsruhe, where an important machine tool factory was destroyed, as well as the main Protestant church and the town's concert hall. But there was no firestorm, and the death toll was just over four hundred.

A week later, during a British night bombing raid on Essen, considerable damage was done to some of the Krupp works that were still in operation. The number of deaths on the ground that night, 463, included eighty-nine prisoners-of-war, thirteen foreign workers, and more than two hundred German criminals who were killed when the city's prison received a direct, though unintentional, hit.

Having left Rastenburg for good, Hitler returned to the headquarters bunker at Bad Nauheim, not far from the River Rhine. He had last used the facilities and shelter of Bad Nauheim during the triumphant days of May 1940. Returning, he approved plans for an attempted German offensive, starting in the Ardennes Forest and driving across the River Meuse to the port of Antwerp. His aim was to seize the port through which was passing – in ever increasing flow – the bulk of the supplies needed by the Allied armies already on German soil.

Hitler told a group of Hitler Youth leaders who came to see him at Bad Nauheim on December 10 that he hoped it was possible to 'decimate this enemy also at the very gates to the Fatherland'. Germany would 'turn the tide' on the Western Front and 'split the American-British alliance once and for all'. But he also seems to have sensed that the time of warmaking in Europe, and enthusiasm for war, was drawing to a close. Two days after his confident assertions to the Hitler Youth, he told a group of generals who came to his new headquarters: 'You can't extract enthusiasm and self-sacrifice like something tangible, and bottle and preserve them. They are generated just once in the course of a revolution, and will gradually die away. The greyness of day and the conveniences of life will then take hold on men again and turn them into solid citizens in grey flannel suits.'

The day of the 'grey flannel suits' had not yet arrived. On December 16, six days after Hitler's reflective prediction of such a return to a peaceful era, the German army launched its counter-offensive to drive through the Ardennes forest to Antwerp. While German troops did break through the American lines – a quarter of a million German troops against 80,000 unsuspecting Americans – and did drive forward almost to the River Meuse, they suffered their first and unexpected setback at the very outset. A parachute drop behind the American lines just north of the breakthrough was a failure. Within twenty-four hours most of the parachutists had been captured, without having disrupted American communications in the rear.

In its first days, however, the German thrust in the Ardennes seemed the prelude to a substantial renewal of the German offensive. Just inside the Belgian border, on the slopes of the Schnee Eifel, nearly nine thousand Americans surrendered. It was the largest single mass surrender by United States forces since Bataan.

More than 19,000 Americans were killed during the German Ardennes offensive, and tens of thousands taken prisoner. There were also episodes when American soldiers were murdered after being captured. At Malmédy an SS unit commanded by SS Lieutenant-Colonel Joachim Peiper took seventy-two American prisoners-of-war into an open field, lined them up and opened fire with a machine gun. Sixty of the Americans were killed. Twelve managed to escape and find shelter in a café. The SS men set the café on fire and shot the men down as they fled the flames – a technique the SS had used many times behind the lines on the Eastern Front.

A year earlier, Peiper had been awarded the Oak Leaves to his Knight's Cross for commanding a partisan sweep in Russia in which 2,500 Russians had been executed, and only three taken prisoner. At ten other places along his line of march in the Ardennes, a further 308 American soldiers and more than a hundred Belgian civilians were killed after having been rounded up. Not far from Malmédy, in the village of Stavelot, a further 130 Belgian civilians were killed – 60 men, 47 women, and 23 children.

News of the Malmédy massacre spread rapidly through the American lines. When, on December 21, German soldiers emerged from a burning house holding up a Red Cross flag, American soldiers opened fire on them as they stood near the doorway, and twenty-one were killed.

In Antwerp, the objective of the attack, a V2 rocket hit a crowded cinema on the first day of the German advance through the Ardennes, killing 567 people, of whom almost three hundred were Allied servicemen. In all, 3,752 Belgian civilians and more than seven hundred Allied servicemen were killed by the rockets sent against Antwerp. The German hopes of reaching Antwerp and the River Scheldt were not to be fulfilled, however. The American troops in and around the town of Bastogne, which the Germans had hoped to overrun on the first or second day, although surrounded and outnumbered, refused to surrender.

The senior American officer in Bastogne, Major-General Anthony C. McAuliffe, when asked to surrender by the Germans, and given by them two hours to contemplate 'annihilation', replied in the single word 'Nuts!' On being asked what 'nuts' meant, the Germans were told that it meant: 'Go to hell!'

Shortly after this brief exchange a German major, flanked by two captains, and by two soldiers carrying a large white flag, approached the American lines and asked for a formal answer to their call for surrender. McAuliffe then had it written out and handed it to the major. It read:

> To the German Commander:
> NUTS.
> Signed,
> The American Commander.

Realizing that the sweep to Antwerp was beyond his powers, Field Marshal von Rundstedt asked Hitler if he could withdraw into the Eifel Mountains. Hitler refused. He had faith in his troops, and above all in the commandos led by Otto Skorzeny who, having successfully infiltrated through the American lines, were causing havoc. The men chosen for this commando raid were English speaking, wore American uniforms, and drove in captured American jeeps and trucks. They blew up bridges, and when confronted with genuine American soldiers gave orders that sent the genuine soldiers away from the battlefield.

It was Allied air bombardment that made it impossible for the Germans to continue their advance through the Ardennes, or even to hold on to what they had conquered in the sweep forward. Railway yards and railway lines in the area leading to the battlefield were subjected to a massive bombardment. Allied fighters struck at the German tanks as they approached to within five miles of the River Meuse, but were more than sixty miles from Antwerp. They failed even to reach the Meuse, as German aircraft were outnumbered by the Allied planes over the battlefield, and were ordered back to Germany by the air force commander.

Skorzeny's commandos were beginning to fall into American hands. Because they were wearing American uniforms they were treated not as soldiers but as spies, and eighteen of them were shot. The appearance over the battlefield on December 24 of sixteen German jet aircraft – the first jet aircraft to go into action as a unit in modern warfare – came too late. There were too few of them to affect the battle in the air.

On December 29, a top secret German Air Force message reported that the impact of the Allied bombing raids throughout the region through which reinforcements to the Ardennes must come had not only destroyed roads and railways on a massive scale, but had eliminated the telephone facilities needed to re-route supply trains. This message, decrypted by the Allies, made it clear that the Ardennes offensive was over, and that there could be no further German forward movement in the West.

On the Eastern Front, which had moved forward to the Vistula and the Danube, several hundred thousand German soldiers were trying to beat back a Russian onslaught on the Hungarian capital, Budapest. As the battle continued in the suburbs, the Fascist Arrow Cross tried to murder Jews in the streets and in their homes. Foreign diplomats, Raoul Wallenberg among them, did their utmost to frustrate these efforts by offering the Jews of the capital protective documents and safe houses protected by Swedish, Swiss, Spanish and Portuguese flags. Wallenberg even intervened to try to prevent Jews being marched away to a concentration camp in Austria under armed German guard. Several hundred of the marchers were allowed back to the city, and to safe houses, as a result of his intervention.

The Red Cross was also active in Budapest in giving its protection to Jews. But the Arrow Cross was as determined as the Germans had been to kill Jews. Hundreds of Jews were slaughtered in the streets, even as the capital awaited the inevitable arrival of the Soviet forces. In one Arrow Cross swoop, Jews in hospitals and old people's homes were attacked, and more than three hundred killed. On December 27 the Arrow Cross executed two Hungarian Christian women, Sister Sara Salkhazi and Vilma Bernovits, who had hidden Jews.

The Hungarian government, like the Roumanian and Bulgarian governments before it, feared for its future once the Soviet army was in control, and contemplated, as the Roumanians and Bulgarians had done, changing sides. In Eastern Poland and throughout Roumania, those who were considered enemies of Communism were being arrested. The Soviet army was handing power, not to local civilians but to Soviet commissars – the long-established political arm of Stalin's military machine. A major stimulus to a Hungarian decision to change sides came on December 29, when the Germans shot two Soviet emissaries who came into their lines under a white flag of truce to discuss the terms for a German surrender.

Realizing that the Germans would fight to the last both around the capital and inside it – as Hitler had ordered them to do – on December 31 the Hungarian Government broke away from the Axis and declared war on Germany.

Even in countries on which not a single enemy soldier landed, or a single bomb fell – most notably Canada and the United States – the nature of the war affected daily life, not by rationing or the often terrifying hardships of occupation and bombardment, but by fears for the soldiers who had crossed the Atlantic or Pacific ocean to fight; fears for a future without the bread-winner; and uncertainty as to when and how the war would end, with what further unknown losses along the way, and with question marks over what the future of the post-war world would be.

The scale of Allied losses up to the end of 1944 was announced early in the New Year by both Washington and London. Those who lived farthest from the enemy were no less the victims of global war. From the time of the Japanese attack on Pearl Harbor and Hitler's declaration of war on the United States at the end of 1941, 138,393 Americans were known to have been killed on land, at sea and in the air, and a further 73,594 were missing, presumed dead. Within the British Commonwealth, the Canadian death toll thus far was 28,040, of whom more than half were pilots and air crew. The Australian death toll stood at 18,015; that of New Zealand at 8,919; and that of South Africa at 5,783.

In addition, 17,415 Indian soldiers had been killed, many of them fighting on the Indian-Burmese border to keep the Japanese out of the subcontinent.

The British war dead numbered 199,497. Tens of thousands more British civilians had been killed by German air bombardment and, most recently, by the V1 flying bombs and the V2 rockets. Behind the statistics lay a vast, uncharted sea of suffering. But the war remained one which, for the Allies, had to be fought. 'Many a home across Canada had been darkened by these tragic losses,' wrote the Canadian military historian Colonel Stacey three years after the end of the war, 'but the bereaved were not without consolation. A tyranny, callous and cruel almost beyond belief, which had menaced the whole free world, had been brought down in ruin; and the way lay open – if men were wise enough to see it – to "broader and better days".'

The war was not yet over: in German-occupied Holland the winter brought with it great hardship to the civilian population. Ration scales, always low, fell repeatedly, until they reached a starvation level of 340 calories per day. During the winter months, 20,000 people died of hunger. Tens of thousands more suffered from severe malnutrition. There was no fuel, no gas and no electricity. At the same time the Germans carried out manhunts in search of forced labourers, setting a target of half a million. From Rotterdam alone 50,000 men were taken.

Of the torment of Holland, a Dutch eye-witness, Hen Bollen has written: 'Tens of thousands of city dwellers, despite being seriously weakened, roamed the countryside, paying exorbitant prices or swapping valuables and textiles for food. Many of them spent days on the road north or east, when ecstatic with some grain, a piece of bacon, or potatoes, they would return home. Those returning would then often fall prey to the Dutchmen of the Economic Control Council or the *Landwacht* (Dutch Nazi Police) who would confiscate the goods which had already cost so much pain and money.'

The Germans were determined not to give any respite. At the port of Delfzijl they prevented the docking of Swedish ships bringing flour, oats and margarine under the auspices of the Red Cross.

In their planning for the future phases – and final phase – of the Pacific War, the United States Joint Chiefs of Staff were continually revising, and as they saw it perfecting, their plans. On December 1 an important forward planning policy was laid down which envisaged American ground forces landing on the Japanese Home Islands. The plan involved an intensified sea blockade and air bombardment in order to create a situation 'favourable to' an assault on Kyushu Island. Such an assault was itself intended to establish a tactical situation that would favour 'the decisive invasion of the industrial heart of Japan through the Tokyo Plain'.

Throughout the Far East the Japanese occupation had stimulated national forces determined not to allow the colonial powers to regain control, but to set up their own sovereign entities as soon as the Japanese were gone. In Vietnam, Vo Nguyen Giap tried – at the time of the Normandy landings in June, when the liberation of France was suddenly in prospect – to embark on a full-scale guerrilla uprising in the northern provinces of Vietnam. But his political chief, Ho Chi Minh, who was then in China, returned and countermanded Giap's orders, warning that such an uprising was premature.

Ho Chi Minh proposed another tactic, about which he gave Giap orders on December 19: the establishment of the first small, compact and highly trained political-military unit, whose aim was to spread Communist ideals and influence village by village. Known as the Vietnam Propaganda and Liberation Units, they were to evolve into the People's Army of Vietnam, led by Giap and charged by Ho Chi Minh with seizing power wherever the Japanese were to withdraw. The first of these units was activated on December 22. It consisted of thirty-four men. Two days later, on Christmas Eve, it went into action, attacking two small Vichy French military outposts.

Giap's tactic on that occasion was to disguise his men as pro-French partisans, and to enter the outposts by the main gate. They were successful, overrunning the outposts for long enough to get away with arms and ammunition. In future years the day of that Christmas Eve action was to be celebrated in North Vietnam, and eventually in both north and south, as the 'birthday' of the Vietnamese armed forces.

Also on Christmas Eve, Winston Churchill flew to Athens to try to secure an all-Party government and prevent a Greek Communist attempt to seize power in the capital. Three weeks earlier twenty-three citizens had been killed in a clash between Communist and non-Communist Greek forces: at the funeral the next day the words on the mourning banners had been written in the blood of the victims. Arriving by air from London as fighting between the Greek factions erupted around him, Churchill took refuge on a British warship anchored off Piraeus. During two days of talks, first on board ship and then in the British Embassy in Athens – which he reached in an armoured car – Churchill was successful in persuading the Greek Communist leaders, who were encouraged to come to terms with him by Stalin's emissary, Colonel Popov, to call a halt to their battle against their fellow Greeks, and to join an all-Party government. For the time being, amid world war, civil war was averted. As the scourge of Nazi rule was being lifted throughout Europe, the imposition of Communist rule was being challenged in Europe's most southerly region.

CHAPTER SEVENTEEN

1945

THE FINAL EIGHT MONTHS OF WAR

> You were our liberators, but we, the diseased,
> emaciated, barely human survivors were your teachers.
> We taught you to understand the Kingdom of Night.
>
> ELIE WIESEL

FEW YEARS OF THE TWENTIETH CENTURY were to see such dramatic and long-lasting changes as 1945. Yet it was a year which began, like each of the four preceding years, with a pattern of world-wide activity related to previous dark ages. There were still men – and women – in combat, lives lost by their thousands each day in the grimmest circumstances, the daily creation of widows and orphans, the fate of masses of men, women and children in the balance, and the future of great nations and widely scattered peoples at risk of turmoil and disintegration.

The opening days of 1945 saw the execution, on January 4, of Fritz Elsas, who had been mayor of Berlin when Hitler came to power. Because of his Jewish descent he had been forced out of public life in 1933. During the witchhunt after July 1944 he was among those suspected of anti-Nazi machinations. His close friend and fellow mayor – of Leipzig – Carl Goerdeler, a leading supporter of the anti-Hitler conspirators, who had been betrayed, was already being held prisoner. Elsas was taken to Sachsenhausen concentration camp, where he was executed.

By that first week of January the German army had been forced back both in the West, where the Americans had begun to regain the ground lost in the Ardennes, and in the East, where just over three million German soldiers faced six million Russians. In the Pacific, the most notorious Japanese weapon was the kamikaze pilot, but the deaths which the pilots inflicted, several thousand during the course of January, could not halt the steady movement of American forces from island to island. Nor could the Japanese retain the stranglehold on supplies to China which they had held since May 1942 with the occupation of Burma and the cutting of the Burma Road. A new road was being built linking China with India through northern Burma, from the Chinese city of Yunnan, through the north Burmese city of Myitkyina, to Ledo. The first convoy set off from Ledo on January 28. It was to prove a vital, and unbreakable link.

Inside the United States, scientific developments were being pushed forward that would dramatically affect the outcome of the war. On January 6 the President of Harvard University, James B. Conant, whom Roosevelt had put in charge of research on the atom bomb, noted that it was expected to be able to drop such a bomb that autumn. Three days later American troops landed on Luzon, from which they had been driven three years earlier.

On the Eastern Front the Soviet forces launched their winter offensive on January 12. Against 180 Soviet divisions the Germans could put only seventy-five. Tens of thousands of German troops that might have been able to help strengthen the defensive line in the East were trapped elsewhere: thirty divisions in two pockets on the Baltic, around Memel and in Kurland, and twenty-eight divisions in and around Budapest, trying to prevent the Soviet thrust from reaching Vienna.

Hitler, seeking to direct his armies in such a way as to hold the line wherever possible, could not keep up with the pace of the Soviet advance. On January 14 he ordered a Panzer corps to move from East Prussia southward, to defend the town of Kielce, which the Russians were attacking in force. But by the time the tanks were within eighty miles of their intended positions, Kielce was already in Russian hands.

Realizing that he could no longer direct the war from either front – the lines were moving so swiftly against him – Hitler set off on January 15 by train from Bad Nauheim to Berlin. During the journey one of his staff, an SS colonel, commented wrily: 'Berlin will be most practical as our headquarters: we'll soon be able to take the tram from the Eastern to the Western Front!' Hitler laughed at the colonel's sense of humour. Henceforth the Chancellery – and in due course the bunker under it – was to be the centre of his military directives and daily life.

On January 17 Soviet forces entered Warsaw. Of all the capital cities that had been under German rule it was the one that had been the most devastated during more than five years of occupation and struggle: first by the heavy German air bombardments of September 1939. Then came the starvation, destruction and physical levelling of the ghetto; then the crushing of the Polish Uprising. And at every stage there were the continual street executions of individual Polish patriots, and of groups of men and women in mass reprisals. The Jewish fate had been daemonic: of the half million Jews who lived in Warsaw before the war, only two hundred were alive in the city on the day of liberation. One of them, Chaim Goldstein, later recalled the day of liberation: 'We have no need to go back down into the bunker. Our cries of "We are free" have reached the ears of our comrades, who now came out into the street one by one. We fall into each others arms and kiss one another.'

The moment of the liberation of Warsaw – as of every occupied capital, town and village, was one of rejoicing. But Goldstein, like all survivors of the Nazi racial policy and its barbarous manifestations, could never forget those nearest and dearest to him who had been murdered. His seventy-seven-year-old mother had been killed in 1942 during a deportation to Treblinka. His brother had been shot dead while trying to help her. His two sisters were both dead, though, as he later wrote – and this was true of so many millions of those Jews and other civilian victims of Nazism – the 'time and place of death remain unknown'.

As Soviet military units entered Warsaw, others were approaching Auschwitz. In the barracks at Birkenau were 15,000 Jews, for whom a new terror was about to begin: long marches on foot, in freezing weather, away from Auschwitz and into Germany – moving from camp to camp. During these marches anyone who was too weak to continue was shot by the ever-vigilant guards. In one column of 800 men, only 200 were alive at the end of eighteen days of marching and the brutality of their guards. In another column of 2,500, a thousand were shot during the first day's march. These 'death marches' became yet another terrible feature of the final months of the war. More than 100,000 Jews, survivors of the camps, died on the roads and roadsides of Germany, or in open railway wagons in which they were transported without any heating in temperatures sometimes far below zero. Of four thousand men – most of them former Auschwitz inmates – who were sent from the nearby slave labour camp at Gleiwitz by train to Nordhausen slave labour camp, six hundred died on the journey. Most of them had frozen to death. Following these marches, 100,000 more deportees were to die in the slave camps to which they were sent, or in the concentration camps in which they were dumped: camps whose names, as a result of this final, six-month-long stage of the war, became synonymous with evil: most notably Dachau and Belsen.

Also on the roads that winter, being taken westward by the Germans in the hope that they would not be liberated by the Soviets, were several thousand Allied prisoners-of-war, and hundreds of thousands — eventually millions — of German civilians who wanted to move as far away as possible from the advancing Russians. Ben Helfgott, a Jewish slave labourer at Schlieben, a camp near Dresden, recalled the fear of the German women working alongside him, that they would be raped en masse, and raped again and again. This was indeed most probably their fate, as it was the fate of innumerable German women of all ages — even women in hospital — in the first days and weeks after Soviet soldiers reached their town or village.

Countess Maria von Maltzan, who had been active in the German resistance to Hitler, and had personally saved the lives of dozens of Jews during the war, later described how Soviet soldiers raped a fourteen-year-old Jewish girl whom the Countess herself had earlier saved from deportation and brought up as her own daughter. 'She screamed for weeks on end, every night. I had to give her the strongest sleeping pills I could find to try to calm her down.' Shortly afterwards, because the girl was Polish-born, the Soviet authorities took her back to Poland.

German refugees were beginning to crowd the roads, hurrying westward. The Germans were also moving their Allied prisoners-of-war westward, away from the advancing Russian armies. A British prisoner-of-war, Sergeant Webster, noted in his diary on January 20: 'Marching all night to cross the Oder before the bridges blown. Intense cold, six refugee children died on route — many falling out of ranks exhausted — frostbite gets a grip.'

On January 18, one day after the Soviet entry into Warsaw, 62,000 German soldiers trapped inside Budapest surrendered. After five days and nights of continuous street fighting, more than 35,000 of their comrades-in-arms lay dead in the streets. Seven of the capital cities which Hitler had overrun between March 1939 and April 1941 were in Allied hands: Warsaw, Paris, Brussels, Luxembourg, Belgrade, Athens and Budapest. Four cities awaited liberation: The Hague, Copenhagen, Oslo and Prague.

On January 20 the Russians entered East Prussia in force. On the following day German troops pulled out of Tannenberg, the scene of their great victory over the Russians thirty years earlier. Before they left they disinterred the bodies of President Hindenburg and his wife, who were buried there, and sent them back to Berlin for re-burial. On January 22 Hitler bowed to the desperate need for troops elsewhere and ordered the evacuation of Memel by sea. He no longer asked his troops there, as he had done in every other besieged city, to fight to the last man. But even as the evacuation of Memel started, the Russians made their most impressive forward push thus far of the 1945 campaign; north-west of Oppeln they crossed the River Oder. Other Russian troops further north, fighting their way through the Polish frontier town of Rawicz, reached Göben, the first German village west of the border. They were less than 150 miles from Berlin.

Hitler watched his army's withdrawal with an eagle eye. When he felt a withdrawal was not justified he took immediate and drastic action. When, on January 23, the German Fourth Army, which had been guarding the frontiers of East Prussia, withdrew from the fortress of Lötzen rather than be encircled by the Russians, Hitler dismissed the army commander and all his staff. Lötzen had barred the way to Rastenburg. With the capture of Lötzen the Russians entered Hitler's former headquarters, where three and a half years earlier he had celebrated his early triumphs against Russia. Within twenty-four hours of the loss of Rastenburg, there was worse news to come for Hitler when, on January 26, Russian troops reached the Prussian Baltic coast, at the town of Elbing. By doing so they cut off more than half a million German soldiers from the embattled heartland of the Third Reich.

In Berlin, executions were still taking place each week of men and women accused of taking part in the July bomb plot. Among those executed in January was Helmuth James Count von Moltke, the leader of the Kreisau Circle, at which officers and aristocrats who were distressed by Nazism had held many of their early discussions. Before his arrest von Moltke was the legal adviser to the German High Command, another of Hitler's hated aristocratic 'vons' inside the military hierarchy. Von Moltke's parents were both Christian Scientists. His great-grand-uncle, Field Marshal Helmuth von Moltke, had been instrumental on the battlefields of 1866 and 1870 in helping to create the Second Reich. At the time of his execution, Hitler's latest victim was thirty-seven-year old.

Three days after von Moltke was hanged in Berlin, the SS shot Violette Szabo in Ravensbrück concentration camp north of the city: she had been parachuted into German-occupied France at the time of the Normandy

Landings and been captured four days later. For her bravery, she was post-humously awarded the George Cross.*

Soviet soldiers advancing through southern Poland reached the German border just east of Auschwitz on January 25. There were still 6,150 Jews in the camp, and 1,200 Poles. That day the SS shot 350 Jews, of whom two hundred were women. They then set fire to twenty-nine of the thirty-five enormous storehouses in which they had sorted the belongings of their victims, blew up the last remaining gas chamber and crematorium, and left. The dead and the dying awaited liberation. One of those waiting was Primo Levi. He later recalled: 'We lay in a world of death and phantoms. The last trace of civilization had vanished around and inside us. The work of bestial degradation, begun by the victorious Germans, had been carried to its con-clusion by the Germans in defeat.'

On the night of January 26 one of Primo Levi's friends, a Hungarian Jew, died in the barracks. He was carried out on a stretcher. Levi later wrote: 'He was very light. We overturned the stretcher on the grey snow.' At that moment the first Russian soldiers arrived at Auschwitz. As well as the survivors, they found the charred ruins of the twenty-nine storehouses and the contents of the six that the SS had not had time to burn. In them were 836,255 women's dresses, 348,000 sets of men's suits, and 38,000 pairs of men's shoes.

At every point on the disintegrating Eastern Front, German soldiers and civilians were fleeing. Tens of thousands made their way by sea from the Baltic enclaves. On January 30 – the twelfth anniversary of Hitler coming to power – eight thousand soldiers and refugees from East Prussia reached Kiel harbour on board the transport ship *Wilhelm Gustloff*, named, as several factories had been, after the Nazi leader in Switzerland assassinated by a Jew before the war. As the ship entered the harbour a Soviet submarine attacked it with its torpedoes. More than six thousand of those on board were drowned. It was the highest maritime loss on a single ship throughout the Second World War.

The Western Allies were about to launch a sustained attack on the German defences along the Rhine. As they prepared to do so, Soviet tanks crossed the Oder on January 31 and seized the town of Kienitz, less than fifty miles

* The other British woman agent posthumously awarded the George Cross was Noor Inayat Khan.

from Berlin. So swift and unexpected was their crossing that they found German soldiers strolling in the streets of the town and trains still running on the Kienitz-Berlin line.

That day, January 31, the British Chiefs of Staff discussed a request from the Soviet High Command for British and American air forces to assist the Russian offensive in Silesia. The Russians hoped that the Western Allies would be willing to rearrange their bombing priorities in order to bomb strategic targets – including German tank factories – on the Eastern Front, both in and around Berlin, and between Berlin and the Silesian front. To meet the Russian request, the British Chiefs of Staff proposed a series of Allied bomber attacks on four cities, Berlin, Dresden, Leipzig and Chemnitz.

Urgency was given to the Russian request for air support when the Ultra decrypts revealed a series of German messages transferring as many as twenty-nine divisions from the interior of Germany, the Western Front, Norway and Italy to the Eastern Front in Silesia. Stalin and the Soviet High Command feared a sustained German counter-attack that might push the Russians back, and wanted heavy bombing on German lines of communication running from west to east, along which the transferred divisions would be moved.

In greeting Churchill and Roosevelt at Yalta on February 4, Stalin asked the Deputy Chief of Staff of the Soviet forces, General Antonov to set out Soviet needs with regard to the Silesian Front. The Russian bomber forces, Antonov explained, did not have the resources to stop the transfer of large numbers of German troops to Silesia. Even without the imminent reinforcements, the Germans had halted the Soviet offensive at several points. For the Russians, an Anglo-American bomber assault was essential.

The Allies had already agreed to help. When the British, American and Soviet Air Staffs studied the problem that week, they confirmed that Leipzig and Dresden would both be targets. The British would bomb by night and the Americans by day. Up till then Dresden, a city of Baroque palaces, art galleries and opera houses – where Schiller once lived, Wagner composed and Dostoevksy gambled – had not been the target of a British or American bombing raid.

The first part of the raid on Dresden took place on the night of February 13/14, when 245 British bombers struck at the city, dropping their bombs during the course of an hour. They were followed three and a half hours later by 529 more British bombers. Their target was the city's railway marshalling yards, through which the German divisions would have to pass on their way to the Eastern Front. During the first of the two attacks a massive firestorm was started, as ferocious as that in Hamburg two years earlier. Eleven square miles of the city were burned out.

On the morning of February 14, according to plan, the Americans bombed the burning city: 450 bombers struck again at the marshalling yards. Of the total of 1,200 British and American bombers that flew over the city, only eight were shot down. Most of Dresden's mobile anti-aircraft guns had been sent to the Ruhr to help against the Allied air raids there. Chemnitz was also bombed by the British on the night of February 13/14, and Chemnitz and Magdeburg were both bombed by the Americans on the morning of February 14. The citizens of Chemnitz and Magdeburg were fortunate that no firestorms started.

Some of the fires in Dresden were still burning seven days after the raids. The death toll may never be ascertained. It definitely exceeded Hamburg in 1942, where more than 40,000 Germans were killed. It may have been as high as 80,000. The number of bodies officially identified and registered by the city officials was 39,773. At least 20,000 more bodies were buried under the ruins or incinerated beyond recognition – even beyond recognition as bodies. The inscription on the mass grave in Dresden's main cemetery addresses the question of how many died with two short sentences:

How many died?
Who knows the number?

On February 2, another of Hitler's opponents, Carl Goerdeler, the former Mayor of Leipzig, had been executed at Plötzensee Prison in Berlin. It was he whom the July conspirators had decided to appoint as Chancellor in Hitler's place. The process of denunciation – as in Goerdeler's case – arrest and execution was unending.

While they were still at Yalta, Churchill and Roosevelt obtained an assurance from Stalin that he would allow free elections in Poland. It was the German invasion of Poland that had extinguished Polish independence and all its trappings – the judicial system, parliamentary elections, the Parliament itself, the difficult balance of minority needs and rights, and the search for economic self-sufficiency. All this had to be refashioned, if only agreement could be reached by the Big Three.

Churchill and Roosevelt obtained Stalin's signature at Yalta on a declaration promising democratic elections in all the former Axis countries that had been overrun. The fact, however, that without exception those countries were falling into the Soviet sphere, made the declaration dependent on Stalin's goodwill. Churchill and Roosevelt had no secret weapon to ensure that goodwill. The defeat of Germany was absorbing all their military capabilities. They certainly could not impose the declaration by force, assuming that Stalin broke it.

The ultimate weakness of the West in the face of Soviet power was already becoming evident. On the Western Front seventy-eight Allied divisions faced an equal number of German divisions, albeit less well equipped and lacking adequate air support. On the Eastern Front, eighty German divisions faced 180 Soviet divisions. The balance of military power, then and in the future, was clear. Soviet goodwill was the only thing on offer to help Poland, Roumania, Hungary, Bulgaria, Yugoslavia, Albania and Czechoslovakia emerge, or re-emerge, as democracies after the war.

Churchill had wanted to hold the Yalta conference in the late autumn of 1944, before the Soviet army had entered any of these countries. But Stalin did not want to try to settle the future of Europe until he was in a much stronger military position in Eastern Europe and the Balkans. He therefore contented himself, at a meeting with Churchill in Moscow in October 1944, with putting a tick on a brief note from Churchill, indicating respective spheres of influence: a proposal that would, for example, have given Britain and America a fifty-fifty share in post-war Yugoslavia, instead of the 100 per cent which Russia had acquired by the time of Yalta as a result of the advance of her armies.

At Yalta, Stalin, Roosevelt and Churchill – the 'Big Three' – and their large teams of advisers were discussing the future of Europe after their victory; and Stalin was extracting from Roosevelt promises for Soviet territorial gains from Japan in the Far East: Port Arthur, South Sakhalin and the Kurile Islands. In Berlin, Hitler was examining an architectural model showing the reconstruction and beautification of his beloved Linz once the war was over. To the head of the Reich Central Security Office, Ernst Kaltenbrunner, who came to see him on February 9 to report a sharp drop in public morale in Germany, Hitler remarked: 'Do you imagine I could talk like this about my plans for the future if I did not believe deep down that we really are going to win this war in the end!'

That week, in Norway, thirty-four Norwegian patriots were executed by the Gestapo. In Berlin, a Swedish diplomat, Count Folke Bernadotte, who was negotiating with the SS for the release of several thousand Jewish women from Ravensbrück concentration camp, noted that the people of Berlin 'gave the impression of being utterly sick of the war and completely dominated by the wish to see it end quickly'. The erection of barricades in the streets had begun. 'There was no panic, but neither was there any enthusiasm.' In the central parts of the city 'four houses out of every five appeared to have been destroyed by the terrific bombardments'.

In the Pacific War, following the strategic decision to prepare for the invasion of mainland Japan, a wider range of targets was established for the American bomber forces, starting with aircraft engine and airframe factories. The first of the new set of raids was launched on January 19 against the two engine and airframe factories near the town of Akashi. Fifty-six bombers made the attack; all returned safely to their base. Only eleven Japanese fighters were available to intercept: four were shot down. The mission planner, General Haywood S. Hansell, described the raid as a 'magnificent success'. Production in the plant was cut by 90 per cent, and never recovered.

Each American advance was shadowed by the deaths of Allied prisoners-of-war and civilian internees. In one of the Japanese civilian internment camps on Sumatra, seventy-six Dutch, Australian and British women internees died from starvation and disease during January. In Borneo, where two thousand Australian and five hundred British prisoners-of-war faced death marches and mass executions, only six of them survived.

The Japanese treatment of Korean and Filipino women and girls had a savagery of its own. On February 9 more than twenty Filipino girls were rounded up in Manila and sent to a military brothel. During three days, some were raped more than thirty times. It was only a chance hit on the building by American shells that enabled some of the girls to escape from the continuing ordeal. One of them gave testimony about the rapes at the Tokyo War Crimes Trials after the war.

In Manchuria, the increased American bombing made no difference to the cruelty of the Japanese occupation. Indeed, as Jung Chang has written, 'The Japanese were becoming more and more edgy':

One day one of my mother's schoolfriends got hold of a book by a banned Chinese writer. Looking for somewhere quiet to read, she went off into the countryside, where she found a cavern which she thought was an empty air-raid shelter. Groping around in the dark, her hand touched what felt like a light switch. A piercing noise erupted. What she had touched was an alarm. She had stumbled into an arms depot. Her legs turned to jelly. She tried to run, but got only a couple of hundred yards before some Japanese soldiers caught her and dragged her away.

Two days later the whole school was marched to a barren, snow-covered stretch of ground outside the west gate, in a bend of the Xiaoling River. Local residents had also been summoned there by the neighbourhood chiefs. The children were told they were to witness 'the punishment of an evil person who disobeys Great Japan.'

Suddenly my mother saw her friend being hauled by Japanese guards to a spot right in front of her. The girl was in chains and could hardly walk. She had been tortured, and her face was so swollen that my mother could barely recognize her. Then the Japanese soldiers lifted their rifles and pointed them at the girl, who seemed to be trying to say something, but no sound came out. There was a crack of bullets, and the girl's body slumped as her blood began to drip onto the snow.

'Donkey,' the Japanese headmaster, was scanning the rows of his pupils. With a tremendous effort, my mother tried to hide her emotions. She forced herself to look at the body of her friend, which was lying in a glistening red patch in the white snow.

She heard someone trying to suppress sobs. It was Miss Tanaka, a young Japanese woman teacher whom she liked. In an instant 'Donkey' was on Miss Tanaka, slapping and kicking her. She fell to the ground, and tried to roll out of the way of his boots, but he went on kicking her ferociously. She had betrayed the Japanese race, he bawled. Eventually 'Donkey' stopped, looked up at the pupils, and barked the order to march off.

My mother took one last look at the crooked body of her teacher and the corpse of her friend and forced down her hate.

Both Germany and Japan had been put on notice by the Allies two years earlier that war crimes would be judged and punished. At the time when the threat of punishment was first made it must have seemed a very remote possibility to either set of perpetrators – whether in Europe or the Far East – that they could ever be brought to justice. With the victory of the Allies in both spheres a growing possibility, the crimes continued. The threat of punishment seemed to have as little deterrent effect in the imminence of defeat as at the time of mastery and domination.

Not only would war crimes be punished if the Allies were to triumph, but on February 10, while still at Yalta, Churchill, Roosevelt and Stalin agreed that Germany must pay reparations for the damage done in all the occupied countries as a result of the occupations.

As the participants of the Yalta conference returned to their respective capitals, American carrier-based aircraft attacked the Japanese Home Islands for the first time. They had been brought to the sea off Honshu Island on the most powerful war making naval force that had ever put to sea, in the twentieth or any other century – a force of twenty aircraft carriers escorted by ninety warships. As the aircraft bombarded military targets in the cities of Honshu, American forces were fighting in the Philippines, seeking to drive the Japanese out of Manila. It proved a savage killing ground, as the Japanese soldiers turned against the local Filipinos, strapping down hospital patients to their beds and then setting the hospitals on fire, and making no distinction for age or sex. One Japanese soldier noted in his diary on February 17: 'In various sectors we have killed several thousand (including young and old, men and women), and Chinese.'

A Japanese Fleet Order first issued on 23 December 1944, and updated as late as 14 February 1945, stated: 'When killing Filipinos, assemble them together in one place, as far as possible, thus saving ammunition and labour. The disposal of dead bodies will be troublesome, so either collect them in houses scheduled to be burned or throw them into the river.' This was done. Many hundreds of Filipinos were shot and bayoneted to death, in buildings which were then set on fire, including fifty civilians – young and old – who had taken shelter in the headquarters of the Filipino Red Cross building, which was clearly marked with the Red Cross sign. Young girls who had taken refuge inside the cathedral were dragged outside and raped. They were then shot.

Before the Japanese soldiers retreated inside Manila's ancient walled city, almost 100,000 Filipinos had been killed. Inside the walled city, the Japanese took with them 5,000 Filipino hostages. Refusing repeated American calls to surrender, they fought to almost the last man, and to almost the last hostage. In the Philippine countryside, the Japanese revenge against Filipino guerrillas was unrestrained. After eleven Filipino guerrillas had been captured while attacking a Japanese air depot, one of the Japanese soldiers ordered to execute them wrote in his diary of how the captives were taken to a nearby coconut grove:

They had no strength left as they had eaten nothing for the last three days since their capture. Their hands were tied behind their backs and they were made to stand in front of the holes with their heads slightly bent downwards. It seemed that their minds were clearly made up that they would be killed, for they said nothing. Their hair was very bushy. I was irritated. Later, one by one the members of our section bayoneted them.

The first one was bayoneted by Suzuki. *My turn* came next. The moment I bayoneted him the victim cried 'Ah' and fell into the hole behind him. He was suffering but I had no emotion at all, that may be because I was so excited. After bayoneting them we covered the bodies with soil and laid coconut leaves on top.

We then returned to the company at 2200 hours singing a marching song.

Another diary of a Japanese soldier found after the fighting contains an entry for February 13: 'Enemy tanks are lurking in the vicinity of Banzai Bridge. Our attack preparation has been completed. I am now on guard duty at the Guerrilla Internment Camp. While I was on duty ten guerrillas tried to escape. They were all recaptured and bayoneted. Later. At 1600 hours all guerrillas were burned to death.'

One Japanese soldier expressed in his diary the unease that he felt at the action he and his fellow-soldiers were taking:

Every day is spent in hunting guerrillas and natives. I have already killed well over one hundred. The innocence I possessed at the time of leaving the homeland has long since disappeared. Now I am a hardened sinner and my sword is always stained with blood.

Although it is for my country's sake, it is sheer brutality. May God forgive me. May my mother forgive me.

To bomb the Japanese mainland most effectively, the Americans needed to use the airfield on the eight-mile wide, barren island of Iwo Jima. The landing took place on February 19, but although the American flag was raised on the island's highest point, Mount Suribachi, on the third day – resulting in one of the most famous photographs of the war – it took fifty more days of violent fighting for them to conquer the island. The death toll was high: 6,821 American marines and 20,000 Japanese soldiers. Nine hundred American sailors were also killed in the battle for Iwo Jima, 218 of them when the escort carrier *Bismarck Sea* was sunk by a Japanese suicide aircraft. Of the six flag raisers in the famous photograph, three were among the American dead. The photograph was turned into a postage stamp almost immediately, and in due course into a massive metal memorial.

Nine days after the Stars and Stripes was raised on Iwo Jima, American forces landed at Puerto Princesa on Palawan island. They were in search of a small group of American prisoners-of-war, held there for the previous three years, whom they hoped to liberate. All they found were some identity discs and personal belongings. Two weeks later they discovered seventy-nine skeletons, twenty-six of them in a mass grave. Bullets had pierced the skulls, which had also been crushed by blunt instruments.

In Europe, the German province of Pomerania, on the road from Warsaw to Berlin, was under Soviet attack. Hitler's military advisers urged him to abandon it and concentrate on the defence of Berlin, but he refused to do so. On the night of February 23/24 there was a massive Anglo-American bombing raid over railway yards, canals, bridges and vehicles throughout Germany. Nine thousand bombers took part, attacking without pause for twenty-four hours. At Pforzheim, where the British dropped 1,825 tons of bombs in twenty-two minutes, a firestorm was caused which killed 17,600 people. This was the third highest death toll during the bombing of a German city after Dresden and Hamburg. Eighty-three per cent of Pforzheim's built up area was destroyed, the largest percentage in any single British bombing raid over Germany.

As the raids of February 23/24 were still taking place, Hitler met his Gauleiters in Berlin. They were the stalwart Nazi Party functionaries who had governed the provinces loyally and with discipline, some of them since 1933. Hitler told them: 'You may see my hand tremble sometimes today, and perhaps even my head now and then; but my heart – never!'

The Gauleiters returned home. They were confronted for the most part with more Allied air attacks and widening devastation. They had also to read of the thirteen-day battle that began on February 26 – in which Canadian troops took a prominent part and suffered heavy losses – to drive a sixteen-mile corridor to the River Rhine. In hand-to-hand combat that day in the village of Mooshof, Sergeant Aubrey Cosens, from the remote rural townlet of Porquis Junction in Northern Ontario, killed more than twenty German soldiers and took another twenty prisoner before being shot down. He was twenty-three years old. Posthumously he was awarded the Victoria Cross. His fellow soldiers fought on, one of them recalling how, when given the next day's objective, 'We thought, Jesus Christ, haven't we done enough?'

On February 27 a British bombing raid on Mainz, in which much industry as well as many historic buildings were destroyed, killed at least 1,122 people, including 647 women, among them forty-one nuns killed when their convent was hit. When Cologne was bombed by a force of 834 British bombers on March 2, the death toll could not be ascertained: the city was virtually in the front line and there was no possibility of an official register of the dead. American troops, entering the city four days later, cleared four hundred bodies from the streets.

Among those killed in February was Jacques Doriot, a French Communist who before the outbreak of war had moved to the far right and founded a pro-German political movement. When, in September 1944, the Vichy Government fled from France to Sigmaringen, in south-west Germany, to escape the advancing Allied armies, Doriot had gone with them. Two years earlier he had helped to raise 4,000 French volunteers to fight on the Eastern Front, and had himself served in the East, wearing the uniform of a German lieutenant. He was killed in a British strafing attack on a German road on February 22.

The German rocket bomb attacks on England continued throughout the winter, with 585 civilians being killed in January and 483 in February. On March 3, the day after the final British bombing raid on Cologne, the flying bomb attacks, which had ceased since the previous September – the launching sites had to be moved from France to Holland – were resumed. In the new assault, some of the flying bombs were launched from aircraft. In an attempt to forestall further rocket bomb attacks, on March 3 the British sent a bomber force to destroy the launch sites near The Hague. Many bombs fell wide of the target, hitting a residential area and killing 520 Dutch civilians.

Two days later, in London, a rocket bomb fell in the middle of Smithfield meat market. More than a hundred people were killed: butchers, market porters, buyers and passers-by. Twelve days later, 134 Londoners were killed when a rocket bomb hit a block of flats in Stepney. But the time had come when the armies advancing in Northern Europe were reaching the launching sites. The last rocket bombs were fired on March 27. One fell on Antwerp, killing twenty-seven people. Another, falling on Orpington in Kent a few moments later, killed one person, Ivy Millichamp, a thirty-four-year-old housewife. She was the last person to die from the terror weapon that Hitler thought could break public morale.

The V2 'reprisal' weapon had killed 2,855 people in Britain and 4,483 in Belgium. It had destroyed several thousand homes. But it had failed to affect the course of the war, serving only to intensify anti-German feeling and to strengthen the belief that it was a 'just war'.

Starting at the beginning of March, the American bombing raids on Japan were able to use Tinian Island – and later Iwo Jima – as their base. A raid against an aircraft factory in Tokyo on March 4 was the last precision bombing raid. Henceforth the method used was 'carpet bombing', putting down as dense a pattern of bombs over a city as could be prepared for it. The firestorms which had devastated the German cities of Dresden and Pforzheim in the previous weeks were to be repeated in Japan, and on an even greater scale.

On March 9 more than three hundred American bombers, flying from Tinian Island, dropped two thousand incendiary bombs on Tokyo. The raid lasted for less than three hours. When it was over a firestorm greater than that in Dresden was raging. Sixteen square miles of Tokyo were burned out. The first official death toll was put at 83,793. Later, when the burned embers had been searched and many more charred remains discovered, that total was put at 130,000.

In the following three months, five more Japanese cities were to face the terrifying rigours of firestorm and mass destruction. The Japanese civilians did not even have the benefit of a competent anti-aircraft defence – the bombers flew too high for the guns the defenders could deploy. In the whole campaign, 243 American airmen were killed, the same number that had been killed in a single night during a British air raid over Berlin a year and a half earlier. Japanese deaths, when the carpet bombing raids came to an end, were more than a quarter of a million. But no amount of bombing, deaths and destruction was able to shake the determination of the Japanese war leaders to continue the war, or to push the Emperor and his government towards peacemaking.

On the day of the Tokyo raid of March 9 the Japanese finally decided that they must take full control of the Vietnamese provinces of French Indo-China. Since 1941 Indo-China had been under Vichy rule. As the Germans had done in Hungary a year earlier, the erstwhile ally became the occupying power and enemy. That day the Japanese seized the French administrative buildings and took over the governing instruments of the country. At Lang-son sixty French soldiers and Foreign Legionnaires refused to give in to Japanese orders to surrender the fortress. Almost all of them were killed when, finally, their fortress was overrun. A few managed to survive the battle. After being captured they were put up against a wall and machine-gunned. After the volley of fire the Japanese soldiers bayoneted any who showed signs of life.

Three of the defenders of Lang-son managed to get away, a Greek legionnaire and two Frenchmen. They were caught three days later. One of the Frenchmen was the commander of the garrison, General Emile Lemonnier. The Japanese demanded that he sign the instrument of surrender. The penalty for not signing, he was told, was decapitation. He refused to sign – twice – and his head was cut off. The other Frenchman, and the Greek legionnaire were then decapitated in their turn.

General Lemonnier's posthumous citation read: 'Rather than forfeit his honour, he remains before history a remarkable example of what constitutes the will and character of a Frenchman.' These words are inscribed today on the wall plaque at the start of the short road which bears his name in Paris, running between the Louvre and the Tuileries.

The Vietnamese Communists took immediate advantage of what the Japanese had done in taking over the French security system that had been used so often and so effectively against them. They also took advantage of the Japanese decision to leave the countryside to its own devices, and maintain control primarily over the towns and main communications routes. This enabled Ho Chi Minh to intensify both propaganda and recruiting among the peasantry. Within three months an army of 10,000 men had been created, and had established Communist control in the countryside north of the city of Thai Nguyen. In the main, the Communists avoided fighting, having as their objective control of as large a land area as possible, and its governance.

In what remained of German-occupied Europe, the pattern of reprisals was still in force. After an attack on March 6 on a senior SS officer in Holland, 263 Dutchmen, including many resistance fighters who were being held in prison as hostages – so-called 'Death Candidates' – were shot. That day, news reached London and Washington of a shooting of quite a different kind, a terrible bridge between a war that was ending and a conflict (sometimes close to war) that was about to begin. The news was that at least four thousand Poles loyal to the London Government or active in the Home

Army against the Germans had been deported by the Soviet occupation authorities from Poland to labour camps in the Soviet Union. As many as six thousand more Home Army officers, all of whom had likewise fought against the Germans, had been arrested and were being held in a camp near Lublin run by Soviet officials. The report of March 6 stated: 'Prisoners are treated badly and many are removed every few days to an unknown destination.' That destination was Siberia. For the first time, Stalin was asserting the power of Soviet tyranny beyond the borders of the Soviet Union.

American troops reached the River Rhine on the morning of March 7, at the small town of Remagen, south of Bonn. The citizens of Remagen had put out white flags. There was no fighting. To the surprise of the American soldiers, the bridge over the river was intact. It was the Ludendorff Bridge, one of the railway bridges built over the Rhine during the First World War. As the Americans approached it, German army engineers on the far side set off their explosive charges. Some of the smaller charges exploded, doing little damage. The main charge failed to go off. The bridge remained in place. One of the first Americans to cross it, Sergeant Alexander A. Drabik from Ohio, later recalled: 'We ran down the middle of the bridge shouting as we went. I didn't stop because I knew that if I kept moving they couldn't hit me. My men were in squad column and not one of them was hit. We took cover in some bomb craters. Then we just sat and waited for the others to come.'

By nightfall a hundred American soldiers had crossed the Rhine. No previous army had crossed the Rhine into Germany since Napoleon in 1805. That night Hitler dismissed Field Marshal von Rundstedt from his post as Commander-in-Chief of the German Army in the West. Hitler commented when one of his staff began to talk about the Field Marshal: 'He is finished. I don't want to hear any more about him.' Four days later Hitler was driven from Berlin to the River Oder to watch the construction of last-minute defences. He then returned to Berlin for the last time. Never again would he journey out of his capital.

British and Canadian forces reached the Rhine on March 9. Germany's western maritime highway was under Allied control. In the struggle to secure the river 10,333 British soldiers, 7,300 Americans and 5,655 Canadians had been killed. The German losses were far higher: 45,000 in the area facing the Americans and a further 22,000 among those facing the British and Canadians.

*   *   *

On March 12, the day after returning to Berlin from the River Oder, Hitler learned that the Americans, who controlled the whole west bank of the Rhine as well as the Remagen bridgehead, had taken 343,000 German prisoners-of-war. Two days later he learned that both the Americans and British were using a new type of bomb, larger than any hitherto used in war, to attack railway marshalling yards and bridges throughout the Ruhr. The bomb weighed 22,000 pounds. It was named 'Grand Slam'.

One area in which Hitler might have gained the initiative was that of building an atom bomb. But German atom bomb research – which had always been far behind that of the United States – was finally brought to a complete halt by an Allied bombing raid on March 15. American bombers, with precise instructions which they carried out to the letter, dropped more than 1,200 tons of high explosives and incendiary bombs on the German thorium ore processing plant at Oranienburg, north of Berlin, on which future German atom bomb development depended.

Among the Allied soldiers killed that day in eastern France was an American infantryman, Edward Keith Hudson. Thirty years later, his friend and fellow-soldier, Paul Fussell, who was next to Hudson when he was killed, dedicated his book *The Great War and Modern Memory* to him. Fussell later recalled: 'My platoon sergeant, an older man (I was twenty) was killed, and we had been very close. I was persuaded that if I'd been leading better as a young officer, he might have, like me, survived – not to mention the others killed and maimed on that occasion. To this day, I've not got over this "survivor's guilt," if that is what it is. There's shame mingled with it too.'

In Berlin the relentless execution of the 'enemies of the Third Reich' continued. On March 19 General Fromm was put before a firing squad and shot. After the July plot he had been ruthless in condemning the conspirators – his most dramatic gesture of loyalty to Hitler being the arrest of von Stauffenberg on the night of the Rastenburg bomb – but the long arm of enquiry had eventually shown that General Fromm himself had earlier intimated that he would join the conspiracy once he could be convinced that it would succeed.

On March 21 General Guderian, whose blitzkrieg technique had brought Germany so many victories between 1939 and 1941, went to see Hitler to impress on him the need to conclude an immediate armistice with Britain and the United States. Germany could then use all its remaining military resources to keep the Russians away from Berlin and central Germany.

Guderian's appeal came on the day when British and American aircraft, in a coordinated attack, made almost all the German jet airfields unusable. But Hitler refused to contemplate making peace in the West. Britain and the United States had become his implacable enemies; he saw behind them a mythical 'world Jewish conspiracy' determined to destroy Germany for all time, just as he had wanted to destroy 'world Jewry' for all time – or, as he once expressed it, for 'at least for a thousand years'.

Had Hitler sought an armistice, the Allies would certainly have insisted that no negotiations could begin with Hitler himself, and that the only negotiations that would succeed would be those which were essentially an acceptance of immediate unconditional surrender. Nor would the western Allies allow any separate peace with Germany: they were committed to acting in tandem with the Soviet Union, and would certainly have done so. Neither Churchill nor Roosevelt would allow any discussions of a separate peace, even on a theoretical basis. Guderian's proposal for an armistice in the West alone could not therefore have worked.

Hitler retained his confidence that some weapon would turn what looked like impending defeat into astounding victory. The rocket bombs had failed to do so, but the jet fighter might still succeed. The German jet fighters, however, whose development Hitler had long neglected, were proving inadequate to redress the balance of Allied air superiority. In a German attack on the Remagen bridgehead, sixteen of the twenty-one attacking aircraft were shot down. At least half of them were jets. The whole exercise – which included trying to hit the bridge with V2 rockets – showed just how pitiful German air power had become. The once boastful Goering was still Commander-in-Chief of the German Air Force, but he had long since become a recluse and a buffoon, grossly overweight and unable to repeat, except in his imagination, the air triumphs of the opening phases of the war.

On March 22 the total inadequacy of the German air defences, for which Goering was ultimately responsible, was shown when 227 British bombers attacked Hildesheim. Only four were lost. The railway yards there, the target of the attack, were severely damaged, as was 70 per cent of the town. Three thousand blocks of flats, containing more than 10,000 apartments, were destroyed or made uninhabitable. In the old town, the cathedral and most of the churches were destroyed. The death toll: 1,645 people.

The bombing of German cities created no upsurge inside Germany in public demands for an armistice, or for surrender. The Gestapo system still worked night and day to curb any expression of what was denounced as 'defeatist' opinion. Nor were any of the belligerents in a mood to parley. When General Patton secured two more bridgeheads across the Rhine, seventy miles south of Remagen – whose bridge had collapsed from fatigue, killing twenty-five American engineers – he telephoned the commander of the million-and-a-half strong 12th Army, General Omar N. Bradley, to tell him of his success, and added: 'Don't tell anyone, but I'm across. I sneaked a division over last night. But there are so few Krauts about there, they don't know it yet.'

Hitler had abandoned the Rhine, but still hoped to hold the Oder, although that river had also been crossed, and in more places than the Rhine. On the Rhine itself, where it marked the western edge of the Ruhr, British and Canadian forces under Montgomery's command made the crossing on the night of March 23. To blind the German soldiers on the far bank, Montgomery brought up specially designed searchlights, mounted in tanks, and shone their extremely powerful lights – capable of thirteen million candle power – straight across the river into the eyes of the defenders. As a tribute to their commander, the attacking force called the lights 'Monty's Moonlight'. It was entirely effective. Within twenty-four hours Hitler ordered a German counter-attack. His order, with its precise details of place and time and scale, was decrypted by British Intelligence through Ultra, and the counter-attack driven back. Hitler never learned that his most secret and most frequently used communication system from the Chancellery to the German commanders in the field – his *Geheimschreiber* teleprinter – was totally insecure.

The advance of the Allies into the centre of Germany was accelerating. On March 25 American forces overran the principal German jet airfields near Darmstadt and Frankfurt-on-Main, and crossed the Frankfurt-Cologne autobahn. That day Churchill himself crossed the Rhine at Büderich, where the 21st Army Group had crossed two days earlier. Three days after his return to Britain he was given news from Poland that once again presaged conflict once the war was over. From Warsaw, a group of sixteen Polish political leaders – non-Communists – had gone to the small town of Pruszkow, under a promise of safe conduct, for consultations with senior Soviet officers. On reaching Pruszkow they were arrested and flown to Moscow, where they were denounced as enemies of Poland and imprisoned.

Stalin had lost no time in removing those who might serve as the representatives of the democratic Poland to which he had given his public support at Yalta. Six weeks later Churchill told the British Foreign Secretary, Anthony Eden: 'The perfidy by which these Poles were enticed into a Russian conference and then held fast in the Russian grip is one which will emerge in great detail from the stories which have reached us, and there is no doubt that the publication in detail of this event upon the authority of the great Western Allies, would produce a primary change in the entire structure of world forces.'

Churchill's forecast was correct. The arrest of the sixteen Poles destroyed the Yalta pledge and was a pointer to the divisions and confrontations that were about to emerge from the ashes and euphoria of victory. A pointer to where those divisions would actually fall geographically came on March 28, when Eisenhower gave up Berlin as the main objective of his armies, and directed Montgomery to advance northward instead, to the Danish border and north-east to the Baltic Sea. Stalin would have the first chance to capture Berlin. Eisenhower regarded the defeat of the German army in the field, not the capture of cities, however prestigious they might be, as his principal task. 'The idea of neglecting Berlin and leaving it to the Russians to take at a later stage,' Churchill protested to his own Chiefs of Staff when Eisenhower's decision was conveyed to him, 'does not appear to me correct. As long as Berlin holds out and withstands a siege in the ruins, as it may easily do, German resistance will be stimulated. The fall of Berlin might cause nearly all Germans to despair.'

On March 29 the first Soviet troops crossed the Hungarian border and entered Austria. They were only fifty miles from Vienna. On the following day, after almost a week of street fighting, Danzig surrendered to the Russians. The British journalist Alexander Werth, recalled: 'The beautiful medieval city had been reduced by then to a smoking ruin, but the Polish flag was solemnly hoisted on what was henceforth to be known as Gdansk. Ten thousand German prisoners were taken, but many more than that were dead. Many civilians in and around Danzig committed suicide, so great was their fear of falling into Russian hands.'

As the Allied armies entered the heartlands of the Third Reich the Gestapo had no compunction in carrying out thousands of acts of revenge. At Flossenbürg concentration camp several dozen Allied agents, most of whom had been captured a year or more earlier in German-occupied Europe, were taken to the scaffold and hanged. Before their execution, the Frenchmen among them sang the Marseillaise. Among the British agents hanged that day was Captain Isadore Newman, who, in the weeks after the Normandy landings, had transmitted from behind German lines hundreds of messages to and from Supreme Allied Headquarters, and members of the French Resistance awaiting their sabotage tasks.

On March 25 the Japanese Imperial General Staff gave orders to the Japanese air force 'to concentrate its full strength to attack and crush the American navy.' For the first time the Japanese air force was being instructed to put its resources at the disposal of the navy. This order was carried out primarily through the instrument of kamikaze suicide attacks. Three days after the General Staff order, a kamikaze volunteer, Hajime Fujii, made his attack. He had earlier been refused permission to fly as a kamikaze because he was a married man with children. His wife, seeing how sad he was not to be able to undertake a kamikaze mission, drowned herself and their three daughters so that he could 'fulfil his destiny as kamikaze'. Her self sacrifice is commemorated in the shrine in Tokyo dedicated to the Japanese war dead of all Japan's wars.

Before going into action at Okinawa, attacking the United States navy radar ships steaming at sea that were serving as protective lookouts for the American troops going ashore, a twenty-two-year-old kamikaze pilot, Heiichi Okabe, wrote in his diary – it was the last entry before he was killed in action:

> What is the duty today? It is to fight.
> What is the duty tomorrow? It is to win.
> What is the daily duty? It is to die.

Japanese suicide pilots launched almost two thousand kamikaze attacks, and sank thirty-four American warships. Even suicide pilots, however, could not make any serious dent in America's hard-won naval mastery. Nor could Japanese ground forces in the Pacific prevent the steady conquest of island after island, although they could fight relentlessly for every mile.

On April 1, Easter Sunday, 50,000 American troops landed on Okinawa, the final stepping stone for the invasion of the Japanese Home Islands. They were opposed by twice that number of Japanese defenders. After twelve days of mostly hand-to-hand fighting the Americans had gained less than two miles. More than 100,000 American combat troops were hurried to the island as reinforcements, with a further 368,000 in support. Okinawa is less than sixty miles long and seldom more than seven to ten miles wide. It became the scene of horrendous fighting, with repeated bayonet charges and individual hand-to-hand combat. Almost every American soldier who was captured on Okinawa was killed after having surrendered.

In the battle for air supremacy above Okinawa the extraordinarily high number of 5,900 Japanese combat planes had been shot down, for the loss of less than eight hundred American planes. On one occasion, instead of sending a single kamikaze pilot, or even a group of ten or twelve, into action at one time against the American warships off Okinawa, the Japanese High Command ordered 355 suicide pilots into the air at the same time, in a collective operation. The tactic was successful, with two American ammunition ships, two destroyers and a tank landing ship being sunk. The cost: all 355 Japanese aircraft and their pilots.

Even warships were enlisted into suicide attacks. On April 7 the largest battleship ever built, the 72,800-ton *Yamato*, armed with nine massive eighteen-inch guns – the largest British or American naval gun was of fifteen-inch diameter – set sail for Okinawa with an escort force of eight destroyers, with only enough fuel to reach the island. Had she reached the island, she might have wreaked havoc among the American warships there. But she was destroyed far short of Okinawa by American torpedo bombers, and 3,063 of her crew were drowned. Her commander, Admiral Seiichi Ito – who was a graduate of Yale University, and the organizer of earlier air kamikaze attacks – locked himself in his cabin so that he would go down with his ship. The escort ships lost 1,187 officers and men. This suicidal destruction is recalled every year at a ceremony held on April 7 at the Tokyo shrine for the Japanese war dead.

On April 1, at the start of the Okinawa landings, Hitler moved his offices in Berlin from the Chancellery, where they had been for the previous twelve years, to the underground bunker deep below it. The battle for the German capital was about to begin. In Moscow, Stalin asked his military commanders that day: 'Well now, who is going to take Berlin, will we or the Allies?' Giving his own answer, Stalin set April 16 as the day for the start of the Berlin campaign.

The German ability to continue fighting was increasingly in doubt. On April 2, Soviet and Bulgarian forces captured the Hungarian oil fields at Nagykanizsa, cutting off the Third Reich from its last supply of fuel oil. Hitler ordered General Kurt Student – the victor of the Crete campaign in 1941 – to retake the oil fields. The general replied that he could not do so: his tanks did not have enough fuel oil to undertake the task. Hitler's order and General Student's reply were both read by the Allies through Ultra, confirming the desperate state of Germany's combat abilities.

On April 3, Montgomery's forces completed their encirclement of the Ruhr and were taking between 15,000 and 20,000 German soldiers prisoner every day. Whole regiments were surrendering without a fight. The white flag had become a familiar sight to the advancing armies. Among those captured were many boys of sixteen and some of fifteen: every German boy born in 1929 had been ordered to take up arms.

On the day of the encirclement of the Ruhr, April 3, an American armoured division, advancing almost a hundred miles further east, noticed a number of emaciated figures walking along the road. 'Cadaverous refugees' was how an American war correspondent, Meyer Levin, described them. 'They were like none we have ever seen. Skeletal with feverish sunken eyes, shaven skulls.' The refugees, speaking almost incoherently of 'people buried in a big hole' and 'death commando', urged the soldiers to come to the camp where they had been held prisoner.

On the following morning American troops entered the site of which the refugees had spoken. Its name was Ohrdruf. Hundreds of corpses were piled up at the entrance. Each one wore a striped uniform and had a bullet hole at the back of the skull. In one of the huts of the camp were more bodies, naked. It emerged that more than four thousand prisoners had died at Ohrdruf in the previous three months. Hundreds had been shot as the Allied armies drew near. Some were Jews, others were Poles and Russian prisoners-of-war. They had been employed building a vast underground telephone exchange intended for use by the German army.

General Eisenhower was called to the mass murder scene, and sent photographs of the emaciated corpses to Churchill, who circulated them to the British War Cabinet. It was the first visual evidence of its kind. The nature of the evil perpetrated in Germany under Nazi rule had been seen and recorded by the western Allies. It could no longer be hidden by Hitler and his followers behind the secrecy of war. The idea which Hitler had espoused five years earlier of consigning his victims to the 'night and fog' of death and oblivion had been exposed to the light of day.

Even as American forces were coming into contact with the horrors of the concentration camps, another aspect of Nazi rule was being exposed: the loot and plunder taken from those who had been conquered or murdered. On April 7 the Americans entered the Kaiseroda coal mine at Merkers. This enormous working had first been dug in the 1870s. By 1945 there were more than 500 kilometres of tunnels and chambers. During the Second World War it had been turned into a bomb-proof storage area. 1,600 feet underground.

The American soldiers who entered the Kaiseroda mine were guided by British prisoners-of-war who had been employed putting the treasures – most of them brought from Berlin that February – into place. One of them, Sergeant Walter Farager, had been a prisoner-of-war since June 1940. In one of the chambers were thousands of sacks of gold coins from various countries, and twenty-seven rows of gold bullion. Elsewhere in the mine were works of art taken from their Jewish owners and from art collections in every occupied country; as well as hundreds of crates of paintings from German museums, and 140 rolls of oriental rugs and tapestries, sent to the mine to escape Allied air raids.

Among the many American soldiers who wrote home on April 7 was Joseph Patrick Kelly. In a letter to his sister he described what he and his fellow-soldiers were experiencing:

> We are deep into Germany in many sectors now and the local civilians still appear to be in a state of shocked disbelief that such a thing could happen to the Reich. The speed of our advances since the crossings of the Rhine has been amazing and most encouraging. It is apparent now that Germany is defeated beyond any hope for recovery and, from a military standpoint, her situation is hopeless.
>
> Any responsible government in a similar situation would surrender to save itself further destruction, but the Nazi fanatics that still control what is left of Germany, knowing that they themselves are doomed, are apparently determined to drag all of Germany with them into complete chaos.
>
> The destruction of German cities by our bombers has to be seen to be fully appreciated. Every city I have seen that was a profitable target for strategic bombing has been completely smashed into rubble. Many of the smaller towns and cities that were not manufacturing or transportation centers are relatively untouched, having been taken without opposition.
>
> The contrast in standards of living between France, Belgium and Holland on the one hand and Germany on the other are quite marked. In general the German is relatively well-fed, well clothed and in many cases well housed. In the cities that have been bombed badly, of course, the housing situation is critical, to say the least. Also, in the areas where heavy

fighting has taken place, the civilians left there are not in particularly
envious circumstances. On the whole, however, up until the present time
they have not suffered as have the rest of Europe.

Now, for the first time in over a century, they are learning at first hand
what war really is like and they don't like it.

Where Hitler's – and Himmler's – orders still ruled, the executions continued. On April 9 Johann Elser, the carpenter who had tried to assassinate
Hitler in Munich in November 1939, was executed at Dachau. That day,
at Flossenbürg, several more of the July plotters and other leading anti-Nazis
were ordered to strip, led down a flight of steps under the trees to a secluded
spot where a scaffold had been erected, and hanged. Among them were
Pastor Dietrich Bonhoeffer, Admiral Wilhelm Canaris and General Hans
Oster, former Chief of Staff of the German High Command's counter-
intelligence department. Oster was one of several high-ranking officers who,
as practising Christians, hated the anti-Christian ideals and practices of the
Nazis. He had been dismissed from the army in 1943 for his undisguised
opposition. As the hangings at Flossenbürg took place, American troops
were only 150 miles away.

On the Eastern Front, the fighting for Königsberg was at its height
throughout the first week of April. During the battle, the Soviet artillery
officer, Alexander Solzhenitsyn, was summoned from his battery by the
commander of his division, General Travkin, and ordered to hand over his
revolver. Two officers then stripped Solzhenitsyn of his badges of rank and
of his military decorations. As he was led away, under arrest, General Travkin
shook his hand. Solzhenitsyn later wrote:

That handshake was one of the most heroic acts I had seen during the
whole course of the war. I was arrested because of my naïve and childish
ideas. I knew that it was forbidden to write of military matters in letters
from the front, but I thought it was permitted to think and reflect on
events.

For a long time I had been sending a friend letters clearly criticizing
Stalin though without mentioning his name. I thought he had betrayed
Leninism and was responsible for the defeats of the first phase of the war,
that he was a weak theoretician and that his language was primitive. In
my youthful recklessness I put all these thoughts down on paper.

Solzhenitsyn was taken to Moscow, and confined in the Lubyanka prison.

On the evening of April 9 the fortress commander of Königsberg, General Otto Lasch, ordered his troops to surrender. At Hitler's orders they had fought to prevent the Soviet forces who were besieging them from breaking through the siege lines protecting the most impressive of all Germany's Baltic cities. In human terms it had been a costly defence, with 42,000 German soldiers and 25,000 civilians killed during several weeks of intense and unceasing artillery bombardment. Sufficient German air power no longer existed to counteract such a pounding. On learning that Königsberg had surrendered, Hitler telegraphed to the few German military radio units that were still operational in East Prussia: 'General Lasch is to be shot as a traitor immediately.' It was an order that could not be obeyed: Lasch was already a prisoner-of-war.

On the day after Königsberg's surrender, Soviet troops reached the centre of Vienna, the capital city that had been Hitler's first – and bloodless – conquest. That day the Gestapo headquarters at Weimar telephoned to nearby Buchenwald to order the concentration camp to be blown up. The telephone call came too late: the camp administration had fled and the inmates were in control. A few hours later the Americans arrived. One of those whom they liberated, Elie Wiesel, later wrote: 'You were our liberators, but we, the diseased, emaciated, barely human survivors were your teachers. We taught you to understand the Kingdom of Night.'

Most of the American liberators who entered Buchenwald that day were members of the 761st Tank Battalion, an all-Black unit, which had seen 183 days of unbroken combat. More than half its members had been killed or wounded. No other American army unit had fought so long without respite. One of its number, Staff Sergeant Johnnie Stevens, the grandson of a slave, recalled fifty-three years after entering the concentration camp: 'We were not prepared for what we found. We saw a big, long building and another high white building. After we took the area, the infantry went in and started bringing people out. We didn't know what they were – they were just skin and bones, wearing these crazy striped uniforms. They looked up at us in our tanks, they stretched out their hands to me. Some tried to give a half-hearted salute. My people have suffered segregation, discrimination, you name it, but this was the worst thing I'd ever seen.'

Inside Buchenwald more than five thousand inmates had died of illness, starvation and brutal treatment during the previous month. The Americans found 77,000 prisoners, many of them on the verge of death. Among those liberated at Buchenwald was the former Commander of the French Land Forces, General Gamelin, who had been imprisoned there for more than two years, having earlier been interned by the Vichy regime and found guilty, at a show trial, of having 'weakened the spirit of the French armies'. Gamelin had been among many hundreds of prisoners in Buchenwald, of many nationalities, who had been held there as 'prominent' personalities, in hard but not cruel conditions, as potential hostages. They were liberated before they could be used, or killed.

On April 12, Canadian troops advancing through Holland reached the last working V-1 rocket launching site, ending the threat of Hitler's final secret weapon. In the Far East that day a new Japanese suicide weapon was used for the first time. This was a flying bomb with a pilot on board who directed the bomb on to its target and was blown up with it. It was known as the *Ohka* ('cherry blossom') and was designed to be launched from a twin-engined bomber twenty miles away from its intended target. The explosive charge weighed 2,340 pounds. In its final dive it could reach 570 miles an hour. The diving speed propulsion was based on data provided by a German engineering firm. The first target to be hit and sunk by a suicide flying bomb on April 12 was the United States destroyer *Mannert L. Abele*. It was on picket duty off Okinawa. Eighty-one officers and men were killed.*

That day, as American sailors faced a new weapon in the Pacific, and as American soldiers overran much of central Germany, their Commander-in-Chief, President Roosevelt, died in the United States. He was sixty-three-years old, and had been ill for a long time, but the seriousness of his illness had been withheld from the public. Even Churchill had been shocked to see just how ill the President looked when they met at Yalta in February.

Roosevelt's death brought tears to the eyes of many battle-hardened American soldiers. 'This evening we spent five minutes in silence for our President,' twenty-three-year-old Henry Schwab wrote home from Germany. 'Believe me, the news shocked us as much as it did you. I consider this the worst thing which could have happened to us at this stage of the war. There is so much work to be done immediately after this war is ended and Roosevelt will be missed. I only hope that our leaders in Washington will carry on the work which Roosevelt had planned.'

---

* The ship was named after Lieutenant-Commander Mannert L. Abele, of Quincy, Massachusetts, who had been drowned together with his crew of sixty-five when the submarine he commanded was lost in the Pacific in 1943.

On the day of Roosevelt's death, Gene Currivan, a journalist with the American troops in Germany, reported to the *New York Times*:

Death is commonplace to combat troops, but today those of them who heard of the death of their Commander in Chief were visibly affected. Sincere sorrow permeated the ranks from Lieut. Gen. George S. Patton Jr. right down to the last doughboy.

When General Patton arrived at his staff conference this morning there was a hushed tone about the room that in itself was fitting eulogy. In the absence of a chaplain, the commander asked that everyone bow his head for a minute in respectful reverence to the memory of the Chief.

Throughout the Third Army front little cliques were gathered, discussing the death that had shocked them all. Some of the younger soldiers, especially those not yet of voting age, had never known another President, and to them the realization of his passing was particularly affecting.

Private First Class Albert M. Osborn, of Bowling Green, Ohio, told Gene Currivan: 'I can remember the President ever since I was a little kid. America will seem a strange, empty place without his voice talking to the people whenever great events occur. He died fighting for democracy, the same as any soldier.'

Among those who expressed his sorrow publicly on April 13 was a member of the House of Representatives for Texas, Lyndon Baines Johnson. Speaking to reporters with tears in his eyes, he told them: He was the one person I ever knew – anywhere – who was never afraid. Whatever you talked to him about, whatever you asked him for, like projects for your district, there was just one way to figure it with him. I know some of them called it demagoguery; they can call it anything they want, but you could be damn sure that the only test he had was this: was it good for the folks?'

For Goebbels, who was sharing Hitler's life in a bunker under Berlin, Roosevelt's death seemed to offer the hope of a way out of Germany's predicament: the new President would agree to a separate peace and then both the Americans and Germans, with the British and French at their side, could fight against the Soviet Union, saving Berlin and pushing the Soviet forces out of Germany. The leader of the Hitler Youth, Alfons Heck, who – at his home in Wittlich – was already far behind the Allied lines, later wrote of his feelings when he heard of Roosevelt's death: 'I shared Josef Goebbels' short-lived illusion that his demise might persuade his successor

Harry Truman to settle for an armistice or even to join us against the Soviets.'

That the war would continue to be fought with ferocity by the Western Powers was, however, evident on the night of April 14/15, when 500 British bombers, flying to Potsdam, sought to destroy the army barracks there. The people of Potsdam had not been badly bombed before, and when the air raid sirens sounded many of them assumed, as they had correctly assumed many times before, that Berlin, not Potsdam, was the target. Thus there was no rush to the shelters, and as many as 5,000 civilians were killed. Only one British bomber was lost.

Harry S. Truman, the new American President, was as determined as his predecessor to see Germany – and Japan – totally defeated. The almost daily revelation of Nazi atrocities only served to strengthen that determination among all the Allies. On April 15 the British entered the concentration camp of Belsen, coming upon scenes as horrific as those which had confronted the Americans at Buchenwald. There were 35,000 unburied bodies at Belsen, a sight that turned the hair white of some of those men who saw it. There were also 30,000 prisoners still alive in the camp, of whom 1,500 were Jewish survivors of Auschwitz. There were also a thousand German prisoners at Belsen who had been incarcerated for anti-Nazi activities. Prisoners of every nationality in what had been German-occupied Europe were found there, including 160 Luxembourg civilians who had been active opponents of German rule in the small principality.

Many of the surviving inmates of Belsen were so near to death – from starvation and from typhus – at the time of the arrival of the British that, despite all medical efforts to save them, three hundred died each day in the week following liberation. Hundreds more died in the weeks ahead, among them, on the eighth day after liberation, a French woman, Yvonne Rudellat, codename Jacqueline, who had been smuggled by boat from Britain to France in the summer of 1942 and had worked as a liaison with the French Resistance for eleven months before being arrested.

Other concentration camps were not yet liberated. At Ravensbrück, north of Berlin, 40,000 men and 17,000 women were assembled on April 15 to be marched out of the camp, and away from the approaching Russians. Guarded by SS men and SS women, this mass of sick and starving inmates were forced to march westward. Those who fell down and could not get up were shot by the wayside. Others were killed when Allied bombs exploded among them: the planes had been trying to hit German road and rail communications.

On April 16 American troops reached the German rocket factory at Nordhausen, in the Kohlstein mountains. Deep underground the V2 rockets were still being assembled. As well as the vast factory, the Americans found 4,000 slave labourers who had been working underground. The three main tunnels in which they worked were each a kilometre long, with forty-two connecting tunnels. As at each slave labour camp which the liberators overran, the Americans were shocked by the conditions which they found, and propelled forward with a renewed anger at the 'master race'.

On the morning of April 16 the Soviet forces on the River Oder opened their offensive against Berlin. Three thousand Soviet tanks crossed the Oder bridges, as more than sixty German suicide planes tried to crash into the bridges and destroy them. The tactic failed. From Berlin, Hitler tried to assert his authority through threats, issuing a directive that day to his commanders on the Eastern Front: 'He who gives the order to retreat will be shot on the spot.'

In an air battle above Berlin on April 16, American aircraft shot down twenty-two German jet aircraft. They were almost the last German jets capable of action. Most of the German munitions factories and ammunition dumps had been overrun. American troops were in the suburbs of Nuremberg, subjecting the city's defenders to a devastating barrage of artillery fire. On April 17 American bombers destroyed 752 German aircraft on the ground. This was virtually the last of the German air force. The planes had been on the ground because they lacked sufficient fuel to fly more than a few hours every day. An American bombing raid on Dresden that night caused further damage to the railway mashalling yards, through which the last available reinforcements for the Eastern Front were being transferred.

The Eastern Front was only twenty miles from Dresden. American troops were approaching from the west. Germany was in imminent danger of being cut in two. Outside the disintegrating Third Reich, the Germans were still fighting in northern Italy. When General von Vietinghoff, the commander of the German forces in Italy, sought Hitler's permission to withdraw northward into Austria, Hitler refused.

In the Pacific, on April 18, during a lull in the battle for the ten-square-mile island of Ie Shima − needed for its airstrip − Ernie Pyle, one of the most popular of America's war correspondents, was driving in a jeep with a Colonel in search of a site for a regimental command post. As they crossed the island a Japanese machine gunner opened fire. The Colonel, Pyle, and those with them, jumped out of the jeep and took cover in a ditch. After a few moments Pyle raised his head. The machine gunner fired again and Pyle was killed, hit in the temple just below the line of his helmet. His body was recovered, still under fire, by some of the infantrymen whose daily existence in war he had tried to convey to the American public.

In Pyle's pocket was found the draft of a newspaper column he had intended to publish as soon as the end of the war in Europe was announced. In it he wrote of how, in the 'joyousness of high spirits' brought about by victory, 'it is easy for us to forget the dead' and he reflected:

Those who are gone would not wish themselves to be a millstone of gloom around our necks.

But there are many of the living who have had burned into their brains forever the unnatural sight of cold dead men scattered over the hillsides and in the ditches along the high rows of hedge throughout the world.

Dead men by mass production – in one country after another – month after month and year after year.

Dead men in winter and dead men in summer.

Dead men in such familiar promiscuity that they become monotonous.

Dead men in such monstrous infinity that you come almost to hate them.

On April 19, American troops entered Leipzig. Like the Russians, they were within a few days' fighting from the Elbe. That day, in Dachau, the SS executed eleven Czech and four French officers who had been captured several years earlier on secret missions to German-occupied France and Czechoslovakia. That same day, the Gauleiter of Bavaria, Fritz Waechtler, one of those Party loyalists upon whom Hitler had depended for the previous decade for the efficiency of Party discipline, was accused by the SS of defeatism and executed in Bayreuth.

On April 20, in his bunker beneath Berlin, Hitler celebrated his fifty-sixth birthday. The Americans were bombing Berlin that day, but during a lull between attacks Hitler came up from his bunker to inspect the teenage soldiers of the Hitler Youth, as well as some much older men who had been conscripted into a newly formed SS division. Returning to his bunker, and to the birthday tea party, he spoke to his guests – among them Himmler – of his determination not to allow Bohemia and Moravia, Norway or Denmark to be overrun.

The terror system over which Himmler presided was in operation even as Hitler's birthday celebrations continued. At Neuengamme concentration camp near Hamburg, twenty Soviet prisoners-of-war and twenty Jewish children – each of whom had earlier been taken away from Auschwitz for medical experiments – were taken to the Bullenhauser Damm School in Hamburg, together with the children's four adult attendants. There, in the basement, the Soviet soldiers and the four attendants were hanged. Then the children were injected with morphine and hanged. Those whose bodies were too light to be strangled by the noose were seized by the legs by an SS man who then pulled them down with his own weight until they were dead. The two youngest children – Mania Altman and Eleonora Witonska – were five years old, originally from Radom, in Poland. The twelve year olds – a girl and a boy – Jacqueline Morgenstern and Georges André Kohn, had been on the very last of the deportations from Paris to Auschwitz in August 1944. The man who had experimented on the children, and who ordered their deaths, was a medical doctor, Kurt Heissmeyer. After the war he practised medicine in the East German town of Magdeburg for nineteen years, before being arrested and sentenced to imprisonment for life.

The Soviet prisoners-of-war and the Jewish children were murdered on April 20 in an attempt to cover up the traces of crime. The killing on April 21 of more than 170 Italian partisans in the region around Gorizia was an act of vengeance by soldiers who no longer had any hope of maintaining control of the region. That day Hitler despatched SS General Steiner to push the Soviet forces back from the River Oder north-east of Berlin. He told Steiner: 'You will see, the Russians will suffer the greatest defeat of their history, before the gates of Berlin.' He also warned the general: 'It is expressly forbidden to fall back to the West. Officers who do not comply unconditionally with this order are to be arrested and shot immediately.'

'Arrested and shot immediately': these few words summed up what the ambitions and aspirations of the Thousand Year Reich had been reduced to. The autobahns linking Berlin with the Crimea and the Caucasus, the new generation of 'pure Aryan' youth, the monumentally rebuilt Berlin, the great 'ideal' cities of Trondheim and Linz, the SS town of Zamosc in Poland (already renamed Himmlerstadt), the much-vaunted 'Jew free' towns and villages, the world-wide respect for German discipline and manhood – all encapsulated at this desperate moment, for Hitler and his regime, in the words 'arrested and shot immediately'.

Hitler's fear that his armies would simply dissolve was not a fanciful one. In the Ruhr pocket, which Montgomery's 21st Army Group had surrounded, 325,000 German soldiers were called upon to surrender. The message stating the surrender terms was dropped by parachute in a container together with a carrier pigeon, National Pigeon Service ring number 43.29018 – known to its handlers as Ruhr Express. A hungry German soldier nearly ate the pigeon before it was taken to command headquarters. Once the message was read and accepted, the pigeon was released: it flew back to its homing base in Britain, a journey of three hundred miles, with the German answer. For this service it was awarded the animal Victoria Cross, the Dickin Medal.

Thirty German generals were among those who surrendered in the Ruhr on April 21. That day, Soviet troops advancing south of Berlin overran Zossen, the headquarters of the German high Command. Specially established 'battle groups' of fifteen and sixteen year olds, the generation of Hitler Youth whose whole lives had been spent in the Nazi system, were assembled in Berlin and sent to hastily constructed defensive positions around the capital. One such group of seventy youngsters, who had been issued with only three anti-tank guns between them, was sent to at Eggersdorf, less than twelve miles east of Berlin, where they were mown down by the Russian tanks and artillery ranged against them.

At Hitler's insistence, despite the unease of those generals who were still fighting, Himmler was appointed commander of both the Rhine and Vistula armies. Travelling to Lübeck on April 22 he held the second of two meetings with the head of the Swedish Red Cross, Count Folke Bernadotte, and offered to surrender both his armies to the Western Allies. If their surrender was accepted, Himmler explained, they would continue fighting against the Russians 'until the front of the Western powers has replaced the German front'.

The Western powers had no intention of turning against the Soviet Union or of embarking on separate negotiations with the Nazi leaders. Any surrender had to be without conditions: the total and complete surrender of all the armies on all fronts. In telling Stalin about Himmler's approach, Churchill assured the Soviet leader that 'the attack of the Allies upon them, on all sides and in all theatres where resistance continues, will be prosecuted with the utmost vigour'.

It was the German armies that no longer possessed the means or the will for such 'utmost vigour'. On April 22 Hitler learned that SS General Steiner, whom he had despatched to the Elbe with such high hopes of halting the Russian advance, had failed to persuade a single unit to take the offensive. The sweep of the Soviet forces south of Berlin was about to reach the Elbe. At Treuenbrietzen the Russians liberated a prisoner-of-war camp in which, among the thousands of soldiers being held there, was Major-General Otto Ruge, the Commander-in-Chief of the Norwegian Army who had been captured five years earlier. For more than a million Allied prisoners-of-war, captivity was coming to an end.

Nazi vengeance continued to be exacted, most ferociously in Berlin itself. On the night of April 22 an SS firing squad executed Rüdiger Schleicher, whose office in the Institute of Aviation Law at the university of Berlin had been a meeting place for German anti-Nazis. His two brothers-in-law, Pastor Dietrich Bonhoeffer and Hans von Dohnanyi, had already been executed for their part in the anti-Nazi movement. It was Dohnanyi who, shortly before his execution earlier that month, had smuggled out a note to his wife: 'Sometimes I have faith that I will win through, even if the world is full of devils.' Those 'devils' had been too swift.

During April 22 three of Hitler's most senior generals, Keitel, Jodl and Christian, urged him to leave Berlin. For three hours they sought to persuade him to go to the more secure mountain redoubts of southern Bavaria. Shouting at them that he was 'deserted', Hitler insisted on remaining in his capital, and in his bunker. He would remain 'and there meet the end when it came'. But anyone who wanted to leave, he said, was free to go – Goering had left Berlin two days earlier, never to return. Three other absentees, Himmler, Ribbentrop and Doenitz, telephoned to the bunker and urged Hitler to leave. He reiterated his determination to stay.

On April 23 Berlin radio announced that Berlin and Prague were the 'inviolable twin citadels' of the Reich and would be defended to the last. That day Hitler took personal command of the defence of Berlin; but he never emerged above ground. That day two more imprisoned Germans were executed a mere hundred yards away from the Führer bunker, at Gestapo headquarters in the Prinz Albrecht Strasse: one was Dietrich Bonhoeffer's brother Klaus and the other the distinguished geographer Albrecht Haushofer, who in the summer of 1944 had let it be known to the conspirators that he supported their aims, and that he favoured the restoration of the German monarchy once Hitler was overthrown.

On the night of April 23/24 British bombers again attacked the German capital. One result of the raid was that the Propaganda Ministry went up in flames. Even as the capital was being pulverized by British bombers from the air and by Soviet artillery from the ground, SS, Gestapo and Hitler Youth formations – including the uniformed Werewolf shock groups which had been set up to act as guerrilla formations behind Allied lines – were fighting street by street, and exacting a terrible vengeance on those who would not fight. A recent historian of Berlin, Alexandra Richie, has written of that tragic time:

> The young Berliner Helmut Altner remembered being pulled from his bed by the SS and ordered to fight; he also recalled that when his platoon leader refused to go into battle he 'was strung up on the nearest tree by a few SS and an SA man – but then he was already fifteen years old'.
>
> The suburbs were filled with such victims, many of whom were murdered only minutes before the Russians arrived; near the Berliner Strasse, according to one woman, 'a soldier in underpants is hanging, a sign saying "Traitor" dangling from his neck'. He was hanging so low that the young boys of the neighbourhood played by twisting him by his legs, winding the rope and spinning the dead man around.
>
> Similar signs scrawled on pieces of cardboard and hung around the wretched victims read I HAD NO FAITH IN THE FÜHRER, or ALL TRAITORS WILL DIE LIKE THIS.
>
> There were many tragic cases of boys being killed while trying to find food for their families, or of sick or old men being shot as 'shirkers' simply because they looked 'too healthy'. Margret Boveri watched in horror as a man was killed on 24 April in front of her house: 'Yesterday was the first day of the Wehrwölfen in our district: a professor . . . tried to throw his local Party uniform in the Lietzensee, he was captured and his throat was cut. The pool of blood was 100 metres in front of our house.' The word 'traitor' was left on the site.

Alexandra Richie also told of how Lothar Rühl, then a teenager, remembered being picked up by the SS:

> They told me to go along with them and said that all cowards and traitors would be shot. On the way, I saw an officer, stripped of his insignia, hanging from a streetcar underpass. A large sign hung around his neck

read, 'I am hanging here because I was too much of a coward to face the enemy.'

The SS man said, 'Do you see that? There's a deserter hanging already'.

Recognizing that the fall of Berlin could no longer be averted, Goering had flown south, to Berchtesgaden. There, however, on the morning of April 25, he was forced to take shelter as more than three hundred British bombers attacked Hitler's mountain retreat.

In Berlin, Hitler fulminated against Goering's treachery – he had let it be known that he was willing to succeed Hitler as Chancellor – and removed him from his twin positions as political successor and as German Air Force supremo. Goering was replaced as Hitler's successor by Admiral Karl Doenitz, who was then at German Naval Headquarters at Flensburg, a few miles from the Danish border. Goering was also replaced, as Commander-in-Chief of the German Air Force, by one of Germany's most highly decorated air aces, Robert von Greim, then commanding the air forces on the Eastern Front.

Greim was summoned by Hitler to Berlin to receive his new assignment, and to be promoted Field Marshal. He flew to Berlin – which was almost completely encircled by Soviet troops – in a tiny plane, accompanied by the woman test pilot Hanna Reitsch. As they flew into the capital, Greim was wounded by Russian artillery fire. He and Reitsch then made their way to Hitler's bunker, but they failed to persuade Hitler to leave with them, and to seek at least temporary safety in either the south or the north. They themselves left, precariously, in the same light plane in which they had arrived, and, flying through air space in which both Soviet and British air power was virtually supreme, managed to reach Admiral Doenitz at Flensburg.

Near the village of Leckwitz, on the western bank of the Elbe, an American army officer, Lieutenant Albert Kotzebue, chanced upon a Soviet soldier. Both men were foraging for food. It was April 25. Together they crossed the river to the eastern bank, where, near the village of Stehla, they found a Soviet encampment. Two great attacking armies had linked up. Germany was cut in two. Four hours later another American patrol came across a group of Soviet soldiers who had crossed the Elbe and were in the village of Torgau. In Moscow, a 324-gun salute was fired to celebrate the coming together of the two armies. In New York crowds gathered in Times Square to sing and dance through the night. On April 26, units of the Soviet army entered Potsdam, completing the encirclement of Berlin. That day the SS warned Himmler that food supplies for the German population still under German control could not last more than another two weeks.

In Washington, President Truman was contemplating another war zone and another war ending. The atom bomb was so near to being perfected that a special Target Committee was looking at possible cities on which to drop it. Tokyo was ruled out because, as the committee noted on April 27, 'it is now practically all bombed and burned out'. The committee concluded: 'Hiroshima is the largest untouched target. Consideration should be given to this city.'

Field Marshal Goering was already under arrest when Hitler learned of Himmler's negotiations with Count Bernadotte. Himmler too – the valued instrument of terror and SS chief – was immediately dismissed from all his posts. Himmler's representative in Hitler's bunker, SS Lieutenant-General Hermann Fegelein, had slipped away to his home in the Berlin suburbs. He was sent for, stripped of his insignia, taken up to the Chancellery yard, and shot. The fact that he was the brother-in-law of Hitler's close companion, Eva Braun, could not save him.

That day, at the lakeside village of Dongo in northern Italy, Hitler's once triumphant Axis partner, Mussolini, was seized by Italian partisans. He had sought to disguise himself in a German air force greatcoat and helmet, but was recognized. On April 28 he was shot dead. He was sixty-one years old. He was shot together with the Secretary of the Fascist Party and four Cabinet Ministers. Mussolini's mistress, Clara Petacci, was also shot. She had insisted on being with him to the last. Her body and that of Mussolini were then taken by truck to Milan and hung up by the heels in the Piazzale Loreto, to be spat upon by the crowds that had once been so full of enthusiasm. Perhaps the individuals who spat had always been opponents. But with the fall of the dictators, few could be found to admit to having applauded them when times were good.

On the morning of April 29, German officers representing General von Vietinghoff signed the unconditional surrender of all German troops in Italy – more than a million men. As Mussolini's body was being taken from Dongo to Milan, Hitler was in his bunker in Berlin writing his political testament and making plans to marry Eva Braun. In his testament he wrote that he was expelling both Goering and Himmler from the Nazi Party, and setting up a new Government, with Admiral Doenitz as President and Dr Goebbels as Chancellor.

In his testimony, Hitler insisted that neither he nor 'anyone else in Germany' had wanted a second war against Britain and the United States. 'Centuries will go by,' he wrote, 'but from the ruins of our towns and monuments the hatred of those ultimately responsible will always grow anew against the people whom we have to thank for all this: international Jewry and its henchmen.' Hitler then stated that the war had been caused solely by those international statesmen 'who either were of Jewish origin or worked for Jewish interests'. The Jews were 'the real guilty party in this murderous struggle' and would be 'saddled' with the responsibility for it. Hitler added, with a reference to his published warnings of 1939 and 1941: 'I left no one in doubt that this time not only would millions of children of European Aryan races starve, not only would millions of grown men meet their death, and not only would hundreds and thousands of women and children be burned and bombed to death in cities, but this time the real culprits would have to pay for their guilt even though by more humane means than war.'

The 'more humane means' had been the gas chambers. That afternoon, American forces entered Dachau, where yet more evidence of atrocities so horrified the soldiers that they killed three hundred of the SS guards. Some of the 33,000 liberated inmates – those among them who had sufficient strength and will for revenge – killed two hundred more. As at Belsen, privation continued to take its toll at Dachau long after liberation, with 2,466 of the camp inmates dying in the following month and a half.

On the day of the liberation of Dachau, SS snipers continued to harass the American troops in the area around the camp. After an American soldier was shot dead by a sniper in the village of Webling, five miles from Dachau, all seventeen SS men who then surrendered were lined up and shot. That same day, April 29, near Buchenwald concentration camp, the Americans discovered a vast underground quarry filled with Nazi treasures: the looted belongings of those whom the Germans had conquered. According to the official listing, the items discovered in the quarry included 'bars of gold, US currency, US gold coins, diamonds, various precious stones, boxes of silver spoons, watches clocks and various other items of property'. Among the boxes were hundreds of gold wedding rings and thousands of gold teeth. There was also 600 pounds weight of fountain pens, wrist-watch straps and novelty jewellery. The silver spoons and other silver tableware weighed 17,000 pounds.

The total value of the hoard discovered on April 29 was estimated at $500 million, the equivalent fifty years later of more than $3 billion. Of this amount, $25 million in German monetary gold was allocated nine months later as an initial installment 'for the rehabilitation and resettlement of non-repatriable victims of German action'. Almost all of those eligible were Jews, but five per cent of the fund was set aside for non-Jews.

On the afternoon of April 29, deep in his bunker, Hitler awarded two Knight's Crosses. The presentations were made by the Citadel Commandant of the bunker, SS Major-General Mohnke, who in May 1940 had been involved in the massacre of British prisoners-of-war at Paradis, near Dunkirk. One of those being honoured was a French SS volunteer, Eugene Vaulot, who on the previous day had commanded an anti-tank unit that had destroyed six Russian tanks in the centre of Berlin. On the following morning, April 30, Hitler learned that American troops had entered Munich, the scene of so many of his early struggles and successes, the city in which he had volunteered in 1914 to serve as a front line soldier, and where, in 1923, he had tried to seize power.

At half past two that afternoon a Soviet soldier waved the Red Banner from a second floor window of the Reichstag building, less than a mile from Hitler's bunker. An hour later, having finished his lunch and said goodbye to those who were with him in the bunker – among them Goebbels – Hitler retired to his room with Eva Braun. Those waiting outside heard a single shot. Hitler had killed himself. When they entered the room, Eva Braun was also dead. She had swallowed poison.

With Soviet shells falling all around, Hitler's body was taken up to the Chancellery courtyard by his devoted staff, doused with petrol and set on fire. The man who had unleashed so many hatreds, and so much bloodshed, was dead. The war that had been as much his responsibility as that of any other single person, continued to be fought, mostly in Berlin, and in isolated pockets in northern Germany, Bohemia and Moravia, Croatia, and the Austrian Alps, for another eight days.

A radio signal was sent from the bunker to Admiral Doenitz at Flensburg, to tell him that he was Chancellor. The warmaking activities, and the future existence, of the Third Reich had become his responsibility. In the Führer bunker in Berlin, above which lay Hitler's body, Goebbels arranged for his six children to be given a lethal injection by an SS doctor, and then had himself and his wife shot by an SS orderly.

On the morning of May 2, Marshal Zhukov accepted the surrender of Berlin. In northern Italy and southern Austria, more than a million German soldiers had laid down their arms. German scientific and Intelligence experts hastened to surrender to the Western Allies and to offer their services. On May 2 the two most senior members of the German rocket bomb research team surrendered to the Americans in southern Germany. They were hurried away to Paris and then to the United States. One of them, Wernher von Braun, later commented: 'We were interested in continuing our work, not just being squeezed like a lemon and then discarded.'

Not rocket bombs to bring more deaths to London and Antwerp, but rockets to put a man on the moon, became the focus of Wernher von Braun's work in the New World. He crossed from one master to another in impressive company. Among those who also brought their expertise from Germany to the United States was Hans von Ohain, the man who had built the first jet engine to power an aircraft in flight – on 27 August 1939. During the war he had continued with his research on jet engines, devising one that was superior to the British and American prototypes in speed, climb rate, service ceiling and armaments. Hitler, who failed to grasp the importance of this for air combat, and for air mastery, ordered the use of jets to be restricted to ground attack. Von Ohain had no problems in putting his expertise at the disposal of the United States.

In order to transfer not only the personnel but the material needed for rocket research, an American officer, Major William Bromely, was given the task of seeking out German rocket equipment from the underground factory at Nordhausen in which it was being manufactured, and in getting it to the United States before the Russians could reach it. He succeeded in finding and transferring four hundred tons, and in requisitioning the railway wagons needed to transport it to Antwerp for shipment across the Atlantic, where it found a new home at the atomic research centre and testing grounds at White Sands, New Mexico.

It was not only scientists who gave themselves up to the Americans. One of those who made certain he fell into American and not Russian hands was Reinhard Gehlen, one of Hitler's most senior surviving Military Intelligence officers. In due course, with American approval, he was to return to Intelligence work against the Russians in post-war Western Germany.

The war in Europe continued for more than a week after Hitler's death. On May 2 the German Foreign Minister, Count Schwerin von Krosigk, broadcast over Berlin radio: 'In the East the iron curtain behind which, unseen by the eyes of the world, the work of destruction goes on, moves steadily forward.' *The Times*, in reporting this remark on the following day, used the word 'iron curtain' – it was the first time it appeared in English as a description of what the Soviets were establishing across Europe.*

On the day of Schwerin von Krosigk's warning of dire events in the East, a group of 850 Jewish women – survivors of Stutthof concentration camp – were trying desperately to leave Lübeck and to find safety elsewhere. They managed to find a barge and go out to three large refugee ships in Lübeck harbour, where ten thousand refugees were on board, hoping to sail to the safety of a neutral Swedish port. But the women were refused permission by the German ships' captains to go on board. They therefore returned to the shore in the barges that had taken them out. As they tried to land, SS men, Hitler Youth and German marines opened fire on them, and more than five hundred of the women were killed.

The three refugee ships remained in the bay. But on the night of May 2/3, before they could sail, there was a heavy British air raid on Kiel. The aim was to prevent German ships from taking troops to Norway, where it was thought the Germans might try to continue fighting. Some of the bombers that were instructed to hit ships in Kiel harbour flew – in error – to Lübeck, which was also at the head of an estuary, but thirty-five miles to the south-east, and dropped their bombs on the harbour there.

Two of the three refugee ships were sunk. On one that was hit, the *Thielbeck*, 2,750 refugees were killed. On the other, a former banana boat, the *Cap Arcona*, more than 4,500 refugees were killed, among them seven hundred gravely ill refugees on the lower deck who were burned to death, and several hundred Russian prisoners-of-war who had been locked in the hold in the ship's banana coolers.

For British Bomber Command, in the words of its diarist, 'there had been a final small tragedy' when two bombers on that final raid to Kiel were lost, and thirteen airmen were killed. The two bombers had apparently crashed into each other while on their bomb runs. One of those killed was a volunteer from the Irish Republic, which had remained neutral throughout the war, and whose President, Eamon de Valera, on learning of Hitler's death, called on the senior German diplomat in Dublin to express his condolences – as one Head of State acknowledging the death of another, it was explained from Dublin.

*   *   *

* On 25 February 1945, five weeks before the German Foreign Minister's broadcast, the phrase 'iron curtain' had been used in German (but not reported in English) by Dr Goebbels, who spoke on the radio of 'ein eiserner Vorhang'.

In the Far East, a risky British military strategy was paying off. This was the decision, made at the start of the year, to continue the campaign in Burma through the monsoon weeks of March and April. The heavy fighting that took place was a triumph for the planning and execution of the British Commander-in-Chief, General Sir William Slim. In the last days of April, with Rangoon as the goal, a seaborne amphibious landing was about to be launched in which Indian troops would have been the major force. It proved unnecessary: the Japanese had already evacuated the city, which was entered on May 3. Since the start of hostilities in Burma in December 1941, 6,000 British and Commonwealth troops, and 36,000 Japanese troops had been killed.

In northern Europe, on the day of Rangoon's liberation, two senior German officers from Admiral Dönitz's headquarters at Flensburg – in effect, the new Reich Chancellery – arrived at Montgomery's headquarters on Lüneberg Heath. When they were shown into Montgomery's presence he asked the officer who had brought them in, 'Who are these men? What do they want?' With those two curt questions began the five day process that was to end with the German surrender.

One of the 'men' was Dönitz's successor as Chief of the German Naval Staff, Grand Admiral Hans Georg von Friedeburg. The other was the Chief of Staff to the German North West Army Command, General Hans Kinzel. They brought with them a proposal not dissimilar to that which Himmler had presented to Count Bernadotte ten days earlier: the surrender to the western Allies of all the German armies then facing the Russians. Montgomery rejected the offer. The only armies they could surrender, he said, were the ones facing him: that is, the German forces in north-west Germany and Denmark, and those still holding out in Holland, behind his lines. A similar surrender of specific forces had been made by the German commanders in Italy three days earlier.

The two German emissaries prepared to return to Flensburg to seek instructions from Doenitz. Before they left Montgomery told them that if his conditions were not acceptable 'I shall go on with the war, and will be delighted to do so, and am ready. All your soldiers will be killed.' The emissaries left, and, returning the following afternoon, May 4, they signed the instrument of surrender.

That day, in Austria, both Salzburg and Innsbruck surrendered to the Americans, who entered Berchtesgaden, Hitler's mountain retreat, at which so many fateful decisions had been made, the fruits of which had all turned rotten. Also on May 4, American troops entered Flossenbürg concentration camp, yet another camp where the Allied soldiers were horrified by what they encountered – the sights and smells of death and starvation.

Among the tens of thousands of prisoners of the Third Reich who were liberated at Flossenbürg were Pastor Martin Niemöller, the former leader of the German Confessional Church who had spoken out courageously against Nazi persecution; Kurt von Schuschnigg, the former Austrian Chancellor who had challenged Hitler in 1938 by calling a plebiscite; and Léon Blum who, when Prime Minister of France before the war, had formed a government which favoured a common European front against aggression. Like the 'prominent' prisoners at Buchenwald, those at Flossenbürg had been kept in relatively tolerable conditions, as potential hostages.

As German soldiers continued to fight in an ever-contracting area, it was the future of the Soviet Union in Europe that dominated Churchill's concerns. In a telegram to Truman on May 4, he pointed out that by the time all the German armies had surrendered – most probably within the next few days – the area under Soviet control 'would include the Baltic Provinces, all of Germany to the occupational line, all Czechoslovakia, a large part of Austria, the whole of Yugoslavia, Hungary, Roumania and Bulgaria, until Greece in her present tottering condition is reached'. Churchill noted that Soviet control would include 'all the great capitals of middle Europe, including Berlin, Vienna, Budapest, Belgrade, Bucharest and Sofia'. He did not mention, though he might have done, Warsaw, Kovno, Riga and Tallinn further to the east, and Tirana to the south.

The spread of Soviet control, Churchill warned – in words which foreshadowed the events and conflicts of the coming four decades – 'constitutes an event in the history of Europe to which there has been no parallel, and which has not been faced by the Allies in their long and hazardous struggle'. The Soviet demands on Germany 'for reparations alone will be such as to enable her to prolong the occupation almost indefinitely, at any rate for many years, during which time Poland will sink with many other States into the vast zone of Russian-controlled Europe, not necessarily economically Sovietized but police-governed'.

Concern about the Soviet Union was overshadowed for the Western Allies by the speed of the German collapse. On May 5 the German forces in southern Germany surrendered, as did the German army in Holland, replaced by Canadian and British soldiers who entered the Dutch cities with their bands playing. A Dutch eye-witness, Hen Bollen, has written:

The impatient population received the liberators with exultant and chaotic joy. They were hugged, kissed and cajoled and smothered in offers of flowers and fruit, by a dancing and jubilant crowd. Down to the very smallest village ecstatically joyous jubilation was in progress. The Netherlands was no longer itself.

At long last we were free again, our happiness and joy abounded.

A few moments after midnight on May 5, the citizens of Prague rose up against their German occupiers. In doing so they found a strange ally: General Vlasov, the most senior Soviet army officer to have thrown in his lot with the Germans. A year earlier, Vlasov had established the Committee for the Liberation of the Peoples of Russia (KONR). Commanding two divisions of former Soviet soldiers, mostly Ukrainians, he had fought against the Russians on the Eastern Front, and had retreated with the Germans. After hearing a radio appeal by Czech patriots on the morning of March 6, he decided to change sides again, to join the Czech insurgents, and to fight against his German masters. Like the Czechs, he hoped to drive the Germans out of Prague before the Russians arrived – much as the Poles had hoped to do in Warsaw nine months earlier.

The Germans fought back, opening fire on the centre of the city from their positions on Castle Hill. In the fighting that followed, more than three thousand Czechs were killed. German SS troops fought in the streets against the men of Vlasov's army, who, until a few days earlier, had been their comrades-in-arms. As they did so they were astonished to find, at Czech patriot headquarters, a United States Army captain. He had just reached the city – on the afternoon of May 6 – at the head of an American armoured reconnaissance column. The captain explained that he was not the vanguard of the approaching American army, but had been sent ahead of the main American force – which had driven the Germans out of western Czechoslovakia – to see if the insurgents were able to hold Prague by themselves until it could be handed over to the Soviet Union. Such a handover was in accordance with an agreement earlier concluded between Stalin and the United States. Having seen that Vlasov's army was supporting the Czechs – though somewhat puzzled by the fact that Vlasov's men were still wearing German uniforms – the American captain and his column withdrew. Within a few hours, as Soviet troops approached Prague, Vlasov's troops in the city deemed it prudent to seek safety in the American lines. Most of its senior officers never reached the Americans: on their way west they were captured by Czech partisans and killed.

American military units were already in possession of large areas of German-held western Bohemia. In each Czech town through which they had advanced during the previous ten days, including the city of Plzen, they had been rapturously greeted as liberators by the Czechs. Under the previously negotiated Soviet-American agreement, however, they had to withdraw, to enable the whole of Czechoslovakia to come within the Soviet sphere.

During May 6 the German forces which had been besieged by the Russians inside Breslau for more than a month raised the white flag. Half an hour later General Alfred Jodl, who had served since 1939 as Chief of the Operations Command of the German Armed Forces, flew from Flensburg to Reims to sign the final act of surrender of all the German armies, navies and air forces still in action.

Jodl tried, as Himmler and Admiral von Friedeburg had done before him, to limit the surrender to those forces facing westward. But General Eisenhower, who listened to this request, rejected it outright. Jodl then sent a radio signal to Flensburg asking Doenitz what he should do. Doenitz – who had been Chancellor of Germany for a mere six days – replied with authorization for Jodl to sign the total and unconditional surrender of all German forces on all fronts. Jodl did so at once, in the presence of a Soviet general, Ivan Susloparov. It was 1.41 in the early hours on May 7.

The Second World War in Europe was over. But the aftermath of war contained many agonies. On May 7, the first day after the German unconditional surrender, thousands of Dutch gathered in the centre of Amsterdam to celebrate the victory and to await the arrival of the first Allied troops. Following the capitulation two days earlier of the German forces in Holland, armed and uniformed German soldiers had been stationed in the city, serving with Allied approval as a police force until the Allied troops arrived. As the enthusiastic crowds gathered to welcome their liberators, the German soldiers in one part of the city centre, Dam Square, frightened by the size of the growing crowd, and fearing an attack on themselves, opened fire. Thirty-one Dutchmen were killed.*

*   *   *

* This incident was witnessed by fifteen photographers who were waiting in the square to photograph the arrival of the Allied troops. An exhibition of their photographs, organized by the Netherlands Photo Archives, was held in London in 1998.

Following the signature of the German surrender at Reims, May 8 was declared VE-Day – Victory in Europe Day. During May 8 a Soviet general took the surrender of the German troops who had continued to fight in and around Prague. German troops who had been cut off in northern Latvia for some months were also ready to surrender.

Shortly before midnight on May 8 there was yet another surrender ceremony, when, in Berlin, Admiral Friedeburg, who had also signed the Lüneberg Heath and Reims surrenders on May 4 and 7, added his signature to the final formal surrender document. The other German signatories were Hitler's chief military adviser throughout the war, Field Marshal Wilhelm Keitel, and Goering's successor as head of the German Air Force, General Hans-Jurgen Stümpff. Marshal Zhukov signed for the Soviet Union.

In San Francisco on May 8, the Foreign Ministers of the victorious powers were establishing the ground rules for the United Nations Organization. Among the delegates was Clement Attlee – Britain's Deputy Prime Minister and leader of the Labour Party – who recalled: 'While we were at the Conference the news came through that the war against the Nazis had ended. We gathered to celebrate the event in a room at the top of a skyscraper. In San Francisco the Japanese War was nearer and of greater concern to the citizens than the European contest and we were sorry not to be at home for the celebrations.'

One of the delegates at San Francisco, the South African Prime Minister Jan Christian Smuts, had taken a leading part in the founding of the League of Nations immediately after the First World War. It was he who drafted the preamble setting out the aims of the new world organization. The United Nations was to be a forum in which every sovereign State, including in due course the defeated nations, would have a place and a voice; but the leading Allied powers still insisted upon a veto in any discussion about the use of force against a member State.

As the talks in San Francisco proceeded, the Soviet Foreign Minister, Vyacheslav Molotov, told his American and British opposite numbers – Edward Stettinius and Anthony Eden – that sixteen members of the all-Party Polish Government in Warsaw, who had gone to Moscow at the request of the American and British governments to negotiate a peace treaty, were all in prison. In the *Daily Herald* a future leader of the British Labour Party, Michael Foot, who was in San Francisco as a journalist, described the impact on the conference of Molotov's announcement. The distressing news, wrote Foot, came 'almost casually' towards the end of an otherwise cordial dinner.

Molotov 'could hardly have caused a greater sensation if he had upset the whole table and thrown the soup in Mr Stettinius's smiling face.'

The Communist-controlled Lublin Radio accused the sixteen arrested Poles of high treason, and demanded that they be brought to trial.

Another young journalist who sent a report from San Francisco on Europe's day of victory had fought in the Pacific War. A biographical note in the *New York Journal-American* explained: 'John F. Kennedy, one-time Navy lieutenant in command of a P-T boat, decorated for bravery in action, is covering the San Francisco United Nations conference from a serviceman's viewpoint.' In his despatch on May 8, Kennedy wrote: 'San Francisco took VE-Day in stride. This city overlooks the Pacific and to the people here "the war" has always been the war against the Japanese. The servicemen who crowd the streets have taken it calmly too. The war in the Pacific is the only war that most of them have ever known – and when you have just come home from long months of fighting and are returning to the war zones in a few days, it is difficult to become excited about "the end of the war". V-Day for them is a long way off.'

In his despatch of May 8, Kennedy reported on the impact of the Soviet presence in San Francisco:

Molotov's work was about done. He leaves the other delegates divided in their attitude toward him and the entire Russian policy. Some are extremely suspicious, while on the other hand there is another group which has great confidence that the Russians in their own strange and inexplicable way really want peace.

The arguments of these delegates boil down to this: it starts with the assumption a nation can usually be depended upon to act in its own best interests. In this case, Russia needs peace more than anything else. To get this peace, she feels she needs security. No one must be able to invade her again. The Russians have a far greater fear of a German come-back than we do. They are therefore going to make their western defences secure. No governments hostile to Russia will be permitted in the countries along her borders. They feel they have earned this right to security. They mean to have it, come what may.

There were those on May 8 for whom neither the celebrations of VE-Day nor the worries about Soviet intentions were to be the dominant memory.

At Fort Oglethorpe, Georgia, a few minutes after Colonel Howard Clark, the commanding officer, had addressed his men to announce the end of the European war, he was handed a War Department telegram announcing that his youngest son, First Lieutenant William A. Clark, had been killed in action on Luzon three weeks earlier. The war in the Pacific continued to cast its shadow. In New York, as hundreds of thousands of people filled the streets to celebrate the victory, wall posters exhorted them: 'We still have to beat Japan. Let's keep on buying war bonds.'

For the Soviet Union, the day chosen for victory day was May 9. That day also saw the surrender of several remote German garrisons, which had been left by both the Germans and the Allies to manage as best they could when the front lines swept past: the garrisons on the Channel Islands, on several Aegean island, on the Baltic island of Bornholm, and in the vicinity of Danzig. Only in western and central Czechoslovakia, and in parts of Silesia, did German generals continue to exhort their men to fight, and resist all attempts to dislodge them. More than six hundred Soviet soldiers were killed on May 9 fighting against the German troops in Silesia: they were killed while, in Moscow, their fellow countrymen celebrated the end of war and the end of killing.

'May 9 was an unforgettable day in Moscow,' Alexander Werth recalled. 'The spontaneous joy of the two or three million people who thronged the Red Square that evening – and the Moscow River embankments, and Gorki Street, all the way up to the Belorussian Station – was of a quality and a depth I had never seen in Moscow before. They danced and sang in the streets; every soldier and officer was hugged and kissed; outside the US Embassy the crowds shouted "Hurray for Roosevelt!" (even though he had died a month before); they were so happy they did not even have to get drunk, and under the tolerant gaze of the militia, young men even urinated against the walls of the Moskva Hotel, flooding the wide pavement.'

The last isolated German garrison to surrender was that of Dunkirk, the perimeter of which had been guarded by Czech troops since the previous September. On May 9 it flew the white flag. To the surprise of the Czech, British and French officers who gathered that day to witness the signature of the surrender document which they had prepared, the German fortress commander, Vice-Admiral Friedrich Frisius, arrived at Allied headquarters outside the town with his own surrender document already signed.

Two days later there were still some German troops in action, east of Plzen, in Bohemia, where they were surrounded by Soviet troops; and in Slovenia, near Maribor, where they were fighting the Yugoslav forces loyal to Marshal Tito. As these last battles were taking place – and Yugoslavia, with Soviet support, was demanding the Italian region of Venezia Giulia – Churchill was setting out his concerns about the future of Europe in a telegram to Truman, sent from London on May 12. It was the Soviet Union that was uppermost in his mind. 'I feel deep anxiety,' he told Truman, 'because of their misinterpretation of the Yalta decisions, their attitude towards Poland, their overwhelming influence in the Balkans, excepting Greece, the difficulties they make about Vienna, the combination of Russian power and the territories under their control or occupied, coupled with the Communist technique in so many other countries, and above all their power to maintain very large armies in the field for a long time.' Churchill went on to ask Truman: 'What will be the position in a year or two, when the British and American Armies have melted and the French has not yet been formed on any major scale, when we may have a handful of divisions, mostly French, and when Russia may choose to keep two or three hundred on active service.' Churchill then set out his deeper worries:

An iron curtain is drawn down upon their front. We do not know what is going on behind. There seems little doubt that the whole of the regions east of the line Lübeck–Trieste–Corfu will soon be completely in their hands. To this must be added the further enormous area conquered by the American armies between Eisenach and the Elbe, which will, I suppose, in a few weeks be occupied, when the Americans retreat, by the Russian power.

All kinds of arrangements will have to be made by General Eisenhower to prevent another immense flight of the German population westward as this enormous Muscovite advance into the centre of Europe takes place. And then the curtain will descend again to a very large extent, if not entirely. Thus a broad band of many hundreds of miles of Russian-occupied territory will isolate us from Poland.

Meanwhile the attention of our peoples will be occupied in inflicting severities upon Germany, which is ruined and prostrate, and it would be open to the Russians in a very short time to advance if they chose to the waters of the North Sea and Atlantic.

Churchill ended his telegram to Truman: 'The issue of a settlement with Russia before our strength has gone seems to me to dwarf all others.' Truman shared Churchill's sense of urgency, and of the need for joint Anglo-American action, starting with the need for a firm response to Yugoslav demands for Venezia Giulia. 'If it is handled firmly, before our strength is dispersed,' Truman replied that same day, 'Europe may be saved another bloodbath. Otherwise the whole fruits of our victory may be cast away and none of the purposes of World Organization to prevent territorial aggression and future wars will be attained.'

The final surrenders of the war in Europe took place on May 14, when 150,000 Germans surrendered to the Soviet army in East Prussia and 180,000 in northern Latvia; and on the following day, when the remnants of the German forces in Yugoslavia capitulated. In the previous two months the Germans fighting on Yugoslav soil had lost almost 100,000 men killed in action. The Yugoslav military deaths were also high: 30,000. But the largest number of victims in Yugoslavia were the civilians – those who had been killed in the aerial bombardment of Belgrade in 1941, or murdered by German SS reprisal squads, or driven from their villages in anti-partisan sweeps and killed by German military units, or been the victims of Croat Ustashi forces. The Yugoslav civilian death toll has been put at no less than 1,700,000.

Allied prisoners-of-war were on their way home. Axis prisoners-of-war would have longer to wait in captivity. Churchill had seen Roumanian prisoners-of-war toiling by the roadside on his drive through the Crimea to Yalta. Hundreds of thousands of German prisoners-of-war were in camps in Siberia. Hundreds of thousands of Displaced Persons – known universally as DPs – many of them Jewish survivors, awaited in DP camps – including in the huts of what had been the evil Belsen. They needed to be fed, clothed, nourished, and sent either home or to new lives in lands far from the scenes of their suffering. Millions of citizens in a dozen European nations looked at the rubble of their cities and the ruins of their homes and tried to imagine how, and when – if ever – this vast destruction could be repaired. Thousands of British, Commonwealth and American troops saw in prospect, instead of long-awaited demobilization, their transfer, possibly within a few weeks, to the Far East and Pacific war zones.

In the Pacific the war continued without respite. On Luzon the Japanese soldiers who barricaded themselves in caves to avoid capture continued to face death by flame throwers and explosives thrown into the mouths of the caves. On Okinawa terrifying scenes unfolded. One American Marine, William Manchester, later recalled how, when a popular company commander, Bob Fowler, bled to death after being hit in action, his orderly 'who adored him snatched up a submachine gun and unforgiveably massacred a line of unarmed Japanese soldiers who had just surrendered'.

Another event from Okinawa of war's descent into the grotesque was also recalled by William Manchester. It concerned eighty-five Japanese student nurses whose task was to tend the wounded and comfort the dying. As the battle raged around them, 'terrified, they had retreated into a cave. Marines reaching the mouth of the cave heard Japanese voices within. They did not recognize the tones as feminine, and neither did their interpreter, who demanded that those inside emerge at once. When they didn't, flame-throwers, moving in, killed them all.'

At sea off Okinawa, Japanese suicide planes continued to attack American warships. On May 4 these attacks had led to the deaths of 446 sailors. Seven days later a further 396 men were killed on the aircraft carrier *Bunker Hill*, three times the number of Americans who had died in the battle in 1775 after which the carrier was named. On May 14 the 19,800-ton aircraft carrier *Enterprise* was the target of a kamikaze attack. An eye-witness, George Blond, later described the scene as the attack began:

The Japanese machine approached from the rear. It was still not to be seen, as it was hidden by the clouds. Guided by radar, the five-inch guns continued to fire at it, and soon the 40-mm machine-guns began to fire as well. It was very strange to see all these guns firing relentlessly at an invisible enemy.

The Japanese aircraft emerged from the clouds and began to dive. His angle of incidence was not more than 30 degrees, his speed approximately 250 knots. There could be no doubt – it was a suicide plane. It was approaching quite slowly and deliberately, and manoeuvring just enough not to be hit too soon.

The pilot knew his job thoroughly and all those who watched him make his approach felt their mouths go dry. In less than a minute he would have attained his goal; there could be little doubt that this was to crash his machine on the deck.

All the batteries were firing: the five-inch guns, the 40mm and the 20mm, even the rifles. The Japanese aircraft dived through a rain of steel. It had been hit in several places and seemed to be trailing a banner of flame and smoke, but it came on, clearly visible, hardly moving, the line of its wings as straight as a sword.

The deck was deserted; every man, with the exception of the gunners, was lying flat on his face. Flaming and roaring, the fireball passed in front of the 'island' (the single superstructure housing funnels, bridges, etc.) and crashed with a terrible impact just behind the for'ard lift.

The entire vessel was shaken, some forty yards of the flight deck folded up like a banana-skin: an enormous piece of the lift, at least a third of the platform, was thrown over three hundred feet into the air. The explosion killed fourteen men; those boys would never laugh and joke again. The last earthly impression they took with them was the picture of the kamikaze trailing his banner of flame and increasing in size with lightning rapidity.

The mortal remains of the pilot had not disappeared. They had been laid out in a corner of the deck, next to the blackened debris of the machine. The entire crew marched past the corpse of the volunteer of death. The men were less interested in his finely modelled features, his wide-open eyes which were now glazed over, than in the buttons on his tunic, which were to become wonderful souvenirs of the war for a few privileged officers of high rank. These buttons, now black, were stamped in relief with the insignia of the kamikaze corps; a cherry blossom with three petals.

When the destroyer *Drexler* was hit by a kamikaze pilot on May 29, 158 men were killed. The American naval historian Samuel Eliot Morison has written: 'Few missiles or weapons have ever spread such terror, such scorching burns, such searing death, as did the kamikaze in his self-destroying onslaughts on the radar picket ships. And naval history has few parallels to the sustained courage, resourcefulness and fighting spirit that the crews of these vessels displayed day after day in the battle for Okinawa.'

In Europe there were those who sought out their persecutors and killed them. But in the main those who had committed war crimes were either arrested and put on trail, or disappeared into towns and cities where their past was not held against them, or where they hid their past from all around them. Some of those who were being sought by the Allies evaded judicial proceedings and possible imprisonment or even execution by killing themselves before they could be arrested or brought to trial. One of these was Konrad Henlein, whom Hitler, as a reward for his stirring up of Nazi enthusiasm among the Germans of the Czech Sudetenland, had made Governor of Bohemia and Moravia (subordinate to the German Protector). The German ruler of Norway, Josef Terboven — whose wedding Hitler had attended in 1934 — was blown up with a stick of dynamite: it was widely assumed that this was suicide. Another Norwegian, Jonas Lie, who as wartime Minister of Police had helped to establish the Norwegian SS — and had fought with it both on the Leningrad front and in Greece — killed himself on May 11 rather than surrender to the Norwegian troops who had surrounded his bunker.

When SS General Richard Glueks, the Inspector of the Concentration Camps since 1940, was found dead in the German naval hospital at Flensburg it was not known whether he had killed himself or been murdered by a Jew seeking revenge for all that Glueks had inflicted on the Jewish people for more than five years. Perhaps it was not even Glueks whose body was lying dead at Flensburg. He was in hospital being treated for shock after one of the last Allied air bombardments; some people believed that he simply vanished without trace. The air ace Field Marshal von Greim, who had tried to persuade Hitler to leave Berlin in the last week of April, took his own life in an Allied prison cell in Salzburg on May 24 — a month after his would-be rescue mission.

Himmler, who had wandered about northern Germany for several days after the final surrender, went into a British army camp and gave himself up. He was identified and then kept under guard until he could be taken away for interrogation. On reaching the interrogation centre he bit on a cyanide capsule that he had concealed in his teeth. He died a few moments later.

On May 23, at Russian insistence, the British arrested Admiral Doenitz — who still regarded himself as German Chancellor — and the members of his government, as they sat in their offices at Flensburg, where they had maintained a shadow government since May 7. Admiral von Friedeburg, who had been a signatory of three separate instruments of surrender, killed himself as the British troops arrived to take him away.

Three weeks after the surrender of the Doenitz government, Ribbentrop, Hitler's Foreign Minister, was arrested in a Hamburg boarding house. He was taken under guard to the Palace Hotel at Mondorf, in Luxembourg, where those former German leaders who were to be charged with war crimes were being assembled.

It was not only Germans for whom trial and punishment was the new prospect. As a result of Soviet insistence, the British had agreed to send back to the Soviet Union all Soviet citizens who were within the British zones of occupation. Stalin exploited this agreement, seeing in it a chink in the Western armour through which he could get hold of his ancient enemies, the fiercely independent Cossacks of southern Russia and the Caucasus. Many of these Cossacks had fought in German units or alongside the Germans, or were inter-war refugees from Soviet Communism, who had been captured by the British forces in southern Austria. At Yalta, Stalin had threatened not to release Allied prisoners-of-war who had been liberated by Soviet troops unless the Cossacks were sent back. The word used was 'repatriation'; the reality, for many thousands, was labour camp and death.

Millions of Germans and German-speaking peoples were also on the move, expelled by the Soviets, Poles and Czechs from areas in which they had lived for many generations. East Prussia was being cleared of its German inhabitants in preparation for Russian and Polish partition and settlement. The Sudetenland was being purged of its Sudeten Germans so that Czechs could live there. Starting on June 11 the Czech authorities began the mass expulsion of more than 700,000 Sudeten Germans.

'I cannot live in such a world,' wrote the painter Oscar Kokoshka when he learned of the expulsion of tens of thousands of people from his native Bohemia on the sole grounds that their language was German. 'I feel individually responsible for the crimes of a society of which I am a member.' As a Jew, Kokoshka was fortunate to have left Prague for Britain before the war.

A swathe of German territory – Danzig and the German provinces east of the River Oder – was being resettled by Poles. As many as three million Germans had become refugees from these regions, and from the Sudetenland, and were moving westward with whatever possessions they could put together in hand-held bundles and small carts.

For a few diligent servants of the Nazi regime, a bright future beckoned. Two months after the defeat of Germany, the United States Joint Chiefs of Staff authorized Operation Overcast, a top secret attempt to find those German scientists of 'chosen, rare minds, whose continuing intellectual productivity we wish to use' and to take them to the United States. Some of these scientists were working at German rocket establishments at Nordhausen and Bleichrode which the Americans had overrun in the last days of the war, but which were due to be transferred to the Soviet Union under the agreement reached at Yalta to divide Germany into four military zones, administered respectively by the United States, Britain, France and the Soviet Union.

Only a few hours before the Russians were due to take over in Nordhausen and Bleichrode, a train left for the American zone, taking the last scientists and their families to the West. By the time Operation Overcast had been completed, 350 German and Austrian scientists were in the United States.

The British had also launched their own top secret Operation Surgeon, designed to 'cut out the heart' of German aviation expertise before it, too could fall into the hands of the Soviet Union. The centre of German Air Force research at Volkenrode was in the British Zone: some twenty German aviation experts were duly assembled and began work on the most recent aviation developments at the Royal Air Force Research Establishment at Farnborough.

In the New Mexico town of Los Alamos, the American top-secret Target Committee, which had earlier discussed Hiroshima as a possible location for the dropping of the atom bomb, heard on May 14 from the nuclear scientists on the committee that the hills around Hiroshima were 'likely to produce a focusing effect which would considerably increase the blast damage'. This made it an attractive target to consider, There was, however, a drawback. The committee was told that Hiroshima's rivers meant that the city was 'not a good incendiary target'.

On May 24, sixteen days after the end of the war in Europe, the American bomber offensive against the Japanese reached a climax with the despatch of more than four hundred bombers against central Tokyo and the industrial areas south of the city. In all, 3,646 tons of bombs were dropped, and more than a thousand Japanese were killed. Also killed were sixty-two Allied airmen who were being held as prisoners-of-war in the city. It was later alleged that they were locked in a wooden cell block when the raid began, while the other prisoners and their jailers went to a proper air raid shelter.

Planning for an American invasion of the most southern Japanese island, Kyushu, had begun on the day after the Tokyo raid of May 24. The date set for the invasion was November 1. There seemed, however, to be a way to curtail the human destructiveness of an actual landing. On May 31, at a meeting in the Pentagon, the American atomic scientist Robert Oppenheimer spoke of the 'neutron effect' of the explosion of a single atom bomb as 'dangerous to life for a radius of at least two-thirds of a mile'. Those present, including the Secretary for War, Henry Stimson, understood that 'dangerous to life' was euphemism for causing death.

The main discussion on May 31 concerned what the targets might be. It was agreed, Stimson concluded at the end of the discussion, 'that we could not give the Japanese any warning' and that 'we should seek to make a profound psychological impression on as many of the inhabitants as possible'. At the suggestion of the President of Harvard, Dr Conant, Stimson agreed 'that the most desirable target would be a vital war plant employing a large number of workers and closely surrounded by workers' houses'.

Japan, like Germany six months earlier, was facing continual retreat in all the regions which it had conquered. In China, where the fighting was about to enter its eighth year, the Nationalist forces had taken the offensive, forcing the Japanese to withdraw from Nanning on May 26, and thereby cutting the Japanese land link with its forces in Indo-China. In an attempt to harass the Japanese forces inside Indo-China, the United States parachuted a military mission to Ho Chi Minh's Communist headquarters, to coordinate and enhance the Communist resistance. Ho Chi Minh took advantage of the presence of the mission to try to obtain a copy of the American Declaration of Independence, on which he wished to model his own imminent declaration of independence against the French, once the Japanese were driven out of Indochina.

The massive bombing of Tokyo on May 24 had brought home to the Emperor and his government the possibility of the ever-increasing destruction of every Japanese city. But on June 8 the Japanese Cabinet decided 'to prosecute the war to the bitter end'. That decision was carried out with tenacity on every island where the flag of the Rising Sun still flew, and with a bitterness that defied the comprehension of the American soldiers, sailors and airmen as they watched the suicide pilot and suicide air squadrons operating with total disregard to the life of the self-proclaimed heroic attacker, and with constant danger to the ship that was being attacked. Two days after the Japanese decision to continue the fight regardless of loss, Australian troops landed on Labuan Island, the first stage in driving the Japanese from North Borneo. They too were met by a tenacious Japanese defence.

The American soldiers in the Pacific, who knew nothing of the atom bomb, were contemplating the fight to land on the Japanese Home Islands, and to conquer them, an enterprise that would be of a far greater order of magnitude than the Normandy landings a year earlier. An American officer, Henry Miller, who was then in the Philippines, later wrote: 'It was in late

June or July, while working on the plans for invading Japan that I was shocked to read an estimate by our medical staff that we could expect 900,000 American and three million Japanese casualties! I recall trying to frame in my mind a concept of 900,000 killed or wounded US soldiers – like ten times the capacity of the huge Los Angeles Coliseum. It was awful to contemplate.'

The Emperor Hirohito also understood the nature of the struggle that was about to begin, and the effect it would have on Japan. On June 20 he summoned his senior Cabinet ministers and military chiefs to the Imperial Palace in Tokyo and asked them to embark on all possible diplomatic means to end the war. The Japanese Foreign Minister, Shigenori Togo, sent a top secret signal to the Japanese ambassador in Moscow to approach the Soviets and to ask them (they were still neutral with regard to Japan) to act as intermediaries with the Americans.

This top secret signal was read by both British and American Intelligence. While it was clear that Japan wanted to negotiate peace with the United States, it was also clear from the message that she would not accept unconditional surrender, only a negotiated peace and no Allied occupation of the Japanese Home Islands. This meant that the Allies would neither be able to dictate the terms of peace nor to occupy Japan. The Japanese initiative, known only in utmost secrecy to a tiny handful of senior military and political figures in London and Washington, was dismissed, and the plans both to invade Japan by land, and to drop an atom bomb, continued.

On June 21, the day after Hirohito's initiative in seeking peace, the battle for Okinawa was reaching its end. That day American forces reached the Japanese command cave. During the night the two senior Japanese officers in the cave, General Ushijima and General Sho, dressed in full ceremonial uniform with their medals and ceremonial swords, were served a special feast, and then, kneeling on a clean sheet with their faces towards Hirohito's palace in Tokyo, killed themselves using a specially sharpened sabre.

On the battlefield of Okinawa, 107,500 Japanese soldiers were killed in just under four weeks' fighting: their bodies were counted on the battlefield. A further 20,000 Japanese are believed to have died in the caves into which they fled: caves into which American assault teams advanced using flame-throwers and explosives. Many local Okinawans were also killed in the fighting: the lowest estimate is 80,000. The American losses were lower, but formidable: 7,613 Americans were killed on land and a further 4,907 were killed at sea as a result of air, and mostly kamikaze, attacks. In the air, 7,800 Japanese war planes had been shot down over Okinawa, for the cost of 763 American aircraft.

A small island had changed hands in battle, and more than 200,000 human beings were dead. Every day saw more loss of life on the battlefields of the Pacific and the Far East, and after the battle. In North Borneo, when an Allied landing was imminent, the Japanese ordered 2,000 Australian prisoners-of-war to march from the prison camp in which they were being held at Sandakan to another camp at Ranau, 165 miles inland. They were sent in groups of fifty, in three separate marches, under heavy guard. Many were suffering from malnutrition, malaria and beri-beri. Those who collapsed on the march were shot or beheaded where they fell. Six managed to escape. There were no other survivors.

Bill Moxham, one of the six escapees, later recalled: 'Once you stopped, you stopped for good. The Japs had no time for the sick.' Captain Takuo Takakuwa, who was in charge of one the three marches, told a war crimes tribunal:

> The orders I issued were that as the enemy would be landing and advancing quickly those PoWs who could not go on any more and were likely to die would hamper the Japanese army and could be put out of their misery by being shot.
>
> On 1 August 1945 I issued orders that all the PoWs were to be killed.
>
> This order was entirely based on the necessity of war operations. I decided to dispose of them as they were becoming cumbersome.

In San Francisco, on June 26, the United Nations Charter was signed. Even as bloody battles were being fought in the Pacific and the Far East, a blueprint for avoiding future war had been agreed upon by the victorious powers. But the power of the gun and tank was still determining territorial change. Three days after the Charter was signed the new Czechoslovak government signed a treaty with the Soviet Union, ceding its eastern province of Ruthenia. The citizens of Ruthenia, having been annexed by Hungary during the war, became Soviet citizens, subjected overnight to the harsh panoply of Soviet Communism.

Inside the Soviet Union yet another wave of purges had begun, in which even army officers who were believed to be out of sympathy with the full rigours of Communism were arrested. Among those brought to trial was the artillery officer, Captain Alexander Solzhenitsyn, who had been under arrest for the previous six months. He was sentenced on July 5 to eight years hard labour.

On American Independence day, July 4, General MacArthur announced the liberation of the Philippines. There were still a few isolated but determined pockets of Japanese resistance, but, starting on July 11, these were attacked from the air using a new weapon, the napalm bomb, the petroleum component of which burned with a tenacious and terrifying fierceness on buildings and human beings. Ten days later, on July 14, as the napalm bomb attacks were reaching their destructive and effective climax, there began the first bombardments of the Japanese coast by United States warships, as a prelude to the November 1 landings: that first day's targets included the Imperial Ironworks at Kamaishi. Also on July 14 the first transfer began of United States troops from the European to the Asian war zone. They too were to be trained and made ready for the amphibious landings of November 1.

In preparing to repel the November landings – though the Japanese did not know their exact date – several new suicide weapons were being designed in Japan. As well as many thousands of men being trained as suicide pilots, training was also under way for torpedo suicide missions: a torpedo on which a man would be strapped and which he would then guide on to its target. A third suicide weapon was also being developed, specifically to stop the coastal landings as the invading troops approached the shore in their troop transports and landing craft. This was the suicide mine. A 'crouching dragon' – a Japanese soldier – would be attached to a mine and would fix it to the hull of the ship, then detonate it.

Experiments were being made with a fourth suicide device: sunken concrete shelters in which six-man squads of crouching dragons would be waiting offshore, just beneath the water, waiting to detonate themselves as the invasion barges passed over them and the invading troops prepared to wade ashore.

These plans were about to become otiose. On July 16 the first atom bomb test was carried out near Alamogordo, in the desert of New Mexico. So intense was the heat of the explosion that the 100-foot steel tower on which the bomb had been placed was transformed into gas which then dispersed. Hard steel had literally vanished into thin air. The sand under the blast was turned into a green glass. Within a mile radius of the explosion, all plant and animal life was killed.

Secretary of War Stimson, who was attending the Allied conference which had just begun at Potsdam, received a coded message: 'Operated on this morning. Diagnosis not yet complete, but results seem satisfactory and already exceed expectations.' At lunch that day he handed Churchill a note which read: 'Babies satisfactorily born.' When Churchill expressed himself mystified by the message, Stimson told him outright: 'The atomic bomb is a reality.' Churchill went at once to see Truman. Three years later he recalled the impact that the news had on them both:

> Up to this moment we had shaped our ideas towards an assault upon the homeland of Japan by terrific air bombing and by the invasion of very large armies. We had contemplated the desperate resistance of the Japanese fighting to the death with Samurai devotion, not only in pitched battles but in every cave and dug-out. I had in my mind the spectacle of Okinawa Island, where many thousands of Japanese, rather than surrender, had drawn up in lines and destroyed themselves by handgrenades after their leaders had solemnly performed the rite of hara-kiri.
>
> To quell the Japanese resistance man by man and conquer the country yard by yard might well require the loss of a million American lives and half that number of British – or more if we could get them there: for we were resolved to share the agony.
>
> Now all this nightmare picture had vanished. In its place was the vision – fair and bright indeed it seemed – of the end of the whole war in one or two violent shocks. I thought immediately myself of how the Japanese people, whose courage I had always admired, might find in the apparition of this almost supernatural weapon an excuse which would save their honour and release them from their obligation of being killed to the last fighting man.

Japanese troops were retreating throughout the South-East Asian and Pacific war zones. They were not being allowed to retreat without a heavy cost. In Burma, where more than 100,000 Japanese troops had been killed in combat, and thousands of others had died of jungle diseases, those who were trying to reach Moulmein were attacked by British bombers making more than three thousand sorties against them. In nine days of continuous bombardment from the air, at least ten thousand Japanese were killed. There had been no similar unequal contest between men in retreat and air power since General Allenby ordered the destruction of the German and Turkish forces fleeing down the Wadi Fara to the Jordan Valley in the last months of 1918.

Behind the lines in Burma, the Burmese nationalist leader General U Aung San offered his services and those of his armed followers to the British, to fight against the Japanese. Eager to see an end to British imperial rule, Aung San had earlier cooperated with the Japanese against the British. But the harsh nature of Japanese occupation had disillusioned him with his would-be anti-British protectors. One of his followers told the British commander-in-chief in Burma: 'If the British sucked our blood, the Japanese ground our bones.'

Helped by British military advisers, Aung San succeeded in driving the Japanese from Loilem in the Shan mountains. His troops found the fullest support from the Burmese villagers, whose lives were often made unbearable by the Japanese. In July a raid by the Japanese on Kalagon village, north of Moulmein, failed to find any guerrillas. Instead, the Japanese military police rounded up the villagers and machine-gunned them: 637 were killed. Four men and a fifteen-year-old girl survived, crawling out at night from under the dead and dying.

Half way through the Potsdam Conference, Churchill returned to Britain to learn the results of the General Election which had been called after the defeat of Germany. The Conservative Party had been defeated and he, its leader, was no longer Prime Minister. The leader of the Labour Party, Clement Attlee – Churchill's wartime Deputy Prime Minister – was the new Prime Minister of Britain. It was Attlee who returned to Potsdam, and on whom the burden of the final decisions fell.

Under the Potsdam Agreement, both Germany and Austria were divided into Soviet, American, British and French zones of occupation. Berlin and Vienna were placed under joint Four-Power control. Poland lost the eastern third of its pre-war territory – including the predominantly Polish cities of Vilna and Lvov – to the Soviet Union. In return it gained a substantial swathe of territory taken from the eastern areas of Germany: the whole industrial region of Silesia, the whole coastal region of Pomerania, and the southern half of East Prussia. The Soviet Union acquired the northern part of East Prussia, including its main city, Königsberg (which was renamed Kaliningrad, after the Soviet President).

The Potsdam conference specifically agreed to 'the removal of Germans from Poland, Czechoslovakia and Hungary'. These Germans were already on the move, a vast array of refugees. As a result of the Soviet annexation of eastern Poland, millions of Poles were also going westward, into those parts of Germany which had been transferred to Poland. German cities became Polish cities. As well as being repopulated, they were renamed. Stettin became Szczecin; Breslau became Wroclaw. Rastenburg, Hitler's former wartime headquarters, became Ketrzyn.

The decisions reached at Potsdam were agreed upon without any German representatives being present or consulted. Unlike the Versailles Treaty of 1919, the Germans were not even asked to append their signatures.

The war against Japan was also discussed at Potsdam. Stalin confirmed the commitment he had made earlier, at Yalta, to enter the war against Japan within two to three months of the end of the war in Europe. At the same time, Britain and the United States, together with the Chinese representative at Potsdam, agreed on a message to Japan – the Potsdam Declaration – warning of 'the inevitable and complete destruction of the Japanese forces, and just as inevitably the utter devastation of the Japanese homeland'. They then set out what they called 'an opportunity to end the war'.

The Allied conditions included the complete disarmament of all Japanese forces, the limitation of Japanese sovereignty to the four main islands of Japan and 'such minor islands as we determine', the establishment not only of freedom of speech, religion and thought but also 'respect for fundamental human rights'. In return, Japan would be allowed 'such industries as will sustain her economy'. She would also be permitted 'eventual participation in world trade relations'.

'We shall brook no delay': with these five words the Allies put the Japanese on notice that they could expect the conflict to intensify. The offer ended: 'We call upon the Government of Japan to proclaim now the unconditional surrender of all the Japanese armed forces, and to provide proper and adequate assurances of their good faith in such action. The alternative for Japan is complete and utter destruction.'

Preparations to drop the atom bomb on Japan continued, with much discussion as to what the target should be. On July 24, the day on which the warning message was agreed at Potsdam – it was only made public two days later – Truman confided in his diary that 'the weapon is to be used against Japan between now and August 10'. He added that he had instructed Stimson 'to use it so that military objectives and soldiers and sailors are the target and not women and children. Even if the Japs are savages, ruthless, merciless and fanatic, we as the leader of the world for the common welfare cannot drop this terrible bomb on the old capital or the new.' The target would be 'a purely military one', Truman added, 'and we will issue a warning statement asking the Japs to surrender and save lives'.

Neither the old Japanese capital, Kyoto, nor the new one, Tokyo, was chosen as the first target, but the city of Hiroshima, which contained many more women and children than soldiers and sailors. On the day that the Potsdam Declaration on Japan was made public the American cruiser *Indianapolis* arrived at Tinian Island carrying the atom bomb, ready to be transferred to an aircraft. On the following day, July 26, the Japanese Prime Minister, Admiral Kantaro Suzuki, rejected the Potsdam Declaration. It was the decision of his government, he said, 'to ignore it entirely and fight resolutely for the successful conclusion of the war'.

The *Indianapolis*, having landed its atom bomb on Tinian, set sail for a new assignment. She was torpedoed, and blew up before she could send out a distress signal. More than 350 of her crew of 1,169 were killed in the explosion. A further 484 died in the water as they struggled to keep afloat on the wreckage of the ship, were eaten by sharks, or succumbed to heat and thirst. The American naval command had no idea that the *Indianapolis* had been hit. When rescue eventually came only 318 sailors were still alive.

In all, 834 of the crew of the *Indianapolis* had died. It was the worst disaster at sea in the history of the United States navy. The commander of the Japanese submarine that had secured this triumph later recalled how, a day later: 'We celebrated our haul of the previous day with our favourite rice with beans, boiled eels, and corned beef (all of it tinned).'

As Western eyes focused on the battle against Japan, there was an echo of the war in Europe on July 27 – almost three months after that war had ended – when a memorial service was held in London for Dietrich Bonhoeffer, one of Hitler's German and Christian victims. Bonhoeffer's friend and biographer, Eberhard Bethge, commented: 'The announcement of this public remembrance of a German and the broadcast by the BBC of the function was an unusual event in those months. For the reports of the appalling discoveries in the Bergen-Belsen concentration camp had reached the British public only after the cessation of hostilities and made it very difficult not to make a sweeping judgement concerning the conquered country.'

Among those who spoke at Bonhoeffer's memorial service was Bishop Bell, earlier an outspoken opponent of the Allied bombing of German cities.

Bonhoeffer's death, he said, 'is a death for Germany – and indeed for Europe too'. In Berlin, however, Bonhoeffer's church protested, in a pastoral instruction, against the conspiracy of July 1944 of which Bonhoeffer had been a part, and in the town of Bielefeld the pastors objected to the municipal authorities naming a street after Bonhoeffer 'because', they explained, 'we don't want the names of our colleagues, who were killed for their faith, lumped together with a political martyr'.

On August 4, at the naval base in Singapore, the Japanese executed seven captured American airmen. A Japanese cook at the base, Oka Harumitzu, later gave evidence against the five perpetrators at a British Military Court, telling the tribunal:

> ... about two o'clock that afternoon when the five petty officers had returned I heard them discussing the morning's events. 'It was difficult to cut today,' one of them said.
>
> 'In Hikiji's demonstration the neck was cut perfectly,' said another, and a third remarked that one of the airmen ran off so he had to go after him to cut his head off.
>
> It appeared that about twenty-five of them had taken part in the execution, and that after the instructor in swordsmanship had given a demonstration the others were allowed to try their hand at it.

The senior naval officer charged with executing the captured American airmen was Lieutenant-Commander Okamoto. He made a statement under oath, which was read out to the court, explaining his action:

The general factors influencing the decision to kill them were:
(1) We could not send them back to Japan.
(2) We could not guard them indefinitely, and
(3) Although the general policy was to send POWs back to Japan or hand them over to the Army authorities, the orders of Fleet HQ had to be carried out.

As far as I know Admiral Imamura never objected to these orders for the execution of any of the prisoners-of-war, neither did Captain Matsuda, nor Captain Saito, nor myself. I thought at the time that the affair was a bad thing and as a private individual thought these things were pitiful; but I could do nothing against orders from Fleet HQ.

I was not anxious to have the men disposed of. I was interested in the matter only because Lieutenant Kobayahi was unable to guard the men because of his operational duties.

On August 4, the day of the Singapore executions, the Japanese army in Manchuria came to the conclusion that no Soviet participation in the war was possible before September. In Japan, several thousand suicide pilots, 'human torpedoes' and 'human mines' were under training. If the American invasion were to come in November, they would be met with a determined resistance.

In Washington, discussions took place during August 5 at the Pentagon as to whether the war against Japan – that is, the existing conventional war – would be more easily brought to an end by blockading the Japanese Home Islands or invading them. The blockade plan would, it was felt, take too long to bring to success – at least a year and possibly more – during which many millions of Japanese would die of starvation. As the meeting drew to a close it was clear that invasion was the option preferred.

The United States had sixteen million fighting men in uniform, Japan only six million. The Americans had suffered 291,557 deaths in action, the Japanese more than 1,270,000. The Japanese had also lost 241,309 civilians killed in conventional American air raids. No American civilians had been killed by bombing in the continental United States, and less than a thousand on the Pacific Islands. The balance of demography and death was in favour of the United States. The date of November 1 for the first landings was confirmed. The meeting had set the seal on what would be the largest amphibious landings ever undertaken.

Eight divisions had landed in Normandy; fourteen would land on Kyushu. Four months later, twenty-five divisions would land on Honshu. Even the names of the landing beaches had been chosen, not individual American States as at Normandy (Utah, Omaha) but the leading Hollywood 'sweater girls' – the pin-ups of millions of soldiers – Grable, Sheridan, Hayworth, Sims and Lamour.

That night, the night of August 5/6, as the planners of the amphibious invasion slept, a total of seven separate groups of American bombers set off from Tinian Island northward across the Pacific Ocean to their different targets. Six of the targets were conventional ones, typical of the almost nightly air offensive being launched against Japan – industries on mainland Japan and shipping targets in the Inland Sea. Several thousand bombs would be dropped on these during the course of the morning. The seventh target was Hiroshima, above which a single bomb would be detonated.

Flying from Tinian, the specially-adapted B-29 bomber *Enola Gay* dropped its single atom bomb in the early hours of August 6. Among the messages scrawled on the casing of the bomb was one which read: 'Greetings to the Emperor from the men of the *Indianapolis*.' The bomb was detonated 1,885 feet above the ground. As the crew of the *Enola Gay* looked back and saw the blinding flash of the explosion they heard their commander's remark: 'My God, look at that son-of-a-bitch go!' A caption to the photograph of the mushroom cloud – a photograph reproduced around the world – read: 'Atomic fungus seen over Hiroshima after explosion.'

The word fungus held a sinister reality. No single man-made blast had ever killed so many people. Within two weeks of the atom bomb explosion the death toll at Hiroshima reached 92,233. Many more died in the years that followed from the effects of radiation. By 1986 the cenotaph in Hiroshima listed 138,890 victims. Of the city's ninety thousand buildings, sixty-two thousand were completely destroyed. Of the two hundred doctors in the city when the bomb was dropped, a hundred and eighty were killed or were too badly injured to attend to the other sufferers. Seven American airmen who had been shot down over the city eight days earlier, and were being held as prisoners-of-war – fearful for their lives at the hands of their captors – were also killed.

One of the first Japanese pilots to fly into Hiroshima after the atom bomb exploded was Captain Mitsuo Fuchida, who had led the attack on Pearl Harbor almost four years earlier. He was depressed and exhausted by the terrifying scenes and – write the historians Gordon Thomas and Max Morgan-Witts – 'continued to wander aimlessly through the wasteland which three years, seven months and twenty-nine days later was a grim reminder that surprise in war can be a two-edged sword.'

On August 8, two days after the Americans dropped the atom bomb on Hiroshima, the Soviet Union declared war on Japan. Two million Soviet soldiers crossed rapidly into Manchuria. They were faced by 700,000 Japanese troops, and drove them southward in a series of ferocious encounters.

President Truman had agreed that if the Japanese did not accept unconditional surrender by August 11, a second atom bomb would be dropped that day. But the weather forecast for August 11 was bad – from the perspective of bomber attacks over Japan – and the date for the second bomb was brought forward two days, to August 9. This gave the Japanese three days rather than five in which to surrender. But they were not told either about the second bomb or the change in date.

In the early hours of August 9, as the usual heavy bomber missions again took off from Tinian Island, a second specially-adapted B-29 bomber, *Bock's car*, took off from Tinian with its single atom bomb. Its objective was the city of Kokura. But when the pilot reached his target it was covered in industrial haze. His orders were only to bomb a visual target. He therefore flew on to the city of Nagasaki, ninety miles to the south-west, and dropped his bomb there. Forty thousand people were killed within a few minutes. Five thousand more were to die in the next three months. Thirty years later the final death toll was calculated at 48,857. Thousands of buildings were completely destroyed, and tens of thousands severely damaged, among them the Urakami Catholic Cathedral, the Chinzei Christian Mission School, and the oldest Christian place of worship in Japan.

At the very moment of this second atom bomb explosion the Japanese Supreme War Direction Council, meeting in Tokyo, was discussing the Potsdam Declaration call for unconditional surrender. The Prime Minister, Baron Suzuki, and the Foreign Minister, Shigenori Togo, both argued in favour of surrender. The Minister of War, General Korechika Anami, argued against, telling the Council: 'It is far too early to say that the war is lost. That we will inflict severe losses on the enemy when he invades Japan is certain, and it is by no means impossible that we may be able to reverse the situation in our favour, pulling victory out of defeat.'

The Council was divided, three for surrender and three for fighting on. That evening, as news of the catastrophic destruction of the second atom bomb reached Tokyo, Suzuki and Togo persuaded Hirohito to call a further meeting of the Council, and to preside over it himself. He agreed to do so. The meeting was held shortly after midnight in the Emperor's bomb shelter. Hirohito spoke of how he was doubtful that Japan could continue to wage effective war, or to defend 'its own shores' in the event of invasion. He therefore authorized the Prime Minister to accept unconditional surrender. In the early hours of August 10 a telegram was sent to the Japanese ambassadors in Switzerland and Sweden: 'The Japanese Government are ready to accept the terms enumerated in the Joint Declaration which was issued at Potsdam on 26 July . . .'.

The Second World War might have ended at that moment. But the second part of the Japanese government's telegram of surrender stated that it was made 'on the understanding that the said Declaration does not comprise any demand which prejudices the prerogatives of His Majesty as sovereign ruler.' While the Soviet army drove the Japanese back deeper into Manchuria, diplomatic exchanges were taking place between Japan and the United States about whether the Emperor could keep his sovereign prerogatives.

On August 10 the future of one area of the Japanese Empire – Korea – was being discussed in Washington by the State Department, War Department and Navy Department's Coordinating Committee. One of the members of the committee was Dean Rusk, a future Secretary of State. Late that night the committee came to the conclusion that, with the surrender of Japan imminent, the United States should be a party to the occupation of Korea. The 38th Parallel seemed as good a divide as any: if the Soviet Union occupied the country north of the parallel and the United States took the southern half, then the capital, Seoul, would be within the American zone.

No American troops were near enough to Korea in the immediate future to land there and take up their occupation duties in the south. But when the partition plan was put to Stalin he accepted it. Had he refused, and insisted on occupying the whole of Korea, there was nothing that the United States could – or would – have done that could have prevented the whole of Korea from coming within the Soviet Communist sphere. The American decision of August 10 to take up occupation duties in southern Korea ensured, inadvertently, that a new conflict, and a new war, would take place within five years on the eastern rim of Asia.

On August 12, the third day of the Japanese-American surrender negotiations being conducted through intermediaries in Switzerland, Japanese infantrymen in Manchuria were being employed as suicide squads against Soviet tanks. But Soviet tank power was overwhelming. When a thousand Japanese infantrymen were brought up by train as reinforcements, Soviet tanks opened fire on them, killing nine hundred.

American bombers were also still in action against Japan. On the morning of August 14 there was an 800-bomber raid against military installations on Honshu. The United States had, meanwhile, agreed that, in the event of a Japanese surrender, the Emperor could remain sovereign and continue to rule Japan, albeit under a Supreme Commander appointed by the Allied powers. Once this American concession had been made, the Japanese Government and the Emperor agreed to surrender.

An announcement was made over Japanese radio that imperial acceptance of the Potsdam Declaration would be broadcast that night, August 14. During the afternoon a thousand Japanese soldiers attacked the Imperial Palace, hoping to find the surrender proclamation there and to destroy it, so that the war could continue. The soldiers killed the commander of the Imperial Guards Division, but were then attacked and driven away by troops loyal to the Emperor. Hirohito had in fact already recorded the surrender message. It was to be broadcast at midnight. Shortly before the broadcast, General Anami, who still wanted Japan to fight on, committed suicide.

At midnight on August 14 a Japanese radio announcer asked all listeners to stand respectfully in front of their radio sets. They then heard, for the first time in Japanese history, the broadcast voice of their Emperor. The enemy, he said, 'has begun to employ a new and most cruel bomb'. Its power to do damage was 'indeed incalculable, taking the toll of many innocent lives'. That, he explained, was why he had accepted the Potsdam Declaration.

As Hirohito's thin, reedy voice came to an end of its dramatic announcement, the Second World War was over. As had happened three and a half months earlier, there were victory parades in every Allied city. In Chicago the banner of the marchers was succinct: 'Japs licked.' A series of grim realities – far worse than most nightmares – was at an end.

Historians, novelists, dramatists, film makers, painters, composers and poets are among those who, since 1945, have sought in their work to convey the episodes and even the essence of the Second World War. Fighting and destruction, courage and hardship, on such a scale defies easy portrayal. The range of combat zones is too large, the nature of the fighting too diffuse, the perils on land, sea and air too varied, the burdens of occupation and belligerency are too crippling, and the desperation of human suffering and loss are too intense, for easy summation.

The torments of the Second World War destroyed millions of lives, and scarred many millions more, with physical and mental scars that they were never to lose, and which were in many instances transmitted to the next generation. Many of the children of those who survived the German concentration camps or the Japanese prisoner-of-war camps, and other incarcerations, carry some of the burdens that their parents carried: uncertainty, guilt, fear, nightmares, unfulfilled hopes; characterized by the breach of trust in their fellow human beings.

When the Second World War came to an end, scarcely twenty years had passed since 'the war to end all wars' had also ended; since the memorials of the First World War had begun to be unveiled. Some of those memorials were still being unveiled in the middle and late 1930s. A few were not yet completed when the Second World War began. The solemn ceremonial unveilings of the monuments to the Unknown Soldier of the First World War were not yet completed when the Second World War broke out.

Monuments had been erected after 1918 in all the belligerent capitals: in London and Paris, in Berlin and Vienna, in Washington and Ottawa, in Belgrade and Rome, in Canberra and Auckland. It was the Unknown Soldier who had served since 1918 as the representative of those millions of men whose pulverized bodies were never identified on the battlefield, and whose sacrifice was thought – for almost two decades – to have made all such future sacrifice unnecessary. In 1941, in the midst of the Second World War, a New Zealand-born poet, Douglas Stewart, who had lived in Australia since 1938, wrote in one of his *Sonnets to the Unknown Soldier*:

> We did not bury him deep enough: break up the monument,
> Open the tomb, strip off the flags and the flowers
> And let us look at him plainly, naked Man.
> Greet him with silence since all the speeches were lies,
> Clothe him in fresh khaki, hand him a rifle
> And turn him loose to wander the city streets
> Where eyes so quickly inured to death's accoutrement
> Will hardly spare him a glance, equipped to die for us.
>
> You see that fellow with the grin, one eye on the girls,
> The other on the pub, his uniform shabby already?
> Well, don't let him hear us, but he's the Unknown Soldier,
> They just let him out, they say he lives for ever.
> They put him away with flowers and flags and forgot him,
> But he always comes when they want him. He does the fighting.

Unknown Soldiers and unknown places: most of the places where the battles had been fought between 1939 and 1945 were tiny villages, featureless ridges, nondescript valleys; their names are often hard to find even on the most detailed map. For no more than a day or two – a week at most – these places made an impact on people thousands of miles away; but they were to cast a shadow, sometimes of fear and sometimes of inspiration, across the next half century and beyond. The inhabitants of so many of the places that were fought over also suffered; those who survived the fighting could not forget the ravages of war.

Throughout Europe and Asia, in North Africa and North America, wherever those who survived chose to put up a sign in remembrance, the war memorials and memorial plaques listing the military and civilian dead have the power to make sane people doubt the sanity of the world.

PART THREE

CHAPTER EIGHTEEN

1945
AUGUST TO DECEMBER

More than an end to war, we want an end to the
beginnings of all wars – yes, an end to this brutal,
inhuman and thoroughly impracticable method of
settling the differences between governments.

FRANKLIN D. ROOSEVELT
(draft speech, written shortly before his death)

THE EMPEROR HIROHITO had spoken and the war was over. A spate of
suicides followed. Hardly had Hirohito finished his broadcast than Vice
Admiral Takijiro Onishi, the 'father' of the kamikaze pilots – 3,000 of whom
had killed themselves in action – killed himself. He used his sword to make
the traditional crosswise incision into his stomach. It was not immediately
successful, and as he refused to allow his aide, Yoshio Kodama, to carry out
the equally traditional final blow, it took him twelve hours to die. In a final
dictated message, the admiral apologized 'to the spirits of these dead flyers
and their bereaved families'. His final exhortation: 'Do not forget your rightful pride in being Japanese.'

The funeral casket containing Admiral Onishi's body 'was made by soldiers', Yoshio Kodama recalled, 'but because of a shortage of planks, the
casket was five inches too small for the admiral. The naval authorities, who
had lost all their dignity and presence of mind as a result of the defeat, did
not have the sincerity to provide a casket for one of their own comrades who
had committed suicide out of a realization of his responsibilities. Neither
did they have the magnanimity to provide him with a funeral hearse'.

Despite Hirohito's broadcast ending hostilities, fighting continued in

Manchuria. The Soviet Union, which had entered the war against Japan seven days earlier, was not going to be cheated of its prize. For another week the Soviet and Japanese armies were in violent combat. When that struggle ended on August 20 more than 40,000 Japanese and 8,219 Soviet soldiers had been killed. Once again, to avoid the disgrace of capture, and despite the Emperor's proclamation that the war was over, hundreds of Japanese soldiers blew themselves up with grenades. On August 23 the Russians occupied Port Arthur, which they had lost to the Japanese in the last Russo-Japanese war in 1905. It had taken forty years to reverse the shame of that defeat. What the Tsar had lost, Stalin had secured. He had also regained Southern Sakhalin, which the Tsar had lost to Japan in 1905, and acquired the Kurile Islands from Japan.

The ending of the war in Manchuria brought with it, as had the ending of the war in Europe, innumerable acts of retribution. Most were never recorded or recalled. Jung Chang's mother was a witness to such acts in Chinchow immediately after Hirohito had broadcast the surrender and P'u Yi had abdicated as the ruler of Manchukuo:

> People crowded in the streets in a state of high excitement. My mother went to her school to see what was happening there. The place seemed dead, except for a faint noise coming from one of the offices. She crept up to have a look: through the window she could see the Japanese teachers huddled together weeping.
>
> She hardly slept a wink that night and was up at the crack of dawn. When she opened the front door in the morning she saw a small crowd in the street. The bodies of a Japanese woman and two children were lying in the road. A Japanese officer had committed *hara-kiri*; his family had been lynched.

'All over' Chinchow, Jung Chang relates, 'Japanese were committing suicide or being lynched.' Japanese houses were looted 'and my mother noticed that one of her poor neighbours suddenly had quite a lot of valuable items for sale. Schoolchildren revenged themselves on their Japanese teachers and beat them up ferociously. Some Japanese left their babies on the doorsteps of local families in the hope that they would be saved. A number of Japanese women were raped; many shaved their heads to try to pass as men'.

In Chinchow the 'looting, raping and killing' of the Japanese continued for eight days, until the arrival of Soviet troops. But it was not long before the liberators themselves dismantled the two local oil refineries and removed them to the Soviet Union as 'reparations'. The Russian soldiers took other confiscatory action as well. 'Russian soldiers would walk into people's homes and simply take anything they fancied – watches and clothes in particular,' writes Jung Chang. Stories about Russians raping local women swept the city 'like wildfire. Many women went into hiding for fear of their "liberators". Very soon the city was seething with anger and anxiety'.

On the day after Japan's surrender, from his base in Yenan, Mao Tse-tung had ordered his troops to advance 'on all fronts' and to disarm all Japanese troops they encountered. He was determined not only to establish a Chinese Communist presence in Manchuria, but to extend Communist authority as widely as possible beyond the areas of China already under Communist control. So successful was he in overrunning large areas of northern China that the Nationalist troops could only be moved by air between the cities they controlled. At the end of August, Mao Tse-tung went to Chungking to negotiate with the Nationalists. But although some form of negotiations continued for a year and a half, it soon became clear that there would be no outcome, no solution, and no prospect but that of civil war.

Shortly before his death in April 1945, President Roosevelt had drafted a speech that he would have made on the day after he died. It included the sentence: 'More than an end to war, we want an end to the beginnings of all wars – yes, an end to this brutal, inhuman and thoroughly impracticable method of settling the differences between governments.'

How far the postwar years would see that vision fulfilled was not clear. In the immediate aftermath of Hirohito's radio broadcast to the people of Japan, Allied prisoner-of-war camps had to be found and liberated. In many of them were former captives who died before medical help could reach them, or were already – as so many of the German concentration camp victims had been at the moment of liberation – beyond the healing resources of medical help.

The first of the Allied soldiers of what would have been the invasion army set foot on Japanese soil on August 28: he was Colonel Charles Tench, the first of a small task force of 150 men sent by General MacArthur to set up the authority of the victorious powers. The Colonel landed at an airfield near Yokohama. 'No hostile action encountered,' was his welcome signal to MacArthur. On the following day an American airborne division landed at Yokosuka naval base. The American occupation of Japan had begun.

The formal signatures of surrender had also to be obtained. At a ceremony held on board the American battleship *Missouri* in Tokyo Bay on September 2, General MacArthur supervised the signing. Standing behind him as he put his own name to the instrument of surrender were two Allied generals who had been captured early in the war: the British General, Arthur Percival, who had been held captive since the fall of Singapore in February 1942, and the American General, Jonathan M. Wainwright, who had been a prisoner of the Japanese since the fall of Bataan three months later. The Japanese signatories were the newly appointed Foreign Minister, Mamoru Shigemitsu, and the Chief of Staff of the Japanese Army, General Yoshijiro Umezu.

Two days later, on September 4, the Japanese soldiers on Wake Island accepted the surrender and laid down their arms. For two years they had been far behind the advancing American front line in the Pacific, left to their own devices rather than engaged in what would have been a costly battle for no strategic gain. During those two years, these conquerors of a small American island, almost two thousand miles from home, had been unable to receive food from Japan: 1,300 of them had died of starvation and a further 600 from the occasional American bombing raid.

The Atomic Age had begun. At its outset, given the Hiroshima and Nagasaki bombs, it was predominantly an American age. Forty years later the American historian Bartley F. Smith reflected: 'The transcendent display of determination and power seemed to announce to a battered and war-scarred world that the young giant, America the invincible, had taken the fate of the world and indeed the very atomic stuff of the universe, into its hands.' In quoting this, another American historian, Scott L. Bills, noted that 'much more arresting than the flattening of Japanese cities was the flamboyant imagery of cosmos grasped, thresholds crossed and new eras begun. The Atomic Age became the metaphor of the day. The twin August flashes above Japanese cities proclaimed to all the pervasive prowess of distant, smokestack America'.

New conflicts were emerging without pause on the ashes of the old, into which the Americans were to be drawn, initially as outsiders, eventually as participants and sufferers. On August 16, the day after the Japanese surrender, the Vietnamese Communist leader, Ho Chi Minh, ordered a 'general insurrection' throughout Vietnam. 'Many oppressed peoples the world over are vying with each other in the march to win back their independence,' he wrote in an open letter to the people of Vietnam. 'We cannot allow ourselves to lag behind.' Reflecting on this attitude, and that of millions of Asians in a dozen colonial territories that had been overrun by Japan less than four years earlier, the American journalist Martha Gellhorn summarized in one sentence the thought process of those who were being told to accept the return of their former colonial masters: 'The tall white man had been conquered and debased by short yellow men; why should anyone accept the white man as master again?'

Under the command of General Giap, Vietnamese Communist troops – the Vietminh – moved from the countryside which they had been controlling for the previous six months towards the city of Thai Nguyen. Two days later, Vietminh troops entered Hanoi. The Japanese had gone and the French had not yet returned. On August 19 Giap took full control of the city, as his forces took over large areas of central and southern Vietnam.

The French did not intend to allow the Vietnamese Communists a victory. Three days after Giap's forces had taken control of Hanoi, and Ho Chi Minh, pushing swiftly southward, had declared an interim Vietnamese government in Saigon, British military aircraft parachuted a Free French military team into southern Indo-China. The Communists took what they hoped would be a decisive step, issuing on September 2 the Declaration of Independence of the Democratic Republic of Vietnam.

Basing its first lines on the American Declaration of Independence, which members of the United States' mission had acquired for him that summer, Ho Chi Minh proclaimed:

All men are created equal; they are endowed by their Creator with certain unalienable Rights; among these are Life, Liberty, and the pursuit of Happiness.

This immortal statement was made in the Declaration of Independence of the United States of America in 1776. In a broader sense, this means: All the peoples on the earth are equal from birth, all the peoples have a right to live, to be happy and free.

The Declaration of the French Revolution made in 1791 on the Rights of Man and the Citizen also states: 'All men are born free and with equal rights, and must always remain free and have equal rights.'

Those are undeniable truths.

Nevertheless, for more than eighty years, the French imperialists, abusing the standard of Liberty, Equality, and Fraternity, have violated our Fatherland and oppressed our fellow citizens. They have acted contrary to the ideals of humanity and justice.

In the field of politics, they have deprived our people of every democratic liberty.

On September 8 – six days after Ho Chi Minh issued this Declaration of Independence, and scarcely three weeks after the ending of the war with Japan – French, British and Indian troops were landed in Indo-China to re-install the French colonial administration which the Japanese had ousted four years earlier, and to forestall the Communists. Because the number of Allied forces was limited, the local French and British commanders enlisted the help of more than two thousand Japanese troops who had surrendered to them, and who had so recently been the hated occupying power.

The new task of the Japanese soldiers was to help secure French authority. In response, Ho Chi Minh and the Communist leaders called upon the people to give whatever gold they possessed to national defence. 'Gold Week' was proclaimed in Hanoi on September 17. 'Well-off families' were asked to make a special effort. But before the end of the month the French had overthrown the interim Vietnamese government which had been set up by the Communists in Saigon.

The Communists took a swift and violent revenge, killing more than a hundred Westerners, including the commander of the American forces who had, from behind enemy lines, been helping them in the fight against the Japanese occupation. The allies of one war were thus becoming enemies, and a conflict began which, over the next forty years, was to bring death to hundreds of thousands of people – many of them civilians – and to ravage large areas of Vietnam.

Korea was another area in which the defeat of Japan created new problems and uncertainties for the victorious powers. The Cairo Declaration of 1943, supported by Britain and the United States, had promised that Korea should become independent 'in due course'. With the defeat of Japan and the collapse of the Japanese Empire – of which Korea had been a part since 1905 – the first United States troops to take up their role as the occupying power south of the 38th Parallel did so as the harbingers of liberty. But they found themselves without enthusiasm with regard to the Koreans for whose well-being they had become temporarily responsible. Indeed, the first American reaction was to allow the Japanese soldiers and police to remain in charge of law and order, and to confirm the Japanese colonial officials in their positions of authority. The Americans did not have the manpower, while the Japanese did have the experience.

On September 11 General MacArthur ordered the removal of all Japanese officials in Korea, but H. Merell Benninghoff, the political adviser to the United States Military Government in southern Korea, told Washington four days later: 'The removal of Japanese officials is desirable from the public opinion standpoint, but difficult to bring about for some time. They can be relieved in name but must be made to continue in work. There are no qualified Koreans for other than the low-ranking positions, either in government or in public utilities and communications.'

Washington urged an end to reliance upon the Japanese, and in the course of four months 70,000 Japanese colonial civil servants and 600,000 Japanese soldiers and civilians were sent back to Japan. Many had to leave homes, businesses and the possessions of a lifetime behind them. Many of the Koreans to whom the Americans handed over responsibility were those who had collaborated longest and most eagerly with the Japanese, and were hated by their fellow-Koreans for having done so. The Americans had turned to them because of their experience.

A main American fear was the emergence of a Communist government in Korea. To combat this, the United States supported the emergence as leader in the south of Dr Syngman Rhee, who had been imprisoned by the Japanese in 1899 – at the age of twenty-four – for five years, because of his agitation for Korean self-government. After obtaining his doctorate at Princeton University – the first Korean to receive an American doctorate – he had spent most of the next thirty-five years in the United States, urging American support for Korean independence. He had also made the case for Korea's part in America's global strategy: in 1944 he had told the State Department: 'The only possibility of avoiding the ultimate conflict between the United States and the Soviet Union is to build up all democratic, non-communistic elements wherever possible.'

The American military commander in Korea, General John R. Hodge, not only supported Syngman Rhee's return to Korea, but informed MacArthur that he was taking action against one of the main local political Parties which 'will constitute in effect a "declaration of war" upon the Communistic elements in Korea, and may result in temporary disorders. It will also bring charges of political discrimination in a "free" country, both by local pinkos and by pinko press'. MacArthur replied 'I am not sufficiently familiar with the local situation to advise you intelligently, but I will support whatever decision you may take in this matter.'

Korea south of the 38th Parallel was to become, under Syngman Rhee, a bastion of anti-Communism, both real and imaginary, local and regional. North of the 38th Parallel, the Soviet Union – with its own Korean nominee, Kim Il Sung – was installing and sustaining a Communist regime. Ironically, General Hodge was not enamoured of the task he had set himself, informing MacArthur on December 16: 'Under present conditions with no corrective action forthcoming, I would go so far as to recommend we give serious consideration to an agreement with Russia that both the US and Russia withdraw forces from Korea simultaneously and leave Korea to its own devices and an inevitable internal upheaval for its self-purification.'

Hodge's pessimism was overruled, and with Truman's approval, South Korea was built up as a front line State along the Iron Curtain.

In China, the East-West divide was also being sharpened. For the previous four years a number of small but effective American Special Service teams had been assisting the Nationalists in their struggle against the Japanese. One of these teams, four men in all, headed by Captain John Birch, was ordered to halt by a Chinese Communist patrol. Shots were fired and Birch was killed. In the United States a nationwide society was set up in his name – the John Birch Society – which became a leading opponent of Communism wherever in the world it had come to power, or sought to do so.

Members of the society called Captain Birch, with pride, 'the first casualty in the Third World War between Communists and the ever shrinking Free World'.

Formal Japanese surrenders were still taking place almost a month after the Emperor's broadcast. In Singapore, the instrument of surrender was read out and signed on September 12. One of the senior British commanders present was General Slim, whose armies had carried out the conquest of Burma, and seen at the end of it the terrible conditions in the prisoner-of-war camps. Slim later wrote of how, as he looked at the 'dull, impassive masks that were the faces of the Japanese generals and admirals seated opposite', he was strangely untouched with any sort of sympathy. 'Their plight moved me not at all.'

Recalling his own military service in the First World War, Slim reflected on his attitude to the Japanese officers facing him: 'For them, I had none of the sympathy of soldier for soldier, that I had felt for the Germans, Turks, Italians, or Frenchmen that by the fortune of war I had seen surrender. I knew too well what these men and those under their orders had done to their prisoners. They sat there apart from humanity.'

On September 18, in Tokyo, General MacArthur established the Supreme Command Allied Powers. Nine days later he was visited by a chastened and humbled Emperor Hirohito who, to the surprise of those present who knew what divinity and power he had wielded scarcely a month earlier, said meekly to MacArthur: 'You are very, very welcome, Sir!'

Both in Germany and Japan, the Allies were preparing to conduct war crimes trials. An International Military Tribunal was set up, with two centres, one in Nuremberg and the other in Tokyo. A large-scale search was ordered for witnesses to the crimes committed against soldiers and civilians, and for the perpetrators to be found and held until they could be put on trial. Many escaped formal accusation by killing themselves, as Himmler had done immediately after his arrest in May. On October 6 Dr Leonardo Conti, one of the German medical doctors who had carried out experiments on concentration camp inmates, killed himself in his prison cell at Nuremberg.

Robert Ley, the head of the German Labour Front – who in May 1942, during a speech at Karlsruhe, had declared: 'It is not enough to isolate the Jewish enemy of mankind, the Jews have got to be exterminated' – had, while awaiting trial, protested to G.M. Gilbert, the Nuremberg prison psychologist: 'How can I prepare a defence? Am I supposed to defend myself against all these crimes which I knew nothing about? Stand us up against the wall and shoot us – you are the victors.' A few days later, Ley committed suicide in his cell. In his suicide note he wrote that he was unable any longer to bear the shame.

The former French Prime Minister, Pierre Laval, tried to kill himself after he had been found guilty of treason by a court in Paris. His suicide bid having failed, he was executed by a French firing squad on October 15. Nine days later Vidkun Quisling, who had been found guilty by a court in Oslo of 'criminal collaboration' with the Germans, was executed by a Norwegian firing squad.

As the Allies made their preparations to bring so-called 'major' war criminals to trial, a meeting of German churchmen and intellectuals met in Stuttgart and discussed Germany's – and their own – responsibility for the atrocities which had scarred Europe, affecting German and foreigner, Christian and Jew, soldier and civilian, adult and child. On October 19 the meeting ended with the publication of the Stuttgart Declaration of Guilt. Among the signatories was Martin Niemöller, who had been a prisoner of Hitler and the Nazis from 1937 to 1945.

Following the Stuttgart Declaration of Guilt, Niemöller began a life of indefatigable travels, including journeys throughout the length and breadth of the United States, describing in his lectures the failure of morality in the war years by those who had been the bystanders of evil. He would end most of his lectures — one of which this writer heard in South Carolina twenty years after the war — with the statement:

First they came for the socialists, and I did not speak out —
   because I was not a socialist.
Then they came for the trade unionists, but I did not speak out —
   because I was not a trade unionist.
Then they came for the Jews, and I did not speak out —
   because I was not a Jew.
Then they came for me —
   and there was no one left to speak out for me.

Those who had committed their wartime crimes in one particular country were to be tried and punished in that country. Those who were thought to have committed criminal acts spanning the whole of Europe, or to have precipitated the coming of war to Europe, were to be tried collectively by all four principal Allies.

Four indictments had been prepared to be used against the German leaders when they were brought to trial at Nuremberg. These were wide-ranging in scope but succinctly expressed:

1. A common plan or conspiracy to seize power and establish a totalitarian regime to prepare and wage a war of aggression.
2. Waging a war of aggression.
3. Violation of the rules of war.
4. Crimes against humanity, persecution and extermination.

The Allies moved quickly to bring these charges and to start the trials. Twenty-two Nazi leaders were indicted on October 20 — the day after the Stuttgart Declaration of Guilt. Nuremberg was chosen as the location of the trials because there was no courthouse or set of public buildings large enough in Berlin that had not been seriously damaged during the Allied bombing raids.

Among the organizations that were found guilty at Nuremberg of collective responsibility for war crimes was the SS. But despite the strenuous efforts of the prosecution, and in particular of the chief United States prosecutor, Telford Taylor – a wartime Intelligence analyst – no collective charge was proved against the German General Staff and High Command. This was a disappointment to the Allies, who had hoped to be able to condemn the military leadership, which had enabled Germany to launch five wars since 1864.

Although the case against the General Staff was lost, Taylor did succeed in showing – in the words of his obituary in *The Times* on 25 May 1998 – 'that the leadership was more than a gaggle of tactical geniuses, and that many of its most admired commanders had been waist-deep in war crimes'.

Trials were held not only at Nuremberg but in specific concentration camps where atrocities were committed by commandants and guards. The first of these began at Dachau on November 15, under American military auspices, with a full array of lawyers and a panel of judges. The accused were forty guards – the survivors of more than 350 guards who had been shot at the moment of the camp's liberation by incensed liberators – and one civilian doctor. The doctor, Karl Klaus Schilling, was a former distinguished professor of parasitology at the university of Berlin and, before the war, a member of the Malaria Commission of the League of Nations.

At his trial, Dr Schilling requested that he be allowed time to write up the results of his medical experiments, in the interest, he explained, of medical science. He had carried out those experiments on human beings. The court was as amazed by his request as it was horrified by what he had done. He was sentenced to death, and hanged.

At Lüneberg, the British army conducted a trial of the commandant of Belsen, Josef Kramer, who had earlier been an official at Auschwitz, Mauthausen and Dachau. After Kramer had described to the court how he had taken part in the gassing of eighty Jewish women at Auschwitz in 1943, he was asked what his feelings about it had been at the time. 'I had no feelings in carrying out these things,' he told the court, 'because I had received an order.' Kramer added, defiantly: 'That, incidentally, is the way I was trained.' He was sentenced to death and hanged.

There was to be no delay in the search for justice. The Nuremberg trials began on November 20. In an attempt to present enough evidence to make the charges effective, more than 100,000 documents, captured by the Allies as they had occupied Germany, were examined. Of these, four thousand were translated into English, French and Russian, for use at the trial. As the

Nuremberg trial began, other trials were taking place that by their nature did not have to take so long. On December 10 a Canadian court martial, held at Aurich, not far from the Dutch border, charged SS General Kurt Meyer with the massacre of at least forty-one Canadian prisoners-of-war in June 1944, immediately after D-Day.

An Englishman was brought to trial in London that November. He was John Amery, the son of L.S. Amery, a leading member of the wartime British government, and the brother of Julian, who had fought with the Albanian partisans behind German lines. John Amery pleaded guilty of trying, while living in wartime Germany, to persuade British prisoners-of-war to join a British Free Corps and fight alongside the Germans against the Russians. The court felt a deep sympathy for his father's anguish, but, as John Amery had pleaded guilty, it had no option but to sentence him to death. He was hanged on December 19.

One set of postwar trials led to violence. From the earliest days of the war the Bengali nationalist Subhas Chandra Bose had dreamed of using Britain's wartime weakness, and possible defeat, to win freedom for India by force of arms. His Indian National Army, which he had offered to Hitler in vain, had been welcomed by the Japanese and had fought alongside the Japanese forces in Burma, and on the frontier of India. Bose had allied his army with Japan, something that the leader of Indian nationalists, Jawaharal Nehru, himself an advocate of early Indian independence, rejected utterly. But Gandhi had written of Bose's followers: 'India adores these men', and when they were put on trial by the British in November 1945 even Nehru described what they had done as 'a brave adventure' that had arisen from 'a passionate desire to serve the cause of India's freedom'.

Bose had been killed in an air crash over Formosa in the closing days of the war. Three of his followers were brought to trial in Delhi. They were found guilty of waging war against King George VI and sentenced to transportation. There were protests against the sentences in Calcutta, Bombay and Delhi. Hindus and Muslims joined forces (Bose was a Hindu) to set lorries and trams on fire. In Calcutta, where British-officered Indian troops opened fire on the rioters, forty-five Indians were killed.

The British recognized the strength of Indian national sentiment and their own inability to curb it by harsh measures, however justified those measures seemed to be by the courts and laws in force at the time. The sentences on the three men were remitted, and they were set free. Within three months,

11,000 Indian National Army soldiers had been released from internment. They were welcomed back in their towns and villages as heroes of India's struggle for independence, leading Gandhi to reflect that their 'hypnotism' – as he called it – 'has cast its spell upon us'.

The war had ended with Soviet troops in occupation of Czechoslovakia, Prague being the last of the capitals occupied by Hitler to be liberated. By the end of the autumn the United States troops who had driven the Germans from western Czechoslovakia had withdrawn. The pre-war borders of Czechoslovakia were restored, with the exception of Ruthenia in the east, which was annexed to the Soviet Union.

On October 28 Eduard Benes, who had returned to Prague from his exile in Britain eight days after its liberation, addressed the Czechoslovak provincial Assembly. Although the rule of Communism was inevitable under the shadow of Soviet guns, yet still the spirit of independence was strong. Benes, symbol of pre-war independence, spoke with emotion of what Czechoslovakia had gone through, and what she had survived:

> Today we, the Czechoslovak nation, are again standing with all our moral strength in our own free Prague, hallowed by great and glorious history, and we are looking across to shattered Berlin and Munich and to the ruins of the Third Reich, our heads high, our conscience clear, in the knowledge of a great historic victory and in the knowledge that our great democratic national truth has prevailed, conscious of the unity of our national State and with great moral and political satisfaction for all that happened at Munich and afterwards.
>
> And Germany, with all her grandiose plans and her historical falsehoods about our lands falling legally under Germany, is lying in ruins, destroyed, shattered, in chaos, with her people crushed and morally shattered. It may take generations for her to recover.
>
> At this moment it is we who call to our nation and to the other nations: 'Yes, there stood Hitler and his Third Reich with all they stood for, and here stand we.' And things have indeed been decided between us by a life-and-death struggle, by the victory of all honest people over the most infamous evil – judgment of the world, of history, and of Providence.

It was a bold man who called upon providence, nor was there any guarantee that providence would respond. The Soviet Union was determined not to relinquish its control, not only over the roads and railways and airfields and industries, but over the political alignments and minds of those in whose lands its armies stood.

For many of the Jewish survivors of the concentration camps – less than 100,000 men, women and children – a return to their homes in eastern Europe was impossible. Other people – including former neighbours – had entered them and taken them over, mostly when the Jews had been thrown out of their houses and apartments in 1940 and 1941 and sent to ghettos, or had been rounded up for deportation in 1942 and 1943. Many Jews were physically and brutally attacked when they tried to go back to their home towns. Some were killed when they tried to enter their family homes, or to take possession of their shops.

Although some Polish Jews were able to return to their homes and rebuild their lives in Poland, more than 1,500 – survivors of the Nazi torments – were killed when they tried to return home. Each spate of killings stimulated a greater exodus. The borders between Poland and Germany, Germany and Austria, and Austria and Italy, were the scene of an ever-flowing stream of survivors trying to get to Italian ports and from there, by clandestine means and on clandestine boats, to reach Palestine.

On November 13 Ernest Bevin, the new British Foreign Secretary and a former Trade Union leader, announced that only 13,000 Jews would be allowed into Palestine that year. His announcement caused anger among the survivors who were at that very moment trying to get to Palestine. These were mostly Polish and Hungarian Jews, but also Jews from every European country that had been occupied by Germany. Those who made this journey were almost all intercepted by British warships off the shore of Palestine, and taken to an internment camp in Palestine, where they were held for up to a year before being allowed to settle in the country legally. While in internment, husbands and wives were kept in separate barracks.

It was a tense period, exacerbating relations inside Palestine between the British Mandate authorities and the pre-war Jewish community, numbering more than half a million, many of whom had served in the Allied armies. There was an upsurge in Jewish terrorism. Not only did the demand grow to let in the survivors; the demand also grew for the British to leave, and to allow the creation of a Jewish State.

More than five months after the end of the war in Europe there was a striking example of successful wartime production when, on October 30, the last of the Liberty Ships was launched in an American shipyard. In all, 2,742 of these prefabricated ships had been manufactured in the United States to enable transatlantic shipping to be replenished after each submarine sinking. More than two hundred had been sunk by the Germans.

No longer needed for the task that had ended, the new ship, together with many more, took part in bringing home the Allied prisoners-of-war and civilian internees from the Far East. Their plight was regarded as the most urgent. Regular soldiers could wait a little longer, until the great ocean liners that had been converted into troopships – including the *Queen Mary* and the *Mauretania* – could be made ready to bring them home.

The death tolls of the Second World War were still being calculated as 1945 came to an end, and were never finally ascertained. As many as fifteen million soldiers, sailors and airmen had been killed in action.* At least ten million civilians had been murdered in deliberate killings – six million of them Jews. Between four and five million civilians had been killed in air raids. Four million prisoners-of-war had been killed or allowed to die in situations of the utmost cruelty after capture – three and a half million of them Soviet soldiers in German captivity. Millions more, soldiers and civilians alike, had been physically maimed and mentally scarred.

These figures do not take into account the death tolls before September 1939 in the Sino-Japanese War. Between 1939 and 1945 disease and hunger had also taken their toll, with war conditions making it much harder to organize alleviation. In Bengal a million and a half Indians had died of starvation. In Egypt, Algeria and Morocco, fifty thousand people had died of typhus. Almost unnoticed in the newspapers reporting the daily struggles on the battlefields, seven thousand Africans had died of meningitis in Tanganyika in 1942.

The prevention of disease, as much as the prevention of war, was on the agenda of the new United Nations. Whether the material and moral resources of the world – so seriously depleted by war – could cope with the challenges ahead was unclear. The Cold War, the divisions between the Communist and non-Communist worlds, and the continuing conflicts of colonialism, cast shadows over every hopeful forecast. The South African leader, General Smuts – who held the honorary rank of Field Marshal in the British Army – proposed creating a storage base for atomic weapons in British-occupied

* The United States Army and Army Air Force deaths totalled 234,874.

Libya. He was concerned that, in a future atomic war, the democracies would be at a disadvantage, setting out his innermost fears in a letter to the British Cabinet on September 25:

> If Washington suspected that Moscow could as easily drop an atomic bomb on New York as she could on Moscow, would America dare to use it? And in such a case would not the final test of power lie with that country which was prepared to use the bomb and pay the least regard for human life and the destruction which it would create?
>
> Again, is not the menace of the bomb greatest to the densely populated countries, where liberal ideals prevail, while being of lesser concern to those more sparsely populated countries of great area, where authoritarianism is in force?

The capacity for human regeneration was as remarkable as the capacity for self-destruction. Twelve weeks after the end of the war in Europe, at a time when Berlin was still in ruins and many of its inhabitants on the verge of starvation, the *Berliner Zeitung* listed, as part of the cultural activities available on the afternoon of August 27 – starting at 4.40 p.m. because of the continuing shortage of electricity – two concerts, eight plays, nine cinemas – mainly showing Russian films – four operettas, seven variety shows, two cabarets and a circus.

The impact of the Second World War remained a point of thought and reflection for the following half century: with every decade its impact has been debated and its effects analyzed. M.R.D. Foot, who had served with British Army Intelligence, working with both the commandos and the Special Air Services, reflected thirty-two years after the guns had fallen silent:

> The war saw the end, or at least the diminution, of a number of social prejudices: that women are in any sense the inferior sex; that government always knows best; that there is anything admirable in empire, or ranting, or slaughter.
>
> Enormous social sacrifices had been made to get rid of fascism and Nazism, and the revelations concerning the concentration camps in the closing weeks of the European war satisfied everybody that this war, at least, had been one worth fighting.
>
> Those who fought learned something about courage, and comradeship,

and the worth of joint action. On the whole, those who learned most, and were most frightened, say least about it.

'And now it is all over,' wrote Kurt von Schuschnigg in the autumn of 1945. The former Chancellor of Austria had been Hitler's prisoner from 1939 to 1945. A free man once more, he was on the Italian island of Capri, having just finished writing his memoirs. 'Humanity holds its breath, the old world together with the new, perhaps for the first time in history,' he reflected. 'Humanity waits for the sunrise. For it was a long and bitter night, in which Lucifer once more tried his strength against God. It was a night which divided mankind into supermen and lower creatures, wilfully forgetting that man is God's creation and creation's destiny. The damage wrought will be irreparable for many years to come. Some of it can never be repaired.'

CHAPTER NINETEEN

1946

> Consent to evil a little, and a great evil will
> overwhelm us, till no tongue crying out against it will
> be heard any more.
>
> ALAN PATON

W HEN THE Christian New Year opened on 1 January 1946 the Second
World War had been over for three and a half months in Asia, and for more
than half a year in Europe. Knowledge of its horrors had only just begun
to be felt across the globe, and would continue to reverberate for many
decades to come. The process of relegating the past to a distant limbo was
also continuous. In the early months of 1946, Primo Levi, who had been a
slave labourer at the Monowitz synthetic oil factory in 1944, wrote a volume
of poems about his experiences. At the time his book was being written, he
later reflected, 'Nazism and fascism seemed truly faceless: they seemed to
have returned to nothingness, vanished like a monstrous dream, justly and
deservedly, the way ghosts disappear at cock-crow. How could I have cultivated rancour, wished for revenge, against a multitude of ghosts?'

Inside Germany there was the beginning of questioning and speaking of
guilt, but it did not always strike a welcome chord. In the first week of
January, during a pastoral visit to German students in several universities,
Pastor Niemöller told a large gathering of 1,200 students at Erlangen of
how he had recently met a German Jew whose parents, bothers and sisters
had all been murdered. 'I could not help myself,' Niemöller told the students.
'I had to tell him, "Dear brother, fellow man, Jew, before you say anything,
I say to you: I acknowledge my guilt and beg you to forgive me and my
people for this sin."'

Hearing this – from a man who was both a pastor and a First World War
naval hero – the students booed. Niemöller was also jeered when, to students

at Marburg and Göttingen, he said: 'We must openly declare that we are not innocent of the Nazi murders, of the murder of German Communists, Poles, Jews, and the people in German-occupied countries.' But Niemöller persevered, telling students in Frankfurt-on-Main on January 6: 'The guilt exists, there is no doubt about that – even if there were no other guilt than that of the six million clay urns containing the ashes of incinerated Jews from all over Europe. And this guilt lies heavily upon the German people and the German name, even upon Christendom. For in our world and in our name have these things been done.'

From the earliest post-war months, aspects of the aftermath of the war impinged on the lives of those who, slowly and often with considerable difficulties, tried to redress the balance of its destruction. On Corregidor, fought over so savagely in 1942, the American Army's Graves Registration Company was working to identify the bodies and to prepare a gravesite for them. As they pursued their sombre task – which was being replicated all over Europe and the Far East – one of the soldiers in the company saw in the distance a line of about twenty Japanese soldiers coming towards him. They were clearly waving pieces of white cloth, and proceeded to surrender to the astonished Americans.

For three and a half months these Japanese soldiers had been unaware that the war was over – no radio enabled them to listen to Hirohito's announcement of the surrender. They had been living and hiding from their imagined enemy in one of the deep underground shelters with which the island was honeycombed. It was only when one of them had crept out at night to look for water that he had found a newspaper from which it was clear that the war was long over.

The contrast between the cost of warmaking and the needs of the postwar world were pointed out in the early months of 1946 by Emery Reves in *The Anatomy of Peace* – first published in the United States – in which he argued in favour of 'universalism and the imperative need for universal law', and for the creation of a world government that would have to rise 'above dogmatic nation-centric conceptions'. Reves' book had been written before the dropping of the first atom bomb, but published a few weeks later. In the New Year printing he wrote: 'Two per cent of the money and effort spent for research and production of the atomic bomb would be sufficient to carry out an educational movement that would make clear to the people what the virus of war is, and how peace can be attained in human society.'

Reves, a Hungarian-born refugee who had been injured in the first German air raid on London, argued that there was 'very little' time left 'to prevent the next war and to stop the drifting towards totalitarianism'. His mother, a Hungarian Jew, had been among those murdered by the Nazis. He dedicated the book to her memory, 'atrociously and senselessly assassinated, like countless other innocuous victims of the war, whose martyrdom can have meaning only if we who survive learn how to prevent the tragedy of future wars'.

In Europe the pattern of retribution which had been established in Europe from the day of Germany's defeat continued throughout 1946. The first person to be hanged in the New Year, on January 3, was William Joyce, who had broadcast from Berlin from the very first days of the war mocking Britain's losses.

Trials and executions were a regular occurence in 1946. In Prague, the former Nazi Chief of Police, Karl Hermann Frank, was found guilty of several hundred charges of murder and hanged. Five thousand people watched his execution. In Poznan, which had been returned to Polish rule after five and a half years of German occupation, the wartime Gauleiter of the region, Artur Greiser, was paraded around the city in a cage before he, too, was hanged – in the square in front of what had earlier been his own official residence. A former commandant of Majdanek concentration camp, Max Koegel, was tried by a British military tribunal set up to prosecute the camp staff at Ravensbrück. Another Majdanek commandant, Martin Weiss, was tried by the Americans as part of the Dachau trial. Both men were sentenced to death and executed. Also executed as a result of another British trial – that of the killers at Neuengamme concentration camp – were Anton Thumann, who had earlier been one of the chief SS guards at Majdanek, and Josef Trzebinski, the Majdanek camp SS doctor.

In Strasbourg, Robert Wagner, the head of the German civil administration in Alsace during the war, was sentenced to death by a French military court, and hanged, for carrying out the deportation of Jews to Vichy controlled camps in the Pyrenees, from where most of them were later deported to Auschwitz. Also in France, Jacques Desoubrie, one of that subsequently excoriated group of collaborators who had betrayed their fellow-Frenchmen and women to the Gestapo, was also tried and hanged. Other collaborators in many lands were not given the benefit of a trial before their execution.

In Tokyo, the International Military Tribunal, Far East, was formally set up on January 19. The prosecutions were to involve eleven nations whose citizens had suffered at the hands of the Japanese occupation forces. As in Europe, other trials were held before the international tribunal began its work, in places where atrocities had been committed. In February an American Army military tribunal tried and convicted General Tomoyuki Yamashita of brutality against both American prisoners-of-war and Filipinos during the occupation of Bataan. He was hanged. A week later, in the same courtyard in which General Yamashita had been hanged, General Masaharu Homma, found guilty by the same tribunal of responsibility for the Bataan Death March, was executed by firing squad.

The British also took independent action in Singapore, where Major-General Shempei Fukuei was found guilty of ordering the execution of Allied prisoners-of-war, taken to the precise spot where one of these executions had been carried out, and shot by a firing squad. By the end of the year, British tribunals sitting in South-East Asia had imposed 221 death sentences, and Australian tribunals in the South Pacific 124 death sentences, for crimes against Allied prisoners-of-war and civilian detainees.

Apparent leniency could create popular unease in both Britain and the United States; it did so in April when one of the four Japanese officers found guilty of executing three American airmen shot down over Tokyo was sentenced to nine years in prison, and his three fellow-executioners to five years.

As the echoes of a world that had been at war for more than half a decade continued to reverberate, the demands and aspirations of the postwar world were beginning to make themselves heard. At the centre of the Labour Party's electoral victory in Britain the previous summer, under Clement Attlee's leadership, was its promise to secure a wider scope of social justice. This promise encompassed greater economic security for the working class, wider opportunities in education, fuller employment, and the application of national resources to rebuild the shattered homes and cities on the basis of social equality.

Although wartime rationing had to be kept in place in Britain during a period of continuing economic hardship, even rationing represented the application of fair dealing, while the Labour Government's legislative programme reflected this egalitarian aspiration. The emphasis of the legislation was on a National Health Service – introduced in 1948 – whereby medical attention and treatment would be free, on cheap and subsidized housing, and on a much higher taxation of wealth.

At the time of its victory the Labour Party had not been in effective power for fourteen years. In 1929 it had won twenty-five more seats than the Conservatives. In 1945 it had a majority of 146. Being out of power for so long had helped to create a bitterness which permeated the political system and affected the legislation. When Churchill asked the economist J.M. Keynes how he explained the punitive nature of some of the taxation, Keynes replied in one word: 'Envy.' But for many Labour activists the desire for a decent life for every citizen was a driving force that, despite the political conflicts which it created, offered the prospect of a Britain in which class divisions would have less influence, the traditional ruling classes less power, and the population at large a greater sense of participation and prosperity. Churchill understood this aspiration. When his doctor spoke to him after the Labour victory of the electorate's 'ingratitude', Churchill answered: 'Oh no, I wouldn't call it that. They've had a very hard time.'

As well as seeking a way forward to greater domestic equalities, the Labour Government also sought to take a lead in international reconciliation. It fell to the sovereign, who was still both King and Emperor, to set the tone. At a banquet held in London on January 9 to celebrate the first meeting of the General Assembly of the United Nations Organization, King George VI told the delegates that 'in the long course' of British history 'no more important meeting' had ever taken place within the boundaries of London. He then set out his hopes for their deliberations, in the context of what had gone before:

> The year 1945 brought the end of the sternest, most widespread, and most dangerous conflict of all ages; it brought final victory over the enemies of the liberties of mankind. But that victory was won at a grievously heavy price; it has left, in its aftermath, a no less heavy responsibility on the victors, now joined together in this organization of the United Nations. It is, in fact, in your hands to make or mar the happiness of millions of your fellow-men, and of millions yet unborn.
>
> It is for you to lay the foundations of a new world, where such a conflict as that which lately brought our world to the verge of annihilation must never be repeated; where men and women can find opportunity to realize to the full the good that lies in each one of them.

The opening session of the General Assembly was held at Central Hall, Westminster, on January 10. It was twenty-six years to the day since the creation of the League of Nations. During the sessions of the League, the national flags of each of the participating States had been predominant. The United Nations had its own symbol — a strange sight at first — which was described at the time as 'a novel aerial projection of the world spread out from the North Pole, in gold and encircled by olive branches'. It was soon to become an accepted symbol of international conciliation and hope.

Fifty-one nations were represented at the opening session of the United Nations Organization. Neither Germany nor Japan had yet been accepted into the governing comity of nations. The delegates had high hopes for what they could achieve, hopes which Attlee expressed succinctly when he said: 'The United Nations Organization must become the over-riding factor in foreign policy' — in the foreign policy of all nations. An immediate breach in the general sense of amity and unanimity was caused, however, at the very outset by the Soviet Union. As many of the nations present had wondered just how the Communist giant would fit into the new organization and carry out its responsibilities, the episode created a disturbing hint of what might be in store.

It had been widely assumed that the first President of the new organization would be the Belgian Foreign Minister, Paul-Henri Spaak. But before he could be nominated the head of the Soviet delegation, Andrei Gromyko, rose to nominate someone else — the Norwegian Foreign Minister, Trygvie Lie. The Soviet Union wanted to make it clear that its wishes had to be heard, and could prevail. Most delegates were shocked into silence by Gromyko's unexpected intervention. He was immediately seconded by the representative of the Ukraine, one of the three delegates — the third was the Byelorussian — who represented the Soviet Union (this triple representation had been a wartime gift to Stalin by President Roosevelt). The Ukrainian delegate went so far as to propose that Trygvie Lie should be elected at once, by acclamation. After many angry delegates insisted on a secret ballot, Paul-Henri Spaak was elected by 28 votes to the 23 cast for Trygvie Lie. The Soviet viewpoint had not been without its supporters. The seeds of a conflict sown during the war had already begun to germinate.

Trygvie Lie was appointed Secretary-General of the organization. As had happened during the early days of the League, a search was made at this first meeting for a mechanism whereby the prevention of war could lie within the powers of the United Nations. Under the aegis of the Security Council a Military Staff Committee was set up, to coordinate international military action in the event of an aggression taking place. An Atomic Commission was also established, with a view to devising a method of controlling scientific discoveries in the nuclear age. The United States, which took the lead in this, wanted all phases of the development and use of atomic energy to be under a single United Nations authority – the International Atomic Development Authority.

The Americans urged all member States, working in unison, to move towards the renunciation of the atom bomb as a weapon, to be followed by the creation of 'an adequate system of control'. Above all, the United States insisted, 'there must be no veto to protect those who violate their solemn agreements not to develop nor use atomic energy for destructive purposes'. In the aftermath of Hiroshima and Nagasaki, this was a powerful statement that atom bombs need not be the arsenal of the future. How far the American wishes would be met was not clear. None of those present at the London meeting, at which these peaceful sentiments with regard to the atom bomb were expressed and endorsed, knew that the Soviet Union was already at work making atom bombs of its own. Even the Soviet, Ukrainian and Byelorussian delegates may not have known.

Also established during the London meeting was an Economic and Social Council, created to coordinate the problems of the reconstruction of twenty or thirty countries whose economies and infrastructures had been shattered by the war. There was also the resolution of the refugee problem to be studied – a problem that was then thought to be solvable, but which, in the years ahead, was to assume almost unmanageable proportions. Other issues which the Economic and Social Council was asked to examine were given special Commissions, each with its own staff and status. One commission was given the task of looking into the illegal trade in narcotic drugs. Another was asked to examine the issue of Human Rights. Employment was allocated a commission of its own, as was transport and communications. Among the sub-commissions established in London was one on the Status of Women: this was quickly given a commission of its own.

Several pre-war elements of the League of Nations were to be retained by the United Nations. These included the International Labour Office at Geneva and the International Court of Justice at The Hague. Fifteen judges were elected during the London conference to sit on the court, among them a British, American and Soviet judge. The League of Nations Mandates Commission had been transformed into a trusteeship Council (Mandates had come to be associated with colonialism, and were beset, as in Palestine, by continual conflict). In order to show its confidence in the newly established

United Nations Trusteeship Council, Britain offered to place under its auspices three British Mandated territories – each of which had been German
until 1918 – Tanganyika, the Cameroons and Togoland.

The work of the London Conference was caught, within three weeks, by
an international crisis that involved the calling of the Security Council, for
the first time since it had been established almost a year earlier. The issue
was a charge by Iran that the Soviet Union was interfering in its internal
affairs. When the British Foreign Secretary, Ernest Bevin, was arguing that
the Iranian claim should be taken seriously, the Soviet representative, Andrei
Vyshinsky, interrupted to say that the claim should be dismissed. But the
presence of Soviet troops – which the Soviet Union claimed was necessary
to keep order – in the north-western Iranian province of Azerbaijan was
regarded by the Security Council (other than the Soviet representative) as
not only unnecessary, but as a clear derogation of Iranian sovereignty.

In a challenge to Britain's championing of Iran, Vyshinsky raised the
question of the presence of British troops in Greece, which was, he said,
endangering the peace of the world, and he demanded Britain's 'quick and
unconditional withdrawal'. Bevin was outraged. The real danger to the peace
of the world, he countered, was in the 'incessant propaganda' of Moscow
and of the Communist Party in every country where it was active, against
the British people and government.

The Soviet Union eventually withdrew its troops from Azerbaijan. Britain
also withdrew its troops from Greece, having ensured that the general election
there was not marred by local Communist violence. Britain also provided
Greece with a substantial interest-free loan to enable it to stabilize its currency and proceed with post-war reconstruction. The first repayments of the
loan did not have to begin for five years.

One more issue intruded on the much-wished-for unanimity of the first
session of the United Nations. Representatives of Syria and Lebanon had
brought to London their governments' complaints about the continued presence of French and British troops on their soil. Both representatives
demanded that these troops should be withdrawn at once. When the Security
Council discussed the issue, the Soviet Union – in order to indicate its
independent stance in the debate – abstained from voting. This constituted
an effective veto, and no decision could therefore be reached.

Seizing the opportunity to secure an agreement without Soviet participation, the British and French delegates at once declared that their two
countries would act in accordance with the majority on the Security Council

and withdraw their troops. The Soviet veto was not to be so easily circumvented, or so smoothly, in future crises. For the second time in the course of a single meeting of the new world body, it was made clear that the Soviet Union would be an awkward partner in the work of international agreement.

Armies still had a part to play in the imposition of the rules and settlements of the Allied victory. In Dachau, which since the arrival of the American liberators nine months earlier had been serving as home for tens of thousands of refugees and displaced persons, there was an ugly incident on January 19 when five hundred United States and Polish troops used tear gas against 339 Soviet citizens who, having served in the German army during the war, were to be repatriated under the inter-Allied agreement reached at Yalta. On the following day the *New York Times* reported that when the American guards broke in to one barrack, whose door had been barricaded, they found that ten of the Russians had killed themselves: some had cut their own throats, others had used pieces of clothing with which to hang themselves. The Russians who continued to resist were overcome by the tear gas and by Polish and American military police. Eisenhower wanted the repatriation scheme abandoned, but he was overruled by the State Department.

Repatriation had been insisted upon by Stalin. Many of those Allied soldiers who had to use force against the Russians were uneasy. When confronted by physical resistance and suicides, they began to question whether everyone being sent back ought to be forced to return to what would clearly be hardship, imprisonment, labour camp and even execution. This unease was particularly strong with regard to the thousands of Cossacks – men, women and children – who were ordered by British troops to leave their camps near Klagenfurt, in the British Zone of Occupation in Austria, and return to Russia. Considerable force had to be used to make them go back.

One group of those being repatriated was taken to Odessa on board the British ship *Empire Pride*. Several of them were extremely ill, and had been looked after in the ship's hospital. An Englishman who was present when they docked noted that the Soviet port authorities 'refused to accept any of the stretcher cases as such and even the patients who were dying were made to walk off the ship carrying their own luggage'. One man who tried to kill himself 'was very roughly handled and his wound opened up and allowed to bleed. He was taken off the ship and marched behind a packing case on the docks. A shot was heard but nothing more was seen'.

The Englishman added that thirty-one other repatriates were taken under

Soviet armed guard behind a dockside warehouse. Fifteen minutes later machine-gun fire was heard.

In a speech in Moscow on February 9, Stalin issued an unexpected and formidable warning that no peaceful international order was possible. For that reason, Soviet production of iron and steel – 'the base materials of national defence' – must be trebled, and consumer goods inside Russia 'must wait on rearmament'.

The senior American diplomat in Moscow, George F. Kennan, was asked by the State Department to comment on Stalin's words. On February 22 Kennan telegraphed to Washington with a warning. 'Wherever it is considered timely and promising,' he said, 'efforts will be made to advance official limits of Soviet power. For the moment, these efforts are restricted to certain neighbouring points conceived of here as being of immediate strategic necessity, such as Northern Iran, Turkey, possibly Bornholm. However, other points may at any time come into question, if Soviet political power is extended to new areas.' Kennan went on to elaborate his warning. A 'friendly' Persian Government, he explained, 'might be asked to grant Russia a port on Persian Gulf. Should Spain fall under Communist control, the question of Soviet base at Gibraltar Strait might be activated. But such claims will appear on an official level only when unofficial preparation is complete'.

Soviet power, Kennan continued, 'unlike that of Hitlerite Germany, is neither schematic nor adventuristic. It does not work by fixed plans. It does not take unnecessary risks. Impervious to logic or reason, it will withdraw – and usually does – when strong resistance is encountered at any point. Thus, if the adversary has sufficient force and makes clear his readiness to use it, he rarely has to do so. If situations are properly handled there need be no prestige-engaging showdowns'. Gauged against the Western World as a whole, Kennan believed that the Soviet Union was 'still by far the weaker force'. Its success 'will really depend on the degree of cohesion, firmness and vigor which Western World can muster. And this is factor which it is within our power to influence'.

Six days after Kennan's telegram was sent from Moscow, the United States Secretary of State, James F. Byrnes – who from 1943 to 1945 had been Director of War Mobilization – spelled out the emerging doctrine in a speech in New York on February 28. It was the day before which, had it not been for the atom bomb, the United States would have launched the invasion of Honshu Island. 'If we are to be a Great Power,' Byrnes said, 'we must act as a Great Power, not only to ensure our own safety but to preserve the peace of the world.'

Six days after Byrnes had spoken, Winston Churchill – then leader of the Conservative opposition – who was in the United States, and to whom Truman had shown George Kennan's telegram, set out, at Westminster College, Fulton, Missouri, what he saw as the reality of the division of Europe which had followed the defeat of Germany. 'From Stettin in the Baltic to Trieste in the Adriatic, an iron curtain has descended across the Continent,' he said. 'Behind that line lie all the capitals of the ancient States of Central and Eastern Europe. Warsaw, Berlin, Prague, Vienna, Budapest, Belgrade and Sofia, all these famous cities and the populations around them, lie in what I must call the Soviet sphere, and all are subject in one form or another, not only to Soviet influence but to a very high, and in many cases, increasing measure of control from Moscow.'*

President Truman shared Churchill's sense of alarm. In common with Churchill, he did not advocate military force to push back the newly established frontier of Communist rule. Churchill had expressed their joint feelings at Westminster College when he said: 'I do not believe that Soviet Russia desires war. What they desire is the fruits of war and the indefinite expansion of their power and doctrines. But what we have to consider here today, while time remains, is the permanent prevention of war and the establishment of conditions of freedom and democracy as rapidly as possible in all countries.'

The method which both Churchill and Truman favoured later became known as deterrence. It involved the maintenance of military strength, and clear warnings that force would be used if aggression took place. As to those countries that had already fallen under Communism, there was to be no war and no violence against them in order to impose – or to restore – democratic systems or national independence. Nor was it clear how, or when, the Communist regimes would fall. Perhaps they would last for as long as the Soviet Union had already lasted – almost thirty years – and perhaps much longer. Those who studied in depth the nature of Soviet Communist rule and control recognized the all-pervasive impact of a monolithic education system, and the unimpeded power of the State to arrest and imprison all opponents of the Communist ideology and system.

The first serious peacetime difference between the Soviet Union and the Western Powers had come at the Security Council in January, when the

---

* Churchill might have added Bucharest, Tirana, Reval (Tallinn), Riga and Vilna.

presence of Soviet troops on Iranian soil had been the point of dispute. Within six months several other geographical areas of tension – potential flashpoints of violent confrontation – had been revealed. An attempt was made, at a meeting of Foreign Ministers in Paris in June, to resolve them, but it failed. The British government had wanted navigation on the Danube to be 'free and open' for all States, so that aid to the Danubian States could be moved to them without hindrance. In support of the British position, Byrnes proposed an international commission to supervise freedom of movement on the waterway. The Soviet Union rejected this. As its armies stood along the whole length of the river from its mouth at the Black Sea to Linz in Austria, there was no means other than persuasion that could achieve what Bevin and Byrnes wanted. But the Soviet Union was not open to persuasion: that became clearer with every issue that was in dispute.

Another area of conflicting aims was on the Yugoslav-Italian border. The Soviet Union wanted to extend the border in Yugoslavia's favour to such an extent that more than half a million Italians would come under Yugoslav rule. The Russians had gone so far as to propose that the port of Trieste, with a majority of Italian inhabitants, should be handed over to Yugoslavia, thereby giving the Soviet Union – to which the Yugoslav Communists were at that time almost totally beholden – a potential naval base at the head of the Adriatic Sea. Bevin successfully resisted this demand, and was able to do so because British and American troops were then in occupation of Trieste. They were to remain there for the next nine years, as a guarantee of Italian sovereignty. Most of the hinterland of Trieste, however, as well as the whole of the Istrian peninsula, including the naval base at Pula – where Yugoslav soldiers were in occupation – became part of Yugoslavia.

Another Soviet demand was that Britain – which had been allocated a United Nations Trusteeship over Libya, should hand Libya back to the Italians, who had themselves conquered it from the Turks before the First World War. Under the Trusteeship, Libya had been promised its eventual independence, and the immediate 'Libyanization' of the public services. The Soviet proposal would have had the effect of prolonging colonial rule, and also, had Moscow maintained good relations with Rome, given the Soviet Union a possible naval outlet in the Eastern Mediterranean. During the Yalta conference a year earlier, Stalin had tried to secure the port at Dedeagatch as a Soviet outlet on the Aegean Sea, but this had been rebutted by both Churchill and Roosevelt.

Another area of dispute concerned Austria. Britain and the United States were keen to proceed as quickly as possible with a treaty that would give Austria its independence and detach it permanently from Germany, as well as guaranteeing its neutrality. The Moscow Declaration of 1943, of which the Soviet Union had been a signatory, stated that Austria had been Hitler's 'first victim'. This gave the Austrians, some of whom had been among Hitler's most loyal supporters and collaborators, a way forward from guilt by action and association, to independence and neutrality.

The Soviet Union did not want to withdraw its troops or lose control of its part of the zonal system that had been established in Austria. This gave the Soviet Union control of the eastern provinces of the country, as well as of Vienna – the centre of which was, however, under Four-Power control – and several hundred miles of the Danube. The Russians avoided discussing the question of Austria at the London conference by refusing to put it on the agenda.

Stalin made no secret of his intentions with regard to the countries bordering on the Soviet Union. In an interview published in *Pravda* on March 13 – in answer to Churchill's remarks about an 'iron curtain' – he pointed out that in 1941 the Germans had invaded the Soviet Union through Finland, Roumania, Bulgaria and Hungary, and that they had only been able to do so because governments hostile to the Soviet Union were in power in those countries. He went on to ask his interviewer: 'Was it surprising that in her desire to safeguard her future, Russia was trying to secure in neighbouring countries governments loyal to the Soviet Union?'

President Truman intended that a main instrument of American power in the face of Soviet Communist ambitions would be the atom bomb which had led to the precipitate surrender of Japan. As far as the United States knew the Soviet Union did not possess the knowledge of how to make the bomb or the raw materials to manufacture it. On July 1, within a year of the atom bomb having been dropped on Hiroshima and Nagasaki, the first American post-war atom bomb test took place on Bikini Atoll, in the Marshall Islands. A 'Guinea Pig' fleet was assembled, of several dozen Second World War vessels: they were destroyed in the explosion, which created an astonishing cloud 2,000 feet across at base and 5,000 feet into the sky. It was to be two years before photographs of the explosion were made public.

There was another aspect of America's post-war involvement in European and Asian affairs that contrasted so strongly with the isolation that had flourished after the First World War. A sense of responsibility towards those who had suffered had been stimulated by the personal experiences of several million United States soldiers, in all the war zones, who were returning home after the Second World War. They had seen the poverty and desperation of countries that had come under occupation, or been the scene of battles.

One manifestation of the new American commitment was the establishment of Fulbright Scholarships. Under the vision of Senator J. William Fulbright, legislation had been approved by Congress whereby American wartime surplus could be sold, and the proceeds go towards scholarships in educational exchange agreements, and the education inside the United States of students from all over the world. The precedent which Senator Fulbright had in mind, he told his colleagues, was the Boxer Indemnity of 1901, imposed by the United States on China after the Boxer rebellion, the surplus money of which was returned to the Chinese Government in 1908 and placed in a trust fund for the education of Chinese youth. Fulbright explained to the Senate:

> This act of friendship has had a very great influence in the promotion of the good will and friendly relations that have prevailed between the people of America and the Chinese. I do not think that one can deny that the exchange of students has been one of the most successful of our international policies.
>
> The foresight of our Government, nearly fifty years ago, has paid great dividends in our relations with the people of Asia. The good will and understanding created by the exchange of students has been our greatest bulwark against unfriendly criticism of our policies in the Far East. Many students of the Chinese and other Asiatic peoples agree that our enlightened attitude toward China was our greatest defense to the propaganda of the Japanese in recent years and is to a great extent accountable for the loyalty of these people during the recent war.
>
> I think it is reasonable to assume that if a similar program can be intelligently administered among the several nations contemplated by this bill, that a great contribution will have been made to the future peace of the world.

The first three of more than sixty States to sign into the Fulbright scholarship programme were China, Greece and the Philippines. The Philippines, which had been granted full independence from the United States on American Independence Day, July 4, was the first of the countries that had been occupied by Japan to achieve statehood; an outcome that, in the first months of the war, the Japanese had themselves appeared to support, but which, as the occupation continued, had become a receding dream.

From the vast regions that had been overrun by Japan, large numbers of Japanese were being repatriated to the Home Islands. Many came from the Chinese cities which they had conquered and settled since 1937; others from the former German Pacific islands which they had acquired as Mandates from the League of Nations after the First World War; others from the Philippines, the Dutch East Indies, Malaya, Burma and Singapore. In all, an estimated 4,226,477 Japanese returned in the course of the year: some were second and even third generation Pacific islanders. A photograph published in the British and American newspapers on August 30 showed one young Japanese child in transit, wearing an oversize coat, with the caption: 'Lost in Pacific. Found under coat.'

On the day after this photograph was published, the New Yorker published an article which revolutionized thinking about the Pacific War, and about the possible future face of war. Under the heading 'A reporter at large' it published John Hersey's account of the fate of Hiroshima. A note by the editors set the tone: 'The New Yorker this week devotes its entire editorial space to an article on the almost complete obliteration of a city by one atomic bomb, and what happened to the people of that city. It does so in the conviction that few of us have yet comprehended the all but incredible destructive power of this weapon, and that everyone might well take time to consider the terrible implications of its use.'

Hersey's article, harrowing in the extreme, was based on interviews with survivors. 'The crux of the matter,' he wrote after his searing portrayal of the impact and terrors of Hiroshima, 'is whether total war in its present form is justifiable, even when it serves a just purpose. Does it not have material and spiritual evil as its consequences which far exceed whatever good might result? When will our moralists give us a clear answer to this question?'

The willingness of the American government – and people – to make contributions to the restoration of a damaged world was reflected by Congressman Lyndon Baines Johnson when he told Congress on June 4, during the Fulbright scholarship debate: 'We in America are the fortunate children of fate. From almost any viewpoint ours is the greatest nation; the greatest in material wealth, in goods and produce, in abundance of things that make life easier and more pleasant.' Nearly every other people in the world, Johnson pointed out, 'are prostrate and helpless. They look to us for help – for that inherent courageous leadership', and he went on to declare, in a clarion call for United States participation in world affairs: 'If we have an excuse for being, that excuse is that through our efforts the world will be better when we depart than when we entered.'

The United Nations was also active in trying to set up instruments of global amelioration. One such, the United Nations International Children's Emergency Fund (UNICEF) was formally inaugurated on December 11. Its initial aim was to give aid to mothers and children who were in need, as a result of the war. The United States, by reason of its national wealth, was the largest single financial contributor to the Fund.

Internally, the problems confronting returning American servicemen, particularly to the southern States, included the perennial racism which blighted so many towns and brought unpleasantness and fear to so many lives. Among the returning soldiers was Staff Sergeant Johnnie Stevens, the slave's grandson who had been among the liberators of Buchenwald. He later recalled both the pre- and post-war problems of being Black:

As a Black soldier, I felt a sense of pride in doing something they said we couldn't do. They said Black soldiers didn't have the skills to fly a plane or be a tankist. People wondered why we fought as hard as we did. But we had to prove something to the American people.

I've seen Black people killed and beaten for no reason at all. When I was ten years old, I saw local rednecks and the Klan break into a house, hang a Black man, and nothing was ever done about it.

Even after the war, I came home with a chestful of medals and I still had to ride in the back of the bus.

The Paris Peace Conference of 1919 had devised the peace treaties that created many of the national borders overrun by the German army between 1938 and 1941. Between 1938 and 1941 those borders had been altered to suit the territorial demands of Germany and her Axis partners – Italy, Hungary, Slovakia and Croatia – as well as, under the Nazi-Soviet Pact of August 1939, the Soviet Union.

A second Paris Peace Conference opened on 29 July 1946. Twenty-one States were present – the victorious powers of the Second World War. Britain, the United States, the Soviet Union, France and China constituted the principal powers. Two other Communist States represented the triple-strength that was to serve as the Soviet Union's international presence for the next forty-five years: Ukraine and Byelorussia. The British Commonwealth was represented by Australia, Canada, New Zealand and South Africa. Also present in Paris was India, scarcely a year away from independence and partition; and Belgium, Czechoslovakia, Greece, the Netherlands, Norway, Poland and Yugoslavia – countries that had been occupied by Germany; and Ethiopia, which had been occupied by Italy. Brazil, which had declared war on both Germany and Italy in August 1942 – and two years later had sent troops to fight alongside the Allies in Italy – was also a participant.

The conference was in session for two and a half months. At its conclusion, five draft treaties were ready for signature. The principal loss of territory was that of Italy, which had to renounce all her African colonies, cede her Adriatic islands and most of the Venezia Giulia province to Yugoslavia, and transfer a few small frontier areas in the Alps, mostly around Mont Cenis, to France. Upper limits were set for her armed forces, and reparations fixed to be paid by Italy to Yugoslavia, Greece, Ethiopia and Albania.

In Central Europe, Hungary had to return the Slovak regions that she had acquired from Czechoslovakia between 1938 and 1940, and had also to cede to Czechoslovakia a small strip of territory on the right bank of the River Danube opposite Bratislava. Roumania got back Transylvania from Hungary, but the Soviet Union acquired both Bessarabia and Bukovina from Roumania. The Soviet Union also acquired the port of Petsamo from Finland, which thereby lost its only outlet on the Arctic Ocean.

The Paris Peace Conference completed its deliberations on October 15. Two weeks earlier, on October 1, the International Military Tribunal at Nuremberg, which had been in session for fourteen months, had completed its main work. 'Months of academic argument, or blunted sensibility, or the dispassionate legal atmosphere of the court,' wrote the journalist R.W. Cooper, 'could not obscure the stark murder that flowed like a river of crimson through almost every phase of the inquiry.' Twelve German wartime leaders were sentenced to death. One of them, Field Marshal Goering, cheated the hangman by swallowing poison in his cell. It later emerged that a sympathetic American guard had provided him with the poison.

On October 16, the day after Goering's suicide, the other eleven German leaders were hanged. Among them was Field Marshal Keitel, whose 'Commissar Order' at the end of 1941 had been used to justify the killings of hundreds of thousands of Russian civilians, including Jews and Gypsies. Also executed that day were Hans Frank, ruler of the General Government, and Ernst Kaltenbrunner – Heydrich's successor at the head of the Reich Central Security Office – who had been in charge of the concentration camp system in 1943 and 1944. Another of those executed on October 16 was Fritz Sauckel, the German Plenipotentiary-General for Labour Mobilization. Between March 1942 and the closing stages of the war he had been responsible for the deportation of five million people from throughout German-occupied Europe to slave labour tasks for the German war economy. In his defence he said that he had known nothing of the concentration camps, but was 'shocked in his inmost soul by the crimes that had been revealed in the course of the trial'.

Also executed on October 16 were Julius Streicher, whose magazine *Der Stürmer* had been a major factor in stirring up hatred against the Jews in the early years of the Nazi regime; Joachim von Ribbentrop, Hitler's Foreign Minister, who argued in his defence that 'war in 1939 was not considered an international crime against peace'; and General Jodl, Chief of the Operations Staff of the High Command of the German Armed Forces from 1938 to 1945, who had advocated 'terror attacks' on the British population in 1940 to 'paralyze the will of her people to resist and finally force the government to capitulate'. It was Jodl who, at Reims on 7 May 1945, had signed the unconditional surrender of all the German armed forces.

Twenty-five days after the conclusion of the Nuremberg Trials, new indictments were issued for a second set of trials. These were also held at Nuremberg and began on December 9. They too were under the auspices of the International Military Tribunal. The accused were doctors and scientists, charged with carrying out medical experiments on Jews, Gypsies and Russian prisoners-of-war. The evidence presented to the court was horrific. When the trial ended on 19 July 1947, of the twenty-three defendants, seven were sentenced to death by hanging.

Among those sentenced to hang was Victor Brack, the Chief Administrative Office of Hitler's Chancellery, who had been at the forefront of the euthanasia programme in which so many Germans were killed in 1939 and 1940, and who subsequently coordinated from Berlin the experiments carried out in the concentration camps. On the scaffold, Brack, who held the rank of Colonel in the SS as well as his medical doctorate, began to speak. 'This is nothing but political revenge,' he said. 'I served my Fatherland as others before me – '.

At that point the black hood was placed over Brack's head and he was hanged. Also hanged that day were Hitler's personal physician, SS Major-General Dr Karl Brandt – who had also been Minister for Health and Sanitation – and Dr Karl Gebhardt, Chief Surgeon of the SS and President of the German Red Cross. One result of the second Nuremberg Trial was the formulation, immediately after the executions, of the Nuremberg Code, designed to make all future 'murderous and torturous' experiments on human beings illegal in international law.

As those who had participated in mass murder went to the scaffold, those who had survived the killings were still on the move. Many of the Jewish survivors were still trying, as they had the previous year, to make their way to Palestine. On July 4 – the day on which the Philippines achieved its independence – forty-two Jews had been murdered in the Polish town of Kielce. Two of the victims, Duczka and Adas Fisz, were children. Four of those killed were teenagers, who were only in Kielce because it was on their route out of Poland to Palestine.

Seven of the victims of the 'Kielce pogrom' had no identification papers and could not be named. The only 'identification' one of the seven possessed was an Auschwitz tattoo number on his forearm. This, as a result of the Gestapo's own careful records, indentified him as one of at least a thousand Jews on a deportation train that had reached Auschwitz from Radom – a town fifty miles from Kielce – on 2 August 1944. Beyond that, nothing could be ascertained about him. He lies with the other victims in a communal grave in the Jewish cemetery in Kielce.

Following the 'Kielce Pogrom', as it quickly became known, there was an upsurge in many of the surviving Jews trying to leave Poland, mostly for Palestine, but many to any destination overseas as long as it was beyond Europe. Tens of thousands of those Jews – whose home towns had been taken over by the Soviet Union after the Nazi-Soviet partition of Poland in October 1939 – had found safety in Soviet Central Asia during the war. Among their new destinations were the United States, Canada, Latin America and Australia.

Those European Jews who made their way to Palestine – more than ten thousand were intercepted by the British in the first six months of 1946 – found a country in turmoil. The Jewish struggle to remove the British from Palestine altogether had been intensified. A small group of Jewish extremists, whose actions in killing both British soldiers and Arab civilians had been denounced and even vilified by the Palestinian Jewish leadership, were brought into a united Jewish Resistance Movement under the senior Jewish political figure in Palestine, David Ben-Gurion.

The most effective action following this agreement took place on the night of June 16/17 when Palestine was isolated from both Egypt and Lebanon by the blowing up of ten road and rail bridges. Twelve days later, on June 28, the British retaliated by arresting all the Jewish leaders – except Ben-Gurion who happened to be in Paris at that moment – and some six thousand other Jews, among them three future Prime Ministers of an independent Israel, including the twenty-four-year-old Yitzhak Rabin. On the following day, British troops raided a kibbutz and seized six hundred rifles, light machine guns, pistols and small mortars that had been hidden there.

More violence followed, with the blowing up by one of the extremist groups, the Irgun – headed by another future Prime Minister, Menachem Begin – of the King David Hotel in Jerusalem. The wing that was blown up was the one in which many British administrators and soldiers had their offices. The blast was so strong that it killed many people passing by in the street. In all, ninety-one people were killed: forty-one Arabs, twenty-eight Britons, seventeen Jews, two Armenians, one Russian, one Greek and one Egyptian. The British dead included the Postmaster-General of Palestine, G.D. Kennedy, who was a veteran of the British army's retreat from Mons in 1914.

Another of the dead in the King David Hotel was a Jewish pre-war refugee from Nazism, Dr Wilhelm Goldschmidt, who had worked for almost a decade for the Mandate authorities as a legal draftsman. The Arab dead included seventeen-year-old Jamil Bader, the son of the hotel's main door-keeper, who had accompanied his father to work that morning for the first time. Donald Thompson, a fifty-five-year-old British civil servant who was on the eve of retirement was dug out alive from the rubble after thirty-one hours without food or water: he died on the day after his rescue.

The King David Hotel bomb served to heighten the hostility of Palestine Jewry towards the terrorists in their midst. 'What next?' asked the Hebrew-language newspaper *Mishmar*. 'Are we to leave the fate of our people in the hands of an evil gang of fascists? Is it not our duty to purge our own camp before it is too late?' The bombing also intensified the hostility of British soldiers and officials towards the Jewish desire for Statehood, even in that portion of Palestine – less than half of the country west of the River Jordan – which had a predominantly Jewish population. On July 30 the British Cabinet decided to deport to detention camps on the island of Cyprus all 'illegal' Jewish refugees whom it could catch. An estimated 100,000 Jews were refused permission to leave their Displaced Persons camps in Europe and make their way legally to Palestine.

The American government under President Truman was pressing the British to allow the 100,000 Displaced Persons to enter Palestine. To advise on their future, an Anglo-American Committee of Inquiry was set up. It went first to the Displaced Persons camps in Europe and then to the British detention camps in Cyprus and Palestine, seeking to find a way out of the impasse between those who wished to live in Palestine and those who wished to keep them out. One member of the Committee was a British Labour Member of Parliament, Richard Crossman, who noted in his diary, after a visit to a Displaced Persons camp in southern Germany: 'They were not Poles any more; but, as Hitler had taught them, members of the Jewish nation, despised and rejected by "civilized Europe". They knew that far away in Palestine there was a National Home willing and eager to receive them and to give them a chance of rebuilding their lives, not as aliens in a foreign State but as Hebrews in their own country.'

Reflecting on a frequent British criticism that the move to Palestine was being pushed forward artificially by Zionist emissaries, Crossman wrote: 'How absurd to attribute their longing for Palestine to organized propaganda! Judged by sober realities, their only hope of an early release was Palestine.' The British Government asked other countries to take in Jewish refugees. But on April 6 the British Consul-General in Madagascar reported that whereas that French overseas territory was willing to take in two hundred immigrants 'of the peasant class' to engage in farming, the French wanted what were described as 'the right type of colonists in the first instance, and not city-bred Jews who were worn and emaciated through long confinement in concentration camps'.

In Britain, the government agreed to a request by a leading Jewish philanthropic organization, the Central British Fund – which had provided financial assistance for several thousand German Jewish children before the war – to bring in and look after as many as a thousand teenage concentration camp survivors, most of them born in Poland, some in Hungary. The first group had been flown, a year earlier, in ten British bombers, from Prague to the

Lancaster, and then taken by bus to a former Ministry of Aircraft Production establishment at Windermere, in the Lake District, where they were gradually nursed back to physical health and mental vigour.

One group of teenage survivors, some four hundred, were given Palestine certificates and allowed to emigrate there. But the gates of the Displaced Persons camps remained shut for almost all those who had fixed Palestine as their destination. On August 12 the British Government announced its intention to adopt 'firm measures' to halt the immigration to Palestine of all Jews who had not received Palestine Certificates.

Several thousand Jews, undeterred by the threat of detention in Cyprus, continued to make their way 'illegally' on small and often barely seaworthy vessels through the Adriatic and the Mediterranean. But the power of the Royal Navy to intercept their fragile craft once they approached the shore of their Promised Land was asserted to the full, and, in the course of fifteen months, more than fifty thousand were taken under escort to detention camps on Cyprus. Also in Cyprus were more than five thousand German prisoners-of-war, awaiting repatriation to Germany. Before they were shipped back home they were employed by the British to build a light railway from the island's capital, Nicosia, to the main camp at Caraolos where the Jewish detainees were being held.

Briefly, the leaders of two national movements – on the western and eastern rims of Asia – found themselves together by chance in Paris. One was Ho Chi Minh, who was leading the struggle for the autonomy of the Vietnamese in French Indo-China, and was in Paris negotiating an agreement with France for an armistice between his Vietminh soldiers and the French colonial forces. Staying at the same hotel was David Ben-Gurion. It was the week in which all Ben-Gurion's colleagues in Palestine had been arrested by the British and were being held in detention, and he was understandably cast down. Ho Chi Minh and Ben-Gurion fell into conversation. Ben-Gurion explained the Jewish predicament and Ho Chi Minh, in the fullness of his own hopes, offered Ben-Gurion a Jewish national home in the highlands of Vietnam. Ben-Gurion politely declined: explaining that he would continue the struggle to achieve statehood in Palestine, despite the current setback.

Ben-Gurion returned to Palestine and Ho Chi Minh returned to Vietnam. Towards the end of the year such hopes as Ho Chi Minh had taken to Paris of a negotiated settlement with France collapsed. On November 20, even while armistice negotiations between the Vietnamese Communists and the French were still taking place, the French attacked a junk in Haiphong harbour which they believed was carrying arms and munitions to the Vietminh. In fierce fighting Vietminh soldiers took over the port. There was a brief ceasefire on the following day, during which the French ordered the Vietminh to leave Haiphong. When the Vietminh refused the French bombarded the port from both land and sea, with artillery, tanks and naval guns. Several thousand Vietminh soldiers were killed in the bombardment.

On December 19 a unit of Vietnamese Communist troops opened fire on a group of French soldiers. Four Frenchmen were killed. They had been part of a small, non-combatant military unit that was examining the grave sites of both the French and Vietnamese who had been killed by the Japanese occupation forces two years earlier. The French responded by demanding that the Vietminh soldiers in Hanoi be disarmed. The Vietminh refused. In two weeks, more than two hundred French soldiers were killed.

As the war spread throughout Vietnam the French secured control of the main cities and the roads between them. The Vietminh moved their forces and their administrative structure – the Communist government – to the area north of Hanoi and near the Chinese border where they had been active since 1944.

Following the defeat of Germany and Japan, and the collapse of their empires, colonial unrest was renewed. As in Vietnam, this unrest was made easier to express by the ending of the rigours of wartime military rule and discipline. In Indonesia, fighting between the Dutch and the Indonesian nationalists, in which the Dutch received British military help, could not curb the Indonesian demand for independence from Holland, whose rule had been destroyed within a few weeks by the Japanese in 1942. In Madagascar, the Hova people, whose dynasty had been suppressed by the French before the First World War, rebelled against the civil administration. As in Vietnam, the French sought to maintain their authority by force.

In India, rebellion broke out among the ranks of the Royal Indian Navy after a British officer allegedly remarked to the ratings at the Royal Indian Navy School of Signals, a shore station in Bombay: 'You are the sons of coolies and bitches!'

There had been discontent for some time among the Indian sailors that as many as four hundred British officers were about to be appointed: the feeling among the ratings was that the time had come for Indian officers to be trained for the task of leadership at sea. The naval ratings had also been as angered by the trials of members of the Indian National Army, and by the use by the British of Indian units to fight against the anti-Dutch insurgents in Indonesia. They had also been stirred by an upsurge in recent nationalist utterances: at a mass rally in New Delhi on January 26, Nehru, while advocating non-violence as 'the only rightful way', had declared that independence was 'not far off now'. News of the mutiny in Bombay was sent by the mutineers from the Royal Indian Navy School of Signals to six other naval stations around the coast. In each of them 'Strike Committees' were set up.*

Led by Leading Signalman Punna Khan, the Bombay mutineers rampaged through the streets, crying out 'Long Live Gandhi' and 'Victory to the Revolution'. 'They ran wild', recalled Percy Gourgey, himself a young Indian naval officer and an eye-witness, 'singling out Britons for attack, stopping buses and private cars and hauling both British and Indian drivers of Service vehicles from their seats. Civilians were forced to remove ties and sun topees – seen as symbols of alien dress smacking of alien rule – and these were burned in a huge bonfire at Flora Fountain, the very heart of Bombay's main banking and insurance centre.' Stone-throwing and bottle-throwing continued all day. 'Bombay went to bed that night with revolution in the air,' Gourgey recalled, 'rioting, looting and acts of violence having broken out in all parts of the city.'

That night troops were ordered to Bombay from the barracks at Poona. In Calcutta, the home of the Indian National Army leader, Subhas Chandra Bose – who had been killed in a plane accident at the very end of the war – the flag of mutiny was raised at the naval base. In Karachi, fire was exchanged between naval ratings on the *Hindustan* and the military police; and later between the mutineers, using naval guns, and troops ashore. Four of the mutineers were killed before the rest raised the white flag of surrender. In Bombay, the cause of the mutineers was taken up in the streets by crowds which, on their rampages, burned down four branches of the Imperial Bank: in the two-day riot that ensued, sixty rioters were killed, and four policemen.

---

* These establishments were in Karachi and Cochin (on the east coast), and Calcutta, Chittagong, Vizagapatam and Madras (on the west coast).

The cruiser *Glasgow* and two destroyers were despatched to Bombay. On the fifth day of the revolt, the mutineers surrendered. A few days later they were rebuked by Gandhi, who said: 'In resorting to mutiny, the Royal Indian Navy ratings were badly advised. If it was for a grievance, fancied or real, they should have waited for the guidance and intervention of the political leaders of their choice. If they mutinied for the freedom of India they were doubly wrong. They could not do so without a call from a prepared revolutionary Party. They were thoughtless in believing that by their might they would deliver India from foreign domination.'

The Indian 'nation', Gandhi asserted, had 'to play the game', and he added: 'If it does, the barricades must be left aside, at least for the time being.'

The British Government realized that the naval mutiny was but a small facet of deep and growing Indian nationalist discontent. The wartime Cripps Mission, although it had not gone far enough for the nationalist leaders, had promised India serious progress towards independence once the war was over. This had become a matter of urgency, if mounting civil unrest was to be averted.

On March 14 the British Prime Minister, Clement Attlee, told the House of Commons – through whom any legislation about the future of India would have to pass – that if India exercised the right for full independence, even outside the British Commonwealth, Britain would not only accept this, but also assist India in the transition to full independence. A British Cabinet delegation travelled to India to discuss the nature of that independence: on April 15 it held an eighty-five minute talk with Gandhi and Nehru, who hoped to retain a united India under a single Indian sovereign authority. Elections to the provincial legislatures – already controlled by Indians without British restraint – revealed the strengthening of the respective ascendancy of the Congress Party and the Muslim League at the expense of the smaller political groupings.

The Muslim League, led after the war, as before it, by Mohammed Ali Jinnah – known to his followers as Quaid-i-Azam: The Great Leader – was demanding the establishment of a separate Muslim State, to be set up in the predominantly Muslim areas of the Punjab, Kashmir, the North-West Frontier Province, and large parts of Assam and Bengal, with the name: Pakistan. This was strenuously opposed by the Congress Party which, despite its significantly Hindu base, hoped to maintain a united India, with Britain replaced by a single sovereign authority, and with Hindus and Muslims working in a single governing instrument.

Jinnah had earlier espoused the idea of a united India, leading the call for Hindu-Muslim unity as early as 1916, and had not entirely abandoned the idea thirty years later. Indeed, his demands for a separate Muslim entity in 1946 may well have been a tactical move intended to gain him greater political leverage within an undivided India. But the passions aroused by the demands for a separate Muslim entity were to sweep aside the possibility of any such subtle intention and outcome. 'In the end,' writes the historian Antony Copley, 'the rhetoric got out of hand and he had created a Franken-stein's monster, a surge of support for Pakistan from below.'

In his negotiations with the British, Jinnah continued to seek a formula that would preserve the unity of India, and gain the maximum benefits for the Muslims who would form such a large majority within it. A turning point, however, which exacerbated Hindu-Muslim relations, came on July 29 in Bombay, when the Muslim League voted in favour of complete sovereign authority in Pakistan – in both North-East and North-West India – and authorized 'direct action' to achieve it. The decision when to launch this civic disobedience, and the inevitable strife that would follow from it, was to be under Jinnah's direction. Hitherto, for a quarter of a century, the Muslim League and the Muslim leadership, including Jinnah, had followed the path of constitutional behaviour and moderation, something which had marked them out in contrast to the Congress Party. The decision of July 29 appeared to change that overnight. If it was intended as a tactical move to extract more from the British and from Congress, it backfired.

As a first sign that 'non-cooperation' was to be the new Muslim weapon, several prominent Muslims who were at the Bombay meeting went up to the platform and 'renounced' the knighthoods that had been conferred on them by the King-Emperor. To bring the Congress and the League back to the negotiating table, the British Viceroy, Lord Wavell – who five years earlier had commanded British and Indian forces in the Western Desert – encouraged talks between Nehru, who had just been re-elected President of the Congress Party, and Jinnah, with a view to securing a coalition between the two leaders. As the talks began, Wavell reported to London that it was the Congress, not the Muslim League, that was rejecting a compromise that might lead to maintaining a united India.

'Gandhi's objective and the objective of the majority of Congress,' Wavell wrote on September 26, was to 'establish themselves at the Centre, and to suppress, cajole or buy over the Muslims, and then impose a Constitution at their leisure.' Wavell added: 'The Congress have not lifted a finger in helping me in getting Jinnah into the Interim Government and though I think they are right in theory on the nationalist Muslim issue, they are dangerously complacent about the probable results of leaving the League out.'

The Muslim League sought guarantees that, within a single Indian entity, their rights would be fully protected and their regions would be autonomous. On October 2 Wavell found Jinnah 'anxious for a settlement if it can be done without loss of prestige'. The talks broke down after Congress turned down the Wavell coalition plan.

Jinnah felt betrayed by the Congress rejection of a coalition. In protest at the failure of an agreement favourable to Muslim demands, the Muslims in Bombay and Calcutta declared a *hartal* – a day of mourning and the closure of shops and offices. When the *hartal* began there were violent clashes between Muslims and Hindus, and in Calcutta that day, August 16, fifty people were killed. This led to an intense flare-up of violence, during which 4,000 people were killed in four days.

Hindus and Muslims were in conflict throughout the sub-continent. One of the Muslim nominees for the Viceroy's Executive Council, Sir Shafa'at Ahmed Khan, narrowly escaped assassination when he was stabbed while on his evening walk at Simla, where the council was to meet. In eastern Bengal, a predominantly Muslim area, tens of thousands of Hindus, particularly those living in villages, were driven from their homes and fled as refugees to the larger towns. Many were killed as they fled. As a reprisal, the Hindus of the predominantly Hindu province of Bihar turned upon the Muslim minority in their midst, killing more than seven thousand.

Gandhi, whose voice for almost three decades had been that of moderation and communal amity, pleaded for an end to the killings. Communal conflict continued, however, boding ill for the unity of India once Hindus and Muslims had achieved statehood. Working together to remove the British had, in the past, created significant areas of Hindu-Muslim cooperation. But with the British having made it clear that they would leave, and do so quickly, communal violence intensified. Each side was trying to stake out its claim on the map.

Indefatigable in his quest for reason and sanity, Gandhi embarked on an arduous 'peace' tour through the Noakhali District of eastern Bengal, travelling on foot from village to village, trying to persuade the Muslim majority and Hindu minority of the district to live together in friendship and mutual respect. It was, he later wrote, the most 'difficult and complicated' mission of his life.

Despite the inter-communal violence, independence for India could not be long delayed. On September 3 the British agreed to replace all the members of the Viceroy's Executive Council with nominees of the Indian National Congress and the Muslim League. The Vice-President of the Council, the number two to the Viceroy, would be given all the powers accorded to a Prime Minister in the White Dominions. In November the British government announced that no more British personnel would be recruited, even temporarily, in the higher echelons of the Indian Civil Service, and that no more British officers would be recruited in the Indian army, navy or air force.

Ceylon and Burma were also in the process of being granted independence. In Burma, the British were pushing for early autonomy for the Anti-Fascist Peoples' Freedom League, headed by General U Aung San, who had thrown in his lot with the British against the Japanese at a crucial moment in the war against Japan. Over considerable areas of Burma, however, the forces of law and order were little in evidence. Following the Japanese surrender, large quantities of discarded arms and ammunition were being held by gangs of disaffected Burmese throughout the country, with the result that there was an increase in the number of well-organized armed robberies.

The British did not intend to re-impose imperial control, and on December 20, in an announcement similar to that which he had made about India at the beginning of the year, Attlee told parliament that it was the British government's desire that the people of Burma obtain self-government by 'the quickest and most convenient path' possible. Churchill was indignant, criticizing what he called 'the appalling haste' of the government's policy of 'scuttle' while the unrest and lawlessness inside Burma continued. Churchill argued that it was Britain's responsibility to restore law and order before power could be transferred. But the Labour Government, with its large parliamentary majority, had decided to accept the desire of both the Indians and the Burmese to rule themselves.

There would be no attempt by the government in London to retain any element of imperial control, or to delay the transfer of power, however disturbed or uncertain the internal situation might be in either India or Burma.

*   *   *

In October the United Nations – which had opened its first Assembly in London at the beginning of the year, reconvened in New York, which was henceforth to be its home. The first meetings were held at a temporary location on Long Island – Lake Success – while building began in Manhattan at a site on the East River that had been donated by the American philanthropist, John D. Rockefeller. There was some amusement when the delegates from the self-proclaimed 'Godless' Soviet Union attended mass at St Patrick's Cathedral, and when several members of the Ukrainian delegation were the unwitting witnesses of an armed hold-up in a New York delicatessen store.

During this session, four new States – Sweden, Iceland, Afghanistan and Iran – were admitted to the United Nations. This raised the membership to fifty-five. As none of them had been among the 'united nations' fighting Germany and Japan during the war, this opened the possibility of all States being members in the near future. Not every State was to be admitted, however. As a sign of moral disapproval of Franco's regime in Spain the Mexican delegation had earlier proposed the exclusion from the United Nations of any country whose regime had come to power with the help of the armed forces of States that had fought against the United Nations. Spanish republicans, exiled from Spain for more than six years, and with no end in sight to their exclusion from Spain, had helped draft the Mexican resolution. They recalled that Franco himself had withdrawn Spain from the League of Nations in May 1939 in solidarity with the Axis.

The United Nations Assembly decided by 34 votes to six, with thirteen abstentions, to debar Spain from all the United Nations' activities. Members who had not yet broken off diplomatic relations with Spain were urged to do so. It was assumed by many opponents of Franco, and even by some of his supporters, that this resolution marked the beginning of the end of his dictatorship, and that, in order to obtain international legitimacy for Spain, the monarchy would be restored. But Franco refused to be influenced by the United Nations vote, which had been far from unanimous. He denounced the 'campaign of defamation' against him and declared that Spain under his leadership and philosophy was 'holy, warlike, artistic, generous, honourable and marvellous'.

Franco also drew encouragement from a statement by Ernest Bevin that the British government would 'take a favourable view if steps are taken by the Spanish people to change their regime, but His Majesty's Government are not prepared to take any step which would promote or encourage civil war in that country'. Franco's Spain was to be isolated, but his rule would not be challenged.

Post-war France was entering into a period of political and governmental instability. General de Gaulle had been elected head of a provisional Government on 13 November 1945, amid apparent national unanimity. It was therefore a shock when, within a year, the forces of the Left were able to make it impossible for him to govern at the head of an essentially all-Party government. On 20 January 1946 he broadcast his resignation. It was a speech as full of sorrow as his appeal in 1940 to all Frenchmen and women to unite against Nazism had been full of determination. After a few days during which France was without a government, a Cabinet was formed by the Socialist leader Félix Gouin, who was dependent for his Cabinet majority on five Communist Party members. As President of the Republic, a leading Socialist party member, Vincent Auriol, was elected.

De Gaulle retired from political life and left the Parisian political scene altogether, seeking solitude first at Marly-le-Roi to the west of Paris, and then at his more distant country house at Colombey-les-deux-Eglises. When the first anniversary of the defeat of Germany was celebrated on May 10 by a victory parade in Paris, de Gaulle refused to participate, going instead two days later – the Feast of Joan of Arc – on a personal pilgrimage to Clemenceau's tomb at Colombier, in the distant La Vendée.

Under Gouin's predominately Socialist government, coal, gas, electricity, and the nine main insurance groups were all nationalized. When elections were held on June 2 for the Constituent Assembly, the Communists received 26 per cent of the vote and the Socialists 21 per cent. Georges Bidault succeeded Gouin as Prime Minister on June 24. That summer the main focus of political debate was on the creation of a new constitution. The final draft gave the dominant legislative powers to the National Assembly, and fewer powers to the President of the Republic than de Gaulle had urged. A referendum confirmed the constitution on 13 October 1946, bringing the Fourth Republic into being, although, as a sign of popular malaise, more than 30 per cent of those eligible to vote abstained.

At the general election held on November 10 the Communists emerged as the largest single political Party in France, with 163 seats in the National Assembly. The second largest Party was the Catholic Centre Party (the MRP) – with 160 seats. The Socialists secured 93. Other Parties held 158 between them. The Communists could not form a government without entering into a coalition. As their conditions of doing so, they insisted that a Communist be given the office of Prime Minister, and asked the Socialist Party to join in the formation of 'a democratic, secular and social government under Communist aegis'. The Socialist Party refused. For fifteen days there was deadlock. It was only resolved when the President, Vincent Auriol, asked the elder statesman of the left, Léon Blum, to form a government. Blum, old and unwell after his long wartime internment in Germany, was not a member of the Assembly. But the deputies voted almost unanimously (575 to 8) to make him Prime Minister, and he accepted. For four days he tried to form a Government of National Union, based on all the political Parties. But his proposal to appoint a Communist as Minister for Defence was resisted by the army, which withdrew its support.

Blum, even before being able to form a government, resigned, but he was persuaded to take the task back on his shoulders. On December 16 he succeeded in forming an all-Socialist administration. Although his was intended to be – and was – very much an interim government (it lasted less than five weeks) it did bring into effect a number of measures which helped to lower the cost of living. The first 'price-reduction drive' was launched in December 31.

The politicians and people of the Fourth Republic faced formidable problems of postwar reconstruction, and of rebuilding a society in which the wartime divisions could be bridged and the wartime hatreds assuaged. At Colombey-les-Deux Eglises, de Gaulle listened on his wireless with deepening anger at the political debates, frustrated that he was no longer in control of the destiny of France. In the privacy of his drawing room, while his wife knitted, he denounced the politicians who had ousted him as 'eunuchs', 'gigolos', 'sodomites', 'eaters of their own vomit' and 'drinkers of their own urine'.

The Italians, like the French, were struggling to find a form of government that would enable the damage and deprivation of war to be repaired. The loss of territory imposed by the Paris Peace Conference had to be accepted: that was the price of defeat, even if the country had changed sides a year and a half before the end of the war. The Italian Communist Party exploited the sense of loss by mockingly announcing that the British would not even leave the Italians with handkerchiefs to cry in. Local elections had been called in February, the first since 1920. They showed an almost even divide between the Christian Democrats and the Socialist-Communist bloc. As both groups were in favour of a republic, King Victor Emmanuel, whom the

Allies had allowed to remain on the throne after Mussolini's fall, abdicated on May 9 and left the country for Egypt and exile.

Victor Emmanuel's son proclaimed himself king as Umberto II. In Rome there were demonstrations in his favour, but the police broke them up. Elections on June 2 showed a massive majority in favour of the Parties calling for a Republic, but final results were not expected for another two weeks or more. Umberto, meanwhile, refused to abdicate. There were pro- and anti-monarchist riots in several cities, and bloodshed in Naples and Taranto. On June 11 the Cabinet authorized the Prime Minister, Alcide de Gasperi, to assume the powers of head of State until the Constituent Assembly could meet and resolve the issue. Umberto, protesting that the government had arbitrarily assumed powers that did not belong to it, flew from Rome to Lisbon, and to exile in Portugal.

On June 18 the detailed referendum results were published. They were closer than had earlier been assumed, but decisive. Casting their vote for a republic were 12,717,923 Italians. Those voting for the monarchy: 10,719,284. This was a majority of 1,998,639 for a republic. Almost a million and a half votes were blank or deliberately spoiled. Even deducting these – which was not necessary under the terms of the referendum – the republicans had a majority of 500,000. At less than three per cent of the total votes cast, this was a narrow majority, but it was a victory nevertheless for a republic.

Italy's post-war economy flourished. Industry was working at three-quarters capacity after having fallen well below half, and exports grew rapidly. Thanks to the hydro-electric plants in northern Italy, the cotton and wool industries did well. The fruit and vegetable harvest was also good, with Britain proving a main purchaser of Italian almonds, lemons and tinned tomatoes. These might seem minor items, but they gave Italy a chance to recover from the war in a way that was being denied the Eastern Bloc countries. To supplement domestic food needs, the United Nations Relief and Rehabilitation Administration (UNRRA) was active throughout Italy, as it was in many of the war ravaged regions of Europe. The United States also made its contribution, in the form of the reimbursement of moneys advanced to the Italian armed forces in 1943 and 1944, and in payments to cover the expenses incurred by the United States occupation forces.

Compared with its former Axis partner Germany, Italy was fortunate. Her change of sides in 1943 had made it possible for her to emerge after the war on the right side of the balance sheet of victor versus vanquished.

Economic life in Germany was at a virtual standstill throughout 1946. Several million burned out buildings, the shells of houses standing row upon row and mile after mile, had to be demolished, and the rubble cleared. In most towns there was near starvation, and in some cases actual starvation. The number of German refugees who had arrived in Germany from the areas in the east occupied by Poland and the Soviet Union was enormous. They came into the Western zones of occupation with virtually no possessions, in urgent need of a roof over their heads and food.

More than three million of these refugees came into the British Zone, and a further 1,800,000 into the American Zone. As many as three million also made their way across the River Oder into the Soviet Zone. Nowhere was the soubriquet 'the century of the refugee' illustrated more graphically in 1946 than between the Oder and the Rhine.

More than thirty volumes of accounts of the plight of the German refugees were published in postwar West Germany by the Federal Ministry for Expellees, Refugees and War Victims, which was set up to help them. A typical eye-witness account refers to an expulsion from the Sudeten town of Brno (in German, Brünn) which began on June 21 and lasted for seven days:

First, we spent four days in the assembly camp, in destitution and degradation, but without brutalities. Food was insufficient. Luggage and bodies were searched. Not only money was taken away (500 Reichsmarks were handed out per person) and all jewelry which might have been salvaged up to then, but also personal documents, family photographs and harmless private letters. Underwear, etc., was spoiled by being stamped with 'Trvale evakuován z republiky Ceskoslovenské' (permanently expelled from the Czechoslovak Republic).

The transport took place in 44 lorries. One third of each lorry was filled with luggage, prams, etc., some thirty persons had to find room in the space which was left. From 24 to 27 June, three days and three nights, they had to stay there, mostly in a squatting position.

The door was closed and there were no windows. It was raining and the water was dripping through the roof (at least in the lorry in which I travelled with my ill wife). The air was foul, the smell unbearable – an open bucket in the lorry had to be used as a lavatory. We were all glad when we arrived in Furth im Wald.

The arrival of the German refugees from the East affected the whole social fabric of the regions into which they came. Towns and regions that had been predominantly Protestant for generations were within a few months predominantly Catholic. Areas which had consisted almost entirely of industrial workers were filled with peasants from the agricultural regions of East Prussia, Pomerania and Posen.

Another influx into the food-starved towns with their chronic shortage of homes was the returning prisoners-of-war. A year after the war had ended they began to return, and for several years were to bring back with them their own often acute sense of defeat and isolation. A total of seven million German soldiers had been taken prisoner during the war. A million were returned from France during 1946, 350,000 from Britain and 50,000 from the Soviet Union – where 3,500,000 remained as prisoners in Siberian labour camps.

Another million people languished in the Displaced Persons camps in the British, American and French Zones. Many of these were survivors of Nazi racial persecution, people uprooted from their homes in central and eastern Europe and brought to Germany as slave labourers, but having no homes that they could return to. Most of them were described as 'irrepatriable'. The Jews among them, about 100,000 in all, made their way slowly either towards Palestine – where, if caught trying to land, they continued to be interned by the British on Cyprus – or to more distant lands. Others had nowhere that would take them in. Gypsies in particular were regarded as pariahs almost as much by those among whom they wished to live as among those who had sought to uproot and destroy them.

An aspect of German life that boded well for the future of Europe was the political system being put in place. Under the Potsdam Agreement, new provinces were being put on the German electoral and administrative map – with Prussia eliminated altogether as a geo-political concept. Of the old, and historic, regions, only Bavaria and Saxony were allowed to remain intact on the map and by name. Berlin formed a separate unit, under a Four-Power administration, divided into four zones, an island of accessibility inside the Soviet Zone. Inside the Soviet Zone, a single political monolith was created with the fusion of the Social Democrats and the Communists. Their union, the United Socialist Party, was a powerful force for discipline and loyalty to the Soviet occupier. In the three Western Zones, the predominant political Parties were the Christian Democrats (in Bavaria the Christian Social Union), the Social Democrats and the Liberal Democrats. In all the elections in the western Zones in 1946 the Communists came in fourth place. In the Bavarian parliament they failed to reach the minimum number of votes needs to win a single seat.

Democratic elections in the Western Zones led to the re-emergence of democracy for the first time in twenty-three years. It was a formidable achievement for the German people. But there was unease, and even resentment, at the Allied determination to question everyone about his or her Nazi past, and to remove from participation in public life those who had been members of organizations which the Nuremberg Tribunal had declared criminal. This 'denazification' process was accelerated by the creation of Denazification Courts, the workings of which were the responsibility of Germans in each locality. Supervision by the military Government was inevitably less than thorough. While many industrialists and officials were removed from their posts, others were needed as experts and were essential – in the words of one British commentator – 'for the sake of efficiency'. To expedite matters, five grades of guilt were established, from 'chief culprits' to mere 'camp followers'. Exclusion from work was one punishment, monetary fines another. Millions of Germans came within the audit of the Denazification Tribunals, but, as the months passed, fewer and fewer found themselves called to account. The economic and social life of the nation had to go on.

Reconstruction was a massive and long drawn out task. As university courses were reinstated, most of them in temporary and prefabricated buildings, university students had to share in the work of reconstruction. Millions of bricks were moved by hand from the ruins of buildings to special sites from which they could then be taken away by truck. In the restoration of university life, the occupying powers played their part. The French were active in their zone in helping to restore both the buildings and teaching structure at the University of Mainz. The British did the same with the University of Göttingen. In Munich the Americans encouraged the establishment of a 'Forum Academicum' in which the teaching of democratic values – through debate rather than diktat – was a central feature. In the Soviet Zone a different set of values was being inculcated: the ideological divisions of the Cold War, which were to dominate the coming four decades of the Twentieth Century. They were evident from the earliest classroom discussions.

The system in East Germany provided for indoctrination from the age of six. As an added inducement to ideological conformity in the Soviet Zone,

Russian became the second language, not only superceding English and French as a spoken language but also as the language which could be used as a vehicle for ideas through newspapers, books and magazines. *Pravda*, not the *New York Times*, *Le Monde* or even radical British newspapers such as the *Manchester Guardian*, constituted the foreign source of news and views not only in East Germany, but in Poland, Czechoslovakia, Hungary, Yugoslavia, Albania, Roumania and Bulgaria – not only 'from the Baltic to the Adriatic', in Churchill's phrase – but from the Baltic to the Black Sea.

The Western Allies, like the Soviet Union, had established their right to reparations from Germany, and this was exacted. In Hamburg several war factories and shipyards were dismantled and sent to Britain. Others were blown up, so that the Germans could not use them. The German merchant marine was divided among fifteen Allied nations, with the Soviet Union receiving a third (which it promised to share with Poland), Britain a half, and the three next largest tranches to Norway, France and Greece. There was a similar distribution of German machine tools. German trade secrets and patents were likewise distributed. But within a year this policy was reversed, as the need to put the German economy on its feet became an Allied priority. The iron curtain, running as it did through Germany, was a constant reminder to the Allies of the 'other' Germany, daily falling more tightly under Communist control.

The existence of the three Western Zones was beginning to be seen in the West as a bulwark against any possible Soviet attempts to expand towards the North Sea and even the Atlantic. It was certainly in the power of Britain, France and the United States to give Western Germany the incentives to remain a capitalist and democratic society. It was the Americans who first declared that they were stopping reparations deliveries in order to safeguard the German economy. The British and French followed. In order to prevent a further cause for economic hardship, the American and British Zones were 'fused' economically on December 3.

The Russians had no such inhibitions, and continued to remove complete industries. From the town of Jena they took the C. Zeiss optical works to Russia 'lock, stock and barrel', including almost the entire German personnel.

The future of Austria as an independent State had been assured by the Moscow Declaration of 1943, which stated that Austria had been Hitler's first territorial victim. The welcoming crowds and the warm endorsement of annexation by the Cardinal Archbishop were relegated to the forgotten elements of history, just as, fifty years later, even the Second World War and the Cold War were being relegated in importance in the public mind in favour of the technological revolutions of the century's end. In the year following the war, a balance was being struck between the catastrophes that had just passed and the need to recreate a pattern of daily life beset, not by bombs and bullets, but by the rebuilding of ruins – physical and psychological. Austria was fortunate in this balance to be allowed to stand outside the newly created eastern ring of dictatorship.

At the very beginning of 1946, on January 7, the four Occupying Powers – the Soviet Union, the United States, Britain and France – issued a joint declaration recognizing Austria as a State with the same frontiers as in 1937. This meant that the South Tyrol would remain inside Italy, a decision which, despite an Italian pledge with regard to the virtual autonomy of the German-speaking people there, caused bitterness within Austria. Many Austrians – particularly in the provinces – were also disturbed by the large number of Jews who fled into Austria during the late summer and autumn after the Polish pogroms, even though most of these Jews were seeking to go through Austria to Italy and Palestine. Age old anti-Semitism, mixed with more recent indoctrination, created a situation fraught with tension.

As part of the Allied Declaration of January 7, diplomatic relations were restored between Austria and the rest of the world. An Austrian Government was given sovereign authority, the only Allied condition being that no monarchist party would be allowed. It was almost thirty years since the Habsburgs had been deposed: they were not to be allowed to return. The Habsburg heir, Archduke Otto, turned his attentions to working for the cause of a united Europe – in which he eventually rose to high office.

An intensification of the East-West conflict broke out in Austria when, on July 6, the Soviet authorities, without consulting the three other occupying Powers, confiscated £5 million worth of industrial property in their Zone as reparations. The Austrian government opposed the confiscation, arguing that the industries that had been confiscated were Austrian property that had been stolen by the Germans after 1938. The American member of the Allied Council, General Mark Clark, also protested to the Soviets. As a gesture of support for Austria, on July 12 the United States handed 280 former German factories to the Austrian government. The Austrian parliament then passed a Bill nationalizing many of the industries that the Soviets had seized. The Russians eventually agreed that the confiscated factories could remain in Austria, be run under Austrian law, and supply the Austrian market.

The Soviet Union watched over the domestic political developments of all its 'satellites' – as they became known in the West – and interfered where it felt it was necessary to ensure the maximum compliance to Communist doctrine and authority. In Czechoslovakia, Eduard Benes, the pre-war democratic leader, and wartime guardian of the Czech cause while he was in exile in Britain, had been re-elected President. But following elections in which the Communists obtained the largest single vote (though not an absolute majority) the Czech Communist leader, Klement Gottwald, became Prime Minister.

One of the early acts of Gottwald's administration, in which Communists held the majority of Cabinet positions, was to break off negotiations with Washington for a $50 million loan on the grounds that 'the United States of America was using credits and loans to further a policy of economic imperialism'. A $19 million loan from Canada was accepted, as was a smaller loan from Britain.

In Hungary, a political clash between the Communist and Smallholder deputies in the Parliament was resolved by the expulsion of the Smallholders as 'reactionaries'. A similar political offensive was mounted against both the Boy Scouts and the Catholic Youth, the Catholic Youth being denounced as 'saturated with reactionary and illegal Fascist elements'. Wartime and even pre-war leaders faced the supreme penalty for their alliance with Germany. Two former Prime Ministers – Dr Bela Imredy (1938–39) and Lazlo Bardossy (1941–42) – were executed at the beginning of 1946, as was the head of the Arrow Cross, Major Ferenc Szalasi, whose thugs had murdered several thousand Jews in the final days of German control of Budapest. A Hungarian Jew, Matyas Rakosi, who in 1946 was Deputy Prime Minister, emerged as the most powerful political figure in the Communist hierarchy.

In Roumania, the opposition Parties agreed to join a Communist-led coalition. Such influence as they hoped to wield as a result was rapidly eroded. When elections were called in October, the British and American governments protested at the widespread Communist intimidation and violence during the campaign, which led to several deaths, including that of local Opposition Party leaders, and an attempt on the life of the Secretary-General of the National Peasants Party. When the election results were announced, giving the Communist Party an overwhelming majority of the parliamentary seats (339 of the 414) the Americans protested again, stressing that the franchise had been denied to important sections of the population, that 'methods of terrorism' had been employed to keep people away from the polling booths, and that the election result did not reflect the national view. In a local gesture of protest as courageous as it was futile, the two main Opposition Party members boycotted the parliamentary session.

The new ruler of Yugoslavia, Marshal Tito, on a visit to Moscow in May, was received personally by Stalin: a rare honour that was given great prominence in the Yugoslav newspapers. He returned to Belgrade bearing a wide-ranging Yugoslav-Soviet agreement on cultural and economic matters, as well as a promise from the Soviet Union to supply Yugoslavia with arms and munitions on long-term credit.

In Bulgaria, the British and American representatives on the Allied Control Commission tried to secure a promise of fair play for the opposition Parties during the elections that were held that October. The Soviet chairman of the Commission vetoed their efforts. Many voters were prevented from reaching the polling booths. When the results were announced, the Communist Party had secured a majority. The opposition parties, which won 101 of the 465 seats, expected some positions of authority within the governing coalition, but when, in November, the Communist leader, Georgi Dimitroff, became Prime Minister, he made it clear from the outset that the Communists did not intend to share power with the opposition. Having established that fact, Dimitroff left Sofia for Moscow, where he too was received by Stalin.

The Kings of Yugoslavia and Bulgaria had been deposed, as was the King of Albania. Control of Albania, as in Yugoslavia, went to the wartime Communist partisan leader. In Albania, this was General Enver Hoxha, a veteran of the Spanish Civil War. Five weeks after Hoxha came to power, the execution of two former Regents and a former Prime Minister marked his determination to make an unambiguous break with the past.

In Poland, under careful Soviet scrutiny, the Communist Party dominated a coalition of Communists, Socialist, Peasant Party, Democratic Party and Catholic Labour Party members. Armed opponents to Communism carried out violent attacks on government installations and even on military barracks. Using this civil unrest as a pretext, on the eve of an election to be held on June 30 the government arrested as many as ten thousand politically active Poles, including many election candidates, particularly those of the Peasant Party, whose leader, Stanislaw Mikolajczyk, had been Prime Minister of the Polish government in exile in London during the war.

Power in Poland was firmly in the hands of the Communist leaders who had been brought at the end of the war from Moscow: among them the President, Boleslaw Bierut and the Prime Minister, Eduard Osobka-Morawski. Opening a new university in the Silesian city of Breslau – renamed Wroclaw and resettled by Poles mostly from the eastern provinces taken over by the Soviet Union – the new authorities took steps to ensure that Communist doctrine would predominate. Education was replacing armies as the main vehicle of political uniformity.

The explanation of Communist success was examined during the year by two Western writers. One of them, the British Socialist thinker Harold Laski warned that the Communist Parties outside the Soviet Union 'act without moral scruples, intrigue without any sense of shame, are utterly careless of truth, sacrifice, without any hesitation, the means they use to the ends they serve'. The 'unstated purpose' of all their thinking was 'the need for crisis, in order when the battle has been joined, to establish dictatorship of the proletariat'. The American liberal, Arthur M. Schlesinger Jr, expressed his feelings in *Life* magazine on July 29. 'The total assimilation of the individual to the party creates selflessness and consecration,' he wrote. 'Like a platoon isolated behind enemy lines, the Communists perform marvels of daring at their leaders' word, each acting as if he embodies the impersonal force of history. Their fearlessness has impressed thousands of workers with the invincible determination of the Party.'

The Soviet Union had been terribly scarred by the war, yet its internal system had emerged unscathed. During 1946 there was one curious cosmetic change: the title of Commissar, for many years the symbol of Communist rule, was abolished. The Council of People's Commissars which had ruled since the revolution was replaced by the more democratic sounding Council of Ministers. Stalin's power was unaffected by this change. He made himself chairman of the Council of Ministers and also retained the Secretaryship of the Central Committee of the Communist Party.

Reparations from the countries that had participated in the invasion of the Soviet Union in 1941 were extracted in the form of raw materials, industrial plant, railway rolling stock, trucks and cars. Although the Soviet Union would not allow any outside inspection, it was clear that far more had been taken than had been envisaged at the wartime conferences when reparations had been discussed. Four countries, each of them within the Soviet bloc, were forced to transfer masses of material: East Germany, Austria, Hungary and Roumania. Goods in considerable quantities were also taken from Poland, which had been Hitler's first victim. With the Soviet army stationed to its west, as well as on Polish soil, and along its northern, eastern and southern borders, Poland had no choice but to comply, its Communist Ministers being little more, in this as in many other regards, than tools of Soviet power.

The American Secretary of State, James Byrnes, protested to the Soviet Union on July 23 about the way the Soviet authorities in Hungary had stripped the country of food and industrial materials in the last half of 1945. This included the removal of four million tons of grain and almost all the meat available to the Hungarian population over a six month period. In reply, Stalin denied that more than three per cent of the Hungarian harvest and been shipped to the Soviet Union. Byrnes, whose sources were good, was sufficiently angered by this mendacity to broadcast over the radio his detailed rebuttal. He went even further, 'reminding' the Soviet government – which was accusing the United States of seeking to enslave Europe economically – that the United States had advanced to the Soviet Union more than $10,000 million in Lend-Lease during the war for the purchase of arms and equipment.

Rebutting the frequent claim being made over Radio Moscow, that the Soviet Union was in danger of encirclement, Byrnes referred to the Soviet acquisition of territory on the Baltic, on the Polish and Finnish frontiers, and in the Pacific, where the Soviet Union had acquired territory from Japan, and he went on to comment: 'Certainly the Soviet Union is not a dispossessed nation.'

The Soviet Union was indeed neither encircled nor dispossessed; but it was to need many years before it could repair the ravages of the war. Of seventy-five coal mines in the Donbass, only four had started production again fourteen months after the war had ended. With the ending of the war, there had been hopes throughout the Soviet Union that the rigours of Stalinist control might be relaxed. But after a year it was obvious that this would not be. In August the Soviet newspapers began to list breaches of collective farm practice and to describe the severe measures that would be taken to put an end to them.

In Soviet schools a campaign was begun to eliminate from the text books any favourable references to what might have been achieved in Russia during the time of the Tsars (agricultural improvements, industrial growth, etc.). Aspects of the pre-Soviet years which had been stressed during the war to evoke a patriotic response (such as the military achievements of Peter the

Great) were removed from the curriculum. A cult of Stalin was begun on a level hitherto unseen: songs, poems, doggerel, wall posters, street slogans, radio programmes, films, plays – all had to sing Stalin's praises.

The imperial aspect of the Soviet Union was also strengthened after 1945, with many of the national groups within the vast country being further encouraged to see Russian as their language, Cyrillic as their alphabet, atheism as their creed, and Moscow as their capital. At the end of the war the population of the Soviet Union stood at 193,000,000. Only a minority were Russians. But Stalin – who was himself a Georgian – ensured that national aspirations were closely monitored, and where they were seen to be thriving, even clandestinely, they were rapidly suppressed.

In the Baltic States, which had been annexed from 1940 to 1941 and then re-annexed in 1944, Soviet soldiers were in armed conflict throughout 1946 with local nationalist forces. In Lithuania, 145 local partisans were killed in clashes that cost the lives of 215 Soviet troops. Armed clashes also took place between Soviet troops and Ukrainian nationalists in the western Ukraine, where more than eight thousand anti-Communist partisans were killed or captured, and arms and ammunition seized, including 20 machine guns, 700 sub-machine guns, and 2,000 rifles. In combating the nationalist forces, two hundred Soviet troops had been killed. Stalin ordered Lavrenti Beria, his secret police chief, to 'finish off the outlaws in the shortest possible time'. It was to take five years before his order was finally carried out.

An element of lawlessness also perturbed the apparently settled routine of Soviet life. In 1946 Stalin was told that the security police had arrested 10,563 pupils who had run away from Factory Training Schools, as well as from trade and railway schools. According to a report from the Minister of the Interior, S.N. Kruglov: 'Many crimes had been committed, including robbery and gangsterism', by students from the schools. Kruglov also gave Stalin the reason. 'The living conditions in the schools are unsatisfactory,' he explained. 'They are unsanitary and cold, and often without electric light.'

It was not only the discipline of trainees that Stalin sought to tighten. Disciplining the intelligentsia was another task that he set himself. The instrument of his will was A.A. Zhdanov, his lieutenant on the ideological front, who called a special conference of writers, artists and composers – including Shostakovich, Prokofiev, and Khatchaturian – to warn them of the folly of independent thought, in music as much as in writing and art. The Soviet Writers' Union met with Stalin's particular anger for what he saw as repeated attempts at independent expressions of opinion. The poet

Anna Akhmatova was among those expelled from the Union in 1946. Such expulsion meant an end to the right to publish – a writer's means of livelihood. When the satirist Mikhail Zoshchenko was likewise expelled from the Union, accused both of having abandoned Leningrad during the wartime siege and of slandering its defenders, his wife Vera wrote to the head of Stalin's office: 'There was never a question of his running away from Leningrad. He was working on his book on partisans right through the winter of '44. There is no trace of slander or malevolence in his books.'

Stalin read the letter but refused to rescind the expulsion order – despite Vera Zoshchenka's opening appeal: 'The greatest joy in my life has been the thought that you exist in the world, and my greatest wish is that you should go on living for as long as possible.' Stalin had long since ceased to heed such honeyed words, if he had ever heeded them. Those writing to him knew, however, that nothing less was expected of them.

In order to develop a Soviet atom bomb, Stalin arranged that prisoners in the Siberian labour camps were put in special camps within camps, to build the facilities needed. Those Soviet scientists who had been sent to labour camps several years before, on spurious charges of anti-Soviet behaviour, were taken from one place of incarceration and sent to another. They were despatched to their new place of work together with the tarpaulin needed for their tents and the barbed wire with which to surround them. In October a report was sent to Stalin about the special sites that had been set aside for atomic research, informing him that as many as 37,000 workers were busy preparing them. In December 1946 Soviet scientists achieved their first chain reaction.

The resources for destruction and for recovery were being developed side by side. On December 11 the United Nations had established the Children's International Emergency Fund (UNICEF) to help mothers and children who were in need as a result of the deprivations of war. The nature of the ideological and spiritual world in which those children would grow up was far from clear. The painter Oscar Kokoshka, who had been an exile in London for eight years, wrote a letter on July 4 to Fritz Schalecker, a German prisoner-of-war who was still in a prisoner-of-war camp in Britain. Schalecker had submitted some of his drawings for Kokoshka's comment. 'Like many of your fellow-Germans,' Kokoshka wrote, 'you were abused in your early youth by a criminal demagogy and thrown into a war of aggression, during which the authority of human precepts was thoroughly and totally suspended, and which appears even now to threaten the future validity of those same precepts.'

Kokoshka warned that a 'sentimental outlook' was 'just as sure to lead to waste and failure as the entire order that is collapsing before our eyes today'. That order, he went on to explain, 'sprang from individual egoism, and was helped to ripen by nationalistic narrow-mindedness. Humanism was believed dispensable. This materialistic attitude found its complete embodiment in Fascism'. Koskoshka added:

> Bear in mind that your personal need and poverty, both physical and spiritual, are nevertheless infinitesimal compared to the need and poverty of the children abandoned to savagery in today's world. If your heart turns in hope to the work of rebuilding, because you are young and want to do good, you must help to make a better world for these children.
>
> You saw for yourself that what was achieved by the sword came to nothing in the end, therefore take up your pencil in the hope of doing better.

Kokoshka went on to tell his German interlocutor:

> If we are warmed by love, the sight of our neighbour, other people, a foreign nation, another race, will enable us to shape a new image of the world, in the contemplation of which the isolation of the individual and his nameless torment in a ruined world will give way to the splendour in which the embrace of love will illumine the choice, form and shape of a new order of humanity.

'Man overthrows the dictates of physical laws and the dominion of blind elements,' Kokoshka believed, 'and by that means fights his way up from the subjection of blind obedience to human freedom.'

Many efforts were made in the aftermath of the Second World War by artists, writers, philosophers and social reformers to relegate the cruelties of the previous decade to the past, and to create new alliances of thought and international amity. One such sustained effort took place in the late summer of 1946 when Germans and Britons, Christians and Jews, met in England under the auspices of the Society for Christians and Jews, to discuss how to combat the racism that had scarred the previous decade. Among those present was Alan Paton, a South African opponent of racial segregation and race hatred, who wrote to his wife on August 7, the day after the conference ended: 'The terrible horror of Nazism is brought home, & it is just as terrible to hear that anti-semitism is not dead in Europe, but that it is being increased by the tens of thousands of homeless Jews drifting across Europe. It seems as if man cannot learn . . .'

In an article which was published in South Africa on September 13, Paton warned his fellow South Africans against anti-semitism. 'We are not a cruel or unjust people,' he wrote, 'but we are criminally careless in our entertainment of anti-Jewish prejudice, which, seized upon by those ready to exploit it, could bring even us to disaster.' From this line of thought, Paton drew a universal conclusion:

> Consent to evil a little, and it will grow. Consent to evil a little, and a greater evil will overwhelm us, till no tongue crying out against it will be heard any more. That of which we should have been master will be the master of us. No shame or remorse will save us then. Therefore consent not to this evil at all.

Before returning to South Africa, Paton went to Norway, and there, at the end of September, began to write a book about South Africa. Stressing the social and moral disintegration of South African society, the book was to serve as a beacon for those who were searching for change and reform. In portraying the conflict between Black and White culture in South Africa, Paton also envisaged their eventual reconciliation. One of the books that influenced him was *Black Boy*, by the Black American writer, Richard Wright. Published a year earlier, *Black Boy* was an outspoken cry of pain against oppression and poverty in the American south. Wright had been born in Memphis, Tennessee.

As Paton worked on his book, which he was to call *Cry, the Beloved Country*, he visited the United States, writing to his wife from Atlanta, Georgia: 'It is strange after New York to ride in buses where Whites sit in one place & Negroes in another. It is just like being in South Africa.'

Injustice has never been deterred by national borders.

CHAPTER TWENTY

1947

The mass madness that can turn man into less than a
brute.

MAHATMA GANDHI

At the beginning of 1947 the former Chief of Staff of the United States
Forces, General George C. Marshall, who was about to become Secretary of
State, concluded a year-long mission to China. He had been instructed by
President Truman to find the best way of helping China recover from the
ravages of almost a decade of war, and an even longer period of spasmodic
but often violent civil war. Marshall's report, made public on January 7,
was emphatic. There was no way, he concluded, that the United States, or
any other power or group of powers, could act as a mediator to help settle
China's internal problems.

The Chinese Government and the Chinese Communists had been expected
to enter into negotiations for a compromise. The United States had been
willing to try to act as an honest broker. Marshall reported, however, that
there was no way for any outsider to overcome 'the complete and almost
overwhelming suspicion with which the Communist Party and the Kuomintang regard each other'. Marshall observed that 'on the side of the Government, which is in effect the Kuomintang, there is a dominant group of
reactionaries who have been opposed to almost every effort I have made to
influence the formation of a genuine coalition Government.' This group, he
added, 'were quite frank in publicly stating their belief that co-operation by
the Communist Party in the Government was inconceivable, and that only
a policy of force could definitely settle the issue.'

Force it was to be, and through force China was to fall, like the Soviet
Union and the Soviet satellites, into a one-Party system that crushed all

dissent. In the Soviet Union, Stalin and Molotov were photographed that year casting their votes in the General Election: but there was only one Party on the ballot paper and no opposition to vote for. The photograph was an exercise in political propaganda, not in democracy. The publication that year of David J. Dallin and Boris Nicolaevsy's book *Forced Labour in Soviet Russia* gave a stark portrayal of the dark side of Soviet life. 'If the Soviet system of forced labour is progress,' they asked in their Preface, 'what is reaction? If the Soviet system is "economic democracy", what is slavery?'

China, like the Soviet Union – the two countries between them covering more than a third of the earth's surface – sought to create an ideological uniformity making use of a monolithic educational system, isolation from the rest of the world, censorship and repression. The process was rapid, though at first it was far from clear that the Communists could gain the upper hand. In March more than twenty thousand Communist soldiers were killed in Manchuria, trying to capture Changchun. But in April they succeeded in cutting the Peking-Hankow railway line, and in June they cut the line from Peking to Tientsin. Throughout Jehol and Manchuria the forces of Chiang Kai-shek, while holding on to the main towns and the railway links between them, saw all authority in the countryside around them go over to the Communists.

In June, Chiang Kai-shek ordered the arrest of Mao Tse-tung, the Communist Party Chairman, on charges of organizing an illegal political Party and instigating rebellion. Mao Tse-tung evaded capture, but hundreds of Communist activists were arrested in the principal Kuomintang cities, including Shanghai and Chungking. In November, Chiang Kai-shek held elections throughout China – the first in its history. The Communist Party was excluded from them. Of the 2,337 candidates, all but 497 were members of the Kuomintang. The Communists denounced the elections as a fraud, and continued to make their plans to defeat the Kuomintang and extend their control throughout China.

China was wracked by shortages of food, continuous military clashes between the Communists and the Kuomintang, and the imprisonment, torture and execution of those suspected by either side of being secret opponents. Jung Chang has recorded her mother's recollections of the winter in the Manchurian city of Chinchow, which was then under Kuomintang control:

In mid-December a crowd of 20,000 people raided two well-stocked grain stores.

One trade was prospering: trafficking in young girls for brothels and as slave-servants to rich men. The city was littered with beggars offering their children in exchange for food. For days outside her school my mother saw an emaciated, desperate looking woman in rags slumped on the frozen ground. Next to her stood a girl of about ten with an expression of numb misery on her face. A stick was poking up out of the back of her collar and on it was a poorly written sign saying 'Daughter for sale for 10 kilos of rice.'

Among those who could not make ends meet were the teachers. They had been demanding a pay rise, to which the government responded by increasing tuition fees. This had little effect, because the parents could not afford to pay more.

A teacher at my mother's school died of food poisoning after eating a piece of meat he had picked up off the street. He knew the meat was rotten, but he was so hungry he thought he would take a chance.

The aftermath of the civilian massacres of the Second World War was marked throughout 1947, as it had been the previous year, by trials and executions. On January 16 General Helmuth von Pannwitz was hanged in Moscow for his part in the murder of tens of thousands of Russian civilians behind the lines on the Eastern Front in 1941. On March 3 the Polish authorities sentenced Josef Meisinger to death for mass murder. He had been arrested by the Americans at Kawaguchi, near Tokyo, within a month of Japan's surrender, having ended his career as the head of the Far Eastern Gestapo. He was executed four days after being sentenced. Also executed, after being tried in Cracow, were Arthur Liebehenschel, the last commandant of Majdanek, and Erich Muhsfeldt, the crematorium supervisor there.

On April 7 Rudolf Hoess, the former Commandant at Auschwitz, was hanged at Auschwitz (in Polish, Oswiecim) next to the house inside the camp where he had lived during the war years with his wife and five children. Five days later, in Belgium, sixteen Belgians who had participated in sadistic tortures at Breendonk camp near Antwerp were executed. Because of the nature of their crimes the court ordered that they should be shot in the back. On May 4, Paul Rafaelson, a former labour camp prisoner and a Jew, was sentenced to death in Prague and hanged for cruelties perpetrated on his fellow prisoners. A press agency report noted: 'He is the first Jewish criminal to be hanged for atrocities.'

Another of those executed in 1947 was Karel Curda, the Czech whose treachery had led to the death of his fellow Czechs who had assassinated Heydrich in 1942. After a trial in France, Max Knipping, the French police chief in northern France who had been responsible for the murder of the former French Minister of the Colonies, Georges Mandel, was sentenced to death and shot. Mandel had been one of the Jewish members of the pre-war Reynaud government, and one of those who had wanted to cross to French North Africa and carry on the war from there.

Not all those sentenced to death for war crimes were executed. Field Marshal Albert Kesselring was sentenced to death by a British court-martial on May 6 for having allowed the shooting of 335 Italian civilians as a reprisal against an Italian partisan action. His death penalty was commuted to life imprisonment. Five years later he was pardoned and freed. Less fortunate than Kesselring was another senior German officer, General Friedrich-Wilhelm Müller, the recipient of the prestigious Knight's Cross with Oak Leaves and Swords, who was found guilty by a Greek court of brutality towards civilians in Greece. Müller was executed in Athens on May 20. That same day Bruno Brauer, a former Governor of Crete, who had waged a ruthless war against the Cretan partisans, was also executed in Greece.

Another of those executed in 1947, in Belgrade, was General Löhr, architect of some of the most savage reprisals in both Serbia and Greece. SS Lieutenant-Colonel Walter Blume, who had been responsible for the deaths of thousands of Greek civilians, though sentenced to death at one of the Nuremberg trials, had his sentence commuted to life imprisonment, and was then released after serving three years in Landsberg prison, where Hitler had written *Mein Kampf*. For his part in the deportation of Jews from Athens, Blume was never brought to trial.

In May, at Britain's initiative, the first of 82,000 German prisoners-of-war were sent back to Germany from camps in Egypt. The 5,000 'who are still enthusiastic Nazis and Fascists,' reported the *Palestine Post*, 'will be the last to be removed'. In seeking to prevent a third war with Germany as their adversary, the French and British Governments signed a treaty binding the two signatories to come to each other's aid if attacked by Germany. The treaty was signed on March 4 at Dunkirk, the scene of the near destruction, and remarkable evacuation of the British Expeditionary Force – and many French soldiers – in 1940.

One of the more sombre aftermaths of war took place on October 25, when the coffins of 6,248 American war dead reached New York on board ship, for reburial in the United States. The bodies had been brought from their graves in France and Germany on board the transport ship *Joseph V. Connolly*. It was decided to hold a memorial service in Central Park, and to take for the service a single coffin from among the many thousands. Four hundred thousand people lined the streets as this one coffin was taken along the route from the docks to Central Park, escorted by six thousand servicemen and veterans. At the service in Sheep Meadow, Central Park, wrote Meyer Berger in the *New York Times*, 'chaplains of three faiths prayed for the soldier dead. Their words, and the choking sadness of Taps, suspended in quivering, unseasonal heat, evoked women's sobs and caught at men's throats'. Berger's account continued:

> In the dead quiet, the strains of the dirge 'Dolore', played by the Fort Jay band with muted brass – a kind of sobbing in music – lay in the heated air. The band and the paratroops escort of honor came down a wide grassy aisle with heartbreaking slowness of tread. Everywhere on the Meadow tears started and women stifled their weeping.
>
> In a front row seat, a woman started up. She stretched out her arms and screamed the name 'Johnny'.

A second ship with the coffins of several thousand more dead American servicemen on board arrived in New York harbour five days later. This time there was no parade and no public service. In Britain a Missing Research and Enquiry Service, staffed by more than a hundred 'searchers', had been set up to try to locate the bodies of British aircrew killed in action over Europe. Of the 42,000 airmen reported missing, almost 20,000 were still unlocated four years after the end of the war.

A collective act of peacemaking was concluded in Paris on February 10. This was the formal signing of treaties of peace negotiated the previous year between the former Allies and their former adversaries Italy, Roumania, Bulgaria, Hungary and Finland. The United States and the Soviet Union put their respective signatures on each of these treaties. A series of decisions, some of which had been made at the time of the Axis surrenders, were signed on the basis of negotiations between sovereign States rather than impositions by the victors.

Italy renounced all her African colonial territories, recognized the independence of Albania and Ethiopia, ceded Istria and most of her Adriatic islands to Yugoslavia, and ceded the Dodecanese Islands to Greece. Hungary returned

Transylvania – which she had acquired under the Nazi-inspired Vienna Award in 1940 – to Roumania. Bulgaria returned to Greece and Yugoslavia the territories she had seized from them in 1941, and which had already been physically reclaimed by those from whom they had been taken. Finland accepted that the land gained by the Soviet Union in the Winter War of 1939/40, including the city of Viipuri on the Gulf of Finland, would be annexed in perpetuity by the Soviet Union. Each of the powers agreeing to these terms accepted that during the Second World War it had cast its lot with 'Hitlerite Germany' – a phrase introduced by the Soviet drafters of the agreements.

Despite the joint signatures of the United States and the Soviet Union on the Paris Treaties, the year was dominated by the ideological differences between them. At the beginning of the year a series of American proposals for cultural exchanges between the two countries – proposals that had earlier received Stalin's apparent approval – were ignored or rejected. After elections had been held in Poland on January 19, in which the opposition Parties were allowed virtually no room for campaigning, the United States protested. Its protest was based on a detailed report from the American Ambassador in Warsaw that the elections had been characterized 'by large-scale arrests, intimidation of Opposition voters, invalidation of registers, and forced voting of Government and factory employees'. The British Ambassador noted that in areas comprising some 22 per cent of the electorate the Opposition list of candidates had been suppressed altogether. More than two thousand Peasant Party members, most of them local Party activists, were in prison on election day.

Two weeks after the Polish election, in a wide-ranging survey, the United States Under-Secretary of State, Dean Acheson, described Russia's foreign policy as 'aggressive and expansionist'. Nor did the United States intend to adopt a mere theoretical standpoint of verbal protest. When Britain announced that it could no longer be responsible for the physical security or economic viability of Greece after March 31, Truman immediately took up the challenge. In telling Congress on March 12 that the United States would do all it could to sustain Greek political independence and financial solvency, he added that similar support would be available to Turkey. American civilian and military personnel would help to supply military and economic aid and to train Greeks and Turks to defend themselves. The 'broad implications' of such a pledge were, Truman admitted, serious, but the alternative to such action was, he said, 'much more serious'.

Truman's speech launched what became known as the 'Truman Doctrine'. Some American newspapers regarded Truman's speech as 'the first shot of

World War III'. But as a sign that the doctrine was acceptable to the legislature, Congress gave its support to the Greek-Turkish Aid Bill, which received the President's signature on May 22. A week later a coup in Budapest brought the Hungarian Communist Party into full power, and confirmed the perspective of the government in Washington that the divide was as geographically stark and as ideologically deep as Churchill had portrayed it in his Fulton speech more than a year earlier. At a specially summoned press conference, Truman called the Communist seizure of power in Budapest an 'outage', offered asylum to the Hungarian President, Zoltan Tildy, and protested against the clear evidence of direct Soviet involvement. The Prime Minister, Ferencz Nagy, who was in Switzerland at the time of the coup, resigned by telephone.

Even as the Communists took power in Budapest, intensifying the East-West divide, the new United States Secretary of State, George C. Marshall – who as Chief of Staff of the American armed forces had been one of the main architects of the Allied victory two years earlier – was putting the finishing touches to what became known as the 'Marshall Plan'. He was encouraged in this task by President Truman, who on February 18 invited several new Republican Congressmen, including Richard M. Nixon, to the White House and – Nixon recalled – 'spoke very earnestly of rehabilitating Europe and emphasized his concern that peaceful German production should be encouraged'.

As Marshall developed his plan he also found support from the American diplomat George F. Kennan, who, on March 28, shortly after his return from Moscow, warned the National War College: 'Remember that in abandoning Europe we would be abandoning not only the fountainheads of most of our own culture and tradition; we would also be abandoning almost all the other areas in the world where progressive representative government is a working proposition.'

Marshall made Kennan the head of his planning staff. The aim of their endeavours, Marshall told his staff, was that the European States themselves would 'contribute constructively to the programme as well as profiting from it'. Speaking at Harvard on June 5, Marshall set out a 'One World' financial aid programme for the recovery of all the nations of war-devastated Europe: former Allies, belligerents and neutrals. His plan was intended, he stressed, to help every European nation – including the Soviet Union – that had suffered damage and privation during the war, on both sides of the Iron Curtain, with the exception of Europe's one pariah nation, Spain.

For Britain, the Marshall Plan was welcomed by Ernest Bevin. In a speech to the Foreign Press Association in London on June 13 he described Marshall's Harvard speech as 'one of the greatest speeches made in world history'. He praised the fact that the plan included the Soviet Union, and also saw in it a chance for Britain to be more closely associated with Europe. 'We are more than ever linked with the destinies of Europe,' he told the journalists. 'We are in fact, whether we like it or not, a European nation and must act as such.' As an adjunct to the plan, Britain would serve as 'a link and bridge between Europe and the rest of the world'.

On June 27 Marshall's proposals were debated in Paris by the Foreign Ministers of Britain, France and the Soviet Union – Bevin, Bidault and Molotov. To the distress of Bidault and Bevin, Molotov opposed the plan, arguing that it was an attempt by the United States to provide financial credits to countries that would then have to use the credits to buy American goods. Molotov went so far as to warn Britain and France that the result of the Marshall Plan would have 'nothing in common with the real interests of the peoples of Europe'. Bidault rebutted this argument with vigour, and went on to 'caution' Molotov 'against a decision which would result in dividing Europe into two groups'.

That division was already almost fully in place. When Molotov warned Britain and France of the 'grave consequences' that would confront them if they went ahead with their support for the Marshall Plan, Bevin replied: 'My country has faced grave consequences and threats before, and it is not the sort of prospect which will deter us from doing what we consider to be our duty.' Molotov then left Paris; with him departed all hope that the Soviet Union would participate in a 'One World' structure that many of Marshall's listeners felt was suddenly in the realm of reality. Following Molotov's departure, Britain and France invited all the European countries in need of financial help for reconstruction to a conference at which a Committee of European Economic Cooperation would supervise the work, and where four sub-committees would be set up to examine the immediate need: the four areas were food and agriculture, fuel and power, iron and steel, and transport.

Under strong Soviet pressure, the French Communist Party – a powerful participant in the French governing coalition – left the government in protest at France's acceptance of the Marshall Plan. Not one of the countries of the Soviet bloc agreed to accept Marshall's offer. The Foreign Minister of Czechoslovakia, Dr Vladimir Clementis, wanted to participate: this was later made into one of the charges against him when he was tried and shot. Stalin also forbade Finland, which had avoided Soviet occupation in 1945 at the price of an uneasy pro-Soviet neutrality, to participate in the plan. In its place the Soviet Union created a Council for Mutual Economic Understanding (Comecon), which quickly became an instrument for systematically bleeding the economies of the satellite States. The one-sided nature of Comecon's economic advantages was to be a strong factor in the growth of anti-Moscow feeling throughout the Soviet bloc.

The first meeting of the fifteen countries that agreed to participate in the Marshall Plan was held on July 12 in Paris.* Bevin described Marshall's Harvard speech as 'continent speaking to continent'. The British government would not only put its own resources behind the plan, he said, but would enlist the help of the British Commonwealth in the work of reconstruction. He also said that the door was 'open' for the countries of Eastern Europe to participate. But speed was essential if the work was to succeed. The work of the four sub-committees began three days later. The plan was a simple yet decisive one: over the coming four years the needy countries of Europe would receive from the United States both the essential supplies to restore their economic life, and the essential dollars with which to buy those supplies. It was also the intention of the plan that the European countries should work together to restore the fortunes of the continent: to this end, the possibility – and desirability – of creating a European Customs Union was at the forefront of all the discussions.

The clash between the United States and the Soviet Union over the Marshall Plan was yet another sign of the widening gulf between their respective outlooks and political systems. Marshall spent forty-six days in Moscow negotiating and explaining. But the Russians had no intention of participating in any way in the work of reconstruction, or in allowing the countries of Eastern Europe that were under their sway to be beneficiaries of the American, British, British Commonwealth or French efforts. Declaring in frustrated tones that 'if the doctors deliberate too long the European patient will die', Marshall urged his fellow-Americans to put the Marshall Plan into effect at once and to make it work. His advice was heeded. Just as in 1941 Lend-Lease (which Marshall had also strongly supported) enabled

* The participating countries were Austria, Belgium, Denmark, Eire, France, Greece, Holland, Iceland, Italy, Luxembourg, Norway, Portugal, Sweden, Switzerland and Turkey.

the warring States of Europe, including the Soviet Union, to continue to confront Hitler with a greater chance of success, so in 1947 the Marshall Plan enabled the ravaged States of Western Europe – despite the Soviet Union's hostility – to contemplate the reconstruction and renewal of the economic fabric of their national life.

On December 19 Truman introduced to Congress the economic measures essential to the Marshall Plan, in the form of an Economic Cooperation Bill. 'Our decision will determine in large part the future of the people of Europe,' he said. 'It will also determine in large part whether the free nations of the world can look forward with hope to a peaceful and prosperous future as independent States, or whether they must live in poverty, and in fear of selfish totalitarian aggression.'

Moscow and Washington had replaced London, Paris, Berlin and Rome as the cities in which the future of the world would principally be decided. Disputes all over the world – from Albania to Korea – found their loudest echoes in the corridors of American and Soviet policymaking. The disputes between the two Super Powers matched in intensity anything that had thrown the Great Powers against each other before 1914.

When the United States – and also Britain – protested to the Soviets at the dissolution of the Agrarian Party in Bulgaria and the execution of its leader, Nikola Petkov, their protests were rejected. In September, partly as a counter to American protestations of Communist breaches of human rights, and partly as a response to the Marshall Plan, the European Communist Parties set up, at Moscow's urging, a Central Information Bureau: the Cominform. As well as the seven countries within the Soviet sphere, the French and Italian Communist parties were also represented. At its first meeting, held in Belgrade, the Cominform denounced the attempts by the United States and Britain to 'strengthen imperialism and strangle democracy'.

Stalin kept a close personal watch on the activities of the Cominform, which he put under the firm control of Zhdanov, through whom Stalin's orders and instructions were issued to the Communist Parties of Eastern and Western Europe. He even chose the name of the Cominform journal, *For a Lasting Peace and a People's Democracy*, and there was no one bold enough – or rash enough – to tell him that this was too long a name to catch popular attention. The journal was put on sale in all the Western capitals, while at the same time the sale of non-Communist Western newspapers was strictly curtailed in the Soviet Union and within the Soviet bloc.

Communist control in Eastern Europe was seen to be tightening throughout the year. In Roumania the veteran anti-Fascist politician and former Prime Minister, Julius Maniu, was brought to trial on October 29, accused by the Communist government of having put himself at the disposal of the 'imperialist camp' which allegedly sought to transform Roumania into a base for launching an armed attack on the Soviet Union. He was sentenced to hard labour for life. At the end of the year it was announced from Bucharest that King Michael – who had just represented Roumania at the wedding in London of Princess Elizabeth – had abdicated, and that Roumania had become a People's Republic.

In the Far East, Korea, having been liberated from forty years of Japanese occupation at the end of 1945, was divided almost in half by the victors. North of the 38th parallel of latitude the Soviet Union held sway. South of the 38th parallel the United States was in control. Talks between the United States and the Soviet Union on Korean unification had broken down in May 1946 after only six weeks. When talks were renewed a year later, on the initiative of George Marshall, there was disagreement on what constituted 'democratic government' – the phrase to which both the United States and the Soviet Union were committed under the terms of the Moscow Declaration of December 1945 on a future unified Korea.

In the northern zone of Korea the Russians had introduced compulsory military service. There were rumours of a substantial army being created. When, in September, the Russians proposed the withdrawal of both American and Soviet armed forces, it seemed that their intention was to dominate both sides of the 38th parallel using the new Korean conscripts. The Americans countered by proposing national elections throughout Korea, to be held under United Nations auspices. This the Soviets rejected. The two occupying powers in Korea were on a collision course.

At the very moment when the United States was emerging as the leading and most active anti-Communist Power, the British Empire was on the wane. At a conference in London which came to an end on January 28, negotiations between Britain and Burma reached what was called an 'agreement to part'. During the negotiations, the head of the Burma Executive Council, General U Aung San, leader of the Anti-Fascist People's Freedom League, persuaded the British Cabinet to agree to the rapid evolution of the independence of Burma, through a careful but brisk timetable of peaceful constitutional change. The first stage was to be the election of a Constituent Assembly. This took place within two and a half months of the London meetings. Aung San's Party, which favoured the transfer of power being carried out peacefully and through negotiations won a clear and overall majority (173 seats out of 210).

Not all Burmese wanted to trust to time and talking, however. Even as Aung San made rapid progress towards his goal – achieving a British pledge on July 8 that even if Burma left the Commonwealth it would be Britain's objective to maintain good relations – his enemies prepared to strike. They did so swiftly. On July 19 five men armed with sten guns entered the Secretariat where the Executive Council was meeting, and shot Aung San dead.* Six other members of the Council were also killed. For a few hours it looked as if the forces of moderation would be swept aside, but one member of the council, Thakin Nu, who by chance had been outside the Council Chamber when the assassins struck, was able to form a government.

Thakin Nu ordered the arrest of Aung San's assassins, headed by a former Prime Minister, U Saw – the very men who opposed him politically. At their trial, the man who had been given the task of killing Thakin Nu gave evidence against his co-conspirators. They were sentenced to death. The first to be hanged was U Saw.

Despite the murders in Rangoon, the path to independence proceeded as Aung San had intended. In September the Constituent Assembly approved a constitution, although the five Karen members representing the Karen people boycotted the vote. They wanted an autonomous Karen State set up immediately. Within a month of the constitution being adopted, a Burmese-British Treaty, signed in London on October 17 between Attlee and Thakin Nu, covered all the issues relating to the transfer of power. Ten days later a Bill was presented to the British parliament whereby Burma would become 'an independent country, neither forming part of His Majesty's Dominions nor entitled to His Majesty's protection'. The Bill added that Britain would recognize Burma as 'a fully independent sovereign State'.

The first British annexation, in Lower Burma, had taken place more than a hundred and twenty years earlier, in 1826. The rest of Burma had been annexed to the British Empire in 1885. In the debate on the second – and crucial – reading of the Bill in the Commons on November 5, Attlee pointed out that the British Commonwealth was 'an association of free peoples, and

---

* At the time of Aung San's assassination, his daughter Suu Kyi was two years old. A future champion of democracy and human rights in Burma, she was awarded the Nobel Peace Prize in 1991, while being held in Rangoon under house arrest.

not a collection of subject races', and urged his fellow parliamentarians to welcome the Bill. He had, however, one exceptionally outspoken opponent, Winston Churchill, Leader of the Opposition.

Churchill's father, Lord Randolph Churchill, as Secretary of State for India, had been the prime mover in the annexation of Upper Burma in 1885. Sixty-three years after his father's proud imperial accession, Churchill looked with deep sorrow on its loss. During the debate he warned in grave tones that the Bill was only a prelude to the 'bloody welter' which would soon begin in Burma. As leader of the opposition he could not allow the opposition to be compromised or disgraced by taking part in 'the fearful retrogression of civilization which the abandonment by Great Britain of her responsibilities in the East' was bringing about.

Despite Conservative opposition, the Labour Government had a clear majority, and the Burma Independence Bill passed its second reading by 288 votes to 114. After proceeding with relative ease through its other constitutional stages, it received the Royal Assent on December 10, to come into force in the first week of 1948. The first constitutional step on the final path to Burmese independence had preceded that for India, but only just. On February 20 – three weeks after Britain and Burma had announced their 'agreement to part' – Attlee had told the House of Commons that British rule in India would end no later than June 1948. An attempt to challenge his decision was made by the Conservatives. Churchill, as Leader of the Opposition, and as an opponent of the India Bill of 1935, warned that the period leading up to Britain's departure would be a period of preparation for civil war, and he added: 'It is with deep grief that I watch the clattering down of the British Empire, with all its glories.'

Attlee was adamant that the British must leave and that the Indians – of whatever religion or status – must govern themselves. 'We can help them,' he said. 'We cannot take their burdens on ourselves.' The House of Commons approved his course by 337 votes to 185. Two months later, as a result of negotiations between the new Viceroy, Viscount Mountbatten, who assumed office on March 23, and the Indian leaders, a much closer date was given for the end of British rule: 'somewhere about August'. This would be on the basis of a partition between the predominantly Hindu and the predominantly Muslim regions of the subcontinent.

India was the most populous region of the British Empire, the one for which the Suez Canal lifeline had been created, the one to which several generations of Britons had been drawn as soldiers and administrators. British rule was soon to come to an end. This was not happening to a defeated imperial power, but to one which had emerged victorious against two major enemies. Within India, however, the will to independence was stronger than any loyalty to the King-Emperor among whose armies Indians had served with distinction in both World Wars.

Inside India, the question of partition bedevilled all debate throughout the spring. Gandhi opposed partition in principle, calling it 'vivisection'. In order to avoid bloodshed, he argued, the Muslims must be given 'all they asked'. During February and March, as Muslims feared that they would be put under Hindu rule, there were riots throughout the North-West Frontier Province and the Punjab. At the end of March several hundred Hindus and Sikhs were murdered in Rawalpindi.

On April 18 Nehru stated that both the Punjab and Bengal would have to be divided, with the predominantly Hindu areas being separated from the Muslim areas. On April 23 Jinnah told Mountbatten that his aim, and that of the Muslim League, was not partition, but 'parity in all-India arrangements', including parity between Muslim and Hindu areas 'over external defence'. Jinnah explained that he envisaged a Union Government with provincial – that is Hindu, Muslim and Sikh – provincial autonomies. Nehru rejected this, and on the following day Jinnah appealed to his Muslim followers to be calm, telling them that he was convinced that Mountbatten 'was determined to play fair' to Muslim aspirations.

Mountbatten was the servant of the British Government. Returning to London he found that, within Attlee's Cabinet, the desire to leave India was paramount, and that partition, for all its immediate dangers, was seen as the easiest and quickest solution. A single All-India Government would involve too many complexities and the prospect of endless Hindu-Muslim violence within it. Mountbatten returned to India from London on May 30. He had been instructed to hurry. At ten in the morning of June 2 he presented the Congress and Muslim leaders, and one Sikh leader, with Britain's partition plan. There was, he told them, a 'terrific sense of urgency' about accepting it.

Jinnah asked for a week in which to get his League Council's decision. Mountbatten said that he could not wait for a day. 'Since you will not accept for the Muslim League,' he told Jinnah, 'I will speak for them myself.' On the following day, despite Jinnah's stated unease at committing himself and his people to what he called 'a truncated or mutilated and north-eastern Pakistan' – and despite what must have been his lingering hopes for a united

India with proper Muslim autonomy – the partition plan was accepted. The Viceroy was still the ruler of India.

On July 1 a Partition Council was set up under Mountbatten's chairmanship, with predominantly Hindu and Muslim representation. Many groups felt under-represented. The Sikhs were particularly angered at having, as they felt, their interests ignored: there had been talk of a 'Sikhistan', with its capital at Amritsar, to take its place as a third independent entity alongside India and Pakistan.

The Partition Council set the date of August 14 for the transfer of power to the two incipient sovereign States, India and Pakistan. Details were worked out for the partition of the existing Indian armed forces, in a proportion of roughly two for India and one for Pakistan. India and Pakistan would each become a Dominion (as Canada had been since 1867) and part of the Commonwealth. Jinnah would become Governor-General of the British Dominion of Pakistan – and King George VI would be nominally King of Pakistan but with no constitutional powers. India and Pakistan would both be fully independent of Britain. A leading British Liberal statesman, Lord Samuel – a former High Commissioner for Palestine – called the Indian Independence Act 'a moral to all future generations, a Treaty of Peace without a War'.

With India about to be detached from the imperial crown, Britain's new concept of empire was to evolve through the existing and possibly expanding Commonwealth, which was edging towards the idea of equality between what had hitherto been the 'mother' country and the countries of the Commonwealth and Empire. Attlee made it clear that there was to be no coercion at the time of independence with regard to membership of the Commonwealth. His words were brief and unambiguous: 'We want no unwilling partners in the British Commonwealth.' Even the word 'British' was soon to be dropped in the title of the organization. The first beneficiary of the new policy was Ceylon, whose independent parliament was opened on November 25 amid considerable ceremonial and fanfare.

Among all the countries most closely linked with Britain through ties of empire, language and emigration over many years, Canada was the one emerging as the most independent country on the world stage. The Canadian Prime Minister, William Mackenzie King, described Canada, when speaking at the annual Toronto Trade Fair, as 'among the foremost of the lesser world powers'. This was recognized internationally that year when Canada was given a seat on the Security Council. It was a Canadian initiative that led to the emergence of a compromise resolution on Palestine at the United Nations.

Britain was dependent on Canada in several ways. In the previous year, 57 per cent of the British wheat and flour ration had come from Canada, and large percentages of other foodstuffs. If Britain were to decide to manufacture her own atom bomb – something which the Attlee government was considering in deepest secrecy – Canadian uranium would be a crucial component.

South Africa, which King George VI, Queen Elizabeth and their two daughters (Princess Elizabeth and Princess Margaret Rose) visited that year was also the destination that year of 25,000 British immigrants. The South African government was eager to bring in as many European – that is, White – immigrants as possible, and the chairman of the Immigrants Selection Board visited Holland, Belgium, Italy, Norway and Sweden to encourage further immigration. The large number of applications led the Prime Minister, General Smuts, who wanted to see the primacy of the Whites retained, to speak of his hopes that the following five to ten years would see 'very substantial changes in the right direction'. But Smuts was vexed when Nehru – soon to be the first Prime Minister of independent India – expressed his dissatisfaction with the restriction imposed on Indians with regard to land ownership: restrictions that were based on colour. When Nehru urged Smuts to repeal the Asiatic Land Tenure Act, in which the inequalities were given legal and binding form, Smuts refused.

Britain was still the ruling power in Palestine, where the British Mandate had been in place for a quarter of a century. But the British will to rule had gone: Jewish terror and heightened national aspirations, and Arab determination not to allow a Jewish State to emerge, created a situation where the British Army could no longer maintain control. A severe economic crisis in Britain added to the determination of the government in London not to be saddled with a growing burden, involving extra troops, mounting expenditure, and the anger of the British public that the terrorists and the agitators were not being crushed, or even curbed. If India and Burma could be given up, where Britain had been responsible for far greater numbers of people over a much longer period of time, and had been faced with problems on a much larger scale, then so could Palestine be given up. Attlee and his Cabinet decided to hand the problem to the United Nations.

The British government in London had reached the end of its tether.

Throughout the year there had been killings everywhere in Palestine which shocked both British and Jews. Two Jewish terrorist organizations, the Stern Gang and the Irgun, although both were denounced by the Jewish Agency for Palestine – which represented the mass of Palestinian Jewry – carried out acts of violence against British soldiers, officials and installations. No more than 12,000 of the half million Jews in Palestine were believed to be members of the two terrorist organizations. But 100,000 British soldiers were deployed searching for them. The Jewish Agency's own defence organization, the Hagana, also found itself in a series of confrontations with the British. For their part, British soldiers were frequently called upon to help Jews who were being attacked by Arabs.

When 4,000 Jewish immigrants – many of them survivors of Nazi persecution – were intercepted by the Royal Navy on board their ship the *President Warfield* and sent back to Germany, and to Displaced Persons camps there, the anti-British feeling was not confined to the Jews of Palestine or even only to Jews. The act was portrayed in many countries as a cruel one. The fact that the would-be immigrants had renamed their ship the *Exodus* added poignancy to their forcible return to Europe – and was later to provide the American novelist Leon Uris with the title of a book that served for two decades as a clandestine rallying point to the national aspirations of tens of thousands of Russian Jews.

The climax of Britain's discomfiture came after the sentence of death was passed on a Jewish terrorist, Dov Gruner, and two of his companions, who had taken part in a raid on Acre Prison whereby 180 Arab and 33 Jewish prisoners had been able to escape. The Irgun retaliated by kidnapping two British sergeants – Clifford Martin from Coventry and Mervin Paice from Bristol – and announcing that if the three terrorists were killed the two sergeants would also be killed. The three terrorists were hanged in Acre Prison on July 29. Two days later the bodies of the two sergeants were found hanged in a eucalyptus grove, their bodies booby-trapped with mines. When the bodies were being taken down a British soldier was injured by the mines.

There was indignation and an upsurge of anti-Jewish feeling in Britain when the fate of the two sergeants was widely and angrily publicized. On Merseyside, Jewish-owned shops were attacked and looted and the words DEATH TO ALL JEWS painted on the entrance to the Canada Dock. In Palestine itself, during the course of an upsurge in terror and counter-terror, eighty-nine British soldiers and policemen were killed, as were thirty Jewish civilians, twenty-four Arab civilians, eighteen Jewish terrorists and four

British civilians. Amid this killing and near chaos, at Britain's request a United Nations 'Committee of Study' worked from May to September to propose a solution. Its members were drawn from a wide spectrum of member States.*

In their final report the Committee of Study advocated the termination of the British Mandate and 'independence for Palestine at the earliest possible date'. There should be both a Jewish and an Arab State in a partitioned Palestine. Following this report, another committee was established, the United Nations Special Committee on Palestine (UNSCOP). Its purpose was to discuss how to implement the partition proposal. At its first meeting, at Flushing Meadows, New York, on September 25, it was addressed by the British Colonial Secretary, Arthur Creech Jones, who gave his support to the Committee of Study's recommendations of independence and an end to the Mandate. He added that Britain was not prepared to try to impose any solution by force of arms. If partition led to violent disputes, Britain did not want to be a part of them. He had been instructed by his government colleagues in London 'to announce with all solemnity that they have consequently decided that in the absence of a settlement they must plan for the early withdrawal of the British forces and British Administration from Palestine'.

Both the United States and Soviet delegates spoke in favour of allowing the Jews to have a State in a partitioned Palestine, and of the creation of two States, one Jewish the other Arab. The Palestinian Arab representatives rejected any division of the land or the creation of a Jewish State in any part of it. The United Nations decided to call for a vote, which was held on November 29, when thirty-three nations voted in favour of a Jewish and an Arab State in a partitioned Palestine. Thirteen nations voted against, including all the Arab States. The four non-Arab States that voted against partition were Cuba and Greece, and the newly independent India and Pakistan, whose respective independence and statehood had emerged only three months earlier as a result of partition. Ten nations abstained on the vote, including Britain.

As soon as news of the passing of the partition resolution reached Palestine, the Jews there rejoiced at the imminent coming of statehood and danced in the streets. The Palestinian Arabs took up arms against the Jews. Although British rule still had six months to run, Jewish buses were ambushed and

---

* From Australia, Canada, Czechoslovakia, Guatemala, India, Netherlands, Persia, Peru, Sweden, Uruguay and Yugoslavia.

passengers killed. The British authorities were powerless to restore law and order. As the year drew to a close the killings and counter killings intensified. On December 2 a crowd of two hundred Arabs attacked the Commercial Centre in Jerusalem, looting and burning dozens of Jewish-owned shops. An attack by armed Arabs from Jaffa against Tel Aviv was beaten off by the Jewish defenders, leaving almost seventy Arabs dead. On December 13, members of the Jewish terrorist Irgun group threw two bombs into an Arab market in Jerusalem. Five Arabs were killed. The Jewish Agency, which was the government-in-waiting for the Jewish area of partitioned Palestine, denounced the Jewish terrorist bombings as 'spectacular acts to gratify popular feeling'. But the bombings continued: Arabs killed Jews and Jews killed Arabs in a spiral of escalating destruction that could not be halted.

Not only in Palestine, but throughout the Muslim world, there were demonstrations of protest against any future Jewish State. On December 9, eighty-two Jews were killed in British-ruled Aden when local Muslims attacked the Jewish shops and homes. In Tripolitania – the former Italian colony then under British rule – more than 130 Jews were murdered. Jewish houses were looted and synagogues attacked in Syria and Egypt. An Arab Liberation Army was formed inside Syria, and prepared to resist any Jewish State by armed intervention. The Jordanian Arab Legion, commanded by British officers, held aloof from the fighting for two weeks: then a group of Legionnaires ambushed a convoy on its way to a Jewish youth village and fourteen members of the convoy escort were killed. On December 30, during an Arab attack on the oil refinery at Haifa, forty-one Jewish workers were killed before the British were able to bring the attack to an end. Britain was no longer governing Palestine, but maintaining a precarious and constantly broken ceasefire between two potential belligerents.

On August 14, as India awaited the imminent hour of independence, Nehru spoke in Delhi to a crowd of more than 100,000 people. 'Long years ago,' he said, 'we made a tryst with destiny, and now the time comes when we shall redeem our pledge, not wholly or in full measure, but very substantially. At the stroke of midnight, when the world sleeps, India will awake to life and freedom.' A few hours later, as August 15 began, India became independent.

It had been necessary to set aside the original transfer date of August 14, as it was deemed an inauspicious day by those millions of devout Hindus for whom such considerations were vital. The secular Nehru accepted this, so that it was not until one minute past midnight, as August 15 began, that the long-awaited, much dreamed of transfer of power could finally take place. It did so smoothly, without violence, as the departing British administrators handed over their offices, their files – and their responsibilities for the life and livelihood of hundreds of millions of people – to their incoming Indian counterparts.

For many of the British in India it was a moment of sorrow and even anguish, the end of a historical era with many points of pride. The first British annexations had taken place two hundred years earlier. The province of the Punjab had been annexed in 1849. The British crown had taken over the government of India from the East India Company in 1858, the year after the Indian Mutiny. Queen Victoria had been proclaimed Empress of India in 1877. In the seventy years since then British rule in India had created a largely beneficent administration dedicated to the welfare of the people of India. It had built a vast infrastructure of road and rail communications. It had promoted irrigation and afforestation. It had advanced not only education but the means – through education and access to all modes of Western thought – whereby the Indian national movement could flourish. It had also imposed restraints and restrictions, penalties and imprisonment, on those who taught or stimulated violence in advocating the overthrow of this imperial – and sometimes imperious – structure. Those on whom the burden of independence had fallen were mostly men who had been imprisoned at various times by the British, as Nehru himself had been several times, and Gandhi even more often.

The worst problem confronting the partitioned subcontinent would be the conflict between Hindus and Muslims. Churchill had warned of this in the 1930s and wanted Britain to retain sufficient powers to be able to influence moderation, and protect those who were the victims of the conflict. The Partition Council had worked to devise a geographic line that could be accepted by both Hindus and Muslims. In the weeks before independence, as it became clear that the Sikhs of Amritsar – their Holy City – would be coming under either Hindu or Muslim rule, there were violent clashes. The Sikhs had always harboured hopes of restoring their own early nineteenth-century kingdom – the Khalistan of later nationalist manifestations. The line of partition cut right across the historic Sikh heartland of Ranjit Singh's 1805 confederation. But it was the fear of Muslim, rather than Hindu rule, that predominated in the Sikh violence of 1947.

On August 2 a group of armed Sikhs attacked a Muslim village, killing sixteen villagers. Within two weeks, almost a thousand people had been killed in the rural areas around Amritsar. In Lahore – where both Sikhs and Muslims expected to be put under Muslim rule, the death toll was sometimes as high as a hundred a day. In Calcutta, violence between Hindus and Muslims led to an even higher death rate than in the Punjab. Louis Fischer, an American journalist who had befriended Gandhi, recalled the scene in Calcutta 'where the inhabitants are squeezed together herring-barrel fashion in filthy slums' and where 'a little Moslem girl pulling a Hindu girl's hair or a Hindu boy calling a Moslem boy names might precipitate a mortal riot'. Fischer added: 'Passion and poverty converted men into tinder. On this inflammable material, Gandhi undertook to sprinkle the sweet waters of peace.'

On August 15 Gandhi pitched his tent in Calcutta, in the vast open space in the centre of the city, the Maidan. 'By his presence,' wrote a British eye-witness, Alan Campbell Johnson, 'he helped to ensure that the communal mayhem and violence did not spread to Bengal.' Mountbatten called Gandhi a 'one-man peace-keeping force' – the military equivalent in the outgoing Viceroy's view of four divisions of an army.

The award of the Partition Council was announced two days after independence. With regard to the disputed cities on the margin of the Hindu-Muslim partition lines, India would receive Calcutta and Amritsar, and Pakistan would receive Lahore, as well as most of the area between the River Sutlej and the River Chenab. The two-day-old Government of Pakistan at once protested at what it claimed was the 'injustice' of the awards, under which, from the perspective of Pakistan, too large an area of the Punjab had been handed to India. The Sikhs, who remembered that they had been the rulers of the Punjab when the British took over, felt cheated of their own religious and national control.

The communal violence which had begun in the weeks before independence, escalated. When Calcutta descended into bloodshed, Gandhi – who held no official position in the new Government of India – announced that he would fast 'to the death' unless the killings ceased. After three days the violence subsided. But in the Punjab it not only spread, but created a massive exodus of Hindus and Muslims moving in opposite directions, driven by fear. More than seven million people were on the move. Repeated butchery took place as they fled. At least a quarter of a million people were killed, as they crowded the roads and trains, seeking desperately to move into the newly-declared national territory of their co-religionists. A specially created Punjab Boundary Force, originally set up in order to police the newly delineated border, was too small and too weak to intervene effectively. When both Hindus and Muslims accused it of unfairness, it was disbanded.

Among the British eyewitnesses of the human tragedies that came with partition was Penderel Moon, a British administrator who on August 25 was driving through a predominantly Muslim area to the town of Hasilpur, to which he was told many Hindus had fled. He had never heard of Hasilpur before:

We were shown the general direction in which it lay and were soon bumping along a sandy, sunken and twisty lane that was said to lead to it. I thought we were never going to reach it; and then, almost unexpectedly, we suddenly came upon it – a small but ancient village, rising up on a slight eminence, but concealed from view by big clumps of tall-growing reeds. Along its curving western side there was a belt, fifty to one hundred yards wide, of open sandy ground between the houses and the cultivated fields.

Our road took us along this western side with the sandy belt on our left. As we drove along, I thought I saw well ahead of us some heaps of manure scattered about on this stretch of sand and nearer, though about seventy yards off and close to the edge of the fields, a couple of men seemed to be lying on the ground. I glanced towards Gurmani, murmuring, 'Why are those men lying over there?' and saw on his face a look of incredulous horror as he gazed out of the window of the car.

'They're corpses,' I exclaimed, answering my own question; and now, to my amazement, the heaps of manure took shape as heaps of human bodies. In twos and threes and sixes and tens, more and more came into view as we rounded the curve of the village, till at the north-western corner, close to the main entrance leading up into it, they lay 'Thick as autumnal leaves that strew the vale of Vallombrosa'.*

Men, women and children, there they were all jumbled up together, their arms and legs akimbo in all sorts of attitudes and postures, some of them so life-like that one could hardly believe that they were really dead. I was forcibly reminded of pictures that I had seen as a child of Napoleonic

* Milton wrote: 'Thick as autumnal leaves that strow the brooks in Vallombrosa. (*Paradise Lost*)

battlefields; and there was perhaps some reason for this in that all these people had in fact been shot down by rifle fire.

We got out of the car and walked slowly up into the village, too stunned to speak.

Another British eyewitness of the civil war in the Punjab was Lieutenant-Colonel James Bell, who had served in India for the previous twenty years, first as a private soldier and later as an officer with the Frontier Force Regiment. During the Second World War he had fought with his Indian troops in Abyssinia, in the Western Desert and in Italy. In the midst of the violence provoked by partition he wrote to a friend:

> Nothing you have read about the Punjab is half as bad as what has really been happening. Thousands of towns and villages burnt and destroyed; thousands and thousands of men, women and children slaughtered in a most ferocious and brutal manner. Trains have been regularly stopped and everyone of the wrong community dragged out and hacked down, including women – if they're not stripped, raped and then left to roam naked.
>
> My own train when I came up in August after a few days leave, was stopped just short of Ludhiana and every Muslim, except about ten in our carriage, slaughtered.

In fact, Colonel Bell himself had hidden the ten Muslims in the washroom of his compartment. Later Bell, whose regiment at the time of Partition contained Muslims, Sikhs, Hindus and Pathans, made himself personally responsible for the safe conduct of 350,000 refugees.*

The plight of the refugees was often cruel and dire. The arrival of the survivors, many of them seriously wounded, all of them bringing stories of slaughter, inflamed the passions of those to whom they came. This was particularly true when a mass of Hindu refugees reached Delhi. Local Hindus and Sikhs attacked Muslims throughout the city. After several days of violence in the streets, almost all Delhi's Muslims fled. An ancient fort, Purana Quila, hitherto – and since – a tourist attraction, was turned into a vast

* In 1948 James Bell transferred to the Pakistan Army, where he served for twelve years, first as Commandant on the Frontier Force Regimental Centre in Abbottabad, and subsequently as Administrative Officer of the Pakistan Air Force public school.

refugee camp. Within two weeks it housed, in conditions of considerable privation, 50,000 Muslim refugees. The new administration of the United Provinces was able, by a supreme effort of diligent military and police work, to prevent the scale of killings that had taken place in the Punjab. But when Hindus killed Muslims the savagery was as intense as when Muslims killed Hindus. They were also examples of courage and humanity.

'A Hindu gave shelter to a Moslem friend the other day,' Gandhi wrote to a friend on October 15, about an incident in Bombay. 'This infuriated a Hindu mob who demanded the head of the Moslem friend. The Hindu would not surrender his friend. So both went down literally in a deadly embrace. This was how it was described to me authentically. Nor is this the first instance of chivalry in the midst of frenzy. During the recent blood bath in Calcutta, stories of Moslems having, at the peril of their lives, sheltered their Hindu friends and vice versa were recorded.' Gandhi added: 'Mankind would die if there were no exhibition at any time and anywhere of the divine in man.'

Philip Mason, who was an eye witness of the killings near Delhi, later wrote:

In the village near Delhi where the Hindus killed the Muslims, race – in the sense of physical difference – was not involved. In that part of Northern India, you could tell a man's religion or caste by the way he tied his headcovering or trimmed his beard, but no one could distinguish a hundred newborn Hindu babies from a hundred Muslim; there are some castes of which there is virtually a Hindu branch and a Muslim branch.

There are villages – this was one – where the Muslims have lived alongside the Hindus in their own quarter peacefully for centuries. But change was in the air and change meant insecurity, and there was fear of the future. There was no danger of Muslim rule in this part of India; there was little prospect of getting the land the Muslims had tilled, which in the end went to Hindu refugees from the West.

Calculated advantage played little part. There was a generalized picture in the mind of the Hindu villager of 'the Muslim' – someone unclean, a 'mlechcha'. Muslims were people who killed cows and ate beef, who pulled down temples and destroyed the images of the gods.

This generalized picture was obliterated as a rule by the figure of the Karim or Haidar or Bashir whom they knew, whom they saw moving inoffensively about the village every day, who might have lent them a hand when the bullocks could not get the cart out of the hole at the corner of the road in the last rains. But the hated picture grew bigger and covered the faces they knew when they heard the Muslims were killing Hindus at Noakhali.

Gandhi had gone to Noakhali when the killings had broken out there nine months before independence. On the day he left by train from Delhi, thirty-two people had been killed in Hindu-Muslim fighting in Calcutta. Driving through the riot-torn areas of Calcutta, Gandhi wrote of how he was overcome by 'a sinking feeling at the mass madness that can turn man into less than a brute'.

Noakhali was a rural area in which Muslims had killed Hindus, burned Hindu homes, forcibly converted Hindus to Islam, and raped Hindu women. 'It was the cry of outraged womanhood,' Gandhi told a prayer meeting before setting off, 'that has peremptorily called me to Noakhali.' He would not leave Bengal, he said, 'until the last embers of the trouble are stamped out. I may stay on here for a whole year or more. If necessary, I will die here. But I will not acquiesce in failure. If the only effect of my presence in the flesh is to make people look up to me in hope and expectation which I can do nothing to vindicate, it would be far better that my eyes were closed in death'.

In the neighbouring province of Bihar, with a population of thirty-one million Hindus and five million Muslims, the events in Noakhali and neighbouring Tippera had incensed the Hindus, thousands of whom had marched through the streets of Patna and other towns shouting 'Blood for blood'. In a single week 'the number of persons officially verified as killed by rioters', wrote the Delhi correspondent of *The Times*, was 4,580. Gandhi later put the total at more than ten thousand, most of them Muslims. 'My present mission', Gandhi wrote in a letter from Noakhali, 'is the most difficult and complicated one of my life . . . I am prepared for any eventuality. "Do or Die" has to be put to the test here. "Do" here means Hindus and Mussulmans should learn to live together in peace and amity. Otherwise, I should die in the attempt.'

Gandhi visited and stayed in forty-nine villages during his Noakhali pilgrimage. 'He would rise at four in the morning,' wrote Louis Fischer, 'walk three or four miles on bare feet to a village, stay there one or two or three days talking and praying incessantly with the inhabitants and then trek to the next village. Arrived in a place, he would go to a peasant's hut, preferably a Moslem's hut, and ask to be taken in with his companions. If rebuffed he would try the next hut. He subsisted on local fruits and vegetables and goat's milk if he could get it. . . . He had just passed his seventy-seventh birthday.'

After Gandhi had left Noakhali, Louis Fischer commented:

He promised to return some day. He promised to return because his mission had not been completed. He had not established the brotherhood of Hindus and Moslems in Noakhali. Relations had improved perceptibly but insufficiently.

Gandhi's task in Noakhali consisted in restoring inner calm so that the refugee Hindus could return and feel safe and so that Moslems would not attack them again. The malady was deep; the violent eruptions, however, were infrequent and ephemeral. Gandhi, therefore, did not despair. He felt that the local communities, undisturbed by outside political propaganda, could live in peace.

The call of Noakhali had been insistent. Gandhi might have sent a message from Delhi or preached a sermon. But he was a man of action, a Karma yogi. He believed that the difference between what we do and what we could do would suffice to solve most of the world's problems. All his life he endeavoured to eliminate the difference. He gave his maximum.

The human suffering of so many tens of thousands of lives destroyed in India in a few months – of the Hindu, Sikh and Muslim refugees, of families uprooted, of culture and continuity impeded – deeply affected the first years, and indeed the first decades, of India and Pakistan. 'People die, and the fact of killing, though painful, does not upset me,' Nehru declared of the widespread communal violence in his home province of the United Provinces. 'But what does upset one is the complete degradation of human nature and, even more, the attempts to find justification for this.'

Within a month and a half of independence more than a million and a half refugees had left their homes for their respective new countries. Another half million were on their way to the partition line. In due course, as many as ten million people had fled from their homes and made their way as refugees, some with their pitiful possessions on carts or in bundles, others with nothing at all but the clothes they stood up in. Disease and flooding caused hardship and death on the march. In one dramatic and successful move 200,000 refugees, most of them Sikhs, were transferred in a single column from the district in which they lived across the border into India, escorted by Gurkha troops.

Mountbatten's Press Attaché, Alan Campbell Johnson, who flew along some of the main refugee routes on September 21, recorded in his diary: 'Today we saw for ourselves something of the stupendous scale of the Punjab upheaval. Even our brief bird's-eye view must have revealed nearly half a million refugees on the roads. At one point during our flight Sikhs and Moslem refugees were moving almost side by side in opposite directions. There was no sign of clash. As though impelled by some deeper instinct, they pushed forward obsessed only with the objective beyond the boundary.'

Despite the Hindu-Muslim violence, the governments of India and Pakistan were resolute in seeking to avoid conflict. On September 21 they issued a joint statement that 'any conception of a conflict between India and Pakistan is repugnant'. The two governments, the statement added, 'will therefore work to the utmost of their capacity to remove the causes of conflict'. One serious problem for Pakistan was the remoteness of East Pakistan – with its capital Dacca – from the rest of the country. Famine conditions there exacerbated the situation. It was almost a thousand miles between the two halves of Pakistan.

Another problem confronting India and Pakistan was that of Kashmir, where a Hindu ruler – whose family had been placed on the throne as a result of British influence a century earlier – governed a large Muslim majority. As Muslim tribesmen from outside his borders attacked in force, the Maharaja asked to join India, as a matter of urgency. India accepted Kashmir's inclusion on October 26. The Muslim attackers redoubled their efforts and reached the outskirts of the capital, Srinagar. Indian troops were flown in, and British subjects living in the city were evacuated. The capital remained under Indian control, but large sections of Kashmir were occupied by Muslim troops – both Pathan tribesmen and a Kashmiri Muslim force known as Azad Kashmir – against whom India did not have sufficient manpower to move with any reasonable hope of driving them out.

In a radio broadcast to the people of India on November 2, Nehru declared that he was prepared to have a referendum in Kashmir under United Nations auspices, but that meanwhile 'we have given our word to the people of Kashmir to protect them against the invader, and we will keep our pledge'. Nehru was true to his word: India remained in control of the capital and much of the country. A year later a United Nations Commission organized a cease-fire.

In Vietnam, the French had no intention of acting as the British had done in India and Burma. For them, the French 'civilizing mission' was not over. For the French psyche, the colonies were far more an integral part of France than even India had been part of Britain for the British. As seen by the government in Paris, the Vietnamese Communist movement and its Viet-minh armed forces were an irritant to be crushed and eliminated. More than 115,000 French troops, well-armed, with armoured vehicles, artillery and air support, confronted a combined military and guerrilla force of about 100,000, ill-armed and with no air power.

The French were certain that they could overcome this challenge to their rule. The French general in Vietnam, Jean Etienne Valluy, was a combat veteran. He had joined the French army in 1917 and fought in the trenches of the Western Front. He had been taken prisoner by the Germans in 1940, was repatriated, and fought against the Germans again in 1945. He was certain that he could defeat the Vietminh forces, whom he regarded as an undisciplined rabble. He told his superiors that he was confident that he 'could eliminate all organized resistance in three months'.

On October 7 General Valluy launched Operation Lea, designed to seize the Communist governmental and military headquarters at Bac Kan, seventy-five miles north of Hanoi. The operation began with a parachute drop on Bac Kan itself. The drop came as a complete surprise to the Vietminh and was nearly a complete success. Ho Chi Minh and General Giap were both at headquarters as the parachutists came down. They managed to jump into a camouflaged hole in the ground just before French troops began to search the bushes above it. Neither leader was caught, although the French captured the letters that were on Ho Chi Minh's desk.

General Phillip B. Davidson, a United States army officer who has chron-icled the Vietnamese war in all its phases, has reflected: 'The lucky escape of Ho and Giap underscores the fact that the destiny of nations – like that of individuals – sometimes turns on nothing more than the accidents of fate. Had the French captured these two men, would Vietnam have been spared thirty years of bloodshed and destruction? Would France and the United States have escaped the divisiveness of national spirit and the trauma of defeat? Unfortunately history never answers these "what-if" questions.'

Within a few days of the escape of Ho Chi Minh and General Giap, the

French parachutists in Bac Kan were themselves surrounded by the Vietminh. For nine days the two relief columns sent to liberate them were harassed, forced again and again to come to a halt. On October 19 the besieged parachutists were finally reached and rescued. The Vietminh disappeared northward to their bases nearer the Chinese border. Operation Lea had failed. Two further French offensives before the end of the year were likewise unable to capture the leaders or to destroy the Vietminh. To carry out these military operations, France diverted monetary and human resources badly needed for its own domestic recovery.

As most of the world's nations continued to struggle to recover from the ravages of prolonged war – for many of them the second war of the century – and as the Cold War threatened yet another potential conflict, the daily life of hundreds of millions was quiet, calm and unexceptional. The hardest task was to earn a reasonable living, and to have the opportunity of work and education for one's children. Legislation that made progress to that end – such as the introduction of the Welfare State in Britain, with its National Health Service as a central element of social fairness – was what seemed to matter most. The deliberations of the United Nations or the Cominform, or the conferences and committees through which so many global issue were being discussed, were remote to the mass of mankind, however much their outcome might affect them.

Echoes of the past abounded. On February 3 a German V2 rocket was loaded on board ship at the London Docks on its way to the Australian War Memorial at Canberra, as an exhibit. Like many such institutions, including the Imperial War Museum in London, the Australian War Memorial had been set up to commemorate the First World War: its area of concern was necessarily being extended.

Shadows of the past still needed to be lifted. Under a constitutional referendum held in Japan on May 3, Japan renounced the use of war. By the vote of the people who for almost four consecutive years had been portrayed by their enemies as cruel barbarians, it seemed that an important step forward had been made in the world. An equally important step in the evolution of new and potentially beneficial forces came in 1947 when Sir John Cockroft, Director of the British Atomic Research Station at Harwell, gave the World Power Conference at The Hague the first public description of the use of atomic energy as a source of domestic fuel.

As well as the beneficial advances of science, there was the endless struggle to obtain military advantage: a struggle far older than the century, and conducted in the strictest secrecy. On October 14 an American pilot, Chuck Yeager, broke the sound barrier. It was the first time that this had been done. Above the Edwards' Air Force base in California, Yeager reached a speed of 1,126 kilometres an hour. The project was so secret – part of the intensifying Cold War search for predominance – that news of its success was withheld from the public for eight months.

CHAPTER TWENTY-ONE

1948

Our first goal is to secure fully the human rights of
our citizens.

PRESIDENT HARRY S. TRUMAN

THE INDEPENDENCE of India and Pakistan represented the fulfillment
of the national aspirations of several hundreds of millions of people. But the
violence which had accompanied it during its first days continued for many
months. On 12 January 1948, Gandhi, who was living in part of the garden
of Birla House in Delhi, announced that he was starting yet another fast
until the killing stopped. For six days he ate nothing, and drank only small
quantities of sweetened water. As he became weaker and weaker, the leaders
of all communities promised him that they would carry out his prescription
for the restoration of communal harmony, and begged him to end his strike.
He agreed to do so. On January 28 Mountbatten's Press Secretary, Alan
Campbell Johnson, wrote in his diary:

Rejoicings over Gandhi's survival from his fasting ordeal ware marred
today by a bomb incident in the garden of Birla House. The bomb, a
home-made affair, went off during the first Prayer Meeting which Gandhi
had attended since the ending of his fast. The force of its explosion,
however, was broken by a wall, which was slightly damaged.

No one was hurt, and there was no panic, Gandhi continuing to conduct
the meeting without showing any sign of awareness that anything
untoward had happened. Indeed, Lady Mountbatten, who went straight
round to visit him, found him wholly unperturbed. He told her he thought
that 'military manoeuvres must have been taking place somewhere in the
vicinity'.

Two days later, on January 30, as Gandhi was walking in New Delhi to the garden of Birla House, in order to hold his regular prayer meeting, a young man greeted him, and then fired three shots. Within a few minutes Gandhi was dead. Shock and bewilderment spread throughout India. The scene in Gandhi's bedroom, to which his body had been taken immediately following the assassination, was witnessed by Alan Campbell Johnson:

> Everyone was in tears. Just outside were numerous sandals which people had taken off before entering the room.
>
> In the far corner was the body of Gandhiji. At first I thought it was completely covered in a large blanket, but then I realized that his head was being held up by one of about a dozen women who were seated round him chanting prayers and sobbing in a plaintive rhythm. Gandhi's face was at peace, and looked rather pale in the bright light. Also they had taken away the steel-rimmed glasses which had become almost an integral part of his features.
>
> The smell of the incense, the sound of the women's voices, the frail little body, the sleeping face and the silent witnesses – this was perhaps the most emotionally charged moment I have ever experienced. As I stood there I felt fear for the future, bewilderment at the act, but also a sense of victory rather than defeat; that the strength of this little man's ideas and ideals, from the very force of the devotion he was commanding here and now, would prove too strong for the assassin's bullets and the ideas they represented.
>
> After standing for some time in silent homage, we moved out into the main hall. As the evening drew on the crowds outside multiplied; one could see their faces pressed against the windows, and they banged insistently upon the glass.

Gandhi's assassin, Nathuram Vinayak Godse, was the editor of a Poona newspaper. A Hindu extremist, he was fiercely opposed to Gandhi's message of reconciliation with Muslims and of cooperation with Hindu untouchables. 'Gandhiji has been killed by his own people, for whose redemption he lived,' the *Hindusthan Standard* wrote. 'This second crucifixion in the history of the world has been enacted on a Friday – the same day Jesus was done to death one thousand nine hundred and fifteen years ago. Father, forgive us.' The *New York Times* reflected this Christian theme, telling its readers: 'He tried, in the mood of the New Testament, to love his enemies, and to do good to those who despitefully used him. Now he belongs to the ages.'

The Government of India reacted to Gandhi's assassination by declaring all private armies illegal, whether Hindu or Muslim. But despite the assassination, the progress of statehood continued uninterrupted. On June 21 the former British Viceroy of India, Lord Mountbatten, who on independence had become Governor-General, was succeeded by an Indian politician, Chakravarti Rajagopalachari, who took the oath of office wearing the simple, white homespun clothing that Gandhi had advocated for all Indians. In his speech of acceptance he made a strong plea for the toleration that Gandhi had espoused, telling his fellow-Indian subjects: 'India is unchangeably committed to the policy of making everyone within her borders find pride and joy in citizenship irrespective of caste, creed, or race.'

In British India, in addition to the provinces, there were 244 Princely States whose rulers had direct treaties with Britain. With the coming of independence each of these States had to join the larger Indian or Pakistani sovereignty. In one of them, the small State of Junagadh, the Muslim ruler, the Nawab, had declared for Pakistan. His decision violated the twin principles, inherent in partition, of contiguity and communal majority. After a series of complicated negotiations, India took over the State. A plebiscite was then held in Junagadh in which 190,779 of the inhabitants voted for accession to India and only ninety-one for accession to Pakistan. Today, fifty years after the vote, the Nawab's palace is deserted and desolate.

In two of the Princely States – the largest two – Kashmir and Hyderabad, there were disputes which involved fighting and bloodshed. Kashmir had been effectively divided before the end of 1947 as a result of the advance of the respective Indian and Pakistani armies, and during 1948 a cease fire was negotiated through a United Nations Commission. Fifty years later Kashmir was still divided, its conflict unresolved despite repeated military confrontations and diplomatic efforts.

The rulers of the Princely States were allowed to retain their 'titles and dignities', their residences – often substantial palaces – and their private fortunes, which were sometimes considerable. But their political power, which until 1947 had been exercised through British Residents appointed by the Viceroy, was taken away from them in its entirety. The Government of India was emphatic in this respect, informing each prince and ruler in July 1948: 'There is, however, one essential condition which the Government of India have attached to all schemes recognized by them relating to the future set-up of the States, namely, transfer of full power from the Rulers to the people. They have firmly declined to be a party to any arrangements relating to the States unless they expressly provided for the establishment of responsible government.' The Princes and Rulers had no choice but to accept.

In Hyderabad, the Nizam, a Muslim prince who was a direct descendant of the Moghul Emperor's Viceroy, refused either to accede to the Indian Union or to grant immediate responsible government. His country would, he said, remain independent. Nehru was emphatic, however, that 'Hyderabad, situated as it is, cannot conceivably be independent, and India can never agree to it.' The State, surrounded on all sides by India, was 86 per cent Hindu. But from within it a Muslim para-military group, the Razakars, began to carry out terrorist attacks across the border into India.

Under pressure from India, on June 15 the Nizam agreed to hold a plebiscite. But the Government of India refused his request to retain economic and fiscal freedom in any future association with India. On September 7 the Government of India demanded the disbandment of the Razakars and the right of Indian troops to be stationed in Secunderabad, the principal military cantonment in the kingdom. The Nizam refused both demands and on September 11 he appealed to the United Nations. Nehru replied that the dispute between India and Hyderabad was 'a purely domestic issue' over which the United Nations had no jurisdiction. Then, on the morning of September 13, Indian troops crossed into Hyderabad at five separate points in the north, south, east and west. The operation was under the control of Vallabhai Patel, the 'strong man' of Congress, whom Nehru had made Home Minister.

The two senior Indian generals whom Patel appointed to take charge of the military operation had both seen distinguished service in the Second World War as commanders of Indian armoured regiments. One of them, General Rajendrasinji, had fought both in the Western Desert, where he had led his men out of a German encirclement, and in Burma, where he had taken part in the advance on Rangoon. Four and a half days after the attack was launched the Nizam accepted India's demands and ordered a ceasefire. General Rajendrasinji was appointed military governor of Hyderabad. The Razakars, maintaining themselves as an underground resistance, were hunted down. Their prowess at the time of the invasion had been much feared, and even vaunted by the Indian Army, leading Eric Britter, the Delhi correspondent of *The Times* to write, on the day of the Hyderabad's surrender:

As for the Razakars, whose fanaticism, offensive spirit, military organization, and equipment have been greatly exaggerated by Indian propagandists in recent months, they have proved the broken reeds that anyone who knew much about them always thought they would be. As reported by your Correspondent several months ago, not more than five per cent of their total number (which was also wildly exaggerated) were armed with firearms, mostly old muzzle-loaders, while the remaining ninety-five per cent carried staves and spears.

Naturally, they could do little against Indian armoured divisions.

During the course of five and a half days of battle 286 Muslim Hyderabadi soldiers and just over a hundred Indians had been killed.

In Pakistan the presence of more than five million refugees from India placed a heavy burden on the economy of the newly independent State. On August 27 Mohammad Ali Jinnah – who had become Governor-General at Pakistan's independence – was forced to declare a state of emergency. Almost half a million refugees then in West Punjab were ordered to move to other provinces. The tribes of the North-West Frontier were also a source of aggravation for Jinnah and his government, which wanted to demobilize them, but feared that it would be unable to do so. In an attempt to secure the loyalty of the tribes, Jinnah made a strenuous tour of the frontier, but was taken ill, and died on September 11 – two days before Indian troops marched into Hyderabad.

Jinnah's death caused a surge of grief throughout Pakistan. But his legacy of secular leadership was under stress. One area which at the time of his death had already emerged as a source of future problems for his country was a move towards the Islamicization of the State. The organization of orthodox Muslim opinion, the Shariat Movement, demanded a much greater and specifically Muslim content in civil law and education.

Each postwar year until the end of the century saw repercussions from the Second World War; 1948 was no exception. On February 5, in his prison cell in Nuremberg, the Commander of the German forces in Holland at the time of the German surrender, General Johannes Blaskowitz – who in 1939 had protested to Hitler about Nazi atrocities in Poland – killed himself shortly before he was to be brought to trial. On the following day, in the Cherche-Midi Prison in Paris, the first Military Governor of Paris, Otto von Stuelpnagel, likewise committed suicide rather than face trial for his actions while he was ruler of the French capital. Among those who did not escape execution was Elsa Ehrich, the chief female SS guard at Majdanek: she was hanged in Lublin, near the scene of her crimes.

Not all war criminals who were sentenced to death for mass murder were hanged. On May 28 the United States military commander in West Germany, General Lucius D. Clay, wrote in a private memorandum:

> As a result of delays in review, stay of sentence pending possible appeal to the Supreme Court, et cetera, the death sentences imposed by military courts on Germans charged with the murder of concentration camp inmates, prisoners of war, et cetera, has accumulated until there are now in excess of five hundred awaiting execution. If and when the status of appeals to the Supreme Court is finally determined, we will then be confronted with this mass execution . . .
>
> I find it difficult to adjust my own mental processes to requiring what looks to be almost a mass execution of more than five hundred persons. I believe it also gives an appearance of cruelty to the United States even though there is no question in my mind that the crimes committed fully justify the death sentence. Moreover, more than three years have elapsed since the crimes were committed.

Some sentences were carried out. Others were commuted to life imprisonment. When Pope Pius XII suggested to Clay that he should exercise clemency for all war criminals without exception, Clay rejected the suggestion. A number of German bishops were successful, however, in prevailing upon Clay to set aside the death penalty on Willi Seifert, who had been found guilty of mass murder with the Special Task Force killing squads on the Eastern Front in 1941.

By 1948, the historian Richard Evans has written, 'the eagerness of the Western Allies to prosecute, condemn, and execute Nazi war criminals was diminishing. The new priorities of resisting Communism and fighting the Cold War were casting the crimes and criminals of the Third Reich into a new light'. Evans added: 'The inhabitants of the Western zones of Germany had to be given responsibility for their own affairs and encouraged to stand up for "Western" values against the threat from the East. In these circumstances, the Allies' military courts began to wind down their activities. The task of prosecuting German war criminals was gradually passed over to the Germans themselves, as was the administration of justice in general.'

The Polish Government continued to find, extradite and bring to trial those Germans who had committed crimes on Polish soil. In August Dr Josef Bühler, who had carried out the 'special pacification operation' of May-June 1940 in which 3,500 Polish intellectuals were killed, was brought to trial in Cracow – the scene of his wartime power – found guilty and executed.

On November 12, in the former War Ministry building in Tokyo, before the International Military Tribunal, Far East, seven Japanese wartime leaders, including General Hideki Tojo, were found guilty of war crimes. All seven were sentenced to death, and sixteen others to life imprisonment. The sentences were reviewed by General MacArthur two weeks later and upheld in their entirety. The death sentences were carried out, by hanging, on December 23.

The echoes of the past were never entirely silenced, but the demands of the postwar world were loud and claimant. In his State of the Union address to Congress on January 7, Truman stressed his desire to facilitate the admission into the United States of more than 200,000 Displaced Persons then in Europe, and to give priority to the legislation needed to institute the Marshall Plan. 'Twice within our generation,' he said, 'world wars have taught us that we cannot isolate ourselves from the rest of the world,' and he went on to explain his purpose:

> When the European economy is strengthened, the product of its industry will be of benefit to many other areas of economic distress. The ability of free men to overcome hunger and despair will be a moral stimulus to the entire world.
>
> We intend to work also with other nations in achieving world economic recovery. We shall continue our cooperation with the nations of the Western Hemisphere. A special program of assistance to China, to provide urgent relief needs and to speed reconstruction, will be submitted to the Congress.
>
> Unfortunately, not all Governments share the hope of the people of the United States that economic reconstruction in many areas of the world can be achieved through cooperative effort among nations. In spite of these differences we will go forward with our efforts to overcome economic paralysis.
>
> No nation by itself can carry these programs to success; they depend

upon the cooperative and honest efforts of all participating countries. Yet the leadership is inevitably ours.

On the day after Truman's speech, Marshall himself testified before the Senate Foreign Relations Committee that his plan – it was put before Congress as the European Recovery Plan Bill – needed to be brought in quickly. 'Either undertake to meet the requirements of the programme,' he said, 'or don't undertake it at all.' To be 'quite clear', he added, 'this unprecedented endeavour of the New World to help the Old is neither sure nor easy. It is a calculated risk. But there can be no doubts as to the alternatives. The way of life that we have known is literally in balance. Our country is now faced with a momentous decision. If we decide that the United States is unable or unwilling effectively to assist in the reconstruction of western Europe we must accept the consequences of its collapse into the dictatorship of police States'.

Marshall and his plan were opposed publicly by a former President, Herbert Hoover, who had spearheaded massive American relief programmes after the First World War. Hoover wanted a fifteen month rather than a four-year commitment. He urged cutting even the fifteen month contribution by more than a third, and described anything greater than short-term relief as 'drain on the American economy'.

The European Recovery Plan Bill suffered only marginally from the opposition of Hoover, and those Senators who still hankered after isolationism and monetary caution. In place of Marshall's request for an initial $6,800 million over fifteen months, the Senate proposed $5,300 million for an initial twelve-month period. As is the inevitable fate of all Bills presented to Congress, the procedural element ensured delay, but the concept had been accepted.

In his State of the Union message Truman – who had to face re-election that year – also stressed that he wanted a major forward leap in economic reforms. These included the conservation of human and natural resources, cheap public housing, control of wages, prices and rents, more electrification in the farming areas, a rise in the legal minimum wage, and an increase in the taxes on corporations. Republicans disliked the essentially interventionist and, as they decried it, socialist tone of the speech. Southern Democrats were disturbed by Truman's pledge on civil rights when he declared: 'Our first goal is to secure fully the human rights of our citizens.'

Three weeks after this challenge, and without conferring with his own

Democrat congressional leaders, Truman sent a civil rights message to Congress. This was the first time that an American President had sent a special message on this divisive and yet humanitarian domestic theme. 'Not all groups are free to live and work where they please, or to improve their conditions of life by their own efforts,' he said. 'Not all groups enjoy the full privileges of citizenship. The Federal Government has a clear duty to see that the Constitutional guarantees of individual liberties and of equal protection under the laws are not denied or abridged anywhere in the Union. That duty is shared by all three branches of the Government, but it can be filled only if the Congress enacts modern, comprehensive civil rights laws, adequate to the needs of the day, and demonstrating our continuing faith in the free way of life.'

The issue of discrimination was one on which Truman felt strongly. His call was not only for a change in attitudes but for legislation. He wanted a Federal law against 'the crime of lynching, against which I cannot speak too strongly'. Discrimination in interstate travel by rail, bus and aeroplane should be ended. The right to vote should be protected. Black soldiers serving in the army should not be subjected to racial abuse. When a group of southern Democrats told him privately that his re-election prospects in the South would be better if he 'softened' his views, he replied that although his own ancestors were Confederates 'my very stomach turned over when I learned that Negro soldiers, just back from overseas, were being dumped out of army trucks in Mississippi and beaten. Whatever my inclinations as a native of Missouri might have been, as President I know this is bad. I shall fight to end evils like this.'

Truman was ahead of his time: in the course of his civil rights message of February 2 he asked Congress to act on the claims of the Americans of Japanese descent who had been forced to leave their homes during the war, and had been kept in confinement 'solely because of their racial origin'. It was to be four decades before Congress rectified the wrongs done to this group, some of whom had fought alongside their fellow-Americans in the battles in Europe in 1944 and 1945.

Truman's principal overseas concern during 1948 was the continuing intensification of the Cold War. On March 5 General Clay reported from Germany that there was 'a new tenseness in every Soviet individual with whom we have official relations'. But it was the fate of Czechoslovakia that was the dominant factor in the ringing of alarm bells in Washington, and accelerated the final passage through Congress of the Marshall Plan.

The Czech Cabinet had originally voted unanimously in favour of accepting the Marshall Plan. But after the Czech leaders were summoned to Moscow, they announced that they had decided to turn it down. The death on March 10 of the Czech Foreign Minister, Jan Masaryk – the son of Thomas Masaryk, the founder of independent Czechoslovakia – also deeply affected American opinion. It seemed certain that he had either been driven to suicide, or murdered, by Communist pressure or design. Four days after Masaryk's death the Senate passed the Marshall Plan under a new title, the Economic Cooperation Act. No one recalling the isolationism of the pre-war years, and the isolation of several of the Senators supporting the plan, could doubt – wrote the British historian H.G. Nicholas – 'that in the Senate's vote of 69 to 17 he was witnessing one of the great reversals of American foreign policy'.

Truman felt a deep pride in what had been done. 'In all the history of the world we are the first great nation to feed and support the conquered,' he wrote privately shortly after the Bill became law, and he added, casting the net of American achievement to two even wider spheres: 'We are the first great nation to create independent republics from conquered territory, Cuba and the Philippines. Our neighbours are not afraid of us. Their borders have no forts, no soldiers, no tanks, no big guns lined up.' That was true of both Canada and Mexico, America's two continental neighbours.

As an additional sign of the new United States commitment to postwar Europe, the House of Representatives added to the Marshall Plan package a further $60 million for the United Nations International Children's Emergency Fund. A sense of imminent conflict with the Soviet Union over-shadowed, however, any comforting contemplation of longer-term improvements in Europe. On March 16 many American newspapers warned of a possible war between the United States and the Soviet Union. What the *New York Times* called 'Russo-Communist aggression' had, the newspaper wrote in an editorial that day, 'overrun Czechoslovakia and is threatening Italy'. The editorial continued:

Such optimism as the present situation warrants must be based chiefly on two assumptions. The first is that the masters of the Kremlin are, if not less fanatical, at least more realistic than was Hitler. The second is that the Western nations can quickly overcome the initial handicap of the democratic process, which demands agreement before action, and, fortified against a fear which leads to inaction or panic, can so organize their defences that Russia will be deterred from further challenges to their security.

Of these two conditions the second is by far the more important. In other words, the main hope for a long continued peace lies in the quick restoration of a better balance of power, in order to stop Russia from trading on Western weakness.

On March 17 Truman asked Congress to bring back universal military training and the restoration of the draft – which he described as 'temporary selective service' – telling Congress that since the end of the Second World War 'the Soviet Union and its agents have destroyed the independence and democratic character of a whole series of nations in Eastern and Central Europe. It is this ruthless course of action, and the clear design to extend it to the remaining free nations in Europe, that have brought about the critical situation in Europe today.' The point had been reached 'at which the position of the United States should be unmistakably clear'. There were times in world history 'when it is far wiser to act than to hesitate'. Truman went on to explain:

The issue is as old as recorded history. It is tyranny against freedom.

Tyranny has, throughout history, assumed many disguises, and has relied on many false prophecies to justify its attack on human freedom. Communism masquerades as a doctrine of progress. It is nothing of the kind. It is, on the contrary, a movement of reaction. It denies that man is master of his fate, and consequently denies man's right to govern himself.

And even worse, Communism denies the very existence of God. Religion is persecuted because it stands for freedom under God.

In ringing tones, which set out the dangers inherent in the defence of democratic values, Truman declared: 'This threat to our liberty and to our faith must be faced by each one of us.' He went on to warn Congress:

We will have to take risks during the coming year – risks perhaps greater than any this country has ever been called upon to assume. But they are not risks of our own making, and we cannot make the danger vanish by pretending that it does not exist. We must be prepared to meet that danger with sober self-restraint and calm and judicious action if we are to be successful in our leadership for peace.

The people of the United States have learned that peace will not come in response to soft words and vague wishes. We know that we can achieve the peace we seek only through firm resolution and hard work.

We can have confidence in the righteousness of our cause. The great ideals of liberty and justice are powerful forces in the hearts of men in every country. The faith in God which sustains us, also sustains man in other lands. Together we can erect an enduring peace.

'We must be prepared to pay the price for peace,' Truman ended, 'or assuredly we shall pay the price of war.' Ten years earlier, in the aftermath of the Munich crisis, Churchill had written: 'War is horrible but slavery is worse.'

On May 4 the American Ambassador in Moscow, Bedell Smith, having warned Molotov not to 'underestimate' the resolution of the United States, told him that 'the door always remains open for the discussion and settlement of our differences'. Responding five days later, Molotov accused the United States of seeking the 'encirclement' of the Soviet Union. The Soviet accusation included the American military occupation in South Korea. This occupation was ended on July 24, when Syngman Rhee was inaugurated as President, and the Stars and Stripes replaced on public buildings by the flag of the South Korean Republic.

American troops remained in South Korea, as a protective force; forty of them were killed in a train crash in September. Despite the establishment of the republic, the Americans were not abandoning South Korea. In his speech at the inauguration of Syngman Rhee in Seoul, General MacArthur declared: 'An artificial barrier has divided your land. This barrier must and shall be torn down.' That barrier was strengthened, however, six weeks later when, on September 9, the Communist-led Democratic People's Republic of Korea was established, with its capital in Pyongyang, under the leadership of Kim Il Sung.

In South Korea, Syngman Rhee's government was not only anti-Communist, it was also a repressive police State in which dissent was continually suppressed. When an army unit was sent on October 19 to attack another army unit that had gone over to the Communists, a thousand Koreans were killed in the clashes that followed. Both the Soviet and United States forces withdrew, leaving the two Koreas facing each other, both poorly armed and ill-organized, but both representing a potential source of conflict that could have implications far beyond the Korean peninsula.

*   *   *

On May 14 the British Mandate in Palestine came to an end. Eleven minutes later President Truman announced that the United States recognized the new State of Israel. The Soviet Union also hastened to give its recognition. The Arab States bordering on the new country launched an immediate attack. Egyptian aeroplanes bombed Tel Aviv. The Transjordanian Arab Legion, and the Syrian-based Arab Liberation Army, both advanced into the area allocated to the Jews by the United Nations. Arab Legion artillery bombarded the Jewish Quarter of the Old City of Jerusalem – a city in which the Jews had been the majority for a hundred years. Egyptian troops reached the southern Jewish outskirts of Jerusalem. In the centre of the country, troops from Iraq attacked Israeli positions.

A war had begun that was to continue for nine months, until both sides were exhausted. The temporary ceasefire lines marking the points at which the fighting ended were to serve as the basis of the borders of Israel for almost twenty years. The main area of Palestinian Arab settlement in Palestine – on the West Bank of the Jordan – was occupied and annexed by Transjordan (the country changing its name to Jordan), which also occupied – and deliberately demolished – the Jewish Quarter of the Old City. Only two countries recognized Transjordan's annexation of eastern Jerusalem and the West Bank: Britain and Pakistan. Egypt occupied the Gaza Strip.

During the course of the war, two ceasefires had been negotiated by the United Nations mediator, Count Folke Bernadotte, a Swedish diplomat who had helped rescue several thousand Jewish women from the Nazi concentration camps in the last weeks of the war. Although, with independence, the Israeli Prime Minister David Ben-Gurion had sought to amalgamate all the Jewish armed forces into one, the Stern Gang terrorists had continued to act independently, and on September 17 they murdered Bernadotte, accusing him of seeking to exclude Jewish sovereignty from the Jewish sector of Jerusalem. Ben-Gurion denounced the assassination, and declared his own war on the Stern Gang. But in Western eyes the damage done to the image of the new State by the murder of Bernadotte was considerable.

During the Israeli War of Independence, 6,000 Jews had been killed, one per cent of the Jewish population of Israel. In the immediate aftermath of the war more than a million Jews reached the country from Europe, and from Muslim lands throughout North Africa and the Middle East. The Jewish survivors of Nazi persecution whom the British had interned on Cyprus made the short journey across the eastern Mediterranean to the new State. Some of them arrived in time to fight – and to be killed – on the first Arab-Israel battlefields. Hundreds of thousands of Arab refugees had fled the battleground or were encouraged by Israel to leave – some were forcibly ejected from their villages, which were then demolished. Crossing the borders to the north, east and south, well over half a million Arabs were placed in refugee camps inside Jordan, Lebanon, Syria and Egypt. Several thousand Arab homes in Jerusalem were taken over by the Jewish newcomers, many of whom were new arrivals who had themselves been driven out of their homes in Arab lands.

The plight of the Arab refugees was described by the first United States Ambassador to Israel, James G. McDonald, who before the Second World War had been the League of Nations High Commissioner for refugees from Germany, most of them Jews. The Arab refugees, he wrote, were a 'huge and pitiful multitude, uprooted, exploited and helpless'. They received 'scant sympathy from the Arab Governments in whose territories they were squatting, with almost no prospect of work and – with few exceptions – the gates of Israel closed against them. Their life was tragic and bitter. UN assistance, and that from some of the Arab States locally, was so meagre as to sustain life, but not more'.

Inside Israel, 160,000 Arabs remained, or returned within a few months of the war. They became Israeli citizens, living for the first decade of statehood under Israeli military administration, but in due course voting in the elections, represented in the parliament, and obtaining their rights as citizens. Fifty years after Israeli statehood was declared, these Israeli Arabs – their numbers grown to more than half a million – constituted more than twenty per cent of the Israeli population.

The future of Germany was causing continual conflict between the three Western occupying powers – Britain, the United States and France – and the Soviet Union. Britain, the United States and France had began to pump money into their zones of Germany in order to accelerate reconstruction. They were also eager to establish a democratic political system in those parts of Germany under their control, such as had already been established in Italy, where the Soviet Union had no part in the postwar occupation. An attempt by the Western Powers to establish a unified currency for the whole of Germany having been rejected by the Soviets, they announced in March that they would take independent action. The Soviets counter-charged that the Western Powers were trying to 'plunder' their respective zones of Berlin.

The war of words accelerated, but was not new. On April 1, however, the Russians imposed stricter controls than hitherto on all Western Power traffic going by road or rail to Berlin. Foodstuffs, freight, and Allied military cargoes, were allowed to pass into the city only after specific Soviet authorization. Soviet air vigilance was imposed on all Allied air traffic. On April 5 there was a mid-air collision between a Soviet fighter plane and a British air liner near Gatow Airport, on the outskirts of Berlin. The fourteen people on the British plane, and the pilot of the Soviet fighter, were killed.

In May, the Soviet Union continued to denounce all Allied economic improvements in western Berlin, insisting that Berlin was economically part of the Soviet Zone. The Western Powers disputed this. On the wider constitutional issue, the divergence of views between the Western and Eastern blocs reached its climax on June 7 when, at the end of a conference held in London, a six-power Pact was signed, under which a constituent assembly and a federal government would be established in western Germany, based upon democratic values and institutions. As well as Britain, France and the United States, three other Western victims of Nazi aggression, Holland, Belgium and Luxembourg also signed the Pact.

On June 23 the Soviet Union countered this Western initiative by calling a conference in Warsaw, attended by all the Communist bloc States, at which the London Pact was condemned. Delegates demanded the demilitarization of Germany, four-power control of the Ruhr – from which Russia was excluded under the Potsdam agreement – and the setting up of an all-German provisional government. The Western Powers saw the Warsaw agreement as an attempt to extend Communist control to the whole of Germany.

The Cold War had emerged again as the dominant element in international affairs. On June 24 Britain, France and the United States found their road and rail access to the former German capital blocked by Soviet troops and tanks. Their only remaining access to Berlin was by air. In order to supply their own forces and administrators, and to feed the German population in the Western sectors of the city, a massive air lift was begun. It was quickly to become a symbol of Western resistance to Communist threats. It was effective, the two million inhabitants of western Berlin were fed, and the Soviet blockade, though it was kept in place, served more as a symbol of the East-West divide than as a threat to the maintenance of the Four Power system. By keeping the blockade in place for fifteen months, the Soviet Union ensured that Western hostility was kept at a high level. Western newspapers and newsreel films portraying the skill and tenacity of the pilots who flew the precious cargoes in, brought the harsh realities of the East-West divide to the attention of millions of people.

The division of Berlin into two sectors and two systems was rapidly effected. There were two Mayors and two municipal administrations, two different currencies, two sets of postage stamps, two electricity supply systems and two police forces. American determination not to give in to the attempted Soviet stranglehold on Berlin was stressed by George Marshall when he spoke at the United Nations Assembly in Paris on September 23. The United States, he warned, would 'not compromise on essential principles'. During his speech, Marshall spoke of the human rights aspects of the conflict:

> It is not only fundamentally wrong that millions of men and women live in daily terror of secret police, subject to seizure, imprisonment, or forced labour without just cause and without fair trail, but these wrongs have repercussions in the community of nations. Governments which systematically disregard the rights of their own people are not likely to respect the rights of other nations and other people, and are likely to seek their objectives by coercion and force in the international field.
>
> The maintenance of these rights and freedoms depends upon adherence to the abiding principles of justice and morality embodied in the rule of law. It will, therefore, always be true that those members of the United Nations which strive with sincerity of purpose to live by the charter, and to conform to the principles of justice and law proclaimed by it, will be those States which are genuinely dedicated to the preservation of the dignity and integrity of the individual.

As the American presidential election drew near, a particularly strong stance with regard to the Soviet Union was promised by Truman's Republican challenger, Thomas E. Dewey, who made considerable political capital out of a leaked suggestion by Truman that the United States Chief Justice go to see Stalin – as the President's personal representative – in an attempt to work out a solution to the East-West divide.

The two leading opinion pollsters both predicted a victory for Dewey, Dr Gallup giving him a 50:45 lead and Elmo Roper an even larger one, 53:38. Several newspapers led their early editions with the confident prediction that Dewey had actually won. The *Chicago Daily Tribune* headline was an emphatic three words: DEWEY DEFEATS TRUMAN. In the event Truman was re-elected by a margin of more than two million votes. Reaching St Louis on his way to Washington by train after the election, Truman was handed the *Chicago Daily Tribune* and held it aloft triumphantly. More than three quarters of a million people thronged the streets around the White House to welcome him back to Washington.

In the Congressional results, wherever 'internationalists' confronted 'isolationists' the victory went to those who favoured the Truman-Marshall interventionist approach. That approach was not only confrontational, as over Berlin, but intended to involve the United States in a wider, ameliorative role. As a culmination of three years work in which the United States had taken a major part – led by Roosevelt's widow Eleanor – on December 9 the United Nations approved a Universal Declaration of Human Rights.

Among the many rights which, as a result of this Declaration, were henceforth enshrined in international law was the right to leave any country, and the right to go to any country. Borders were to serve as the facilitators to movement, not as barriers. Also approved that day was the United Nations Convention on Genocide, setting out the imperative for the future prevention and punishment of genocide wherever it should occur. The convention was intended to place any repetition of the racial mass murders of the Second World War beyond the pale of legality – and, as the framers of the convention hoped, of possibility.

The convention outlawing genocide had still to be ratified by all the member States of the United Nations. Meanwhile, the broad sweep and ambitious intentions of the United Nations Declaration on Human Rights were being challenged by actual violations. The first of these took place on December 27 when, in response to the refusal of the Hungarian Catholic leadership to make concessions to the Communist regime there, the government arrested Cardinal Mindszenty. His right to leave Hungary was immediately curtailed. Anna Kethly, the veteran Hungarian Social Democrat leader, was imprisoned.

From the Western perspective, the Cold War was essentially a defensive exercise. It would require considerable expenditure on arms, a build-up of military resources, the development of the latest technology, and constant vigilance through open and secret Intelligence work. But it was not an interventionist creed. The Berlin blockade showed clearly that there were no plans to take aggressive action. Those who advocated bombing Moscow – and there were people both in Washington and London who did so vocally – were in a tiny minority, ignored by the political and military establishments.

The same non-interventionist creed on the part of the Western democracies was seen with regard to China, where the Nationalists were being pushed back by the Communists at every point of conflict. In May the Communists announced the establishment of a North China People's Government which encompassed seven provinces and forty-four million people. By the end of June the Communist National Liberation Armies drove the Nationalist forces back to the Yellow River. American military equipment was still reaching the Nationalists, but American observers in China reported that no sooner was it reaching them than they were selling it to the Communists. For those involved in this trade, money had a greater lure than national fervour.

In October the Nationalists lost their remaining strongholds in Manchuria. One of the last cities to fall was Chinchow, which was encircled by Communist troops on October 1 and besieged. Nationalist reinforcements sent from Huludao were driven off. As the siege continued, Communist artillery bombarded the city without respite. Jung Chang has described her mother's reaction: 'When my mother first heard the whine of the shells flying over, she was a little frightened. But later when the shelling became heavier, she got used to it. It became like permanent thunder.' Jung Chang added: 'A kind of fatalistic indifference deadened fear for most people.' During the siege the family's donkey was killed by a piece of shrapnel, 'so they ate it'.

On October 14 the Communists launched a determined assault on Chinchow, starting with a massive artillery bombardment. After thirty-one hours of bombardment, and then of hand-to-hand fighting, they took the city. Jung Chang recorded the moment when, after the Nationalist forces had finally gone, her mother's aunt opened the front gate of their home. 'Several corpses were lying right outside,' she wrote. 'My mother heard her shriek and went to have a look. Corpses were lying all over the street, many of them with their heads and limbs missing, others with their intestines pouring out. Some were just bloody messes. Chunks of flesh and arms and legs were hanging from the telegraph poles. The open sewers were clogged with bloody water, human flesh, and rubble.'

An estimated 20,000 Nationalist soldiers had been killed in the day and night battle for Chinchow. Among the 80,000 captured were eighteen generals. A Nationalist attempt to retake the city was unsuccessful. The Communists moved on to the last two remaining Nationalist strongholds, Changchun and Mukden. They too were unable to hold out against the sustained bombardment, and the massive infantry assault that followed. By

November 2 the Communists were in control of Manchuria, the fourth rulers of the province in three years.*

At the end of November, the State Department warned all American citizens that it was unsafe to remain anywhere in China except the far south and the island of Taiwan. When Chiang Kai-shek's wife reached Washington on December 1 to appeal for American intervention on behalf of the Nationalist cause she was met with words of sympathy but no promises and no action. An hour-long meeting with Truman produced nothing of comfort for her: the official communiqué after her visit stated merely that Truman had 'listened sympathetically'. On December 16 the State Department announced that American policy towards China – defined as a 'hands-off' policy – would not change.

The Soviet Union had continued to absorb its territorial gains of 1945. Lithuania proved the most difficult of the new Soviet Socialist Republics to bring within the rigours of the Communist system. On March 24 a decree was issued in Lithuania imposing the collectivization of all farms there. Similar decrees were issued in Latvia and Estonia. Two months later there was a campaign in Lithuania against what the local newspapers called an 'underground movement' based upon 'bandit gangs' whose aim was characterized as murder, sabotage and terrorism by 'enemies of the people'. Lithuanian Catholic priests were denounced for 'educating the youth in a spirit of opposition to the State'. In Latvia and Estonia, at harvest time, many farmers were arrested and sentenced to a year or two 'deprivation of liberty' for having refused to deliver their quotas to the State.

The wartime return to patriotic and traditional Russian art and music was to be reversed. Sentiment was no longer needed as a unifying force for the peoples of the Soviet Union. On February 10 the Central Committee of the Communist Party issued a decree on music, accusing Shostakovich, Prokofiev and Khatchaturian of 'losing touch with the masses' and of falling victims to 'decadent bourgeois influences'. The three made an immediate confession of their 'errors' and promised to mend their ways – and amend their music – in future. Newspapers also fell under the displeasure of the more rigorous ideological scrutiny. The satirical magazine *Krokodil* was censured by

---

* The Japanese had been driven out in 1945 by the Russians. The Russians had withdrawn three months later. The Kuomintang had seized control of most of the cities by the first months of 1946. The Communists had driven out the Kuomintang by the end of 1948.

the Central Committee for its 'lack of militancy' in portraying the evil ways of capitalism. The Academy of Social Sciences, which had been established after the war, was reorganized to provide a more rigorous ideological training for Party and State officials.

With Stalin's personal sanction, a ferocious newspaper campaign was launched against two declared enemies of Soviet Communism, 'bourgeois nationalism' and the 'survival of religious prejudice'. Some indication of how deeply religious feeling must have survived after thirty-one years of Communist rule was seen in the calls in *Pravda* for a more vigorous anti-religious propaganda. In Byelorussia and the three Baltic States – all of them Soviet Republics since 1945 – the Roman Catholic Church was singled out for denunciation.

In the Central Asian Republics of the Soviet Union, Islam and the Mullahs were accused of encouraging polygamy, bride-barter and the wearing of veils. Another accusation against the predominantly Islamic Soviet Republics was that religious festivals were reducing the productivity of collective farms. There were even accusations that Communist Party members, and Young Communists, had helped to build mosques and had taken part in religious services. Jews were also denounced for continuing to conduct religious services in private homes.

Stalin's own attitude towards the Jews was hostile in the extreme. Many of the early Bolshevik leaders whom he had purged and shot a decade earlier were of Jewish origin. Trotsky, axed to death in Mexico on Stalin's orders during the Second World War, was the son of a respected Jewish family, the Bronsteins. In 1948 all manifestations of Jewish cultural and national pride were under attack. Most cruelly, the leading Jewish actor and theatre director, Solomon Mikhoels, was murdered, on Stalin's secret orders, and then given a public funeral. Mikhoels had been a member of the Jewish Anti-Fascist Committee which Stalin had set up during the war to take pro-Soviet propaganda to the West and to win support for the Soviet struggle against Hitler. After the war the Committee had set about compiling a volume of facts and documents on the Nazi Holocaust on Soviet soil. The book was prepared for publication in Russian, Yiddish and English. On Stalin's order publication was refused and the printing presses smashed.

On November 8 Molotov's wife Polina, herself Jewish, and a member of the Anti-Fascist Committee, welcomed Golda Meir, the Israeli ambassador to Moscow, to a diplomatic reception as an honoured guest. Twelve days later, on November 20, the Anti-Fascist Committee was dissolved. Almost all its members were arrested, and in due course most of them were shot. Dozens of Soviet writers who were Jews, and who wrote in the Yiddish language – which was the lingua franca of more than a million Russian Jews – were arrested. Polina Molotov was imprisoned.

On Stalin's instructions the Soviet newspapers attacked Jewish culture and Jewish 'characteristics'. Jews were condemned as 'rootless cosmopolitans', alien to the Russian way of life and hostile to Russian needs. Jewish theatre critics were denounced as an 'anti-Party group', the newspapers printing their Russian-sounding names and then, in brackets, their original Jewish names, which every non-Jew in Russia could recognize as Jewish (Epshtein, Goldshtein, Grinberg, etc.). The question was then asked, how could anyone with such a name give a true verdict on Russian literature and culture. A new enemy had been singled out, and the Jews of Russia could only wait in fear and trembling for new indignities and harsh decrees. Stalin even arrested two of his relatives by marriage: 'they were both connected,' writes Stalin's biographer Robert Conquest, 'through Jewish friends, to the new Jewish conspiracies.' Both were sentenced to ten years imprisonment for espionage – and only released after Stalin's death six years later.

Soviet links with the new Communist States that formed a swathe of territory between Russia and western Germany, Austria and Italy, were maintained by the presence of large numbers of Soviet troops, and were strengthened by formal agreements. On February 4, during the signature of a Soviet-Roumanian Treaty, Molotov – who had concluded his semi-eponymous treaty with Ribbentrop nine years earlier – spoke of how important the new treaty was 'at a time when the new war-mongers in the imperialist camp are patching together military-political blocs directed against the Soviet Union'. Considerable stress was laid on the threat to the Soviet Union of American military might, assisted by various 'lackeys of imperialism', of whom Britain was usually portrayed as the second – and sometimes even as the principal – villain.

The Soviet treaties with her neighbours were quickly extended: Hungary signed on February 18 and Bulgaria on March 18. Poland was already signed up. On April 6 non-Communist Finland signed a treaty with the Soviet Union promising to repel any direct aggression on Finland by Germany or any State allied to Germany. One wartime ally and associate of the Soviet Union had begun, however, to resist the pressures from Moscow: President Tito of Yugoslavia. His partisan forces had been as instrumental as the Soviet

Army – if not more so – in driving the Germans from his country. Tito courageously broke with Stalin and sought to maintain his own form of Communism. On March 27 Stalin sent Tito a letter, signed by himself and Molotov, warning of the dangers of the breach. At the heart of it was the sentence: 'We think Trotsky's political career is sufficiently instructive.' But Tito would not allow himself or his country to be browbeaten. At a meeting of the Cominform in Budapest in June, which Yugoslavia declined to attend, the senior Soviet representative told the other Eastern European and Western Communist delegates: 'We possess information that Tito is an imperialist spy.'

On June 28, reflecting the exchange of letters between Tito and Stalin, the Cominform published a resolution calling on the people of Yugoslavia either to force their government to support the Soviet Union, or to form a new government that would do so. Vladimir Dedijer, who had fought at Tito's side throughout the war, and whose wife Olga, herself a partisan, had been killed in action against the Germans, later recalled how the Cominform resolution was received in Belgrade:

> The great majority, which had not been conversant with the letters, simply could not believe their eyes. There were people who cried from despair in the streets that morning. But that was the first reaction. After the first pain came a wave of indignation, and pride. The whole country united as one man. Feelings rose high. Men in the street were proud of their country. The air was charged with feeling as before, during the greatest events in the modern history of Yugoslavia.
>
> From many parts of Yugoslavia cables reported: 'People feel as they did on March 27, when Yugoslavia broke the Axis yoke and challenged Hitler.'

Following Yugoslavia's ejection from the Communist bloc, the Soviet Union had only Albania as a compliant outlet on the Adriatic. But as a result of Tito's independent stance, Albania had no direct overland link with the rest of the Soviet bloc.

The last action Tito had taken in conjunction with the Soviet Union had been to approve a Soviet proposal for the exclusive control of the River Danube below Linz by the countries along its banks. This convention was signed in Belgrade on August 19. Britain, France and the United States refused to sign: they had been promised rights of their own during the Potsdam Conference in the summer of 1945, but under the new convention these were rescinded.

Within Western Europe there was a revival of the call for European unity. It was a call which had been heard on several occasions before the Second World War but had then seemed almost utopian. An important step forward was made in 1948, when, on March 17, a treaty was signed in Brussels by five powers – Britain, France, Belgium, the Netherlands and Luxembourg – for the creation of a Consultative Council which would meet whenever there seemed to be a threat to peace. A month later, on April 17, the five Foreign Ministers of the Brussels Treaty powers met in Paris and established a Permanent Commission, with its seat in London, to monitor any threats to peace and the security needs of the treaty powers. Its mandate was quickly enlarged to consider economic and financial measures of mutual interest. A Military Committee – later renamed the Defence Committee – was also established, and held its first meeting in London on April 30.

In parallel with the governmental work of the five Brussels Treaty powers, an International Committee of the Movements for European Unity, which had been set up at the end of 1947, was active throughout the early months of 1948. Among its component parts were the United Europe Movement of which Winston Churchill was chairman; the French Council for United Europe headed by a former French Prime Minister Edouard Herriot; and the Economic League for European Cooperation led by the Belgian statesman Paul van Zeeland.

Encouraged by the Brussels Treaty, but hoping to go beyond it with regard to European cooperation and unity, the International Committee convened a Council of Europe meeting at The Hague in May. The object of the meeting was, in the words of its manifesto, to 'affirm the urgent need for close and effective unity among the peoples of Europe'. All of Europe was intended to participate, including, when political developments allowed, Eastern Europe. More than 750 delegates were present, including several former Prime Ministers. In his address, the seventy-three-year-old Churchill – who had entered Parliament in Britain just after the turn of the century – set out his vision of what a United Europe could be. His words were to inspire the delegates and those whom they represented to persevere with their goal of a united Europe, and to prevail. If the cause of United Europe 'was academic', Churchill told them, 'it would wither by the wayside; but if it was the vital need of Europe and the world in this dark hour, then the spark would start a fire which would glow brighter and stronger in the hearts and the minds of men and women in many lands'.

This, Churchill pointed out in his speech at The Hague, 'is what has actually happened. Great governments have banded themselves together with all their executive power. The mighty republic of the United States has espoused the Marshall Plan. Sixteen European States are now associated for economic purposes; five have entered into close economic and military relationship.' He hoped that 'this nucleus' would in due course be joined by the peoples of Scandinavia and the Iberian peninsula, as well as by Italy.

Addressing himself to what was – and was to remain – a crucial question with regard to European unity, the question of a united Europe and national sovereignty, Churchill commented: 'It is said with truth that this involves some sacrifice or merger of national sovereignty. But it is also possible and not less agreeable to regard it as the gradual assumption by all the nations concerned of that larger sovereignty which can also protect their diverse and distinctive customs and characteristics and their national traditions, all of which under totalitarian systems, whether Nazi, Fascist, or Communist, would certainly be blotted out for ever.'

The Council of Europe was determined to see western Germany take its place around the European discussion tables. Churchill strongly supported this aim, welcomed the German delegation 'into our midst', and told the Hague Congress: 'The German problem is to restore the economic life of Germany and revive the ancient fame of the German race without thereby exposing their neighbours and ourselves to any rebuilding or reassertion of their military power of which we still bear the scars.' Churchill then spoke of the aim of United Europe in its human dimension, recalling the efforts of his wartime American partner to set out the objectives of the war itself:

President Roosevelt spoke of the Four Freedoms, but the one that matters most today is Freedom from Fear.

Why should all these hard-working families be harassed, first in bygone times, by dynastic and religious quarrels, next by nationalistic ambitions, and finally by ideological fanaticism?

Why should they now have to be regimented and hurled against each other by variously labelled forms of totalitarian tyranny, all fomented by wicked men, building their own predominance upon the misery and the subjugation of their fellow human beings?

Why should so many millions of humble homes in Europe, aye, and much of its enlightenment and culture, sit quaking in dread of the policeman's knock?

That is the question we have to answer here. That is the question which

34. Paris, August 1945: American soldiers celebrate victory over Japan.

35. Tokyo Bay, September 1945: General MacArthur signs the Japanese surrender terms on the USS *Missouri*. Behind him are General Wainwright who surrendered to the Japanese after Bataan and Corregidor and General Percival who surrendered at Singapore.

36. A souvenir on its way to a museum: a German V2 rocket leaves London for the Australian War Memorial in Canberra, February 1947.

37. On his retirement as Chief of Staff General George S. Marshall receives a medal from President Truman, November 1945.

38. (*below*) Bikini Atoll, in the Pacific: an atomic test, 1948.

39. Stalin and Molotov cast their vote in the Soviet General Election, December 1947.

40. Alexander Solzhenitsyn as an artillery officer of the Russian Army.

41. Ho Chi Minh in 1945, preparing for a mission against the French in Vietnam.

42. Refugees from the fighting in Kashmir, February 1948.

43. Nehru and Gandhi
at the All-India Congress
meeting in Bombay at
which Nehru took office
as President of the
Congress, July 1946.

44. Residents of Calcutta
celebrate Indian
independence, August
1947.

45. American bombers attacking North Korean targets, 1950

46. *(above)* Ichon immediately after its American capture, September 1950.

47. *(right)* A railway marshalling yard in North Korea is hit by a salvo of American bombs.

48. Korea, 1950: an American soldier takes a Communist prisoner.

50. An American soldier using a flame-thrower to burn down possible hiding places for snipers (March 1951).

49. A United Nations cemetery near Pusan, South Korea.

perhaps we have the power to answer here. After all, Europe has only to arise and stand in her own majesty, faithfulness and virtue, to confront all forms of tyranny, ancient or modern, Nazi or Communist, with forces which are unconquerable, and which if asserted in good time may never be challenged again.

In a peroration which pointed the way forward both to an active United Europe movement and to Britain's participation in it, Churchill first warned and then encouraged his listeners and fellow-Europeans:

A high and solemn responsibility rests upon us here this afternoon in this Congress of a Europe striving to be reborn.

If we allow ourselves to be rent and disordered by pettiness and small disputes, if we fail in clarity of view or courage in action, a priceless occasion may be cast away for ever.

But if we all pull together and pool the luck and the comradeship – we shall need all the comradeship and not a little luck if we are to move together in this way – and firmly grasp the larger hopes of humanity, then it may be that we shall move into a happier sunlit age, when all the little children who are now growing up in this tormented world may find themselves not the victors nor the vanquished in the fleeting triumphs of one country over another in the bloody turmoil of destructive war, but the heirs of all the treasures of the past and the masters of all the science, the abundance and the glories of the future.

Two days later after his speech at The Hague, Churchill went to Amsterdam, where he told an open air meeting: 'I am not the enemy of any race or nation in the world.' Speaking of Britain's two former adversaries on the battlefield, the Germans and the Japanese, and of the Russians, he declared: 'We all understand their toils and sufferings', and he added that it was not against any race or nation 'that we range ourselves. It is against Tyranny, in all its forms.'

The belief that individual efforts by those who were better-off could benefit those who were poor was seen in February when the first charity shop was opened in Britain, by Oxfam. Its initial aim was to acquire clothing which it could then ship to needy people overseas. The Palestinian Arab refugees were among its first beneficiaries.

Even in capitalist countries State intervention was often seen as the way forward for national prosperity, despite warnings from economists such as John Jewkes of Manchester University, in his book *Ordeal By Planning*, of 'the incipient evidence of totalitarian fervour for doing good to other people at whatever the cost to them'. In Britain the Labour Government had nationalized the railways, the electricity industry and the gas industry, and on July 5 established a National Health Service with free medicine, and free medical treatment, for all. Inventions that had been developed for warmaking were turned to peaceful uses. Radar was used for the first time in Britain to supervise merchant shipping approaches to a port – Liverpool – in thick fog. Medical advances, which in wartime had been another arm of warfare, were put at the disposal of general medicine. Three new antibiotics, that could combat trachoma, typhoid and TB, were in preparation. In the world of entertainment, the first long-playing gramophone record, released by the Columbia Record Company, heralded a cultural revolution.

In North America and Western Europe, television was beginning to take its place as a purveyor of news and entertainment. New games and customs proliferated. In 1948 the word game Scrabble was launched in the United States, as was the drive-in hamburger café, by Richard and Maurice McDonald, whose surname and distinctive red-and-yellow logo were, five decades later, to adorn shopping malls throughout the world, including Moscow and Jerusalem.

There was a reminder in 1948 of how far the Twentieth Century had come in its inventions: January 30 – the day on which Gandhi was assassinated in India – was also the day on which Orville Wright died in the United States. It was Wright who, with his brother Wilbur, had designed the first aircraft engine, and made the first power-driven flight in 1903. The adaptation of flight to warfare had brought death to as many as a million people between 1937 and 1945. With the advent of the jet engine, itself an essentially wartime invention, the myriad benefits of long distance travel were to be brought to many thousands of millions of people. And yet, amid the scientific and technical advances which were to benefit so many, the curse of racism – which in Europe had so recently erupted into mass destruction – remained elsewhere in ugly contrast to the four freedoms of which Roosevelt had spoken with such passion.

In South Africa the segregation of Whites from the majority Black and Coloured population headed the agenda of the opposition Nationalist Party, and of the smaller but vociferous Afrikaner Party. Their attitude was challenged that year, not on the streets or in the courts, but in a book. It was the novel by Alan Paton, *Cry, The Beloved Country*, subtitled 'A Story of Comfort in Desolation'. One passage read:

Your brother has no use for the Church any more. He says that what God has not done for South Africa, man must do. That is what he says.
— This is a bitter journey.
— I can believe it.
— Sometimes I fear — what will the Bishop say when he hears?
One of his priests.
— What can a Bishop say? Something is happening that no Bishop can stop. Who can stop these things from happening? They must go on.
— How can you say so? How can you say they must go on?
— They must go on, said Msimangu gravely. You cannot stop the world from going on. My friend, I am a Christian. It is not in my heart to hate a white man. It was a white man who brought my father out of darkness. But you will pardon me if I talk frankly to you. The tragedy is not that things are broken. The tragedy is that they are not mended again. The white man has broken the tribe. And it is my belief — and again I ask your pardon — that it cannot be mended again. But the house that is broken, and the man that falls apart when the house is broken, these are the tragic things. That is why children break the law, and old white people are robbed and beaten.
He passed his hand across his brow.
— It suited the white man to break the tribe, he continued gravely. But it has not suited him to build something in the place of what is broken. I have pondered this for many hours and must speak it, for it is the truth for me. They are not all so. There are some white men who give their lives to build up what is broken.
— But they are not enough, he said. They are afraid, that is the truth. It is fear that rules this land.

The Nationalist Party, committed as it was to apartheid, did not fear the words of a novel. Patiently they worked through the parliamentary system, introducing in February a motion to cancel the representation of Indians in the parliament. The motion was defeated, but the thrust towards separation was gaining momentum. A General Election was held on May 26, when Dr

D.F. Malan's Nationalist Party won more seats than Jan Christian Smuts' United Party, which, as the ruling instrument for many years, had been as close to liberalism as an essentially White-supremacist Party could be. Together with the Afrikaner Party, the Nationalists won 79 seats, as against 74 for the United Party and its Labour Party allies.

The new Government was formed on June 4, with Malan as Prime Minister, and with the support of the Afrikaner Party headed by N.C. Havenga, who became Minister of Finance. A priority for the new government was to turn the system of apartheid from one of social separation to legal separation. For the rest of the year and throughout the following years, in measures reminiscent of the Nuremberg Laws of 1935 – whereby German Jews were made second class citizens – a series of legislative acts defined three categories of citizen: White, Coloured and African. Marriages were prohibited between European (that is White) and non-European (Blacks and Asians). Under the Immorality Act, sexual intercourse between 'Europeans and Coloureds' (that is, between Whites and Indians) was also forbidden.

Once legalized, the separation of people by colour led to terrible abuse throughout South Africa, sustained by police coercion, and a vigorous secret police and informant system which, in maintaining unjust laws, undermined the rule of law.

At eleven in the morning of June 21 six young scientists in the electrical engineering department at Manchester University contemplated the success of an experiment on which they had been working with the patience that is as essential for science as is inspiration. Nine times that morning they had put a series of programmes through a computer – named Baby – and on the tenth try the computer worked. It could 'remember' and calibrate any number of digits that were fed into it. Mathematical problems could be solved 10,000 times faster than hitherto. The team that carried out the successful experiment was led by Freddie Williams and Tom Kilburn, both of whom had worked on radar during the war.

Fifty years later, Tom Kilburn told a journalist, Jane Kelly, who visited him at his house in the suburbs of Manchester, that there had been little public interest in their research in its early days, 'but when the Baby worked we were immediately visited by two top people in the Government who gave us £1 million for five years' further work'. The team in Manchester had helped to usher in the computer age.

Public enthusiasm for sport was heightened during the Olympic Games, which had last been held in Berlin twelve years earlier. London was the site for the new Games, which opened on July 29. Austerity in Britain was such that no stadium or special facilities could be built. Wembley Stadium, built for the Empire Exhibition in 1924, was the main scene of the competitive events. Most of the accommodation for the athletes was in the Royal Air Force wartime barracks at Uxbridge. The United States won by far the largest number of gold medals, thirty-eight in all. Sweden was next in the league table with sixteen. Germany, which at the previous Olympics had sought to vaunt its national and racial superiority, won none. Nor did Britain, the host nation.

Visiting Britain that year, an Australian cricket side, captained by Don Bradman, won twenty-five of their thirty-four games, and lost none. In his last Test Match innings before his retirement, Bradman was dismissed without scoring a run – though his average Test score was 99.94. Returning home, he received the first knighthood ever awarded to a playing cricketer.

Towards the end of 1948 there was another echo and remembrance of the Second World War. On November 2, All Souls' Day, a memorial was unveiled to the west of London, near Northolt aerodrome, to the 1,241 Polish airmen who had been killed in action after taking off from British airfields. Many of them had fought in the Battle of Britain, including Sergeant Michal Brzozowski, killed on the decisive day, 15 September 1940. The Polish historian Bohdan Arct, writes: 'In numerous military cemeteries all over Great Britain graves of the Polish winged warriors are scattered. Looked after with great care, they are beautifully kept. Graves of young men, full of enthusiasm and patriotism, who left their country to fly, fight and win under the foreign sky. Alas! they did not survive to see the historical day of May 8th, 1945.'

Every year, on Armistice Day, fresh flowers are placed around the monument, which is surmounted by an eagle perched ready to take off for flight.

CHAPTER TWENTY-TWO

1949

A flaw in the pattern . . . a stain that must be wiped out.

GEORGE ORWELL

THE RULE OF STALIN was in its third decade, overshadowing every aspect of Soviet life, tyrannical and malign. In a courtroom in Paris in January 1949 the nature of the Soviet system was under scrutiny. The court case and the trial arose as a result of the publication, two years earlier, of a book, *I Chose Freedom*, by Victor Kravchenko, a former Soviet official who had defected to the United States during the Second World War.

In the book, which was widely read in the West, Kravchenko gave details of Soviet violations of human rights, and, as he had done at the time of his defection – in the words of the *New York Times* of 4 April 1944 – 'denouncing the Stalin regime for failure to grant political and civil liberties to the Russian people'. A left-wing French magazine, *Les Lettres française*, suggested that the text must have been written by American agents. Kravchenko sued in the courts. Witnesses who were sent from Moscow to denounce the book, were confronted by witnesses sent from Washington.

During the trial, details emerged about the harshness of the Soviet labour camp system, in which millions of people suffered privation, indignity and pain, unable to gain redress, cut off from all contact with family and friends, never knowing for certain if their harsh incarceration would end when their sentences ended, or be arbitrarily prolonged. The truth of these details was upheld by the court. For Jean-Paul Sartre, who attended the trial, the existence of such crimes could no longer be denied: the decision for him and Communist sympathizers like him was whether to justify those crimes, remain silent, or become public critics of the Soviet system. Sartre chose first to remain silent, and then to suggest that the Soviet proletariat could be trusted to get rid of the 'anomalies' in the Soviet system when the time was right to do so.

The harsh reality of which Kravchenko had written was far from over. In the four-day period between March 25 and 28 a virtually continuous convoy of thirty-three trains left Latvia for 'special settlement areas' in Siberia. On board were 43,000 Latvian civilians, of whom more than 10,000 were children. This was part of Operation Tidal Wave, under which almost 100,000 people were deported from the three Soviet Baltic Republics – Latvia, Lithuania and Estonia.

Among more than five million Soviet citizens imprisoned in labour camps in Northern Russia, across Siberia and in Central Asia, or in enforced exile, in conditions of utmost hardship, were 503,375 women: this precise figure was given to Stalin by the Minister of the Interior. One such of those accused and sentenced – her case was typical – was a woman who, while queuing for milk in Moscow, had told those around her that she understood from her son in the Red Army in Vienna that people were no longer queuing for milk in the West. She was at once denounced by the whole queue, and sentenced to ten years in labour camp.

Tens of thousands of women prisoners had been sent away from their homes together with their children. When the Soviet Deputy Prime Minister, Georgy Malenkov, informed Stalin that the cost of maintaining children in the camps was estimated at 166 million rubles a year, Stalin agreed that women with children under the age of eleven should be released. Such mothers, Stalin decreed, must nevertheless continue to do forced labour, but they could do it in their home towns. Women who had been sentenced for 'counter-revolutionary activity', however, must remain in the camps with their children. Such were the discussions and decisions of the Soviet leader in his seventieth year.

President Truman's decisions were of a different order. Elected by popular vote to the Presidency for the first time – he had earlier succeeded automatically on Roosevelt's death – he presented at his inaugural address in Washington on January 20 the epitome of a liberal-minded, socially progressive, democratic programme. Described by Truman himself as the 'Fair Deal', its aim was to extend social security, raise the minimum wage, greatly increase federal house-building and – under the Housing Act passed six months later – provide federal funds for both slum clearance and building low-cost housing for the poor.

Inauguration Day itself was a moment of triumph for American democracy. More than a million people filled the streets of Washington to watch or share in the festivities. It was also the first inauguration ceremony to be broadcast live on the television screens of the nation, in front of which an estimated ten million more Americans were gathered: the largest number of people until then to watch a single event. Another hundred million listened to the inaugural proceedings on the radio. Among those present at the ceremony itself were ninety-eight veterans who had served in Truman's artillery battery on the Western Front during the First World War.

It was not only the domestic challenges, but the overseas burdens, that were a feature of the words and commentary that accompanied the inauguration celebrations in Washington. The period ahead, Truman said in his speech, 'will be eventful, perhaps decisive, for us and for the world'. Much of the speech turned on the foreign policy of the United States. As he spoke – his biographer David McCullogh has written – 'he looked solemn and determined as he read from a loose-leaf note book. The voice was surprisingly strong. There was no hesitation, no stumbling over words. It was plain that he had worked on all of it, knew every line. Those close by the platform could see his breath frosting the air'.

Foreign policy dominated the speech and the concerns of the President. Central to those concerns was his understanding of the basic difference between the democratic and Communist systems that confronted the world. Truman set out those differences with clarity and determination:

> Communism is based on the belief that man is so weak and inadequate that he is unable to govern himself, and therefore requires the rule of strong masters.
>
> Democracy is based on the conviction that man has the moral and intellectual capacity, as well as the inalienable right, to govern himself with reason and firmness.
>
> Communism subjects the individual to arrest without lawful cause, punishment without trial, and forced labour as the chattel of the State. It decrees what information he shall receive, what art he shall produce, what leaders he shall follow, and what thoughts he shall think.
>
> Democracy maintains that government is established for the benefit of the individual, and is charged with protecting the rights of the individual and his freedom in the exercise of those abilities.

During his address, Truman did not mention the Soviet Union by name, but he told his many millions of listeners in the most unambiguous of tones: 'The actions resulting from the Communist philosophy are a threat to the efforts of free nations to bring about world recovery and lasting peace'.

A Washington newspaper, the *Evening Star*, commented: 'Clearly he was conscious of the terrible responsibility his victory had won him. His would be decisions affecting, possibly, the very future of mankind. Ahead of Harry Truman's America, nameless, half-imagined dangers lurked in every shadow. None knew this better than he.' Within three months of Truman's inauguration the North Atlantic Treaty was signed in Washington, establishing the North Atlantic Treaty Organization (NATO). Twelve nations subscribed to the treaty: the United States, Canada, Britain, France, Luxembourg, Belgium, the Netherlands, Italy, Portugal, Denmark, Iceland and Norway. The basis of their coming together was to provide for mutual military assistance in the event of aggression. The potential aggressor was no longer Germany, but the Soviet Union.

Western Germany was not a party to the North Atlantic Treaty, but her political postwar regeneration was more and more in accordance with the western democratic ideals which underpinned the NATO concept. On May 23 the Federal Republic of Germany (also known as West Germany) came into existence with the approval of the Western Allies. Its capital was to be Bonn. On September 12, following free and openly contested elections, Theodor Heuss was elected President and Konrad Adenauer Chancellor. Neither had been members of the Nazi Party. Both had opposed the excesses of the Hitler regime. In 1933 Adenauer had been dismissed as Chairman of the Prussian State Council because of his opposition to Nazism, and had been twice imprisoned – in 1934 and 1944.

Nine days after the elections, Allied Military Government came to an end, replaced by an Allied High Commission. At a ceremony in Bonn the black-red-gold flag of the Federal Republic was raised, and Adenauer told the assembled Allied dignitaries that while Germany was 'still not wholly free' she would do her utmost to use the political powers that had been given to her. Referring to the millions of Germans who had been expelled to the West from former German lands in the East, Adenauer declared that 'not until they had succeeded in converting the flotsam millions of refugees into settled inhabitants would Germany enjoy internal stability.' He also spoke of the need to create a 'viable European federation' that would embrace the basic industries of all the European countries. He ended by speaking of the deeper spiritual change that was needed both in Germany and Europe, telling his listeners: 'If we return to the sources of our European civilization, born of Christianity, then we shall succeed in restoring the unity of European life in all fields of endeavour.'

The Soviet Union could do nothing to impede the emergence of democracy in West Germany. Within three weeks of the German elections, Stalin called off the Berlin blockade. The American commander of West Berlin, General Lucius D. Clay – who had been fighting against the Germans four years earlier – was awarded the freedom of the city he had helped to sustain. By means of an incredible 277,264 separate flights, the citizens of West Berlin had been fed and supported, and the presence of the Western Allies in the city upheld. Forty-three British servicemen had been killed in accidents during the breaking of the blockade. East Germany and the Soviet sector of Berlin remained under tight Communist control.

The Communists sought allies wherever they could be found. At a special World Peace Conference held in Paris, it was the Black American singer and actor Paul Robeson who gave them the greatest fillip when he said, in defence of the Soviet Union: 'It is unthinkable that American Negroes will go to war on behalf of those who have oppressed us for generations against a country which in one generation has raised our people to the full dignity of mankind.'

As the new confrontations and conflicts pitted the Communist and non-Communist worlds against each other in Europe and Asia, the old confrontations and conflicts continued to make an impact. On January 28, after a British military trial in Hamburg, Fritz Knoechlein, who had been responsible for the execution of British prisoners-of-war at Paradis in northern France in 1940, was hanged in the British garrison prison. The appeal of his defence counsel – 'Spare the life of the accused. He has a wife and four children who are dependent upon him for support. Consider the fact that he is a soldier, and the Court is composed of members of the British Army' – had been in vain.

Also executed on January 28 was Joseph Kieffer, Knoechlein's deputy at Gestapo headquarters in Paris in 1943 and 1944. He had been found guilty of the execution of British paratroopers in Normandy in 1944. It was Kieffer who had interrogated and tortured Noor Inayat Khan, the British agent captured in France in 1943: following her interrogation she had been sent to Dachau and shot.

*   *   *

After two decades of violent turmoil, the political future of China was about to be resolved. The Communist forces were everywhere in the ascendant. The Nationalist forces defending the lower Yangtze were surrounded, and could neither break out nor defeat their People's Liberation Army adversaries. The threat of widespread military defeats divided the Nationalist Kuomintang leadership. Some wished to open negotiations with the Communists with a view to a ceasefire, and the emergence of some form of territorial compromise, perhaps even a joint Communist-Nationalist administration. The leader of this group was the Vice-President of the Kuomintang, General Li Tsung-jen. Others were convinced that no compromise was possible.

Hoping at least to gain time, on January 8 Chiang Kai-shek asked the United States, Britain, France and the Soviet Union to 'mediate' between the two warring sides. As he waited for the Four-Power response, he saw his own military and political control disappear over thousands of square miles of China. On January 11 the Nationalist forces, surrounded on the lower Yangtse, were defeated. On January 12 the Four Powers collectively rejected Chiang Kai-shek's appeal for mediation. Recognizing that he could not resist a renewed Communist attack, the Nationalist commander in north China, General Fu Tso-yi, surrendered.

Outside Peking, only three towns in the north remained under Nationalist control: Taiyuan, Tatung and Tsingtao. On January 14, speaking with the authority of virtual military mastery over north China, Mao Tse-tung broadcast the conditions under which he would agree to negotiate with the Kuomintang – with whom two decades earlier he had worked in tandem. He would agree to a coalition government, but the Nationalists would have to purge all 'war criminals' from it. He then produced a list of these war criminals, which was headed by Chiang Kai-shek and General Li Tsung-jen.

Faced with the loss of control even in southern China, on January 19 the Nationalist leaders debated their course. A majority, led by one of Mao Tse-tung's 'war criminals', General Li Tsung-jen, decided to approach the Communists and seek a cease fire. Chiang Kai-shek thereupon stood down from the Presidency and Li Tsung-jen became acting President, with a mandate to open negotiations. As a gesture of sincerity, his first step was to issue a decree abolishing both the martial law system and the special courts on which the Kuomintang had relied in order to assert its authority.

On the battleground, fighting continued throughout these internal debates, offers and decrees. On January 22 the Communist forces entered Peking. In east and central China the Nationalists fell back below the

Yangtse. Divisions inside the Kuomintang led to delays in the opening of ceasefire talks, with Chiang Kai-shek waiting in the wings – at his birthplace, Fenghua – in the hope that the talks would fail. Peace talks began in Peking of April 1. The Communist delegation was headed by Chou En-lai. For three weeks the negotiations continued, but the Communists adopted a position based upon confidence in even greater military successes, and no agreement was possible.

On April 20, in preparation for a major offensive across the Yangtse, Communist artillery bombarded the Nationalist-held shore in the region of Chingkiang, fifty miles east of the Nationalist capital, Nanking. A British frigate, *Amethyst*, which was steaming up river with stores for the British Embassy in Nanking, was damaged by Communist artillery fire and grounded. Seventeen members of her crew were killed, including her commanding officer, Lieutenant-Commander B.M. Skinner. Among those seriously wounded – he lost a leg – was Stoker Ronald Fletcher, who during the Second World War had seen action at Narvik, Crete and the Normandy Landings. Also killed by Chinese Communist gunfire were nine members of the Royal Navy destroyer *Consort* that had tried, in vain, to take *Amethyst* in tow.

Fifty miles down river at Kiangyin, two more British warships, the cruiser *London* and the destroyer *Black Swan*, were alerted for action. A garbled, incomplete message from *Amethyst* reported that she was under fire, had many casualties, and had run aground. The radio then went dead. *London* and *Black Swan* immediately made their way down river in the direction of Nanking, towards *Amethyst*, hoping to be able to pull her clear and escort her back. 'It was a perfectly glorious morning,' one of those on board the two warships later recalled, 'with blazing sun and much too warm for the blue uniforms being worn; the slight morning haze was just lifting and all looked peaceful. The ships were at action stations, tin hats being worn for the first time since the war ended in 1945. All the White Ensigns and white flags were hoisted, enormous Union Flags painted on canvas hung on each side of the hulls.'

Within five minutes of getting under way, both warships were fired on by Communist batteries on the north bank of the river. *London* was the first to be hit, followed by *Black Swan*. They continued on their path, but were hit again; the Navigating Officer and the Chinese pilot of *London* were both killed. It was clear that the two ships could proceed no further without risk of being sunk, and they turned back. At the suggestion of the commander of the *Black Swan*, Captain A.D.H. Jay, medical supplies were dropped to the grounded warship by a Royal Air Force transport aircraft. Diplomatic efforts were then made to persuade the Communist authorities to give the *Amethyst* safe conduct down the river, but this was refused.

By the time *London* and *Black Swan* reached the safety of Shanghai, the total death toll on all four British warships stood at forty-six, as well as two dead Chinese pilots. On April 21, the day after the attack on the British warships, the Communists began their military offensive across the Yangtse. It was swiftly successful, with Nanking being occupied on April 24. On the following day Mao Tse-tung set out an eight-point proclamation with regard to Communist rule. 'Bureaucratic capital' would be confiscated. Those who tried to 'create trouble' – the 'counter-revolutionary elements' – would be severely punished.

In an attempt to win nationalist followers to his side, Mao Tse-tung promised that private schools, hospitals and churches would be protected, and that Kuomintang officials would be 're-employed' according to their capacities. The 'petty bourgeoisie, national bourgeoisie and patriotic democratic elements' would, he said, together with the working class and the peasantry, form part of the People's Democratic United Front. Industrialization, without which true socialism was impossible, would bring 'benefits to both labour and capital'.

While setting out promises and prospects for China, Mao Tse-tung continued to supervise the advance of his armies. After the fall of Nanking on April 24, Hangchow, Hankow, Nanchang, Shanghai and Ningpo fell to the Communists in rapid succession. Sian was occupied on May 20, enabling the People's Liberation Army to turn westward. At the same time, the last three Nationalist pockets in north China – Taiyuan, Tatung and Tsingtao – were also overrun. Hundreds of millions of Chinese, who four years earlier had been in the grip of Japanese occupation, came under Chinese Communist rule.

In June and early July heavy rains and severe flooding impeded the Communist military advance in the south. But there seemed no doubt as to what the military outcome would be. When Mao Tse-tung spoke on July 1 it was with a harsher tone than at the end of April. 'The reactionaries must be deprived of the right to voice their opinion,' he declared. The 'people' must be in control of the army, the police and the courts. Once possessing this control the people need not be afraid 'of the national bourgeois class'.

By the third week of July the Communist forces were ready to move forward again. Their success was swift, with Changteh, Changsha and the coastal city of Fuchow falling to their advance. On June 15 a triumphant Mao Tse-tung announced that he was 'willing to negotiate the establishment of diplomatic relations with any foreign government on the basis of the principles of equality, mutual benefits, and mutual respect'. His own course was clearly set. On July 1, the twenty-eighth anniversary of the founding of the Communist Party of China, he stressed that the world was divided into two systems, one imperialist, one socialist. 'A third road does not exist.' The Chinese Communists, he added, 'ally ourselves with the Soviet Union'.

Relations with the West worsened on July 30. That day the new commanding officer on the *Amethyst*, Lieutenant-Commander J.S. Kerrans, having been held with his ship and crew under Communist control for more than three months, managed to take his ship downstream in darkness and escape. At one point during his seven-and-a-quarter-hour dash he was under the point-blank fire of Communist shore batteries. He replied with his own guns and steamed on, breaking through a boom across the river at Kiangyin, and joining the British fleet at sea. The last of a series of ten messages from the fleeing frigate was: 'Have rejoined the Fleet south of Woosung. No damage or casualties. God save the King.'

On August 28, Mao Tse-tung announced the establishment of a Manchurian People's Government. On September 21, as fighting continued in the south, the Chinese Communist Party held a meeting of 662 delegates in Peking, at which Mao Tse-tung proclaimed the establishment of the People's Republic of China. The new government set as its main aim 'opposing imperialism, feudalism, and bureaucratic forces', while at the same time 'eliminating counter-revolutionary forces'. The 'people's democratic dictatorship' would be led by the working class, 'based on the alliance of workers and peasants'.

Mao Tse-tung became Chairman, and Chou En-lai was appointed Prime Minister and Foreign Minister of the new government. The tasks facing the Communists were formidable: in the north, half a million peasants were in urgent need of relief, especially food. The coastal cities were also suffering from widespread hunger, American shipments of wheat and flour having been stopped at the beginning of the year. The battle against the Nationalists had also still to be finally won.

Peking having been declared the new capital, the official work of government began there on November 1. In the south, the Nationalists continued to be driven back from their last strongholds. Following the fall of Nanking the Nationalist government – like the French government in 1940 – had withdrawn its capital from city to city as its armies fell back. The first temporary capital was set up at Canton, then moved to Chungking – the capital during the Second World War – and then to Chengtu.

On November 20 General Li Tsung-jen left mainland China for medical treatment in Hong Kong: on December 5 he left Hong Kong by air for the United States. Two days later, on December 7, the Nationalist government left mainland China for the island of Taiwan. It was never to return to the mainland. A Nationalist naval blockade against Shanghai was effective for a while, but the few air raids mounted from Taiwan were not. On December 16 Mao Tse-tung travelled to Moscow, where he had talks with Stalin and the Soviet leaders.

Mao Tse-tung had never been outside China before. Stalin's biographer Dmitri Volkogonov has commented with his usual wryness: 'Even their Marxism gave them little in common, since Mao was fond of mixing his with Confucianism, while Stalin generally confined himself to quoting his own works.' As Stalin and his visitor talked and ate, and Mao Tse-tung regaled Stalin with ancient Chinese folklore, their respective officials were drafting a thirty-year Treaty of Friendship, Alliance and Mutual Assistance. A new axis was being formed whose control was to stretch from the Baltic Sea to the South China Sea.

One area of Chinese Communist activity that rang alarm bells in the West was Vietnam. As Chinese Communist forces, in their accelerating advance against the Nationalists, approached the northern border of Vietnam, it seemed to the French rulers there that Ho Chi Minh and his Communist Vietminh government might be considerably strengthened in their struggle against France by their proximity to China. In an attempt to counteract this, France decided to make concessions to the former Emperor, Bao Dai – who had been in exile for the previous three years – in order to attract the Vietnamese people to a non-Communist regime.

Bao Dai visited Paris in March and reached a series of agreements with the French government, whereby the three entities of Vietnam – Tonkin in the north, Annam in the centre and Cochin China in the south – were united into a single State of Vietnam. This State would be autonomous, with its own army, full internal sovereignty, and full civil, commercial and penal jurisdiction. French military, naval and air bases would remain, and French culture would be encouraged. In return, France would propose Vietnam for membership of the United Nations. Vietnam would remain within the French Union, as would the other two former protectorates of French Indo-China – both of them integral parts of the Indo-Chinese Union of 1886 – Laos and Cambodia.

In April, Bao Dai returned to Vietnam. He was confident that as a result of the agreement with France, which had been signed on March 8, he could offer the people of Vietnam an attractive alternative to the Communist regime which had been established by Ho Chi Minh. Under the agreement, Vietnam became 'independent within the French Union'. This was the furthest extent of decolonization that the government in Paris – then headed by Henri Queuille – would permit. Since the resignation of de Gaulle three years earlier, France had been governed by eight different administrations (and Queuille himself was to be Prime Minster twice more). Maintaining a colonial presence, and emphasizing the permanence of the French Union overseas, was a political commitment of successive French governments.

Boa Dai arrived in Saigon on June 13. On the following day he was proclaimed Chief of State of the new State of Vietnam. The reaction of the Vietminh was immediate. The Supreme Commander of the Communist Armed Forces, General Vo Nguyen Giap, called for a vigorous military offensive against the Vietnamese forces loyal to Bao Dai, and against the French lines of communication. The scale of opposing forces grew. At the time of Bao Dai's return it was estimated that the Vietminh had 82,000 men under arms. The French and Bao Dai forces numbered 110,000. Within a few months, extra French troops raised this figure to more than 130,000. Many of the French forces were sent to Tonkin to act as a barrier against any possible Chinese Communist incursion across the northern border.

Inside France many Socialists argued that Bao Dai did not and could not represent the Vietnamese people, and that France must negotiate with Ho Chi Minh. On December 27 the French newspapers published a letter signed by sixty-five professors, parliamentarians and others declaring that Bao Dai had failed, and calling for a truce with the Vietminh and elections in which the Vietminh would be allowed to take part, supervised by the United Nations. But three days later Bao Dai strengthened his position as the sole and legitimate ruler of Vietnam when he signed an agreement with France transferring even more powers to his government than under the agreement of the previous March. The United States had recognized the Boa Dai government on June 21. Towards the end of the year Britain intimated that it might be prepared to do likewise. India, however, whose support Bao Dai badly wanted, declined to give it. Meanwhile, the Communist forces of General Giap continued to attack the French, as Ho Chi Minh publicly denounced Bao Dai's regime.

Two countries appeared to the Western world to be acting as barriers to the onward march of Communism in Asia: Japan and South Korea. Through the supervision of General MacArthur, the United States still watched over all political development in Japan, and was helping to create the conditions that would enable Japan to be built up economically, hoping by the stimulation of Japanese economic progress to inhibit the growth of the Japanese Communist Party. In May, as the Chinese Communists were advancing south of the Yangtse, the United States decided that no further reparations would be taken from Japan until she had been able to stabilize her economy and move towards self-support. At the same time, American aid of $400 million a year would continue.*

The efforts by Japan to put the war years behind it were successful. MacArthur added to the transformation by announcing on several occasions that democracy was 'now well-rooted' in Japan. Japanese self-esteem was boosted when a Japanese swimming team, competing in Los Angeles, broke nine world records. This triumph was followed by the equally gratifying award of the Nobel Prize for Physics to Professor Yukawa as a pioneer in modern theoretical physics. Fourteen years earlier he had postulated the existence of a nuclear particle hundreds of times heavier than the electron. This had been verified by experiments in Britain immediately after the war.

Something of Japan's re-found confidence was shown during the negotiations for a peace treaty with the Soviet Union, when the Japanese Prime Minister, Shigeru Yoshida – who had been Japanese ambassador in London before the war – announced that if the Russian offer was too unfavourable Japan could always walk out of the negotiations. Although he immediately withdrew his statement, Yoshida had given a clear indication of the return of an independent Japanese cast of thought.

In Korea, the North Korean Communist forces had begun to mount armed attacks across the 18th Parallel into South Korea. In the course of the year more than two thousand armed Communist infiltrators were killed by the

* The equivalent in 1998 of more than $5,000 million (the largest recipient of United States aid in 1998, Israel, received just over $3,000 million).

South Korean army. While the North Korean leader, Kim Il Sung, was supported in the maintenance of Communism in the north by the Soviet Union, the government in the south was sustained by American aid, which President Truman announced would continue, at an initial $150 million for the year beginning in June 1949. As the last American troops left, they transferred considerable quantities of military equipment to the southern army. But unlike the Soviet Union, which sent tanks, artillery and a hundred modern military aircraft to North Korea, the United States set limits on the nature of the arms it was prepared to provide to South Korea, and refused to give South Korea the means of making effective war on the north.

Efforts by the United Nations to open trade between north and south were a failure. South Korean politicians who favoured closer trade and contacts with North Korea were imprisoned by Syngman Rhee for 'unpatriotic activity'. A leading opposition figure in the south, seventy-four-year-old Kim Ku, who wanted to open discussions with the north, was assassinated in June by a South Korean army officer.

As the military attacks from the north continued, it was announced from the southern capital, Seoul, that Soviet officers and soldiers had taken part in them. Syngman Rhee appealed to Chiang Kai-shek and to the Philippines government to help establish a Pacific Union, specifically to oppose further Soviet and Communist encroachment. He also appealed to the United States for an assurance of American military help in the event of foreign aggression or 'foreign-inspired' domestic unrest. But there were outside observers who saw any direct involvement by the United States as unwise. One of these was a British army officer, Major J.R. Fergusson, who informed the Foreign Office in London in December, in the course of its inquiry into War Office opinion:

> In the past it has always been our view that irrespective of strengths the North Korean forces would have little difficulty in dealing effectively with the forces of South Korea should full-scale hostilities break out. This somewhat naturally (since they raised, equipped and trained South Korean forces) was not the American view. Recently, however, they have been coming round to our way of thinking regarding the capabilities of the respective forces . . .
>
> On the question of aggression by the North, there can be no doubt whatever that their ultimate objective is to overrun the South; and I think in the long term there is no doubt that they will do so, in which case, as

you so aptly remark, the Americans will have made a rather handsome contribution of equipment to the military strength of Asiatic Communism.

As to their method of achieving their object, short of World War III beginning, I think they will adopt the well-tried tactics of preparing the country from within rather than resort to open aggression, although 'frontier incidents' will doubtless continue.

'Whilst being in no doubt about future North Korean (or Soviet) plans regarding South Korea,' Major Fergusson added – expressing the considered view of the British War Office – 'we think an invasion is unlikely in the immediate view'. However, if it did take place, 'I think it improbable that the Americans would become involved. The possession of South Korea is not essential for Allied strategic plans, and though it would obviously be desirable to deny it to the enemy, it would not be of sufficient importance to make it the cause of World War III. Meanwhile, we must accept an uneasy status quo and hope for the best.'

The Soviet Union and the Soviet bloc, although signatories to the United Nations Declaration of Human Rights – to which all the governments east of the Iron Curtain had appended their signature in 1948 – continued to disregard those rights. On the twentieth anniversary of the start of the collective farm system in the Soviet Union there was an intensification of moves against peasant landholders in areas annexed in 1945 – chiefly the Baltic Republics – which had hitherto escaped the full rigour of collectivization. One area that was seriously affected was Ruthenia, which had belonged to Czechoslovakia between the wars. In Lithuania 130,000 peasant farms were incorporated into the collective farm system in 1949. Collectivization was not as violent as it had been before 1939, but it disturbed agricultural production and created animosity and resistance to the orders from Moscow.

In the arts, a campaign was launched against 'rootless and homeless cosmopolitanism'. Writers, artists and musicians were among those singled out for attack. The first shot was fired in an article in *Pravda* on January 28 with the headline: 'About a Certain Anti-Patriotic Group of Theatre Critics.' It was alleged that cosmopolitanism was a 'plot' to undermine Soviet theatre by replacing national, patriotic and Socialist plays and productions with 'decadent bourgeois' ones. The literary pseudonyms of those who were considered guilty of the 'crime' of cosmopolitanism were widely printed, together with their real names, which were often recognizably Jewish.

A Soviet soldier, Marshal Konstantin Rokossovski, a veteran of the Spanish Civil War – who had been born in Warsaw and was of Polish origin – arrived in the Polish capital in February accompanied by three Soviet generals. Their visit followed immediately after the arrest of hundreds of former officers of the wartime underground army, the Armia Krajowa, which had been loyal to the London government – at that time the only legitimate Polish government. Further measures followed that marked a closer working partnership with the Soviet Union. The independent-minded Polish Communist Party leader, Wladyslaw Gomulka, who had already been removed from his position of power, was cut off altogether from any political influence and then expelled from the Party's governing body. At the end of March measures were introduced by the Ministry of Justice which effectively abolished trial by jury. The measures were justified on the grounds that they were for 'improving and simplifying court procedure'. In a series of political trials, the accused were said to have been the agents and tools of Western imperialism.

On November 7 the Soviet Marshal, Rokossovski, was created a Marshal of Poland and made Minister of Defence in the Polish government. On the following day it was announced that he had accepted Polish citizenship. It was Rokossovski who had refused during the Warsaw uprising of 1944 to give landing facilities on Soviet controlled airfields for British, American or Polish pilots. In an Order of the Day on the anniversary of the Bolshevik revolution of 1917 he called on the Polish armed forces 'to tighten the ties of brotherhood with the powerful Soviet Army and the armies of the People's Democracies' – something that he proceeded to do. He also ensured that part of the Polish Army's task was to attend to Communist political work as well as, and even instead of, military training.

In Czechoslovakia the Communist system was imposed at every level of society: characterized by the ignoring of human rights. Men were taken for forced labour and for ideological re-education. Women were forced to work in industry. Children were made to join Party organizations. Newspapers were strictly controlled, and several perceptive foreign correspondents were expelled. As in Poland, citizens innocent of wrong-doing were brought to trial and accused of spying for the Western Powers. It was like the Soviet spy trials of the 1930s repeated. Plunder also played its part: the Soviet Union was insisting on the massive export to Russia of Czech railway rolling stock, armaments, machine tools, industrial instruments and uranium. In return the Soviet Union provided some food (about 40% of the return) and raw materials (57%) which the Czechs had then to transform into manufactured goods that could be re-exported to Russia.

Within a year of the Czech Communist coup of February 1948 the Party and its ideology were established as the predominant authority and ethos across the whole range of administrative functions. In the words of the Minister of the Interior, Vaclav Nosek, at the beginning of 1949: 'Our State apparatus will no longer be a non-Party body, but a creative part of our Socialist endeavours. We shall put in key positions people devoted to Socialism – as far as possible from the ranks of the working class. A positive attitude to the working class must be apparent at first sight to anyone approaching an official.' Even the Czech capital, Prague, was, in the words of the Party newspaper *Rudé Pravó*, 'to be purged of bourgeois elements and given to working people'. This was not mere verbal bluster: by the end of the year at least 5,000, and possibly as many as 40,000 Czech citizens had been arrested without charge and sent without trial to forced labour camps throughout the country. Even the Editor-in-Chief of *Rudé Pravó*, Vilem Novy, a member of the Central Committee of the Czechoslovak Communist Party, was dismissed from his post. Held in custody for five years and subsequently rehabilitated, he became a vigorous supporter of the Communist regime and Soviet influence.

The Catholic Church was also under constant and mounting pressure. After Archbishop Josef Beran denounced the Government's attempt to set up an independent, pro-Communist Catholic hierarchy – having earlier issued a pastoral letter with an injunction addressed to himself: 'Don't remain silent, archbishop! You can't remain silent! – he was confined to his palace and forbidden access to his followers.* In retaliation, a Papal decree was issued from Rome excommunicating all church members who were active supporters of the Communist party. In November a law was passed giving the Czech State full control over the appointment of the clergy and the payment of their salaries.

The most publicized political trial of 1949 was in Hungary. It opened in Budapest on February 3, when the Hungarian Communist authorities accused Cardinal Jozsef Mindszenty, the Prince-Primate of Hungary, of spying on

---

* From 1950 to 1963 Archbishop Beran was under house arrest in the Archbishop's Palace in Prague. After his release he was forced to live outside Prague, in southern Bohemia. When, in January 1965, he was named Cardinal by the Pope, he was permitted to go to Rome, but on the condition that he did not return to Czechoslovakia. He died in Rome in 1969, and is the only Czech, and non-Pope, to be buried in St Peter's in the Vatican.

behalf of the United States and of seeking the restoration of the Habsburgs (he had met the heir to the Habsburgs in Chicago in 1948). The Cardinal's arrest caused indignation among Hungarian Catholics; his trial caused consternation. Throughout it, he was outspoken in his criticism of Communism. Found guilty of 'organizing conspiracy against the Republic', he was sentenced to penal servitude for life. A senior Catholic university professor, Dr Jusztin Baranyi, who was charged with him, was sentenced to fifteen years in prison.

A second trial that year in Hungary struck at the inner circle of the Communist regime itself. One of the accused was the former Minister of the Interior and Foreign Minister, Lazlo Rajk. Another was the Chief of the General Staff. They were accused of planning a military coup and the assassination of the other leaders, to be followed by an alliance with Tito's Yugoslavia in a war against the Soviet Union, and the establishment of Hungary as a 'colony of American imperialist interests'. As with the Soviet purge trials in the 1930s, the charges were absurd and the rule of law noticeably absent in the way the cases were conducted. All the defendants were found guilty and executed. The British historian C.A. Macartney wrote at the time:

> The real purpose of the trial seems to have been multiple: to provide occasion for publishing 'revelations' about Marshal Tito (to a garbled description of whose war-time activities much of the evidence was devoted) which could be used later, if required, as a *casus belli* by the USSR or its ventriloquist's dummies, to terrorize the people of Hungary, and to provide excuses for further tightening up of the dictatorship; and incidentally to get rid of a man who, although a ruthless fanatic, did not entirely fit in with the rest of the ruling clique, being neither Moscow-trained nor a Jew, and may perhaps really have wanted to preserve for his country a shred of independence.
>
> At any rate, the affair was followed by another grand purge in the political parties, Ministries, and other posts of national importance, an increasing number of which were being taken over, at the end of the year, by Soviet citizens.

The Hungarian Communist Party still had, however, to provide the bulk of the personnel, and following the purges a big organized drive was opened to raise the 'ideological level' of the survivors. According to the plans of the Ministry of Enlightenment, five hundred selected future instructors were to be given a two years' course and all Party functionaries a three months' course; while ordinary Party members had to attend seminaries and evening schools until they had thoroughly absorbed 'Marxism-Leninism'.

Several British and American subjects were arrested in Hungary that autumn and winter and falsely accused of espionage. One of them was a Hungarian-born British subject, Dr Edith Bone. She was sixty-one years old. Arrested on October 1, she was kept in solitary confinement for fourteen months. When she refused to confess to spying − of which she was innocent − she was put into a windowless cell for six months. She called it her 'flea circus'. In response to the arrest of Dr Bone the British government broke off the Anglo-Hungarian commercial and financial talks that were then taking place in London, and the State Department forbade American citizens from visiting Hungary. On December 28 the Hungarian government nationalized all foreign-financed trading and industrial enterprises, and all privately owned shops and factories employing more than ten people.

The Roumanian Government was equally thorough in its imposition of Communist rule. On January 14 a law was promulgated whereby those found guilty of minor economic offences against the State were liable to the death penalty. In February the middle-class-based National Popular Party was dissolved. In March, a Land Act enforced the collectivization of farms without compensation to landowners or farmers. Peasants were warned that failure to cooperate in the collective farm programme would debar them from receiving tractors and other agricultural equipment from the government stores which alone could provide them.

The two remaining non-Communist Cabinet Ministers in positions of authority in Roumania were removed in April, with additional powers being transferred to the Communist Foreign Minister Anna Pauker − who, being Jewish, also provoked considerable anti-Semitic reaction among those hostile to the regime. Organized religion was also under the strongest pressure, with both the Roumanian Orthodox Church and the Greek Catholic Church being made subservient to the State system. The Roman Catholic Church fought a tenacious rearguard action, with the result that in June the Roman Catholic bishops of Alba Julia and Jassy were arrested, and on August 1 all Roman Catholic congregations were dissolved by State decree.

Soviet influence was asserted during the year through a number of joint Soviet-Roumanian companies, each controlled by their respective State authorities. Natural gas, metal, coal, shipbuilding and insurance were among the enterprises which came under joint control, giving the Soviet Union a voice in the daily running of the Roumanian economy. Roumania had also to give the Soviet Union priority over the exports of Roumanian oil and timber. In a parallel move, the diplomats of Western countries were refused permission to visit several Roumanian provinces, and could not even leave Bucharest without permission. Similar restrictions throughout the Soviet satellites made it almost impossible for accurate accounts of these Communist regimes to reach the West.

The Yugoslavs under Tito, having broken with the Soviet Union, found that, briefly, Bulgaria was also taking a somewhat independent line on foreign policy, and was advocating a federation of European socialist States. In an attempt to end any idea of an independent foreign policy, even within the Communist system, Stalin invited them both to send delegations to Moscow. On February 10 he presided in the Kremlin over a joint meeting – his idea – between them. After having abused both for their respective disobedience to the true tenets of Communism, Stalin suggested that they form themselves into a Bulgarian-Yugoslav Federation. Both delegations rejected this idea. Later, in a twenty-five page letter to Tito, Stalin denounced Yugoslavia's continuing independent stance as 'deviation ' and 'treachery'. Bulgaria, with her Black Sea shore vulnerable to Soviet naval pressure, had meanwhile returned to the fold of orthodoxy and obedience. Yugoslavia pressed ahead with its independent activity. When Stalin summoned its leaders to a Cominform meeting in Bucharest they refused to go.

In Bulgaria, the brief effort at a quasi-independent foreign policy having been firmly rebuffed by Stalin, the year was marked by a strengthening of Communist Party control. Treason trials were held against non-Communist politicians and church leaders, one of whom, Vassil Ziapkov, the head of the Congregational Church, was sentenced to life imprisonment. Strong British and American protests against the trials of the Protestant church leaders were contemptuously rejected by the Bulgarian Government. In January, religious schools had been abolished. In April, the British Government brought before the United Nations the question of the suppression of religious freedom in Bulgaria. The treason trials continued. The Soviet Minister of Defence, Marshal Nikolai Bulganin, visiting Sofia in September, explained publicly that 'treason' meant any act that weakened the ties of friendship between the Soviet Union and Bulgaria.

Another feature of Communist rule was revealed in Bulgaria in the summer: the purging of senior members of the Party and the intensification of party discipline and control. The Chief of the General Staff, General Kinov, was among those arrested and dismissed. On December 7 a public trial opened in Sofia, again reminiscent of the public purge trials in the Soviet Union more than a decade earlier. A leading Central Committee member, Traicho Kostov – the former Chairman of the Committee for Economic and Financial Affairs – and ten other leading Communist figures, were accused of plotting to allow Yugoslavia to annex Bulgaria, of having committed treason over many years, and of attempting to sabotage trade agreements with the Soviet Union. All the defendants except Kostov confessed, Soviet-style, to these imaginary crimes, implicated Kostov, and were sentenced to long terms of imprisonment. Kostov protested his innocence, and his impeccable Communist credentials, throughout the trial. He was found guilty, and executed on December 16, nine days after the trial had begun.

On December 21 Stalin celebrated his seventieth birthday. In Moscow a gala performance was given in his honour by the Bolshoi Ballet. Among those present were Mao Tse-tung, Dolores Ibarruri, and the ruler of East Germany, Walter Ulbricht.

The imposition of Communism in Eastern Europe was relentless. But Churchill, who had been leader of the Conservative Opposition in Britain for the past three years, expressed long-term optimism at the prospects for freedom in the countries where the rule of law was being perverted. Speaking at the Massachusetts Institute of Technology on March 21, he said: 'Laws, just or unjust may govern men's actions. Tyrannies may restrain or regulate their words. The machinery of propaganda may pack their minds with falsehood and deny them truth for many generations of time. But the soul of man thus held in trance or frozen in a long night can be awakened by a spark coming from God knows where and in a moment the whole structure of lies and oppressions is on trial for its life.' Churchill concluded: 'People in bondage need never despair.'

This forecast seemed hopelessly optimistic in the light of events in the Soviet Union and Eastern Europe that year, dominated as they were by the successful Soviet testing of an atom bomb. News of this test was made public, not by the Soviets, but by the American, British and Canadian Governments, who released the information on September 23. Within two months, on November 10, Andrei Vyshinsky, who had become Soviet Foreign Minister earlier that year, explained to the United Nations in New York that atomic energy was being used in the Soviet Union, not as part of any military arsenal, but 'for razing mountains, irrigating deserts, cutting through jungles, and spreading life, prosperity and happiness in places where human footsteps had not been in a thousand years'.

No one knew whether the possession by the Soviet Union of the atom bomb would lead to a more aggressive Soviet foreign policy, or whether the threat of atomic war would force a standstill in conflict between the United States and Russia for fear of mutual destruction. Also unknown at that time outside a tiny circle was the fact that Britain was in the process of manufacturing its own atom bomb. A new era was in the making, haltingly and surreptitiously. 'Proliferation' was as yet not a word known to the international political dictionary. On August 1 the United States Atomic Energy Commission submitted a report to Congress stressing the positive aspects of the development of atomic energy as an alternative domestic fuel and power source. The report also doubted – wrongly as subsequent research was to show – that there had been any increase in the incidence of cancer in either Hiroshima or Nagasaki as a result of the atom bombs exploded there four years earlier.

The science of flight, which had been an integral part of the destruction of Hiroshima and Nagasaki – as well as of Tokyo, Dresden, Hamburg, Belgrade, Coventry, Warsaw, Guernica and Nanking – had begun to re-establish itself after the Second World War as the facilitator for international business and holiday travel. During 1949 a United States B-50 bomber made the first non-stop flight around the world, refuelling in the air four times – above the Azores, Dharan, the Philippines and Hawaii. Its average speed was almost 250 miles an hour. The jet engine was also showing its potential. Five months after the record breaking flight of the B-50, a British de Havilland Comet jet airliner flew 2,980 miles, from London to Castel Benito, Tripoli, at an average speed of 450 miles an hour. This was the fastest flight by any commercial air liner at that time. Another development, the use of turbines to drive aircraft engines, was used that year in a civilian airliner for the first time, designed to fly almost two thousand miles at a cruising speed of more than 300 miles an hour.

In the United States, those who feared Communist subversion were encouraged on October 17 when a guilty verdict was passed against eleven leaders of the American Communist Party. They had been charged with 'conspiracy to teach the overthrow of the United States Government by violence'.

Recognition of the Black American contribution to the society of the

United States was making slow but steady progress. The first opera by a Black American composer to be performed by a company of standing – the City Center Opera Company of New York – received its world premier in the spring of 1949. It was *Troubled Island,* by William Grant Still, the story of the overthrow of the Haitian Emperor Dessalines in 1806. Almost twenty years earlier, Still's pre-war *Afro-American Symphony,* composed in 1931, had led him to be hailed by music critics as the 'dean of America's Negro composers'. The very word 'Negro' was to be replaced half a century later by 'Afro-American' as the name for his people in the United States.

In South Africa, the first riots against apartheid since the triumph of the Nationalist Party the previous year broke out in Johannesburg. But at a luncheon club in New York on October 19, one of the most vocal White South African opponents of apartheid, Alan Paton, spoke hopefully. 'I look for the day,' he said, 'when in South Africa we shall realize that the only lasting and worth-while solution of our grave and profound problems lies not in the use of power, but in that understanding and compassion without which human life is an intolerable bondage, condemning us all to an existence of violence and misery and fear.'

'Understanding and compassion' did not yet seem to be the predominant moods of the mass of mankind. Indeed, a grave warning of the way in which the world might go was published that year, in the form of a novel, by George Orwell, *Nineteen Eighty Four.* The novel was set in the imaginary totalitarian world of Oceania, where the official language was Newspeak. It was intended that the language of the free world, Oldspeak, would have disappeared altogether by the year 2050. The very word 'free' was part a problem: 'The word *free* still existed in Newspeak, but it could only be used in such statements as "This dog is free from lice" or "This field is free from weeds". It could not be used in its old sense of "politically free" or "intellectually free", since political and intellectual freedom no longer existed even as concepts, and were therefore nameless.'

Total control over the mass of the people of Oceania was exercised with vigilance and psychological cunning: 'If human equality is to be for ever averted – if the High, as we have called them, are to keep their places permanently – then the prevailing mental condition must be controlled insanity.' When Winston Smith, Orwell's hero, dares to exclaim, 'Down with Big Brother!' his interrogator smiles at him and says: 'You are a flaw in the pattern, Winston. You are a stain that must be wiped out.'

CHAPTER TWENTY-THREE

1950

Who are those who are really disloyal? Those who
inflame racial hatreds, who sow religious and class
dissensions. Those who subvert the Constitution by
violating the freedom of the ballot box.

HENRY STEELE COMMAGER

THE TRIUMPH of the Communists in China brought Mao Tse-tung to
the centre of the world stage. On January 6, while he was still in Moscow,
his government was recognized by Britain. Fear of a vastly extended Communist bloc, the continuing Communist propaganda against the West, and the
knowledge that the Soviet Union not only possessed the atom bomb but
was manufacturing it in quantities, led to an extension of the North Atlantic
Treaty Organization (NATO) by means of a series of bi-lateral defence
agreements between the United States and each of the NATO countries.

These agreements were signed on January 27. Four days later, in strictest
secrecy, President Truman instructed the United States Atomic Energy Commission to begin work on a bomb that could cause far more devastation than
the atom bomb – it was called the hydrogen bomb. On February 14 the
thirty-year Treaty of Friendship, Alliance and Mutual Assistance negotiated
by Mao Tse-tung and Stalin was signed in Moscow between the Soviet Union
and China. The Cold War had acquired a new axis. But from his position
as Leader of the Opposition in Britain, Churchill – nine days before a General
Election which he hoped, in vain, would return him to office – set out a
vision of international amelioration. 'The idea appeals to me,' he told the
citizens of Edinburgh on February 14, 'of a supreme effort to bridge the
gulf between the two worlds, so that each can live their life, if not in
friendship, at least without the hatreds of the Cold War.' Then, using for
the first time the word 'summit' to describe a meeting of world leaders 'at

the top', he declared: 'It is not easy to see how things could be worsened by a parley at the summit, if such a thing were possible.'

No such 'summit' was in the offing; tension between West and East remained high. On February 20, after Bulgaria refused to withdraw charges against the American diplomat Donald Heath of conspiring with the disgraced Communist leader Traicho Kostov, the United States broke off diplomatic relations with Bulgaria. On March 1 the atomic scientist Klaus Fuchs – a pre-war German refugee who had been living and working in England and the United States – was sentenced by a British court to fourteen years in prison for betraying atomic secrets to the Soviet Union. A week later, on March 8, the Soviet Defence Minister, Marshal Kliment Voroshilov, announced publicly that the Soviet Union possessed the atom bomb. Three days later, following the shooting down of a private American plane over Soviet air space in Latvia, the Soviet Union stated that the plane was a bomber – which it was not – and protested vehemently.

In an effort to reduce the feeling of disintegration in international affairs, on June 6 the recently re-appointed Secretary General of the United Nations, Trygvie Lie, announced a twenty year 'peace programme'. His idea was to institute more regular meetings of Foreign Ministers, to create a permanent United Nations military force, to admit more members to the United Nations, and to extend more aid to poorer countries. It was a path along which the United Nations travelled, but the goal was to take many years. As a first step to the widening of the membership of the United Nations, on November 4 the General Assembly revoked the four-year-old ban on Spain becoming a member. There were to be no pariah nations.

Fear of Communist expansion and subversion led to an extraordinary episode in the public life of the United States. It took the form of a witchhunt against alleged Communists in the administration. On January 9 Senator Joseph McCarthy alleged that 205 Communists were working in the State Department. So emphatic and widely publicized were his charges that the Senate Foreign Relations Committee was instructed to investigate them. For almost four years, 'loyalty oaths' had been demanded by tens of thousands of employers who were frightened of Communist subversion. It was Truman himself who had formulated the Loyalty Oath in March 1947. Many municipalities had taken them up and supported them, including the New York City Council. Many newspapers supported them, including the influential Hearst press.

The loyalty oaths were attacked in *Harper's* magazine by the constitutional historian Henry Steele Commager, who called them 'an abuse of power that violated the Constitution'. Those who refused to sign these oaths were often forced to leave their jobs. This, wrote Commager, was unlawful. 'In the making,' he warned, 'is a revival of the Red hysteria of the early 1920s, one of the shabbiest in the history of American democracy; and more than a revival, for the new crusade is designed not merely to frustrate Communism but to formulate a positive definition of Americanism, and a positive concept of loyalty.'

Commager went on to ask:

Who are those who are really disloyal? Those who inflame racial hatreds, who sow religious and class dissensions. Those who subvert the Constitution by violating the freedom of the ballot box. Those who make a mockery of majority rule by the use of filibuster. Those who impair democracy by denying equal educational facilities. Those who frustrate justice by lynch law or by making a farce of jury trials. Those who deny freedom of speech and of the press and of assembly. Those who demand special favours against the interest of the commonwealth. Those who regard public office merely as a source of private gain. Those who would exalt the military over the civil. Those who for selfish and private purposes stir up national antagonisms and expose the world to the ruin of war.

For a while it seemed as if Commager's was a voice in the wilderness. As the anti-Communist crusade gained in momentum, the Republican-dominated Congress passed an Internal Security Bill (also known as the McCarran Act) requiring all Communist organizations to register, and forbidding the employment of Communists in companies doing defence work. Truman vetoed the Bill, but it was passed into law over his veto.

On January 25 a senior United States diplomat, Alger Hiss, who had accompanied Roosevelt to the Yalta Conference, and in 1947 had become President of the Carnegie Endowment for International Peace, was found guilty of perjury for concealing membership of the Communist Party. He was sentenced to five years in prison.

In portraying the witchhunt that followed McCarthy's accusations, an American cartoonist, 'Herblock' (Herbert Lawrence Block) coined the term 'McCarthyism', which quickly entered the language. Not since Quisling had the name of an individual come to convey such odium. The McCarthyites suffered a setback in late July, however, when the Senate accepted a Foreign Relations Committee report that the State Department had not been subjected to 'Communist infiltration'. But when the previous year's conviction of eleven American Communists on charges of 'conspiracy to teach and advocate the overthrow of the government' was sent for appeal, it was sustained by one of America's leading jurists, Judge Learned Hand, whose record fifty-two year service as a Federal judge ended only with his death eleven years later.*

Among the lawyers who defended those accused of being Communists or perjurers, and who also defended those who refused to testify, was Telford Taylor, the former chief American prosecutor at the Nuremberg trials. Taylor was denounced for his courageous stand by one of the Hearst newspapers, the *Chicago Tribune*, which argued that he had 'served Moscow' at Nuremberg by prosecuting 'good Germans'. When the lawyers who had defended the American Communist Party were themselves accused by the judge of contempt of court, and threatened with disbarment, Telford Taylor defended them. He also defended Junius Scales, who was imprisoned for membership of the Communist Party despite the fact that the prosecution was unable to show that he shared, or even knew, of its aims. In later years Taylor used to point out that Scales had been convicted on a standard of guilt that the Nuremberg trial judges had rejected for major war criminals.

In a display of public defiance, Telford Taylor argued, most forcibly in a speech at West Point, that McCarthy's inquiry into Communist subversion at an army camp, Fort Monmouth, New Jersey, had undermined army morale and values far more than any actual subversion could have done. By way of reply, McCarthy attacked Taylor publicly in the pages of *Newsweek*, and twice subpoenaed him, but Taylor could not be silenced; indeed, in a book which he wrote about the witchhunts, *Grand Inquest*, he made McCarthy look not only absurd but a major influence in seeking to pervert American constitutional and moral values.

Another work that upheld freedom of expression, and sane rather than insane inquiry, was Arthur Miller's play *The Crucible*. Drawing on the destructive interrogations and burning of alleged witches in Salem, Massachusetts, in the seventeenth century, Miller gave courage not only to Americans who were under attack, but – in the years to come – to people under tyranny

---

* Judge Learned Hand, wrongly described in some books (including volume one of this book) as a native American, was descended from colonial Puritan stock.

everywhere, including Poland and China. Of the origin of his play he later wrote, after describing the 'depressing' spectacle of the McCarthy witchhunts:

> Perhaps more disturbing to me than all the rest was the atmosphere being created, a pall of suspicion reaching out not only to radio and television and movie studios but into Holy Trinity Church in Brooklyn Heights, whose Minister, Reverend William Howard Melish, was hounded out of his pulpit, and his family out of their home, by an anti-Communist campaign among a divided vestry.
>
> While his aged father, John Howard Melish – in former years the handsome, popular minister of this immense and beautiful Episcopal church, the clergyman who for decades had sworn New York's mayors into office – lay bedridden on the top floor, the son and his family were put out in the street.
>
> As head of a section of Russian War Relief, he had become a rather naive believer in the goodness of Soviet aims, if not of the system. That he had never ceased being a devout Christian no one seemed to question, and over the many long months of his self-defence, ending in a civil court case upholding his bishop's right to fire him, I could only conclude that the country was intending to become a philosophical monolith where no real differences about anything important would be tolerated.

The impact of *The Crucible* spread far beyond the United States. Thirty years later Arthur Miller was in Shanghai. 'The writer Nien Chang,' he wrote, 'who spent six and a half years in solitary confinement and whose daughter was murdered by the Red Guards, told me that after her release she saw the Shanghai production and could not believe that a non-Chinese had written the play. "Some of the interrogations," she said, "were precisely the same ones used on us in the Cultural Revolution". It was chilling to realize what had never occurred to me until she mentioned it – that the tyranny of teenagers was almost identical in both instances.'

The nature of Communist ideology and practice was under scrutiny during 1950 not only in the hysterical atmosphere of American courts, but in the mental ferment of the Western literary and intellectual world. Six former Communist intellectuals or Communist sympathizers cooperated in the publication of a book that year, edited by Richard Crossman, a British Labour Member of Parliament, entitled *The God that Failed: Six Studies in Communism*. The contributors included the American journalist – and biographer of Lenin

– Louis Fischer, the French writer André Gide, and the Hungarian-born novelist and broadcaster Arthur Koestler. Each explained how and when he had became disillusioned with Communism. 'Death came to Spain in open combat in the sun,' Fischer wrote, recalling the late 1930s. 'Death stalked Russia in the cellar.'

André Gide had lost faith after his visit to the Soviet Union in 1937. 'The Communist spirit has ceased being in opposition to the Fascist spirit, or even differentiating itself from it,' he had written then in his journal. In 1950 he was outspoken in his censure:

Although the long-heralded Dictatorship of the Proletariat has not materialized, there is nevertheless dictatorship of one kind – dictatorship of the Soviet bureaucracy. It is essential to recognize this and not to allow oneself to be bamboozled. This is not what was hoped for – one might almost say that it is precisely the last thing in the world that was hoped.

The workers have no longer even the liberty of electing their own representatives to defend their threatened interests. Free ballot – open or secret – is a derision and a sham; the voters have merely the right of electing those who have been chosen for them beforehand. The workers are cheated, muzzled and bound hand and foot, so that resistance has become well-nigh impossible.

The game has been well played by Stalin, and Communists the whole world over applaud him, believing that in the Soviet Union at least they have gained a glorious victory, and they call all those who do not agree with them public enemies and traitors. But in Russia this has led to treachery of a new sort. An excellent way of earning promotion is to become an informer, that puts you on good terms with the dangerous police which protect you while using you.

Once you have started on that easy, slippery slope, no question of friendship or loyalty can intervene to hold you back; on every occasion you are forced to advance, sliding further into the abyss of shame. The result is that everyone is suspicious of everyone else and the most innocent remarks – even of children – can bring destruction, so that everyone is on his guard and no one lets himself go.

Arthur Koestler expressed the anguish of all six men – and tens of thousands of other former Communists – when he wrote of Communism's victims and the failure of fellow Communists – himself included – to speak out:

Every single one of us knows of at least one friend who perished in the Arctic subcontinent of forced labour camps, was shot as a spy or vanished without trace. How our voices boomed with righteous indignation, denouncing flaws in the procedure of justice in our comfortable democracies; and how silent we were when our comrades, without trial or conviction, were liquidated in the Socialist sixth of the earth.

Each of us carries a skeleton in the cupboard of his conscience; added together they would form galleries of bones more labyrinthine than the Paris catacombs.

At no time and in no country have more revolutionaries been killed and reduced to slavery than in Soviet Russia. To one who himself for seven years found excuses for every stupidity and crime committed under the Marxist banner, the spectacle of these dialectical tight-rope acts of self-deception, performed by men of good will and intelligence, is more disheartening than the barbarities committed by the simple in spirit.

'Having experienced the almost unlimited possibilities of mental acrobatism on that tight-rope stretched across one's conscience,' Koestler added, 'I know how much stretching it takes to make that elastic rope snap.

But snap it had: each essayist in *The God that Failed* had horror stories enough to show the miseries of false moral indignation, conformity and turning a blind eye. In an attempt to create an intellectual front against Communist uniformity and distortions, a Congress for Cultural Freedom was called: it met in West Berlin, almost within sight of one of the most westerly points of the Communist world.

Inside the Communist world, however, the repressions and trials of previous years continued. Jan Masaryk's successor as Czechoslovak Foreign Minister, Dr Valdimir Clementis, was forced to resign in May because, although a Communist, he had opposed the Nazi-Soviet Pact in 1939 and the Soviet invasion of Finland later that same year. This opposition constituted, according to the public denunciation against him, failures of a particularly serious order, leading to the conclusion that 'there must have existed germs of distrust towards the USSR and comrade Stalin before 1939 if that failure could happen.' Dr Clementis was a Slovak. Several leading Slovak Communists, including Dr Novomesky, the Commissioner for Education, Art and Science, were accused of 'bourgeois nationalism' and dismissed.

In June the rule of law reached a low point when a new Penal Code for Czechoslovakia was introduced, specifically warning relatives not to protect those closest to them. 'Kinship with the guilty party,' the code laid down, 'does not exculpate people who become accomplices in or fail to report a crime if that crime is high treason, sabotage or espionage, for the principle is established that the interests of the working people's State hold precedence over family ties.' In Hungary, the Security Police, more than 25,000 strong, was made an autonomous force directly responsible to the Cabinet. In the Hungarian Army, several Soviet officers obtained senior positions. Later in the year, on September 7, a Hungarian government decree led to the closing down of most religious orders, the shutting down of their buildings and the eviction of their members.

In Roumania, in June, the Vicar-General of the Diocese of Alba Julia, who was the last bishop of the Latin rite still conducting worship in public, was arrested. He was not allowed to continue preaching. Two months later the regime further strengthened its powers by introducing the death penalty for 'negligence by workers leading to public disaster, theft, and destruction of military equipment', as well as for espionage. Eight death sentences were announced before the year ended on Roumanian citizens allegedly working for foreign powers. Roumania had become as loyal to the Soviet system and method as any satellite country. Albania, not to be outdone, announced that in its elections in May the Communist Democratic Front obtained 98.99 per cent of the vote. A month later Albania joined the Cominform and signed a treaty of friendship with the Soviet Union.

Yet another show trial was under way in the Soviet Union. Stalin had decided to remove a group of senior officials who had always been hard working, and loyal to him as their leader. All of them were from Leningrad, a city he feared all his life as a potential centre of dissent, of rivalry, and of independence. The first to be arrested was Nikolai Voznesensky, a member of the Politburo. He had been one of the most effective organizers of the wartime Soviet economy. If he had a 'fault' in the eyes of the Soviet system, it was one that theoretically ought to have been a valued Communist quality: he had always tried to bring the workers of any factory into the process of planning and management, and into the discussions about the aims of the enterprises in which they worked.

Once more a search was on for 'spies' and 'enemies of the people'. Once more those caught up in the net and arrested had never been spies or enemies. All of them were members of the Communist Party at its highest echelons. In bringing Nikolai Voznesensky to trial Stalin also brought accusations against Voznesensky's brother Alexander – the rector of Leningrad University

– and his sister Maria, a Communist Party worker. All three accused were found guilty and shot. Only Nikolai Voznesensky appears to have been kept in prison first, for three more months, before being taken by truck to Moscow wearing only light clothes, in mid-winter. Stalin's biographer Dmitri Volkogonov commented: 'Either he died on the way, or was shot.'

In the cause of European Union, there was a breakthrough on March 21 when the West German Chancellor, Konrad Adenauer, proposed publicly that there should be an economic union between West Germany and France. On May 9 an announcement in Paris launched the Schumann plan, which placed the French and German coal industries, and all French and German iron and steel production, under a single authority. The plan envisaged other countries joining. Thus for the second time within seven weeks, France and Germany – three time military adversaries in the previous eighty years – took a positive and practical lead in the move towards a united Europe. With negotiations starting in June and ending in September, a European Payments Union (the EPU) was established between fifteen European countries, and Britain and the sterling area, to settle and regularize trade deficits and surpluses over the coming two years. Once again the instinct for cooperation, even if limited to the economic sphere, indicated a willingness to work together that went further than anything seen before the war.

On June 15 West Germany was admitted to the Council of Europe. Propelled forward by the East-West divide, the cause of European unity was gaining momentum, and the recovery of western Europe separating it economically as well as ideologically from its eastern neighbours. When the Consultative Assembly of the Council of Europe met in August, Churchill was among those who supported a motion for the creation of a European Army. The motion was passed by 89 votes to five. In October the French Prime Minister, René Pleven, announced the creation of a European Military Community which would include a European Army. This became known as the Pleven Plan.

Repercussions of the emergence of independence in South-East Asia continued to bedevil life throughout the region. In Burma the year began with half a dozen different rebellions in different parts of the country, bringing hardship and the devastation always caused by fighting to areas that had been ravaged only eight years earlier during the Allied struggle with the Japanese. Only the lack of cooperation between the rebel groups gave the

Burmese Government a chance to move against them one by one. The government was further helped by a tendency among the rebel groups to turn against each other. The most active were the Karens. Other rebel groups included the White Flag Communists, the Red Flag Communists, and the Army Mutineers. In the Tavoy district, Communist rebels brought the British-owned tin mining enterprises to a halt. In the far east of Burma, Chinese Kuomintang soldiers who had fled from China to escape capture by the Communists were roaming the countryside and surviving by the ancient devices of pillaging and looting.

The first military operations by the Burmese Government against the insurgents were launched from Rangoon at the beginning of March, when the Karens were driven out of several towns and finally from their headquarters at Toungoo, where their broadcasting equipment was captured. The Karens did not give up their fight, however, but withdrew to the hill country east of Toungoo and in the Irrawaddy Delta. Later in the year the Karen rebellion suffered another blow when its leader, Saw Ba U Gyi, was killed. Also killed with him was a former British army officer, Captain David Vivian, whom the Karens had released from a Burmese jail after he had been imprisoned for his part in the murder of the Burmese Ministers in 1947. Vivian had then helped the Karens with the manufacture of arms.

After taking the Karen capital, the government forces marched against the city of Prome, where several of the other rebel groups had their headquarters. This too was overrun. It was the Karens who managed to regroup most effectively. As their new leader they chose Colonel Saw Min Maung, who had won the Military Cross fighting for the British against the Japanese five years earlier. The Colonel was the son of a Karen Anglican priest. Unable to track him down or enter his strongholds, the Burmese government began negotiations. The Karens, mistrustful, acted warily and maintained their fighting capacity.

The fighting in Burma had a deleterious effect on the economy, with the amount of rice available for export falling to a million tons, compared with an average of three million tons a year before the Second World War. Help came from the British Commonwealth, with Britain providing a loan of £3,375,000, India £1 million, Pakistan and Australia £500,000 each and Ceylon £250,000. It was the first exercise in collective Commonwealth assistance since the independence of India, Pakistan and Ceylon four years earlier.

In Indonesia, the republican government that had emerged after the Japanese defeat and the withdrawal of the Dutch was beset with problems. Seeking to unify the vast country under a single political system, in Java it faced two sources of violent rebellion. One was headed by an extreme Muslim group, Dar-ul-Islam, whose leader was Andi Abdul Aziz. The other was led by a rebel Dutchmen, 'Turk' Westerling. Other outbreaks of violence took place on the islands of Borneo, the Celebes and Sumatra.

In the South Moluccas rebels declared the independence of the islands and seized the capital city of Ambon. It took more than seven months before government forces were able to dislodge them. The fighting that continued on many of the Indonesian islands was initially supervised by three separate federal authorities. But on May 15 a unitary Republic of Indonesia was agreed upon. It came into being three months later, on August 17, which was henceforth celebrated as Indonesian Independence Day.

In the Philippines, the Communist-led Hukbalahap rebellion gained in strength during the year. There were numerous rebel raids on provincial towns, and many casualties. Large amounts of American aid – which over five years totalled $2,000 million dollars – were funnelled into the fight against the rebels, or into the personal coffers and bank accounts of the leaders. Corruption had become an integral part of foreign aid. 'Much of that money has not been used as wisely as we would have wished,' Dean Acheson commented at the beginning of the year.

In Japan, still under American military occupation, the essentially conservative government remained subordinate to General MacArthur, the Supreme Commander Allied Powers (SCAP). The main government initiative, which MacArthur approved, was the suppression of Communism in Japan. In June the Communist Party's Central Committee members were forbidden to take any further part in public life. This ban was later extended to thirteen of the Party's thirty-six elected Members of Parliament. Throughout Japan, Communist Party newspapers were suppressed. At the same time Communist civil servants were dismissed and the Communist-dominated Federation of Trade Unions dissolved.

Unimpressed by the flight of the Japanese Communist leadership underground, the Cominform, on Moscow's initiative, expressed severe criticisms of the strategy of the Japanese Communists, who, already demoralized by their own government's actions, were further cast down by Moscow's censure. One Communist leader in South-East Asia who appeared to be able to control an increasingly large area was Ho Chi Minh. On January 14 he asked the world to recognize his Vietminh regime as the legitimate and sole ruler of

Vietnam. Four days later Communist China gave its recognition, followed on January 30 by the Soviet Union. France was contemptuous of Ho Chi Minh's pretensions, however, and confident that despite the setbacks of previous years it could defeat him on the battlefield.

On February 2 the French government concluded an agreement with Vietnam, Cambodia and Laos, whereby they were recognized as 'Associated States within the French Union'. Each would continue to be ruled through its own leaders and with its own parliaments, in the case of Vietnam by the pro-French Bao Dai. On February 7 Britain and the United States recognized this constitutional arrangement. Ho Chi Minh denounced it. The future of Vietnam, and the ability of the rulers whom Europe supported being able to prevail over the local Communist forces — themselves drawing inspiration from Peking and Moscow — was unclear and full of foreboding.

In the Far East, a new war was about to break out, less than five years since the defeat of Japan. At four in the morning of June 25, a North Korean artillery and mortar barrage was the signal for the North Korean armed forces to invade South Korea. The invading forces had at their disposal 150 Soviet-built T-34 tanks. They quickly crossed the border — the 38th Parallel which had been the dividing line between North and South Korea since the defeat of Japan five years earlier. Within six hours the North Koreans had occupied the border town of Kaesong, the medieval Korean capital.

When President Truman was told the news of the North Korean attack he feared — his daughter Margaret later recalled — 'this was the opening of World War III'. On the following morning Truman flew back to Washington from Missouri. He later wrote of his thoughts during that journey. The pre-war fate of Manchuria and Ethiopia were both on his mind. 'I remembered how each time that the democracies failed to act it encouraged the aggressors to keep going ahead,' he later wrote. 'If the Communists were permitted to force their way into the Republic of Korea without opposition from the free world, no small nation would have the courage to resist threats and aggression by stronger Communist neighbours. If this was allowed to go unchallenged, it would mean a Third World War, just as similar incidents had brought on the Second World War.'

Reaching Washington, Truman told one of those who met him at the airport, 'By God, I am going to let them have it.' The United Nations Security Council, meeting that day, passed a resolution by nine votes to nil demanding the withdrawal of North Korean forces. There was no Soviet

veto, as the Soviet delegate, Yakov Malik, had walked out of the Security
Council five months earlier in protest at his colleagues' refusal to give Communist China the Chinese Nationalist' place on the Council.

The North Korean Government ignored the Security Council resolution
and continued to order the southward sweep of its forces. Truman took one
other step that day to shore up the anti-Communist forces in South-East
Asia, announcing that 'the despatch of military aid to the forces of France
and of the Associated States in Indochina will be accelerated, and a military
mission will be sent to Indochina to work closely with those forces'. The
principal 'Associated State' was Vietnam. The American military mission
arrived there within a month.

On June 27, following the United Nations resolution demanding the withdrawal of North Korean forces from South Korea, Truman ordered all American naval and air forces based in Japan, as well as those on Okinawa and in
the Philippines, to be put on the alert for action. That same day, the United
Nations Security Council called on all member States of the United Nations
to 'render such assistance to the Republic of Korea as may be necessary to
repel the armed attack and to restore international peace and security to the
area'. Sixteen member States responded to the call for troops.

By far the largest contingent came from the United States, although the
American army had been drastically reduced in size and armaments in the
previous three years. Britain also made its contribution, starting in the first
days with the dispatch to Korean waters of the eight warships of her small
Far East fleet that were nearest to hand. Australia sent air forces from the
outset. A full-scale armed confrontation of Communist and non-Communist
States seemed imminent.

Canada was among those countries pledged to contribute to the defence
of South Korea, but hoped to restrict its contribution to three destroyers
and an air-transport squadron. The United States subsequently put pressure,
through the United Nations, for Canada to do more. The problem was not
so much one of political will as of the weak state of Canada's armed forces.
Within seven weeks of the outbreak of war, Canada agreed to contribute
troops. Rearmament measures were announced from Ottawa and a Canadian
Army Special Force set up to prepare the Korean expedition.

By the time all the United Nations forces were assembled the numbers
involved were considerable. The United States and the other participating
anti-Communist countries, including South Korea, could put 775,000 men

into the field and had 1,060 aircraft available for combat. The Communist forces in the region, including those in China and the Soviet Far East, were estimated at just over three million, with 4,825 combat aircraft. Whether either the Soviet Union or China would enter the war was, however, unknown. There might be neither time nor cause for either of them to do so. On June 26 a report sent from General MacArthur, who was in Tokyo, to the Joint Chiefs of Staff in Washington, on South Korean resistance, stated: 'Our estimate is that a complete collapse is imminent.'

At a meeting of his senior advisers that night in the White House, Truman said that even if it was decided to commit American ground troops to Korea – and he had not yet done that – no action should be taken north of the 38th Parallel. Emphatically, Truman told those with him, 'I don't want to go to war'. But it was difficult to see how war could be avoided, once Truman authorized, as he did that night, American air and naval support to the South Korean forces. As the meeting ended Truman told his advisers: 'Everything I have done in the past five years has been to try to avoid making a decision such as I had to make tonight.'

On June 27, advance units of North Korean troops and tanks entered the South Korean capital, Seoul. As they did so the North Korean leader, Kim Il Sung, announced that his Communist forces would quickly 'crush' South Korea. The name of Kim Il Sung was unfamiliar to most of those in the West who found themselves following a new conflict with a new cast of characters. Kim was not yet forty. While still a student he had been trained in Communist ideology and techniques in Moscow. During the Japanese occupation of Korea he had built up an effective resistance force, the Korean People's Revolutionary Army. Returning to Russia, he had entered North Korea in August 1945 as a major in the Soviet Army. In July 1946, with Soviet support, he had become Prime Minister of the People's Democratic Republic of Korea, and Supreme Commander of the North Korean armed forces. His rule over North Korea was to span four decades, to cause great suffering, and to outlast even the existence of the Soviet Union from which he had derived his initial support and power.

On June 27 Truman received the support of the leaders of Congress for American military involvement in Korea. In a statement to the newspapers that day he declared: 'The attack upon Korea makes it plain beyond all doubt that Communism has passed beyond the use of subversion to conquer independent nations and will now use armed invasion and war.' By a vote of 315 to four the House of Representatives agreed to extend the draft law by a year. In the United Nations the American decision for military intervention was supported and adopted. The Soviet delegates had continued to absent themselves from the debate.

By June 28 most of the South Korean army had been destroyed. No American ground troops had yet been in combat: indeed, MacArthur had not received permission from the Joint Chiefs of Staff in Washington to send his men into action. Air action was in a different category. On June 30, with Washington's approval, MacArthur authorized the commander of the United States Air Forces in South Korea, General George E. Stratmeyer, to extend his air operations into North Korea 'against air bases, depots, tank farms, troop columns, and other purely military targets such as key bridges or highway and railway critical points'. Stratmeyer was instructed to make sure that he kept all his air operations 'well clear of the frontiers of Manchuria and the Soviet Union'. Neither China nor the Soviet Union were to be tempted or forced to intervene. Truman also made a direct personal request to the National Security Council in Washington that the bombing of North Korea was 'not indiscriminate'. As a result of this Presidential request, MacArthur instructed Stratmeyer to bomb only 'purely military targets' in North Korea.

On June 29 MacArthur drove towards the battlefield to inspect the South Korean troops guarding the Han River. He was shocked by what he found, and, hurrying back to Tokyo by air, asked the Joint Chiefs to allow American ground forces to be sent into action. The South Korean Army, he explained, was down to no more than 25,000 effective fighting men. It had not engaged in serious combat with its northern adversary, and lacked effective leadership. Nor had it made any plans for the defence in depth of South Korea. He thought the chance of it holding the Han River line was 'highly problematical'.

MacArthur recommended a full American military commitment, using two divisions of United States troops then under his command in Japan, and seeking to secure the region between Seoul and the 38th Parallel. 'Unless provision is made for full utilization of the Army-Navy-Air team in this shattered area,' he told the Joint Chiefs, 'our mission will at best be needlessly costly in life, money and prestige. At worst, it might even be doomed to failure.'

The urgency of MacArthur's recommendation was understood in Washington. Even while he was speaking to the Chief of Staff at 3 a.m. Washington time on June 30, a telephone call was put through from the Chief of Staff's office to the Secretary for the Army, Frank Pace, who immediately telephoned

Truman. It was 4.47 a.m.; Truman, who was already up and shaved, took the call at his bedside. MacArthur wanted two divisions of American ground troops to be sent to Korea and to enter combat. Truman's biographer David McCullough comments: 'Truman never hesitated. It was a moment for which he had been preparing himself for days and he made his decision at once.'

At 9.30 that morning Truman formally acceded to MacArthur's request. From that moment the United States was committed to a full-scale land war, under the military commander who had been the single most important victor over Japan. In his diary Truman noted later that day: 'Must be careful not to cause a general Asiatic war.'

The first United States troops to arrive in South Korea, under the flag of the United Nations as well as their own, landed at Pusan, at the south-eastern corner of the peninsula, on July 1. Six days later the Security Council instructed the United States to appoint a Supreme Commander of all the United Nations forces in South Korea. A day later, MacArthur was appointed to the task.

On July 3, in the first of several efforts to make sure that neither the Soviet Union nor the Chinese were provoked into intervention, General Stratmeyer issued specific orders to all United Nations' pilots not to fly over the Chinese or Russian borders.

Pushing south of Seoul, across the Han River, North Korean forces reached and crossed the 37th Parallel. That day the British government appealed to Moscow to use its influence with the Communist government of North Korea to stop the war. The Soviet Union declined to intervene. American troops, flown from Japan four days earlier, were rushed to the front line. The first four hundred were sent to Osan, fifty miles south of Seoul, with instructions to hold the line north of the town. They believed that within a week the very presence of American forces would send the North Koreans hurrying back across the border. The historian Max Hastings has written of the experiences of these four hundred men on the way to the front: 'They had been strafed by presumed North Korean Yaks, which they later discovered were Australian Mustangs. They had watched an ammunition train explode, and a South Korean officer without explanation force one of his own men to his knees and shoot him in the back of the neck.'

On the night of July 4 – American Independence Day – the four hundred Americans dug in, on a rocky hillside, in the rain. They had neither the training, combat experience nor equipment to stand up to the North Korean forces. Within hours of the battle beginning on the following day they were outgunned, outnumbered and outflanked. Their artillery pieces did not have the fire power to halt the North Korean's Soviet-built T-34 tanks which were driving through their position. A precipitate retreat began, bewildering for those who carried it out, amid fear, danger, injury – and the death of their colleagues. One of those in action in that first engagement, Lieutenant Philip Day, later recalled, as the retreat began:

Guys fell around me. Mortar rounds hit here and there. One of my young guys got it in the middle. My platoon sergeant, Harvey Vann, ran over to him. I followed. 'No way he's gonna live, Lieutenant.'

Oh, Jesus, the guy was moaning and groaning. There wasn't much I could do but pat him on the head and say, 'Hang in there.'

Slowly the governments that were committed to sending troops to Korea persuaded their Cabinets and parliaments of the rightness of the cause. 'I think that no one can have any doubt whatever that here is a case of naked aggression,' the British Prime Minister, Clement Attlee, told the House of Commons on July 5. 'Surely, with the history of the last twenty years fresh in our minds, no one can doubt that it is vitally important that aggression should be halted at the outset.'

A larger American force was waiting for the North Koreans on July 6. It too was forced to retreat. That day, in Washington, the American National Security Council was given a briefing on the number of troops capable of being sent into action. The figure showed a strong imbalance: 90,000 North Koreans, 25,000 South Koreans and 10,000 Americans. On July 7 fresh American troops, advancing from their headquarters at Taejon, pushed the Korean line back on the western side of the peninsula, helped by American air strikes. But that same day, on the eastern side, North Korean troops advanced rapidly, their artillery bombarding three British supply bases along the coast, at Chumunjin, Samchok and Posham. Sketch maps published daily in the Western newspapers showed the bold arrows of the 'Red advance' and 'New thrust by Reds'.

More United States troops were flown from Japan into the south-eastern port of Pusan on July 8. Some were thrown into the battle, others placed in a defensive line along the Kum River, north-west of Taejon. The American advance on the western side of the peninsula was short-lived. On July 11 the North Koreans renewed their offensive towards Taejon and drove the Americans back. One battalion managed to fight its way out of a pincer attack. Another was cut off and surrendered. Air attacks by both United States and Australian warplanes were unable to prevent a flank attack on South Korean troops holding the Han River line. Once this was overrun, the American defenders of Taejon were in peril. On the eastern side of the peninsula, despite the naval bombardment by Anglo-American naval patrols on July 11, the attackers came to within sixty miles of Pusan and continued their advance towards it.

On the eastern side of the peninsula the initiative in the war at sea lay with the United Nations forces. On July 12 a British warship was able to silence three of the four guns of a North Korean heavy artillery battery at Inchon. That same day, Wonsan, a strategically important North Korean port, was attacked by almost fifty American heavy bombers. On land, however, a renewed North Korean advance on July 12 saw the breakthrough of 20,000 North Korean soldiers towards Taejon. An American 'line of no retreat' was set up on the Kum River. As the line held against heavy tank and artillery attack, a North Korean communiqué spoke of the 'stiff resistance' that its forces were facing. MacArthur also issued a communiqué. 'By one of the most skillful and heroic actions in American history,' he declared, 'American troops in Korea have provided the time needed to rush up reinforcements.' But after a thirty-six hour tank battle, in which the North Koreans had the numerical superiority, the Americans were forced to pull back.

The North Korean successes had not only been rapid, but also shocking to those for whom possible Communist aggression was the nightmare facing them in many other regions bordering on China and the Soviet Union, and even beyond those borderlands. Tibet was believed to be in danger of a Chinese attack. The Yugoslav Communist leader, Marshal Tito, was thought to be vulnerable to a sudden Soviet offensive. On July 12 – as American troops were battling north of Taejon – the United States sent a warning to the Soviet Union not to attempt to make war on Yugoslavia. Greece was also believed to be in imminent danger of a Soviet-inspired attack from Bulgaria. Five days after the American warning to the Soviet Union about Yugoslavia, the United Nations Balkan Committee asked the Secretary General to warn member States that the Cominform countries 'may be preparing to attack Greece'. False charges emanating from Moscow that Britain and the United States were encouraging Greece to attack Albania and Bulgaria were denounced by the Balkan Committee as a 'screen' to justify an anti-Greek offensive.

At his first press conference since the outbreak of war, President Truman declared that in spite of their early reverses the Americans would not be driven out of South Korea. However much the North Koreans might continue to advance, the American servicemen would be able to retain a foothold. 'And they will be able to carry that foothold as far north as the 38th parallel', he said. 'We have never had the tar licked out of us – and it won't happen this time.' That day the United States Air Force announced a plan to accelerate reinforcements. Ninety-three commercial transport planes were being chartered to operate an airlift to the Far East.

The American armed forces, even as they were being pushed back to Taejon, celebrated their first recommendation of the war for a Silver Star. It went to Sergeant J.R. Glaze, a Texan. As one of his comrades-in-arms told the newspapers:

> We were in a tank when we met a big Russian-built tank carrying an 88-mm. gun. We fired four rounds at it, but nothing happened, so Glaze told me to take over, got out in spite of artillery and machine-gun fire, grabbed a bazooka from a GI and went after that Russian job.
>
> He cut through the woods and came out about twenty yards to one side of it and let fire. From the way he stood there exposed to every North Korean infantryman in the place you would have thought he was on manoevres.
>
> His bazooka caught the tank right on the turret and blew it off. So he went after the second tank, stalking it from behind bushes along the side of the road. Then he ducked out from behind them and fired again and set the second tank on fire.

In reproducing these remarks, a British newspaper, the *Daily Graphic*, commented: 'And this man shows the spirit that will win.' The bravery of individual members of the United Nations force could not, however, at that particular moment, halt the numerically superior North Korean forces, who were themselves buoyed up by the prospect of a rapid and total victory.

The reality on the battlefield was harsh for the American forces, who had even found that the Red Cross symbol used to protect the wounded was serving no purpose. On July 18 a United Nations war correspondent, Robert Miller, reported:

Mercy is just about unknown.

The percentage of casualties among doctors and orderlies is the same as among the troops, and in many cases is higher.

The enemy expects no quarter and gives none.

The Americans entered the war with polished bright crosses on their ambulances and flags flying from their litter jeeps.

Orderlies who attended the wounded wore armbands and carried no weapons.

'What a bunch of innocents we were!' one of them said to me yesterday.

For there is no front-line orderly who has not been under fire at one time or another. Several collecting stations have been overrun and the wounded murdered.

At least two doctors have been killed while tending the wounded at front-line hospitals.

One of the first things the orderlies did was to paint out the red cross insignia.

One told me: 'We tried leaving it on the roof for air identification, but that just drew more fire.

'So we painted those out, too.'

Captain Donald Duerk, a medical officer, said his medical company had been shot to pieces.

'The infiltrating enemy have no respect for the Red Cross and often seem to wait until we get our load of wounded aboard before they attack us,' he said.

'The real heroes of the war are the jeep drivers who drive through enemy road blocks and fighting areas to bring out the wounded.

The North Koreans continued their advance, fighting street by street for Taejon and driving the American and South Koreans out of the city. During the battle, as Taejon burned, the commander of the American 24th Division, General William F. Dean, disappeared. He was last seen, according to one account, facing a North Korean tank with his revolver in hand. He was never seen again.

An American hospital train tried to leave Taejon on July 18. The city was then virtually surrounded. The train was only able to make its way south after an American sergeant, Elmo Smallwood, shot the Korean driver who did not want to continue, and himself took over the controls. That night Truman broadcast a message from MacArthur in which the general declared: 'We are now in Korea in force, and with God's help we are there to stay until the Korean Republic is fully restored.'

Every effort was made to impede the North Korean advance. On the eastern side of the peninsula American troops landed on July 19 at Pohang-Dong, and rushed northward to Yongdok. But having formed a defensive line, they were pushed back. That day MacArthur promised that the United States would make a 'superhuman effort' to pour in to South Korea the men and guns needed to drive the North Korean forces out. The cost of fulfilling that pledge was formidable. On July 19 Truman sent Congress a military budget with an emergency appropriation of $10 billion that raised the total peacetime military expenditure for the fiscal year 1950–51 to more than $48 billion. In the following fiscal year it was to rise even further, to $60 billion.

On the day of his military budget proposals – which Congress approved – Truman also made a television address to the people of the United States. Whereas, in 1938, Neville Chamberlain had spoken of Czechoslovakia as 'a far away country of which we know nothing', Truman said in 1950: 'Korea is a small country thousands of miles away, but what is happening there is important to every American.'*

The United States forces were fighting under the United Nations flag, Truman said, to resist an act of 'raw aggression'. It was this fact that made the war a 'landmark in mankind's long search for a rule of law among nations'. Three days later the United States Defence Department announced that it needed 547,000 men to join up without delay. By normal procedure, the quickest this could be authorized by Congress was three days. The Senate, determined not to cause even a three-day delay, abandoned the accepted procedure and approved the Bill in the space of a few minutes. The House of Representatives did likewise. At the same time, thirty-two warships that had served in the Second World War, including a dozen troopships, were ordered to be taken out of the 'mothball' fleet and brought back into service. A contract for the mass production of new tanks was placed with the Cadillac motor car division of General Motors.

Reflecting on the burdens which the United States had taken on, the American diplomat George Kennan wrote: 'Today we have fallen heir to the problems and responsibilities the Japanese had faced and borne in the

---

* London is 650 miles from Prague. Korea is more than 5,500 miles from the western seaboard of the United States.

Korean-Manchurian area for nearly half a century, and there is a certain perverse justice in the pain we are suffering from a burden which, when it was borne by others, we held in such low esteem.'

In Britain, mobilization orders had begun to go out to several thousand reservists. At the same time, national servicemen were being alerted to an extension of their time under arms. The British Chiefs of Staff favoured a conventional air offensive against North Korea. Echoing the arguments used by Bomber Command in the Second World War, they suggested that heavy bombing might of itself bring North Korea to the negotiating table. 'We shall be no worse off if it did not,' was their argument.

In their survey of the options available, the British Chiefs of Staff ruled out the use of the atom bomb. 'We assume there will be no question of using the atomic bomb in Korea,' they wrote. 'This weapon must in our view be kept in reserve for use in the proper place in the event of a major war with Russia. Anyway there are no suitable objectives for it in North Korea. This is a United Nations police action, and we do not want to kill thousands of civilians and create a radio-active shambles, but with the minimum loss of life and expense on either side, to restore the status quo and the integrity of South Korea.'

Taejon, so recently held by American troops, was bombed by American bombers on July 21 and a North Korean ammunition train destroyed. Railway marshalling yards in Seoul were also hit from the air. But the American bombers were not unchallenged, being attacked by North Korean pilots flying Soviet-made Yak fighters. That day, after a sixteen-hour battle, American troops retook Yechon, a town held by the North Koreans. The victors were men whom the British newspapers described as 'coloured troops' and 'Negro GIs'. 'It was the first sizable US ground victory so far,' reported the *Daily Graphic*.

The news from the war reaching the United States was at times horrific. One report on the front page of the *New York Times* told of the bodies of seven American soldiers, who had been taken prisoner by the North Koreans, found at the roadside. They had been shot through the face. Their hands had been tied behind their backs.

As American troops struggled to hold the line at Yechon, and to regroup south of Taejon, North Korean troops swept southward along the west coast. On the east coast Yongdok was overrun. There were fears that Pusan itself, the south-eastern port and main landing place for United Nations troops and supplies, would fall. Acts of bravery were everywhere recorded, and exhorted. Major-General Hobart Gay, commander of the United States 1st Cavalry Division, promised 'a decoration and champagne' to every American GI who destroyed a North Korean tank. A British pilot, Lieutenant Peter Cane, flying an amphibious aircraft, rescued the first American naval pilot shot down over the sea by North Korean anti-aircraft fire.

Lieutenant Cane and his navigator, Flight Sergeant G.C. Onion, flew their rescue mission from a British cruiser. The pilot they rescued was Lieutenant Wendell R. Muncie, who had spent two and a half hours in the sea.

On July 23 the Parliament of Thailand – which had officially changed the country's name from Siam in 1939 – met in secret session, and agreed to send troops as part of the United Nations contingent in Korea. This commitment was much appreciated by the United Nations, so much so that it appointed Thailand as a member of its recently established Commission for the Unification and Rehabilitation of Korea. The government of India, in a gesture of neutrality verging on support for the Communists, had refused to serve on the Commission.

Thailand was already the recipient of $10 million in United States aid 'to resist Communism', and of United States arms and munitions under a Military Assistance Programme authorized by Congress. In a sustained attempt to prevent the Chinese minority in Thailand from siding with the Communist cause, immigration of Chinese was curtailed and government control over Chinese schools was enforced. The King of Thailand also issued a proclamation giving the government the power to mobilize troops in the event of a Communist uprising. One young Thai officer who was about to leave for Korea was expecting to become a father any day; his regimental commander suggested the child's name, Chalermsuk – 'Celebrated War'. The boy was born two days after his father left for the war. His, he later reflected, was 'a unique name'.

The Thai military contingent for Korea was raised by a call for volunteers. It was intended to raise 4,000 men, but 11,000 men volunteered. Due to the difficulties in providing training and equipment, however, only 1,200 men were sent to Korea. With the war intensifying in Korea, there were fears among many Thais of an attempt by local Chinese to seize power in Bangkok. Arms being smuggled into Thailand from China were seized, and the number of trades in which Chinese could participate was curtailed.

On July 25 the American defensive perimeter at Yongdok was overrun. The North Koreans had pushed the South Korean and American troops back to the south coast and south-east corner of the Pusan perimeter. Only a quarter of South Korea remained under the control of the United Nations forces. That day Bolivia offered to send thirty officers and several hundred men to join the United Nations line.

A 'last ditch' defence triangle was established on July 26, running from Pohang on the Sea of Japan, through the railway junction of Taegu and then south to Masan. But the American troops had no intention of withdrawing so far back, and made strenuous military efforts to push back the North Koreans. That morning American troops east of Yongdok launched a counter-attack in which cooks, clerks and drivers fought alongside the regular infantrymen. After visiting the front line, General MacArthur declared: 'There are heartaches and setbacks ahead. But I was never more confident of victory.' That night American troops on the south coast pulled back twenty-five miles towards the 'last ditch' perimeter at Masan. The North Korean artillery barrages were both intense and accurate, causing one American lieutenant-colonel to describe them as 'sheer butchery' to his troops. 'It is now our job,' another American officer commented on July 28, 'to see that the situation does not become disastrous.'

Following the Thai and Bolivian decisions to send combat troops to Korea, the British Government − which already had naval and air forces fighting in Korea − decided at the end of July to send combat troops as well. The need was urgent if the United Nations cause was not to be lost altogether. On July 29 the United States Eighth Army commander, General Walton H. Walker, issued an order that Pusan must not fall. 'There are no lines behind which we can retreat,' he said. 'This is not going to be a Dunkirk or Bataan. A retreat to Pusan would result in one of the greatest butcheries in history. We must fight to the end. We must fight as a team. If some of us die, we will die fighting together.'

Pusan did not fall. The establishment of a 130-mile defensive perimeter around the port enabled the North Korean forces to be kept at bay, albeit with heavy casualties. United Nations air forces were able to strike with considerable effect at the long North Korean supply lines. Pusan itself became the port of disembarkation of a growing influx of American arms and armour. The battle of the Pusan perimeter began on July 31. Only by holding the perimeter could the United Nations effort in Korea be sustained. The alternative was the evacuation of Korea, or surrender and massacre if evacuation proved impossible. Watching the conflict intensify, the Indian Prime Minister, Jawaharlal Nehru, told the parliament in New Delhi on August 3: 'As we face the world situation today it looks as though the fate of the world seems to hang, in regard to peace and war, by a thread which might be cut down by a sword or blown off by a gun.'

On August 5 the North Korean troops broke across the Naktong River. But they failed to push further forward, and were themselves driven back across the river twelve days later. Despite renewed North Korean assaults, the Pusan perimeter held, and was being reinforced daily. But the ugliness and demoralization of war was everywhere apparent. 'Everything seemed in turmoil,' one American marine recalled of his brigade's arrival. 'There were too many people with a wild stare in their eyes.' The knowledge that some units had abandoned their dead, and even their wounded, on the battlefield was further cause for unease. 'We realized something was radically wrong the moment we arrived,' another American recalled. 'We could see our advance party sitting on the quay, silent and unmoving. Our unit really was unfit to go at all. We had been told we would have three or four months in the country to train before we were committed to combat. Instead, on the quayside, we were just told to uncrate the weapons and get ready to go into line.'

Containing almost 100,000 armed men, the Pusan perimeter continued to hold, but there was no certainty that it could hold for much longer. The need to take more active measures was obvious to all the supporters of the United Nations' effort. In London the House of Commons held an emergency session on September 9, when measures were passed for more active British participation in the war. Two days later Truman appointed the Second World War Chief of Staff, and post-war sustainer of Western Europe, General Marshall, as Secretary of Defence.

On September 12 the first British troops took up their position in the front line in the Pusan perimeter, west of Taegu. Further American reinforcements also arrived. Despite renewed North Korean attacks at almost every point, the perimeter was maintained. In the rest of South Korea, an estimated 26,000 South Korean civilians were executed by the North Korean army and police within their zone of conquest. On public buildings and in city streets the portrait of Stalin hung next to that of Kim Il Sung.

The South Korean Government, trapped in the perimeter, and cut off from its main sources of manpower, conscripted teenagers and old men. After being shown how to use a weapon these conscripts were sent to the front line. Once in the line – a British war correspondent, James Cameron, recalled – they were 'at most times heavily outnumbered, and their casualties were enormous. The intake was vast, the training almost unbelievably cursory. The man was drafted at the age of eighteen. On the Sunday he might be at work in the paddies or the shop; by the following Sunday he was in the line; in next to no time he was either a veteran or a corpse'.

Morale inside the Pusan perimeter was at a low ebb. Many of the defending troops were ill-trained and poorly equipped, fearful of the apparent endless waves of North Koreans attacking them, unused to the terrain, uncertain as to the cause for which they were being asked to fight and die. MacArthur was determined to change this, and to do so by a dramatic military initiative. Even as the battle for the Pusan perimeter offered the daily spectre of defeat for the United States forces, he was putting forward a proposal to his military, naval and air commanders for a surprise amphibious landing. It would take place at Inchon, a city on the west coast, only twenty-five miles from Seoul, and two hundred miles from Pusan.

The plan for the Inchon landing was MacArthur's brainchild. The capture of Inchon, so far up the west coast of the peninsula, would immediately disorient the North Korean hold on South Korea. There had been a successful military landing at Inchon once before: in 1904, by the Japanese. The new landing was to be an amphibious one on a massive scale, involving 262 ships and 70,000 American troops – half as many as were struggling in the Pusan perimeter. No other United Nations participant in the war was capable of such a commitment, or of such a daring, risky enterprise. But when MacArthur set out the plan in detail on August 23 at his Tokyo headquarters, to a galaxy of military chiefs and commanders, there was consternation. The Army Chief of Staff, General Lawton J. Collins, spoke of the fears of the army about the effect of withdrawing the United States Marine brigade from Pusan, MacArthur's essential prerequisite for the Inchon landing.

During the meeting of August 23, Admiral Forrest Sherman urged a 'safer' landing much further south, at the port of Kunsan. Admiral James H. Doyle told the meeting: 'All I can say is that Inchon is not possible.' MacArthur – seventy years old, a master of emotional presentation – then answered the critics and doubters. One of those who was present later recalled:

He spoke with that slow, deep resonance of an accomplished actor. 'Admiral, in all my years of military service, that is the finest briefing I have ever received. Commander, you have taught me all I had ever dreamed of knowing about tides. Do you know, in World War I they got our divisions in Europe through submarine-infested seas? I have a deep admiration for the navy. From the humiliation of Bataan, the navy brought us back.'

Then – literally with a tear in his eye – he said: 'I never thought the day would come, that the navy would be unable to support the army in its operations.'

It was a great theatrical performance. MacArthur's peroration embraced the communist threat to Korea: '. . . It is plainly apparent that here in Asia is where the Communist conspirators have elected to make their play for global conquest. The test is not in Berlin or Vienna, in London, Paris or Washington. It is here and now – it is along the Naktong River in South Korea . . .'

He summoned up the ghost of his hero, General Wolfe, whose assault upon the heights of Quebec had also been opposed by his staff. He asserted the very implausibility of his own plan as its strongest argument for surprise, and thus success: 'The very arguments you have made as to the impracticabilities involved will tend to ensure for me the element of surprise. For the enemy commander will reason that no one would be so brash as to make such an attempt.'

Then, finally: 'I can almost hear the ticking of the second hand of destiny. We must act now or we will die . . . We shall land at Inchon, and I shall crush them.'

The deep voice fell away to a whisper. After forty-five minutes of oratory such as the world seldom sees save from the stalls of a theatre, the Supreme Commander returned to his chair. The Chief of Naval Operations stood up and declared emotionally: 'General, the navy will get you to Inchon'.

On August 28 the Joint Chiefs of Staff gave its approval to the Inchon landing. To make the authorization for the enterprise undisputed, Truman was asked to give his support in writing, and did so.

MacArthur was concerned, as the final stages of preparation went ahead, that a landing at Inchon might bring in Chinese – and even Soviet troops – in order to prevent the North Koreans from being pushed back across the 38th Parallel. He believed, however, that he could secure the city and make rapid progress before the Soviet or Chinese leaders realized what had happened. He was right. When the landings took place on September 15 the North Koreans were quite unprepared for an attack so far behind the front line. The scale of the attack was formidable: almost two hundred

American ships took part, as well as twelve British, three Canadian, two Australian, two New Zealand, one French, one Dutch and fifteen South Korean warships.

The initial naval bombardment was massive. One American ship fired 165 rounds at a single North Korean gun emplacement – 'the economics of plenty' was the British journalist, James Cameron's, wry comment as he witnessed the scene. Inchon, a city of a quarter of a million people, fell after a day of fighting. Cameron witnessed during the immediate aftermath 'the consolidation, the flattening of ruins, concealment of corpses, tending of wounds, the sifting of friends from enemies, the quick from the dead, the simple from the suspects'. His account continued:

There was quite a lot of Inchon still standing; one wondered how. There were quite a number of citizens still alive. They came stumbling from the ruins – some of them sound, some of them smashed, numbers of them quite clearly driven into a sort of numbed dementia by the night of destruction. They ran about, capering crazily or shambling blankly, with a repeated automatic gesture of surrender. Some of them called out as we passed them their one English phrase, as a kind of password: 'Sank you!' 'Sank you!'; and the irony of that transcended the grotesque into the macabre.

The pacification and securing of the town was the task of the South Korean militia; this they undertook with violent and furious zeal.

There was yet more to see of the aftermath of battle:

Here and there prisoners waited crouched on the ground with their hands round their necks; they were naked. The dead were arranged by the road-side, the wounded lay in groups beside them, and American medical corpsmen were moving methodically among them. One of them moaned quietly, like a dog; he was a collander of bullet holes; once again a Korean mutilated to a degree that would have meant death to a European – yet continued to live. The doctor came over to give him morphia; he crushed the needle of the omnopon capsule three or four times against the Korean's arm without making a puncture.

'It sure is the damnedest thing,' he said. 'The Gook has genuinely got a thicker skin than any other guy, in a strictly physical sense.'

The soldier suddenly sat up briskly and began to explain something rapidly to the doctor. He spoke urgently, shaking his head. 'Let's have the interpreter,' said the doctor, but the Korean attempted one gesture too many with his shattered arm, and died in mid-sentence.

I got a lift back to Red Beach in an Amptrack; it was like riding in some gigantic clockwork toy.

Advancing from Inchon, American troops reached the Han River opposite Seoul within eleven days of the landing. The success at Inchon was followed by the second part of MacArthur's plan, the breakout from the Pusan perimeter. The breakout was not without its particular tragedies as well as triumphs for the Americans and the other United Nations forces. On September 23 a British force which had just taken a strategic hill across the Naktong River was attacked in error by American aircraft with cannon fire and napalm, and driven off the hill. When the British force retook the hill, seventeen men were killed in the assault, including its commander, Major Kenneth Muir, who was awarded a posthumous Victoria Cross.

On September 25 the Americans reached the outskirts of Seoul, and were engaged in street-by-street fighting. 'The battle for Seoul became a source of lasting controversy, and deep revulsion to some of those who witnessed it,' the historian Max Hastings has written. 'It provided an example of a form of carnage that would become wretchedly familiar in Indochina a generation later – allegedly essential destruction in the cause of liberation. It was passionately argued by some correspondents and not a few soldiers that the civilian casualties and wholesale destruction could have been avoided by an effective enveloping movement, rather than a direct assault supported by overwhelming air and artillery support.'

MacArthur had set September 25 for the capture of Seoul – it being three months to the day since the North Korean invasion – and he did not want the delay that a pincer movement would entail. The battle therefore continued in the streets of the city, as 20,000 North Korean troops tried to delay its capture for as long as possible. The battle lasted for three days. When it ended, MacArthur flew to Seoul from Tokyo to take the salute and plaudits. Syngman Rhee told MacArthur: 'We love you as the saviour of our race.' Briefly the Stars and Stripes was raised on the Capitol building in Seoul, but it was soon lowered, and replaced by the United Nations flag.

Following the American entry into Seoul, the breakout from the Pusan perimeter was intensified. As it proceeded, more than half of the North Korean army was trapped in a massive pincer movement. Its surrender was announced on September 27. That same day Truman decided to allow MacArthur to advance beyond the 38th Parallel, but he insisted that the general first assure himself that there was no sign of a substantial Chinese or Soviet military intervention. Truman added that MacArthur must not carry the war into China or the Soviet Union.

From Seoul, the American troops swept northward. Driving the North Korean forces before them, on October 1 they reached the 38th parallel. South Korea was again under its own sovereignty. 'Well and nobly done,' Truman telegraphed to MacArthur – who was back in Tokyo. It was Mac-Arthur's finest hour since he had taken the surrender of Japan in Tokyo Bay five years earlier. That same day, October 1, impatient to exploit his success, MacArthur ordered the South Korean and American troops to cross the 38th Parallel and move into North Korea. His own instructions from Washington were: 'The destruction of the North Korean armed forces'.

During the swift advance to the 38th Parallel, every effort had been made to avoid provoking the Chinese. After an American bomber crew made a navigational error on the night of September 22/23 and bombed a Chinese airstrip across the North Korean border, strict briefings were given to every bomber crew to stay clear of the border altogether. With the land forces poised to advance north of the 38th Parallel, the danger of an inadvertent air strike north of the Yalu River intensified. On October 8 two American pilots – 'whose zeal' in the words of the official history, 'surpassed their navigational prowess' – flew over and repeatedly strafed a Soviet airfield north of the Manchurian-Chinese border. An apology was issued to the Soviets, and the two pilots were court-martialled, although the court-martial refused to convict them.

The North Koreans were moving hundreds of Americans – prisoners-of-war and civilian internees – northward, away from the battle zone and towards the Yalu River border. As on Bataan in 1942 and in Germany in 1945, death marches were under way with all their cruelties and torments. Larry Zellers, a Methodist missionary who had been teaching at Kaesong when he was captured, was on a march that covered more than a hundred miles of rough terrain in winter weather. As many as a hundred American prisoners-of-war and civilian captives were shot on that march because they were too weak to continue, or as a punishment for an alleged infringement. Among the episodes Zellers later recalled was the first in which the North Korean commander of the march – the Tiger – displayed his authority:

We had travelled for only a short distance when several American military prisoners fell out of march and were left by the side of the road. The Tiger was so angry that he called the march to a halt. He ordered the ranking officer, Maj. John J. Dunn, and all officers who were group leaders and had permitted men to drop out to report to him. When five officers stepped forward, The Tiger lined them up by the side of the road.

'I will shoot these five men for disobeying my orders,' he announced.

'Commissioner, try to save us', the men pleaded.

When Commissioner Lord tried to reason with The Tiger, he was ordered not to speak: 'Shut up, or I will shoot you too. You are only the translator.'

Herbert Lord was a British Salvation Army missionary: Commissioner was his Salvation Army rank. He tried to explain that the guards had given permission to leave the men by the road:

'Where are those guards? Show them to me!' ordered The Tiger. It was obviously an impossible demand under the circumstances.

'Honorable Leader,' Commissioner Lord continued, 'it is unjust to punish these men for doing what they thought was permitted.'

'Then I will shoot the man whose group lost the most men. Who is that leader?'

Lt. Cordus H. Thornton of Longview, Texas, stepped forward. He stood tall and erect, as he did throughout his entire ordeal. 'Save me if you can, sir,' he whispered to Commissioner Lord. At that point The Tiger was in no mood to listen to anyone; he ordered Lord not to speak under the threat of being shot.

'Death is the penalty for disobedience in wartime,' he informed Lieutenant Thornton. 'Isn't that true in the American army as well?'

'In the American army, sir, I would have a trial.'

The Tiger turned around and for the first time surveyed the curious onlookers who had gathered on the public road. In that group were a number of North Korean soldiers who were moving in our same direction, away from the front lines. They were a seedy-looking lot. Having been beaten in the war at this point, they were probably in retreat to some staging area where they would be regrouped. Their uniforms were tattered. Most had no hats. Only one or two carried weapons, and all appeared haggard and exhausted.

These men would be Lieutenant Thornton's jury. 'What is to be done to a man who disobeys the lawful order of an officer in the Korean People's Army?' asked The Tiger.

'Shoot him!' they all shouted.

'There, you have had your trial,' The Tiger announced.

'In Texas, sir, we would call that a lynching,' Lieutenant Thornton responded.

'What did he say?' The Tiger demanded. Commissioner Lord had not translated the last remark. On hearing the translation, The Tiger made no comment but proceeded swiftly about his business of preparing for an execution. He asked Thornton if he wished to be blindfolded. Hearing an affirmative answer, The Tiger handed a small towel to a guard. Another towel was used to tie the victim's hands behind his back. The Tiger's moves were fast and efficient. He threw off the large padded coat he was wearing, revealing his rank . . .

'You see,' The Tiger said, pointing to the epaulettes on his shoulder, 'I have the authority to do this.' He moved smartly to face the victim and ordered him to turn around. Pausing for a moment, The Tiger pushed up the back of Thornton's fur hat . . .

I had seen too much already; my eyes snapped shut just before The Tiger fired his pistol into the back of Thornton's head.

In Britain, the ruling Labour Party was confronted with considerable grass roots opposition to British participation in the war in Korea. Traditional anti-Americanism had been refuelled by resentment at Britain's dependence on Marshall Aid, and by reluctance to be seen to be a partner in an 'American' war. The Labour Government was determined, however, to support the United States and United Nations effort in Korea, and had already committed troops, ships and planes to the conflict. On October 2 the Foreign Secretary Ernest Bevin, speaking at the Labour Party Conference, chastized those fellow-Socialists who argued that Britain did not have to become involved. 'Do you think we like it?' he asked. 'Do you think, after all the years of fighting we have done in the labour movement in the hope of getting a peaceful world, that we like having to do it? Is there any Minister who likes to go down to the House of Commons to ask for £3,600 million for war?'

Bevin then linked the United Nations efforts in Korea with the failed efforts at united action on the eve of the Second World War:

Is there any delegate in this conference who would go back to his constituents and say we are doing wrong in paying the proper insurance premium
now for our security? We blamed the Conservatives for knowing Hitler
was on the move and not making adequate preparations . . . because they
would not go in for collective security . . .

We are in office now, and shall we refuse to do what we called upon
others to do which would have prevented the 1939 war if they had only
done it.

On October 6 the United Nations approved the advance north of the 38th
Parallel. The aim of the continuing military operation, it declared, was 'to
ensure the conditions of stability throughout Korea'. A series of earlier
messages from the Chinese Foreign Minister, Chou En-lai – the most direct
sent four days earlier through the Indian Ambassador in Peking, K.M.
Pannikar – stated that if the United Nations forces crossed the 38th Parallel
the Chinese would send troops into North Korea. These messages were
regarded by the American policymakers as a bluff. On October 9 the Americans crossed the 38th Parallel into North Korea. For a week they were
confronted by a tenacious North Korean military resistance, but when this
broke they advanced rapidly northward in swift pursuit.

On October 15 President Truman flew more than 14,000 miles to meet
General MacArthur on Wake Island. To reach Wake, MacArthur flew two
thousand miles from his Tokyo headquarters. The two men had never met
before. During an encounter which lasted less than three hours Truman
stressed that the war must remain 'limited'. MacArthur expressed his confidence that all 'formal resistance' by the North Koreans throughout North
Korea would end 'by Thanksgiving' – in five weeks' time. He also told
Truman that the Chinese were not likely to intervene. 'They have no Air
Force,' MacArthur said, and he added: 'Now that we have bases for our Air
Force in Korea, if the Chinese tried to get down to Pyongyang there would
be the greatest slaughter.' MacArthur added that if the Soviets intervened
to help the Chinese with air support, their competence was so limited 'that
I believe the Russian air force would bomb the Chinese as often as they
would bomb us'.

On October 19, four days after the Truman-MacArthur meeting, American
and South Korean forces captured Pyongyang, the capital of North Korea.
On the following day, MacArthur gave orders for the 'maximum effort' to

advance to the border of North Korea, along the Yalu River. A day later he told his commanders that they were 'authorized to use any and all ground forces as necessary, to secure all of North Korea'. The British government was uneasy at any military advance up to the Chinese border, and proposed instead the creation of a buffer zone south of the Yalu. On hearing this, MacArthur was scathing. 'The widely reported British desire to appease the Chinese communists by giving them a strip of North Korea finds its historic precedent in the action taken at Munich on 29 September 1938,' he reported to Washington. 'To give up any portion of North Korea to the aggression of the Chinese communists would be the greatest defeat of the free world in recent times. Indeed, to yield to so immoral a proposition would bankrupt our leadership and influence in Asia, and render untenable our position both politically and morally.'

The spectre of 'Munich' was to be used many times by men and governments unwilling to compromise. Even when, as in the Korean case, the enemy had in fact been driven out of the territory he had invaded, making the comparison with the transfer of the Sudetenland to Hitler an inexact one, the very word 'Munich' was meant to send a shudder of shame through the recipients.

It was not Chinese intervention to help the North Koreans that followed the American advance towards the Yalu, but Chinese military action elsewhere. On October 22, Chinese forces entered Tibet. Communist China had acquired a new border with independent India.

Three days after the Chinese advance into Tibet, the first South Korean troops reached the Yalu River. A bottle was filled with its water and sent to Syngman Rhee. But Chinese troops had begun to enter North Korea and join in the battle. Large numbers had crossed the border and reached the hydroelectric installations around the Chosin reservoir. A British officer, Lieutenant Colin Mitchell, was one of the first of the United Nations troops to encounter the new combatants:

> They were unlike any enemy I had seen before. They wore thick padded clothing, which made them look like little Michelin men. I turned one body over with my foot, and saw that he wore a peaked cap with a red star badge. These soldiers were Chinese.
>
> I then turned over another and, as I looked down at him, he opened

one eye and looked up at me. I shot him with my Luger, shouting to the platoon, "they're alive!"

It was quickly over, and all the enemy lay dead.

The world focus on the Korean war, with its new Chinese dimension, and on the Chinese invasion of Tibet – which provided newspapers with yet another area to portray in sketch maps marked with graphic arrows – was briefly but dramatically overshadowed on November 1 when two armed Puerto Ricans tried to kill President Truman in Washington. One of the men was shot dead and the other seriously wounded by the police and presidential guards before they could reach the President, who was then living at Blair House, and had been having a short afternoon nap. A presidential guard, Private Leslie Coffelt, was killed in the shoot-out. There is a plaque to Coffelt's memory – dedicated by Truman himself – on the Blair House railings near the spot where Coffelt died.

The two Puerto Ricans were protesting against continuing United States rule over Puerto Rico, which had been ceded to the United States by Spain in 1898. The would-be assassin who survived the shoot-out, Oscar Collazo, told his questioners that Truman had been chosen as their target because he represented the 'system'. As Collazo expressed it: 'You don't attack the man, you attack the system.' Yet Truman believed that the people of Puerto Rico should have the right to determine their political relationship with the United States. He had extended the American social security system to the island, and had appointed the first native Puerto Rican as governor.

Collazo was sentenced to death. Truman commuted the sentence to life imprisonment. After twenty-nine years in prison, Collazo was pardoned by President Jimmy Carter.

On November 7, Tibet appealed to the United Nations against the Chinese aggression. But the United Nations was too deeply involved in Korea to have the energy for a new area of conflict, despite considerable anguish among many members that Tibet was falling under Chinese and Communist control. The Tibetan army, which was no match for its adversaries, accepted defeat. It could not expect succour from the outside world.

As United Nations forces moved deeper and deeper into North Korea, and more than 60,000 North Korean troops were being held by the United Nations as prisoners-of-war, there were signs of increasing Chinese military involvement in the fighting. On November 1 a number of American units found themselves under sustained attack by Chinese troops and fled southward. The Chinese assault was accompanied by the blowing of bugles. One of the Americans caught by this unexpected Chinese intervention, Private Carl Simon, later told Max Hastings: 'There was just mass hysteria on the position. It was every man for himself. The shooting was terrific, there were Chinese shooting everywhere, I didn't know which way to go. In the end, I just ran with the crowd. We just ran and ran until the bugles grew fainter.'

On November 15 MacArthur reported to Washington that Chinese troops already inside North Korea were 'massing' in substantial numbers. There were at least 30,000 of them already in Korea, and 700,000 more on the Manchurian side of the border. In Washington the Joint Chiefs suggested to MacArthur that he might consider not trying to advance as far as the border, but halt his troops somewhere short of it to avoid the risk of clashes with Chinese forces. MacArthur replied that it would be 'utterly impossible' to halt his troops except along the border itself. If peace and unity were to be restored in Korea, he insisted, it would be necessary to destroy all 'enemy forces' within the borders.

On November 24, under MacArthur's confident command, the United Nations forces launched an offensive into north-east Korea. It was the day before Thanksgiving, the day by which MacArthur had earlier forecast that North Korean resistance would have come to an end. 'If this operation is successful, I hope we can get the boys home by Christmas,' was his new forecast to newspaper reporters. Two days later Chinese troops entered the war in even greater force. It had been thought at first in Washington that the Chinese aim was to establish a buffer zone along the southern side of the border. Hence the Joint Chiefs earlier suggestion that MacArthur should leave an area free between his troops and the border. But this was a misapprehension. The Chinese intention was not a mere buffer zone. They had entered the combat with a view to securing a victory, and fought accordingly.

One feature of the Chinese attack of November 26 that astounded the Americans and other United Nations forces was the appearance of jet fighters. These were Soviet-built MiG-15s. In the November battles fifty MiGs fought, flown by both Chinese and Soviet pilots. They flew from air bases on Chinese soil north of the Yalu that were immune from United Nations attack. Within twenty-four hours of the Chinese attack, the United Nations forces – which included American, British, Turkish and South Korean units – beat a swift retreat southward. Near Kunu-ri an American column retreated through six miles of Chinese fire, at heavy cost.

As the retreat from Kunu-ri continued, and panic and fear began to overtake all organization and discipline, the order went out: 'Every man for himself.' Lieutenant Colin Mitchell, the British officer who had been among the first to encounter Chinese troops, later recalled an episode during the retreat, when as he put it, 'it was pointless to stand and fight':

> I remember one of my company headquarters, a quiet, reliable chap, who was sitting on the ground near me, about to open a tin of baked beans. He suddenly stood up and screamed. He ran wild-eyed into the middle of a paddy-field ignoring the sergeant-major's shouted orders to come back.
>
> I walked after him and he stood there waiting for me, holding the tin of beans like a grenade, shouting, 'don't come any nearer!' I did, and he flung the tin at me, but missed. When I came up to him, I just told him that I knew exactly how he felt, because I felt like that too, but we were all in this together and just had to stick it out or go under.
>
> At this he broke down and sobbed, then walked back with me to our position and resumed his place with the battalion.

By the last week of November more than 200,000 Chinese soldiers had crossed the Yalu River. On November 27 American forces holding part of the defensive perimeter around the Chosin reservoir were attacked by a far larger force of Chinese. That day the American commander, General Edward M. Almond – who had earlier commanded the Inchon landing – flew by helicopter to the Chosin reservoir airstrip at the town of Hagaru. His words to the men at Hagaru were pugnaciously confident: 'We're still attacking and we're going all the way to the Yalu. Don't let a bunch of Chinese laundrymen stop you.'

At first the Americans around the Chosin reservoir held the line, but the Chinese kept attacking, undeterred by the heavy casualties inflicted on them, and fighting almost entirely at night. After three successive nights of unequal combat, the Americans began to move southward, fighting rearguard actions as they sought to extricate themselves. 'The Chinese have come in with both feet,' MacArthur reported to Washington on November 28. That was the day, Truman later wrote, 'when the bad news from Korea had changed from rumours of resistance to certainty of defeat'. United States forces were in retreat.

MacArthur pressed Washington to authorize further withdrawals. The United Nations Command, he warned, was 'facing the entire Chinese nation in an undeclared war'. His own troops were 'mentally fatigued and physically

battered'. After consultations with Truman, the Joint Chiefs informed Mac-
Arthur: 'We consider that the preservation of your forces is now the primary
consideration.'

General Marshall was particularly emphatic, at a meeting of the National
Security Council in Washington on November 28, that for the United States
to get into a war with China 'would be to fall into a carefully laid Russian
trap. We should use all available political, economic and psychological action
to limit the war'. Dean Acheson, the Secretary of State, described as the
'imperative step' for MacArthur's forces that they 'find a line that we can
hold, and hold it'.

At a press conference on November 30, Truman said that the United
States 'will take whatever steps are necessary to meet the military situation,
just as we always have.' He was asked if that included the atom bomb. 'That
includes every weapon we have', he replied. Hitherto the use of the atom
bomb had not been a subject for public discussion. Caught unawares by the
line of questioning, and unable to break off the discussion, Truman was
drawn deeper into speaking about the unspeakable. 'There has always been
active consideration about its use,' he said. He then shook his head and told
the assembled journalists: 'It is a terrible weapon and it should not be used
on innocent men, women, and children who have nothing whatever to do
with this military aggression. That happens when it is used.'

Truman was then asked by Merriman Smith, the White House correspondent for the United Press – who imagined that the President would use the
question to answer in the negative – if the use of the atom bomb in the
Korean conflict was 'under active consideration'. Truman replied: 'Always
has been. It is one of our weapons.' The outcry was immediate. That evening
in the British House of Commons a leading member of the Conservative
opposition, R.A. Butler, spoke of 'the horror that many of us would feel at
the use of this weapon in circumstances which were not such that our own
moral conscience was satisfied that there was no alternative'. Churchill, who
within a year was to be Prime Minister again, warned that the United
Nations 'should avoid by every means in their power becoming entangled
inextricably in a war with China'. It was in Europe, Churchill stressed, 'that
the world cause will be decided. It is there that the mortal danger lies'.

Hoping to restrain the United States in a policy that had not in fact been
adopted, Clement Attlee flew to Washington. There he told Truman that
Britain was concerned at the dangers of a direct attack on China. It might
bring in the Soviet Union under the Sino-Soviet Friendship Treaty, which

had been negotiated between Stalin and Mao Tse-tung at the end of 1949. Should that happen, remarked one of Attlee's delegation – the Chief of the Imperial General Staff, Field Marshal Slim, victor of the 1944–45 Burmese campaign – 'we should have to say good-bye'.

In order to hold the line west and south of the Chosin reservoir as long as possible, while ten thousand American troops pulled back, a British Royal Marine unit was sent towards Hagaru, which was still under American control. On reaching Hagaru they fought alongside the Americans to hold it for as long as possible. The American Marines proved tenacious defenders, despite the rigours of winter and the lack of much-needed supplies and transport. When a group of war correspondents was flown into Hagaru on December 4, the American Marine commander, General Oliver P. Smith, told them: 'Gentlemen, we are not retreating. We are merely advancing in another direction.'

Following the entrance of Chinese troops into the Korean War, there was deep anxiety inside the United States. 'I've worked for peace for five years and six months, and it looks like World War III is here,' Truman wrote in his diary on December 4. 'I hope not – but we must meet whatever comes, and we will.' On the following day the North Korean capital, Pyongyang, was abandoned by those who had entered it in triumph only forty-seven days earlier. 'The Korean situation is tragic,' General Eisenhower – who in 1944 had commanded the armies that drove the Germans from Normandy to the Elbe – wrote in his diary that day, 'although I still believe that MacA can stabilize the situation if he comes back far enough to stretch the hostile lines and expose their communications to incessant air attack.'

The retreat from Hagaru began on December 6. As they pulled back, the American and British troops were ambushed by the Chinese in what was quickly named 'Hellfire Valley'. The retreating force took with it 160 Chinese soldiers who had been captured further north. As the ambush began, these captives made a run towards the Chinese lines. The American soldiers opened fire on them, and all but thirteen were shot down.

On December 7, the second day of the retreat from Hagaru, the United Nations in New York condemned the Chinese action in crossing into North Korea. The United Nations Commission for the Unification and Rehabilitation of Korea (UNCURK) reported: 'On the basis of existing evidence the commission has come to the conclusion that Chinese forces in great strength are attacking the United Nations forces in North Korea and that these

Chinese forces form part of the armed forces of the People's Republic of China.' This was indeed the case. When General Collins flew from Washington to Tokyo to confer with MacArthur, at Truman's request, the question he wanted answered was whether there was any way in which the mass of Chinese troops could be prevented from taking over the whole of North Korea.

MacArthur saw only one way of at least weakening the tide of Chinese troops pushing southward. That was the bombing of Chinese troop concentrations while they were still on the Chinese side of the border. He was later to write: 'If I had been permitted to bomb them before they crossed the Yalu, they would never have crossed.' Strategically such bombing made sense, whatever its adverse political repercussions might be within the United States. MacArthur had the means to bomb the Chinese supply lines leading through Manchuria to the border, and to bomb the Chinese bases inside China that were providing the essential war supplies for the invading troops. Unless he could do so, he told General Collins, his forces would sooner or later be forced to withdraw from the Korean peninsula altogether.

General Emmett O'Donnel, commander of the American Far East Air Forces, supported MacArthur. Later he was to tell a Congressional Inquiry: 'I was all for the bombing of Manchuria and I wanted very badly to do it as soon as we recognized the Chinese Communist forces . . . as bona fide forces.' Had the bombing been authorized then – in the last week of November, or at the time of General Collins' visit to Tokyo – 'I think we could have gotten in and for very small cost in casualties we could have really hit them hard and perhaps even stopped them.'

The numbers of Chinese troops inside North Korea by the beginning of the second week of December was not known for certain by the United Nations, but was estimated at between 400,000 and 450,000 men. Further United Nations withdrawals were therefore imperative, and MacArthur ordered them. On December 10 the troops who had been fighting their way south from the Chosin reservoir reached the port of Hamhung. Hundreds had been killed during the retreat, thousands were wounded or suffering from frostbite. Elsewhere on the peninsula, retreat and defeat had become synonymous terms; in ten days some American units retreated 120 miles. On December 15 the American forces, pushing ever southward, retreating even more swiftly than they had marched northward in triumph, crossed back over the 38th Parallel.

On December 16 a State of Emergency was proclaimed throughout the continental United States. There would be federal controls on prices and wages, and an addition of $50 million to the already increased defence spending. A new Office of Defence Mobilization was set up. The United States was preparing for a long and arduous war. General Marshall later recalled: 'We were at our lowest ebb.'

There were those among the American commanders who wanted to hold a perimeter around Hamhung, as had earlier been done around Pusan. But MacArthur ordered the port's evacuation. In all, in the course of ten days, 100,000 fighting men were taken off by sea. It was like Dunkirk and Bataan over again – the historic precedents MacArthur had sworn not to see repeated. On December 24, as the last ship left, American naval guns opened fire on the port, destroying such storehouses and dock installations which not been blown up during the evacuation.

Throughout China a campaign had been launched 'To Resist America and Aid Korea'. Almost every factory in north-east China had drawn up 'anti-American aggression emulation targets'. On December 27, three days after the Americans had evacuated Hamhung, the Chinese Government refused a United Nations offer of a cease fire. A day later, Chinese troops, advancing southward in force, crossed the 38th Parallel into South Korea. The American and South Korean forces had retreated three hundred miles in thirty days, fighting every mile of the way in temperatures far below zero. American bomber pilots struck at American supply depots that had been abandoned in the retreat, determined to deny the Chinese use of them. At MacArthur's specific request, Korean villages suspected of sheltering Chinese troops were a particular target. In the last two weeks of December an estimated 6,694 Chinese troops were killed in aerial attacks.

Frustrated at the continual withdrawal of his troops, MacArthur pressed his superiors in Washington for direct action against China itself. On December 30 he proposed that the United Nations should recognize a state of war with China, and then authorize the United Nations Command – of which he was head – to blockade the Chinese coast, destroy through naval gunfire and air attack China's industrial capacity to wage war, and authorize Chiang Kai-shek's forces in Formosa, who were under a specific ban in this regard, to take 'diversionary actions against vulnerable areas of the Chinese mainland'.

MacArthur went further, arguing – no doubt plausibly from a technical standpoint, but ignoring the possibility of Soviet nuclear retaliation – that if between thirty and fifty atom bombs were dropped on Manchuria and the cities of mainland China, the war would be over. When the Joint Chiefs agreed that the atom bomb was the only weapon that could effectively defeat the Chinese, Truman refused to contemplate such a course. The man who had authorized the dropping of two atom bombs on inhabited cities was not going to authorize the dropping of a third. The Korean War would continue to be fought as it had been fought for the past six months, as a struggle between infantry, artillery, tanks and aircraft.

Dean Rusk, the Assistant Secretary of State, later recalled a discussion about bombing a large dam on the Yalu River. The Air Force Chief of Staff, General Hoyt S. Vandenberg, 'had gone to Korea, flown a plane over the dam, and dropped our biggest conventional bombs on it. It made only a little scar on the dam's surface. He returned to Washington and told us that we could knock the dam out only with nuclear weapons. Truman refused.'

The tensions created by the military setbacks in Korea, and the continuing Chinese advance into Tibet, led the North Atlantic Treaty powers, meeting on December 19, to create an integrated defence force. It was to be under the supreme command of General Eisenhower. The new 'enemy' which it felt had to be more effectively confronted – the Soviet Union – had its troops stationed along the Elbe, and commanded military resources even greater than those which the previous enemy – Germany – had been able to deploy six years earlier.

The war in Korea had provided the main Far Eastern focus of attention and concern during 1950. But in Vietnam, as fighting between the French and the Vietminh intensified, the French were forced to pull back from the northern frontier areas, and to take up defensive positions in the Red River Delta. Among the towns which the French had evacuated by the end of October was Lang-son, where they abandoned vast quantities of equipment, including 940 machine guns, 450 vehicles, four thousand new machine guns, more than eight thousand rifles and a thousand gallons of fuel oil, all of which became part of the growing armoury of the Vietminh.

On October 8, as 3,500 French soldiers were trapped in the fortress of Cao Bang, the Vietminh attacked. As the main French force – which included three battalions of Moroccan troops – pulled back, their French commander commented: 'We shall never come back.' In the course of the retreat, 2,500 French soldiers were killed or taken prisoner. The Moroccan troops, attacked by wave after wave of Vietminh soldiers, had broken in panic and fled. In their terror many of them went berserk. It was the worst disaster in eighty

896 · DESCENT INTO BARBARISM

years of French colonial history. In Paris the socialist leader Pierre Mendès-France argued that the only way to secure Vietnam was by a greatly increased military effort which would harm the French economy at home. He therefore suggested opening negotiations with Ho Chi Minh. The government rejected this.

On October 17 a State of Emergency was declared in Tonkin. Arms, equipment and medical supplies began to arrive from the United States, but there was no chance of reversing the humiliation of the withdrawal from the border forts. The Vietminh had considerably extended the area of its control. The French military commander, General Marcel Carpentier, regarded the situation as so grave that he drew up plans to withdraw to the 18th Parallel, leaving all of Vietnam north of that line, including Hanoi and Haiphong, to the Vietminh. This was only a plan, devised in a moment of panic – but it reflected the hopelessness of controlling an increasingly hostile countryside by force of arms.

On November 22, in the Chamber of Deputies in Paris, the French Government secured a majority of 337 to 187 'to reinforce the army as required'. The motion also appealed for help to the United States, not naming America as such, but stating that the Government 'should make clear to the free world the international and anti-Communist nature of the war in Vietnam.'

As the Second World War continued to impose its legacy of guilt and denial, the Interior Ministry of the West German province of Württemberg was asked to recognize the Gypsies as candidates for compensation. Details of their persecution during the war were well documented: many thousands of Gypsies had been murdered alongside Jews in the gas chambers. But the appeal for compensation was turned down, the Interior Ministry explaining, on May 9: 'It should be borne in mind that Gypsies have been persecuted under the Nazis not for any racial reason but because of an asocial and criminal record.'

In Poland, the search for wartime documentation was rewarded on December 1 when building workers, digging in the ground of what had once been the Warsaw ghetto to set the foundations of new blocks of flats, discovered a metal milk churn containing part of an eye-witness report of the mass murder of Jews at Treblinka. The milk churn had been hidden in the ground by the historian Emanuel Ringelblum, who had been betrayed while in hiding after the ghetto uprising of 1943, and killed by the Gestapo.

The perpetrators of war crimes continued to seek an escape from justice. On December 19 a ship left the German port of Bremerhaven for St John, New Brunswick. Among the passengers was Helmut Rauca, who had taken the leading part in selecting for death many thousands of Jews in the Kovno ghetto, in German-occupied Lithuania. Rauca reached Canada and became a Canadian citizen. But in doing so, he lied about his Nazi past, and because of this, when discovered and exposed thirty-three years later, he could be extradited to Germany. He died in a prison hospital in Frankfurt-on-Main while awaiting trial.

Five years after the end of the Second World War, the painful burdens of the past were in contrast to the bright opportunities of the present. The steady postwar growth of middle class prosperity and consumer spending was typified on July 31 when one of the first self-service shops was opened in Britain, the brainchild of J. Sainsbury; and when, in the United States, the first modern charge card was issued, by Diners' Club in New York.

It was not only former wars, but wars still being fought, that were eclipsed by improvements in the daily lives of millions of people. Even as American troops were fighting in the mud and ice of the Korean peninsula, popular entertainment in the United States reached several milestones, including the first performance of Irving Berlin's musical *Call Me Madam* in New York on October 12, and the premier, also in New York, of the Frank Loesser and Abe Burrows musical *Guys and Dolls*, on November 24. That year at La Scala, Milan, Maria Callas, a Greek soprano, made her operatic debut.

The end of 1950 marked the end of the first half of the twentieth century. In the United States, television had begun regular transmissions in colour. The new medium was recognized as a harbinger of change in the habits of millions of people. In an article in the *Manchester Guardian*, the American commentator Alistair Cooke wrote, from New York: 'The movies were trembling at the gargantuan birth of television and wondering if that was what had robbed the movie box office of about one-fifth of its annual revenue. Television, incidentally, now came on every day from morn to midnight and, though much of it is mediocre when it is not infantile, American television has begun to set a standard in spot-news reporting, in comedy shows, and in group discussions.'

On the last day of the half-century Marshal Tito announced that he was giving a New Year's Amnesty to 11,327 prisoners. Some were political prisoners and many were peasants who had been imprisoned for failing to deliver their grain quotas. It was with the burdens of Communism and the

East-West divide uppermost in its mind that an editorial writer in the *News Chronicle* wrote:

> ... at the turn of the half-century it is worth recalling how swift has been the triumph of the idea of 'government of the people, for the people, by the people' through the Western world. And the most remarkable thing of all is the way it has penetrated the ancient East and captured India.
>
> The very speed of this transformation should be a warning to us. We have already paid a heavy price for the incredible momentum of social and scientific change. The great moral values which sustained our forefathers have been all but swamped by the swift tide of material progress.

Reflecting on the importance of maintaining the achievements which the defeat of Nazi tyranny and Japanese militarism five years earlier were a central part, and of which the United Nations military action in Korea was, at that very moment, an integral element, the *News Chronicle* writer continued:

> Democracy is essentially a creative idea. During this half-century we have seen it groping after, reaching out to its highest aspiration, a unified world in which men will live at peace with one another.
>
> The first of these attempts was the League of Nations. It failed. The United Nations represents the rebirth of the hope. So long as the idea of democracy exists, it will, out of its inner necessity, be always striving to set the world free from the curses of war, hate and tyranny, and unify the peoples in a world self-government.

CHAPTER TWENTY-FOUR

1951

> ... even if the differences between West and East are,
> for the time being, intractable, the creation of a new
> atmosphere and climate of thought, and of a revived
> relationship and sense of human comradeship, would, I
> believe, be an enormous gain to all the nations.
>
> WINSTON S. CHURCHILL

IN THE OPENING DAYS of 1951 there was no improvement in the fortunes of the United Nations forces in Korea. On January 1 the North Korean and Chinese troops broke through the United Nations line that had been temporarily re-established on the 38th Parallel, and pushed southward, making a mockery of MacArthur's earlier and much vaunted confidence in victory by Christmas. On New Year's Day, as a British brigade was going forward to the front line, American soldiers going south called out to the tank crews: 'You're going the wrong way, buddy!'

The Englishmen took up their positions, fought, and were forced back. One of them, Lieutenant Bill Cooper — who when recalled to the army had asked himself 'What would people say if I didn't go?' — later recalled: 'I was shaken at the speed it all happened: the red in a stream with bodies in it, the great trails of blood in the snow as if a snail had crawled across it.' That day an order was issued to all Chinese troops in Korea to collect prisoners as a New Year gift for Mao Tse-tung. Units were encouraged to compete for the largest number of prisoners they could take.

On January 4 the South Koreans and Americans were driven out of Seoul, as they had been six months earlier in the first days of the war. Once more the Americans were retreating towards Pusan. On January 7 an American soldier, Private James Cardinal, whose unit was holding a mountain pass sixty miles north-west of Taegu, through which thousands of troops were retreating, wrote to his parents in the Bronx:

> It looks like the beginning of the end. The Chinese are kicking hell out of the US Army, and I think we are getting out, at least I hope so. I think they are going to evacuate all UN troops from Korea soon, as it's impossible to stop these Chinese hordes. There's just too many of them for us to fight in Korea. If the big wheels in Washington decide to fight here it will be the biggest mistake they ever made, as I don't think we can hold the Chinks. Anyway, let's hope they decide to evacuate us.
>
> When you get complaining and bitching letters from me, remember every soldier over here feels that way. The troops over here are mad, mad at America, Americans and America's leaders. We all feel we've been let down, by our incompetent blundering leadership, from the White House down. It seems to me to be – to hell with the troops in Korea.
>
> If we must fight communism, let's do it in Europe which is the cradle of western culture and our own civilization. It seems to me that's more worth fighting for than some barren oriental wasteland, with uncountable hordes of savage warriors.

A more vigorous state of mind was about to impinge and dominate the American troops in Korea. On 23 December 1950 General Walker had been killed when his jeep was in collision with a South Korean army truck. His replacement was General Matthew B. Ridgway, a veteran of the fighting in the Ardennes in the Second World War, where a severe reversal had been met and countered. Within a few weeks Ridgway's fighting qualities and professionalism had begun to influence every branch of his troops, including those in retreat. Under his initiative, a United Nations counter-offensive was planned, making use of the overwhelming American air superiority and the American ability, if this was made a priority, to obliterate the Chinese supply routes. On 13 January 1951 Truman sent MacArthur a telegram reiterating the American position that the war in Korea was meant 'to demonstrate that aggression will not be accepted by us or by the United Nations'.

With Churchill's caution – that the United Nations should 'avoid by every means in their power becoming entangled inextricably in a war with China' – and Attlee's recent visit to Washington in mind, Truman sought, however, to impress upon MacArthur that 'great prudence' was needed in the future conduct of the war. 'Steps which might in themselves be fully justified and which might lend some assistance to the campaign in Korea,' Truman explained, 'would not be beneficial if they thereby involved Japan or Western Europe in large-scale hostilities.' By Japan, Truman meant the American occupation authorities and forces in Japan, over which MacArthur was the supremo. 'In the worst case,' Truman continued, 'it would be important that, if we must withdraw from Korea, it be clear to the world that that course is forced upon us by military necessity and that we shall not accept the result politically or militarily until the aggression is rectified.'

'. . . if we must withdraw from Korea . . .' These six words were the harbingers of a change in United States policy. On January 13, the day of Truman's telegram to MacArthur, the Political Committee of the United Nations Assembly approved a plan – put forward by a three-man committee consisting of a Persian, a Canadian and an Indian member – for an immediate ceasefire and the withdrawal of all foreign forces from Korea 'by appropriate stages'. The Americans expressed their willingness to consider these proposals seriously. The Chinese rejected them, stating on January 17 that they had been put forward solely to help the American troops then fighting, and falling back, in front of the Chinese onslaught.

The soldiers who were fighting in Korea were as far removed from these diplomatic manoeuvres as it was possible to be. Colin Mitchell later recalled a typical incident, as seen from a British officer's perspective:

We had, without knowing it, deployed on an old battlefield fought over at the very beginning of the campaign. The corpses were those of both armies who had obviously been killed in and around this minefield during the initial North Korean attack. The rats had grown fat on them. I wirelessed back the state of affairs and after a couple of hours a party of American engineers came trailing up the ridge.

The sergeant, a huge negro, seemed unconcerned at my warning that the place was full of anti-personnel mines and must be strewn with trip flares. His white subordinates were less confident so they left him to wander off on his own. He had not gone twenty yards when there was a dreadful bang and I turned to see the wretched man with half his head blown away.

That was the end of it. The place was clearly untenable and a few hours later we were withdrawn from the position while someone in Brigade Headquarters drew a circle round it on the map and no one went near that nightmare area again.

Following the Chinese rejection of a Korean ceasefire, the American House of Representatives adopted by acclamation – and the Senate by a unanimous vote – a series of resolutions branding China as the aggressor. The United States wished to go further, and to obtain United Nations condemnation of China for its military intervention into Korea. Britain, France and Australia urged a more cautious approach. Attlee told the House of Commons on January 23 that while Britain condemned China's military intervention in Korea, any consideration by the United Nations of military action against China would 'close the door to a negotiated peace'. Britain and the United States were at odds. To the distress of Washington, the British government wanted to explore a Chinese proposal for a seven-Power conference, to be held on Chinese soil, to consider a 'limited' ceasefire.

At the United Nations the Chinese proposal for a seven-Power conference gained momentum, strongly supported by the senior British delegate, Sir Gladwyn Jebb. Twelve Arab and Asian States, headed by India, gave the proposal their support. Canada also put its weight behind the ceasefire concept. A 'Good Offices Committee' was established to try to reach an 'accommodation' with Peking. The process of moving towards a ceasefire had begun.

While seeking a compromise that would avert war with China, the British government was emphatic in its opposition to Soviet foreign policy. On January 26, in a public speech outside London, Attlee warned that in order to stand up to Russian intentions it was necessary to ensure a substantial British rearmament which would require of the British people 'great exertions and serious sacrifices':

> Our way of life is in danger, our happiness and the happiness and future of our children are in danger; and it is both our privilege and our duty to be ready to defend them if they are attacked.
>
> War would bring our standards crashing down: defeat would destroy and obliterate them forever. Make no mistake about that.
>
> So far as we are able we shall distribute the burden with equity and fairness. I have no fear whatever about the response we shall get.

Attlee went on to say that the Soviet rulers had inherited imperialism from the Tsars and added to it ideological imperialism. The 'arid and unattractive doctrines' of Marxism-Leninism were about as distant as they could be from 'true' Socialism, but they were held by men who controlled 'great armies', and who 'rejected the moral values on which civilization is based'. Attlee then quoted from a Geneva-born philosopher, Henri Frederic Amiel (1821–1881), who, having visited Russia in the second half of the nineteenth century, warned:

What terrible masters these Russians would be if they should ever spread their rule over the countries of the South. They would bring us a Polar despotism – tyranny such as the world has never known, silent as darkness, rigid as ice, insensible as bronze, decked with an outer amiability and glittering with the cold brilliancy of snow: slavery, without compensation or relief that is what they would bring us.

Inside the Soviet Union, the pressures for artistic uniformity were evident throughout the year. Shostakovich, who had been censured three years earlier for his 'bourgeois formalistic tendencies' found his most recent works, the oratorio *Song of the Forests* and his music for the film *Fall of Berlin* both lavishly praised. Soviet songwriters were warned to avoid 'decadent café banality' and to express instead 'the healthy outlook of modern Soviet man'. The hallmark of an acceptable song was that it should be 'courageous, hearty, lyrical and sincere'.

It was not always easy for Soviet writers and producers to get it right. A Soviet opera set in the collectivized countryside, *From the Bottom of My Heart*, which was widely praised for its realism when it was first produced in January, was condemned in *Pravda* in April, after Stalin had attended a performance, as 'untrue to life' and with 'feeble and colourless music'. The chairman of the government's own Committee for Artistic Affairs, as well as the director of the Bolshoi theatre, were immediately dismissed, and the composer of the opera, G.L. Zhukovksy, who had earlier been awarded the prestigious Stalin prize, had the prize taken away from him.

History, the writing of which had always been an instrument of Soviet policy, was again being rewritten from yet another ideological perspective. Caucasian and Central Asian rebels against Tsarist imperialism, hitherto heroes of Soviet history, were denounced as 'feudal reactionaries'. Local national pride was to be replaced by love of Moscow and devotion to Stalin. In July two Ukrainian writers (A. Korneichuk and Wanda Wasilewska) of impeccable Communist Party standing were ordered to revise their libretto for the opera *Bogdan Chmelnitsky* on the grounds – made public by *Pravda*

– that it had not satisfactorily assessed the Russian contribution to the seventeenth century Ukrainian leader's struggle against the Poles.

In August the Azerbaijan Communist Party had to announce the banning throughout Azerbaijan and Soviet Central Asia of sections of the patriotic national poem *Dede Korkut,* which, it was suddenly alleged, was 'an instrument of bourgeois nationalist and pan-Turanian propaganda. To discredit the poem still further, it was stated that 'German scholars' had taken a hand in compiling it.

Also in August, *Pravda* expressed indignation at a statement in which the British Foreign Secretary, Herbert Morrison, speaking in Edinburgh, deplored the fact that Soviet citizens were restricted in their access to information about foreign countries, in their contacts with foreign citizens, and in their right to travel abroad. If he were a Russian, Morrison declared:

> I would find no rule of law, no political and religious freedom and equality, no sort of constitutional safeguards, no right to turn the Government out of office, or even to vote for any candidate not hand-picked by the Kremlin.
>
> I would find a Parliament which is very rarely allowed to meet, and is then the tool of the government.
>
> I could not criticize or agitate against the Government except from time to time to denounce a few of the lower ranks of the bureaucracy.
>
> My working conditions would depend on the whim of trade unions under the thumb of the State, and I would have no freedom to choose my own job or to improve my position by taking such work as I liked at home or overseas.
>
> I could certainly look to comprehensive social security and health services, and to fair shares of necessities and special allowances for children, but at a much lower standard than here.
>
> My opportunities for higher education would also be worse.

Throughout the Communist bloc the repressions of previous years continued. In Poland, where the Roman Catholic Church served as a focal point of opposition to Communism, a number of priests were brought to trial, and there were further attempts to secularize education. In Hungary, Archbishop Grösz, the acting head of the Roman Catholic Church – Cardinal Mindszenty being under house arrest – was arrested and brought to trial with eight other religious leaders. The archbishop was found guilty of a number of specious charges and sentenced to fifteen years in prison. A campaign then began against 'class-alien and unreliable elements' in the capital, especially those suspected of still adhering to the 'rotten Liberal attitude' of the past.

As many as fifty thousand people were forced to leave Budapest, most at only a few hours notice, and without being able to take with them more than they could put in their hand luggage. Some were sent to do rural work, others to forced labour camps. Aristocrats, former Cabinet Ministers, generals, bankers and intellectuals were among those deported. They included several widows bearing famous names, invalids, and a woman aged 102. When both Holland and Sweden offered to take in the deportees, their offers were greeted with derision by the Communist Party newspapers.

In the Soviet Union the labour camp system was as strict and as demoralizing as it had ever been, after thirty years of the exercise – the perfection – of Communist punishment. The Party punished its own as harshly as it punished its enemies, who were seldom vocal enough to be found. Alexander Solzhenitsyn, who had been a prisoner in the Gulag for the previous five years, later wrote a novel about the torment of Gulag life, *One Day in the Life of Ivan Denisovich*. In one scene Solzhenitsyn recalled the opening months of 1951. Among the characters in the novel was Tsezar – described by Solzhenitsyn as 'a hotch-potch of nationalities: Greek, Jew, Gypsy, you couldn't make out which' – and Captain Buinovsky, a former naval commander. Both were prisoners. Lieutenant Volkovoi was the camp security chief. Shukhov was the surname of Ivan Denisovich, the novel's hero:

. . . Volkovoi told the guards to take the name of anyone who might be wearing extra garments – the culprits were to surrender them in person at the camp-stores that evening with a written explanation of how and why they had hidden the garments.

Shukhov was in regulation dress. Come on, paw me as hard as you like. There's nothing but my soul in my chest. But they made a note that Tsezar was wearing a flannel vest and that Buinovsky, it seemed, had put on a waistcoat or a cummerbund or something. Buinovsky, who'd been in the camp less than three months, protested. He couldn't get rid of his commander's habits.

'You've no right to strip men in the cold. You don't know Article Nine of the Criminal Code.'

But they did have the right. They knew the code. You, chum, are the one who doesn't know it.

'You're not behaving like Soviet people,' Buinovsky went on saying. 'You're not behaving like communists.'

Volkovoi had put up with the references to the criminal code but this made him wince and, like black lightning, he flashed:

'Ten days in the cells.'

And aside to the sergeant:

'Starting from this evening.'

They didn't like putting a man in the cells in the morning: it meant the loss of his work for the whole day. Let him sweat blood in the meantime and be put in the cells in the evening.

Deportation, labour camps and internal exile did not require the vastness of a country like the Soviet Union in order to be practised. In Roumania, as in Hungary, they became a well-tried method of repression. As many as ten thousand of the Serb minority living near the Yugoslav border with Roumania were deported to labour camps in the Roumanian interior. In the campaign against Roman Catholicism, the eighty-one-year-old Bishop of Timisoara was tried by a Roumanian military court on charges of spying 'in the service of the Vatican'. He was sentenced to eighteen years solitary confinement. To deter Jewish immigration to Israel, for which pressure had been growing, a hundred of Roumania's leading Zionists were arrested. There was also a sustained campaign of Russification, with as many as ten thousand workers being made to learn Russian, and to use textbooks that would serve as 'a day-to-day guide and material factor in the formation of the workers' Socialist conscience'.

In Czechoslovakia, Communist Party rule was tightened by a series of purges. The culmination came when the Party's Secretary General, Rudolf Slansky, was dismissed from his post, and, after a brief spell as Deputy Prime Minister with no real authority, charged with being an enemy of the people, an imperialist spy, and the agent of 'Jewish capitalism', which he intended to restore. A purge trial reminiscent of earlier Soviet trials, was in the offing.

In Korea, American troops, having been driven back so decisively from the Yalu River and the 38th Parallel in the previous months, began advancing northward again on January 25. The United States Eighth Army under General Ridgway had found a commander who had the personality and drive to inspire his men to reverse the tide of withdrawal and demoralization. Ridgway, like General Montgomery and his Eighth Army in the Western

Desert almost a decade earlier, understood that the needs of his men must be taken care of, and seen to be taken care of, as one of the priorities of war. As well as a much improved use of air power and artillery in striking at the Chinese and North Korean positions, and improved communications, Ridgway instituted a regime of better quality food, warmer clothing for the fiercesome Korean winter, and improved Mobile Army Surgical Hospitals (MASH) for the sick and wounded.*

In Vietnam, a number of sustained military assaults were carried out by General Giap on French fortified positions north of Hanoi. This was the start of what the Vietminh called the General Counter-offensive. Its philosophy was set out by one of the leading theorists of the Vietnamese Communist struggle, Truong Chinh:

> As a result of the long war the enemy troops became weary and discouraged, and are tormented by home-sickness. The French economy and finances are exhausted; supplying the army is difficult, the French troops have put up with privations and the French people do not want the war in Vietnam to go on any longer . . .
>
> As for us, although our material resources are not yet adequate, our fighting spirit soars constantly higher . . .
>
> During this stage, the enemy surrenders many positions and withdraws to entrench himself in the big cities . . . As for us, our consistent aim is that the whole country should rise up and go over to the offensive on all fronts – completely defeat the enemy and achieve true independence and unification.

The first battle of the General Counter-offensive took place at Vinh Yen, only twenty-five miles north west of Hanoi. More than 20,000 Vietminh troops attacked the 6,000 French defenders, who included many Senegalese and Algerian troops. As the Vietminh appeared to be gaining the advantage, the new French commander of the forces in Vietnam, General de Lattre de Tassigny – France's most senior and experienced general – flew in a light aeroplane to Vinh Yen and personally took charge of the defence. He also

---

* One of the historians of the Korean War, Max Hastings, wrote in 1987: 'Popular awareness of the Korean War today centres upon the television comedy show MASH, which dismays most Korean veterans because it projects an image of Korea infinitely less savage than that which they recall.'

called in reinforcements from throughout Vietnam including the south, and organized air strikes.

It was the use of French air power that was decisive. The most effective weapon proved to be the napalm bomb – a development of Second World War flame-throwing devices – which ignited the fields, trees and attackers in one indiscriminate blaze. The Vietminh retreated, leaving at least 6,000 dead on the battlefield. The French losses were 700. General Giap's much-heralded General Counter-offensive had failed. General de Lattre followed his success in building a defensive line (the 'De Lattre Line') around the Red River Delta. Six hundred small fortified military posts were in place by the summer and a further six hundred by the end of the year. De Lattre's hope was that a Vietnamese National Army could be set up by Bao Dai and used to take over the defence of the line from the French and French colonial troops. To this end de Lattre persuaded Bao Dai to introduce conscription. But in the event the full burden of the defence of the line fell on the French.

Despite the heavy setback at Vinh Yen, General Giap ordered an attack on March 23 on the village of Mao Khe, near the Gulf of Tongking. Three French destroyers took part in the battle, pounding the attackers from their anchorage in the Da Bac River. The heavy naval gunfire, and further use of napalm by the French air force, prevented the destruction of the French defences. In the final battle inside Mao Khe, more than 3,000 of the Vietminh attackers were killed. A third and final offensive that year was against the French fortified positions on the Day River, south-east of Hanoi. The battle began on May 29 and lasted for three weeks. Support was given to the attackers by two areas of Vietminh guerrillas inside the Delta.

As many as fifteen thousand Vietminh troops were involved in the attack, assisted by forty thousand porters carrying ammunition and food. The Vietminh succeeded in crossing the river, but French naval and air counterattacks, helped by the local Vietnamese Catholic militia, broke their lines of supply and forced them back. As the retreat was in progress, the French counterattacked with heavy air bombardment, and napalm bombs. As many as nine thousand Vietminh troops were killed.

Waiting until the monsoon had passed, on November 14 General de Lattre took the offensive beyond his defensive line, seeking to drive the Vietminh from the Black River and the area around it, on which the Vietminh were dependent for their rice supplies. The assault was successful, the area secured, and a sustained Vietminh counterattack on December 9 was driven off. In one village alone, Tu Vu, more than 400 of the Vietminh attackers were killed. De Lattre, by then mortally ill with cancer, had won a final victory.

The dominance of the United States in the councils and defence of the West was seen most clearly on February 22, when it was announced in the British House of Commons that an American admiral would be given command of the North Atlantic Treaty Organization forces in the Atlantic. Many British parliamentarians were indignant at what seemed a derogation of British naval power – the power on which a hundred years of British commercial and imperial supremacy had been based. Attlee explained four days later that the predominant need was the ability to secure 'a speedy transition to war' should the need arise. In this context, the only enemy envisaged was the Soviet Union. The primacy of the United States was again made clear on March 12 when the British Admiralty spokesman, James Callaghan – who was to become Prime Minister a quarter of a century later – explained that while Britain had 150,000 naval personnel, the United States had more than 850,000.

Pressure from the Soviet Union increased when, on February 4, Stalin gave an interview to *Pravda* – such interviews by the Soviet leader were rare – warning that the United Nations, 'set up as a bulwark for the preservation of peace, is becoming an instrument of war, a means of unleashing a new world war'. He was particularly indignant at the United Nations declaration that China had been an aggressor in sending its troops into Korea. 'One has to lose the last remnants of conscience,' Stalin said, 'to assert that the United States, which has seized Chinese territory – the island of Taiwan – and has invaded Korea up to the borders of China, is the side defending itself, while the Chinese People's Republic, which is defending its borders, and is trying to regain the island of Taiwan, seized by the Americans, is the aggressor.'

Stalin went on to warn that there was an 'aggressive nucleus' of powers within the United Nations, made up of the ten North Atlantic Treaty countries and the twenty Latin American republics, that was seeking to 'take the inglorious path of the League of Nations'. No doubt Stalin recalled all too well that the very last collective act of the League of Nations, before it was overtaken completely by the Second World War, was to expel the Soviet Union for its invasion of Finland at the end of 1939.

Following Stalin's interview, the Soviet Union gave both material and moral support to North Korea and to the Chinese forces fighting in Korea. But it made no move to commit a single Soviet soldier to the battle. It was believed by many Western observers that Stalin refrained from sending 'volunteers' to Korea because he was contemplating military action against Tito's Yugoslavia.

On the battlefield, the influence of General Ridgway was everywhere apparent. In the last two weeks of February so much ground had been recaptured that a senior British officer, Air Vice-Marshal Cecil Bouchier – a Battle of Britain veteran – reported to the Air Ministry in London: 'The myth of the magical millions of the Chinese in Korea has been exploded. In the last United Nations offensive, the Americans have learned how easy it is to kill the Chinese, and their morale has greatly increased thereby.'

On February 21 the Canadian forces in Korea were in action for the first time. Together with British and Australian troops, and supported by New Zealand artillery, they took part in an advance that was to drive the Chinese back fifteen miles. On the Canadian contingent's second day in action, four Canadian soldiers were killed.

On March 14 the United Nations forces retook the South Korean capital, Seoul. It was remarked with some acerbity in Washington that 'while General MacArthur was fighting the Pentagon, General Ridgway was fighting the enemy.' Within two weeks, on March 27, South Korean troops reached the 38th Parallel and crossed it, pushing northward. Ridgway had no plans to retake Pyongyang or to press as far as the Yalu River. Instead, he formed a defensive line 115 miles from coast to coast, and made preparations to hold it against what his Intelligence reports indicated to be an imminent Chinese offensive.

From his headquarters in Tokyo, MacArthur continued to advocate air strikes against Chinese targets in Manchuria and China proper. Even Ridgway's line seemed at variance with MacArthur's strategic vision. A month earlier he had said publicly: 'The concept advanced by some that we establish a line across Korea and enter into positional warfare is wholly unrealistic and illusory.'

But Washington no longer took MacArthur's advocacy seriously. When he put forward the need to 'sever' Korea from Manchuria, and thereby prevent the arrival of any further Chinese reinforcements, by laying down along the length of the Yalu River a zone of radioactive wastes – 'the by-products of atomic manufacture' – his request was rejected out of hand. The fact that Ridgway was able to secure military successes on the battlefield seemed to give the lie to MacArthur's insistence that victory could only come if drastic measures were adopted, or if China herself was attacked.

In the third week of March, Truman began to work out proposals for a ceasefire agreement which he hoped to put to his United Nations allies. He first approached MacArthur for his comments, but MacArthur refused to enter into the discussion, other than to oppose what he called 'further military restrictions' on his command. On March 21 Truman sent his ceasefire proposal to the other United Nations participants in the war. On the previous day the Chiefs of Staff in Washington had informed MacArthur that, in answer to his recent requests for a more active war north of the Yalu River, there must be no 'all-out war' with China.

Angered, MacArthur decided to take his own initiative, and did so at the very moment that America's United Nations allies were studying Truman's ceasefire proposals. On March 24 MacArthur issued a proclamation in which he stated that the Chinese 'must by now be painfully aware that a decision of the United States to depart from its tolerant effort to contain the war to the areas of Korea, through an expansion of our military operations to his coastal areas and interior bases, would doom Red China to the risk of imminent military collapse'. To avoid this, MacArthur said, he offered the Chinese truce negotiations.

When MacArthur's bellicose proclamation – of discussions under the threat of all-out war – was read in Washington, it created outrage. On March 29 the Chinese rejected the offer. Three days later the Indian government made a public appeal for a truce. Britain, a participant in the United Nations war effort, followed on April 2. The momentum for a compromise was in stark contrast to MacArthur's threat of a wider, and potentially nuclear, war.

For more than two weeks Truman had seethed with anger at MacArthur's pronouncement, and on April 10 he acted. He did something that had not been done since Abraham Lincoln sacked General George B. McClellan almost a century earlier – he sacked a Commander in Chief. McClellan had commanded the Army of the Potomac. MacArthur commanded the American forces in Japan and the United Nations Forces in Korea. Ironically, McClellan's fault had been his refusal to attack. MacArthur's fault was his desire to attack above and beyond the limits assigned him.

There was an outburst of indignation among the Republicans in Washington when MacArthur's sacking was announced half an hour after midnight on April 10 – that is, in the early hours of April 11. As calls were heard for the impeachment of the President, Senator Nixon urged the Senate to censure Truman, and to call upon him to 'restore' MacArthur to command. Truman's action, Nixon declared, had both heartened and 'appeased' the Communist world. Nixon called in the press photographers to see, and to photograph, two large piles of telegrams which he had received, protesting against the dismissal of MacArthur.

Truman ignored the outcry. 'We do not want to widen the conflict', he explained to the American people in a short broadcast on the night of MacArthur's removal. The United States was ready, he said, at any time 'to negotiate for a restoration of peace in the area' – a 'real' peace, he explained, not one based on appeasement.

Truman – who was at the start of his seventh year as President – appointed General Ridgway as MacArthur's successor, and gave Ridgway his full support. MacArthur, returning to the United States, was welcomed by many as a hero. In a provocative speech to Congress on April 19 he denounced Truman's policy of restraint. The policy of limiting the war to Chinese aggression in Korea, he said, was to follow the path of 'prolonged indecision'. He had wanted 'every available means' used to bring victory, he explained, though he made no mention of his desire to use the atom bomb on Chinese cities, or to create a radioactive belt between Korea and Chinese Manchuria.

As April came to an end there was no clear sense of direction among the commanders of the United Nations force. When General Ridgway's successor as commander of the Eighth Army, General James Van Fleet, was asked at his first press conference, on April 22, 'What is our goal in Korea?' he replied: 'I don't know. The answer must come from higher authority.' In Washington, the military defeat of the North Korean and Chinese forces on North Korean soil was the overriding objective. War on Chinese soil had to be avoided.

On the Korean battlefield the struggle continued without pause or amelioration. On April 24 Canadian troops were in action north of Kapyong, at a position being held by American, Australian, British and South Korean troops. As the Chinese attacked, the first Canadian platoon to face them was partially overrun, but managed to extricate itself and fall back to join the rest of the Canadian battalion. When the battalion was surrounded, and ammunition ran low, supplies were dropped in by parachute. Ten Canadians were killed before the battalion was able to withdraw. Henceforth the Canadians were to be in many fierce actions: in all, 516 of them were killed, their names inscribed in Ottawa in the Korean Book of Remembrance.

On the night of April 24/25 a Japanese American soldier, Corporal Hiroshi H. Miyamura, from Gallup, New Mexico, protected his squad from an attack by vastly superior numbers of Chinese, killing more than sixty attackers with his machine gun and, when his ammunition ran out and he was severely wounded, resorting to hand to hand combat with bayonet, thereby enabling his fellow Americans to withdraw. His citation for the Medal of Honour described how 'when last seen he was fighting ferociously against an over-whelming number of enemy soldiers'.

In the air, the daily American bombing and strafing missions were unham-pered by opposition. During April 25 more than 764 sorties were flown and an estimated 1,500 Chinese and North Korean troops were killed or wounded. Lieutenant Archie B. Caldwell, of San Bernardino, California, reported of the air attack which he led on troops near Kaesong: 'We worked them over with our napalm and our machine guns.'

The need to increase defence spending in order to continue at war in Korea led the British Labour government to impose charges on people using the National Health Service – a central aspect of the post-war Welfare State which the Labour Party had pioneered. The government insisted that the charges were essential if Britain was to fulfil its defence commitments in Korea and in Western Europe. In protest at this, on April 22 two members of the government resigned. One of them, Aneurin Bevan, was the founder of the Health Service. The other, one of the youngest members of the administration, was Harold Wilson – who was to become Prime Minister thirteen years later.

On April 22, after darkness fell, the Chinese launched a new offensive in Korea. Some of the few Chinese soldiers who were taken prisoner as the offensive began spoke of how their commanders – or, more accurately, their political commissars – had told them that they would be celebrating May Day in Seoul. The shock of the initial Chinese assault drove back the United Nations line in many places, but did not break it. New Zealand, Australian, Canadian and British troops were among those who took the brunt of the attack, and stemmed the tide.

On the Imjin River, British troops, together with a Belgian unit, were in hand to hand combat with the Chinese during a four day battle. As the Chinese attacked, Padre Sam Davies of the 1st Battalion, The Gloucester Regiment – known as the Glosters – was listening to the battalion radio reports. 'Standing in the sunny hollow where main Headquarters lay,' he later wrote, 'I tried to realize the position. We were isolated by Chinese hordes intent on the kill. It was simply a matter of hours before darkness fell, and the lonely battalion would be assaulted on all sides in the nightmarish moonlight. Gloucester was 11,000 miles away. I longed to be able to say "Stop" to the rushing minutes: to prolong this quiet sunny afternoon indefinitely.'

The battle when it came was one of the highest courage and hopeless resistance. The Chinese numbers were overwhelming. Three Filipino light tanks that tried to reach the surrounded British infantry positions and give them cover were unable to break through. Because the American artillery liaison officer had been withdrawn a few days earlier to another part of the front line, heavy artillery support was not available. Orders to withdraw came on the night of April 24/25, and were a relief to those under fire. But they were also surrounded; some Chinese snipers were shooting at their transport vehicles four miles behind their positions. Those units that could break out did so, losing heavily on the way, with more than sixty men being killed. The main body of the Glosters, however, were trapped. The battalion adjutant, Captain Anthony Farrar-Hockley, has recorded a conversation between the battalion's commanding officer, Colonel Carne, and his adjutant. Carne had just been listening to the battalion radio:

'You know that armour/infantry column that's coming from 3 Div to relieve us?'
'Yes sir.'
'Well, it isn't coming.'
'Right, sir.'

In was in the early hours of April 25, while it was still dark, that the Glosters heard the bugle of the Chinese sounding the attack. In an act of defiance, and with morale-boosting wit, Captain Farrar-Hockley ordered his own Drum Major, Philip Buss, to return the bugle call with a sequence of British army orders: 'Reveille', 'Cookhouse', 'Defaulters' and 'Officers Dress For Dinner'.

The battle that followed was an unequal one. Some of the British soldiers had not eaten for forty-eight hours. The riflemen were left with just three rounds of ammunition each; the bren gunners had only a magazine and a half each. No one could maintain more than a minute of fire. Forty men managed to wend their way out of the trap. Some of those who stayed were so tired that they lay down to await capture. Others, their weapons at the ready, tried to fight their way out, but were confronted by sustained Chinese machine-gun fire. Farrar-Hockley – who had fought bravely in Europe in the Second World War – was forced to accept that the situation was hopeless. 'Feeling as if I was betraying everything that I loved and believed in, I raised my voice and called "Stop!".

The Glosters were led off into captivity. Farrar-Hockley was to make three attempts to escape in the days ahead, but was recaptured each time. Another captive, Major Guy Ward, had been a prisoner of the Germans from 1941 to 1945. His first thought when he saw the Glosters surrounded by Chinese was 'Oh my God, here we go again'. Captivity in North Korea, and also on Chinese soil, was a cruel experience, one about which many men would not speak in later years, or would do so – like many of the Allied prisoners of the Japanese in the Second World War – only in muted tones.

In the Second World War the fate of the Allied prisoners-of-war held by the Japanese, and the Russian prisoners-of-war held by the Germans, had been tragic. The fate of the prisoners-of-war held by the Chinese during the Korean War was equally so. Of the 7,140 Americans who fell into Chinese hands, 2,701 died in captivity. Of the 1,188 British and Commonwealth prisoners, fifty died. During the North Korean retreat early in the war, a hundred American prisoners-of-war had been driven into a railway tunnel and killed. In the camps, the cruelty of the north Korean guards was the most feared. There were savage interrogations, especially of air crew. Solitary confinement was a much-dreaded punishment. Hunger and starvation were daily enemies. Another implacable enemy was dysentery. Some men drowned when they fell into the open latrines. An American prisoner, Lieutenant Walt Mayo, told Max Hastings: 'It was easier to die than it was to live.'

On April 25, as a by-product of the war in Korea, the United States Congress passed the Servicemen's Indemnity Act, whereby the United States Treasury would provide $10,000 each to survivors of combatants killed in Korea, and in any future conflicts.

On May 15 a renewed Chinese offensive succeeded in driving back the South Korean troops facing it for as much as thirty miles. American troops of the 2nd Infantry Division who were in the line of attack did not pull back, despite heavy casualties. Their divisional history described the battle:

Artillery, crashing into the ground forward of the lines, took a terrific toll
of the attackers, while other hundreds died in the minefields checkered
with barbed wire. The groans of the wounded, screams of the attackers
and the blast of bugles mingled with the clattering roar of battle as waves
of Chinese pushed against the lines . . .

Searchlights were turned on to illuminate the battle area and aid the
defenders in locating and slaughtering the onrushing Chinese.

The Chinese failed in their objective, the recapture of Seoul. Eleven days
after the Chinese offensive began, the United Nations forces once again
crossed the 38th Parallel and were on North Korean soil.

Whether the Korean War could remain confined to the Korean peninsula,
or would become a wider, and even a global – and nuclear – war, continued
to be the subject of much discussion, and of much fear in many parts of the
world that were as yet in no way directly affected by it. In May, Fritz
Sternberg, a pre-war German refugee from Nazism, then living in London,
wrote in the epilogue of his book *Capitalism and Socialism on Trial*, that
while the war in Korea would most probably remain a 'localized' one, and
even be ended by means of an armistice, 'the danger of a third world war
remains, and it might break out at any time'. Nevertheless, Sternberg added,
'in view of the fact, appreciated by the leaders of both sides, that a new
world war would result in a tremendous amount of devastation in the world,
and in particular in Russia and the United States, it is quite possible that peace,
or rather, the period of armistice in which we are now living, will be maintained
for quite a long period, and that, in fact, it may never end in war'.

By the time of MacArthur's removal more than 10,000 American soldiers
had been killed in Korea. The North and South Korean, and the Chinese
death tolls had been far higher.

On June 23 the Soviet delegate at the United Nations, Yakov Malik,
announced his government's decision to propose a ceasefire, and to seek an
armistice that would lead to a mutual withdrawal of forces on either side of
the 38th Parallel. In Peking, the *People's Daily* supported the Soviet proposal.
Two days later, at a speech at Tullahoma, Tennessee – on the first anniversary
of the start of the Korean War – Truman said that he was willing to negotiate
a settlement of the war on the basis of a Korea divided as hitherto along
the 38th Parallel. He also spoke of the Communist intentions when the war
began, and of his own reactions:

We remembered Japan and Manchuria, Italy and Ethiopia and Hitler and the Saar Basin. For the first time in history a world organization of nations took collective military action to halt aggression. And, acting together, we halted it.

A year ago today Korea looked like an easy conquest to the Soviet rulers in Moscow and their agents in the Far East. But they were wrong. Today, after more than a million Communist casualties – after the destruction of one Communist army after another – the forces of aggression have been thrown back on their heels. They are back behind the line where they started.

Things have not turned out the way the Communists expected.

The United Nations has not been shattered. Instead it is stronger today than it was a year ago.

Truman's thoughts were much focused on the pre-Second World War era, and even pre-First World War eras. 'The Kaiser and Hitler,' he said, 'when they started their great wars of aggression, believed that the United States would not come in. They counted on being able to divide the free nations and pick them off one at a time. There could be no excuse for making that mistake today.' As to the future, Truman added:

Of course, we cannot promise that there will not be a world war. The Kremlin has it in its power to bring about such a war if it desires. It has a powerful military machine, and its rulers are absolute tyrants.

We cannot be sure what the Soviet rulers will do.

But we can put ourselves in a position to say to them: Attack – and you will have the united resources of the free nations thrown against you; attack – and you will be confronted by a war you cannot possibly win.

If we could have said that to the Kaiser, or to Hitler, or to Tojo, the history of the world would have been very different.

It hasn't been easy to bring the free nations together into the united effort to resist aggression. It hasn't been easy to work out these alliances, and to build up our defenses, and to hold the line against great odds and discouragement in Korea. It hasn't been easy – but it is a record of tremendous progress in man's age-old struggle for peace and security.

Responding directly to the Soviet request for an armistice, General Ridgway offered, on behalf of the United Nations forces in Korea, to meet his Communist opposite number to discuss an end to hostilities. Both the Chinese and the North Koreans accepted the Soviet request.

Armistice negotiations opened on July 10 at Kaesong, inside the only area south of the 38th Parallel still held by Communist forces. As the talks continued so did the fighting. By mid-August the American death toll had reached 13,822. This was already a quarter of the United States dead in the First World War. Truman was filled with anguish at the heavy loss of life. He remembered all too well the First World War battlefields on which he had served as an artillery officer. Yet he could only wait, like everyone, to learn the outcome of the ceasefire talks, and read in the newspapers story after story of suffering and pain.

Sometimes the stories Truman read concerned events far from the battle-field. David McCullough, Truman's biographer, has recorded how, one August morning, the President read in the newspapers that the body of an American soldier killed in action, Sergeant John Rice, had been brought home for burial in Sioux City, Iowa, 'but that at the last moment, as the casket was to be lowered into the grave, officials of the Sioux City Memorial Park had stopped the ceremony because Sergeant Rice, a Winnebago Indian, was not "a member of the Caucasian race" and burial was therefore denied. Outraged, Truman picked up the phone. Within minutes, by telephone and telegram, it was arranged that Sergeant Rice would be buried in Arlington National Cemetery with full military honours and that an Air Force plane was on the way to bring his widow and three children to Washington.' McCullogh comments: 'That, as President, was the least he could do.'

The American bombing missions over North Korean and Chinese-held pos-itions continued throughout the ceasefire talks. In the first year of the war the United States Far Eastern Air Force, during the course of almost a quarter of a million sorties, had dropped 97,000 tons of bombs and 7,800,000 gallons of napalm on their adversaries. They had killed tens of thousands of Korean and Chinese soldiers, for the loss of 187 airmen.

On August 22 the Communists broke off the ceasefire talks at Kaesong, claiming that a United Nations aircraft had attacked the conference area. When the United Nations asked to be allowed to investigate the charge, the Communists refused to let them do so. To avoid a similar incident, General Ridgway asked for the talks to be moved to a place that was not wholly under Communist control. The Communists agreed to this, and on

October 25 the talks were started again at the village of Panmunjom, in no-man's land.

As the renewed ceasefire talks continued, the gulf between the two sides seemed unbridgeable. The Communists wanted the 38th Parallel to be restored as the border between North and South Korea. But to do this would mean that the United Nations forces, and the South Koreans, would have to give up 2,000 square miles of North Korean territory which they had overrun in the final phase of the war. Another unacceptable Communist demand was that all United Nations forces must leave Korea before any political settlement was reached. This would mean leaving South Korea to fend alone against North Korean and Chinese Communist political pressure.

On November 27 the Communist delegates at Panmunjom agreed that the existing ceasefire line should be the approximate future border between North and South Korea. This decision also constituted part of the ceasefire agreement and a victory for the United Nations in the bargaining that had continued – parallel with the fighting – since July. To the distress of the United Nations, however, the North Koreans refused to let the International Red Cross visit the prisoner-of-war camps in the north. The United Nations had a list of 132,471 men who were believed to be in captivity. The North Koreans issued a list of 11,559 names. This discrepancy was deeply distressing to the Americans and their Allies.

Following the ceasefire accord, the North Koreans began to build a fortified defensive position across the Korean peninsula. It was 155 miles from coast to coast, and virtually immune from destruction by the heaviest artillery fire. The depth of the position varied from fifteen to twenty-five miles, and was guarded by 855,000 men. It made the Iron Curtain border in Europe look almost flimsy.

In Britain, the Labour Government decided – while fighting still continued in Korea – to mark a definite break with the post-war years of austerity and brooding on the past, and to do so by holding a Festival of Britain. It was declared open by King George VI as he stood on the steps of St Paul's Cathedral on May 3. Funfairs, a specially built concert hall on London's badly bombed South Bank – the Royal Festival Hall – and myriad entertainment during the summer, expressed confidence in Britain's ability to flourish, and to be a leader in the world, in the second half of the century. Much of the preliminary planning was undertaken by a senior Labour Cabinet Minister, Herbert Morrison, whose grandson Peter Mandelson was to be in charge of the Millennium celebrations, and London's Millennium Dome, fifty years later.

The Festival of Britain took place a hundred years after the Great Exhibition of 1851, and like its predecessor its purpose was to celebrate achievement. A Dome of Discovery had an educational aspect that gave many hundreds of thousands of schoolchildren – this author among them – a glimpse into the modern age. The activities of the Festival of Britain, which took place throughout the country, would 'add up', according to the official handbook, 'to one united act of national reassessment, and one corporate re-affirmation of faith in the nation's future'. Among the long-term activities was the laying, in London, of the first stone of the National Theatre. The national mood was also buoyed up by international sporting successes, when England's football team beat Argentina, Scotland beat Denmark, and Wales beat Portugal in the World Cup.

Clement Attlee's Labour Government had introduced numerous social reforms, but at the cost of increased taxation and social divisions. Despite the uplift of the Festival of Britain and the sporting success, austerity remained. The national indebtedness created by five-and-a-half years of war, and the continuing cost of the reconstruction of battered cities, was still damaging to the national economy. Socialism, for all its ideological and practical appeal, had not proved the panacea many had hoped it would be. When a General Election was held in October the Labour Government, already with a narrow majority, was defeated – losing twenty seats – and the Conservatives were returned to power.

Churchill was again Prime Minister. As a former negotiator with the Soviet Union at the highest level, he brought with him the hope, which he had expressed publicly while Leader of the Opposition, that it might be possible to build bridges with Stalin's Russia. 'The realities which confront us are numerous, adverse and stubborn,' he said on November 6, in his first speech to parliament after returning to office. 'We must be careful not to swing on a wave of emotion from despondency to over-confidence; but even if the difference between West and East are, for the time being, intractable, the creation of a new atmosphere and climate of thought; and of a revived relationship and sense of human comradeship, would, I believe, be an enormous gain to all the nations.'

For the following three-and-a-half years Churchill was to work, despite a near-crippling stroke in 1953, for a drawing together of the Soviet Union and its former wartime Allies. He had already coined the word 'summit' for the type of meeting he had in mind, first between him, the American President and Stalin. Churchill pushed hard for such a meeting: but the United States Government proved reluctant to follow his lead, and the Soviet Union was unwilling to put its beliefs and ambitions to the test of face-to-face discussion.

In the Middle East, the frustrations that followed the ending of the first Arab-Israel war led to deep resentment among many Palestinian Arabs that they had been denied a State of their own. A Palestinian State in part of Palestine had been the decision of the United Nations in November 1947, but much of that part of Palestine had been occupied by Jordan in the final phases of the war, and Jordanian rule, based on Amman, had been imposed throughout the area-known as the West Bank (Egypt was in occupation of the other main Palestinian Arab area, the Gaza Strip). A young Palestinian Arab decided to express his grievance against Jordan through violence, and on July 20, assassinated King Abdullah of Jordan as he was about to pray in the Al-Aksa mosque in Jerusalem. The assassination was witnessed by Abdullah's seventeen-year-old grandson, Hussein, who was later to rule Jordan for half a century. The assassin claimed that his quarrel with the Abdullah was the King's willingness to come to a peace agreement with Israel. No such agreement proved possible until Hussein himself negotiated it in 1994.

It was not only the Palestinian Arabs who had a grievance that extremists among them sought to demonstrate through assassination. On March 7 the Prime Minister of Iran, General Ali Razmara, had been shot and killed by Islamic fundamentalists who wanted Iran to be an Islamic republic. On July 15 the Lebanese Prime Minister, Riad Bey e-Solh, had been assassinated in Beirut by a member of a Syrian extremist group that wanted Lebanon to be part of Syria. It was while attending a memorial service for Riad Bey that Abdullah had been assassinated in Jerusalem.

Further assassinations marred both colonial and national rule that year. On October 6 the British High Commissioner for the Federation of Malaya since 1948, Sir Henry Gurney, was assassinated by Malayan Communists. During a thirty year career as a Colonial civil servant he had served in Kenya, Jamaica, the Gold Coast and Palestine. Ten days after Gurney's assassination the Prime Minister of Pakistan, Liaquat Ali Khan, was assassinated by an Afghan fanatic. Liaquat Ali Khan had been an active member of the Muslim League in the struggle for independence since 1923 and Prime Minister of Pakistan since independence.

On December 24 Libya, which had been an Italian colony since Italy's victory over the Turks before the First World War until her defeat during the Second World War, became independent. The British military administration withdrew, and the local chieftain, Idris, became King. As Britain's withdrawal came as a result of a United Nations resolution – of 21 November 1949 – Libya was the first independent State to be created by the United Nations.

The East-West divide affected every region of the globe. On September 1 the United Nations Security Council discussed a complaint by Israel that the Egyptian refusal to allow ships bound for Israel to use the Suez Canal was adversely affecting the Israeli economy, and the stability of the whole region. France, Britain and the United States called on Egypt to end the restrictions. Three Powers refused to condemn Egypt: the Soviet Union, China and India. In its determination to maintain neutrality in world disputes, India was increasingly aligning itself against the Western powers.

Alignments for defence proliferated, and served to demarcate the world into more and more rigidly defined blocs. On September 1 the United States, Australia and New Zealand signed a Pacific Security Agreement, under which each of the signatories pledged to come to the help of the other in the event of a military attack. Other alignments were emerging that drew together hitherto separate and disparate nations and peoples, determined to have a voice in the counsels of the world. On February 9 a World Muslim Conference opened in Karachi, seeking to establish world-wide Muslim unity. One of the resolutions passed at the conference stated that an act of aggression against any one Muslim State would be considered an act of aggression against them all.

On March 29 a Congress of the International Council of Women opened in Athens. It too sought to establish the right of a particular group – in this case women – to have a recognized voice, a common policy, and an influence in the council of nations. These were early days in the cause of women's rights worldwide, but the basis had been established almost half a century earlier, when the campaign for votes for women had begun to make its mark. Individual women had also served as beacons for the emergence of a specifically women's movement: the efforts of President Roosevelt's widow Eleanor were important in this regard, as she campaigned – within the framework of the United Nations – for improved working conditions for women throughout the world.

Many disparate groupings hastened to gather together and to formulate their demands. In Hamburg on September 21 the sixth congress of the European Movement voted to urge the inclusion of Germany 'on terms of equality' in any European Community. The French delegate, not yet willing to make the leap forward into reconciliation, voted against. Meeting in San Salvador on October 8, the Foreign Ministers of El Salvador, Nicaragua, Guatemala, Costa Rica and Honduras established a Union of Central American States, to secure their own common interests and to set up a mechanism of consultation.

Many of the groups that came together did so through fear of the Great Power alignments and the build-up of armaments – including atomic weapons – which the Cold War had generated. It was from among the Great Powers themselves, however, that the most dramatic proposal for amelioration was put forward. On November 7 the United States, Britain and France produced a disarmament plan which they intended to introduce at the United Nations Assembly. The plan was a comprehensive one, covering the regulation, limitation and balanced reduction of all armed forces and all armaments. The atom bomb was included in the scheme. The three governments made clear that 'a first and indispensable step is disclosure and verification'. There must be international inspection of all armed forces, para-military forces, security forces and police forces.

On the evening that this proposal was made public, President Truman spoke on the radio. 'This is a proposal,' he said, 'for lessening the burden of armaments which now bears so heavily upon the world. It is a common-sense way of getting started toward the regulation and balanced reduction of all armed forces and all implements of war, including atomic weapons. We hope the General Assembly will consider this proposal as an urgent and important matter.' Truman then spoke of his hopes for the future, once arms reduction had been achieved:

New hope and opportunities would be given everywhere for better conditions of life. There would be greater freedom – greater production – greater enjoyment of the fruits of peaceful industry. Through the United Nations we could wage the only kind of war we seek – the war against want and human misery.

In the lifetime of our own generation, we could bring about the greatest period of progress for the world in all recorded history.

This is our vision. This is our hope. This is what all free people have been striving for. We are determined to gain these tremendous opportunities for human progress. We are determined to win real peace – peace based on freedom and justice.

We will do it the hard way if we must – by going forward as we are doing now, to make the free world so strong that no would-be aggressor will dare to break the peace.

But we will never give up trying for another way to peace – the way of reducing the armaments that make aggression possible.

That is why we are making these new proposals to the United Nations. We offer them in good faith and we ask that they be considered in good faith.

We hope all other nations will accept them – and will join with us in the great enterprise for peace.

On the day after Truman's broadcast, Dean Acheson told the United Nations Assembly that it was Soviet policies that were forcing the Western powers to increase their armaments. If the Three-Power proposals for arms reduction were accepted, 'the huge military expenditure now burdening most nations could be largely ended'.

The American appeal was rejected by the senior Soviet delegate and former Foreign Minister, Andrei Vyshinsky. One Western observer called Vyshinsky's speech a 'cataract of abuse'. Mocking the Three-Power disarmament proposals as insincere, Vyshinsky said that 'the mountain had given birth to a mouse, and a dead mouse at that'. After reading the Western proposals for the first time the previous night he had been 'unable to sleep for laughing'. What was urgent, he insisted, was for United Nations forces in Korea to leave within three months. He added that membership of the North Atlantic Treaty Organization was 'incompatible' with membership of the United Nations.

The Western States worked tirelessly to ensure that they were in a position to face the Communist bloc militarily. Central to their activity were increased armaments, an increased proportion of their budgets allocated to military expenditure, and a tightening of the alliance system that had grown up around the North Atlantic Treaty. On December 30, in Paris, the Foreign, Finance and Defence Ministers of France, Italy, Luxembourg, Belgium, the Netherlands and West Germany announced that the proposed European defence force would be called the European Defence Community (EDC) and that in due course it would be superseded by a federal body. Another step had been taken on the road to European unity, under the impetus of national defence. On the following day, December 31, the Economic Cooperation Administration of the Marshall Plan was replaced by a Mutual Security Agency. The East-West divide was further accentuated.

When 1951 opened, more than five-and-a-half years had passed since the end of the Second World War in Europe. But war crimes trials continued to be held. On January 15, Ilse Koch was sentenced to prison in West Germany for the second time. Four years earlier she had received a four-year sentence for her sadistic actions at Buchenwald, where she had been the wife of the camp commandant, Karl Koch, whom the SS had themselves executed for corruption in 1944. In her second trial Ilse Koch was sentenced to life imprisonment. Sixteen years later, she killed herself in prison.

Three weeks after Ilse Koch's second sentence the American High Commissioner in Germany, John J. McCloy, anxious to see West Germany take its place among the Western Powers in the East-West divide, issued an amnesty for all convicted industrialists who had used slave labour, and for all generals. Among those released as a result of the amnesty was Alfred Krupp von Bohlen, whose Krupp factories had employed, and terribly ill-treated, slave labour, on a vast scale. Originally sentenced at Nuremberg in July 1948 to twelve years' imprisonment, Krupp became a free man two-and-a-half years later.

In Brussels, General Alexander von Falkenhausen, the former German Military Governor of Brussels, was found guilty on March 7 of ordering the execution of several hundred Belgian hostages, and of the deportation of 25,000 Belgian Jews to Auschwitz. He was sentenced to twelve years' imprisonment, but was released after three weeks as an act of clemency, and in recognition of the fact that he had also protected many individual Belgians from the SS. Indeed, in July 1944 he had been imprisoned by Hitler for alleged leniency as Military Governor, and when he was liberated by the Americans in Dachau in May 1945 he was about to be executed by the SS for having sympathized with the organizers of the July Plot. Between his arrest by Hitler in July 1944 and his release by the Belgians in April 1951 he had been confined in forty-three different prisons.

Oswald Pohl, who had been in charge of the disposal of the possessions of the murdered concentration camp victims, and who had supervised the melting down of gold teeth taken from the corpses of the dead at Auschwitz, was tried by a United States military tribunal, found guilty, and hanged on June 8. The place of his execution was Landsberg Prison, where Hitler had been confined in 1923 and where he had written *Mein Kampf*. On the day of Pohl's execution, Otto Ohlendorf was also hanged. He had been in charge of several Special Task Force killing squads in German-occupied Russia which had murdered 90,000 people, most of them Jews. In his defence he cited the historical precedence of the killing of Gypsies in the Thirty Years' War (1618–1648). Also executed by the Americans on June 8 was another Special Task Force commander, Wernher Braune. Following his execution the Bavarian welfare authorities gave him the status of 'war victim', thereby qualifying his widow for an automatic pension.

There was another execution on September 8, that of the commander of the SS troops who had suppressed the 1943 Warsaw Ghetto uprising, Jürgen Stroop. He was executed in Warsaw. The site chosen for his execution was amid the rubble of the former ghetto, which was in the process of being transformed into a series of housing estates. Before being extradited from Germany to Poland, Stroop had already been sentenced to death by an American military tribunal for shooting American pilots and hostages in Greece.

During 1951 the United Nations presented for the signature of individual States the International Genocide Convention which had been promulgated three years earlier. A petition signed by almost a hundred United States citizens, among them Paul Robeson, and handed in to the United Nations Secretariat in Paris, urged the United Nations to consider that White America was carrying out genocide against the Black population, and listed some twenty cases each year since 1945 when Blacks had been killed in circumstances claimed to be purely, and savagely, racial.

The Genocide Convention created an international framework for the outlawing of the destruction of 'national, religious, ethnic or racial groups'. Six years after the end of the mass murder of Jews, the concept of the deliberate destruction of a whole group of people because of their collective origins had been given international condemnation. The German Federal Republic accepted this, and announced its adherence to the Convention.

There was an echo of an even more distant past that year when, on November 11 – still celebrated as Armistice Day after thirty-three years and a Second World War – the French President, Vincent Auriol, unveiled a statue in the heart of Paris to Marshal Ferdinand Foch, the generalissimo of the main Allied armies – French, British and American – in the final struggle of the First World War. Since his death in 1929, Foch's body had lain in the chapel of Les Invalides, near the tomb of Napoleon.

*   *   *

The first fifty years of the Twentieth Century, so many of them years of war and years of turmoil, never lost their cruel fascination for those who had lived through them, or who recognized in them so many causes of later distress. The future also troubled many minds as the century advanced into its second half. One aspect of the future that gained in importance every year – decade after decade until the century's end – was the plight of refugees. From July 1947 until December 1951 the main burden of refugee resettlement had been undertaken as an emergency and temporary measure, at the request of the United Nations, by the International Refugee Organization (IRO). The IRO was equipped with its own fleet of forty ships, a staff of more than five thousand, and a yearly budget of between $100 and $150 million, with the United States contributing more than half the operating costs. The Soviet Union and its Eastern European satellites refused to participate in any way. 'This,' writes the IRO's historian, Tommie Sjöberg, 'contributed to making that organization the first truly effective international refugee organization.' His comment is a reminder of the wide repercussions the East-West divide was having, and the dissention Soviet participation was causing, even on good deeds. In the four-and-a-half years of its work, the IRO resettled a million refugees in sixty-five different countries. The five main countries of resettlement were the United States (329,000 refugees), Australia (182,000), Israel (132,000), Canada (123,000) and Britain (86,000).

To put the work of the International Refugee Organization on a permanent basis, in 1951 the United Nations High Commission for Refugees was set up. From the day of its establishment it was immediately responsible for almost two million refugees worldwide. Fifty years later it was to be responsible for the well-being of more than ten million refugees, all of whom had been displaced from their homes, some by war, others by civil war. In the ongoing discussion as to whom the century can be said to 'belong', there were many who call it the century of the refugee.

MAPS

Legend:
- European frontiers 1920-1937

Lake Ladoga

FINLAND
Viipuri
Helsinki
Leningrad
Hango
Tallinn
ESTONIA

NORWAY
Oslo
SWEDEN
Stockholm
Riga
LATVIA

Scapa Flow

North Sea
DENMARK
Baltic Sea
Memel
LITHUANIA
Kovno
Vilna
Danzig
EAST PRUSSIA

GREAT BRITAIN

The Hague
Rotterdam
Copenhagen
Lübeck
Stettin
Bielsk
Hamburg
Berlin
Warsaw
Poznan
RUHR
GERMANY
Breslau
Radom
POLAND
Cologne
Prague
Chropaczowa
Cracow
Lvov
LUXEMBOURG
CZECHOSLOVAKIA
RUTHENIA
London
English Channel
BELGIUM
Reims
Paris
SAAR
Nuremberg
Vary
Versailles
Melun
Strasbourg
MAGINOT LINE
Munich
Vienna
Budapest
Zurich
SWITZERLAND
AUSTRIA
HUNGARY
ROUMANIA
FRANCE
Geneva
Lyon
Evian
SOUTH TYROL
Riva
Trieste
Zagreb
Belgrade
Bucharest
Turin
Milan
Venice
BULGARIA
Marseille
Nice
Genoa
Rapallo
Florence
YUGOSLAVIA
Sofia
SPAIN
Barcelona
CORSICA
Rome
ITALY
Dubrovnik
Mlini
Skopje
THRACE
Foggia
Durazzo
ALBANIA
Bari
Tirana
Salonika
MAJORCA
MINORCA
Naples
Taranto
Brindisi
IBIZA
SARDINIA
GREECE
BALEARIC ISLANDS
CORFU
Aegean Sea
Mediterranean Sea
Adriatic Sea
SICILY
Reggio di Calabria
Athens
Piraeus
Tunis

0 kilometres 500
0 miles 250

© Martin Gilbert 1998

1. Europe, 1933–1937

2. Germany, 1933–1937

3. Central Europe, 1933–1937

SCOTLAND

NORTHUMBERLAND
Newcastle
Hebburn
Durham

Calder Hall
Windermere

Douglas
ISLE OF MAN

Irish Sea

Lancaster
Warton
Freckleton

Liverpool
Birkenhead
Huyton
MERSEYSIDE

Manchester

Sheffield

Criccieth

W A L E S

E N G L A N D

MIDLANDS
Birmingham
Coventry

SOUTH WALES
Swansea
Cardiff

Castlemartin

Gloucester

Bristol
Bath

Imber
Down

Bletchley
Stoke Mandeville
Brize
Norton
Oxford

Harwell
Aldermaston

Harlow

River Thames

Northolt
Uxbridge
London
Lewisham
Croydon
SURREY

Aldershot

Biggin Hill
Westerham

Southampton
Weymouth
Portland
Bill

Petworth

ISLE OF WIGHT

Dartmouth
Slapton
Sands

North
Sea

Fylingdales
Moor
Scarborough

York

Leeds

Hull

Norwich

EAST ANGLIA

Cambridge

Martlesham

Dovercourt
Harwich

Deptford
Greenwich
Orpington
Strood
Farnborough

Dover

Calais
Pas-de-
Calais

Boulogne

English Channel

© Martin Gilbert 1998

0   kilometres   100

0   miles   60

4. Britain

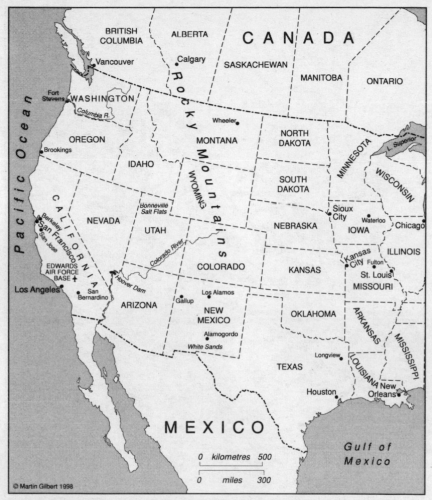

5. The western United States and Canada

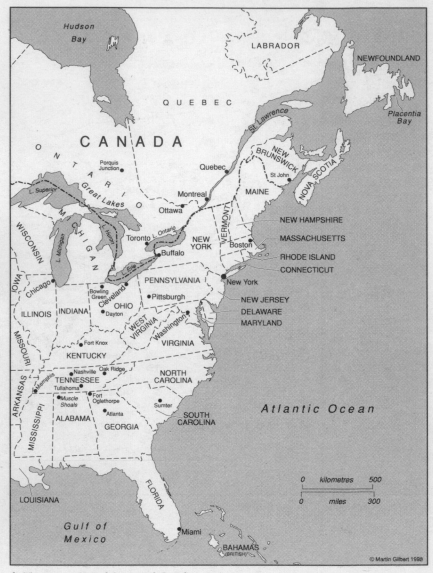

6. The eastern United States and Canada

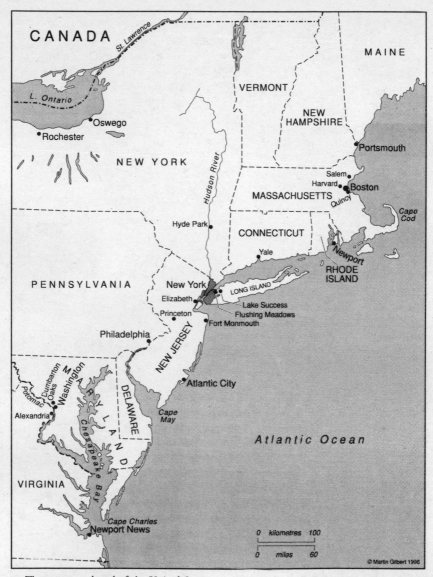

7. The eastern seaboard of the United States

Caribbean Sea

CURACAO
DUTCH

WEST INDIES

BARBADOS *BRITISH*

Atlantic Ocean

PANAMA

Caracas •

TRINIDAD *BRITISH*

VENEZUELA

GUIANA *BRITISH*
GUIANA *DUTCH*
GUIANA *FRENCH*

Panama
Canal

Bogota •

COLOMBIA

EQUADOR

Quito •

River Amazon

A M A Z O N I A

PERU

Pernambuco
(Recife) •

Lima •

B R A Z I L

Bahia •

BOLIVIA

La Paz •

Pacific
Ocean

PARAGUAY

GRAN
CHACO

C
H
I
L
E

Rio de Janeiro •

Sao Paulo •

JUAN
FERNANDEZ
CHILE

Valparaiso •

Cordoba •

Santiago •

Buenos Aires •

• Montevideo

URUGUAY

ARGENTINA

Puerto Saavedra •

PATAGONIA

South Atlantic Ocean

FALKLAND ISLANDS
BRITISH

0   kilometres   1000

TIERRA DEL
FUEGO

0   miles   500

Cape Horn

© Martin Gilbert 1998

8. South America

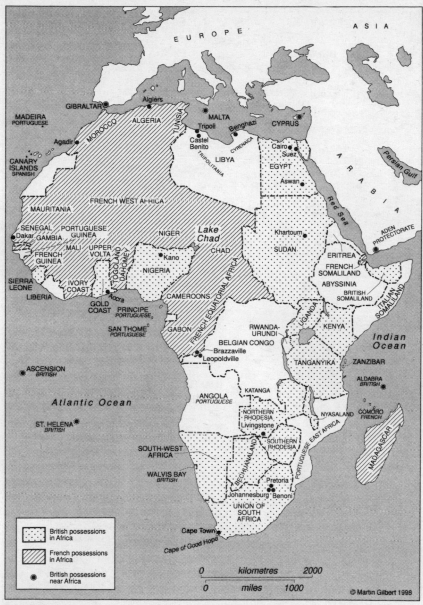

EUROPE   ASIA

GIBRALTAR
MADEIRA
PORTUGUESE   Algiers   MALTA
                MOROCCO   ALGERIA   TUNISIA   Benghazi   CYPRUS
    Agadir   Tripoli
CANARY   Castel   CYRENAICA   Cairo
ISLANDS   Benito   Suez
SPANISH   TRIPOLITANIA   LIBYA   EGYPT

                    FRENCH WEST AFRICA   Aswan

MAURITANIA

SENEGAL   PORTUGUESE   NIGER   Lake   Khartoum
Dakar GAMBIA GUINEA   Chad
        MALI UPPER   CHAD   SUDAN   ADEN
FRENCH   VOLTA   PROTECTORATE
GUINEA   TOGOLAND Kano   ERITREA
SIERRA   IVORY DAHOMEY NIGERIA   FRENCH
LEONE   COAST   SOMALILAND
LIBERIA GOLD Accra   CAMEROONS   ABYSSINIA
        COAST PRINCIPE   BRITISH
        SAN THOME PORTUGUESE   SOMALILAND
        PORTUGUESE   GABON   FRENCH EQUATORIAL AFRICA
                                                UGANDA KENYA
                        RWANDA-
                        URUNDI
ASCENSION   BELGIAN CONGO   Indian
BRITISH   Brazzaville   Ocean
            Leopoldville   TANGANYIKA ZANZIBAR
Atlantic Ocean   KATANGA   ALDABRA
                                              BRITISH
ST. HELENA   ANGOLA   COMORO
BRITISH   PORTUGUESE NORTHERN NYASALAND FRENCH
                          RHODESIA
                          Livingstone
SOUTH-WEST   SOUTHERN
AFRICA   RHODESIA
                  BECHUANALAND
WALVIS BAY
BRITISH   Pretoria
                  Johannesburg Benoni
                  UNION OF
                  SOUTH
                  AFRICA
            Cape Town
        Cape of Good Hope

Legend:
::::: British possessions in Africa
//// French possessions in Africa
• British possessions near Africa

0   kilometres   2000
0   miles   1000

© Martin Gilbert 1998

9. Africa, 1933–1960

SOVIET UNION

VOLGA
GERMAN
REUBLIC

UKRAINE

ROUMANIA

Odessa

River Volga

Sofia
BULGARIA

River Don

SOVIET

Caspian-Black Sea
Canal

KAZAKHSTAN

Sebastopol

Black Sea

Istanbul
(Constantinople)

GREECE

Athens

Aegean

Izmir

Sochi

CENTRAL

Mineralniye
Vody

ANATOLIA

Ankara

ABKHAZIA

CHECHNYA

Batum

GEORGIA

Caucasus

Caspian Sea

ASIA

CRETE

RHODES

TURKEY

Erzincan

Tbilisi

AZERBAIJAN
SOVIET REPUBLIC

Baku

CYPRUS

Iskenderun

ARMENIA

KURDISTAN

TURKESTAN

Mediterranean Sea

Latakia

LEBANON

SYRIA

AZERBAIJAN
IRAN

Alexandria

Acre
Haifa

Cairo

PALESTINE

JORDAN

H3

Baghdad

Teheran

Meshed

Habbaniya

Sinai

EGYPT

IRAQ

Basra

IRAN
(PERSIA)

KUWAIT

AFGHANISTAN

HEDJAZ

SAUDI

DAHRAN

BAHRAIN

Persian Gulf

Medina

Red Sea

Riyadh

QATAR

BRITISH
INDIA

SUDAN

Mecca

ARABIA

Khartoum

Keren

Massawa

ERITREA

Adowa

YEMEN

San'a

OMAN

Ogaden Desert

Gondar

TIGRE

ADEN
PROTECTORATE

Arabian

Sea

DJIBOUTI

Aden

Addis Ababa

Djibouti

Gulf of Aden

ETHIOPIA

BRITISH
SOMALILAND

ITALIAN
SOMALILAND

SOKOTRA
BRITISH

0   kilometres   400

0   miles   250

© Martin Gilbert 1998

10. The Middle East and Ethiopia

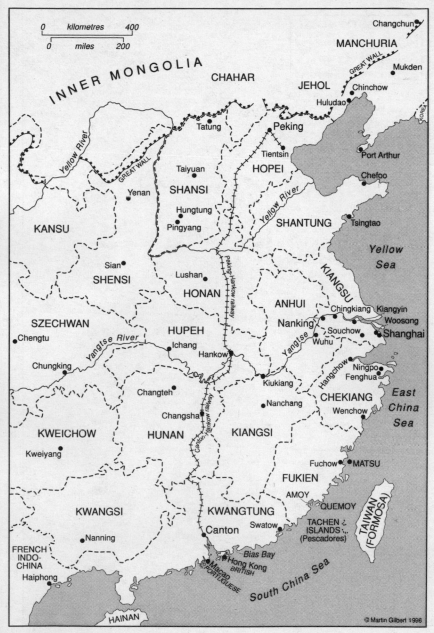

11. China

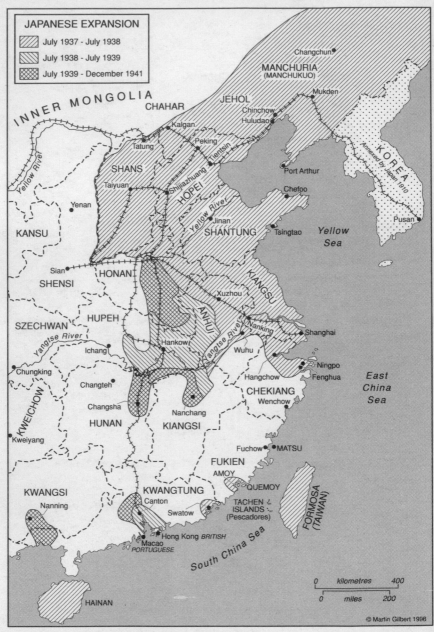

JAPANESE EXPANSION

- July 1937 – July 1938
- July 1938 – July 1939
- July 1939 – December 1941

INNER MONGOLIA

CHAHAR

JEHOL

MANCHURIA
(MANCHUKUO)

Changchun

Mukden

Chinchow
Huludao

Kalgan

Peking

Tientsin

Tatung

Port Arthur

KOREA
Annexed by Japan 1910

SHANS

Taiyuan

Shijiazhuang

HOPEI

Chefoo

Yenan

Yellow River

Jinan

SHANTUNG

Tsingtao

Yellow
Sea

Pusan

KANSU

Sian

HONAN

KIANGSU

SHENSI

Xuzhou

SZECHWAN

HUPEH

ANHUI

Nanking

Shanghai

Yangtse River

Ichang

Hankow

Yangtse River

Wuhu

Ningpo
Fenghua

Chungking

Changteh

Hangchow

East
China
Sea

KWEICHOW

Changsha

Nanchang

CHEKIANG

Wenchow

Kweiyang

HUNAN

KIANGSI

Fuchow

MATSU

FUKIEN

KWANGSI

AMOY

QUEMOY

Nanning

KWANGTUNG

Canton

Swatow

TACHEN
ISLANDS
(Pescadores)

FORMOSA
(TAIWAN)

Hong Kong BRITISH

Macao
PORTUGUESE

South China Sea

HAINAN

| 0 | kilometres | 400 |
| 0 | miles | 200 |

© Martin Gilbert 1996

12. The Japanese advance through China, 1937–1941

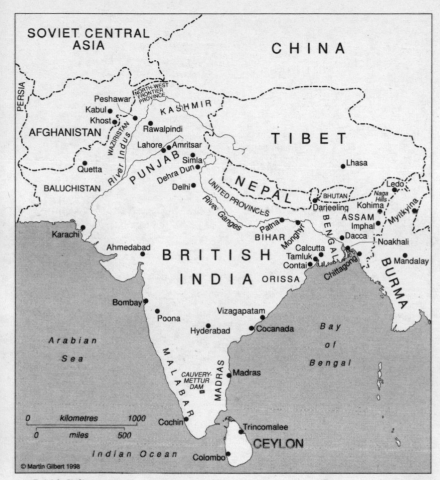

13. British India

Map 1: Spain

- Bay of Biscay
- FRANCE
- Pyrenees
- San Esteban
- Gijon
- Santander
- Guernica
- La Coruna
- Grado
- Oviedo
- Bilbao
- BASQUE REGION
- Durango
- GALICIA
- ASTURIAS
- Pamplona
- NAVARRA
- Tremp
- Cape Finisterre
- Vigo
- Leon
- Burgos
- Saragossa
- River Ebro
- Camarasa
- Balaguer
- CATALONIA
- Barcelona
- Vallvidrerea
- Oporto
- Salamanca
- ARAGON
- Brihuega
- Jarama River
- Tarragona
- P O R T U G A L
- Madrid
- Vinaroz
- Teruel
- River Tagus
- Toledo
- Castellon
- MAJORCA
- Sagunto
- Lisbon
- ESTREMADURA
- Valencia
- BALEARIC ISLANDS
- IBIZA
- Almaden
- FORMENTERA
- Merida
- S P A I N
- Alicante
- Cordoba
- Cartagena
- Huelva
- Seville
- Granada
- Mediterranean Sea
- Cape St. Vincent
- Malaga
- Almeria
- Cadiz
- GIBRALTAR BRITISH
- Atlantic Ocean
- Tangier FREE ZONE
- Ceuta SPANISH
- Tetuan
- Melilla SPANISH
- SPANISH MOROCCO
- © Martin Gilbert 1998
- 0 kilometres 100
- 0 miles 160

14. Spain

- Atlantic Ocean
- SPAIN
- Cadiz
- GIBRALTAR BRITISH
- Tangier
- Mers-el-Kebir
- Oran
- Zeralda
- Chenoua
- Algiers
- Philippeville
- Bizerta
- Cape Bon
- SPANISH MOROCCO
- Orléansville
- Constantine
- Tunis
- Sakiet Sidi Youssef
- Casablanca
- Meknes
- Fez
- Taza
- MOROCCO
- ALGERIA
- TUNISIA
- Oued Zem
- Marrakech
- Atlas Mountains
- Sahara Desert
- Agadir
- Anti-Atlas
- LIBYA
- © Martin Gilbert 1998
- 0 kilometres 400
- 0 miles 200

15. French North Africa

16. Austria, 1933–1937

Map 17 labels

SAXONY

Lignite: fuel basis of Czech railways and domestic heating
Sugar beet

Chemical Works

Breslau

GERMANY

SILESIA

POLAND

Hops for Pilsen breweries

Copper mines

A

Brux

Aussig

Main railway line broken

Textiles

Coal

Rail link to Poland broken

Trinec Steel Works (to Poland)
Korvinna coal basin (half to Poland)

Saaz

Karlovy Vary (Karlsbad)

Prague

BOHEMIA

Teschen

Plzen (Pilsen): Skoda arms works kept by Czechoslovakia

MORAVIA

Klatovy (Klattau)

Railway traffic broken

Brno

SLOVAKIA

Graphite

Machine tools

Frontier fortifications essential for Czech defence

River Danube

Bratislava

Vienna

A = Aš(Asch)
C = Cheb (Eger)

GERMANY
AUSTRIA

Slovakian iron ore (to Hungary)
Slovakian sugar beet (to Hungary)

Budapest

HUNGARY

—— The borders of Czechoslovakia, 1918 1938

Czech territory ceded to Germany at Munich, 30 September 1938

Czech territory given to Hungary by Germany and Italy at Vienna 2 October 1938

Czech territory siezed by Poland in September 1938 and formally annexed on 1 November 1938

Percentage of Czech industrial output lost:
Lignite   93
Coal mines   55
Electrical energy 46

0 kilometres 35
0 miles 25

© Martin Gilbert 1998

17. Czechoslovakia partitioned, September–November 1938

18. The conquest and partition of Poland, September–October, 1939

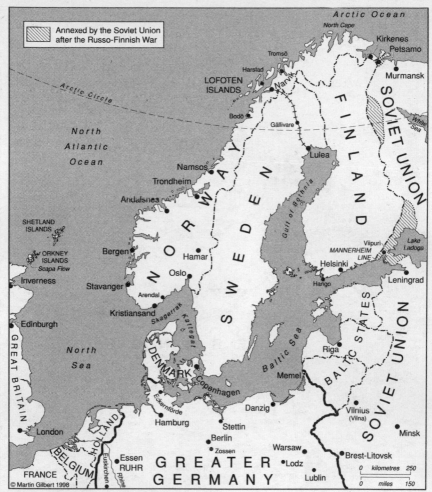

19. Scandinavia and the Baltic, April–May 1940

20. The German invasion of Belgium, Holland, Luxembourg and France, May–June 1940

21. Europe, 1940–41

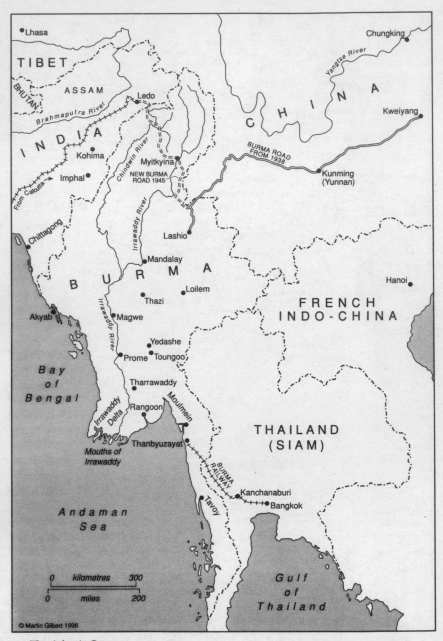

Lhasa

Chungking

TIBET

BHUTAN

ASSAM

Ledo

CHINA

Yangtse River

Brahmaputra River

INDIA

Kohima

Chindwin River

Myitkyina

NEW BURMA
ROAD 1945

BURMA ROAD
FROM 1938

Kweiyang

From Calcutta

Imphal

Lashio

Kunming
(Yunnan)

Chittagong

B   U   R   M   A

Irrawaddy River

Mandalay

Loilem

Hanoi

Akyab

Magwe

Thazi

FRENCH
INDO-CHINA

Irrawaddy River

Yedashe

Prome   Toungoo

Bay
of
Bengal

Tharrawaddy

Irrawaddy
Delta

Rangoon

Moulmein

THAILAND
(SIAM)

Thanbyuzayat

*Mouths of
Irrawaddy*

Andaman
Sea

BURMA
RAILWAY

Kanchanaburi

Tavoy

Bangkok

0   kilometres   300

0   miles   200

Gulf
of
Thailand

© Martin Gilbert 1998

22. **The Atlantic Ocean**

23. The Balkans, April–June 1941

24. Hitler's plan, 11 June 1941

SWEDEN
FINLAND
Gulf of Finland
Lake Ladoga
Lake Onega
Tallinn
ESTONIA
Gatchina
Leningrad
Kingisepp
Mga
Chudovo
Luga
Lake Peipus
Luga
Baltic Sea
Lake Ilmen
Riga
LATVIA
Pskov
Kalinin
LITHUANIA
Nevel
Rzhev
Danzig
Tilsit
Kedainiai
Polotsk
Moscow
Rastenburg
Kaunas
(Kovno)
Vilna
Vitebsk
Vyazma
Marienwerder
Ponar
Smolensk
Venev
GREATER
Marcinkance
River Dnieper
BALTIC REGION
WHITE
Minsk
Maly
Trostenets
Yelnya
1 September 1941
Bialystok
RUSSIA
Nieswiez
GERMANY
Baranovichi
Bryansk
Brest-
Litovsk
Bobruisk
Lublin
River Vistula
River Bug
Lutsk
Hitler and Mussolini's journey 28 August 1941
Lvov
Zhitomir
Kiev
Kharkov
SLOVAKIA
EASTERN GALICIA
Drohobycz
Proskurov
Berdichev
1 September 1941
Buczacz
BUKOVINA
Kamenets-
Podolsk
Kremenchug
DONETZ
River Donetz
BASIN
H U N G A R Y
Uman
Dnepropetrovsk
Jassy
BESSARABIA
Kishinev
Krivoi Rog
Zaporozhe
Nikolayev
River Dnieper
Mariupol
Kherson
Odessa
Sea of
Azov
R O U M A N I A
Kerch
0   kilometres 150
Black
Sea
CRIMEA
0   miles   100
© Martin Gilbert 1998
Sevastopol

25. The German invasion of the Soviet Union, June–September 1941

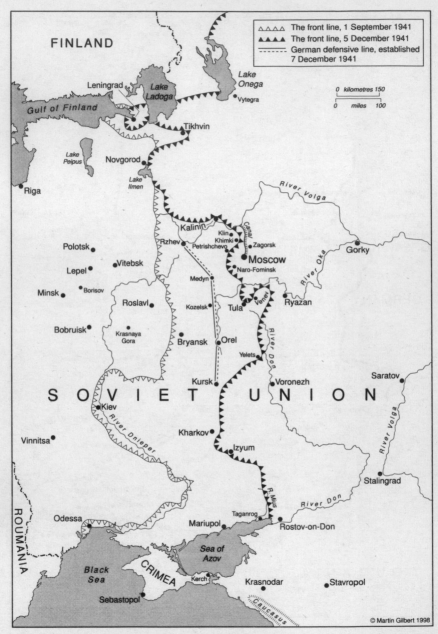

26. The war in the Soviet Union, September–December 1941

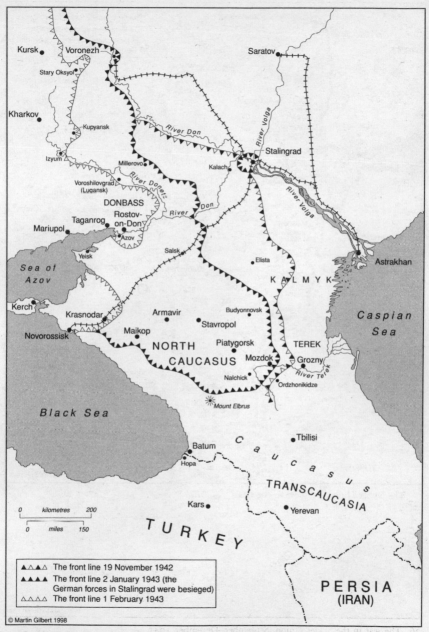

27. Southern Russia and the Caucasus, November 1942–February 1943

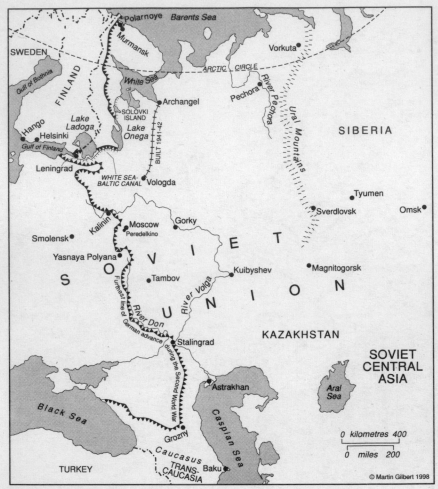

28. The Soviet Union: Moscow to the Urals

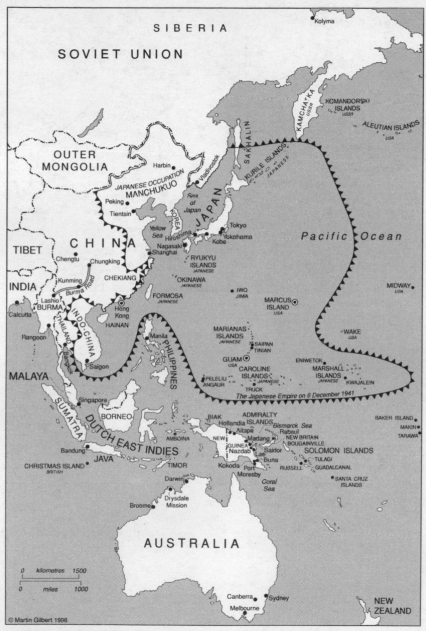

The Japanese Empire on 6 December 1941

29. The Japanese Empire on 6 December 1941

© Martin Gilbert 1996

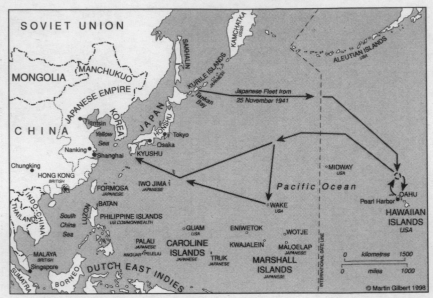

30. Pearl Harbor and the war in the Pacific

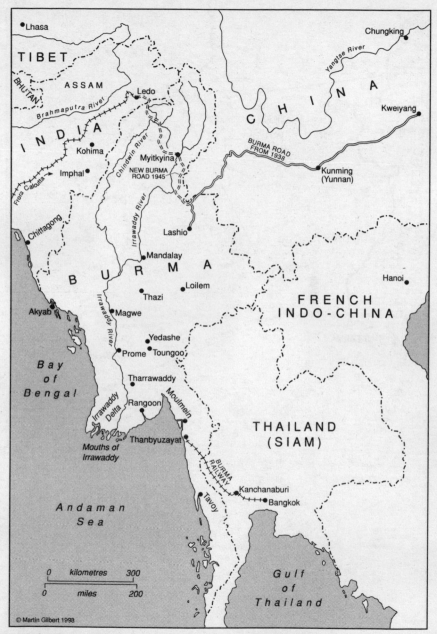

31. India, Burma, Thailand, the Burma Road and the Burma Railway

Baltic Sea

EAST
Rastenburg
PRUSSIA

Nevel

Rzhev

Vitebsk

Moscow

Smolensk

Grodno

Minsk

Orsha

Yelnya

Bialystok

WHITE
RUSSIA

Mogilev

Roslavl

5 July 1943

14 September 1943

Bryansk

Orel

GREATER

Klintsy

Prokhorovka

RUSSO-POLISH BORDER, 1921-1939

Gomel

GERMANY

Chernigov

Kursk

Voronezh

VOLHYNIA

Konotop

'Panther Line' Defence,

Zhitomir

Kiev

Sumy

Belgorod

River Dnieper

Kharkov

EASTERN
GALICIA

5 July 1943

Vinnitsa

Poltava

13 March 1943

Kremenchug

BUKOVINA

RUTHENIA

Dnepropetrovsk

HUNGARY

BESSARABIA

Krivoi Rog

Zaporozhe

Taganrog

Odessa

Melitopol

ROUMANIA

Sea of
Azov

CRIMEA

0   kilometres   150

0   miles   200

Black Sea

→ Hitler's journey by air, 13 March 1943

▲▲▲▲ The front line on 5 July 1943

.... Russo-Polish border, 1921-1939

© Martin Gilbert 1998

32. The Eastern Front, 1943

33. The Eastern Front, December 1943–January 1944

34. Allied deception plans, January–June 1944

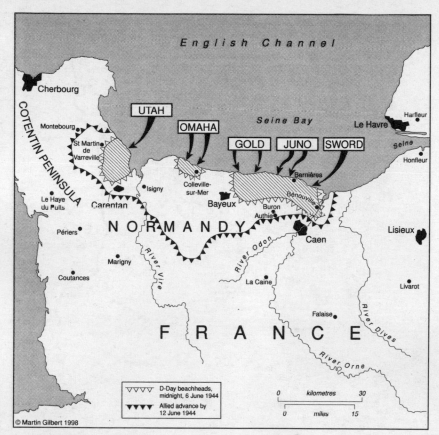

35. The Normandy landings, June 1944

The front line 13 August 1944
The front line 26 August 1944
The front line 3 September 1944

North Sea

GREAT BRITAIN

Westerbork

Bletchley

Amsterdam

London

The Hague

HOLLAND

WALCHEREN

River Rhine

RUHR

Gelsenkirchen

Westerham

Dunkirk

Antwerp

Zelzate

Cologne

Calais

BELGIUM

Roetgen

Bad Nauheim

Boulogne

Watten

Brussels

Slapton Sands

English Channel

Dieppe

Ascq

River Meuse

GREATER

Cherbourg

Arras

Cambrai

Sedan

GERMANY

Somme

Le Havre

Amiens

Honfleur

Rouen

Beauvais

Marival

Luxembourg

COTENTIN

Caen

Soissons

Reims

Verdun

Metz

Coutances

Lisieux

La Roche Guyon

Falaise

Nucourt

Strasbourg

Seine

Paris

Nancy

St. Malo

Trappes

Mar-ly-le-Roi

Natzweiler

Rennes

Le Mans

Etampes

Sens

Colombier

Lorient

Orléans

Seine

Belfort

German Defence Line 18 August 1944

Dijon

Colmar

Nantes

Saumur

Tours

SWITZERLAND

River Loire

Poitiers

Saint-Amand

La Rochelle

River Rhône

Bay of Biscay

Oradour-sur-Glane

Limoges

Annecy

AUVERGNE

Tulle

Lyon

Izieux

Voiron

Bordeaux

RHONE VALLEY

Grenoble

Rhône

PROVENCE

Toulouse

Avignon

Cannes

Bagnères de Bigorre

Marseille

Toulon

SPAIN

Pyrenees

Mediterranean Sea

0 kilometres 150
0 miles 100

© Martin Gilbert 1998

36. The liberation of France, June–September 1944

37. The Western and Italian Fronts, October–November 1944

38. The Eastern, Italian and Balkan Fronts, June–December 1944

North
Sea

DENMARK

SWEDEN

Copenhagen

BORNHOLM

Baltic Sea

HELIGOLAND

Flensburg

Kiel

Rostock

Kolberg

POMERANIA

Lübeck

Stettin

Hamburg

Neuengamme

Bremen

Lüneberg
Heath

River Elbe

Ravensbrück

Poznan

Allied advance by 19 April 1945

Belsen

Sachsenhausen
Oranienburg

Gatow

Berlin

Kienitz

Potsdam

Frankfurt-on-Oder

Harz Mountains

Magdeburg

Treuenbrietzen

Eggersdorf
Zossen

Duisburg

RUHR

Schlieben
Stehla
Leckwitz

River Oder

Düsseldorf

Nordhausen

Torgau

Colditz

Leipzig

Görlitz

Bonn

Eisenach

Buchenwald

Breslau

Remagen

Merkers

Ohrdruf

Weimar

Dresden

Western Neisse

Russian forces 19 April 1945

River Rhine

THURINGIA

SUDETENLAND

Wittlich

19 April 1945

Theresienstadt

River Elbe

Bayreuth

Plzen
(Pilsen)

Prague

Olomouc

Nuremberg

Flossenburg

BOHEMIA

Brno

MORAVIA

Pforzheim

BAVARIA

Stuttgart

WURTTEMBERG

River Danube

Von Greim's
journey

Webling

River Danube

Bratislava

SLOVAKIA

Dachau

Linz

Vienna

Munich

River Inn

AUSTRIA

Zurich

Salzburg

Berchtesgaden

STYRIA

River Enns

Innsbruck

SWITZERLAND

TYROL

Graz

HUNGARY

CARINTHIA

Nagykanizsa

SOUTH
TYROL

River Adige

Maribor

Dongo

SLOVENIA

YUGOSLAVIA

VENEZIA GIULIA

0   kilometres   100

Gorizia

0   miles   75

Trieste

Milan

ITALY

Adriatic
Sea

© Martin Gilbert 1998

39. The defeat of Germany, January–May 1945

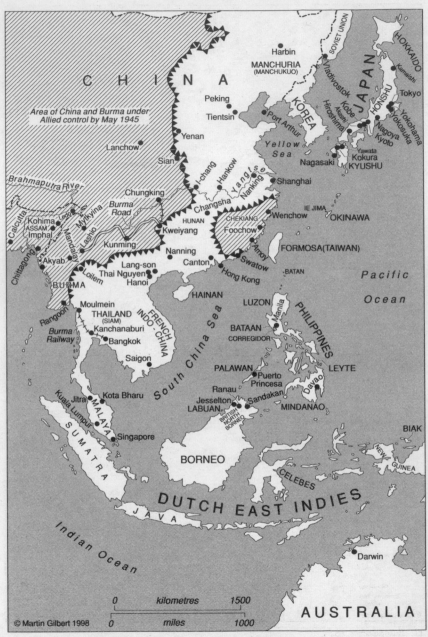

40. The defeat of Japan, May–August 1945

41. Europe after 1945

42. French Indo–China

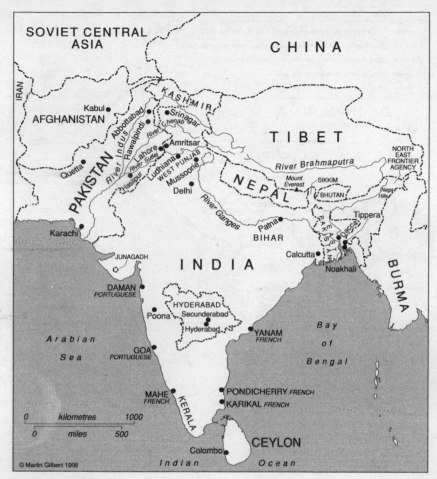

SOVIET CENTRAL
ASIA

CHINA

IRAN

AFGHANISTAN
Kabul

Abbottabad
Rawalpindi
Srinagar

KASHMIR
River Chenab

River Indus

Quetta

PAKISTAN

Hasilpur
River Sutlej
Lahore
Amritsar
Ludhiana
WEST PUNJAB
Mussoorie

Delhi

TIBET

River Brahmaputra

NORTH
EAST
FRONTIER
AGENCY

Mount
Everest

NEPAL

SIKKIM

BHUTAN

Naga
Hills

Karachi

River Ganges

JUNAGADH

INDIA

Patna
BIHAR

Calcutta

Tippera
Dacca

PAKISTAN

Noakhali

BURMA

DAMAN
PORTUGUESE

Poona

HYDERABAD

Secunderabad

Hyderabad

Bay

of

Bengal

Arabian

Sea

GOA
PORTUGUESE

YANAM
FRENCH

MAHE
FRENCH

KERALA

PONDICHERRY FRENCH

KARIKAL FRENCH

0   kilometres   1000

0   miles   500

Colombo

CEYLON

© Martin Gilbert 1998

Indian   Ocean

43. India and Pakistan

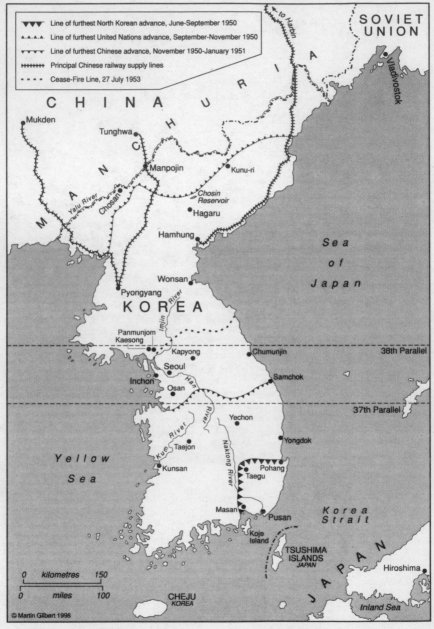

Legend

Symbol	Description
▼▼▼	Line of furthest North Korean advance, June-September 1950
▲▲▲	Line of furthest United Nations advance, September-November 1950
▼▼▼	Line of furthest Chinese advance, November 1950-January 1951
++++++	Principal Chinese railway supply lines
- - - -	Cease-Fire Line, 27 July 1953

SOVIET
UNION

to Harbin

Vladivostok

C H I N A

M A N C H U R I A

Mukden

Tunghwa

Manpojin

Kunu-ri

Yalu River

Chosan

Chosin
Reservoir

Hagaru

Sea

of

Japan

Hamhung

Wonsan

Pyongyang

K O R E A

Imjin River

Panmunjom
Kaesong

Kapyong

Chumunjin

38th Parallel

Seoul

Inchon

Han River

Osan

Samchok

37th Parallel

Yechon

Yongdok

Kum River

Taejon

Naktong River

Kunsan

Pohang

Yellow

Sea

Taegu

Masan

Pusan

Korea
Strait

Koje
Island

TSUSHIMA
ISLANDS
JAPAN

Hiroshima

J A P A N

| 0 | kilometres | 150 |
| 0 | miles | 100 |

© Martin Gilbert 1998

CHEJU
KOREA

Inland Sea

44. The Korean war, 1950-53

BIBLIOGRAPHY OF BOOKS CONSULTED

Reference books and documents:

Herbert Aptheker, *A Documentary History of the Negro People in the United States*, volumes five (1945–1951) and six (1951–1959), Citadel Press, New York, 1993.

Marcel Baudot (and others), *The Historical Encyclopedia of World War II*, Facts on File, New York, 1980.

Margaret Carlyle (editor), *Documents on International Affairs, 1939–1946: Volume II, Hitler's Europe*, Oxford University Press, London, 1954.

Henry Steele Commager (editor), *Documents of American History since 1898*, Appelton-Century-Crofts, 7th edition, New York, 1963.

Cook's Continental Time-table, Steamship and Air Services Guide, London, Thomas Cook and Son, August 1939.

R.E.G. Davies, *A History of the World's Airlines*, Oxford University Press, London, 1964.

I.C.B. Dear (general editor), *The Oxford Companion to the Second World War*, Oxford University Press, Oxford, 1995.

Lucjan Dobroszycki (editor), *The Chronicle of the Lodz Ghetto, 1941–1944*, Yale University Press, New Haven, Connecticut, 1984.

M. Epstein, and others (editors), *The Annual Register, A Review of Public Events at Home and Abroad*, Longmans, Green, London, 1934–1966.

Richard Fuller (editor), *Shokan: Hirohito's Samurai*, Arms and Armour, London, 1991.

George C. Kohn (editor), *Encyclopedia of Plague and Pestilence*, Facts on File, New York, 1995.

Paul Johnson, *A History of the Modern World: From 1917 to the 1980s*, Weidenfeld and Nicolson, London, 1983.

Harold Josephson (editor-in-chief), *Biographical Dictionary of Modern Peace Leaders*, Greenwood Press, Westport, Connecticut, 1985.

Geoffrey Nowell-Smith (editor), *The Oxford History of World Cinema*, Oxford University Press, Oxford, 1996.

William Outhwaite and Tom Bottomore, *The Blackwell Dictionary of Twentieth Century Social Thought*, Blackwell, Oxford, 1993.

Alan Palmer, *Dictionary of the British Empire and Commonwealth*, John Murray, London, 1996.

Alan Palmer, *Who's Who in World Politics From 1860 to the Present Day*, Routledge, London, 1996.

Winston G. Ramsey (editor), *The Blitz Then and Now*, three volumes, Battle of Britain Prints International, London, 1990.

Philip Rees, *Biographical Dictionary of the Extreme Right since 1890*, Simon and Schuster, New York, 1990.

Cesare Salmaggi and Alfredo Pallavisini (editors), *2194 Days of War: An Illustrated chronology of the Second World War*, Windward, London, 1979.

T.R. Sareen (editor), *Select Documents on Indian National Army*, Agam Prakashan, Delhi, 1988.

Thomas Schieder (editor), *The Expulsion of the German Population from Czechoslovakia*, Federal Ministry for Expellees, Refugees and War Victims, Bonn, 1960.

Horatio Smith (General Editor), *A Dictionary of Modern European Literature*, Oxford University Press, London, 1947.

Louis L. Snyder, *Encyclopedia of the Third Reich*, Robert Hale, London, 1976.

H.R. Trevor-Roper, *Hitler's War Directives, 1939-1945*, Sidgwick and Jackson, London, 1964.

Philip Waller (editor), *Chronology of the 20th Century*, Helicon, Oxford, 1995.

Robert Wistrich, *Who's Who in Nazi Germany*, Weidenfeld and Nicolson, London, 1982.

Contemporary Works (in chronological order of publication):

Edgar Ansel Mowrer, *Germany Puts The Clock Back*, John Lane, The Bodley Head, London, 1933.

Heil! A Picture Book, Compiled from Authentic Material, John Lane, The Bodley Head, London, 1934.

J.A. Spender, *These Times*, Cassell, London, 1934.

Arnold J. Toynbee, *Survey of International Affairs, 1933*, Oxford University Press, London, 1934.

B.T. Reynolds, *The Saar and the Franco-German Problem*, Edward Arnold, London, 1934.

Stefan Lorant, *I was Hitler's Prisoner: Leaves from a Prison Diary*, Victor Gollancz, London, 1935.

Sidney and Beatrice Webb, *Soviet Communism: A New Civilisation?*, two volumes, Longmans Green, 1935.

Alan Campbell Johnson, *Peace Offering*, Methuen, London, 1936.

Lieutenant-Commander Tota Ishimaru, *Japan Must Fight Britain*, Hurst and Blackett, London, 1936.

H.A.L. Fisher, *A History of Europe*, Edward Arnold, London, 1936.

John Gunther, *Inside Europe*, Hamish Hamilton, London, 1936.

Allen W. Dulles and Hamilton Fish Armstrong, *Can We Be Neutral?*, Harper and Brothers, New York, 1936.

Martha Gellhorn, *The Trouble I've Seen*, Putnam, London, 1936.

André Gide, *Back from the USSR*, Secker and Warburg, London, 1937.

Francis W. Hirst, *Armaments: The Race and the Crisis*, Cobden-Sanderson, London, 1937.

George Steer, 'Guernica', *London Mercury*, volume XXXVI, May-October 1937, London, 1937.

G. Ward Price, *I Know These Dictators*, George G. Harrap, London, October 1937.

Stephen Roberts, *The House that Hitler Built*, Methuen, London, 1937.

F.A. Voigt, *Unto Caesar*, Constable, London, 1938.

Genevieve Tabouis, *Blackmail or War*, Penguin, London, 1938.

Oswald Dutch, *Thus Died Austria*, Edward Arnold, London, 1938.

Eugene Lennhoff, *The Last Five Hours of Austria*, Rich and Cowan, London, 1938.

Harold John Timperley, *Japanese Terror in China*, Modern Age Books, New York, 1938.

George Orwell, *Homage to Catalonia*, Secker and Warburg, London, 1938.

S. Grant Duff, *Europe and the Czechs*, Penguin, London, 1938.

Charles W. Domvile-Fife, *This is Germany*, Seeley Service, London, 1938.

Thomas Mann, *The Coming Victory of Democracy*, Secker and Warburg, London, 1938.

G.E.R. Gedye, *Fallen Bastions, The Central European Tragedy*, Victor Gollancz, London, 1939.

Martha Dodd, *My Years in Germany*, Victor Gollancz, London, 1939.

Louis Macneice, *Autumn Journal* (poems), Faber and Faber, London, 1939.

Francis Yeats-Brown, *European Jungle*, Eyre and Spottiswoode, London, 1939.

Hermann Rauschning, *Germany's Revolution of Destruction*, William Heinemann, London, 1939.

Norman Angell, *Must It Be War?*, Labour Book Service, London, 1939.

E.M. Forster, *Two Cheers for Democracy*, Harcourt, Brace and World, New York, 1939.

John Steinbeck, *The Grapes of Wrath*, William Heinemann, London, 1939.

J. Gunnar Andersson, *China Fights for the World*, Kegan Paul, Trench, Trubner, London, 1939.

Documents Concerning German-Polish Relations and the Outbreak of Hostilities between Great Britain and Germany on September 3, 1939, His Majesty's Stationery Office, London, 1939.

H.G. Wells, *The Common Sense of War and Peace: World Revolution or War Unending*, Penguin, London, 1940.

John F. Kennedy, *Why England Slept*, Wilfred Funk, New York, 1940.

M. Polanyi, *The Contempt of Freedom: The Russian Experiment and After*, Watts, London, 1940.

T.R. Fyvel, *The Malady and the Vision, An Analysis of Political Faith*, Secker and Warburg, London, 1940.

E.H. Gombrich and E. Kris, *Caricature*, Penguin, London, 1940.

Carl J. Hambro, *I Saw It Happen in Norway*, Hodder and Stoughton, London, 1940.

Walter Tschuppik, *The Quislings, Hitler's Trojan Horses*, Hutchinson, London, 1940.

Alexander Werth, *The Last Days of Paris: A Journalist's Diary*, Hamish Hamilton, London, 1940.

Lothrop Stoddard, *Into the Darkness: Nazi Germany Today*, Duell, Sloan and Peace, New York, 1940.

F.B. Czarnomski, *They Fight for Poland, The War in the First Person*, George Allen and Unwin, London,1941.

Arthur Koestler, *Darkness at Noon*, Macmillan, London, 1941.

Harold Butler, *The Lost Peace, A Personal Impression*, Faber and Faber, London, 1941.

Alexander Werth, *Moscow '41*, Hamish Hamilton, London, 1942.

The Persecution of the Catholic Church in the Third Reich, Facts and Documents Translated from the German, Catholic Book Club, London, 1942.

R. Coupland, *The Cripps Mission*, Oxford University Press, London, 1942.

Roy Fuller, *The Middle of a War* (poems), Hogarth Press, London, 1942.

Leon Blum Before his Judges, At the Supreme Court of Riom, March 11th and 12th, 1942, The Labour Party, London, 1943.

Tosha Bialer,' Behind the Wall (Life – and death – in Warsaw's Ghetto)', *Collier's*, New York, 20 and 27 February 1943.

George Rodger, *Red Moon Rising*, Cresset Press, London, 1943.

Edward R. Stettinius Jr., *Lend-Lease, Weapon for Victory*, Macmillan, New York, 1944.

Arieh Tartakower and Kurt R. Grossman, *The Jewish Refugee*, Institute of Jewish Affairs, New York, 1944.

A.G. Russell, *Colour, Race and Empire*, Victor Gollancz, London, 1944.

Penderel Moon, *Strangers in India*, Faber and Faber, London, 1944.

Edgar Snow, *People On Our Side*, Random House, New York, 1944.

Reginald Coupland, *India, A Re-Statement*, Oxford University Press, London, 1945.

Bill Mauldin, *Up Front* (text and pictures), World Publishing Company, Cleveland, Ohio, 1945.

A.P. Herbert, *Light the Lights* (poems), Methuen, London, 1945.

Padre J.N. Duckworth, *Japanese Holiday* (broadcast), 12 September 1945 (Kwai Railway Memorial, Three Pagodas Group, 1997: bruce@computer4u.com)

John Hersey, 'Hiroshima', *New Yorker*, 31 August 1946 (published later that year in book form by Alfred Knopf, New York).

Zorach Warhaftig, *Uprooted: Jewish Refugees and Displaced Persons After Liberation*, Insititute of Jewish Affairs, New York, November 1946.

Emery Reves, *The Anatomy of Peace*, George Allen and Unwin, London, 1946.

Harold J. Laski, *The Secret Battalion: An Examination of the Communist Attitude to the Labour Party*, Labour Publications Department, London, 1946.

R.W. Cooper, *The Nuremberg Trial*, Penguin, London, 1947.

Treaties of Peace with Italy, Roumania, Bulgaria, Hungary and Finland, His Majesty's Stationery Office, London, 1947.

Victor Kravchenko, *I Chose Freedom, The Personal and Political Life of A Soviet Official*, Robert Hale, London, 1947.

John Jewkes, *Ordeal By Planning*, Macmillan, London, 1948.

David J. Dallin and Boris I. Nicolaevsky, *Forced Labor in Soviet Russia*, Yale University Press, New Haven, Connecticut, 1947.

Alan Paton, *Cry, the Beloved Country: A Story of Comfort in Desolation*, Scribner, New York, 1948.

George Orwell, *Nineteen Eighty Four*, Secker and Warburg, London, 1949.

Richard Crossman (editor), *The God That Failed*, Harper and Brothers, New York, 1950.

Fritz Sternberg, *Capitalism and Socialism on Trial*, Victor Gollancz, London, 1951.

Letters, Diaries, Speeches and Dispatches:

Eberhard Bethge, *Dietrich Bonhoeffer, Letters and Papers from Prison* (third edition, revised and enlarged), SCM Press, London, 1967.

Alan Campbell-Johnson, *Mission with Mountbatten*, E.P. Dutton, New York, 1953.

William E. Dodd and Martha Dodd (editors), *Ambassador Dodd's Diary, 1933–1938*, Victor Gollancz, London, 1941.

Hugh Dormer's Diaries, Jonathan Cape, London Cape, London, 1947.

Etty: A Diary 1941–43, Jonathan Cape, London, 1983.

Bernard B. Fall (editor), *Ho Chi Minh on Revolution, Selected Writings, 1920–66*, Frederick A. Praeger, New York, 1967.

Robert H. Ferrell, *The Eisenhower Diaries*, W.W. Norton, New York, 1981.

Generalissimo Chiang Kai-shek, *Resistance and Reconstruction: Messages During China's Six Years of War, 1937–1943*, Harper and Brothers, New York, 1943.

Olda Kokoshka and Alfred Marnau (editors), *Oscar Kokoshka Letters, 1905–1976*, Thames and Hudson, London, 1992.

Julian Eugeniusz Kulski, *Dying, We Live: The Personal Chronicle of a Young Freedom Fighter in Warsaw (1939–1945)*, Holt, Rinehart and Winston, New York, 1979.

Hubert G. Locke, *Exile in the Fatherland, Martin Niemöller's Letters from Moabit Prison*, William B. Eerdmans Publishing Company, Grand Rapids, Michigan, 1986.

Lucy Moorehead (editor), *Freya Stark, Letters, volume four, Bridge of the Levant, 1940–43*, Michael Russell, Salisbury, Wiltshire, 1977.

David Nichols (editor), *Ernie's War: The Best of Ernie Pyle's World War II Dispatches*, Randon House, New York, 1986.

William L. Shirer, *Berlin Diary, The Journal of a Foreign Correspondent, 1934–1941*, Hamish Hamilton, London, 1941.

Herbert Wegener (editor), *Thomas Mann, Letters to Paul Amann, 1915–1952*, Secker and Warburg, London, 1961.

B.D. Zevin (editor), *Nothing to Fear: The Selected Addresses of Franklin Delano Roosevelt, 1932–1945*, Hodder and Sroughton, London, 1947.

Memoirs:

José Antonio de Aguirre, *Freedom was Flesh and Blood*, Victor Gollancz, London, 1945.

A. Anatoli (Kuznetsov), *Babi Yar*, Jonathan Cape, London, 1970.

Eduard Benes, *Memoirs of Dr Eduard Benes: From Munich to New War and New Victory*, George Allen and Unwin, London, 1954.

Count Folke Bernadotte, *The Curtain Falls, Last Days of the Third Reich*, Alfred A. Knopf, New York, 1945.

Edith Bone, *Seven Years Solitary*, Hamish Hamilton, London, 1959.

James Cameron, *Point of Departure: Experiment in Biography*, Arthur Barker, London, 1967.

Lord Casey, *Personal Experiences 1939–1946*, Constable, London, 1962.

Jung Chang, *Wild Swans, Three Daughters of China*, HarperCollins, London, 1991.

General Mark W. Clark, *From the Danube to the Yalu*, Harper and Row, New York, 1954.

Milovan Djilas, *Land Without Justice, An Autobiography of his Youth*, Methuen, London, 1958.

Milovan Djilas, *Conversations with Stalin*, Harcourt, Brace and World, New York, 1962.

Anthony Farrar-Hockley, *The Edge of the Sword*, Frederick Muller, London, 1954.

Louis Fischer, *Men and Politics, An Autobiography*, Jonathan Cape, London, 1941.

Saul Friedländer, *When Memory Comes*, Farrar, Straus and Giroux, New York, 1979.

Martha Gellhorn, *Travels with Myself and Another*, Dodd, Mead, New York, 1979.

Joseph C. Grew, *Turbulent Era, A Diplomatic Record of Forty Years, 1904–1945*, two volumes, Hammond and Hammond, London, 1953.

George F. Kennan, *Memoirs, 1925–1950*, Little, Brown, New York, 1967.

Victor Klemperer, *I Shall Bear Witness: The Diaries of Victor Klemperer, 1933–41*, Weidenfeld and Nicolson, London, 1998.

Primo Levi, *The Drowned and the Saved*, Michael Joseph, London, 1988.

James G. McDonald, *My Mission in Israel, 1948–1951*, Victor Gollancz, London, 1951.

William Manchester, *Goodbye, Darkness: A Memoir of the Pacific War*, Little, Brown, New York, 1979.

Vladka Meed, *On Both Sides of the Wall*, Ghetto Fighters' House, Tel Aviv, 1972.

Pierre Mendes-France, *The Pursuit of Freedom*, Longmans, Green, London, 1956.

Arthus Miller, *Timebends, A Life*, Methuen, London, 1987.

Lieutenant-Colonel Colin Mitchell, *Having Been A Soldier*, Hamish Hamilton, London, 1969.

Richard M. Nixon, *The Memoirs of Richard Nixon*, Sidgwick and Jackson, London, 1978.

Matthew B. Ridgway, *The War in Korea*, Barrie and Rockliff, London, 1968.

Antoine de Saint-Exupéry, *Wind, Sand and Stars*, William Heinemann, London, 1939.

Kurt von Schuschnigg, *Austrian Requiem*, G.P. Putnam's Sons, New York, 1946.

Sir Georg Solti, *Solti on Solti: A Memoir*, Chatto and Windus, London, 1997.

Stephen Spender, *World Within World*, Hamish Hamilton, London, 1953.

Telford Taylor, *The Anatomy of the Nuremberg Trials: A Personal Memoir*, Bloomsbury, London, 1993.

980 · DESCENT INTO BARBARISM

George Weidenfeld, *Remembering My Good Friends, An Autobiography*, HarperCollins, London, 1995.

Elie Wiesel, *Night*, MacGibbon and Kee, London, 1960.

Elizabeth Wiskemann, *The Europe I Saw*, Collins, London, 1968.

Richard Wright, *Black Boy: A Record of Childhood and Youth*, Harper and Brothers, New York, 1945.

Larry Zellers, *In Enemy Hands, A Prisoner in North Korea*, University Press of Kentucky, Lexington, Kentucky, 1991.

Biographies:

Jonathan Aitken, *Nixon, A Life*, Weidenfeld and Nicolson, London, 1993.

Peter F. Alexander, *Alan Paton, A Biography*, Oxford University Press, Oxford, 1994.

James Bentley, *Martin Niemöller*, Oxford University Press, Oxford, 1984.

Nicholas Bethell, *Gomulka, His Poland, His Communism*, Longmans, London, 1969.

Eberhard Bethge, *Dietrich Bonhoeffer: Theologian, Christian, Contemporary*, Collins, London, 1970.

Mary Bosanquet, *The Life and Death of Dietrich Bonhoeffer*, Hodder and Stoughton, London, 1968.

Gordon Brook-Shepherd, *Dollfuss*, Macmillan, London, 1961.

Dr Melvyn H. Brooks (editor), *Dr Hannah Billig, 1901–1987, The Angel of Cable Street: Memories*, privately printed, Karkur, Israel, 1993.

Andrew Brown, *The Neutron and the Bomb, A Biography of Sir James Chadwick*, Oxford University Press, Oxford, 1997.

Alan Bullock, *Ernest Bevin: Foreign Secretary, 1945–1951*, Heinemann, London, 1983.

Hubert Cole, *Laval, A Biography*, Heinemann, London, 1963.

Robert Conquest, *Stalin, Breaker of Nations*, Weidenfeld and Nicolson, London, 1991.

Vladimir Dedijer, *Tito Speaks: His Self Portrait and Struggle with Stalin*, Weidenfeld and Nicolson, London, 1953.

Louis Fischer, *The Life of Mahatma Gandhi*, Jonathan Cape, London, 1951.

Jean Overton Fuller, *Madeleine* (the story of Noor Inayat Khan), Victor Gollancz, London, 1952.

Sarvepalli Gopal, *Jawaharlal Nehru: A Biography, Volume One, 1889–1947*, Jonathan Cape, London, 1975 (volumes two and three, 1979 and 1984).

Ronald Hayman, *Writing Against: A Biography of Sartre*, Weidenfeld and Nicolson, London, 1986.

Konrad Heiden, *Der Fuerher: Hitler's Rise to Power*, Victor Gollancz, two volumes, London, 1944.

Walter Isaacson, *Kissinger, A Biography*, Faber and Faber, London, 1992.

Doris Kearns, *Lyndon Johnson and the American Dream*, Harper Row, New York, 1976.

Lord Kinross, *Atatürk, The Rebirth of a Nation*, Weidenfeld and Nicolson, London, 1964.

Robert Low, *La Pasionaria: The Spanish Firebrand*, Hutchinson, London, 1992.

Compton Mackenzie, *Dr Benes*, George G. Harrap, London, 1946.

David McCullough, *Truman*, Simon and Schuster, New York, 1992.

Denis Mack Smith, *Mussolini*, Weidenfeld and Nicolson, London, 1981.

H. Montgomery Hyde, *Stalin: The History of a Dictator*, Rupert Hart-Davis, London, 1971.

Evgeny Pasternak, *Boris Pasternak, The Tragic Years, 1930–60*, Collins Harvill, London, 1991.

Paul Preston, *Franco, A Biography*, HarperCollins, London, 1993.

Ralf Georg Reuth, *Goebbels, The Life of Joseph Goebbels, The Mephistophelean Genius of Nazi Propaganda*, Constable, London, 1993.

Christopher Sykes, *Orde Wingate*, Collins, London, 1959.

James Tobin, *Ernie Pyle's War: America's Eyewitness to World War II*, Free Press, New York, 1997.

Olivier Todd, *Albert Camus: A Life*, Chatto and Windus, London, 1997.

Dmitri Volkogonov, *Stalin, Triumph and Tragedy*, Grove Weidenfeld, New York, 1988.

E.P. Wigner and R.A. Hodgkin, *Michael Polanyi*, Royal Society, London, 1977.

John Evelyn Wrench, *Francis Yeats-Brown, 1886–1944*, Eyre and Spottiswoode, London, 1948.

General books:

Noel Annan, *Changing Enemies: The Defeat and Regeneration of Germany*, Norton, New York, 1996.

Yitzhak Arad, *Ghetto in Flames: The Struggle and Destruction of the Jews in Vilna in the Holocaust*, Yad Vashem, Jerusalem, 1980.

Bohdan Arct, *Polish Wings in the West*, Interpress, Warsaw, 1971.

John A. Armstrong (editor), *Soviet Partisans in World War II*, University of Wisconsin Press, Madison, Wisconsin, 1964.

Max Arthur, *The Royal Navy, 1914–1939, A Narrative History*, Hodder and Stoughton, London, 1996.

982 · DESCENT INTO BARBARISM

Sidney Aster, *1939, The Making of the Second World War*, Andre Deutsch, London, 1973.

Albert Axell, *Stalin's War Through the Eyes of His Commanders*, Arms and Armour, London, 1997.

Ralph Barker, *Children of the Benares, A War Crime and its Victims*, Methuen, London, 1987.

Wladislaw Bartoszewski and Zofia Lewin (editors), *Righteous Among Nations: How Poles Helped the Jews, 1939–1945*, Earls Court Publications, London, 1969.

Hilary Beckles, *A History of Barbados: from Amerindian settlement to nation-state*, Cambridge, 1990.

Antony Beevor, *Crete: the Battle and the Resistance*, John Murray, London, 1991.

Ralph Bennett, *Ultra and Mediterranean Strategy, 1941–1945*, Hamish Hamilton, London, 1989.

Leslie Bethell (editor), *The Cambridge History of Latin America*, Volume Six, Cambridge University Press, Cambridge, 1994.

Scott L. Bills, *Empire and Cold War: The Roots of the US-Third World Antagonism, 1945-47*, Macmillan, London, 1990.

Leslie Blau, *Bonyhád: A Destroyed Community, The Jews of Bonyhád, Hungary*, Shengold Publishers, New York, 1994.

William B. Breuer, *Retaking the Philippines: America's Return to Corregidor and Bataan, October 1944-March 1945*, St Martin's Press, New York, 1986.

Gordon Brook-Shepherd, *Anschluss, The Rape of Austria*, Macmillan, London, 1963.

George Bruce, *The Warsaw Uprising, 1 August – 2 October 1944*, Rupert Hart-Davis, London, 1972.

Robert Buderi, *The Invention that Changed the World: The Story of Radar from War to Peace*, Simon and Schuster, New York, 1996.

Olaf Caroe, *Soviet Empire, The Turks of Central Asia and Stalinism*, Macmillan, London, 1953.

Raymond Carr, *Spain 1808–1975*, Clarendon Press, Oxford, 1966.

Raymond Carr, *The Spanish Tragedy: The Civil War in Perspective*, Weidenfeld and Nicolson, 1977.

Peter N. Carroll, *The Odyssey of the Abraham Lincoln Brigade: Americans in the Spanish Civil War*, Stanford University Press, Stanford, California, 1994.

Connery Chappell, *Island of Barbed Wire: Internment on the Isle of Man in World War Two*, Robert Hale, London, 1984,

Iris Chang, *The Rape of Nanking, The Forgotten Holocaust of World War II*, Basic Books, New York, 1997.

Anne Chisholm, *Faces of Hiroshima*, Jonathan Cape, London, 1985.

Alan Clark, *Barbarossa: The Russian-German Conflict, 1941–1945*, Hutchinson, London, 1965.

Thurston Clarke, *By Blood and Fire, The Attack on the King David Hotel*, Hutchinson, London, 1981.

Richard Cobb, *French and Germans, Germans and French: A Personal Interpretation of France under Two Occupations, 1914–1918/1940–1944*, University Press of New England, Hanover, New Brunswick, 1983.

Robert Conquest, *The Great Terror: Stalin's Purge of the Thirties*, Macmillan, London, 1968.

Charles Cruikshank, *Deception in World War II*, Oxford University Press, Oxford, 1979.

M.N. Das, *The Political Philosophy of Jawaharlal Nehru*, George Allen and Unwin, London, 1951.

Phillip B. Davidson, *Vietnam at War, The History. 1946–1975*, Sidgwick and Jackson, London, 1988.

Gavan Daws, *Prisoners of the Japanese, POWs of World War II in the Pacific*, William Morrow, New York, 1994.

T.K. Derry, *The Campaign in Norway*, His Majesty's Stationery office, London, 1952.

John Dunstan, *HMS Black Swan, her part in The Yangtze Incident, April 1949*, Black Swan Association, 1998.

Major L.F. Ellis, *The War in France and Flanders, 1939–1940*, Her Majesty's Stationery Office, London, 1953.

Eloise Engle and Lauri Paananen, *The Winter War: The Russo-Finnish Conflict, 1939–40*, Sidgwick and Jackson, London, 1973.

Richard J. Evans, *Rituals of Retribution, Capital Punishment in Germany, 1600–1987*, Oxford University Press, Oxford, 1996.

Joachim C. Fest, *The Face of the Third Reich*, Weidenfeld and Nicolson, London, 1970.

Joachim C. Fest, *Plotting Hitler's Death, The Story of the German Resistance*, Henry Holt, New York, 1996.

M.R.D. Foot, *SOE in France: An Account of the Work of the British Special Operations Executive in France, 1940–1944*, Her Majesty's Stationery Office, London, 1966.

Paul Fussell, *The Great War and Modern Memory*, Oxford University Press, London, 1975.

Robert Frank Futrell, *The United States Air Force in Korea, 1950–1953*, revised edition, Office of Air Force History, United States Air Force, Washington DC, 1983.

John and Carol Garrard, *Inside the Soviet Writers' Union*, The Free Press, New York, 1990.

John Garrard, *The Brest Ghetto Passport Archive*, 1998, www1.jewishgen.org/databases/brest.htm

Martha Gellhorn, *The Face of War*, Atlantic Monthly Press, New York, 1959.

Patricia Giesler, *Valour Remembered: Canadians in Korea*, Directorate of Public affairs, Veterans Affairs, Ottawa, Canada, 1982.

John Gittings, *The Role of the Chinese Army*, Oxford University Press, London, 1967.

Daniel Jonah Goldhagen, *Hitler's Willing Executioners: Ordinary Germans and the Holocaust*, Little, Brown, New York, 1996.

Percy S. Gourgey, *The Indian Naval Revolt of 1946*, Orient Longman, Hyderabad, 1996.

Samuel B. Griffith II, *The Chinese People's Liberation Army*, McGraw Hill, New York, 1967.

Theodore S. Hamerow, *On the Road to the Wolf's Lair, German Resistance to Hitler*, Belknap Press (Harvard University Press), Cambridge, Massachusetts, 1997.

Major General Haywood S. Hansell Jr, *Strategic Air War Against Japan*, Airpower Research Institute, Maxwell Air Force Base, Alabama, 1980.

Max Hastings, *The Korean War*, Michael Joseph, London, 1987.

R.E.M. Irving, *The First Indochina War, French and American Policy, 1945–54*, Croom Helm, London, 1975.

Ayesha Jalal, *The Sole Spokesman: Jinnah, the Muslim League and the Demand for Partition*, Cambridge University Press, Cambridge, 1985.

Kenneth N. Jordan, Sr, Forgotten Heroes, *131 Men of the Korean War Awarded the Medal of Honor, 1950–1953*, Schiffer Military/Aviation History, Atglen, Pennsylvania, 1995.

George F. Kennan, *American Diplomacy, 1900–1950*, Secker and Warburg, London, 1952.

Serge Klarsfeld, *French Children of the Holocaust, A Memorial*, New York University Press, New York, 1996.

H.W. Koch, *The Hitler Youth: Origins and Development, 1922–1945*, Stein and Day, New York, 1976.

Dan Kurzman, *Left to Die: The Tragedy of the USS Juneau*, Simon and Schuster, New York, 1994.

Leopold Labedz (editor), *Solzhenitsyn: A Documentary Record*, Allen Lane, The Penguin Press, London, 1970.

Raymond Lamont-Brown, *Kamikaze, Japan's Suicide Samurai*, Arms and Armour, London, 1997.

Kenneth Scott Latourette, *A History of Modern China*, Penguin, London, 1954.

Robert Leckie, *Conflict: The History of the Korean War, 1950–53*, Putnam, New York, 1962.

Cecil Lee, *Sunset of the Raj: Fall of Singapore, 1942*, Pentland Press, Edinburgh, 1994.

I. E. Levit, *Ashes of Past Beat into our Hearts: Holocaust*, Jewish Cultural

Society of the Republic of Moldova (and others), Chisinau (Kishinev), 1997.

Robert Jay Lifton, *The Nazi Doctors, Medical Killing and the Psychology of Genocide*, Basic Books, London, 1986.

Wm Roger Louis, *Imperialism at Bay, 1941–1945: The United States and the Decolonization of the British Empire*, Clarendon Press, Oxford, 1977.

Hugh Lunghi, *The Common Cause Story: Freedom, The Common Cause of Mankind*, Common Cause, Fleet, Hampshire, 1995.

Noel Malcolm, *Kosovo: A Short History*, Macmillan, London, 1998.

Arthur Marwick, *The Explosion of British Society, 1914–62*, Pan, London, 1963.

Philip Mason, *Common Sense About Race*, Victor Gollancz, London, 1961.

Mark Mazower, *Inside Hitler's Greece: The Experience of Occupation, 1941–44*, Yale University Press, New Haven, Connecticut, 1993.

Martin Middlebrook, *The Nuremberg Raid*, Allen Lane, London, 1973.

Martin Middlebrook, *The Berlin Raids: RAF Bomber Command Winter 1943–44*, Viking, London, 1988.

Walter Millis, *This Is Pearl! The United States and Japan, 1941*, William Morrow, New York, 1947.

Penderal Moon, *Divide and Quit* (India 1947–1948), Chatto and Windus, London, 1961.

Samuel Eliot Morison, *History of United States Naval Operations in World War II*, Oxford University Press, London, 1958.

Jawaharlal Nehru, *The Discovery of India*, Meridian Books, London, 1946.

John North, *North-West Europe, 1944–5, The Achievement of 21st Army Group*, His Majesty's Stationery Office, London, 1953.

Stanley G. Payne, *A History of Fascism, 1914–1945*, University of Wisconsin Press, Madison, Wisconsin, 1995.

Cathy Porter and Mark Jones, *Moscow in World War II*, Chatto and Windus, London, 1987.

David Pryce-Jones, *The Hungarian Revolution*, Ernest Benn, London, 1969.

David Pryce-Jones, *Paris in the Third Reich: A History of the German Occupation, 1940–1944*, Holt, Rinehart and Winston, New York, 1981.

David Rees, *Korea: The Limited War*, St Martin's Press, New York, 1964.

P.R. Reid, *The Colditz Story*, Hodder and Stoughton, London, 1952.

Alexandra Richie, *Faust's Metropolis, A History of Berlin*, Carroll and Graf, New York, 1998.

John Robertson, *Australia at War, 1939–1945*, William Heinemann, Melbourne, 1981.

Hans Rumpf, *The Bombing of Germany*, Frederick Muller, London, 1963.

Lord Russell of Liverpool, *The Knights of the Bushido, A Short History of Japanese War Crimes*, Cassell, London, 1958.

Harrison E. Salisbury, *The 900 Days: The Siege of Leningrad*, Martin Secker and Warburg, London, 1969.

Gaetano Salvemini, *Prelude to World War II*, Victor Gollancz, London. 1954.

Gerhard Schoenberner, *The Yellow Star: The Persecution of the Jews in Europe 1933–1945*, Transworld, London, 1969.

Gerhard Schoenberner, *House of the Wannsee Conference, Permanent Exhibit*, Haus der Wannsee-Konferenz, Berlin, 1996.

Robert Service, *A History of Twentieth-Century Russia*, Allen Lane/The Penguin Press, London, 1998.

Hugh Seton-Watson, *The Pattern of Communist Revolution: A Historical Analysis*, Methuen, London, 1953.

Ellen Schrecker, *Many are the Crimes: McCarthyism in America*, Little, Brown, New York, 1998.

David Sibley, *The Behar Massacre: The execution of 69 survivors from the British Merchant Ship 'Behar' in 1944 by the Imperial Japanese Navy*, A. Lane, Stockport, 1998.

Tommie Sjöberg, *The Powers and the Persecuted: The Refugee Problem and the Intergovernmental Committee on Refugees*, Lund University Press, Lund, Sweden, 1991.

Bartley F. Smith, *The War's Long Shadow: The Second World War and its Aftermath: China, Russia, Britain and America*, Simon and Schuster, New York, 1986.

Ronald H. Spector, *Eagle Against the Sun: The American War with Japan*, Viking, London, 1984.

Jonathan D. Spence, *The Search for Modern China*, W.W. Norton, New York, 1990.

Colonel C.P. Stacey, *The Canadian Army, 1939–1945, An Official Historical Summary*, Ministry of National Defence, Ottawa, 1948.

George H. Stein, *The Waffen SS, Hitler's Elite Guards at War, 1939–1945*, Cornell University Press, Ithaca, New York, 1966.

Gerald Emanuel Stern, *Broken Image, Foreign Critiques of America*, Random House, New York, 1972.

Gustav Stolper, Karl Häuser and Knut Borchardt, *The German Economy, 1870 to the Present*, Weidenfeld and Nicolson, London, 1967.

Rita Thalman and Emmanuel Feinermann, *Crystal Night, 9–10 November 1938*, Thames and Hudson, London, 1974.

Gordon Thomas and Max Morgan-Witts, *Voyage of the Damned: The Voyage of the St Louis*, Hodder and Stoughton, London, 1974.

Gordon Thomas and Max Morgan-Witts, *The Day Guernica Died*, Hodder and Stoughton, London, 1975.

Gordon Thomas and Max Morgan-Witts, *Ruin from the Air: The Atomic Mission to Hiroshima*, Hamish Hamilton, London, 1977.

Hugh Thomas, *The Spanish Civil War*, Eyre and Spottiswoode, London, 1961.

Hugh Thomas, *Cuba, or the Pursuit of Freedom*, Eyre and Spottiswoode, London, 1971.

Christopher Thorne, *The Far Eastern War: States and Societies, 1941–45*, Hamish Hamilton, London, 1985.

Tzvetan Todorov, *A French Tragedy: Scenes of Civil War, Summer 1944*, University of New England Press, Hanover, 1997.

H.R. Trevor-Roper, *The Last Days of Hitler*, Macmillan, London, 1947.

Barry Turner, . . . *And the Policeman Smiled: 10,000 Children Escape from Nazi Europe*, Bloomsbury, London, 1990.

Adrian Walker, *A Barren Place: National Servicemen in Korea, 1950–1954*, Leo Cooper, London, 1994.

Lawrence D. Walker, *Hitler Youth and Catholic Youth, 1933–1936, A Study in Totalitarian Conquest*, Catholic University of America Press, Washington DC, 1970.

John W. Waller, *The Unseen War in Europe: Espionage and Conspiracy in the Second World War*, Random House, New York, 1996.

Walter Warlimont, *Inside Hitler's Headquarters, 1939–45*, Weidenfeld and Nicolson, London, 1964.

Alexander Werth, *Russia at War, 1941–1945*, Barrie and Rockliff, London, 1964.

Rebecca West, *Black Lamb and Grey Falcon, A Journey Through Yugoslavia*, 2 volumes, Macmillan, London, 1942.

W. Denis Whitaker and Shelagh Whitaker, *Rhineland: The Battle to End the War*, Stoddart, Toronto, Canada, 1989.

Novels and poetry:

Vasily Grossman, *Life and Fate*, Collins Harvill, London, 1985.

Primo Levi, *Shema: Collected poems of Primo Levi*, Menard Press, London, 1976.

Jean-Paul Sartre, *The Reprieve*, Hamish Hamilton, London, 1947.

Alexander Solzhenitsyn, *One Day in the Life of Ivan Denisovich*, Victor Gollancz, London, 1963.

Articles in Journals and Magazines:

Laurie Barber, 'Jitra: The Forgotten Battle', *Journal of the Society for Army Historical Research*, No. 75, London, 1997.

Denis C. Bateman, 'Incident at Imber', *After the Battle*, No. 49, 1985.

Hen Bollen, 'Canadian Campaigns in Holland, 1944–1945', *Victory Parade: Canadian War Artists in Holland, 1944/45*, Legermuseum, Delft, 1990.

988 · DESCENT INTO BARBARISM

Christopher R. Browning, 'Germans and Serbs: The Emergence of Nazi Antipartisan Policies in 1941,' Michael Berenbaum (editor), *A Mosaic of Victims, Non-Jews Persecuted and Murdered by the Nazis*, New York University Press, New York, 1990.

John Haag, 'A Woman's Struggle Against Nazism: Irene Harand and *Gerechtigkeit*, 1933–1938, *The Wiener Library Bulletin*, volume XXXIV, numbers 53/54, London, 1981.

Mushirul Hasan, 'Partition, The Human Cost', *History Today*, (India and the British), volume 47 (9), London, September 1997.

John Higgins, 'Partition in India', Michael Sissons and Philip French (editors), *Age of Austerity, 1945–51*, Hodder and Stoughton, London, 1963.

Carolsue Holland and Thomas Rothbart, 'The Merkers and Buchenwald Treasure Troves', *After the Battle*, No.93, London, 1996.

Peter Kenez, 'Soviet Film Under Stalin', Geoffrey Nowell-Smith (editor), *The Oxford History of World Cinema*, Oxford University Press, Oxford, 1996.

David Leitch, 'The Explosion at the King David Hotel', Michael Sissons and Philip French (editors), *Age of Austerity, 1945–51*, Hodder and Stoughton, London, 1963.

Peter Malina, 'Eduard Pernkopf's atlas of anatomy or: The fiction of "pure science"', *The Middle European Journal of Medicine*, volumes 4–5, Vienna, 1998.

Charles Musser, 'Engaging with Reality', Geoffrey Nowell-Smith (editor), *The Oxford History of World Cinema*, Oxford University Press, Oxford, 1996.

Thomas Powers, 'The Conspiracy That Failed', *The New York Review*, 9 January 1997.

Eric Rentschler, 'Germany: Nazism and After', Geoffrey Nowell-Smith (editor), *The Oxford History of World Cinema*, Oxford University Press, Oxford, 1996.

Francis Robinson, 'The Muslims and Partition', *History Today*, (India and the British), volume 47 (9), London, September 1997.

Andy Saunders, 'John Gillespie Magee', *After The Battle*, No. 63, London, 1989.

Fritz Saxl, 'The History of Warburg's Library (1886–1944)', E. H. Gombrich, *Aby Warburg, An Intellectual Biography*, Phaidon, Oxford, 1970.

Evelyne Shuster, 'Fifty Years Later: The Significance of the Nuremberg Code', *The New England Journal of Medicine*, volume 337, number 20, Boston, 13 November 1997.

Christian Streit, 'The Fate of the Soviet Prisoners of War', Michael Berenbaum (editor), *A Mosaic of Victims, Non-Jews Persecuted and Murdered by the Nazis*, New York University Press, New York, 1990.

Nechama Tec and Daniel Weiss, 'A Historical Injustice: The Case of Masha Bruskina', *Holocaust and Genocide Studies*, London, winter 1997.

Newspaper articles:

Elena Becatoros, 'Discovery of sub wreck confirms survivor's tale, *Sunday Times*, 18 February 1998

Ian Brodie, 'Pride of Pacific battle found', *The Times*, 21 May 1998.

Roger Boyes, 'Nazi to be tried for killing 500 in death camp', *The Times*, 5 March 1998.

Joan Breckenridge, 'Remembering the heroes of yesterday, A couple lobby for a memorial in Normandy to Canadians who helped liberate Europe', *Globe and Mail* (Toronto), 20 May 1998.

Jay Bushinsky, 'Latvian president asked to apologize for murder of Jews', *Jerusalem Post*, 23 February 1998.

David Childs, 'Otto Ernst Remer', *Independent*, 9 October 1997.

Susan Fishkoff, 'Witness who won't stay silent' (Johnnie Stevens), *Jerusalem Post*, 5 January 1998.

Ruth E. Gruber, 'Ex-Nazi sentenced to life for Italy's worst massacre,' (Erich Priebke) *Jewish Chronicle*, 13 March 1998.

Alan Hamilton, 'Veterans honour the Slapton victims', *The Times*, 28 April 1994.

Simon Hayden, '"Neutral" Sweden's role in war,' Reuters, *Hong Kong Standard*, 8 January 1998.

Jane Kelly, 'The shy genius who changed all our lives' (Tom Kilburn), *Daily Mail*, 18 June 1998.

Wim van Leer, 'After the deluge' (Berlin in August 1945), *Jerusalem Post*, 17 January 1986.

Christopher Munnion, 'S. Africa searches for lost war hero honoured by navy', *Daily Telegraph*, 25 April 1998.

James Pringle, 'Christians keep faith in China's "secret houses"', *The Times*, 1 June 1998.

Byron Rogers, 'When the Hood blew up without trace', *Sunday Telegraph*, 24 May 1998.

Denis Staunton, 'Countess Maria von Maltzan, In defiance of fascism', *Guardian*, 18 November 1997.

Stuart Wavell, 'A blond bombshell for Sweden', *Sunday Times*, 30 October 1997.

Guy Yeoman, 'Sinking of "Khedive"', *The Times*, 24 February 1994.

Michel Zlotowski, 'Silence is broken over round-up of children', *Jewish Chronicle*, 29 August 1997.

Unpublished manuscripts:

Eda Shapiro and Rick Kardonne, Victor Kugler, 'The Man Who Hid Anne Frank, His Memoirs In His own Words', Toronto, 1996.
Martin Gilbert, 'War of the 38th Parallel', Korean War Scrapbook, June-July 1950.

I have also drawn on documentary material in the following of my own books: *Britain and Germany Between the Wars*, Longmans, 1964; *Plough My Own Furrow, the Life and Letters of Lord Allen of Hurtwood*, Longmans, 1966; *The Holocaust, The Jewish Tragedy*, Collins, London, 1986; *Second World War*, Weidenfeld and Nicolson, London, 1989; *The Day the War Ended: VE-Day in Europe and Around the World*, HarperCollins, London, 1995; *The Boys, Triumph over Adversity*, Weidenfeld and Nicolson, London, 1996; *Holocaust Journey, Travelling in Search of the Past*, Weidenfeld and Nicolson, London, 1997; *Israel: A History*, Doubleday, London, 1998; and volumes five to eight of *Winston S.Churchill*, Heinemann, London, 1976–1988.

INDEX

compiled by the author

Dunlop, Colonel Edward: witnesses an atrocity, 431–2

Dunn, Major John J.: a prisoner-of-war in Korea, 884

Durango (Spain): bombed, 136; recalled, 137

Düsseldorf (Germany): bombed, 355, 466, 509; protests in, 491

Dutch: 'bludgeoned', 308; German rule over, 319

Dutch East Indies: 26, 331, 389, 406; overrun, 412, 419; Japanese repatriated from, 742; nationalist uprisings in, 750

Dvinsky, B. A.: and Soviet Intelligence, 253

Dybenko, General: his fate, 144, 209

Dzhugashvili, Yakov (Stalin's son): captured, 389

EAM (National Liberation Front): in Greece, 518

EDES (National Republic Greek League): 518

ELAS (Greek People's Liberation Army): 518

Eagle (British aircraft carrier): brings reinforcements, 445

Eaker, General Ira C.: and a bombing appeal, 581

earthquakes: 51, 74, 289

East Africa: troops from, drowned, 544

East Anglia (Britain): and a deception, 561, 562, 571; air missions from, 614

East Germany: and the Soviet Union, 767; and Communist control, 836

East Pakistan: famine in, 799

East Prussia: 10, 16, 104, 251, 265, 276, 278, 336, 375, 378, 579, 584; Russians reach, 621, 626; German troop movements from, 636; cut off from Germany, 639; refugees from, drowned, 640; final surrender in, 686; Germans expelled from, 690, 761; divided between Russia and Poland, 697

East Upper Silesia (German-annexed Poland): 281

Easter Rebellion (1916): 191

Eastern Galicia (Poland): 273, 386, 540, 557

Eberl, Dr Irmfried: and mass murder, 417, 457, 459

Ebro River (Spain): 214, 215

Eckernförde (Germany): and the German invasion of Norway, 299

Economic and Social Council (of the United Nations): 734

Economic Control Council (wartime Holland): 632

Economic Co-operation Bill (USA): and the Marshall Plan, 782, 812

Economic League for European Co-operation: 825

Eddy, Nelson: an echo of, in Germany, 107

Eden, Anthony: and Abyssinia, 68, 71, 110; and the Rhineland, 99; and German fears, 227; and the mass murder of Jews, 477; and Poland, 543, 656, 682; and a bombing appeal, 581

Eder Dam (Germany): bombed, 504

Edgers, Dorothy: and a fateful translation, 407

Edinburgh (Scotland): the call for a 'Summit' from, 854–5; criticism of the Soviet Union in, 904

Edwards' Air Force base (California): sound barrier broken above, 802

Eger (Czechoslovakia): see index entry for Cheb

Eggersdorf (near Berlin): fate of Hitler Youth at, 669

Egypt: independent, 122; and Palestine, 217; and a non-stop flying record, 222; Roosevelt's question to Hitler concerning, 243; fighting in, 341, 350, 355, 369; a bomber base in (against Roumania), 450; bombers diverted to, 450; Germans driven from, 465–6; typhus in, 725; isolated from Palestine, 747; German prisoners-of-war return from, 776; violence against Jews in, 791; and Israel, 815, 922; Palestinian Arab refugees in, 816

Ehrich, Elsa: hanged near scene of her crimes, 808

Eicke, Theodor: 'to incarcerate or annihilate', 265; and daily executions, 269; and the German invasion of Russia, 375

Eichmann, SS Lieutenant-Colonel Adolf: at Wannsee, 420; orders deportations, 451, 484; in Hungary, 554–5; his work cut short, 582

Eifel Mountains (Germany): no withdrawal to, 629

Einsatzgruppen: see index entry for Special Task Forces

Einstein, Albert: xx, 18, 60, 127, 279

Eire: see index entry for Irish Free State

Eisenach (Germany): 685

Eisenhower, General Dwight D.: and a new 'hero' (MacArthur), 432; and the battlefield at Falaise, 605; and the psychological burdens of continuous combat, 619–20; gives up Berlin as main objective, 636; called to a scene of mass murder, 659; and Germany's surrender, 681; and the 'iron curtain', 685; and the Korean War, 892; and NATO, 895

Eisenstein, Sergei: a propaganda film by, 65

El Salvador: 923

Elbaz brothers: deported, 498

Elbe River: 111, 579, 685

Elbing (East Prussia): 16; Russians reach, 639

Elbrus, Mount: Swastika flies on, 465

Elizabeth, Princess: a wedding guest of, forced to abdicate, 783; visits South Africa, 788

Elizabeth, Queen (wife of George VI): visits South Africa, 788

Elsas, Fritz: executed, 635

Elser, Johann Georg: a would-be assassin, 283; executed, 661

Elton, Geoffrey: interned, 326

Emden (German cruiser): sailors injured on, 268

Emergency Relief Appropriations Act (United States): 218

Emergency Rescue Committee (United States): 359

Emilia: dies, 549

Empire Pride (British ocean liner): and repatriation scenes, 736–7

Empire Training Scheme (Canada): 478

Empress of Canada (ocean liner): sunk, 490

Enabling Law (1929): extended by Hitler, 149

'enemy aliens' (in Britain): interned, 325–6; on the high seas, 328–9

Engel, Major: Hitler confides in, 404–5

'England's Difficulty': 72

England Football Team: beats Argentina, 920

Enigma (Signals Intelligence): 295–6, 356, 364, 365, 375, 432, 465, 466, 487, 488, 501, 502, 503, 506, 533, 630

Eniwetok Atoll (Pacific): Americans land on, 545

Enola Gay (American bomber): drops atom bomb, 702

Enterprise (American aircraft carrier): and a kamikaze attack, 687–8